MAO: THE REAL STORY

ALEXANDER V. PANTSOV

WITH STEVEN I. LEVINE

SIMON & SCHUSTER

NEW YORK   LONDON   TORONTO   SYDNEY   NEW DELHI

Simon & Schuster
1230 Avenue of the Americas
New York, NY 10020

Copyright © 2007, 2012 by Pantsov A.V.
Introduction copyright © 2012 by Pantsov A.V.
English language translation copyright © 2012 by Steven I. Levine

Originally published in a different version in 2007 in Russian by Molodaia Gvardiia as *Mao Tszedun.*

First Simon & Schuster hardcover edition October 2012

SIMON & SCHUSTER and colophon are registered trademarks of Simon & Schuster, Inc.

For information about special discounts for bulk purchases, please contact Simon & Schuster Special Sales at 1-866-506-1949 or business@simonandschuster.com.

The Simon & Schuster Speakers Bureau can bring authors to your live event. For more information or to book an event, contact the Simon & Schuster Speakers Bureau at 1-866-248-3049 or visit our website at www.simonspeakers.com.

Designed by Nancy Singer

Maps by Paul Pugliese

Manufactured in the United States of America

10   9   8   7   6   5   4   3   2

Library of Congress Cataloging-in-Publication Data
Pantsov, Alexander, date.
    [Mao Tszedun. English]
    Mao : the real story / Alexander V. Pantsov with Steven I. Levine.
—1st Simon & Schuster hardcover ed.
        p.   cm.
    Originally published in Russian: Moskva : Molodaia Gvardiia, 2007, under title Mao Tszedun.
    Includes bibliographical references and index.
1. Mao, Zedong, 1893–1976.   2. Heads of state—China—Biography.   3. China—Politics and government—1949–1976.   I. Levine, Steven I.   II. Title.
    DS778.M3P287613   2012
    951.05092—dc23
    [B]   2011053113
ISBN 978-1-4516-5447-9
ISBN 978-1-4516-5449-3 (ebook)

To the memory of my grandfather,

Georgii Borisovich Ehrenburg (1902–1967),

A Russian Sinologist,

One of the first biographers of Mao Zedong,

And the author whose works inspired me greatly

—ALEXANDER V. PANTSOV

CONTENTS

Cast of Characters   IX

Note on the Spelling of Chinese Words   XVIII

Introduction: Myths and Realities   1

PART ONE: THE APPRENTICE

1   The Foster Child of the Bodhisattva   11

2   On the Threshold of a New World   21

3   "I Think, Therefore, I Am"   31

4   The Sound of Footsteps in a Deserted Valley   47

5   Dreams of a Red Chamber   56

6   The Great Union of the Popular Masses   68

7   Breathing World Revolution, or The Magic of Dictatorship   85

8   "Following the Russian Path"   98

9   The Lessons of Bolshevik Tactics   107

PART TWO: THE REVOLUTIONARY

10   Entering the Guomindang   119

11   Hopes and Disappointments   131

12   Playing with Chiang Kai-shek   143

13   The Collapse of the United Front   161

14   The Path to the Soviets   185

15   Red Banner over the Jinggang Mountains   200

16   A Single Spark Can Start a Prairie Fire   216

17 UNDER THE COMINTERN'S WING 233

18 DOG EAT DOG, COMMUNIST-STYLE 254

19 THE LONG MARCH 275

20 THE XI'AN INCIDENT 289

21 THE FLIRTATIOUS PHILOSOPHER 305

22 CONSOLIDATING CONTROL OVER THE CCP 322

23 STALIN, MAO, AND THE NEW DEMOCRATIC
REVOLUTION IN CHINA 343

PART THREE: THE DICTATOR

24 VISIT TO THE RED MECCA 363

25 THE KOREAN ADVENTURE 374

26 THE CONTRADICTIONS OF NEW DEMOCRACY 390

27 SOCIALIST INDUSTRIALIZATION 400

28 THE GREAT TURNING POINT 413

29 THE EMANCIPATION OF CONSCIOUSNESS 424

30 THE GREAT LEAP FORWARD 449

31 FAMINE AND FEAR 470

32 "THE DISMISSAL OF HAI RUI FROM OFFICE" 491

33 TO REBEL IS JUSTIFIED 507

34 THE RED GUARD TRAGEDY 522

35 THE MYSTERY OF PROJECT 571 540

36 DEATH OF THE RED EMPEROR 555

EPILOGUE 573

ACKNOWLEDGMENTS 579

ILLUSTRATION CREDITS 581

APPENDIX 1: MAO ZEDONG'S CHRONOLOGY 583

APPENDIX 2: MAO ZEDONG'S GENEALOGY 589

NOTES 593

BIBLIOGRAPHY 675

INDEX 715

CAST OF CHARACTERS *

Bo Gu (real name: Qin Bangxian) (1907–1946). General secretary of CCP Central Committee, 1931–35. One of Mao's main antagonists.

Bo Yibo (1908–2007). China's finance minister, 1949–53. Deputy premier, 1956–75.

Borodin, Mikhail Markovich (alias Bao Luoting, Bao guwen; real surname: Gruzenberg) (1884–1951). Main political adviser to Guomindang Central Executive Committee and Comintern representative in China, 1923–27.

Braun, Otto (alias K. O. Wagner) (1872–1955). Military adviser to CCP Central Committee, 1932–35. Mao's opponent.

Brezhnev, Leonid Ilich (1906–1982). First (general) secretary of the Soviet Communist Party, 1964–82.

Bukharin, Nikolai Ivanovich (1888–1938). Soviet Communist Party Central Committee Politburo member, 1924–29. Member of Presidium of Comintern, 1919–29.

Cai Hesen (alias Cailin Bin; real name: Cailin Hexian) (1895–1931). Mao's close friend. Member of CCP Central Executive Committee, 1927–28, and Politburo, 1931.

Chen Boda (1904–1989). Mao's secretary, 1939–58. Head of the Central Cultural Revolution Group, 1966. Arrested, 1970, and imprisoned.

Chen Duxiu (alias T. S. Chen, Tu-siu Chen, the Old Man) (1879–1942). Founder of the Chinese communist movement, leader of CCP, 1921–27.

Chen Yi (1901–1972). Joined communist movement in 1922. Deputy premier, 1954–72. Foreign minister, 1958–72. PLA marshal from 1955. Opposed Cultural Revolution, February 1967.

---

* Only the names of the more important individuals are given, and not all pseudonyms are included.

Chen Yun (real name: Liao Chenyun) (1905–1995). Joined communist movement in 1925. Deputy premier, 1954–75, 1979–80. Economic specialist.

Chen Zaidao (1909–1993). Commander of Wuhan and Hubei military districts, 1955–67.

Chiang Kai-shek (1887–1975). Commander in chief of Guomindang National Revolutionary Army from 1926. Head of Guomindang regime from 1928.

Deng Xiaoping (alias Deng Xixian; real name: Deng Xiansheng) (1904–1997). Deputy premier, 1952–68, 1973–76, 1977–80. Central Committee general secretary, 1956–66. Purged in Cultural Revolution, but returned to power in 1978 and reversed Mao's policies.

Deng Zhongxia (alias Deng Kang) (1894–1933). One of the first Chinese communists. Labor movement organizer.

Deng Zihui (1896–1972). Head of CCP Central Committee Rural Work Department, 1953–62. Deputy premier, 1954–65.

Dimitrov, Georgii (alias G. M.) (1882–1949). General secretary of Comintern Executive Committee, 1935–43.

Ehrenburg, Georgii Borisovich (1902–1967). Soviet Sinologist. Author of the first biographic sketch of Mao Zedong, 1934.

Engels, Friedrich (1820–1895). Cofounder of Marxism.

Ewert, Arthur Ernst (alias Harry Berger, Jim, Arthur) (1890–1959). Comintern representative in China, 1932–34.

Gao Gang (1905–1954). Chairman of Northeast regional government, 1949–52. Deputy premier, 1949–54. Head of State Planning Commission, 1952–54. Expelled from CCP, 1955.

Gromyko, Andrei Andreevich (1909–1989). Soviet foreign minister, 1957–85.

He Long (1896–1969). An organizer of Nanchang Uprising, 1927. Deputy premier, 1954–69. PLA marshal from 1955.

He Shuheng (alias Bewhiskered He) (1876–1935). Mao's friend. Cofounder of the Hunan communist movement and CCP, 1921.

He Zizhen (alias Guiyuan, Wen Yun) (1909–1984). Mao's third wife.

Hu Shi (1891–1962). Chinese liberal philosopher.

Hua Guofeng (1921–2008). Mao's successor, 1976.

Jiang Qing (alias Li Yunhe, Lan Ping, Marianna Yusupova; real name: Li Shumeng) (1914–1991). Mao's fourth wife. Head of the Central Cultural Revolution Group from 1966. Member of the extreme leftist Gang of Four. Arrested, 1976, and imprisoned.

Kai Feng (1906–1955). Secretary of Communist Youth League Bureau, 1932–35. Mao's opponent during Zunyi Conference, 1935.

Kang Sheng (alias Zhao Yun; real name Zhang Zongke) (1898–1975). Mao's chief spymaster.

Kang Youwei (1858–1927). Chinese philosopher and politician, constitutional monarchist.

Karakhan, Lev Mikhailovich (1889–1937). Soviet ambassador to China, 1923–26.

Khrushchev, Nikita Sergeevich (1894–1971). First secretary of the Soviet Communist Party, 1953–64. Chairman of the Soviet Council of Ministers, 1958–64.

Kim Il Sung (1912–1994). North Korea's premier, 1948–72, and president, 1970–94. Head of the Korean Workers' Party, 1949–94.

Kissinger, Henry A. (b. 1923). U.S. national security advisor, 1969–75. Secretary of state, 1973–77.

Kosygin, Alexei Nikolaevich (1904–1980). Chairman of the Soviet Council of Ministers, 1964–80.

Kovalev, Ivan Vladimirovich (1901–1993). Stalin's representative in China, 1948–50.

Kuai Dafu (b. 1945). Red Guard leader at Tsinghua University, 1966–68.

Lenin, Vladimir Ilich (1870–1924). Leader of the Russian Socialist Revolution, 1917. Head of the Russian Bolshevik party, 1903–24.

Li Da (1890–1966). Cofounder of CCP, 1921.

Li Dazhao (alias T. C. Li, Ta-chao Li) (1889–1927). Chief librarian at Peking University from 1918. One of the first Chinese communists. Member of CCP Central Executive Committee, 1922–27.

Li Fuchun (1900–1975). Deputy premier and head of State Planning Commission from 1954. Politburo member, 1956–69. Opposed Cultural Revolution, February 1967.

Li Hanjun (1890–1927). Cofounder of CCP, 1921.

Li Lisan (real name: Li Longzhi) (1899–1967). An organizer of the Chinese labor movement from 1921. De facto head of CCP, 1928–30. Instigated the so-called Li Lisan adventurist line, 1930.

Li Min (aka Jiaojiao, Tanya Chao Chao) (b. 1937). Mao's eighth child, a daughter from He Zizhen.

Li Na (b. 1940). Mao's tenth child, a daughter from Jiang Qing.

Li Shaojiu (1903–1935). A Red Army commissar and Mao's loyalist. Organized the purge of party and army cadres in Futian, Jiangxi province, December 1930.

Li Weihan (alias Luo Mai, Luo Man) (1896–1984). Member of Renovation of the People Study Society, 1918–19. Head of CCP Central Committee United Front Department, 1948–64.

Liang Qichao (1873–1929). Chinese philosopher and politician, constitutional monarchist.

Lin Biao (alias Li Ting) (1907–1971). PLA marshal from 1955. China's minister of defense, 1959–71. Mao's designated successor, 1969–71. Tried to escape to the Soviet Union but died in a plane crash, September 1971.

Lin Liguo (alias Laohu) (1946–1971). Lin Biao's son. Tried to escape to the Soviet Union but died in a plane crash, September 1971.

Lin Liheng (alias Doudou) (b. 1944). Lin Biao's daughter.

Liu Shaoqi (alias Liu Weihuang) (1898–1969). A leading Chinese communist. Deputy Chairman of CCP Central Committee, 1956–66; Chairman of the PRC, 1959–68; and Mao's designated successor, 1961–66. Main victim of the Cultural Revolution.

Lominadze, Vissarion Vissarionovich (alias Nikolai, Werner) (1897–1935). Comintern representative in China, 1927.

Lu Dingyi (1906–1996). Head of CCP Central Committee Propaganda Department, 1945–66.

Luo Fu (Zhang Wentian) (1900–1976). General secretary of CCP Central Committee, 1935–40. China's deputy foreign minister, 1954–60.

Luo Yigu (1889–1910). Mao's first wife.

Luo Zhanglong (alias Tate Uchirō) (1896–1995). Member of Renovation of the People Study Society, 1918–20. One of the first Chinese communists.

Mao Anqing (alias Mao Yuanyi, Yang Yongshu, Nikolai Yongshu, Kolya) (1923–2007). Mao's second child, a son of Yang Kaihui.

Mao Anying (alias Mao Yuanren, Yang Yongfu, Sergei Yongfu, Yong Fu) (1922–1950). Mao's first child, a son of Yang Kaihui.

Mao Yichang (1870–1920). Mao's father.

Mao Yuanxin (b. 1941). Mao's nephew.

Mao Yuanzhi (1922–1990). Mao's niece.

Mao Zedong (1893–1976). Cofounder of CCP, 1921. Leader of the Chinese communist movement from 1935. Chairman of CCP Central Committee from 1945; Chairman of the PRC, 1954–59.

Mao Zemin (alias Yang Ze, Zhou Den) (1896–1943). Mao's younger brother.

Mao Zetan (1905–1935). Mao's youngest brother.

Maring (alias Ma Lin, Mr. Anderson, Philipp; real name: Hendricus Josephus Franciscus Marie Sneevliet) (1883–1942). Comintern representative in China, 1921–22.

Marx, Karl (1818–1883). Cofounder of Marxism.

Mif, Pavel (alias Petershevskii) (1901–1938). Rector of the Communist University of the Toilers of China, 1927–29. Comintern representative in China, 1930–31.

Mikoyan, Anastas Ivanovich (alias Andreev) (1895–1978). Soviet people's commissar (minister) of internal and foreign trade (supply), 1926–49, 1953–55. First Deputy Chairman of the Council of Ministers, 1955–64.

Montgomery, Bernard Law (1887–1976). British field marshal from 1944.

Nie Rongzhen (1899–1992). Deputy premier, 1956–75. PLA marshal from 1955. Opposed Cultural Revolution, February 1967.

Nie Yuanzi (b. 1921). Red Guard leader at Peking University, 1966–68. Author of the first *dazibao* (big character poster) of the Cultural Revolution, 1966.

Peng Dehuai (1898–1974). Commander in chief of China's troops in Korea, 1950–53. Minister of defense, 1954–59. Criticized Great Leap Forward, 1959.

Peng Gongda (1903–1928). Secretary of Hunan party committee, August–November 1927.

Peng Pai (1896–1929). First organizer of the communist peasant movement in China.

Peng Zhen (1902–1997). First secretary of Beijing Municipal Committee, 1949–66. Mayor of Beijing, 1951–66.

Qu Qiubai (1899–1935). De facto head of CCP, 1927–28. Head of CCP delegation to the Comintern Executive, 1928–30.

Rao Shushi (1903–1975). Headed CCP Central Committee Organizational Department, 1953–54. Purged with Gao Gang, 1955.

Ren Bishi (alias Zheng Ling, Chen Lin) (1904–1950). Opponent of Mao in Central Soviet Area, 1931–33. CCP representative to Comintern, 1938–40. Member of CCP Central Committee Secretariat, 1941–50.

Roy, M. N. (1887–1954). Comintern representative in China, 1927.

Shi Zhe (1905–1998). Mao's interpreter who accompanied him to the Soviet Union, 1949.

Smedley, Agnes (alias Anna) (1892–1950). American left-wing journalist.

Snow, Edgar (1905–1972). American left-wing journalist, author of *Red Star Over China*, 1937.

Snow, Helen Foster (alias Peg, Peggy, Nym Wales) (1907–1997) American left-wing journalist, Edgar Snow's first wife.

Song Qingling (alias Madame Suzy, Leah) (1893–1981). Sun Yat-sen's widow. Left-wing Guomindang member, collaborated with the CCP and the Comintern.

Stalin, Joseph Vissarionovich (alias Filippov, Feng Xi) (1879–1953). General secretary of Bolshevik party, 1922–34. Secretary of Bolshevik party from 1934. Chairman of USSR Council of People's Commissars from 1941.

Sun Yat-sen (real name: Sun Wen) (1866–1925). Father of the Chinese republic. Founder of Guomindang, 1912. Formed a united front with the communists.

Tan Pingshan (1886–1956). A leader of the Chinese Communist Party, 1923–27.

Tan Yankai (1880–1930). Hunan governor, 1911–13, 1916–17, 1920. Chairman of Guomindang government, 1928–30.

Tan Zhenlin (1902–1983). Deputy premier, 1959–75. Opposed Cultural Revolution, February 1967.

Tang, Nancy (real name: Tang Wensheng) (b. 1943). One of Mao's interpreters.

Tang Shengzhi (1889–1970). Hunan militarist who backed Northern Expedition, 1926. Commander of Western column of Guomindang National Revolutionary Army, 1927.

Tang Xiangming (nicknamed Butcher Tang) (1885–1975). Hunan military governor, 1913–16.

Tao Yi (1896–1931). Mao's first love.

Tian Jiaying (1922–1966). Mao's secretary. His support of the peasants' contract system infuriated Mao in 1962.

Vladimirov, Petr Parfenovich (1905–1953). Soviet intelligence officer in CCP Yan'an headquarters, 1942–45.

Voitinsky, Grigorii Naumovich (alias Wu Tingkang; real surname: Zarkhin) (1893–1953). Comintern representative in China, 1920–21.

Wang Hairong (b. 1938). Mao's grandniece. Deputy chief of Protocol Department, Ministry of Foreign Affairs, 1971–72. Deputy foreign minister, 1974–76.

Wang Hongwen (1935–1992). Shanghai rebel chief and member of the extreme leftist Gang of Four during Cultural Revolution. Mao's designated successor, 1972–76. Arrested, 1976, and imprisoned.

Wang Jiaxiang (alias Communard, Zhang Li) (1906–1974). Opponent of Mao in Central Soviet Area, 1931–34. Supported Mao during Long March and Zunyi Conference, 1934–35. Director of International Liaison Department from 1951.

Wang Jingwei (1883–1944). Leader of "Left" Guomindang. Head of Wuhan government, 1927.

Wang Ming (real name: Chen Shaoyu) (1904–1974). De facto head of the CCP, 1931. One of Mao's main antagonists. Lived in Moscow, 1931–37, and from 1956.

Wang Zuo (1898–1930). Bandit chieftain in Jinggang Mountains, collaborated with Mao from 1927.

Wen Qimei (alias Wen Suqin) (1867–1919). Mao's mother.

Wu Han (1909–1969). Playwright and deputy mayor of Beijing. Criticism of his play *The Dismissal of Hai Rui from Office*, 1965, ignited the Cultural Revolution.

Wu Peifu (1874–1939). Hubei militarist in the 1920s.

Xiang Jingyu (1895–1928). Mao's friend and Cai Hesen's wife. An organizer of Chinese women's movement.

Xiang Ying (1898–1941). Acting secretary of the Central Committee Bureau for the Soviet areas, 1930–31.

Xiang Zhongfa (1879–1931). General secretary of the CCP Central Committee from 1928. Executed by Guomindang police.

Xiao San (alias Emi Siao; real name: Xiao Zizhang) (1896–1983). Mao's schoolmate and friend. Chinese writer.

Xiao Yu (real name: Xiao Zisheng) (1894–1976). Mao's schoolmate and friend. Author of *Mao and I Were Beggars,* 1959.

Xu Teli (1877–1968). Mao's teacher at the Provincial First Normal School in Changsha. Famous communist activist.

Yang Changji (alias "Confucius") (1871–1920). Mao's mentor at the Provincial First Normal School in Changsha and father of Yang Kaihui.

Yang Kaihui (alias Xia, "Dawn," "Little Dawn") (1901–1930). Mao's second wife.

Yang Shangkun (1907–1998). Head of the General Affairs Department of the Central Committee, 1949–66. An early victim of the Cultural Revolution, 1966.

Yao Wenyuan (1931–2005). Shanghai party journalist and member of the extreme leftist Gang of Four during the Cultural Revolution. Arrested, 1976, and imprisoned.

Ye Jianying (1897–1986). PLA marshal from 1955. Opposed Cultural Revolution, February 1967. Minister of defense, 1975–78.

Ye Qun (1917–1971). Lin Biao's wife. Died in a plane crash trying to escape to the Soviet Union.

Ye Zilong (1916–2003). One of Mao's secretaries.

Yuan Shikai (1859–1916). Powerful warlord. President of China from February 1912.

Yuan Wencai (1898–1930). Bandit chieftain in Jinggang Mountains, collaborated with Mao from 1927.

Yudin, Pavel Fedorovich (1899–1968). Stalin's envoy in China who reviewed Mao's Marxist credentials, 1950–52. Soviet ambassador in China, 1953–59.

Zhang Chunqiao (1917–2005). Member of the extreme leftist Gang of Four during Cultural Revolution. Arrested, 1976, and imprisoned.

Zhang Guotao (1897–1979). Cofounder of the CCP, 1921. One of Mao's main antagonists. Quit the party, 1938.

Zhang Jingyao (1881–1933). Hunan military governor, 1918–20.

Zhang Yufeng (alias Xiao Zhang, Little Zhang) (b. 1944). The last of Mao's favorite woman intimates and his Secretary for Essential and Confidential Matters.

Zhang Xucliang (1901–2001). Manchurian warlord known as "The Young Marshal," who attempted to arrest Chiang Kai-shek in December 1936, instigating the so-called Xi'an Incident.

Zhao Hengti (1880–1971). Hunan military governor, 1920–26.

Zhou Enlai (alias Moskvin) (1898–1976). A leading Chinese communist who often opposed Mao, 1927–34, and then became Mao's right-hand man and staunch supporter. Premier from 1949. Mao's designated successor, 1972.

Zhu De (alias Danilov) (1886–1976). Mao's closest associate during the civil and anti-Japanese wars, 1928–45. Commander in chief of the Red Army, Eighth Route Army, and People's Liberation Army.

The English spelling of Chinese words and names used in this book is based on the pinyin system of romanization (use of the Latin alphabet) to represent the pronunciation of Chinese characters. We follow the modified pinyin system used by the Library of Congress, which replaces an older system with which readers may be familiar. Thus, for example, we spell the name of the subject of this biography as Mao Zedong, not Mao Tse-tung. (Both romanizations yield the same pronunciation: *Mao Dze-doong*.) For the same reason we spell the name of China's capital as Beijing, not Peking. Following accepted practice, however, we use the traditional English spelling of the names Sun Yat-sen and Chiang Kai-shek and the city Canton, as well as the names of famous institutions such as Peking University and Tsinghua University.

The pronunciation of many pinyin letters is roughly similar to English pronunciation. However, some letters and combinations of letters need explanation. These are listed below.

VOWELS:

a   like *a* in *father*

ai   like the word *eye*

ao   like *ow* in *cow*

e   like *e* in *end*

i   like *i* in *it*

ia   like *ye* in *yes*

o   like *o* in *order*, except before the letters *ng*, when it is pronounced like the two *o*'s in *moon* u like the second *u* in *pursue* when it follows the letters *j, q, x,* and *y;* otherwise, like the double *o* in *moon,* except in the vowel combination *uo,* the *u* is silent

ü like the second *u* in *pursue*

ya like *ya* in *yacht*

ye like *ye* in *yet*

yi like *ee* in *feet*

When two separately pronounced vowels follow each other, an apostrophe is inserted to indicate the syllable break between them. Thus, *Xi'an,* for example, is two syllables while *xian* is just one.

CONSONANTS:

c like *ts* in *tsar*

g like the hard *g* in *get*

j like *j* in *jig*

q like *ch* in *cheese*

r in initial position, like *s* in *vision;* at the end of a word, like the double *r* in *warrior*

x like *s* in *soon*

xi like *shee* in *sheet*

z like *dz* in *adze*

zh like *j* in *jockey*

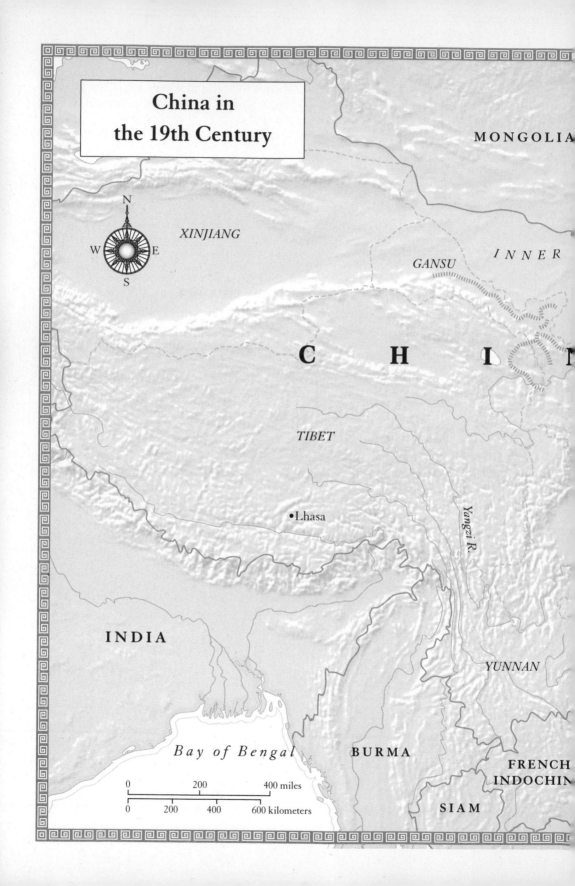

China in
the 19th Century

MONGOLIA

XINJIANG

GANSU

INNER

C H I N

TIBET

Yangzi R.

•Lhasa

INDIA

YUNNAN

Bay of Bengal

BURMA

FRENCH
INDOCHIN

| 0 | | 200 | | 400 miles |
| 0 | 200 | 400 | | 600 kilometers |

SIAM

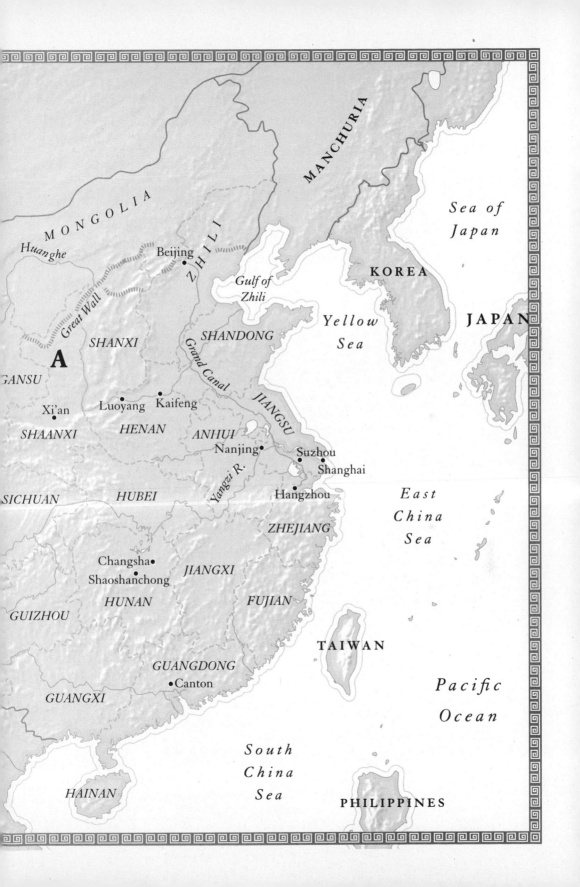

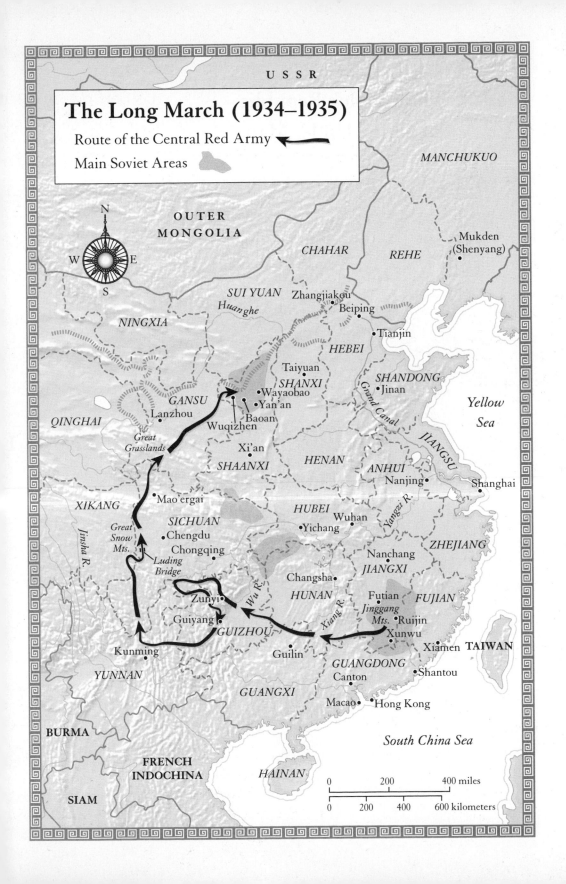

The Long March (1934–1935)

→ Route of the Central Red Army

Main Soviet Areas

USSR

OUTER MONGOLIA

MANCHUKUO

CHAHAR

REHE

Mukden (Shenyang)

SUI YUAN

Huanghe

Zhangjiakou

Beiping

NINGXIA

Tianjin

HEBEI

Taiyuan

SHANXI

Wayaobao

Yan'an

SHANDONG

Jinan

Grand Canal

Yellow Sea

GANSU

Lanzhou

Baoan

Wuqizhen

Great Grasslands

Xi'an

SHAANXI

HENAN

ANHUI

Nanjing

Shanghai

JIANGSU

QINGHAI

XIKANG

Mao'ergai

Great Snow Mts.

Jinsha R.

SICHUAN

Chengdu

Chongqing

Luding Bridge

HUBEI

Wuhan

Yichang

Yangzi R.

ZHEJIANG

Nanchang

JIANGXI

Changsha

Zunyi

Wu R.

HUNAN

Futian

Jinggang Mts.

Ruijin

FUJIAN

Guiyang

GUIZHOU

Xiang R.

Xunwu

Xiamen

TAIWAN

Kunming

Guilin

Shantou

YUNNAN

GUANGDONG

Canton

BURMA

GUANGXI

Macao

Hong Kong

FRENCH INDOCHINA

HAINAN

South China Sea

SIAM

| 0 | 200 | 400 miles |

| 0 | 200 | 400 | 600 kilometers |

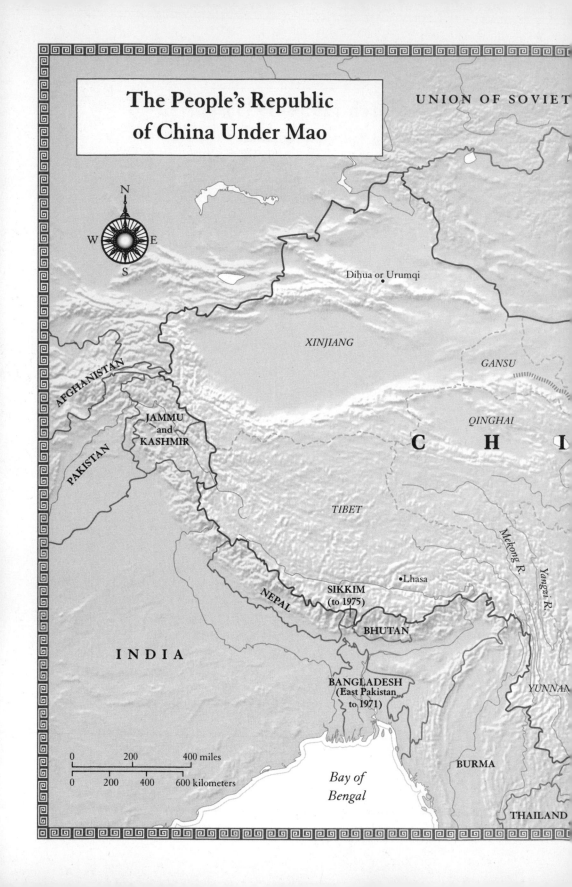

The People's Republic of China Under Mao

UNION OF SOVIET

AFGHANISTAN

PAKISTAN

JAMMU
and
KASHMIR

NEPAL

SIKKIM
(to 1975)

BHUTAN

BANGLADESH
(East Pakistan
to 1971)

INDIA

Dihua or Urumqi

XINJIANG

GANSU

QINGHAI

C H I

TIBET

Lhasa

Mekong R.

Yangzi R.

YUNNAN

BURMA

THAILAND

Bay of
Bengal

0   200   400 miles

0   200   400   600 kilometers

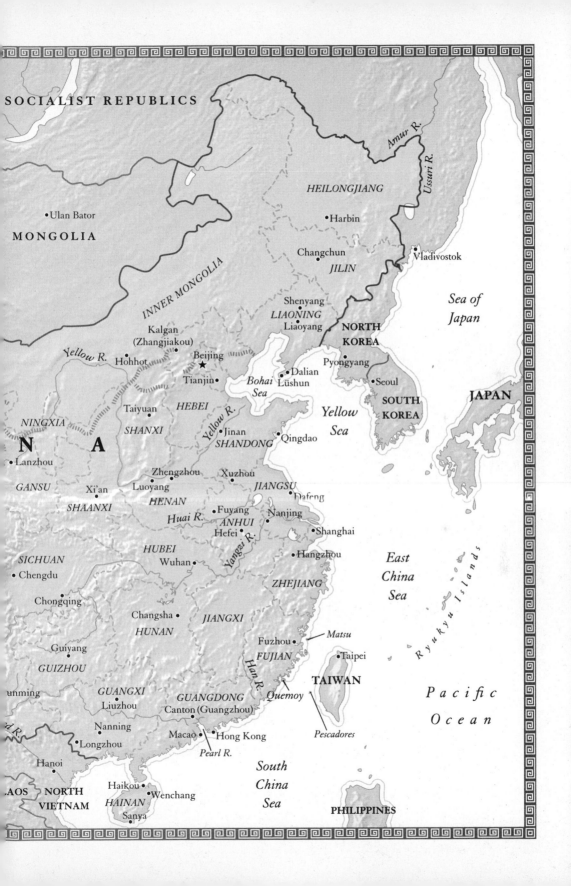

MAO

MYTHS AND REALITIES

Historical figures merit objective biographies. Yet the challenge of writing such biographies is daunting even under the best of circumstances. The biographer must pursue a seemingly endless trail of published and unpublished sources, often in a variety of languages, exhaust the contents of numerous archives, winnow truth and fact from rumor and falsehood, strike the right balance between the public persona and the private person, and judge the wisdom and folly of the subject over the span of a lifetime. Such difficulties are multiplied when the subject of the biography is the leader of a closed society that jealously guards its secrets. This is certainly the case with Mao Zedong, the founder of modern China. But now, more than thirty-five years after his death in 1976, with the release of important new documents from China and exclusive access to major archives in the former Soviet Union, a clearer, more nuanced, more complete portrait of the most important Chinese leader in modern times can be drawn. That is the aim of this biography.

To be sure, Mao has been the subject of numerous biographies in Western languages since the American journalist Edgar Snow first wrote down Mao's life story just past its midpoint, in July 1936. A year later Snow published that story as the centerpiece of *Red Star Over China,* an influential book that helped shape history and remains in print to this day. For what it tells about the lineage of Western-language Mao biographies—a lineage from which our own biography significantly departs—it is worth relating why that encounter between the guerrilla commander cum leader of the Chinese Communist Party and the young American reporter took place.

Already a well-known journalist by the mid-1930s, Snow was extremely sympathetic to the Chinese communist movement, although he was not a Marxist. Among the mainstream media for which he wrote, including the *New York Herald Tribune, Foreign Affairs,* and the *Saturday Evening Post,* he enjoyed a reputation for being independent-minded, unlike many other leftist reporters in China, who openly paraded their pro-communist views.

It was precisely this reputation that attracted the attention of the leaders of the Chinese Communist Party, including Mao Zedong. They intended to make use of the thirty-one-year-old American to improve their public image and expand their political influence. Snow had his own reasons for seeking out Mao. An ambitious journalist with an instinct for the big story, he jumped at the opportunity for a sensational scoop. Each man intended to use the other for his own purposes. Snow arrived in Baoan, in northern Shaanxi province, on July 13, 1936, just two days after Mao Zedong himself set up camp in that remote and desolate town. Mao was fleeing from Generalissimo Chiang Kai-shek, head of the National Government and the leader of the Nationalist Party (the Guomindang, or GMD), whose forces had inflicted a serious defeat on the Chinese Red Army.

Mao granted Snow's request for a series of interviews, in which he first spoke at length about his childhood and youth before outlining his career as a communist revolutionary. The communists had made a shrewd choice picking Snow. The impressionable American came to view Mao as a wise philosopher-king, Lincolnesque in appearance, perspicacious, easygoing, and self-confident. "He certainly believed in his own star and destiny to rule," Snow recalled.[1] Transcribing Mao's monologue into his notebook during long nights in the candlelit cave where they met, Snow was sooner Mao's amanuensis than a critical journalist. Once his mission was accomplished, Snow returned to Beijing with his precious notes and began working on the manuscript that became *Red Star Over China.*

Just as Mao and Snow had hoped, *Red Star Over China* created a sensation, particularly among liberal intellectuals and leftists in the West. Its intimate portrayal of Mao as a romantic revolutionary struck a sympathetic chord with Western readers disillusioned with the austere figure of an increasingly authoritarian Chiang Kai-shek. Snow's pioneering work set the tone for many subsequent books by authors who were equally or even more sympathetic in their depictions of Mao. There was only one major point on which these later works differed from Snow's. While Snow viewed Mao as a faithful follower of Soviet Marxism, other writers asserted that as early as the late 1930s, the Chinese Communist Party (CCP) under Mao's leadership had become autonomous and self-reliant. According to this view, Mao, an independent thinker and actor, had basically distanced himself from Moscow, unlike the dogmatic Chinese Stalinists whom he had bested in intraparty struggles. Mao stood tall; he was his own man, an authentic Chinese revolutionary, not Stalin's stooge.

This was Mao's main attraction for authors trying to explain the Chinese revolution to American readers.

As early as the late 1940s and early 1950s, leading American China scholars including John King Fairbank, Benjamin I. Schwartz, Conrad Brandt, and Robert North propounded what became the classical formulation about Mao's "independence," both with respect to his relations with Stalin and his views of China.[2] They wrote that Stalin mistrusted Mao and considered him a "peasant nationalist" rather than a communist. Furthermore, the upsurge of the Chinese revolution in the countryside under the leadership of Mao seemed to disprove the orthodox Marxist view regarding the "historic role" of the working class. China's "peasant revolution" was the opening act in what promised to be a dramatic era of peasant revolutions throughout the postcolonial world. After the split between the Soviet and Chinese communist parties in the early 1960s, Russian and Chinese authors followed a similar line.

Meanwhile, Mao underwent a permutation from down-to-earth revolutionary commander into what one biographer in the early 1960s called the "emperor of the blue ants," in reference to the blue clothing all Chinese wore.[3] After proclaiming the establishment of the People's Republic of China (PRC) on October 1, 1949, Mao moved into the Forbidden City in Beijing, the former imperial quarters. As the cult of his personality developed in the following years, he became inaccessible except to his close colleagues and members of his entourage. His public appearances were carefully stage-managed and his interviews and pronouncements assumed an increasingly Delphic character. The Western-language biographies of Mao published during his lifetime, including the best one, by the prominent China scholar Stuart R. Schram in 1967,[4] were constructed largely on the basis of published Communist Party documents; Mao's published writings, speeches, and statements; impressions of foreigners who had been granted audiences with Mao; a few memoirs by political acquaintances and adversaries; and a variety of other scattered sources. The thesis of Mao's independence and creative adaptation of Marxism to Chinese circumstances continued to occupy center stage.

At first glance, this thesis seems well-founded. Until the end of 1949, Mao never visited Moscow even once, and Stalin did not know him personally. At the same time, negative reports calling Mao "anti-Leninist" and accusing him of the cardinal sin of "Trotskyism" regularly reached the Kremlin from various sources of information inside and outside the Chinese Communist Party. Thus Khrushchev's assertion that Stalin considered Mao a "cave Marxist" appears logical.[5] In the late 1950s, after the Twentieth Congress of the Soviet Communist Party condemned Stalinism, Mao himself often recalled that he sensed Stalin's mistrust of him.[6]

On closer inspection, however, the received wisdom regarding Mao's relationship to Stalin and the Soviet Union turns out to be wrong. In reality, as newly available Soviet and Chinese archives reveal, Mao was a faithful follower of Stalin who took pains to reassure the Boss of his loyalty and who dared to deviate from the Soviet model only after Stalin's death.

This revelation is one of many reasons why a thorough reassessment of Mao is warranted. The truth has long reposed in the secret archives of the CCP, the Soviet Communist Party, and the Communist International (Comintern). Only recently have these archives become available, in whole or in part. The most interesting of innumerable revelations regarding Mao's policies, outlook, and personal life are contained in unpublished documents regarding Mao, his enemies, and his friends, preserved in the former Central Party Archive of the Central Committee of the Soviet Communist Party in Moscow. The Bolsheviks began to organize the archive shortly after the October Revolution of 1917. From the very beginning its main task was to collect documents not only on the history of the Bolshevik party, but also on the history of the international labor and communist movements. After the liquidation of the Comintern in 1943, all of its documentary collections were transferred to the Central Party Archive. In the 1950s the archives of the Communist Information Bureau (Cominform) were also deposited there. Finally, in June 1999, the former Communist Youth League Archives were merged into the collection. Today these consolidated archives are known as the Russian State Archive of Social and Political History. A brief survey of the contents of these archives highlights their importance as a source of new information that we have thoroughly mined for this biography of Mao Zedong.

First, they are the biggest depository of documents in the world on the international communist movement and the history of the Communist Party of the Soviet Union (CPSU). They house about two million written documents, 12,105 photographic materials, and 195 documentary films, which are organized in 669 thematic collections. A core component of the archives is an extensive collection of papers related to the Chinese communist movement. These include voluminous files of the CCP delegation to the Executive Committee of the Comintern (ECCI); the CCP Central Committee's various accounts and financial receipts; the Comintern and the Bolshevik party's directives to China; the papers of Lenin, Stalin, Trotsky, and other Bolshevik leaders; secret reports of Chinese communist and Chinese nationalist representatives to the Comintern; and personal dossiers on many leading Chinese revolutionaries.

The collection of private documents relating to the Chinese communists is of particular interest. Unlike many other archival materials, these were not opened to most scholars even during the brief period of the Yeltsin ideological "thaw" in the early 1990s. This collection has always been secured in a top-secret section of the archives. Even today public access to the files is highly restricted. Only a very few specialists, including one of us, Alexander V. Pantsov, have been permitted access to these materials and continue to enjoy such access on the basis of personal ties with archivists and scholars in contemporary Russia. This restricted collection comprises 3,328 personal dossiers, including those of Mao Zedong, Liu Shaoqi, Zhou Enlai, Zhu De, Deng Xiaoping, Wang Ming, and many other top members of the CCP leadership.

The dossier on Mao Zedong is the most impressive. It contains fifteen volumes of unique papers, including his political reports; private correspondence; stenographic records of meetings between Mao and Stalin, Stalin and Zhou Enlai, and Mao and Khrushchev; Mao's medical records, compiled by his Soviet physicians; secret accounts by KGB and Comintern agents; personal materials regarding Mao's wives and children, including the birth certificate of his previously unknown ninth child, born in Moscow; accusations against Mao written by his political enemies within the CCP leadership; and a variety of Soviet embassy and KGB secret messages related to the political situation in the PRC from the late 1950s to the early 1970s. *We are the first biographers of Mao to make use of all these materials—materials that proved invaluable in reassessing Mao's private and political life.*

Supplementing the Russian and Chinese archival sources is a large volume of biographical material, reminiscences, and handbooks published in recent years in the PRC. Among them are memoirs and diaries of Mao's secretaries, paramours, relatives, and acquaintances that are also helpful in our reinterpretation of Mao's life.

No less important are documents from the still highly restricted collections of the Central Committee of the CCP in Beijing, recently made known through the efforts of Chinese historians. These archival materials include a thirteen-volume set of Mao Zedong's manuscripts, starting from the founding of the PRC; a seven-volume chronicle of the Mao clan based in Shaoshan; records of Mao's private talks; and various collections of Mao's previously unknown draft papers, speeches, comments, critiques, notes, and poetry.

Our biography of Mao Zedong is based upon all of these unique archives and newly available documents as well as many interviews with people who knew Mao. As such it is up-to-date. A recent biography of Mao by Jung Chang and Jon Halliday, *Mao: The Unknown Story,* was criticized in the academic community on the grounds of unreliability and distorted judgments.[7] We tried to avoid these shortcomings by making careful and discriminating use of a wider array of sources than any other biographer, weighing evidence carefully, and presenting sound and forceful judgments unmarred by political considerations. This dispassionate attitude allows us to present the Great Helmsman as the multifaceted figure that he was—a revolutionary and a tyrant, a poet and a despot, a philosopher and a politician, a husband and a philanderer. We show that Mao was neither a saint nor a demon, but rather a complicated figure who indeed tried his best to bring about prosperity and gain international respect for his country. Yet he made numerous errors, having trapped himself in a cul-de-sac of a political and ideological utopia, and basking in his cult of personality while surrounding himself with sycophantic courtiers. Without a doubt he was one of the greatest utopians of the twentieth century, but unlike Lenin and Stalin, he was not only a political adventurer but also a national revolutionary. Not only did he promote radical economic and social reforms, but he also brought about a national revolution in former semicolonial China and he united mainland China, which had been engulfed in a civil war. Thus it was Mao who renewed the world's respect for China and the Chinese people, who had long been despised by the developed Western world and Japan. Yet his domestic policies produced national tragedies that cost the lives of tens of millions of Chinese.

We also tried to write a lively and interesting human story that devotes a lot of attention to Mao's character and his personal and family life as well as to his political and military leadership. It is filled with fascinating stories from memoirs and interviews that present Mao as son, husband, father, friend, and lover, as well as strategist, theorist, statesman, and political infighter. From many angles we show Mao as a man of complex moods, subject to bouts of deep depression as well as flights of manic exaltation, a man of great force of will and ambition who achieved virtually unlimited power during his leadership of the Chinese Communist Party and of the People's Republic of China. Our goal was to draw a living portrait that we hope will engage even readers who know little about Mao and China. We also tried to describe the kaleidoscopic array of people Mao encountered and the places in China where he lived, studied, worked, and relaxed, from his native village of Shaoshanchong to the Forbidden City in Beijing, where he lived as a virtual emperor. Our book, which tells the history of modern China through the life of its most important leader, tries to convey the feel, smell, and texture of China.

Our research has also uncovered many new and startling facts about Mao's life that require us to revise commonly accepted views of the history of the Chinese communist movement, of the history of the PRC, and particularly of Mao himself. On the basis of extensive research, we document the continuing financial dependence upon Moscow of the CCP from its founding in 1921 through the early 1950s. Careful attention to the life of Mao suggests that the history of the CCP at the time can be understood only if one takes into account its continuing dependence on Moscow for authoritative policy guidance and direction. Archival materials on major figures such as Zhang Guotao, Zhou Enlai, Liu Shaoqi, Cai Hesen, Qu Qiubai, Deng Zhongxia, Wang Ruofei, Chen Yu, Li Lisan, Gao Gang, Yu Xuxiong, and others also suggest that the CCP remained subordinate to Stalin and his lieutenants, who controlled the Comintern and held the fate of CCP leaders in their hands. This is demonstrated, for example, by reference to the countless humiliating interrogations and self-criticism that leading Chinese communists were forced to undergo because of alleged mistakes or "Trotskyist activity." There is even evidence suggesting that in 1938 Stalin was planning a major show trial of Comintern officials, including Zhou Enlai, Liu Shaoqi, Kang Sheng, Chen Yun, Li Lisan, and some others. Had he not backed away from this plan, many top leaders of the CCP might have become his victims. Some documents, however, suggest that he murdered most of the CCP delegates to the Seventh Comintern Congress, held in July–August 1935.

Stalin did not include Mao Zedong on his "blacklist." Indeed, it was Stalin himself and the Comintern that assisted Mao's rise to power in the Chinese Communist Party. To be sure, Mao was not like East Germany's Walter Ulbricht, Bulgaria's Todor Zhivkov, or other dependent leaders of Central and East European communist parties, but there can no longer be any doubt that he was loyal to Stalin, whom he looked to for guidance as well as support. (Our treatment of the Mao-Stalin meetings in December 1949–January 1950 is revealing in this respect. Equally germane is our account of Mao's uneasy relations with Stalin during the Korean War. Stalin did not try to unite Korea but rather attempted to weaken the United States by involving it in a conflict not only with North Korea, but also with China. By doing so Stalin tried to provoke revolutions across the globe.) It was only after Stalin's death in March 1953 that Mao began to distance himself from the Soviet leadership. He came to view Khrushchev as an untrustworthy buffoon and deliberately treated him with contempt. We show that personal enmity between Mao and Khrushchev was one of the main reasons for the Sino-Soviet rift. By the late 1960s this rift had escalated to a degree that has often been underestimated. Drawing upon the former Soviet secret archives we demonstrate that in the late 1960s Sino-Soviet relations became so tense that the Soviet leadership had even begun to consider armed intervention in the affairs of the PRC, such as undertaking an atomic attack against the PRC's industrial centers or blowing up Chinese atomic sites.

We also tried to present a vivid and objective portrait of the aging Mao from the late 1950s to his death in September 1976, a period marked by Mao's audacious attempts to remold Chinese society along the lines of a uniquely Maoist socialism during the Great Leap Forward (1958–61) and the Cultural Revolution (1966–76), efforts that caused tragedy on a vast scale. All these events are examined on the basis of the new archival materials and with the aim of identifying the overarching objectives and personal rivalries among top leaders whom Mao, increasingly paranoid as he aged, skillfully manipulated to advance his aims.

In contrast to conventional views, we show that the Cultural Revolution was not merely Mao's final struggle for power, but rather a serious if tragically flawed effort to achieve his utopian vision of creating a new, ideal citizen in a new, ideal society. By the mid-1960s Mao had come to believe that the socialist reconstruction of sociopolitical relations was insufficient. Even after the construction of socialism people would remain inert and egotistical. Each person would harbor a greedy ego dreaming of returning to capitalism. Thus, if things were just allowed to slide, even the Communist Party itself could degenerate. That is why he arrived at the conviction that it would be impossible to build communism without first destroying the old, traditional values of Chinese culture. However, he obviously underestimated human nature. That misjudgment caused the failure not only of the Cultural Revolution, but also of the entire Maoist project. The system of barracks communism, a stark and regimented society, that Mao envisioned died with Mao himself.

In conclusion, our task as historians was neither to blame nor to praise Mao. It is far too late to settle any scores with Mao. He is dead and answerable only, as he himself said, to Karl Marx. The task we set ourselves, rather, was to portray in all essential details one of the most powerful and influential political leaders of the twentieth century. It is our hope that this book will help readers to achieve a deeper and more accurate understanding of Mao, of the times and country that produced him, and of the China he created.

PART ONE

THE APPRENTICE

THE FOSTER CHILD OF
THE BODHISATTVA

The South China village of Shaoshanchong, in Xiangtan county, Hunan province, sits in a narrow valley squeezed between hills covered with evergreen trees and rice paddies, the blue sky above. In the distance looms Shaoshan Mountain, which gave its name to the village and is particularly revered by Buddhists. A branch railroad runs from Changsha, the provincial capital, to the nearest town, which is also called Shaoshan. It takes the local train about three hours to traverse the hundred-mile distance. A line of buses parked in the broad square fronting the railway station awaits visitors. "Chairman Mao's birthplace! Chairman Mao's birthplace!" cry the conductors. A jolting, half-hour ride brings you to a village street, which takes you past flooded rice fields and lotus-filled ponds to a large, thirteen-room brick house cum museum. To the left and right are similar or slightly smaller typical peasant dwellings. The atmosphere is that of a typical rural community. A small village like so many others in Hunan, it is distinguished by being the birthplace of a man who changed the history of his country and whose influence is still felt throughout the world long after his death.

Many of the inhabitants of the village within this valley were surnamed Mao. This was where their clan had settled. All of the people named Mao traced their lineage back to the bold warrior Mao Taihua, a native of neighboring Jiangxi province who had left his native region in the mid-fourteenth century to take part in the campaign of the imperial army in Yunnan province against the Mongols, who had ruled China since the 1270s. The Mongols' main force was defeated by the rebel army of the monk Zhu Yuanzhang, who in 1368 proclaimed himself the emperor of a new Chinese dynasty, the Ming. There in distant Yunnan, Mao Taihua married a local girl and in 1380 took her and their children to Huguang (now known as Hunan), where they settled in Xiangxiang county, south of Xiangtan. Some ten years later two of his sons moved north to Xiangtan county and made their homes in Shaoshanchong. They were the progenitors of the Mao clan in Shaoshan.[1]

The future supreme leader of China was born into one such family, that of Mao Yichang, on the nineteenth day of the eleventh month of the Year of the Snake according to the lunar calendar. By the official dynastic reckoning, this was in the nineteenth year of the reign of Emperor Guangxu, of the Qing (Manchu) dynasty, which had ruled China since 1644. The Guangxu (Bright Beginning) era had begun in 1875, proclaimed in the name of the young emperor Zaitian, who was then four years old, by his maternal aunt, the Empress Dowager Ci Xi. According to the Western calendar, the birth of a son, a joyful event in any Chinese family, occurred in the family of Mao Yichang on December 26, 1893.

Mao's father could hardly contain his happiness, but his mother was worried. The baby was very big, and she was afraid she might not be able to nurse him. She had already given birth to two sons who had died in infancy. Wrapping the newborn in swaddling clothes, she set off to see a Buddhist nun who was living in the mountains, and with tears in her eyes, asked her to look after the infant. But the nun refused. The baby looked very healthy, and there was no need to worry over him. The hermit nun, after recommending prayers to ensure the child's well-being, advised the distraught mother to keep her son. Snatching up her baby, the mother rushed off to her father's house in a neighboring district. There she stopped in front of a small temple perched atop a twelve-foot high rock dedicated to the Bodhisattva Guan Yin, the Goddess of Mercy. Prostrating herself, physically and emotionally exhausted, she prayed that the Bodhisattva would agree to become her son's foster mother.[2]

In keeping with tradition, the parents of the birth mother were quickly informed of the birth of the boy and a rooster was presented to them. If it had been a girl, they would have been given a hen.

The Chinese considered the nine months spent in the womb as the first year of life, so a baby was considered to be one year old at birth. An ancient ritual required that the newborn be swaddled in cloths sewn from his father's old trousers. More old trousers, supposed to absorb any kind of contagion, were hung above the cradle. The infant was bathed only on the third day, in the presence of guests who were allowed to view him for the first time. On the day of the infant's first bath, the father presented sacrifices to the spirits of the ancestors, and put an onion and ginger into the infant's hot bathwater, symbolizing mind and health. Picking up the infant, the mother handed him to the midwife who had assisted in the delivery. Holding the onion root to the baby's head, the midwife intoned, "First, be smart, second, be wise, third, be cunning." Afterward she pressed a lock or a bar against the infant's mouth, arms, and legs, and said, "Be quiet." A scale was placed on the infant's chest so that he would weigh a lot, and boiled eggs were placed against his cheeks for happiness. A red string from which silver coins dangled was tied around the infant's wrist. After a month the infant's head would be shaved, leaving locks of hair at the temples and the nape of the neck. This was an important event at which the infant was given a name. Guests again gathered, bringing gifts of money, pork, fish, fruit, and decorated eggs.

From time immemorial, parents had chosen names for their newborns with the aid of Daoist fortune-tellers. In accordance with tradition, Mao Yichang consulted the local geomancer, who advised him of the need to use the "water" sign in his son's name, because this was lacking in his horoscope.[3] The wishes of the geomancer dovetailed with the imperatives of the clan's genealogical chronicle. Each generation had specific Chinese characters allotted to it that were supposed to be used in the given names of all the males of that particular generation. The given names themselves could be quite different, but all of them had to contain these common characters that denoted membership in the generation to which they belonged. In the generation of Yichang's newborn son (the twentieth generation of the Mao clan), this signifier was the character ze, the left side of which contains the three strokes of the "water" element. The character ze had a dual meaning: it signified moisture and to moisten as well as kindness, goodness, and beneficence. Mao Yichang chose dong, meaning "east," as the second character of the infant's given name. The name Zedong was unusually beautiful—"Benefactor of the East!" At the same time, again in accordance with tradition, the child was given a second, unofficial name to be used on special, ceremonial occasions: Runzhi, which means "Dewy Orchid." Mao's mother gave him yet another name, shi, or stone, which was supposed to protect him from all misfortunes and hint at his kinship with the Bodhisattva. Since Mao was the third son in the family, his mother called him shisanyazi, literally the Third Child Named Stone.

Mao Zedong was born into a small household. Besides his father and mother there was only his paternal grandfather. (Mao Zedong's paternal grandmother, named Liu, had died nine years before his birth, on May 20, 1884, when she was thirty-seven years old.) The family occupied only half of the house, the eastern or left wing. Neighbors lived in the other half. In front of the house were a pond and rice paddy and in back, pine and bamboo groves. Almost everyone in the village of some six hundred households was poor. Hard and exhausting work on tiny plots of land yielded little income.

Mao Zedong's paternal grandfather, Mao Enpu, had been poor his entire life, leaving his son debt-ridden. Mao Zedong's father, Mao Yichang, however, was able to wrench himself loose from poverty. An only child, Yichang was born on October 15, 1870. At the age of ten he was betrothed to a girl three and a half years older than him, named Wen Qimei. They were married five years later. Soon afterward, on account of his father's debts, Yichang was drafted into the local Xiang Army. (Xiang, the traditional name of Hunan, was named after the Xiang River, which flows through the province.) When Mao Yichang returned after a long absence, by spending his accumulated army pay he was able to redeem the land his father had lost, and became an independent cultivator. He was crude and irascible, but very hardworking and frugal. According to Mao Zedong's daughter, who evidently heard this from her father, Mao Yichang often repeated, "Poverty is not the result of eating too much or spending too much. Poverty comes from an inability to do sums. Whoever can do sums will have enough to live by; whoever cannot will squander even mountains of gold!"[4] Yichang's wife, who was known in the village as Suqin ("Simple Toiler")[5] because of her industry and goodness, helped him make his way in the world. By the time Mao Zedong was ten, the year his grandfather died, Mao Yichang by dint of incredible exertions had managed to save up some money and acquire a bit more land.[6] Eight years earlier, a younger brother, Zemin, was born, and a year after the grandfather's death, a third son, named Zetan. In addition to these children and the two sons who had died prior to Mao Zedong's birth, Mao's parents also had two daughters, but both of them died during infancy.

Mao's mother tried to imbue her sons with her own religious feelings. During his childhood and adolescence, Mao often accompanied his mother to a Buddhist temple, and she dreamed that her eldest son might become a monk. Mao's father, however, did not share her wishes, but neither did he object very much. He treated Buddha with secret respect, although he gave no outward signs of this. It happened that once, not far from the village, he had encountered a tiger on the road. Mao's father was terrified, but apparently so was the tiger. Man and tiger ran off in opposite directions. Mao's father interpreted this as a warning from on high. Always a religious skeptic until then, he now began to fear excessive atheism.[7]

Although Mao Yichang respected and feared Buddha, he thought it more useful for his eldest son to grasp the wisdom of Confucianism, the traditional philosophy derived from the sayings of the ancient philosopher Confucius (551–479 BCE) and his followers. China's political system was based on Confucian principles that demanded moral perfection from humanity. According to Confucius, people had to fulfill the sacred covenants (*li*) bestowed by Heaven, among which the most important were humanity (*ren*), filial piety (*xiao*), and virtue (*de*). Only by observing these Heavenly laws could one achieve the highest ethical ideal, the goal that Confucianism strived for.

Individual conscience determined whether one actually followed the teachings of Confucius, but as a practical matter it was impossible to have a career without knowledge of the sayings of the philosopher. An ability to juggle quotations from Confucius was necessary in order to receive an official post. Anyone who was unfamiliar with the *Analects* of Confucius and the other books of the classical canon, including the *Mencius,* the *Great Learning,* and the *Golden Mean,* was considered uneducated.

Therefore, not surprisingly, Mao's father, who had only two years of schooling, was eager for his eldest son to master Confucian learning. Yichang had lost a lawsuit regarding a hilly parcel of land because he had been unable to bolster his case with citations from Confucius. The court instead ruled in favor of the defendant, who had demonstrated his deep knowledge of the classics. Mao's daughter writes that her grandfather decided at that point, "Let my son become just such an educated man and stand in on my behalf."[8] Accordingly, Mao Zedong was sent to a private elementary school in Shaoshan, where he was required to memorize the Confucian classics.

Mao memorized the sayings of the revered philosopher for purely utilitarian reasons, to vanquish others in arguments by introducing an apt quotation at precisely the right moment, but the moral-ethical precepts of Confucius seem to have left not a trace in his soul. Mao's daughter recounts how her father once bested his own teacher in an argument. "One hot day," she writes,

> when the teacher was absent from school, Father suggested to his classmates that they go swimming in a pond. When the teacher saw his students bathing in their birthday suits, he considered this extremely indecent and decided to punish them. But Father parried with a quotation from the *Analects* in which Confucius praised bathing in cold water. Father opened his book, located the needed quotation, and read the words of Confucius out loud. The teacher now remembered that Confucius really had said this, but he could not lose face. Infuriated, he went to complain to Grandfather.
>
> "Your Runzhi is absolutely unbearable. Once he knows more than me, I will no longer teach him!"

Mao was equally adept at deploying quotations from Confucius in his private disputes with his father, who constantly cursed his son for being disrespectful and lazy. Sometimes Mao won out, but usually the disputes ended badly for him. His father, who prized filial piety above all other Confucian principles, would thrash his son when he dared to contradict him. "I'll kill you, such a mongrel who respects no rules whatsoever," he shouted at Mao.[9] He also whipped his two other sons. Mao's mother trembled over her darlings and tried to defend them, but usually failed.

The family conflicts, the cruelty of his father, and the defenselessness of his mother, whom he greatly loved and pitied, inevitably affected the character of Mao. He grew into a passionate and proud rebel no less stubborn than his father, whom he greatly resembled.[10] Although irritated by his father's stern temper, Mao himself became increasingly harsh, bitter, and headstrong.

His stubbornness may have had ethnopsychological as well as family roots. The Hunanese, who season their food with liberal doses of hot red pepper, are famous throughout China for their hotheaded temperament. "Hot like their food," is the way they're usually characterized.

Many years later Mao provided a semifacetious Marxist explanation for the conflicts within his family. In July 1936, when he granted the American journalist Edgar Snow's request for an interview, he said:

> As middle peasants then my family owned fifteen *mou* [1 *mou* or *mu* is one-sixth of an acre] of land . . . my father accumulated a little capital and in time purchased seven more *mou,* which gave the family the status of "rich" peasants. . . .
>
> At the time my father was a middle peasant he began to deal in grain transport and selling, by which he made a little money. After he became a "rich" peasant, he devoted most of his time to that business. He hired a full-time farm laborer, and put his children to work on the farm, as well as his wife. I began to work at farming tasks when I was six years old. My father had no shop for his business. He simply purchased grain from the poor farmers and then transported it to the city merchants, where he got a higher price. In the winter, when the rice was being ground, he hired an extra laborer to work on the farm, so that at that time there were seven mouths to feed. . . . He gave us no money whatever, and the most meager food. . . . To me he gave neither eggs nor meat.

Somewhat later, Mao, laughing, added,

> There were "two parties" in the family. One was my father, the Ruling Power. The Opposition was made up of myself, my mother, my brother, and sometimes even the laborer. [Mao was referring to his brother Zemin, since his brother Zetan had not yet been born.] In the "United Front" of the Opposition, however, there was a difference of opinion. My mother advocated a policy of indirect attack. She criticized any overt display of emotion and attempts at open rebellion against the Ruling Power. She said it was not the Chinese way. . . . My dissatisfaction increased. The dialectical struggle in our family was constantly developing.

Quarrels between a father and his eldest son were uncommon. Mao even got into fierce disputes with his father in the presence of others, an unthinkable display of impudence. In his interview with Snow, Mao said of his father, "I learned to hate him." [11]

Mao's thrifty father gradually made his way in the world, buying up the land deeds of other peasants and managing to amass a rather considerable fortune, some two to three thousand Chinese silver dollars. The majority of Chinese peasants lived in grinding poverty. Generally speaking, late-nineteenth and early-twentieth-century Qing China was an extremely backward, wild, and medieval country. Capitalism was just in its infancy and had not yet made a serious impact on society. Contemporary capitalist enterprises were established in places like Shanghai, Tianjin, and Wuhan, far from Shaoshan. Only in these few cities was there growing economic prosperity. In the villages life went on as it had since ancient times. The vast majority of peasants expected no benefits from the market. In the autumn they typically had to sell part of the grain they needed themselves, at heavily discounted prices, to profiteers like Mao's father to pay off their debts. In the spring, when prices had risen, they then had to buy back a like amount of grain, suffering severe financial losses in the process, just in order to avoid famine.[12] Paupers and the rural underclass, including vagabonds, homeless beggars, and other riffraff, who made up a significant part of the population, roughly 40–45 million out of a total population of about 400 million, were particularly ill-disposed to ordinary businessmen and traders. A full tenth of the Chinese population was poor and unemployed.[13] These were the people who contemptuously referred to peasants like Mao's father as *tuhao* (masters of land) or bloodsuckers. Since in the cities there were few modern enterprises that could offer employment to those who wanted it, the great mass of the population was confined within its native places. There at least some of them could find odd jobs, especially during the rice-planting and rice-harvesting seasons. But most of them had no such luck. Hordes of ragged and filthy people wandered along the rural roads, begging for alms. In the market squares one often saw peasants holding signs, offering to sell their young daughters, and sometimes their sons, whom they had brought with them in woven willow baskets.

Many peasants joined mafia-type bandit gangs like the Triad Society and engaged in robbing the *tuhao*. Cruel insurrections were a common occurrence not only in Hunan, but in other provinces as well.

In the cold winter of 1906, the district of Pingxiang, about 150 miles from Shaoshan, was in the throes of a vast insurrection begun by the Hongjiang (Prosperity) society, a branch of the powerful Hongmeng (Red Brotherhood), which had branches in many provinces in south and southeast China. Particularly active on the border between Hunan and Jiangxi, between Shaoshan and Pingxiang, it sought to overthrow the alien Manchu dynasty (Qing), which had conquered China in the middle of the seventeenth century, and restore the previous Ming dynasty. The members of the society—the "Brotherhood of the Sword," as they styled themselves—were bound by a unique religious ritual that was kept hidden from the uninitiated. They were obligated to help each other in all circumstances, and they believed in magical Daoist and Buddhist exorcisms as well as in shamanism and sorcery. They practiced martial arts in the belief that a series of physical and spiritual exercises (*wushu* and *qigong*) would render them invulnerable.

Staging an insurrection in Pingxiang, the Hongjiang society openly proclaimed its goals via two slogans: 1) "Overthrow the Qing and restore the Ming," and 2) "Destroy the rich, help the poor." Rumors about the uprising quickly spread through the neighboring districts of Jiangxi and Hunan. Armed with sabers, spears, and swords, the rebels terrorized the surrounding districts, attacking the homes of the *tuhao* and pillaging the *lieshen* (literally, the evil literati), the term the poor peasants applied to the wealthy rural gentry. They made off with the money and supplies of the relatively prosperous peasants and held wild orgies in their homes. A portion of the stolen goods was distributed to the poor. After ten days government troops suppressed the uprising, but the local people were unable to calm down for a long time. Zhang Guotao, a native of Pingxiang, who was then nine years old and who became later one of the founders of the CCP and Mao's chief rival in a power struggle, sympathized with the insurrectionists, but was terrified nonetheless. He remembered the scene this way:

People came and went on the road—some empty-handed, others carrying things—all in silent haste. But we three youngsters encountered nothing exceptional as we trudged along. After five *li* [a *li* is about .3 miles] we arrived at a small general store that the Wens owned . . . the shopkeeper cautioned us against walking it alone . . . Since he tended the shop alone and could not leave it to accompany us, he suggested that we eat there and spend the night. We were only too happy to accept his warm invitation.

It must have been about midnight when a crowd of hefty drunken men carrying sabers dragged us from bed and stood us on a counter . . . brandishing sabers at us. "Chop off the kids' heads and wet our battle flags in their blood," some yelled. "They'd be nice to try our sabers on," bawled others. "Don't kill them," still others suggested. "Tie them up and cart them off, and let their families ransom them back with big shiny silver dollars."

The shopkeeper tried desperately to save us. Pleading that we be allowed to go back to sleep, he promised them wine, food, and everything else in the shop. And because he belonged to their gang, as we learned later, they listened to him. Pandemonium continued for a while; but they left us alone at last, and we crept back to the bedroom. As our terror gradually subsided, we reentered the village of slumber.[14]

Similar rebellions occurred in other places, including Changsha, the Hunan provincial capital. In Shaoshan members of the Elder Brother Society, soon joined by other poor peasants, rose in rebellion. Demanding relief from the rich peasants, they began a movement under the slogan "Eat rice without charge!" "My father," Mao recalled, "was a rice merchant and was exporting much grain to the city from our district, despite the shortage. One of his consignments was seized by the poor villagers and his wrath was boundless. I did not sympathize with him. At the same time, I thought the villagers' method was wrong also."[15]

The rebels were brutally suppressed. A new governor quickly ordered the arrest of the leaders of the uprising, many of whom were decapitated, their heads displayed on poles for the edification of future would-be rebels. Troops were also sent into action against the Elder Brother Society in Shaoshan. Their leader was caught and also decapitated.

Executions in China were public. Criminals were dressed in sleeveless vests on which "bandit" or "murderer" was written in black characters. Their arms were tied behind their backs and they were paraded around the city or the countryside in open carts, preceded by soldiers bearing arms or sabers. People crowded around both sides of the procession. Many of them accompanied the cart along its entire route. Escorting the condemned in this fashion, the soldiers finally threw the condemned from the cart onto the jam-packed square. One of the soldiers, handing his saber to a comrade, would approach the criminal, kneel before him, and ask forgiveness for what he must now do. This was to protect himself from possible revenge by the soul of the imminent victim. This ritual also allowed the condemned to preserve face by giving him a last modicum of respect. The condemned man was now made to kneel, and the soldier cut off his head with one swift blow. After this, the crowd dispersed. Village life was rather dull, so a spectacle like a public execution was of genuine interest. It was particularly appreciated if during the procession the condemned exhibited bravery by singing songs or shouting slogans. Then someone in the crowd would be sure to say, "Hao! Hao!" ("Bravo! Bravo!").

Violence begot violence. It was in such an atmosphere, in a society where human life was worth nothing, where people labored unceasingly day after day just to make ends meet and in the hope of escaping poverty, that the character of Mao Zedong, Zhang Guotao, and many other future communist revolutionaries was forged. Peasant rebellion, as Mao himself acknowledged, produced an indelible impression on him during his childhood and influenced him throughout his life.[16]

According to Mao himself, Chinese literature, above all historical novels dealing with uprisings, rebellions, and insurrections, also had an enormous influence on his worldview and consciousness. He read over and over again such works as *The Biography of the Ever Faithful Yue Fei, Water Margin, The Romance of Sui and Tang, The Three Kingdoms,* and *Journey to the West,* books describing the feats of legendary knights, warriors, and adventurers as well as the leaders of popular rebellions. They praised the ideals of brotherhood among warriors and affirmed the cult of physical strength. Their heroes sounded the call to rise up against traditional ways.[17]

Mao's mother prayed in vain to the Bodhisattva. Her beloved son will not follow the holy noble path of the Most Gracious Buddha, but rather the road of blood, violence, and revolution. The ethical philosophy of Confucius, the great humanist, will also leave him cold. "I knew the Classics, but disliked them," confessed Mao to Edgar Snow.[18] Already in early childhood, under the influence of his despotic father, incendiary literature, and his surroundings, he concluded that open rebellion was the only way to defend one's rights. If you remained humble and obedient, you would be beaten over and over again.[19]

2

ON THE THRESHOLD
OF A NEW WORLD

Mao left school at the age of thirteen. His stern teacher had used harsh methods of instruction and often beat his pupils. Mao could no longer endure such abuse and his father had no objection to his quitting school. "I didn't want you to become a *xiucai*," he said, referring to the lowest degree one could receive in imperial China by passing the district examination. "In any case, the imperial exams* had already been abolished, and it made no sense for the boy to continue his studies. There's much work to be done, so come back home," he is reported to have said.[1] Mao Yichang supposed that his son would attend to the family's business, and in particular that he would take care of the bookkeeping chores, but Mao wanted to continue his studies on his own. A passion for reading consumed him. He avidly devoured everything that came into his hands, with the exception of classical philosophical texts. He usually read at night, covering the window of his room with a blue homespun sheet to prevent his father from seeing the light of the oil lamp by which he read. His father would fly into a rage whenever he saw his son with a book, even if Mao was reading during his free time.

It was at this time that Mao came across a book that aroused his interest in politics. Written by the great reformer Zheng Guanying (also known as Zheng Zhengxiang), *Words of Warning to an Affluent Age,* published in 1893, summoned Chinese to study "the science of wealth and power," that is, to apply the lessons of European industrialization to the task of modernizing China. It spoke of the need to establish a British-style constitutional monarchy in the Middle Kingdom. The author came out against the traditional Confucian order and in favor of limited bourgeois reforms aimed at strengthening the state.[2]

To understand the role this book played in the life of the adolescent Mao, we must briefly examine the situation in China at that time. At the beginning

---

* The imperial exams were the primary path to official service in China during the dynastic era.

of the twentieth century, China was in a state of semicolonial economic dependency as a result of the aggression of the developed capitalist countries. The two Opium Wars (1839–42 and 1856–60), the first waged against China by England, which craved the legalization of free trade, and the second by England in league with France, forced the Middle Kingdom to conclude unequal treaties with the "hairy foreign devils," as the Chinese called the white colonialists. The victors seized control of China's tariffs and China lost its economic independence. Foreign merchants were exempted from paying domestic custom duties (*lijin*) upon crossing provincial boundaries, which put Chinese merchants at a disadvantage. Foreigners secured the right to establish settlements in the growing number of ports that were open to foreign commerce. They enjoyed the right of extraterritoriality, in other words, they were not subject to Chinese courts.

Cheap Western goods began to flood Chinese markets, resulting in the bankruptcy of millions of handicraft workers. The tax burden rose sharply. Defeated in a series of wars, China was forced to pay indemnities to the victors.

China's inclusion in the world economy led to a profound economic and social crisis. The country was shaken by a huge anti-Manchu uprising, the Taiping Rebellion, in which many destitute peasants and handicraft workers took part. (*Taiping* means "great peace.") The leader of the rebellion, Hong Xiuquan, a rural teacher from Guangxi in South China, called for the creation of a Taiping Heavenly Kingdom based on the principle of equality. Inspired by Christian precepts, in particular Baptist and Puritan teachings, Hong claimed that in a dream God the Father had revealed to him that he was the younger brother of Jesus Christ. The Heavenly Kingdom of Great Peace would be celebrated on the ruins of the corrupt Qing dynasty. With fire and sword the rebels would clear a path to ideal peace and justice, plundering and killing not only the Manchus but also the *tuhao* and the *lieshen*.

More than twenty million people were killed during the civil war. The country teetered on the brink of collapse, but the dynasty survived. Between 1861 and 1894, the Manchu court, headed by Empress Dowager Ci Xi, attempted to implement a series of state-building reforms under the rubric of self-strengthening. Ci Xi and her lover Prince Gong, together with influential Chinese dignitaries and conquerors of the Taiping, tried to industrialize and modernize China in order to transform it into a strong military power. They began to build industrial enterprises, arsenals, and wharves, construct railroads, open modern universities, and publish newspapers and journals. Capitalism, however, developed very slowly in China. Although the state formally ceased interfering in private business, corrupt government officials and local bigwigs continued to restrict the initiative of individual private entrepreneurs in order to stop competition. Most industrial enterprises belonged to bureaucratic capital and to regional oligarchs, the most powerful of whom controlled their own private armies. From its very beginning capitalism in China was monopolistic. At the start of the twentieth century there were slightly more than twelve million nonagricultural workers, of whom three-fourths, or around nine million, worked in large enterprises that employed more than five hundred workers. Favorable conditions for the growth of small- and medium-scale native entrepreneurs did not develop.

Progressive patriots, among them Zheng Guanying, who supported self-strengthening, criticized the monopolistic economic policy of high government officials. They advised against restricting small and medium business, promoted reform and, to a certain extent, radical reform, and occasionally voiced democratic ideas. Many of their proposals addressed the need for political as well as economic reforms, and for liberalizing the judicial system as well as the state system. But they were ignored and the reform program failed.

In 1885 China lost another war with France; in 1895, in the Sino-Japanese War, it was humiliated by Japan. Although this defeat ignited an even greater flare-up of patriotic feeling, the plans of the reformers were doomed to failure. The leaders of the new reform movement, Kang Youwei and Liang Qichao, who were leading philosophers and men of letters, called on the young and progressive-minded emperor to emulate Peter the Great and initiate reform from above. They urged him to introduce a constitutional monarchy, Westernize the army and the educational system, and encourage entrepreneurship. The emperor attempted to institute new reforms during a hundred-day period in 1898. Hoping to remove the empress dowager from affairs of state, he turned for help to Yuan Shikai, a powerful general, but in vain. Ci Xi learned about the plot. She promptly had her nephew declared insane, removed him from power, and put him under house arrest. Many reformers were executed; Kang Youwei and Liang Qichao fled abroad.

Civil society did not exist in China. Since all opposition political activity was suppressed inside China, advocates of change were forced to pursue their political activities abroad. One such person was Sun Yat-sen (real name Sun Wen), a native of Guangdong province in the south, and a student of Zheng Guanying. Sun was born in 1866, and educated in Hawaii, Canton, and Hong Kong. In 1892 he graduated from medical school. Disillusioned with the reformist movement, Sun left China in 1894, relocating to Hawaii, where his elder brother lived. There, in Honolulu in November 1894, he founded the first Chinese revolutionary society, the Xingzhonghui (China Revival Society). Unlike the reformers, Dr. Sun Yat-sen demanded the revolutionary transformation of China along republican lines. In January 1895 a branch of the society was established in the British colony of Hong Kong and soon afterward in the nearby metropolis of Canton, where Sun himself moved shortly thereafter. That autumn, members of the society mounted their first anti-Manchu uprising in Canton, which failed. Sun was forced to flee with a high price on his head. He spent sixteen years in exile and did not return to his homeland until two months after the antimonarchical revolution had taken place.

Despite its crushing defeat, the China Revival Society survived and soon resumed its revolutionary activity. During the period 1901–1904 new revolutionary organizations appeared in China. In 1905 many of them combined to form the Zhongguo geming tongmenghui (Chinese Revolutionary Alliance), known by its shorter name as the Tongmenghui (Revolutionary Alliance) and founded in Tokyo. As president of the Revolutionary Alliance, in the first issue of *Minbao* (The People), the main organ of the Revolutionary Alliance, Sun Yat-sen proclaimed a radical political program of the Three Principles of the People: Nationalism, Democracy, and People's Livelihood.

By Nationalism Sun meant the overthrow of the Manchu monarchy, by Democracy the establishment of a republic. The third principle, People's Livelihood, meant the so-called equalization of land rights, that is, the nationalization of the basic means of production in China in the interest of strengthening the regulatory role of the state in the Chinese economy. Sun Yat-sen's political program guaranteeing the primacy of the state in the economy was directed against oligarchic capitalism, which created conditions for the exclusive enrichment of those who had already risen to the top. His objective was to use state power to promote the development of a middle class in China. Sun supported a progressive land tax that could facilitate the creation of a "just society" with equal opportunities.

Meanwhile, another powerful peasant uprising was occurring in north China, aimed against the "hairy foreign devils." The uprising was led by a secret religious society, the Yihequan (Fists of Righteousness and Harmony), comprising mostly martial arts masters. Like the members of the Brotherhood of the Sword, the warriors of the Yihequan believed that physical and spiritual exercises as well as magic and sorcery would render them invulnerable to enemy bullets, missiles, and sabers. Their mode of fighting resembled fisticuffs, and so the first foreigners who clashed with them called them Boxers. The uprising began in 1898 in Shandong and Zhili provinces. On June 13, 1900, the rebels seized Beijing, the capital, plundered the wealthy merchants' quarter, torched thousands of houses, and laid siege to the foreign diplomatic compounds. Their anger was directed mainly against missionaries and Chinese Christians.

Improbably, Ci Xi supported the Yihequan uprising. The story went that she decided to conduct an experiment and invited a group of "invulnerables" to the Forbidden City. At her command, soldiers from her personal guard lined up the Boxers against a wall and unleashed a volley of gunfire at them. None of the Boxers was even wounded. Stunned by this miracle, on June 21, 1900, Ci Xi declared war against the whole world.

The miracle was short-lived, however. A joint eight-power army consisting of the major Western powers, including the United States, and Japan defeated the Boxers and the Qing forces. In Beijing on September 7, 1901, the Chinese government signed a new unequal treaty that bound China to pay 450 million ounces of silver as an indemnity over the next thirty-nine years, the equivalent of $301.5 million U.S. gold dollars at the time. Chinese troops had to leave Beijing and foreign troops were quartered in the capital. Thus, at the beginning of the twentieth century, China was fully dependent economically, and partly dependent politically, on foreign powers. Foreign businessmen dominated the Chinese market. The Middle Kingdom occupied a third-tier position in the international division of labor. China's dependence on the imperialist powers increased over the next decade. By 1912 China's national debt was 835 million ounces of silver. By then, 107 treaty ports were open to foreigners. The socio-political crisis was deepening.

In 1901, after the suppression of the Boxer Rebellion, the Qing again turned to reform. The court began to discuss the possibility of introducing a constitution, undertook measures to stimulate private entrepreneurship, and established a new army consisting of thirty-six battle-worthy modern divisions. At the high point of the reformist movement, the emperor, who had never been released from house arrest, passed away on November 14, 1908, preceding by just one day the death of his power-hungry aunt, Empress Ci Xi.

Big changes were in the air. The country's new rulers, acting on behalf of the new, three-year-old emperor, Pu Yi, took measures to introduce a constitution. In 1909 elections were held for provincial consultative committees in preparation for the constitution. They became foci of liberal opposition. It was announced that elections for a parliament would be held in 1913.

The adolescent Mao knew almost nothing of these developments. Whatever he may have heard of them made no impression on him. The great events of the day passed him by. We may suppose that no one told the young Mao about the Boxers; Shaoshan was a backwater where nobody read newspapers. Even news of the death of the emperor and the empress dowager did not reach Shaoshan until two years after Pu Yi had ascended the throne.[3] But Mao must certainly have been told about the Taipings. The Taiping Rebellion had rolled through the province only forty years before his birth, and there were many surviving eyewitnesses of those terrible events. Moreover, Mao's father served in the Xiang Army in the 1880s, the same army that had suppressed the Taiping Rebellion twenty years earlier.

A new conflict with his father flared up, intensified by his parents' decision to have him marry. In either late 1907 or 1908, they picked out a suitable girl for him. She was a distant relative of Mao Zedong. The girl, named Luo Yigu ("First Daughter"), was four years older than Mao. (She was born on October 20, 1889.) Her father, Luo Helou, was a rural intellectual, a *shenshi*, but he was basically a farmer. The family was very poor and unfortunate. Luo Helou and his wife had had five sons and five daughters, but all the sons died in infancy and only three daughters survived. The death of their sons was a heavy blow, since in China sons alone were considered a blessing. After growing up, a girl had to marry, that is, she would leave her family which, moreover, was obligated to provide a rich dowry. But a son would stay at home as an heir and successor. His duties included taking care of his parents in their old age and, after their passing, to put the souls of the dead at ease and regularly perform at their graves the traditional ceremonies. Luo Helou was happy to present his eldest daughter to the family of Mao Yichang, whose wife, Wen Qimei, was in need of a helper because her health, undermined by heavy labor, had deteriorated.

In keeping with tradition, matchmakers were sent to the bride's house. It was considered improper to accept the proposal right away, so the match-making took quite a while. Finally, both sides exchanged gifts and concluded a marriage contract, which was considered inviolable. Even should the bride die before the wedding, a tablet with her name on it would be brought to the groom's home and placed on the family altar. If the groom died, the bride had to go to her "husband's" home as his widow.

Mao Zedong and his bride met only on the day the marriage contract was drawn up.[4] We don't know whether he was pleased with Luo Yigu;* in any case he wanted to study, not get married. Unfortunately, he had no choice but to bow to the will of his parents. By the time he learned of their intentions, it was already too late. The marriage contract had been signed, the wedding date set, and Mao Yichang had delivered a bride-price and other ritual gifts to Luo Helou.

Following the local custom, the wedding feast, to which numerous rela-tives and friends were invited, began in the groom's home a day before the wedding itself. On the wedding day, the bride, dressed in red, was carried in a red palanquin to the home of the bridegroom. Her face was covered with a red veil and her lips crimsoned with red lipstick. The girl was supposed to ex-press her unhappiness, to cry, and to accuse her future husband of his failings, calling him a "hairy insect," a "ravenous, lazy, and tobacco-addicted dog," a "drunkard," and so forth. A fireworks display was arranged at the bridegroom's home. Then the bridegroom and the bride prostrated themselves before the ancestral altar of the bridegroom, before the spirits of Heaven and Earth, the Sun and the Moon, the "sovereign and the elements of Water and Earth," and, finally, before the spirits of the deceased ancestors. Then they bowed to each other, concluding the wedding ceremony. The guests continued to feast for two more days and presented gifts, usually money, to the newlyweds. Then a

---

* Most likely Mao was not impressed. According to his granddaughter, Kong Dongmei, at this time the fourteen-year-old Mao Zedong was in love with another girl, his cousin Wang Shigu, but unfortunately for him, their horoscopes did not match and the local geomancer would not allow the marriage.

"viewing" of the young couple took place. As a joke this was called "making a commotion in the bridal chamber." A master of ceremonies, his face painted black and wearing a costume festooned with leaves, conducted guests into the bridal chamber, where they made indecent gestures or sang obscene verses. To put an end to these improprieties the young husband had to bribe the guests. The new bride had to show her mother-in-law the bloodstained sheet from her wedding night as proof of her virginity.

Mao Zedong endured all these ceremonies with difficulty. According to him, he did not sleep with his bride and he refused to live with her.[5] Mao accorded so little significance to this, his first marriage, that he couldn't even remember how old his wife had been when they were betrothed. Mentioning his wedding in passing to Edgar Snow, he said, "My parents had married me when I was fourteen to a girl of twenty."[6] In fact, Luo Yigu was eighteen. It's hard to believe that a fourteen-year-old adolescent boy refused to share his bed with an eighteen-year-old girl, but we have no evidence that Mao spoke untruths to Edgar Snow, provided one does not consider the strange note in the *Chronicle of the Shaoshan Mao Clan* that Mao Zedong and Luo Yigu supposedly had a son named Yuanzhi, who, for some reason, was handed over to be raised by a family named Yang.[7] No one knows whether this is so, but most likely the scribe who compiled the *Chronicle* got something mixed up. There is no other evidence for the birth of this child.

Soon after his wedding, Mao ran away from home and lived for a year in the house of an unemployed student, also in Shaoshan. He continued his avid reading, devouring the *Records of the Grand Historian* by the ancient Chinese chronicler Sima Qian and the *History of the Former Han Dynasty* by Ban Gu. These books described the deeds of the great rulers of ancient China—heroes and antiheroes, generals, politicians, and philosophers. He also was attracted to contemporary books and articles, immersing himself in *Personal Protests from the Study of Jiao Bin,* compiled in 1861 by Feng Guifen, another leading reformer. It recounted the foreign aggression against China and counseled self-reliance by borrowing foreign techniques and technology but not altering the foundations of China's ideological-political system.[8] Mao also read a pamphlet by the young Chinese revolutionary Chen Tianhua, which, he claimed, produced a particularly strong impression upon him: "I remember even now that this pamphlet opened with the sentence: 'Alas, China will be subjugated!' It told of Japan's occupation of Korea and Formosa, of the loss of suzerainty in Indo-China, Burma and elsewhere. After I read this I felt depressed about the future of my country and began to realize that it was the duty of all the people to help save it."[9]

Poor Luo Yigu. "Neither a married woman nor a maiden," is how they talked about her in the villages. She bore her humiliation in silence. Philip Short, one of Mao's biographers, writes that some villagers in Shaoshan believed she remained in her new family as a concubine of Mao's father.[10] Whether or not this was true, she had not long to live. On February 11, 1910, she died of dysentery.[11] She was barely past her twentieth birthday.

Surprisingly, Mao's father forgave his "ungrateful son" for having shamed him in front of the entire village. Evidently, Mao Yichang wasn't nearly as bad as Mao later recalled. In the fall of 1910, Mao Yichang's obstinate son asked for money to continue his education and the older man grudgingly agreed. He had to fork out quite a lot of money, some 1,400 copper cash or one Chinese silver dollar for five months of tuition, space in a dormitory, and use of the library. The school Mao Zedong chose—the Dongshan Higher Primary School—was located some fifteen miles from Shaoshan and taught contemporary subjects, including the natural sciences.

At this time Mao was sixteen and a half. For the first time in his life, he left his native place, in the company of an older cousin, Wen Yunchang, nine years his senior, who attended the same school and had persuaded Mao to enroll there. His hated father and all his other relatives escorted Mao to the edge of the village,[12] and when Mao Yichang returned home he found the following verses written by the prospective student of the Dongshan School:

Full of resolve your eldest
sets out from his native place.
My studies will bring me glory;
And I'll never return to this place.
Wherever my bones may be buried
will make no difference at all.
Wherever one goes in the valley
The mountains are equally tall.[13]

Already he burned with a desire to leave his mark on history. Books about the great Chinese emperors, two of whom, Liu Bang of the Han dynasty (256 or 247–195 BCE) and Zhu Yuanzhang of the Ming dynasty (1328–1398), were sons of the poorest of the poor, whirled about in Mao's youthful head. It is just such a passion to attain glory that animates the children of ordinary families to become leading scientists, writers, and politicians. Patriotic feelings summoned Mao to great deeds. The proud soul of the provincial youth propelled him forward.

The path to glory, however, was difficult. In his new school, the poorly dressed, thin, and lanky peasant boy was greeted with hostility by his fellow classmates. (At five foot nine inches Mao was unlike the typically short southerners.) Most of them were the sons of rich landlords; moreover, unlike Mao they were from Xiangxiang district. They were bursting with arrogance, and they had only contempt for the interloper who had just one decent suit of clothes. They found everything about him irritating, including his dialect. In many parts of China even people in neighboring districts speak different dialects. This was the case in the neighboring districts in Hunan that were separated only by Mount Shao—Xiangtan where Mao was born, and Xiang-xiang, his mother's home district and the place where Dongshan School was located.[14] The people in these two neighboring districts could understand each other, but not easily.

Only a few of his fellows showed Mao any sympathy. The student clos-est to him, apart from his cousin, was Xiao Zizhang (or Xiao San). Later, in 1920, Xiao left China to work and study in France, where he joined the Euro-pean branch of the Chinese Communist Party. Subsequently, in 1927, he set off for the Soviet Union, where he stayed for many years, and under the nom de plume of Emi Siao became a well-known writer and poet and one of the first biographers of Mao Zedong. One friend and one cousin were not enough. Mao, with his overbearing character, suffered from the hostility of most of his classmates. "I felt spiritually very depressed," he recalled later.[15]

This situation only intensified his desire for success. Insults irritated his willful and unruly spirit, steeled his will, and deepened his hostility toward anyone who surpassed him in one way or another. Ultimately, he succeeded in winning the teachers' respect through his efforts. Mao was able to compose essays in the classical style and was industrious and hardworking. He con-tinued to be a voracious reader. During his time at the Dongshan School, he maintained his interest in history, particularly the history of ancient Chinese rulers, including the legendary sage-kings Yao and Shun, the bloodthirsty em-peror Qin Shi Huangdi, and the famous Han emperor Wu Di, who was the first Chinese ruler to pacify the northern Xiongnu nomads (Huns) and bring east-ern Turkestan, Vietnam, and Korea under Chinese control. For the first time Mao became acquainted with geography and began to read foreign history. A book called *Great Heroes of the World* drew his attention, and he learned about Napoleon, Catherine the Great, Peter the Great, Wellington, Gladstone, Rous-seau, Montesquieu, and Lincoln.[16] He wanted to be like them.

His most important reading at the time was material about Kang Youwei and the reform movement of 1898, including a copy of the *Xinmin congbao* (Renovation of the people) journal published by Liang Qichao in Yokohama. He was shaken by these works, which his cousin had passed along to him. "I read and re-read these until I knew them by heart," he said subsequently. Liang Qichao's book, *On Renovation of the People,* published in *Xinmin congbao* in 1906, was a treasure trove of knowledge for him. In this philosophical treatise, the famous reformer, in his own words, "wanted to search for the primary cause of the decay and backwardness of the people of our state and compare this with the progress of other countries, so that the people, learning of our defects, would take precautions against disaster, and hasten to progress of their own accord."[17]

Liang Qichao's arguments about the progressive role of constitutional monarchy and the regressive influence of despotic monarchy made the greatest impression upon Mao. After reading the chapter "On State Ideology," Mao wrote the following note:

> In a constitutional state, the constitution is created by the people; the monarch enjoys the love of the people. . . . In a despotic state, the monarch lays down the law, and one bows down before the monarch, not the people. . . . England and Japan are examples of the first type, the various dynasties that have pillaged China over several thousand years are examples of the second type.[18]

Mao literally prayed for Kang Youwei and Liang Qichao, believing that an "honest, good, and wise" emperor would summon Kang and Liang to his aid, and would bestow a constitution upon the country. Nationalistic feelings that had already stirred him were strengthened by reading the works of the re-formers. Both Liang and Kang were extremely chauvinistic. China's revival on an Anglo-Japanese model would, they believed, lead to the Middle Kingdom's victory in the global competition among nations and the establishment of Chinese hegemony. Otherwise, the two ideologues of reform asserted, China would perish.

In school Mao learned about Japan's victory over Russia in 1905. He and other students were excitedly informed of this by a young teacher of music and English who had studied in Japan. Mao was proud of the Japanese victory, and many years later he was able to sing for Edgar Snow the Japanese song "Battle of the Yellow Sea," which his teacher loved. "At the time I knew and felt the beauty of Japan, and felt something of her pride and might, in this song of her victory over Russia," said Mao.[19] He sympathized with the Japanese, but not because he rejoiced at the victory of "the yellow race over the whites," as some of his biographers assert.[20] It is doubtful that Mao can be accused of racism. At the time, Mao was a patriot, not a racist. The victory of the Land of the Rising Sun in the war with czarist Russia evoked his delight only because it demonstrated the superiority of constitutional monarchy over despotism. It likewise confirmed the ideas of his beloved reformers that an Asian country that had set out on the path of political modernization could reduce to ashes a mighty European power that was bound by the chains of absolutism.

He remained at the Dongshan School for just seven or eight months. In early 1911, Mao decided to go to Changsha, the capital of Hunan province, to enroll in a middle school that was accepting students from the district of Xiangxiang. He received a letter of recommendation from one of his teachers, gathered together his few belongings, and set off on foot in the early spring to the large and unfamiliar city. He left behind his childhood and adolescence; the Dongshan School encircled by a high, fortresslike wall; and his arrogant classmates and supportive teachers. An alluring and frightening new world awaited him.

3

"I THINK,
THEREFORE, I AM"

Mao, who lived in Changsha for more than seven years, was overwhelmed by the first city he had ever encountered. Never before had he seen urban streets, two- and three-story houses, and countless junks bobbing on the waves at stone wharves. In the early twentieth century Changsha, with a population over 200,000, was considered one of the best cities in China.[1] Located on the right bank of the Xiang River, it was surrounded by an impressive stone wall with lofty turrets that towered above seven tunnel-like passageways shut at night with huge gates. Everything in the city amazed Mao: the broad stone-paved streets, the unique long stone embankment, the electric lights in the palace of the governor and other luxurious houses, and two yellow-tiled Confucian temples. But most impressive of all was the railroad, constructed just three years earlier, which ran alongside the city wall on the eastern outskirts of Changsha. Mao saw for the first time that marvel of Western technology, a locomotive. The rows of shops, one after another, with their enormous signboards hanging like banners from long poles along the walls, also impressed him. The stores were filled with all manner of domestic and foreign goods. No wonder Changsha was considered one of the liveliest commercial centers in China. The many people, the noise and din were unbearable. "[T]his city was very big, contained many, many people, numerous schools, and the yamen of the governor. It was a magnificent place altogether!" Mao reported ecstatically to Edgar Snow.[2]

The city had been founded three thousand years before. During the third century BCE it was conquered by the ruler of Qin, who as Qin Shi Huangdi became the first emperor of China. It was he who bestowed the name Changsha (Long Sands) upon the city. Directly across from the city walls, Orange Island, a long and narrow sandy spit of land, densely covered with orange trees, lay in the Xiang River. In 1664, Changsha became the capital of the newly established province of Hunan.

Beyond Orange Island, on the left bank of the river rises Yuelu Mountain.

It is less than 800 feet high, but, like Mount Shao, it is sacred. On the eastern side of the mountain was the famous Yuelu Academy, founded during the Song dynasty, where Zhu Xi (1130–1200 CE), the leading Confucian philosopher, taught. In 1903, shortly before Mao came to Changsha, the academy was reorganized into the Hunan Institute of Higher Education, a modern educational institution.

A small number of foreigners who had settled on Orange Island lived in Changsha. Americans who had founded a branch of Yale University and a hospital there in 1906 made up the largest contingent. Changsha had been opened to foreign trade rather late, in July 1904, and the local inhabitants were not yet accustomed to foreigners in their midst. Anti-foreign sentiments were very strong. This is how Edward Hume, an American physician at the Yale Hospital, described the reaction of the locals to the appearance of foreigners on their streets: "Mothers pushed their little children behind them as they saw us coming, to hide them from the 'evil eye.' Some held their noses as we passed. The amah told us once that the smell of the Westerner was so characteristic that Chinese recognized our presence without even seeing us. Some of the youngsters . . . followed the sedan chairs shouting 'foreign devil.' " [3]

Mao had a kaleidoscope of impressions from the city. The young man was worried that he would be refused entry into this "great" urban school, but to his surprise he was admitted. This time, too, he stayed only a few months. In October 1911, an antimonarchical revolution suddenly broke out. It was rather bloodless, and had almost no impact upon the broad masses of the peasantry. [4] It was touched off on the night of October 10 by an uprising of the Eighth Engineer Battalion of the New Army, stationed in Wuchang in Hubei province. A majority of the soldiers in this battalion were members of a revolutionary organization, the Progressive Society (Gongjinhui), which had close ties with the Revolutionary Alliance. By the morning of October 11, the whole city was in the hands of the insurgents. The following day Manchu power was overthrown in the adjacent cities of Hankou and Hanyang. Thus, the tricities of Hankou, Hanyang, and Wuchang, which comprised Wuhan, were at the center of the revolutionary events. This spontaneous occurrence evoked an explosion of anti-Manchu sentiment in many cities throughout the country, but it caught the leaders of the Revolutionary Alliance unawares. Sun Yat-sen learned of the uprising from the newspapers while he was traveling by train from Denver to Kansas City. He went straight to Washington and then to London, hoping that with the help of friends he could collect the financial resources the Revolutionary Alliance urgently needed. In contrast, the local Wuhan constitutional reformers, headed by a thirty-seven-year-old politician named Tang Hualong, quickly sized up the situation. They not only went over to the side of the revolution; they took over its leadership. On October 11, a military government for Hubei province was established, headed by a conservative general, Li Yuanhong, the forty-seven-year-old commander of the Twenty-First Brigade of the New Army. Tang Hualong was named the civil governor.

By the end of November, fifteen of China's eighteen provinces had overthrown Qing authority. In the majority of these, civilian authority had passed into the hands of the former constitutional reformers, who systematically excluded the genuine revolutionaries from leadership roles. Military administration wound up in the hands of the commanders of the local detachments of the New Army. One after another, the newly established provincial governments declared their independence from the central authorities.

Changsha, some 250 miles to the south, learned of the events in Wuhan on October 13, when representatives from Li Yuanhong arrived in town. The director of the school where Mao was enrolled allowed one of these representatives to deliver an incendiary speech to the students. His speech had an electrifying effect on many of the students, including Mao, who by this time had already evolved from patriotic monarchist to confirmed revolutionary. His worldview was influenced by the first newspaper he ever read, the *Minli bao* (People's independence), one of the organs of Sun Yat-sen's Revolutionary Alliance. From this paper, the young Mao learned about the leader of the Chinese democratic movement and his Three Principles of the People. Mao became an ardent supporter of Sun. Swayed by what he had read, Mao decided to write an article, which he posted on one of the walls at his school where everyone could see it. "It was my first expression of a political opinion, and it was somewhat muddled," he later admitted. "I had not yet given up my admiration of K'ang Yu-wei [Kang Youwei] and Liang Ch'i-chao [Liang Qichao]. I did not clearly understand the difference between them. Therefore in my article I advocated that Sun Yat-sen must be called back from Japan to become President of a new Government, that K'ang Yu-wei be made Premier, and Liang Ch'i-chao Minister of Foreign Affairs." [5] At this point he really didn't understand anything, neither the reformism of Kang Youwei and Liang Qichao nor the revolutionary thought of Sun Yat-sen. He was drawn to these persons only from his thirst for heroic deeds.

Having chosen the path of revolution, Mao cut off his queue, or pigtail, even before news of the Wuchang uprising. This was an act of rebellion, since every subject of the Qing Empire had to wear a long pigtail as a sign of submission to the Manchus. One fellow student followed his example, but the rest were too frightened. Stirred by the impassioned speech of Li Yuanhong's representative, Mao and several of his classmates soon decided to run off and join the insurrectionists, but they were unable to leave the city. On Sunday, October 22, soldiers of the Forty-Ninth Regiment, quartered not far from Changsha, mutinied. With support from soldiers from the Fiftieth Regiment, the mutineers entered the city and seized all of the strategic points. That same day a military government of Hunan was established, headed by two young extremists, Jiao Dafeng and Chen Zuoxin, who were closely linked to the mafia-like Elder Brother secret society. The administration of Jiao Dafeng and Chen Zuoxin did not last long. Just nine days later, on October 31, a coup d'état occurred, again organized by soldiers of the Fiftieth Regiment. Jiao and Chen were killed and power wound up in the hands of moderate liberals led by the former chairman of the Hunan provincial assembly, the thirty-two-year-old millionaire Tan Yankai.

Classes were suspended, so Mao decided to enroll in the revolutionary army and make his contribution to the revolution. Victory was still not assured. The Qing court was negotiating with General Yuan Shikai, commander of the powerful Beiyang Army, trying to convince him to put down the rebellion. However, Yuan Shikai wanted total power and temporized. Meanwhile, thousands of Manchu families, fearing reprisals, fled to their historic homeland in Northeast China. On November 2, the Qing court appointed Yuan Shikai prime minister while Mao Zedong's idol, the constitutional monarchist Liang Qichao, was appointed minister of justice. The new prime minister contacted the heads of the rebellious provinces and several leaders of the Revolutionary Alliance, but negotiations were fruitless, because the military governors and revolutionaries demanded the overthrow of the Qing monarchy while Yuan Shikai sought a compromise with the court. At the height of these events, Sun Yat-sen finally returned to China, on December 25. The leader of the Revolutionary Alliance, not wishing to negotiate with Yuan Shikai, opted for a military showdown. On December 29, in Nanjing, the former capital of the Ming dynasty, delegates of the rebellious provinces declared themselves the National Assembly and chose Sun as the provisional president. On January 1, 1912, Sun assumed his post and proclaimed the founding of the Republic of China.

The country was split. In Beijing, power remained in the hands of the emperor and Yuan Shikai. In Nanjing, Sun Yat-sen was in charge. Civil war appeared inevitable. Eighteen-year-old Mao Zedong, acting courageously, joined the Hunan Army as it prepared to invade the north.

As it happened, the young recruit saw no military action. As the country fell apart, armies rapidly began to play a more important role, but Sun Yat-sen had no professional army and quickly lost any real power. Most of the National Assembly delegates who had voted for Sun sought a compromise with Yuan Shikai and were simply playing Sun as a trump card in a game with the commander of the Beiyang Army. Essentially quite moderate, they wanted a cautious politician as president rather than someone like Sun Yat-sen, who would trample upon tradition. Many of them were powerful oligarchs who feared the implementation of Sun Yat-sen's third Principle of the People (People's Livelihood), aimed at establishing state control of the economy. In their eyes, Yuan Shikai was ideal. They needed Sun Yat-sen as provisional president only in order to exert pressure upon the indecisive general, and they succeeded. Finally realizing that the majority in the National Assembly in Nanjing regarded Sun

Yat-sen merely as a transitional figure, Yuan Shikai transmitted his terms for the abdication of the Manchu boy emperor to the court. On February 12, 1912, the six-year-old emperor Pu Yi formally abdicated. The revolution had triumphed! On February 14, Sun Yat-sen submitted his resignation, which the National Assembly accepted unanimously. The following day the delegates, again unanimously, chose Yuan Shikai as the provisional president of the country.

After six months in the Hunan Army, Mao decided to return to his studies to complete his formal education. His request to be discharged was granted and he came away with an excellent impression of the army. For the first time in his life he had had enough of everything. He had received a very respectable salary of seven silver dollars a month. (Recall that in the Dongshan Higher Primary School, he paid less than one dollar for five months of tuition, room, and library fees.) He had lots of free time, and he lived very comfortably. He differed from the general mass of soldiers, most of whom were illiterate paupers who had joined the army because they had nothing to eat. The proud student who knew his own worth could not help but condescend toward such persons. "I spent two dollars a month on food. I also had to buy water," he later recalled to Edgar Snow. "The soldiers had to carry water in from outside the city, but I, being a student, could not condescend to carrying, and bought it from the water-pedlars."[6]

What an interesting revelation from the leader of the working people. How alike they all were—Lenin, Stalin, Mao. Fighting for social equality, they did not think of themselves as on the same plane as others and raised themselves above the crowd.

Mao now found himself at a crossroads. He had a passion for learning, but he didn't know what he wanted to become. He began to read student recruitment advertisements in the newspapers. At first he was attracted to a police school, but he soon had a change of heart and enrolled in a school for soap making. Then, influenced by a friend, he decided to become a jurist, and he registered in a law school, then in a commercial middle school, and then in a higher commercial public school. Mao was young and, like many eighteen- and nineteen-year-old youths, he wanted everything at once. The higher commercial public school required a good command of English, but Mao had no talent for languages. After studying at the commercial school for just one month, Mao left in the spring of 1912 and entered the Hunan Higher Provincial Middle School, which was soon renamed the Provincial First Middle School.

Here, too, he didn't stick it out very long. "I didn't like the First Middle School," he recalled. "Its curriculum was limited and its regulations were objectionable."[7] Disillusioned with teachers and with schools, Mao decided to study on his own. For half a year he went daily to the Hunan provincial library, where he spent most of his time reading up on geography, history, and Western philosophy. Liberalism, to which he was now attracted, had come to China from

Europe and America along with capitalism. The schools he had attended had taught nothing about foreign countries. At the age of nineteen he first saw a world map and was astonished by it. He began studying the foundational works of contemporary Western democracy, including Adam Smith's *The Wealth of Nations,* Charles Darwin's *On the Origin of Species,* Montesquieu's *On the Spirit of Laws,* as well as books by John Stuart Mill and Herbert Spencer. He found in the library collections of foreign poetry, ancient Greek myths, and works on the history and geography of Russia, America, England, France, and other countries.

His father had cut him off. Mao Yichang was unhappy with his grown son hanging around in the city without a job, changing schools almost monthly, and demanding financial support. Each time Mao enrolled in a new school, he wrote to his father, imploring this "ancestor" whom he despised to send him money, from which one silver dollar went for his registration fee. Living in Changsha was not cheap. Why did Mao prefer to lean on his father rather than get a job? In a big city like Changsha there were many opportunities for work even though many of these jobs were menial. In the provincial capital new homes were being built, streets were being laid out, and commerce was thriving. He probably could not have gotten a job as a coolie (a porter or a stevedore) since mafia-like organizations controlled that kind of labor, but he could have been a private tutor or an ad writer. Mao, however, didn't even consider such possibilities. As a student, a potential member of the gentry, an intellectual, he felt he belonged to a higher class than these soldiers, peasants, and coolies. Of course, Mao was not the only one guilty of such feelings toward labor. His arrogance was endemic to his social group. Not only Mao but other young Chinese intellectuals from commoner backgrounds who had only a primary education felt they were special in a society where virtually everyone was illiterate. Thirty years later, reminiscing about his life in Changsha in a public speech to his comrades in the Communist Party, Mao himself acknowledged,

> I began life as a student and at school acquired the ways of a student; I then used to feel it undignified to do even a little manual labor, such as carrying my own luggage in the presence of my fellow students, who were incapable of carrying anything, either on their shoulders or in their hands. At that time I felt that intellectuals were the only clean people in the world, while in comparison workers and peasants were dirty. I did not mind wearing the clothes of other intellectuals, believing them clean, but I would not put on clothes belonging to a worker or peasant, believing them dirty.[8]

Wandering about the city streets, Mao often came across coolies, construction workers, stevedores, itinerant peddlers, and other unfortunate people. Countless beggars asked for alms from passersby. The revolution had brought no changes to such people. Workers toiled from dawn to dusk till they dropped from exhaustion. From morning to night the streets swarmed with porters dressed in pitiful rags—short pants that came to just below the knee, and baggy shirts. Some carried goods on long carrying poles; others pushed wheelbarrows with small wooden boards strapped to each side. These vehicles were the main form of urban transport. A coolie harnessed himself to the back of the cart, throwing a thick strap around his neck and gripping long bamboo shafts in both hands. Passengers sat on either side of the wheel on wooden planks while the coolie pushed the conveyance forward, straining every muscle in his body. The faces of the porters and transport workers were emaciated from their heavy, stupefying labor. Only now and then could these people take a short break to drink a cup of green tea, eat a small dish of boiled rice, or grab a smoke.

Mao Zedong as yet felt no sympathy toward the sufferings of the working class. He was more concerned about the profound problems of China's national revival. Life without money, however, was not conducive to philosophical ruminations. His implacable father promised financial support only if his son settled down. Finally, Mao decided to become a teacher. In the spring of 1913 he became a student at the newly opened Hunan Provincial Fourth Normal School.

Xiao San, his friend from Dongshan, was already studying there and had convinced him to attend.[9] It was a tuition-free educational institution with about two hundred students. One year later, in March 1914, the provincial authorities decided to merge this school with the larger and better-established Provincial First Normal School, which enrolled more than a thousand students. Mao, like the other students, was automatically transferred to the new school. The First Normal School was well-known in Changsha and had been founded toward the end of the Qing dynasty, in 1903. Its building was the most modern in the city, and people in Changsha called it the "Western palace" because it was built in a European style of architecture. The railroad ran right past the campus, and beyond flowed the majestic Xiang River, on whose sandy banks students spent their free time in hot weather.

Mao quickly befriended Xiao Zisheng (Xiao Yu), the older brother of his friend Xiao San. Xiao Yu, in his third year, was considered the best student in the school, but respected the newcomer from the outset. Mao and he were very close for a long time, and not until 1921 did their paths diverge, when Xiao Yu opposed the establishment of the Chinese Communist Party. Later, in 1959, Xiao Yu, an exile in Uruguay, published his reminiscences of Mao's childhood and youth under the title *Mao Tse-tung and I Were Beggars.*[10]

Xiao described his initial impressions of the new student: "A tall, clumsy, dirtily dressed" Shaoshan fellow, whose shoes badly needed repairing,

Mao was not unusual in appearance, as some people have maintained, with his hair growing low on his forehead, like the devils pictured by old-time artists, nor did he have any especially striking features. . . . To me he always seemed quite an ordinary, normal-looking person. His face was rather large, but his eyes were neither large nor penetrating, nor had they the sly, cunning look sometimes attributed to them. His nose was flattish and of a typical Chinese shape. His ears were well-proportioned; his mouth, quite small; his teeth very white and even. These good white teeth helped to make his smile quite charming, so that no one would imagine that he was not genuinely sincere. He walked rather slowly, with his legs somewhat separated, in a way that reminded one of a duck waddling. His movements in a sitting or standing position were very slow. Also, he spoke slowly and he was by no means a gifted speaker.[11]

Most of the students at the Normal School, who judged others not on appearance, but on content, immediately took a liking to Mao. It is true that Mao was not a very diligent student. He thought he had earned the right to study only those subjects, like the social sciences and literature, that he found interesting and came easily to him. English, arithmetic, natural sciences, and drawing left him cold. Writing was considered the most important subject, and he always received the highest grades on his compositions. Therefore, in spite of everything, Mao was in good standing. His passion for reading did not desert him. "Mao Zedong was addicted to reading Chinese and European philosophers and writers, summarizing and expanding upon their thoughts in his diaries," recalled Xiao San. "He wrote quickly as if sparks were flying from his writing brush. His class compositions were posted as examples on the walls of the school. He could read two or three times faster than anyone else. In the library he was always surrounded by a wall of books."[12]

Mao became close friends with another student in the school, who went by the name of Cailin Bin. His real name was Cailin Hexian, but he had chosen the pseudonym Bin ("Refined Politeness") upon entering the school, as something that precisely fit his character. Cailin Bin had a piercing native intelligence. As tall as Mao, with a thick shock of hair and sad, thoughtful eyes, he stood out from the others. Books were his passion. He could go for days without washing his face, and months without shaving or changing his clothes. Later, under the name of Cai Hesen, he would become one of the main organizers of the communist movement in China. There can be no doubt that contact with new and interesting people like Cai Hesen enriched Mao's life. It was Cai who over the course of two or three years convinced Mao of the importance of the "worker question" and explained the need to organize a communist party.

The greatest influence on Mao at the Provincial First Normal School was four of his teachers. The First Normal School was famous for its teaching staff, many of whom had been educated abroad and were fluent in English, French, and Japanese. Several of them were later invited to teach at the best universities in China, including Peking University and Peking Normal University. One of his teachers, Yuan Jiliu (or Yuan Zhongqian), whom everyone called Yuan the Big Beard, taught Mao to write brilliant essays. Others, like Xu Teli and Fang Weixia, members of the Revolutionary Alliance who had taken part in the 1911 Revolution, instilled in Mao faith in republican principles and strengthened his patriotic consciousness. So enthusiastic was Mao that he literally bowed down to Xu Teli. During the struggle to introduce a constitution, Teacher Xu had cut off his finger as a sign of his sincerity and resoluteness, and with the blood trickling out of his wound had written a petition to the delegates of the Qing National Assembly imploring them to persuade the Qing court to hold parliamentary elections. Both Xu and Fang later became important figures in the CCP.[13]

But the main influence in Mao's student life was meeting Professor Yang Changji, an elegant gentleman just past forty. He impressed his students with his extensive knowledge of Chinese and Western philosophy and ethics. In 1898 he had taken part in the reform movement, and he was acquainted with many well-known Chinese educators. Yang left China in 1903 and spent many years abroad, studying in Japan, Scotland, and Germany. He came to Changsha in 1913 and was immediately invited by Governor Tan Yankai to serve as head of the Department of Education.[14] He politely refused, preferring the modest position of teacher in the Provincial First Normal School to high government office. He also taught at the Fourth School, where Mao Zedong first met him in the autumn of 1913, until it merged with the First. Thus began a seven-year friendship between teacher and student that lasted until Yang Changji's death in mid-January 1920.

They shared a mutual affection and respect. This is what Mao told Edgar Snow about Yang Changji: "The teacher who made the strongest impression on me was Yang Chen-ch'i [Yang Changji], a returned student from England. . . . He taught ethics, he was an idealist, and a man of high moral character. He believed in his ethics very strongly and tried to imbue his students with the desire to become just, moral, virtuous men, useful in society."[15] And this is Yang Changji's assessment of his favorite pupil:

> Student Mao Zedong said that he comes from a locality on the boundary between Xiangtan and Xiangxiang. . . . His hometown is in the high mountains, where people live together by clans. Most of them are peasants. . . . His father, too, was previously a peasant, but has now become a trader. His younger brother is likewise a peasant. His mother's family is from Xiangxiang, and they are also peasants. And yet it is truly difficult to find someone so intelligent and handsome [as Mao]. . . . [M]any unusual talents have come from peasant families.[16]

Professor Yang Changji was known at school as "Confucius" because of his education and erudition. In addition to ethics, he taught logic, philosophy, and pedagogy.[17] He was an adherent of Western liberalism, which he saw as akin to the teachings of the famous Ming dynasty Confucian philosopher Wang Yangming (1472–1529), and another great Confucian, Wang Chuanshan (1619–1692), two of a small number of Chinese thinkers who regarded the individual as of paramount importance.[18]

Yang Changji's students were eager to listen and converse with him for days on end. They even gathered at his home on Sundays. Among them were Mao, the Xiao brothers, and Cai Hesen. Such ideas as liberalism and individualism should have opened for Yang's students the path to the liberal-democratic reconstruction of Chinese society. In discussing the ideas of Wang Yangming and Western philosophers, however, what Professor Yang focused on was not the abstract idea of universal freedom, but individualism in a wholly utilitarian manner within the framework of the "hero and the crowd." What China needed, he asserted, was strong personalities, and he called upon his students to seek to persist in self-cultivation every day. "You spend too much time in self-denial and too little in mindfulness cultivation," he told them.[19] Yang Changji believed that strong individuals had the right to elevate themselves above the morality of the crowd. From the viewpoint of Mao's teacher, ethics should be directed toward one goal: the self-actualization of the individual.

Under the influence of his mentor, Mao read a Chinese translation of *System der Ethik,* a work by the nineteenth-century German philosopher Friedrich Paulsen, who asserted that the activity of a person who was totally focused on the achievement of a carefully defined goal was the highest and most absolute value. This teaching convinced Mao that the inflexible will of a great person trumped all other ethical principles. Such an ideology, expressed in the familiar slogan "The end justifies the means," accurately reflected the inclinations of Mao himself, a proud and stubborn provincial who dreamed of glory. He made an enormous number of marginal notes in his copy of *System der Ethik;* they total more than twelve thousand words in all. Here are just a few of the more typical notes:

> [P]urpose is unrelated to knowledge and is related only to feeling and will. . . . Morals are not prescriptive; they are descriptive. . . . In the broad sense there is no universal human morality. . . . Morality differs with the times, but it none the less remains morality. . . . Morality is different in different societies, and with different persons. . . . Since human beings have an ego, for which the self is the center of all things and all thought, self-interest is primary for all persons. . . . The starting point of altruism is the self, and altruism is related to the self. It is impossible to say that any mind is purely altruistic without any idea of

self-interest. Nothing in the world takes the other as its starting point, and the self does not seek to benefit anything in the world that is totally unrelated to the self. . . . Paulsen, too, takes individualism as his foundation. This is an individualism of the spirit, and may be called spiritual individualism. . . . Blind morality has no value at all. . . . In the realm of ethics, I advocate two principles. The first is individualism. Every act in life is for the purpose of fulfilling the individual, and all morality serves to fulfill the individual. Expressing sympathy for others, and seeking the happiness of others, are not for others, but for oneself. . . . I suspect that natural instincts are not necessarily false, and that the sense of duty is not necessarily true. . . . [W]e have a duty only to ourselves, and have no duty to others.[20]

Only one conclusion was possible from all this, and Mao drew it: "Some say that we must believe that the moral law comes from the command of God, for only then can it be carried out and not be despised. This is a slavish mentality. Why should you obey God rather than obey yourself? You are God. Is there any God other than yourself?"[21] A strong individual was not bound by moral principles and strived for the achievement of a great goal. The dictatorship of the will and unlimited power. What a novel interpretation of liberalism. Not freedom for everyone, but everyone a law unto himself.

As in Descartes's formula, "I think, therefore, I am," Mao placed his emphasis on the pronoun "I." He was just a step away from "class morality" and "class struggle." He already sensed his own greatness. Thus, he wrote,

The truly great person develops the original nature with which Nature endowed him. . . . This is what makes him great. . . . The great actions of the hero are his own, are the expression of his motive power, lofty and cleansing, relying on no precedent. His force is like that of a powerful wind arising from a deep gorge, like the irresistible sexual desire for one's lover, a force that will not stop, that cannot be stopped. All obstacles dissolve before him.[22]

Mao had no doubt that the masses must blindly follow the directions of the great man. He supposed that people in general and Chinese in particular were stupid and ignorant. In June 1912, Mao had written a short essay referring contemptuously to the "ignorance" of the Chinese people, who were unable to judge properly the merits of what Mao deemed the progressive actions of Lord Shang, a fourth-century BCE minister of the ancient Chinese state of Qin, and founder of the Legalist school of philosophy. "Shang Yang's laws were good laws. . . . How could the people fear and not trust him. . . . From this, we can see the stupidity of the people of our country."[23] Mao was not the least bothered by the fact that Shang Yang was one of the bloodiest ministers in ancient China and established a cruel dictatorship. What mattered to Mao was that Shang Yang had elevated himself above the crowd, had been able to achieve power, and that his drastic reforms had strengthened the state of Qin.

The idea of self-improvement, of physical and spiritual training, likewise occupied Mao in these years. He and his classmates were ardent national-ists who were seeking to save their country and were animated by a thirst for struggle and heroic self-sacrifice. Seized by an abnormal self-conceit, they be-lieved in the unrestricted priority of the will and of reason. They denied the existence of God, and were convinced that they had a right to do whatever they pleased. He and his friends trained themselves for future battles.

"We also became ardent physical culturists," Mao said to Edgar Snow.

In the winter holidays we tramped through the fields, up and down mountains, along city walls, and across the streams and rivers. When the sun was hot we doffed shirts and called it a sun-bath. In the spring winds we shouted that this was a new sport called "wind bathing." We slept in the open when frost was already falling and even in No-vember swam in the cold rivers. All this went on under the title of "body-training." [24]

It was no accident that the first article Mao published was called "A Study of Physical Education." It was published in the leading Shanghai journal *Xin qingnian* (New youth) in April 1917 under the pseudonym "Twenty-Eight Stroke Student," referring to the number of strokes it took to write the three characters of his name, Mao Zedong. Yang Changji had submitted it to the journal.[25] Mao asserted: "Our nation is wanting in strength; the military spirit has not been encouraged. The physical condition of our people deteriorates daily. These are extremely disturbing phenomena. . . . If our bodies are not strong, we will tremble at the sight of [enemy] soldiers. How then can we at-tain our goals, or exercise far-reaching influence?"[26] Mao offered his readers a program of physical training he himself had devised. He believed that sports would not only make the nation healthy, but also temper the will of the people. "The will," he emphasized, "**is the antecedent of a man's career.**"[27] After read-ing Paulsen's book in early 1918, Mao wrote another essay. This one was called "The Energy of the Mind." Unfortunately, this work has not survived, but we know that Professor Yang loved it.[28]

Mao's desire to become a strong, willful, and purposeful hero, not bound by any moral chains, is understandable. The examples of great men made his brain whirl. But this is not a sufficient explanation for his beliefs. Intellectuals of his generation experienced the degraded condition of their country as trag-edy. Not only Mao, but many of his peers, too, dreamed of themselves as giants smashing the greedy foreign powers and local tyrants that were exploiting China. How they yearned to defeat the haughty British and Americans, to put an end to the arbitrary rule of the corrupt officials, militarists, and oligarchs, in order to provide a better life for the people.

Overcome by patriotic zeal and wishing to learn more about the life of the people, in the summer of 1917 Mao set off with his friend Xiao Yu to travel around Hunan. They roamed more than three hundred miles on foot along dusty rural roads, meeting peasants, local officials, gentry, and merchants. Mao wore an old, light-colored robe and carried an umbrella and a small pack in which he kept a change of underwear, a towel, notebook, a writing brush, and ink. These last items were indispensable, as students were able to earn money along the way by writing signs, announcements, and poetic inscriptions at the request of local people. By this time, Mao's attitude toward work had changed. The peasants fed and sheltered him and Xiao Yu. Closely observing the joyless life of the rural folk, Mao probably recalled his own difficult childhood. Of all the great heroes of the past the one that he now wanted to emulate was Liu Bang, the peasant's son who had organized poor people to rebel and founded the great Han dynasty. Many years later Xiao Yu recalled that while wandering the roads of Hunan he and Mao talked about Liu Bang.

> "Liu Pang [Liu Bang] was the first commoner in history to become Emperor," he continued thoughtfully. "I think he should be considered to be a great hero!"
>
> "Oh no," I remonstrated. "Liu Pang was a bad man. . . . He was too selfish, too self-centered to be an emperor." I explained, "He was really nothing more than a man with political ambitions who was successful. . . . [H]e got rid of one despot only to become another himself. . . . Remember the friends and generals who risked their lives fighting for him? When his armies were successful, these men became famous leaders and he became afraid that one or another of them might try to usurp his throne; so he had them all killed. . . ."
>
> "But if he hadn't killed them, his throne would have been insecure and he probably wouldn't have lasted long as Emperor," said Mao.

"So in order to be successful in politics, one must kill one's friends?" Xiao Yu exclaimed in astonishment. But Mao did not wish to prolong the conversation. "We both knew," Xiao Yu concluded, "that he was identifying himself with Liu Pang in his ambition."[29]

Back at school, Mao again immersed himself in the social sciences. He continued to read newspapers and magazines very closely, especially *New Youth* and *The People,* Sun Yat-sen's journal.

The situation in China was growing ever more tense. On June 6, 1916,

Yuan Shikai died. This general-turned-politician had tried to rule China the old way, relying upon his loyal Beiyang Army. He was a stranger to new and democratic ideas. Soon after he had been chosen as the provisional president of the Republic of China, he began to institute an openly dictatorial order in the country. He was opposed not only by Sun Yat-sen's revolutionaries but also by local military oligarchs who did not wish to disband their troops and submit to him. In the winter of 1912–13, Sun Yat-sen's Revolutionary Alliance, which was renamed the Guomindang (Nationalist Party), won a resounding victory in parliamentary elections. Yuan Shikai felt threatened. Having secured the support of the Western powers, which had extended him an enormous loan of 25 million pounds sterling (around 100 million U.S. dollars), Yuan Shikai began to prepare for civil war. In March he ordered the assassination of Song Jiaoren, the Guomindang leader in parliament. Beiyang Army troops began to be redeployed to strategic centers in central China. An anti–Yuan Shikai uprising, the so-called second revolution, flared up in the eastern province of Jiangxi, with Guomindang members playing an active role. A number of other provinces supported the revolt, but troops loyal to the president suppressed it. In November 1913 Yuan Shikai outlawed the Guomindang, dispersed the parliament, and suspended the constitution. Sun Yat-sen was again forced to flee to Japan. A new constitution effectively placed all power in the hands of the president, and parliament, which reconvened in December 1914, bent to Yuan Shikai's will, and declared him president for life.

By 1915, however, Yuan Shikai's authority had been substantially undermined as a result of his capitulation to Japan's increasingly aggressive policy toward China. Soon after the start of World War I, Japan, as a member of the Entente, occupied Germany's colony in China, the port of Qingdao and the Jiaozhou Bay district on the southern coast of the Shandong peninsula. At the same time, the Japanese seized a railroad built by the Germans that linked Qingdao with Jinan, the capital of Shandong province, as well as mines belonging to the Germans. On January 28, 1915, Japan presented an ultimatum to Yuan Shikai, the so-called Twenty-One Demands, acceptance of which would have turned China into a Japanese colony. News of this impudent demand infuriated the Chinese intelligentsia. On May 7, Yuan Shikai, fearing that Japan might dispatch troops, accepted most of the demands, but even the usually supine parliament refused to ratify the agreement. Thus, on May 25, 1915, Yuan Shikai affixed his own seal to the agreement. An anti-Japanese movement began in China. Young people were especially indignant. Mao Zedong expressed his feelings in the following sentences: "The 7th of May dishonors our Motherland. How can we students take revenge? With our very lives!"[30]

In late December 1915, on the advice of his American adviser Frank Goodnow, Yuan Shikai announced the restoration of the monarchy and proclaimed himself the new emperor. This action further incensed public opinion.

The three southwestern provinces of Yunnan, Guangxi, and Guizhou declared their independence. Civil war flared up, and in the midst of it Yuan Shikai unexpectedly died of uremia at the age of fifty-six. He was succeeded by General Li Yuanhong, who had taken part in the Wuchang uprising of 1911.

All these events impacted social and political conditions in Mao's home province of Hunan. The provincial governor Tan Yankai joined the Guomindang in 1912, thinking to strengthen his position as a member of the most popular political party in the country. In 1913 he supported the "second revolution" by proclaiming the independence of Hunan, but he miscalculated. Yuan Shikai dispatched troops, which occupied Changsha and relieved Tan Yankai of all his posts. He barely escaped with his life. Yuan's protégé, the conservative general Tang Xiangming, was installed in power in Changsha, where he established a reign of terror in the province and tried to eradicate the weakly developed roots of democracy. He banned every kind of political activity, including student meetings in schools and colleges.[31] During the three-year reign of Butcher Tang, as he was known in Hunan, from five to ten thousand people were executed for political reasons. The terror stopped temporarily only after Li Yuanhong came to power in Beijing. In June 1916, Butcher Tang fled to Shanghai disguised as a peasant.[32] Tan Yankai briefly returned to power, but after a year he was replaced by General Fu Liangzuo. Soon after a new regime of terror was instituted in Changsha by General Zhang Jingyao, whom the Hunanese called "Zhang the Venomous."[33]

After the death of Yuan Shikai, as central power imploded, Hunan, like all of China, became mired in chaos. The armies of numerous militarists, their ranks filled with déclassé peasants and other unemployed men, ignited fratricidal civil wars. The Western powers, interested in selling China arms and receiving additional economic privileges, encouraged this development.

In sum, Mao had more than sufficient reason to be concerned about the fate of his country. He pondered the great and invincible rulers of antiquity, owing to whose energy and will his motherland had inspired fear and trembling in its neighbors and earned the proud name of Zhongguo, or Middle Kingdom. Mao became convinced that only force merited respect and only a despot would be able to unite and revive China. It is striking that Mao respected not only the emperor Liu Bang, but also the hated Hunanese tyrant Tang Xiangming. After Tang's downfall, Mao wrote a bitter letter to his friend Xiao Yu:

> I still maintain that Military Governor Tang should not have been sent away. . . . Tang was here for three years, and he ruled by the severe enforcement of strict laws. . . . Order was restored, and the peaceful times of the past were practically regained. . . . The fact that he killed well over ten thousand people was the inescapable outcome of policy. . . . Without such behavior the goal of national protection

would be unattainable. Those who consider these things to be crimes do not understand the overall plan.[34]

Later, Mao would note, "This . . . does not mean that all homicide is wrong. . . . What we call evil is only the image, not the essence."[35] Such reasoning sends shivers down the spine.

It was now the autumn of 1917. Mao Zedong was in his twenty-fourth year and so far he had not accomplished much of anything. He greedily devoured his books, seeking to find the truth in their pages, but it was now time for action. Finally, he grasped what he needed to do. His soul thirsted for battle, for war, for revolution. "[A] long period of peace, pure peace without any disorder of any kind, would be unbearable to human life," he wrote,

> and it would be inevitable that the peace would give birth to waves. . . . [H]uman beings always hate the chaos and hope for order, not realizing that chaos too is part of the process of historical life, that it too has value in real life. . . . When they come to periods of peace, they are bored and put the book aside. It is not that we like chaos, but simply that the reign of peace cannot last long, is unendurable to human beings, and that human nature is delighted by sudden change. . . . The destruction of the universe is not an ultimate destruction . . . because from the demise of the old universe will come a new universe, and will it not be better than the old universe![36]

It was then he confessed his desire to burn all Chinese anthologies of prose and poetry that had been written since the Tang and Song dynasties. Evidently he thought they were not progressive enough. He passionately informed his friends of the need to smash traditional family ties and to effect a revolution in the relations between teachers and students.[37]

Many years later he translated these youthful feelings into a formula that the entire world took as his political credo: "To rebel is justified." Meanwhile, he continued to dream with his friends, but his dreams were acquiring ever clearer shape. On a warm September day in 1917, when his friends, who were picnicking with him on a hill behind the school, began to argue about what should be done to save the nation, Mao said firmly, "Imitate the heroes of Liangshanbo!"[38] These were the rebellious peasants in his favorite novel, *Water Margin*.

4

THE SOUND OF FOOTSTEPS
IN A DESERTED VALLEY

In May 1918, Professor Yang Changji received an irresistible job offer from the rector of Peking University, the well-known educator Cai Yuanpei. Peking University was considered the best and most liberal of Chinese universities. At the beginning of June, Mao Zedong and Yang Changji parted, but by the end of the month, Professor Yang wrote to his favorite student, urging Mao to join him in Beijing. A group of young men and women in Beijing was preparing to journey to France, where they would combine work with study. Professor Yang advised Mao and his friends to take advantage of this opportunity to learn about the world.[1]

By then Mao was busy with political and organizational activities. He had already demonstrated his organizational abilities in the autumn of 1915 when he sent a notice to several schools in Changsha inviting young people interested in patriotic work to contact him. In his words, he "ardently desired to make friends." Mao wanted to widen his circle of acquaintances to include those who "were tempered by suffering and fully determined to sacrifice everything for the sake of their country." He signed the notice with the pseudonym we have already encountered, the "Twenty-Eight Stroke Student."[2]

Five or six people replied, but only three expressed an interest in joining the patriotic circle.[3] One was Luo Zhanglong, a nineteen-year-old who introduced himself by the Japanese name Tate Uchirō ("Knight-Errant"). He had heard of the declaration from a friend, and immediately wrote to Mao. Several years later, Luo became one of the leading members of the Chinese communist movement, but he was expelled from the CCP in 1931 because he opposed its Stalinist leadership. Two other young people who joined Mao's circle subsequently became ultrareactionaries.

Mao received one other reply, or "half a reply," from Li Longzhi, a sixteen-year-old student at a middle school in Changsha, whom Luo Zhanglong had advised to meet Mao. According to Mao, "Li listened to all I had to say, and then went away without making any definite proposals himself, and our friend-ship never developed."[4] Li Longzhi, who had just come to Changsha from the countryside, later said that Mao seemed so well educated that he simply felt ter-ribly inadequate.[5] This feeling would fade five or six years later when Li Long-zhi, under his new name of Li Lisan, became one of the leading organizers of the Chinese labor movement. In 1928 he became the de facto head of the Com-munist Party and until late 1930 the dominant figure in the CCP leadership whom Mao himself had to obey.

But that was in the future. Meanwhile, Mao, with the help of Luo Zhang-long and several other classmates, managed to cobble together a group of patriotic youth. There were some amusing incidents along the way. The ad-ministration of the local women's college interpreted Mao's declaration as the attempt of a dissolute youth to find a bed partner. However, the leadership of the First Normal School vouched for Mao.[6] After a while, several individuals had gathered around Mao.[7] One of them told Mao, "[Your letter was like] the sound of footsteps in a deserted valley; at the sound of your feet my face shone with joy."[8]

This is how Mao remembered this circle:

> It was a serious-minded little group of men and they had no time to discuss trivialities. Everything they did or said must have a purpose. They had no time for love or "romance" and considered the times too critical and the need for knowledge too urgent to discuss women or personal matters. I was not interested in women. . . . Quite aside from the discussions of feminine charm, which usually play an important role in the lives of young men of this age, my companions even re-jected talk of ordinary matters of daily life. I remember once being in the home of a youth who began to talk to me about buying some meat, and in my presence called in his servant and discussed the mat-ter with him, then ordering him to buy a piece. I was annoyed and did not see this fellow again. My friends and I preferred to talk only of large matters—the nature of men, of human society, of China, the world, and the universe![9]

In June 1917, Mao Zedong was named the best student in the school. This honor was awarded every year at the end of the spring semester. On this occa-sion a majority—forty-nine people—voted for Mao.[10] Soon afterward he again demonstrated his organizational ability. In September 1917, he founded an association of Xiangtan natives in the school and became more active in the Student Union, which soon chose him as its leader.[11]

The most important undertaking of the Student Union was to revive an evening workers' school that had been started at the Normal School six months earlier, but had shut down by the fall of 1917. Through Mao Zedong's efforts, classes resumed on November 9, with 102 students, most of whom were unemployed laborers who had come to the city to search for work.[12] By this time Mao Zedong had changed his view of ordinary people. He had matured, and although he still felt superior to them in social status, he no longer disdained them. "Plants and trees, birds and animals all nurture and care for their own kind," he reasoned. "Must not human beings do the same? . . . Some of them [the worker students] are out of school simply because there is some lack in their natural endowments, or they come from less fortunate circumstances. It is precisely for such people as these that the humane person should show sympathy, rather than shift the responsibility to them."[13] In this school the "lover of humanity" Mao Zedong acquired his first experience of teaching by giving lectures on Chinese history.[14]

In November 1917, Mao played an active role organizing a student volunteer guard. These were troubled times in Hunan, like everywhere else in China. Civil war raged. Soldiers often occupied the college buildings and behaved improperly toward the students, especially the females. This produced indignation and protests. During the rule of Governor Fu Liangzuo, beginning in November 1917, the Provincial First School was able to stand up to the demands of the army, which wanted to turn the educational institution into a barracks. It was Mao who organized the defense, in the words of Xiao San, taking "charge as though he had received the sanction of the Ministry of War."[15] Unlike the teachers and the other students, he had some slight military experience. In November the situation grew more tense. After the rout of Fu Liangzuo's army the retreating soldiers terrorized the local population and threatened to attack the school. Mao again demonstrated initiative by contacting the local police, several of whom responded to his call for help. A student self-defense force was organized, although armed only with wooden rifles and bamboo sticks.

As not only an ex-soldier but also chair of the Student Union, Mao took personal command. The students and the police waited until the soldiers had come right up to the school gates; then Mao ordered the police—the only ones with real rifles—to open fire. Then the students began to light firecrackers in empty jerry cans and loudly shout, "If you hand over your weapons there will be no trouble!" The soldiers took fright and surrendered.[16] The school journal for November 1917 contained the following entry: "The fighting in southern Hunan is critical, and there is a great disturbance. The students have organized a garrison force for day and night patrols. Guard duty is extraordinary."[17]

Xiao San recalled that Mao was particularly interested in military issues at this time.[18] Not only China, but the whole world, was at war. Mao closely followed events in the European theater, reading the daily Beijing, Shanghai, and Hunan newspapers, some of which he subscribed to himself. By his own reckoning, he spent a third of the money his father sent him on books and periodicals.[19] He had a strange habit: after reading the newspaper from cover to cover, he cut off the white margins of the pages and sewed them together with thread. Xiao San tells us, "He picked out geographic place names from the newspaper and wrote them down on these white margins."[20]

In the winter of 1917, Mao and his friends thought of organizing a tightly centralized group of like-minded persons. "I built up a wide correspondence with many students and friends in other towns and cities," Mao said to Edgar Snow. "Gradually I began to realize the necessity for a more closely knit organization."[21] It was finally established in April 1918, and called Xinmin xuehui (Renovation of the People Study Society). Mao and his fellows obviously borrowed the name from Liang Qichao's journal (*Xinmin congbao*—Renovation of the people), which the Chinese reformer published in Yokohama. Xiao Yu suggested the name, and everyone happily agreed to it.[22]

The founding meeting of the society took place on Sunday morning, April 14, 1918, in Cai Hesen's home in the village of Yingwan on the left bank of the Xiang River. Thirteen men assembled in a small, poorly furnished shack hidden in the shade of dense trees. "The weather was bright and clear," recalled Mao. "Gentle breezes caressed the azure waters of the river and the emerald grass along its banks. This left an indelible impression on all those who attended the meeting."[23] In addition to the host and Mao, others present were their old friends: the Xiao brothers, Luo Zhanglong, and others. There were also some new faces, including forty-two-year-old He Shuheng, with whom Mao had entered the Provincial Fourth Normal School in 1913. He Shuheng graduated after just a few months and had been teaching Chinese in a primary school in Changsha since July 1914. He was short and broad-shouldered, very serious and modest, wore large round eyeglasses, and enjoyed the unbounded respect of his younger comrades. They jocularly called him Bewhiskered He, because of his black whiskers, which made him look like a member of the classical gentry. He was actually a rural intellectual who at age eighteen had passed the first level of the old imperial examination system and become a *xiucai*. Mao and Xiao Yu became friendly with him during summer vacation in 1917, when they visited Bewhiskered He in his native village of Ningxiang during their wanderings through the province.[24] This selfless, unusually energetic man with a piercing gaze played a large role in Mao's life. He became Mao's closest assistant in organizing a communist circle in Hunan in 1920, and he took part in the First Congress of the Chinese Communist Party in 1921.[25] He Shuheng considered Mao an "extraordinary man" and despite their significant difference in age, He always respected Mao greatly and never disputed his superiority.[26]

Those assembled in the woods discussed the bylaws of the organization, a draft of which Mao Zedong and another member of the society had drawn

up in March. It said, in part, "The main goals of the society are to reform academic studies, to temper the character of its members, and to ameliorate the
human heart and customs. . . . All members must abide by the following rules:
1. Do not be hypocritical; 2. Do not be lazy; 3. Do not be wasteful; 4. Do not
gamble; [and] 5. Do not consort with prostitutes." Anyone could join the society upon the recommendation of five or more existing members, payment of a
one-silver-dollar membership fee, and approval of his candidacy by more than
half the members of the organization. Everyone was required to pay annual
membership dues, which were also one silver dollar.[27]

After the bylaws were adopted the leadership was selected. Xiao Yu was
named general secretary. According to his younger brother Xiao San, the position of general secretary was first offered to Mao, but he declined, and agreed
only to serve as one of two deputies to Xiao Yu.[28] Eventually about seventy to
eighty persons joined the society, including several girls: Li Si'an, a student at
the Canye School in Hunan; Tao Yi, a student at the First Normal School and
one of Professor Yang Changji's favorites; Cai Chang, who was Cai Hesen's
younger sister; and Xiang Jingyu, a female friend of Cai's. Many members of
the organization later became leading figures in the Chinese communist movement, and most of these laid down their lives in struggles for a new China.[29]

All of the members tried to achieve the following dream: "To improve the
life of the individual and of the whole human race." This is why they called
their society the Renovation of the People Study Society. Although they rejected "romance," they were romantics themselves. "[A]t that time the new
thought and new literature had already sprung up in the country," wrote Mao
Zedong, "and we all felt that in our minds the old thought, the old ethics, and
the old literature had been totally swept away. We came to a sudden realization
that it was all wrong to lead a quiet and solitary life, and that on the contrary
it was necessary to seek an active and collective life. . . . [W]e formed a view of
life that emphasizes continual striving and improvement."[30]

The members of the society soon introduced changes in the organizational goals. They were no longer satisfied with the restructuring of academic
studies and moral education. Now they wanted nothing less than the "transformation of China and the whole world,"[31] and they sincerely desired to begin
by transforming themselves. Apart from the noble intentions of becoming better, purer, and smarter, and the desire to bring joy to humankind, for the time
being they had no concrete ideas at all. "We started out as members of a petit
bourgeois intellectual organization, striving for 'self-improvement' and 'mutual assistance,' " recalled Li Weihan, one of the members of the group. "A majority of the members were young people who believed in reform, and ardently
desired progress. But how should we bring about these reforms? How should
we achieve progress? Groping our way forward, we still had not even come to
this point."[32] In Xiao San's words, the program, on the whole, "was a mixture

of Confucianism and Kantianism."³³ Mao Zedong's assessment was essentially the same. "At this time," he said, "my mind was a curious mixture of ideas of liberalism, democratic reformism, and Utopian Socialism. I had somewhat vague passions about 'nineteenth-century democracy,' Utopianism and old-fashioned liberalism, and I was definitely anti-militarist and anti-imperialist."³⁴

In June 1919 Mao graduated from the Normal School. As his daughter put it, he was at a crossroads.³⁵ There was either no work or he didn't want to look for a job. Along with several friends, among them Cai Hesen, he settled on the left bank of the Xiang River and dreamed about creating a commune there, some sort of "work-study society of comrades," to work the land together and grasp the nature of science.³⁶ He was almost broke, but this didn't bother him. His friends teased him, saying "not a penny in his pocket, a concern for all the world!"³⁷ He spent whole days in thought, wandering around the environs, and feasting his eyes upon nature.

There was a magnificent view of Changsha from the summit of Mount Yuelu. The curved golden roofs of the Confucian temples shimmered under the hot sun; the eight towers of the fortress thrust majestically upward. Below, the Xiang River flowed unhurriedly at the foot of the mountain. Mao felt happy. He had many friends who viewed him as their leader. Several years later, in the autumn of 1925, Mao, who liked to write verse, would revisit these haunts and, recalling the past, would write the following lines:

> Standing alone in the cold autumn,
> where the Hsiang [Xiang] River flows north,
> on the tip of Orange Island,
> looking at thousands of hills,
> red all over,
> row after row of woods, all red,
> the river is green to the bottom,
> a hundred boats struggling,
> eagles striking the sky,
> fish gliding under the clear water.
> All creatures fight for freedom
> under the frosty sky.
> Bewildered at empty space,
> I ask the great, gray earth:
> who controls the rise and fall?
>
> Hundreds of friends used to come here.
> Remember of the old times—the years of fullness,
> when we were students and young,
> blooming and brilliant

with the young intellectuals'
emotional argument,
fist up, fist down,
fingers pointing
at river and mountain,
writings full of excitement,
lords of a thousand houses merely dung.
Remember still
how, in the middle of the stream,
we struck the water,
making waves which stopped
the running boats? [38]

During this period of relative inactivity Mao Zedong received the letter from his teacher concerning the recruitment of a group of young men and young women to travel to France. He shared this news with Cai Hesen, the Xiao brothers, and other friends. Cai Hesen and the older Xiao brother—Xiao Yu—were particularly excited by this opportunity. They had long dreamed of traveling abroad to study and considered France an ideal destination. It was a democratic country with solid revolutionary traditions. A meeting of the society was quickly called, at which "it was considered essential to have a movement to study in France and to make every effort to promote it." [39] The vast majority of those present expressed a desire to go to France. [40] Xiao Yu wrote to Yang Changji right away to find out more about the group in Beijing. One week later a reply arrived. Professor Yang said that he had met with the rector of Peking University, Cai Yuanpei, who had approved the participation of the young Hunanese in the work-study program. [41]

This program, first developed in 1912, was conceived by two anarchists, Li Shizeng and Wu Zhihui, who were among the first to receive an education in France. They were followers of the French anarchist theorist Élisée Reclus, who believed in a dialectical connection between education and revolution, as did his Chinese disciples. With good reason they supposed that revolutionary progress in society was impossible without the broad development of science and education. In 1905 Li Shizeng and Wu Zhihui established the first Chinese Anarchist Group in Paris, and in 1912 they organized the Chinese Society for Frugal Study in France, whose objective was to promote inexpensive means of receiving an education. They proposed that newcomers would pay their expenses by working in French enterprises and fund their own education on the principle of "one year of work, two years of study."

The society shouldered the task of attracting young Chinese to study in France and helping them find work. The core idea was to take advantage of the superiority of the Western educational system to educate a "new" man and a "new" woman, both workers and intellectuals. Only such persons, the anarchists thought, could regenerate China. Over the course of two years, 1912 and 1913, they sent one hundred Chinese students to France. At the end of 1913, however, the Chinese Society for Frugal Study in France was forced to cease operations. Yuan Shikai asserted that it made no sense for Chinese students to study in Europe.[42] The movement received a new lease on life in August 1917, however, when China entered the world war on the side of the Entente. The Chinese did not take part in the fighting, but per an agreement with the French, China sent 140,000 laborers to France, most engaged in digging trenches.[43] This reenergized the Chinese anarchists. Li Shizeng began to devote all his efforts to organizing a mass Chinese youth work-study movement in France. He contacted Cai Yuanpei, the rector of Peking University, and public figures in France, and soon established the joint Sino-French Study Society to facilitate the development of a system for educating Chinese in France as well as strengthening Sino-French cultural ties. The anarchists wanted to attract Chinese students to Europe in order to promote an amalgamation of "intellectuals" with the workers' movement. Branches of the organization were established in Beijing, Canton, and Shanghai. Preparatory schools for those intending to go on work-study to France were established in Beijing, Chengdu, Chongqing, and Baoding in 1918 and early 1919. The schools enrolled students from fourteen years old and up.[44]

European education appealed to Chinese youth for several reasons. Cai Yuanpei explained that there was a dearth of higher educational institutions in China and the level of existing ones left much to be desired. Second, there was not enough highly qualified teaching staff in China. Third, the Chinese Ministry of Education and associated institutions lacked the resources to organize effective practical studies for students, because of the paucity of libraries, museums, and botanical and zoological gardens.[45]

After receiving the letter from Professor Yang, Cai Hesen set off for Beijing, where he met with Yang Changji, Li Shizeng, and Cai Yuanpei. On June 30, he sent a letter to Mao Zedong and other members of the society confirming the possibility of traveling to France. He urged his friends to hurry to Beijing.[46]

Mao, however, first had to attend to some family matters. His mother, Wen Qimei, had been seriously ill since 1916. She had long suffered from stomach ulcers, and now she had contracted inflammation of the lymph nodes. Mao loved his mother very much and felt sorry for her. While studying in Changsha he periodically visited her. Over the past few years his parents had had a falling-out, for reasons unknown. Rumors circulated that Wen Qimei could not forgive her husband for having taken his son's wife as his concubine, but the disagreement may have been about something else. Mao's father became more cantankerous as the years passed, and she may simply have found living with him unbearable. Finally, she gathered up her belongings and moved in with her older brothers in her native village of Tangjiatuo. Mao Yichang, a traditionalist, probably found it hard to bear his spouse's rebellion, which violated the canons of Confucian morality.

As always, Mao was wholly on his mother's side. In early August 1918, he paid her another visit, this time at his uncles' house. He tried to persuade his mother to go with him to the provincial capital for medical tests. However, she refused, probably because she didn't want to burden her beloved son. Back in Changsha, Mao wrote to his uncles, again expressing the hope that his mother would still come to the city. He counted on her coming in late autumn, accompanied by his brother Zemin. In this same letter, he informed his relatives that he intended to go off to Beijing. He said nothing about traveling to France, assuring them that "sightseeing is the only aim of our trip, nothing else."[47] In reality, he simply didn't want to upset anyone. He had no reservations about traveling to France with his comrades and was excited at the prospect of the forthcoming adventure.[48]

On August 15, Mao left Changsha for Beijing with twenty-five of his comrades. They traveled to Wuhan on a small riverboat, then continued their journey by rail. It was Mao's first train ride, and a long one, some eight hundred miles.

They were delayed for two days in the small city of Xuchang in Henan province because the Yellow River was in flood. Mao was actually quite pleased. Xuchang was the site of the ancient Chinese kingdom of Wei, founded by Emperor Cao Pi, one of the persons who figured in his favorite novel, *Romance of the Three Kingdoms*.[49] At Mao's suggestion, the friends decided to explore the old city. They learned that the ruins of the ancient settlement were beyond the fortress wall. It's easy to imagine how excited Mao must have been. He was on his way to subdue the world, and a chance visit to a historic place that was steeped in the glory of past centuries was naturally full of symbolism. It was as if the famous heroes of antiquity were spurring him on to achieve great things for the glory and power of his country.

5

DREAMS OF A
RED CHAMBER

Mao and his friends arrived in Beijing on August 19, 1918, and set off at once for the home of Yang Changji, who lived in the northern part of town, not far from the city gates. Yang was overjoyed to see them, and offered to accommodate four of them, including Mao.[1] Yang; his wife, Xiang Zhenxi; his twenty-year-old son, Yang Kaizhi; and his seventeen-year-old daughter, Yang Kaihui (literally, "Opening Wisdom") lived in the small house located on a narrow and dirty alley.[2] Mao was already acquainted with his teacher's family since he had often visited Yang Changji in Changsha. At the professor's invitation, in the summer of 1916 Mao had even spent several days as his guest in Yang's native town of Bancang. Mao recalled how he had walked more than twenty miles in his straw sandals to the unprepossessing brick house.[3] At that time, Yang Kaihui, who was affectionately called Xia ("Dawn" or "Little Dawn"),[4] was only fifteen (she was born on November 6, 1901), and the bashful Mao had not exchanged a single word with her. Nor had he spoken with his hostess. It was considered improper to converse with women whom you barely knew, so he had simply bowed his head as a token of respect. But he fully indulged his desire for conversation with his teacher, whose enormous library also delighted him. He and Yang Kaihui had seen each other subsequently, but Mao, it will be recalled, was not interested in women and apparently did not even notice that the young girl had blossomed into a young woman.

Now, seeing her again, Mao could not contain his emotions. Standing before him was a beautiful young woman with sensuous lips and attentive dark eyes. Mao's friends were equally impressed. "She was rather small in stature and round-faced. She looked somewhat like her father," recalled Xiao Yu, "with the same, deep-set, smallish eyes, but her skin was quite white."[5] Meanwhile, "Little Dawn" was captivated by this "intelligent and well-mannered" Shaoshan native whom her father had often praised. "I had fallen madly in love with him already when I heard about his numerous accomplishments," she recalled many years later. "Even though I loved him, I did not display my feelings. . . . I was firmly convinced that people had to come to love on their own. Nonetheless, I did not stop hoping and dreaming. . . . I decided that if nothing came of this, I would never marry anyone else."[6]

To Yang Kaihui's disappointment, their relationship did not develop smoothly. Two and a half years passed before their fates became intertwined. Mao was too shy, and he also had no money to go courting. His pride would not allow him to live off Yang Changji. After several days relaxing at the Yangs', Mao and his friends thanked their hosts and moved into a small apartment consisting of three tiny rooms.* They were too poor to afford anything else.[7] The one-story little wooden house with its large, paper-covered windows housed four other friends as well. Every night the eight men somehow managed to fit onto a single *kang*—a low, flat platform that occupied almost half the room, stretching from wall to wall. Serving as a heated bed in traditional Chinese homes, in cold weather the *kang* is warmed by hot smoke from a hearth built into one of its sides. The smoke circulates throughout the *kang*, filling all the cavities, and exits through an aperture in an outside wall. The friends, however, could not afford to heat the *kang*, so they slept close together for warmth. There was only one padded cotton coat among the eight, so on cold winter days they took turns going outside. Only after four months could they afford to buy two more coats. They cooked on a small stove inside the room.[8]

The tiny house with its minuscule interior courtyard was on a narrow alley in the Three-Eyed Well district of Beijing, quite close to Peking University. It was also near the famous artificial lake Beihai (North sea), located in a park of the same name, as well as the Forbidden City, the permanent residence of the former emperor Pu Yi.

Mao often wandered along Beijing's dusty streets and unpaved alleys. Unlike Changsha, Beijing was not a large commercial center and its commercial streets were not marked by a profusion of signs and advertisements. Yet many of the streets, the main shopping street of Wangfujing above all, were packed with people. Five times as many people lived in Beijing as in Changsha, around one million in all.[9] Large numbers of rickshaws, always being pulled at a fast clip, crowded the streets and alleys.[10] Almost one out of every six Beijing men between the ages of sixteen and fifty earned his livelihood as a rickshaw puller. An efficient rickshaw man could net more than fifteen silver dollars a month after deducting payment for the rickshaw, which most pullers rented from special garages—this at a time when an assistant librarian at Peking University earned only eight.[11]

Automobiles, still a rarity, rolled along the wide avenues, honking their

---

* Later, conversing with Edgar Snow, Mao reduced the number of rooms to just one, probably to impress upon Snow just how poor he had been at the time.

horns. Coachmen shouted at passersby to make way for their carriages, pulled by shaggy Mongolian ponies. Pullers with empty rickshaws hustled for fares, shouting raucously above the roar, "Mister! Mrs.!" The din was unbearable; it deafened every traveler in Beijing. One could often see camels on the streets as goods caravans arrived in Beijing from the Mongolian steppe. Their appearance only added to the chaos.[12]

Nevertheless, the city produced a surprisingly favorable impression. It was impossible not to be delighted with its magnificent architectural monuments, its unique palace complexes and temples, harmoniously placed in parklike settings. Mao, too, sensed the profound poetic charm of the capital. "[I]n the parks and the old palace grounds I saw the early northern spring," he said. "I saw the white plum blossoms flower while the ice still held solid over the North Sea [Beihai]. . . . The innumerable trees of Peking [Beijing] aroused my wonder and admiration.[13]

Beijing is one of China's oldest cities. It was founded four or five thousand years ago during the time of the legendary Yellow Emperor and initially called Yudu (Peaceful capital). Its current name of Beijing (Northern capital) dates from 1403 CE and was bestowed by the Ming emperor Yongle, who in 1421 transferred the capital here from Nanjing (Southern capital). It was on Yongle's command that a grandiose palace complex, occupying more than seventeen hundred acres, was built in the center of Beijing, officially called the Purple Forbidden City. In the southern part of Beijing, Yongle erected the stunningly beautiful Temple of Heaven (Tiantan), intended for imperial sacrifices to the ancestors.

The Manchus captured Beijing in 1644, and constructed the elegant Summer Palace in the northwestern outskirts of the city. This palace, located in the center of an enormous 840-acre park, Yuanmingyuan (Park of perfect splendor), stood until 1860, when the "civilized" Anglo-French forces that invaded Beijing during the Second Opium War pillaged and torched it in barbaric fashion. Deciding against restoring the palace, the empress dowager instead ordered the refurbishing of another grandiose summer residence in a nearby park, the Yiheyuan (Good health and harmony park).

Unfortunately, Mao could not enjoy the beauties of the Yiheyuan, since the entrance fee was so high that not even many rich Beijing residents could afford to visit the emperor's palace. But Mao was not depressed. What he did see was quite enough for a first visit.

In the early twentieth century, Beijing was also China's cultural and intellectual center. It was there in 1898 that a modern pedagogic institute was established and which, soon after the 1911 Revolution, was renamed Peking University, or Beida as Chinese usually call it. After the appointment of the liberal Cai Yuanpei as rector in the fall of 1916, a "New Culture" movement unfolded at Beida and many other educational and scholarly institutions throughout the country. The initiators of this movement were like the eighteenth-century French philosophes, who proclaimed the cult of reason instead of the traditional cult of faith, this time in Chinese society. The Enlightenment had finally come to China and Peking University was its bastion. The New Culture Movement inspired the new Chinese intelligentsia to search for new theoretical approaches that might help to solve China's economic, political, and social crises.

The mouthpiece of the movement was *Xin qingnian* (New youth), the same journal that published Mao Zedong's essay on physical culture in April 1917. Its editor in chief was Chen Duxiu, the dean of the College of Letters at Beida. *New Youth* had initiated the New Culture Movement, which targeted traditional Confucian ideas, and became one of the most influential publications disseminating such Western ideas as democracy, humanism, and the latest scientific theories. Its pages popularized anti-Confucian morality and Western individualism and liberalism, and sounded a clarion call for the spiritual renewal of society. The journal likewise played a major role in disseminating the new literary language of *baihua* (common speech) in place of the ancient classical Chinese language, which was too difficult for the broad mass of the Chinese people to learn to read.

The ideals that *New Youth* and Cai Yuanpei stood for were naturally close to the heart of young Mao Zedong. He admired Rector Cai, Beida professors Li Dazhao, Hu Shi, and other leaders of the popular movement, and he simply idolized Chen Duxiu. Peking University, or more precisely its newly constructed main building on Shatan (Sandbar), was just a fifteen-minute walk from Mao's quarters in the Three-Eyed Well. The tall, four-and-a-half-story building attracted Mao like a magnet. He already knew that the students and teachers had named it the Red Chamber (*hong lou*), after the eighteenth-century novelist Cao Xueqin's famous novel *Dream of the Red Chamber,* because the three upper stories of the building were clad in dark red bricks.

Mao must have been overjoyed when, in October 1918, Professor Yang Changji found him a job in Peking University. Yang gave him a letter of recommendation to Li Dazhao, professor of economics and director of the Beida library.

Li, like Mao, was from a prosperous peasant family, and only slightly more than four years older than Mao. He had been born not far from Beijing, in the small village of Daheito, on October 29, 1889. He had gone to a private village school, where, like Mao, he had studied the Confucian classics, and in 1907 he entered the Beiyang Political-Legal Academy in Tianjin, the large commercial city near Beijing. By the eve of the 1911 Revolution, he had already become politically and socially active. In 1913 the twenty-four-year-old published pa-

triotic verses and articles that attracted the attention of thoughtful intellectuals. After graduating in 1913, Li decided to continue his education abroad and
soon enrolled in Waseda University, a famous Tokyo institution. He returned
to China in May 1916 and immediately became involved in the New Culture
Movement. Li was invited to join Peking University in November 1917 and
took up his duties as professor of economics and head of the library in January
1918. Soon after, at Chen Duxiu's suggestion, he became a member of the editorial board of *New Youth*.[14] At the end of December 1918, he and Chen Duxiu
founded another journal, *Meizhou pinglun* (Weekly review), which addressed
political issues in an even sharper manner than *New Youth*.

Li was a tall, smiling, and amiable person who wore round metal-rimmed
glasses and cultivated a long mustache.[15] He was precise in manner and elegantly dressed, and unlike many other Beida professors, he liked on occasion
to wear Western suits, a tie, and white shirts with high starched collars. He was
someone whom people noticed.

Li offered Mao a position as assistant to the librarian at a salary of eight
dollars a month.[16] This was not much money, but Mao was not worried by material problems. He happily accepted the offer, and for the first time in his life
he had his own desk. Later, with pride in his voice, he would tell his relatives
that he worked on the staff at Beida.[17]

Director Li was even better read than Chen Duxiu and Cai Yuanpei, especially in the areas of contemporary Western philosophy, politics, and economics. He was the first person to show a serious interest in what for China were
the new teachings of Marxism. Before him almost no one in China knew anything about Marx, even though the earliest news about Marxian socialism appeared in the Middle Kingdom toward the very end of the nineteenth century.
In early 1903 a brief excerpt from *The Communist Manifesto* was first published in China in the form of a quotation cited in *Contemporary Socialism*,
a book published in China by the Japanese author Fukuda Shinzō. In January
1908, Chinese anarchists published a translation of Friedrich Engels's preface
to the 1888 English edition of *The Communist Manifesto* in their journal *Tianyi
bao* (Heaven's justice). This was the first work by the founders of Marxism published in China in complete form. At this time, the overwhelming majority of
Chinese intellectuals were unclear as to what Marxism actually was and failed
to differentiate Marx's socialism from all the other socialist teachings.[18] This is
what Mao himself said in April 1945:

> Apart from a small number of students who had studied abroad, no
> one in China [in those years] understood [Marxism]. I myself did not
> know that there had been such a person as Marx either. . . . At that
> time we . . . knew nothing about the existence in the world of imperi-

alism or any kind of Marxism. . . . Earlier there had been people like Liang Qichao and Zhu Zhixin who had referred to Marxism. They say there was also someone who translated Engels' *Socialism: Utopian and Scientific* in a journal. Generally speaking, at the time I didn't see [these editions], and if I did, I just skimmed over them, and paid them no heed.[19]

Li Dazhao was the first in China to draw attention not only to Marxism, but also to the worldwide significance of the Bolshevik experience. Embracing the Bolshevik positions, in 1918 he began to propagandize Russian communism on a wide scale. As early as July 1918, in his article "Comparing the French and Russian Revolutions," Li Dazhao wrote,

> The Russian revolution marks a change in the consciousness not only of Russians, but of all mankind in the 20th century. . . . We must proudly welcome the Russian revolution as the light of a new civilization. We must pay close attention to the news from Russia which is building upon the principles of freedom and humanism. Only thus can we keep pace with world progress. And we should not despair over occasional disorders in today's Russia![20]

Such were the dreams born in the stillness of the Red Chamber.

Shortly after Mao joined the library staff, Director Li himself acquainted him with the rudiments of Bolshevik ideology. "Capitalists," he suggested, "comprise an insignificant minority of mankind while workers are the overwhelming majority. . . . Anyone who does not work, but who consumes that which others produce is a thief." We must put an end to "injustice," Li argued. "We must . . . provide everyone an opportunity to become workers, not thieves." How can this be done? Through the path of a world socialist revolution, which the Russian communists have begun. "The Bolsheviks," he explained,

> grounded their actions in the teaching of the German economist, the socialist Marx; their goal is to do away with state boundaries that currently are an obstacle to socialism, to destroy the regime of capitalism by which the bourgeoisie accumulates profits. . . . The Bolsheviks recognize the existence of class warfare, the war of the world proletariat against the world bourgeoisie. . . . They propose to establish a federal democratic republic of Europe as the foundation of a world federation. . . . This is the new credo of world revolution in the 20th century.

Intoxicated with his new faith, Li Dazhao wrote:

One can understand that Trotsky sees the Russian revolution as the
fuse that will ignite the world revolution. . . . Numerous popular
revolutions will erupt one after the other . . . these are revolutions on
the Russian model, revolutions of the 20th century. . . . The tocsin of
humanism has sounded. The dawn of freedom has arrived. The future world is the world of the red flag. . . . The Russian revolution . . .
heralds changes on the earth. . . . [T]he victory of Bolshevism is the
victory of a new spirit based on the general awakening of mankind in
the 20th century.[21]

Li soon tried to draw his assistant into actual political activity. He invited
Mao to a meeting of the preparatory committee to organize a patriotic society
called Young China, the goals of which coincided with those of the Renovation of the People Study Society. In late November 1918, Mao attended another
meeting called by Li Dazhao at Beida, which resolved to found a Marxist Study
Society.[22]

Of course, prior to meeting Li Dazhao, Mao had already heard about the
Russian Revolution from the Chinese local and national press. On November
17, 1917, the Changsha *Dagong bao* (Justice) carried a story about the events in
Russia and Mao certainly knew the name of the leader of the Bolshevik party.[23]
In November 1917, Mao could read brief accounts of the speeches by Trotsky
and Lenin at the Second All Russian Congress of Soviets, in the pages of *Minguo shibao* (Republic news) and *Shishi xinbao* (Factual news). They reported
Lenin's proposals to end the world war promptly, to give land to the peasants,
and to tackle the economic crisis. Information about Lenin, Trotsky, Bolshevism, and the October Revolution appeared often in the Chinese press in 1918
and evoked considerable interest. But Mao could not have imagined that this
was the "light of a new era."[24] Everything that Li Dazhao said was new to him.
He realized his education thus far was insufficient, so he decided to attend
lectures at Peking University.

Toward this end, in early 1919 Mao joined three university societies:
philosophy, modern literature, and journalism.[25] In the latter he became acquainted with the important publisher and publicist Shao Piaoping, who had
founded the Chinese information agency and the popular Beijing newspaper
Jing bao (Capital news). This was a very useful contact. Shao inducted Mao
into the world of authentic journalism. At a meeting of the Young China society, Mao's attention was drawn to Deng Kang, a student in the Department of
Literature at Peking University. A tall, thin, jovial youth with a kind smile and
mischievous eyes, he was dressed in a traditional Chinese gown from which
his long neck protruded. Mao may have turned to him because of his Hunan

accent. In any case, the two young men, who were almost the same age, shared basically the same ideals and soon became friends. Like Mao's old friend Cai Hesen, Deng played an important role in Mao's life and under the name of Deng Zhongxia became one of the first organizers of the workers' and communist movement in China, and a leading figure in the CCP.

Yet the man who, in Mao's own words, "influenced" him "perhaps more than anyone else" was Chen Duxiu.[26] In 1936 Mao was not shy about confessing this even to Edgar Snow, an American journalist whom he did not know, despite the fact that by then Chen Duxiu, after a rather tortuous life journey, had become the main Chinese Trotskyist. Mao must really have respected Chen Duxiu to make such a confession during the heat of the paranoid anti-Trotskyist campaign that Stalin was conducting in the international communist movement.

Chen Duxiu's personality had a hypnotic effect on other people as well. As early as 1917 Mao and his friends at the Normal School discussed that Chen meant as much to China as Tolstoy did to Russia, and that, like the Russian writer, he was someone who in his personal life and in his writings has "sought after truth and abided in the truth, not caring what others might say."[27] Chen Duxiu enjoyed enormous respect on the part of the patriotic intelligentsia even though he was still rather young. Born on October 8, 1879, in 1918 he was just thirty-nine.

A native of Huaining (now Anqing) in Anhui province, as a child Chen had received a classical Confucian education. Between 1900 and 1902 he gained some knowledge of Western sciences by visiting contemporary educational institutions in China and Japan. Returning to China in the spring of 1903, he was drawn into intensive revolutionary activity, participating in the founding of progressive newspapers and magazines in Shanghai and in Anhui province. It was Chen Duxiu who in mid-September 1915 founded the journal *Qingnian* (Youth) in the International Settlement of Shanghai. A year later it was renamed *Xin qingnian* (New youth). Chen Duxiu was invited to join Peking University at the end of November 1916, and was soon appointed dean of the College of Letters.[28]

Like Li Dazhao, at the time Chen enjoyed occasionally dressing in Western clothes. His three-piece gray suit, perfectly starched shirt, and tie gave him the look of an American professor at a business school. But his appearance was deceptive. He was extremely sociable, both sharp-tongued and funny and sometimes peremptory in debate, but he was never contemptuous toward others. Despite the ten years between them, Chen Duxiu and Li Dazhao became friends, and Chen greatly respected his younger colleague.

Chen treated Mao Zedong, who was not even officially a student, in the same democratic spirit he treated Li Dazhao. Mao could not help but fall under his spell. "We regard Mr. Chen as a bright star in the world of thought," he wrote after several months. "When Mr. Chen speaks, anyone with a reasonably clear mind assents to the opinions he expresses."[29] Unlike Li Dazhao, however, Chen Duxiu was not yet a supporter of either Bolshevism or Marxism. Responding to a reader of *New Youth*, he said it made no sense to talk about socialism in China since industry was so little developed in the country.[30] He continued to advocate personal freedom, democracy, and humanism.

Chen Duxiu's ideological position meant a lot to Mao Zedong. The assistant librarian respected Director Li, but he implicitly believed in Professor Chen. Therefore, he was still quite skeptical about Bolshevism. Of the various communist currents, Mao was most interested in anarchism, with its strong emphasis on individualism, the more so since both Chen Duxiu and Li Dazhao were sympathetic toward anarchist ideas.[31]

Between 1916 and 1920 anarchism was enormously popular in China, including at Peking University. Anarchism was the first Western social philosophy to attract followers in China, and it was the anarchists who first paid attention to the workers' situation and who began to organize the first trade unions. Among the Chinese anarchists were supporters of various teachings, such as Kropotkin's mutual aid, Bakunin's spontaneous revolution, Proudhon's anarcho-syndicalism, and the theories of some Japanese anarchists who advocated the reconstruction of society by establishing isolated, self-supporting new settlements in mountainous and forest districts. Kropotkin enjoyed the greatest influence. He advocated the transformation of state and society via decentralization on the basis of the free self-organization of people in a federated union of communist communities. Chinese anarchists typically intertwined various strands of anarchist thought and strived above all for absolute personal freedom, which they understood to entail a total rupture with contemporary society.

Mao was able to find quite a few anarchist works in the Beida library. He became acquainted with and was attracted by a number of them.[32] After all, he had come to Beijing to take part in the "work-study movement in France" headed by anarchists. Recalling his life in Beijing, Mao said, "My interest in politics continued to increase, and my mind turned more and more radical. . . . But just now I was still confused, looking for a road. . . . I read some pamphlets on anarchy, and was much influenced by them. With a student named Chu Hsun-pei [Zhu Qianzhi], who used to visit me, I often discussed anarchism and its possibilities in China. At that time I favored many of its proposals."[33] Kropotkin had the greatest influence on Mao. Obviously, Mao's dreams were no less fantastic than those of Li Dazhao.

Of all the members of the Renovation of the People Study Society, Mao alone found work at Peking University. The others made ends meet through casual earnings. They all enrolled in training classes at various educational institutions that were preparing candidates for the trip to France. Several of them enrolled in a school attached to Peking University, others in a school located in Baoding, a city about a hundred miles southwest of the capital; Cai Hesen began to study at a school south of Baoding. In addition to these young men and young women, two older persons were preparing seriously for the journey. We have already met one of them, Xu Teli, a professor at the First Normal School in Changsha. The other was Cai Hesen's mother, Ge Jianhao, also known as Ge Lanying. The main subject of study was French, and results on the exams were the basis on which persons were selected for the journey. Candidates had to pass an oral conversation test in French and submit to a health test.[34]

Having gotten his bearings in Beijing, Mao changed his mind about going to Paris. What was he thinking? In his conversations with Edgar Snow, he said, "Although I had helped organize the movement . . . I did not want to go to Europe. I felt that I did not know enough about my own country, and that my time could be more profitably spent in China."[35] Why, then, did he have to go to Beijing? Why start working in the library? Mao's statement is very dubious. Let us recall how happy he had been to receive news from Yang Changji about the recruitment of students for France. Most likely there were other reasons Mao did not go to France. He had no money, but he could have got his hands on some. Professor Yang would certainly have lent the necessary sum to his favorite student. No, it was not a question of money. None of Mao's friends had any, and ultimately the expenses of the trip were covered by contributions.[36] The problem was a different one. Mao, who had absolutely no talent for languages, simply couldn't pass the French language exam. During his time at the Normal School every morning he learned English by rote,[37] but the result still was next to nothing. Could it have been any different with French? Even if he had been accepted to study in France, he would not have been able to feel confident in a foreign country. He was not one to accept second-class status.

The main reason for Mao's decision not to go to France was pride. Mao, a proud and imperious individual, did not want to feel that he was worse than the others. Even in Beijing, the elitist capital, he didn't always feel at ease.

Of course, Li Dazhao, Chen Duxiu, and Shao Piaoping treated him well, but even so, he could not help but feel like a poorly educated provincial. Even though he was almost the same age as Li Dazhao, there was a huge gulf between them. During the five months he worked at Beida he felt constantly humiliated. Yet in Changsha he had been the best student of all, and recognized as the leader. "One of my tasks was to register the names of people who came to read newspapers," Mao recalled, "but to most of them I didn't exist as a human being. . . . I tried to begin conversations with them on political and cultural subjects, but they were very busy men. They had no time to listen to an assistant librarian speaking southern dialect."[38]

As is so often the case, it was young people who had merely reached the threshold of success in society and politics who displayed such haughtiness. For the leaders of the Beida Student Union, Fu Sinian and Luo Jialun, the library assistant from Hunan was an invisible man. Hu Shi, already a well-known professor of philosophy, and who was just two years older than Mao, likewise ignored him.[39] At meetings of the journalist society Mao became acquainted with Chen Gongbo and Tan Pingshan, who were soon to play an important role in the creation of the CCP, but they also paid him little heed. Zhang Guotao, who by the beginning of 1919 had made a name for himself among Beida students through his patriotic activity, was indifferent to Mao. In his memoirs, which were written in the 1950s and 1960s, Zhang did not even recall his first meeting with Mao, but Mao remembered it very well, and he did not forget how Zhang had brushed him off.[40]

In January 1919, Xiao Yu was the first to leave for France, and in March the other Hunanese were ready for the journey. Just then Mao Zedong received news that his mother's health had further deteriorated. In his own words, he "had to rush back home to look after her."[41] His was a strange sort of haste. He left Beijing on March 12, but didn't arrive in Changsha until April 6, and not till April 28 did he write a letter informing his uncles that he was on his way. All this time he was thinking of everything but his ill and much-beloved mother. Mao first went to Shanghai with a group of students who were ready to depart for France, and hung around there for twenty days. "I was detained there on business," he explained to his uncles.[42] What sort of business? All he did was wait to say good-bye to his dear friends who were sailing for France. Meanwhile, his mother was growing sicker by the day. A strange sort of behavior for a devoted son.

Why did he suddenly exhibit such callousness? We can understand this only if we again recall the insults Mao endured in the capital. Psychologically, he needed to accompany his friends on the trip to Shanghai. Moreover, now that general secretary Xiao Yu was gone, he again began to play the role of leader, escorting the members of the group that he led on this important political enterprise. He wanted so much to feel like an important person again, the leader, a political activist. He passionately desired fame and power. But he probably also felt guilty, which is why in his interview with Edgar Snow he falsely asserted that his mother had died in 1918, before he had gone to Beijing.[43] His conscience may have tormented him, but his vanity and lust for power trumped his conscience.

Mao Zedong's unhappy mother died on October 5, 1919, at the age of fifty-three. Burdened with grief and possibly shame, Mao arrived home to bid her farewell on her final journey. Standing in front of her grave, he recited verses that he had composed himself:

> *From her sickbed Mother calls her sons.*
> *Her love is boundless.*
> *I suffer endless pangs of conscience*
> *from failing to express my gratitude.*
> *Throughout her life, and now again, she seeks the Buddha.*
> *I know her time on earth is short.*
> *I grieve, but know not where to find her loving face.*
>
> *Spring winds scatter the sunlight on distant southern shores.*
> *The autumn rains of Shaoshan shed endless tears.*[44]

Less than four months later, Mao's father died of typhus at the age of forty-nine. He was buried in the same grave with his wife.[45] By then Mao was back in Beijing, preoccupied with important political issues. He did not attend the funeral.

6

THE GREAT UNION OF
THE POPULAR MASSES

Back in Changsha, Mao felt himself in his element. Here, unlike in Beijing, he didn't have to prove himself to anyone. He was already widely respected by many educated people and, in the absence of Xiao Yu, he was seen as the leader of the Renovation of the People Study Society.

He easily secured a position teaching history at Xiuye Primary School. As always in China, this came about through connections. An old friend, Zhou Shizhao, recommended Mao to the school where Zhou himself taught. Mao had a light load, just six classroom hours a week and lots of free time. He received a minuscule salary of around four yuan (equal to four silver dollars) a month, but it was enough to keep him fed. He lived at the school, in keeping with the prevailing practice.[1] Principles of pedagogy required that teachers not only give lectures, but also model proper behavior for their students.

The spring of 1919 was a troubled time. In late April, soon after Mao returned to Changsha, the political situation in Hunan and throughout China became extremely tense. In January a conference of the twenty-eight victorious powers in World War I had convened in Paris to draw up a peace treaty with Germany. Chinese public opinion was outraged by the refusal of the representatives of the Entente powers to honor the just demands of the Chinese delegation, namely, that the Chinese port of Qingdao and the surrounding territory on Jiaozhou Bay, which had been seized by the Germans in 1898 and then by the Japanese in November 1914, be returned to China, which had joined the war against Germany as of August 1917. The Japanese, however, wanted to retain the former German colony for themselves. The Chinese representatives at the conference were profoundly disappointed that the delegates from the leading Western powers supported Japan. England, France, and Italy, bound by the secret treaties they had concluded with Japan in February–March 1917, wanted no conflicts with their wartime ally. These agreements accorded Japan recognition of its right to German holdings in China in exchange for its help to the Entente. Moreover, Western leaders were counting on Japan to play a significant role in a new war against Soviet Russia. The American delegation tried to find a compromise, but failed.

The peace conference that the Chinese expected to recognize China as an equal member of the new, postwar international system merely resolved to restore to China some ancient astronomical instruments seized by the Germans during the Boxer Rebellion. The Chinese were understandably insulted. Students were particularly indignant. "Japan will possess Qingdao and Jiaozhou while we Chinese will do what, gaze at the stars?" raged the students. A telegram from Wang Zhengting, a Chinese delegate to the conference, to a Shanghai newspaper in late March 1919 added fuel to the fire. It said:

> We insisted ... that the Twenty-One Demands and other Secret agreements be annulled. ... [W]orst of all was that among the Chinese were some who made concessions for their own mercenary reasons. ... These are henchmen of traitors to our nation. We express the hope that public opinion throughout the country will rise up in struggle against these traitors and create the opportunity to annul the treaties that were thrust upon us.[2]

Wang Zhengting's call fell upon fertile soil. An anti-Japanese patriotic movement began to develop in China and a search commenced for the traitors whom Wang Zhengting had written about in his telegram. Suspicion fell upon the leading Japanophiles: Cao Rulin, the minister of communications; Zhang Zongxiang, the Chinese minister to Tokyo; and Lu Zongyu, the director of the Chinese Mint.

The situation grew tenser by the day and finally exploded. On Saturday evening, May 3, student activists gathered at Peking University and decided to organize a large demonstration the following day, Sunday, on Tiananmen Square, in front of the entrance to the Forbidden City. One law student gave a fiery speech at the meeting, slashed his finger with a knife, and wrote in his blood on a piece of white cloth, "Return Qingdao to us!" He raised his slogan high above his head and the hall erupted in applause.[3]

At 10 A.M. on May 4, more than three thousand students from various educational institutions in Beijing gathered on the square. Everywhere white flags could be seen—white is the color of mourning in China—along with maps of Qingdao and incendiary placards. Despite exhortations by a representative of the Ministry of Education, the Peking garrison commander, and the chief of police, the demonstrators moved toward the nearby Legation Quarter. Still believing in "Great America," they wanted to submit a petition to the U.S. minister in the name of 11,500 students in Beijing. The basis of their faith was President Woodrow Wilson's message to Congress on January 8, 1919, in which he had set forth his Fourteen Points for "universal peace," condemning secret treaties and calling for a "free, open-minded, and absolutely impartial adjustment of all colonial claims." The guards at the Legation Quarter refused to allow the students to enter. They permitted just four representatives to meet with an official of the American embassy.

This refusal roused the crowd to a fever pitch. Then someone suggested settling scores with the traitors. So they set off for the nearby house of Cao Rulin, burst into it, and went on a veritable rampage. Whatever they didn't smash, they dumped into a pond in the courtyard. Cao Rulin managed to escape, but Zhang Zongxiang, who happened to be present, was grabbed and savagely beaten by the students, who dispersed around 5 P.M. after setting fire to Cao's house.[4] What had begun nobly as a series of patriotic speeches wound up as pure hooliganism. The police arrested thirty-two people, but under the pressure of liberal public opinion they were quickly released.

This was hardly the end. Throughout May and into June, Beijing students were up in arms. They held strikes, demonstrations, and meetings, but they committed no more outrages. News about the events of May 4 spread throughout the country. In Shanghai and many other cities, not only students but also many merchants, gentry, and even workers expressed solidarity with the students in Beijing. Filled with patriotic feelings, the rickshaw pullers unanimously refused service to Japanese. In many places, residents expressed their anti-Japanese feelings through demonstrations and strikes. Shipping came to a halt along the Yangzi River as dockworkers went on strike. Posters saying, "Return Qingdao to us!" "Wipe Away the National Shame!" and "Down with the Three Minister Traitors!" appeared everywhere. In response to a call by the Central Chamber of Commerce in Beijing, a campaign to boycott Japanese goods developed throughout China. Crowds smashed the windows of stores trading in Japanese manufactures, seized Japanese goods, and burned them on the streets. Newspaper editors refused to accept and print Japanese advertisements, the sailing schedules of Japanese ships, or even information about exchange rates for the Japanese yen.[5] The president of China, Xu Shichang, was forced to compel the resignation of Cao Rulin, Zhang Zongxiang, and Lu Zongyu, but the disturbances did not die down until June 28, when news came that the Chinese delegates had refused to sign the unjust Treaty of Versailles, which the Entente powers had concluded with Germany.

Students in Changsha also attempted to organize an anti-Japanese demonstration in solidarity with the students in Beijing. On May 7, several thousand people came out on the streets of Changsha. They were supported by the merchants.[6] The demonstration was quickly dispersed, however, by troops under General Zhang Jingyao's command, that same "Zhang the Venomous" who had established a reign of terror in the city one year earlier. It is not known whether Mao Zedong took part in this demonstration. Most likely not; otherwise the Maoist chroniclers would not have missed an opportunity to glorify his participation.

Of course, Mao could hardly fail to take an interest in the student struggle, but spontaneous acts of protest did not appeal to him. He believed in the need to channel spontaneity. More than anything else an organization was necessary, a vanguard firmly welded together by the will of a great leader. Mao had not read Friedrich Paulsen in vain. "A moral action depends on feeling and will, which must precede the moral action." Mao never betrayed this credo.[7] In early May 1919 he began seriously considering the creation of an effective organization that could lead the patriotic student movement in Changsha. The Renovation of the People Study Society, which had only about seventy members in May 1919, many of whom were now in France, had proved to be ineffective.[8] In mid-May Mao discussed the situation with Deng Zhongxia, who had come to Changsha from Beijing and gave Mao a detailed report on the student activities there. Mao, Deng, and Bewhiskered He (He Shuheng) decided to organize a broadly based Hunan student association, following the example of similar organizations in a number of cities and provinces.[9] The members of these student unions advanced a strikingly expressed political goal: "To employ . . . all the power that students can muster" to "restore national sovereignty and punish those who had betrayed the motherland."[10]

On May 25 a conference of more than twenty Changsha school representatives, many of them members of the Renovation of the People Study Society, convened in He Shuheng's apartment. Mao Zedong introduced Deng Zhongxia, who recounted the events of May 4 and expressed the hope that Hunan students would declare a general strike in solidarity with the students of Beijing. Deng's speech made their heads spin and the orator himself, young and intelligent-looking, produced quite an impression. Life now had real meaning. It demanded struggle, self-sacrifice, and glory. Three days later the Hunan Students Association was formally established. Peng Huang, a student at the Hunan School of Commerce who was a close friend of Mao's, was selected as chair of the association.

On June 3 the Hunan Students Association declared a citywide strike in which students from twenty schools in Changsha took part. This unprecedented strike inspired the local newspaper, the *Justice*, to publish the appeal of the striking students on June 4: "Diplomacy has failed, the country has been broken apart, and unless timely measures are taken to save the state, it will perish." The appeal also called upon the government not to sign the Versailles Treaty and to annul the Twenty-One Demands.[11] The situation was very tense. Conflict with the authorities was avoided only because summer vacation soon began. Many students left for home, but the organization continued to function. Students returning home were organized into propaganda squads that were tasked with using lively and accessible means to spread the idea of a boycott of Japanese goods in the villages. At this time, one-act patriotic skits, rather primitive in nature, and which the students themselves composed, became very popular in China. They produced an enormous impression upon their illiterate peasant and urban audiences.

A number of students signed up for the inspection squads along with representatives of the merchants' guilds that were enforcing the boycott. On July 7, the union and the merchant corporations jointly held another massive demonstration, this time carefully planned, calling for the destruction of Japanese goods. Zhou Shizhao, who took part in it, recalled:

> In front, columns of marchers carried banners saying "Meeting to burn Japanese goods," and "Countrymen, be vigilant! Do not buy Japanese goods under any circumstances." All of the students carried some sort of Japanese goods on their shoulders, and behind them followed shop assistants from silk goods stores. Members of the Union to Defend Native Goods and the Student Association brought up the rear, carrying the banners of their unions. Parading along the noisy streets, the column stopped in front of the Education Committee. The students unloaded the Japanese goods, soaked them with kerosene, and set them ablaze. Only after the goods were reduced to ashes did the demonstrators disperse to their homes.[12]

Two days later, on the initiative of the leaders of the Students Association, a general meeting of representatives from public organizations was held, and it was decided to establish a united Hunan association embracing all sectors of the population.[13]

From Mao's perspective, all of this was not enough. He had become convinced that propaganda was the most effective means of influencing the masses. Mao, following Lenin, whom he scarcely knew about at the time, could say, "In our opinion, the starting point of all our activities, the first practical step towards creating the organization we desire, the thread that will guide us in unswervingly developing, deepening and expanding that organization, is the establishment of a . . . political newspaper."[14] Neither Mao nor his comrades had the means to start a newspaper; therefore, they decided to establish a Hunan-wide student information journal along the lines of Chen Du Xiu's and Li Dazhao's *Weekly Review*. Mao Zedong defined its aims in florid and enthusiastic words: "The vast and furious tide of the new thought is already rushing, surging along both banks of the Xiang River."[15]

The first issue of the *Xiangjiang pinglun* (Xiang River review) was composed in about ten days and appeared on July 14, 1919. The Manifesto on the Founding of the *Xiang River Review*, which Mao wrote as editor in chief, said, "Unfettered by any of the old views or superstitions, we must seek the truth. In dealing with people, we advocate uniting the popular masses, and toward the oppressors, we believe in continuing the 'sincere admonishment movement.' " In the category of "oppressors," in addition to bureaucrats and militarists he included capitalists. The months he had spent in Beijing had not been in vain. He was still strongly attracted to anarchism, and Li Dazhao's lectures on socialism had likewise left their mark. He was still rather cautious, did not advocate violence, and called only for democracy and liberalism. "We put into practice the 'cry of revolution'—the cry for bread, the cry for freedom, the cry for equality—the 'bloodless revolution,' " he asserted. "Thus, we will not provoke widespread chaos, nor pursue the ineffectual 'revolution of bombs,' or 'revolution of blood.' " Even with respect to the Japanese, Mao still considered most effective the adoption of such means as "boycotting classes, merchants' strikes, workers' strikes, and boycotting Japanese products."[16]

The first issue of the journal published Mao's pointed article on the arrest of his idol Chen Duxiu by the Beijing militarists. Chen had been taken into custody during the student movement on June 11, 1919, for distributing a leaflet he had written called "Declaration of the Citizens of Beijing," in which he had sharply criticized the domestic and foreign policies of the Chinese president and prime minister over the "Shandong question." He spent eighty-three days in prison, after which he left Beijing and settled in Shanghai. Shaken by Chen's arrest, Mao accused all of Chinese society:

> The danger does not result from military weakness or inadequate finances, nor is it the danger of being split up into many small fragments by domestic chaos. The real danger lies in the total emptiness and rottenness of the mental universe of the entire Chinese people. Of China's 400 million people, about 390 million are superstitious. They superstitiously believe in spirits and ghosts, in fortune-telling, in fate, in despotism. There is absolutely no recognition of the individual, of the self, of truth. This is because scientific thought has not developed. In name, China is a republic, but in reality it is an autocracy that is getting worse and worse as one regime replaces another. . . . [The] masses of the people haven't the faintest glimmer of democracy in their mentality, and have no idea what democracy actually is. Mr. Chen has always stood for these two things [science and democracy]. . . . For these two things, Mr. Chen has offended society, and society has repaid him with arrest and imprisonment.[17]

As a mark of solidarity with his teacher, Mao reproduced Chen Duxiu's antigovernment leaflet in his article.

In this same issue Mao first published a brief note about the Bolsheviks. He didn't offer any judgment; he merely called on the Chinese public to study the Russian experience: "Each of us should examine very carefully what kind of thing this extremist party [the Bolshevik party] really is. . . . In the twinkling of an eye, the extremist party, to everyone's amazement, has spread throughout the country [Russia], to the point that there is no place to hide from them." [18]

Two thousand copies of this maiden issue were quickly distributed and soon, at the end of July, an additional two thousand copies were sold in just three days. On July 21, there appeared simultaneously a special supplement to the first issue as well as the second issue in a press run of five thousand copies. A week later five thousand copies of the third issue appeared. For Hunan these were enormous numbers. Of the nine daily newspapers in Changsha only the *Justice* had a circulation of as much as 2,300 to 2,400 copies. The others sold between one hundred and five hundred copies. [19] Mao managed to compose five issues of the journal, but only four of them were distributed. The fourth issue went on sale August 4, also in a print run of five thousand. The fifth issue had already been typeset when it was confiscated at the printer's by Zhang Jingyao's soldiers. [20]

The journal was Mao Zedong's brainchild. According to Zhou Shizhao, Mao literally spent every spare moment in working on the journal. "Awaking late at night, I would see a light in his room through a crack in the wall," Zhou recalled. "After writing an article, he then edited it, composed the printer's dummy himself, proofread it, and sometimes even sold copies of the journal on the street." [21]

The journal also published brief factual summaries, most of which Mao himself wrote, under the titles "Survey of Events in the West," "Survey of Events in the East," "International Notes," "Xiang River Notes," and "New Literature and Art." From his writing brush flowed the article that brought him national attention, "The Great Union of the Popular Masses." Broad in scope and characteristic of his thinking at the time, it took up almost the entirety of three issues of the weekly paper, from the second through the fourth. He attempted to answer a basic question that had tormented a generation of revolutionaries: what could be done when "the decadence of the state, the sufferings of humanity, and the darkness of society have all reached an extreme."

Mao's solution left no doubt that his vision of revolution was still moderate. Starting from the supposition that the reason for all of China's woes, as well as those of other countries, was that the oppressors of the people, that is, the aristocrats and capitalists of various countries, were united against the popular masses, he proposed to "fight fire with fire." Only a "great union of the popular masses," a great unity directed against the violence of the "oppressors," he wrote, could save the country. In essence, he proposed the establishment of trade unions of all the oppressed strata in society, including peasants, workers, students, women, primary school teachers, policemen, and rickshaw coolies. Mao placed all these people into the class of the "poor and the weak," who were opposed by the "rich and the strong." Small professional organizations of the oppressed, he believed, would help to catalyze the "great union" of all unfortunate people. Once united, the popular masses of China would easily crush the aristocrats and the capitalists, whom they outnumbered many times over. The popular masses need only unite, rise up, and cry out in full voice, then "the traitors will get up and tremble and flee for their lives."[22]

The article was steeped in Kropotkin's ideas of "mutual aid," although Mao also credited the struggle of a "hundred thousand brave Russian warriors [who] suddenly exchange the imperial standard for the red flag." He called on Chinese soldiers who were serving the militarists to follow this example. The time will come, he wrote, when Chinese soldiers will realize that they are the "sons, brothers, or husbands" of ordinary people. "[T]hey will join hands and turn the other way instead, becoming together valiant fighters resisting the aristocrats and the capitalists." Just as in Russia and a number of other European countries, a social revolution will occur in China that will be part of the global struggle of the oppressed. Under the influence of Li Dazhao, Mao wrote,

> As a result of the World War and the bitterness of their lives, the popular masses in various countries have suddenly undertaken all sorts of action. In Russia, they have overthrown the aristocrats and driven out the rich, and the toilers and peasants have jointly set up a Soviet government. The army of the red flag surges forward in the East and in the West, sweeping away numerous enemies. . . . We know it! We are awakened! The world is ours, the state is ours, society is ours. . . . We must act energetically to carry out the great union of the popular masses, which will not brook a moment's delay![23]

These words may well seem naïve. But if one recalls that the "great union" of the May Fourth students in Beijing had forced the retirement of the "national traitors" Cao Rulin, Zhang Zongxiang, and Lu Zongyu without any bomb-throwing, it is not hard to understand what inspired Mao. His understanding of social revolution did not involve bloodshed, but rather the concerted and peaceful action of the "great union of the popular masses," who would deafen the oppressors with their "great and mighty roar." But perhaps he was closer to the truth than at any other time. "We accept the fact that the oppressors are people, are human beings like ourselves. . . . [If] we use oppression to overthrow oppression . . . the result [will be] that we still have oppression," he wrote.[24] Yet less than nine months later Mao fundamentally betrayed his youthful ideals and unconditionally accepted the radical concepts of Marx and Lenin.

For the time being everything was fairly peaceful. "The great union of the popular masses" seemed quite attainable. The first step was to assemble a small but closely united group of like-minded individuals around the principle of mutual aid. Toward the end of 1919, Mao revived his old idea of establishing an agricultural commune on the left bank of the Xiang River, across from Changsha. The hold of anarchism upon him, particularly the communistic ideas of Kropotkin concerning mutual aid, strengthened his desire "to build a new village at the foot of Mount Yuelu." He counted upon the help of his friends. He wanted to open a village school to teach social science and educate the "new man." Of course, nothing came of this, but Mao continued to cherish the dream for several months.

The *Xiang River Review,* particularly Mao's article, "The Great Union of the Popular Masses," was enthusiastically greeted by democratically inclined people in several Chinese cities. Even such intellectuals as Hu Shi and Luo Jialun, who nine months earlier would have nothing to do with the librarian's assistant, praised it fulsomely.[25] One can imagine Mao Zedong's exultation. The young provincial had stepped into the national political arena. People were reading him; people were talking about him. The confiscation of the fifth issue only increased his popularity. He had become a victim of the crude authorities.

He had not been imprisoned, however, and was able to continue his political activity. In mid-August 1919, Mao and other leaders of the Hunan Students Association decided to try to unite various public groups under an anti-Zhang banner. The governor of Hunan, Zhang Jingyao, was behaving like a real bandit. He and his three brothers, who held high office in his military administration, along with their soldiers went around robbing peasants, looting the public treasury, extorting tribute from merchants, kidnapping and killing people, raping women, trading in opium, and withholding salaries from teachers. They treated Hunan like a conquered province. The people lived in fear, trade dried up, prices skyrocketed. "If 'Zhang the Venomous' is not uprooted, Hunan will perish," people were saying.[26]

At the beginning of September, Mao Zedong was invited by the Sino-American hospital Xiangya to serve as editor in chief of its weekly journal, *Xin Hunan* (New Hunan). Six issues had already appeared, but it had yet to find its voice. Mao accepted on condition that he would define the journal's direction. The Americans had been impressed by his fight for liberal values, so they agreed. Mao defined his goals in the first issue he edited: "1) to criticize society, 2) to reform thought, 3) to introduce [the new] learning, 4) to discuss problems." He continued, "Naturally we will not be concerned with 'success or failure, or whether things go smoothly or not.' Still less will we pay attention to any power (authority) whatsoever. For our credo is: 'Anything may be sacrificed save principle, which can absolutely not be sacrificed.' "[27] It was hardly surprising that after four weeks this journal, too, was shut down.[28]

The romantic aura of a fighter against tyranny, his obvious journalistic talent, and his growing national popularity combined to make the handsome twenty-five-year-old Mao Zedong particularly attractive to women. Yang Kai-hui was far off and flesh would have its due. In the fall of 1919 Mao began an affair with Yang Changji's favorite female student, Tao Yi. She was three years younger than Mao and distinguished from the many other girls he knew by her sense of purpose and her wit. Passion overwhelmed him, and he was unable to master it. Love "is an irresistible natural force," he exclaimed in a burst of enthusiasm. "The power of the human need for love is greater than that of any other need. Nothing except some special force can stop it. . . . [The only thing able] to block this surging tide of the need for love, is none other, I believe, than 'superstition.' "[29]

The affair was stormy but brief; it flamed out as suddenly as it had flared up, in the late summer of 1920. The two lovers separated for ideological reasons. By then Mao had begun to lean toward communism, and Tao Yi could not accept the doctrines of Bolshevism. Soon after they split up, Tao Yi left Changsha for Shanghai, where she founded a women's school. She died in 1930, before her thirty-fifth birthday.[30]

In the autumn of 1919 there were as yet no portents of this lovers' drama. Both Tao and Mao believed in liberalism, democracy, and free love. It was at this time that Mao wrote a series of articles on problems of love and marriage that were published in the pages of Changsha's leading newspaper, *Justice*. The occasion was an incident that had shaken the whole town. On November 14, a girl named Zhao Wuzhen, given by her parents to become the concubine of a rich and elderly merchant, committed suicide by slitting her throat with a razor while being carried in a red palanquin to her bridegroom's house. The horror that everyone awaiting her arrival experienced is impossible to describe and for many days no one in town spoke of anything else. Many people condemned the girl for violating the canons of Confucianism, but there were also many who sympathized with her. Naturally, Mao, Tao Yi, and all of their comrades took the side of Zhao Wuzhen. Mao was particularly indignant. "The background to this incident," he wrote, "is the rottenness of the marriage system, and the darkness of the social system, in which there can be no independent ideas or views, and no freedom of choice in love."[31]

The problems of love and marriage, no matter how serious, could not deter Mao and his friends from pursuing their main goal of getting rid of the governor and his criminal clique. Throughout the fall Mao worked to turn as many people against Zhang as he could. In the spirit of the "Great Union of the Popular Masses," Mao thought Beijing might be persuaded to recall Zhang if Hunan demonstrated its unanimous refusal to accept this bloody oligarch. Meanwhile, he continued the active propaganda campaign to boycott Japanese goods via the Hunan Students Association, which operated underground after Zhang had banned it following his confiscation of the *Xiang River Review*.

In mid-November Mao also called a meeting in an attempt to revive the

Renovation of the People Study Society. The internal structure of the society was reorganized by creating two departments: a "consultative department" (in essence, legislative) and an "executive department" consisting of several subdivisions: school, editorial, women's, and overseas education. An Executive Committee was also established. What had been an amorphous society began to acquire the character of a centralized political party. Bewhiskered He was chosen as the chair of the Executive Committee. Mao Zedong, Tao Yi, Zhou Shizhao, and several others became part of the Consultative Department.[32] Unfortunately, the projected transformation failed. Shortly after the November meeting, many members were drawn into tumultuous public events and some were forced to leave Changsha.

The organization became paralyzed for almost a year. At the end of November, public opinion was agitated by news of clashes between Japanese soldiers and patriotic Chinese students in coastal Fujian.province. Changsha students decided to hold a demonstration of solidarity and planned to put on another grand anti-Japanese show. Just then the local committee to defend native goods discovered a large quantity of contraband Japanese piece goods during its inspection of a warehouse in Changsha. The committee decided to confiscate them and burn the goods in public. On December 2, a crowd of some five thousand students, teachers, workers, and shop assistants moved through the streets of the city to the building of the Education Committee. Zhou Shizhao recalled the occasion:

> The weather was clear that day. . . . The winter sun shone on the faces of the young people, but their hearts were overflowing with rage and indignation. . . . When the crowd passed by the stores selling foreign goods, loud cries of "We shall destroy contraband goods" and "Down with merchant traitors" thundered forth. . . . At 1:00 P.M. the column of demonstrators arrived at the doors of the Education Committee. They piled up the Japanese fabric, and the crowd of students and onlookers, now some ten thousand strong, circled around the pile, waiting for it to be torched.
>
> Just at th[is] moment . . . the chief of staff of Zhang Jingyao's troops, his younger brother Zhang Jingtang, who was prancing about on a horse and waving a saber, summoned a company of soldiers and a platoon of mounted cavalry into the square. He ordered his soldiers to surround the students in a tight circle. He climbed up on the platform and shouted, "Arson, the burning of goods, is banditry. So the students are bandits. And how does one talk with bandits? They understand only one language. They need to be beaten and destroyed!" Having spoken, he ordered the cavalrymen to drag the students off

the stage and beat them. He continued to shout, "Students! Go back where you came from. . . ." Several hundred soldiers pointed their bayonets at the students, and forced us to leave the square. We returned to our schools seething with indignation. . . . But we did not know what to do.[33]

Mao Zedong and the other leaders of the patriotic movement reacted instantaneously. On the following day, December 3, an emergency meeting of the Renovation of the People Study Society and activists from the Hunan Students Association was held outside the southern gates of the city. They decided to declare a general strike and demand the immediate recall of Zhang Jingyao. A follow-up meeting on December 4 resolved to send special delegations to Beijing, Tianjin, Shanghai, Hankou, Changde, Hengyang, and Canton to launch a national campaign to remove Zhang.[34]

The strike began on December 6. Seventy-three of the city's seventy-five schools shut down. Some 1,200 teachers and 13,000 students went on strike. "We will not return to class until 'Zhang the Venomous' is removed from Hunan," they declared.[35] That same day Mao and several other local activists set off for Beijing. Mao took only an oiled paper umbrella to shield him from the sun and rain, a change of underwear, and a few books.[36] The trip took almost two weeks. On December 18, Mao was once again in Beijing.

Apparently not much had changed in the city since his departure. There were no signs of the recent student fervor. Life had reverted to normal. Chen Duxiu, who had been forced to leave for Shanghai, no longer taught at Peking University, but Li Dazhao still headed the library. But tragedy had struck the Yang Changji family. Several months before Mao's arrival, it was discovered that the venerable professor had inoperable stomach cancer. He was placed in an excellent German hospital, but his condition steadily worsened; he was dying.[37] Mao rushed to see him soon after he arrived, and tried to cheer up his beloved teacher, but Yang knew his end was near.

Mao again met Yang Kaihui at her father's bedside, but they were both so burdened with grief that they didn't talk at all about themselves. There was really nothing between them. Later, Kaihui would assert that during their time apart, Mao was constantly writing her "love letters," but who knows whether this is really true.[38] No such letters have survived. Moreover, Mao had been under the spell of Tao Yi, who enchanted him not only with her womanliness, but also because he considered her "a very enlightened and purposeful person."[39] We know that he wrote to her and even made plans for the future.[40]

Yang Changji died at dawn on January 17, 1920, leaving his family in pitiful financial circumstances. The talented teacher had not earned much money. His older son was still a student and could not support his mother and sister.

Friends and students of the deceased assumed the burden of looking after his family. Naturally, Mao Zedong was among the most active of those who established a fund to support the family of the esteemed professor.[41]

Mao did not forget why he had come to Beijing. The Hunan delegation bombarded the administration of the president, the cabinet, the ministers of foreign affairs, finance, agriculture, and trade with requests. They beseeched the government to dismiss and punish Zhang Jingyao promptly "so as to maintain the law and rescue the people from calamity."[42] The delegation enumerated basic crimes committed by the Hunan governor and his brothers. "Since coming to Hunan last year, Zhang Jingyao has unleashed his troops of hungry wolves," Mao Zedong wrote on behalf of the delegation, "raping, burning, looting, and killing, and has given free rein to his government, a fierce tiger that pillages, plunders, cheats, and exacts taxes."[43]

But it was all in vain. The corrupt, mafia-like government had no intention of dealing seriously with the question of Zhang Jingyao. The only thing that Mao and his partners achieved was a promise from government officials to send "someone" to conduct a "secret investigation."[44] Mao was deeply disappointed. The "Great Union of the Popular Masses" had proved powerless before the provincial oligarch, who was well connected to the cabinet. When Zhang Jingyao cleared out of Hunan in June 1920, his departure was a result of the usual game of musical chairs among warlords. Once again Changsha was occupied by Tan Yankai, who reclaimed his governorship.[45]

Military power alone had meaning in China. The rifle was the midwife of power. But Mao still didn't fully grasp this, although he saw what was going on. Despite his youthful romanticism, he was a rather sober person overall. He was hot-tempered, and in letters to his friends he sometimes accused himself of being "too emotional and . . . vehement," but hysterical exaltation sickened him.[46] He was not one to cut his finger and write patriotic slogans with his blood. He still sincerely believed in the priorities of science, education, and culture, and in the possibility of disinterested journalism and activity in the public realm. This conviction would pass in a few years, but for now Mao continued to "dwell in the clouds." It is noteworthy that having learned of the flight of Zhang Jingyao, Mao Zedong demonstrated the height of naïveté in writing, "The people of Hunan should take another step forward and work for a 'movement to abolish the military governorship.' . . . The Hunan people's expulsion of Zhang was their own decision, and it is not tied to any of the dark forces. If they are really awakened to the need to abolish the military governorship, they can simply kick it out themselves."[47] In reality the people in Changsha sat at home, not daring to show their faces on the street, while Zhang Jingyao's army withdrew from the city. Could they really rise up against whoever occupied the position of military governor?

During this winter Mao met frequently with Li Dazhao and Deng Zhongxia, from whom he learned a lot about Bolshevik Russia, where a full-scale civil war was raging. There the enigmatic extremist party, having united workers and peasants under its red banners, was struggling against the aristocrats and plutocrats whom Mao Zedong hated. At Professor Li's recommendation he resumed reading communist literature. He already knew that under Li Dazhao's influence Chen Duxiu had migrated to the communist position. As early as April 20, 1919, Chen had published a note about the Bolshevik Revolution in the journal *Weekly Review,* in which he said that this revolution was "the beginning of a new era in the history of mankind." Mao was pushed toward taking this new doctrine more seriously than before.

Since he knew no language other than Chinese, he could read Marxist works only in translation, but there were few of these in China. The only available writings of Marx were an abbreviated version of *The Communist Manifesto* published in the *Weekly Review* and *The Critique of the Gotha Programme,* openly polemical leftist brochures that called for the violent overthrow of bourgeois rule and the establishment of a dictatorship of the working class. Among Lenin's writings, he had access only to "Political Parties in Russia and the Tasks of the Proletariat," written by the Bolshevik leader in early April 1917. There was also a translation of the "Manifesto of the Communist International to the Proletariat of the World," written by Trotsky for the First Congress of the Comintern, the world communist organization created by the Bolsheviks in March 1919.

Mao also carefully read several other works that explicated communist ideas, including *Class Struggle* by the German Marxist Karl Kautsky and *A History of Socialism* by the British philosopher and Fabian socialist Thomas Kirkup. "During my second visit to Peking [Beijing]," he later told Edgar Snow,

> I had read much about the events in Russia, and had eagerly sought out what little Communist literature was then available in Chinese. Three books especially deeply carved my mind, and built up in me a faith in Marxism. . . . These books were *The Communist Manifesto,* translated by Chen Wang-tao [Chen Wangdao], and the first Marxist book ever published in Chinese; *Class Struggle,* by Kautsky; and a *History of Socialism,* by Kirkupp [Kirkup]. By the summer of 1920 I had become, in theory and to some extent in action, a Marxist, and from this time on I considered myself a Marxist.[48]

Mao embellished the facts when he related his ideological transformation to Snow. Everything was more complicated, and it goes without saying that the aforementioned works did not effect an instantaneous transformation of his consciousness. Moreover, the translation of *The Communist Manifesto* by Chen Wangdao did not appear in print until August 1920, so Mao could not have read it by that summer.* The writings of Li Dazhao and Chen Duxiu, who were popularizing the October experiment, filled out the picture that was taking shape in Mao's mind.[49] His conversations with Professor Li, his contacts with Deng Zhongxia, who had already accepted the views of the Bolsheviks, and with other young intellectuals in the capital all served to influence his thinking.

After May 4, 1919, the mood of the students in Beijing changed. Wartime illusions about Anglo-American liberalism that Chinese patriots had shared now evaporated. This led to a crisis of liberal thought in China as a whole and particularly in the capital. The drawing of ideological and political lines within the intelligentsia intensified.[50] Just then, industrial workers entered upon the stage of Chinese history for the first time. Some hundred thousand workers had taken part in the May Fourth Movement. Their awakening appeared to those Chinese revolutionaries who were already acquainted with Marxism as a clear affirmation of the truth of Marxist theory concerning the "world historical mission of the working class."[51] But the more critical factors determining the interest of Chinese public opinion in Marxism were the triumphant character of the October Revolution in Russia, the radically anti-imperialist and anticapitalist policy of the Soviet government, and the successes of the Red Army in its struggle against the imperialist interventionists and domestic counterrevolutionaries. "With the Russian Revolution, Marxism demonstrated that it was a force that could rock the world," Li Dazhao emphasized in 1919.[52] He was essentially correct.

The achievements of the Russian communists evoked a desire to understand the ideology that guided their actions. Patriotic Chinese intellectuals began to study the Bolshevik experiment, searching for a theory they could use as a lever to move China. Marxism began to be disseminated and accepted in China through the prism of the Bolshevik experiment. Many years later Mao wrote, "It was through the Russians that the Chinese found Marxism. . . . Follow the path of the Russians—that was their conclusion."[53] Most leading Chinese intellectuals borrowed only Bolshevism from among the broad spectrum of Marxist tendencies. Its adherents were distinguished by their voluntarist outlook regarding the laws of social development, their underestimation of the principles of the natural historical evolution of human society, their tendency to treat the role of the masses and of class struggle in history as absolutes, their total negation of the rights of property and of the individual, their apologia for violence, and likewise their denial of universal human values, in-

----

* In fairness we should note that Mao might have become acquainted with another translation of *The Communist Manifesto*, which, according to the memoirs of Luo Zhanglong, was mimeographed by students at Peking University. But whether this is really true is not known for certain.

cluding generally accepted concepts of ethics and morality, of religion, and of civil society. They possessed a simplified and superficial understanding of the socioeconomic, political, and ideological structures of capitalist and precapitalist societies, failing to take into account the diversity of social systems. Their views on world development were globalist in nature; the only thesis they were willing to accept was the inevitability of a world socialist revolution.

Some Chinese youth, who keenly felt their country's weakness and humiliation, were particularly attracted by the Bolsheviks' iron will. They viewed Lenin's policy of unfettered proletarian terror as a manifestation of invincible power. And power was precisely what the Middle Kingdom lacked. Bertrand Russell, the liberal British philosopher who visited China in early 1920, was profoundly struck by the degree to which so many young Chinese were "in love with terror." Russell came to China after first visiting Soviet Russia. The notes on his Russia trip were published by Chen Duxiu in one of the issues of *New Youth*.[54] He described the actions of the Russian communists objectively and thoroughly.[55] As a man on the left, his lectures and writings underlined the "enormous significance of the Bolshevik experiment for world development," arguing the need for all socialists to support Soviet Russia. At the same time, as a liberal, he was horrified by the actions of the Bolsheviks, which he deemed incompatible with the principles of democracy, and by the terror they had unleashed. Speaking in China, Russell condemned the dictatorship of workers and peasants, although he referred rather positively to the idea of communism. He argued that the rich should be convinced through education to change their ways. Then it would not be necessary "to limit freedom or to have recourse to war and bloody revolution."[56] His Chinese students, however, greedily imbibed precisely that for which Russell censured the Bolsheviks.

Mao's sojourn in Beijing in the winter and spring of 1920 did not lead to any fundamental change in his consciousness. To be sure, Marxism and especially Bolshevism impressed him with its apologia for being iron-willed, and made him think more about Russian communism. But Mao had not become any sort of Marxist by the spring of 1920. This is what he wrote to his friend Zhou Shizhao in mid-March 1920: "To be honest, I still do not have a relatively clear concept of all the various ideologies and doctrines."[57] His thinking was still a mishmash. He already considered Soviet Russia the "number one civilized country in the world," but he still dreamed of going off somewhere with his comrades and founding a "Self-Study University." He drew up detailed assignments for everyone in this utopian commune, and argued that "all proceeds will be held entirely in common. Those who earn more will help those who earn less; the goal is subsistence."[58] Under the influence of everything he had read and heard about the Land of Soviets, he wanted to go there, and in February 1920 he even obliquely broached to Tao Yi the possibility of their going there together in a year or two. However, suddenly, at the end of June

1920, he declared that "a tiny blossom of New Culture has appeared in Russia, on the shores of the Arctic Ocean. For several years, fierce winds and heavy rains have been testing it, and we still do not know whether it will develop successfully or not." [59]

In a letter to his old teacher Li Jinxi in early June he wrote, "Recently I have been concentrating on the study of three subjects only: English, philosophy, and newspapers. For philosophy, I have started from the 'three great contemporary philosophers,' and will gradually learn about the other schools of thought." By the "three great contemporary philosophers" he was referring not to Lenin and company, but rather to Bertrand Russell and to those other liberal intellectuals Henri Bergson and John Dewey. [60] He confessed to experiencing a "hunger and thirst for knowledge," but his studies were disorderly and his reading without purpose. "I cannot calm my mind down, and I have difficulty in persevering. It is also very hard for me to change. This is truly a most regrettable circumstance!" [61] He sampled everything. Philosophy, linguistics, even Buddhism, attracted him. Despite the lessons from Professor Li, he still had not accepted Bolshevism as the only true worldview.

Mao left Beijing on April 11. As he had done the year before, he set out on a journey. This time he went first to Tianjin, a two-to-three-hour ride east of Beijing, and then to the capital of Shandong province, Jinan, famous for its springs. After this Mao found time to stop at the birthplace of Confucius, the picturesque town of Qufu, and then to climb to the summit of the nearby sacred mountain of Taishan, from where one could admire the beautiful sunrise. After descending the mountain he visited Zoucheng, the birthplace of Mencius, another great ancient philosopher. Then he traveled to Shanghai by way of Nanjing. In Shanghai he had business to attend to. His journey took twenty-five days. That was enough time to rest and gather his strength for the coming political battles.

7

BREATHING WORLD REVOLUTION, OR THE MAGIC OF DICTATORSHIP

Arriving in Shanghai on May 5, 1920, Mao lodged with Hunanese friends in a small two-story house on a dirty street in the western part of town. There he stayed for two and a half months.[1] As always, Mao was almost broke, as were his friends. In order to make ends meet, he had to jettison what he called his "intellectual's habit" and engage in physical labor. Mao wound up washing other people's laundry.[2] His work as a laundryman occupied only "half-time" and he spent his free hours politicking and wandering about town.[3]

He managed to have a good look around Shanghai. Located on the banks of the Huangpu, one of the tributaries of the Yangzi River, Shanghai was already the largest industrial and commercial center of China and in all of East Asia. Starting in 1842, the year the British arrived on the scene, Shanghai had been transformed by 1920 from a town of 230,000 into a giant metropolis with no fewer than two million residents, twice as many as in Beijing. The city was the main open port of the country. Countless wharves and warehouses stretched along the left bank of the Huangpu River.

Shanghai was divided into six main districts. Five of them—Nandao, Zhabei, Wusong, the International Settlement, and the French Concession—were located on the left or west bank of the Huangpu, and one—Pudong—on the right or east side. Close to the northern railroad station, on the left bank of the Wusong (also known as Suzhou Creek), a small river that was a tributary of the Huangpu, lay the industrial, workers' quarter of Zhabei. This was a new district dating from the mid-nineteenth century. Nandao, the oldest part of Shanghai, dating from the Tang dynasty (618–906 CE), lay between the southern railroad station and the Huangpu. South of Zhabei and north and west of the Huangpu stretched the International Settlement, which was governed by the British. Adjoining the International Settlement to the south was the French

Concession. Thus the foreign concessions bisected the left bank of Shanghai, forming two broad swathes squeezed in between the Chinese districts of Nandao and Zhabei. To the west of the International Settlement and the French Concession, on the upper reaches of Suzhou Creek, was the remaining Chinese district of Wusong.

Of the city's thirty-five square miles, more than a third belonged to foreigners. Foreign law prevailed on the territory of the settlements (the concessions), and foreign troops and police were stationed there. Chinese were allowed to live in these districts. Wealthy Chinese and intellectuals opposed to the Chinese authorities took advantage of this opportunity. In fact, the number of Chinese living in the International Settlement and the French Concession was many times greater than the number of foreigners.* The political atmosphere was much more liberal than anywhere else in China, and in the International Settlement, the standard of living significantly higher. The stores that lined Nanking Road were unique in China. Branches of the largest European and American banks were located in the International Settlement and the French Concession, along with expensive hotels and villas. Shanghai's architectural profile contrasted sharply with those of other Chinese cities. The quay made a particularly strong impression with its massive stone skyscrapers and sharp spires thrusting into the sky. Life bubbled up all around, advertisements blazed, cars careened along the streets, rickshaw pullers rushed to and fro, ships from every nation were loading and unloading in the harbor, elegantly dressed ladies accompanied by refined gentlemen promenaded along the central part of the quay or Bund in the shade of the trees. Crowds of people jostled each other along Nanking Road and nearby streets and alleys. Numerous shops and restaurants, movie theaters and casinos attracted an affluent public.

In Shanghai one could hear English, French, and even Russian spoken everywhere. In 1925 there were 2,766 Russians in Shanghai, no fewer than 6,000 British, about 1,500 Americans, and more than 1,000 French. In all, there were 37,758 foreigners of various nationalities in the city. Japanese composed the majority; in 1925 there were 13,804 Japanese,[4] but owing to the presence of the Russians, British, and French who put their stamp on the city, Shanghai had the flavor of a European capital. The architecture of its international quarters differed little from New York or London.

Mao Zedong could not help but notice how un-Chinese it seemed even though he lived rather far from Nanking Road and the Bund. He could always use that technological wonder, a tram, which ran through the International and French settlements. He also rode the tram to reach his clients, picking up

---

* In 1885, for example, the ratio of Chinese to foreigners in the International Settlement was 35 to 1, and in the French Concession there were 25,000 Chinese and 300 foreigners.

dirty laundry and delivering freshly washed bundles. These trips, he said, used up a large part of his minuscule income.[5]

By now quite a few of the anti-Zhang activists were gathered in Shanghai. The Association for the Revival of Hunan, a public organization established by wealthy emigrants from the province, had begun functioning in Shanghai in December 1918. Other Hunanese fraternal societies that demanded the ouster of Zhang also operated in Shanghai. The most influential was the Society of Hunanese Residing in Shanghai. In the spring of 1920, Xu Fosu, a famous son of Hunan, who was president of the parliament of the Republic of China and an opponent of Zhang Jingyao, stayed in Shanghai.[6]

All the efforts of Mao and other patriotic Hunanese in Shanghai were in vain, yet Mao Zedong continued tilting at windmills. To be sure, he now approached the struggle in a more sophisticated way. He sought not only to get rid of the corrupt bosses, but to change the vicious system that produced such despots. In proclamations that he wrote between the spring and autumn of 1920, Mao, displaying a utopian fervor, favored Hunanese popular self-rule. He proposed separating Hunan from China, which was mired in filth; declaring Hunan's complete independence; and introducing a local constitution and an elected, genuinely democratic form of governance. Mao recalled, "Disgusted with the Northern Government, and believing that Hunan could modernize more rapidly if freed from connections with Peking [Beijing], our group agitated for separation. I was then a strong supporter of America's Monroe Doctrine and the Open Door."[7] This is a strange confession on the part of a man who told Edgar Snow that by the summer of 1920 he had become a Marxist.

The idea of an "independent Hunan" was not new. On the eve of the 1911 Revolution, the Hunanese revolutionary democrat Yang Shouren had insisted that a free Hunan could become a model for all the other provinces in China, which would ultimately unite around new, federalist principles, leading to the renaissance of the Chinese nation.[8] Naturally, this idea had not the slightest connection with Marxism or Bolshevism, but it fit well into the traditions of several Western European countries as well as that of the United States. Mao did not accept it immediately. In March 1920 he still expressed doubts about the possibility of separating Hunan: "[S]ince it is a province within China, it would not be easy for Hunan to establish its independence, unless . . . our status becomes like that of an American or German state."[9] Soon, however, he became a passionate advocate. He started from the premise that "China is so vast. Each province differs greatly from the others in sentiments, interests, and the level of popular wisdom. . . . [At the same time] Hunan's geography and the nature of its people have great potential. If they are mixed up in the nationwide organization, their particular strengths will be undermined, and they will be restrained from further progress."[10]

Mao counted upon the creative energy of the citizens of his native province. "If the Hunan people can take the lead now, then Shaanxi, Fujian, Sichuan, and Anhui provinces, having similar conditions, will follow, and then some ten to twenty years later, they may join together in providing a general solution to the problems of the whole country."[11] He wanted to establish a kind of special "Hunanese civilization," a society of free people who would govern their own country without a military governor or an army, and would promote education, industry, and trade.[12] He also compared Hunan with Switzerland and with Japan.[13] Mao counted especially upon the citizens of the provincial capital to be the vanguard in the movement for independence and democratization. "[T]he responsibility has inevitably fallen on the shoulders of our 300,000 citizens of Changsha," he wrote.[14]

In June 1920, Mao presented his plan for the revival and reconstruction of Hunan to the person whom he respected most, Chen Duxiu.[15] Chen was then living in a small, traditional Chinese brick house on a quiet lane in the French Concession where the editorial office of *New Youth* was also housed. What Chen replied is unknown, but most likely he showed no interest in this naïve project. Otherwise, Mao Zedong would surely have made mention of his response in one of his speeches. Instead, Chen Duxiu tried to set Mao onto the "true path" of Marxism. "I had discussed with Chĕn [Chen], on my second visit to Shanghai, the Marxist books that I had read," Mao later recalled, "and Chĕn's own assertions of belief had deeply impressed me at what was probably a critical period in my life."[16]

Chen Duxiu was busy establishing the first Bolshevik cell in China. Soviet communists, members of the Communist International (Comintern), provided him with direct financial and ideological assistance. Created on Lenin's initiative in March 1919, the Comintern united and coordinated the efforts of all radical revolutionary parties that adopted Bolshevik principles. It was the headquarters of world revolution, the main ideological and organizational center of the world communist movement. It was also a powerful intelligence service, dispatching agents and saboteurs to various countries. An elected Executive Committee (ECCI), with its own bureaucratic apparatus staffed by foreign as well as Soviet communists, directed the Comintern. From its headquarters on Moscow's Sapozhnikovskaia Square across from the Kremlin, the ECCI sent its representatives to the far corners of the earth, carrying instructions, directives, and, most important, money and valuables that the Bolsheviks had expropriated from the former Russian aristocracy and the bourgeoisie. This money created communist organizations in Europe and Asia, in Africa and America, opened underground presses and party schools, and paid striking workers and professional revolutionaries. The Bolshevik leaders Lenin, Trotsky, Zinoviev, and Stalin did not stint on supporting the communist movement outside of Soviet Russia. In the early years of Soviet power they linked their hopes for the construction of socialism in backward Russia to the victory of proletarian revolution on a world scale.

Naturally, their attention was also drawn to China. During the years when civil war was raging in Russia, one couldn't reach China from Moscow. Therefore, in the spring of 1920 a group of Bolsheviks from the Soviet Far East, headed by Grigorii Voitinsky, was dispatched to China. Voitinsky, whom Chinese called Wu Tingkang, was a tall, smart, and energetic twenty-seven-year-old with dark, curly hair and sad, thoughtful eyes. He pleasantly surprised people with his native intelligence, tact, and gentle, dignified manner. Moreover, he spoke English fluently, a great asset, since many radical Chinese intellectuals knew Western languages, particularly English and French, but not Russian. Meeting Voitinsky, it was impossible to imagine that this charming young man was one of the main organizers of the communist movement in Siberia and the Russian Far East, a rock-solid Bolshevik who was merciless toward the enemies of the revolution.[17]

Voitinsky, whose real name was Zarkhin, was accompanied on his trip by his wife, also a Bolshevik, Maria Kuznetsova, whose party alias was Nora. Voitinsky's traveling party also included a Chinese interpreter, Yang Mingzhai, a former worker who subsequently became an accountant, and who had lived in Vladivostok since 1901. The Comintern agents arrived in Beijing in April 1920. Before them lay an especially conspiratorial task: to establish regular ties with radical Chinese activists in order to help them organize communist circles. They had sufficient money for this subversive work.

They got lucky right away. Through a teacher of Russian literature at Peking University, a Russian émigré named Sergei A. Polevoi, who was sympathetic toward Soviet Russia, Voitinsky was able to make contact with Li Dazhao. The Soviet Bolshevik presented to Professor Li a breathtaking plan to create a communist party in China, but although Li accepted the idea wholeheartedly he advised Voitinsky to discuss the plan first with Chen Duxiu. Yang Mingzhai, who had heard about Chen Duxiu from the Russian émigrés, proffered the same advice to Voitinsky. Carrying a letter of recommendation from Li Dazhao, the trio of Voitinsky, Kuznetsova, and Yang arrived in Shanghai at the end of April.

In China, not only money but also personal connections were important. Thus Voitinsky's approach, skillfully making use of Polevoi and Li Dazhao, was effective. A group of Soviet communists already in Shanghai established contact with Voitinsky's group and together they all began to "cultivate" Chen, who was already prepared for an alliance with Soviet Russia. It was decided to make use of *New Youth* as a tribune for the dissemination of communist ideas, with the objective of uniting all radical revolutionary forces around the journal.[18]

It was just then that Mao Zedong visited Chen. Their conversation confused Mao, who trusted Chen but didn't want to abandon his plan to unite the popular masses of Hunan in support of proclaiming the province's independence on the basis of self-rule and progress. In early July he returned to Hunan still in a state of confusion.

Mao conceived the idea of jointly investing with his friends to establish the first cooperative bookstore in China that would distribute social and political literature. The store, called the Cultural Book Society, opened for business in September with the aim of selling all kinds of worthwhile books, journals, and newspapers at affordable prices, thereby making a notable contribution to the enlightenment of the Hunanese people.[19] The initiative attracted the attention of many public figures. It is worth noting that the Chinese characters for the store's signboard were written by Tan Yankai himself, although only after he was forced to step down in late November 1920 from his position of provincial governor of Hunan.[20] The store was located in a small two-story building consisting of three rooms that Mao and his comrades rented from the Sino-American Xiangya Hospital. Its initial capital was only 519 yuan, but by the end of October 1920, Mao and his friends were able to stock 164 book titles for sale, including works by Russell, Kropotkin, Darwin, Plato, Hu Shi, Kirkup's *History of Socialism,* which Mao liked so well, and many others.[21] The store also sold as a separate brochure Marx's preface to the first edition of *Capital* and a book by the journalist Shao Piaoping called *A Study of the New Russia,* which was essentially the first detailed account by a Chinese author of the history of the Russian communist movement over the past seventeen years.[22] The store also distributed forty-five journals and three newspapers, including the communist media published by Chen Duxiu, Li Dazhao, and several other socialists: *New Youth, Workers' World, The Workers, Workers' Tide,* and *Young China.* By April 1921 branches of the Cultural Book Society had opened in seven districts in Hunan, and kiosks were installed at four educational institutions in Hunan.[23]

In late August 1920, under the influence of his conversations with Li and Chen, Mao founded the Russia Studies Society in Changsha.[24] For tactical reasons, Jiang Jihuan, a well-known liberal, was chosen as general secretary, but Mao was really in charge. The society had ambitious goals: individual and collective study of Soviet Russia, collecting accessible literature, publishing research and reviews about the Land of Soviets, and sponsoring a special Russian class to prepare people who wanted to travel to Moscow to study. The society was located in the same quarters as the bookstore.[25]

Mao himself dreamed of going to Russia. In Beijing he consulted with Li Dazhao and several other comrades about this and even took some classes with the Russian professor Polevoi.[26] When he was in Shanghai, he had wanted to continue his study and for some time looked for another Russian émigré who would agree to teach him Russian. An entire campaign of work and study in Soviet Russia whirled in his head along the lines of the "diligent work and frugal study" movement initiated by the anarchists in regard to France.[27] He undoubtedly received news of the active preparations along these lines that Chen Duxiu and Voitinsky were undertaking in Shanghai. In September 1920 Chen and Voitinsky organized a Foreign Language School for socialist-minded youth who wanted to study in Moscow.[28] Once a week, Chen Wangdao, the translator into Chinese of *The Communist Manifesto,* gave them lectures on Marxism.[29] Voitinsky supplied graduates with funding to pay for their travel to Russia.

All this made an impression on Mao, yet he was not quite ready to embrace Bolshevism. He respected Li Dazhao and Chen Duxiu deeply and was attentive to their point of view, but it was terribly difficult for him to shed his liberal and anarchist ideas. Striving to advance the cause of popular enlightenment in order to awaken the creative forces of Hunanese, in the summer and autumn of 1920 Mao took part in organizing several other societies both in Hunan and in his native district of Xiangtan.[30] He continued to agitate for Hunan self-determination in articles he published in the local press, and he petitioned the governor and spoke in public. In early October he chaired a public meeting in Changsha at the Education Committee, where he organized a signature drive for a petition he had drafted calling for the convening of a People's Constitutional Assembly in Hunan. The petition was signed by 430 persons, including journalists, scientists and educators, businessmen, and even workers.[31] On October 10, China's national day, the resolution was delivered to Tan Yankai during a grandiose, ten-thousand-person demonstration.[32] On November 7, during another massive demonstration in Changsha, Mao carried a large banner reading "Long Live Great Hunan!"[33]

But nothing came from his ventures for independence. Individual demonstrations and meetings, even massive ones, did not lead to revolution. Reminiscing about this many years later, Mao noted with bitter self-irony, "T'an Yen-k'ai [Tan Yankai] was driven out of Hunan by a militarist named Chao Hêng-t'i [Zhao Hengti], who utilized the 'Hunan independence' movement for his own ends. He pretended to support it, advocating the idea of a United Autonomous States of China, but as soon as he got power he suppressed the democratic movement with great energy."[34]

To be fair, on January 1, 1922, Zhao Hengti would become the only militarist in China to grant a constitution to his province; however, as Mao correctly noted, he did this only because he lacked sufficient military power to play the role of a national leader. The constitution, which masked his military dictatorship, bore no relationship to the kind of people power Mao advocated. "The life span of the Provincial Constitution is definitely limited," Mao prophesied. "Realization of a federation of self-ruled provinces is even less of a possibility under any circumstances."[35]

Confronting these difficulties for the first time, many of Mao's formerly active supporters began to abandon the movement for popular self-rule. Those who earlier had shouted louder than anyone else now preferred to sit at home. Everything that Mao had long stood for now collapsed. What disturbed Mao most of all and contributed to his profound sense of disillusionment was the apathy of the population. The people whom he had counted upon turned out to be so passive that Mao simply lost heart. He poured out his rage in a letter to a friend from his youth, Xiang Jingyu: "In the last few months, I have seen through the Hunanese: muddle-headed with neither ideals nor long-term plans. In political circles, they are lethargic and extremely corrupt, and we can say there is absolutely no hope for political reform."[36]

This is when he began to think seriously about what Li Dazhao and Chen Duxiu had said to him. Yes, he decided, "We can only . . . carve out a new path, and create a new environment."[37] Cai Hesen, who had studied French at a men's college in Montargis, France, also appealed to him. Cai had become an ardent Bolshevik under the impression of everything he had seen in Europe. He wrote to Mao:

> I believe that a contemporary world revolution is the only way to achieve victory. I now see clearly that socialism is a reaction to capitalism. Its basic mission is to destroy the economic system of capital by means of the dictatorship of the proletariat. . . . I think the principles and methods of socialism are completely applicable for the future reconstruction of China. . . . [O]ur first order of business is to organize a party, a communist party, inasmuch as it is the initiator, propagandist, vanguard, and headquarters of the revolutionary movement.[38]

Just then Chen, Voitinsky, and Li were working at creating such a party. In May 1920 Chen and Voitinsky had established the so-called Revolutionary Bureau, which also included three people who were close to Chen.[39] It began working to create party circles. On July 19, 1920, a meeting of the most active comrades took place in Shanghai, at which it was decided to organize a communist cell headed by Chen Duxiu.[40] On August 22, the Shanghai Socialist Youth League was formed, and similar organizations soon appeared in Beijing, Tianjin, Wuchang, and several other cities. In October a Beijing communist group headed by Professor Li was formed, and in November the Socialist Youth League of China was officially proclaimed.

This first score of Chinese communists were all students, young teachers, and journalists. There were no workers or peasants among them. The oldest,

Chen Duxiu, just forty-two, was known as "the Old Man." The youngest was the eighteen-year-old Beida student Liu Renjing, who knew a little Russian. What united them was a passionate desire to achieve in their own homeland by whatever means possible and as quickly as possible what had occurred in Russia. In November 1920, Chen began to publish in Shanghai a quasi-legal journal, *Gongchandang* (Communist), in which he persistently propagated the idea of establishing a communist party. The journal published Comintern documents as well as articles about the prospects for a Bolshevik revolution in China. He also began publishing a magazine for workers, *Laodongjie* (Workers' world), which in simple and accessible language explained the Marxist theory of capital and surplus value to poorly educated persons.

Mao Zedong also understood the need to create a "group of people bound together by an ism."[41] He never had any doubts about the importance of a highly cohesive political organization, but the Renovation of the People Study Society had always been rather amorphous and the Hunan Students Association had long since ceased to exist. He had to start over again. Mao decided to reorganize the Renovation of the People Study Society along Bolshevik lines. He shared his ideas with Luo Zhanglong, who had already joined the Bolshevik circle in Beijing:

> We really must create a powerful new atmosphere. . . . To create such an atmosphere naturally requires a group of hardworking and resolute "people," but even more than that, it requires an "ism" that everyone holds in common. Without an ism, the atmosphere cannot be created. I think our Study Society should not merely be a gathering of people, bound by sentiment. . . . An ism is like a banner; only when it is raised will the people have something to hope for and know in what direction to go.[42]

Mao began to rectify the amorphous character of the society while he was still in Shanghai, in May 1920. He called a meeting of the twelve members of the group who were then in Shanghai and they adopted new principles aimed at strengthening the organization. But there was no discussion of any "common ism."[43]

At this point the situation changed dramatically. Mao had become convinced of the need to draw a clear line of demarcation between those who only paid lip service to radical change and those who were prepared to act upon their convictions at whatever cost. He had had enough of amorphousness and inclusivity. By November 1920 Mao had fixed on Bolshevism, with its program of world socialist revolution, as the "ism" of choice. Not all of his old friends agreed with Mao. Xiao Yu, who had returned from France in October 1920, did not accept the Bolshevik program. In a letter to Mao he noted bitterly, "We do not regard it as permissible to sacrifice part of the people in exchange for the welfare of the majority. I advocate a moderate revolution, a revolution with education as its instrument, which seeks to promote the general welfare of the people and carries out reforms through the medium of trade unions and cooperatives. I do not think the Russian-style Marxist revolution is justified." [44] But Mao's mind was made up. He had been attracted both to anarchism and liberalism, and had reaped only disappointment. He might still agree in principle with Xiao Yu that it was a good thing "to seek the welfare of all by peaceful means," but he now considered all these notions as utopian fantasies. He expressed his position as follows: "[M]y present view of absolute liberalism, anarchism, and even democracy, is that these things sound very good in theory, but are not feasible in reality." How could one depend upon the reeducation of the exploiters, he wondered, if education in the contemporary world was in the hands of these very same capitalists? The bourgeoisie owned the factories and the banks, controlled parliament, the army, and the police. Where was there room for the communists? No, he objected, only "A Russian-style revolution . . . is a last resort when all other means have been exhausted. It is not that some other better means are rejected and we only want to use this terrorist tactic." [45] In other words, let it be Bolshevism rather than a better way out of the situation; "charity" got you nowhere. "[I]n my opinion," Mao summed up, "the Russian Revolution, and the fact that radical Communists in various countries are daily growing more numerous and more tightly organized, represent simply the natural course of events." [46]

His approach to Bolshevism was deliberate. He chose "terrorist tactics" under the pressure of circumstances, having become disillusioned with the creative power of the people and their capacity for self-government. Bolshevik-style totalitarianism, with its denial of civic freedom, its appeal to an all-around dictatorship of the communist party, its fanaticism and uncompromising character was the logical solution to the problem for the young radical. It also fit his purely personal needs: we may recall that in Mao's consciousness, "will" and "power" trumped all other concepts.

It was not the romance of universal equality that enticed him to embrace communism. What attracted him was the apologia for violence, the triumph of will, and the celebration of power. Finally, he had made his choice. It was immoral, but understandable. How could one speak of liberalism or democracy in a state where civil society was absent, where 390 million of 400 million were illiterate, in which even though the emperor's power had been abolished in 1912 "there are very few citizens who really know what a republic is." [47] It was a country where capitalism had still not penetrated all aspects of public life, and in which every economic structure known to history was represented.

It was a savage, patriarchal country. What kind of force was needed to move such a country out of its profound torpor?

What attracted Mao to Bolshevism also attracted other radical Chinese revolutionaries. Swept off their feet by the October Revolution, they embraced the Bolshevik experiment practically without any critical understanding. Even those who had read the works of the founders of classical Marxism and who could, therefore, discern a distinct divergence between the theory and the practice of the Bolsheviks on one hand and Marx's materialist concepts on the other, were still inclined to view the actions of the Russian communists as real "Marxism," and concluded that there were "defects" in Marx's historical materialism. As to the teachings of Marx and Engels themselves, Chinese radical youth most easily grasped the strongly revolutionary ideas of class struggle of the workers against the capitalists, of an anticapitalist social revolution, and of the dictatorship of the proletariat.[48] Among the classics of Marxism with which they were familiar, the young Chinese intellectuals singled out *The Communist Manifesto*, the pamphlet written by the young Marx and Engels that was openly propagandistic and political in tone, and exceptionally passionate in calling for direct revolutionary action. They were attracted by its extremism, which was reminiscent of the radicalism of the Bolsheviks. It was precisely in the *Manifesto* that Chinese supporters of communism found their confirmation of the authentically Marxist character of Bolshevik theory. Typical in this connection are Chen Duxiu's lectures "A Critique of Socialism," which he published in the July 1, 1921, issue of *New Youth*. Abundantly quoting from the *Manifesto* as well as from *The Critique of the Gotha Programme*, Chen Duxiu concluded, "Only in Russia was the true essence of Marx's teaching revived and given the name of communism. . . . Only the Russian communist party, in both words and deeds, is truly Marxist."[49]

The Chinese followers of the Bolsheviks agreed that the immediate goal of their movement was to prepare their own October Revolution. China's proletarian revolution, they thought, should not only destroy the rule of feudal-militarist forces, but also put an end to the development of capitalist relations in their country. It should be aimed at the old exploiting classes as well as against the new, including the national bourgeoisie. At the same time, it was also anti-imperialist, aiming at overthrowing the sway of foreign capital in China. Naturally, the result of such a revolution in China would be the establishment of a dictatorship of the proletariat.[50]

Ultimately, Mao Zedong arrived at similar conclusions. Once he accepted Bolshevism he no longer had any doubts. In mid-November 1920, Mao turned to the task of establishing underground cells in Changsha. In October he had already received the statutes of local Socialist Youth Leagues from Shanghai and Beijing.[51] Therefore, he started with organizing just such an association.

From the beginning of the school year he had been working as the director of a primary school attached to the Provincial First Normal School, so that he was in contact with young people.*

The first person Mao spoke to concerning the "search for comrades" to undertake appropriate work was his former student from the Xiuye Primary School, Zhang Wenliang.[52] At the time Zhang was already a student in the Provincial First Normal School; he was, apparently, following in the steps of his teacher. Mao began to look for suitable young persons among students at the Hunan Commercial Institute and the First Middle School in Changsha.[53] He acted cautiously, and he advised Zhang Wenliang to do likewise. "He also talked [with me] about the Youth League," Zhang Wenliang wrote in his diary, "saying that emphasis should now be given to looking for real comrades, and that it was better to go slowly, and not advance too hastily."[54] By early December they had succeeded in recruiting more than twenty young people, and soon after, on January 13, 1921, the Hunan branch of the Socialist Youth League was officially established.[55]

Sometime in November 1920, Mao received a letter from Chen Duxiu advising him to organize a communist group in Changsha like the one in Shanghai.[56] Chen's suggestion evoked not only Mao's interest, but also that of Bewhiskered He, Peng Huang, and another friend of Mao's, He Minfan of the Chuanshan Municipal Middle School. For reasons of security, the friends met in a cemetery. A start had been made. What lay ahead was convincing other members of the Renovation of the People Study Society to accept Bolshevism, and thereby transform an existing organization that had not yet defined its political position into a communist one.

For the time being everything was going well, and Mao hoped to win over additional members of the society, at least those who were in Changsha. Things were also looking up in his personal life. At the end of September he began seeing Yang Kaihui, the daughter of the late Yang Changji. She had returned to Changsha with her mother and brother in January 1920 after the death of her father. According to custom, the family conveyed the coffin of the deceased to his native place. In Bancang, a little town some twenty miles north of Changsha, the ashes of the revered Professor Yang were interred. After observing the stipulated period of mourning, Kaihui moved to Changsha to continue her studies.[57] At first the young people were shy with each other, and they went for walks along the river accompanied by Zhang Wenliang and Tao Yi, who apparently had completely cooled off toward Mao. Mao already had experience with girls, but it took him a long time to overcome his shyness toward Kaihui.

---

* The Chinese system of education in the 1920s had some unique features. There were three levels in primary school—lower, middle, and high. Therefore, graduates of the highest level of primary school might be in the sixteen- to seventeen-year-old age range.

Instead of love, they spoke often of politics. Mao told her about Soviet Russia and the Bolshevik revolution, and acquainted her with the ABC's of Marxism, to the degree that he was acquainted with them. Under his influence Kaihui joined the Socialist Youth League. But in the end the feelings growing in both of them burst into the open. "I saw his heart," Kaihui later recalled, "and he clearly saw mine."[58]

Evidently, they were made for each other. But what had happened to Mao's naïve faith in free love? In the winter of 1920 he and Kaihui were married.[59] The young couple was of one mind in rejecting a traditional marriage ceremony. They did without a dowry and without a red palanquin. They dismissed all this as petty bourgeois philistinism.[60]

Both before and after her wedding Kaihui was extremely jealous of her husband's relationship with Tao Yi. It seemed to her that that old romance was still going on.[61] Her fears intensified when she did not see her beloved for a long time. They lacked the money to rent their own room, so they continued to live apart as before, seeing each other only on Sundays. Only on their honeymoon in Shaoshanchong, which lasted just a few days, were they together. They arrived there in early February 1921, to celebrate Chinese New Year's with Mao's brothers; his second cousin Zejian, whom Mao's parents had adopted as their daughter in 1912;[62] and Mao's sister-in-law Wang Shulan, the wife of his brother Zemin.[63] Not until October 1921 were they able to rent a small three-room wooden house on the edge of a pond in the suburb of Qingshuitang, just beyond the eastern gates of the city. Kaihui brought her mother, Xiang Zhenxi, there from the village. It was the custom in China to share a home with parents. It was thought that several generations should live under one roof.[64] Mao got the money to pay the rent from party funds. By this time he had succeeded not only in communizing the Renovation of the People Study Society, but also in expanding underground Bolshevik activity in many directions.

8

"FOLLOWING THE RUSSIAN PATH"

Early on the morning of January 1, 1921, more than ten people gathered on the top floor of a small house in the center of Changsha at No. 56 Chaozong Street, the premises of the Cultural Book Society. Members of the quasi-legal Renovation of the People Study Society, they had assembled in response to a call from their leaders, He Shuheng and Mao Zedong. Over the next three days they discussed the following vital questions: What should be the general goal of the organization? What methods should they use to reach that goal, and what should they do to get started right away? The meeting was chaired by Bewhiskered He.

Mao Zedong was the first to speak. He said,

> some members proposed organizing a Communist Party, while others wanted to practice a work-study philosophy and to transform education. . . . [T]here are two schools of thought in China today about how to resolve the problems of society. One advocates transformation, while the other wants reform. The former is that of Chen Duxiu and others; the latter is that of Liang Qichao, Zhang Dongsun [Liang Qichao's adherent] and others.[1]

The debate over the issues engendered heated disputes. Everyone understood that the future political program of the organization would depend on how the majority voted. The main question was whether to accept Bolshevism. The entire first morning was spent on discussion of general problems, and the meeting never got around to the core issue. At 11:30 A.M. the meeting broke up; the key disputes were carried over to the next day. At 9:00 A.M. on January 2, everyone was present, including some new people who had heard of the interesting discussion. Eighteen people were gathered in the room. Bewhiskered He again presided.

As the first order of business a majority voted to maintain the previous formulation of their general goal, which was "the transformation of China and the whole world." Then they moved to the next item. Again Mao spoke first. He reminded everyone that in addition to the revolutionary Leninist solution there were other ways of addressing social problems including "social policy," "social democracy," "the moderate type of communism (the doctrine of Russell)," and "anarchism." Then he suggested they go round the circle and take turns declaring themselves. "I advocate radicalism," began Bewhiskered He. "One moment of upheaval is worth twenty years of education." At once Mao supported his elder comrade:

> Social policy is no method at all, because all it does is patch up some leaks. Social democracy resorts to a parliament as its tool for transforming things, but in reality the laws passed by a parliament always protect the propertied class. Anarchism rejects all authority, and I fear that such a doctrine can never be realized. The moderate type of communism, such as the extreme freedom advocated by Russell, lets the capitalists run wild, and therefore it will never work either. The radical type of communism, or the ideology of the workers and the peasants, which employs the method of class dictatorship, can be expected to achieve results. Hence it is the best method for us to use.

Most of those present agreed that the Russian variant of socialism should be adopted, because "in China, society [is] apathetic and human nature is degenerate. . . . Chinese society lacks organization and training." The young Hunanese radicals favored the extreme formula "If the people are not able to make themselves happy, let's drag them into happiness with an iron hand." In the end, twelve of the eighteen present voted for Bolshevism.[2]

Mao had reason to celebrate. He had played the key role in the creation of a communist organization in Changsha, but as often happens to many people, right after this success he fell into a depression. It appears that he had a nervous breakdown from the tension of the preceding few days. Earlier, too, he was given to self-analysis, and now he was in the depths of despair. In a letter to Peng Huang that he wrote at this low point, he discovered eight "defects" in himself that he believed would keep him from becoming a truly exceptional person, a great leader, which is what he had always passionately desired to be. These were his "defects": 1) too emotional, always in the grip of feelings; 2) prone to subjective judgments; 3) somewhat vain; 4) too arrogant; 5) rarely self-analytic, too quick to blame others and unwilling to recognize his own blunders; 6) good at big talk, but weak in systematic analysis; 7) values himself too highly and is too facile in self-appraisal; 8) "weak-willed."[3] He was particularly ashamed to confess this last "very great defect," because he had so assiduously cultivated an iron-willed spirit. Mao concluded his letter to his old friend with a frank admission that what motivated him was the fact that "I do not want to sacrifice my true self, I do not wish **myself** to turn myself into a puppet."[4] Mao's self-deprecation passed as quickly as it came. He never again doubted his right to power. The only surprising thing is that the letter has survived.

By the summer of 1921 there were already six communist cells in China. In addition to Shanghai, Beijing, and Changsha there were also party groups in Canton, Wuhan, and Jinan. A tiny cell was also organized in Japan by two members of the Shanghai circle who had gone there to study. Chen Duxiu circulated a letter to all these organizations to set "an agenda for a [united] conference as well as a time and place."[5] Shanghai was chosen as the venue for the founding congress of the Communist Party of China.

On June 3, 1921, a new Comintern representative arrived in China. Maring, the pseudonym under which he was listed in the Comintern Executive Committee archives, was a Dutch Jew from Rotterdam and one of the oldest activists in the Dutch social democratic and communist movements. The thirty-eight-year-old Maring, or Ma Lin as the Chinese called him, was known by many different names and had come to Shanghai as a Mr. Anderson. His real name was Sneevliet—Hendricus Josephus Franciscus Marie Sneevliet. Unlike Voitinsky, who had left China by this time, the new ECCI emissary was not known for his tact. He knew his own value as a special agent of Moscow, and he had walked the halls of the Kremlin with Lenin, Trotsky, and Zinoviev. He had already proven himself an outstanding labor organizer not only in the Netherlands, but also in Java, in the Dutch East Indies between 1913 and 1918. There he had been active in the initial stages of the Indonesian national liberation struggle. It was this experience that commended him to Comintern leaders. When he arrived in Moscow in June 1920 he was welcomed into important Kremlin offices, and at the Second Comintern Congress in July–August 1920, Maring served as secretary of the Commission on National and Colonial Questions. He was also chosen as a member of the ECCI, the leading organ of the Comintern, and easily outranked Voitinsky.

Maring was disliked by many Chinese communists because of his lack of civility. An elegant and rather pompous gentleman who dressed in a gray three-piece suit and bow tie, Maring reminded people of those same haughty colonialists against whom he himself had struggled. At least, this was the impression he made upon Zhang Guotao, who at their first meeting sized up this "foreign devil" as "aggressive and hard to deal with. . . . He saw himself coming as an angel of liberation to the Asian people. But . . . he seemed endowed with the social superiority complex of the white man."[6]

Vladimir Neiman (alias Vasilii Berg), another Soviet emissary, known in China as Nikolsky, arrived with his wife in Shanghai from Irkutsk as an agent of the Far Eastern Secretariat of ECCI, the special regional organ of the Communist International that had been established in January 1921.[7] Chen Duxiu, however, was not in Shanghai. In December 1920, he had accepted an invitation from the southern Chinese militarist Chen Jiongming, who had seized power in Guangdong province two months earlier, to assume the chairmanship of the Guangdong Provincial Education Committee in Canton. For tactical reasons General Chen Jiongming was masquerading as a liberal and swearing his fealty to democracy. He succeeded in fooling not only Professor Chen, but also Sun Yat-sen, who had returned to China after more than two and a half years of exile in Japan only after the death of Yuan Shikai in June 1916. Sun had settled in Canton. Meanwhile, the new president of China, General Li Yuanhong, who initially had tried to restore the constitution that his predecessor had trampled upon, under pressure from northern militarists had himself dissolved the parliament. In June 1917, exasperated by the conduct of the president, the deputies started gathering in Canton where they rallied around Sun Yat-sen and reconstituted the parliament in September 1917. A dual power formally came into being in the country. (In reality, as we know, the situation was much more complicated. China disintegrated, and every local militarist considered himself de facto independent.) On October 3, 1917, Sun was chosen as the generalissimo of South China. But this time, too, lacking an army of his own, he was soon forced to retire to Shanghai at the insistence of yet another militarist. There he stayed until November 1920, when Chen Jiongming, a member of Sun's own party, who had seized power in Canton in late October, invited the hapless generalissimo to return. On April 7, 1921, Sun was proclaimed the extraordinary president of the Republic of China. In reality, he only controlled Canton and environs. Proclaiming himself a revolutionary, Chen Jiongming even managed to fool the worldly wise agents of the Communist International, including Voitinsky.[8] (Not a year and a half would pass before, in June 1922, Chen Jiongming would rebel against the unfortunate Sun Yat-sen, forcing the latter to flee once more to Shanghai two months later.)

For the time being, however, it seemed that a new era had dawned in Canton, which is why Chen Duxiu had accepted Chen Jiongming's offer to serve in his government. Following a proposal by the ECCI representatives, it was decided to hold the founding congress of the Chinese Communist Party (CCP) without Chen. Li Dazhao, burdened with work at Beida, also could not come to Shanghai, but even this did not bother Maring and Nikolsky. In June 1921, a member of the Shanghai communist nucleus, Li Da, substituting for Chen Duxiu, sent a notice to all communist organizations throughout the country inviting them each to send two representatives to the congress in Shanghai.[9] Soon after, on July 9, Maring sent a secret dispatch to Moscow: "I hope that the conference that we intend to convene at the end of July will prove very useful to our work. The small groups of comrades will be united. After this we can begin centralized work."[10] By July 23, everything was ready. Twelve delegates, two each from Shanghai, Beijing, Wuhan, Changsha, and Jinan, and one each from Canton and Tokyo, assembled. Among them were Mao Zedong and Bewhiskered He.

Mao and He left Changsha by steamer on the evening of June 29 and arrived in Shanghai a week later. They were met by the Shanghai liaison, Li Da's wife,

Wang Huiwu, who was in charge of making arrangements for the delegates. She put up the delegates in the empty dormitory of the Bowen Women's Lycée in the French Concession. The director was her acquaintance, a Mrs. Huang Shaolan, who suspected nothing and was glad to get some extra income. Wang Huiwu told her that a group of professors and students in town for a scholarly symposium needed temporary quarters. The visiting "professors and students" slept on the floor because there were no beds in the dormitory.[11]

Fifteen people participated in the congress, which opened on July 23 in another room of this same dormitory.[12] In addition to the twelve delegates, Maring and Nikolsky attended along with Bao Huisen, a special representative from Chen Duxiu. Two days after the congress opened it was shifted to the nearby home of Li Hanjun, one of the participants. Maring chose this place for reasons of security. Li Hanjun was the younger brother of Liu Shucheng, one of the wealthiest persons in Shanghai. The families of Liu and Li owned two adjoining private houses in the French Concession. The sessions of the founding congress of the CCP continued in No. 106 Wangzhilu (it is also No. 3 Shudelu Lane). Maring hoped that secret agents would not poke their noses in there. Li Hanjun's house is now the Museum of the First Congress of the CCP.

At the end of July 1921, the prospects for a rapid seizure of power in China were nil. At the time there were only fifty-three people in the ranks of the CCP.[13] Those assembled in Li Hanjun's house could only dimly discern the contours of the future bloody battles for a socialist revolution. Zhang Guotao, a delegate from Beijing whom we have already encountered, was chosen as chair of the congress.[14] Mao Zedong and Zhou Fohai, who had come from Japan, were asked to serve as secretaries. Busy with matters of protocol, Mao was not very active. He spoke only once, delivering a brief report on the Bolshevik group in Changsha. According to Zhang Guotao's reminiscences, Mao was "pale-faced," but he displayed a "rather lovely temperament. . . . [I]n his long gown of native cloth [he] looked like a Taoist [Daoist] priest out of some village. His fund of general knowledge was considerable. . . . A good talker, Mao loved an argument, and while conversing, he delighted in laying verbal traps into which his opponents would unwittingly fall by seeming to contradict themselves. Then, obviously happy, he would burst into laughter."[15]

Zhang, along with Li Hanjun, Bao Huisen, and Liu Renjing, displayed the greatest enthusiasm. A majority of the congress with the exception of their host stood firmly for the dictatorship of the proletariat as the central tenet of their new faith. The cautious Li Hanjun, who was quite familiar with Marx's economic teachings and, therefore, advised against trying to expedite a socialist revolution in a backward country, was quickly overwhelmed. The "pure breath" of Bolshevism emanates from the congress documents that were prepared by an editorial committee. The programmatic principles of the CCP were defined as follows:

A. With the revolutionary army of the proletariat to overthrow the capitalist classes, to reconstruct the nation from the labor class, until class distinctions are eliminated.

B. To adopt the dictatorship of the proletariat in order to complete the end of class struggle—abolishing the classes.

C. To overthrow the private ownership of capital, to confiscate all the productive means, such as machines, land, buildings, semi-manufactured products, etc., and to entrust them to social ownership.

D. To unite with the Third [i.e., Communist] International.[16]

This course also defined the tactical line endorsed at the congress: "Our Party, with the adoption of the Soviet form, organizes the industrial and agricultural laborers and soldiers, preaches communism, and recognizes the social revolution as our chief policy; absolutely cuts off all relations with the yellow intellectual class, and other such parties."[17]

The latter thesis was further developed in the "Decision as to the Objects of Communist Party of China":

Towards the existing political parties, an attitude of independence, aggression and exclusion should be adopted. In the political struggle, in opposition to militarism and bureaucracy and in demanding freedom of speech, press, and assemblage, when we must declare our attitude, our party should stand up in behalf of the proletariat, and should allow no relationship with the other parties or groups.[18]

The members of the Communist Party also adopted this isolationist position with regard to the Chinese nationalist revolutionaries headed by Sun Yat-sen. The delegates of the congress emphasized that Sun's government in Canton was no better than the government of the northern militarists,[19] despite the fact that Chen Duxiu was one of its ministers. This assertion of "revolutionary purity" demonstrates just how much these leftist Chinese radicals, who had just officially broken with liberalism, wanted to declare their ideological and organizational autonomy.

Even Maring and Nikolsky were giddy with revolutionary fervor. Maring spoke about his activity in Java, which involved promoting cooperation between the Social Democratic Association of the Dutch East Indies and local nationalists.[20] He explained that there are many different kinds of democrats, and to bolster his point of view he cited the basic resolutions on the national and colonial questions adopted at the Second Comintern Congress one year earlier.[21] As early as late November 1919, Lenin and other revolutionary leaders in Moscow realized that the attempt to disseminate Bolshevik theories beyond the eastern borders of Soviet Russia faced serious obstacles. Apart from a small number of leftist radicals, it seemed that no one in the East was eager to embrace Bolshevism. Most intellectuals adhered to nationalist views. The ideas of nationalism, rather than the abstract idea of internationalism that the Comintern supported, were also more easily accepted by the masses.

By the summer of 1920, Lenin understood that "pure" Bolshevik tactics aimed at preparing for socialist revolution were unlikely to be successful in the East. This forced the Russian communists to consider how to adapt their theories to countries that were even more backward industrially than Russia or that were either colonies or semi-colonies. They began to view world socialist revolution not only, or not so much, as the struggle "of revolutionary proletarians in all countries against their own bourgeoisie," but as rather the struggle "of all the oppressed people in all the colonies, countries, and dependencies against international imperialism."[22] Such thinking was incorporated into the new Comintern policy in China based on the theory of anticolonial revolution that Lenin had formulated in 1920.

In essence Lenin argued that the precondition for the emancipation of the working masses—mostly peasants—of industrially backward colonial and semi-colonial countries of the East was the overthrow of foreign imperialist domination in these countries. Revolutions in the East, therefore, including China, would be nationalist, not socialist, in nature. In order to garner significant popular following, local communists would have to support the bourgeois liberation movements of colonial and dependent nations. By participating in these democratic movements rather than isolating themselves, the communists should assume the leadership of the masses, and transform the nationalist movements into revolutions of a new type by propagating the idea of peasant soviets and soviets of exploited workers. Where conditions allow, they should attempt to establish soviets of the working people.

Speaking at the Second Comintern Congress in 1920, Lenin emphasized the temporary and purely tactical character of the new course. He asserted that the communists should provide support only to genuine nationalist revolutionaries. Such persons would allow the communists to educate and organize the broad masses in a more revolutionary, that is, communist, spirit, and support their struggle against landlords and all manifestations of feudalism. Lenin insisted upon preserving the organizational independence of the proletarian movement, even in its rudimentary form. He added that if the "bourgeois democrats" impede the communists' organizational work then the communists would have to struggle against them.[23] In plain English, it meant that we will support the national revolutionaries, but only when they do not get in the way of our organizing the masses to struggle against these very same national revolutionaries. Linked to this concept was the idea that the victory of anticolonial revolution in the countries of the East would switch them onto some sort of "noncapitalist" path of development.

Maring tried to convey all of this esoteric theorizing to the assembled delegates, emphasizing that the policies of the Bolsheviks in China must be flexible, but his speech made no impression upon them. They found it extraordinarily difficult to understand the need simultaneously to grasp the theory of class conflict of the proletariat against the bourgeoisie and the concept of anti-imperialist cooperation. They also were unable to comprehend that all of Bolshevism was founded on a lie. For the time being the "right to dishonesty" preached by the apologists of Leninism confused them. They were attracted to communism largely by its revolutionary allure, the romanticism of class conflict, and its egalitarian ideals.

The congress participants were ready to sum things up when suddenly, on the evening of July 30, a middle-aged man in a black robe looked in on the room where they were meeting. Asked to identify himself, the stranger muttered something about looking for the director of a publishing house, a Mr. Wang. (Wang, the most common surname in China, is the equivalent of Smith in America). He vanished at once, but Maring was very agitated and ordered everyone to disperse. Only the host and his friend Chen Gongbo, the delegate from Canton, remained. Not a quarter of an hour passed before the French police burst into the house. "Who is the owner?" asked the inspector in French. "I am," replied Li Hanjun, who knew French quite well.

"Who was at the meeting in your house?"

"There was no meeting," Li objected. "A few professors from Peking University were discussing plans of the *New Epoch* publisher." (Such a publisher really had existed since June 1921; it was legal and officially had no relationship with the communists, although it was secretly financed by the Comintern.)

"Why are there so many books in this house?"

"I am a teacher. I need these books for my work."

"Why do you have so many books about socialism?"

"I work concurrently as an editor. Whatever they send me I read."

"There were two foreigners here. Who were they?"

"Two Englishmen, professors from Beida. They came here on summer vacation and dropped in to chat."

Then the inspector began to interrogate Chen Gongbo in English. Chen did not know French.

"Are you Japanese?" he asked for some reason.

"No," replied Chen. "I came from Guangdong."

"Why did you come to Shanghai?"

"I am a professor at the Guangdong Institute of Jurisprudence. It's my summer vacation, and I came to Shanghai to have a good time."

"Where are you staying?"

"Here."

Hanging around a while longer, the police conducted a search of the house, but evidently they didn't try very hard, because they found nothing.

This saved Li Hanjun and Chen Gongbo. In one of the drawers in Li's bedroom desk was a draft of the "Program for the Communist Party of China."

Late at night the conspirators gathered at the home of Chen Duxiu, where Li Da and Wang Huiwu were staying. It was understood that continuing the congress in Shanghai was impossible. Mao thought that they needed to go somewhere far away, but Wang Huiwu proposed that they relocate to her native town of Jiaxing, on the shore of Lake Nanhu, about thirty-five miles to the south, in Zhejiang province. There they could rent a boat and hold the final session on the lake. Almost everyone agreed, but for various reasons several people decided not to go. Chen Gongbo, for example, was terribly frightened. He had come to Shanghai with his young wife, and now it seemed their honeymoon might have a tragic ending. After talking it over with Li Da, he and his wife promptly departed for several days to Hangzhou, in Zhejiang province, more than one hundred miles south of Shanghai. Because the police were watching his house Li Hanjun could not leave the city. Maring and Nikolsky also decided not to go outside of Shanghai, so as not to draw attention to themselves.

The next day, July 31, the remaining participants in the forum, including Mao, set out by train for Jiaxing, accompanied by Wang Huiwu. Mao's old friend Xiao Yu, who was in Shanghai and had heard about the congress from Mao, decided to see how things would wind up. Wang put everyone up in an expensive local hotel with a name that was quite inappropriate for the occasion—*Happy Couples*. They also rented a boat from this hotel. After washing up and eating breakfast, Mao and the others, minus Xiao Yu, went out on the lake around 10 A.M. The boat was quite roomy and had a large cabin. They all seated themselves and headed for the middle of the lake. They were in luck. The weather was not very good and it was drizzling, so there were very few vacationers out on the water. After lunch almost no one was around.

In the absence of the Comintern representatives the delegates adopted a program, a Decision about the Objectives of the CCP, and a manifesto all in extreme leftist, ultrarevolutionary versions. It seems they felt like heroes and feared no one. Then they unanimously selected Chen Duxiu as secretary of the Central Bureau of the party. (In 1922 the position of secretary was changed to chairman of the Central Executive Committee, and in 1925 was renamed general secretary of the CEC; Chen Duxiu would occupy this position until July 1927.) Two more persons were chosen for the Central Bureau: Zhang Guotao in charge of organizational work, and Li Da in charge of propaganda. In Chen Duxiu's absence, the duties of secretary were assigned to Zhou Fohai.

It was already 6 P.M., but nobody wanted to return to shore. Sitting in the boat, the young people shouted out, "Long live the Chinese Communist Party! Long live the Third International! Long live communism, the liberator of humankind!"[24] We do not know whether there was an answering echo.

9

THE LESSONS OF
BOLSHEVIK TACTICS

That the delegates at the congress had acted contrary to the directives of the Comintern representatives reached Maring's ears at once. He refused to tolerate disobedience from a bunch of political adolescents. Thus he demanded that Chen Duxiu quickly return to Shanghai and assume direct leadership of the party.[1] Even though Chen had his own plan—he was thinking of moving CCP headquarters to Canton[2]—he was compelled to submit. In September 1921 he resigned his post as chairman of the Guangdong Provincial Education Committee and came to Shanghai.

Meanwhile, Maring, ignoring the resolutions of the CCP Congress, left for South China to gauge the prospects for organizing an anti-imperialist united front between the CCP and Sun Yat-sen. At the end of December 1921 he met with Sun in Guilin, in Guangxi province.[3] They discussed the possibility of establishing a secret alliance between the Guomindang and Soviet Russia. Moreover, Maring proposed reorienting the Guomindang to support the masses, establishing a school to train military cadres for the Chinese revolution, and transforming the Guomindang into a strong political party that would bring together representatives of various sectors of society. He delivered a speech about Soviet Russia to military officers who were loyal to Sun.

Maring's conversations with Sun and other Guomindang leaders, as well as with Chen Jiongming, and his new knowledge of the Guomindang's achievements in organizing the workers' movement strengthened his resolve to steer the CCP leaders away from their "exclusive attitude towards the KMT [Guomindang]." A more cooperative stance toward the Guomindang would make it easier for the CCP to forge ties with the workers and soldiers of South China, where Sun Yat-sen's supporters held power. Maring emphasized that the CCP did not have to "give up its independence, on the contrary, the comrades must together decide which tactics they should follow within the KMT. . . . The prospects for propaganda by the small groups [of communists], as long as they are not linked to the KMT, are dim," he concluded.[4] Maring's initiative to have communists enter the Guomindang was approved by Sun Yat-sen and several other Guomindang leaders, who assured him that they would not obstruct communist propaganda inside their own party. However, Sun Yat-sen was pessimistic about the prospects for interparty cooperation between the Guomindang and the CCP.[5]

Returning to Shanghai, Maring related his conversations with Sun to the leaders of the CCP and advised them to consider his new proposal for developing the CCP within the Guomindang. Maring's proposition horrified Chen Duxiu and the other CCP leaders. Indeed, it was dead on arrival, as Chen Duxiu immediately notified Voitinsky, who was in Moscow at the time.[6] Infuriated by Chen's action, Maring left for Moscow at the end of April 1922 to complain. He didn't even bother to say good-bye to any of his Chinese acquaintances, except for his short-term Shanghai girlfriend.[7]

In the disputes about a united front Mao Zedong stood foursquare with his teacher Professor Chen as did all the other communists from Changsha. The party cells in Guangdong, Shanghai, Beijing, and Hubei—the overwhelming majority of Chinese Bolsheviks—rejected any form of cooperation with the Guomindang.[8] Their main goal was to establish their own party organizations and develop a workers' movement under the aegis of the Communist Party.

After he arrived in Changsha, Mao too became active in party and trade union organizing. He returned home only in mid-August, having stopped for several days in Nanjing, where Tao Yi was taking preparatory courses at Southeastern University.[9] (There is no way of knowing whether Kaihui's suspicions that her husband was still having an affair with Tao Yi had any foundation.) In Changsha he quickly established the Hunan branch of the All-China Workers' Secretariat, whose headquarters had just been established in Shanghai according to a resolution of the founding congress of the CCP.[10] He immediately contacted the local anarchists who were the true pioneers of the workers' movement in Hunan. Their leaders were Huang Ai and Pang Renquan; the union they had organized in November 1920 was the Labor Association. The anarchists published a popular journal, the *Laogong zhoukan* (Labor weekly). Workers who had participated in a two-thousand-person strike at the No. 1 Cotton Mill in Changsha in April 1921 were among their most active members.[11]

Understanding that he could not possibly compete with such an influential union, Mao did the only sensible thing under the circumstances: he tried to win over Huang and Pang to his side. At the end of November 1921, Mao wrote an article for the anarchist journal under the revealing title "My Hopes for the Labor Association," in which he brazenly declared that he had sympathized with this organization for a year already, and then he tried to push his Bolshevik ideas: "The purpose of a labor organization is not merely to rally the laborers to get better pay and shorter working hours by means of strikes. It should also nurture class consciousness so as to unite the whole class and seek the basic interests of the working class. I hope that every member of the Labor Association will pay special attention to this basic goal." [12]

Using flattery and persuasion, Mao ultimately induced Huang Ai and Pang Renquan to join the Socialist Youth League in December 1921, but in January 1922, both leaders of the Labor Association were seized by thugs working for Zhao Hengti and executed on the charge of "buying firearms, colluding with bandits, and agitating for a strike at the mint at the end of the year when any stoppage of work was simply out of the question, as the copper money to be coined in the mint was required for the soldiers' pay and rations." [13] The executions of Huang and Pang played into Mao's hands. Only now was the Hunan branch of the All-China Secretariat of Trade Unions (formally Workers' Secretariat) able to take charge of the workers' movement in the province.

The individual who assisted Mao greatly in organizing communist unions was his old acquaintance Li Lisan, the same shy young man who in the autumn of 1915 had been unable to overcome his embarrassment before the "omniscient" student from the Provincial First Normal School and had not joined Mao's circle for that reason. Since then Li had had many experiences. He had seen the world as a member of the Diligent Work and Frugal Study movement in France, had sampled socialist ideas, and, after returning to Changsha in November 1921, had turned up at Mao's house, where he was greeted cordially. In France Li had befriended Cai Hesen, and this was enough for Mao to change his opinion of Li. "A guest returns to Dongting Lake," he said in greeting Li Lisan, inviting him to continue the poetic stanza he had begun. This was the custom that existed among educated persons at the beginning of the century. "At Xiao and Xiang I come upon an old friend," Li replied elegantly. [14]

They did not become friends, but for a time they developed comradely relations. Entering the Communist Party soon thereafter, Li proved to be a passionate orator and a resolute man very popular among workers. In late December 1921, Mao and Li traveled together to the coal mines at Anyuan, located in western Jiangxi province near the border with Hunan, to launch a workers' movement. Seeing a great opportunity, Mao asked Li to remain in Anyuan to undertake the organization of the local workers, which he did. [15]

Meanwhile, Mao focused on organizing unions in Changsha and other cities in Hunan. Under Marx's influence, Mao at this time considered workers to be the main force of the future revolution, and he was not at all disconcerted that there was virtually no industrial working class in his native province. In all of Hunan there were only three large industrial enterprises, and in one of these, the First Silk Factory, a significant percentage of those employed were children between the ages of nine and fifteen. There were also small nonferrous metal workshops, but these employed very few workers. Most of the workers whom the Chinese communists initially considered the working class were temporary or seasonal laborers in the handicrafts industry who had only recently arrived from the countryside, along with coolies and rickshaw pullers. From Mao's perspective, generally, "most people are workers who work with their hands or their minds."[16] Of course, in a strictly sociological sense, this was not so.

By the middle of 1923, Mao and his comrades had succeeded in organizing twenty-two trade unions, many of which were called workers' clubs, consisting of miners, railway workers, typographers, municipal service workers and employees of the mint, rickshaw pullers, barbers, and others.[17] In eight of these unions Mao was chosen as secretary.[18] In all, these organizations included about 30,000 people, although the majority of the unions were quite small and bore no comparison to the Anyuan workers' club founded by Li Lisan. At a time when the latter, established on May 1, 1922, numbered 11,000 members, the strongest of the Changsha unions, the Rickshaw Pullers Union, had only about 2,000.[19] Nonetheless, under the influence of communist propaganda all these unions actively engaged in class struggle. In Changsha and elsewhere, in early 1922 "a vigorous labor movement began," Mao Zedong recalled.[20] It reached its peak in the autumn of 1922, when, according to Mao's figures, more than 22,000 workers took part in strikes.[21]

Mao was directly involved in the overwhelming majority of these strikes. He rushed about all over northeastern Hunan and western Jiangxi, often accompanied by his pregnant wife, Kaihui, who had joined the CCP in 1921. He gave speeches in workers' auditoriums at the lead and zinc mine at Shuikoushan, the Anyuan coal mine, the Xinhe and Yuezhou railroad stations, and at factories in Changsha and Hengyang.[22] He also drew his own relatives into the workers' movement. In addition to Kaihui he was assisted by his younger brother Zetan, who had been living with him in Changsha since 1918; his second cousin Zejian; and a girlfriend of Zetan's, Zhao Xiangui. At the end of 1921, Mao persuaded Zetan, who was studying at a primary school attached to the Provincial First Normal School, and his second cousin Zejian, who was attending a municipal girls' school in Changsha, to join the Socialist Youth League. In March 1923, Mao sent Zetan to the workers' club at the Shuikoushan lead and zinc mine, where he joined the CCP in October. Returning to Changsha later in the year, Zetan became the secretary of the municipal committee of the Chinese Socialist Youth League. Then, in 1923, Mao Zejian and Zhao Xiangui also joined the party. Zhao married Zetan the following year.[23]

Even the middle brother, Zemin, who had always been distinguished by his sobriety and good sense, and on whom had rested the entire burden of the household in Shaoshan after the death of their father, succumbed to his older brother's blandishments. He rented out all his land, left his home, and in February 1921 came to Changsha, where he plunged into politics. Mao arranged for Zemin to be the bursar in the primary school attached to the First Normal School that he himself directed at the time, and gave him a room in a dormitory. Through many long evenings Mao explained the ABC's of politics to Zemin and his young wife, Wang Shulan. In the fall of 1922 Zemin joined the CCP and soon thereafter Mao sent him off to Li Lisan, at the Anyuan colliery. There the thrifty Zemin served as director of the miners' consumer co-op. Unfortunately, Shulan could not accompany her husband: half a year earlier, on May 5, 1922, she had given birth to a daughter. Thus Mao acquired a niece, Mao Yuanzhi, and since that time Shulan had lived permanently in Shaoshan.[24]

Under Mao's direction, many Hunanese communists were engaged in agitation among the working people and in organizing trade unions. Their efforts bore fruit. Nine out of ten large-scale strikes that took place in 1922 and the first half of 1923 ended in the complete or partial victory of the workers. The strikes on the Wuchang–Changsha and Zhuzhou–Pingxiang railroads were particularly powerful, as was the strike at the Anyuan mines, which took place in September.

The overwhelming majority of strikes were economic in nature. The strikers demanded an eight-hour day, higher wages, and improved working conditions. They asked for nothing out of the ordinary. Life for them was unbearable. Workers toiled for twelve to thirteen hours a day, lived in filthy barracks, and were paid a pittance. They had no interest in politics and no intention of overthrowing anyone. Quite the contrary. One of their most popular demands was the establishment of so-called arbitration commissions to resolve disputes with the entrepreneurs under the aegis of the authorities.[25] The strikes were usually quite peaceful; rarely did they lead to bloody clashes with the bosses.

These successes strengthened Mao's influence among the workers. The authority of the Hunan branch of the All-China Secretariat of Trade Unions grew correspondingly. On November 5, 1922, a broader organization, the Hunan Federation of Trade Unions (HFTU), was established on its foundation with Mao as its general secretary.[26] Now even Governor Zhao Hengti had to reckon with him. In mid-December, Mao, representing the HFTU, met with the governor for an hour and a half to discuss several urgent problems, primarily economic in nature, affecting workers. The upshot was that Zhao was forced to recognize the constitutional right of workers to organize and to strike. Mao immediately published a report on this meeting in *Justice*.[27]

What Mao and his comrades failed to do was to instill a communist consciousness in the minds of the workers. Even though Mao declared in his meeting with the governor that "what the workers wished for was socialism, because socialism was really beneficial to them," this was not so.[28] The same situation prevailed everywhere in China, including Shanghai. Chen Duxiu reported to Moscow, "The majority of the workers are artisans who still work in old craft shops. . . . They are apolitical. The number of modern workers is very small. . . . If we try talking to them about socialism and communism, they are scared off. . . . Only a handful of them enter our party and then only because of ties of friendship. Even fewer understand what communism and the communist party are."[29]

Mao was eager to radicalize the labor movement, but nothing came of his efforts. Nevertheless, doggedly persisting in his efforts to unite the workers' daily struggle with opposition to the militarist regime, Mao believed that the governor of Hunan had "betrayed all the ideas he had supported, and especially he violently suppressed all demands for democracy."[30] This despite the fact that Zhao Hengti tolerated him, allowed him to publish, received Mao at his residence, and when he met with Mao even stated that "socialism might be realized in the future."[31] Unable to rely upon the labor movement to oppose the governor, Mao made use of the provincial party and Socialist Youth League organizations that he devoted great efforts to building up.

Officially, the Hunan committee of the CCP was established on October 10, 1921, which, according to the calendar adopted after the 1911 Revolution, was the tenth day of the tenth month of the tenth year of the republic. Naturally, Mao was chosen as secretary. The party committee was located at his house in the suburb of Qingshuitang, not far from the eastern railroad station. At the end of May 1922, upon the motion of the Central Bureau of the CCP, a Special Xiang District Committee was formed, uniting the more than 30 communists from Hunan and western Jiangxi. Mao also became the secretary of this committee.[32] He also headed the Executive Committee of the Socialist Youth League of Changsha, which was established in mid-June 1922.[33] Thus he concentrated in his own hands the leadership of the underground Bolshevik movement in the region. Soon CCP and Chinese Socialist Youth League cells existed in a number of schools in Changsha as well as in the cities of Hengyang, Pingjiang, Changde, and in the Anyuan colliery.[34] In all of them the "iron will" of the rising communist leader was evident. By November 1922, there were already 230 communists and young socialists in Hunan at a time when there were only 110 in Shanghai. There were even fewer, only 40, in Canton, 20 in Jinan, and 15 in the eastern province of Anhui.[35]

Obviously, Mao had too much to handle. He still hoped to go study in Russia[36] in three or four years, but he was inundated with work. Instead of learning Marxism himself, he had to teach others. In August 1921, he and Bewhiskered He founded a school in Changsha to train cadres for the Communist Party. The school operated legally under the title of Self-Study University, and with the help of local intellectuals Mao even succeeded in getting a subsidy of some four hundred Chinese dollars from the hated Zhao Hengti's government.[37] Mao became the general manager and his brother Zemin served as bursar. Both of them resigned their positions at the primary school attached to the First Normal School.[38]

Meanwhile, significant political changes were taking place in the Chinese Communist Party. In early 1922, a number of Chinese political figures accepted an invitation from the Bolshevik leadership to visit Moscow and Petrograd. Among them were five delegates to the First CCP Congress, including Zhang Guotao and Bewhiskered He. They attended the first Congress of the Peoples of the Far East, which was sponsored by the Comintern. The congress, dedicated to the problems of a national united front in the colonies and semi-colonies, had an enormous impact upon the Chinese communists. The Comintern leaders impressed on the minds of the delegates the idea of cooperation between communists and nationalist revolutionaries. The chairman of the Executive Committee of the Comintern, Grigorii Zinoviev, was particularly impassioned. He flatly asserted that the Chinese, Korean, and Japanese communists "were a very small group for now" and therefore they had to "not stand apart, not look down on those sinners and publicans who had not yet become communists, but to get into the thick of things, to engage the tens of millions of people who were struggling in China, people who were struggling for national independence and emancipation."[39] This was Lenin's message, too. He met with a group of congress delegates including Zhang Guotao, another communist named Deng Pei, and Guomindang representative Zhang Qiubai. Lenin raised the possibility of cooperation between the Guomindang and the Chinese Communist Party, and elicited the views of Zhang Qiubai and Zhang Guotao on this issue.[40]

Of course, the leaders of the CCP had to reconsider. Zinoviev and Lenin were not the likes of Maring. They were leaders, teachers, mentors. Therefore, Zhang Guotao, He Shuheng, and the other communists at the forum voted for the "Manifesto of the Congress of the Peoples of the Far East" that contained a call for the unity of all anti-imperialist revolutionary forces.[41] Returning to China in March 1922, Zhang Guotao informed the Central Bureau of the CCP about the results of his trip:

> [M]ost leaders in Moscow thought that the Chinese revolution was opposed to imperialism and to the domestic warlords and reactionary influences that were in collusion with it. . . . [T]his Chinese revolution must unite the efforts of all the different groups of revolutionary forces in all China. In the final analysis there must be cooperation between the KMT [Guomindang] and the CCP. Lenin himself had emphatically brought out this point.[42]

Chen Duxiu was confused by this report. It was necessary to resolve this problem.

Thus, in early May 1922, the First Congress of the Chinese Socialist Youth League, which took place legally in Canton, cautiously expressed the view that it was necessary to support the revolutionary struggle against imperialism and militarism and for the achievement of national independence and civil freedoms.[43] This resolution could not have passed without Chen Duxiu's approval. A month later, on June 15, Chen himself published the first "State-ment of the Chinese Communist Party on the Current Situation," in which he acknowledged that Sun Yat-sen's government in Canton enjoyed the support of the workers of South China, and that "of all the political parties that pres-ently exist in China, only the Guomindang is comparatively revolutionary and more or less democratic. . . . [T]he Chinese Communist Party proposes . . . to call upon the Guomindang and other revolutionary democratic groups as well as all organizations of revolutionary socialists to convene a joint conference aimed at creating a united democratic front."[44]

Of course, this was written with a heavy heart. It was no accident that in place of the Comintern's definition of a national front, Chen substituted a democratic front, which had a more radical ring to it. Soon, on June 30, he wrote a new letter to Voitinsky saying that the CCP "very much hoped" that the Guomindang would be able to "recognize [the need] to reorganize [i.e., uniting with the communists and political radicalization] and would go forward with us hand-in-hand. However, there is little chance of this happen-ing."[45] This was certainly an original interpretation of the Comintern's pol-icy. Moscow believed not that the Guomindang should march hand in hand with the communists, but that the communists, of whom there were just 195, should form an anti-imperialist alliance with the more powerful party of Sun Yat-sen, with its 10,000 members.

Nevertheless, some positive changes took place, and the CCP's new line was confirmed in the documents of its second congress, held in Shanghai July 16–23, 1922. This meeting took place without Mao's participation. Although he had come to Shanghai, he didn't make it to the congress. In his own words, he "forgot the name of the place where it was to be held, could not find any comrades, and missed it."[46] This is rather strange since Mao at least should have remembered Chen Duxiu's address; he had been there numerous times. But there is no more persuasive explanation of his absence available.[47]

Mao had no recourse but to return to Changsha, which must have been a matter of regret since the congress was very important. The delegates reorga-nized the leading organs of the party, selected a Central Executive Committee, headed by Chen Duxiu, in place of the bureau, and founded a new party organ, a journal called *Xiangdao zhoukan* (Weekly guide). They discussed the main ques-tion of forming a united "democratic" front. Of the twelve persons present, five had participated in preparations and proceedings of the Congress of the Peoples of the Far East. Zhang Guotao gave a report to the congress on the Comintern summit, after which the congress registered its agreement with the decisions taken in Moscow and Petrograd, and affirmed the secret resolution about the "democratic united front" and the manifesto.[48] Both documents justified the need to establish an interparty bloc of the Communist Party and the Guomin-dang.[49] In class terms, the united front was depicted as a "temporary alliance" of the proletariat and the poor peasantry with the national bourgeoisie, groups that, as the manifesto asserted, were "able to unite their strength to resist foreign imperialism and the corrupt Peking [Beijing] government."[50] The congress ignored Maring's earlier suggestion that communists enter the Guomindang.

Soon after, on August 12, 1922, Maring returned to China. He could not help feeling victorious. He flourished two papers with which to silence those in the CCP who were ill-disposed toward him. The first was an instruction written by the secretary of the Executive Committee of the Comintern, Karl Radek, that wholly supported Maring's initiative regarding the entry of communists into the Guomindang. It emphasized that the Chinese Communist Party should preserve its complete independence within the Guomindang and remain there only until such time as the CCP developed into a mass political organization. The second paper was a directive from Voitinsky, who was now the head of the Far Eastern Bureau of the ECCI. It stated flatly, "The Central Committee of the Communist party of China according to the decision of the Presidium of Comintern of July 18 must . . . do all its work in close contact with Comr. PHILIPP."[51] (This was one of Maring's many pseudonyms.)

Right after he returned to Shanghai, according to Zhang Guotao, Maring informed the leadership of the Communist Party that "the Comintern endorsed the idea of having CCP members join the KMT [Guomindang] and considered it a new route to pursue in achieving a united front."[52] On August 25, he visited Sun Yat-sen, who was again in Shanghai, having been chased out of Canton by Chen Jiongming, who had unexpectedly betrayed Sun. Sitting in Sun's cozy office, the ECCI emissary informed the Guomindang leader that Moscow had advised the Chinese communists to unite with his party. He counseled Sun to devote more attention to the mass anti-imperialist movement of the workers and peasants.[53] Disoriented from the betrayal by his militarist ally Chen Jiongming, Sun was ready to accept Maring's recommendation and agreed to reorganize the Guomindang. In those days he was pondering the fate of the Chinese revolution and, in his own words, "disappointed in everything he had previously believed." Right after the coup by his former comrade in arms Chen Jiongming, he became "convinced that Soviet Russia was the only real and true friend of the Chinese revolution."[54]

Maring had good reason to celebrate, but Chen Duxiu did not want to capitulate so easily. Neither did the members of the Central Executive Committee of the party chosen at its Second Congress who supported their chairman, including Zhang Guotao; Cai Hesen, who had returned from France in early 1922; Gao Junyu, the editor in chief of the newly created CCP organ *Weekly Guide;* and Li Dazhao, who was a candidate member of the CEC. Soon, at Maring's request, they convened for a meeting on August 29 in Hangzhou. There the participants rented a boat and for the next two days, with time off for eating and sleeping, they sailed on picturesque West Lake, at the edge of the city, encircled by fantastical hills dotted with elegant medieval pagodas. On this occasion, the tranquil waters covered with bright red lilies did not evoke peace. The boat glided gently between small islands covered in bamboo groves, but the meeting, which was attended by Maring's interpreter Zhang Tailei, along with Maring himself and the members of the CEC, was stormy and dramatic. Judging by Chen Duxiu's recollection, all of the members of the Central Executive Committee present at the meeting opposed the proposal of Maring, who peremptorily demanded the implementation of the ECCI resolution. At first, only Zhang Tailei, who was not a member of the CEC, supported the Kremlin's representative. Maring was furious. All his arguments encountered hostility. Finally, unable to restrain himself and determined to alter the course of the discussion, he threatened to expel the dissidents from the Communist International. He categorically demanded that the assembled submit to Comintern discipline.[55]

Suddenly, Chen Duxiu understood. There was no point even in dreaming about equality with the Moscow Bolsheviks. His infant party was wholly dependent upon Moscow, which demanded one thing only—absolute obedience. Before the establishment of the CCP, Chen Duxiu had sought most of the funds needed for the functioning of the Bolshevik circles from publishing activities, but with the formation of the CCP there was a catastrophic shortage of funds. The expenditures of the communists were constantly growing, and if, at the beginning of 1921, they amounted to only 200 Chinese dollars, by the end of the year they had reached almost 18,000![56] For a time the leaders of the CCP tried to preserve their innocence, naïvely believing they could do without subsidies from the Comintern.[57] However, this proved impossible. In 1921, the Comintern provided the CCP 16,650 Chinese dollars at a time when the party was able to raise only 1,000 dollars on its own. In 1922 the Chinese communists were unable to scrape together any money at all while they received 15,000 dollars from Moscow by the end of the year.[58] They were not in a position to demur. The Kremlin funded not only Chen Duxiu, whose monthly payment was thirty dollars, but also the regional party organizations, so it became a very straightforward choice: either they capitulated to Moscow's authority and continued to receive financial support as before, or they crossed Moscow and got nothing. Rethinking their position, the participants came to the only reasonable conclusion: they unanimously agreed to enter the Guomindang.

They must have felt sick at heart. It is unlikely that the beauty of the lake could have lifted their gloom. At the northwestern shore of the lake towered a stone statue of Yue Fei; the great general of the Southern Song dynasty who had found his final resting place here gazed silently at them. What an irony that this fateful meeting, which turned the CCP into an obedient instrument of foreign politicians, had taken place near the grave of a fearless warrior renowned for his patriotism.

PART TWO

THE REVOLUTIONARY

10

ENTERING THE GUOMINDANG

Sun Yat-sen endorsed the decision of the CCP Central Executive Committee to enter the Guomindang.[1] At Chen Duxiu's request, Li Dazhao and Lin Boqu, a Communist Party activist who had extensive ties with the Guomindang leadership, began negotiations with Sun Yat-sen. Recalling these later, Li Dazhao wrote that they discussed "the question of the rebirth of the Guomindang in order to achieve the rebirth of China." In other words, they discussed reorganizing the Guomindang in both a political and organizational sense, including admitting communists into its ranks. In early September 1922, Sun welcomed Chen Duxiu, Li Dazhao, Cai Hesen, and Zhang Tailei into his party.[2]

On September 4, 1922, a meeting of Guomindang central and provincial leaders in Shanghai discussed the question of reorganizing the party. Communists also took part. Sun Yat-sen appointed a special nine-member commission, including Chen Duxiu, to compose a draft program and statutes for the Guomindang. Meanwhile, Sun entered into intensive correspondence with Adolf Joffe, a leading Russian Bolshevik who had come to Beijing in August at the head of a Soviet diplomatic mission.

The Comintern also strived to soften the negative attitude of the communists to the Guomindang. In the fall of 1922, Chen Duxiu was summoned to Moscow in the company of the effusive leftist Liu Renjing. They attended the Fourth World Congress of the Communist International, held in November and December. Chen and Liu met with the leaders of the ECCI and discussed the tactics of the anti-imperialist united front. Trying to change Chen's mind, Comintern officials even elected him a member of the congress's Commission on the Eastern Question.[3] The upshot was that soon after Chen Duxiu and Liu Renjing returned to China, the Chinese communists retired the slogan "democratic front" and replaced it with a call to establish an "anti-imperialist, national revolutionary front."

On January 1, 1923, Sun Yat-sen published a declaration on reorganizing the Guomindang. The next day a meeting was convened in Shanghai on party affairs and the party program and statutes were published. Sun Yat-sen's famous Three Principles of the People were given a new and more radical formulation. Sun stressed anti-imperialism, defense of the rights of workers, and the democratic transformation of China.[4] He invited Chen Duxiu, Zhang Tailei, Lin Boqu, and the Cantonese communist Tan Pingshan, who had also earlier been a member of the Revolutionary Alliance, to work in the central and regional apparatuses of the Guomindang.

On January 26, Sun and Joffe issued a joint declaration in which the Soviet representative assured Sun that in the struggle for national renewal and full independence "China enjoys the widest sympathy of the Russian people and can count on the support of Russia." Both sides expressed their "complete agreement on Chinese-Russian relations" and emphasized that "at present the communist order or even the Soviet system cannot be introduced into China" because of the absence of the necessary conditions.[5] Sun's rapprochement with the CCP and Soviet Russia continued with growing intensity as the troops of local militarists who were loyal to him drove the forces of Chen Jiongming, who had betrayed Sun, out of Canton into the eastern part of Guangdong. In February, Sun returned to Canton to head a southern Chinese government there.

Although these events shaped the context of his subsequent rise to power, Mao played no part in them. He continued working in Hunan until April 1923, organizing strikes and workers' demonstrations in Changsha and neighboring districts. On October 24, 1922, Kaihui gave birth to their firstborn, whom they named Anying. Mao himself selected the name when Kaihui returned home with the newborn. Looking happily at his wife, he asked, "Well, what shall we name the baby?" Then, without awaiting her answer, he said, "Let him be Anying." (*An* means "the bank of a river"; *ying* means "hero.") "The Hero Who Reaches the Shore of Socialism. What do you say?"[6] Kaihui agreed. She was happy.

Mao had no time, however, to take care of his son. Party work fully occupied him. The situation in China changed dramatically when on February 7, the militarist Wu Peifu, who had masqueraded as a "friend of the workers," carried out a bloody reprisal against striking railroad workers. Thirty-two people were killed and more than two hundred wounded. A wave of "white" terror engulfed Henan and Hebei provinces. Many trade unions and workers' clubs were smashed. Mao had to react. Demanding that the guilty be punished, on February 8 he organized a general strike on the Changsha–Wuchang railroad. On the same day a memorial meeting was held that attracted more than twenty thousand workers and students. Meetings were also held in many urban trade unions and a large demonstration took place at the Anyuan mines.

On March 29, the Special Xiang District Committee, headed by Mao, and public organizations in Changsha sponsored a large-scale anti-Japanese demonstration. Some sixty thousand people paraded along the streets of the city that day as part of a national campaign coinciding with the expiration of the Japanese lease of the Chinese ports of Lüshun (Port Arthur) and Dalian. Once again Chinese public opinion demanded the annulment of the extortionate Twenty-One Demands.[7]

Mao's actions stretched the patience of the Hunan governor beyond his breaking point. In April, Zhao Hengti cracked down on the union leaders and issued a separate order for the arrest of Mao Zedong.[8] Mao had to flee.

Happily, in January 1923, the Central Executive Committee of the CCP had already decided to recall Mao from Changsha. Chen Duxiu invited him to work in the central party apparatus in Shanghai. Both Maring and Chen were extremely satisfied with Mao's activities in Hunan and awarded him this promotion. In a November 1922 letter to Zinoviev, Joffe, and Voitinsky, Maring praised the party organization in Hunan as the best in China.[9] Now Mao faced the task of disseminating the Hunan experience throughout the country.

Li Weihan, Mao's old friend from the Renovation of the People Study Society, was appointed in his place. Packing his few belongings, Mao left for Shanghai by boat. He was loath to part with his wife and son. Kaihui was pregnant again and no one knew how long they would be parted.

When Mao arrived in Shanghai a week later, Chen Duxiu was not there. He had left for Canton in March to establish direct links with Sun Yat-sen. Mao headed for the Central Executive Committee in Zhabei, the dirty, smoky, and noisy workers' district of Shanghai. The CEC was also preparing to move. The Comintern had decided that the central apparatus of the party should relocate to Canton, following its chairman. In early June, Mao, accompanied by Maring, set off for the south.[10]

There, sheltered by Sun Yat-sen, the Chinese communists were able to operate openly for the first time. For Mao, it seemed, the secret meetings and passwords were a thing of the past. He was now preoccupied with legal work connected to establishing the united front. In Changsha, influenced by telegrams and letters from the Central Executive Committee, Mao had already begun to change his negative attitude toward the Guomindang. Practical experience was also decisive. Mao had been shaken by the bloody carnage inflicted upon the Hankou railway workers by Wu Peifu and the crushing of the trade union organizations in Hubei, Henan, and Hebei. He was particularly affected by the collapse of the workers' movement in Hunan as a result of Zhao Hengti's reactionary policies. He could not help but notice that Sun Yat-sen and his Three Principles of the People were sympathetic to the workers' movement. In January 1922, Sun's Canton government had provided considerable assistance to striking Chinese workers and seamen in Hong Kong. The seamen's strike, which was anti-imperialist in nature, relied on the solidarity of the entire population of Guangdong province, including the national bourgeoisie, and achieved partial success. The Hankou railway workers, who were spurred on by the communists, received no support from other social forces and were defeated.

For the first time Mao publicly expressed his support for the anti-imperialist alliance, on April 10, 1923, several days before departing Changsha. On the pages of *Xin shidai* (New age), the journal published by the Self-Study University, he said:

> If we analyze the influential factions within the country, there are only three: the revolutionary democratic faction, the non-revolutionary democratic faction, and the reactionary faction. The main body of the revolutionary democratic faction is, of course, the Guomindang; the rising Communist faction is cooperating with it. . . . The Communist Party has temporarily abandoned its most radical views in order to cooperate with the relatively radical Guomindang. . . . This [situation] is the source of peace and unification, it is the mother of revolution, it is the magic potion of democracy and independence. Everyone must be aware of this.[11]

However, Mao did not become a staunch advocate of the united front like Maring and the ECCI. For now he said nothing about the entry of communists into the Guomindang. But the isolation of the Communist Party and the workers, and the profound crisis of the trade union movement, plunged him into depression; he saw the alliance with the Guomindang, even though not ideal, as a way out of the situation. Meeting with Maring in Shanghai, Mao could not restrain his gloomy thoughts. Maring reported that Mao was depressed by the fact that in all of Hunan with its population of thirty million, there were no more than thirty thousand organized workers. Maring wrote that Mao was "at the end of his latin with labororganization [sic] and was so pessimistic that he saw the only salvation of China in the intervention by Russia," proposing that Soviet Russia should build a "military base" in northwest China. Moreover, he supposed that "in Chinese conditions the old tradition of a patriarchal society still strong. . . . [W]e cannot develop a modern mass party neither comm[unist] nor nationalist."[12]

In Canton, however, Mao cheered up. The turning point was the Third Congress of the Communist Party, held legally from June 12 through June 20, 1923, in the eastern outskirts of Canton. Chen Duxiu chaired the forum while Maring played an active role. The 40 delegates who assembled in this quiet setting, in what looked like an uninhabited house, represented 420 members of the CCP, of whom one-quarter (110) were in prison.[13] Since the Second Congress the party had more than doubled in size, adding 225 members. The CCP was mostly male—there were only 19 women in it—and dominated by intellectuals. There were just 164 worker members. Party cells were operating in Guangdong, Shanghai, Beijing, Changsha, Anyuan, Tangshan, Jinan, Hangzhou, Hankou, at the Changxingdian railroad station near Beijing and the Pukou railroad station near Nanjing, and also overseas in Moscow.[14] (The Moscow cell was composed of Chinese students at the Communist University of the Toilers of the East [KUTV in Russian abbreviation], a special educational institution established by the Comintern in 1921.)[15] Mao's was the most active of all the cells and the largest, containing more than half the party members. It was the only one that merited praise from Chen Duxiu, who singled it out in his report: "We may say that only the comrades from Hunan have done good work."[16]

There were particularly heated disputes over the tactics and form of the united front, and Mao had to delve deep into the details, which he found difficult at first. In Hunan there had been far fewer members of the Guomindang than there were communists, and no one had been working on the united front. In China generally, in most of the places where the CCP was active, the influence of the Guomindang was minuscule. Sun Yat-sen's party was based in Canton and had a relatively large organization in Shanghai, but elsewhere the members of the Guomindang were few and far between. Sun was a "big cannon," said representatives from the periphery. He produced a loud noise, but little else.[17] Why, then, did everyone have to join the Guomindang? Just what organization would they join when Guomindang branches could be counted on the fingers of one hand? It would be foolish for the communists themselves to establish Guomindang organizations and then join them.

Important figures in the party, including Zhang Guotao and Cai Hesen, voiced these arguments. They no longer objected on principle to the tactic of entering the Guomindang, but, as Cai Hesen later recalled, they didn't want "to go too far in that direction." Completely at odds with them were Maring, supported by Chen Duxiu, Li Dazhao, Zhang Tailei, and several other delegates obedient to Moscow. They believed it necessary "to criticize the Guomindang for its feudal tactics," but at the same time they should "push and guide this party onto the path of revolutionary propaganda, and form a left wing of workers and peasants inside it." Thus it was necessary "to develop the Guomindang throughout the whole country."[18] Maring and Chen Duxiu advanced the slogan "Let everyone work in the Guomindang."[19]

On this issue Mao supported Zhang Guotao and Cai Hesen.[20] He had been friends with Cai for many years and was influenced by Cai to a certain degree. Moreover, at the beginning of the congress he was unable to shake his pessimism regarding the prospects for the development in China of mass parties and the workers' movement. Yet his position was not as uncompromising as that of Zhang and Cai, and for now he was obviously ambivalent. During the discussion he asserted that the "Komintan [Guomindang] is dominated by Petit-Bourgeoisie. . . . Petit-Bourgeoisie can for the present time lead [the revolution]. That is why we should join Komintan. . . . We should not be afraid of joining."[21] Yet, at the crucial moment during the roll call, he voted against the resolution of Chen Duxiu. When the resolution obligating the communists to help expand Guomindang organizations throughout China was adopted by a vote of twenty-one for and seventeen opposed, he "lightheartedly announced his acceptance of the decision of the majority."[22] This despite the resolution's emphasis on the need to "establish a strongly centralized party as the head-quarters of the national revolutionary movement" and acknowledgment that only the Guomindang could play that role. The Communist Party, the resolution declared, could not turn into a mass organization in the near future "since the working class was not yet a powerful force."[23]

That Mao in the end withdrew his objections was not forgotten. Evidently at the initiative of Maring and Chen Duxiu, for the first time Mao was made a member of the Central Executive Committee, consisting of nine members and five candidate, or nonvoting, members. During the election for members of the CEC he received thirty-four votes. Only Chen, who was elected unanimously, and Cai Hesen and Li Dazhao received more votes than Mao.[24] Moreover, Mao joined the exclusive Central Bureau, consisting of just five persons, a kind of Politburo headed by Chen.[25] Most important, Mao was chosen as head of the Organizational Department and secretary of the CEC. In the latter capacity he replaced Zhang Guotao, who was dropped because of his sharp opposition to the line of the ECCI. In other words, Mao was the second leading figure in the party.

For the first time in his life he was on an equal footing with his teacher. Now he was not only a journalist but also a communist functionary on a nationwide scale. He became known in Moscow as "unquestionably an able worker," as Solomon Vil'de (pseudonym Vladimir), a Soviet agent in Shanghai, wrote in a letter to Voitinsky.[26]

At this congress Mao first became seriously engaged with the peasant question, an issue that was entirely new to him, but one that was to become indissolubly linked with his name. Of course, he was well acquainted with the destitute life of Chinese villages, but until then he had never been seriously involved with organizing the peasantry. In Hunan, only twice under his leadership had attempts been made to organize landless peasants against large landowners, but without results. He and Tan Pingshan were included on a commission charged with drafting a resolution on the peasant question. He also took part in discussions concerning the party's policy regarding the peasantry. Unlike many others at the congress, Mao unexpectedly manifested a keen understanding of the problem. He asserted, "[I]n any revolution the peasant problem was the most important problem. . . . The KMT [Guomindang] had built something of a foundation in Kwangtung [Guangdong] . . .

due to its possession of armies composed of peasants. If the CCP would concern itself with the peasant movement and mobilize the peasants, it would not be difficult for the Party to build a situation similar to that in Kwangtung."[27] At the time almost no one paid attention to these prophetic words. The resolution adopted by the delegates was amorphous and pretentious. "The resolution of the Third Congress of our party," it declared, "asserts the necessity of uniting small peasants, renters, and agricultural laborers to struggle against the imperialists who control China, to overthrow the militarists and the venal officials, to crush local bandits and *lieshen* [evil gentry] in order to defend the interests of the peasantry and advance the cause of the national revolutionary movement."[28] A directive from the ECCI to the Third Congress, sent from Moscow on May 24 but not received until July 18, soon confirmed that the peasant movement had to be engaged seriously. It stated in unambiguous terms that "the central issue in politics is precisely the *peasant question*."[29]

This formulation was the work of Nikolai Bukharin, a candidate member of the Bolshevik Politburo who was actively involved in the work of the Comintern. For now, however, this was only a paper declaration; the Chinese communists did not translate it into action. For some time even Mao's speech on the peasant question at the Third Congress remained inconsequential.

The only Chinese communist sympathizer who had begun to organize the peasantry as early as the spring of 1922 was Peng Pai, from Guangdong. "It is a useless waste of effort," his friends argued; "the peasantry is extremely dispersed and incapable of being organized and impervious to propaganda because of their ignorance."[30] Peng Pai succeeded in founding several peasant unions in eastern Guangdong, but when they launched a rent reduction campaign in 1923 Chen Jiongming crushed them.[31]

After the Third Congress, in the aftermath of the defeat of the workers' and peasants' movements, many though not all communists were attracted by the idea of working in the Guomindang. The CEC of the CCP even drafted a plan to extend Guomindang party organizations to all important points in north and central China.[32]

Mao, too, was apparently euphoric about creating a united front. While the Third Congress was still in session, during free moments he along with Li Dazhao and Zhang Tailei began to talk with Tan Yankai about the possibility of forming an alliance.[33] Tan, the former governor of Hunan who was a sworn enemy of Zhao Hengti, lived just a two-minute walk from where the congress was meeting; he had a luxurious three-story house. He was a Guomindang member in good standing with Sun Yat-sen. Therefore, an alliance with him would be very advantageous to the Chinese communists. Soon after the Congress, Mao himself joined the Guomindang.[34] He also enthusiastically supported the idea of sending Tan Zhen, one of Sun Yat-sen's comrades in arms, to

Hunan to organize Guomindang cells there. He sent a directive to Li Weihan, via Tan Zhen, insisting that the Xiang district Communist Party committee provide full assistance to Sun's emissary.[35]

The Soviet Bolsheviks likewise actively assisted the formation of an anti-imperialist front in China. In March 1923, Moscow fulfilled Sun Yat-sen's request by providing two million gold rubles in financial assistance "to work for the unification and national independence of China." On May 1, Joffe so informed Sun Yat-sen, emphasizing that Moscow requested the head of the South China government to "preserve the strictest confidentiality regarding all of our assistance."[36] In June 1923, the first group of five military advisers left the USSR for Canton. Their task was to help Sun Yat-sen create his own Guomindang army. From the perspective of CCP leaders, including Mao Zedong, this should be a "new" and genuinely "people's" army that employed "new methods and a new spirit of friendship to defend the republic." They called on Sun Yat-sen to do this.[37]

On July 31, at Stalin's suggestion, the Politburo of the Russian Communist Party (Bolshevik) decided to send Mikhail Borodin, an old Bolshevik and leading member of the ECCI, to China as political adviser to Sun Yat-sen.[38] He was to synchronize his position of "high adviser to the Guomindang" with his responsibilities as the Comintern's new representative to the CEC of the CCP, replacing Maring.

Mikhail Borodin was born in 1884, and became a member of the Bolshevik party in 1903. He knew Lenin well, fought in the first Russian revolution (1905), and took part in the Fourth Congress of the Russian Social Democratic Labor Party, held in Stockholm in 1906. Afterward, he and his family emigrated abroad, first to England and then the United States, until 1918. From living abroad Borodin conveyed the impression of being very Westernized. "A tall, commanding presence with a leonine head," is how Song Meiling, Sun Yat-sen's sister-in-law, remembered Borodin, drawing attention to the impeccable good manners that marked his appearance. He was a man "with a shock of neatly coiffed, long, slightly wavy dark brown mane that came down to the nape of his neck," she recalled, "with an unexaggerated but ample mustache that French generals of that time feigned. . . . Speaking in a resonantly deep, clear, unhurried, baritone voice of mid-America intonation without a trace of Russian accent, he lowered still more his voice into a slow basso profundo when emphasizing the importance of a certain point he was making. He was a man who gave the impression of great control and personal magnetism."[39]

"A man of few words, he preferred to listen than to speak, and he offered his point of view to others in brief phrases and rejoinders," is how Sergei Dalin, a secret agent for Soviet Russia, remembered him.[40] Unlike Comrade Philipp (Maring), Borodin was more patient with the Chinese communists. In this way, according to Zhang Guotao, "he was not to be taken on the same level as

Maring."[41] Borodin's real surname was Gruzenberg, but like everyone in the Comintern he changed his name many times. The Chinese would call him Bao Luoting or Bao guwen (Adviser Bao).

On August 16, Sun Yat-sen dispatched a special mission to the USSR headed by Chiang Kai-shek, a man he trusted, an energetic general and member of the republican movement from the days of the Revolutionary Alliance. Also sent on the mission were another Guomindang member and two communists, including Zhang Tailei. The delegation arrived in Moscow on September 2, and over the next three months became acquainted with the structure of party organs, including the Central Committee of the Russian Communist Party; studied the functioning of the soviets; visited military units; and met with leading figures in the Soviet Union, including Trotsky, Zinoviev, Lev Kamenev, and Georgy Chicherin.[42] General Chiang, thirty-six years old, trim, smart, and well educated, made a very positive impression on the Moscow leaders. He held leftist views at the time and strived to demonstrate his "closeness" to the Bolsheviks.[43] Realizing that his mail was being inspected by the Russian authorities, in one letter to his wife he made a point of mentioning that he was reading Marx's *Capital* in his spare time. "I find the first half of this work very heavy-going," he noted, "but the second half is both profound and entrancing." In another letter, he enthused, "I enjoyed Mr. Trotsky, whose essential qualifications for being a revolutionary are patience and activity." After this, Comintern officials clearly intimated their hope that Chiang would become a member of the Communist Party. Not objecting in principle, Chiang replied he would first have to obtain permission from Sun. (He had no intention of joining any communist party, although he really was a leftist at this time.)[44]

At Chiang's request, in November 1923 the ECCI drafted a new resolution on the national question in China and on the Guomindang, incorporating a new interpretation of Sun Yat-sen's Three Principles of the People. The Comintern offered the Guomindang a logical program for an anti-imperialist, national democratic revolution, the key feature of which was the call for a radical agrarian revolution and the nationalization of industry.[45] After the ECCI adopted this resolution on November 28, it was transmitted to Chiang Kai-shek. Chiang submitted it to Sun Yat-sen, who, at least formally, accepted almost all of the Comintern's recommendations, with the exception of the proposal on the agrarian question. Sun used the ECCI resolution as the basis of the second section of the manifesto that would be approved at the First Congress of the Guomindang in January 1924.

Borodin and Lev Karakhan, the Soviet government's envoy to the Beijing government, arrived in China at the end of August 1923. Karakhan remained in Beijing while Borodin proceeded to Canton via Shanghai, arriving in early October. Soon additional Soviet political and military advisers arrived to serve the government of South China.[46] In discussions with them Sun Yat-sen displayed a lively interest in the experience of party, state, and military construction in Soviet Russia as well as in Russia's position in international affairs. Borodin made a particularly positive impression upon him. The result was that in November, Sun published the Manifesto on Reorganizing the Guomindang and a new draft party program. On December 1, at a conference in Canton, he spoke about reorganizing the Guomindang into a mass party that relied not only on the army, but also on the civilian population. He said, in part:

> Now our good friend Borodin has come to us from Russia. . . . [T]he Russians succeeded in the course of one revolution of fully realizing their ideas, the creation of a revolutionary government that grows stronger by the day. . . . They were victorious, because the entire party, assisted by the army, took part in the struggle. We must learn from Russia its methods, its organization, its way of training party members; only then can we hope for victory.[47]

By this time Mao Zedong had left Canton. At the end of July, at Chen Duxiu's request he returned to Shanghai. Along with his friends Cai Hesen, Luo Zhanglong, and Xiang Jingyu, he settled in Zhabei, in the northern part of town, on a small lane near Xiangshanlu (Aromatic mountain street), which was anything but aromatic. In early September the Central Executive Committee of the party returned to Shanghai from Canton. Despite growing cooperation with the Guomindang, Chen Duxiu preferred to keep his distance from Sun Yat-sen,[48] obviously not wishing to turn the CEC of the CCP into "a vassal of the KMT [Guomindang]."[49] The CEC was located in the same house where Mao, Cai, Luo, and Xiang were living.

As before, all of Mao's energies were absorbed in the work of the united front. "The present political problem in China," he wrote, "is quite simply the problem of the national revolution. To use the might of the people to overthrow the warlords and also to overthrow foreign imperialism, which colludes with the warlords in their evil acts—such is the historic mission of the Chinese people. . . . We must all have faith that the one and only way to save oneself and the nation is the national revolution."[50] In mid-September, Mao went to Changsha to help establish a branch of the Guomindang.[51] In the two and a half months since Tan Zhen, Sun Yat-sen's emissary, had arrived in Hunan, nothing had happened. The Hunanese communists had sabotaged the attempt to establish a Guomindang organization there. Even Mao found it difficult to overcome the resistance of his old comrades. Among other things, he lacked the means to conduct organizational work, and he needed "at least about a hundred yuan a month."[52] His task was further complicated by the outbreak of a new war between Zhao Hengti and Tan Yankai. In September the situation further deteriorated when General Wu Peifu intervened in the conflict on the side of Zhao. Mao, of course, sympathized with Tan, but Tan lost. The province once more plunged into an abyss of terror. Zhao Hengti declared martial law, closed the Self-Study University, and dispersed the Federation of Trade Unions. He personally ordered the arrest of Mao Zedong and other leaders of the labor movement.[53] Working deep underground, Mao was forced to use one of his pseudonyms, Mao Shishan ("Stone Mountain"), a variant of one of his childhood names.[54] The only source of joy for Mao was his family. Anying was a healthy growing boy and on November 13, Kaihui gave birth to another son, whom they named Anqing ("The Youth Who Reaches the Shore of Socialism").

While Mao was in Changsha, the November 1923 plenum of the CCP Central Executive Committee was held in Shanghai. The plan to establish Guomindang party organizations in north and central China had failed. Only one had been established, in Beijing. The membership of the Communist Party itself had contracted by three-fourths; only about one hundred members remained. Chen Duxiu himself acknowledged that the party was going through a crisis. The plenum condemned "leftist distortions" of the united front policy and adopted a resolution concerning the actual participation of communists in the reorganization of the Guomindang. A resolution approved by the plenum, titled "A Plan for Developing the National Movement," emphasized that communists should join existing Guomindang organizations while retaining their membership in the CCP and establish Guomindang organizations where none existed, especially in north and central China.[55]

The plenum also demanded that communists and Socialist Youth League members create their own clandestine organizations within the united front, the members of which were obligated to follow the leadership of the CCP in all of their political statements and actions. The communists' task was to struggle to "occupy a central position in the Guomindang."[56]

The effort to reorganize the Guomindang slowly moved forward as Sun prepared to hold a Unification Congress of the GMD in late January 1924. By this time, thanks to Mao's efforts, a Guomindang organization had finally been established in Hunan, with three local cells: one in Changsha and two others, in Ningxiang and Anyuan.[57] By the end of December there were already some five hundred Guomindang members in Hunan, but among them the Communist Party members were the most active. They were also the overwhelming majority of the members of the executive committee of the provincial organization, seven of nine.[58] It was no accident, therefore, that at the end of the year Mao was picked as one of the delegates from the Hunan Guomindang organization to the party congress.

Again he had to leave his family and, as before, it pained him to say goodbye to his wife. But this time his melancholy was even stronger. On the eve of his departure there had been some sort of unpleasant scene between him and Kaihui; something had happened, but what it was we do not know. He boarded the steamship for Shanghai and gazed at Changsha fading into the distance. His lips whispered:

> With a wave of my hand I'm off.
> How painful to exchange glances.
> Bitter feelings torment us still.
> Your brow betrays the residue of anger
> Hot tears linger in your eyes.
> I know that letter is the cause of our estrangement.
> But clouds and fog don't last forever,
> and you and I, the two of us together,
> are all that matter in this world.
> That people often suffer in this world is true.
> What concern is that of ours?
> Does Heaven know or care?
> This morning hoarfrost paves the eastern road,
> A sliver moon illuminates the pond and half the sky.
> And yet alone and desolate am I.
> The ship's horn cleaves my heart in two.
> I journey solo to the farthest climes.
> Let's cut the bitter threads of melancholy.
> Forceful as an avalanche on Kunlun* or a cleansing wind,
> Let us unfold our wings once more
> and soar into the azure sky.[59]

---

* Kunlun is a mountain range in southwestern China.

11

HOPES AND
DISAPPOINTMENTS

In the early and mid-1920s, Canton under the liberal rule of the Guomindang was as striking as Shanghai, though in an entirely different way. "In the south . . . the atmosphere was different," wrote Sergei Dalin. "Workers' unions, the communist party, and the Socialist Youth League all functioned legally." [1] The air smelled of revolution. Meetings, assemblies, and demonstrations were going on constantly. "Political life was in full swing," recalled another emissary of the Kremlin, Vera Vishniakova-Akimova. "All the open places on walls and columns were plastered with placards and handbills, flags were hung from poles fastened above the heads of the passersby, narrow strips of material covered with slogans were stretched across the streets." [2] The revolutionary upsurge was particularly noticeable during the preparations for the First Congress of the Guomindang. "People were busy with preparation for the Congress," wrote Zhang Guotao, "and there were even more banquets than usual. The situation was somewhat like that in a large family when some great festive occasion is about to be celebrated." [3] The old city with its more than two-thousand-year history seemed to have been reborn.

Situated on the left bank of the wide Pearl River, whose waters were stained with red silt, some ninety miles upriver from the British colony of Hong Kong, Canton was rightly considered the capital of South China. It was large, populous, and bustling. Life seethed along its twisting commercial streets, its noisy markets, and in its smoky port. Unlike Shanghai, however, it had almost no modern industry. There were just several dozen small-scale silk-weaving plants and a multitude of primitive handicraft shops in which all kinds of items were produced, from mother-of-pearl ornaments to lacquerware statues.

The city was christened Canton by French travelers in the eighteenth century, according to their transliteration of the South Chinese pronunciation of the provincial name, Guangdong. The name stuck. There were far fewer foreigners in Canton than in Shanghai. Beginning in 1842 only one foreign concession existed in Canton, a joint Anglo-French concession consisting of the tiny island of Shamian, on White Goose Bay where the Pearl River divides into two arms. Separated from the main part of town by a strait barely twelve feet wide, this district is still distinguished by its elegant Western architecture, and its symmetrically laid out streets and squares, heavily shaded by gardens and parks. It provided a sharp contrast to the other—Chinese—Canton, flooded by sunlight, diverse, and crowded. A contemporary observer wrote, "Canton is like an enormous market, lively, mobile, which never closes even at night. As in all Chinese cities from time immemorial, the streets were very narrow, two or three meters wide. One was struck by the almost complete absence of signs in English. . . . The streets were always noisy, Chinese music was heard everywhere, and on the quay, which was the main street of Canton, there were many painted ladies."[4]

In the early 1920s more than half a million people lived in Canton, no fewer than two hundred thousand on boats in the water, the so-called sampans, meaning literally "three boards." Hundreds of sampans in rows three to four deep were lined up along the shore. An eyewitness recalled, "They all looked very poor. . . . Whole families took shelter in them, and little kids craned their tiny heads in our direction with interest. The young ones were fastened by the leg with a rope or wore on their backs a peculiar life belt—a dry log."[5]

In mid-January 1924, Mao returned to Canton as a delegate to the Guomindang congress. He went straight to Wenminglu (Civilization Street) in the city center, where this most important forum was scheduled to open on January 20. Mao had a few days to look around. Downtown Canton presented quite a spectacle. The narrow and filthy streets that ran alongside the broad and well-lighted Wenminglu were filled with homeless beggars, coolies, and petty merchants. Late at night when the city quieted down, they spread mats on the sidewalks and lay down to sleep. Some improvised shelters out of crates; others slept on the stoops of houses. There were many such destitute people in other cities in South China, including Changsha. One can hardly suppose that any of them, even had they known about the Guomindang congress, would have expected it to effect any change in their lives. The revolutionary atmosphere that permeated public opinion was alien to the urban slums.

Wandering the streets Mao could not help but notice these things. His conviction grew that "[n]o Bourgeois Revolution is possible in China. All antiforeign movements were (are) carried on by those who have empty stomach but not Bourgeoisie."[6] He had mentioned this at the Third Congress of the party, and from then on the thought had not left him alone. He supported the alliance with the Guomindang, but he understood its limits and its tactical flexibility. Sometimes he was carried away by the developing cooperation with the nationalists, but such periods alternated with doubts and disappointments. The firm conviction that only a dictatorship of the proletariat could save China never left him.

When he arrived in Canton, there were more than 11,000 members of the Guomindang from Guangdong, Jiangxi, Hunan, and Hubei. (Figures were unavailable for the rest of the country.) Canton had the largest number, 8,218 members; Jiangxi more than 2,000, mostly in Shanghai; there were roughly 500 in Hubei, about 500 in Hunan, and more than 300 in Hankou.[7] Meanwhile, the CCP had only slightly more than 100 members. In other words, even if one supposes that by the Unification Congress of the Guomindang most communists had already joined the GMD, which was actually not so, the Communist Party would still seem like a small, local branch of the Guomindang, less than 1 percent of the party of Sun Yat-sen.

But the communists were extremely active both inside and outside the hall where the congress took place from January 20 to January 30. Of the 165 of the 198 delegates actually present, 23 were members of the CCP, or almost 14 percent. Among them were such well-known communists as Chen Duxiu, Li Lisan, Lin Boqu, Li Weihan, and Xia Xi, and even the leftist Zhang Guotao. Li Dazhao, Tan Pingshan, and Mao Zedong were the most active of all. Communists were represented in all the organs of the congress about which we have information.[8]

Judging by the composition of the presidium and the commissions, the balance of forces between rightists and leftists (including communists) was roughly equal. A fierce battle resolved the question of communist membership in the Guomindang. At a banquet on the opening day of the congress, the right-wing Guomindang member Mao Zuquan declared, "If the communists accept our program, they should leave their own party." In the commission on rules, a right-wing delegate named He Shizhen proposed unsuccessfully that Guomindang members be prohibited from belonging to other parties. Finally, in debates on the party rules, Fang Ruilin and Feng Ziyou, fervid anticommunists, advocated excluding members of other parties from membership in the Guomindang. Li Dazhao replied with the following, obviously hypocritical, words:

[I]n our country . . . only the Guomindang can become a great and mass revolutionary party and achieve the task of freeing the nation, establishing people's power, and asserting the people's livelihood. . . . We enter this party in order to make our own contribution to this enterprise and thereby to the cause of the national revolution. . . . That we are entering the party is proof that we accept its program. . . . Look at the newly worked out program of this party, and you will see there is not an iota of communism in it.[9]

At the same time, Li Dazhao did not hide the fact that in the united front the Communist Party, as a section of the Comintern, would act as an autonomous force. But he claimed this was even an advantage for the Guomindang since the CCP could serve as the connecting link between the party of Sun Yat-sen and the world revolutionary movement. A delegate from Tianjin disputed Li Dazhao, but the right wing was in the minority.[10] Many delegates openly opposed the right, including old comrades in arms of Sun Yat-sen like Liao Zhongkai, Wang Jingwei, and Hu Hanmin.[11] Liao Zhongkai said, "The time has come to understand that only in unity with other revolutionary parties can we victoriously conclude the revolution."[12]

Sun Yat-sen's position was decisive. During the congress, he pursued a policy of transforming the Guomindang. He attempted to apply the experience of Soviet Russia and the Russian Communist Party and spoke in favor of accepting communists into the Guomindang.[13] Consequently, the overwhelming majority favored admitting communists into the Guomindang, stressing only that they observe intraparty discipline. Ten communists were chosen for the Central Executive Committee (CEC) of the GMD, which consisted of forty-one individuals (twenty-four members and seventeen candidate members).

Li Dazhao, Tan Pingshan, and another communist, Yu Shude, representing the Beijing organization, became full members of the CEC. Tan even became a member of the highest organ of the party—the Standing Committee (Politburo). He headed one of the key departments of the CEC—the Organizational Department. Mao and six other communists were chosen as candidate members of the Central Executive Committee. Among these persons who, like Mao, had no voting rights on the CEC were Lin Boqu and Zhang Guotao, whom we have already met, and the still young but extraordinarily active journalist Qu Qiubai. At this time the twenty-four-year-old was just beginning to impress Chinese public opinion. His success was considerably facilitated by the trust the ECCI reposed in him. (Qu had worked in Moscow as a correspondent for the popular Beijing newspaper *Chenbao* [Morning news] for more than two years from January 1921 through the spring of 1923.) Comintern officials took note of this clever young Chinese who joined the CCP in Moscow in the spring of 1922 and was soon assigned to help Chen Duxiu and Liu Renjing in connection with the Fourth Comintern Congress. Chen took to him, selected Qu as a delegate to the Third Congress of the party, and appointed him chief editor of *New Youth* and of the newly established party organ, the journal *Qianfeng* (Vanguard). In the summer of 1923, Qu, along with Zhang Tailei, served as secretary to Maring.[14] When Mikhail Borodin arrived in China in late August 1923, Qu became one of his interpreters and assistants.*

The formation of a united front based on admission of communists to the

---

* An entire company of Chinese communists who knew Russian served Borodin. Working with Qu were Zhang Tailei and his wife, and graduates of Moscow's Communist University of the Toilers of the East: Li Zhongwu (a nephew of Liang Qichao), Huang Ping, Fu Daqing, and Bu Shiji.

Guomindang was the most important outcome of the First All-China Congress of the Guomindang, which issued a new manifesto on this occasion. Many communists, Mao included, were extremely satisfied with these results. They were energized as a result of the successful development of the united front. Borodin explained to his Chinese comrades that "the creation of Guomindang organizations, the larger the better, is the chief task of communists."[15]

Soviet money, which flowed into the CCP in an ever-increasing stream, facilitated the acceptance of Borodin's directives. Having yielded to Kremlin pressure during the meeting at West Lake, the Chinese communists quickly adapted to these circumstances. They accepted the unequal relationship with Moscow, and they were very active regarding the financial side of their ties with the Comintern. The lessons in cynicism taught by Maring had not been in vain. After West Lake the Chinese communists were not at all shy about asking Soviet and Comintern officials for more and more money. According to Maring's data, at most one-tenth of the members of the party paid membership dues at a time when a majority of the communists worked only for the party.[16]

"We have already started the anti-imperialist work according to your instruction," Chen Duxiu wrote in English in early November 1924 to the Soviet ambassador in Beijing, Lev Karakhan, "but we have not received the necessary fund which you promised to pay. Our budget for Shanghai is $600. Please let us know as soon as possible. With communist greetings. T. S. Chen,* Secretary of E[xecutive] C[ommittee] CCP."

"Dear Comrade," echoed Li Dazhao in a letter in English to this same Karakhan:

> The local [CCP] committee in Kalgan [Zhangjiakou] asks the Northern Committee to give the monthly living expenses for Comrades Tian-Ten-Sou, Ma-Je-Liang and Fu-En-Tsu who are working in Pa-to [Baotou] for the newspaper, the "Si-pe-min-bao." The Northern Committee considers that the funds for those three comrades whom were sent for military work were supported since a long time from your side. Therefore, please, you arrange and give an answer to their demand. With comrade[ly] greetings. The Northern Committee of the CCP. Secretary: T. C. Li.[17]

---

* In these years, it was customary for Chinese intellectuals to sign their names using the Latin alphabet in the Western fashion, using only initials for their personal names and placing these before their family names. They employed the transliteration system then in use, the so-called Wade-Giles system named after its creators, the British professors Thomas Francis Wade (1818–1895) and Herbert Allen Giles (1845–1935). It is substantially different from the system adopted by the UN in the early 1970s. In the Wade-Giles system, T. S. Chen means Tu-siu Chen, T. C. Li is Ta-chao Li, and T. T. Mao is Tse-tung Mao.

Many more examples could be cited. The result of such parasitism was that until the mid-1930s, the CCP was able to function only by relying on the Kremlin's help to the tune of 30,000 U.S. dollars a month.[18] Soviet financial support was truly all-encompassing and detailed down to the penny. It is evident that Comintern agents and the Soviet embassy were even paying for the office help of party organizations who were working for wages.

The Young Communists did not lag behind the party. (At the beginning of 1925, the Socialist Youth League had been renamed the Chinese Communist Youth League.) "To step up our work, [the league] needs appropriate financial support," Ren Bishi, secretary of the CCYL, who had studied in Russia in the early 1920s, wrote in Russian on February 2, 1926, to Soviet ambassador Karakhan. "We have already accumulated debts of about 500 Chinese dollars that need to be repaid as soon as possible. . . . It is desirable that you provide us material assistance monthly as well as on this one-time basis."[19]

Wholly dependent upon Soviet financial support, the leaders of the CCP were unable to stand up to the Soviet emissary Mikhail Borodin. For example, in a conversation with Borodin in January 1924, during the Guomindang congress, all the communists present expressed "full unanimity" that the time was not ripe for radical agrarian revolution.[20]

Mao, who returned to Shanghai from Canton in mid-February, supported this "rightist" course. On February 25, 1924, he and several other Guomindang activists established a Shanghai Bureau of the GMD in the French Concession, at No. 44 Huanlong Street, not far from where Sun Yat-sen lived. After receiving a substantial bribe, the local French police inspector promised to give the Guomindang advance warning of any possible actions the French authorities might take against them.[21] In addition to acting as secretary for the Communist Party, Mao also began working in the Shanghai Bureau of the GMD. At its first session he was chosen as secretary of the Organizational Department, and soon he began to perform the duties of head of the record-keeping office. Soon he joined the staff of the standing committee of the bureau as a candidate member.[22] There was more than enough work for him. In March, as a representative of the CCP Central Executive Committee, he took part in a plenum of the CEC of the Socialist Youth League. Here he met the Communist Youth International representative Sergei Dalin, who later wrote that what struck him was Mao's unbridled optimism with regard to the Guomindang. Not sharing Mao's enthusiasm, Dalin reported to Voitinsky right after the plenum,

You will hear such things from Mao, the secretary of the C[E]C (none other than Maring's protégé), such things that will make your hair stand on end. For example, the idea that the Guomindang is a proletarian party and should be admitted into the Comintern as one of its sections. On the peasant question, he says that the class line should be discarded, that there's nothing we can do with the poor peasants and that we must link up with the landlords and the officials (*shenshi*), etc. This guy was the party's representative in the Youth League and he tried insistently but unsuccessfully to push this point of view at the plenum of the League. I sent a letter to the C[E]C of the party requesting that they appoint a new representative.[23]

Dalin was upset over nothing; at that time almost all the leaders of the CCP under Borodin's influence entertained pretty much the same notions. In February 1924, the CCP Central Executive Committee even approved a special "Resolution on the National Movement," which posited the expansion of the Guomindang and rectification of its "political errors" as the communists' main tasks as well as expansion of the Guomindang's mass base by attracting workers, peasants, and representatives of the urban middle classes into its ranks. The CCP itself should transition to an illegal position within the Guomindang and secretly prepare to take over the leadership.

The ECCI reacted sharply to this "deviation" and undertook to correct it. In April 1924, the Comintern dispatched Voitinsky to China to explain to the CCP leadership that working inside the Guomindang was "a means, not an end" toward strengthening the Communist Party and preparing it for the subsequent battle for power in the country outside of the Guomindang and against the Guomindang.[24] The May 1924 enlarged plenum of the CCP Central Executive Committee that Voitinsky arranged and attended repudiated the CEC's February resolution.[25]

After this directive the leaders of the party veered off in a completely different direction. On July 13, 1924, Chen Duxiu wrote to Voitinsky, who had already returned to Moscow:

As regards the current situation in the Guomindang, we find there only rightists and anti-communists; if there is a small number of leftists, then they are our own comrades. Sun Yat-sen and several other leaders are centrists, not leftists. . . . Thus, supporting the Guomindang now only means supporting the Guomindang rightists, since all the organs of the party are in their hands. . . . You must promptly send a telegram to Comrade Borodin requesting that he give a report on the actual situation; we expect that a new Comintern policy will be developed on that basis. In our opinion, support [of the Guomindang] should not be shown in the previous form, and we must act selectively. That means that we should not support the Guomindang without any conditions or limitations, but support only certain aspects of its activity that are in the hands of leftists; otherwise we will be aiding our enemies and buying ourselves opposition.[26]

Then, on June 21, Chen Duxiu and Mao Zedong, at their own peril and on their own initiative, distributed a secret circular to lower-level party organizations that said:

> At present only a few Guomindang leaders, such as Sun Yat-sen and Liao Zhongkai, have not yet made up their mind to separate from us, but they also certainly do not wish to offend the right-wing elements. . . . For the sake of uniting the revolutionary forces, we must absolutely not allow any separatist words or actions to emerge on our side, and we must try our best to be tolerant and cooperate with them. Nevertheless, considering the Guomindang's revolutionary mission, we cannot tolerate the non-revolutionary rightist policies without correcting them. . . . We must strive to win or maintain in our own hands "the real power of leading all organizations of workers, peasants, students, and citizens."[27]

Thus the enthusiasm of CCP leaders for organizational work in the Guomindang lasted just a few months and did not exert any serious influence on the GMD. Certain that the Comintern, in the person of Voitinsky, was supporting them, they began to torpedo Borodin's instructions, insisting on the need to "cast off Canton now" in order gradually to prepare a "general uprising of workers, peasants, and soldiers." This mood was expressed most sharply by Mao's friend Cai Hesen.[28]

Again the ECCI hastened to intervene. Moscow was extremely interested in maintaining the anti-imperialist united front after having invested so much effort and money in establishing it. In 1923 the USSR had begun supplying Sun Yat-sen with weapons, military supplies, and money. In 1924, some twenty Soviet military advisers worked in Canton, many helping the Guomindang organize a military academy to train officers for a new "party army." The Soviet government transferred 900,000 rubles to Sun Yat-sen for this academy, which officially opened on June 16.[29] The Whampoa Academy, as it became known in Chinese history, became an important source of cadres for the Guomindang National Revolutionary Army. Sun Yat-sen appointed Chiang Kai-shek its commandant and Liao Zhongkai as commissar of the academy. The youthful communist Zhou Enlai, who had just returned from France, was appointed head of the Political Department. Only twenty-six, Zhou was already well known as an activist in the May Fourth Movement, a student leader in Tianjin, the founder in 1919 of the patriotic Juewu (Awakening) society, and one of the organizers of the European branch of the CCP in 1922–23. The tall and well-built young man with European-looking features impressed everyone as a steady and serious worker. He was very well educated, knew Japanese and three European languages (French, German, and English), and was modest but very dignified. He was immediately recognizable as an outstanding person.

From May to July 1924 the group of Soviet advisers was headed by Pavel Pavlov, who died in a tragic accident. In October a new chief military adviser arrived as his replacement, Vasilii Bliukher, an important commander and future marshal of the Soviet Union. He and Sun Yat-sen began to consider plans for military campaigns aimed at uniting all of China under Guomindang rule. He remained in Canton until July 1925, when he returned to the Soviet Union for medical treatment.[30] Naturally Moscow did not wish to encourage the CCP's excessive "leftism." In November 1924 Voitinsky was sent back to China to cool the ardor of Chen Duxiu and his comrades. With this goal in mind, the Fourth Congress of the CCP assembled in Shanghai.

By this time serious contradictions between the communists and the followers of Sun Yat-sen had surfaced. They were especially deep-seated in Shanghai, and the Communist Party CEC, which was again located there, was well aware of them. Mao reacted to the change of circumstances in a particularly sharp way. Difficult work inside the Guomindang had quickly exhausted him. By May he felt unwell, both physically and spiritually. By July the "friction" with the Guomindang intensified to such a degree that his nerves were shot, and he resigned from the post of secretary of the Organizational Department.[31] At that time, according to the reminiscences of the communist Peng Shuzhi, "He looked in pretty bad shape. His thinness seemed to make his body even longer than it actually was. He was pale, and his complexion had an unhealthy, greenish tinge. I was afraid that he had contracted tuberculosis, as so many of our comrades had done."[32]

Throughout the spring and into the early summer he lived in dirty and smoky Zhabei in the residence of the CCP Central Executive Committee. In early June, Kaihui, her mother, and their two children came to Shanghai. Xiang Jingyu who served as CEC property manager allotted Mao and his family a separate wing, but it was still crowded. Ultimately, they had to move and, fortunately, it was to a much better place, in a quiet lane in the International Settlement. Kaihui did all she could to help her beloved husband in his work. During the evenings she found time to teach in a workers' night school.[33] In Shanghai for the first time, she could not refrain from some innocent temptations. The luxurious city offered an endless number of attractive services; however, all she wanted was the pleasure of having a photograph taken with her children. This black-and-white photo has survived. Kaihui looks calm though a bit sad. Anqing is seated on her knees, quite small, with a funny tuft of hair on his head, and Anying is standing next to her, a sturdy lad with chubby cheeks and a decisive gaze. There is a strong resemblance to his father.

Meanwhile, by mid-autumn Mao's condition had become unbearable. He began to suffer from attacks of neurasthenia. On October 10, the national holiday, at a meeting organized by the Shanghai bureau, two Guomindang rightists initiated a brawl, throwing punches at the leftists. The incident deepened the gulf between the communists and the followers of Sun Yat-sen.[34] Moreover, the flow of financial support from Canton ceased. The result was that the work of the bureau came to a halt. At the end of December Mao requested medical leave of the CCP Central Executive Committee. Chen Duxiu agreed and Mao and his family finally left unloved Shanghai for Changsha. From there they headed straight to his mother-in-law's home in Bancang, and then in early February proceeded to Shaoshan. He, Kaihui, and the children were accompanied on their journey home by Zemin, who two months earlier had left Anyuan for Changsha because of an attack of appendicitis. Not long after, their younger brother Zetan and his young wife, Zhao Xiangui, joined them in Shaoshan.[35]

Mao spent seven full months at home. How tired he was with the irritating daily chatter about the united front, diplomatic negotiations with the "bourgeois nationalists," and political games and squabbles. His initial euphoria had passed, followed by depression. It was not by chance that he didn't remain in Shanghai even for the Fourth Congress of the CCP, which took place just two weeks after his departure, on January 11–22, 1925. He was, after all, the secretary of the CEC and the number-two man in the party. Yet, he dropped everything and ran off.

Evidently, he was simply not up to bearing responsibility for the "ruinous" policy. The constant interference by Moscow may have irritated him, too. We know he was noted for excessive impulsiveness. He would have derived little pleasure from sitting at the congress and listening to the "wise" Voitinsky brainwash Chen Duxiu yet again. So he requested "leave." This was hardly the action of a careerist.

The Fourth Congress took place under Voitinsky's leadership. The flexible Chen again had to submit and correct his "errors." The position of the "leftists" was subjected to sharp criticism, yet very few of the twenty delegates, who represented 994 members of the party, dared to utter any protest. Those who expressed disagreement were quickly labeled as agents of "Trotskyism," since the battle with Trotsky was coming into style in the Comintern.[36] Mao was not reelected to the new CEC. Qu Qiubai, who was considered Borodin's "right-hand man," was elected in Mao's place. Qu was also placed in the exclusive Central Bureau of the CEC, along with Chen Duxiu, Zhang Guotao, Cai Hesen, and Peng Shuzhi, one of the former leaders of the Moscow branch of the CCP.[37] Peng now headed the Propaganda Department of the CEC. Qu Qiubai also founded the new party organ, the weekly newspaper *Rexue ribao* (Hot blood). Both the Propaganda Department and the newspaper did everything they could to push Moscow's policy.

But these changes as yet affected Mao very little. He was enjoying peace and quiet in the bosom of his family. Of course, because of his active nature he couldn't simply sit still with his arms folded. For many years now he had been accustomed to being an organizer. At first it was not easy for him to overcome his intellectual's contempt for his neighbors, who had been tilling the soil since time immemorial. He had left the village many years ago and had long thought of his fellow countrymen as "stupid and detestable people."[38] Marxism had taught him to respect urban workers, the "liberators of mankind," not destitute peasants. Working among the peasants held no attraction for Mao. "Until we are sure that we have a strong cell in the countryside and until we have conducted agitation for a long period of time," said Mao during the First Congress of the Guomindang, "we cannot resolve to take a radical step against the wealthier landowners. In China generally [class] differentiation has not yet reached a point where we can initiate such a struggle."[39] Moreover, one should not forget that Mao himself was a landowner—though by no means a large one—who ever since he had left home lived to a significant degree on the labor of farmworkers and renters.* His mother-in-law also had a bit of land, in Bancang, a little town in Changsha district. Of course, as a communist he should have had sympathy for the village poor, and as someone who had come from this milieu he could not fail to understand peasant problems. Still, it was harder for him to associate with the downtrodden and ignorant peasants than with the workers who had tasted city life. Just like the first peasant agitator Peng Pai, whom the peasants themselves had initially taken for a madman,[40] Mao had to experience everything himself.

With the help of a distant relative, Mao Fuxuan, who was apparently able to convince his fellow countrymen that Yichang's eldest son had his head screwed on right, Mao finally succeeded in making contact with his neighbors. He began to explain Marxist political economy and Bolshevik strategy to them in simple and accessible terms. He met with them at his home or in secluded places such as family ancestral temples that were scattered about the neighboring hills. That most of the peasants in the vicinity belonged to his clan was a great help to him. (Even now more than 60 percent of the inhabitants of Shaoshan are surnamed Mao.)[41] As much as they could, his wife, Kaihui; his youngest brother, Zetan; his sisters-in-law Shulan and Xiangui; as well as middle brother Zemin (who, however, did not linger long in the village) helped Mao with his work. In May 1925, Zemin was ordered by the Xiang District Committee to return to Changsha, and in July he was sent to Canton for a short-term course in the Peasant Movement Training Institute that had been

---

* It will be recalled that Mao's father owned 22 *mu,* or about 3.5 acres of land. After his death the land was inherited by his three sons.

set up at the end of July 1924 by the Guomindang CEC, at the suggestion of the CCP. The institute trained agitators and organizers for the peasant unions.

According to Mao Zedong, he and his comrades succeeded in establishing more than twenty peasant unions in the region in the spring of 1925.[42] That was certainly an impressive result. Until then there had been only one peasant union in the Xiangtan district, organized in February 1925. Then, in July, a peasants' night school was established in Shaoshanchong, in which Kaihui taught Chinese and arithmetic. Shulan was the first to sign up, after which both sisters-in-law succeeded in winning over several more people. They went from house to house declaiming the following:

> A peasant's life is hard
> We will not give our grain to the landlord
> We work all year round
> Yet the grain bin is empty.[43]

Such simple forms of agitation worked better than any party resolutions. Around the same time Zetan organized another night school for peasants in a small neighboring village. In mid-July, Mao established a CCP cell in Shaoshanchong and put Mao Fuxuan at the head of it. He also established a small Young Communist group.[44] Unexpectedly, working with peasants attracted him. He acquired new experience that would turn out to be invaluable in the near future. Although he did not begin to have greater respect for the ignorant, illiterate rural toilers, he became convinced that the revolution could succeed only by relying upon the countless unfortunate peasantry.

1 2

PLAYING WITH
CHIANG KAI-SHEK

Enormous changes were occurring in the world outside Shaoshan. On March 12, 1925, Sun Yat-sen died from liver cancer in Beijing, where he had gone to take part in a peace conference to unify the country. He was invited there by Feng Yuxiang, a former client of Wu Peifu, who turned against his patron in October 1924. Feng declared his support for Sun, renamed his own separate army the Guominjun (Nationalist Army) after the Guomindang (Nationalist Party), occupied Beijing, and called for an end to the civil war. Turning to Moscow for help, he was supplied by the Kremlin with a number of well-known Soviet military advisers.

Sun Yat-sen's death was a great loss, but it did not further complicate the general situation in China. A factional struggle for power erupted within the Guomindang, but very quickly the Guomindang "leftists" triumphed. Wang Jingwei, one of Sun's closest collaborators, chief of the Guomindang "leftists," and head of the Propaganda Department of the CEC, became the leader of the Guomindang and head of the Canton government. Cordial relations continued to develop among General Feng, the Guomindang, and the USSR. At the end of March the "party army" of the "leftist" Chiang Kai-shek established the Canton government's control over eastern Guangdong province, and in June suppressed an uprising by Yunnan and Guangxi troops. Chiang Kai-shek's star was swiftly rising.

On May 30, 1925, an incident in Shanghai provoked a surge of nationalist feeling in China unseen since the May Fourth Movement. British troops fired upon a crowd of Chinese on Nanking Road who were protesting the killing of a communist worker, Gu Zhenghong, by a lone Japanese. The murder of the unfortunate Gu had aroused the whole city. Workers in many factories went on strike and students boycotted classes. On May 24, the day of Gu's funeral, tens of thousands of people held an anti-Japanese demonstration. Everything might have blown over, but in Qingdao on May 28, Chinese militarists, responding to the request of Japanese entrepreneurs, opened fire on workers who had come out in the streets in solidarity with the textile workers of Shanghai. Two demonstrators were killed and sixteen wounded. The reprisal in Qingdao ignited a firestorm. On May 30, about two thousand students gathered on Nanking Road in the center of the International Settlement, shouting, "Down with imperialism!" "Shanghai for the Chinese!" "Return the Settlement!" and "Everyone in China unite!" A number of people were arrested, but around 3 P.M. a large crowd gathered in front of the police station demanding the release of the detainees. The officer in charge snapped and gave the order to fire on the crowd. Ten were killed and dozens wounded.[1] This action evoked a storm of indignation. At a conference of Shanghai trade union activists on May 31, a municipal General Trade Union Council was established, headed by Li Lisan. At his call about two hundred thousand Shanghai workers laid down their tools. In response twenty-six foreign warships entered the Huangpu River and American, British, and Italian marines landed. New bloody clashes resulted in the deaths of 41 Chinese and the wounding of 120.[2]

The Shanghai massacre marked the beginning of the May Thirtieth Movement, the beginning of the nationalist revolution. Demonstrations, protest meetings, and strikes occurred at foreign enterprises. The public again resorted to a boycott, this time of foreign goods in general. On June 19, workers in Hong Kong came out in support of those in Shanghai and two days later so did the workers in Shamian. More than 250,000 people were on strike. This action was followed by the mass exodus of working people from these colonial centers to Canton and environs. The Guomindang government began to support the strikers. A blockade of Hong Kong and Shamian was declared, and a Hong Kong–Shamian Strike Committee was formed under the leadership of the Workers' Department of the GMD Central Executive Committee. Its chairman was Su Zhaozheng, a Guangdong native, who had just joined the CCP on the eve of the strike, in the spring of 1925. His deputy was Deng Zhongxia.

The anti-imperialist struggle intensified daily, with Canton as its center. The National government of the Republic of China, under the chairmanship of Wang Jingwei, was officially proclaimed on July 1, on the foundation of the Canton government. Wang Jingwei also became the head of the Military Council of the government and the troops loyal to the Guomindang were united into a single National Revolutionary Army (NRA), initially consisting of six corps. Chiang Kai-shek became the commander of the First Corps, composed of Whampoa Academy cadets, and Tan Yankai, the former governor of Hunan, commanded the Second Corps. Zhou Enlai was appointed head of the Political Department of the First Corps. There were quite a few communists in the other corps as well.[3] As a revolutionary upsurge swept throughout the country, the CCP-Guomindang alliance began to solidify into an irresistible force.

By July the wave of the patriotic movement reached Shaoshan. Mao quickly organized an "Avenge the Shame Society" on the foundation of the peasant unions, although he did not invent this name. Similar associations were popping up everywhere. In Changsha the organization had been established in early June at a huge anti-imperialist meeting of more than two hundred thousand people. In early July, Mao revived the Shaoshan district branch of the Guomindang that had started the previous year.[4] At the same secret meeting a district-level "Avenge the Shame Society" was formed from more than twenty small unions. Mao deployed it to wage an intensive anti-imperialist propaganda campaign. He and his comrades organized youth agitation brigades that went to the villages and introduced to peasant audiences the idea of boycotting foreign goods.[5]

In late August, however, Governor Zhao Hengti issued a new order for Mao's arrest. It was less Mao's revolutionary agitation that irked the governor than the campaign Mao had organized against a local bigwig named Chen. Because of a drought in Shaoshan, the peasants, fearing a crop failure, requested that Chen sell them grain from his reserves. Chen refused since he counted on selling his grain at a high price in the city. Mao immediately convened a joint meeting of the communist cell and the peasant union. Two activists were sent off to have a discussion with Chen, but nothing much came of it. Chen was ready to load the grain on a barge bound for Xiangtan. Then, under Mao's command, more than a hundred peasants armed with hoes, wooden staves, and bamboo poles moved under cover of night to the warehouse of the "bloodsucker" Chen. They demanded that the granary be opened and the grain sold at a reasonable price. Chen capitulated but immediately informed the governor. Again Mao had to flee. Friends warned him he would be arrested. By a stroke of good luck, a well-disposed employee in the district administration came across a telegram that his superior had received from Zhao Hengti saying, "Arrest Mao Zedong at once. Execute him on the spot." He informed Mao. On Shulan's advice Mao left Shaoshanchong in a closed palanquin, disguised as a doctor. Before his departure he strictly instructed his younger brother Zetan not to wait until Zhao Hengti issued an order for his arrest, but to follow him quickly to Canton.

A day later Mao was in Changsha, and in early September he left for the south. He began to be tormented again by an attack of nerves. Succumbing to fear, at one of his night lodgings he burned all of the notes he had made on the road. In the middle of September he finally arrived in Canton, where he spent the next two weeks recuperating in the Dongshan Hospital; his nerves were shot.[6] Soon Mao Zetan arrived in the southern capital, where he began to work at the Whampoa Academy and in the Guangdong committee of the CCP.[7]

In addition to all the other setbacks, Mao experienced a new blow in October. Friends of his youth Cai Hesen and Xiang Jingyu separated. The scandal had a negative impact on the moral climate in the party as a whole. The union of Cai and Xiang had always been considered a model in the CCP. Mao's friends were among the first who, disdaining bourgeois morality, began living together without any sort of marriage ceremony, long before such free love became fashionable among liberal Chinese youth. They were both reserved, businesslike, serious, and insufferably moral. Many female communists, who were lively and flirtatious, were afraid of Xiang Jingyu, who constantly lectured them about morality. During party meetings, Xiang sometimes publicly scolded Chen Duxiu himself, who was fond of dirty jokes. The women dubbed her "Granny of the Revolution." Qu Qiubai's wife, the charming Zhihua, who had ditched her unloved first husband for Qu, especially feared Xiang. So the split was like thunder in a clear blue sky. In the middle of September, when Cai was in Beijing, Xiang Jingyu, to her own surprise, was unfaithful to him with the handsome Peng Shuzhi. Zheng Chaolin, Peng's secretary, remembered:

> On the evening of the Mid-Autumn Festival we threw a sumptuous dinner. . . . After the guests had left, I returned to my pavilion room to sleep, but Xiang Jingyu stayed in Peng Shuzhi's room. It was a hot night, and the doors . . . had been left ajar. I awakened to hear Xiang Jingyu . . . telling Peng Shuzhi that she loved him.
>
> Presently, she went up to the second floor. Peng came to my room and said, "Something really strange has happened!" He repeated to me what I had just heard Xiang saying.
>
> "I would never have dreamed it," he told me.
>
> "Don't carry it any further," I told him. "It could harm the functioning of the organization." . . .
>
> From that day on, Xiang frequently came down from the second floor to talk to Peng Shuzhi, often for hours on end. . . . [H]e did not discuss the situation with me. He had accepted Xiang Jingyu's love.[8]

Nevertheless, word got out. Xiang herself admitted her infidelity to Cai, who could think of nothing better than to bring up the matter at an expanded session of the Central Executive Committee. The sensational news struck the leading members of the Chinese Communist Party with such force that, according to Zheng Chaolin's reminiscences, at first Chen Duxiu, Qu Qiubai, Zhang Guotao, and other leaders of the CCP were speechless. Finally, Chen Duxiu decided to terminate the affair. The CEC sent Cai and Xiang to Moscow, Cai as CCP representative to the Comintern Executive Committee and Xiang Jingyu to study at KUTV (Communist University of the Toilers of the East). At the end of the session, Chen Duxiu had everyone pledge to keep mum about what had occurred. He especially warned Qu Qiubai to say nothing to Zhihua, but Qu was unable to control himself. Soon the entire party knew. Most of the women, colleagues of Xiang Jingyu, gloated over her misfortune. The opinions of the men were divided. Qu Qiubai and Zhang Guotao conceived a hatred for Peng Shuzhi and demanded he be expelled from the Central Executive Committee, while Chen Duxiu leaned toward the adulterer and took him under his wing.

There was no repairing this broken cup. As soon as they arrived in Russia, in December 1925, the aggrieved Cai ditched Xiang Jingyu and became infatuated with the wife of Li Lisan. Li Lisan and his wife had accompanied the "model couple" on their journey from Shanghai to Moscow, where Li and Cai were supposed to take part in the Sixth Enlarged Plenum of the ECCI. Along the way, the naïve Li asked his wife to be a bit friendlier to the cuckolded Cai. He got more than he bargained for. The result was that Cai and Li's wife began openly living together, Li returned to China by himself, and Xiang Jingyu ultimately took up with a Mongol from KUTV.

None of this would have mattered had it not destabilized the upper echelon of the party, straining personal relations between Cai Hesen on one hand and Peng Shuzhi and Li Lisan on the other.* There is a sequel to the story. After his mistress's departure, the grief-stricken Peng began drinking and perhaps would have become an alcoholic had not a new passion entered his life in the form of the enchanting Chen Bilan. Unfortunately, before she met Peng she had been involved with another party heavyweight, Luo Yinong, the secretary of the Jiangsu-Zhejiang Regional Party Committee. From then on the spurned Luo became an enemy of Peng Shuzhi.[9] These personal squabbles distracted the leaders of the CCP from more urgent matters. But the "steadfast communists" who preached "free love" were human beings after all, and the human factor was far from the least important in politics.

Mao Zedong could not help but react to this situation. We don't know if he castigated Xiang Jingyu, but there is no doubt that he empathized with his close friend Cai and condemned Peng Shuzhi. He must have sided with Cai, too, in his clash with Li Lisan. In any case, the love scandal did not help Mao's recuperation. He continued to suffer attacks of nerves. Fortunately, at the very end of December, Kaihui came to Canton with her mother and their children, and they settled into a quiet neighborhood in Dongshan.[10] Mao began to feel like his old self again.

It was impossible for him to play the sick man for long, and even before

---

* Following this, rumors circulated within the CCP for a time that Li Lisan, hoping to get rid of his wife, had encouraged her to seduce Cai Hesen. At this time he was supposedly madly in love with her younger sister. Whether this was really true we don't know, but it is a historical fact that Li and Cai hated each other.

Kaihui's arrival Mao left the hospital in early October and immersed himself in political activity. Again, as in early 1924, he was overcome by an irrepressible patriotic impulse, again viewing the goals of the nationalist revolution as primary and relegating the tasks of social transformation to the back burner. In the fall of 1925 Mao formulated his political credo as follows:

> I believe in Communism and advocate the social revolution of the proletariat. The present domestic and foreign oppression cannot, however, be overthrown by the forces of one class alone. I advocate making use of the national revolution in which the proletariat, the petty bourgeoisie, and the left wing of the middle bourgeoisie cooperate to carry out the Three People's Principles of the Chinese Guomindang in order to overthrow imperialism, overthrow the warlords, and overthrow the comprador and landlord class (that is to say, the Chinese big bourgeoisie and the right wing of the middle bourgeoisie, who have close ties to imperialism, and the warlords), and to realize the joint rule of the proletariat, the petty bourgeoisie, and the left wing of the middle bourgeoisie, that is, the rule of the revolutionary popular masses.[11]

In early October, Wang Jingwei invited him to work in the CEC of the Guomindang and to assume his duties as head of the Propaganda Department. Wang knew Mao as a talented journalist and agitator. Mao soon began to edit the journal of the Propaganda Department, *Zhengzhi zhoubao* (Political weekly), which he used to disseminate his views on problems of the united front and the national revolution and to attack "rightist" elements in the Guomindang.[12]

The positions he defended dovetailed with those expressed by the leadership of the CCP. He had no disagreements with Chen Duxiu or other members of the CCP Central Executive Committee. Like other leaders of the CCP, periodically he tacked from side to side. It was difficult to work out the politics of the optimal combination of national and social elements. In 1925 the tactical zigzags of the leaders of the CCP generally began to acquire the character of a certain political line, which, naturally, was defined and conceptually grounded in Moscow. Chen Duxiu and the other Chinese communists merely had to submit to it.

The essence of the new policy was as follows. According to the Kremlin theoreticians, from now on the Chinese Communist Party should use its sojourn within the Guomindang not only to transform itself into a mass political organization, but also to radically transform the Guomindang's class and political character by having Guomindang leftists and communists seize power inside the party. Within the framework of the new policy the members of the

CCP should use their presence in the GMD to transform this organization into as "leftist" a party as possible, into a "people's (worker-peasant) party." They should do this first by ousting "representatives of the bourgeoisie" from leading posts and then purging them from the Guomindang. Then they should subject their "petty bourgeois" allies to their influence in order finally to establish the "hegemony of the proletariat" in China, not directly through the Communist Party but via the Guomindang.

The outlines of this new tactical line were sketched in the spring of 1925 by Voitinsky. In itself there was nothing new in Voitinsky's proposal. The leaders of the Chinese communists themselves were the first ones to advocate this line in February 1924. However, they were put in their place then, as Voitinsky himself was not yet ready to approve this policy. Now he believed that a favorable situation had been created inside the Guomindang as a result of the struggle of various intraparty factions over Sun Yat-sen's legacy. In April 1925, Voitinsky was able to present his views to Stalin. He summarized the conversation for the Soviet ambassador in China, Karakhan, on April 22, 1925: "He [Stalin] was very surprised when we explained to him that the communist party has its own organization . . . that the communists enjoy the right to criticize inside the Guomindang, and that most of the work of the Guomindang itself is being conducted by our comrades."[13] Taken aback by what Voitinsky had told him, Stalin soon provided his assessment of the prospects for the national-revolutionary movement in China. Needless to say, he did not credit Voitinsky for his "revelations." The authorship of the new concept had to belong to the Leader, not to some mere clerk. The Leader ascribed a universal meaning to his theory, advancing it as a panacea not only for the solution of the problems of China but of the East in general. Precisely as a maneuver that would facilitate the establishment of the hegemony of the Communist Party in the nationalist movement, he began to think of transforming the Guomindang and several other nationalist revolutionary parties of the East into "worker-peasant" or "people's" parties.

It was from this angle of vision that he analyzed the draft resolution of the Fifth Enlarged Plenum of the Executive Committee of the Communist International (March–April 1925) on work in India. (The plenum did not adopt a special resolution on China.) In his remarks on that document he singled out the issue of establishing the hegemony of communists in a future Indian "people's party."[14] Stalin's directives were immediately executed by the ECCI, which quickly conveyed them to China as well.

In May 1925, Stalin addressed this problem openly in a speech at the anniversary of the Communist University of the Toilers of the East:

> In countries like Egypt and China where the national bourgeoisie is already split into a party of revolution and a party of appeasement . . .

the communists must switch from a policy of a national united front to a policy of a revolutionary bloc of workers and the petty bourgeoisie. . . . [T]his bloc can take the form of a single party, a worker-peasant party **like the Guomindang** provided, however, that this unique party *in reality* represents a bloc of two forces—the communist party and the party of the revolutionary petty bourgeoisie. Such a composite party is necessary and expedient if . . . it facilitates the actual leadership of the revolution by the communist party.[15]

Once more the Executive Committee of the Comintern responded immediately, taking Stalin's ideas as its guide. In this spirit, the Sixth Plenum of the ECCI (February–March 1926) adopted a special "Resolution on the Chinese Question."

The political emergence of the proletariat provided a powerful impetus to the further development and strengthening of all revolutionary democratic organizations of the country, and in the first place the **people's revolutionary party, the Guomindang** and the revolutionary government in Canton. The Guomindang . . . represents a revolutionary bloc of workers, peasants, the intelligentsia and urban democracy . . . in the struggle against foreign imperialists and the military-feudal life-style and for the independence of the country and united revolutionary democratic power.[16]

Perhaps Stalin thought he was just developing the previous line. In reality, he was revising it to the point of absurdity. His theory meant that intraparty cooperation with the Guomindang became an end in itself. Stalin figured that the communists would ultimately succeed in ousting "representatives of the bourgeoisie" from leading posts and then from the Guomindang itself, but if a favorable concatenation of circumstances did not occur, that is, if the Guomindang elements turned out to be stronger than the communists, then the communists would have to make concessions to the leaders of the GMD, which would restrict their autonomy and their political independence. All this for the sake of remaining within the Guomindang, the "people's" party, for to exit the Guomindang would be to bury their hopes for transforming this party into a "worker-peasant party."

This conception of a united front was purely bureaucratic, based almost entirely on armchair calculations about the balance of forces in the Guomindang. As someone extremely skilled in intraparty intrigues, Stalin must have been convinced of the inevitable success of his policy, as he was then occupied with getting rid of his chief antagonists from the leadership of the Bolshevik party. However, this policy could not be effective in China, which was consumed by the flames of nationalist revolution. Unlike the degraded Russian Communist Party, the Guomindang was a revolutionary party and the anticommunist military faction within it was popular not only in the officer corps, but also among significant segments of Chinese society. It was simply impossible to squeeze the members of the group out of their own political organization.

The Chinese communists objectively were the hostages of Stalin's line. They were unable not to accept it, for they were totally dependent upon Soviet financial assistance. However, it was likewise impossible to implement the orders to communize the Guomindang without risking a rupture of the united front.[17] Judging by the reminiscences of Zhang Guotao, a majority of the leaders of the CCP eventually understood this, and therefore was compelled to maneuver, bluff, and twist about.[18] But this did not always help, and the only possible result was defeat.

Initially, nothing presaged such a dramatic turn of events. It seemed that the communists and the Guomindang "leftists" had a real chance to transform the party into a "worker-peasant" party. An anti-imperialist movement gripped the country, the workers' struggle was intensifying, and the apparently "leftist" leaders of the GMD were emphasizing their interest in developing good relations with the CCP, the USSR, and the Communist International. Even though practically the entire officer corps of the NRA and a majority of the GMD leadership belonged to the landlord class, no one even interfered with Mao's radical propaganda inside the Guomindang that the landlord class should be destroyed.[19] It is true that on August 20, the Guomindang "leftist" leader Liao Zhongkai was assassinated by a terrorist, but this only weakened the position of the "rightists." In response to the killing, Wang Jingwei advanced the slogan "Those who wish to make revolution should move toward the left!"[20] The disheartened "rightists" tried to split the Guomindang, convening a separate conference that they called the Fourth Plenum of the Guomindang CEC in the Western Hills outside of Beijing, but nothing came of this. Wang Jingwei, Chiang Kai-shek, Tan Yankai, and many other party leaders, who were supported by the communists, spoke out against the rightists. On November 27, in the name of the Guomindang CEC, Mao drafted an appeal to all comrades in the party that sharply criticized the Western Hills group. On December 5, this appeal was published in the first issue of the *Political Weekly*. With Bolshevik cynicism it declared that "today's revolution is an episode in the final decisive struggle between the two great forces of revolution and counterrevolution in the world. . . . We must recognize that in today's situation, he who is not for the revolution is for counterrevolution. There is absolutely no neutral ground in the middle."[21]

Mao expounded his views much more systematically in a major work, "Analysis of Classes in Chinese Society," which was published December 1,

1925, in *Geming* (Revolution), the official journal of the Second Corps of the NRA. Despite its title, the article was hardly a scholarly sociological analysis. At that time no one in the CCP could have seriously analyzed the class structure of China, as there were no leading sociologists or major economists in its ranks.[22] But Mao aspired to nothing of the sort. His strictly propagandist article had the concrete political objective of demonstrating that the enemies of the revolution were few in number because of the very nature of Chinese society, and that consequently the "leftist" bloc would inevitably be victorious. For simplicity's sake he divided society into five categories: the large, medium, and petty bourgeoisie, the semiproletariat, and the proletariat. He ignored the fact that he was applying to Chinese society a scheme of class relations in developed capitalist societies that did not fit. He posed a purely political question, "Who are our enemies, who are our friends?" and in the end he answered:

> All those in league with imperialism—the warlords, the bureaucrats, the comprador class, the big landlords, and the reactionary intellectual class, that is, the so-called big bourgeoisie in China—are our enemies. All the petty bourgeoisie, the semiproletariat, and the proletariat are our friends, our true friends. As for the vacillating middle bourgeoisie, its right wing must be considered our enemy; even if it is not yet our enemy, it will soon become so. Its left wing may be considered as our friend—but not as our true friend, and we must be constantly on our guard against it [in another part of the article he wrote: "They are now still in a semi-counterrevolutionary position."].

Mao also considered the lumpen proletariat (vagabonds) to be "true friends." He pointed out: "This group of people can fight very bravely; if we can find a way to lead them, they can become a revolutionary force."

The result was an impressive picture: 395 million friends versus 1 million enemies and 4 million vacillators.[23] Mao did not bother with statistical data concerning the actual composition of various social groups. All of the figures were gross estimates and even his figure for the overall population of China was arbitrary, 400 million, when according to the postal census of 1922 actually it had already reached 463 million. Nor did he burden himself by explaining the actual economic role of various social classes in the system of production relations.[24] Nevertheless, the article was popular precisely because of its political character. In February 1926 it was reprinted by the Peasant Department of the Guomindang CEC in its journal *Zhongguo nongmin* (Chinese peasant).

Mao took an active part in the preparations and proceedings of the Second Guomindang Congress, held in January 1926 soon after Chiang Kai-shek's forces had routed the remnants of the local militarists and occupied all of

Guangdong province. He was a member of the credentials commission as well as of the commission drafting resolutions on propaganda and the peasant question. He delivered an extensive report on the results of party propaganda over a two-year period.[25] Thus he could take some credit for the fact that the Second Congress took place under the slogan of the ever-strengthening unity of the Communist Party and the "left wing" of the Guomindang. In elections to the new Central Executive Committee Mao was again chosen as a candidate member. The number of communists in this highest organ of the Guomindang increased from ten to thirteen, and seven members of the CCP enjoyed full voting rights compared to only three in the CEC chosen at the First Congress. This was done at the personal instruction of Wang Jingwei. The CCP leaders themselves suggested only two communists for the CEC. Two members of the communist party—Tan Pingshan and Lin Boqu—became members of the Standing Committee of the CEC. One more communist was included in the Central Control Commission of the GMD.

   Nothing, it seemed, foreshadowed any complications. During the entire congress, Wang Jingwei "was even more 'left' than the Communists," recalled Soviet agent Vera Vishniakova-Akimova.[26] Wang's report asserted that both communists and noncommunists were shedding their blood together on the field of battle, that they were united as one and that nothing could divide them.[27] The Soviet agent was delighted that "[b]efore the close of the congress one of the members of the presidium unfurled a red banner with a gold inscription, 'Oppressed peoples of the world unite and throw off the yoke of imperialism'—a gift from the Third International. The ovation continued for several minutes. . . . The routed rightists kept their silence."[28] Soon after the congress, Mao was confirmed in his post as acting director of the Propaganda Department of the CEC.[29] This "leftist celebration" continued right up to the end of March 1926, culminating with a speech by Hu Hanmin, one of the leaders of the GMD, at the Sixth Plenum of the ECCI in Moscow on February 17. This old comrade in arms of Sun said, "There is only one world revolution and the Chinese revolution is a part of it. The teachings of our great leader Sun Yat-sen coincide on essential matters with Marxism and Leninism. . . . The slogan of the Guomindang is: For the popular masses! This means that workers and peasants must take political power into their own hands."[30] That very month the Central Executive Committee of the Guomindang even addressed an official request to the Presidium of the ECCI asking that the GMD be accepted into the Comintern. The letter stressed that "[t]he Guomindang strives to achieve the task that has confronted the Chinese revolution for thirty years already, namely, the transition from the nationalist to the socialist revolution."[31]

   It was enough to make one's head spin. In February 1926, leaders of the Soviet Communist Party and the Executive Committee of the Communist International seriously examined this request, and a majority of the Politburo of the Central Committee even expressed approval of accepting the GMD as a sympathetic party.[32] However, caution prevailed; an evasive reply was drafted to the GMD Central Executive Committee and transmitted to Hu Hanmin.[33] It noted that the Presidium of the ECCI "views the Guomindang as a real ally in the struggle against world imperialism," and promised to include the question of the Guomindang's entry into the Comintern on the agenda of the forthcoming Sixth Congress of the Communist International if the GMD Committee insisted on pressing the issue.[34]

Events, however, did not develop in the direction that the Comintern officials and the CCP were pushing them. On the contrary, implementation of the Comintern resolutions aimed at communizing the Guomindang inevitably led to an anti-leftist military coup in Canton, led by Chiang Kai-shek, who in early 1926 began a swift rightward evolution.

Chiang's anticommunist outburst took place on March 20, five days after the end of the Sixth Plenum of the ECCI. The general, whom just three years earlier Comintern officials had invited to join the Communist Party, had long been dubious about the activities of the Soviet and Chinese communists in China. His trip to Russia in the fall of 1923 had led him to the conclusion that the Bolshevik "brand of internationalism and World Revolution are but Czarism by other names, the better to confuse and confound the outside world." [35] Returning to China in late December 1923, Chiang reported to Sun that, "[a]s regards their policy in China, I feel . . . they wish ultimately to Sovietize it." [36] Yet, for the time being he wisely concealed his feelings from the public, particularly since he received no response from Sun Yat-sen. Chiang acted so skillfully that even the savvy Borodin considered him among his friends.[37] By the spring of 1926, however, Chiang had run out of patience with the activities of a number of Soviet specialists, many of whom behaved arrogantly. He was especially irritated by Corps Commander Nikolai V. Kuibyshev, chief of the South China group of advisers, whose pseudonym in China was Kisanka. Apparently, this Soviet adviser was an arrogant and dull-witted veteran who was intoxicated with his own enormous power. Kisanka, according to Vishniakova-Akimova, openly despised the Chinese military, ignored diplomatic etiquette, and shamelessly tried to place the NRA under his own strict control.[38] He ignored Chiang Kai-shek and preferred to deal with Wang Jingwei on all military matters. For his part, Wang used Kisanka to discredit General Chiang. Behind their screen of unity the two leaders of the Guomindang shared a deep mutual antipathy. Chairman Wang could not stand the crude soldier Chiang. The latter was literally nauseated by the full-cheeked blatherer with his heavily pomaded hair. Only Borodin somehow succeeded in maintaining a delicate balance of power in the Guomindang CEC. The misfortune of the Chinese communists derived from their unequivocal support of Wang and Kisanka.

Beginning in late February, those dissatisfied with the "leftist" direction of the government began grouping around Chiang Kai-shek. Thus the personal conflict between General Chiang on one side and Wang Jingwei, Kuibyshev, and Kisanka on the other began to acquire a political coloration. On March 20, Chiang struck. He declared martial law in Canton, arrested a number of communists, and sent troops to surround the residences of the Soviet military advisers. He had deliberately provoked the incident by ordering the commissar of the warship *Zhongshan,* the communist Li Zhilong, to bring the vessel to the Whampoa Academy. When Li sailed into the roadstead near the school, he was suddenly declared to be a "mutineer," and a story about a "communist plot" was concocted.[39] All over Canton, Chiang's proclamations were posted saying, "I believe in communism and am almost a communist myself, but the Chinese communists have sold out to the Russians and become 'their dogs.' Therefore, I oppose them."[40] What he achieved at once was the removal of Kisanka and his deputies and the return of Bliukher, whom he trusted. The incident ended peacefully. Having achieved his aim, Chiang freed the detainees and even apologized to the remaining Soviet specialists in Canton. At the end of May 1926 Bliukher returned.

Nevertheless, Chiang Kai-shek's coup, unmistakably aimed against both the Chinese and the Soviet communists, signified the establishment of an almost undisguised military dictatorship of the Guomindang "rightists" and centrists in the territory controlled by the National government. Consequently, the position of both the communists and the Guomindang "leftists" grouped around Wang Jingwei was significantly weakened. Wang, reportedly ill, was forced to go abroad. In the villages of Guangdong the peasant unions began to be disarmed. The most serious consequence for the Chinese Communist Party came in the form of a series of demands by Chiang aimed at restricting the political and organizational autonomy of the communists inside the Guomindang. Chiang Kai-shek introduced these demands at the May 1926 plenum of the Guomindang CEC. These included a prohibition on criticizing Sun Yat-sen and his teachings, a limit of one-third on the number of communist members of the CEC and of provincial and municipal Guomindang committees, a prohibition against communists heading departments of the Guomindang CEC, and a prohibition on members of the Guomindang joining the CCP.[41] Soon after the plenum, Chiang gathered all the threads of power in his own hands. He occupied the post of chairman of the Standing Committee of the Guomindang CEC, and he headed the Military Council of the National government and the Department of Military Cadres of the Guomindang CEC. Most important, he was proclaimed the commander in chief of the National Revolutionary Army.[42]

On the eve of the May plenum, already knowing that Chiang would raise the question of the future status of the CCP in the Guomindang, the Chinese communists asked Moscow, "What is to be done?" Chen Duxiu was inclined to exit the Guomindang, not wishing to sacrifice the independence of the Communist Party. Voitinsky, Trotsky, and Zinoviev agreed, but not Stalin. He rejected any such proposal because it would wreak havoc with his tactical scheme. From the perspective of the Kremlin leader, just a couple of weeks earlier the communists in the "worker-peasant Guomindang" had been on the verge of seizing power. How could one so easily surrender the positions that had been conquered? In Stalin's logic this was tantamount to an unjustifiable surrender to the Guomindang "rightists."[43] Moscow directed the CCP to slow down the tempo of the offensive inside the Guomindang in order to regroup the forces. Stalin recognized the need for "internal organizational concessions to the *Guomindang leftists* in the sense of reshuffling personnel."[44] It was only a matter of the "leftists."

The Soviet Politburo viewed Chiang's coup as a conflict between the communists and those who objectively were their allies. (At this time no one in the Soviet leadership viewed Chiang Kai-shek as a "rightist.") Borodin himself, who recognized that the Soviet and Chinese communists had overreached, understood that Chiang Kai-shek's demonstration was in order. He shared his thoughts in a private conversation with Zhang Guotao: "Had Dr. Sun been alive, he would also have taken certain measures to restrain the activities of the CCP."[45] Again the Chinese communists had to submit, the more so since in May 1926 the Soviet Politburo had directed the ECCI and the Soviet government "to step up assistance—personnel and financial—to the Communist party of China by all means available."[46]

Mao, like fellow communists Tan Pingshan and Lin Boqu, who also headed departments of the Guomindang CEC, had to resign his post. According to Zhang Guotao's memoirs, Mao was particularly unhappy and blamed Borodin for this policy of retreat. In a private conversation with Zhang Guotao, Mao referred to Borodin as a "foreign devil."[47] The Propaganda Department and the Peasant Department were now headed by men considered Guomindang "leftists," while Chiang Kai-shek himself headed the Organizational Department.[48]

Mao did not remain without work. In mid-March, four days before the coup, he had been appointed director of the Sixth Session of the Peasant Movement Training Institute, which, as a result of reorganization, now recruited students from all over China. On May 3, a festive ceremony was held to register the new students, of whom there were 327, and on May 15 classes began. Starting in early April he also lectured on the peasant question to classes of party and youth agitators from Guangdong province.[49] Mao could now devote himself fully to what for all practical purposes had become his main work since the summer of 1925, namely, organizing the Chinese peasantry.

The appointment was not fortuitous. Since his return from Shaoshan, Mao had tirelessly addressed the problems of the peasant movement, written about them in Guomindang publications, and raised them in his speeches. He asserted that

[w]e have concentrated too much on city people and neglected the peasantry. . . . [T]he more the oppression of the peasants is relieved, the quicker the national revolution will be accomplished. . . . If we wish to consolidate the foundation of the national revolution, we must, once again, first liberate the peasants. . . . Only those who endorse the liberation movement of the Chinese peasants are faithful revolutionary members of the party; if not, they are counterrevolutionaries.[50]

Within the Communist Party, Mao had come to be viewed as a real expert on the peasant movement. Even the leaders of the Guomindang, including those of "rightist" orientation, considered the "king of Hunan" (as Mao was jokingly called in CCP circles) an "expert on the peasant question." In Borodin's words, they themselves "proposed him for membership in the commissions on peasant questions."[51] As early as January 1926, Mao had published a short article, "Analysis of Various Classes of the Chinese Peasantry and Their Relationship to Revolution," in the journal *Chinese Peasant*, directly addressing the situation of the Chinese peasantry. Although this article repeated, sometimes literally, many of the arguments in his previous article on classes in Chinese society, the left wing of the Guomindang welcomed it. Revolutionaries did not need a scholarly treatise but rather a politically pointed, militant, and clear proclamation, which is just what it was. Moreover, unlike the December publication, this article described the social structure of the Chinese village much more clearly. Instead of five categories (large, medium, and petty bourgeoisie, semi-proletariat, and proletariat), Mao now divided rural society into eight parts: large and small landlords (as before he related them directly to the large and the petit bourgeoisie), owner-peasants (petit bourgeoisie), semi-owner peasants (who rented part of their land), sharecroppers (renters with their own agricultural implements), poor peasants (renters lacking their own agricultural implements), farm laborers (for some reason Mao included handicraftsmen in this group), and vagrants. This picture was closer to reality, although it was still far from being accurate. Mao still did not realize that he had exaggerated the degree of capitalist development in the Chinese countryside.

There was one new element in the article. This time Mao spoke with special sympathy about the millions of vagrants who were forced to engage in banditry, to beg alms, or to serve in the armies of militarists. As before, he considered them allies, capable of "fighting very bravely," but he didn't limit himself to general phrases. "As for the vagrants, we should exhort them to side with the peasants' associations and to join the great revolutionary movement in order to find a solution to the problem of unemployment," he asserted. "We must never force them to go over to the side of the enemy and become a force in the service of the counterrevolutionaries."

He still placed his main hope on a "single organization" of five categories of peasants (owner-peasants, semi-owner peasants, sharecroppers, poor peasants, and farm laborers and handicraftsmen). He demanded that they struggle against the entire class of landlords, not just against the largest landowners. (The latter, incidentally, he categorized as those owning more than 500 *mu*, or about 80 acres, of land.) "Toward the landlord class, we adopt in principle the method of struggle, demanding from them economic and political concessions. In special circumstances, when we encounter the most reactionary and vicious local bullies and evil gentry who exploit the people savagely . . . they must be overthrown completely." [52]

Around the same time, in a January 1926 article published in *Political Weekly*, the journal that he edited, Mao again emphasized that the entire landlord class was in the camp of the enemy, along with imperialists, bureaucrats, militarists, and compradors. "Only the alliance of the three classes of the petty bourgeoisie, the semiproletariat, and the proletariat is truly revolutionary," he summarized, including the vagrants this time in the category of proletariat. The whole article was pointed against the landlords. Mao excoriated the petty "landlords" who, he said, "want revolution in order to get rich, while other classes want revolution to relieve suffering; they want revolution in order to make themselves into a new class of oppressors, while other classes want revolution to achieve their own liberation and to ensure that in the future they will be forever free from class oppression." [53]

Such leftism, it will be recalled, was characteristic of this period. Chiang Kai-shek's coup d'état was still more than two months distant. Many CCP leaders agreed with Mao. In October 1925, an enlarged plenum of the CEC of the Chinese Communist Party had defined the course precisely as sharpening "class struggle" in the villages. [54] This plenum was the first in the history of the party that gave serious attention to agrarian problems and it also resolved to establish a special department on the agrarian question within the Central Executive Committee. (The department was not established until November 1926.) [55]

In the middle of February 1926, pleading illness, Mao turned over the Propaganda Department to his deputy Shen Yanbing, who was later to become famous as the writer Mao Dun, and for the next two weeks conducted an investigation of the peasant movement in northern Guangdong and southern Hunan. Following this activity he gave a speech on problems of the peasantry to cadets of the officers' school of the Second Corps of the Guomindang army. [56]

Having pruned back the communists and the "leftists," Chiang Kai-shek prepared in earnest to carry out the Northern Expedition, a military campaign conceived by Sun Yat-sen with the aim of subduing the militarists and unifying China. Bliukher, with whom Chiang and the other Chinese generals got on famously, provided the greatest assistance in this matter.

At the end of March, while immediate preparations for the Northern Expedition were under way, Mao had taken part in a meeting of the Peasant Department of the Guomindang CEC, which department at this time was still directed by the communist Lin Boqu. Understanding that the appearance of the NRA would inevitably attract millions of peasants to the national revolution, Mao proposed a resolution committing the activists in the peasant movement to devote more attention to those areas through which the army of the Guomindang would have to pass, including the provinces of Jiangxi, Hubei, Zhili, Shandong, and Henan.[57] For some reason he didn't mention his native province of Hunan, perhaps because the need to organize the peasant movement in the province directly bordering Guangdong was something nobody doubted.

At the beginning of July, the troops of the National Revolutionary Army, totaling about 100,000 officers and men, moved north. The 150,000-strong Nationalist Army, commanded by Feng Yuxiang, who had declared his support for Sun in October 1924, was objectively their ally. In May 1926, Marshal Feng had even joined the GMD; however, he was unable to help his party comrades because three and a half months before the Northern Expedition he had suffered a stinging defeat at the hands of the northern militarists. Three groups of militarists opposed Chiang Kai-shek. Chief among them, in central China, was Wu Peifu, who had ordered the shooting of the striking Hankou workers on February 7, 1923. In eastern China was Marshal Sun Chuanfang and in northern and northeastern China was Marshal Zhang Zuolin. Wu's and Sun's armies each numbered some 200,000 while Marshal Zhang could field 350,000 men. The forces were obviously unequal, but Chiang Kai-shek was lucky. As early as February 1926, a split occurred in the army of Zhao Hengti, the Hunan governor, which was part of Wu Peifu's group. Tang Shengzhi, the commander of the Fourth Division, rose in rebellion and threw in his lot with the Canton government. Enlisting the support of Canton, Tang attacked General Zhao, forcing him to flee Changsha. At the end of March 1926 Tang proclaimed himself governor of Hunan but was unable immediately to fortify his position in the provincial capital. General Wu moved troops against him, and Tang was forced to abandon the city.

In these circumstances Chiang Kai-shek took the only correct action. On May 19, he sent a 2,000-man regiment—the only one in the Guomindang army led by a communist—into Hunan. This regiment helped Tang Shengzhi master the situation. In early June, Tang's division was reorganized as the Eighth Corps of the NRA. This predetermined the initial success of the Northern Expedition. Just two days after it started out, on July 11, the combined forces of the Fourth, Seventh, and Eighth Corps again seized Changsha. In mid-August, at a meeting between Tang Shengzhi and Chiang Kai-shek, it was decided to continue the Northern Expedition in two columns. The objective of the western column was Wuhan; the eastern column would head for Nanchang, the capital of Jiangxi province. Chiang Kai-shek himself would lead the eastern column; Tang Shengzhi the western. On August 17, the Northern Expedition resumed.[58]

The unification of the country had begun, but Mao remained in Canton. He could not go to his native Hunan, which had already been liberated by the NRA, because he was overloaded with work. He was constantly being asked to speak about the peasant movement at various meetings. Everyone was expecting a massive revolutionary upsurge in the countryside. Over a period of four months in the Peasant Movement Training Institute, Mao took up three themes: the "peasant question" (23 hours a week), "educational work in the countryside" (9 hours), and geography (4 hours). At the invitation of the peasant committee of the Guangdong provincial party committee of the Guomindang, he lectured on the agrarian question and on the history of the Comintern and the USSR at courses the committee sponsored for military officers. For a week in July, along with the auditors of the Peasant Institute, he was busy with agitation-propaganda work among peasants in northern Guangdong on the border with Hunan; in mid-August in Haifeng district in the east of the province he spent fourteen days supervising students' practical work. At the beginning of September he lectured the cadets at the Whampoa Academy. At the same time, he was editing and preparing for publication a series of brochures on "The Peasant Question."[59]

He did not change his radical views. He still called for the overthrow of the entire class of landlords, notwithstanding the fact that landlords' sons were heading the armies of the Northern Expedition. "The peasant problem is the central problem of the national revolution," he affirmed.

> If the peasants do not rise up, if they do not join the national revolution and support it, then the national revolution cannot achieve success. . . . The greatest enemy of revolution in an economically backward semi-colony is the feudal-patriarchal class in the countryside. . . . If the peasants do not rise and do not struggle in the countryside against the privileges of the feudal-patriarchal landlords, it will be impossible to end the power of the militarists and the imperialists.

The conclusion followed that the main task at present must be "the rapid development of the peasant movement."[60] This is what he taught his listeners; this is what he devoted all his efforts to. Nothing, it seemed, could darken the prospects that opened up before the revolution. Millions of oppressed peasants, so it seemed, were ready to smash All Under Heaven.

THE COLLAPSE OF
THE UNITED FRONT

By the fall of 1926, the western column of the NRA had arrived at the Yangzi River valley after routing Wu Peifu's forces in Hunan and Hubei. On September 6 Hanyang was taken, on September 7, Hankou, and on October 10, Republic Day, Wuchang. These three cities, collectively known as Wuhan, were now in the hands of the National Revolutionary Army. Wuhan was one of the largest centers in China, with a population of roughly one and a half million people. Its geographical position on the central China plain, at the intersection of the most important transport arteries in the country, the Yangzi flowing from west to east and the north-south Beijing–Hankou and Wuchang–Changsha railroads, accounted for its strategic importance. In the late nineteenth century Wuhan was opened to foreigners, who established their concessions in Hankou. The city quickly developed into the most important commercial port in central China. Industrial enterprises appeared in Hankou as well as in neighboring Hanyang. The center of public and cultural life in the tricities, however, remained Wuchang, the capital of Hubei province.

The capture of Wuhan constituted a great victory on the part of the Guomindang army. In early November the Political Council of the Guomindang CEC adopted a resolution to move the seat of the National government from Canton to Wuhan, and a month later some of the ministers, mostly the leftists, along with Borodin moved to their new location. On January 1, 1927, Wuhan was officially proclaimed the capital of Guomindang China.[1] The nationwide victory of the Guomindang over the reactionary militarists was imminent.

In early November, Mao Zedong also left Canton, but the path he took led him to Shanghai, not Wuhan. The CCP Central Executive Committee had again assigned him to work in the central party apparatus, this time to head the newly created Committee on the Peasant Movement and to work in tandem with Peng Pai, the best-known organizer of peasants in Guangdong, who had already joined the party. In all, six people, each with a proven talent for rural work, would be working under Mao.[2] Mao shared their background, even though his actual experience of working with peasants was considerably less than that of, for example, Peng Pai. He was distinguished by his ability at theoretical generalization from the facts, his talent for expressing his thoughts crisply and clearly and artfully putting them into a conceptual form, and his enormous talent as a publicist. His views on peasant problems accorded with those of many CCP leaders who were themselves quite leftist. In September 1926, for example, Qu Qiubai, a member of the Central Bureau of the CCP, advised the Propaganda Department of the CEC to base their work on Mao's thesis concerning the peasants' struggle against "the greatest enemy of the revolution," "the feudal-patriarchal class of the landlords." Qu Qiubai as well as Voitinsky may have been instrumental in arranging Mao's appointment as secretary of the Committee on the Peasant Movement.[3]

From June 1926, Voitinsky was stationed in Shanghai as chairman of the newly organized Far Eastern Bureau of the ECCI. When the Northern Expedition was launched, acting on his own authority and at his own risk, Voitinsky induced the CCP Central Executive Committee to conduct a consistently radical policy on the peasant question.[4]

It is not known whether the general secretary, Chen Duxiu, opposed Mao's appointment. Probably not. The "Old Man" continued to enjoy enormous respect among the party leadership, and it is doubtful that Mao could have received the position without his approval. Chen, who himself held leftist views, was maneuvering as always. Even as he listened to the leftist Voitinsky he assured Stalin that extremism, which threatened the united front, would no longer be countenanced. Soon after the start of the Northern Expedition, Chen convened another plenum of the Central Executive Committee in Shanghai, which, in Zhang Guotao's words, adopted a "flabby" resolution on the peasant movement.[5] It now merely called on the peasants to struggle for rent and interest reduction, easing of the tax burden, and a prohibition on speculation. The resolution said, "Peasants! Rise up as one to struggle against corrupt officials, *tuhao* and *lieshen*, against excessive taxes and endless extortions levied by the militarist governments!"[6] That was all.

Qu Qiubai, Zhang Guotao, Tan Pingshan, and many other communists were dissatisfied. Even Chen Duxiu's own son, Chen Yannian, who headed the Guangdong provincial party organization, was opposed to the general secretary at this time. These leaders demanded that "in conjunction with the successful development of the Northern Expedition," the "slogan of the agrarian revolution 'divide the land among the peasants' " should be raised, "in order to mobilize the peasants to carry out the campaign."[7] But the general secretary, responsible for the flawless execution of Stalin's policy in China, was powerless to do anything himself. Perhaps he agreed to Mao's appointment, secretly hoping that with the help of this well-known "expert" on the peasantry he could "push" a "leftist" course, bypassing the Comintern.

It is doubtful that Mao had any sense of these maneuvers. The Sixth Session of the Peasant Movement Training Institute had completed its studies two months before he was invited to Shanghai, so he could take up his new assignment with a light spirit. His family left Canton at the same time. Kaihui was five months pregnant and by mutual agreement it was decided that she, her mother, and the children would return to Changsha.[8] They were separated again, but Kaihui did not complain. She understood that the revolution needed Mao.

After Mao caught up on intraparty intrigues, he didn't tarry long in Shanghai. The situation in the CEC apparatus was very tense, and the party leadership was split by squabbles. Moreover, the balance of forces between radicals and moderates in the CCP leadership had recently shifted. While Mao was en route to Shanghai, Voitinsky received a shocking directive from Moscow. Fearing for the outcome of the Northern Expedition, Stalin ordered the CCP to switch to a tactic of further retreat, this time making concessions even to the Guomindang "rightists." Stalin figured that the evolving military situation in China created a balance of forces in the GMD that was increasingly unfavorable to the CCP, which is why the party had been unable to purge the Guomindang of "anticommunists." On October 26, the Politburo of the Soviet Communist Party adopted a directive prohibiting the development of a struggle in China against the bourgeoisie and the feudal intelligentsia, that is, against those whom the Comintern had heretofore viewed as "rightists." Neither Stalin nor his supporters abandoned their hopes for the communization of Chiang Kai-shek's party. It was only a question of changing tactics, or so they said. In fact, the directive of October 26 signified a new policy toward China, which is precisely how the Far Eastern Bureau interpreted it.[9]

Immediately after receipt of the directive, on November 5–6, on the eve of Mao's arrival, the Far Eastern Bureau and the CCP Central Executive Committee considered the evolving situation. Chen Duxiu could note bitterly that in his game with the Comintern he had been correct. Had he followed the advice of Voitinsky and Qu Qiubai, he would immediately have been scapegoated. Now, on Voitinsky's initiative, it was decided to "push the Guomindang left onto the path of revolution . . . in such a way that it would not panic prematurely or run away." Put simply, it was impossible under any circumstances to radicalize the peasant movement. A resolution was promptly sent to Moscow assuring headquarters that they would only demand the confiscation of land from the largest landlords, the militarists, and the *lieshen* as well as public lands for subsequent transfer to the peasants. But Stalin balked even at such a moderate resolution and insisted on substituting the meaningless wish for the political confiscation of land belonging to counterrevolutionaries.[10]

This is what Mao encountered in Shanghai. He had no intention of renouncing his views, but neither did he want to make waves. At this point in his rise to power it would have been foolhardy to do so. He soon called a routine meeting of his department, at which he proposed to devise a concrete "Plan to Develop the Peasant Movement at the Present Stage," based on the ideas he had expressed in late March 1926. The plan committed the CCP "to adopt the principle of concentrating its efforts on developing the peasant movement." In other words, it demanded that priority be given to organizing peasants not only in Guangdong, but also in districts where the Guomindang army was operating, specifically the provinces of Hunan, Hubei, Jiangxi, and Henan. Moreover, "significant efforts" should also be applied to organizing peasants in a number of other places, including Sichuan, as well as Jiangsu and Zhejiang, where the NRA would be fighting very soon.[11] This was meant to ensure that the chance to assume the leadership of the revolutionary masses was not lost.

On November 15, 1926, the Central Bureau of the CCP adopted the plan, and by the end of November Mao was on board a ship traveling from Shanghai to Wuhan to represent the Committee on the Peasant Movement in Hankou. Before leaving he submitted to *Guide Weekly,* the central party journal, an article about the peasant movement in Jiangsu and Zhejiang in which he now spoke only of a struggle against the *tuhao* and the *lieshen,* not against the entire class of landlords.[12] He was passionate about taking action, but Comintern instructions restrained him. The revolution was blazing up all around, the Guomindang army was taking city after city, victory seemed near, and his fertile imagination probably conjured up crowds of peasants rising up, revolutionary courts for the "bloodsucking" landlords, the collapse of the power of the imperialists, the usurers, and the landowners.

In Hankou, however, his mood improved. The atmosphere here was even more leftist than in Canton. "Except for the quiet foreign concessions, the old city that was Hankow [Hankou] had donned the new clothes of revolution," an eyewitness recalled. "The [Guomindang] flag with the blue sky and the white sun was fluttering everywhere. . . . Revolutionary organizations of all descriptions mushroomed, emerging from underground, one after another. . . . Even the big bosses of industry and trade would shout, 'Long live the world revolution!' "[13]

Soon Borodin, too, arrived in Wuhan. He seemed irritable. Stalin's October directive had mixed up all his cards. In early October, he had devised a plan to curb the absolute power of Chiang Kai-shek, by now the standard-bearer of the Guomindang "right." Borodin, unable to forget the events of March 20, had long since turned against Chiang. In the second half of October, Borodin had arranged a joint session of the Guomindang CEC along with representatives of provincial and special municipal party committees attended mostly by "leftists." Mao was a participant. The meeting adopted a new program for the Guomindang that included most of the moderate CCP demands on the peasant question, including rent and interest reduction. In addition, an appeal was made to Wang Jingwei, then living in France, to return from his "leave." The blow against Chiang Kai-shek was precisely aimed, and Borodin now wanted to build upon his success. As soon as Borodin arrived in Wuhan, disregarding Moscow's directive he met with Tang Shengzhi, the commander of the western column of the NRA, and informed Tang that he no longer trusted Chiang Kai-shek but only him. "Whoever can faithfully carry out the proposals of Dr. Sun Yat-sen will become the greatest figure in China," he said to the flattered general. Tang replied, "I am ready to follow all your directives." [14] Borodin now became obsessed with his struggle against Chiang Kai-shek and no longer heeded Stalin's October directive.

Meanwhile, Borodin encountered major problems in Wuhan. As the units of the militarists—Tang Shengzhi first among many—joined the Guomindang army, its officer corps, never a bastion of liberalism, became increasingly conservative. General Tang himself was by no means a "leftist." He only played at revolution, hoping with the help of the CCP and the Guomindang "left" to oust Chiang Kai-shek and become commander in chief. Thus the change in the composition of the NRA actually facilitated the rapid increase of "rightist" influence in the Guomindang. Borodin was powerless against them. As Zhang Guotao brilliantly stated, the situation in the city could best be described as "the beautiful dusk." [15] The flurry of leftist phrases bore no relation to the actual balance of forces.

In November 1926, Chiang Kai-shek took Nanchang and, inspired by success, confronted Borodin directly. In response, on Borodin's initiative a so-called Provisional Joint Assembly of Party and Government Organizations was convened in Wuhan on December 13 and assumed all power in the Guomindang-controlled areas. In addition to the Guomindang "leftists," three communists joined this body. There were posters everywhere proclaiming, "Increase the Authority of the Party!" "Demand Wang-Chiang Cooperation!" and "Welcome Wang Jingwei's Return to China!" No one seemed bothered by the fact that Wang had still not returned to China. Slogans such as "We support Commander in Chief Chiang!" that had earlier adorned the city were replaced with the call "We support the leadership of the central government!" [16] A rupture between "leftist" Wuhan and "rightist" Nanchang had become inevitable.

The evolving situation was discussed at a meeting of members of the Central Bureau of the CCP along with Voitinsky and Borodin on the evening of December 13. Most of the top party leaders, including Mao, were present. It was a stormy meeting. Chen Duxiu delivered the political report, which, in the spirit of the October directive, pointed out the "extremely serious" danger of a split in the united front. He asserted that "now most of the GMD's political and military strength is in the hands of the right," which, although it "desperately wants to calm down the workers' and peasants' movement . . . has not openly obstructed the anti-imperialist movement." Chen proposed doing everything to "save the rightists now" and convince them "to unite the armed forces with the people." In this connection, he sharply criticized those who had committed "leftist errors," and called for toning down class conflict in the cities and countryside and withdrawing the most radical slogans that might irritate the Guomindang. "We should try to explain to shop clerks and workers that they should not raise excessively high demands," he asserted. "The current struggles over rent- and interest-reduction are more pressing for the peasantry than solving the land problem," he added.[17]

Mao was deeply depressed by the content of his teacher's report, which seemed unthinkable from a communist perspective. Did he know that Chen, forced to persuade his comrades to accept what he himself did not believe, felt disgusted? Sooner or later, however, all communists, not just those in China, had to learn the simple art of hypocrisy.

For now, however, Mao was not ready to surrender without a fight. Although Chen did not criticize him personally, Mao flew into a rage. Chen's proposals also provoked objections from representatives from Guangdong and Hunan, who spoke of the need to mobilize the masses. Mao Zedong came to their defense, but their views were rejected by a majority of those present.[18] The resolution adopted at the end of the meeting pointed to two dangerous deviations in the united front, namely "the irrepressible leftward movement of the unfolding mass movement, [and] . . . the unrestrained rightward movement of the military authorities and their fear of the mass movement." Therefore, the CCP must exert pressure on the Guomindang government, "compelling it to shift to the left" and at the same time attract the masses, compelling "them to lean slightly to the right."[19]

None of this, however, could alter reality. Voitinsky held talks in Nanchang with Chiang Kai-shek that achieved nothing. Returning to Hankou, he told Zhang Guotao that the "situation was hopeless."[20] On December 31, 1926, Tan Yankai, the head of the National government, and other conservative ministers who did not want to relocate from Canton to "leftist" Wuhan joined Chiang Kai-shek in Nanchang. Although the "leftists" proclaimed Wuhan the new capital of Guomindang China, the "right" wing of the Guomindang continued to grow stronger daily. On January 3, 1927, Chiang and his supporters decided to establish an anti-Wuhan center of power, the Provisional Central Political Council. In the beginning of February, Chiang demanded from Moscow Borodin's prompt recall and replacement by someone to Chiang's own liking (Chiang named Karl Radek or Lev Karakhan).[21]

By this time Mao had already left Wuhan to speak at the First Peasant Congress of Hunan. The situation in the upper echelons of the party depressed him, and so the timing of the trip was opportune. On December 17 he arrived in Changsha, where a grand reception had been arranged for him. Here in his native place they remembered him, respected him, and valued him, especially because communists still dominated the local Guomindang organizations and most of them respected Mao as a highly successful fellow countryman. After all, Mao had been a candidate member of the Central Executive Committee of the Guomindang, which is to say, he had entered the leadership cohort. "You possess rich experience in the peasant movement," the organizers of the congress, most of whom were CCP members, wrote to him in the telegram of invitation. "We await your return to Hunan impatiently, and we cherish great hopes for the leadership you will provide here for everything." [22]

Three days later Mao Zedong delivered a key speech at a joint session of the delegates of the peasants' and workers' congresses of Hunan. More than three hundred people crowded into the small auditorium of the local theater to hear him. Mao was introduced as "leader of the Chinese revolution." His speech, however, was less revolutionary than the great majority of the extremely left-ist delegates would have liked. But what could Mao say in public after Stalin's October directive and the December resolution of the CCP Central Executive Committee? Moreover, a representative of the Far Eastern Bureau of the ECCI was on the presidium of the congress. (He was Boris Freier, called Bu Lici [Boris] by the Chinese.) Mao's message was basically as follows: "[T]he time for us to overthrow the landlords has not yet come. . . . [N]ow is the time to knock down the imperialists, the warlords, the local bullies [tuhao] and bad gentry [lieshen], to reduce land rents, to reduce interest, and to increase the wages of farm laborers. . . . [I]n the period of the national revolution we do not intend to take the land for ourselves." Naturally, as he had done earlier he em-phasized the significance of the peasant struggle. "The national revolution is the joint revolution of all classes, but there is a central problem of the national revolution, which is the peasant problem. Everything depends on the solution to this problem. . . . If the peasant problem is solved, the problems of the workers, merchants, students, educators, and others will likewise be solved." [23]

Mao's speech pleased the Soviet representative, [24] but the Hunanese com-munists were obviously disappointed. As radicals, they had wanted to hear a call to a "redistribution of the land by the people themselves."

Yet, neither in Hunan nor in Hubei nor in Jiangxi had the peasants risen up against the landlords on their own. In the wake of the advance of the col-umns of the National Revolutionary Army, it was not a spontaneous move-ment of the peasant toilers that gained strength in the countryside; rather, it was a disturbance of the rural lumpen proletariat, that is, that part of the rural population that the peasants themselves from time immemorial had viewed as the most destructive factor in society. One of the characteristic features of village life in China was the division of society not into gentry and peasantry, as in the West, but into two deeply antagonistic parts: those who had land, in-cluding not only the rich but all who could feed themselves, and those without land, the rural lumpen proletariat. Because of the enormous agrarian over-population in China there was not enough land for everyone, so that even a tenant farmer, no matter how poor he may have been, felt happy in comparison with the ragged folk who tramped the rural roads. The gulf between working farmer and the rural lumpen proletariat was enormous, a hundred times greater than that between rich and poor peasants. An important reason for this was that in China there had never existed formal class distinctions like that between "peasant" and "landlord." Farmers were distinguished from each other solely in terms of the level of the income their property produced and were categorized as either large or small landlords (*dizhu*) or peasants (*nong-min*). Of course, this did not mean that there were no contradictions within the class of landowners itself, but all these usually paled in comparison with the danger of the lumpens. The crime and violence of these latter made them a menace to all farmers, which is why even landless tenants usually lined up on the side of the landholders.

The situation was exacerbated by the strong clan divisions in the villages. The peasants lived in communities bound internally by strong traditional bonds. Within the communities everyone was related, closely or distantly, and all bore the same surname. Moreover, they were often all members of the same secret society. Naturally, the position and incomes of various members of the clan differed, and within the community there were both large property own-ers as well as poor tenants. Such circumstances usually did not create much discord in the course of daily life. The blood relations among the peasants were stronger than was class consciousness. This was the more so since the wealthier clan members of the community did not exploit the tenant members badly and, as a rule, rented them land on favorable terms. Not infrequently, the poorer relatives had the right to rent land belonging to the clan on advanta-geous terms. They also received protection from armed militia, the so-called *mintuan*, which were supported by the village leaders.

This protection was particularly important not only in the event of clashes between the peasants and rural bandits, but also in case of fierce interclan conflicts. Such conflicts occurred quite frequently, especially in those regions in southern China where society was traditionally divided between rich and poor clans. The latter were usually composed of lineages that had moved from the north to the south many centuries earlier but had not assimilated either in a cultural or social sense with the local inhabitants. Even in the twentieth century southerners contemptuously called them Hakka, the pronunciation of *kejia* (guest) in the dialect of the newcomers. The same term was also applied to other settlers, not only those from the north. In China as a whole there were more than thirty million Hakkas, but their clans were scattered throughout a vast territory of southern China, from Sichuan in the west to Fujian in the east. The imperious local clans (the *bendi*, or "core inhabitants") did not give the migrants access to fertile lands, so the Hakka were forced to live in hill country that was poorly suited to agriculture. Consequently, from generation to generation they were forced to rent land from the old residents who took advantage of the migrants.

Roughly a quarter of the new arrivals had no work and either turned to banditry or begging. Poverty among the Hakka was so great that in most Hakka families even rice was considered a delicacy. Even worse than their indigence was the daily humiliation to which they were exposed. The indigenous people despised them on many counts—because they spoke in their own dialect, because their women never bound their feet, but most of all because ages ago the Hakka "betrayed" their own small homeland. "By leaving their native lands, they showed disrespect to the memory of their ancestors," asserted the *bendi*. Therefore, it is understandable why from time to time the oppressed clans rebelled, and then it was a war to the death, often resulting in the total extermination of the weaker lineage.*

As a rule, neither the rural lumpen proletariat nor the members of the subordinate clans demanded any land redistribution. What they strived for, in a word, was power. They wanted to dominate, humiliate, and grind into the dirt everyone who was even slightly better off than they. The rural lumpen proletariat were simply not interested in the means of production, and the members of the poorer communities were convinced that the only way to solve their problems was by exterminating the wealthy clans to the last person. Unlike in the West, there was no baronial land in China. All land was either worked by the peasant proprietors themselves or rented out. In this situation, a blanket redistribution of land to everyone on an equal basis threatened sharecroppers and poor peasants by inevitably shrinking the parcels of land from which they fed their families, perhaps even leading to the total loss of their land. The only ones inclined to a total redistribution were the destitute paupers, who, unlike the bandit and rural lumpen proletariat, had not yet lost the habit or taste for productive labor. But many of them, too, bound by patriarchal-clan concepts of life, rarely lifted a hand to work on the land of the landlords. In the best—or, more accurately, the worst—case, they identified with the rural lumpen proletariat, attacking the wealthy to grab their money and provisions.

The danger posed by the rural lumpen proletariat and paupers naturally mitigated the interclan contradictions, but it certainly did not eliminate them. Life in China did not turn into an unending clan war because, in addition to the rural lumpen proletariat, all the peasants had another common enemy, the government. Everyone—both landowners and tenants—suffered from the government's taxes, corrupt officials, and militarist oligarchs. When the tax

---

* Hakka rebellions in China were infrequent. The most famous of them was the Taiping Rebellion (1851–1864) as a result of which more than twenty million people perished.

burden was increased, taxpaying landowners were forced to raise rents. Relying upon armed force, the militarists were literally plundering the rural population. Taxes, not simply the land tax, but dozens of supplementary ones, including an irrigation tax, a tax to deal with natural disasters, and dozens of others were levied, often several years in advance.* The peasants were also forced to present gifts to officials, arrange expensive dinners, and fulfill other duties as well. The only immunity was among that stratum of the village elite who because of their family or other ties enjoyed the protection of bureaucrats or army officials.[25]

Obviously, the problems were immense and difficult to resolve. The objective allies of the communists in the Chinese countryside were the rural lumpen proletariat, as Mao had long understood. Thus in January 1926 he had called for the admission of this group into the peasant unions. But he must have known that the rules of the unions forbade admission to vagrants and people of unknown occupation. The peasants did not want an influx of rural lumpen proletarians into their organizations, so the Guomindang, meeting them halfway, even adopted special resolutions closing the doors of the unions to "bandit elements." The rural lumpen proletarians themselves were not clamoring to enter the peasant unions since the union members had pledged not to gamble.[26] In addition to these outcasts of society, the CCP could unconditionally count upon support from the dependent Hakka clans. It could also count upon the sympathy of a part of the poorest peasants who belonged to wealthy lineages, but this sympathy demanded a particularly skillful sort of propaganda. Thus the question the CCP faced was, Either we fight for hegemony in the revolution, in which case we need to stir up the paupers, the rural lumpen proletariat, and the poor lineages against the rest of the peasantry, or we submit to the Guomindang, which is fighting the militarists but defending both the rights of the peasant proprietors and the privileges of the landlords.

It is understandable, therefore, that prior to Stalin's October directive the local communists, including those in Hunan, wanting to establish a future communist dictatorship, consciously lighted the flames of fratricidal warfare in the countryside. Mao himself contributed to the instigation of mass carnage. He rejected the notion that the paupers and rural lumpen proletariat were creating a problem for the united front that was no less serious than that of the "rightist" NRA officers.

In Hunan during the initial period of the Northern Expedition, the peasants were passive and showed little real support for the troops of the NRA. After the establishment of the new government, however, the mass move-

---

* In Hunan province, for example, there were 23 supplementary taxes while in neighboring Hubei there were 61. In the eastern province of Jiangsu there were no less than 147.

ment grew exponentially, due in large part to incitement by the communists. (Toward the end of 1926 some 110 communist organizers but only 20 from the Guomindang were working in the Hunan countryside. In addition, there were many members of the Communist Youth League.)[27] Moreover, the communists' appeals and slogans electrified the atmosphere, facilitating the upsurge of a spontaneous movement even in places communists were physically unable to reach. All the prohibitions barring the rural lumpen proletariat from joining the peasant unions were discarded. The result was that many of the peasant unions were taken over by bandit secret societies such as the Red Spears and the Elder Brother Society, which groups always inspired terror among respectable rural inhabitants.[28] Entire villages, including the members of poor clans, enrolled en masse.

"Class organizations of the peasants" grew like mushrooms after a rain. In July 1926 there were 400,000 members of various peasant organizations in Hunan, and by December that number had grown to more than 1.3 million.[29] Taking advantage of the situation, the rabble took to destroying the homes of the rich, and the communists were gleeful. Here was class struggle in the countryside! "[I]n Hunan, the out-of-work peasants are the bravest and most heroic vanguard," wrote members of a peasant association controlled by the communists. "They fiercely attack the oppressing classes [with methods] such as wearing high hats, parades, fines of money, fines of food and drink, beating, and settling accounts. . . . Now the feudal class has risen in great panic."[30] The same sort of "revolutionary" upsurge was observed in other provinces occupied by the NRA. An explosion of banditry occurred on a massive scale. There were terrible clashes between poor and rich clans in which entire villages were slaughtered.

In December 1926, all this had to be stopped just because the policy of the Comintern had changed. Could one really explain to the "warriors of the revolution" who were drunk on blood that their enemies were really their friends? And who should explain this new party policy? Mao Zedong certainly did not want to get involved with this, but he needed arguments to convince the leadership of the party and, if possible, Stalin that the policy of retreat vis-à-vis the rightists was mistaken. He decided to investigate several districts in Hunan to gather data to confirm his radical views. Several years later, with reference to an analogous situation, he would say, "Without investigating you have no right to speak," unmistakably hinting that other "theorists" would profit by spending less time in their offices.[31]

He spent from January 4 to February 5, 1927, on his investigation and gathered an enormous amount of material on the development of the mass movement in the five districts in Hunan. Among those with whom he spoke were, in his own words, "experienced peasants" and "comrades in the peasant movement." The result was a comprehensive *Report on an Investigation of the Peasant Movement in Hunan,* which he began writing in Changsha. Kai-hui helped him work up the material; it would be difficult to overestimate her contribution. The children were being looked after by a nurse whom Mao and Kaihui had hired in December.

Mao was living not far from the center of Changsha, in the remarkable old district of Wangluyuan. The small wooden house stood on a hill from which one could view majestic Mount Yuelu rising above the opposite bank of the Xiang River. The scenery could inspire any poet to write noble verses about love and bliss. Mao, however, was not feeling poetic. Anger and fury drove his writing brush as he wrote his manifesto in defense of the agrarian revolution of the unfortunate masses.

"I saw and heard many strange things of which I had hitherto been un-aware," he declared in the beginning of his report. Then he presented his main thesis:

> [A]ll criticisms directed against the peasant movement must be speed-ily set right, and the various erroneous measures adopted by the revolutionary authorities concerning the peasant movement must be speedily changed. . . . In a very short time, several hundred million peasants in China's central, southern, and northern provinces will rise like a fierce wind or tempest, a force so swift and violent that no power, however great, will be able to suppress it. They will break through all the trammels that bind them and rush forward along the road to liberation. . . . All revolutionary parties and all revolutionary com-rades will stand before them to be tested, to be accepted or rejected as they decide. To march at their head and lead them? To stand behind them, gesticulating and criticizing them? Or to stand opposite them and oppose them? Every Chinese is free to choose among the three, but by the force of circumstances you are fated to make the choice quickly.

What "peasants" was Mao talking about? Just whom did he wish to lead?

> Those people in the countryside who used to go around in worn-out leather shoes, carry broken umbrellas, wear green gowns, and gamble—in short, all those who were formerly despised and kicked into the gutter by the gentry, who had no social standing, and who were completely deprived of the right to speak, have now dared to lift their heads. Not only have they raised their heads, they have also taken power into their hands. They are now running the township peas-ant associations (the lowest level of peasant associations), and have

turned them into a formidable force. They raise their rough, black-ened hands and lay them on the heads of the gentry. They tether the bad gentry with ropes, crown them with tall paper hats, and parade them through the villages. . . . Every day the coarse, harsh sounds of their denunciation pierce the ears of these gentry. They are giving orders and running everything. They, who used to rank below everyone else, now rank above everybody else—that is what people mean by "turning things upside down."

The well-to-do farmers branded such "peasants" as riffraff. After all, the paupers who flooded the peasant associations mistreated even those villagers who were not very rich. Under various pretexts the paupers did not even let them join the peasant associations. Mao himself reported: "They coined the phrase: 'If he has land, he must be a bully, and all gentry are evil.' In some of the places even those who own 50 mu [8.15 acres] of fields are called local bullies, and those who wear long gowns are called bad gentry." Not only did the lawless mob impose fines and indemnities on everyone whom they arbitrarily labeled "bully" and "evil gentry," but they also beat those who used sedan chairs, believing they exploited carriers. (All well-to-do peasants and landlords used sedan-chairs when they had to travel.) The mob also swarmed into the houses of relatively wealthy neighbors, slaughtered their pigs, and consumed their grain. "They may even loll on the ivory-inlaid beds belonging to the young ladies in the households of the local bullies and bad gentry." The mob did not even shrink from killing the rich. The paupers also took delight in mocking the wealthy and desecrating hallowed sites that had been off-limits to the likes of them. "The women of Baiguo in Hengshan *xian* [county] gathered in force and swarmed into their ancestral temple," Mao wrote, "firmly planted their backsides in the seats and joined in the eating and drinking, while the venerable clan bigwigs had willy-nilly to let them do as they pleased. At another place, where poor peasants had been excluded from temple banquets, a group of them flocked in and ate and drank their fill, while the local bullies and bad gentry and other long-gowned gentlemen all took to their heels in fright."

Mao's conclusion was as follows:

[T]he privileges the feudal landlords have enjoyed for thousands of years are being shattered to pieces. Their dignity and prestige are being completely swept away. With the collapse of the power of the gentry, the peasant associations have now become the sole organs of authority, and "All power to the peasant associations" has become a reality. . . . It is fine. . . . To give credit where credit is due, if we allot ten points to the accomplishments of the democratic revolution, then the achievements of the city dwellers and the military rate only three points, while the remaining seven points should go to the achievements of the peasants in their rural revolution.

Just seven years after maintaining that violent and bloody revolutions were ineffectual, the enthusiastic young man who had believed in liberalism spilled so much hatred onto paper that reading his venomous outpouring is enough to send chills down one's spine:

[A] revolution is not like inviting people to dinner, or writing an essay, or painting a picture, or doing embroidery. . . . A revolution is an uprising, an act of violence whereby one class overthrow the power of another. . . . It was necessary to overthrow completely the authority of the gentry, to knock them down and even stamp them underfoot. . . . To put it bluntly, it is necessary to bring about a brief reign of terror in every rural area. . . . To right the wrong it is necessary to exceed the proper limits; the wrong cannot be righted without doing so.[32]

The report was almost ready, and it was time for Mao to return to Wuhan. Leaving Changsha he hastened toward the unknown. Once again he was going to "swim against the current," but he didn't want to retreat. He had now identified those whose anger born of desperation would help him on his ascent.

He returned to Wuhan on February 12, and four days later delivered a preliminary report to the Central Executive Committee of the CCP. "All actions of the peasants against the feudal landlord class (*dizhu*) are correct. Even if there are some excesses, they are still correct."[33] After his presentation, he again returned to finishing the *Report*. Soon Kaihui arrived with the children and the nurse. They all moved into a spacious house in Wuchang. For a while several of his friends from the party lived there, too.[34]

Toward the end of February Mao finished his *Report* and presented it to the party leadership. The unexpected happened. Not only was the radical document accepted and highly praised by a majority of the members of the Central Bureau of the CCP, but it was also warmly greeted in Moscow itself. In March 1927, the first two chapters of the *Report* (there were three chapters in all) were published in the main party journal, *Guide Weekly*. The complete text began to be published in the Hunan communist weekly *Zhanshi* (Warrior). Excerpts from the *Report* also appeared in the left Guomindang press, and in April a Hankou publisher issued it in a pamphlet edition with a preface by Qu Qiubai. Moreover, in May and June 1927, the first two chapters of the *Report* were reprinted in Russian and English in *Kommunisticheskii Internatsional* (Communist International), the political organ of the ECCI. Following this the same chapters were published in *Revoliutsionnyi Vostok* (Revolutionary East), the organ of the Soviet Asian Studies Association. Finally, in May 1927, Bukharin, who was then Stalin's closest associate and in essence the number-two man in the Kremlin, gave a positive assessment of Mao's *Report* at the Eighth Plenum of the ECCI.

There was a simple explanation for this reaction. While Mao was traveling in Hunan, Moscow decided to halt the retreat in view of the intensifying power struggle between Tang Shengzhi and Chiang Kai-shek. The CCP was instructed not to fear the possibility of sharpening class conflict in the countryside. Stalin pressured the Seventh Enlarged Plenum of the ECCI (November 22–December 16, 1926) to adopt an aggressive resolution on the situation in China. Although this document did not yet refer to an imminent agrarian revolution, it spoke of the need to place the question in "a prominent place in the program of the national revolutionary movement." It even emphasized there was no need to fear this might weaken the anti-imperialist united front.[35] The new tactics were embodied in a concrete directive to China, sent to Borodin on December 17, 1926.[36] Moreover, exactly two months later Stalin attempted to launch an offensive policy inside the Guomindang. The general strike of Shanghai workers on February 19, 1927, under the leadership of the CCP, forced his hand. Within three days the strike had grown into an armed uprising against the militarist Sun Chuanfang. Even though it was suppressed two days later it seemed that the general situation in the country had become sharply radicalized.

In February the Politburo of the Soviet Communist Party facilitated the prompt return to China of Wang Jingwei, leader of the Guomindang "leftists," in the hope of strengthening the "leftist" faction within the Guomindang. Wang returned to China via Moscow, where Comintern officials were ready to discuss Chinese affairs with him.[37] The new tactics led to the following:

> Energetically place the peasant, petty bourgeois, and worker base under the left Guomindang . . . aim to get rid of the Guomindang rightists, discredit them politically and systematically remove them from leading positions . . . aim to take over important positions in the army . . . intensify the work of Guomindang and communist cells in the army . . . work toward arming the workers and peasants, *transform the local peasant committees into de facto organs of power and armed self-defense*. . . . A policy of voluntary semi-legality is unacceptable; *the communist party must not act as a brake on the mass movement*. . . . Otherwise the revolution will face enormous danger.[38]

In brief, Mao was lucky. His *Report* concurred with Moscow's new resolutions. Yet, it was too early to celebrate. The political situation in Wuhan remained unstable, and the radical peasant movement, of course, did not help to normalize it. In the spring of 1927, it burst all bounds and, in the words of Zhang Guotao, one of the few members of the CCP Central Executive Committee who was skeptical of Mao's *Report,* the peasant movement reached a "stage of madness." No less extreme were the actions of members of the so-called workers' pickets that were operating in a number of cities. The riffraff that flocked into these organizations even attacked the relatives of influential Guomindang members and communists. In Changsha the son-in-law of Tan Yankai was arrested and fined even though Tan had distanced himself from Chiang Kai-shek in February 1927 and gone over to the "left" in Wuhan. Even the father of General Tang Shengzhi, who was considered the bulwark of the "left" Guomindang, was subjected to persecution.* It comes as no surprise, then, that General Tang, who visited Changsha in February 1927, let slip the following irritated remark in an informal conversation with the Japanese consul: "[A]lthough the provincial government is temporarily in the hands of the communists, they and the strife they have brought about will be dealt with and their excesses curbed. As a result their regime will end and a new government will come in." [39]

The Third Plenum of the Guomindang CEC, held in Wuhan from March 10 to 17, 1927, added fuel to the fire. Responding to pressure from the "leftists" and the communists, the plenum stripped General Chiang of all his top posts in the party, including the chairmanship of the Standing Committee of the CEC. It also resolved to reshuffle the composition of the National government and offer two posts to communists. Mao Zedong, who, along with the other five candidate members of the CEC, had been accorded voting rights, actively participated in the meetings of the plenum and spoke several times during the debates. He and two Guomindang "leftists" helped draft the resolutions on the peasant question and the plenum's appeal to peasants. He was responsible for their radical tone, especially of the latter document, which directly summoned the peasants to agrarian revolution, that is, to the further development of the peasant movement not only against "warlords, imperialists, local bullies and bad gentry," but also against the privileges of the entire "feudal landlord class." [40]

Chiang Kai-shek, not present at the plenum, was forced to declare his support for its decisions, but he was simply waiting for the moment to strike a decisive blow against the entire "Wuhan gang." The Wuhan group was likewise waiting for an opportune moment to deal with Chiang Kai-shek. Immediately following the plenum they issued a secret directive to General Cheng

---

* Persistent rumors circulated in Wuhan that in Liling county, Hunan, the peasant union had executed the father of Li Lisan, a rural teacher, as a *tuhao* and *lieshen.* Fortunately, this information proved to be wrong.

Qian, who commanded NRA troops on the right bank of the Yangzi, to arrest Chiang Kai-shek at the first opportunity.[41] Thus, following the plenum the polarization within the Guomindang only intensified.

Suddenly a new popular uprising erupted in Shanghai on March 21, and this time it succeeded in toppling the local warlord Sun Chuanfang. On the evening of March 22, NRA troops entered Shanghai, which had already been liberated by workers' militias. The next day Nanjing was taken. This was all so unexpected that for an instant everyone in Wuhan thought that the victory of the Guomindang was imminent. On April 1, Wang Jingwei returned from Europe to liberated Shanghai, where he was warmly greeted by the public. On April 10 he arrived in Wuhan.

Like everyone else, Mao rejoiced at the successes of the GMD army, but he remained focused on the countryside. In early March the Central Peasant Training Institute was established in Wuchang and the Guomindang CEC appointed him one of its leaders. He was constantly busy, preparing lesson plans, hiring instructors, dealing with financial matters, and teaching his favorite courses on "The Peasant Question" and "Educational Work in the Countryside." He also scheduled the daily life of the more than eight hundred students, three times as many as there had been in Canton.[42] On top of that, he continued to work in the CCP's Committee on the Peasant Movement, delivered lectures, and provided reports to the General Political Administration of the NRA and other organizations. In late March, Mao was chosen as among the leaders of the newly created All-China Peasant Association, at a preparatory conference in Hankou to convene a National Congress of Peasant Unions, and headed its Organizational Department. The All China association brought together peasant unions operating in seventeen provinces throughout the country.[43]

At this conference, in the presence of Peng Pai, Fang Zhimin, who was one of the organizers of the peasant movement in Jiangxi province, and "two Russian communists, York and Volen,"* Mao advocated "a widespread redistribution of land." Apparently no one objected to such an extreme project. The members approved a resolution endorsing Mao's proposal and notified the Central Executive Committee of the CCP. The conference requested that the Chinese communists examine this question at their forthcoming Fifth Congress.[44] On April 2, a meeting of the Standing Committee of the Guomin-

---

* These were the China specialists Evgenii Sigismundovich Iolk (1900–1937 or 1942), who worked in China under the pseudonyms Johan and Johanson, and Mikhail Volin (real name Semen Natanovich Belen'kii (1896–1938). In 1926–27 they were on Borodin's staff and were working on agrarian issues in China. In early 1927 they even published a two-volume documentary study in English, edited by Borodin, called *The Peasant Question in Guangdong*. Moreover, Volin reviewed Mao Zedong's "Analysis of Classes in Chinese Society" in *Canton*, the journal of the Soviet advisers.

dang CEC included Mao in the membership of the Land Committee of the CEC to help in working out measures to implement "the transfer of land to the peasants." Everything seemed to be going his way.

Just then Mao's family had a new addition. On April 4, 1927, Kaihui gave birth to their third son. His father first named him Anmin ("People Who Reach the Shore of Socialism"), but then changed the name to Anlong ("Dragon Who Reaches the Shore of Socialism"). By "dragon" he meant the peasant movement, which, like the mighty hero of Chinese folk tales, "shook Heaven and Earth."

Soon, however, disturbing news began to reach Wuhan. On March 24, Nanjing, which had been occupied by troops of the NRA, was subjected to shelling from British and American ships in response to attacks against the residences of foreigners during which several persons, including the British consul, had been wounded. Chiang Kai-shek, who arrived in Shanghai soon afterward, was obviously preparing for a repetition of the events of March 20, 1926, but this time with a much tougher ending. Voitinsky had already informed Moscow of Chiang's intentions as far back as late February.[45] Clashes between units of Chiang Kai-shek's army and armed worker and peasant formations increased in frequency. In a number of places Chiang's forces crushed trade union organizations. Stalin, afraid of provoking Chiang Kai-shek, again retreated. In late March 1927, the Soviet Politburo decided on new concessions to Chiang. Directives were sent to the Central Executive Committee of the CCP "to avoid clashes with the National Army and its leaders in Shanghai at any price."[46] But it was already too late. Stalin's policy was totally bankrupt. On April 12, having secured the support of prominent Shanghai businessmen and the chiefs of the municipal mafia groups, the Qingbang (Green Gang), Chiang Kai-shek unleashed a bloody white terror in Shanghai and other parts of east China. As a result of the joint actions of Chiang's soldiers and the gangsters, more than five thousand people were executed and about as many arrested during just the first two days of the coup, April 12 and April 13.

Ironically, April 12 was the day that Mao spoke at a session of the Land Committee of the Guomindang CEC, calling for the prompt implementation of agrarian revolution. Perturbed by the outbreak of riffraff banditry, Chiang Kai-shek's officers were crushing the communists, but Mao continued to insist upon the radicalization of the movement. He apparently rejected the new Stalinist directive. "The so-called confiscation of land," he declared, "simply means not paying rent, that's all. At present the peasant movement in Hunan and Hubei has already reached the point where the peasants themselves have stopped paying rent and have seized power. It is first necessary to solve the agrarian problem in reality and then work out the legal framework."[47]

News about the events in Shanghai only poured oil on the fire. On April 15 came news of an anticommunist coup in Canton. The local generals had

chosen the path of Chiang Kai-shek. Three days later Chiang Kai-shek proclaimed the establishment of a new National government in Nanjing. Mao became more agitated than ever. At meetings of the Land Committee, and with
the support of several Guomindang extreme "leftists," Mao began drafting a
resolution aimed at solving the agrarian question. His draft was criticized,
however, by Wang Jingwei, Tan Yankai, and General He Jian, who deemed it
necessary to avoid "excesses" in the peasant movement, so all the work done
by the committee was in vain.[48] The Land Committee was forced to note, "The
problems are so great and intricate that without [analysis] of materials on the
situation in various provinces and without taking into account various points
of view it will be impossible to resolve them. . . . A fundamental resolution of
the agrarian problem is not within the competence of [this] C[E]C meeting."[49]
Mao was extremely dissatisfied with this outcome. "The Guomindang leaders
cover up their complete unwillingness and inability to satisfy the demands of
the peasants with empty, puffed-up phrases," is how he summed things up.[50]

To a degree Mao's mood accorded with Stalin's new directives that the
Comintern had sent to China shortly after Chiang Kai-shek's coup. Stalin now
demanded that the CCP effect the prompt radicalization of the Guomindang
"left," and that the Chinese communists do everything possible to urgently
"push" the supporters of Wang Jingwei toward organizing a real social transformation. In implementing this new policy Stalin invested particular hopes
in the Comintern's new representative in China, the Indian communist M. N.
Roy, a member of the ECCI who had been sent to China in March 1927. The
energetic Roy, who arrived in Hankou in early April, quickly began to express
a series of radical ideas to Borodin and the leaders of the CCP.[51] (The Central
Executive Committee of the Communist Party had relocated to Hankou after
Chiang Kai-shek's coup.) Naturally, Roy immediately came into conflict with
Borodin, who intuitively grasped that any extremist demarche on the part of
the communists could precipitate the "leftist" Guomindang generals into the
anticommunist camp. Borodin was supported by Chen Duxiu, who also understood that an attempt to implement Stalin's new policy could only result in
a bloody denouement. After April 12, Chen "spent whole days thinking and
worrying and working diligently; but the ogre of melancholy always held him
tight."[52] He knew he faced a reckoning with Stalin for everything that would
inevitably come to pass regarding the Communist Party. Perhaps better than
anyone else in the CCP, Chen understood that Stalin's policy in China, which
he had had to follow all these years, was doomed to failure from the very beginning. "He tried his best to produce a remedial program; but his strength was
inadequate, and no miracles dropped from heaven," recalled Zhang Guotao.[53]

In these circumstances, the Fifth Congress of the Communist Party began
its sessions in Wuchang on April 27, two weeks after the Shanghai coup. It
started off as a grand show. Many leaders of the "left" Guomindang and the

National government, including Wang Jingwei, Tan Yankai, Xu Qian, and Sun Ke, came to greet the communists. There were lots of speeches. This was the largest congress the CCP had held so far, with eighty delegates and more than twenty guests gathered in a hall festooned with banners and pennants. The delegates represented 57,967 members of the party. (During the Fourth Congress in January 1925, the CCP had only 994 members.) The growth in the ranks was impressive indeed, but the data announced at the congress did not take into account that in the two largest cities, Shanghai and Canton, the party organizations of the CCP had been almost wholly destroyed on the eve of the congress. There was nothing much to celebrate. The situation was catastrophic, and there was nothing the congress could do about it. This is how Mao remembered the sessions:

> When the Fifth Conference was convened in Wuhan . . . the Party was still under the domination of Chên Tu-hsiu [Chen Duxiu]. Although Chiang Kai-shek had already led the counter-revolution and begun his attacks on the Communist Party in Shanghai and Nanking, Chên was still for moderation and concessions to the Wuhan Kuomintang [Guomindang]. . . . I was very dissatisfied with the Party policy then, especially towards the peasant movement. . . . But Chên Tu-hsiu violently disagreed. . . . Consequently, the Fifth Conference, held on the eve of the crisis of the Great Revolution, failed to pass an adequate land programme. My opinions, which called for rapid intensification of the agrarian struggle, were not even discussed, for the Central Committee, also dominated by Chên Tu-hsiu, refused to bring them up for consideration. The Conference dismissed the land problem by defining a landlord as "a peasant who owned over 500 *mou* [82 acres] of land"—a wholly inadequate and unpractical basis on which to develop the class struggle.[54]

Not everyone in the inner circle of party leadership supported Chen Duxiu. As always, Qu Qiubai was on Mao's side. During the Congress Qu had distributed a brochure, "Disputed Issues in the Chinese Revolution," that was directed against "right opportunism." He didn't attack Chen by name, but the entire work was pointed against Peng Shuzhi, who was close to Chen, and who as director of the Propaganda Department fiercely defended the policy of concessions. Mao's closest friend Cai Hesen likewise heatedly defended Mao.

With the support of such influential people, the Central Bureau chose Mao as a candidate member of the Central Committee of the CCP. (The congress passed a resolution renaming the highest organ of the party from Central Executive Committee to Central Committee.) Mao occupied the thirty-second position in the party hierarchy and after the congress he no longer headed the Committee on the Peasant Movement.

The "betrayal" by Chiang Kai-shek and the Cantonese generals had a deeply personal as well as public and political meaning for Mao. During the April 12 coup, one of his brothers, Zemin, was in Shanghai, and his other brother, Zetan, in Canton. Mao could not help but worry about them. Zemin had been working in the proletarian district of Zhabei since November 1925, after graduating from the Peasant Movement Training Institute in Canton. He headed the Publication and Literature Distribution Department of the Central Committee of the CCP and served as director of the party printing house and of its bookstore. He was living in Shanghai under the pseudonym Yang Ze with his second wife, a young departmental coworker named Qian Xijun.

As for Zetan, in April 1927 he was working in the peasant union in Guangdong. He was also married a second time. In October 1925, his first spouse, Zhao Xiangui, on assignment from the party, had left Changsha for Moscow to study at the Comintern's newly established educational institution for Chinese revolutionaries, the Sun Yat-sen University of the Toilers of China.[55] (One hundred and eighteen young Chinese communists and members of the Guomindang, including Chiang Ching-kuo, Chiang Kai-shek's sixteen-year-old son from his first marriage, also left then for the "Red Mecca.") Zetan remained in Canton, and he was not one to live alone. In the summer of 1926, sixteen-year-old, round-faced Zhou Wennan, Zetan's close acquaintance from the Socialist Youth League, came with her mother from Changsha to Canton at his request. She had already caught the eye of Mao's younger brother a year before Zetan's wife had gone to Moscow. There in Canton, after four or five months, they got married. (At this time the revolutionary youth paid no heed to such archaic concepts as official divorce, so that once his wife left for Moscow, Zetan felt completely free.) Half a year after their marriage, his new flame joined the Communist Youth League, and soon after, the CCP. In April 1927 she was five months pregnant.

Happily, everything turned out well for Mao's brothers and their wives. They managed to elude the "white" generals who were in power in Shanghai and Canton, and ultimately wound up in Wuchang, where Mao Zedong and Kaihui greeted them warmly. Soon after his arrival, Zemin began working as the managing editor of the left Guomindang newspaper *Hankou minguo ribao* (Hankou Republic daily), and Zetan, with the rank of captain, was sent to the Political Department of the Fourth Corps of the NRA, which corps had the largest number of communists.[56]

Meanwhile, the situation continued to deteriorate badly for the CCP. At the end of April it was reported from Beijing that on April 28, Li Dazhao had been executed by order of a military court. He had been arrested on April 6 by

Chinese police not far from the Soviet legation in the territory of the Legation Quarter. In addition to Li Dazhao, nineteen leaders of the Northern Bureau of the CCP and of the Guomindang, among them one woman, were tortured and executed.[57] Mao was grief-stricken. He had always treated Professor Li as his own teacher. Two and a half weeks later, on May 13, the Fourteenth Independent Division under General Xia Douyin, which had been considered totally loyal, rose up against the Wuhan government. General Xia attacked Wuhan and was repelled only through superhuman efforts. (Incidentally, Mao Zedong took part in the defense of Wuhan; he organized armed self-defense units from auditors of the Central Peasant Training Institute.)[58] On May 21 a new uprising occurred, organized by Xu Kexiang, the commander of one of the regiments of the NRA stationed in Changsha, who unleashed a bloody bacchanalia in the capital of Hunan.

Unable to restrain his irritation, Stalin demanded the impossible of the CCP, namely, to direct the "left" Guomindang to unleash an agrarian revolution in all provinces, take measures to organize "eight or ten divisions" of revolutionary peasants and workers "as the Wuhan guard," and to convince the supporters of Wang Jingwei that if they did not "learn to be revolutionary Jacobins, they would perish for the people and the revolution."[59] Stalin simply failed to understand the real correlation of forces in China, and therefore he insisted,

> Without an agrarian revolution victory is impossible. . . . We firmly stand for the seizure of land from below. . . . We need to draw into the Central Committee of the Guomindang additional new peasant and worker leaders from below. . . . We must change the current structure of the Guomindang. We must refresh the upper echelon of the Guomindang and recruit into it new leaders emerging from the agrarian revolution, and we must expand the periphery with millions from the workers and peasant unions. . . . We must end our dependence on unreliable generals. . . . It is time to act. We must punish the bastards.[60]

According to Zhang Guotao, when one of Stalin's telegrams was read at a meeting of the Politburo of the Central Committee, "everyone present had the reaction of not knowing whether to cry or to laugh. . . . How could we talk at this time of eliminating unreliable generals?"[61] Chen Duxiu could only shake his head. "Earlier Zinoviev ordered us to help the bourgeoisie, and now Stalin tells us to carry out an agrarian revolution in the next twenty-four hours."[62]

In this troubled time Mao Zedong gathered his brothers together to discuss the situation. To avoid upsetting Kaihui, they pretended to play mahjong; in fact, they were deciding what to do next. Realizing that Wang Jingwei would soon follow in the footsteps of Chiang Kai-shek, Mao said, "We cannot wait around until they kill us; we must either depart with the army [just then elements of the Fourth Corps were commencing a campaign against Jiujiang, southeast of Wuchang on the Jiangxi-Hubei border] or we must return to Hunan." It was decided that the older brothers would ask to be sent on a mission to Hunan while Zetan left with the Fourth Corps. They also resolved that Zetan's pregnant wife, along with Kaihui and Mao's sons, would leave Wuchang for Changsha as soon as possible.[63]

Soon after this meeting Mao Zedong asked Chen Duxiu to send him to Hunan to try to salvage whatever might still be rescued. Cai Hesen supported Mao's request, suggesting that the Hunan party committee be reorganized with Mao as its secretary. Chen, however, wanted to send Mao to do party work in Sichuan, but Mao refused. On June 24, the Politburo Standing Committee adopted Cai's resolution, and Mao left for Changsha, soon joined by Zemin.

Meanwhile, the united front was unraveling in front of everyone's eyes. In mid-June it became known that Feng Yuxiang, whom the Guomindang "leftists" and the Comintern considered one of the most reliable military commanders, was making active preparations to follow the path of Chiang Kai-shek. A few days later Feng carried out a coup in Zhengzhou, the capital of Henan. In Wuhan itself the situation was growing increasingly complicated. Business was paralyzed, shops were closed, and factories shut down. Wuhan was being threatened from all sides. The dissatisfaction of the population steadily increased, prices spiraled upward, inflation grew, the political scene was chaotic. Most members of the CCP Central Committee had the sensation of "lingering in a leaky house with a rain-storm raging at night."[64]

Under these circumstances, ten days after the resolution about party reorganization in Hunan, Chen Duxiu summoned Mao back to Wuhan. In Mao's words, Chen was afraid that Mao's radical actions would trigger an uprising by Tang Shengzhi.[65] Chen still hoped to keep things from falling apart; he convened an enlarged meeting of the Central Committee and the Politburo at Borodin's house in Hankou, and discussed the situation with M. N. Roy and Borodin. But all was in vain. Under pressure from Moscow he was forced to step down on July 12; just three days later Wang Jingwei broke with the communists. The defeat of the Chinese Communist Party and with it the Stalinist line on China became a reality.

Mao was shocked. What was he thinking at the time? That everything might be saved if only the party gave the land to the peasants? That the peasants and workers should be armed? That the party should leave the Guomindang? Probably all three of these. Perhaps he remembered how happy he had been when the troops of the NRA had taken Shanghai and Nanjing. Or perhaps how he had rejoiced when his beloved "Little Dawn" (Kaihui) had given birth to their third son? Back then, in March and April, everything had seemed possible, everything had symbolized victory. It was then, in the fullness of spring, replete with joyful hopes about the future, that he had ascended the Yellow Crane Tower, which thrust up into the sky not far from his home. For a long time he had gazed into the distance at the flood tide of the boundless Yangzi River. Like hundreds of poets before him, he could not contain his feelings, which formed themselves into verses:

> *Nine vast rivers rush through central China,**
> *an iron line plunges north to south.†*
> *Rain, mist, gray, immense gray.*
> *Turtle and Snake Mountains‡*
> *Block the great Yangtze [Yangzi] River.*
>
> *Where has the Yellow Crane flown?*
> *Only the place for travelers remains.§*
> *Lifting the cup of wine to the pouring River,*
> *my heart's tide surges wave-high.*[66]

---

* The reference is to the nine tributaries of the Yangzi.

† The reference is to the Beijing–Hankou railroad and the Wuchang–Changsha railroad, which intersect in Wuhan.

‡ Turtle Mountain and Snake Mountain are two hills on opposite sides of the Yangzi. The former is located in Hanyang, the latter in Wuchang. It is on Snake Mountain that the Yellow Crane Tower rises.

§ The legend goes that long ago in Wuchang a young man named Xin had a wine shop. One day Xin, a well-known and well-liked fellow, gave wine to a wandering Daoist monk. In gratitude on the wall of the shop the monk drew a picture of a crane that turned out to be magical. Every time when someone clapped their hands the crane would perform graceful dances. The young man was ineffably happy for now his shop was always crowded with people who wanted to gaze upon the miraculous crane while downing a cup or two. But after ten years the Daoist monk again showed up in Wuchang. He dropped in to Xin's shop, drew forth a flute, played upon it, mounted the crane, and flew off to heaven. To commemorate these happenings Xin's family built the Yellow Crane Tower upon the site of the shop. According to historical data, the tower was built in 223 CE.

THE PATH TO THE SOVIETS

The main cause of the defeat of the Chinese communists was that throughout all the years of its existence the CCP had remained tightly bound to the Soviet Communist Party and under its powerful control and ideological pressure. Chen Duxiu and the Central Committee lacked freedom of maneuver. In everything they had to ask for instructions from Moscow or, if the situation demanded an immediate resolution, from its representatives such as Voitinsky, Maring, Borodin, or Roy. The Russian bosses, with little understanding of Chinese problems, scanted the opinions of their Chinese colleagues and issued directives concerning core questions about the Chinese revolution. Only the Chinese were bothered. The Comintern moguls prided themselves on being specialists on the revolutionary movements of all countries. Zhang Guotao wrote, "[W]e resented this procedure, feeling that it was unreasonable; but since from the beginning the CC of the CCP had followed the tradition of paying respect to Moscow, we accepted it with silent resignation. . . . The directives of the Comintern were complied with in all matters whether large or small."[1] These directives were often simply impossible to implement. A particularly critical situation developed now when Stalin demanded that the CCP carry out a decisive attack against the "left" Guomindang.

Another factor that accelerated the defeat of the CCP at this time was the explosion of mostly communist-inspired pauper–lumpen proletariat terror in the countryside. The barbaric action of crazed crowds that pillaged and killed both the innocent and the guilty was undoubtedly a serious factor in undermining the united front. These actions were mostly aimed against the petty and medium landlords who were the foundation of the Guomindang, including the "left." Thus the uprising of Guomindang officers whose families had suffered from the "red" terror was inevitable.

A "white" terror, no less deadly than the "red" terror, now shook Chinese society. The officer corps of the NRA, supported by peasant self-defense forces (*mintuan*) and members of secret societies that had swung over to their side, carried out the cruelest measures, dreaming only of revenge. In Hunan, Hubei,

Jiangxi, Guangdong, and other Guomindang-controlled provinces, rivers of blood flowed. In just the twenty days following Xu Kexiang's coup, more than ten thousand persons were killed in Changsha and surrounding areas.[2] Among the victims were many local leaders of the CCP and the peasant associations. Another ten thousand were executed in the counties of Xiangtan (Mao's native place) and Changde. In Xiangtan, the executioners "beheaded the chief of the . . . general labor union and kicked his head about with their feet, then filled his belly with kerosene and burned his body." Peasants in Hubei who belonged to wealthy clans exterminated entire villages with the help of Guomindang troops. They gouged out the eyes of victims, cut out their tongues, cut off their heads, smashed their bones, drew and quartered them, cut off their legs, doused them with kerosene and burned them alive, and branded them with red-hot irons. "In the case of women, they would run string through their breasts and parade them around naked in public, or simply hack them into pieces." In just three counties of Hubei thousands of people were killed in the first weeks after the coup.[3]

From a Western perspective, revenge often took the most improbable forms. Thus General He Jian, whose father had been arrested by the peasant union, sent soldiers to Shaoshan in late 1927 to dig up the bones of Mao's parents from their grave and scatter them on the slopes of the mountains. According to ancient popular belief, this was supposed to have a devastating effect on Mao's own feng shui. He Jian's troops, however, didn't know where Mao's parents were buried so they had to ask for help from the local peasants, who flatly refused to cooperate. When the soldiers threatened them, one local person simply deceived them. He led the punishment squad to the grave of the ancestors of a local *tuhao,* which they then proceeded to exhume.[4]

The weakly organized and poorly armed peasant unions collapsed at the first onslaught of Guomindang troops. The peasants who had joined the unions out of fear of the rural lumpen elements that controlled them had no desire to fight against the Guomindang armies for interests that were not their own. At the first favorable opportunity they threw down their pikes and fled. Xu Kexiang was able to establish control over the entire Changsha area even though he had only a thousand troops at his disposal because the multimillion-member peasant unions turned out to be "paper tigers."[5]

In this time of troubles, Mao turned out be almost the only major leader of the CCP who assessed the situation soberly. This was his most important contribution to the communist rise to power. His brief trip to Hunan in late June and early July 1927 convinced him that the communists' struggle for power in China could succeed only on condition that the Communist Party create its own military force. All of the political games, the united front, and the mass movement were no more than a farce if that was forgotten. In a militarized China, "political power is obtained from the barrel of the gun."[6] One should not play at rebellion, but retreat in order to organize a Red Army. Where would the communist troops come from? Mao had answered this a long time ago. Naturally, it was those who were capable of "the most steadfast struggle," the paupers and rural lumpen proletariat.

At a meeting of the Politburo Standing Committee in Hankou on July 4, Mao, just back from Hunan, suggested that one possible way to save the party was to order the Hunan peasant union to "go to the mountains," because in the mountains "it would be possible to establish a military base." "As soon as the situation changes [Mao was hinting at the inevitable coup by Wang Jingwei] we will be powerless if we don't have armed forces." Right after the meeting he discussed this question with his closest friend, Cai Hesen. "We can't sit around and wait until somebody works everything out," he said excitedly. Cai was suffering from asthma, but he shared Mao's indignation. On Mao's initiative he promptly wrote a pointed letter to the Standing Committee of the Politburo demanding that it "work up a military plan."[7]

This initiative failed. Chen Duxiu was still in power, and his depression peaked in early July. One more woe was added to his burden. On July 4, his eldest son, Chen Yannian, was executed by the Guomindang in Shanghai. After this Chen faced "an expanse of darkness, and so he himself would have to resort to the course of giving up his position to more capable persons," wrote Zhang Guotao, who was precisely one of those "capable persons."[8]

After Chen's retirement, the new party leadership (Provisional Bureau of the Central Committee) was headed by Mao's protector, Qu Qiubai.* Happily for Mao the leaders reexamined his idea of "going to the mountains," but approved it only as a backup. In the critical situation of summer 1927 the communists needed to retreat. Any attempts to organize a near-term counterattack could only result in new victims, but most of the leaders of the CCP, including Qu Qiubai, still seething with anger, were inclined to action, however foolhardy it was. In mid-August they decided to mount a series of armed ventures in rural Hunan, Hubei, Guangdong, and Jiangxi as well as in the famous Fourth Corps of the Guomindang army. Their desire to spill Guomindang blood was overwhelming.[9]

The Comintern itself insisted upon the speedy organization of armed uprisings. For the time being its directives spoke not of purely communist ventures, but rather about the need to "raise the masses of the left Guomindang against the upper leadership." Moscow emphasized that "[o]nly if the revolutionary transformation of the Guomindang turns out in reality to be hopeless, and if this failure coincides with a new and serious upsurge of revolution," only then would it be necessary to "build soviets."[10] In other words, Moscow

---

* In addition to Qu, the new leadership was made up of Zhang Guotao, Zhang Tailei, Li Weihan, Li Lisan, and Zhou Enlai.

demanded an uprising against the "traitor" Wang Jingwei under the slogans of the "left" Guomindang.

Such directives must have seemed absurd to any sensible person, but the leadership of the CCP was forced to accept them. The party's catastrophic defeat had not emancipated it from Stalin's influence. On the contrary, the weakened CCP became even more dependent upon Moscow as Stalin laid most of the blame on the CCP leadership. "There is *not a single* Marxist mind in the Central Committee [of the CCP] capable of understanding the underpinning (the social underpinning) of the events now occurring," he wrote to his comrades Vyacheslav Molotov and Nikolai Bukharin in early July 1927. At one point Stalin even mused about fortifying the CCP with a special system of "party advisors" attached to the CCP Central Committee and each provincial party organization. From Stalin's perspective, these "nannies" were "necessary at this stage because of the weakness, shapelessness and political amorphousness, and lack of qualification of the current Central Committee [of the Chinese Communist Party]."[11]

At the end of June, Stalin had sent one of his most trusted confidants, a Georgian named Lominadze, to China to replace M. N. Roy.[12] He no longer trusted either Roy or Borodin. Bliukher served as the conduit through which Moscow supplied its Chinese wards with money until the end of August, when the duties of "financier" passed to Lominadze after Bliukher's departure.[13] Stalin's new emissary had arrived on July 23 and immediately held talks with Qu Qiubai and Zhang Guotao, who many years later remembered them as "the worst conversation."

Vissarion V. Lominadze was a tough character who had joined the revolution at the age of fifteen. A professional revolutionary, he struck everyone who knew him by his disdain for death—his own or others. He entered Stalin's inner circle very early and with his support rose quickly to become a leading figure in the Comintern. Just shy of thirty, he had already savored and been corrupted by the taste of bureaucratic power. Around six feet tall, solidly built, and with thick black hair, Lominadze was an impressive figure even though he blinked very often, whether from nearsightedness or some other reason.[14] Yet Lominadze's bureaucratic manner and his habit of ordering the CCP leaders about alienated them immediately. Nikolai (or Werner, the two names he used in China) was utterly devoid of Eastern politesse, and he immediately unleashed upon Qu Qiubai and Zhang Guotao a torrent of baseless accusations. "Lominadze first stated that he was the plenipotentiary of the Comintern, ordered here to correct the many mistakes committed in the past by the personnel of the Comintern and the CC of the CCP in the Chinese revolution," wrote Zhang Guotao. Lominadze "immediately declared that the CC of the CCP had committed the serious error of rightist opportunism and had violated the directives of the Comintern."[15] He demanded that an emergency party conference be convened as soon as possible to reorganize the party leadership.

Naturally, this demand infuriated Qu Qiubai and Zhang Guotao, but what could they do? Comintern discipline bound them hand and foot, and they were desperately in need of Moscow's money. Moreover, they needed Soviet arms for the uprisings they were planning. Luckily, just then the Soviet Politburo adopted a resolution to provide assistance to the CCP, "enough to supply about one corps." They allotted 15,000 rifles, 10 million rounds of ammunition, thirty machine guns, and four mountain artillery with 2,000 shells, to the tune of 1.1 million rubles. The arms were supposed to be shipped from Vladivostok to a Chinese port that the communists would seize as a result of their armed uprisings.[16] Therefore, Qu and Zhang had to swallow Lominadze's insult.

That same evening the Central Committee received a letter from the local provincial committee in Hunan. The situation in the province continued to deteriorate despite efforts by the secretary of the party committee, Yi Lirong, an old friend of Mao's, to stabilize it somehow. "After the departure of our secretary Mao Zedong . . . the situation in all departments of the provincial committee has become critical," wrote members of the party committee; "we are hoping [only] for the return of Mao Zedong."[17] But Qu Qiubai did not want Mao to leave, because he required his support at the upcoming party conference. He needed Mao as an authority on the peasant question. In late July and early August feverish preparations for armed peasant actions were under way in the Central Committee, and, of course, Mao took part in the planning. The idea was for poor peasants to rise up directly against the landlords during the autumn harvest, when the tenants were theoretically obligated to settle accounts with the landowners. The communists wanted to seduce the poor peasants with the simple, albeit illegal, idea of not paying their debts.

Meanwhile, on the night of July 31–August 1 a carefully prepared CCP uprising took place among NRA troops quartered in Nanchang. These were independent units of the Second Front Army of the NRA, under the overall command of the "left" Guomindang general Zhang Fakui. General Zhang himself, of course, did not participate in the action. Just two days earlier he had attended a meeting of "left" Guomindang members where it was decided to purge the communists from the Second Front Army. Party leadership of the uprising was exercised by Zhou Enlai, as always self-disciplined, energetic, and businesslike, assisted by Zhang Guotao, Peng Pai, and others. (At the time Zhou headed the Military Committee of the CCP Central Committee.) In direct command of the mutineers were the commander of the Twentieth Corps, He Long, an ex-bandit from western Hunan who was now sympathetic to the communists; Ye Ting, a communist and former commander of the famous Independent Regiment of the Fourth Corps; and the head of the Municipal Political Security Bureau, the commander of the Training Regiment of the Ninth Corps, the communist Zhu De.

The twenty thousand or so insurgents succeeded in seizing the city, but they did not intend to remain there. Following the plan developed by the Provisional Bureau of the CCP Central Committee, they were supposed to set off immediately to attack Guangdong and proclaim a new revolutionary government there. On August 3, the insurgent troops, reorganized into the so-called Second National Revolutionary Army under the overall command of He Long, left the city of Nanchang, but their advance south was difficult. In late September and early October 1927, the insurgents suffered a crushing defeat near Swatow in eastern Guangdong, where they had gone to receive arms from the USSR. After this their army disintegrated. He Long fled to Hong Kong; Ye Ting and Peng Pai escaped to Lufeng county in Guangdong province to establish a military base; and Zhu De led a thousand men on a difficult march to the Guangdong-Jiangxi border.

Mao Zedong did not take part in preparations for the Nanchang Uprising, but once he learned about it he was eager to join the insurgents. In early August he even proposed to the Central Committee that he organize a "peasant army" under his command to aid He Long. On August 3, Qu Qiubai promptly appointed him secretary of the Special South Hunan Committee, but later that same day Qu revoked his decision. Further reflection suggested that Mao's plan was unrealistic.[18]

So the "King of Hunan" had to stay in Wuhan. Soon, on August 7, he took part in the Extraordinary Conference of the Central Committee of the CCP, held under conditions of utmost secrecy in the apartment of one of the Soviet advisers to the Wuhan government, Mikhail Razumov, who with his wife was living in the territory of the former Russian concession in Hankou in a quiet neighborhood inhabited mostly by foreigners. (The USSR maintained relations with the Guomindang for a while after the rupture of the united front between the GMD and the CCP, and there were Soviet representatives and even consulates in a number of cities, including Hankou, Changsha, and Canton.) The Razumovs' apartment was on the second floor of a large three-story European-style house. It was to this apartment that Mao Zedong came early on the morning of August 7. Qu Qiubai, who ran the meeting, looked unwell. He had long suffered from tuberculosis, and that illness as well as the events he had just experienced had completely exhausted him. He sprayed saliva when he spoke, as he always did when he was agitated, so it seemed that in the room there was "a thick mist of tuberculosis bacteria."[19] Counting Mao, Lominadze, and Qu Qiubai, altogether twenty-five persons took part in the conference, including two other Soviet comrades in addition to "Nikolai." The room was crowded, stuffy, and hot.

Those present constituted less than 30 percent of the leadership of the party. Chen Duxiu was not invited to the conference even though he was still in town.[20] Instead, three members of the Communist Youth League, one staff member of the Military Committee of the Central Committee, and two local representatives from Hunan and Hubei were invited.[21] Most of the participants were people Mao had known for a long time. Only a few may have been unfamiliar. Among these was a new head of the technical secretariat of the Central Committee, a modest but very capable young man of twenty-three who was so diminutive that at scarcely five feet he only came up to Mao's shoulder. A year earlier he had returned to China from the Soviet Union, where he had spent some time studying at the Communist University of the Toilers of the East, and then spent several months at the Sun Yat-sen University of the Toilers of China. Earlier he had worked and studied in France, where he had gone when he was still a youth. His real name was Deng Xiansheng (Deng "Who Surpasses the Sage"), but at five years old he received a new name—Deng Xixian (Deng "Aspiring to Benevolence"). After arriving in Wuhan to engage in clandestine work, he changed his name to Deng Xiaoping (Deng "Little and Plain"), a very ordinary Chinese given name that was unlikely to attract much attention. Probably Mao paid no attention to this squat little man.[22] But even had his gaze lingered on him, he could not possibly have imagined that after Mao's death this unprepossessing man, the son of a family from eastern Sichuan, would play a decisive role in the fate of Mao's main creation, socialist China.

Presiding over the conference was Li Weihan, a member of the Provisional Bureau and former secretary of the Hunan party committee whom Mao had known for many years. Speaking first, Lominadze sharply criticized the Chinese communists for having committed "major errors," the roots of which went "very deep." Then Li Weihan asked those present to express their views.

Mao spoke in support of the Comintern representative. He had long demanded the radicalization of party policy and had often opposed Chen Duxiu. Everyone knew how fiercely he had fought for a thoroughgoing agrarian revolution. Now it seemed his hour had come. He referred to the "errors" of the previous leadership regarding the peasant movement. "The broad masses inside and outside the Party want revolution," he said, "yet the Party's guidance is not revolutionary; there really is a hint of something counterrevolutionary about it." To his credit, he never mentioned Chen Duxiu by name. In fact, none of the Chinese at the conference criticized Chen personally. Despite Stalin's negative view of him, Chen remained the "head of the family" in their eyes. Only Lominadze attacked Chen by name. After finishing his critique, Mao addressed the basic tasks of the party. Here for the first time at such a high official level, he voiced his inner thoughts about what had been worrying him most recently, namely, the need to devote exceptional attention to the military factor.

[W]e used to censure [Sun] Yat-sen for engaging only in a military movement, and we did just the opposite, not undertaking a military movement, but exclusively a mass movement. . . . At present, although we have paid some attention to it, we still have no firm concept about it. The Autumn Harvest Uprising, for example, is simply impossible without military force. Our conference should attach great importance to this issue. . . . From now on, we should pay the greatest attention to military affairs. We must know that political power is obtained from the barrel of the gun.[23]

This was hardly a trivial statement then, and even sounded somewhat un-Bolshevik. The Comintern had always taught communists that in the revolutionary movement they must primarily rely on the masses, first the industrial workers and then the poor peasants. This accorded with the canons of Marxism. The actual Bolshevik experience of revolution and civil war suggested just the opposite, but the decisive importance of the military factor was ignored. The "great social revolution of the multi-million masses of the Russian proletariat" could not be depicted as some sort of military coup.

After everyone at the conference had spoken, Qu Qiubai delivered a self-critical report. Then they turned to a discussion of three resolutions: on the peasant struggle, the workers' movement, and organizational questions as well as a rather lengthy "Appeal to All Party Members," which Lominadze had drafted and Qu Qiubai had already translated. Then Mao took the floor again. He spoke for only about five minutes, but his speech had enormous importance because Mao expressed his basic views on the peasant question more holistically than ever before:

1. A criterion must definitely be fixed for big and medium landlords [dizhu]. Otherwise, we will not know who is a big or medium landlord. In my opinion, we could take fifty mu [8.15 acres] as the limit; above fifty mu, whether the land is fertile or barren, it should all be confiscated.

2. The question of small landlords is the central problem of the land question. The difficulty is that, if we do not confiscate the land of the small landlords, then since there are many localities where there are no big landlords, the peasant associations would have to cease their activity. Hence, if we wish basically to abolish the landlord system, we must have a certain method for dealing with the small landlords. At present we must resolve the small landlord question, for this is the only way we can satisfy the people.

3. The problem of owner-peasants. The land rights of rich peasants and

middle peasants are not the same. The peasants want to attack the rich peasants, so we must adopt a clear orientation.

4. The bandit problem is an extraordinarily great problem. Because such secret societies are uncommonly numerous, we must have tactics [for dealing with them]. There are some comrades who hold that we can simply use them; this is [Sun] Zhongshan [Sun Yat-sen]'s method, which we should not follow. It suffices that we carry through the agrarian revolution, and then we will certainly be able to lead them. We must definitely regard them as our brothers, and not as guest people [Hakka].[24]

This is how Mao set forth the essence of his basic program for the revolutionary struggle. What he said boils down to this: we must create an army out of bandits, the poorest peasants, paupers, and rural lumpen proletarian elements whom we can attract to our side only by confiscating the land of both the landlords and the peasants. (In the eyes of the rural lumpen proletariat any working farmer might be viewed as a "rich peasant.") Several months later he would express these thoughts in the laconic formula "Drawing on the plentiful to make up for the scarce, and drawing on the fat to make up for the lean." He would follow this formula his whole life, with certain variations, of course.

Mao's extremism was so cynical that even Lominadze, hardly noted for being softhearted, objected. "We need to neutralize the urban petty bourgeoisie," he declared. "If we start to confiscate all the land, the urban petty bourgeoisie will vacillate and turn against us. . . . As for the question of secret societies raised by Dong [Mao Zedong], we . . . will not make use [of such societies].[25]

Lominadze's criticism was offered in a friendly spirit. "Comrade Dong" went a bit too far, but still he was a genuine leftist. He was not like the opportunist Chen Duxiu. The others responded similarly. Cai Hesen, gasping for breath from an attack of asthma, even went so far as to defend his childhood friend. He suggested inducting Mao into the Politburo as a person who "had not agreed with the CC policy on the peasant question" and was "a representative of the tendency that demanded the prompt carrying out of an agrarian revolution." Therefore, Mao's name was added to the list of members and candidate members for the Provisional Politburo that Lominadze had compiled. Mao was elected as a candidate member of this organ, which was supposed to guide the party until the convening of the regular Sixth Congress, supposedly in six months. Fifteen others were elected to the Provisional Politburo, nine full members and six candidate members, including such familiar names as Qu Qiubai, Li Weihan, Peng Pai, Deng Zhongxia, Zhou Enlai, Zhang Tailei, Zhang Guotao, and Li Lisan. It is interesting to note that Cai Hesen was not among them.[26]

Qu Qiubai could be satisfied. The change of leadership had gone smoothly. Chen had been removed once and for all and nobody had openly opposed Lominadze. The majority of communists were accustomed to subordinating themselves to Moscow. Yet many of them were unable to overcome their ingrained reverence for Chen Duxiu, so they merely formally accepted Lominadze's criticism of the founder of the party. Meanwhile, unbeknown to Lominadze, Qu himself secretly visited the "Old Man" late at night to seek his advice on how to handle matters.[27]

Soon after the conference, Qu met with Mao and asked him to move to Shanghai and work on the Central Committee. The ECCI, proceeding from a classical Marxist conception of the "world historical role" of the working class, had decided that working-class Shanghai should again become the headquarters of the party. Mao, however, asked to be sent to Hunan. "I don't want to go off to a big city and live there in a big hotel," he said. "It's better if I go to the countryside, climb up a mountain, and make friends with the forest brothers."[28] According to Zhang Guotao, Mao "ran a great risk in voluntarily going to Hunan." The majority of CCP leaders had no burning desire to go to that province.[29] On August 9, the question of Mao's assignment was finally resolved when Qu sent him as a special representative of the Central Committee to organize the Autumn Harvest Uprising. The core action was planned for southern Hunan and a special South Hunan Committee was organized that Mao headed. The newly appointed secretary of the Hunan party committee, the energetic young Peng Gongda, who was also a candidate member of the Provisional Politburo, traveled with Mao. He had made his name by proposing to Chen Duxiu, right after Xu Kexiang's bloody coup, a plan to attack the capital of Hunan with a force of 300,000 armed peasants.

Arriving in Changsha on August 12, Mao found Xu Kexiang engaged in extirpating communism. Of three thousand party members in the local party organization no more than a hundred remained alive.[30] "There is only one way to deal with the Communists," Xu would say many years later, recalling the past: "namely with toughness, because force is the only thing they understand and of which they are really afraid."[31] Mao had no time to feel his way forward. He had to carry out the specific directive of the party leadership: "Begin uprisings with the aim of bringing about an agrarian revolution and overthrowing the reactionary regime."[32] He had to coordinate with the new Soviet consul in Changsha, who was the local Comintern representative, Vladimir Kuchumov (pseudonym Mayer, Chinese called him Ma Kefu).* Kuchumov had come to China from Moscow along with Lominadze.[33]

One of the first things Mao did upon arriving in Changsha was meet secretly with the former secretary of the party committee, Yi Lirong. Yi was

---

* This name is sometimes erroneously transliterated as Meyer.

under attack by his comrades because he was one of the few communists who had dared to openly accuse the Comintern of lacking the courage to admit its "opportunistic" errors in China.[34] Naturally, Lominadze was particularly ill-disposed toward him, but Mao saw no reason to break with an old friend. They agreed to convene a meeting of the provincial committee in the very near future. Then Mao went to Bancang, where his wife and children were living after their return from Wuchang. He tarried there longer than he should have and did not return to Changsha until August 16 or 17. The members of the party committee, who had been vainly awaiting him in the city, finally held the meeting without him on August 16.

When Mao came back to Changsha he was accompanied by his wife, sons, and the old nanny who took care of the children and also looked after Kaihui. This time "Little Dawn" did not want to let him go alone. She may have intuited that not much time remained for them to be together. All six of them returned to the city and settled in Kaihui's father's old house.[35]

Immediately upon his return, Mao convened a new meeting of the provincial party committee and delivered a speech outlining the main tasks for organizing the uprising. As he had at the August 7 conference in Hankou, he argued that the main slogan of the CCP should be the total confiscation of the land.

> In China there are only a few big landlords, but quite a number of smaller landlords. If we confiscate only the big landlords' land, few landlords will be affected, and the amount of land confiscated will be extremely small. The number of poor peasants demanding land is very great, and if we confiscate the land of the big landlords alone, we cannot satisfy the demands and needs of the peasants. If we want to win over all the peasants, we must confiscate the land of [all] the landlords and distribute it among the peasants.[36]

At this meeting he said nothing about the need to confiscate the land of peasant proprietors, but he had not rethought his position. The very next day, in a letter to the Central Committee of the CCP, he insisted,

> [T]he Hunanese peasants definitely want a complete solution of the land question. . . . I propose . . . [to] confiscate all the land, including that of small landlords and owner-peasants, take it all into public ownership, and let the peasant associations distribute it fairly to all those in the village who want land, in accordance with the two criteria of "labor power" and "consumption" (in other words, the actual amount of consumption for every household, calculated on the basis of the number of adults and children in the household).[37]

He insisted on doing things his way even though he knew very well that the majority of peasants and his beloved rural lumpen proletarians were not demanding land at all. The former dreamed only of reducing taxes and rent; the latter sought to divide other people's belongings. It is possible that he posed the question of a "radical land distribution" only to satisfy part of the neediest paupers, the poorest tenants, and members of the indigent Hakka clans. There were plenty such people in the Chinese countryside; there were 30 million Hakka alone. Nevertheless, this was not the main point. By 1927, Mao's personality was set and he had acquired the habit of leadership. Like many bosses accustomed to giving orders, he had absolutely no doubt about his right to decide the fate of everyone below him. Mao was completely convinced that he knew what was needed better than any peasant. That is why only several days after the idea of the total confiscation of land had been criticized by Lominadze, Mao returned to it, this time in the presence of the Comintern's representative in Hunan, Kuchumov/Mayer. He was already certain at this time that China was ripe for its version of the Bolshevik Revolution.[38] Therefore, there was no need to "indulge" the "landlords" and the "bourgeoisie."

Mao would continue to push his left radical views in the future. Of course, he would have to maneuver, accommodate, and make detours, but he would never betray his utopian ideals of universal equality. As if insuring himself against the possibility that the "dull-witted" peasantry might actually not respond to his call, at this meeting Mao raised the question of the special importance of the military factor.

[I]f we wish to create and unleash this uprising, it will not do to rely on the power of the peasants alone. There must be military support. With the help of one or two regiments, the uprising can take place; otherwise, it will fail in the end. . . . If you want to seize political power, to try to do it without the support of military forces would be sheer self-deception. Our Party's mistake in the past has been that it neglected military affairs. Now we should concentrate 60 percent of our energies on the military movement.

In conclusion, Mao again invoked a favorite formula: "We must carry out the principle of seizing and establishing political power on the barrel of a gun."[39]

A majority of the members of the Hunan party committee supported their trusted fellow countryman. Only Yi Lirong expressed caution. "If we confiscate their [the small landlords'] land at the present time," he explained, "they will certainly join the big landlords in the counterrevolutionary camp. Thus, now is not the time to confiscate the land of the small landlords."[40] But no one wanted to listen to him. Everyone was convinced that now was the time to play the populist card. "The slogans to establish a democratic revolutionary government have turned sour," they asserted. The communists wanted to rise up under their own banner, not that of the "left" Guomindang, to proclaim the establishment of soviets, and to cut off the heads of anyone who could be considered a landowner. They were completely uninterested in whether the peasants needed this or not. "Our method was to pursue the revolution from above and to extend it from the military to the peasants rather than the other way around," acknowledged Peng Gongda.[41]

However, the Provisional Politburo, which Lominadze controlled, came out against this. In an urgent letter to Hunanese comrades it characterized Mao's viewpoint regarding the relationship between the military factor and the mass movement as "military adventurism," adding, "the CC believes that we must rely on the masses. The military should play a secondary role." Mao's idea of an immediate and full redistribution of land was again rejected. "The main slogan at present is the confiscation of the land of big landlords," the letter said. The Provisional Politburo also demanded that all work should continue under the banner of the "left" Guomindang. Instructions to change the slogans had not yet arrived from Moscow. Not a single person in the Hunan party committee agreed with this policy, but only when the Politburo categorically demanded the execution of its directives did Mao and his supporters yield.[42] As further events demonstrated, however, they had done so only formally.[43]

Meanwhile, preparations for the Autumn Harvest Uprising were proceeding at full speed. At the very end of August the Hunan party committee decided to strike the main blow in the central part of the province with the combined forces of a "peasant army," the remnants of which were located in counties east of Changsha; a regiment of Guomindang troops that was commanded by a member of the Communist Party; and unemployed miners from the Anyuan colliery. The slogans of the uprising were extremely simple: "Execute local reactionaries, confiscate their property, burn down their houses, and destroy traffic and communication services." The main goal was the seizure of Changsha. A majority of the communists who had been inculcated with the Russian experience could not conceive of revolution without an urban base. Did Mao himself want to attack the provincial capital? Most probably not. According to Peng Gongda's memoirs, Mao insisted on limiting the scale of the uprising.[44] He was not interested in the uprising itself; he had long since understood that the current phase of the communist revolution had failed, and that it was past time to gather one's forces and head for the hills. But he had to subordinate himself to the decisions of the Politburo. Not until much later would he be able to impose his own will on his comrades irrespective of what they themselves thought.

Two committees were established to guide the uprising: a Front Committee, which was concerned with purely military matters, and an Action Committee, which coordinated the party committees in the counties where the uprising was to take place. Mao headed the Front Committee, Yi Lirong the Action Committee. At dawn on August 31, Mao left Changsha for the border region between Hunan and Jiangxi where the uprising was slated to begin.

In a rush, he embraced Kaihui for the last time. They agreed that she, the children, and their nanny would go to her mother in Bancang. Before parting she gave him a new pair of straw sandals and asked him to take care of himself. She was concerned because several days earlier, when they had traveled together from Bancang to Changsha, Mao had hurt his leg and was still limping. She didn't accompany him to the train station. Her younger cousin Kaiming volunteered to escort Mao. Did they somehow intuit they would never meet again? Did they understand that on that early morning they were parting forever? Mao left for the Changsha station, where an express train would whisk him away to a new life in which he would become the "great savior of the nation," "the teacher," and the "leader." Kaihui would remain in the past.

For some time she and the children managed to live in comparative safety in her old Bancang home. She was protected by her membership in a respected local clan. None of the local officials or military officers dared to touch the daughter of Yang Changji, the respected teacher and educator. She had little money and occasionally received remittances from Mao's brother Zemin in Shanghai. She pined for her husband and poured out her feelings in verse.

> Gray skies, north wind rising, the cold invades my bones.
> I think of you always, my lonely wayfarer;
> Calm waves can erupt into towering billows.
> Has your bad leg fully healed? Do you have warm clothes?
> Who will attend your lonely sleep? Who share your sorrow?
> Not a letter or even a note from you. No one to ask how you are.
> If I had wings, I'd fly to see you.
> To pine forever for one's love is torture.
> When shall we two meet again?[45]

Only when the Red Army headed by Mao really began to irritate the Hunanese authorities did they arrest her. In August 1930, soon after the communist troops seized Changsha, General He Jian, the commander of the Guomindang army in Hunan, issued an order for her arrest. A reward of one thousand yuan was offered for her head, and on October 24, 1930, she was behind bars. Her oldest son, Anying, who had just turned eight, was also arrested, along with the devoted family nanny. While she was being arrested, the middle son, Anqing, cried bitterly and clutched the soldiers' overcoats with his small hands. Then one of the soldiers struck him on the head with a heavy object. Poor Anqing fell down and suffered a serious brain concussion. He never recovered from this encounter with the soldiers.

He Jian demanded of Kaihui only that she renounce her husband. He believed that if Mao's wife did this publicly, many communists would surrender to the police. But she refused to betray her beloved. Therefore, she was remanded to a military tribunal despite an appeal for pardon by Cai Yuanpei, the renowned former rector of Peking University, who had responded to a request from Kaihui's mother. The court deliberated for fewer than ten minutes. After asking several formal questions, the judge dipped his writing brush in red ink, made a mark on the protocol of interrogation, and threw it onto the floor. This was the procedure in Chinese courts announcing a death penalty. On the morning of November 14, 1930, they came to her cell to take her to her execution. Anying, who was with her, burst into tears, but she said to him, "What's the matter with you? You are my Hero! My precious, tell papa not to grieve over my death. He should do everything to hasten the victory of the revolution!" Then she added, "I hope that after my death my relatives will not give me a bourgeois burial."

She was executed by a firing squad in a cemetery in Shiziling, a suburb of Changsha lying to the north of the city gates. This was the same place where her cousin Kaiming had been executed nine months earlier. Eyewitnesses reported she had been conveyed to the place of execution in a rickshaw and that armed soldiers had trotted along on both sides. When she fell, struck by many bullets, one of the executioners quickly removed her shoes and threw them as far as he could. This was always done in China so that the deceased, God forbid, would not come back to haunt his or her killers. Afterward the soldiers returned to their barracks to eat. But suddenly one of the townsmen who had witnessed the execution ran up to say that the "deceased" was showing signs of life. Interrupting their meal, seven of the executioners returned to the execution ground and finished her off. They watched silently as the dying woman convulsively scratched at the black earth with her trembling fingers.

In the evening her body was turned over to her relatives, who conveyed it to Bancang. She was buried not far from her parents' home, on a slope planted in cotton in the shade of young pines. Soon the local underground communists freed Anying and his nanny by bribing the prison guards. A month later, after learning of the death of his wife from the newspapers, Mao sent his mother-in-law thirty silver yuan to erect a gravestone. "The death of Kaihui," he wrote, "cannot be repaid even should I die a hundred deaths."[46]

By this time, however, he had long since been living with another woman, whom he had met just two months after his departure from Changsha. It will be recalled that "the power of the human need for love" was for Mao "greater than that of any other need." And nothing "except some special force" could stem in him "this surging tide of the need for love." In the spring of 1929, this new woman gave birth to a daughter. Thus the thirty pieces of silver he had sent for the headstone were purely symbolic.

15

RED BANNER OVER THE JINGGANG MOUNTAINS

Seated on the train on August 31, 1927, Mao first headed for the small town of Zhuzhou, south of Changsha. There he discussed plans for the uprising with members of the local party committee. The communists of Zhuzhou would begin the uprising by blowing up a railway bridge across the Xiang River and creating a series of diversions along the rail line. Then Mao arrived in Anyuan for an important military conference in the village of Zhangjiawan. There the party activists decided to form the so-called First Division of the First Corps of the Workers and Peasants Revolutionary Army, numbering about five thousand men.

Then, overflowing with heroic feelings, Mao set out for Tonggu, north of Anyuan, to inform the pro-communist soldiers and poor peasants of the decision to reorganize their detachments into the Third Regiment of the First Division. He already envisioned himself the leader of the rebels. New verses formed in his mind:

> Ours is the Peasant-Worker Revolutionary Army,
> on our banners the axe and the sickle emblazoned!*
> We shall not halt at the Lushan Mountains,
> we'll march to the Xiao River and on to the Xiang.
> With all their power the dizhu oppress the people,
> the peasants hate them back in kind.
> When we gather the harvest, autumn clouds will thicken,
> thunderbolts will herald the uprising.[1]

---

* At the time the hammer on the flag of the CCP was indeed commonly mistaken for an axe.

Everything seemed to be going well, but along the road, Mao and the county party secretary were stopped unexpectedly by a detachment of local peasant militia (*mintuan*). The militia had no idea whom they had picked up, but in any case they decided to bring them to their chief. The situation appeared dire. The white terror was still raging, and the two men might simply be shot. This is how Mao recounted this incident to Edgar Snow:

> I was ordered to be taken to the *min-t'uan* [*mintuan*] headquarters, where I was to be killed. Borrowing several tens of dollars from a comrade, however, I attempted to bribe the escort to free me. The ordinary soldiers were mercenaries, with no special interest in seeing me killed, and they agreed to release me, but the subaltern in charge refused to permit it. I therefore decided to attempt to escape, but had no opportunity to do so until I was within about two hundred yards of the *min-t'uan* headquarters. At that point I broke loose and ran into the fields.
>
> I reached a high place, above a pond, with some tall grass surrounding it, and there I hid until sunset. The soldiers pursued me and forced some peasants to help them search for me. Many times they came very near, once or twice so close that I could almost have touched them, but somehow I escaped discovery, although half a dozen times I gave up hope, feeling certain I would be recaptured. At last, when it was dusk, they abandoned the search. At once I set off across the mountains, traveling all night. I had no shoes and my feet were badly bruised. On the road I met a peasant who befriended me, gave me shelter and later guided me to the next district. I had seven dollars with me and used this to buy some shoes, an umbrella and food. When at last I reached the peasant guards safely, I had only two coppers in my pocket.[2]

The carefully prepared uprising, which began on September 9, ended, as could have been expected, in a crushing defeat. Neither the passive peasantry nor the demoralized railroad workers and miners offered any practical support to the rebellious soldiers and officers. "The peasants did not rise up, as their leaders lacked determination," Peng Gongda wrote.[3] Under these circumstances, on September 15 Mao and the members of the Hunan party committee decided on their own not to attack the provincial capital. Senseless actions like that promised nothing but more casualties. It was time to retreat, and not play at being heroes.

Gathering the remnants of their forces in a little town, Wenjiashi, about sixty miles east of Changsha, Mao announced his intention of striking through to the south along the Hunan-Jiangxi border, in the direction of the high mountainous region of Jinggang (literally "wells and ridges").[4] This inaccessible massif in the central part of the Luoxiao range had long served as a sanctuary for rebels and bandits. Mao considered it "an excellent base for a mobile army."[5] The distinguishing feature of this place was the fantastic combination of mountain peaks jutting into the sky and deep precipices plunging sharply downward, which made it an ideal refuge.

On September 21, the fifteen hundred exhausted fighters, all that remained of the First Division, with red ribbons tied around their necks as the sign of rebellion, set out on their difficult journey. "Discipline was poor, political training was at a low level, and many wavering elements were among the men and officers. There were many desertions," recalled Mao.[6] One of the rank-and-file soldiers painted an equally gloomy picture: "Our units were not familiar with the surroundings and lacked adequate preparation. Epidemics of fever, marching during the hottest time of the year, and the lack of bases all led to great losses."[7] Not until October 27 did Mao's detachment, having lost a third of its men en route, finally reach the town of Ciping, the main settlement of the Jinggang region. Here they halted at the foot of the tallest mountain in that locale, the 5,700-foot Wuzhishan (Five Peaks Mountain), in a wide valley crisscrossed with rice paddies. All around, wherever one looked, steep mountains covered with evergreens thrust up to the sky.[8]

A month later, on Mao's initiative, two organs of political power were established: a legislative body in the form of an Assembly of Workers, Peasants, and Soldiers' Deputies, and an executive organ, a People's Assembly. For the time being he did not use the word "soviet"—in Chinese, *suweiai*—but these institutions were in essence soviets. Naturally, he immediately encountered a host of problems. He needed to operate in a new and unknown environment amid an alien population that was often hostile toward their uninvited guests and who, moreover, spoke in a dialect that many of the soldiers, including Mao, did not understand.

In this poor area, far from the provincial administrations of Hunan and Jiangxi, people lived according to their own traditional laws. The economy of the region, in Mao's words, was "still in the age of the mortar and pestle."[9] He was referring to the fact that in the mountains a mortar and pestle were used to hull the rice. Only down in the valleys did they have hand-operated mills. Power was exercised by bands of outlaws headed by a certain Yuan Wencai and one Wang Zuo. Six hundred cutthroats armed with ancient pistols, rifles, and swords dominated all of Ningang county, which had a population of 150,000 people.[10] Therefore, before becoming a "citizen of Jinggang," Mao first had to establish friendly relations with the outlaws who were pillaging this region. He succeeded in doing this, and, in his own words, he became "king of the mountain."[11]

The history of Mao's relations with the "brotherhood of the forest" is worth recounting. Yuan Wencai and Wang Zuo belonged to dependent, indigent Hakka clans whose ancestors had settled in this region from Guangdong or Fujian when the fertile valleys had already been assimilated. Thus they were not considered natives even though both of them had been born in Jinggang. As a result, Yuan and Wang were not well-disposed to the people in the valley. The local old-timers treated the newer inhabitants with contempt and exploited them mercilessly. This is why in their early youth Yuan and Wang had joined one of the groups of bandits, the *madaodui*—the Sword Society, composed of "aliens" like themselves. They rose to leading positions in this organization, exacted tribute from the local population, and cruelly punished those who resisted. They decapitated the recalcitrant and displayed the skulls on poles. Yuan played the main role in this society, and Wang respected him as his "elder brother." Their friendship was sealed in blood.

Mao had just entered Jinggang when, in early October 1927, he sent a respectful letter to Yuan Wencai proposing they meet. He expressed his willingness to present Yuan one hundred rifles as a mark of respect if the latter would allow him to settle in these parts. The bandit, who possessed only sixty decrepit rifles, could hardly refuse such a gift, but his pride would not allow him to take possession of the weapons without paying for them. Upon meeting Mao, Yuan paid him a thousand silver yuan. This was a generous gesture, typically Chinese. Tradition demanded that a host who received tribute had to repay the giver a hundredfold. Otherwise he might "lose face" and the guest might think the host was having problems. Mao appreciated this, and his simplicity and courteousness pleased Yuan. The bandit chief was flattered that such an important man—he had heard that Mao was one of the leaders of the Communist Party—was showing him such attention. Deeply moved, Yuan even informed Mao Zedong that he had become a member of the Communist Party the year before. Although there is no way of knowing if this was true, Mao pretended that he believed it. Through Yuan he also established ties with Wang Zuo, to whom he presented seventy rifles and ample ammunition. The communist leader's erudition strongly impressed the poorly educated Wang Zuo. "Commissar Mao is the most educated man," he said. "Just speak with him once and you get the feeling that you spent ten years doing nothing but reading books!"[12] It was Wang who advised Mao to base himself in Ciping, which was under Wang's control. The divisional hospital was established in the neighboring settlement of Maoping, Yuan Wencai's hometown. Since Mao was five years older than Yuan and Wang, they called him Mao *dage* ("Elder Brother Mao"). According to custom, the forming of this bandit brotherhood was celebrated with wine and roast pork.

Not everything went smoothly. Clashes between Mao's troops and Yuan and Wang's bandits occurred. The naturally distrustful Wang Zuo was especially exasperated by these occurrences, and for good reason. "What if Mao robs us of our power," Wang said as he shared his doubts on one occasion with Yuan. "He will swallow us and not even notice." So the cunning Yuan thought of a way to bind Mao to them. He introduced Mao to He Zizhen, the attractive sister of an old friend, and recommended her as a reliable interpreter of the local dialect. The girl was just eighteen years old and had only recently joined Yuan's unit. Yuan treated her well, and He Zizhen was on particularly good terms with Yuan's wife. Wang Zuo was also favorably disposed toward her and had given her a Mauser. Zizhen (literal translation "Treasuring Oneself") had joined the Communist Party at the age of sixteen, and the local party organization had sent her to the Jinggang Mountains soon after the "Whites" had taken power in her home district. She was well read and politically literate, but above all attractive, energetic, lively, and graceful. She had a sweet oval face, large, shining eyes, and delicate skin. Not by accident her childhood name had been Guiyuan ("Round Moon in the Garden of Cassia Trees"). She made a positive impression upon Mao, whom she herself liked even though he was sixteen years older. She knew he was married and had three sons; he had told her so himself. But nothing could stop her; Mao knew how to please women. At the time he was particularly irresistible—very thin, long-haired, with a high forehead and sad, dark eyes. Zizhen was taken with him. He radiated both physical strength and intellectual power, was sensitive, wrote poetry, and was well versed in literature and popular folklore. The youthful He Zizhen had never met anyone like this before. Was this mutual love? Or just sexual attraction? People who knew them are not of one mind.

In the early spring of 1928, Mao asked Zizhen to help him work on some manuscripts. "I can help you only if you don't think my calligraphy is bad," she said. The next day she came to him. (Mao was working then in a monastery in the mountains.) From that time on they began living together. At the end of May, a kind of "wedding" took place in the presence of the matchmaker Yuan Wencai and his comrades. They ate sweets and nuts. They drank tea. They laughed, joked, and made merry. No one, of course, thought about Kaihui, who at the time was still alive.

But, as it happens, Kaihui learned of her husband's betrayal. For long months she had heard nothing from him and now this! The blow was so strong that Kaihui decided to kill herself and probably would have had it not been for the children.[13] She bore this insult for two years, right until the end of her life.

Meanwhile, events in the CCP were unfolding stormily. On September 19, Stalin finally decided to officially withdraw the CCP from the Guomindang and begin the communists' struggle to establish soviets in China. Qu Qiubai received the directives the following day via the Soviet consul in Hankou. At the end of September the leaders of the Chinese Communist Party left Hankou by boat for Shanghai, where they continued their activities deep underground.[14] Lominadze soon joined them. In October, another representative of the ECCI, the German communist Heinz Neumann (alias Moritz or Gruber) arrived in Shanghai, then left for Canton via Hong Kong to prepare a new uprising known to history as the Canton Commune. It likewise ended in defeat. Among its numerous victims was Zhang Tailei, Borodin's former interpreter. The white terror and the CCP's adventurist policy exacted a heavy price. By the end of 1927 it had lost about four-fifths of its membership, from almost 58,000 down to 10,000.

This is why many communists, not just Mao, retreated to the countryside in the winter of 1927–28. In distant and inaccessible regions they launched a new struggle under the slogan of soviets. Moscow had dictated this slogan. Still, Mao was the first and as such encountered many problems: the incomprehension of his comrades, the hatred of jealous persons, reproaches of "left deviation," and accusation of "right deviation." In September Mao had already been subjected to a devastating critique by Kuchumov, the Soviet consul and Comintern representative, for his refusal to attack Changsha. Kuchumov termed the "inaction" of the Hunan party committee an "exceptionally shameful betrayal and cowardice" and demanded that the Politburo promptly replace the provincial party leadership. The Soviet consul was convinced that the uprising in Changsha could have succeeded had Peng Gongda and Mao Zedong not exhibited a "monstrous example of Chinese-style philistinism." In response, Qu Qiubai ordered prompt action in Changsha. Simultaneously, he sent to Changsha his plenipotentiary representative, Ren Bishi, who carried out a reshuffling of the leadership of the party committee, although Peng Gongda remained secretary. Ren's efforts, however, had no effect on the situation, and he himself quickly grasped that the "moment for an uprising" in Changsha had "been lost." [15]

Mao was dealt another blow at an enlarged plenum of the Provisional Politburo in Shanghai, held November 7–14, 1927. Two emissaries from Moscow presided over this meeting—Lominadze, who left for Russia on November 10, before the meeting was over, and a representative of the Red International of Trade Unions, Olga Mitkevich. Their intervention predetermined the degree of punishment that the organizers of the inglorious uprisings incurred. Once more Stalin demanded scapegoats and declined to accept any responsibility for mistakes. A resolution adopted by the meeting, "On Political Discipline," said this about Mao Zedong and his comrades:

> In its leadership of the peasant uprising, the Hunan Provincial Committee completely disregarded the tactics of the CC which repeatedly indicated that the main force of the rebellion in Hunan province must be the peasant masses. The CC likewise directly warned the secretary of the provincial committee, Comrade Peng Gongda, against the error of military opportunism and demanded that the provincial commit-

tee rectify these mistakes. . . . The Enlarged Plenum of the Provisional Politburo of the CC resolves to impose the following correctives on the executive organs of party organizations and on responsible comrades who implemented the abovementioned erroneous policy. . . . The following members of the Hunan Provincial Committee—Peng Gongda, Mao Zedong, Yi Lirong, and Xia Minghan—are relieved of their responsibilities as members of the provincial Party committee. Comrade Peng Gongda is relieved of his responsibilities as candidate member of the Politburo and remains in the party on a six-month probationary status. . . . Comrade Mao Zedong . . . is dismissed from candidate membership in the Provisional Politburo of the CC.[16]

It was at this time that the term "Mao Zedongism" was circulated by the Central Committee as a synonym for "military opportunism."

Mao learned of his dismissal from the Politburo four months later, in early March 1928, when Zhou Lu, a special plenipotentiary from the newly reconstituted party committee of southern Hunan, came to see him. This self-assured young man was convinced of his importance because he headed the South Hunan Military Department.[17] The party committee he represented had been established three months earlier, in December 1927, and the Central Committee had assigned it the task of reorganizing the communist leadership in the Jinggang Mountains. (By this time the All-Hunan Party Committee in Changsha had been almost completely smashed by the Guomindang.)

The leaders in Shanghai could not forgive Mao his independence; on December 31, 1927, they demanded Mao's ouster from the leadership of the Front Committee. The usually restrained Zhou Enlai, secretary of the Military Committee of the Central Committee, expressed particular dissatisfaction with Mao, possibly because he himself was culpable. He had been in charge of the failed Nanchang Uprising. "Mao's troops are just bandits who roam here and there," Zhou asserted, adding, "Such leaders [as Mao] do not believe in the strength of the popular masses and fall into real military opportunism."[18] The remaining members of the Hunan party committee agreed with him, asserting that Mao's army was entirely composed of "vagrants."[19] No less hard (and accurate) were the judgments of Mao's army by the members of the Comintern's Far Eastern Bureau in Shanghai. For example, Alexander Al'brecht, the representative of the secret International Liaison Department of the ECCI, reported to Moscow in late February 1928:

The question of establishing a Red Army is vitally important. Since these armies have neither bases nor supplies, they impose a great burden on the peasantry. Since part of this army is semi-bandit in its origins, for example Mao Zedong's units, with the passage of time they break up and turn the peasants against themselves. Particularly awful is that these armies often go away, leaving the peasants to pay for their attacks against militarist troops.[20]

News of the party sanctions shook Mao to the core, especially because Zhou Lu, trying to discredit Mao entirely, declared that the Central Committee had expelled Mao from the party. This was a bald-faced lie, but Mao was unable to confirm or deny it. The result was that Zhou Lu dismissed Mao from all of his party work and demoted him to the post of commander of the First Division.* As the "nonparty" commander, Mao was unable to decide not only political questions, but military ones as well, since only the party could lead in all areas. Zhou Lu also dissolved the Front Committee and handed party power in the First Division to the commissar of one of the regiments whom he favored, the twenty-two-year-old He Tingying. Evidently the special plenipotentiary figured that the young and inexperienced secretary would be putty in his hands. But he miscalculated. He Tingying, connected to Mao by their joint participation in the Autumn Harvest Uprising and the difficult march from Wenjiashi to Jinggang, treated Mao like the authoritative leader he was.[21] Zhou Lu also failed to consider there were others in the First Division besides the youthful He upon whom Mao could rely.

One of the persons Mao most trusted in the Jinggang Mountains was his younger brother Zetan. On the eve of Wang Jingwei's coup, on Mao's advice, Zetan had left Wuhan and set out with the troops of the Fourth Corps for Jiujiang, on the Jiangxi-Hubei border. That is where news of the purge of communists from the "left" Guomindang and the NRA caught up with him. Danger confronted him, and on the advice of the chief of staff of the Fourth Corps, the communist Ye Jianying, he fled to Nanchang, hoping to link up with He Long's troops, which were engaged in the uprising. By the time he got there the communists were gone and Guomindang troops were everywhere. Zetan was stopped by a patrol at the gates of Nanchang. They released him after a brief interrogation. Departing Nanchang, he headed south, and some 120 miles from the city he caught up with the sentries of the rebel army. They took him to Zhou Enlai, who immediately recognized him as Mao's brother. Zetan was sent to work with Ye Ting in the Political Department. Along with others he took part in the storming of Swatow, and then, joining up with Zhu De's forces, he made the difficult march with the troops to the Guangdong-Jiangxi border. There, in the middle of November 1927, Zhu De's soldiers linked up with fighters from one of the battalions of Mao's division who had been wandering in the mountains after being cut off from the main force by Guomindang troops.

---

* Later, Mao, recalling this time, observed ironically, "So, as soon as I became a democratic figure [i.e., not a communist], they could appoint me division commander."

From them Zhu and Zetan learned about the Autumn Harvest Uprising and about Mao's base area in the Jinggang Mountains. Zhu De decided to establish a link with Mao and sent Zetan to him. A letter from Zhu that Zetan carried said, "We must unite forces and carry out a well-defined military and agrarian policy."[22]

At the end of November, Zetan safely reached Ciping, and the brothers had a warm reunion. Zetan stayed with Mao and helped him with everything. To be sure, for a while he tried to win away He Zizhen, but in vain. Meanwhile, his wife, Zhou Wennan, along with her tiny son, whom she had given birth to six months earlier and had named Chuxiong, was imprisoned in Changsha, where she had been sent after a traitor had denounced her in March 1928. Did Zetan know about this? Perhaps not. But he should have remembered that she was pregnant the last time he had seen her in Wuchang. So he certainly should have assumed that he had become a father sometime in September. The child became seriously ill in prison, was taken from his mother, and placed in the prison clinic to die. However, he survived and several months later was placed in the care of his grandmother. To protect him, the old woman changed his family name from Mao to Zhou. (Only when he turned ten did she tell him who his father was.) Not until July 1930, when Red Army troops briefly seized Changsha, did the wife of Mao's younger brother regain her freedom. By this time the impatient Zetan had already found a new love object. Rejected by Mao's lover, he found solace in her younger sister, the attractive He Yi. In early 1931 they were married.*

Something about the Mao brothers was not conducive to family life. The middle brother, Zemin, was also hardly a model husband or father. He abandoned his first wife, Shulan, and their three-year-old child and never saw them again. She, too, suffered a lot. She was arrested twice, first right after Xu Kexiang's mutiny at the end of May 1927. Fortunately, she was released right away. The local people vouched for her and said she had long since been divorced from Mao Zemin. But in May 1929, she was rearrested and thrown into the municipal prison in Changsha. The Red Army freed her in July 1930, as

---

* It is worth noting that Zhao Xiangui, Zetan's first wife, at just this time was risking her life by engaging in underground work in Changsha. Returning from Moscow in the spring of 1927, she began to put into practice in Hunan what she had learned in Moscow, organizing a peasant movement or, to be more precise, a movement of paupers and rural lumpen proletarians. After Xu Kexiang's mutiny in Changsha on May 21, 1927, she was put behind bars, but she was freed the following January. In early 1931 she left for Wuhan, where for security reasons she changed her name to Zhao Lingying. Subsequently she was sent to work in Shanghai, then in Nanjing, and finally in Jinan, the provincial capital of Shandong. There she married the secretary of the Shandong party committee, but in the summer of 1932 first her husband and then she was seized by the Guomindang and executed.

they had Mao Zetan's former wife. She did not leave prison alone, however. She was accompanied by the nine-year-old son of her cell mate, who had implored her to take and educate the child, who was named Huachu. From then on the three of them, Shulan, her daughter Yuanzhi from Mao Zemin, and Huachu, lived together. Shulan made ends meet by working at odd jobs, but by the end of the summer of 1931 she couldn't manage any longer. She set off with the children for Shanghai, where rumor had it her former husband was living with his new wife. But she failed to find Zemin there. Party acquaintances told her truthfully that Zemin and his wife, Xijun, had gone to Hong Kong in July 1931 on orders from the Central Committee. So Shulan had to return home. She was poor, half starved, and of no use to anyone.*

All this was not simply due to the heartlessness of the Mao brothers. They were not the only ones to behave this way. Polygamy was quite common in China and even the most fervent partisans of women's liberation among the male members of the Chinese Communist Party possessed a rather contemptuous view of the "gentler sex," albeit at a subconscious level. They viewed women not so much as comrades but as sex objects. As for children, who even thought about them? Among the paupers and rural lumpen proletarians whose interests the Communist Party represented, children, especially daughters, were often seen as a burden. Of course, unlike with the poor peasants, the callousness of CCP leaders toward their offspring was not exclusively a matter of economics. They simply had no time for children; they had to focus on the main tasks—revolution, civil war, the emancipation of the oppressed masses. In the great scheme of things, the tears of a child, even their own child, were virtually unnoticeable.

Intraparty struggles took much effort, in Mao's case no less than the revolution itself. His new enemy Zhou Lu showed up in Jinggang in March 1928, intoxicated with power. He ordered Mao Zedong to redeploy his forces from Ciping to southern Hunan to support the local peasant movement there. Mao complied. He did not feel in a strong enough position to openly resist the party's representative. Not till a month later, now in eastern Hunan, was he able to persuade Zhou Lu to turn back. There was no peasant movement in Hunan, but Mao had heard rumors that Zhu De's troops had redeployed from Jiangxi to southern Hunan and now were approaching the spurs of the Jinggang Mountains. He had to set out and meet them as soon as possible.

The idea of linking up with Zhu De had preoccupied Mao. Zhu De was a professional soldier as well as a longtime member of the party and commanded a powerful military force numbering more than two thousand soldiers. Back

---

* She survived until the victory of the revolution. For a while she worked in the Mao Zedong Museum in Shaoshan, and then she moved to Changsha. There she died of illness in July 1964, at the age of sixty-eight.

in mid-December 1927, Mao had introduced his plan for unification to the Hunan party committee, which had approved it, as had the Central Committee, which sent a directive to that effect to Zhu De. But it was only now in April 1928 that the prospects for unification looked promising. The historic meeting of the two leaders took place on either April 21 or April 22, 1928, in the hamlet of Linxian, west of Jinggang. After three or four days their forces were completely merged after the Special Hunan Provincial Committee conferred on them the name of the Fourth Corps of the Chinese Workers and Peasants Revolutionary Army, in honor of the famous Fourth Corps of the NRA.[23] (In June 1928, by decision of the CCP Central Committee, the Revolutionary Army was renamed the Red Army.)

In Zhu De, just seven years older than he was, Mao acquired an ideal comrade. Like Mao, Zhu came from peasant stock, in Sichuan province. His Hakka father was much poorer than Mao's father, so much so that, unable to feed himself and his family, he had had to drown five of his own children in a pond with his own hands.[24] "I loved my mother, but feared and hated my father," Zhu De confessed to the American journalist Agnes Smedley in 1937. "I could never understand why my father was so cruel."[25] Luckily, a well-to-do relative of his murderous father took Zhu De in when he was just six years old. He received a superior education. In 1909, when he was twenty-three, Zhu De entered the Yunnan Military Academy, in the capital city of Yunnanfu (now Kunming). That same year Zhu De joined Sun Yat-sen's Revolutionary Alliance and devoted all his energies to "the struggle for the republic."[26] He also became a member of the secret mafia-type Elder Brother Society, whose well-articulated network penetrated all layers of Chinese society. Zhu De took an active part in the 1911 Revolution against the Qing dynasty and he rose to be a brigade commander in the forces of one of the Yunnan militarists. In September 1921 he was appointed commissioner of police for Yunnan province. "He acquired several wives and concubines and built a palatial home in the capital of Yunnan," Edgar Snow wrote. "He had everything he desired: wealth, power, love, descendants, poppy dreams, eminent respectability and a comfortable future. He had, in fact, only one really bad habit, but it was to prove his downfall. He liked to read books."[27] He became so interested in Bolshevism that he abandoned everything and went to Europe, first to France and then to Germany, where he studied military science. There as well he met Zhou Enlai, who convinced him to join the Communist Party in October 1922. In July 1925, Zhu traveled to the Soviet Union and became a student at the Communist University of the Toilers of the East (KUTV), where, under the pseudonym of Danilov, he began studying Bolshevik sociology and economics. Soon he was transferred to one of the secret Soviet military schools, and after he graduated in the summer of 1926 he returned to China. He took part in the Northern Expedition, after which he made a significant contribution to organizing the Nanchang Uprising under the direction of his old friend Zhou Enlai.

He was physically strong, loved to play basketball, and slept with his soldiers on the damp earth; his manner of living and dress was plain. Everyone who knew him was struck by his modesty and pleasant manner. His main virtue was that he was utterly devoid of political ambition. Zhu De recognized Mao's priority in everything concerning politics, while Mao initially did not dispute Zhu's opinions on military matters. Thus this was an ideal combination from every perspective.[28]

After Zhu and Mao joined forces, they fully agreed on returning to the old Jinggang base in the central part of the Luoxiao range. They established their headquarters in the town of Longshi, north of Ciping. Zhou Lu was no longer an obstacle. Back in Jinggang he had been captured by the Guomindang and executed. The goal that Mao and Zhu De shared was to try to expand their influence into six counties of the Hunan-Jiangxi-Guangdong border region after consolidating their soviet base. In Mao's words, "Our main tasks, as we saw them, were two: to divide the land, and to establish Soviets. We wanted to arm the masses to hasten those processes."[29]

Mao's meeting with Zhu De was also noteworthy because it was from Zhu that he learned no one had expelled him from the party. Moreover, Mao soon received word from the Jiangxi Provincial Committee that he had been appointed secretary of the newly formed Hunan-Jiangxi Special Border Area Committee. With the formation of this committee, he had again concentrated in his own hands all of the political and military power in the Jinggang region. Naturally, he was very pleased. (In November 1928, Mao would further strengthen his power when the Central Committee appointed him secretary of the newly revived Front Committee, a special institution that reported directly to the Jiangxi party committee and ranked above the Hunan-Jiangxi Special Border Area Committee.)

Numerous paupers and rural lumpen proletarians, allies of the communists, arrived in Jinggang along with Zhu De's forces. Together they engaged in looting and killing in southern Hunan for several months. The regional economy was so devastated that Zhu De's troops in southern Hunan could feed themselves only by raising and selling opium.[30] The communists knew it was bad to traffic in narcotics, but they simply had no other recourse. Thus, while continuing to struggle for the rights of the laboring people, they themselves mercilessly poisoned the people. It was because of these economic difficulties that Zhu De ultimately had to withdraw his troops from southern Hunan and go to Jinggang.

By May 1928, some eighteen thousand fighters had assembled in the Jinggang region. Mao considered the majority of them "messy people with very poor discipline."[31] Thus the first order of business was to establish strict control over this armed mob. To do this without the ability to supply them regularly with provisions and clothing was impossible. Medicine was also urgently needed. No less than a third of the troops in Jinggang were sick or wounded. It was also necessary to organize the production of weapons and ammunition. There were only two thousand rifles and a few machine guns for the eighteen thousand troops. Against this background, Mao decided to undertake wide-scale socioeconomic reforms or, to put it more precisely, agrarian revolution. Until then, starting in October 1927, Mao's soldiers along with Yuan Wencai and Wang Zuo's bandits had used old-fashioned means of procuring what they needed. They levied taxes on the inhabitants of the valley and they confiscated from the homes of *tuhao* and *lieshen* everything they could get their hands on. But even by such pillaging Mao was unable to pay his soldiers more than three copper coins a day. This was very little; therefore, new means were essential.

Finally he was able to implement his long-percolating ideas about a just Chinese society. These views were radically egalitarian and, in essence, anti-peasant. In Jinggang all the land belonging to peasants as well as to landlords was confiscated and handed over to the "Border Area Soviet Government of Workers, Peasants, and Soldiers," which, incidentally, was headed by the bandit Yuan Wencai. The land was then distributed among rural inhabitants-supporters of the regime in a strictly egalitarian fashion, according to the number of mouths in a household. The buying and selling of land was prohibited and those who received land "must be compelled to work." All this was done in accordance with personal directives from Mao. A quasi-legislative basis for these measures was provided only one month prior to the departure of the Fourth Corps from Jinggang, in December 1928, when the regional Soviet government retroactively adopted the "Jinggangshan Land Law" that Mao had drafted. Here, too, Mao remained faithful to himself. On April 12, 1927, he had openly asserted, "It is first necessary to solve the agrarian problem in reality and then work out the legal framework." This is just what he did.[32]

Mao's report to the Central Committee of the CCP on November 25, 1928, indicated that by June 1928, most of the land in the region had already been confiscated and redistributed. The remainder continued to be divided through the late fall. Such rough and ready redistribution naturally evoked considerable resistance. It was not only the landlords who loathed egalitarianism, but also the great mass of the peasantry, first of all the peasant proprietors who belonged to the wealthier native clans (*bendi*). Mao acknowledged that "[i]n the countryside, where clan organizations prevail, the most troublesome are not the despotic gentry, but the intermediate classes." It was they who most actively obstructed the redistribution that began only after Red Army soldiers had shot several local people. After that the peasants could either flee from Jinggang or sabotage the implementation of the agrarian revolution. Most of them fled, because they were terrified that the Hakka, aided by the Red Army, would kill all of the indigenous population. "[M]ost of the native peasants defected, put on white ribbons, and led the army to burn down houses and comb the mountains," Mao noted gloomily in his report to the Central Committee. In response, "the settlers hastened to confiscate the pigs, cattle, clothes, and other property of the native peasants."[33] Thereafter, those who remained in the valley cut back on trade and ceased handicraft production. Practically all the markets shut down and daily necessities including salt, cloth, medicines, and many other commodities virtually disappeared. The communists resorted to requisitioning. A political economy based on plunder and murder precluded the possibility of leading a normal life. To supply soldiers the three to five coins they needed daily for food, more than ten thousand yuan per month was required. And "[i]f the captured despotic gentry do not send us money, we have no money to use," Mao reported to the Central Committee. After all, money could be "obtained entirely from expropriating the local bullies, but . . . you can expropriate only once in a given locality; afterward, there would be nothing to take."[34]

The result was that "the struggle in the border area," in Mao Zedong's words, "is almost purely military. Consequently, the Party and the masses must both be militarized . . . and the fighting has come to constitute our daily life."[35] Thus terror became the sole means of survival. "Our overall strategy in the rural struggles now on is: . . . massacre the landlords and the despotic gentry as well as their running dogs without the slightest compunction; threaten the rich peasants by means of the Red terror so that they will not dare to assist the landlord class," Mao wrote. To implement terror in a timely fashion, special "red execution teams" were established from the "bravest workers and peasants" and carried out nighttime guerrilla raids on the villages.[36] Naturally, the Red Army soldiers, who were mostly paupers, rural lumpen proletarians, and Hakka, greeted this policy enthusiastically. "The vagrants are after all particularly good fighters," Mao enthused in his report. "Consequently, not only can we not diminish the vagrants now in our ranks but it is difficult to find more for reinforcements."[37] The Hakka, who were generally a warlike group, fought especially bravely.

As a result of the militarization of life in the region, by late summer the Red Army was even beginning to achieve small victories over individual Guomindang units. The battle of Huangyang Pass, northwest of Ciping, in which the Red Army routed a regiment of the Eighth Corps of the NRA, was particularly impressive. Mao was ecstatic. Looking out over the eternally green mountains, he composed some new verses:

> Below the mountain, their flags flying,
> High on the mountain, our bugles blowing:
> A thousand circles of the enemy around us:
> We will stand unmoved.

Defense is deadly, trench and wall,
The strongest fort is our will.
From Huang-yang-chieh [Huangyangjie] cannon roar,
Crying: the enemy runs away in the night.[38]

But he celebrated too soon. Despite the terror, the problem of acquiring provisions remained acute. The Red Army men ate mostly pumpkin or squash, rice was considered a delicacy, and there was practically nothing else. Accustomed to spicy dishes, the southerners suffered. The fighters unhappily shouted, "Down with capitalism, and eat squash!" Many of them developed stomach problems from such a diet. According to his daughter, Mao himself suffered from constipation. He couldn't stand bland food, and there was none of the red peppers that he loved. He was saved by warm, soapy enemas that He Zizhen administered to him.[39]

This totally anti-peasant policy finally led to a profound crisis. By late autumn, the attempt to introduce "war communism" into Chinese society had isolated Mao's corps and placed it in opposition to the majority of the population. Mao certainly understood what was happening, but he did not want to reexamine his extremist views. His great energy drove him forward. The goal and the romance of struggle blinded him, and his enormous will compelled him to overcome all obstacles while his faith in the power of dictatorship kept him from veering off the path. The difficulties he encountered only strengthened his resolve to carry out his plans to the end, no matter the cost.

For a long time he had felt that he was exceptional and infallible. Was there no basis for this? A peasant's son from the Hunanese boondocks, he had already been able to accomplish so much. He was able not only to make his way in the world, but to compel many of the leading sons of the nation to respect and even fear him. How could he not have faith in himself?

He did not want to leave Jinggang. The region was ideal in a strategic sense, surrounded on all sides by tall, steep mountains and connected by road to two provinces—Hunan and Jiangxi. Here one could defend oneself successfully for a long time without fear of being surrounded by the enemy. In any other place, Mao thought, "a tiger [i.e., the Fourth Corps] on the plain may be attacked by a dog."[40] Nevertheless, in the end he had to leave. By early December 1928, the economic resources of Jinggang were almost completely exhausted. The Fifth Corps of the Red Army, which had been formed several months earlier, arrived in Jinggang in early December. Its soldiers were struck by what they saw. Peng Dehuai, the commander of the Fifth Corps, recalled that at that time "the men of the Fourth Army [Corps] of the Red Army still wore summer clothes and straw sandals. They had no winter clothing, no salt to prepare food, and no money to provide individual soldiers with the three coppers needed for daily meals."[41] Of the eighteen thousand soldiers under Mao's command in May

1928, no more than six thousand remained. It became clear to Mao, Zhu De, and Peng Dehuai that only by leaving this ruined place and finding new places to pillage "could they overcome their difficulties."[42]

In early January 1929, Mao and Zhu resolved to switch their base to southern Jiangxi province, along the Fujian border. Although Mao deemed the new region a remote place, he could not have failed to consider that the Jiangxi-Fujian border region promised the communists numerous advantages. This was a territory more densely populated with newcomers. In China it was even called "Hakka country." There, in the forested districts with a mild and favorable climate, far from the industrial centers that were controlled by the Guomindang, the body of Mao's troops had an excellent chance at creating a strong base area. A majority of the poor local Hakka was sympathetic to the communist revolution; many of them even saw the Red Army as a sort of kindred clan.

On January 14, 1929, Zhu and Mao's troops, numbering barely more than 3,600 men, headed south from Jinggang.[43] They were dispirited and exhausted. They knew that the Jinggang experiment had been a failure. Mao himself acknowledged this in a letter to the Central Committee.[44] At the old base there remained only five companies of Peng Dehuai's Fifth Corps, reorganized as the Thirtieth Regiment of the Fourth Corps; wounded and ill soldiers of the Fourth Corps; and the troops of Yuan Wencai and Wang Zuo. The overall command of these remaining troops was given to Peng, who was appointed as the deputy commander of the Fourth Corps.

Several days prior to the departure of Zhu and Mao's troops from the Jinggang region, during a celebratory meeting dedicated to the unification of the Fourth and Fifth Corps an unpleasant event occurred that many interpreted as a bad omen. A platform that had been hastily constructed for the meeting turned out to be flimsy and collapsed when Mao, Zhu, and other leaders climbed onto it. The people exclaimed, but Zhu De tried as best he could to calm them down. "Never mind! If we fall, we shall rise and fight again. Let's rebuild it."[45] The meeting proceeded, but an unpleasant feeling lingered among the soldiers. New trials awaited them, and now this bad luck seemed to spite them.

He Zizhen accompanied Mao on the campaign. To part would have been dangerous. The sad fate of Kaihui spoke for itself. Later, it is true, in conversations with a friend Zizhen asserted that she had supposedly tried unsuccessfully to remain in Jinggang, since she had long felt that Mao "was unworthy of her." According to her, Mao simply ordered his guards to take her "at any cost"; she sobbed uncontrollably the entire way.[46] This assertion is doubtful. She said this to her friend after she and Mao had separated (their split came in 1937). In January 1929, she was five months pregnant. In such a condition she had no reason to leave her husband.

16

A SINGLE SPARK CAN
START A PRAIRIE FIRE

While Mao and Zhu De were implementing agrarian revolution in the Jing-gang Mountains, Chiang Kai-shek was gradually consolidating his power in China. In mid-1928 the completion of the Northern Expedition resulted in the unification of the country under Guomindang rule. Nanjing became the capital of the Republic of China. Beijing, occupied by Yan Xishan, an ally of Chiang Kai-shek, was renamed Beiping.* Several days earlier, Zhang Zuolin, the head of the Beijing government and boss of Manchuria, was assassinated by the Japanese, who were unhappy with his passivity in the war against the Guomindang.[1] His heir, twenty-seven-year-old Zhang Xueliang, became the new governor of Manchuria and formally recognized the authority of Chiang Kai-shek. On January 1, 1929, the period of military rule was terminated and a new stage of political tutelage proclaimed for the next six years. This was done in accordance with a gradual, three-step transition to genuine democracy—military rule, political tutelage, democracy—a concept developed by the late Sun Yat-sen. Thus the basic ideas of the revolution of 1925–27 had been formally achieved and an all-China government established. To be sure, warlord conflicts continued periodically and only by colossal efforts on the part of his forces did Chiang achieve victory in these internecine conflicts.

Meanwhile, China still remained dependent on foreign powers politically and economically. The unequal treaties, including the right of extraterritoriality, were not abolished, even though between 1928 and 1930 most major coun-

---

* The Guomindang government followed the example of the first ruler of the Ming dynasty, which established its capital at Nanjing (Southern capital) and renamed the former capital Beiping (Northern peace).

tries signed agreements with the Nanjing government, returning to China the right to set its own tariffs.

Significant changes were also taking place in the international communist movement and the CCP. In February 1928, the Ninth Enlarged Plenum of the ECCI convened in Moscow, recognized that the wave of revolution had receded, and declared its opposition to an adventurist policy of uprisings and in support of "painstaking work to win the masses" over to the Chinese Communist Party. Several months later, in June–July 1928, the Sixth Congress of the CCP was convened. Because of the white terror in China, the congress was held in the USSR, in Moscow province. Attending the conference were 118 delegates, of whom 84 were full delegates and 34 were alternates. Among the delegates were such familiar names as Qu Qiubai, Zhou Enlai, Li Lisan, Zhang Guotao, and Cai Hesen. Mao, of course, was not present. He was carrying on his war against "counterrevolutionary" peasants in the Jinggang Mountains. At that point there were no reliable statistics concerning party membership. By a resolution of an enlarged plenum of the Provisional Politburo in November 1927, the system of party membership cards and lists of party members was rescinded. The approximate number of party members was estimated at 40,000–50,000, which was far from reality.[2]

The congress expressed its solidarity with the Ninth Plenum of the ECCI, which had condemned "putschism." The policy of uprisings that the CCP had pursued starting in late 1927 was condemned as "mistaken." Naturally, responsibility for this defective course was placed upon the leader of the party, Qu Qiubai. Stalin and the Comintern again got off scot-free. Under Soviet dictation, the delegates adopted a resolution characterizing the present stage of the Chinese revolution as "bourgeois democratic," notwithstanding the national bourgeoisie's "betrayal" of the revolutionary movement. The point was that in backward "semi-feudal" China, it was impossible to carry out a purely communist policy such as nationalizing the mills and factories, eliminating the petty bourgeoisie and wealthy peasants, "sharpening the struggle" against rich peasants, and so forth. The leaders of the CCP followed their Moscow bosses, who strived to demonstrate their devotion to historical materialism by asserting that a particular country's readiness to undergo communist reforms was determined by its level of socioeconomic development. By saying this they completely forgot that Lenin himself had rejected this interpretation of Marxism. They were fanatically observing a kind of sacramental religious ritual that had nothing in common with how communists acted in practice.

Consequently, delegates at the congress subjected Mao's radical ideas to a firestorm of criticism. One of the Hunanese delegates said,

In Hunan province, I must say . . . there is a deviation, a special theory of Comrade Mao. He has an entire system of ideas. What has he told us? He said that we are now entering directly into the worker-peasant revolution, i.e. the socialist revolution, that the Guomindang banner has become a black banner, that now we must unharness our own red banner. . . . I must also say that Comrade Mao's views that the revolution is already a socialist one have been widely circulated among the masses.[3]

Qu Qiubai himself, most likely with Mao in mind, criticized the position of several "comrades" regarding the agrarian question. "Our slogan for the struggle should not be confiscation of the peasants' land. True, there were such mistaken ideas among our comrades last autumn, but the Central Committee was against this and issued its directives on this question indicating the incorrectness of this view."[4] Yet, the criticism of Mao was not politically destructive. The party leadership had not yet been informed of the policies that Mao was pursuing in Jinggang, and so they were excoriating him for past errors that seemed to be eliminated. "We still do not know," said Zhou Enlai, "what is their [Mao's and Zhu De's] attitude to the agrarian reform and to the organization of the Soviets. . . . We also do not know what forms of struggle Mao Zedong and Zhu De adopted." One delegate simply defended Mao: "At present, the situation regarding Mao Zedong has improved. Before he did not know the CC's line, but now the provincial [party] committee has gotten in touch with Mao Zedong and given him a directive, so they have already begun to do this work. As for the military, it, too, has changed its modus operandi and has begun to mobilize the masses."[5]

This is why Mao not only was not expelled from the party at the Sixth Congress, but was elected in absentia as a full member of the Central Committee. After all, he was the organizer of the first CCP base area, and the Comintern recognized the importance of developing a Chinese Red Army. In addition to Mao, twenty-three others became full members and thirteen candidate members of the Central Committee. Upon the recommendation of the ECCI, forty-eight-year-old Xiang Zhongfa, a leader of the workers' movement, was chosen as general secretary of the Central Committee. He was never considered a leading political figure, but the Comintern supported him because Xiang Zhongfa came from a proletarian background, and at the time Moscow blamed all the disasters of the Communist Party on the fact that it had too many intellectuals among its leaders. Nevertheless, to assist Xiang, the ECCI included such major intellectuals as Zhou Enlai and Li Lisan in the party's top leadership. Qu Qiubai and Zhang Guotao retained their membership in the top party organs, but in punishment for their "putschism" they were made to stay in the USSR. Qu headed the newly reorganized CCP, Communist Youth

League, and All-China Federation of Trade Unions (ACFTU) delegation to the highest organs of the international communist movement. Zhang became his deputy.*

Mao learned about the resolutions of the Ninth Plenum of the Sixth CCP Congress long afterward. Not until November 2, 1928, did he receive the letter from the Central Committee "On the February Resolutions of the Comintern," which had been sent to him on June 4. Only in early January 1929, not long before his departure from the Jinggang region, did the basic resolutions of the Sixth Congress reach him. Despite the fact that the resolutions had repudiated his policies, Mao, politically savvy, simply pretended that he heartily approved of all the party's prescriptions. He had no intention of changing anything. He would continue to act this way vis-à-vis the Party bosses as long as he felt unable to oppose them directly.

He quickly replied to the Central Committee, "We agree completely with the International's resolution on China: at present, China is definitely still at the stage of bourgeois-democratic revolution. . . . [T]he revolutionary tide is ebbing daily in the country as a whole. . . . The resolutions adopted at the Sixth Congress are extremely correct, and we accept them with great joy."[6] He blamed all the excesses on others, of course, primarily on his deceased nemesis Zhou Lu, who, according to Mao, had forced him to adhere to a "leftist" course. "He criticized us," Mao wrote to the committee, "for not burning and killing enough, for not carrying out the policy of 'turning the petty bourgeois into proletarians and then forcing them to make revolution.' " In this connection, Mao observed, "[a]s for not confiscating the land of owner-peasants, the whole of it has already been confiscated in the territory of the independent régime in the border area, so of course the problem will not arise again."[7] In other words, of course I agree with you, but it's too late to change anything.

Upon instituting a new land law in southern Jiangxi in April 1929, Mao introduced at least one basic change in comparison with the "Jinggangshan Land Law." The sentence about the complete confiscation of land holdings was replaced by a thesis stating that only "public land and land belonging to the landlord class" would be expropriated. However, the stipulations banning the purchase or sale of land and requiring egalitarian redistribution of land based principally on the number of mouths in a family were preserved, despite the

---

* Eight persons made up this delegation. Three of them (Qu Qiubai, Zhang Guotao, and Huang Ping) were considered representatives of the CCP to the ECCI, two others (Lu Dingyi and Liu Mingfu) representatives of the Chinese Communist Youth League to the Youth Comintern, and another two (Deng Zhongxia and Yu Fei) representatives of the ACFTU to the Profintern, the international trade union organization. This was the first time such a delegation had been formed. Prior to this, the CCP had been represented in Moscow by unaffiliated individuals.

fact that they were not in accord with the principles of a bourgeois democratic revolution.

The decisions of the Ninth Plenum as well as the resolutions of the Sixth Congress were discussed at meetings of party activists, but Mao did not openly discuss points concerning CCP tactics vis-à-vis the forest brigands contained in two congress resolutions ("On the Peasant Question" and "On the Organization of Soviet Power"). They concerned how to win rank-and-file members of these bands over to the side of the party, while asserting that all of the leaders, including those who had assisted the communists during the uprising, should be liquidated.[8] Mao could hardly announce these points in the presence of Yuan Wencai and Wang Zuo.

Several months after Mao left the Jinggang region, Yuan Wencai somehow managed to get hold of copies of these two resolutions and read the most important points to the illiterate Wang Zuo. He said, "No matter how loyal we were to them, they didn't trust us." Wang flew into a rage. In February 1930, both bandits attacked Peng Dehuai's units in Jinggang. Yuan and Wang engaged them on a pontoon bridge near town. Both bandits were beaten in the brief battle and tried to flee into the hills, but their luck ran out. One of them was killed on the bridge; the other jumped into the water and drowned. Several hundred bandits were taken prisoner by the communists.[9] According to the beliefs of the Hakkas both their souls and their spirits (and each person has three souls and seven spirits) would not be able to find peace, because both Yuan and Wang had met unnatural deaths, and Heaven would not take them in.[10]

Conversing with Edgar Snow in 1936, Mao remembered them with contempt and falsely claimed that Yuan and Wang had been killed by peasants.[11] Yet, many years later, in the early 1950s after the PRC was founded, Yuan Wencai and Wang Zuo were rehabilitated and their names inscribed on the list of revolutionary heroes, which could not have happened without Mao's approval. It seems he still could not forget how much he owed them. On May 29, 1965, on a visit to the Jinggang Mountains, Mao met with Yuan Wencai's widow, Xie Meixiang, and with Luo Xiaoying, one of the widows of Wang Zuo, who had had three wives simultaneously. During this meeting he said, "Yuan Wencai and Wang Zuo contributed to the victory of the Chinese revolution." Afterward, Chinese historians began to write that Yuan and Wang had died as the result of a "traitorous plot."[12] Leaving Jinggang in January 1929, however, Mao could not have imagined that just a year later Yuan and Wang would encounter such a fate. They had parted warmly, on good terms.

Mao and Zhu's troops advanced south quickly. On February 1, 1929, they arrived at the mountainous region of Luofuzhang, located in the very heart of Hakka country, at the intersection of Fujian, Guangdong, and Jiangxi provinces. These were impoverished places where the half-starved tenants made up more than 70 percent of the population.[13] To tarry there would mean an intolerable existence, and the Guomindang troops were following on the Red Army's heels. Trying to shake them, the Red Army turned sharply to the north, then east, and then again south, wandering through the counties of southern Jiangxi and northern Fujian, attacking small cities and settlements, robbing the local inhabitants, and torching their houses. They were unable to establish a permanent base.[14] Everywhere they went the Red Army men, almost half of whom were party members, called upon vagabonds and poor tenants to seize and divide other people's land, not to pay their debts or rent, and to organize guerrilla detachments. They seized all the "reactionaries," mocked and paraded them through the villages in dunce caps, or just killed them without mercy. To intimidate and educate the population, they publicly displayed the bodies of their dead enemies, following the custom of bandits. Other communists in Anhui, Hubei, Guangxi, and Guangdong did just the same. Many acted on the principle of "only killing and arson." The destruction of the "exploiting elements" and the "burning of towns" turned into a kind of standard operating procedure.[15]

Paying no attention to the resolutions of the Sixth Congress, Mao and Zhu intensified the struggle against the petty bourgeoisie, rich peasants, and merchants under the pretext of rooting out "reactionaries." They covered up their banditry with grandiloquent phrases. "The Red Army . . . strives for the well-being of the workers and peasants," Zhu De and Mao wrote in one of their appeals to the inhabitants of a commercial town they had seized.

> It also makes every effort to protect the merchants. It exercises strict discipline and does not encroach upon anyone. Because of the current shortage of food supplies, we are writing to you now to request that you kindly collect on our behalf 5,000 big foreign dollars for the soldiers' pay, 7,000 pairs of straw sandals and 7,000 pairs of socks, 300 bolts of white cloth, and 200 laborers. It is urgent that these be delivered to our headquarters before eight o'clock this evening. . . . If you ignore our requests, it will be proof that the Ningdu merchants are collaborating with the reactionaries. . . . In that case we will be obliged to burn down all the reactionary shops in Ningdu as a warning against your treachery. Do not say that we have not forewarned you.[16]

As before, to fill their coffers, the communists were deeply involved in the opium trade.[17]

In late May 1929, He Zizhen gave birth to a daughter in the town of Longyan, which the Red Army was temporarily occupying but had no possibility of retaining. The enemy was swiftly approaching, and the Mao-Zhu forces had to leave at once. Mao had only enough time to name the newborn Jinhua ("Gold Flower"). Half an hour after she had given birth, at Mao's request He Zizhen handed the infant to a peasant family along with fifteen yuan. In her own words, she didn't even cry.[18] She probably suffered, but she was tough and able to hide her feelings. Soon afterward she changed the character *zi* in her name Zizhen from one meaning "self" to one meaning "child," so that her name now meant "Treasuring the Child." "We will get her back after the victory of the revolution," Mao told his wife, but he was unable to keep this promise. Neither Mao nor He Zizhen was ever able to find her.

Mao had no time for babies, especially when the Red Army was experiencing unprecedented difficulties.[19] In constant battles with government troops and local peasant self-defense units, Red Army forces were quickly melting away. In two months the Fourth Corps lost more than six hundred men. Intraparty intrigues were also causing problems. In April, a letter from Shanghai composed in February by Zhou Enlai arrived unexpectedly, urgently recalling Mao and Zhu from the army, but without providing any reason. The Central Committee also demanded splitting the Fourth Corps into small groups and dispatching them to a large number of places to ignite the agrarian revolution everywhere.[20] Of course, Mao resented the fact that the new leaders in the central party apparatus were afraid of his and Zhu's independence and of their armed forces. "Who knows what they're really up to," was the implicit message in the letter. "Will they flare up and slip out of control? After all, they possess military power. It's better to cut them off at the roots before they turn into new militarists."

Mao grasped this logic instantaneously; therefore, neither he nor Zhu obeyed the order. Dividing the Red Army into small units, he wrote with poorly concealed irritation, "results in weak leadership and organization and inability to cope with adverse circumstances, which easily lead to defeat." In this same letter, Mao acquainted the Central Committee with the principles guiding the guerrilla tactics that he and Zhu had worked out:

> (1) Divide our forces to arouse the masses, concentrate our forces to deal with the enemy; (2) The enemy advances, we retreat; the enemy camps, we harass; the enemy tires, we attack; the enemy retreats, we pursue; (3) To extend stable base areas, employ the policy of advancing in waves; when pursued by a powerful enemy, employ the policy of circling around; (4) Arouse the largest numbers of the masses in the shortest possible time and by the best possible methods.

"These tactics," Mao wrote, "are just like casting a net; at any moment we should be able to cast it or draw it in. We cast it wide to win over the masses and draw it in to deal with the enemy."[21]

These were the principles he would follow for many years; later they were adopted by armed communists in Indochina and other colonial and dependent countries in Asia, Africa, and Latin America, under the name of People's War.

Surprisingly, Mao Zedong's reply did not lead to an intensified conflict with the Central Committee. Once again Mao was lucky. At the end of April, stunning news reached China from Moscow that temporarily softened the committee leaders' attitude. In April 1929, Nikolai Bukharin was fiercely criticized for his "rightist pro-kulak views" and a massive collectivization campaign commenced in the USSR whose main target was peasant-proprietors. Stalin was responsible for all these changes. The new Soviet course naturally influenced the Comintern's agrarian policy. In July Bukharin was dismissed from the Comintern, a month after Stalin had begun to change the CCP's "pro-kulak" policy. However, the Russian term *kulak,* signifying a specific social stratum (the rural bourgeoisie), had no equivalent in Chinese. In the CCP documents it was translated by the two-character phrase *funong,* which connoted only property, that is, "rich peasant." Thus, identifying it as a separate category of the peasantry would inevitably lead to activating the communists' anti-peasant policy. On June 7, the Political Secretariat of the ECCI sent to the Central Committee of the CCP a letter on the peasant question that emphasized the importance of dealing correctly with the kulaks, the issue on which "the Chinese comrades have committed their gravest mistakes." Because the kulaks frequently play an "open or covert counterrevolutionary role in the movement," one must battle them decisively. This letter openly praised the activities of Mao Zedong and Zhu De, whose "guerrilla detachments . . . despite repeated attempts to suppress them on the part of reactionaries, not only have managed to preserve their cadres, but have recently achieved notable successes in Fujian province."[22]

The sharpening of Moscow's struggle against Chinese "kulaks" had far-reaching consequences. In other words, Moscow demanded struggle against not only the *dizhu* (landlords), but also the *nong* (peasants). Whether they were rich or poor was a different question. The Chinese communists themselves were the ones who defined what constituted "wealthy," and we have already seen how they did this in practice.

A translation of this letter was published in China in November 1929, in the CCP journal *Gongchan* (Common property). Mao was ecstatic. On February 7, 1930, buoyed by support from Moscow, he promulgated a new land law, the third of its kind. It was adopted at a joint party conference of the Red Army in the village of Pitou, in central Jiangxi. In addition to the point about confiscating all the immovable property of the landlords, Mao included the following article: "Of land, hills, woods, ponds and houses belonging to owner-peasants, if there is a surplus in excess of what is needed for self-support, after the majority of local peasants demand its confiscation, the soviet should approve the peasants' demand, confiscate the surplus portion and redistribute it." As before, the law established the principle of equal division of the land that Mao expressed in a vivid formula: "Drawing on the plentiful to make up for the scarce." Six months later he added the following phrase: "Drawing on the fat to make up for the lean." [23]

The poor Hakka naturally welcomed such a law, and many of them took part in the agrarian revolution. In Xunwu county in southern Jiangxi, where, by May 1930, 80 percent of the land had already been redistributed, the local activists even composed a song that was popular among the Hakka and others:

> *They put us down. So, let's rise up brothers,*
> *Everyone as one, in a single upsurge*
> *We join the Red Army right away.*
> *Who can obstruct such a force?* [24]

Moscow's support could not have been more timely. From June until November 1929, until Mao learned that the Kremlin approved his position, he had suffered from deep depression. He still had no regular contact with the Central Committee, and for a long time he remained ignorant of the fact that on June 12 the Politburo had repudiated the criticism of Mao it had leveled in its February letter. [25] In June, in addition to all his other difficulties, Mao's relations with Zhu De sharply deteriorated. Zhu unexpectedly expressed his dissatisfaction with Mao's micromanagement of the actions of the armed forces entrusted to his command. The "patriarchal style" of the secretary of the Front Committee also began to irritate him. Several subunit commanders supported Zhu.

They were particularly unhappy with Mao's efforts to employ the officers and men in agitprop work among the people, an activity Mao deemed increasingly important. Unwilling to renounce his egalitarian views and acknowledge mistakes in the conduct of the agrarian revolution, he tried to shift responsibility for the failure of his radical policies onto the shoulders of the peasants, the "dimwitted" bumpkins. Mao was now energetically conducting revolutionary propaganda in southern Jiangxi and western Fujian. There were several hundred propagandists among his troops, but he also made the soldiers participate in this work. Injecting communist revolutionary ideas into the heads of the rural dwellers with the help of the Red Army, Mao hoped that the Jiangxi-Fujian experiment would be successful. He did not care that such propaganda activities were diverting the soldiers from their military tasks.

Mao and Zhu might have settled their differences, but in early May 1929 a special representative from the Military Department of the Central Committee from Shanghai crudely intervened in their slowly smoldering conflict. Liu Angong was a self-assured young man of thirty who had just returned to China from Moscow, where he had spent a year at the Infantry School. Therefore, he considered himself an expert in military affairs as well as a great Marxist theoretician. He acted viciously toward Mao. Without understanding the situation, he gave his unconditional support to Zhu De and affixed upon Mao the deadly political label of "factionalist." Following the lead of several commanders, he accused Mao of propagating a "patriarchal system" in the party organization of the Fourth Corps. Obviously, his Soviet teachers had taught the Infantry School cadet how to struggle against "enemies." As soon as he arrived, Liu Angong, appointed head of the Political Department of the corps, began to ramp up the conflict. What particularly galled Mao was that Liu constantly brandished his "Moscow" education but understood nothing about the situation in Jiangxi. To be sure, he did not bother Mao too long: in October 1929 Liu was mortally wounded in battle.[26] Yet Mao retained hostile feelings to insolent Soviet graduates. He soon dedicated a small work, "Oppose Bookism," to such people as Liu Angong. Written in May 1930, it was published as a pamphlet in August under a different title, "On the Work of Investigation." "How can someone be a Communist, and yet go around with his eyes shut talking nonsense?" he asked, alluding not only to Liu Angong but also to many of the Shanghai leaders. He added, "Surprisingly, when problems are discussed within the Communist Party, there are also people who say, whenever they open their mouths, 'Show me where it's written in the book.' " Of course, he continued, "[w]e need Marxism in our struggle. If we welcome this theory, it has nothing whatsoever to do with any formalistic or even mystical notion of a 'sage.' . . . We must study the Marxist 'books,' but they must be integrated with our actual situation. We need 'books,' but we must definitely correct the bookism which departs from reality."[27]

By mid-June 1929 the conflict had become so intense that Mao decided to announce his resignation from the Front Committee. On June 14, he irritably noted, "I myself am too weak physically and too poor in my wisdom and knowledge, so I hope that the Central Committee can send me to Moscow to study and rest for a while."[28]

His strength really had been undermined by all these quarrels. Soon, physically and psychologically weakened, he contracted malaria. Setting his work aside, at the end of June he and Zizhen sequestered themselves in a small two-story house not far from Gutian in western Fujian, where they spent the remainder of the summer. There he convalesced, read, and wrote poetry. Only occasionally did he take part in party discussions. He remained in the Front Committee but was replaced as secretary by twenty-eight-year-old Chen Yi, an old friend of Zhou Enlai and a party member since 1923. In late July, Secretary Chen set out for Shanghai to report on the situation and seek instructions. At the end of August he reported to the Central Committee on how things were in the Zhu-Mao corps.[29] By this time, as we now know, Zhou Enlai, Li Lisan, and other leaders were already on Mao's side, but Mao still didn't know this. So there was nothing for him to do but wait and worry.

Meanwhile, his troops continued to lord it over Hakka country. Everywhere they went they left a trail of fire and ashes. "Deeds, land titles, debt registers, tax rolls (lists and books), all were completely burned," wrote a contemporary.

> The slogans of "No rent (to the landlords), no taxes (to the Guomin-dang authorities), no debts (to the usurers)" were implemented. All of the old tax offices were destroyed and the tax collectors killed. During the uprising, the workers, peasants, and soldiers used their sharp knives to weed out the *tuhao,* the gentry [*shenshi,* rural intelligentsia], the militarists, the officials, the Guomindang committee members, and the agents of imperialism—priests and the missionaries.[30]

But Mao was still depressed. At the end of August, he and Zizhen moved to a bamboo hut in the mountains, where he continued to convalesce and meditate. Over the doorway of their isolated cottage he hung the words "The book lover's refuge."[31] There was melancholy and sadness; thoughts welled up of his great lost love for his faithful Kaihui. Zizhen, of course, was young and beautiful, but very obstinate. Hakka women were generally distinguished by their independent and proud temper, and she markedly so. "You are iron and I am steel," Mao said to her. "If we clash it will sound like a gong!" Later he would tell their daughter Li Min, who was born in 1937, that their "arguments often escalated into clashes." When this happened Mao "often stood on 'positions of strength,' " trying to put Zizhen down by invoking his "political authority." He shouted and cursed, threatened to expel his insubordinate wife from the party, gave her a "verbal dressing down," but he was usually the first to seek reconciliation. He failed to break Zizhen's spirit.[32]

This is probably why in the wee hours thoughts about the obedient "Little Dawn" (Kaihui) and their sons gave him no peace. "I lost my proud Poplar," he would write many years later in one of his verses.[33] (Kaihui's family name Yang means "poplar" in Chinese.) At the end of November, he sent a letter to Li Lisan in Shanghai asking Li to tell his brother Zemin that he would like Kaihui's postal address. "[A]lthough I am better now," he informed Li Lisan, "my spirits are not yet fully recovered. I often think of Kaihui, Anying, and the others, and I would like to communicate with them."[34] Despite the bitterness of the civil war, Mao was not able to jettison all of his human feelings. Did he have some sort of bad premonition? He remembered his former wife just one year before her tragic death.

Around this time Chen Yi returned from Shanghai with the long-awaited decision of the Central Committee: it recognized Mao's position, not Zhu's, as correct. Chen Yi and Zhu De asked Mao to return, but only after a month of negotiations did he finally leave his mountain hideaway. Once again he headed the Front Committee, and now he concentrated almost unlimited power in his own hands. His opponents were unhorsed, so he decided put the disagreements behind him. Zhu De resumed being obedient and the entire corps subordinated itself to Mao. Many trials lay before them. Revenge could wait. On November 28, 1929, Mao informed Shanghai, "There is absolutely no problem in uniting the Fourth Army [Corps] Party under the correct guidance of the Central Committee. . . . The only problem is that the basic theoretical knowledge of Party members is too low, and we must quickly carry out education."[35] In December 1929, in Gutian in western Fujian, he convened a party conference of the corps at which, even though he sharply criticized "the purely military viewpoint," he at the same time hinted at a way out of the crisis.[36] "Treat the illness to save the patient" is how he later described the method tested in western Fujian.

All this was done in a purely Chinese spirit. "Destroying an opponent does not prove him wrong" is a wise Chinese saying. "You need to make him 'lose face.' If your enemy survives the shame, then you can do with him whatever you will. Only you will decide whether or not to restore his 'face.' This is called giving someone a chance to rectify his ways." For Chinese it was the most skillful method for dealing with opponents. Of course, Mao didn't always act this way; he was not just a Chinese, but also a member of the Communist Party, and as such, acknowledged the "correctness" of Bolshevik methods of bloody executions. But he mainly applied such methods only toward those whom he genuinely deemed "class enemies" beyond redemption. Or toward those who, from his perspective, were of no further use even "without face."

This, incidentally, is also how the Guomindang operated. As a rule, the police who arrested communists always gave them a choice between death and public renunciation. They usually released their prisoner if he chose the shameful path. They might not even demand that the broken man turn in his former comrades.[37] What the Chinese police required was not betrayal but for the communist to "lose face." Many of those who repented were even given work, and even entrusted with very responsible positions. Everyone knew that the person who had shamed himself would serve with exceptional zeal.

After sorting out intra-army relations, Mao was able to concentrate on political questions. The sharpening of the struggle against the "rightists" in the Soviet Communist Party, connected with the full-scale collectivization in the Soviet Union, led the Comintern to radicalize its policy with respect to the worldwide national liberation movement. The resolutions of the Tenth Plenum of the ECCI held in Moscow in July 1929 targeted the "rightist danger" that supposedly threatened all communist parties. The main error of the "rightists" was that they refused to recognize "the symptoms of a new revolutionary high tide [pod'em in Russian]" in the world. In other words, they "lagged behind" the revolutionary masses. The Russian-language resolutions of the plenum, received in Shanghai in late September, caused confusion within the Central Committee of the CCP. According to an eyewitness, "At first a majority of the Central Committee inclined toward a cautious interpretation of this directive. . . . They were afraid that if they gave too leftist an interpretation to the phrase, they might end up cracking their heads against the wall again."[38] The Chinese were confused by the Russian word *pod'em,* with its dual meaning of "high tide" and "on the rise." They wanted to be absolutely certain that this time their Russian bosses would not find fault with them. Suddenly the Comintern was criticizing them not for "putschism" but for passivity. The Tenth Plenum had clearly identified "the rightist danger" as the main one in the international communist movement.

Such was the situation that prevailed among the leadership of the Chinese Communist Party in the early 1930s. One could simply not talk about any degree of independence on the part of the CCP. Complete financial dependence upon Moscow paralyzed the leaders of the communist movement. At most they might oppose Comintern representatives in China, but never the Kremlin itself. The funds transferred to Shanghai, mainly via the special International Liaison Department, grew steadily. By the late 1920s and early 1930s it was hundreds of thousands, even millions of rubles and dollars. Thus, by 1930, the Soviets spent five million rubles on training Chinese revolutionaries in the Communist University of the Toilers of China, which had been founded in 1925 under the name of the Sun Yat-sen University of the Toilers of China.[39] For the seven months from February to September 1930, the CCP received more than 223,000 Mexican dollars from Moscow. (The Mexican dollar circulated in China on par with the yuan.) In October, it received another $10,000 in American dollars.[40] (At this time an American dollar equaled 3.6 yuan.) At the same time, in 1930 the Central Committee of the Communist Youth League received 70,000 yuan from the same source, and the Chinese branch of the International Organization for Aid to Revolutionary Fighters (MOPR in Russian abbreviation), a special Comintern agency that provided support to the families of underground communists and incarcerated revolutionaries, received 11,400 yuan.[41] How could there be any question of disobeying Moscow?

After a thorough discussion of the materials from the plenum on December 8, 1929, the Central Committee issued Circular No. 60, "Practical Implementation of Defense of the USSR," which outlined the contours of a new, aggressive revolutionary policy. The CCP leaders obviously wanted to be "more Catholic than the Pope," in this case, Stalin. They demanded that all party members work to "assist a high tide of revolutionary war" by combining armed struggle in the rural areas with new uprisings in the cities. The goal of these coordinated actions was the "seizure of the largest centers of the country." Li Lisan and Zhou Enlai were chiefly responsible for drafting this circular.

Worldwide trends seemed to confirm the "correctness" of the resolutions of the Tenth Plenum. At the end of October 1929, the New York stock market crashed. The Great Depression, which soon engulfed the capitalist world, planted new hopes in all communists. It seemed that the inevitable downfall of world capitalism was fast approaching. The economic crisis had a direct impact on China's economy. Industrial enterprises shut down and unemployment skyrocketed. Catastrophic inflation occurred, poverty increased, and the gap between rich and poor widened. In addition, the struggle among various intra-Guomindang groups intensified. Wang Jingwei, who was a leader of the "Reorganizationists" group, urgently demanded the reform of the party. In this situation, the Comintern drew the conclusion that China was at "the initial moment of a revolutionary high tide."

In mid-December Shanghai received a new directive from Moscow, a letter from the ECCI that had been drafted on October 26, just when the world financial market had begun to wobble. The new directive called upon party leaders to focus on "the exacerbation of all contradictions" in China. The country was entering a "period of the most profound national crisis," whose special feature was the "revival of the workers' movement which was emerging from the state of depression following the serious defeats of 1927." The authors of the document perceived in this "a true and vital sign of the growing high tide" of the revolutionary movement and therefore demanded that the CCP "begin to prepare the masses to bring about the revolutionary overthrow of the power of the bourgeois-landlord bloc, and look to the establishment of a dictatorship of the working class and the peasantry in the form of soviets, actively developing and constantly broadening revolutionary forms of class struggle such as massive political strikes, revolutionary demonstrations, guerrilla attacks, and so forth." The letter concluded on a threatening note: "The main danger inside the party at present is the mood of right opportunism that . . . underestimates the significance of peasant war, underestimates and applies the brakes to revolutionary energy and initiative, and belittles the independent and leading role of the proletariat and the communist party." [42]

Zealously striving to execute these directives, the Central Committee of the CCP, however, overreached. At the end of February it released a new circular, No. 70, which asserted that "all of China, from Guangdong to Zhili [old name for Hebei], from Sichuan to Jiangsu, is gripped by crisis and by a revolutionary movement. . . . The mass struggle is developing evenly throughout the country. . . . In the present situation it is clear that victory is possible initially in one or several provinces, in particular in Wuchang and adjacent districts." Therefore, the Central Committee considered it necessary to deploy the Red Army to attack and seize large cities. [43]

This resolution was elaborated in a letter from the Central Committee to the Front Committee of the Fourth Corps on April 3, 1930, that developed the idea that it was possible to conquer Jiangxi, Hubei, and Hunan provinces as well as the central city of Wuhan in the very near future. [44] They all desperately wanted to appear as ultraleftists. This task resonated with the proposal that

Mao Zedong himself had expressed more than a year earlier in his letter to the Central Committee: to seize Jiangxi and the contiguous western parts of Fujian and Zhejiang over the course of a year.[45] At the time, the Central Committee, which was critical of Mao, did not respond to this idea. Now it not only returned to it, but expanded upon it. It still was unable to restrain itself from criticizing Mao and Zhu De for "peasant consciousness and banditism," but weren't the leaders of the CCP who were hatching plans for a bloody nationwide slaughter themselves acting like bandits?

Mao was pleased with the new turn of events. He did not repudiate his previous year's intention to conquer Jiangxi, although he made certain changes. "This proposal to take Jiangxi within one year erred only in mechanically setting a time limit of one year," he wrote in early January 1930 in a letter to the talented young commander Lin Biao, who some time back had come to the Jinggang Mountains with Zhu De. "As to the subjective and objective conditions in Jiangxi, they very much merit our attention." In early February, almost three weeks before the appearance of Circular No. 70, and acting on his own initiative, Mao announced at a party conference of the Fourth Corps his decision to attack Ji'an, the largest city in western Jiangxi.[46] Like Li Lisan, Zhou Enlai, and many others, he experienced an enormous rush of excitement, pleasurably anticipating the revolutionary explosion. "All China is spread with dry faggots which will soon be aflame," he wrote to Lin Biao. "The saying 'A single spark can start a prairie fire,' is an apt description of . . . the present situation. . . . It is like a ship far out at sea whose masthead can already be seen at the horizon from the shore; it is like the morning sun in the east whose shimmering rays are visible from a high mountain top; it is like a child about to be born moving restlessly in its mother's womb." [47]

Meanwhile, the leaders of the CCP continued their feverish preparations for revolution. In early March 1930, Zhou Enlai left for the USSR to deliver a report. In China, Li Lisan remained the de factor leader of the CCP. Lively, temperamental, and proactive, he also headed the Central Committee's Department of Agitation and Propaganda. It was at his initiative that an all-China conference of soviets was convened in Shanghai in late May 1930, attended by some forty delegates. By this time, in addition to Jiangxi and Fujian, soviet districts existed in Hubei, Hunan, Guangdong, and Guangxi. Under Li Lisan's influence, the conference called upon Chinese soviet workers to "begin the struggle for socialism" against "counterrevolutionary kulaks" [48] (in other words, the working peasantry). Mao Zedong did not attend the conference* despite Li Lisan's importunate demands that he cast everything aside and come to Shanghai. A trip to the forum would have been risky. Could he be sure

---

* Nevertheless, he and Zhu De, who likewise did not take part in the conference, were elected in absentia as honorary chairmen.

that Li Lisan would not try to detain him? Mao remembered how the Central Committee had tried to recall him and Zhu De from the army. Nevertheless, he had no objections to the conference resolutions.

Of particular significance was the decision to amalgamate individual units of the Red Army by reducing the number of corps and forming four army groups. The First Army Group was entrusted to the leadership of Zhu and Mao. Right after getting this news, Zhu and Mao unified on June 13 all the armed forces that were operating in southwestern Jiangxi and western Fujian. There were about twenty thousand officers and men under their command. Realizing that this was not enough for an army group, Zhu and Mao initially called their troops the First Field Army, but six days later, evidently not wishing to enter into a new conflict with Shanghai, they accepted the name the Central Committee had bestowed upon them: the First Army Group. In addition to the Fourth Corps, commanded by Lin Biao, the Sixth and the Twelfth Corps of the Red Army, which were conducting military actions not far from where the forces of Zhu and Mao were located, were amalgamated into the First Army Group.

Soon after, on June 21, Li Lisan's special emissary arrived in the Zhu-Mao region to inform the commanders of the First Army Group about a sensational new Politburo decision. The resolution, bearing the distinctive title "The New Revolutionary High Tide and an Initial Victory in One or More Provinces," was drafted by Li Lisan and pointed the communists toward unleashing a revolutionary struggle for power in the near term. "China is the weakest link in the ruling chain of world imperialism; it is the place where the volcano of the world revolution is most likely to erupt," the resolution stated.[49]

There was no time to waste. The next day Zhu and Mao issued an order for a campaign to attack Jiujiang and Nanchang, the largest cities in Jiangxi. The "Great Revolution" had begun. It need hardly be mentioned that it failed. They did not succeed in taking Jiujiang, let alone Nanchang. Only the small Third Army Group, commanded by Peng Dehuai and consisting of 7,000–8,000 officers and men, scored some success. They were able to seize Changsha and hold it for ten days, during which time they thoroughly looted it. It was because of the pillaging of Changsha that Kaihui would soon be arrested.

In late August–early September 1930, having linked his army group with Peng Dehuai's forces to form the First Front Army, numbering some 30,000 men,* Mao twice tried to repeat the success of the Third Army Group in the vicinity of Changsha, but neither he nor Peng was able to conquer the capital of Hunan again. The working masses of the city remained absolutely passive,

* Zhu became the commander of the First Front Army, Peng his deputy commander. Mao served as general political commissar.

withholding their support from the communists. The result was that the units of the First Front Army suffered enormous casualties.[50]

The leaders of the CCP, including Mao, completely miscalculated with respect to both political and military matters. There really was a crisis in China, but the CCP was still too weak to seize power. The party had grown in the past three years, boasting some 60,000 members, but this was obviously not enough. The entire Red Army numbered no more than 54,000 men, and only half of them were equipped with rifles.[51] So for Mao, as for Li Lisan, it was too early to proclaim to the whole world that "the gunpowder of the revolution is already exploding, and the light of the dawn of the revolution will quickly arrive."[52] The world revolution was still some distance off. It was necessary to retreat yet again, to reorganize the troops, and, most of all, to shift to a strategy of protracted war. Once more a base area was needed, an inaccessible one like that in Jinggang, only much larger. There was no possibility of feeding themselves in a small territory.

Mao had long understood the need to establish such a base, but many of the field commanders did not support him. Their creed was that of the free-roaming bandit who adheres to a strategy of flying guerrilla raids. Their simple-minded military science consisted of attacking, looting, and burning everything and then going off to a new region. Lin Biao was one such commander. Mao lauded him as a brilliant officer but criticized him all the time for his unwillingness to waste time on building a secure soviet base.[53] "[Y]ou seem to think that . . . to undertake the arduous work of establishing political power would be to labor in vain," Mao wrote to him.

> Instead, you want to extend our political influence through the easier method of roving guerrilla actions and wait until the masses throughout the country have been won over, or more or less won over, before launching a nationwide insurrection which, with the participation of the Red Army, would become a great nationwide revolution. Your theory that we must first win over the masses everywhere on a nationwide scale, and then establish political power, is not, in my opinion, applicable to the Chinese revolution.

No, Mao asserted, only a policy that envisions the systematic creation of organs of soviet power in various parts of the country is correct in semi-colonial China, for which "imperialism is contending in its final stages."[54] Only then could a single spark ignite a prairie fire.

UNDER THE
COMINTERN'S WING

Mao decided to establish the secure base in northwestern Jiangxi. Located in the middle course of the Ganjiang River, this region occupied an advantageous strategic position. It was no farther from there to Nanchang—and in September–October 1930, Mao had not yet refused to attack the provincial capital—than it was from Jinggang, where units subordinate to the First Front Army still operated. The hilly and partially mountainous district was extremely well suited for guerrilla warfare. The densely forested mountains provided sanctuary from which one could emerge at will to strike at opponents who held rich commercial towns and settlements. The center of the region was Ji'an, a commercial city of about fifty thousand, the third largest in Jiangxi, and home to many wealthy people who were attractive targets for plunder. There were many small workshops where weapons could be forged. A powerful soviet area could be established there.

Mao took the town on October 4, 1930, and quickly announced the formation of a Jiangxi Provincial Soviet Government. Finally he could provide his officers and men with everything they needed. After seizing Ji'an, the Red Army extracted eight million Mexican dollars and a lot of gold from the townspeople.[1] It seemed that wonderful prospects opened up before the First Front Army, but Mao and his superiors in the Central Committee soon faced major problems.

In the autumn of 1930, Li Lisan and his colleagues learned that the Comintern was extremely dissatisfied with their adventurist policies. After conversations with Zhou Enlai in Moscow, the ECCI had already begun to suspect that the CCP Central Committee had "gone too far" to the left in interpreting Moscow's directives. Despite its doubts the ECCI did not react at all to the Chinese Politburo's ultraleftist resolution "The New Revolutionary High Tide and an Initial Victory in One or More Provinces." In principle Moscow did not reject the idea of "seizing one or more industrial and administrative centers." It merely saw that goal as dependent upon the strengthening of the Red Army.[2] It was the defeats suffered by the Chinese communists from late July through early September that radically altered the situation. Stalin was not fond of losers and never forgave them. Moreover, just then he was informed of several statements by Li Lisan regarding world revolution that contradicted his own conception about building socialism in one country. In early August, intoxicated with news of the seizure of Changsha, Li Lisan called for the USSR to become directly involved in the revolutionary events in China. His calculation was simple: provoke a world war in which, he was convinced, the Soviet Union would inevitably emerge victorious. Thus the Chinese revolution would serve as the fuse of the "great world revolution." Stalin also learned that within the narrow circle of the party leadership Li had cursed the Comintern and counterpoised loyalty to Moscow against loyalty to the Chinese revolution, saying that "after the seizure of Hankou we'll be able to sing a different tune to the Comintern."

Stalin scented Trotskyism and ordered Li Lisan "to come here [i.e., Moscow] immediately."[3] At the end of September 1930, on orders of the ECCI, an enlarged plenum of the CCP Central Committee was held in Shanghai to "correct its mistakes through collective self-criticism." Qu Qiubai and Zhou Enlai guided the meeting, along with a representative of the Far Eastern Bureau in Shanghai, the German communist Gerhard Eisler. The plenum, however, did not unmask the Li Lisan platform; Li Lisan's authority in the party was so strong that neither Qu nor Zhou nor even Eisler was able to do anything. The plenum listened to Li's "unsparing" self-criticism but retained him as a member of the Politburo, although he was removed from the Politburo Standing Committee, which now consisted of only three persons: Xiang Zhongfa, Qu Qiubai, and Zhou Enlai. In the end the plenum admitted only "partial tactical and organizational errors" in implementing the Comintern's line.[4]

At this point Stalin lost all patience. He immediately dispatched Pavel Mif, whom the Soviet Politburo considered a great China expert, to Shanghai. Mif was a tough and brutal man who had become a China specialist on orders of the party. He was only twenty-nine in 1930, but he had already gained a reputation in the Comintern as well as in the CCP. He had risen rapidly through the ranks and by 1928 had been named rector of the Sun Yat-sen University of the Toilers of China (UTK) in Moscow, which in September 1928 was renamed the Communist University of the Toilers of China (KUTK). Less than a year later, Mif was named head of the Far Eastern section of the ECCI. Mif's rapid ascent went to his head. According to his contemporaries, "the Comintern's chief China specialist" behaved like a haughty, imperious, and self-assured bureaucrat. "He was a very ambitious person . . . and adept in the technique of Stalin's strategy," recalled Zhang Guotao, who branded him "unscrupulous and opportunistic."[5]

Mif arrived in Shanghai in October 1930 under the guise of a German commercial traveler named Petershevskii. (He traveled via Germany, where in the interest of security he underwent plastic surgery.) He immediately assumed the leadership of the Far Eastern Bureau. Flagrantly intervening in the internal affairs of the CCP, he essentially renounced the decisions of the September plenum and in the absence of Li Lisan, who had gone to Moscow "to study," he made active preparations to convene a new party forum. His task was facilitated by receipt on November 16 of a new anti–Li Lisan document, "Letter of the ECCI on Li Lisanism," in which the political line of Li was condemned as "anti-Marxist," "anti-Leninist," "opportunistic," and "in essence" Trotskyist. In contemporary communist parlance that sounded like a verdict. The Central Committee of the CCP was crushed. Mif could do with it whatever he willed.

Convinced that the "salvation" of the party was only possible by means of renewing its leadership, Mif convened a new enlarged plenum in Shanghai in early January 1931. On his own authority he added his former student Chen Shaoyu, who had previously not even been in the Central Committee, to the Politburo. Shen Zemin, another graduate of KUTK, was co-opted into the reconfigured Central Committee as an alternate member. To support these decisions, Mif invited a gaggle of his former Moscow students to the plenum. These young people, none of whom were members of the Central Committee, accounted for one-third of the participants in the forum. In addition to Chen Shaoyu and Shen Zemin they included among others Bo Gu (real name Qin Bangxian), Wang Jiaxiang, and Chen Yuandao.[6] All of them would soon play an important role both in the CCP and in the life of Mao Zedong.

To the Standing Committee Mif added in absentia Zhang Guotao, who had long since opposed the Li Lisan line. Qu Qiubai was excluded from this highest party organ because he had stained his reputation by his "appeasement" of Li Lisan at the September plenum. Qu was also removed from the Politburo, as was Li himself, but both remained members of the Central Committee. Several days after the plenum, Mif, flouting all norms, placed Chen Shaoyu on the Standing Committee. Also, in March 1931, the leading organs of the Chinese Communist Youth League were reorganized at his insistence. Bo Gu became the secretary of the Central Committee of the youth league.

Mif's "revolution" produced far from favorable results for the CCP. The persons he trusted the most, Chen Shaoyu and Bo Gu, were constrained by their Moscow past, particularly the struggle against Trotskyism in the USSR, in which they had all actively participated. Most prominent among them was the broad-browed and stocky Chen Shaoyu, who like Mif was energetic, willful, and uncompromising. Gifted with a flair for foreign languages, Chen learned Russian tolerably just a few months after enrolling in UTK in late November 1925. This became his trump card. While other students were struggling with the Cyrillic alphabet, Chen gained favor with the teachers at the university who did not know Chinese. Despite his youth (he had been born in 1904) and his short time in the party (he joined the youth league in September 1925, and became a party member in 1926), Chen became the assistant to and interpreter for Mif, who was teaching a course on Leninism at the university. In September 1926, Mif nominated him for the post of chairman of the student commune and toward the end of that same year involved him in the struggle against Trotskyism.[7] Ultimately, with Mif's help, Chen and his confederates succeeded in bringing the students at UTK under their sway.

In 1929 Chen went to China. He and his wife, Meng Qingshu, settled in Shanghai, where he got some low-level assignment, but then suddenly his luck turned. Mif, newly arrived in China, decided to rely upon Chen and other graduates of KUTK. The veteran party cadres were quite dissatisfied, but most kept their mouths shut. Those few who voiced their discontent were soon disciplined or even expelled from the party. The result was that the Comintern's power over the CCP peaked in 1931. "After Li Lisan's struggle against the Comintern and the condemnation of Li Lisan's anti-Comintern line," Zhou Enlai recalled, "the Chinese communists considered every word of the ECCI emissaries as absolutely authoritative."[8]

News of the September plenum reached Mao only in early December 1930. He learned about what had taken place at the new January plenum two weeks after it wrapped up, and not until March 1931 did he learn that "Comrade Li" was being subjected to a humiliating course of "study" in Moscow. Mao had his own take on all these events. He had never liked Li Lisan and had no reason to feel sorry for him. Mao remembered all the accusations that this "king for a day" had hurled at him over the past months. Nor had he forgotten Li's demand that he leave his army and come to Shanghai. Especially fresh in mind was the latest letter that Li had written him, dated June 15, 1930, in which Li, intoxicated with unlimited power, had indulged in such rude expressions that Mao naturally took offense. Li had accused Mao, one of the oldest members of the party, of possessing a "peasant mentality," failing to understand the changing political situation, and being unable to follow the directives of the Central Committee. Mao was also heartened by the news that he himself had been made a candidate member of the Politburo at the September plenum and that he had been reelected to that position at the new, January plenum. He was pleased that Zhu De, who was now devoted to him, had been co-opted into the Central Committee, albeit as a candidate member.

But was Mao aware that the decisions of the plenums regarding him had been taken in response to pressure from Moscow? Did he understand that Stalin was beginning to look him over seriously as a possible future leader of the party? Probably not, but he might have guessed at it. At this time Moscow was beginning to give active support to Mao's advancement. Starting in the late 1920s, Stalin's Comintern began to support Mao and even periodically to rise to his defense when one or another CCP leader criticized the obstinate Hunanese. In its reports to the center, the Far Eastern Bureau highly praised the Zhu-Mao army as "the best" in all respects.[9] Reading this information and observing the growth of the Soviet areas, Stalin concluded in July 1930 that under Chinese conditions "the creation of a battle worthy and politically mature Red Army . . . is the first order of business the achievement of which will likely guarantee the powerful development of the revolution."[10] Precisely for that reason he increasingly fastened his attention on Mao. In the USSR there even began a campaign to glorify him, for the time along with Zhu De. This is what the Soviet press wrote about these "two heroes" at the time. These are "two communists, two guerrilla leaders whose names alone make thousands of distinguished Chinese turn pale from anger, indignation, and most frequently from panicky fear. They are also well-known outside of China."[11]

In the summer of 1930 it was Moscow in the form of the Far Eastern Bureau of the ECCI in Shanghai that supported the decision of the Politburo of the CCP to appoint Mao as political commissar of the First Army Group, the most powerful one, and then as general political commissar of the First Front Army. Subsequently, in mid-October, Moscow actively supported Mao's co-optation into the Central Committee Bureau for the Soviet areas, a new party structure that was intended to centralize all party work in rural districts under the control of the CCP.[12] Next, Moscow suggested that Mao be appointed either as chair or as a member of the Central Revolutionary Military Council (CRMC), a kind of provisional government of all of the Soviet areas.*

This is what the Far Eastern Bureau of the ECCI wrote to the CCP Politburo on November 10, 1930:

> The command of our Red Army (Mao Zedong, Peng Dehuai) had no connection with the government. The government is one thing, the army is another. . . . Needless to say, such a situation is unsuitable. We need to arrange things so that Mao Zedong has responsibility not only for the condition and operations of the army, but also participates in

---

* The decision of the Chinese Politburo to establish the CRMC was adopted on October 17, 1930, the same date as the formation of the Bureau of the Central Committee. At that time, Mao Zedong's district was called the Central Soviet Area. Until then, beginning in June 1930, a so-called Chinese Revolutionary Military Council had operated in the Soviet districts in Jiangxi; in August it was rechristened the Chinese Worker-Peasant Revolutionary Council. It functioned as the highest organ of military-bureaucratic power in the territories that Mao controlled, and all the local armed forces of the CCP as well as the Jiangxi Soviet government were subordinated to it. From the very beginning Mao served as chairman. However, he did not concern himself with administrative problems; rather he devoted all his attention to political and military questions.

the government and has partial responsibility for the work of the latter. He must be appointed a member of the government (chairman of the Revolutionary Military Council). There is no need to discuss the advantages of such an arrangement; it is obvious.[13]

At first, until the arrival in Jiangxi of Zhou Enlai, who had been appointed secretary of the Central Committee Bureau for the Soviet areas, and Xiang Ying, another important party leader, Mao, on Moscow's initiative, was even entrusted with leadership of this organ. Naturally, he was gratified by such support and approved the decisions of the plenums.

On the other hand, as one of the founders of the party, Mao must have been hostile to Mif's "clever puppies," who had advanced into the leadership while bypassing all the rules. He generally despised the overly educated graduates of the Soviet international schools. The dogmatic style of the insolent Muscovite students contrasted sharply with his own methods, based in the first instance on painstaking study of conditions in the locale where he was working. "Seek truth from facts," he would write later, at the end of 1943, in effect summing up his entire rural research in the 1920s and 1930s. However, Mao always adjusted his conclusions to fit his radical views. The result was that it was not practice that served as the criterion of truth but rather leftist ideas that were the criterion of reality.

In 1930 Mao conducted seven field studies in villages in southern and western Jiangxi. The results, of course, were identical. The enemies of the revolution were not only the landlords, but also the well-to-do peasants, whom he categorized as those with an "excess of money and land." He acknowledged that unlike the landlords, these peasants got by on their own; they did not force anyone to work for them, they did not rent out land, they got up early and went to bed late, working their small plots by the sweat of their brows. In general, they were very hardworking people. But this was precisely what was wrong with them. Mao believed that the industriousness of these "well-to-do peasants" resulted in their producing more than they needed for their own sustenance. Therefore, they sold surplus grain on the market or loaned it to their poor neighbors. In other words, they stood out from the mass of their half-starved poor fellow villagers, many of whom consequently hated them. "Most of the poor peasants cry out [slogans like] 'equal land' and 'tear up debts' in opposition to this kind of rich peasant," Mao wrote.

If the Communist Party should stop this activity of the poor peasants, those poor peasants could not but hate the Communist Party. Because of this, we know that not only must we decide to strike down these half-landlord-like rich peasants, but moreover we must equalize the rich owner-peasants' land, cancel loans made by the rich owner-peasants, and divide the rich owner-peasants' grain—there is no doubt that we have to do this. We must do it, and then and only then can we win over the poor peasant masses.[14]

His new investigations "confirmed" his oft-repeated thesis about the enormous revolutionary potential of the rural lumpen proletarians, the "outcasts" who "had nothing to wear when it got cold" and who were "very ragged."[15] In the districts seized by the Red Army all these people, including criminals and beggars, "welcome the revolution," Mao noted significantly. "They were extremely happy when they heard that the local bullies were to be overthrown and the land redistributed."[16]

Not all communists shared his conclusion. In 1930–31 Mao confronted the most powerful opposition within the party in all of the time he had been dealing with the agrarian question. Members of the local Jiangxi CCP organization sharply disagreed with his pro-lumpen ideas aimed against the working peasantry. The disagreement became so intense that it led to open armed conflict, the first such bloody struggle between hostile factions in CCP history. This was the Futian Incident, named after the town where, in early December 1930, troops of the Jiangxi faction attacked representatives of Mao Zedong who were busy exposing "counterrevolutionary elements."

The roots of the conflict were first exposed in February 1930, during the joint party conference of the Front Committee of the Fourth Corps, the Special West Jiangxi Committee, and the army committees of the Fifth and Sixth Corps of the Red Army. It was held in the village of Pitou, not far from the major population center of Donggu, in central Jiangxi. It was this conference that on February 7 adopted a land law that established the principle of equal division of the land. "Drawing on the plentiful to make up for the scarce, and drawing on the fat to make up for the lean." That formula is what the local Jiangxi communists condemned as egalitarianism. They called for the division only of land belonging to the landlords, not to peasants, and even then not according to "the number of mouths" in a family, but according to the number of able-bodied laborers per household.[17] Mao viewed this as an obvious "right-wing deviation" that had to be opposed vehemently. "[T]he local leading organs of the Party at all levels are filled with landlords and rich peasants," he concluded, "and the Party's policy is completely opportunist."[18]

He was convinced that he was right, especially since several weeks before the conference he had received the anti-kulak ECCI letter on the peasant question that had been sent to the CCP Central Committee in June 1929. The Jiangxi communists were represented at the conference by the Western Jiangxi Special Committee as well as a number of delegates from the Army Committee of the Sixth Corps. This corps itself included local guerrilla units that had been operating in the province prior to the arrival of Mao's troops. Reorganizing them into the Sixth Corps on instructions from the Central Committee, Mao appointed the forty-year-old Hunanese Liu Shiqi as the corps political commissar and as secretary of its Party Committee, and his own younger brother, Mao Zetan, as chief of the Political Department of the corps. He wanted to place the Jiangxi men, whom he did not fully trust, under reliable control. If the majority of peasants and party members had welcomed the troops of the Fourth Corps in "Hakka land," where southern Jiangxi, western Fujian, and northeast Guangdong came together, the situation was different in the central districts of Jiangxi and the contiguous areas to the west and northwest. There the people considered themselves native Jiangxi people (*bendi*), and their hostility toward the Hakka in the south had persisted for generations. Men from this environment also dominated the local organizations of the CCP, the guerrilla units, and the Jiangxi branches of the Sandianhui (Three-Dot Society), a secret society supported by the communists. Fifty percent of the troops in the Fourth Corps were Hunanese, and another 20 percent men from southern Jiangxi and western Fujian, so the local people viewed them as outsiders, as Hakka, and did not trust them. This is why the Jiangxi party organization adamantly opposed the radical land law that Mao had proposed.[19]

At the conference in Pitou, however, the Jiangxi group was in the minority, the law passed, and Mao began to pursue agrarian revolution in the central and western districts of the province "with fire and sword." He and Zhu De advanced the slogan "Complete physical extermination of the kulaks."[20] This is what led to the exacerbation of the conflict.

The situation was aggravated by the existence of a secret anticommunist group, the AB Corps (AB *tuan*), which had been created by local Guomindang members in 1925–26 and was active in the province. (The letters "A" and "B" denoted different levels of membership at the provincial and district levels.) The main goal of the league was to unmask communist heresy, and they did not shy away from dirty methods, including infiltrating provocateurs and spies into CCP organizations to disrupt the communist movement.[21] Their activity reached its apogee in October–December 1930, just when Chiang Kai-shek was unleashing a powerful offensive against the soviet areas in Jiangxi. This military operation, carried out by troops of the Ninth Corps of the NRA and supplementary units attached to it, with a total force of 100,000, was called the First Bandit Suppression Campaign. Agents of the AB Corps played an important role in it.

Of course, the provocateurs had to be unmasked, but how? It was practically impossible to distinguish friends from enemies. Ferreting out spies required time, but the mortal danger hanging over the Red Army required urgent action. Fear engendered by Chiang Kai-shek's offensive was mounting and relations between the "newcomer" and local communists worsening. Both factions, on the pretext of attacking the AB Corps, were fiercely attacking each other. A wide-scale purge was taking place in the army and the party during which both the innocent and the guilty were seized. Mao played the major role. The Jiangxi communists had no chances against him and his Hakka army. By October 1930, more than a thousand members of the Jiangxi party organization had fallen victim to the terror. One out of every thirty Jiangxi communists was destroyed.[22] Mao believed he was not dealing with "sick" comrades in the party whose "illnesses" he was prepared to treat, but rather with Guomindang spies engaged in deep conspiracies. He began to imagine them literally everywhere. "Recently the entire Party in southwest Jiangxi has been showing signs of a very serious crisis," he reported to the Central Committee in mid-October. "The entire Party leadership is dominated by the rich peasants' line. . . . A majority of the leading organs at all levels, both internal and external, are leading organs filled with AB Corps members and rich peasants.[23] . . . Without a basic transformation of the Party in southwest Jiangxi, this crisis can assuredly not be overcome."[24] The Jiangxi leaders resisted as best they could. "Mao wants to concentrate power in his own hands," they complained to the Central Committee.[25]

The Futian Incident flared up under these circumstances. Early on the morning of December 7, 1930, when the First Army Group was fighting numerically superior Guomindang forces, a company of Red Army troops under the command of Li Shaojiu, a Mao loyalist, entered Futian, a town in the rear area located a mile or so from the east bank of the Ganjiang River. Its assignment was to arrest several local communists suspected of ties to the AB Corps, including the head of the Political Department of the Red Army's Twentieth Corps, based in Futian. (This unit had been formed in June 1930, on the basis of the Sixth Corps, and consisted mostly of Jiangxi men.)[26] Mao's order had been rather laconic: "Do not kill the important leaders too quickly, but squeeze out of them [the maximum] information. . . . [Then], from the clues they give, you can go on to unearth other leaders."[27]

At first everything went smoothly. The headquarters of the Twentieth Corps was surrounded; the suspects were taken into custody and interrogation begun. Naturally, they all denied any guilt. Then Li Shaojiu ordered that they be tortured. Torture of those in detention happened all the time, and the Red Army was no exception. Mao himself later admitted, "In 1930 beating was widely used during interrogation. I myself witnessed how the accused were beaten up."[28]

The evidence extracted from those under arrest exceeded all expectations. It appeared as if many commanders of the Twentieth Corps as well as the entire Jiangxi party committee, the entire provincial committee of the Communist Youth League, and all of the leaders of the provincial soviet government were "members of the AB Corps." Li, certain he had uncovered a huge plot, immediately ordered the arrest of all the delegates appointed to the Jiangxi party emergency conference, scheduled to begin in Futian on December 8. In all 120 men were confined in bamboo cages. The bacchanalia entered its final stage. An eyewitness recounted:

> Li Shaojiu shouted out loudly "You should know that middle peas-ants always may rebel. Your only course is to confess. . . . The party, undoubtedly, will give you an opportunity to rectify your errors." . . . Then they were tortured with kerosene, lighted wicks, etc. They were being tortured and interrogated at the same time. No real interro-gation could take place like this. It was simply torture. Moreover, they were asked, "Do you confess that you joined the AB Corps, when did you join, what kind of organization is it, what are its tac-tics, who are its leaders? Speak the whole truth." If no confession was forthcoming during the interrogation and torture, then the tortures were intensified. . . . The fingernails of the comrades were smashed, their entire bodies burned. . . . All one could hear were the constant screams of the tortured. . . . They were subjected to the most barba-rous tortures. The wives of several leaders were arrested, including the wife of Comrade Bai Fan, secretary of the Southwest Jiangxi Party Committee, and others. They were tortured, stripped naked, beaten on the arms with sharp instruments, burned all over their bodies, in-cluding their genitals, had their breasts sliced off with penknives, and generally subjected to inhuman tortures the mere recitation of which makes one recoil in horror. All of the arrested, those who had been in-terrogated as well as those who had not, were held separately, bound hand and foot. They were surrounded by guards holding rifles with fixed bayonets. A voice had scarcely rung out when the soldiers went to work with their bayonets. The arrested were fed with leavings. . . . Fifty people were taken off to be executed.[29]

Afterward, Li Shaojiu set off for neighboring Donggu, where the purge continued, but his luck ran out. Among those arrested there was Liu Di, a political cadre of the Twentieth Corps, who somehow managed to convince the sadistic Li Shaojiu that he wasn't guilty. Li, displaying his humanity, re-leased Liu. The moral of the story is do not act contrary to your own charac-ter. Having regained his freedom, Liu Di quickly rose in rebellion, arrested Li Shaojiu and his entourage, and attacked Futian on December 12 at the head of a detachment of four hundred men. After the all day and all night battle, Liu Di succeeded in seizing the building where those under arrest were being held and freeing those prisoners who were still alive. More than one hundred guards were killed.

Almost all the officers and men of the Twentieth Corps, more than three thousand in all, supported Liu Di's actions. The emergency conference adopted a resolution to quit Futian for a safer place west of the Ganjiang River. Slogans were put forth: "Down with Mao Zedong who kills, deceives, and oppresses the workers and peasants!" and "Long live Zhu De, Peng Dehuai, and Huang Gonglüe!" (The last was the commander of the Third Corps of the Red Army.) It is striking that they released the bloodthirsty Li Shaojiu and his fellows, evidently figuring that the leadership of the First Front Army would see this as a sign of goodwill.

Several days later the Jiangxi communists informed their party comrades about what had happened and placed the entire blame upon Mao, whom they accused of having "worked out a cunning plan to destroy comrades in the party." Mao "has become a 100 percent right* opportunist and criminal in the unfolding class struggle," they asserted. "Mao Zedong strives to achieve his right opportunist goals, his deserter's ideas, and other dirty and shameless objectives. . . . Mao Zedong has long opposed the Central Committee. . . . Desiring to preserve his position, he purposed to physically destroy the leading party and youth league cadres in Jiangxi province and establish a party bearing the exclusive stamp of the Mao Zedong group to use it as a weapon in his war struggle against the Central Committee."[30]

Mao viewed the events in Donggu and Futian as counterrevolutionary rebellion. Zhu De, Peng Dehuai, and Huang Gonglüe agreed. But the last word belonged to the leaders of the Central Committee and the representatives of the Comintern. Mao, of course, wasted no time in informing them. In January 1931, he sent the party leaders a letter of appeal, which said:

> Their [the rebels'] plot is first to draw in Zhu [De], Peng [Dehuai], and Huang [Gonglüe] to overthrow Mao Zedong, first concentrating their forces to overthrow one person, and then overthrowing the others one by one. Comrades, at this crucial juncture of the decisive class struggle, Chiang Kai-shek is shouting loudly "Down with Mao Zedong" from without, and the AB Corps and the Liquidationists are shouting "Down with Mao Zedong" from within the revolutionary ranks. How they echo each other's voices and copy each other's tastes![31]

A special delegation of pro-Mao communists from southeast Hunan, headed by Liu Shiqi, delivered this message to Shanghai. The documents that the Hunanese communists brought to Shanghai—including Mao's letter of appeal; a manifesto in Mao's defense by Zhu De, Peng Dehuai, and Huang

---

* At the time, it was better to accuse your opponent of a "right" rather than a "left" deviation. It was more of a sure thing.

Gonglüe; and their appeal to the Red Army men of the Twentieth Corps—as well as, no small matter, the 50,000–60,000 Mexican dollars (100,000 by one account) that Mao sent via the delegation to the Central Committee, produced the desired effect. Examining the "Futian issue" in mid-February 1931, the Politburo and Pavel Mif unanimously took Mao's side.[32] A month later the Far Eastern Bureau of the ECCI and the CCP Politburo adopted resolutions regarding this issue.[33]

The person who initially had to deal with the Futian Incident was Xiang Ying, a member of the Politburo who had arrived in the Central Soviet Area in October 1930. He had been dispatched to replace Mao as acting secretary of the Central Committee Bureau for the Soviet areas. (The head of the bureau, Zhou Enlai, remained in Shanghai since Mif and other officials of the Far Eastern Bureau believed that he was "simply indispensable for transforming party work.")[34] Barely acquainting himself with the matter, the new chief declared that what was going on was an unprincipled squabble and that both sides should be punished. "The incident must be settled peacefully," he insisted.[35]

Xiang Ying's conclusion, naturally, could not satisfy Mao Zedong. The commanders of the First Front Army were likewise dissatisfied. Xiang, a thirty-two-year-old textile worker, generally had a very hard time asserting his authority among the troops of the First Front. Fortunately for Mao, a new representative of the Central Committee, Politburo member Ren Bishi, and Wang Jiaxiang, a pupil of Mif's, came to the Central Soviet Area in early April 1931, sent by Zhou Enlai "to sort out the situation."[36] These two men, who along with Zhou Enlai, Zhang Guotao, and Shen Zemin were members of the special commission on the Futian Incident, joined the newly organized Standing Committee of the Central Committee Bureau for the Soviet areas, together with Xiang Ying and Mao Zedong. They strongly condemned the "rebels." Soon the Politburo's decision on the Futian events was received in the Central Soviet Area. Once more Mao was the winner. On April 16 an enlarged conference of the bureau adopted a decision that fully satisfied him.[37] Later, in May 1931, Xiang Ying yielded the post of acting secretary of the bureau to Mao, and at the end of June handed over to Mao the chairmanship of the Central Revolutionary Military Council as well.[38]

The purges continued but were directed now at the organizers of and participants in the "anti-soviet uprising." By the spring of 1932 "over 90 percent of the cadres in the southwestern Jiangxi area were killed, detained, or stopped work."[39] Liu Di suffered a terrible fate. In April 1931, a military tribunal presided over by Zhu De sentenced him to death and he was decapitated.

Naturally, Li Shaojiu emerged unscathed. In January 1932, the Central Committee Bureau for the Soviet areas, now under the leadership of Zhou Enlai, accused him of "going too far," and limited itself to administering a party punishment. Li was demoted and placed under party supervision for the next six months. By June of the same year he was again given a responsible command position in the First Front Army, and in October he was reassigned to work in one of the soviet areas in western Fujian. There in the land of the Hakkas he died, "heroically sacrificing himself" in battle against the Guomindang army.[40]

The higher tribunals could not forgive Liu Di and other rebels for splitting the forces of the Red Army at a moment of mortal danger for the soviet area in Jiangxi. Meanwhile, the First Front Army was successful in its battle against Chiang Kai-shek's punitive expedition. The proven tactics of Mao and Zhu— "the enemy advances, we retreat; the enemy camps, we harass; the enemy tires, we attack; the enemy retreats, we pursue"—demonstrated their effectiveness under new conditions. It was an impressive victory. The First Front Army annihilated more than fifteen thousand enemy officers and men and seized many prisoners, ten thousand rifles, and a radio transmitter, which, however, no one knew how to operate. Even one division commander, named Zhang Huizan, fell prisoner. They cut off his head, fastened it to a board, and floated it down the Hengjiang River, a tributary of the Ganjiang. They figured that the head would eventually float down to Nanchang, straight into the hands of Chiang Kai-shek, who was waiting there.[41]

Celebrating the victory, Mao poured out his joy in new verses:

Immense woods under frost sky,
all blazing red.
Anger of heaven's soldiers
soared up to heaven.
Fog over Lungkang [Longgang],* *a thousand peaks darkened.*
All shout with a single voice:
Far up ahead we captured Chang Hui-tsan [Zhang Huizan].

Two hundred thousand troops
break into Kiangsi [Jiangxi] *again,*
wind and dust rolling half way to heaven.
Millions of workers and peasants aroused,
all struggle with a single heart:
riot of flags around Puchou [Buzhou] *Mountain.*[42]

After the first punitive expedition, the troops of the First Front Army succeeded in repelling two additional expeditions organized by Chiang Kai-shek in April–May and July–September 1931. Chiang Kai-shek threw his best forces

---

* On December 30, 1930, near Longgang village, the decisive battle took place in which the Guomindang punitive forces were defeated and the division commander Zhang was taken captive.

against the "terrorists." The second expedition was led by He Yingqin, the minister of defense; the third was led by Chiang himself, all to no avail. News of the victories of the "communist bandits" sowed terror among the peace-loving citizens, but the Nanjing government could do nothing. The protracted war that Mao had advocated had become a reality.

Yet Mao's socioeconomic policies failed among the hostile population of southwest Jiangxi. As in Jinggang, his new attempt to establish relations with the working peasantry turned into another catastrophe. Perhaps the collapse of the platform under Mao and Zhu De several days before they left Jinggang was a portent.

While the battle against the first punitive expedition was still raging and prior to the Futian Incident, Mao had suggested abandoning the Jiangxi base and heading southeast, in the direction of Fujian (Land of the Hakkas). But several commanders in the Third Army Group of Peng Dehuai opposed it. This began to change at the end of January, when the Central Committee recommended that Mao move "slightly to the south."[43] However, until the Futian Incident was resolved in his favor, withdrawal would have signified Mao's capitulation to the "shameless" Jiangxi men. When Mao learned that the Politburo had ruled in his favor, he felt it was possible to move his headquarters toward the border with Fujian. This may have been when the Red Army men composed the following lively song:

> *The commissar leads us to grain*
> *You may be sure that all will be well*
> *We will still smash the foe*
> *And break through all obstacles.*[44]

The Futian Incident demonstrated that Mao could count on victory only in a favorable social environment and, moreover, in a favorable ethnic setting. Hakka country was ideal on both counts. At the end of March 1931, just before Chiang Kai-shek's second punitive expedition, Mao, Zhu De, and Xiang Ying finally shifted to southeast Jiangxi, first basing themselves at a village with the poetic name of Qingtang (Azure pond). Situated in a deep valley, the village occupied an advantageous strategic position, surrounded on all sides by steep mountains covered with dense subtropical forests. During Chiang's second expedition, however, Mao and Zhu had to abandon it and changed their headquarters several times. After the defeat of the third expedition, in late September they settled in Yeping, a few miles north of Ruijin, one of the key trading centers of Hakka country.

Meanwhile, the situation in Shanghai was steadily worsening. After Mif's departure for Moscow in April 1931, a series of heavy blows fell upon the Politburo and the Far Eastern Bureau of the Comintern. An especially critical situation developed at the end of April with the arrest of Gu Shunzhang, a candidate member of the Politburo who was head of the secret (or special) section of the Central Committee. His department was responsible for organizing the red terror in cities controlled by the Guomindang. Gu, a pupil of the Soviet Union's secret police organs, was directly responsible for the elimination of provocateurs, traitors, and other enemies of the CCP who had been sentenced to death by the Central Committee. His section was also responsible for espionage and for protecting the top party leaders. Gu was arrested on April 24, 1931, in Hankou, where he had gone to prepare an assassination attempt against Chiang Kai-shek. He was recognized by a provocateur in one of the municipal parks, where he was passing himself off as an itinerant juggler named Li Ming. Terrified by a warning shot, this professional killer with the manners of a Shanghai playboy preferred to "lose face."[45] He gave the police all the secret addresses of the Politburo and of the Jiangsu and Hubei party committees. From May to July more than three thousand Chinese communists were arrested and many of these were shot. Xiang Zhongfa, general secretary of the Central Committee, was among the victims. Unable to withstand torture, he gave testimony, although this did not save his life. The Guomindang preferred to execute a man of such distinction, broken as he was.

The communists took terrible revenge on Gu Shunzhang. Unable to punish him directly, they massacred almost his entire extended family, including his wife, father-in-law, and mother-in-law. According to one source, seventeen were killed; according to another the figure was thirty. Even the elderly nursemaid who lived with the family was not spared. This monstrously cruel and senseless order was given by Zhou Enlai, who not long before had condemned Mao and his "bandits" for engaging in "purposeless and indecent pogroms and murders."[46] After the arrest of Gu Shunzhang, Zhou became the head of a newly formed Special Work Committee of the Central Committee; it amalgamated all of the secret services. The quintet of five killers he dispatched to do the deed spared only the twelve-year-old son of the traitor. They lacked the spirit to kill the child.* Gu Shunzhang himself was executed by the Guomindang in December 1934, when they suspected him of playing a double game.

As a consequence of Gu's betrayal, in mid-June the Shanghai municipal police arrested two key officials of the Far Eastern Bureau, both collaborators of the International Liaison Department of the ECCI: Yakov Rudnik and his wife, Tatiana Moiseenko-Velikaiia, who were living in Shanghai under the spousal name of Noulens. They were the conduit through which the Comin-

---

* Many years later one of these subordinates of Zhou gave a simple explanation of the crime. Prior to Gu Shunzhang's betrayal many meetings of the top party leadership had taken place in his home, and so everyone in his household knew the CCP leaders personally. It was impossible to rely upon their keeping silent.

tern supplied the Central Committee and the Far Eastern Bureau with money, via an account with the bogus Metropolitan Trading Company. Thus their arrest undermined the financial security of the party and the Communist Youth League, whose municipal organizations continued to depend upon Comintern funds. From August 1930 to May 1931, every month the ECCI had provided more than US $25,000 worth of gold dollars to the Central Committee.[47] (The monthly payment was raised by $5,000 over what it had been in 1929.)

After a while the Comintern found another means of renewing the cash payments. Just in the period from September to December 1931, the Shanghai party organization alone received US $10,300 from Moscow.[48] Overall until the end of the year direct payments from the ECCI to the Chinese Communist Party totaled more than one million yuan, or about US $280,000.[49] But the white terror totally paralyzed the Far Eastern Bureau, which in midsummer 1931 curtailed its operations. In mid-September, Moscow's main representative, Ignatii Rylsky, decided to reorganize the leadership of the CCP yet again. By then the majority of Politburo members were outside of Shanghai. Some were imprisoned; others were 'conducting underground work in the north. From early April Zhang Guotao was in the soviet area at the juncture of Hubei, Henan, and Anhui provinces north of Wuhan, where he headed the local bureau of the Central Committee. Another Politburo member, the former sailor Chen Yu, represented the CCP on the ECCI starting in June 1931 under the pseudonym of Polevoi. Fearing arrest, Chen Shaoyu tried to escape from China to Moscow. Zhou Enlai recalled, "By order of the ECCI representative a Provisional Central Committee was established in Shanghai to take charge of the work."[50] Following the establishment of the Provisional Central Committee, at the end of September 1931, Chen Shaoyu and his wife quickly left for Moscow, where this "nestling of Mif" headed the new delegation of the CCP. He assumed a pseudonym under which he became well known in the history of the Chinese Communist Party and the Comintern, namely, Wang Ming. (In the coded correspondence with the CCP Central Committee and with other Communist Parties he sometimes used another pseudonym, Vancouver.) Sometime later, Zhou Enlai also left Shanghai, disguised as a priest, and set out to join Mao in southern Jiangxi, where, ultimately, he headed the Bureau of the Central Committee.[51]

While these events unfolded in Shanghai, Mao continued to gather his strength. Having dealt in Stalinist fashion with the "kulak scum" from the Western Jiangxi Special Committee of the CCP and having repelled three punitive expeditions by the Guomindang, he rapidly strengthened his position in the party. The only thing that he needed now was Stalin's blessing, but Stalin had not yet come out decisively in Mao's favor, although he continued to support him. With Machiavellian perspicacity, the master of the Kremlin established a combined leadership of the CCP on the foundation of three groups:

homegrown guerrilla cadres (Mao and his supporters), Moscow graduates (Chen Shaoyu/Wang Ming, Bo Gu), and old Comintern cadres (Zhou Enlai, Zhang Guotao, Xiang Ying). None of these groups was given the opportunity to take the measure of the others.

So Mao had to wait, which he did patiently, like a real gambler. He had his own calculation, but unlike Stalin's it was more precise. He not only had to demonstrate that he was "the most loyal student of Comrade Stalin," but also to push out of the way all his competitors, waiting only for an opportune moment to get rid of them. He was a master of intrigue down to the last detail.

His striving for unlimited dominance consumed him ever more, and his boundless energy pushed him forward. In this daily bloody battle for power he increasingly turned into a victim of his own passion. His struggles against Chiang Kai-shek, the intraparty opposition, class enemies, and "deluded" comrades were killing the last vestiges of human feeling in him. Love, goodness, loyalty, trust were vanishing, dissolving into the strongest emotions that smothered him. The result was that Mao's heart was hardening, and his life turned into the pursuit of a chimera.

His children were under the care of others. How were they faring? What were they feeling? He knew nothing of this. Meanwhile, it was his sons' fate to endure many hardships. After the death of Kaihui, the local underground communists secured the release of his eldest son, the eight-year-old Anying, through bribing his guards. He and his seven-year old brother, Anqing, and three-year old brother, Anlong, then lived with their grandmother in Bancang village, naturally under surveillance. The police hoped to capture Mao via his children, supposing that the father would be concerned about them.

But time passed and neither Mao nor his messengers appeared. Instead, on a Monday evening, right before the Lunar New Year (February 16, 1931), when everyone, including the gendarmes, were preparing for the holiday, a stranger knocked on the door of Grandma Xiang Zhenxi. He carried a letter from Zemin to Li Chongde, the wife of Kaihui's elder brother, who lived in the same house. Mao's brother requested that in the interest of their safety his nephews be brought to him in Shanghai. His wife, the childless Qian Xijun, was very worried about the fate of the children. It was she who persuaded Zemin to write the letter. Li Chongde recalled, "I unwrapped the parcel with a rapidly beating heart under the oil lamp and was astonished to see Mao Zemin's handwriting. He asked me to send Mao Zedong's three sons to Shanghai, giving me date, place and information on how to get in touch with people there." After consulting her relatives, Li decided to comply. For security reasons the children were given new names, which the older boys had to memorize. Anying was called Yongfu ("Always Happy"), Anqing was called Yongshou ("Always Healthy"), and Anlong was called Yongtai ("Always the Utmost"). Their surname, too, was changed from their father's to their mother's, namely, Yang.

Li Chongde then departed with the children for Shanghai, playing the role of their mother. Grandma Xiang Zhenxi accompanied them.

The difficult journey took several days, and when at last the exhausted children arrived at their uncle Zemin's house, they began to cry. They had thought they were being brought to their father, but instead they had to live in a clandestine kindergarten on the territory of the International Settlement. Zhou Enlai had made this decision. This Shanghai shelter, established for the children of CCP officials with funds from the Comintern International Organization for Aid to Revolutionary Fighters, was not exactly an ideal place for children, but there was no other option. At the time about thirty children lived there, including the daughters of Li Lisan and Cai Hesen. One of the governesses was the wife of Li Lisan. But Mao's sons did not want to go there. "I want to be with papa," sobbed Anying. "I must get revenge for mama!" The children clutched Li Chongde's dress, begging her to take them home. "Their crying was like a knife piercing my heart," Li recalled. She tried to calm them, but was crying herself as if possessed of a premonition that for her nephews the worst was yet to come.

Soon after arriving at the shelter little Anlong fell ill. He began to suffer from diarrhea and his temperature spiked. He was diagnosed with a case of dysentery and he soon passed away.* Then, because of Gu Shunzhang's betrayal, the kindergarten was closed. Uncle Zemin and Aunt Xijun left town for one of the Soviet areas. The director of the kindergarten, Dong Jianwu (alias Pastor Wang), who was concurrently an official in the Special Work Committee of the Central Committee, took Mao's sons, whom nobody else wanted, into his own home for a time, but soon he too had to leave for Wuhan. The children remained under the guardianship of his ex-wife Huang Huiguang, who knew nothing of their background and paid little attention to them. She had four children of her own.

Anying and Anqing always hoped for news from their father. They sent a letter to him via Uncle Zemin when Zemin was preparing to leave Shanghai, but their father did nothing to save them even though he actually received their letter. At the end of the summer of 1932 they ran away from Auntie Huang. For four years they wandered the dirty streets, scavenging in garbage bins, collecting leftovers and cigarette butts, earning spare change from shopkeepers, and selling newspapers. They suffered beatings and insults. It was not until the spring of 1936 that members of the Shanghai party organization discovered them. Then the mighty Stalin took an interest in their fate. With his agreement, the Central Committee of the CCP arranged their travel to the Soviet

---

* It is interesting to note that in the mid-1960s in various provinces throughout China there suddenly appeared several dozen "Mao Anlongs." These pretenders, however, were quickly unmasked by the all-knowing security organs.

Union via Hong Kong, Marseille, and Paris. By an irony of fate, it was the same familiar Pastor Wang who was in charge of these arrangements.[52]

Meanwhile, Mao devoted himself entirely to party and military work. In the autumn of 1931, when he received the letter from his children, he simply set it aside. There was too much else to do. He had to strengthen the Central Soviet Area, and make preparations for the First All-China Congress of Soviets. This meeting was to be the venue for the founding of the Chinese Soviet Republic, uniting all of the "red" districts in the country. As chairman of the Central Revolutionary Military Council, Mao was directly responsible for convening and overseeing the congress. Yeping had been chosen as its locale. It was there that more than six hundred delegates assembled, all of whom had to be housed, fed, and guarded. Mao's forces had seized this village, which was located very close to the city of Ruijin, deep in the mountains of southeast Jiangxi and close to the border with Fujian, back in the spring of 1929. Control of the local population had passed back and forth between Guomindang and communists during the intervening two and a half years; now Mao was apparently firmly ensconced in these parts. It was he who, by agreement with Moscow, was slated to become the chairman of the Central Executive Committee and the head of the Council of People's Commissars or, in the terminology then current, People's Committee of the Central Executive Committee of the Chinese Soviet Republic.[53]

By November 7, the anniversary of the October Revolution in Russia, all was ready:

> Over the Congress hall was hoisted the red flag with the hammer and sickle. Inside workers wired the building with electric wires and connected them with the dynamos captured from Kian [Ji'an] in the year before.
>
> When the time came for the electric lights to be switched on, crowds of peasants gathered about, unbelieving. . . . The Congress hall became flooded with light from hundreds of glass lamps.
>
> Some of the weaker peasant women fainted on the spot. . . . After the Congress hall was wired, it was richly decorated with pine boughs, with great banners brought by mass organizations, and with slogans of the Soviets hung on all the big pillars upholding the roof. . . . There were four entrances to the hall, one on each side of the building. The big main entrance was at the front. Outside, above the main entrance, were draped two big red silk banners embroidered with hammer and sickle, one for the soviets, one for the Communist Party. The entire outside front entrance was a mass of green boughs in which two huge five-pointed stars were embedded. The stars were of solid silver, for there was plenty of silver in the soviet regions.[54]

On Saturday, November 7, at seven in the morning, delegates began to enter the hall to the sound of a volley of rifles and the crackle of firecrackers. "[T]he orchestra on the stage began to play the *International*." Dressed in specially tailored suits—Red Army jackets with high collars and blue cotton trousers—the delegates looked very festive. They wore red stars on the left sleeve of their jackets and scarlet silk triangles on the right sleeve with their delegate number embroidered upon it. On the band of their service caps were ribbons inscribed, "First Congress of Chinese Soviets."

Over a fortnight the delegates adopted the basic constitutional program of the Chinese Soviet Republic, a land law that strengthened the equal division of both movable and real property of landlords and the working peasantry,* a law on labor, and several other documents, and chose a provisional All-China Central Executive Committee. A week later, at the first session of the CEC, according to plan, Mao became the chairman of this highest legislative organ. Zhang Guotao and Xiang Ying were designated his deputies. Mao also headed the Council of People's Commissars, in which the post of people's commissar for foreign affairs—an ambitious position for a country that no one recognized—was held by Mif's student Wang Jiaxiang. The post of people's commissar for military affairs, naturally, went to Zhu De, and the post of people's commissar of education to Qu Qiubai. (Qu, however, was still in Shanghai, burning up with tuberculosis, so in his absence, Mao's old teacher from Changsha, Xu Teli, directed people's education in the Chinese Soviet Republic.) Ruijin was proclaimed the capital of the CSR.

After the arrival of communist troops in this ancient city, the population numbered some sixty thousand. Stretching a mile or so from west to east, it was surrounded by mountains. There were several textile and machine workshops, a large market square where peasants from all points around sold their wares, and also numerous local temples that the communists took over to serve as their offices. Although Ruijin was no Shanghai, it was a suitable city for the seat of government.

It seemed that Mao had finally reached the pinnacle of power, but this was not so. A fierce struggle was just getting under way. Wang Ming's iron boys, Bo Gu most of all, who had become the de facto leader of the Politburo after other CCP leaders had gone away, did not wish to yield the victor's laurels to Mao. The twenty-four-year-old Bo Gu, who had joined the Communist Party just

---

* The law did not talk directly about confiscating the land of peasants (other than that of "kulaks"), but that is the only way one can interpret the clause regarding the expropriation not only of *dizhu* land, but also that of "big private owners" who "engaged in working the land themselves." Not a single *dizhu* worked his own land, only peasants did this. The definition of "big," it will be recalled, could not confuse anyone. For the destitute rural lumpen proletariat anyone with land was a "big" landowner.

six years earlier, was no less ambitious than his friend Wang Ming. Very thin and tall, he embodied everything that Mao hated in the Moscow parvenus. Only superficially familiar with Chinese realities, Bo Gu, like other of Mif's people who had returned from Moscow, firmly believed in the all-powerful Soviet experience. Looking at his wild hair sticking up and his enormous eyeglasses, like wheels, that concealed his protruding eyes—he suffered from Basedow's disease—and listening to his nervous laugh and quavering voice, one might take him for a first-class grind who was exhausted from his constant studying, if not for his domineering character and coarse dictatorial manners. He worshipped Stalin, and imitating him, smoked a pipe. Like his Kremlin idol, he placed no value whatsoever on human life. Neither that of the "class enemy" nor of his own comrades in the Communist Party. Unable openly to dispute Moscow's policy of supporting Mao, through his supporters Bo Gu did everything he could to weaken the influence of his rival and lower him in the eyes of Stalin. Bo Gu was obsessed by Mao's aura as the great guerrilla leader.

18

DOG EAT DOG,
COMMUNIST-STYLE

The sign of a new disfavor came in the form of a letter from Shanghai dated August 30, 1931, subjecting Mao to criticism no less sharp than during the era of Li Lisan. The Bureau of the Central Committee, which Mao headed, was accused of committing extremely serious rightist as well as left opportunist errors that demonstrated the "absence" among its leaders of "a clear class line." It's difficult to say who among the top leaders drafted this letter, but the document clearly reflected the views of a new generation of leaders, Mif's people, who were beginning to dominate the party. The main accusation was that Mao had supposedly pursued a "kulak line" in agrarian reform. What the letter writers were referring to was that Mao had implemented the equal division of land according to the principle "Drawing on the plentiful to make up for the scarce, and drawing on the fat to make up for the lean." The new leaders insisted that the kulaks should be given only the worst land, and all of the best land should be given to the poor.

Mao's "guerrilla" tactics also garnered him significant reproaches from the Provisional Politburo, even though these tactics had enabled the Red Army to repulse three Guomindang punitive expeditions. Mao's successes had undermined the authority of the newly risen leaders. They insisted on the "expansion" of the soviet areas by the prompt seizure of, most importantly, "comparatively large cities." [1] By this time, as far back as mid-October 1930, Mao had resolved to reject any further plans to capture overly large centers. [2]

Obviously, the Moscow-returned students were even more leftist than Mao and Li Lisan. That they were doing their utmost to brand others with the charge of Li Lisanism simply meant that Chen Shaoyu/Wang Ming, Wang Jiaxiang, and the others were seizing the moment to consolidate their own power. They commenced their secret struggle against Li Lisan and the other "elders" soon after they had returned to China, and were especially active starting in the summer of 1930. By prior agreement, they began to inundate their former rector Mif with letters written in Russian or English using coded language. It was not the Politburo's adventurism that they disliked. Criticizing Li for leftism was not then in style. Knowing very well what was most despised in Moscow, they consistently accused Li of "right" deviation even when he advocated mad schemes for world revolution. "The right lung is still painful due to a lack of daring and knowledge on the part of the doctors as well as the lack of good medicine," Wang Jiaxiang informed Pavel Mif just three days prior to the CCP Politburo's adoption of an ultraleft resolution on June 11, "On the New Revolutionary Tide." "Can you send some sort of medication?" "Part of the hosts are indeed suffering from pain in the right shoulder," added Chen Shaoyu/Wang Ming in his own name. Their joint letter said:

> The host's ugliness derives from the fact that the right side of his brain is diseased. This disease requires first-class treatment that is very difficult to receive in poverty-stricken China. We hope that *very soon* a good doctor and good medicine will be found to cure the host and improve the position of the co[mpany].[3]

Amusing language, and readily understandable without a translation.

Chen Shaoyu/Wang Ming and the others continued to pursue a provocationist policy even after the "good doctor" (Pavel Mif) carried out the needed "operation." Obviously they believed that the January plenum had not succeeded in excising the entire "diseased portion of the brain." This was the occasion for the August letter.

Soon after its receipt, in mid-October Xiang Ying, Ren Bishi, and Wang Jiaxiang were inserted into the lineup in the Central Soviet Area. In early November, on the eve of the congress of soviets, these representatives of the Provisional Politburo convened a party conference in Ruijin. Then a hailstorm of accusations was loosed upon Mao; he was charged with "narrow empiricism," "extreme right opportunism," "kulak deviation," and "guerrillaism." Mao tried to justify himself, referring to local conditions, but it was all in vain. The majority of conference participants, with the exception of several district secretaries, endorsed the Central Committee letter. Mao was removed from his post as acting secretary of the Central Committee Bureau for the Soviet areas and Xiang Ying was again appointed to replace him.[4]

All of this happened just several days prior to the First Congress of Soviets, at which Mao was slated to be "chosen" as chairman of the Central Executive Committee of the Chinese Soviet Republic (CSR) and of the Council of People's Commissars. A telegram regarding the need to "choose" him, which had been approved by Moscow, was received in Yeping at the very end of October,[5] two to three days prior to the party conference. Why, then, was it necessary to attack someone who, after all, had been prepared to serve as the head of the CSR?

The only explanation is that the leadership in Shanghai and its agents in southern Jiangxi wanted to show the communists that the secretaries of the Central Committee and of the Central Committee Bureau, not the newly chosen Chairman Mao, would control everything as before. The Chairman was just a soldier of the party, and far from the best one at that. Thus, the posts of chairman of the CEC and of the Council of People's Commissars turned into purely nominal positions. In the Chinese Soviet Republic, as in the USSR, the party controlled the government.

Immediately after the congress, on November 25, Mao was also removed from his post as chairman of the Central Revolutionary Military Council, although he remained the chief of its General Political Administration as well as one of its fifteen members. Zhu De became the head of the CRMC. Wang Jiaxiang and Peng Dehuai became Zhu's deputies. At this same time the troops of the First Front Army were reorganized into two army groups (the Third and the Fifth) and five corps, which were directly subordinate to the Central Revolutionary Military Council. The headquarters of the First Front Army was abolished, and with it the posts of general political commissar and secretary of the General Front Committee that Mao had held.[6] This heavy blow sharply curtailed Mao Zedong's influence both in the party and the army.

Mao began to sense a worsening atmosphere around him. Almost none of his close friends remained, apart from his younger brothers and their wives, who, fortunately, were in the Central Soviet Area, but neither Zemin nor Zetan were members of the Central Committee. In early May 1928, Xiang Jingyu, proud, passionate, and insubordinate, was shot in Hankou. Her former husband Cai Hesen, Mao's closest friend, was executed in Canton in early August 1931. His death was particularly cruel. The butchers first subjected him to inhuman tortures, and then crucified him on the wall of his cell. Then, finally, they pierced him through the chest several times with a sharp bayonet. They desisted only when the lifeless body sagged on the iron nails. Two years earlier, in August 1929, Peng Pai had died in Shanghai.

After Zhou Enlai's arrival in Ruijin in late December 1931, the situation grew worse. Replacing Xiang Ying as secretary of the Bureau of the Central Committee, Zhou continued the anti-Maoist line. At the first session of the Bureau of the CC, on January 7, he declared that the Bureau had committed errors in the struggle against counterrevolutionary elements and "should admit its responsibility in the spirit of self-criticism."[7] Mao made no objection, although Zhou's criticism cut him to the quick.

Two days later, Bo Gu and his friend Luo Fu, who was in charge of propaganda for the Provisional Politburo, issued a directive, "On Winning Initial Revolutionary Successes in One or More Provinces." That this title was almost exactly the same as the infamous resolution of Li Lisan likely did not bother them. They demanded that the Red Army again attack Nanchang, Ji'an, and other major cities in Jiangxi, and reminded all of the doubters, "As before, right opportunism remains the main danger. . . . We must direct fire against the rightists."[8]

This enabled Zhou to strike another blow against Mao. Knowing that their fiery Hunanese would be averse to entering into a fruitless discussion, the new secretary of the Bureau suggested to the members of the Bureau of the CC a plan to attack the second largest city of Jiangxi, namely, Ganzhou, which was located between the Central Soviet Area and the Jinggang Mountains, where individual troops of the CCP were still operating. The seizure of this fortified strongpoint would create an opportunity to expand the "Red Zone" significantly, but neither Zhou nor the majority of the leaders of the Bureau seemed to realize how difficult this campaign would be for the Red Army. Mao, naturally, did not agree, and was again subjected to criticism.[9] His enemies could take satisfaction from the fact that their "always wrong" opponent had "lost face."

Mao then decided to "do battle" on questions of international politics. China's international position had drastically worsened due to Japanese expansionism. On September 18, 1931, Japan's Kwantung Army, stationed in Manchuria (Northeast China), provoked the Mukden Incident. Citing an explosion on the South Manchurian Railroad that the Japanese had themselves detonated, the Kwantung Army occupied Mukden, the largest city in Manchuria, and also Changchun, the capital of Jilin province. By late autumn all of Manchuria, with a population of thirty million, was under Japanese control. Chiang Kai-shek, immersed in military action against the soviet area, offered no resistance, but a wide anti-Japanese movement developed throughout the country. The patriotic upsurge was so great that Mao concluded in January 1932 that the CCP should "play" with these events. He calculated that the wave of popular anti-Japanese sentiments could be redirected against Chiang Kai-shek, who had not defended Manchuria. The unexpected uprising in mid-December in the city of Ningdu, in Jiangxi province, of the Guomindang's Twenty-Sixth Army (which Chiang Kai-shek had thrown into battle against the communists) inspired this thought in Mao. The seventeen thousand soldiers of this army rebelled because they were unhappy with Chiang's policy of "appeasement" vis-à-vis Japan. Ningdu, located only about ten miles north of Ruijin, instantly became "red."[10]

In mid-January 1932, at a regular session of the Bureau of the Central Committee, Mao said, "The broad scale incursion of Japanese imperialism into China has brought about an anti-Japanese upsurge. This will inevitably lead to changes in inter-class relations in the country." Understandably, one should take advantage of this development, but precisely how, that was the question that he wanted to discuss. What a row that provoked! The representatives of the Provisional Politburo flared with indignation. They considered it virtually criminal to make use of the Japanese invasion to advance the interests of the Communist Party, especially since, from the perspective of the Comintern, the purpose of the Manchurian events was to prepare a launching pad for the Japanese military to attack the USSR. One of those present attacked Mao for "right opportunism." A deathly silence ensued. Mao was so outraged that his words stuck in his throat.

He did not want to work with the members of the Bureau anymore and after the session he requested "sick" leave. It was an old trick he had employed during his conflict with Zhu De and the Front Committee of the Fourth Corps in June–November 1929. With his wife and bodyguard he left for the mountains, turning his government duties over to Xiang Ying. Then he was struck another blow. Wang Jiaxiang removed him from his last military post, that of chief of the General Political Administration of the Central Revolutionary Military Council (at that time renamed the General Political Administration of the Chinese Worker-Peasant Red Army).

Mao now sank into melancholy. High on the summit of Donghua Mountain, he sat in pitch darkness in a deserted temple for days at a time, playing on a short flute. He had become fond of this ancient eight-holed folk instrument, made from the stem of a bamboo, back in the Jinggang period. It was damp and cold in the temple, however, and He Zizhen insisted that he move to a neighboring cave. Here he continued his musical diversion. Music-making and a rustic life, however, failed to calm his nerves. Neither did poetry help.[11] Pondering what had occurred, Mao came to realize that the new struggle for power would be the most brutal yet.

The latest "leftist deviation" of the CCP leadership was again directly linked to Moscow, as the Chinese communists continued to receive their instructions, both strategic and tactical, from Moscow, where everyone was simply raving about the "rightist danger." After routing Bukharin and his supporters, Stalin purged additional so-called rightists in December 1930. This was followed by the trial of the "Industrial Party," a supposed "rightist" organization of engineers, technicians, and economists who were accused of anti-Sovietism and sabotage. It is not surprising that many in the Comintern believed the "rightist danger" was real, especially since Stalin asserted that class struggle would become sharper and capitalist aggressiveness greater in view of the accelerating construction of socialism in the USSR and the deepening of the world crisis. Based on these premises, the Eleventh Plenum of the ECCI in March–April 1931 emphasized that "[t]he revolutionary upsurge is growing," expressing, inter alia, "the development and strengthening of soviets and of the Red Army in a significant part of the territory of China . . . and the strengthening of the revolutionary movement in the colonies."[12]

On July 31, the ECCI Presidium addressed a special resolution to the CCP

Central Committee pointing out, "At the present stage of the movement when the country is facing a revolutionary crisis and soviet power has triumphed in a number of regions, the outcome of the struggle depends above all directly upon the communist party itself. . . . [T]he Chinese communist party must totally unmask the views of right opportunism along a broad front, and carry out a struggle to the end in both theory and practice."[13]

It was this document that demanded that kulaks and poor peasants not be accorded equal rights to the land, but no criticism was specifically addressed to Mao. The sharpening of the conflict against Mao was the exclusive enterprise of the new CCP leaders. Nothing in the resolution spoke about new attacks upon cities. The plan to seize "one or two urban centers" that was implemented early in 1932 in southern Jiangxi in the bloody battle for Ganzhou was likewise the work of the Shanghai leadership, although they were in line with the viewpoint of the Comintern. Two and a half months after the Provisional Politburo had issued its August directive, Mif himself wrote Stalin advancing the idea of conquering major cities in China.[14] Stalin supported him.

In these circumstances, it was impossible to speak of "guerrilla tactics" in the opinion of the leadership of the Central Committee Bureau. Along with other members of the Bureau, Zhou Enlai conscientiously began to carry out the directive of the Central Committee that the Comintern had essentially approved. Mao opposed this, though not because he was generally against taking cities. Rich commercial centers always attracted his attention. He wanted to emulate his beloved heroes in the novel *Water Margin,* that is, to swoop down on a small, poorly defended city, pillage it, and then retreat to a safe haven. He did not consider it rational to hunker down in large strategic points. It was this view that irritated the leadership, which, as before, believed the Chinese revolution could be victorious only by relying on urban centers. Nevertheless, what a fearless person was Mao, again swimming against the tide. Might he have sensed a kind of force behind him?

This time, too, he was lucky. The effort to capture Ganzhou utterly failed. Many army commanders now understood that Mao had been right in objecting to this offensive. "With 14,000 men, our Third Army Group could certainly not have overcome such a superior force holding strong fortifications," Peng Dehuai recalled later. "It was a grave error to attack a fortified city before finding out the real situation of the enemy troops holding it." The most unfortunate aspect was that the siege of Ganzhou, which lasted for two months (January–March 1932), coincided with a Japanese attack against Shanghai, which was defended by the Guomindang's Nineteenth Army.[15] It appeared that the communists and the Japanese were working in tandem.

The leaders of the Bureau had to swallow their pride. In early March, Xiang Ying, braving a torrential downpour, showed up at Mao's lair and, in the name of the Central Revolutionary Military Council and Zhou Enlai personally, asked him to "return to action" promptly. Mao was barely able to contain his joy. Soaked from the rain and humiliated by his unenviable assignment, Xiang Ying looked pitiful. Gathering their things, Mao and He Zizhen descended the mountain for Ruijin that very night. Mao put his bamboo flute in the pocket of his military-style service jacket. Who knew how often he would be fated to play it? His return from disgrace still meant nothing. The struggle for power continued.

For now, however, he had to proceed immediately for the front, to the district of Ganxian some sixty miles west of Ruijin, and the only thing he managed to do was to give to the members of the Bureau and the government the text of a declaration regarding Japan's incursion into China, which he had outlined back in late January, right after Japan's bombardment of Shanghai. The document was pointed: the Soviet government of China officially declares war upon Japan. Of course, this action was purely formal in nature. The communist armies were operating far from Manchuria and Shanghai. Its political significance, however, was enormous. With the help of propaganda and demagogy and by boldly exploiting the anti-Japanese mood of the people, the CCP was able to transform itself in the eyes of many Chinese patriots into a truly nationalist force, which helped it in its struggle against the Guomindang. After lengthy disputes, the declaration was finally adopted by Mao's "colleagues" on April 15. Six days later it appeared in the pages of *Hongse Zhonghua* (Red China), the official organ of the CEC and of the Council of People's Commissars of the Chinese Soviet Republic.[16]

By then Mao was already far from Ruijin. He spent the remainder of March in southern Jiangxi trying to fix the critical situation, then transferred to Fujian, to Lin Biao's forces. Until the end of June he took part in military operations in the south and southwest of this province. Accompanying the troops, he carried out a difficult raid to the south along mountain roads, more than 150 miles from Ruijin, against the rich but weakly defended commercial city of Zhangzhou, where he was able to enjoy the romance of banditry. After pillaging Zhangzhou and several neighboring towns and villages, Mao turned back to the south of Jiangxi. Along the road, his soldiers, as usual, killed *dizhu* (landlords), *funong* (rich peasants), and ordinary local peasants, or *bendi* (the primordial enemies of the Hakka); burned down their homes; and seized their property. They left a wasteland in their wake. One of Mao's contemporaries, who passed through this region a little over a year later, recalled that "[e]verywhere rice fields were clogged with mud, yam-fields overgrown with weeds, sugar going to seed, and houses burnt to the ground, with hardly anyone in sight."[17]

The manifest success of the operation strengthened Mao's authority in the army. The "heroic" campaign to Fujian, which provided so many pleasant moments to the soldiers and commanders, followed hard upon the unsuccessful siege of Ganzhou, which had been the responsibility of the new leaders.[18]

Yet he still had to hold bitter discussions on tactics with the members of the Bureau. His opponents were not opposed to pillaging and murder; they simply believed it necessary to posit global goals without irritating the enemy in minor battles, and to conduct major operations to seize entire provinces. The discussions turned sharp. An inkling of these events can be derived from a telegram that Zhou Enlai and others sent to the CCP Central Committee on May 3, 1932. They said in part:

> We have disagreements regarding the direction of expanding the [Central] Soviet area and the actions of the Red Army. At a session of the Bureau of the CC CCP of the Soviet areas at the end of last year, Mao Zedong proposed establishing a soviet area in the tri-mountain area along the borders of Fujian, Guangdong, Jiangxi, and Hunan. Communard [Wang Jiaxiang] came out against this plan and asserted that in the current political situation this was a deviation from the seizure of large cities. . . . When Moskvin [Zhou Enlai] arrived, Mao Zedong . . . expressed his opposition to attacks on urban centers. . . . This political line is hundred percent opportunism; it underestimates the current situation and completely contradicts the directives of the CI [Comintern] and the CC [CCP]. . . . We have resolved to struggle against Mao Zedong's mistakes and criticize them in the party organ.[19]

Nine days later, with Mao absent from Ruijin, a session of the Bureau was held at which criticism was again directed against his "defective line." The resolution adopted said, "It is necessary to uproot all of the right opportunist errors that occurred in the past work of the Bureau," meaning, during the period of Mao Zedong's leadership. This was immediately transmitted to Shanghai, and the members of the Provisional Politburo then informed the ECCI about the new disagreements with Mao, certain their protector Mif would finally put an end to this conflict with Mao.[20]

But the response from the center was discouraging. Persons much more powerful than Mif intervened regarding the question of Mao. We can only speculate about why they did this. On May 15, 1932, Otto Kuusinen, Dmitry Manuilsky, Josef Piatnitsky, and Wilhelm Pieck, reliable Stalinists who were members of the highest organ of the ECCI, namely, the Political Commission of the Political Secretariat, examined the conflict in Ruijin. Mao was put under Moscow's protection.[21]

The Provisional Politburo and the Bureau of the Central Committee were forced to retreat, although they didn't want to admit defeat. "All of the issues have been correctly resolved," wrote Zhou Enlai to the CCP Central Committee after receipt of a telegram of June 9, 1932, from the Political Commission that effectively supported Mao. "Our discussion proceeded in a comradely atmosphere and was limited to the members of the Bureau. This did not interfere with Mao Zedong's leading work."[22]

The only thing that could please Bo Gu and his confederates in Jiangxi was that Moscow was defending Mao only from public criticism. It was still not in agreement with his guerrilla tactics. That is why Zhou soon sent another telegram to the Central Committee seeking the leadership's agreement to send Mao away from Ruijin. On June 10 he wrote: "Mao Zedong is physically very weak; he remains at work in the high mountains and suffers from insomnia and a poor appetite. However, when he is with the army he is full of energy and is skilled in conducting military operations. The Bureau of [the CCP Central Committee of the soviet areas] has decided to send him to the front to plan military operations. He likewise wishes to set out for the front."[23]

What a strange telegram. Mao had not yet managed to arrive in the "high mountains" of Ruijin from southern Jiangxi, yet, in Zhou Enlai's words, he was already feeling indisposed and had stopped eating and sleeping. Probably the members of the Bureau were not very happy about the return of the chairman of the CEC and of the Council of People's Commissars. Mao himself did not wish to return to Ruijin. In mid-June he was already in southern Jiangxi with his troops. There he received the news about the reestablishment of the First Front Army by order of the Provisional Politburo. Zhu De was reconfirmed as commander in chief of the army, with Wang Jiaxiang as chief of the General Political Administration. They and Mao were leading the First Front Army against the Guangdong militarists who were attacking the soviet area.[24]

Now Mao had to demonstrate his exceptional diplomatic abilities. Finding himself in the same leadership group as Wang Jiaxiang, one of his main opponents, Mao resorted to the favorite tactic of all politicians, namely, "divide and rule." Mao had paid great attention to Wang, this stoop-shouldered young man in round eyeglasses who was thirteen years his junior, ever since Wang and Ren Bishi had shown up at his home in the village of Qingtang in April 1931. Like all of Chen Shaoyu's crew, Wang Jiaxiang spoke Russian fluently, but unlike the others he was devoid of excessive ambition. A dogmatist who believed fervently in Russian experience, somewhere deep inside he remained an ordinary Chinese peasant. One could find a common language with him even though he could be rude and intolerable on occasion.

Mao already had begun to "court" him in late April, but failed to achieve any substantial results.[25] Now he renewed his blandishments with Zhu De's help. Finally, they succeeded in "winning over" the "stubborn youth." Just then, Zhou Enlai showed up at their headquarters in the latter half of July. At this point Mao went for broke, utilizing every opportunity to "win over" Zhou himself with the help of Zhu De and Wang Jiaxiang. Results were soon forthcoming. Accustomed to playing second fiddle, Zhou Enlai, under constant pressure, could not resist. Mao Zedong overwhelmed him. With Mao, Zhu, and Wang, Zhou now signed a telegram to the Bureau of the Central Committee requesting that it cancel its plan for a new attack upon Ganzhou. That same day, all four addressed the Bureau proposing restoration of the post of general political commissar for the First Front Army, specially for Mao Zedong. They even considered it possible to demand the elimination of the post of chairman of the government (Mao could not combine both positions).[26]

Mao had apparently forgotten all of the insults, but his "winning over" of Wang and Zhou were only steps on the road to the conquest of power. The end justifies the means and for now he needed these two former adversaries. With their help he hoped to break through the ring of alienation that the new party leaders had drawn close around him. But the members of the Bureau who remained in Ruijin, Ren Bishi foremost among them, were under pressure from Bo Gu and Luo Fu and had no desire to ease relations. Accepting the de facto designation of Mao as political commissar, at the same time they continued to condemn his guerrilla tactics and insist upon the seizure of large urban centers.

The conflict intensified. The military views of Ren Bishi, who was blindly executing the directives of the Provisional Politburo, were too much at odds with those of Mao. Then the Bureau of the Central Committee once again raised the question of the "opportunism" of the chairman of the CEC and of the CSR. The criticism directed against Mao reached its apogee. All the Ruijin-based members of the Bureau came out against Mao Zedong. In addition to Ren Bishi there were Xiang Ying; Deng Fa, who headed the secret service of the Central Soviet Area; and Gu Zuolin, the Bureau secretary of the Communist Youth League. They all sharply criticized Mao for proposing to avoid large battles, to go off into the mountains, and to decentralize the army. In other words, he persisted in favoring "defensive tactics rather than any sort of offensive at present."[27] Exasperated with his behavior, in September 1932, Ren Bishi and the others concluded that "Mao Zedong does not understand Marxism."[28] Having decided to remove him and subject him to public criticism, they promptly informed the Central Committee:

> Comrade Mao Zedong is vacillating with regard to expansion of [the Central] Soviet Area, seizure of major cities, and the struggle to achieve initial victory [of the revolution] in one or several provinces. His opportunist line . . . continues and he often tries to push it, ignoring the party leadership, and promoting cadres on the basis of personal connections rather than from [the needs] of public utility. Although Comrade Moskvin [Zhou Enlai] is there [at the front], it is difficult in reality for him to put into practice the views of the Bureau [of the CCP Central Committee] and to radically change their actions. . . . For the sake of achieving unity of views among the military leadership, we

firmly and openly criticize the errors of Comrade Mao [Zedong] and desire that he be recalled to the rear to work in the [central] soviet government.[29]

Without awaiting approval from the Central Committee or the representatives of the ECCI, at the end of September Ren, Xiang, Deng, and Gu went to the front (in Ningdu county) "to convene a plenum of the Bureau." In early October they held their field session in the village of Xiaoyuan, at which they subjected Mao to withering criticism for his "guerrilla mentality" and "right opportunism." They also lit into the "appeasers"—Zhou Enlai, Zhu De, and Wang Jiaxiang—for "not sufficiently believing in the victory of the revolution and underestimating the power of the Red Army." The upshot was that Mao had to abandon the front line, again "on account of illness." Ren Bishi and his confederates happily granted him leave "to recuperate." This time he was taken to a hospital high up in the mountains, more than ninety miles south of Ningdu.

Meanwhile, the leaders of the Provisional Politburo were also meeting in Shanghai. The telegram from Ruijin delighted them since they were very eager to bring Mao down. The meeting in Ningdu apparently provided an opportunity. "We must wage an active struggle inside the party against his [Mao Zedong's] views," enthused Bo Gu. "It would be good to send Zedong to the rear where he can engage in work in the soviets," seconded Luo Fu.[30] The other leaders agreed, but they were worried about how Stalin and the ECCI would react. They dreaded evoking another furious response from Moscow. The solution turned out to be simple. The leaders prepared two variant responses. The first, in Chinese, was sent to the Bureau of the Central Committee. (It was received in Ningdu only after Mao had already departed from there.) The second, in English, was sent to the ECCI, along with a translation of the telegram from the Bureau. (Both of these latter documents arrived in Moscow on October 16.) The version sent to the Comintern emphasized that there should be no "open discussion" directed against Mao, but the version sent to Jiangxi indicated precisely the opposite: "Begin a discussion of Zedong's views."[31]

After receiving the Politburo's response, in Mao's absence Ren Bishi and his confederates removed Mao from his position as general political commissar, thereby depriving him of any influence in the army, and bestowed his duties upon Zhou Enlai. Two weeks later Shanghai confirmed their decision.[32]

Hearing this, Mao lost his self-control. He had been left without real work. Mao did not consider his honorary service in the government as amounting to anything.[33] He Zizhen recalled that he cried, "Dogmatism ruins and destroys people! They have no idea about practical work; they have never had contact with a single worker or peasant, yet they give orders right and left and are preoccupied with purely administrative matters! How can one possibly be victorious in this mode in the battle against the Guomindang? Do they understand why the peasants rose up in revolution?"[34]

The only thing he took pleasure in at this time was the birth of a new son. In early November 1932, Zizhen gave birth to a son whom Mao named Anhong ("Red Army Man Who Reaches the Shore of Socialism"). Cradling him in her arms, the happy mother rejoiced. She was vexed, however, because the doctors would not let her nurse the infant, since she was suffering from malaria. But Mao was not depressed. At his instructions his bodyguards found a nursemaid for the infant, who took him into her care. This simple peasant woman called all her babes-in-arms by the same name, "xiao maomao" (little fur ball or the hairy little one). When Mao Zedong first heard this he was ecstatic. "Just look," he said to Zizhen. "People call me 'Lao Mao' [Old or Honored Mao], and my son is called Xiao Maomao [Little Double Mao]. That means he is much more Mao than I am.* And in the future he'll become even stronger!" Humor alone saved him in this difficult situation. And his old bamboo flute. But the sad melodies that Mao played fed his wife's melancholy.

Once again Moscow came to Mao's rescue. More precisely, rescue came in the form of Moscow's new representatives in China, before whom the likes of Bo Gu and Luo Fu had to snap to attention. In the autumn of 1932 the new ECCI representative arrived in Shanghai along with his wife. He was a German named Arthur Ernst Ewert. Of course, no one in China knew him as Ewert. He entered the country with an American passport under the name of Harry Berger, and in CCP circles he began to use the underground aliases of "Jim" and "Arthur." This forty-two-year-old veteran of the German Communist Party was on very good standing in the Comintern. In 1928, at the Sixth World Congress of the Comintern, he was chosen as a candidate member of its Executive Committee and from 1929 on he was a deputy director of the Eastern Secretariat. Like many Germans, he was punctilious and pedantic. But he was a great drinker. At this critical juncture, Ewert played an important role in Mao's life by providing support in his battle against intraparty enemies despite the fact that he too considered Mao's military tactics "dangerous," "passive," and "deviationist." "Mao Zedong's general approach is mistaken (too much stress on the effectiveness of defense, on concealment in the mountains, etc.)," he reported to the Comintern.

But after learning of the telegram from the Bureau of the Central Committee, he informed Josef Piatnitsky, the secretary of the ECCI, on October 8,

---

* The humor is built upon wordplay. The expression *xiao maomao* actually has a dual meaning. It can be translated either as "hairy little one" or as "little fur ball." Thus many in China affectionately call their newborn babies after the soft, downy hair on their heads, but it can also mean "Little Double Mao" if *Mao* is the character for the surname Mao rather than the character *mao* that means "hair."

1932, that the "leadership of the party in Jiangxi" had decided to remove Mao and subject him to public criticism, without any prior preparation. "Not to mention that such an approach to the situation at present would demonstrate our weakness to the foe," he pointed out, "one should not resort to such decisions without . . . serious preparation (to say nothing of your approval). Mao Zedong remains a popular leader. . . . [W]e have come out against that part of the resolutions, demanded that disagreements within the leading organs be eliminated, and come out against the removal of Mao Zedong at this time."[35] Naturally, Ewert also informed the leadership of the CCP Central Committee of his position.

The result was that Bo Gu and Luo Fu had to retreat, but they would still not let Mao return to military affairs. The leaders of the party apparently could not stand him, but they were unable to avoid dealing with him. In early 1933 they even had to meet with Mao in person, and after that their paths were so interwoven that it became unthinkable to avoid personal contacts. At the end of January 1933, Bo Gu, Luo Fu, and one other member of the Provisional Politburo, the twenty-eight-year-old Shanghai printer Chen Yun (real name Liao Chenyun), were forced to relocate to the Central Soviet Area.[36] Their move, in the words of Wang Ming, was necessitated by a monstrous white terror that "made the existence of the party's leading centers in Shanghai virtually impossible."[37] This led to the liquidation of the Central Committee Bureau for the Soviet areas and the placement of the entire party leadership in the areas in the hands of Bo Gu. In formal terms the Central Committee Bureau and the Provisional Politburo were united into a new party organ dubbed the Central Bureau of the CCP.[38] Real power remained with Bo Gu, who, in accordance with directives from the ECCI, charted the party's basic political line.

Evidently fearing that the move would reignite intraparty conflict, in a telegram to the Central Committee routed via Ewert the Political Secretariat of the ECCI paid special attention to "the question of Mao Zedong": "With respect to Mao Zedong it is necessary to employ maximum patience and comradely influence, providing him full opportunity to engage in responsible work under the leadership of the CC or the CC Bureau of the party."[39] Forwarding this directive to Ruijin, Ewert appended his own commentary: "We ask that you work closely together with Mao Zedong, but that you keep an eye on him so that our military work gets done and is not destroyed by large-scale discussions and vacillation."[40]

Starting in January 1933, however, opportunities for the ECCI and its Far Eastern Bureau to influence the CCP's intraparty life diminished. After the departure of the Provisional Politburo from Shanghai, their links shrank. Radiograms that Ewert sent to Ruijin could not substitute for direct contact between Comintern emissaries and Bo Gu and other party leaders. By early October

1934, after a new, and this time decisive, failure of the Shanghai organization, communist activity in the city practically disappeared. Soon afterward the ECCI closed its Far Eastern Bureau.[41]

In Ruijin the intraparty struggle continually heated up. Bo Gu was so negative toward Mao that initially he tried to avoid any contact with him. In January 1933, passing through the town where Mao was still hospitalized, Bo Gu flatly refused to visit the "sick man." In response to his comrades' plea, "You should drop by and look in on him," Bo Gu snapped, "And just what is there about Mao Zedong that makes it worth my while?"[42] Of course, his ill will served no purpose. The cunning Mao would never indulge in such behavior, because he was simply more cautious.

There was good reason to "look in" on Mao. He was no newcomer to battling the Guomindang, which is why some party officials periodically sought his advice. Among them was Luo Ming, the acting party secretary of Fujian. After one of his visits this fiery partisan of guerrilla warfare succeeded in getting a public endorsement of Mao's tactics from his party committee, which naturally caused a big scandal. In February 1933, the enraged Bo Gu launched a broad intraparty campaign against the so-called Luo Ming line. In the heat of the moment, Mao's younger brother Zetan fell from power. Along with several other active supporters of Mao Zedong, he was criticized no less than Luo Ming, and in May 1933 was dismissed from military work. This was also the fate of most of Mao's other relatives in the Central Soviet Area.

In the spring of 1933, Zizhen, who had been acting secretary of the Council of People's Commissars, lost her job and was sent for "reeducation" at the Central Committee's party school. Her sister He Yi, Zetan's wife, was also sent there, though she was six or seven months pregnant. (He Zizhen, too, was pregnant again; she gave birth to the infant, a boy, in late autumn of 1933, but he lived for only a short time.) They badgered He Yi so much to "unmask" her husband as an "opportunist" that soon after giving birth she fell seriously ill. They thought she was dissembling and Bo Gu himself raised the question of expelling her from the party. Only because Dong Biwu, an old party member who doubled as secretary of the Control Commission and deputy rector of the party school, afforded her protection did the matter fade away. He Yi escaped with a reprimand. Soon, however, Zizhen's elder brother Meixue was removed from his post as acting divisional commander and was also sent to engage in study—at the Red Army Academy. The repression even extended to Mao's father-in-law and mother-in-law, Zizhen's aged parents who were living in the village of Donggu, in the north of the Central Soviet Area. They were both fired from the local party committee where they worked.[43]

Meanwhile, serious charges of "opportunism of the Luo Ming type" were leveled against the former head of the technical secretariat of the Central

Committee Deng Xiaoping, who had been working in various positions in the Central Soviet Area since August 1931. It was then that Mao took notice of this man who had shown his character and not bowed his head before Mao's enemies.[44]

Mao's life turned into a living hell. Returning to Yeping in mid-February during the high tide of the campaign against Luo Ming, Mao felt totally isolated. Only He Yi often called upon him and her sister in their house. She cried and complained about her life. Mao was sympathetic but could do nothing. "They are purging you because of me. They have dragged all of you into my affair," he said bitterly.[45] He was practically barred from all work and was not invited to most sessions of the Politburo. Many feared any contact with him. Mao did not leave his house for days on end, preferring to spend time with his family. Many years later he recalled, "I was immersed in a cesspool like some sort of wooden Bodhisattva, and then dragged out after turning into a stinking doll. At this time not only a single person, but not even a single devil dared to cross the threshold of my house. All that was left for me was to eat, sleep, and shit. At least they didn't cut off my head."[46]

By a happy accident at least they did not touch Mao Zemin and his wife, Qian Xijun. Taciturn by nature, yet businesslike and confident, Zemin had been working in the government. From March 1932 he served as director of the State People's Bank. He did not intervene in any intraparty squabbles. Qian Xijun worked as deputy secretary for the party committee of the government apparatus. Of course, in his heart Zemin deeply sympathized with his brothers, but he was unable to help them.

Zhu De, Zhou Enlai, and Wang Jiaxiang were far from Yeping, away at the front. Starting in late February 1933, fierce battles against Chiang Kai-shek's troops were taking place. In a month of fighting the Red Army repulsed a new Guomindang punitive campaign—the fourth—led by Minister of War He Yingqin. This time the Nanjing government threw half a million soldiers against the communists, and the situation was critical. Zhu, Zhou, and Wang had only one chance to defeat the enemy, namely, to adopt the old Maoist tactic of "luring the enemy in deep." "The enemy advances, we retreat; the enemy camps, we harass; the enemy tires, we attack; the enemy retreats, we pursue." This "magic" formula brought salvation. At the end of March the Fourth Expedition was defeated, but Zhou and Zhu remained with the troops. Wang Jiaxiang moved to Ruijin in early May, but Mao could not speak with him man to man. At the end of April Wang had been seriously wounded in the stomach by shrapnel and the wound had not healed. He had to spend all his time in the hospital and suffered terribly as shrapnel migrated through his body, causing him intense pain. The only thing that helped was opium.

In the autumn of 1933 the German communist Otto Braun, a member of the Far Eastern Bureau, arrived in the Central Soviet Area. He was very much like Ewert and even loved to drink as much as the ECCI representative. He looked like Bo Gu, tall and thin as a lath with big, round eyeglasses, but his hair was light and his eyes were blue. He had the air of a sergeant major in the old German army, did not tolerate dissent, and was very self-assured and rude. He considered himself the main authority in questions of Red Army strategy and tactics even though he had come to Ruijin merely as a military adviser to the CCP Central Committee.

The arrival of Braun, who was, among other things, a secret agent of the IV (intelligence) Section of the Soviet General Staff, did not augur well for Mao since it was in the area of military tactics that the basic contradictions between the guerrilla leader and the Central Committee and the Comintern lay. Braun had already been apprised of Mao's "opportunistic" views when he arrived in Shanghai in the fall of 1932. Bo Gu, with whom Braun became very friendly, had inculcated in the German hostile feelings toward Mao. Thus Braun became an opponent of Mao as well as of the "spineless appeasers" such as Zhu De and Zhou Enlai, who rarely appeared in Ruijin.[47] Although Braun was not the official representative of the Comintern (such as Ewert was until midsummer 1934), with the support of Bo Gu he "usurped the command of the Red Army."[48] That is how he himself, a number of years later, while repenting his "sins" before the Comintern leaders, characterized his own activity. Not knowing Chinese or "the conditions characterizing the Red Army's struggle in China," he maintained ties exclusively with Bo Gu and other graduates of Soviet educational institutions with whom he could speak Russian. Prior to coming to China, Braun had studied in Moscow for four years in the M. V. Frunze Military Academy. Imperious and strict, he began to dispense suggestions on every issue, political as well as military. "Other opinions were suppressed and the initiatives of front-line commanders often disregarded," Braun himself admitted, adding "I was extraordinarily stubborn and rigid . . . and fought for my views without an ounce of self-criticism."[49]

It was only owing to the quiet but palpable support of their leader by army commanders and local party secretaries that Bo Gu and Braun did not succeed in crushing Mao. As always, Moscow's position was of greatest significance despite the weakening of its ties with the CCP Central Committee. There influential forces were not interested in overthrowing Mao, though the situation in the ECCI was complicated by the fact that not all its chiefs viewed Mao as the most important leader of the Chinese Communist Party. The Far Eastern Section of the Eastern Secretariat and its director, Pavel Mif, persistently advanced Chinese graduates of Moscow higher educational institutions to key posts in the CCP. It was with Mif's help that Wang Ming became the head of the CCP delegation to the Comintern in 1931 and Bo Gu the leader of the party. Yet, other Comintern officials, members of the Soviet Central Committee, and the Far Eastern Bureau of the ECCI realized that "Mif's fledglings" lacked practical experience. Some officials relied on such old Comintern cadres as Zhou Enlai, Xiang Ying, and Zhang Guotao. There were several factions in the ECCI apparatus. Behind the scenes these groups fought each other tooth and nail. Nor was there unity among those who oversaw the CCP. For example, conflicts between Mif and the deputy director of the Eastern Secretariat, Ludwig Mad'iar, were frequent.[50] Therefore, various factions in the ECCI supported "their own people" in the CCP. Stalin, it will be recalled, initially did not favor any of the factions in the ECCI or in the CCP leadership. Mao was elevated merely as a counterweight to Zhou Enlai, Xiang Ying, Zhang Guotao, Wang Ming, Bo Gu, and Luo Fu, essentially strengthening his position in the early 1930s.

Not until the mid-1930s did Stalin decisively favor Mao Zedong. In mid-January 1934, on Moscow's insistence, Mao was transferred from candidate to full member of the Politburo at the regular plenum of the CCP Central Committee.[51] This plenum took place in Ruijin, but Mao refused to participate, relying, as always, on "illness." (Bo Gu sarcastically observed to Otto Braun that Mao had a periodic attack of "diplomatic illness.") The Central Bureau of the CCP, as always trying to undermine Mao's authority, decided that the report "On the Soviet Movement and Its Tasks" was to be delivered to the plenum not by Mao Zedong as chairman of the CEC and of the Council of People's Commissars, the normal procedure, but by Luo Fu, the second-ranking person in the party, whom the Bo Gu faction had nominated to replace Mao as the new chairman of the Council of People's Commissars.[52] This is why Mao pleaded "illness." The plenum chose a new Politburo Standing Committee, consisting of seven men: Bo Gu (designated the general secretary), Luo Fu, Zhou Enlai, Chen Yun, Zhang Guotao, Wang Ming, and Xiang Ying.

At the end of January the formal Second Congress of Soviets was convened. Six hundred ninety-three delegates and eighty-three alternates approved all of the resolutions of the party and reelected Mao to the by now meaningless post of chairman of the CEC.[53] Right after the congress, at the first session of the CEC, Luo Fu replaced Mao as head of the Council of People's Commissars of the Chinese Soviet Republic (or the People's Committee of the Central Government, as it was now called).[54] Surprisingly, Mao's replacement took place without the knowledge of Moscow, a unique phenomenon.[55] Not knowing this, Mao felt bad about it.

At the conclusion of the CEC meetings, he again "took ill" and stopped working. Bo Gu, Otto Braun, and their supporters merely rejoiced. In early spring 1934, they informed Arthur Ewert of Mao's "illness." He in turn informed the secretary of the ECCI, Piatnitsky, and Wang Ming: "Mao Zedong has been ill for a long time and requests that he be sent to Moscow. Do you think it possible to send him as a delegate to the [VII] Congress [of the Comintern planned to take place in Moscow in July–August 1935]? In the view of your representative [Ewert] and the Shanghai Bureau [of the CCP Central Committee], it will be difficult to guarantee the safety of his journey. Furthermore, we need to consider the political consequences." [56]

Naturally, the ECCI understood that the idea of sending Mao Zedong to Moscow originated with Bo Gu, who wanted a pretext for getting rid of his obstinate and powerful opponent. In early April, the Political Commission of the Political Secretariat of the ECCI adopted the following resolution:

> His [Mao's] trip to the USSR is considered inexpedient. Every effort must be made to treat him in Soviet China. Only should it prove to be absolutely impossible to treat him in Soviet China can he come to the Soviet Union. . . . [We] are opposed to Mao Zedong's trip, because we don't want to subject him to the risk that a journey entails. It is absolutely necessary to arrange for his treatment in the Soviet area no matter how large the expense. Only if it is completely impossible to treat him locally and the danger of a fatal outcome from his illness presents itself could we agree to his coming to Moscow. [57]

Bo Gu tried to object. At his order the question of Mao was raised again in June 1934 by Gao Zili, the minister of agriculture of the Chinese Soviet Republic, who came to Moscow that month. He conveyed Bo Gu's words to Wang Ming: Mao "makes mistakes on the big issues; he only succeeds in minor matters." [58]

This was precisely the time, however, that Moscow began to propagate a heroic image of Mao. In 1934 the journal *Kommunisticheskii Internatsional* (Communist International) in Russian and *Za rubezhom* (Abroad) published Mao Zedong's report to the Second All-China Congress of Soviets on the work of the CEC and the Council of People's Commissars. Mao's report was simultaneously published as a separate pamphlet in Russian and Chinese in an edition of five thousand copies. Soon the first collection of Mao Zedong's selected speeches and articles was published in the USSR in these same two languages, likewise in an edition of five thousand copies. [59] Finally, in November 1934, the journal *Za rubezhom* published the first sketch of Mao by Georgii Borisovich Ehrenburg in its section "Portraits of Contemporaries." Prior to this, only one article acquainting readers with Mao Zedong had been published in the Soviet Union, in February 1930, by the *Pravda* correspondent in China, Alexei Ivanov, under the nom de plume of Ivin, but in it Mao was presented always in tandem with Zhu De. [60]

Understanding which way the wind was blowing, Wang Ming and Kang Sheng, the leaders of the CCP delegation to the ECCI, in September 1934 advised the CCP Central Committee "to follow the example of Zhu De and Mao Zedong and work directly in the guerrilla detachments." [61]

But Bo Gu and Otto Braun continued to object. Mao still had no voting rights in either military or party affairs. The conflict flourished. Moreover, the military-strategic position of the Central Soviet Area worsened catastrophically. In October 1934 the First Front Army, recently renamed the Central Red Army, suffered a serious defeat at the hands of Chiang Kai-shek's forces.

The communists of the Central Soviet Area had been trying for a year to contain the Guomindang onslaught. This fifth campaign had begun in late September 1933, two to three weeks prior to Otto Braun's arrival. Chiang Kai-shek personally led a million troops into battle against the "Red bandits." His German advisers devised a plan to extinguish the Chinese Soviet Republic by erecting along its borders several thousand blockhouses, powerful stone forts separated from each other at a distance of one to two miles. Deciding to eliminate the CCP once and for all, Chiang was now cautious. His soldiers moved slowly deep into the "red zone," at a rate of barely a mile per day, consolidating their gains at each new line and tightening the ring. One of Chiang's generals characterized the tactics thus: "Drain the pond to catch the fish." Chiang employed not only military means but political as well. He laid special emphasis on the latter, calculating 30 percent military and 70 percent political. In all the newly reconquered territories, the traditional village system of mutual responsibility (*baojia*) was revived, and local peasant self-defense detachments were reestablished. Large rewards were offered for the capture of leaders of the Communist Party. For example, a quarter of a million yuan was offered for Mao's head. Moreover, in 1934, at Chiang Kai-shek's personal initiative, a program of national revival was introduced with the aim of resurrecting the lost Confucian norms of decorum and morality.[62]

These measures produced results. The Red Army was bled white, losing one battle after another. The situation was exacerbated by the senseless tactic of positional warfare that Otto Braun, supported by Bo Gu, imposed on the Red Army under the slogan of "Do not yield an inch of ground!" He was unable to grasp that Chinese conditions differed substantially from those in Russia. In the Frunze Academy, Braun had been taught how to plan offensive operations, and this experience inculcated in him faith in the magical powers of lightning attacks. Repeatedly, he threw Red Army troops against well-fortified enemy positions, into a hail of machine-gun fire, achieving nothing. Deprived of his voice, Mao was powerless to do anything. Having graduated from no academy other than the rigorous school of guerrilla warfare, Mao understood that Otto Braun was wrong. Later he would assert: "[S]o long as we lack superior troop strength or reserves of ammunition and have only one Red army in each soviet area to do all the fighting, positional warfare is basically useless to us. For us, positional warfare is generally inapplicable in attack as well as in defense."[63] Bo Gu and Braun paid him no heed.

Finally, by the early summer of 1934 the situation had become hopeless.

Arthur Ewert wrote: "As a result of constant battles and insufficient war booty our military supplies have significantly dwindled. Our losses have been enormous. Desertion is growing." In May the Secretariat of the Central Committee resolved to begin preparations for the evacuation of the Red Army's main forces from the Central Soviet Area. An urgent telegram was sent to Moscow: "What remains is to defend the CSR to the last possible moment while simultaneously preparing to redeploy our main forces in a different direction."[64] Another telegram followed with a request for material aid to the tune of one million Mexican dollars for the purchase of medicines and uniforms.[65] A trio consisting of Bo Gu, Luo Fu, and Zhou Enlai was established for operational leadership,[66] but actually, according to Otto Braun's memoirs, all the basic problems were resolved "in personal conversations" among Bo, Zhou, and Braun himself.[67]

On June 8 the Political Commission of the Political Secretariat of the ECCI approved a plan by Bo Gu and other leaders of the CCP and emphasized to Ewert that the departure of the main forces from the Central Soviet Area should be considered "temporary," and "in the interest of preserving a vital force from under attack." Instead of a million "Mex," the "Chinese comrades" were sent only 200,000 rubles, which equaled about 150,000 Mexican dollars.[68]

Mao knew nothing of this. The troika kept the evacuation plan secret from him. Even Zhou Enlai, despite the apparently good relations between him and Mao, breathed not a word. Zhou always held his finger to the wind, and in those days the wind was not blowing in Mao's direction. Not until early October, shortly before the withdrawal from Ruijin, did the troika consider it necessary to inform Mao. Mao was then some sixty miles west of the capital, in the village of Yudu, with the troops of the First Corps. From late September he had been suffering from malaria, and was still not in good shape. Illness really had ground him down, and he looked emaciated and worn out.

The ruling troika also informed him of the decision, again taken without his participation, to allow thirty women, the wives of the top party leaders, to follow the army. (Apart from them only twenty other women, most of them nurses and other service personnel, were allowed to take part in the march.)[69] Happily, Zizhen was included among the thirty. She was enrolled in a sanitary brigade in the Chief Medical Administration. But Mao and Zizhen had to part from their two-year-old son, Anhong, "the hairy little one." The troika was firm on this point: no children on the march.

Mao quickly informed his wife of all this by special messenger; she was living with their son at the time in the ancient mountain monastery of Yunshan, some twelve miles southwest of Ruijin. She had moved there in July 1934 along with officials from the CEC and the Council of People's Commissars to escape the raids by enemy aircraft. Mao advised Zizhen to hand over the infant to their wet nurse, who was like a family member, but that woman lived far off in the countryside and Zizhen had no time to bring the child to her. Zizhen consulted her sister, He Yi, who along with her husband, Mao's younger brother Zetan, and her parents did not intend to depart on the march. She and Zetan, like many other party and military officials, were staying at the old base under the command of Xiang Ying and Chen Yi. Zetan was slated to command an independent division.

Zizhen asked her sister to assume responsibility for making arrangements for Anhong. He Yi gladly agreed. "Go away and don't worry about anything," she reassured Zizhen. "I will take care of our parents and my nephew." It was decided that He Yi would deliver the young boy to the wet nurse as soon as possible. Neither Zizhen nor Mao ever saw their son again. Several days later the main force of the Red Army commenced its famous Long March from the Central Soviet Area to the west. On October 25, the army broke through the first ring of encirclement and moved into southern Hunan. By then He Yi had already transported Anhong to the wet nurse in the countryside. He Yi herself was living with her parents for a time in the home of some Red Army man. She was pregnant again and so decided not to risk leaving with her husband for the mountains. Soon afterward, Zetan, fearing for his nephew's safety, decided to arrange something more reliable. Upon his secret directive, the boy was entrusted to the family of one of his guards who lived in Ruijin, to be brought up there. But several months later, in April 1935, Mao Zetan was ambushed and killed. He took to his grave the secret of where young Anhong was living.

After the victory of the revolution, in the autumn of 1949, Zizhen along with He Yi and their older brother, Meixue, unsuccessfully tried to locate the boy. He Yi made a special effort since she felt guilty toward her sister. By some sort of mysterious coincidence, during her search, in the very place where Zetan had died, her jeep overturned on a mountain road and He Yi died without regaining consciousness.[70]

19

THE LONG MARCH

In early November, Red Army units, after breaking through the second line of blockhouses, emerged into southeastern Hunan. They numbered more than 86,000 troops, divided into five army groups (First, Third, Fifth, Eighth, and Ninth) and two so-called field columns—the staff column (whose secret code name was Red Star) and the transport column (whose secret code name was Red Order). The first column included members of the Central Revolutionary Military Council, including Mao Zedong. The second column consisted of members of the Central Committee, Central Executive Committee, and Council of People's Commissars staff members and various service personnel, including the medical company, one of whose nurses, as we know, was He Zizhen. Marching with the second column was the "reserve division," consisting entirely of unemployed peasants who had been drafted as porters for half a yuan per day. These people, in the words of Otto Braun "transported hundreds of bundles of leaflets, chests of silver bullion, and arsenal machinery. . . . Members of the reserve division were, for all practical purposes, unarmed, for the spears, swords, and daggers they carried could hardly be counted."[1] The ratio of fighters to noncombatants was roughly 3:1. For all the soldiers there were forty thousand rifles and more than a thousand light and heavy machine guns. There were also several pieces of heavy artillery, which were soon discarded since they impeded forward progress and for which there were no shells. All the soldiers carried packages of rice and salt, provisions calculated to last for two weeks.[2]

The final goal of the march had not been determined. After they broke through the blockade ring, it was assumed that everything would become clear. There had been no radio contact with the ECCI since early October 1934, after the final collapse of the Shanghai Bureau. After seizing the clandestine apartment of the secretary of the bureau, the Guomindang police confiscated the radio set that had been the sole means of communication among the CCP Central Committee, the Far Eastern Bureau, and the ECCI.[3] There was also no contact with other soviet areas. News reached the Central Committee that troops of the Second and the Sixth Front Army Groups of the Red Army, under the overall command of He Long, were operating somewhere along the juncture of Hunan, Hubei, and Sichuan provinces. The secretary of the CCP committee for these forces was Ren Bishi, who had been sent to join He Long in May 1933. There was also intermittent information about the guerrilla units under Zhang Guotao, the so-called Fourth Front Army, which, it was thought, after being beaten by Chiang Kai-shek in October 1932 had retreated to northwest Sichuan. But no one really knew whether this was really so. Only one thing was more or less clear: the army groups had to move in a westerly direction, to the Guangxi-Hunan-Guizhou border triangle, which, according to available information, as Braun writes, "was free of enemy fortifications."[4] The carefully calculated route traversed areas densely settled by Hakkas,[5] who, naturally, greeted the Red Army as liberators. Their support enabled the Red Army to overcome obstacles and arrive in Guizhou in December. The Guomindang forces did not risk attacking the main force, because they feared an uprising of the Hakka who lived according to their own clan rules and did not recognize the authority of the Guomindang.

Despite their successful breaching of several lines of enemy fortifications and their relatively safe completion of the first stage of what is now known as the Long March, the troops were depressed. Many of the officers and men grumbled and the difficulties of the march intensified their dissatisfaction. Every day the number of deserters and laggards increased. Those who continued were at the end of their rope. This created a unique opportunity for Mao to return to power. By taking advantage of this mood and properly channeling it, he would be able to take revenge on Bo Gu. He had to play the game boldly, setting the members of the leading troika against each other and counterpoising Bo Gu and Otto Braun against the other members of the Politburo. He had to act decisively, but without excessive ego.

Mao managed this task brilliantly. By the time they arrived in Guizhou, he had won over a majority of the members of the party leadership. Almost all the army commanders were on his side. Most important, he concluded a secret alliance with Luo Fu, the former close comrade in arms and devoted friend of Bo Gu. Mao had first met him in Shanghai in the early 1920s, when everyone still knew him as Zhang Wentian, a talented young journalist and novelist who had gone to school in China, Japan, and America, studied Western literature as well as physics and mathematics, and was well versed in the social sciences. Seven years younger than Mao and older than Bo Gu by the same number of years, Luo Fu embodied two epochs in the development of the communist movement. Along with the future creators of the CCP he had taken part in the May Fourth Movement, and together with "Mif's fledglings" he had studied in Moscow from 1925 to 1930 at the Sun Yat-sen University of the Toilers of China. Tall and thin like Bo Gu and Otto Braun, he differed from them in possessing great tact. Behind the thick lenses of his eyeglasses one could see the intelligent eyes of an intellectual.[6]

Mao had begun wooing Luo Fu in the Central Soviet Area several months before the Long March. As the military situation deteriorated, Mao noted that Luo Fu became increasingly nervous and periodically expressed dissatisfaction with the authoritarian methods of Otto Braun and Bo Gu. Mao decided to take advantage of this. Then Luo Fu unexpectedly dropped in to "consult" with Mao about military affairs that he wished to understand better. The conversation was tête-à-tête. After the meeting Mao began deliberately to promote Luo at the rare meetings of the Politburo that he attended. Meanwhile, Luo intensified his dispute with Bo Gu. At the end of April, after the most recent major defeat of the Red Army, Luo Fu caused a real scandal for his old friend by criticizing Bo. Otto Braun supported Bo, while Wang Jiaxiang, who was still in the hospital but closely followed the course of military actions in the Central Soviet Area, supported Luo Fu.[7]

By the beginning of the retreat, relations among Mao, Luo, and Wang had become so solid that when Mao suggested the three of them should be in the same column, his new friends readily agreed.[8] Mao had turned everything around. In Braun's words, by the end of the first stage of the march, under Mao's influence the "conspirators" constituted "the political leadership . . . of the faction which waged a subversive struggle to take over the Party and Army leadership."[9] Each of the three assiduously "cultivated" the army commanders and the members of the party leadership. Wang Jiaxiang, who was always in an extremely irritable state, from his stomach pain or some other reason, was particularly active in this regard.[10] For the time being, Zhou Enlai remained on Bo Gu's side, but he was undependable. Mao had no doubt that this flexible and cautious man would go with whoever was stronger.

Mao was not mistaken. In Liping, the first town in Guizhou seized by the Red Army, during a Politburo meeting Zhou supported Luo, Mao, and Wang when they demanded that Bo convene immediately a plenum of the leadership to discuss the results of the struggle against the Guomindang's fifth punitive campaign. Bo Gu had to agree, although he knew the meeting would be aimed against him and Otto Braun.

During the next three weeks, while the Red Army advanced northward in Guizhou toward Zunyi, the second-largest commercial center in the province, both warring factions prepared for the decisive political battle. It was decided to hold the conference in Zunyi, which, intelligence reports suggested, would not be difficult to occupy. Thus the Red Army soldiers could rest while the leaders engaged in resolving the intraparty disputes.

Zunyi was captured early on a rainy morning, Monday, January 7, 1935. The soldiers, tired, wet, and famished from the march, were happy to get food and shelter. Their two-week supply of provisions had long since been exhausted and the poor Hakka in the villages lacked provisions for themselves. In poverty-stricken Guizhou, located in a mountainous, rain-drenched area unsuitable for agriculture, most rural people were poor. There is a saying, "In Guizhou not three days go by without rain; there are not three *li* of level ground, and you will never find anyone there with three copper coins." After a difficult march of fifteen hundred miles, the soldiers wanted to spend a few warm days in peace. On January 9, Mao Zedong, Bo Gu, and other party and army leaders entered Zunyi. Mao, Luo Fu, and Wang Jiaxiang stayed in its vicinity, in a spacious private house belonging to a commander of the Guizhou army. While Red Army soldiers gorged themselves in the small restaurants on spicy Sichuan cabbage, boiled meat, chicken, and red peppers, the three "conspirators" devised a strategy for the coming conference. Bo Gu was also actively preparing. At his request, Kai Feng, one of the few remaining Bo Gu loyalists, held several "edifying" talks with Nie Rongzhen, an important political commissar in the Red Army, but Nie categorically refused to support Bo.[11]

Everything had been decided in advance. The ground had swiftly eroded under the feet of Bo Gu and Otto Braun. Nevertheless, on the eve of the conference Mao held a secret meeting with his supporters at which the impassioned Wang Jiaxiang dotted all the i's. "We shall throw them out when we meet," he asserted.[12]

Finally, the day of decision arrived. Early on the morning of January 15, nineteen men gathered in a small room on the second floor of the residence of Bai Huizhang, a divisional commander in the Guizhou army. (They were soon joined by one more person.) These were Politburo members and candidate members who had marched with the troops of the Central Red Army as well as several commanders and political commissars of the army groups. Deng Xiaoping, who again became head of the technical secretariat of the Central Committee on the eve of the conference, was present, as were Otto Braun and his interpreter. Everyone, with the exception of Braun and his interpreter, sat around a large rectangular table on which an old kerosene lamp was standing. The conference would probably last a long time, so the lamp would likely be needed. A dim light filtered into the room through a tinted glass window. Outside it was drizzling as usual.

Bo Gu opened the meeting by reading a report on the reasons for the defeat in the battle against the fifth punitive campaign. Zhou Enlai followed with a supplementary report. Both of them tried to justify their actions. Bo laid all the blame on objective reasons, Zhou on subjective ones. Then Luo Fu took the floor, speaking for Mao and Wang Jiaxiang as well as himself, and subjected the military and political line of the general secretary to a withering criticism. When he finished, Mao spoke next for a full hour. In Braun's words, "[i]n contrast to his usual wont, he made use of a painstakingly prepared manuscript." This was hardly surprising; the conference was of vital significance to him. Completely destroying the arguments of Bo and Zhou, he accused them as well as Braun of bearing the main responsibility for the retreat from the Central Soviet Area.

Mao asserted that they initially adhered to "purely passive defensive tactics" and then "switched to positional warfare," after which, at the decisive moment, they "turned and ran." Mao called this kind of conduct a "childish game of war." He also directed "his attack on leadership techniques" of Bo and Braun.[13]

No sooner had he finished than up jumped Wang Jiaxiang, who fully supported Mao and Luo. Many wished to speak. Ultimately, the conference lasted three days. The military methods of Braun and the political leadership of Bo Gu were subjected to particularly sharp criticism in the speeches of Zhu De, Peng Dehuai, Nie Rongzhen, and, especially, Lin Biao, who deemed Braun's tactics simply "clumsy and stupid."[14] The only person who defended Bo Gu was Kai Feng, the Young Communist and one of Mif's people; he leveled the standard accusation at Mao, namely, that he did not understand Marxism-Leninism. Mao recalled,

> During the Zunyi conference Kai Feng said to me "Your methods of warfare are not particularly clever; they are based on just two books, *The Romance of the Three Kingdoms* and Sun Zi's *The Art of War*. How can one wage war by relying on these books?" At the time I had only read *Romance of the Three Kingdoms*, not *The Art of War*. Yet this comrade spoke with such assurance that I had read it! I asked him how many chapters were there in *The Art of War* and what did the first chapter say. But he was unable to reply at all. It was clear that he himself had not read this book. Afterwards, setting aside other things, I made it my business to read *The Art of War*.[15]

During these speeches, Otto Braun sat quietly near the door, chain-smoking. He felt awful, not only because he thought the conference was a "base insinuation" but also because he was suffering from an attack of malaria. Bo Gu felt no better, even though he was not ill. Unbalanced in the best of times, he was continually flashing a nervous smile, baring his large teeth, and surveying everyone with a venomous look. Zhou Enlai instantaneously reoriented himself and, taking the floor for the second time, fully acknowledged the correctness of Mao and his supporters.[16] But Braun, who refrained from saying anything, "requested permission to spend some time with the First Corps" so that he "could better acquaint" himself, "through direct experience at the front, with the Chinese civil war so highly extolled by Mao."[17]

In sum, the Mao Zedong faction achieved total victory. Luo Fu composed a draft resolution that asserted Bo Gu's report was "basically incorrect," and that the main reason for the surrender of the Central Soviet Area was mistakes in military leadership and in the tactical line. It was adopted.[18]

Following the conference the members of the Politburo held a separate organizational session at which Mao was co-opted into the Standing Committee. He was also appointed deputy to general political commissar Zhou, who no longer posed a danger to him. Although Bo Gu retained his former position, the influence of the new troika of Mao, Luo Fu, and Wang Jiaxiang was now dominant.[19]

After the organizational meeting Mao rushed off to Zizhen with a wildly beating heart.

"Is the meeting over? How are you?" she asked excitedly.

At this he broke into a smile.

"Everything went not badly. Now I have the right to speak."

Many years later he told his daughter Li Min how they had celebrated his victory.

> That day your mother waited for me for a very long time. I returned home and had not sat down when she peppered me with questions. I wanted to play a trick on her, but I was bursting with joy. When someone is happy they become talkative. I folded my hands behind my back and began pacing around the room, speaking unhurriedly, "The meeting figured that a Buddha like me might still prove useful, therefore, they dragged me out into the light and put me on the Standing Committee of the Politburo of the Central Committee. This means they still respect old Mao, and suppose that he is still good for something. I am unworthy, yes, unworthy. I understand that they chose me for the leadership of the CC just to fill an empty spot. To be sure, I did not play at modesty; when the fate of the country is at stake every simple peasant has a role to play!"
>
> Your mother looked at me attentively, and was all ears. That evening we were enormously happy.[20]

In speaking to his daughter, Mao omitted only one thing: her mother was expecting another baby and his struggle for power, combined with the hardships of the march, had undermined her health. Zizhen was terribly exhausted. She was due to give birth in a month, and she knew she could not keep the baby. The Long March was continuing, and children were an unnecessary burden. Mao apparently did not think about this. He was intoxicated with victory.

Zizhen gave birth in February 1935, in a small village in the north of Guizhou, in a straw hut belonging to a poor peasant family of the Yi nationality. In this area, as in many border regions in Sichuan and Yunnan, there were many non-Han Chinese. Among them the Yi were the most numerous. They hated the Han Chinese and saw no difference between the Guomindang and the communists, and often attacked small groups of Red Army soldiers. At the approach of large contingents of the Red Army, all of the Yi gathered their cattle and their goods and chattel and went off into the forests and mountains, leaving only empty houses for the Red Army. It was in one such house that Zizhen delivered her baby. The infant girl cried long and loud, but the

exhausted mother tried not to look at her. The commander of the medical brigade recalled: "After the baby was washed off, we wrapped her in a white cloth.
[As for what to do next] I consulted with the venerable Dong.* Dong wrote a
note and attached thirty yuan to it. Basically, what it said was 'The army on the
march cannot take with it this newly born child. We are leaving it for you to
bring up. Let it be like your granddaughter. When she grows up, she will look
after you.' "[21] Placing the infant girl, covered with rags, onto the sleeping bunk
where she had just been born, along with the note and the money, everyone,
including Zizhen, left the house. The "Iron Stream" continued to flow west-
ward. There was no time for emotion.

What happened to the little girl, whom the mother had not even named,
is not known. Rumor has it that after the departure of the communists, the
inhabitants of the house took her into their family and named her Wang Xiuzhen, meaning "Beautiful Treasure Wang," but three months later she died
from a cancerous tumor.[22] No one knows if this is true.

Mao never even saw his new daughter. He had no particular interest in
her anyway. The struggle for power continued. Neither Bo Gu nor Otto Braun
acknowledged their mistakes. Kai Feng vented his aggressive temper. Some
members of the Politburo, even though they accepted the new triumvirate of
Mao, Luo Fu, and Wang Jiaxiang, still did not actively support them. So they
had to act energetically and uncompromisingly. Mao and Luo went for broke.

In early February, at a meeting of the Standing Committee, Luo suddenly
demanded that Bo Gu yield the position of general secretary to him. Mao supported him. Two others present, Chen Yun and Zhou Enlai, did not object. Bo
Gu, who was losing his self-control, capitulated. A month later, on March 4,
the new party leader implemented an important decision via the Revolutionary Military Council: "To establish a special Front Command and to designate
Comrade Zhu De as Front Commander and Comrade Mao Zedong as Front
Political Commissar."[23] Zhu De remained commander in chief of the entire
Central Red Army and Zhou Enlai was formally the general political commissar. The following day, in the name of the Central Revolutionary Military
Council, Zhu De, Zhou Enlai, and Wang Jiaxiang clarified the situation. Only
battle-ready units would come under the direct purview of the Front Command, while noncombatants would be assigned to the operational leadership
of the newly established Field Command.[24]

Finally, Mao had actually recaptured the positions he had lost in Ningdu
in October 1932. Although he did not formally become general political commissar again, most of the power in the army was in his hands as front political
commissar. Standing on the summit, he had to be circumspect, as those who

---

* This was Dong Biwu, secretary of the Control Commission and deputy rector of the
Higher Party School. In the past, he had stood up for He Zizhen's sister, He Yi.

remained below might be jealous. Grasping this, Mao consulted with Luo Fu about appointing another, military, troika to take charge of army matters. He proposed that Zhou Enlai be appointed as chairman, with himself and Wang Jiaxiang as the other members.[25] Notwithstanding Zhou Enlai's nominal leadership, Mao's was the decisive voice in this group. He commanded the army, but both Zhou's and Wang's vanity was assuaged. Both of them could prove useful to him.

Meanwhile, the goal of the Long March gradually came into focus, namely, to unite with Zhang Guotao's forces in northwestern Sichuan. Mao was very excited. In late February or early March, he composed new verses.

> *West wind fierce,*
> *immense sky, wild geese honking,*
> *frosty morning moon.*
> *Frosty morning moon.*
> *Horses hooves clanging,*
> *bugles sobbing.*
>
> *Tough pass,*
> *long trail, like iron.*
> *Yet with strong steps*
> *we climbed that peak.*
> *Climbed that peak:*
> *green mountains like oceans,*
> *setting sun like blood.*[26]

His army marched forward at a rapid pace, some twenty-five to thirty miles per day, but their goal was still distant. Zunyi, ruined and deserted, had long since been left behind. Prior to the departure of the Red Army, in the words of an eyewitness, "[t]he city presented a desolate sight." The once-flourishing commercial center lay in ruins.[27] But Mao was not thinking of the inhabitants of this poor town. What counted was that his army had rested there and replenished its supplies.

Yet officers and men continued to suffer enormous difficulties. There was a shortage of clothing and military supplies. Otto Braun recalled that "marching was done at night because the Kuomintang [Guomindang] air force flew incessant sorties during the day, bombing and strafing us." In one such attack Zizhen was badly wounded. The shrapnel that remained in her body tormented her. (Later, when Zizhen was X-rayed, seventeen pieces of shrapnel were found in her body.)[28] She had to make the rest of the journey by stretcher.

"The advance, flank, and rear guards endured dozens of attacks, occasionally on all sides at once," wrote Braun.

The situation worsened when we crossed the jagged mountains on the Kweichow [Guizhou]-Yunnan border. The narrow path led up and down sheer cliffs. Many horses fell and broke their legs; only the mules kept their footing. Rations were becoming an ever more critical problem as we advanced into Yunnan. There was hardly anything to eat in the mountains. Soldiers sliced flesh from dead horses until nothing but the skeletons remained. Even in the plains few vegetables and little rice were found. . . . One can imagine then what it was like in the Army as a whole. The number of deaths, more from disease and exhaustion than battle wounds, increased daily. Although several thousand volunteers had been enlisted since the beginning of the year, the ranks had visibly dwindled.[29]

Of the 86,000 men who had begun the Long March in the Central Soviet Area, barely 20,000 survived by the time they reached Sichuan.

But these survivors continued to plod forward. In early May they traversed the broad and stormy Jinsha River, as the Yangzi River was called in that place. A month later, passing along the border with Sikang (Tibet), they traversed another mighty mountain stream, the Dadu River. This crossing was particularly difficult. A narrow chain suspension bridge, constructed in the early eighteenth century, linked the northern and southern banks of the seething river, which was squeezed between the mountains. When the CCP troops approached, enemy soldiers removed the plank roadway halfway across, and when the communists started to cross, Guomindang aviation began to bomb them mercilessly. Nevertheless, the Red Army fighters managed to get to the other side.

Afterward their route passed through an uninhabited and trackless mountain wilderness. The Red Army troops were shod in light slippers or straw sandals, and every day it got colder and colder. Only by traversing these mountains could they emerge onto the northwest Sichuan plateau. "Rivers in full spate had to be forded, dense virgin forests and treacherous moors crossed, mountain passes four to five thousand metres high surmounted," Braun recalled. "More and more, our route was lined with the bodies of the slain, frozen or simply exhausted. All of us were unbelievably lice-ridden. Bleeding dysentery was rampant; the first cases of typhus appeared."[30]

Finally, in mid-June, units of the Central Red Army approached one more narrow chain bridge with wooden planking across a small mountain stream, the Fori River, in Maogong County in western Sichuan. Here the long-awaited linkup with the advance guard of Zhang Guotao's army took place. Zhang himself and his staff were in neighboring Maoxian, two days distant. Informed of the joyful reunion, he hurried to meet them. On June 25, Mao and Zhang finally embraced each other. That same night a dinner party was held. No one talked about the Long March or the Zunyi Conference or the adventures of the

Fourth Front Army. "Mao Tse-tung [Mao Zedong], a Hunanese, who was fond of chili, made chili-eating the topic of merry conversation, discoursing at length on the theme that chili-eaters were revolutionaries. He was refuted by Ch'in Pang-hsien [Bo Gu], a native of Kiangsu [Jiangsu] Province, who did not eat chili. Such talk was fun and helped create an atmosphere of light-heartedness."[31] It seemed that the Long March was over, but major trials still lay ahead.

Zhang Guotao, the thirty-eight-year-old veteran of the communist movement, craved absolute power and was averse to compromise. Tall, with high cheekbones and a prominent jaw that jutted slightly forward, he looked pugnacious. He had an explosive temperament and during his long tenure in the CCP he had been in opposition more than once—first vis-à-vis Maring, then Lominadze, and then Qu Qiubai. During the high tide of the struggle against Trotskyism, some people in the ECCI tried to accuse him of links to the Trotskyite underground, but nothing came of their efforts.[32] Overall he was well thought of in the Comintern, and although he was sometimes picked on, this was mostly out of the Bolshevik duty to be eternally suspicious of everyone. He was considered loyal and in November 1927, three years before the "purge," he was even awarded the Soviet Order of the Fighting Red Banner as a "brave warrior of the Chinese Revolution." Nevertheless, former KUTK students Luo Fu, Bo Gu, Wang Jiaxiang, and Kai Feng, assuming that there was no smoke without fire, were suspicious of Zhang Guotao, viewing him as an "old opportunist" and a "covert Trotskyite." He, in turn, as one of the founders of the party, viewed Mif's upstarts with scarcely concealed contempt.

Therefore, the outpouring of "joy" upon meeting could fool no one. A new conflict in the leadership was inevitable and from it only Mao could emerge the winner. The "Moscow students" who wanted to squeeze out Zhang Guotao would have to rally around him. Only Mao, with his ability to weave intrigues and to maneuver in what seemed to be hopeless situations, could guarantee a favorable balance of forces from their perspective.

Mao himself was wary of Zhang. Although for now Zhang did not dispute the decisions taken at Zunyi intended to enhance Mao's authority, Mao anticipated such a challenge. He understood that Zhang considered himself the "master of the situation." He had seven or eight times as many troops as those in the Central Red Army. His soldiers were better armed, better fed, better outfitted, and better shod. They had not lost their fighting spirit, and Zhang enjoyed undisputed authority among the commanders and political commissars of his army. There was no comparison between his troops and the exhausted and ragged units of the Central Army, which had almost completely lost their fighting ability. Moreover, of the ten thousand that had managed to get to Maogong, two thousand were noncombatants.[33]

Under these circumstances the spirit of "spontaneous friendship" quickly dissipated. Zhang began to demand power. In July his troops strengthened the

claims of their leader by provoking a series of military clashes with Mao's de-
tachments.[34] Mao and the other CCP leaders had to back off. In mid-July, Luo
Fu was prepared to hand over the position of general secretary to Zhang, but
Zhang preferred the more important position at the time, general political commissar of the united Red Army, which was soon reorganized into nine corps.
(Four of these were assigned to the First Front Army and five to the Fourth
Front Army.) Zhou stepped down and Mao relinquished the post of front political commissar. Control of the army passed to Zhang Guotao. His commanders
demanded that Zhang also be given the post of chairman of the Central Revolutionary Military Council. Zhang graciously retained Zhu De in that position,
but power in the CRMC was now concentrated in Zhang's hands.[35]

Meanwhile, the Long March continued. The united army moved north to
the juncture of Sichuan, Gansu, and Shaanxi, where the Politburo had decided
to establish a new Soviet area. It was impossible to remain in western Sichuan,
largely because the local tribes detested the communists who had robbed them.
These were wild and dangerous places that suffered from utter deprivation. The
Red Army needed provisions. Therefore, as one of the participants wrote, "for
better or worse, we were forced to take every crumb we found and continuously send requisition parties into the mountains to hunt stray livestock." [36] This
could not go on for long. Aggressive mountaineers increasingly attacked the
Red Army soldiers who had brought them nothing but sorrow.

Just then Mao and Luo Fu decided to strike back at Zhang Guotao. Several days after Zhou Enlai had yielded the post of general political commissar
to Zhang, around July 20 the march halted, and the Politburo gathered for a
crucial meeting. In a calm voice, Luo Fu asked Zhang Guotao to give an account of the work he had accomplished since the time he had left Shanghai for
the soviet region on the Hubei-Henan-Anhui border in April 1931. (Zhang,
facing attacks from Chiang Kai-shek, had been forced to evacuate this region
in October 1932.) After Zhang's report, Mao unleashed a sharp attack against
him, accusing him of committing serious errors in surrendering the old base
area. Zhang rejected all the accusations and the conference ended inconclu-
sively. But the new intraparty conflict had now sharpened. Two weeks later,
Luo Fu accused Zhang Guotao of having abandoned his new base in northern
Sichuan. At this Zhang finally exploded: "And how is it that you, who lost the
entire Central Soviet Area, consider your line correct?" [37] He now grasped that
Mao and Luo Fu were purposely exacerbating the conflict, and he decided to
defer till a more auspicious time any explanation.

For now he suggested dividing the army into two columns and advancing
into southern Gansu. One column would proceed along the left flank of the
swamp that lay before them and the other along the right. There, in Gansu,
about ninety miles from the border with Sichuan, they would reunite. Around
August 10, the left column, headed by Zhang Guotao and Zhu De, set off in the

lead. The right column, including Mao and most of the Politburo members, waited. Zhou Enlai had contracted malaria in July and was in very bad shape. The doctors did all they could, but still it took several days for the crisis to pass.

Finally, at the end of August, the right column set out. Before them stretched an endless, surprisingly beautiful green steppe, but this beauty concealed mortal danger. Otto Braun recalled:

> A deceptive green cover hid a black viscous swamp, which sucked in anyone who broke through the thin crust or strayed from the narrow path. I myself witnessed the wretched death of a mule in this fashion. We drove native cattle or horses before us which instinctively found the least dangerous way. Grey clouds almost always hung just over the ground. Cold rain fell several times a day, at night it turned to wet snow or sleet. There was not a dwelling, tree, or shrub as far as the eye could see. We slept in squatting positions on the small hills which rose over the moor. Thin blankets and large straw hats, oil-paper umbrellas or, in some cases, stolen capes, were our only protection. Some did not awaken in the morning, victims of cold and exhaustion. . . . Our sole nourishment came from the grain kernels we had hoarded or, as a rare and special treat, a morsel of stone-hard dried meat. The swamp water was not fit to drink. Still it was drunk, for there was no wood to purify it by boiling. Outbreaks of bloody dysentery and typhus, which had subsided somewhat in Sikang, again won the upper hand. . . . We were fortunate that the enemy could attack us neither from the air nor on land.[38]

This most difficult crossing took several days. When the utterly exhausted fighters finally stepped onto terra firma, an order arrived from Zhang Guotao, Zhu De, and their chief of staff, Liu Bocheng, to turn back! Their column had gotten stuck in the swamp and was unable to cross one of the mountain streams that was flooding across their path; therefore, Zhang, Zhu, and Liu decided to head back south, and they demanded that Mao's troops do the same. But this was not to be. On September 8, they received a reply from Zhou Enlai, Luo Fu, Mao Zedong, and several other commanders and commissars of the right column, saying "we sincerely hope that you, our elder brothers, will think closely and carefully, and firmly resolve to . . . change your course and move northward."[39] In other words, the Politburo informed Zhang that it did not intend to bow to his orders.

Then Zhang Guotao took a fatal step. He sent a secret telegram to his former fellow officers in the Fourth Front Army, who were now in command positions in the right column, requesting that they "initiate a struggle" against the Politburo.[40] Mao learned of this telegram at once, however, and summoned an emergency meeting of the Standing Committee. They decided to continue the march north to Gansu, after which they issued an "Appeal to All Comrades" in which Mao, Luo Fu, Zhou Enlai, Bo Gu, and Wang Jiaxiang, speaking in the name of the Central Committee, called upon the officers and men of both the right and left columns not to obey any orders to move south, but to march only north in order "to establish a new Soviet Area in Shaanxi-Gansu-Sichuan." Neither side wanted to yield. Enraged, Zhang Guotao turned south while Mao's column entered southern Gansu. The split in the Red Army and in the leadership of the CCP had become a fact.

In mid-September, on the Gansu border, the troops of the right column were reorganized into the so-called Shaanxi-Gansu Brigade, numbering some six thousand men, with Peng Dehuai their commander and Lin Biao his deputy. Mao served as political commissar. A new objective was now defined for the march: to advance not into northeastern Gansu, but farther, to the Soviet border in order to receive essential assistance. Mao asserted that "Zhang Guotao has gone south, thus causing rather heavy losses to the Chinese revolution. Nevertheless, we are definitely not going to be downhearted, but are moving forward in a big way. . . . Northern Shaanxi and northwestern Gansu are the places where we should go."[41]

Thus far there had been no link with Moscow; therefore, on September 20 it was decided to dispatch two party representatives to distant Xinjiang to try to establish a link with the ECCI and to inform the Comintern of the upheavals that had occurred during the Long March. Mao's brother Zemin, who was in the transport column, was chosen as one of these emissaries.[42]

Soon, however, the plans changed sharply and the journey to Xinjiang was put on hold. Mao and his comrades learned to their surprise that a rather substantial soviet area existed in northern Shaanxi, close to the northeast border of Gansu, and that Red Army detachments under the command of a communist named Liu Zhidan were active there.[43] It was no more than 250 miles to this base.

This news was a gift of fate. Mao calculated that the entire Long March could now be presented as an action planned in advance and aimed at bringing the communist bases into areas that were potentially facing the threat of Japanese invasion. By the fall of 1935, the Japanese had greatly increased their pressure on north China. Following their occupation of Manchuria, the Japanese Army had seized Rehe, the province south of Manchuria, and two years later they moved into eastern Hebei. The Imperial Army approached within striking distance of Beiping (Beijing) and Tianjin, another large city in north China. The Japanese plan was perfectly clear: to annex all of north China and convert it into a purportedly "independent" state, as the Japanese had already done in Manchuria. By this time the upsurge of anti-Japanese feeling in China was greater than ever before. By skillfully playing on this sentiment, Mao could kill two birds with one stone. The "Anti-Japanese March" to north China would enable him not only to strengthen the communists' position in their struggle for power against the "corrupt" Nanjing government, but also to crush Zhang Guotao once and for all. After all, the "splitter" had not wanted to go north.

At a leadership conference of the Shaanxi-Gansu Brigade on September 22, Mao declared, "We intended to march north, but Zhang Guotao wanted to go south. . . . The Japanese imperialists were invading China, and we were going north to resist Japanese invasion. We would first go to northern Shaanxi, the home of the Red Army under Liu Zhidan."[44]

This final objective was reached in a month. In mid-October, Mao's troops crossed the border of the north Shaanxi soviet area and entered the village of Wuqizhen, located in a narrow mountain valley. From the local residents they learned that the Red headquarters was located in the district capital Baoan, fifty miles to the east. A detachment was sent out to contact Liu Zhidan.[45] Meanwhile, a meeting of the Politburo was convened on October 22 at which Mao announced that the Long March was over.

Exactly a year had passed since eighty-six thousand officers and men of the Red Army had left the Central Soviet Area. They had traversed eleven provinces, covered more than six thousand miles, crossed over five mountain ranges, forced their way across twenty-four large rivers, and passed through dangerous swamps. The price paid for this success was colossal. No more than five thousand persons made it all the way to northern Shaanxi.

Still, this was a truly heroic "Iron Stream." Proud of what had been accomplished, Mao expressed his sense of triumph:

> The Red Army does not fear
> the Long March toughness.
> Thousands of rivers, hundreds of mountains, easy.
> The Five Ridges
> merely little ripples.
> Immense Wu Meng [Wumeng]* Mountain—
> merely a mound of earth.
> Warm are the cloudy cliffs
> beaten by Gold Sand River.
> Cold are the iron chains
> bridging Tatu [Dadu] River.
> Joy over Min Mountain,†
> thousand miles of snow:
> when the army crossed,
> every face smiled.[46]

---

* The Wumeng Mountains straddle Guizhou and Yunnan.

† The Min Mountains range along the Sichuan-Qinghai-Gansu border.

20

THE XI'AN INCIDENT

As Mao's forces linked up with Liu Zhidan's in Shaanxi, Zhang Guotao was wandering around in northwest Sichuan. After forty days he managed to extricate his forces from the marshy bogs. On October 5 he established a new "CCP Central Committee," a new "Central Government," and a new "Central Revolutionary Military Committee," and "expelled" Mao Zedong, Zhou Enlai, Bo Gu, and Luo Fu from the party.[1] It would be hard to imagine anything more stupid. He also cruelly punished and even shot those commanders and commissars in his column who opposed these actions.[2]

By now the Politburo had settled down in northern Shaanxi. In mid-December 1935, Mao and other leaders relocated to Wayaobao, the only district center, in Braun's words, that was "firmly in the hands of the Red Army. . . . We noted that a poor, partially calcified land lay before us," he recalled.[3] Dozens of hamlets and villages lay in ruins; the fertile land was deserted. The sparse rural population eked out a miserable existence. Years of warlord campaigns, horrific banditry, and terrible harvests and epidemics had catastrophically undermined the local economy. Between 1928 and 1933, several years prior to the arrival of Mao's forces, more than half of the local population had died of famine. In many villages all of the children below age ten had died. Northern Shaanxi was almost depopulated.[4] As was the case everywhere in northern China, there was no distinction here between Hakka and *bendi*, but the terrible poverty of the people, who teetered on the edge of death by starvation, created exceptionally favorable conditions for growth of the CCP, just as in "Hakka country."

Endless narrow ravines and yellow plains scarred with deep canyons stretched in all directions. Lifeless loess hills, in which the survivors of war and famine lived in caves, towered sullenly above this landscape. Practically anyone could dig a cave home in the soft loess soil. The leaders of the CCP, including Mao Zedong and He Zizhen, took up residence in such caves. The dull northern landscape was conducive to melancholy, but Mao was not swayed by emotions. Zunyi and, especially, the rupture with Zhang Guotao had placed him in a position where everyone viewed him as their authoritative leader.

Throughout the fall and winter he was busy establishing organs of power in the new district, devoting most of his attention to strengthening his military forces. After incorporating the local guerrillas, the Red Army numbered 10,410 fighters.[5] In early November, Mao reorganized his forces, restoring the old name of the First Front Army. In Zhu De's absence—Zhu De was still with Zhang Guotao—the position of commander was filled by Peng Dehuai. Mao occupied the position of political commissar. The Northwest Revolutionary Military Council was established to exercise supreme control over the soviet area. Mao became its chairman and Zhou Enlai, who had recovered from his illness, and, in formal terms, Zhu De, became his two deputies. (Mao forgave "Old Zhu," understanding that the professional warrior was accustomed to subordinating himself to party leadership and was therefore unable to stand up to Zhang Guotao.) A government, basically concerned with economic matters, was established called the Northwest Office of the Central Government of the Chinese Soviet Republic. Mao's brother Zemin was appointed minister of economy and foreign trade, while Bo Gu was given the lofty position of chairman. Mao knew how to repair relations with people he needed, including former enemies. The tested principle of "Treat the illness to save the patient" continued to bear fruit. The grateful Bo Gu was happy to serve Mao.

Only with the refractory Zhang was he unable to patch up relations for a whole year. In late November 1936, Zhang, accompanied by Zhu De, showed up in northern Shaanxi seeking reconciliation.[6] By then Zhang had almost entirely lost his army in the swamps and mountains of Sichuan, Xikang, and southern Gansu, where he was engaged in constant battles. Mao greeted him magnanimously. Zhang had "lost face" and was, therefore, no longer dangerous. A loser, no one would have followed him even had he chosen to continue his "anti-party" activity. "We all spoke and congratulated each other," wrote Zhang Guotao. "At that time, we discussed our future, not our past."[7] Mao made Zhang one of his deputies in the Revolutionary Military Council and appointed him general political commissar of the Red Army—Zhu De remained as commander—and appointed him deputy chairman of the government. The split had been overcome. Zhang's capitulation meant that not only the remnants of his Fourth Front Army entered into Mao's forces, but also the troops of the Second Front Army of He Long and Ren Bishi that, in June 1936, after completing their trek to Xikang from the old base area on the Hunan-Hubei border, had joined up with Zhang's forces.

The future began to look bright for the communists. Escalating Japanese aggression fueled the patriotic upsurge of the Chinese people. In December 1935, a wave of powerful anti-Japanese student demonstrations rolled through the country (the so-called December Ninth Movement). Dissatisfaction with the government's policy of appeasement toward Japan arose even in the Guomindang army. Thus the CCP's anti-Japanese stance began to resonate with Chinese public opinion.

Mao continued his anti-Japanese rhetoric, realizing that only by giving voice to strong patriotic sentiments could the communists secure wide popular support. Of course, Mao had no intention of renouncing class struggle, but it was to his tactical advantage to tone down the radical rhetoric. The division of property on the model of bandits had thus far led only to defeat. Although Chiang Kai-shek remained the main enemy, from then on appeals to Chinese patriotism became an increasingly important element in the communist struggle.

Luckily, his new policy was completely in line with that of the Comintern. In the summer of 1935, Stalin, fearing German and Japanese aggression against the USSR, sharply altered his policy. Communists were directed henceforth not to seek the overthrow of the ruling classes, but rather to organize a new united front with them—in the West an antifascist united front and in the East an anti-Japanese united front. In his private calculations, Stalin was not reconsidering the strategic goals of the communist movement, namely, establishing world domination.[8] He was simply maneuvering to attract to his side and, correspondingly, to the side of various communist parties, as many allies as possible. These decisions were taken in Moscow in July–August 1935, at the Seventh Congress of the Comintern. There, on August 1, Wang Ming, speaking in the name of the Chinese Soviet Republic and the Central Committee of the CCP, published a declaration calling upon his fellow countrymen to stop fighting and unite in struggle against Japan. From the circle of "fellow countrymen," however, Chiang Kai-shek and his cabinet members were excluded.[9]

Lacking a link with Moscow, Mao and other Politburo leaders were unaware of these changes and so they acted at their own risk. None of them knew that Moscow was striving to reestablish its severed links with the Chinese communists. Moscow already knew about the Zunyi Conference and wholly supported the decisions taken there. Chen Yun, one of those who had taken part in the conference, conveyed its essential points to Comintern officials after he arrived in Moscow in late September 1935, shortly after the conclusion of the Seventh Congress of the Comintern. Since he did not have a copy of the Zunyi resolution his information could not be verified by documents. Moscow received the text of the resolution later, sometime in 1936. The text of the resolution itself was of no particular importance, however, since Moscow was already positively inclined toward the CCP Politburo's decisions.[10]

By September 1935, the Comintern had already initiated the true cult of personality of Mao. At the Seventh Congress of the Comintern it had pronounced him one of the "standard-bearers" of the world communist movement, along with the general secretary of the ECCI, the Bulgarian communist

Georgii Dimitrov.[11] This was done through the lips of the CCP representative Teng Daiyuan, but without the sanction of the Moscow leadership Teng would not have said what he did. The Seventh Congress devoted special attention to elevating the authority of Communist Party leaders. At a specially convened meeting of the CCP delegation to the Comintern in late August 1935, Wang Ming, the delegation leader, said: "Whose authority should be elevated? Of course, that of the members of the Politburo. . . . Who first? The authority of comrades Mao Zedong and Zhu De."[12]

Wang Ming was not at all devoted to Mao Zedong and fancied himself as leader of the party. Soon afterward Guo Zhaotang (alias Afanasii Gavrilovich Krymov), an official on his staff, with Wang Ming's direct assistance, drafted a special note about Mao Zedong to the Comintern aimed at undermining the positive impression that Stalin was forming about the guerrilla leader. It said,

> Social background—small landowner [someone who read the note placed a question mark in red pencil above this]. No systematic mistakes. A very hard worker, efficient agitator, and organizer, knows how to penetrate into the thick of the masses, a good leader of mass work. Has rich experience in the peasant movement and guerrilla warfare. Can work in hard and very difficult conditions. He is very active and gets the work done well. Personal characteristics—likes to mingle with the masses, do propaganda work, is selfless. In addition to the aforementioned positives are shortcomings, namely, <u>insufficient theoretical preparation; therefore, is inclined to make individual political mistakes, however, easily and quickly corrects his mistakes under correct and firm party leadership.</u> [A large part of the last phrase was underlined by someone in red pencil, bracketed on the side, and a question mark placed in the margin.][13]

A number of members and former members of the CCP delegation to the Comintern, including Li Lisan and Zhao Yimin, informed higher authorities that Wang Ming was "undermining the authority of Mao Zedong among Chinese comrades in the USSR." In conversation with ECCI officials on February 17, 1940, Li Lisan said:

> It seems to me that the main source for spreading the idea that Mao Zedong was not a political leader was Wang Ming. He told me, Xiao Ai [Zhao Yimin], and others that Mao Zedong was a very good person, but very weak when it came to theory. In conversation with me and with Xiao Ai, whom he trusted more, Wang Ming, speaking of Mao Zedong's report to the Second Congress of Soviets, said there were many weak points in the report, but that he had corrected them

and now the report was better. Other documents received from China were similarly corrected, thus, many of these corrected documents were different from their versions in China.[14]

So it was most likely under pressure from the leadership of the Comintern that Wang Ming was forced to elevate the authority of his rival. As before, none of the Chinese communists could dispute these decisions, because the CCP's financial dependence upon the USSR had not eased. Enormous sums of Soviet money continued to flow to the Central Committee of the CCP. On June 8, 1934, the Political Commission of the Political Secretariat of the ECCI decided to send 100,000 rubles from unspent funds of the Chinese Communist Party and 100,000 rubles from a reserve fund.[15] On July 1, 1934, it was decided in Moscow that in 1934 the Chinese Communist Party would receive 7,418 gold dollars monthly.[16]

Following the Seventh Congress a full-blown campaign to exalt Mao Zedong commenced in the USSR. In early December 1935, *Communist International,* the theoretical and political organ of the Comintern, published a long panegyric sketch titled "Mao Zedong—leader of the Chinese working people."[17] The unsigned article was written by Aleksandr Moiseevich Khamadan, deputy director of the Foreign Department of *Pravda.** Soon after, on December 13, 1935, the same author's article about Mao was published in *Pravda.*[18] His biographical sketch, along with biographies he wrote about Zhu De and Fang Zhimin, commander of CCP troops in Fujian, who died in 1935, was later published in a brochure titled "Leaders and Heroes of the Chinese People," issued by the State Social-Economic Publishers.[19]

It was not until mid-November 1935, when an emissary from the CCP delegation to the Comintern, an old Chinese communist named Lin Yuying, a cousin of Lin Biao's whom Mao had long known, arrived in northern Shaanxi, that Mao learned of the resolutions of the Seventh Congress, including, apparently, the praise directed at him.[20] After discussing the materials of the Seventh Congress for several days, the leaders of the CCP concluded that to align with Stalin's new policy, they had to alter their basic political direction. Luo Fu asserted the need to change party policy toward *funong* (rich peasants) and distinguish between them and the *dizhu* (landlords). Lin Yuying agreed. Mao, however, did not want to transform his relationship to the peasantry, although

---

* A. M. Khamadan (real name Faingar) was a Jew born in Derbent in 1908. After working at *Pravda,* he moved to *Novy mir* (New world), where he was deputy to the editor in chief. At the beginning of World War II he was a TASS correspondent. In 1942 he was taken prisoner by the Nazis in Sevastopol, Crimea. He conducted underground work in the POW camp under the Russian name of Mikhailov, and was put into prison and then executed in May 1943.

he acknowledged that a fundamental resolution of the class question in the countryside was not imminent. On December 1, he sent Luo Fu a letter setting forth his view. "I basically agree with changing the tactics toward the rich peasants," he wrote,

> but ... when ... the poor and middle peasants demand the equal distribution of the land of the rich peasants, the Party should support this request. The rich peasants may get land of the same kind as the poor and middle peasants. . . . [T]here should be some difference between the policy toward the rich peasants and that toward the middle peasants. . . . We must point out that when the struggle deepens, the rich peasants are sure to join the ranks of the landlords. This is a peculiarity of the semifeudal rich peasant class in China.[21]

Mao's propositions were only "basically" accepted. Luo Fu disagreed with Mao's main thesis, which was to support the poor and middle peasants if "in the course of struggle" they advocated the equal division of the land of the wealthy peasants. Mao's position sharply contrasted with the Comintern's united front policy. On December 6, while Mao was away with the troops, an enlarged plenum of the Politburo approved Luo Fu's resolution "On Changing Tactics toward the Kulaks."[22] Nine days later, wishing to avoid conflict, Mao issued a corresponding directive in the name of the Central Executive Committee of the Chinese Soviet Republic.[23] However, he did not alter his own views on the problems of the "rich peasants."

Two days later, in Wayaobao, Luo Fu convened a new enlarged meeting of the Politburo that examined general political and military questions connected to the Comintern's new course. This meeting laid the foundations for the CCP's new line, namely, to "unite the civil war with the national" and direct it against both the Japanese and Chiang Kai-shek via the formation of a "revolutionary national united front" of all patriotic forces, including the Guomindang. In keeping with the spirit of the August First Declaration to unite to fight Japan, only Chiang Kai-shek and his closest associates would be excluded.[24] Mao emphasized, "[W]hen the national crisis reaches a crucial moment, splits will occur in the Guomindang camp. . . . Such situations . . . are favorable to the revolution. . . . We must turn to good account all such fights, rifts, and contradictions in the enemy camp and use them against our present main enemy [i.e., the Japanese]."[25]

The leaders of the CCP began working toward this end even before the conference. In late November 1935, Mao first addressed a proposal for a truce and joint action against the Japanese to an officer of one of the Guomindang armies deployed in Shaanxi.[26] This was essentially a goodwill gesture toward Zhang Xueliang, the most prominent military figure in the Northwest. Marshal Zhang, the former Manchurian warlord, whose troops had retreated from Manchuria under Japanese pressure and were now based in south and central Shaanxi, played an important role in China's balance of power. The headquarters of his 200,000-man Northeast Army was in Xi'an, the provincial capital. The Young Marshal—in 1936 he was just thirty-five years old and because of his youth he was called Young Marshal in Chinese political and journalistic circles—was reputed to be a fierce Japanophobe. He had a special score to settle with the Japanese. In 1928, the Japanese intelligence service had assassinated his father, Marshal Zhang Zuolin, for pursuing an independent policy in Manchuria. In 1931, Japan's Kwantung Army, after provoking the Mukden Incident, occupied all the patrimony of Zhang Xueliang, forcing him to flee to Shaanxi. From there he tried to establish good relations with anyone he thought might help him drive the Japanese from Manchuria.

The naïve marshal, who was sympathetic toward the fascists, invested particular hope in Il Duce, believing that only an ironlike totalitarian dictatorship like Mussolini's could rescue China from the crisis. He also counted on help from the Duce's daughter, Edda, the wife of the Italian consul general in Shanghai and future Italian minister of foreign affairs, Count Ciano. Zhang was a ladies' man. Good-looking, youthful, and dark-haired with a bristling mustache, he adored nightclubs and cabarets, was a splendid dancer, and courted women elegantly. The passionate Italian lady could not resist the handsome marshal, whose personal fortune, incidentally, amounted to some $50 million. It is hard to blame her, particularly since Count Ciano slighted her and preferred to linger in Shanghai's bars and houses of prostitution. Edda's romance with Zhang Xueliang continued for only a short time. In 1932, Edda and her husband returned to Rome.

In April 1933, Zhang Xueliang also left for Italy. Mussolini's daughter, although smitten by him, was unable to offer assistance. Her father would not condemn militarist Japan. Disenchanted with Il Duce, Marshal Zhang retained his faith in totalitarianism. He traveled to Germany, where he met with Hitler and Goering, but also got nothing from them. Then he went to France, where he encountered Maxim Litvinov, the Soviet people's commissar for foreign affairs. Hoping he might receive help from the communists, he asked Litvinov to arrange a trip to Moscow for him, but Stalin, not wishing to complicate his relations with Japan, rebuffed him.[27]

Zhang Xueliang, finally understanding he would get no help from abroad, returned to China in January 1934. His chance to take revenge against the Japanese surfaced in November 1935 when Mao proposed a truce to one of his commanders. On April 9, 1936, Zhang began direct negotiations with representatives of the CCP, among them Zhou Enlai, which culminated in Zhang Xueliang agreeing to halt military actions against the communists and even to help supply them with weapons.

This arrangement eased the situation on the borders of the soviet area, but only to a certain degree. In June 1936, Gao Shuangcheng, the commander of the Eighty-Sixth Division of the Guomindang army, on Chiang Kai-shek's order, attacked the communists and seized their capital Wayaobao, forcing Mao, Luo Fu, and the others to flee to Baoan, more than ninety miles west of Wayaobao. Baoan was a tiny, half-abandoned town with just four hundred inhabitants and almost all of its houses in ruins.[28]

Nevertheless, the CCP's policy of creating a united front remained unchanged. Mao asserted this unambiguously to Edgar Snow, who had arrived in Baoan to meet with him. In their first interview, on July 15, 1936, Mao emphasized, "The fundamental issue before the Chinese people today is the struggle against Japanese imperialism."[29]

Mao had good reason for optimism. The loss of Wayaobao had no effect on the strategic situation. The Red Army had steadily grown to twenty-five thousand warriors, and the anti-Japanese front was gradually taking shape. The courtship of Zhang Xueliang was going so well that the communist leaders even began thinking about secretly admitting him to the CCP. (Zhang had expressed the desire to become a communist.)[30] In late June to early July a radio link with Moscow had been reestablished, and in his very first telegram Mao asked Stalin to increase aid to the Communist Party to $2 million Mexican dollars per month. He also requested that Moscow send airplanes, heavy artillery, missiles, infantry weapons, antiaircraft artillery, and pontoons. At the same time, he informed Stalin about Zhang Guotao's "opportunist errors."[31]

Mao would soon receive aid. Stalin would send him two million rubles and, several months later, US $500,000 and 1,166 tons of fuel, military supplies, and other strategic goods.[32] Even earlier, on August 15, he would send a directive in the name of the Secretariat of the ECCI in which he "basically" approved Mao's policies.

The August 15 telegram proposed expansion of the united front. Stalin advised Mao to jettison his negative attitude toward Chiang Kai-shek and "set a course on ceasing military operations" between the Red Army and the Guomindang as a whole, not just with Zhang Xueliang, whose admission into the party, incidentally, he forbade. "We think it is incorrect to place Chiang Kai-shek on the same level as the Japanese aggressors," he indicated, ". . . for Japanese imperialism is the main enemy of the Chinese people, and at the present stage everything should be subordinated to the struggle against it."[33] Stalin's position is easily understood since beginning in 1934, he was regularly receiving information from the Foreign Department of the OGPU (Soviet security police that was the forerunner of the KGB) and from military intelligence about a probable Japanese attack against the USSR. Mao, of course, knew nothing of these secret Soviet intelligence reports, but in any case he raised no objections to Stalin. Ten days later he dutifully sent a letter to the Central

Executive Committee of the Guomindang proposing to end the civil war and begin negotiations.[34] "The core of our policy is to work with Chiang [Kai-shek] to resist Japan," he declared subsequently to the Chinese communists.[35]

But Chiang Kai-shek, not the communists, remained the main player on the Chinese political stage. The Soviet consul in China, Dmitrii Bogomolov, reported Chiang would agree to an alliance with the communists "only on the eve . . . of war with Japan and in connection with an agreement with the Soviet Union."[36] Meanwhile, Chiang was preparing for a new, sixth, campaign against the communists to strengthen his authority as the national leader on the eve of the inevitable large-scale conflict with Japan.

Chiang Kai-shek knew about the negotiations between Zhang Xueliang and the communists and repeatedly warned the Young Marshal that the communists were untrustworthy. But in vain. Therefore, in early December 1936, Chiang decided to meet with Zhang in person, confident that he could make the blundering young man see reason. On December 4, 1936, he flew from his field headquarters in Luoyang to Xi'an. He lodged in the ancient residence of the Tang emperor Xuanzong, located in the picturesque town of Huaqing-chi, enclosed by hills and famed for its mineral hot springs. In the past, the emperor's enchanting and ambitious concubine, Yang Guifei, loved to take the waters here.

Chiang settled into a gloomy one-story pavilion named Wujianting (Five-room pavilion), in the southeast corner of the park complex. There he met Zhang Xueliang, who was accompanied by the commander of the Seventeenth Field Army, General Yang Hucheng, a confederate of the Young Marshal. Zhang Xueliang insisted on the need to unite with the communists in the struggle against the Japanese. Chiang objected, arguing that the destruction of the CCP was the key to successful resistance against foreign aggression. The discussion soon reached an impasse.

On Wednesday, December 9, the atmosphere became even tenser. Responding to new threats against China by Japan's minister of war, more than ten thousand students in Xi'an organized a demonstration. It coincided with the first anniversary of the nationwide anti-Japanese December Ninth Movement of 1935. Students demanded an end to the civil war and the unification of all forces against Japan. Along the road from Xi'an to the district city of Lintong, located not far from Chiang Kai-shek's residence, the students were met by police, who opened fire and wounded two of them. By a twist of fate, the wounded students happened to be the children of a Northeast Army officer.[37]

Zhang Xueliang snapped. At 10 P.M. on Friday, December 11, he issued an order to the top officers of the Northeast Army to arrest Chiang Kai-shek. On December 12 at 5 A.M., a two-hundred-man detachment of troops led by the commander of Zhang Xueliang's personal guard, twenty-eight-year-old captain Sun Mingjiu, attacked the residence of Chiang Kai-shek. Hearing shots,

Chiang jumped out of his bedroom window and hid in a narrow crevice in the surrounding snow-covered hills. He was discovered two hours later, barefoot and in a robe thrown over his nightshirt, shivering terribly and initially unable to utter a word. In his haste, he had forgotten his false teeth. The captain addressed Chiang Kai-shek in accordance with military regulations. Finally, with some difficulty Chiang said, "If you are my comrades, shoot me now and finish it all."

"We will not shoot!" Sun replied. "We only ask you to lead our country against Japan. Then we shall be the first to cheer our generalissimo." (Chiang had been the generalissimo of China's armed forces since 1928.)

"Call Marshal Chang [Zhang] here, and I will come down," said Chiang Kai-shek.

"Marshal Chang is not here. The troops are rising in the city; we came to protect you."

At these words, the generalissimo apparently calmed down and requested that they bring him a horse so he could come down from the mountain.

"There is no horse here," Sun replied, "but I will carry you down the mountain on my back."

And he knelt down before Chiang Kai-shek. Taking his time, the generalissimo scrambled up on the captain's broad back. Having carried the generalissimo to a car, Zhang Xueliang's chief guard finally said to him, "The past is the past. From now on there must be a new policy for China."

"I am sure," said Chiang Kai-shek dryly, "that Marshal Chang has an excellent policy for China."

"This is a time of national crisis," parried Sun. "We hope that the generalissimo will receive the demands of the people."

"I am always ready to consider the demands of Marshal Chang," Chiang declared.

"The one urgent task for China is to resist Japan. This is the united demand of the men of the Northwest. Why do you not fight Japan, but instead give the order to fight the Red Army?"

"I have never said that I would not fight Japan," replied Chiang indignantly.

"But the Tungpei [Northeast] army demands that you fight Japan as soon as possible, for their homes have been seized by the enemy, and all of China suffers because of their loss."

"I am the leader of the Chinese people," Chiang suddenly burst out. "I represent the nation. I think that my policy is right, not wrong."

"If you represent the Chinese people," said Sun, "why do you not resist Japan? This is the demand of the whole Chinese nation. How can you claim to represent them when you do not carry out their demands?"

"I am a revolutionary," the generalissimo said, terminating the dispute. "I am always ready to sacrifice myself. I have never changed my views; and even though you hold me prisoner, my spirit will never submit to another's."[38]

Chiang Kai-shek was transported to Xi'an where Zhang Xueliang, excusing himself for the necessary inconvenience, again demanded that Chiang stop the war against the communists and lead the nationwide resistance to Japan. Meanwhile, Shao Lizi, the civilian governor of Shaanxi who had issued the order to disperse the student demonstration on December 9, was also arrested, along with more than ten persons in Chiang Kai-shek's retinue.[39]

News of Chiang Kai-shek's arrest reached communist headquarters in Baoan on the morning of December 12. Mao Zedong and the other CCP leaders were elated. Mao's secretary recalled:

> Early on the morning of December 12, I was awakened by the duty radio officer. He said that Zhang Xueliang and Yang Hucheng had sent a radiogram to Mao Zedong from Xi'an; it was marked "Extremely Urgent." The radiogram, written in semi-colloquial language, was brief. I remember little of it apart from the two characters "*bing*" (soldiers) and "*jian*" (admonish). I quickly delivered the radiogram to Mao Zedong who had still not gone to bed. After reading it, [he] joyfully exclaimed, "How about that! Time for bed. Tomorrow there will be good news!"[40]

What the two characters signified was Zhang Xueliang's decision to use force to "admonish" Chiang Kai-shek. This is what the Young Marshal transmitted to Mao Zedong. When Mao awoke the entire city was extremely excited. Otto Braun, who lived adjacent to the compound of the Central Committee of the CCP, was also struck by the unusual animation that gripped Baoan. He noted that Mao arose early in the morning, which was very unusual for him since, as a rule, he worked nights, and therefore woke up late. In Mao's cave the field telephone, which connected Mao with other leaders of the party and the government and with army commanders, was ringing continuously. "The news spread with lightning speed throughout the entire place," Otto Braun recalls.

> It produced a genuine rapture, for Chiang Kai-shek was the most hated man in the CCP and the Chinese Red Army. . . . [T]here was an open air meeting . . . of all Party members, Army men, and soviet functionaries in Pao-an [Baoan] and its vicinity. . . . Mao Tse-tung [Mao Zedong] spoke first. . . . The gist of the speeches was . . . that the time had come to settle accounts with Chiang Kai-shek as a traitor to China's national interests and to bring him before a people's court. . . .

The entire nation and all its armed forces should be mobilized for the war against Japan and its accomplices in the KMT [Guomindang].[41]

A huge meeting adopted a resolution to "demand a 'mass trial' of Chiang Kai-shek as a traitor, and there was wild jubilation in the town."[42] At a meeting of the Politburo on the morning of December 13, a very excited Mao described the arrest of Chiang Kai-shek as a revolutionary, anti-Japanese, progressive event.[43] Almost unanimously the Politburo resolved that Chiang Kai-shek should be tried and sentenced to death.[44] Afterward Mao personally informed the Comintern about what had transpired.[45]

News of the events in Xi'an, which reached Moscow that same day, December 13, likewise amazed the Comintern chiefs. Dimitrov was in seventh heaven. "Optimistic, favorable assessment regarding Zhang Xueliang. The Sov[iet] Union needs to be restrained and to respond skillfully to the anti-Soviet campaign in connection with the events in Xi'an," he wrote in his diary.[46] The next day he convened a meeting to discuss Chinese affairs with his most trusted associates. Only afterward did he contact Stalin.

What he heard astonished him. As usual the Boss was laconic: "Advise them [the Chinese Communists] to adopt an independent position, to come out against internal internecine strife, to insist on a peaceful resolution of the conflict, on agreement and joint actions, on a democratic platform for all parties and groups standing for the integrity and independence of China, emphasizing the position adopted by the party in its letter to the Guomindang and in the interview [with] Mao Zedong."[47] Now here was something that no one would have expected. Stalin was demanding that the communists free Chiang Kai-shek. How else could the conflict be resolved peacefully?

Several hours later, at midnight, Stalin suddenly phoned Dimitrov and, without concealing his irritation, asked, "*Who is this Wang Ming of yours? A provocateur? He wanted to file a telegram to have Chiang Kai-shek killed.*"

The flabbergasted Dimitrov answered that he had not heard anything of the sort.

"I'll find you that telegram," said Stalin, throwing down the receiver.[48]

In fact, he did not look for the telegram. Most likely, there simply hadn't been any such thing, and someone had incorrectly informed Stalin. It is also possible that Stalin wanted to frighten Dimitrov, knowing that he was ready to issue an order to have Chiang Kai-shek executed. In any case, the Boss was dissatisfied and did not hide his irritation.

Soon after Molotov phoned.

"*Come to Com[rade] St[alin]'s office tomorrow at 3:30; we'll discuss Ch[inese] affairs. Only you and Man[uilsky], nobody else!*"[49]

What was discussed in Stalin's office is unknown. One may suppose that the Boss expressed his dissatisfaction with the political nearsightedness of

Dimitrov, Mao Zedong, Wang Ming, and officials of the Comintern and the CCP Central Committee. Naturally, Molotov said yes to everything. Stalin's point was that the arrest and execution of Chiang Kai-shek would inevitably deepen the split in Chinese society and make things increasingly difficult for Stalin. In November 1936, just a month prior to the Xi'an Incident, Nazi Germany had concluded an Anti-Comintern Pact with Japan that was aimed at the Soviet Union. Thus, for Stalin, converting Chiang Kai-shek into an ally was a matter of life and death. He knew that emergency meetings of the Standing Committee of the Guomindang Central Executive Committee and of its Political Council, which had convened on December 12, simultaneously adopted resolutions to crush Zhang Xueliang's mutiny by force. He Yingqin, the war minister, who was devoted body and soul to Chiang Kai-shek, was already prepared to give the order to bomb Xi'an and dispatch a punitive expedition there. Guomindang planes had already begun to bomb various populated points in Shaanxi province.

On December 15, the day after his meeting with Stalin, Dimitrov transmitted the Boss's directive about peacefully resolving the incident to officials of the ECCI. The next day he was back in the Kremlin, discussing the text of the Comintern directive to the Central Committee of the Chinese Communist Party with Stalin and his top lieutenants. The directive urged the CCP to stand "decisively for a peaceful resolution of the conflict."[50]

It is easy to imagine Mao Zedong's reaction upon receipt of this instruction. Humiliation. Shame. Disappointment. Most likely, all three. In Edgar Snow's words, Mao "flew into a rage when the order came from Moscow to release Chiang. Mao swore and stamped his feet." An eyewitness whom Snow called "X" informed him of Mao's reaction.[51]

Most humiliating was that Moscow's order came when Mao himself understood the need to resolve the conflict peacefully. For technical reasons Dimitrov's telegram, sent on December 16, did not arrive in Baoan until the morning of the 17th or the 18th, and part of it failed to transmit. Not until December 20 was Mao able to read the full text of Moscow's directive.[52] By then he already knew the Comintern's position from Soviet media reports. Moreover, Mao had received the text of Zhang Xueliang's "Appeal to the Nation" clarifying that Zhang did not seek Chiang Kai-shek's death. The Young Marshal's objective was to force Chiang Kai-shek to resist Japan. Arriving in Xi'an on December 17, Zhou Enlai began negotiations with Zhang and General Yang Hucheng. Chiang Kai-shek refused to meet with them or to discuss Zhang's proposals. "Both for your own sake and for the sake of the nation, the only thing for you to do is to repent at once and send me back to Nanking [Nanjing]," he said to Zhang. "You must not fall into the trap set by the Communists. Repent before it is too late."[53]

The situation was growing tenser. By December 19, Mao realized that the incident had to be settled. Extremely upset, he was unable to control himself at the Politburo meeting that day. Acknowledging that "the issue of the day is mainly that of resisting Japan, not the question of relations with Chiang Kai-shek," he suddenly interjected, "The Japanese say that the arrest [of Chiang Kai-shek] was arranged by the Soviet Union, while the Soviet Union says it was contrived by the Japanese. Both sides are distorting the essence of the matter."[54] The Politburo adopted a resolution aimed at a peaceful outcome to the conflict. Moscow's directive, which had been transmitted by Mao Zedong to Zhou Enlai at 8 P.M. on December 20, changed nothing. From the outside, however, it looked as if Mao had been forced to accept Stalin's orders. Mao needed to report on the implementation of the Comintern's directive, but he did not want to lose face in front of his own party comrades. Therefore, despite the objective circumstances and while formally approving Moscow's directive, Mao went slow on concluding an agreement with Chiang Kai-shek regarding the establishment of an anti-Japanese united front. Chiang, too, was in no hurry to form an alliance with the CCP, even though the British and American military attachés who arrived in Xi'an as mediators requested him to do so.

On December 22, Song Ziwen, who was Chiang's brother-in-law, and the generalissimo's wife, Song Meiling, flew into Xi'an. Only then did the crisis end. Zhang Xueliang, the gallant cavalier, could not resist the charming Song Meiling. On Christmas Day he presented her with a gift: he declared that he himself would escort her and her husband to Nanjing. He was terribly naïve.

After flying into Nanjing, Chiang immediately handed the rebellious marshal over to a military tribunal, which sentenced him to ten years in prison. In July 1937, however, with the start of the full-scale Sino-Japanese War, he was amnestied along with all other political prisoners. But Chiang never forgave him. Zhang was put under house arrest, where he languished for many years. When he fled China in 1949, Chiang took Zhang to Taiwan with him, where his prisoner remained under guard long after Chiang's death in 1975. It was not until 1990 that Zhang Xueliang regained his freedom, at the age of eighty-nine.

Meanwhile, Chiang continued preparations for the sixth anticommunist campaign. At the end of December, new military forces began to assemble along the borders of the soviet area in northern Shaanxi. At this point, on January 6, 1937, Mao could not restrain himself. In a telegram he and Luo Fu sent to Zhou Enlai and Bo Gu, he asserted that it was necessary "to prepare boldly for war" against the Guomindang.[55] This warlike mood in Baoan, however, inevitably drew a swift reaction from the Comintern. On January 16, 1937, Dimitrov gave Stalin the draft of a new directive to the CCP Central Committee. Three days later, on January 19, Dimitrov and Soviet Politburo members Molotov, Andrei Andreev, Andrei Zhdanov, and Nikolai Yezhov gathered in Stalin's office to discuss the situation. The tone of the telegram was rather sharp:

We attach exceptional importance to a peaceful resolution of the events in Xi'an. However, this outcome could be ruined not only by the machinations of the Japanese imperialists and their agents who are trying by every means to ignite civil war, but also as a result of mistaken policies of your party.

Now it is clearer than ever that the party's previous policy was incorrect, namely, to seek to achieve a united front by excluding Chiang Kai-shek and overthrowing the Nanjing government. . . . The party's main task at present is to achieve an effective end to the civil war. . . . [T]he party must openly declare and firmly conduct a policy of supporting all measures of the Guomindang and the Nanjing government that are directed toward . . . uniting all forces of the Chinese people to defend the integrity and independence of China against Japanese aggression.[56]

At Stalin's urging, on January 20 Dimitrov sent Mao a separate letter on the need to change the direction of work in China. In the name of the Secretariat of the ECCI, Dimitrov asked Mao to consider "switch[ing] from the soviet system to a system of people's revolutionary rule on democratic foundations," while preserving "soviets only in urban centers and not as organs of power but as mass organizations."[57]

The categorical tone of Moscow's January 19 telegram convinced Mao of the need once more to reassure the Kremlin of his complete loyalty. Several days later, seeking Dimitrov's advice, he sent him the draft of a CCP Central Committee telegram addressed to the Third Plenum of the Fifth Guomindang Central Executive Committee, due to convene in Nanjing on February 15. Dimitrov forwarded the telegram along with his draft response to the Soviet Politburo, which approved the proposed text with several revisions. On February 5, Dimitrov informed Mao and several days later the CCP Politburo Standing Committee dispatched a telegram to the Third Plenum of the Guomindang CEC reading in part:

Our party sincerely hopes that the Third Plenum of the Guomindang will adopt the following principles as government policy:

1. Complete cessation of the civil war, and the concentration of national forces for unified resistance to external aggression;
2. Freedom of speech, assembly and organization, amnesty for all political prisoners;
3. Convening a conference of representatives of all parties, groups, social strata, and armies, concentration of all the capable persons in the country for joint salvation of the motherland;

4. Rapid and full completion of all preparatory work for the war of
   resistance to Japan;
5. Improvement of the lives of the people.

The CCP Central Committee promised to terminate its policy of armed uprisings aimed at overthrowing the National government on a nationwide basis. It also expressed its readiness to rename the soviet government the government of the Special Region of the Chinese Republic and to rename the Red Army the National Revolutionary Army, which would be directly subordinated to the Central Government of the Guomindang and the Military Council in Nanjing. Moreover, it agreed to introduce a democratic system of general elections in the Special Region and to stop confiscating landlords' land.[58]

Mao had turned forty-four. He had acquired an enormous reputation as a political figure on the national stage and his influence in the party was virtually unchallenged. His dependence on Moscow, however, had not diminished; nor had the CCP's position of subordination to the Comintern. Although the Moscow leadership's conception of the Chinese revolution often changed, as before the Chinese Communist Party remained closely tied to the ECCI and the Communist Party of the Soviet Union (CPSU). Soviet ideological influence on the Chinese communists remained overwhelming. The Xi'an Incident served only to strengthen it. Although Mao began storing up insults and dissatisfaction in his inner self, he still remained an obedient pupil of the great Stalin.

Early in 1937, Zizhen gave birth to their fifth child, a girl. Zhou Enlai's wife, Deng Yingchao, called the baby Jiaojiao ("Beauty"). Later, when his daughter turned thirteen, in accordance with Chinese tradition Mao gave her a new, grown-up name, Min ("Prompt"). He took the Chinese character *min* from a saying of Confucius, "A gentleman should be slow to speak and prompt to act" (*junzi yu na yu yan er min yu xing*). At the same time, he changed her family name from Mao to Li, the character he used in his favorite pseudonym, Li Desheng, meaning "Retreat in the Name of Victory."[59]

Meanwhile, on January 13, 1937, soon after his daughter's birth, and pursuant to an agreement with Zhang Xueliang reached prior to the arrest of the Young Marshal, the Central Committee of the CCP moved from the caves of Baoan sixty miles south to Yan'an, the largest city in northern Shaanxi. Before departing, holding his swaddled baby girl in his arms, Mao said to her, "My Beauty, you are in step with the times. We are going to live in the city."[60]

THE FLIRTATIOUS
PHILOSOPHER

The move to Yan'an brought major changes to Mao Zedong's daily life. He could now enjoy the comforts of real city life. The new "red" capital was nothing like Baoan, a dusty and desolate hamlet where most of the buildings lay in ruins. Yan'an was a very lively place. "Farmers and small vendors sold meat, eggs, vegetables, and other edibles in the open-air market," Otto Braun recalled. "The small shops and restaurants, even some very respectable establishments, remained open to business. In short, Yenan [Yan'an] reflected nothing less than peace and normalcy. We watched what to us was unaccustomed civilian activity." [1]

Located in a long mountain valley, on the south bank of the wide but shallow and rocky Yan River, the city was surrounded by loess hills. Massive fortress walls ran along almost its entire circumference and from these walls jagged rectangular towers thrust upward into the sky. They housed the city gates: northern, southern, and two eastern gates (large and small). There were no gates on the west or southwest sides. There the fortress wall ran along the ridge of the hills, securing the city from any unwanted guests.

The city was an ensemble of narrow and lively streets, long blocks of houses with curved tile roofs, luxurious estates, and private homes that belonged to members of the local elite, but which had been abandoned by their owners. Soaring into the sky above everything else was a graceful nine-story pagoda located on one of the surrounding heights. Yan'an (literally "Long peace"), it seemed, held the promise of a long-awaited respite for Mao and his comrades. Peace with the Guomindang was gradually becoming a reality.

More than three thousand people lived in the town, but there were more than enough empty dwellings so that most of the party leadership were able to find satisfactory accommodations. Mao and He Zizhen, along with other members of the Central Committee and their wives, settled into the western part of town, at the foot of Fenghuangshan (Mount Phoenix), a prestigious neighborhood of wealthy merchants and landowners who, naturally, had fled at the first rumors of the approach of the CCP army. Mao and his wife occupied the home of a well-to-do merchant. The light and spacious rooms were remarkably clean. The yellow loess hills that stretched in humpbacked waves beyond the horizon were clearly visible. Next to one of the windows in a room that served as a combined living room and bedroom stood a large wooden bed and beside another a traditional *kang* heated by smoke from the hearth. A table, some chairs, bookshelves, and an enormous wooden bathtub completed the furnishings. All that was lacking was sufficient cabinets for papers, but Mao improvised with several empty oil drums that his bodyguards brought in for him. (The barrels turned out be from the Standard Oil Company, adding an American touch to the Chinese décor.)[2] Luo Fu, Zhu De, Zhou Enlai, and Peng Dehuai settled into the neighboring houses.

Not far from town, numerous caves were cut into the steep slopes of the loess mountains along both sides of the river. They stretched in long rows north out of the city, and from a great distance they looked like swallows' nests or bats' caves.[3] Most of the officers and soldiers of the Red Army lived there. In addition, several high-ranking leaders of the CCP preferred a spartan existence in the caves to the relative luxury that Mao, Zhou, and others had chosen. Among them was Zhang Guotao, who increasingly sensed the ill will of Mao and his colleagues toward him.

The extreme left-wing American journalist Agnes Smedley, a masculine-looking suffragette of forty-five who despised bourgeois morality and worshipped Stalin, arrived in Yan'an in late January or early February 1937 and was also living in one of the caves. She was not formally a member of any communist party, but prior to her arrival in northern Shaanxi she had maintained secret connections with the Comintern and the Communist Party of the USA (CPUSA). In the early 1930s she played the role of an unofficial representative of the ECCI in China and served as a channel through which Comintern agents occasionally passed money and directives to the Chinese communists. Under the alias of Anna she was also enmeshed in the Soviet spy ring in Shanghai involving the Soviet military intelligence agent Richard Sorge, then living under the alias of Johnson. In 1930, Smedley became one of his many lovers, referring to him as this "handsome Hercules" in a letter to a woman friend. Soon after her arrival in Yan'an, Smedley formally applied for admission to the Chinese Communist Party, but she was politely rejected. This came as a blow, although she accepted the arguments of her Chinese friends who explained that it would be better for the talented journalist to remain formally outside the CCP so she could be of greater use to the communist movement.[4]

In the cave next to Smedley lived her interpreter, Wu Guangwei, an attractive stage actress who had also just recently come to Yan'an. Agnes called her Lily and this name suited her perfectly. With a face like the full moon and elegant as a flower floating on a lake, the twenty-six-year-old Lily was as different from Smedley as she was from all the other inhabitants of Yan'an. Alone among all the women in Yan'an, she used cosmetics, large quantities of which she had brought from Xi'an. She twisted her long black hair, which cascaded down her shoulders in luxuriant strands, and she took meticulous care of her skin and her nails. Not surprisingly, many men, including married ones, began to take notice of her.

Mao, too, would succumb to her charms. At first, his relations with Lily were innocent. He would occasionally call on her and her neighbor, to chat, play cards, drink coffee and sometimes sip rice wine, and munch on soda crackers, which Smedley, who suffered from ulcers, always tried to keep in stock. Several times he stayed on for dinner. By all appearances he simply valued her as a talented actress who was making a noticeable contribution to the revolutionary struggle. At the time Lily was starring on the Yan'an stage in the role of Nilovna in a theatrical adaptation of Maxim Gorky's *Mother.*

As time passed, however, rumors began floating around town. Women, most of them married, were particularly upset. As active party members, they, along with their husbands, had experienced the difficult trials of civil war, the Long March, the Guomindang blockade, hunger, bombardment, and separation from their children. For the most part they considered themselves revolutionary moralists. "Charm" and "femininity" were not in their vocabulary. Colorful clothing, cosmetics, and styled hair evoked their contempt. They looked upon casual conversation with unfamiliar men as akin to adultery. They related to men, including their own husbands, as comrades in the struggle; they dressed like them, cut their hair short, and behaved with extreme modesty and independence—all in all it amounted to a strict guerrilla-style puritanism.

The women of Yan'an also didn't have much time for Agnes Smedley, and not only because she had befriended Lily. Smedley's personal style was not that different from the other women: she never used cosmetics, dressed simply in masculine style, was unpretentious, and passionately loved the Communist Party. But she was rather crude, self-assured, and much too independent. She believed in free "revolutionary" love, rejected marriage, declaring it a means of enslaving women, and campaigned for birth control. (Smedley had had to stop a campaign for douching that she had initiated among local peasant women. The women in Yan'an drank the lemon-scented liquid instead of using it for its intended purpose.) At public meetings, Smedley was excessively outspoken and spent hours on end in her cave interviewing men. Zhu De's wife, the willful and energetic Kang Keqing, particularly despised her, and for good reason. Scarcely had she arrived in Yan'an when Smedley began to work on a biography of Zhu, with whom she had fallen in love. She did not even try to conceal her feelings to Zhu, her "best friend on earth."

Kang Keqing and He Zizhen organized against Smedley and Lily, and soon all of the revolutionary women in Yan'an joined in. Agnes and Lily took little notice, continuing their tête-à-têtes with Zhu and Mao respectively. Two other women joined their dangerous game, the well-known communist writer Ding Ling, also a thoroughly emancipated woman; and, upon occasion, Helen Foster Snow, Edgar Snow's wife, who was known as Peg or Peggy among her circle of friends. (Her nom de plume was Nym Wales.) Helen, like her husband an American journalist, had come to Yan'an at the end of April. She was as enchanting as any Hollywood beauty, but rather modest. Still, she showed up at Smedley's soirées because she saw nothing wrong with them.

Mao's and Zhu's meetings with Lily, Smedley, Ding Ling, and Peggy Snow were not always innocent. Sometimes, in Mao's presence, the women would lightheartedly discuss which of the local men they considered the most handsome (Smedley and Snow could speak a little Chinese). Laughingly, they would reject this one as too fat, that one as too thin, another one as too small. They agreed that the most attractive were Lin Biao, a "classical Adonis," and Xu Haidong, a military cadre whose muscular figure captivated them. They also considered Mao handsome, comparing him to Lincoln. At this moment, they would usually spread their hands apart and say, "These are good men, but alas, we cannot compete with their wives!" Smedley would joke, "If you, the leaders of the CCP, cannot free yourselves from under the heel of women, how can you possibly liberate China?"

Apparently tired of sharing his bed with his wife, Mao was barely able to restrain himself. His rendezvous with the women became more frequent. Almost every evening Mao went to see them, read aloud lyrical verses that he had again begun to compose, and conversed with Smedley about romantic love. (Usually it was Lily who brought them together.) Soon he and Smedley conceived the idea of organizing a dance school. They got hold of an old gramophone and several foxtrot records, and they arranged a musical evening at a church that had been abandoned by missionaries who had fled the city. Scandalized by such overt "debauchery," the wives of the CCP leaders boycotted the dance lessons, but their husbands happily took part. Zhu De, Zhou Enlai, and He Long were especially keen to master the American dances. Even the ascetic Peng Dehuai showed up to observe the goings-on. These lessons continued for several weeks, bringing Mao and Lily even closer together.[5]

Helen Foster Snow recalled what followed:

On May 31, I was invited to visit the American journalist, Agnes Smedley, in her spacious and comfortable cave on the hillside. . . . I roasted two potatoes in a small fire outdoors and ordered my bodyguard to buy two tins of pineapple. Lily Wu cooked peppers and eggs. Agnes Smedley ordered cabbage soup and other dishes from the restaurant.

Mao Tse-tung [Mao Zedong] arrived. . . . He was in high spirits that evening. Mao had a most attractive quality which does not show in photographs, an expressiveness and aliveness. . . . Agnes looked up at Mao worshipfully, with her large blue eyes—which at times had a fanatical gleam. Lily Wu was also looking at Mao with hero-worship. A bit later, I was stunned to see Lily walk over and sit beside Mao on the bench, putting her hand on his knee (very timidly). Lily announced that she had had too much wine. . . . Mao also appeared startled, but he would have been something of a cad to push her away rudely, and he was obviously amused. He also announced that he had had too much wine. Lily then ventured to take hold of Mao's hand, which she repeated from time to time during the evening.[6]

The next day Zizhen learned what had happened. Most likely Mao's bodyguards, who respected Comrade He and detested Lily, who they thought was a bad influence upon Mao, informed Zizhen of Mao's behavior. At the time in China, where social norms were somewhat puritanical, a man and a woman were not supposed to touch each other in public, and yet Lily was openly flirting with a married man, obviously trying to seduce him. Zizhen knew her husband too well to remain unruffled. Mao was complaisant when it came to female caresses. He valued beauty and loved willing women. All this he found in abundance in Lily. Smarting from the insult, Zizhen rushed out of her house and headed straight for the cave section of town.

Night had long since fallen when she arrived at Lily's cave. Zizhen had no doubt she would find her unfaithful husband there. This is how Edgar Snow subsequently described the scene from Smedley's report:

Late one evening after Agnes had already gone to bed . . . she heard the sound of footsteps rushing excitedly up the hill. Then the door of Lily's cave was pushed open and a woman's shrill voice broke the silence. "You idiot! How dare you fool me and sneak into the home of this little bourgeois dance hall strumpet." Smedley leapt out of bed, threw on her coat, and ran next door. There was Mao's wife standing beside the seated Mao beating him with a long-handled flashlight. He was sitting on a stool by the table, still wearing his cotton hat and military coat. He did not try to stop his wife. His guard was standing at attention at the door looking perplexed. Mao's wife, crying in anger, kept hitting him and shouting until she was out of breath. Mao finally stood up. He looked tired and his voice was quietly severe. "Be quiet, Zizhen. There's nothing shameful in the relationship between comrade Wu and myself. We were just talking. You are ruining yourself as a communist and are doing something to be ashamed of. Hurry home before other party members learn of this."

Suddenly Mao's wife turned on Lily, who was standing with her back against the wall like a terrified kitten before a tiger. She railed at Lily, saying, "Dance-hall bitch! You'd probably take up with any man. You've even fooled the Chairman." Then she drew close to Lily and while brandishing the flashlight she held in one hand, she scratched Lily's face with the other and pulled her hair. Blood flowing from her head, Lily ran to Agnes and hid behind her. Mao's wife now directed her anger against Agnes.

"Imperialist," she shouted. "You're the cause of all this. Get back to your own cave." Then she struck the "foreign devil" with her flashlight. Not one to turn the other cheek, Smedley flattened Mrs. Mao with a single punch. From the floor, Mao's wife, more humiliated than hurt, shrieked, "What kind of husband are you? Are you any kind of man? Are you really a communist? You remain silent while I'm being struck by this imperialist right before your eyes."

Mao rebuked his wife, saying, "Didn't you strike her even though she had done nothing to you? She has a right to protect herself. You're the one who has shamed us. You're acting like a rich woman in a bad American movie." Furious but restraining himself, Mao commanded his guard to help his wife up and take her home. But she made a fuss and refused to cooperate, so Mao had to call two more guards, and they finally led Mao's hysterical wife from the room. As they proceeded down the hill, Mao followed in silence, with many surprised faces watching the procession from their caves.[7]

In just a few hours the whole town and certainly all the cave-dwellers knew what had happened. As Smedley and Edgar Snow reported, Mao quickly convened a meeting of the party leadership at which it was resolved to keep this matter secret, forbidding anyone to speak of what had happened. But it was hardly possible to calm He Zizhen. She demanded that the Central Committee punish Smedley, Lily, and Mao's bodyguard, who had been present during the incident. She also accused a bodyguard of plotting against her; after all, he had seen everything, but had not intervened. For days on end she complained to her friends, the wives of the party leaders, about her unfaithful husband, the "shameless hussy" Wu Guangwei (Lily), and the "imperialist procuress" Smedley. Naturally, they were sympathetic, shaking their heads while examining the black bruise about her right eye that Smedley had inflicted upon her.[8]

To cool the anger of his wife, Mao was forced to send Lily away. On a rainy morning in July, she rode off with her theatrical troupe and Ding Ling into Shaanxi province. Before her departure, choking back tears, in the courtyard in front of her cave she burned the papers with Mao's poems that he had presented to her on the happier evenings.

Mao also asked Agnes Smedley to leave Yan'an. Rumors were circulating around town that Zizhen had incited her bodyguards to shoot Smedley, and Mao, unable to quell the rumor, tried to get Smedley to leave town. But he was unsuccessful. Soon after their conversation Smedley injured her spine when her horse stumbled, fell down, and badly crushed her. Confined to six weeks on the *kang*, she was physically unable to leave town until September 10. Three days earlier Peggy Snow had departed the city.[9]

Unable to forget what had occurred, and despite Mao's efforts to stop her, He Zizhen left him and their young daughter, who was just starting to speak, and moved from Yan'an to Xi'an on the pretext that she was in need of qualified medical assistance. The shrapnel she carried in her from the bomb was bothering her, but removing it was not likely the main reason for her leaving; Mao's romantic escapades were.

Meanwhile, political events in the country and in the world were unfolding at a feverish pace. Throughout the first half of 1937, Stalin assiduously pursued the goal of officially establishing a new united front between the CCP and the Guomindang. This required substantial financial sums, and he was not at all stingy as he sought ways to transmit large sums to the Chinese Communist Party. One link in Stalin's financial supply chain was the widow of Sun Yat-sen, Song Qingling, who became involved in the clandestine financial operations of the Comintern. Under the names of Madame Suzy and Leah, she acted as an intermediary, transmitting large sums of money from the Comintern to the leaders of the Chinese Communist Party. She was not an official member of the CCP, but being quite leftist ("almost a communist" in Dimitrov's words),[10] she had maintained unofficial ties with the leaders of the Communist Party from the period of the revolution in 1925–27.* In November 1936, for example, in response to a letter addressed to her from Mao Zedong in which he referred to the financial difficulties of the CCP, she helped Comintern representatives send US $50,000 via the communist Pan Hannian, one of the leaders of the Central Committee Special Sector who conducted secret intelligence operations in the Guomindang territory.[11] A subsequent telegram from the ECCI to the CCP Central Committee, dated November 12, 1936, informed it of the decision to provide the Chinese Communist Party financial aid worth approximately $550,000. The initial part of this sum, $150,000, was transferred to Pan Hannian in Shanghai at the end of November, again via Song Qingling. Then in early March 1937, Moscow promised to increase financial assistance to the CCP in the current year to $1.6 million. All told, the amount of Comintern assistance to the CCP in 1937 approached $2 million.[12]

On March 10, 1937, Stalin ordered Dimitrov to recall to Moscow Chiang

---

* In 1926–27 Borodin even referred to Song Qingling as "the only man in the entire left-wing Guomindang."

Kai-shek's son, Chiang Ching-kuo, a political émigré then living in Sverdlovsk in the Urals where he worked in the local city soviet. He had lived in the Soviet Union under a Russian name, Nikolai Vladimirovich Elizarov, since 1925 when he enrolled at Sun Yat-sen University. He joined the Bolshevik party and even married a Russian woman. Stalin had decided to send him to his father, assuming that Chiang Ching-kuo would have some influence and could convince his father of the need to establish contact with the communists in the interest of repelling Japanese aggression.[13]

An agreement between the Guomindang and the Communist Party was spurred not by Chiang Ching-kuo's return to China, however, but by the domestic political situation. In the spring of 1937, the Japanese increased their forces just a few miles from Beiping. Concerned about this development, Chiang Kai-shek held face-to-face talks in Hangzhou in late March with CCP representatives Zhou Enlai and Pan Hannian. It was agreed that the CCP would maintain control over its own armed forces, consisting of three divisions numbering just over forty thousand troops. As before, the communists would control the government of the region they occupied, but they would obey orders from Chiang's government in Nanjing.[14] In early April, after lengthy consideration, the Politburo of the CCP Central Committee approved this decision.

In exchange for an alliance with the CCP, Chiang wanted to obtain an agreement with the government of the USSR to supply war matériel to the Guomindang. So, on April 3, 1937, Chiang Kai-shek held secret talks in Shanghai with Soviet ambassador Dmitrii Bogomolov.

On May 29, a semi-official delegation from the Guomindang Central Executive Committee visited Yan'an. At a reception in their honor, Mao said, "During the past ten years our parties were not united; now the situation has changed. Now if our parties do not unite, the country will perish."[15] Following a suggestion by the head of the Guomindang delegation, representatives of both groups made a pilgrimage to the grave of Huang Di, the legendary ruler of ancient China, some sixty miles south of Yan'an. Together they cleaned the dust from Huang Di's gravestone as a symbolic gesture that henceforth all the differences between the hostile parties would be ignored. Mao, satisfied with the gesture, said that the visit had given him hope.[16]

The graveside visit marked the formal end of clashes between CCP and Guomindang forces. On June 8, direct talks between Chiang and Zhou Enlai resumed in the resort town of Lushan, in Jiangxi province. The conversations continued until June 15. An agreement was reached on ending the civil war. Sun Yat-sen's Three Principles were accepted as the basis of cooperation.[17]

But only after the outbreak of the full-scale Sino-Japanese War on July 7, 1937, was an anti-Japanese united front finally established. The proximate cause of this unification was Japanese bombardment on August 13 of Shanghai, the center of Chiang Kai-shek's and Anglo-American investors' economic interests. Several days later, on August 22, the generalissimo, whom the Japanese had pushed to his limits, concluded a nonaggression treaty with the Soviet Union, which promised to help China in its struggle against the Japanese onslaught.[18] At the same time he issued an order to include the Red Army in the table of organization of his National Revolution Army. The Workers and Peasants Revolutionary Army was renamed the Eighth Route Army and consisted of three divisions: the 115th under the command of Lin Biao, the 120th under He Long, and the 129th under Liu Bocheng. Zhu De was appointed commander of the army and Peng Dehuai his deputy. Soon the government of the so-called Special Border Region of the Chinese Republic, as the Northwest Office of the Central Government of the Chinese Soviet Republic now came to be called, was confirmed. The region included eighteen counties in Shaanxi, Gansu, and Ningxia provinces.[19] Chiang Kai-shek confirmed Lin Boqu as its chairman. Lin had already been fulfilling this responsibility in place of Bo Gu, who had been transferred to work as the director of the Organizational Department of the Central Committee of the CCP.[20] A month later, on September 22, the Communist Party published a declaration recognizing the leading role of the Guomindang, and on the next day Chiang Kai-shek's statement regarding the establishment of an anti-Japanese united front of all political parties in the country was issued. Stalin had cause to celebrate. Even if only formally, China was now united in struggle against Japan, and this substantially diminished the likelihood of Japanese aggression against the USSR.

There continued to be problems, however, with genuine unification. Neither Chiang Kai-shek nor Mao Zedong trusted the other and neither of them in fact wanted any part of a real united front. Mao agreed to negotiations with Nanjing only under the Stalinist whip. He accepted the policy of the anti-Japanese united front reluctantly, and he acquiesced to it only after he figured out that he could wrest some advantage from it. Some other party leaders shared a different perspective on the united front. Indeed, disagreements within the party were expressed in the varying approaches concerning how to fight Japanese aggression. Mistrusting Chiang Kai-shek and wishing to husband his forces for the coming postwar struggle with the Guomindang for leadership of the democratic revolution, Mao was loath to engage not only in positional or static warfare, in other words, direct confrontation on the battlefield, but generally in any kind of regular or mobile warfare against the Japanese under the leadership of the generalissimo. He did not refuse to assist "friendly regular forces," but from his perspective the Eighth Route Army could and should engage only in purely guerrilla or mobile-guerrilla military actions (what he called "sparrow" war) in the Japanese rear independent of the Guomindang, taking "the initiative into its own hands." Such a method of warfare, he believed, would be "freer, livelier, and more effective." Moreover, he insisted that no more than 75 percent of the main forces of the former

Red Army be sent to fight the Japanese, and that the remaining 25 percent be retained in the Special Region to defend against a possible attack by Chiang Kai-shek. Chiang was not to know about this percentage.[21] Luo Fu, who again became Mao's main ally, completely shared his views.[22]

Zhou Enlai, Bo Gu, Zhu De, Zhang Guotao, and Peng Dehuai viewed the problem differently; they believed that guerrilla warfare alone would not suffice to repel the attacks of the Japanese military machine. They favored close cooperation with the forces of the Central Government, and asserted that the Eighth Route Army was capable of engaging in mobile warfare and inflicting significant losses upon Japanese forces.[23]

An enlarged Politburo meeting convened by Luo Fu and Mao Zedong on August 22, 1937, in a small village near the district town of Luochuan, fifty-five miles south of Yan'an, played an important role in debating the tactics for conducting the war. Twenty-two people took part in the meeting, including important army commanders as well as party leaders. After four days of debates, Mao emerged victorious. A resolution drafted by Luo Fu was adopted pledging that the Eighth Route Army would initially conduct mobile guerrilla warfare in cooperation with other Chinese units in order to win "the trust" of the Nanjing government and the approval of public opinion. In the event of a possible breach in the front by the Japanese, forces under the control of the communists were directed to switch over to independent, guerrilla operations, expanding the scope of their military activities throughout Japan-occupied territory in north China.[24]

Elated by his victory, Mao soon tried to consolidate it further. At a meeting of the Politburo Standing Committee just two days after the Luochuan Conference, he asserted,

> While conducting a joint war of resistance [with the Guomindang] against Japan, we need to combine the national and the social revolutions. During the long period of the united front the Guomindang will try to exert systematic and all-around pressure on the communist party and the Red Army, trying to win them over to its side. We must increase our political vigilance. We must make sure that the peasantry and the petit bourgeoisie follow us. There are some elements inside the Guomindang that waver between the GMD and the CCP. This creates favorable conditions for us to win the Guomindang over to our side. The question of who will win over whom will be decided in a struggle between the two parties.

In conclusion, Mao warned that the main danger within the CCP was now that of "right opportunism."[25] (What he meant was "capitulation" to the Guomindang and a retreat from the struggle for a socialist revolution.)

He repeated the basic theses of this speech several days later at a meeting of higher-level party activists in Yan'an, emphasizing the idea that during the course of the war communists, "after establishing a democratic republic of workers, peasants, and bourgeoisie, must prepare for the transition to socialism." Apparently it was this question rather than the war with Japan that occupied most of his thoughts at this time. "Either we will overcome them [the Guomindang], or they us," he asserted. He never tired of arguing that the CCP troops must engage only in guerrilla warfare in the mountainous areas, "independently and autonomously," husbanding their strength and never becoming puppets in the hands of Chiang Kai-shek. The anti-Japanese war would be protracted, he explained, so it was necessary to be patient and wait until the Japanese army lost its strength.[26] "The enemy advances, we retreat; the enemy camps, we harass; the enemy tires, we attack; the enemy retreats, we pursue," he continued, invoking his favorite formula, which later became a maxim of People's War.

Of course, his words made a lot of sense. Like any other militarist in China, Mao understood that his power and even his very existence wholly depended on the strength of his army. As before, political power grew from the barrel of a gun. In such circumstances, how could he risk subjecting his armed forces to the blows of the Japanese? If he should lose them, Chiang Kai-shek would immediately end the united front and send his troops to crush Mao. It was simply astounding that his opponents did not want to acknowledge the obvious.[27] Following the Luochuan Conference, however, the numbers of his opponents diminished considerably. Zhu De, Peng Dehuai, and many others accepted his "guerrilla" ideas.

Meanwhile, the Guomindang army was retreating, suffering one catastrophic loss after another. In July 1937, Japanese troops took Beiping and Tianjin. In November they captured Taiyuan, the capital of Shanxi province, and then Shanghai. The offensive of the Japanese Imperial Army continued, and it seemed that nothing could stop it. The USSR fulfilled its agreement by providing enormous amounts of aid to Chiang Kai-shek, sending advisers, money, and arms. It did all that it could do, just as it had during the Great Revolution of the mid-1920s. But to no avail. Chiang Kai-shek's army retreated. The only thing that Stalin achieved was Chiang's pledge that he would not sign a separate peace with the Japanese. Chiang was prepared to wage a protracted war.

At this point Stalin, who closely followed the dramatic development of events on the Chinese fronts, understood that it was necessary once again to rethink the CCP's tactics. On November 11, 1937, he met with members of the CCP delegation to the ECCI. Wang Ming, Kang Sheng, and Wang Jiaxiang had requested to see him in connection with Wang Ming's and Kang Sheng's departure for their homeland. Wang Jiaxiang, who had come to Moscow to recuperate from a wound he had suffered in April 1933, remained as the acting head of the CCP delegation to the Comintern under the alias of Zhang Li. Dimitrov also took part in the conversation.

Stalin gave detailed instructions to the departing Chinese. The issues of the anti-Japanese united front and the anti-Japanese war were the first order of business. Judging from Dimitrov's diary, Stalin emphasized that the CCP should play a leading role in a common national resistance war, suspend its revolutionary program, and focus on fighting the external enemy—Japan—rather than domestic opponents. He said that because Chinese were united in opposition to Japan, China was in a more favorable position than Russia had been in 1918–20, when the Bolsheviks were engaged in battling foreign interventionists during the Russian civil war. Therefore, he was confident of China's victory. Stalin promised to help China develop war industry: "If China has its *own military industry,* no one can defeat it."

He also expressed his thoughts concerning the CCP's military tactics, advising the Chinese communists to avoid frontal attacks inasmuch as the Eighth Route Army lacked artillery. "Its [Eighth Route Army] tactics," Stalin said, "should be . . . *harrying* the enemy, drawing him into the interior of the country, and *striking at the rear.* It is necessary to destroy communication, railroads, and bridges [used by] the Japanese army." He demanded expansion of the CCP army to thirty divisions. In conclusion, Stalin said, "*At the Chinese party congress* it is counterproductive to engage in theoretical discussions. Leave theoretical problems for a later period, after the end of the war. The odds of speaking about a *noncapitalist* [i.e., socialist] path of development for China are worse now than they were before. (After all, capitalism is developing in China!)" *[28] In other words, Stalin demanded that the CCP formulate a new political line that excluded a path to socialism until after the war against Japan had been won. The members of the CCP delegation were obliged to report this to their Central Committee and to Mao in person.

On November 14, Wang Ming and his wife, Meng Qingshu (alias Rosa Vladimirovna Osetrova), and Kang Sheng and his wife, Cao Yiou (Russian pseudonym Lina), flew from Moscow through Xinjiang and arrived in Yan'an on November 29. Traveling with them from Xinjiang was Chen Yun, a member of the Politburo Standing Committee who had taken part in the Long March and was considered an energetic comrade. He had worked in Xinjiang from April 1937, as the chief representative of the Comintern and of the CCP Central Committee. It was Wang Ming who, with Dimitrov's blessing, had sent Chen Yun there.

Mao Zedong, Luo Fu, and other party leaders warmly welcomed the guests at the airport, and Mao even called Wang Ming "a blessing from the sky,"[29] but none of this meant anything. Mao understood that Wang Ming was the craftiest, most vicious, and most merciless rival for power of all those he had thus far encountered.

---

* Stalin supposed that the Chinese communists would convene their regular Seventh Congress of the CCP in the coming months.

Proud, egotistical, and power-hungry, Wang was truly Stalin's best pupil. And that is just how he perceived himself. Three days prior to his departure for China, on November 11, 1937, he received direct instructions from Stalin to "take measures" to eradicate "manifestations of Trotskyism in the actions of the CCP leadership." "Using all available means, intensify the struggle against Trotskyites," he suggested to Wang. "Trotskyites must be hunted down, shot, destroyed. These are international provocateurs, fascism's most vicious agents."[30] Stalin entrusted Wang to inform him directly about all questions pertaining to the possibility of a "Trotskyite" degeneration of the communist movement in China, and with Stalin's blessing, Wang had no doubts that he could succeed in bringing the entire party under his control.

As soon as he arrived in Yan'an, Wang Ming informed Mao and the leaders of the CCP of Stalin's latest military and political directives. He demanded an immediate special session of the Politburo to discuss the situation. Mao, Luo Fu, and the others were forced to submit. The meeting lasted six days, from December 9 through 14, and took place under Wang's de facto leadership. How could it be otherwise? After all, he was Stalin's envoy!

Wang unequivocally condemned the decisions of the Luochuan Conference, thereby coming out against Mao's policies. If the war was the main concern of the CCP and the "fight for national independence and freedom, and the unity of the country and the people" was the order of the day, then it followed that all work should be subordinated to the united front.[31] Wang asserted the need to cooperate as closely as possible with Chiang Kai-shek "to mobilize the strength of the Chinese people," avoiding any independent actions that might harm the unity of China in the struggle against the Japanese aggressors.[32]

Wang Ming and Dimitrov were not thinking of the CCP; their main objective was that active resistance to the Japanese in China would, ultimately, help make the Soviet Union more secure. Mao objected and tried to ground his position philosophically. Two months before he moved to Yan'an, he had begun to show a lot of interest in the subject of Bolshevik philosophy, and up till early July 1937, in addition to his beloved poetry, he continued to study it, mainly relying on Chinese translations of two Soviet textbooks and one article published in the *Great Soviet Encyclopedia*. These works were written by officials of the Communist Academy, the Leningrad philosophers Ivan Shirokov and Arnold Aisenberg, as well as the Moscow "leading lights" Mark Borisovich Mitin and Isaak Petrovich Razumovskii.*[33] All were dyed-in-the-wool Stalin-

---

* It is interesting that most scholars erroneously identify the editor of one of the philosophical works that influenced Mao as one M. Shirokov, even though it was the rather well-known philosopher and party official Ivan Mikhailovich Shirokov (1899–1984), who, subsequently, in 1945–46, served as the acting head of propaganda for the Leningrad municipal party committee.

ists who, in the words of Mitin, the most distinguished of them, were "guided by one idea: how best to understand each word and each thought of our beloved and wise teacher Comrade Stalin and how to convert them and apply them to the solution of philosophical problems."[34]

Two textbooks and one article, albeit a very long one, were hardly enough to turn Mao into a great philosopher. But he was a diligent student. He studied the works attentively and appreciated their categorical logic and politicized and didactic method of expression, typical of Stalinist social science. He was particularly impressed by the law of unity and the struggle of opposites that Soviet philosophers defined as the foundation of materialist dialectics.[35] The conclusions that he drew from his reading were entirely in the spirit of Marxism: "The purpose of studying philosophy is not to satisfy one's curiosity but, rather, to change the world."[36] He applied this Marxist formula to the realities of his own country.

In the spring and summer of 1937, Mao even gave a series of lectures on dialectical materialism to the students of the Anti-Japanese Military-Political University, which had opened in Yan'an not long before. Sticking closely to the text and borrowing the basic propositions of the Soviet philosophers entirely without attribution, he again related these to the tasks of the Chinese revolution. "The Chinese proletariat, having assumed at the present time the historical task of the bourgeois-democratic revolution, must make use of dialectical materialism as its mental weapon," he said.[37]

His expansive presentations (each lecture lasted for four hours, and the entire course took more than 110 hours) left an enormous impression on his listeners. Mao gained tremendous respect from his students as a man who had grasped the unfathomable, and soon parts of his lectures were published in the university journal.[38]

Proceeding from his new dialectical propositions, at the December plenum Mao also tried to prove that, "In the united front 'peace' and 'war' represent the unity of opposites. . . . There is a question of who will win over the other, the Guomindang or the communist party. The Guomindang has been politically influenced by the communist party. . . . Speaking in general terms, [we must conduct] an independent and autonomous guerrilla war in the mountainous area under the comparatively centralized command [of the Guomindang]."[39] But Wang Ming's demagogy won the day.[40] With support from Kang Sheng, Chen Yun, and several other members of the Politburo, Wang presented himself as the only true interpreter of Moscow's directives, thereby undercutting Mao's position. Later, Mao recalled that after Wang Ming's return, his own "authority didn't extend beyond" his "cave."[41] (After He Zizhen's departure, Mao often lived in his cave home even though he still had his house in Yan'an.)[42]

Mao noted sarcastically in January 1938, "I am just starting to study military questions, but for the time being I cannot write an article in this domain.

It would be somewhat better [for me] to study philosophical works a while longer before writing anything, and there would seem to be no immediate urgency."[43]

Of course, this did not mean that Mao was conceding the argument to Wang Ming. Quite the opposite. Throughout the winter of 1937–38 and all of the following spring he prepared his counterattack. One reason Mao could focus on intraparty struggles was that Zizhen was far away. In January 1938, she traveled to the Soviet Union via Gansu and Xinjiang. There, under the pseudonym of Wen Yun, she was enrolled in the Chinese party school of the Central Committee of the International Organization for Aid to Revolutionary Fighters of the USSR, located in Kuchino, a little town outside Moscow. At the same time, she underwent a series of tests at the First Kremlin Polyclinic, but the doctors decided that the shrapnel from her Long March wounds was lodged too deeply in her bones and tissue to extract.[44] Moreover, she was expecting another child. She had conceived in August 1937, shortly before her departure from Yan'an. At the time she left town she was unaware she was pregnant.

The baby, a boy named Lyova, was born on April 6, 1938, in the Sechenov Maternity Hospital in Moscow.[45] It was Zizhen's sixth child.[46] Ten months later he died of pneumonia. Grief-stricken, Zizhen had him buried in a common grave in a cemetery near Moscow.[47] All her life she was tormented by the fact that she had been unable to save him. He would prove to be her last child from Mao Zedong.

Mao's thoughts were elsewhere. The struggle for power against Wang Ming fully consumed him. Wang, speaking in Stalin's name, had won the first round, but Mao was determined to subdue this enemy as he had already subdued so many others. Only in late 1937 and early 1938 did he seem to grasp the real meaning of the Stalinist united front policy expressed by the Kremlin dictator on November 11, 1937, in his directives to the CCP leadership. As usual, Stalin's tactics were based upon deception. Stalin wanted the CCP to conduct guerrilla warfare in the Japanese rear and lure the aggressor deep into the interior of China in order to tie down his forces. At the same time the party should propagandize a new path of postwar development for China, namely, a moderate democratic one rather than a radical leftist one that would not be supported by the majority of the population. After all, Stalin plainly asserted that "the odds of speaking" about a socialist path of development for China were "worse" now than ever before. Such a policy would enable the Communist Party to expand its mass base significantly by attracting the many Chinese who opposed any sort of dictatorship, whether communist or Guomindang. Naturally, such a zigzag presupposed that the CCP would ostensibly distance itself from the USSR, which stood for proletarian dictatorship.

Mao correctly understood Stalin and laid out the initial elements of the new CCP theory in early March 1938 in an interview with the English writer and fellow traveler Violet Cressy-Marcks, whom he received in his house in Yan'an. To her question of whether the Chinese Communist Party was modeled on Russian lines, Mao replied, "On Marx-and-Lenin principles, but it is quite separate from Russia. . . . Sun Yat-sen's principles and Lenin's and Marx's doctrines were for the betterment of the people, and so far in China the two principles coincide."

"And if in working out the experiment it was found later that they didn't?" probed Cressy-Marcks.

"Later it must be left to the people to say what they want," Mao replied, for the first time not referring to the development of the democratic revolution into a socialist one.

"Do you think collective farming good?" Cressy-Marcks continued.

"Yes, it would be bound to be good if we had the implements to give the people as in Russia," Mao explained, obviously suggesting that China had a long way to go before it would reach socialism.[48]

Then, at the beginning of May, Mao expressed himself on this subject more definitively in a conversation with an official of the American embassy, the Marine officer Evans Carlson, who was visiting Yan'an. This is what Carlson reported to President Franklin Roosevelt:*

> I had two long talks with Mao Tse-tung [Mao Zedong]. He is a dreamer, of course; a genius. And he has an uncanny faculty of piercing through to the heart of a problem. I questioned him especially about the plans of the Chinese Communist Party when the war shall be over. He replied that the class struggle and the agrarian revolution as such would be given up—until the nation has passed through the preparatory stage of democracy. He felt that the state should own the mines, railways and banks, that cooperatives should be established, and that private enterprises should be encouraged. With regard to foreign capital he felt that those nations which are willing to meet China on a basis of equality should be encouraged to invest. He was very friendly and cordial.[49]

Recalling his conversations with Mao two years later, Carlson added, "[H]e said, 'Communism is not an immediate goal, for it can be attained only after decades of development. It must be preceded by a strong democracy, followed

---

* In the mid-1930s Captain Carlson served as one of Roosevelt's bodyguards and became a friend to the president. Before his departure for China in July 1937, he received a letter from the president requesting that he inform him privately ("just between us") about everything going on in China. For reasons of confidentiality, Carlson had to address his correspondence to the president's secretary, Marguerite "Missy" LeHand.

by a conditioning period of socialism.' " In this connection Carlson wrote: "There was certainly nothing very radical about these points." [50]

Prior to his meeting with Mao, from December 1937 until February 1938, Carlson inspected the troops of the Eighth Route Army that were operating in the Japanese rear in Shanxi province. There he spoke with Zhu De and others close to Mao. He drew just one conclusion from all these meetings: "The Chinese Communist group (so-called) is not communistic in the sense that we are accustomed to use the term. . . . I would call them a group of Liberal Democrats, perhaps Social-Democrats (but not the Nazi breed). They seek equality of opportunity and honest government. . . . [I]t is not Communism according to the connotation with which they are familiar." [51] We do not know if Roosevelt believed his former bodyguard, but it is obvious that a new conception of the Chinese revolution was beginning to take final shape. Along with Zhu De and several other CCP leaders who shared his view, Mao began to disseminate it effectively.

Meanwhile, the situation on the battlefronts continued to deteriorate. On December 13, Nanjing, the capital of the country, fell. Over the next several days more than 300,000 people were killed by Japanese soldiers. Twenty thousand women were raped. The Central Government evacuated to Wuhan.

Soon after, on December 17, Wang Ming, whom the Politburo had chosen to head the Changjiang (Yangzi River) Bureau of the Central Committee, flew to Wuhan as well, creating a power base parallel to that in Yan'an. There he advocated a version of the united front that stressed cooperation with Chiang Kai-shek and the Guomindang rather than Mao's version, which paid lip service to unity but emphasized the domestic struggle for power.[52] Flexible as ever, Zhou Enlai, who had been tasked since 1936 with establishing and strengthening cooperation with the Guomindang, instantly came over to Wang's side, as did Kang Sheng, Zhang Guotao, and Bo Gu. At Yan'an in late February–early March 1938, the members of Wang's faction waged open battle at a meeting of the Politburo against the supporters of Mao Zedong. Neither side, however, was able to best the other. For a time the balance of forces within the party leadership was approximately even.

At this point Mao decided to send one of his closest confidants to Moscow to explain the situation and request instructions. Apparently acting on the rule that "failures add to experience," he chose Ren Bishi. The eternally gloomy Ren, who was always complaining about his health, felt guilty toward Mao for having taken part in the merciless persecution against him in the early 1930s. On March 5, along with his wife, Chen Congying (also known as Zheng Song), and the sister of the deceased Cai Hesen, Cai Chang (Russian name Rosa Nikolaeva), Ren left for Lanzhou, the capital of Gansu province, and from there flew to Moscow in mid-March via Xinjiang. Mao Zedong's fight for undivided power in the CCP had entered its final stage.

22

CONSOLIDATING CONTROL
OVER THE CCP

Despite Wang Ming's ambition, Mao was hardly perturbed. The wily Wang knew how to produce an impression by playing on his Moscow connections, but Stalin did not envision him as the leader of the CCP. The propaganda campaign to exalt Mao in the Soviet Union continued. Still, relations between Mao and Stalin were not always smooth, and during the Xi'an Incident they had even become rather tense. Moreover, Wang Ming skillfully presented himself as the Kremlin's man. Thus, when dispatching his emissary to Moscow, Mao naturally wondered how the "great" Stalin would react to the CCP's intraparty problems.

Ren Bishi was engaged in a delicate mission in Moscow. He could not openly oppose Wang Ming, since he was not certain that Mao's understanding of Stalin's tactic was correct, but he needed to secure decisive recognition of Mao as the main leader of the CCP. He began by stepping cautiously. Shortly after his arrival in mid-April, he presented an extensive report on China to the Presidium of the Comintern. He said that after the arrival of "Comrade Wang," who transmitted the Comintern's instructions, the CCP corrected all its errors and now the Central Committee, represented by Mao, was doing everything right.

He received no reply to his presentation. In mid-May, feeling quite anxious, he delivered a lengthy report to a session of the Presidium of the ECCI in which he increased his praise of Wang Ming and again strived to dissipate any possible doubts of the Comintern leaders regarding Mao Zedong. He conveyed the message that Mao was no less faithful to Moscow than Wang; that he had no problems with the united front; therefore, it was best to make no changes in the leadership of the Chinese Communist Party. Let Mao remain at the helm![1]

The result of his efforts was that the Comintern ultimately adopted the resolution that Mao needed. After Dimitrov consulted with Stalin in mid-June the ECCI declared "its full agreement with the political line of the [Chinese] communist party," and on this occasion even supported Mao Zedong's policy to pursue guerrilla warfare in the Japanese rear and preserve the complete political and organizational autonomy of the Communist Party in the united front.[2] It also approved the choice of Mao as general secretary of the Central Committee, in place of Luo Fu. In early July 1938, Dimitrov transmitted this resolution to Wang Jiaxiang, acting head of the CCP delegation to the Comintern, who was intending to return to China. Ren Bishi, who was succeeding Wang Jiaxiang, was present at the conversation.[3] Dimitrov said,

> You must tell everyone that it is necessary to support Mao Zedong as the leader of the Communist Party of China. He has been tempered in practical struggle. Such persons as Wang Ming should no longer fight for the leadership. . . . Only by unifying the CCP can a [unified] faith be created. In China the key to national resistance to Japan is the anti-Japanese united front and the key to the united front is the unity of the CCP. The victory of the united front depends upon the unity of the party and the cohesion of [its] leadership.[4]

After returning to China, Wang Jiaxiang reported Moscow's decision at a Politburo meeting on September 14.[5] Li Weihan, a participant in the meeting, recalled that "[a]t the meeting Wang Jiaxiang conveyed . . . Dimitrov's point of view [actually, it was Stalin's point of view, Dimitrov only acted as his mouthpiece] which incontrovertibly indicated that the leader of the Chinese people was Mao Zedong. Dimitrov's words produced an enormous impression upon those present. From that time on our party had a better and clearer understanding of Mao Zedong's leading position; the question of a united party leadership was resolved."[6] Mao was pleased. Several years later, in June 1945 at the Seventh Congress of the party, he acknowledged that "[i]f it had not been for the Comintern's instruction it would have been very difficult to solve the problem [of the leadership]."[7] At this time, supporting Wang Jiaxiang's election to the Central Committee, Mao reminded the delegates that "[u]pon his return from Moscow, he succeeded in perfectly conveying the Comintern's line."[8]

At long last he was able to celebrate victory. Thereafter Mao had no more serious rivals in the party. Six months earlier, in April 1938, unable to bear his isolation, Zhang Guotao had fled from Yan'an to Hankou and quit the CCP. Mao, Luo Fu, and other party leaders formally ratified his expulsion from the party and accused the deserter of "opportunism." The Presidium of the ECCI affirmed this decision.[9]

After making his choice in the mid-1930s in favor of Mao Zedong, Stalin continued his efforts to strengthen the vertical control of his favorite over the Chinese Communist Party. Only by transforming the CCP into a Russian-style, leader-focused party (that is, by Stalinizing the party) could its victory in the future civil conflict with the Guomindang be assured. The Stalinization of the CCP required intensification of the cult of the leader-thinker and the complete suppression of intraparty opposition, even if it had to be fabricated in the event that no real opposition existed. In all of this Stalin could help Mao greatly.

In 1938 a campaign to propagate Mao's cult of personality unfolded with renewed vigor in the USSR. The leader of the CCP was presented as a "wise tactician and strategist" who had enriched world military thought with his "brilliant theory" of anti-Japanese guerrilla war. Mao's formula of "the enemy advances, we retreat; the enemy camps, we harass; the enemy tires, we attack; the enemy retreats, we pursue" was even accorded a kind of mystical significance.[10] An abridged translation of Edgar Snow's *Red Star Over China,* from which Mao's self-critical comments about his childhood and adolescence had been excised, was rushed into print. The text of the book was edited to bring out more clearly Snow's main point: Mao Zedong is

> an accomplished scholar of Classical Chinese, an omnivorous reader, a deep student of philosophy and history, a good speaker, a man with an unusual memory and extraordinary powers of concentration. . . . It is an interesting fact that many Japanese regard him as the ablest Chinese strategist alive. . . . He appears to be quite free from symptoms of megalomania, but he has a deep sense of personal dignity, and something about him suggests a power of ruthless decision when he deems it necessary.[11]

Several months earlier, a translation of Mao's autobiography from Snow's book was published in the journal *Internatsional'naia literatura* (International literature).[12] In 1939, the State Publishing Association issued a canonical biographical sketch of Mao, based on newly edited notes of Snow that were partially supplemented by information from the ECCI.[13] A brochure titled "Mao Zedong, Zhu De (Leaders of the Chinese people)" also appeared on Moscow bookshelves. This booklet, written by Emi Siao (Xiao San), Mao's fellow student in Changsha who was then living in Moscow, presented Mao as the "model" leader of the anti-Japanese struggle and of the Chinese communist movement.[14]

Almost immediately after receiving news of Stalin's blessing, Mao engaged in propagating his own cult of personality. An important milestone was the convening in September 1938 of the Sixth Enlarged Plenum of the Central Committee, a prolonged forum that stretched from September 29 to November 6, at which Mao spoke at great length. Numerous problems had to be resolved, foremost among them the task of laying an ideological foundation for his dictatorship. Mao wholly accomplished this task. His lengthy report, which he read over the course of three days, stunned his audience. Everyone was particularly struck by the seventh section, "The Place of the Chinese Communist Party in the National War," in which Mao sketched what was to become the canonical history of the party:

> Broadly speaking, in the last seventeen years our Party has learned to use this Marxist weapon—the method of struggle on two fronts in ideology, in politics, and in work, opposing Right opportunism, on the one hand, and opposing Left opportunism, on the other.
>
> Before the Fifth Plenum, our Party fought Chen Duxiu's Right opportunism and Li Lisan's Left opportunism. . . . After the Fifth Plenum, there were two further historic inner-Party struggles, namely, at the Zunyi Conference and in connection with the expulsion of Zhang Guotao.
>
> Because the Zunyi Conference corrected serious errors of a Left-opportunist character—errors of principle committed in the fight against the enemy's Fifth Encirclement and Suppression campaign—and united the Party and the Red Army, it enabled the Central Committee and the main forces of the Red Army to bring the Long March to a triumphant conclusion.[15]

In sum, the numerous mistakes committed within the party prior to Mao's ascension had now been corrected and the CCP under Mao's leadership was now united around the correct line.

What was demanded now of the party members, in the first instance of the cadres (*ganbu*)? Study, study, and study some more. "Once the political line has been laid down, cadres are the decisive factor," Mao said, quoting Stalin.* "We should not forget this truth. . . . Therefore, it should be our fighting task to train large numbers of new cadres in a persistent and planned way."[16] What should one study? The theories of Marx, Engels, Lenin, and Stalin. But—and here Mao was paraphrasing Lenin—one must bear in mind that "[w]e should not regard their theories as dogma, but as a guide to action." This was the main idea in his report. Mao formulated a thesis about the need to "sinify Marxism," that is, to adapt it to Chinese realities. "The history of this great nation of ours goes back several thousand years," he said, "we must sum it up critically, and we must constitute ourselves the heirs to this precious legacy. . . . There is no such thing as abstract Marxism, but only concrete Marxism . . . Marxism

---

* In a translation of this sentence into Chinese from the late 1940s and early 1950s, this statement is not in quotation marks, that is, it is presented as Mao Zedong's own revelation. In what became the classical formulation, it goes as follows: "Once the political line is established, the decisive factor is cadres."

applied to the concrete struggle in the concrete conditions prevailing in China. . . . Marxism apart from Chinese peculiarities . . . is merely an empty abstraction." * Mao further asserted, "We must put an end to foreign formalism. There must be less repeating of empty and abstract refrains; we must discard our dogmatism and replace it with a new and vital Chinese style and manner, pleasing to the eye and to the ear of the Chinese common people."[17]

The text of the report quickly became known in Moscow (at the end of January 1939, Lin Biao, who had come to the Soviet Union for medical treatment and study, brought it with him),[18] but no negative reaction ensued. Nor could it have. Mao's policy regarding the ideological foundation of "Chinese Marxism" corresponded to Stalin's tactical line. Moreover, it expressed the desire of the newly blessed leader of the CCP to present himself to the members of his party as a great theoretician, something Stalin understood.

Mao's personal life, like his political life, gradually began to fall into place. The harsh winter of 1937–38 passed and with it the bitter aftertaste of his quarrel with his wife, who had left him. What sense was there in crying over the past or passing the days in solitude? Dozens of young women were streaming into Yan'an from every corner of the country, attractive women who were revolutionary-minded and devoted to the party's cause. Among the newly arrived beauties two stood out: the Shanghainese film star Lan Ping ("Blue Apple") and the Cantonese singer Li Lilian. They had come to Yan'an in late August 1937, not long before Zizhen's departure. Mao had paid no attention to them, because he was too deeply immersed in his family drama. Kang Sheng and Otto Braun, however, took advantage of this opportunity. The former already knew Lan Ping; in the early 1930s she had even been his lover. Meeting her in Yan'an awakened old feelings, and Kang began to drop in on his old flame. Braun was interested in Li Lilian. She was married, but this did not bother him. Throughout his sojourn in Yan'an, he suffered terribly from loneliness. He was bitter after his defeat at the Zunyi Conference. Mao, Luo Fu, and the army commanders openly despised him. He shared a small house with the American doctor George Hatem (Ma Haide), who had come to Shaanxi in July 1936 with Edgar Snow and then stayed on with the Chinese communists.[19] It is hard to imagine two people more different than Hatem and Otto Braun, yet the friendly doctor sympathized with his lovestruck housemate. Hatem was sociable and good-hearted with large, "sad, Semitic eyes that were as black as olives."[20] Braun, a typical Aryan, was not known for his complaisance. He

---

* It is worth noting that just a year before the Sixth Plenum, in his lectures on dialectical materialism, Mao expressed precisely the opposite thought. "[We] must," he said then, "struggle with all the outworn philosophies now existing in China, raise the flag of criticism on the ideological front throughout the whole country, and thereby liquidate the philosophical heritage of ancient China." Evidently he did not stay in one place.

spurned all foreigners who came to Yan'an, including Agnes Smedley and Peggy Snow, as agents of the bourgeois special services. The only exception he made was George, with whom Braun not only shared lodging, but also went hunting. He wanted to return to the USSR but Moscow denied him permission. Then he met the lively Li Lilian, who loved good food, Ping-Pong, dancing, and talking about politics and art. In 1938 she deserted her husband and married Otto Braun, who stunned her with his charm offensive.[21]

Lan Ping had her own dreams. She knew she had no future with Kang Sheng, who was married and had no intention of getting divorced. She needed to find something more permanent. The young but already experienced woman decided to go for broke. Her objective was Chairman Mao himself. Lan Ping was ambitious, vain, and purposeful. She was born in March 1914 in Zhucheng, a small town in Shandong province, in the family of Li Dewen, a wealthy carpenter. Her father bestowed her first, child's name, Shumeng, meaning "pure and unsophisticated," but the life that awaited her was neither simple nor serene. Her alcoholic father mercilessly beat her mother until finally mother and daughter fled their home. After ten years of just scraping by, they went to live with the girl's maternal grandfather in Jinan, the large and bustling provincial center of Shandong. The young girl, who at the age of seven had been given a new, grown-up name, Yunhe ("Crane in the Clouds"), retained only one good memory of Zhucheng. The young director of the elementary school where she had studied Confucius for a while was very thin and tall and wore big round eyeglasses. She remembered how he had looked at her, how he had spoken to her, which for some reason made him very anxious, and how he had once invited her and her mother to his house. He needed a housemaid, and after hemming and hawing a bit, he offered the job to Yunhe's mother. The young girl's heart melted from his glances and his words, and her temples throbbed. The director was named Mr. Zhang. Many years later she would meet him in Qingdao, and an irresistible force would fling them together. The former director would then bear a different name, Zhao Yun, which he would soon change again to Kang Sheng. By then Yunhe had turned into a beautiful woman, left home with a theatrical company, and, by the early 1930s, became a well-known provincial actress. She had married, gone through a platoon of lovers, and had been living a Bohemian life. She had only one physical defect—six toes on her right foot.[22] But this seems not to have repelled any of her many admirers.

In Qingdao, Kang Sheng brought Yunhe into the unfamiliar world of revolutionary politics and introduced her to members of underground organizations. She soon remarried, this time to a colleague of Kang's. Under the influence of her communist husband, she became a member of the Communist Party in February 1933. Two months later, when her husband was imprisoned, she fled Shanghai in a panic, and attempting to cover her traces she changed her name again, to Li He. But in the fall of 1934 she, too, was arrested, then released three months later under still mysterious circumstances. Either they "believed in the innocence" of a beautiful woman, as she asserted subsequently, or they received from her the required confession. In any case, she was let go and soon became known on the Shanghai stage and in film by the name of Lan Ping. Her greatest triumph came from her portrayal of Nora, the destroyer of bourgeois values, in Henrik Ibsen's play *A Doll's House.* Her cinematic roles also gained her considerable attention, including in such strikingly anti-Japanese films as *Old Bachelor Wang* and *Twenty Cents.* It seemed that everything was going well for her: she had a new husband, a string of lovers, crowds of admirers, and a splendid lifestyle. But in August 1937, the Japanese attacked Shanghai.

Moved by the patriotic upsurge, the effusive, passionate, and romantic Lan Ping took off for Yan'an with her latest lover, the director of *A Doll's House.* The Communist Party's appeals to organize an anti-Japanese united front resonated with her, as they did with other leftist Chinese artists. In Yan'an she was destined to play her greatest role, as the devoted, tender, and solicitous new lady friend of the Leader. She was a formidably clever and crafty woman, delicate and elegant as a mountain bloom but possessing enormous inner strength and indomitable energy.

Her old friend Kang Sheng greatly assisted her in this undertaking. Soon after Ren Bishi's departure for Moscow, Kang began to build bridges to Mao, and toward this end he decided to make use of his faithful woman friend. At the end of April, a favorable opportunity presented itself. Mao gave a talk at the Lu Xun Academy of the Arts, a new educational institution established to train politically reliable cultural workers. Lan Ping, newly signed up as an instructor at the academy, arrived in time to take a seat in the front row, sporting a thick notebook. She listened avidly to every word spoken by the Chairman, and rapidly wrote everything down in her notebook at almost stenographic speed. Naturally Mao noticed her. Among the sunburned peasant faces her tender little white face stood out clearly.

After the lecture she approached him.

"I still have so much to learn," she said timidly. "But thanks to you, I know that I can deepen my knowledge."

"Well, if there's anything you don't understand, don't be shy. Come visit me, and we'll talk it over," he replied, looking her up and down. She was slender, very modest, wearing two braids tied in back of her head with a ribbon.

Then Kang Sheng took over. Taking advantage of the fact that he and Lan Ping were from the same town, he began praising the excellence of Zhucheng women to Mao Zedong. Several days later he invited Lan Ping to meet with the Leader. But it was not until September 1938, four months later, that Lan Ping became Mao's lover and one of his secretaries. Soon afterward she decided to change her name again. The past was over, and she asked Mao to pick out some characters that he liked. He chose Jiang Qing ("Azure River").* Mao's latest romance, however, engendered terrible gossip in Yan'an. Naturally, the puritanical wives of party officials were scandalized. Again they pitied Zizhen, who had gone through fire and flood with them, immediately conceived a hatred for Jiang Qing, and began to bad-mouth her. A report that the Central Committee received from Liu Xiao, one of the leaders of the party organization in Shanghai, added fuel to the fire. He reported that Yunhe/Lan Ping had behaved "in an unworthy fashion" in prison, and that she might possibly be a "Guomindang spy."

Kang Sheng once again intervened, assuring everyone of Jiang Qing's political reliability. The Chairman himself finally put an end to the dispute. "I will marry her," he said to his comrades in the party. The wedding took place on November 19, 1939.[23] Kang Sheng celebrated: having betrayed Wang Ming, he had now gained the Chairman's full trust via Jiang Qing. He would soon become one of the persons closest to Mao and the man Mao entrusted with leadership of the party's secret services.

Poor Zizhen! Only now did she have to drain the same bitter cup that Kaihui had earlier. When she learned of her husband's new passion, she was stunned. Mao sent her a formal notice of divorce and two years later sent their daughter to her in Moscow. Thus their rupture was now complete. All her hopes were gone. She was overjoyed to meet with her daughter, whom she hadn't seen in three and a half years, but it was a bitter sort of joy. Initially, she and Jiaojiao lived in a rest home belonging to the International Organization for Aid to Revolutionary Fighters in the village of Monino, near Moscow, where Zizhen had been undergoing treatment. She had grown weary of political study as well as with public work, and she didn't want to do anything. Therefore, she only managed a grade of C in her elementary exam on the foundations of Marxism-Leninism.

In the fall of 1941, after World War II had begun, she and her daughter were transferred to the International Orphanage in Ivanovo, where Zizhen started working as a governess and Jiaojiao studied. (In the children's home Mao's daughter was called Tanya Chao Chao.)[24] There too were both of Mao's sons, Anying and Anqing, who had come to Moscow in the fall of 1936. They had traveled for almost six months from Shanghai to the USSR via Hong Kong, Marseille, and Paris. Both of these "heroes" had finally reached "the shores of socialism" in November 1936 and were enrolled in the Ivanovo orphanage under the names of Sergei Yunfu [Yongfu] and Nikolai Yunshou [Yongshou] respectively.[25] They became acquainted with Zizhen in the spring

---

* Many years later, in a conversation with the American writer Roxane Witke, Jiang Qing denied that Mao had thought up her new name. She claimed to have invented it herself. Jiang Qing's assertion, however, contradicts other sources.

of 1938, and thereafter generally got along well with her. They even began to call her "Mother." Then they too received news of their father's new marriage, but didn't know whether these rumors were true or not. In any case they tried not to ask Mama He about them. "We tried to distract her in whatever ways we could," Anying and Anqing recalled later. "We told her all kinds of stories and anecdotes and spoke about the situation in the country and events abroad. But in these conversations there was one name we never mentioned, but which we thought of all the time, namely, Mao Zedong." [26]

Via their sister Jiaojiao, their father sent them a letter dated January 31, 1941. After lamely excusing himself for not having replied to their letters, Mao urged his children to focus their studies on the natural sciences rather than politics. This would earn them the respect of others and make them happy. Perhaps the veteran of bruising intraparty conflicts wanted to spare his own offspring the psychological traumas he himself had endured in the political arena. Asserting that he had no wish "to interfere in your affairs," a rather curious wish for a father who, in the same letter, claimed that he worried a lot about his children, Mao wrote that they were responsible for determining their own futures. With his own father, of course, Mao had had to struggle to escape the orbit of Confucian filial piety, but that was hardly the case with his own children whom he had virtually abandoned to a harsh fate. In place of parental love, of which the letter reveals few traces, Mao promised to send them more books, the treasured companions of his own youth.[27]

This was the second letter from the father to his sons since he had left them early on the morning of August 31, 1927. The first, a brief note of seven lines, he had sent a year and a half earlier, on August 26, 1939.[28] He had sent that one via Zhou Enlai, who had flown to Moscow for medical treatment along with his wife and their adopted daughter.

This was hardly a very warm letter, and it said nothing about his new marriage despite the fact that Jiang Qing had given birth five months earlier to a daughter. On August 3, 1940, Li Na (Li "Slow") was born in a Yan'an hospital. As he did for his older daughter Jiaojiao, Mao gave Li Na the surname of his own pseudonym Li Desheng. He took her personal name from the same Confucian quotation, "A gentleman should be slow to speak and prompt to act" (*junzi yu na yu yan er min yu xing*).[29]

By the time of Li Na's birth, Mao already had complete power over the CCP and his armies controlled several guerrilla areas behind Japanese lines. Almost two years earlier, the Japanese Imperial Army had seized large parts of northern, eastern, and central China as well as several ports in the south and southeast of the country. In late October 1938, both Canton and Wuhan fell, and the Guomindang government moved to Chongqing, in Sichuan province. It had no intention of surrendering but lacked the strength for a large offensive. Mao took advantage of the fact that the front had stabilized to establish communist power in a number of districts located deep in the Japanese rear. The Japanese Imperial Army was only able to occupy the cities and other important strategic objectives as well as the lines of communication. The Japanese only rarely foraged in the countryside for provisions, and Guomindang officials had completely lost control. Mao began to send armed detachments into these rural areas to fill the power vacuum. His strategy was successful. By 1940, more than ten CCP base areas had been established behind Japanese lines—for propaganda purposes, the communists called these "liberated areas"—and new ones were quickly being added.[30]

In Yan'an, meanwhile, Mao formulated the idea of the "New Democratic revolution" as a special stage in the development of the liberation movement in China. He was aided in this effort by his capable secretary Chen Boda, who had come to Yan'an in 1937. In 1938, on Mao's instructions, this "plump, clumsy man in glasses with disproportionately large ears and deeply set eyes"[31] had begun to deal with theoretical questions concerning the Chinese communist movement. Mao first set forth his new theory in mid-December 1939, in an article titled "The Chinese Revolution and the Chinese Communist Party," coauthored with "several comrades," including Luo Fu and Chen Boda. Later, he developed this theme in January 1940, in a special brochure, *On New Democracy*. Mao started with the proposition that because China was a "colonial, semicolonial, and semifeudal" country (the phrase was Luo Fu's),[32] what China needed to achieve was not a socialist but rather what he called a "new-democratic" revolution. Appealing more to the nationalist sensibilities than to the social strivings of his fellow countrymen, he talked about the need for social reforms in the spirit of Sun Yat-sen's Three Principles of the People. He interpreted these principles very broadly, promising to guarantee the right of private property after the revolution, to stimulate national entrepreneurship, and pursue a policy of protectionism, that is, to attract foreign investors under strict state control. He called for tax reduction, the development of a multiparty system, the organization of a coalition government, and the implementation of democratic freedoms. The theory of New Democracy differed from old-style Western democracy, according to Mao, because it would be implemented under the leadership of the Communist Party. However, the party was no longer presenting itself as the political organ of the working class, but rather as the organization of the united revolutionary front striving to unite "all the revolutionary people." The future China, Mao asserted, would not be a dictatorship of the proletariat but "a joint dictatorship of all revolutionary classes"; in the economy of the new country, state, cooperative, and private capitalist property would coexist.[33]

In his struggle with the Guomindang, then, Mao was beginning to lean on the democratic traditions of Chinese society. In the first half of the twentieth century, democracy was hardly an unknown concept in China. At that time,

among the many factors stimulating a significant revitalization of Chinese political culture were the victory of the antimonarchical 1911 Revolution, the
proclamation of a republic on January 1, 1912, the adoption of the Constitution of 1912, elections to the first parliament and parliamentary debates, Sun
Yat-sen's struggle against Yuan Shikai and his plans to restore the monarchy,
the New Culture movement of 1915, the anti-Japanese May Fourth Movement of 1919, the collaboration and confrontation between the CCP and the
GMD during the first united front of 1924–27, and much else. All these events
strengthened the democratic inclinations of the Chinese intelligentsia, the segment of society that was expected to accept New Democracy enthusiastically.[34]

As the foundation of his concept Mao used Stalin's November 1937 directives that he himself had developed in a series of talks in 1938. His new works
expanded upon those talks but contained nothing new in principle. His new
policy fully corresponded with Stalin's geopolitical strategy. It is worth noting
that just when Mao was elaborating his conceptual foundation, Stalin began to
think about dissolving the Comintern.[35] This was not a coincidence.

In the second half of the 1930s, Stalin himself was working very hard to develop new tactics for the international communist movement. His conversation
with Wang Ming and Kang Sheng in November 1937 is just one bit of evidence.
He aimed at deceiving not only the Chinese intelligentsia and Chiang Kai-shek,
but the entire bourgeois West. He wanted them to believe that with the exception of the CPSU, of course, beginning with the Seventh Comintern Congress,
communist parties had dropped the struggle for socialism and had substituted
the idea of building a humanitarian society of "popular democracy." (There was
no essential difference between what Stalin and Mao stood for since the former
spoke of "people's democracy" and the latter of "new democracy.") In their quest
to seize power in the postwar period, communist organizations posing as national "democratic" parties would improve their chances of gaining control of a
broad coalition of nationalist forces. It was precisely because he wanted to "dupe"
the capitalists that Stalin finally dissolved the Comintern. He did this in May
1943, but the idea had germinated already in 1940.[36] It was deception that constituted the foundation of Stalin's "people's democracy," and in his private talks with
his comrades in arms the Bolshevik leader made no secret of it.[37] As always, Mao
was in luck. He proposed his idea of New Democracy at just the right moment,
which further commended him to the Kremlin leader.

Meanwhile, in the early 1940s, Mao was able to return to intraparty matters. He had already established himself as the party's main theoretician, and
now he had to suppress the "opposition" and consolidate his cult. Otherwise,
in the tradition of Stalin, he would not feel that he was a full-fledged dictator.

The easiest thing was to settle accounts with the Trotskyites, but they
had no significance in China. In the late 1930s and 1940s there were only a
few Trotskyist organizations in China, the largest of which, the Chinese Rev-

olutionary Party, numbered all of twenty to thirty persons. Since an actual Trotskyite enemy was illusory, Wang Ming's assignment as Stalin's emissary on Trotskyite matters in China made no sense. The career of "Pavel Mif's fledgling" was nearing its end. Now it became his fate to become the leader of the "opposition" that the new "Great Leader" of the CCP had to crush.

Without Stalin's approval, Mao could not have initiated a campaign against Wang, but soon he received the go-ahead to proceed. In late 1939 and early 1940, the ECCI prepared recommendations regarding the organizational question for the Central Committee of the CCP at the forthcoming Seventh CCP Congress. Zhou Enlai was supposed to deliver these recommendations orally to Mao Zedong and the other members of the Central Committee at the end of March 1940.* In a telegram to Mao dated March 17, 1940, the Comintern chief Dimitrov wrote: "Zhou Enlai will personally inform you about everything we discussed and agreed upon regarding Chinese affairs. You need to seriously consider everything and take decisive measures completely on your own. In case of disagreement with us on some questions, please inform us promptly and tell us your reasons." [38]

A memorandum from the Personnel Department of the ECCI to Dimitrov addressed personnel matters in the CCP:

> One must bear in mind that Wang Ming possesses no authority among the old cadres of the party. . . . He was promoted to the leadership of the party at the Fourth Plenum of the CC [January 1931] under the influence of Mif [at the time of the composition of this memorandum Mif had been arrested by the NKVD (Soviet security police, a successor of OGPU) and shot as an "enemy of the people"]. . . . [I]t is recommended that the leadership of the CCP not place Wang Ming in leading roles and leading positions within the leadership of the party. It is recommended that the leadership of the party not include [current] Politburo member Kon Sin [Kang Sheng] and alternate Politburo member Fang Ling [Deng Fa] as well as Central Committee members Guan Xiangying and Yang Shangkun in the Politburo or the Secretariat and not use them for personnel, organizational, or secret service work.
>   It is recommended that Politburo and Secretariat member Bo Gu, Central Committee members Luo Man [Luo Mai, Li Weihan], Chen

---

* Ren Bishi and his wife returned to Yan'an along with Zhou and his wife. Lin Biao (under the pseudonym of Li Ting), who had come to the USSR for medical treatment in January 1939, stayed on as acting representative of the CCP to the Comintern. He discharged this responsibility until August 1941, after which he too returned to Yan'an. Subsequently, by agreement with the ECCI, the Central Committee of the CCP sent no more representatives to Moscow.

Changhao, Zhang Hao [Lin Yuying], and Kong Yuan not be placed on the Central Committee and not be used in personnel, organization work or in the central organs of the party. . . . From material supplied by the Personnel Department of the ECCI and from conversations with Zhou Enlai, Zheng Ling [Chen Lin, Ren Bishi], Mao Zemin and others, assessments have been compiled of 26 leading members of the CCP (these are attached) who may be promoted to the leading organs of the party at the Seventh Congress. Basically, these are the most trustworthy, experienced, and tempered cadres of the party who have survived difficult underground work and civil war and who are now conducting party, military, and military-political work. Of these 26 comrades the following stand out: Lin Biao, He Long, Liu Bocheng, Nie Yongcheng [Nie Rongzhen], Xiao Ke, Xu Xiangqian, Chen Guang, Deng Xiaoping, and Ye Jianying, all of whom are well-known not only in the party, but throughout the country as leaders and commanders of Eighth Route Army units; Deng Yingchao (female) [the wife of Zhou Enlai], Mao Zemin, Gao Gang, Xu Teli, Chen Yi, Liu Xiao, Zhang Qiqi [?], and Zeng Shan are all wholly tested and experienced party officials. . . .

Mao Zedong is certainly the most important political figure in the CCP. He knows China better than the other CCP leaders, knows the people, understands politics and generally frames issues correctly.[39]

The overwhelming majority of those recommended were supporters of Mao Zedong. Those whom Moscow turned thumbs down on were deemed followers of Wang Ming. Once again, the ECCI and, standing behind it, Stalin himself, helped Mao to consolidate his power. This time they even overdid it. Mao did not view Kang Sheng, who had already openly switched to his side, nor several others of these party officials as his foes. He even tried to defend Kang Sheng in one of his letters to Dimitrov. "Kon Sin [Kang Sheng]," Mao wrote, "is reliable."[40]

Soviet money also assisted in strengthening Mao's authority in the CCP. At the end of March 1940, Zhou Enlai brought Mao US $300,000 from Moscow.[41] But this was far from the final gift. The USSR continued to help the Chinese Communist Party even after Nazi Germany attacked the Soviet Union on June 22, 1941. In the Russian archives, a striking document has been preserved in the special files of the Politburo of the CPSU: a decision of the Politburo from July 3, 1941, to release to the ECCI $1 million in American dollars for assistance to the Central Committee of the Chinese Communist Party.[42] The ECCI had asked the Politburo for $2 million, but had to settle for $1 million.[43] On the very day, July 3, that Stalin first publicly acknowledged the extent of the German onslaught, the Politburo decided to send $1 million to the Central Committee of the Chinese Communist Party.[44]

Meanwhile, in 1941 Mao persisted in rewriting party history to make it serve his cult of personality. The infallible Leader must appear as a kind of savior of the nation, a prophet and a teacher at the most critical moment for the CCP. The advent of the Great Helmsman must be presented as an epochal event for which the entire course of the communist movement served as preparation. Here Mao, as always, followed the bidding of his teacher. "History sometimes demands that it be corrected," Stalin said, letting the cat out of the bag one day.[45] Mao had no doubts on this score. *The History of the Communist Party of the Soviet Union, Short Course,* a translation of which was done in Yan'an in late 1938 and 1939, served as his model.[46]

On September 8, 1941, the Secretariat of the Central Committee, under Mao's leadership, adopted a resolution to organize serious research on problems of party history. The main focus was on the period that had been the most difficult for Mao, namely, from the Fourth Plenum of the Central Committee (January 1931) to the Zunyi Conference (January 1935).[47] Two days later, at an enlarged plenum of the Politburo, Mao delivered a report on the history of intraparty struggle with the focus on dogmatists, subjectivists, and "left opportunists" during the period 1931–34. (Although he did not mention Wang Ming by name, everyone knew whom he had in mind.) In this connection, Mao emphasized, "Only those teachers who can sinify Marxism are good teachers. . . . The study of method of thought of Marx, Engels, Lenin, and Stalin, the study of *The History of the Communist Party of the Soviet Union,* will constitute the heart of our studies, and we should read more antisubjectivist writings."[48] Then he prepared a long article on the theme of "left opportunism" that was so critical that even he dared not risk publishing it. Only his closest confidants became acquainted with the article.[49]

Mao's speeches launched a campaign to reexamine party history with the objective of firmly inculcating the cult of the Leader. This campaign in February 1942 developed into a broad-scale "purge" of the party (*zhengfeng*). Its main target was Wang Ming, whom Stalin threw into the trash. Wang still enjoyed the trust of Dimitrov, who had become good friends with Wang during his work in Moscow. Therefore, the general secretary of the ECCI worried a great deal about the fate of this friend who had been transformed into Mao's main antagonist, but without Stalin's approval, Dimitrov could do nothing to help him.

Bo Gu, Luo Fu, and the other pupils of the "enemy of the people" Mif were targets as well of *zhengfeng,* which also touched Zhou Enlai for his past opposition to Mao. The campaign, however, was nothing like the Soviet purge of 1937. "The present leadership of the CCP," Mao said in January 1943, "considers the past purges in the CPSU mistaken. What is needed is a 'spiritual purge' like that now going on in the Special Region."[50] True to his principle of "treating the illness to save the patient," he didn't initiate arrests and executions, but rather ideological study (one of the witnesses called it "psychological calisthenics").[51] Yan'an was immersed in endless meetings, gatherings, and conferences at which Mao's former opponents, labeled as "dogmatists," engaged in confessions and self-criticism while unrestrainedly praising the "wisdom" of the Leader. They wrote self-denunciations and denunciations of their friends. A special commission to conduct *zhengfeng*, at the head of which Mao placed Kang Sheng, filed and arranged these in the archives.

Liu Shaoqi, who had come to Yan'an at the invitation of the Chairman in December 1942, also played a major role in the new ideological campaign. Mao had long known him but had not had close contacts with him until the early 1940s. They had first met in the summer of 1922, when the twenty-four-year-old Liu, who had just completed his six-month course at the Communist University of the Toilers of the East in Moscow, came to Changsha to do trade union work. Mao sent him to Anyuan, the mining town in western Jiangxi, to serve as Li Lisan's chief assistant in running a workers' club. Liu was just five years younger than Mao and his equal in organizational abilities. Very thin and frail-looking, he had inexhaustible energy, determination, and courage. Like Mao, he came from a peasant family in Hunan. He joined the party in December 1921 in Moscow, while studying there. Liu quickly became one of the major leaders of the national workers' movement and in 1925 he was chosen deputy chair of the All-China Federation of Trade Unions. In 1927 he became a member of the Central Committee of the CCP. At the Fourth Plenum of the Central Committee in January 1931, on Mif's recommendation he became a candidate member of the Politburo. This sponsorship, however, was not reflected in his political positions. In January 1935, during the Zunyi Conference, he supported Mao Zedong, from which time Mao had his eye upon him and appointed him to several responsible positions. After the outbreak of the Sino-Japanese War, Mao sent him to southeast China to conduct political work among communist guerrillas in the Japanese rear there. In July 1939, during one of his visits to Yan'an, Liu delivered two lectures at the Institute of Marxism-Leninism on "How to Be a Good Communist." Like Mao, he called upon all party members to engage in daily self-education, emphasizing that "[t]he test of a Party member's loyalty to the Party, the revolution, and the cause of communism is whether or not he can subordinate his personal interests absolutely and unconditionally to the interests of the Party, whatever the circumstances."[52] Two years later, in July 1941, Liu delivered a report to the party school of the Central China Bureau of the Central Committee titled "On Intra-party Struggle," which was directed against dogmatism. This report elicited special praise from Mao.[53]

It was as a "specialist" in party affairs that Mao invited Liu to Yan'an. In March 1943 his new favorite joined the newly reorganized Secretariat of the Central Committee, along with Ren Bishi. Liu also was appointed Mao's deputy on the Revolutionary Military Council and likewise headed the Organizational Department and the Investigation Bureau of the Central Committee.[54] His influence in the party grew rapidly even though formally he was not a full member of the Politburo. Mao entrusted Liu Shaoqi with major responsibility for preparing for the Seventh Congress of the CCP, originally scheduled for the spring of 1941 but repeatedly delayed and finally convened in April–June 1945. The delegates who arrived in Yan'an in 1941 had to take part over a period of two to three years in all of the activities of the *zhengfeng* movement under the control of Liu Shaoqi and Kang Sheng. The only one who refused to engage in self-criticism was Wang Ming.[55]

In early 1943 Mao increased the pressure on Wang, who had reported sick in order to avoid participating in *zhengfeng*. On January 15, 1943, Dimitrov received a disturbing message from Yan'an that Wang Ming was seriously ill.[56] The message relayed by Soviet intelligence officer Petr Vladimirov reported, "He needs treatment in Chengdu or the USSR, but Mao Zedong and Kon Sin [Kang Sheng] supposedly do not want to let him leave Yan'an, for fear that he will give out unfavorable information about them."[57]

But what could Dimitrov do? He was not an independent actor and he had to carry out Stalin's policy. Was there any way he could risk exacerbating relations with Mao on his own initiative? Trying to stall, he advised the Red Army Intelligence Directorate not to interfere in the internal affairs of the Chinese communists.[58] This, however, could not satisfy Wang Ming. At the end of January 1943, Wang sent a detailed telegram via his Yan'an-based Soviet physician, Dr. Andrei Orlov, and Vladimirov to Stalin and Dimitrov on the theme of Mao Zedong's "anti-Leninist" and "Trotskyite" activity. It was received in Moscow on February 1.[59] On February 3, however, Dimitrov also received a telegram from Mao containing sharp accusations against Wang.[60] Evidently, Mao had learned of his enemy's slanders and hastened to counterattack. The best defense was to attack.

The conflict grew sharper. On February 11, NKVD commissar Vladimir Dekanozov unexpectedly called Dimitrov to talk about Wang Ming. Dekanozov advised Dimitrov to tell Wang he should immediately contact the Soviet ambassador, Alexander Panyushkin, who could ask Chiang Kai-shek to permit Wang to leave China.[61] Apparently Dekanozov had learned through his own sources of Dimitrov's friendship with Wang Ming, and hastened to attend to this matter. Or was this a sudden provocation? It is just too strange a demarche. Why was it necessary to ask permission from Chiang rather than Mao? Most likely Dekanozov was putting Dimitrov to the test: would Dimitrov place his personal relations above the interests of the international communist movement? Dimitrov would have to sacrifice his old friend. He did nothing. Finally, on December 13, 1943, he sent Wang a pessimistic message: "As for your part[y] affairs, do your best to settle them yourselves. Intervening from here is for now inexpedient."[62] It seemed that Wang's fate was sealed.

Literally just days after this pessimistic telegram, on December 22, 1943, Dimitrov sent a personal letter to Mao urgently recommending that he not persecute Wang and requesting that he not touch Zhou Enlai. "I consider politically incorrect the campaign being waged against Zhou Enlai and Wang Ming," he wrote. "Persons such as Zhou Enlai and Wang Ming must not be severed from the party, but protected and used as much as possible for the good of the party."[63] Dimitrov must have received a directive from Stalin, or at least Stalin's approval.

What had happened in these nine days? Why did Stalin decide to protect Wang Ming? Might he have desired to use him as a counterweight against Mao in the future? Or did he recall his "merits" in the struggle against "Trotskyism"? No one knows what moved the Kremlin dictator during these cold days in late December 1943.

Dimitrov's letter of December 22 did not pass unnoticed. Mao dispatched two telegrams in reply, on January 2 and January 7, 1944. In the first he said, "Our relations with Zhou Enlai are very good. We have no intention whatsoever of cutting him off from the party. Zhou Enlai has had great success and made progress." But Mao was unwilling to retreat on the matter of Wang Ming.

> Wang Ming has engaged in various antiparty activities. This has been brought to the attention of all party cadres. But we do not want to make this known to the masses of party members. . . . Among the higher-ranking party cadres the result of studying Wang Ming's errors is that these cadres have rallied even closer together and are more united. . . . I consider Wang Ming unreliable. Wang Ming was arrested earlier in Shanghai. Several persons said that when he was in prison, he confessed to belonging to the communist party. Afterward he was released. They also spoke of his dubious ties with Mif. Wang Ming engaged in a great deal of antiparty activity.

Five days later, however, Mao retreated. He understood very well with whom he was really corresponding.

> Intra-party issues: Policy in this area is aimed at unification, at achieving unity. With respect to Wang Ming we will pursue just such a policy. As a result of the work carried out in the second half of 1943, the situation inside the party, the unity of the party has improved significantly.
>
> Please set your mind at ease. All of your thoughts and all of your concerns are close to my heart, because my thoughts and my feelings are essentially the same.[64]

After receiving the January 7 telegram, which, incidentally, Mao demonstratively sent via Vladimirov rather than his own channels, Dimitrov was finally able to relax. Mao had remained loyal to Moscow. Dimitrov wrote to him on February 25. "I was particularly heartened by your second telegram. I had no doubt you would devote the needed serious attention to my friendly observations and would take the appropriate measures dictated by the interests of the party and our common cause."[65]

On January 19, Dimitrov also sent a telegram to Wang Ming on the subject of his relations with Mao, informing his persecuted friend of his successful negotiations with his enemy.[66] One cannot say that Wang was entirely satisfied. He understood, however, that he could expect nothing more from Stalin and Dimitrov. The Kremlin chieftain did not want to see him as the leader of the CCP, but neither did he intend to let Mao tear Wang to pieces. It was time for him to submit. On March 7, Dimitrov received a reply from his old friend:

Dear G.M. [Dimitrov]!

In December and January I was given your two telegrams.

Thanks for your concerns about the CCP and about me. My relations with Mao Zedong remain as before, inasmuch as I wholeheartedly support him as the leader of the party, regardless of the personal disagreements between us in the past concerning specific aspects of the policy of the anti-Japanese united front and of the most serious campaign conducted against me during the past year on questions of intraparty life.

A comrade told me that he informed you in detail about all these issues.

I don't know what might be of interest to you in this sphere and what questions might be unclear.

Please let me know and I will respond. During the past year a campaign has been going on in the party to reexamine its entire history on the basis of the ideas and activities of Mao Zedong.

He is presented as the main representative of Chinese Bolshevism and of sinicized Marxism-Leninism.

Recognizing that you may be able to elevate the authority of the party, which is particularly important in the absence of the Comintern, I fully support this campaign in a situation in which the emphasis is on the CCP as a national proletarian party.

Toward this end I have already informed Mao Zedong and the CC both orally and in writing that the struggle against Li Lisanism and the advancement of the new policy of the anti-Japanese united front is Mao Zedong's contribution, not mine as I had earlier believed.

I also renounced all political disagreements.

I wholeheartedly thank you and dear Roza [Dimitrov's wife] for your longterm care and education of my daughter.[67]

At the Seventh Congress of the CCP, which finally took place in Yan'an from April 23 to June 11, 1945, both Zhou Enlai and Wang Ming were included as members of the Central Committee, and Zhou Enlai even strengthened his position in the upper echelons of the party. Characteristically, Mao did not open the Seventh Congress until, on his personal orders, the "ill" Wang Ming had been carried into the conference hall on a stretcher. Only then did he open the party forum with these words: "I have invited Comrades Wang Ming and Wang Chia-hsiang [Wang Jiaxiang, who had again fallen ill, was also brought to the hall on a stretcher]. This makes our congress truly a congress of unity!"[68]

The inclusion of Wang Ming and Zhou Enlai did not mean that Mao's power had been curtailed in the slightest. The disgraced Wang was no longer a significant political figure, while Zhou Enlai demonstrated such complete submission that the Great Leader of the CCP had long since realized the value of Zhou's abilities. Mao's victory was complete and decisive. He had attained a height to which no other leader in the CCP could aspire. His cult had fully matured.

It was Mao himself who chose the members of the Central Committee at the Seventh Congress, dominated all of the sessions, and defined the direction of its work and its decisions. He delivered the main report "On Coalition Government," in which he again expounded his program of New Democracy.[69] With the exception of Wang Ming, it seemed that all of the other 754 delegates representing 1.2 million party members sincerely viewed Mao as the conscience of the party. They wholeheartedly believed in their Leader and were ready to die for him.[70]

On the eve of the congress Mao successfully concluded another important forum, namely, the Seventh Enlarged Plenum of the Central Committee, which on his bidding adopted a "Resolution on Certain Historical Questions." In this new, canonical history of the party the chief role, of course, was given to Mao, and the entire course of the CCP prior to the Zunyi Conference was depicted as a chain of continuous deviations from Mao's correct line, first to the right and then to the left. In this connection, all of his real and supposed adversaries (Chen Duxiu, the "putschists," Li Lisan, Wang Ming, Bo Gu, Zhang Guotao, and even his former friend Luo Zhanglong, who in 1931 opposed not Mao but the Politburo) were stigmatized.[71]

An important measure undertaken at the congress was the adoption of a new party constitution. Liu Shaoqi delivered a report on this matter in which he surpassed all the other delegates in his unrestrained exaltation of Mao. The text of the constitution was itself remarkable in naming "Mao Zedong

Thought" as the ideological foundation of the CCP. "The Communist Party of China," it read, "guides its entire work by the teaching which unites the theories of Marxism-Leninism with the actual practice of the Chinese revolution—the Thought of Mao Tse-tung [Mao Zedong]."[72]

The term "the Thought of Mao Tse-tung" or "Mao Zedong Thought" (in Chinese *Mao Zedong sixiang*) had first been advanced by Wang Jiaxiang at the beginning of July 1943. It appeared in Wang's article "The Chinese Communist Party and China's Path to Liberation," published in the newspaper *Jiefang ribao* (Liberation daily). Prior to this, beginning in September 1940, various terms appeared in the party lexicon of the CCP including, for example, "the theories of Comrade Mao Zedong," "the ideas of Comrade Mao Zedong," "the theory and strategy of Mao Zedong," "the theory and strategy of Comrade Mao Zedong," "the viewpoints of Comrade Mao Zedong," "the views of Comrade Mao Zedong," "the policy of Comrade Mao Zedong," "the line of Comrade Mao Zedong," "the path of Comrade Mao Zedong," "the style of Mao Zedong," and even "Mao Zedongism." Wang's formula, however, was the one that took hold, despite the fact that many of the toadies preferred the term "Mao Zedongism."

Four years later, at the Second Plenum of the Seventh Central Committee on March 13, 1949, Mao himself touched upon the question of why the "ideas of the Chinese communists" should not be called an ism:

> Some people say that the ideas of Stalin are called a teaching rather than an ism because of Stalin's modesty . . . [but] modesty is not the explanation. . . . [I]n the Soviet Union there already exists Leninism, and the ideas of Stalin are congruent with this ism, they are its systematic embodiment in practical politics. It is wrong to say that both Leninism and Stalinism exist, that there are two isms. It would be precisely the same if the ideas, line, and policies of the Chinese revolution were seen as an ism. . . . It is better for us to be a branch of Marxism-Leninism.[73]

Of course, another reason was that as long ago as 1927, the term "Mao Zedongism" had been used in the Chinese Communist Party with a very negative connotation as a synonym for military opportunism. The dissident communist Ye Qing had likewise employed the term with a negative meaning when he attacked the CCP in the 1940s from the position of classical Marxism. In his work "The War of Resistance and Culture," Ye Qing asserted there was not an iota of Marxism-Leninism in Mao Zedong, but only one ism, namely, Mao Zedongism, "an ism that represented the peasant petit bourgeoisie."[74] Ye Qing's work was well-known among Chinese communists, and Mao could not ignore this.

The main point, however, was that the final choice of the term reflected the attempt of Mao and his supporters to create a purely Chinese ideology expressing equally the interests of all strata in Chinese society, from the proletariat to a segment of the landlords and of the national bourgeoisie, a kind of ideology of the united front. The term "thought" (*sixiang*) in contradistinction to "ism" (*zhuyi*) perfectly fitted this supraclass Chinese national ideology. In fact, unlike *zhuyi* this term was Chinese in origin. It was borrowed by the Japanese in the nineteenth century from classical Chinese, in which it was used to express "to comprehend," "to think," and "to recollect." The Japanese used it to signify the new Western concepts of "ideology" and "ideas." Enriched by its new content, the term *sixiang* returned to China from Japan. The term *zhuyi*, however, had no roots in Chinese tradition. In the nineteenth century the Japanese concocted the word *zhuyi* from the Chinese characters *zhu* (foundation) and *yi* (meaning) to convey the idea of the Western concepts "doctrine," "principles," and "cause." The term *zhuyi* was transmitted to China as something that was previously unknown. It was natural that *sixiang* (thought) would be much more comprehensible and closer to the broad masses of the Chinese people, who had experienced the heavy burden of the past even in recent times, than the foreign term *zhuyi* (ism).

In China even sacred views that were disseminated and expressed with the aid of new or little-known terminology elicited negative reactions and resistance. At the same time, innovative concepts and doctrines that relied upon a traditional lexicon were recognized and supported by the broad masses. Mao, as we know, had a profound understanding of Chinese political culture. Moreover, as a rule he spiced his works, especially those dealing with New Democracy, with a large number of quotations from the ancient classics that were prized and respected by the Chinese people.[75]

Mao's modus operandi was fully congruent with Stalin's policy and therefore could not evoke any dissatisfaction from that quarter. Quite the contrary. The all-powerful chief of the world communist movement must have been impressed that the Chinese Communist Party was now united around this Leader who loyally grasped his "wise" tactical line and imitated it so faithfully in all respects.

At the First Plenum of the Central Committee following the Seventh Congress, Mao was elected chairman of the Central Committee, of the Politburo, and of the Secretariat, and at the end of August 1945, at an enlarged plenum of the Politburo, he was also elected chairman of the newly reorganized Military Council of the Central Committee. He concentrated all power in his own hands. In early August 1945, the Second Session of the First Plenum of the Central Committee adopted new versions of "The Resolution on Certain Questions of History," and also of the party constitution, in which the role and significance of Mao were presented in an even more vivid fashion.[76] The Chinese Communist Party entered the final phase of the Sino-Japanese War fully armed ideologically, politically, and organizationally.

23

STALIN, MAO, AND THE NEW DEMOCRATIC REVOLUTION IN CHINA

It is quite possible that within his circle of intimates Stalin referred to Mao as a "cave Marxist," just as it is likely Mao had reason to be offended that Stalin did not trust him. But whom *did* Stalin trust? Which of his most devoted henchmen did he not despise? Whom did he consider a great Marxist? All of them were just figures on his chessboard.

Pacing in his office, Stalin simultaneously contemplated his moves in multiple games. In China a complicated and important party was in play; its victory would determine the outcome of his life's work. The triumph of the Chinese Communist Party would radically alter the correlation of forces in the world arena in favor of the USSR. If only he and Mao could succeed in neutralizing America and make Washington and its allies take at face value the New Democratic plans of the Chinese communists. If only Roosevelt, then Truman, would accept the concept of New Democracy and support the Communist Party. Then the CCP would be able gradually to "squeeze" Chiang Kai-shek and his supporters out of positions of power and next, by maneuvering among the Guomindang left and the liberals, ultimately seize power.

The game was played on a vast field. Mao did his part through interviews, articles, and speeches. The books by Edgar and Helen Foster Snow, Agnes Smedley, and other journalists as well as Evans Carlson's dispatches all hit the same target. Rapturous stories about Mao and his comrades by British journalists Freda Utley and Claire and William Band, and by American reporters T. A. Bisson, Harrison Forman, and others, all produced a substantial impression upon the public. With one voice, they all assured the world that the Chinese communists had nothing in common with Marxism-Leninism.[1] The surly dictator Chiang Kai-shek and his regime steadily lost ground in the eyes of many Americans to the "liberal" nationalist Mao and his "people's" government.

The high point of this game came in 1944–45 when Mao, Zhou, Zhu De, and other members of the Chinese communist leadership held direct talks with U.S. officials. They began in late July 1944, when a Douglas C-47 carrying nine passengers touched down at the Yan'an airport. This was the first group of the so-called Dixie Mission, composed of personnel from the State Department, the War Department, and the Office of Strategic Services (OSS), the predecessor of the CIA. It was headed by Colonel David D. Barrett, a chunky man of fifty-four who had once served as the assistant military attaché in Chongqing. He was considered a specialist on Chinese affairs, knew Chinese history and culture well, and spoke Chinese fluently. The second-ranking member was John Stewart Service, second secretary in the U.S. embassy in Chongqing, and whom Ambassador Clarence Gauss called "our government's expert on Chinese communism." In early August, a second contingent of the Dixie Mission arrived, headed by another diplomat, Raymond P. Ludden. After this, Americans came to Yan'an with increasing frequency, and they even organized trips to several "liberated areas." At the end of July 1945 there were thirty-two members of the so-called American Observer Group in Yan'an.[2]

The major conclusion that Barrett, Service, and many other members of the mission arrived at after conversations with Mao and from their personal observations was as follows:

> Politically, any orientation which the Chinese Communists may once have had toward the Soviet Union seems to be a thing of the past. The Communists have worked to make their thinking and program realistically Chinese, and they are carrying out democratic policies which they expect the United States to approve and sympathetically support.
>
> Economically, the Chinese Communists seek the rapid development and industrialization of China for the primary objective of raising the economic level of the people. They recognize that under present conditions in China, this must be accomplished through capitalism with large-scale foreign assistance. They believe that the United States, rather than the Soviet Union, will be the only country able to give this economic assistance and realize that for reasons of efficiency, as well as to attract American investment, it will be wise to give this American participation great freedom. . . .
>
> The *conclusion,* which is the continual statement of the Communist leaders themselves, is that American friendship and support is more important to China than Russian.

The members of the mission advised the American government to change its orientation toward the Chinese communists, warning that they might turn "back toward Soviet Russia if they are forced to in order to survive American-supported Kuomintang [Guomindang] attack." [3]

It is amazing how easily Mao, Zhou, and the other CCP leaders were able to deceive these experienced American intelligence officers. There was nothing they didn't promise them. In order to neutralize Washington, in the summer of 1944 Mao was even prepared to change the name of the Communist Party to New Democratic. In October 1946 this was precisely how the Communist Youth League of the "liberated areas" was renamed, and in April 1949 the entire Chinese Communist Youth League became the New Democratic Youth League. Ultimately, the party was not renamed, but all the other changes played the Americans for fools.

At the same time, Stalin and Foreign Minister Molotov, with equal mastery and cynicism, were manipulating the Americans on the diplomatic front. Molotov told W. Averell Harriman, the American ambassador to the USSR, and General Patrick J. Hurley, the new American ambassador to China, in early September 1944, "The so-called Chinese Communists are not in fact Communists at all. . . . The Soviet Government is not supporting the Chinese Communists." He confirmed this during another meeting on April 15, 1945, this time in Stalin's presence. Hurley immediately reported this to Washington. [4]

Neither Harriman nor Hurley, however, was taken in by Stalin's guile. Nor did the intelligence officers in Washington believe the communists. After analyzing the reports from China of their colleagues as well as an enormous body of other literature about the CCP, in the summer of 1945 officials of the Military Intelligence Division of the U.S. Department of War concluded, "The Chinese Communists *are* Communists. . . . The 'democracy' of the Chinese Communists is Soviet democracy. . . . The Chinese Communist movement is part of the international Communist movement, sponsored and guided by Moscow." [5] Therefore, in the final analysis neither Mao nor Stalin succeeded in deceiving the American leadership.

When World War II ended in mid-August 1945, China was still divided. The Guomindang's Central Government, backed by the United States, controlled only two-thirds of the country. The Communist Party held the Shaanxi-Gansu-Ningxia Special Region embracing thirty counties as well as eighteen large "liberated areas" in the north, east, and south of China with a total population of 95.5 million. [6] Northeast China (Manchuria) was occupied by the Soviet Army. But for the first time in many years there appeared to be a real possibility of a peaceful, democratic reunification of the country. The United States and the Soviet Union did not want a new war in China and feared that a serious conflict there could easily spill over into a much wider war. [7]

In his geopolitical calculations from 1945 to 1949, Stalin had to reckon with the U.S. monopoly of nuclear weapons. Unprepared to withstand a nu-

clear attack by the United States, he had to make every effort to avoid provoking Washington.[8] "The two US atomic bombs shook Stalin, making him
eager for a compromise," Zhou Enlai later recalled.[9] The secret Yalta Agreement, signed by the Great Powers in February 1945, as well as the Soviet-
Guomindang Treaty of Friendship and Alliance, concluded on August 14,
1945, the day Japan surrendered, also constrained initiatives on the part of
the Kremlin dictator. Through them the USSR received vital economic, political, and territorial concessions in the Far East. Particularly important was the
agreement with Chiang Kai-shek that Stalin himself called "unequal."[10] Special
protocols that accompanied the Soviet-Guomindang Treaty gave the Soviet
side the right to maintain a naval base at Lüshun (Port Arthur) for thirty years,
to control the port of Dalian in Northeast China, and to exercise joint management of the Chinese Eastern Railroad.[11] This is why Stalin after World War II
began to voice doubts about the CCP's ability to take power. He did not want to
risk through unconditional support of the CCP what he had already achieved
by aiding the United States and China in the war against Japan. He even advised Mao to come to a "temporary agreement" with Chiang Kai-shek and
insisted that Mao must go to Chongqing for a personal meeting with his sworn
enemy. As an explanation for this he could come up with nothing better than
the assertion that a new civil war might lead to the destruction of the Chinese
nation.[12]

Mao was appalled by Stalin's "treachery," but he had to submit and go talk
to Chiang. "I was compelled to go since Stalin insisted," Mao said later.[13] On
August 23, 1945, at an enlarged meeting of the Politburo, he declared, "The
Soviet Union, acting in the interest of world peace and bound by the Chinese-
Soviet treaty, cannot provide us assistance."[14] On August 28, he flew to
Chongqing with Zhou Enlai even though the Central Committee had received
letters protesting negotiations with the Guomindang from various party organizations.[15] Accompanying the CCP leaders were the Guomindang general
Zhang Zhizhong and U.S. ambassador Hurley, who had arrived in Yan'an the
day before. At the airport Mao smiled while saying good-bye to Jiang Qing and
members of the Politburo, but according to Soviet intelligence agent Vladimirov, it was obvious that he was unhappy. Mao approached the gangway of
the airplane as if "he were going to his execution." Unembarrassed in front of
the others, Mao kissed Jiang Qing on the lips in public for the first time.

The negotiations, however, led nowhere. Mao spent six weeks in Chongqing in meetings with Chiang and other Guomindang leaders as well as with
representatives of liberal public opinion, and even signed a peace agreement,
but he had no intention of abandoning his struggle for power. He was simply
making a concession to Stalin since he knew that the CCP could succeed only
if the USSR provided military and economic aid.

Now he had to wait until Stalin ("this hypocritical foreign devil," as Mao later called him)[16] changed his position. Meanwhile, he had to listen to instructions from Rodion Malinovsky, the Soviet commander in Manchuria. On Stalin's insistence, Malinovsky refused to allow Eighth Route Army forces to occupy the cities of Northeast China until after the Soviet army had withdrawn from them. "We are not interfering in domestic Chinese politics," he said. "The domestic problems of China must be resolved by the Chinese themselves."[17]

Stalin slowly began to get over his "deviation" as soon as Mao Zedong was able to assure him that the CCP could cope with all the difficulties it faced. In the fall of 1945, the Chinese communists on their own initiative managed to defeat some Guomindang troops in two consecutive battles in north China. Stalin began to waver. In October 1945, he decided to transfer to CCP troops in Manchuria part of the arms of the Kwantung Army seized by Soviet soldiers. In this connection, to be sure, he did not want to advertise his participation in the Chinese civil war, although he evidently began to consider it a reality. "All of our officers, liaison personnel, and other persons must be withdrawn from Yan'an and the zones where Mao Zedong's troops are engaged as quickly as possible," he said in reprimanding his assistants at this time. "The civil war in China is taking a serious turn, and I'm afraid that our enemies will subsequently accuse our people in these areas, who actually have no control over anything, of being the instigators of civil war in China. The sooner we withdraw them from there the better."[18]

In February–March 1946, through an irony of fate, it was Chiang Kai-shek himself who, under pressure from rightists, was beginning to conduct a short-sighted policy vis-à-vis the USSR that nudged Stalin toward unconditional support of the CCP. The Guomindang and public opinion began at this time to express dissatisfaction with the conduct of the Soviet Army in Northeast China. It goes without saying that the Soviet occupation forces were engaged in outrageous plunder: they dismantled and shipped to the Soviet Union large-scale industrial enterprises and appropriated the property not only of Japanese but of Chinese citizens as well. The result was that Manchurian industry suffered a loss of $858 million. On March 6, the Ministry of Foreign Affairs of the Republic of China issued a protest in this connection and demanded the immediate withdrawal of the Soviet Army.[19] Did Chiang Kai-shek understand then that the Chinese communists would replace the Russians? Probably not. Relying on U.S. support, he counted on his own forces occupying the cities vacated by the Soviets. But he miscalculated.

A week later, on March 13, Stalin began to withdraw his troops, an operation completed on May 3. At the same time, he called on his Chinese comrades to act vigorously and openly, even criticizing them for their excessive deference toward the United States.[20] In other words, he agreed to the entry of CCP troops into Manchurian cities, and he even insisted that Mao's army occupy them as quickly as possible, having ordered the Soviet Army to cooperate with the Chinese communists in establishing control over the local lines of communication.[21]

By then the Cold War had already commenced and Stalin finally began to provide real assistance to the Chinese communist armies. Manchuria was turned into a base for the CCP. In June 1946, a new full-scale civil war erupted in China.

Initially, it began inauspiciously for the communists. The Guomindang's 4.3 million troops significantly outnumbered the 1.2 million officers and men of the CCP armies. In the first months communist forces were forced to abandon 105 cities and towns. Chiang Kai-shek launched a broad attack along the entire front—from Shaanxi province in the west to the shore of the Pacific Ocean in the east. He also waged war in Manchuria. The Americans, to be sure, considered Chiang's actions "overambitious" and warned him that such a military campaign "would plunge China into economic chaos and eventually destroy the National Government" inasmuch as Chiang, by extending his front, was exposing his "communications to attack by Communist guerrillas," compelling his soldiers "to retreat or to surrender their arms together with the munitions which the United States has furnished them."[22]

But meanwhile the communists were losing one battle after another. On March 12, 1947, Chiang Kai-shek's air force bombed Yan'an itself and the surrounding cave encampment. In the city itself little had remained to destroy after repeated bombing by Japanese planes starting in November 1938. All that was left of Yan'an were its destroyed fortress walls and two or three streets. The party and political leadership had long since moved to caves in the northern outskirts of the city where Mao, too, lived. This was the area subjected to intensive bombardment by the B-24s and P-52s in Chiang Kai-shek's air force. Nonstop flights by about fifty planes continued over the course of a week and Guomindang infantry launched a large-scale attack on the city from the south.[23]

By March 18, Guomindang troops had advanced to within a couple of miles of the city. Mao gave the order to abandon Yan'an and that same evening departed the cave encampment with Jiang Qing and Li Na. Before climbing into his old army jeep, Mao ordered Peng Dehuai, in charge of the evacuation, to make sure that the rooms in all the caves were swept clean and that the furniture was not broken.[24] He did not want the Guomindang troops to think that the communists had fled in a panic.[25]

He set out for northern Shaanxi, where all summer, fall, and winter he led his thoroughly exhausted army along the mountain roads. At the end of March 1947, the army was renamed the Chinese People's Liberation Army (PLA). Mao's eldest son, Anying, who had returned from the USSR to Yan'an in early January 1946, experienced the bitter taste of retreat with him and Jiang Qing.

This tall and handsome youth of twenty-three with kind and sad-looking eyes had experienced a great deal. In May 1942 he had graduated from the International Orphanage; moved by an internationalist impulse, he wrote to Stalin requesting to be sent to the front against the Nazis: "I will seek to revenge the thousands and tens of thousands of Soviets who have been killed."[26] He was sent to study military science and in August 1944, Lieutenant Sergei Yunfu, as he was called, was sent to the Second Byelorussian Front as a probationary officer. He served there for only four months, but long enough to "get a whiff of powder." In November 1944, he was summoned back to Moscow, this time to study in the Institute of Oriental Studies.[27] He repeatedly requested that he be sent to China. Finally, at the end of 1945, he was granted permission. On the eve of Anying's departure, Stalin met with him at the Kremlin, wished Anying a good journey, and presented him with an engraved revolver.[28] Anying flew to Yan'an with the revolver and was never without it thereafter.

His relations with his father were complex. Anying had almost no memory of Mao, felt pity for Mama He, and was always on guard, if not worse, with Jiang Qing, who frequently complained about him to Mao. "Soon disagreements between father and son arose over theoretical issues," we read in the reports of Soviet intelligence officers.

> Mao Zedong deemed his son a "dogmatist" who knew theory, but was unfamiliar with life and working conditions in China. Mao Zedong asserted that his son had been spoiled in the USSR, and he expressed his dissatisfaction with the education he had received. In order to "teach him about life" in China, in April 1946, Mao [An]ying was sent to the countryside to work as a laborer for a rich peasant Wu Ma-you. Mao [An]ying worked as a laborer for about three months.[29]

Only then was his father satisfied. "Everyone should taste some bitterness in his life," Mao said.[30] He added, "Earlier you ate bread and drank milk, but now in China you must try northern Shaanxi millet gruel, it is very good for your health."[31]

After this he sent his son to work in the Propaganda Department of the Central Committee, and in March 1947, Anying, along with other Central Committee workers, left Yan'an and followed Mao into the mountains of northern Shaanxi. Soon Mao's other children, Anqing and Jiaojiao, returned to China from the USSR with He Zizhen. They arrived in Harbin, where they were taken care of by local CCP officials. The children chattered away in Russian (they knew almost no Chinese), but Zizhen was in a terrible state. The last two years in the USSR had been traumatic. In 1945, Jiaojiao suddenly fell terribly ill. She was diagnosed with pneumonia and was thought to be dying. Panic-stricken, Zizhen took her from the hospital, fearing the loss of her last child. The daughter pulled through, but Zizhen was pushed to the brink of insanity. The ordeal had been too much for her. Soon after her daughter's recovery, Zizhen was placed in a psychiatric hospital in the village of Zinovo, about twenty miles southwest of the city of Ivanovo. It was not until March 1947, after repeated requests by Wang Jiaxiang, who was in Moscow for medical treatment, and his wife that Zizhen was released into their care. Only then was she able to see her daughter again. Jiaojiao herself (Li Min) recalled the reunion: "I was conducted into some sort of hotel. Entering the room, I saw a middle-aged woman. I was floored! Was this mama? Pale, thin, worn out! Even her smile was feeble and her eyes were lifeless."[32] Two months later, escorted by Wang Jiaxiang and his wife, mother and children departed for their homeland.[33] Arriving in Harbin, Zizhen began to sob. "Finally, I have escaped those terrible days, from a life dependent on foreigners! Now I am really free!" she asserted.[34]

Meanwhile, in the summer of 1947, Mao carried out a brilliant plan: he dispatched a part of his forces to Chiang Kai-shek's rear to establish a new military base in the high mountain region of Dabie, in the Central Plain. This diversionary maneuver was intended to compel Chiang Kai-shek to redeploy some of his military units from the northwestern and northeastern fronts to defend the major cities of the Central Plain: Wuhan, Jiujiang, Nanchang, Shanghai, and the capital city of Nanjing itself. In this way the generalissimo's strategic plans were ruined. This operation initiated a new phase in the war— the counteroffensive of CCP forces.[35] On April 25, 1948, the communists retook Yan'an. By June 1948, the Guomindang army had contracted to 3,650,000 troops while the armed forces of the CCP had increased to 2,800,000.[36]

In the spring of 1948, after fording the Yellow River, Mao and his troops crossed into Shanxi province and continued into western Hebei at a forced march. The Working Committee of the Central Committee, headed by Liu Shaoqi and Zhu De, had been located here since the spring of 1947. Liu and Zhu lived in the village of Xibaipo, located 350 miles southwest of Beiping in the relatively inaccessible Taihang Mountains. At the end of May 1948, Mao Zedong's forces arrived in Xibaipo, which became the new capital of communist China for almost the rest of the civil war.

In Xibaipo, Mao and Jiang Qing lived in a cozy one-story house with an inner courtyard paved in stone. There was little furniture but Mao was content with the bare necessities. He spent most of his time in his office, sitting at a massive wooden table, in an oval armchair with four crooked legs. Here he met with party comrades, worked on military operations with Zhu De, and drafted party documents. Here, too, in June 1948 he had a disagreeable confrontation with his eldest son that long cast a shadow over their relationship. The straight-talking and rather naïve Anying, in a state of high excitation, accused his father of creating a "cult of the Leader" and even called him a "false Leader." He had already progressed enough in party circles to sense the atmosphere. It is impossible to say how this would have ended had Jiang Qing and Zhou Enlai not criticized Anying and demanded he write an explanation.

Somewhat chastened, the fighter against the cult of personality threw himself on the mercy of the victor. He admitted that "my action . . . has undermined father's authority." He explained that one of the reasons for his "conceit" was the respectful treatment he had received in the USSR, where he had been "treated like a 'little Leader' . . . [and] he had enjoyed comfortable material conditions and had not experienced any difficulties in his life." After Mao, Zhou, and Jiang pondered his case, a resolution was adopted to "utilize Mao [An]ying in low-level technical work in the Central Committee apparatus under the control of [Mao's secretary] Chen Boda." It was stipulated that his "living conditions should not be any different from those of other workers at this level." Mao refused to meet his son until February 1949. Anying was forbidden to show up in his father's house without permission.[37]

His family problems, of course, did not divert the Chairman from his struggle for power with Chiang Kai-shek. There in Xibaipo, Mao, Zhu De, Zhou Enlai, Liu Shaoqi, and other party leaders elaborated measures to rout the armies of Chiang Kai-shek despite the numerical superiority of Guomindang forces, U.S. support for Nanjing, and the PLA's dearth of technology and arms. Over a period of five months, from September 1948 through January 1949, the communists conducted three major strategic operations. The first was in Manchuria, the second in eastern China, and the third in the region of Beiping-Tianjin. More than half a million enemy officers and men were eliminated and several large cities, including Beiping, were taken. Just a year or two earlier, very few people had believed this possible. Back then, Mao's statement "All reactionaries are paper tigers," spoken during an interview with the American correspondent Anna Louise Strong in August 1946, had only elicited smiles.* His assertion that "[w]e have only millet plus rifles to rely on, but history will finally prove that our millet plus rifles is more powerful than Chiang Kai-shek's aeroplanes and tanks" could be taken as an eloquent polemical flourish.[38] Nonetheless, the PLA triumphed. On January 31, 1949,

---

* It is worth noting that several years later, in early 1949, the pathologically suspicious Stalin wrote to Mao, "We have reliable information that the American writer Anna Louise Strong is an American spy. . . . She has long served the Americans as a spy. We advise you not to allow her into your midst or into areas occupied by the CCP." Naturally, this was typical Stalinist gibberish. In reality, Anna Louise Strong was a passionate supporter of the communist movement in China. In 1958 she even moved to the PRC, where she lived out her days. (She died in 1970.) She was buried in Beijing in Babaoshan, the cemetery for heroes, and on her gravestone the following words were inscribed: "Friend of the Chinese people, progressive American journalist." Incidentally, Agnes Smedley, who died in 1950, was also buried at Babaoshan.

per agreement with General Fu Zuoyi, who was defending the city, PLA forces entered Beiping. Nanjing was taken on April 23, Shanghai on May 27, and Qingdao on June 2. The Guomindang government first fled to Canton, then to Chongqing, to Chengdu, and, finally, in early December, to Taiwan. The tens of millions of dollars that the Soviet government had spent on the Chinese revolution had paid off. Mainland China was now in the grip of a communist dictatorship.

What were the reasons for the CCP victory? How did the PLA succeed in making its breakthrough? First of all was the traditional guerrilla method of warfare that Mao's armies actively employed in the initial stage of the conflict. Retreating in the first months, the communists tried to keep the enemy on the run, their purpose being "to tire him out completely, reduce his food supplies drastically and then look for an opportunity to destroy him." Mao called this method the tactics of "wear and tear."[39] As early as the summer of 1947, PLA units began attacking enemy positions.[40]

Second, the Guomindang forces were falling apart and the generals and officers were powerless to improve the situation. The fighting spirit of the soldiers had collapsed while "in the Chinese Communists the fervor became fanatical."[41] Chiang Kai-shek's army demonstrated a complete incapacity to fight. Corruption and localism flourished in all of the units. The vestiges of militarism were also strong. Commanders did not want to risk their units, viewing them primarily as sources of their own political influence in society as well as of enrichment.

Third, the government's inability to stimulate economic development was also quite evident. In 1946 inflation gripped the country. From September 1945 to February 1947 the value of the yuan dropped by a factor of thirty. In 1947 the monthly rate of inflation reached 26 percent. The crisis continually worsened. An eyewitness reported: "Inflation was creating tremendous financial insecurity . . . Inflation was so severe that the pile of money that would purchase three eggs in the morning would buy only one egg by the afternoon. People carried their money in carts, and the price of rice was so high that citizens who in ordinary times would never have dreamed of stealing were beginning to break into grain shops and make off with what they could."[42]

The number of strikes soared. In 1946, in Shanghai alone there were 1,716 strikes. By the spring of 1948 the government was forced to introduce rationing in all the major cities, and in order to increase grain reserves introduced compulsory purchase of grain at reduced prices.[43] This measure alienated the Guomindang's natural ally, the well-to-do peasants. The broad masses of the population grew dissatisfied with Chiang Kai-shek's domestic policies.

The CCP took advantage of the situation and rallied various political forces around itself. It came to power not under the banner of socialism, communism, or Stalinism, but under the slogan of New Democracy, which was of decisive importance.

Fourth, the position of the USSR was also significant. Despite the fact that Stalin initially took a cautious position with respect to the Chinese conflict, he did not seem to oppose the communist revolution in China, as some historians have erroneously suggested.[44] To be sure, at first he spoke of the possible division of China into two parts along the dividing line of the Yangzi River (the CCP in the north, the Guomindang in the south).[45] However, he refused any form of mediation between the warring sides despite several requests from Chiang Kai-shek's government.[46] Although he repeatedly sent categorical directives to his embassy in China demanding that it not intervene in the conflict, he had no desire to rescue the Guomindang.[47] Prior to the fall of Nanjing, it is true that he ordered his ambassador Nikolai Roshchin to follow Chiang Kai-shek to Canton at the same time that the American and British ambassadors remained in the capital, but in his own words, he did this "to secure intelligence, so that he [Roshchin] could regularly inform us [Stalin] of the situation south of the Yangzi, as well as among the Guomindang higher-ups and their American masters."[48] Stalin secretly informed Mao to this effect. As far back as early 1948, that is, before Mao's arrival in Xibaipo, in conversations with Bulgarian and Yugoslav delegations in the Kremlin, Stalin acknowledged that the Soviet side had been mistaken and the Chinese communists correct in their assessment of the prospects for the civil war. He also spoke of this in July 1949 when he met with Liu Shaoqi, who was paying him an unofficial visit. "Did my telegram sent in August 1945 obstruct your war of liberation?" he asked Liu. The answer, of course, was no, but feeling that his interlocutor was merely saying this to please him, and to absolve him of responsibility for his prior cautious policy in China, he added, "Now I am quite old. My concern now is that after my death, these comrades [he pointed to Marshal Kliment Voroshilov, Molotov, and others] will be afraid of imperialism."[49]

Stalin did not want to intervene in the conflict, but he helped out the CCP quite a lot with weapons and advice. He conducted a particularly extensive correspondence with Mao during this period. Maintaining secrecy, he signed his coded telegrams either with the Russian pseudonym Filippov or the Chinese one Feng Xi [Fyn Si] and transmitted them to Mao via his representatives. One of these was Dr. Andrei Orlov and the other was General Ivan Kovalev, who arrived in Xibaipo in January 1949 and had earlier served as people's commissar of communications for the USSR. Stalin's fear regarding the possibility of direct U.S. intervention in China was entangled with his persistent hope of duping the West. Throughout the civil war he outdid Mao Zedong in attempting to demonstrate that the CCP had supposedly distanced itself from the Bolshevik party. Beginning in late 1947, Mao regularly expressed his desire to visit Stalin, but Stalin refused to receive him until military operations in China were basically concluded. He did not want to give the West and Chiang Kai-shek further grounds for labeling Mao a "Soviet agent."

Throughout the 1946–49 civil war in China, Stalin consistently cooled the genuine communist enthusiasm of Mao. The documentary sources demonstrate that during this period Mao Zedong was more radical than Stalin. In 1946–49 Mao already adhered to the concept of New Democracy passively. He changed his attitude to New Democracy as soon as he realized he could defeat the Guomindang. He had developed this line during the Sino-Japanese War for tactical reasons because the CCP was weak, but when he realized that he could defeat Chiang, he began to ask Stalin to let him abandon it. Mao opposed this line not infrequently even though in formal terms he continued to follow it so as not to irritate the Muscovite leader.[50] Stalin's circumspection is explicable not only in terms of his fear of a nuclear conflict with the United States or his desire to deceive Washington. As a Russian national communist, when Stalin thought about the consequences of a CCP victory he must have been concerned about the future emergence of a powerful new center of communist power. A communist China that achieved rapid economic modernization along the Soviet model through dictatorial means might pose a threat to his hegemony in the communist world. By seeking to limit Mao's ambitions to "democratic" goals, Stalin might bind Mao to himself and subordinate the CCP's tactical line to his own political course of action.

At the same time, Stalin's suspicion of Mao grew in proportion to the CCP's success in the civil war. It further intensified after the "Yugoslav shock" of 1948, that is, after Stalin's break with the Yugoslav leader Josip Broz Tito, whom Moscow had considered one of its most loyal satellites until he suddenly became disobedient. Soon after the "Tito affair," in private conversations with his intimate supporters, Stalin began to express his growing anxiety about a possible new threat, this time from China. "What kind of man is Mao Zedong? He has some sort of special views, a kind of peasant's outlook. It's as though he's afraid of the workers and keeps his armies away from cities," he mused.[51] His right-hand man Molotov, whom Stalin asked to visit Mao and see "what sort of fellow" he was, also had doubts about Mao, calling him a "Chinese Pugachev" in conversations with Stalin.* "He was far from a Marxist, of course," Molotov said. "He confessed to me that he had never read Marx's *Das Kapital.*"[52] In early 1949, Stalin even requested a written opinion from Borodin, the former "chief adviser" to Sun Yat-sen and the Wuhan government in 1923–27, regarding Mao. Obviously grasping what the paranoid leader wanted, Borodin wrote:

---

* Pugachev was a famous Cossack leader of a large-scale Russian peasant rebellion in the eighteenth century.

His independence of character and, even more so, his tendency to "go it alone" were already evident in those years. At meetings, it seemed that he was bored and disengaged when others were speaking, but if he was speaking himself, it was as if no one else had said anything before him. . . . Mao Zedong's distinctive characteristic is overweening self-assurance. He has long since considered himself a theoretician who has made his own contributions to social science. . . . He possesses a mistaken view of . . . the superiority of the peasants over other classes . . . and a concomitant underestimation of the leading role of the proletariat. Mao Zedong repeatedly expressed this point of view in personal conversations with me.

KGB colonel Georgii Mordvinov, who had supervised the Chinese Communist Party in the late 1930s and 1940s, also gave an unflattering testimonial regarding Mao Zedong. He emphasized "Mao Zedong's patriarchal inclinations, his pathological suspicion, his extraordinary ambition, his megalomania that developed into a cult."[53] Might this latter characterization have caused Stalin any embarrassment inasmuch as it fit him to a T? Borodin's assessment caused Stalin to sit up and take notice.

Until the situation became clarified, Stalin would not agree to receive Mao, though he permitted Jiang Qing and their daughter Li Na entry into the USSR. The visit was secretive; Jiang Qing traveled under the name of Marianna Yusupova. The formal reason for the journey was illness. Life in the caves of Yan'an and long, exhausting travels through the mountains of Shaanxi, Shanxi, and Hebei had undermined Jiang's health. She was five foot four inches tall but weighed only ninety-seven pounds. This is why Mao thought to send her and their daughter to the Soviet Union for rest and medical treatment.[54] At the same time, Jiang was supposed to explore life in the Soviet Union and make contact with important people. Thus Stalin's and Mao's interest in her visit coincided.

She and Li Na were in Moscow from May through August 1949. On May 18, Jiang Qing first checked into the therapeutic and then the otolaryngology clinic of the Kremlin hospital on Granovsky Street, where she was diagnosed as suffering from general exhaustion. She spent more than a month in the hospital. She complained about weakness, rapid fatigue, stomach pain, intermittent diarrhea, disrupted sleep, and extreme excitability. She requested that the temperature in her room be kept at a constant 65 degrees. She said that she had twice suffered from dysentery, and that since childhood she had several attacks of angina every year. After consulting with professors, on June 13, 1949, Jiang Qing had her tonsils removed, and two weeks later was sent to the Barvikha Sanatorium, outside Moscow. After that she and her daughter rested at a government dacha for a time, and on August 29 she was sent to Crimea. Stalin provided a special railroad car for her trip. By an amusing coincidence, she took her rest in Koreiz, the former home of the famous Prince Felix Yusupov, Rasputin's killer, whose Russian surname she now shared. She occupied the entire lower floor. General Ludvik Svoboda, the future president of Czecho-slovakia, and his wife, Irena, occupied the second floor. Jiang Qing spent most of her time playing billiards with them and strolling in the neighborhood. The Central Committee of the CPSU assigned to her a junior staff member, Anas-tasia Kartunova, who had just graduated from the Moscow Institute of Orien-tal Studies two years earlier.[55]

In July 1949, a CCP delegation headed by Liu Shaoqi came to the USSR on an unofficial visit.[56] At the end of November, at Mao Zedong's request, the Soviet government granted permission for Ren Bishi to enter the country for medical treatment.[57]

As always, Stalin closely followed developments in China. He had his own secret informers even within the Politburo of the CCP, and he was able to exert influence, more or less effectively, on the Chinese communist leadership. For their part, Mao Zedong and the other CCP leaders constantly informed him of their plans and intentions, and regularly consulted with Moscow even on trifling matters. In February 1949, for example, they requested "Comrade Filippov's" opinion on whether they should transfer the capital of China from Nanjing to Beiping. And on September 28, the eve of the proclamation of the People's Republic of China, they expressed interest in his point of view as to whether they should contact all of the countries of the world regarding the restoration of diplomatic relations "via radio in a generic form or to each indi-vidual state via separate telegrams."[58] "Comrade Master-in-Chief" is how Mao Zedong addressed Stalin in his coded telegrams to Moscow. It is quite possible that Mao lacked "much good feeling"[59] toward Stalin, but he understood per-fectly that he had to be especially loyal to him in both words and deeds, par-ticularly since he could hardly help knowing about Stalin's suspicious nature. This is why, for example, in an August 28, 1948, telegram informing Stalin of the questions he would like to discuss with him during his future visit to the Soviet Union, Mao had declared, "We need to come to an understanding so that our political course will fully coincide with that of the USSR."[60]

Instead of an invitation for Mao to visit Moscow, in January 1949 Stalin sent his representative Anastas Mikoyan on a secret mission to Xibaipo to dis-cuss the most important questions. Mikoyan was accompanied by two men with the same surname: Ivan Kovalev, whom we have already encountered, and Evgenii Kovalev, director of the Far Eastern Sector in the International Foreign Policy Department of the Central Committee of the CPSU. "One was a fool, and the other a coward," the dour Mikoyan later told Stalin.

One of the questions Stalin entrusted his representative to discuss with

Mao was the nature of New Democracy in China. In a telegram of November 30, 1947, Mao had written to Stalin: "In the period of the decisive victory of the Chinese revolution, following the example of the USSR and Yugoslavia, all political parties with the exception of the CCP, must leave the political stage; this will significantly strengthen the Chinese revolution."[61] This thesis openly contradicted what Mao had written in "On Coalition Government" and contradicted the entire course of New Democracy, which aimed at creating a multiparty system in China. In a telegram of April 20, 1948, Stalin expressed his disagreement with Mao's proposal.

> We do not agree with this. We think that various opposition parties in China which are representing the middle strata of the Chinese population and are opposing the Guomindang clique will exist for a long time. And the CCP will have to involve them in cooperation against Chinese reactionary forces and imperialist powers, while keeping hegemony, i.e., the leading position, in its hands. It is possible that some representatives of these parties will have to be included into the Chinese people's democratic government and the government itself has to be a coalition government in order to widen the basis of this government among the population and to isolate the imperialists and their Guomindang agents.[62]

Mao, apparently, wholly accepted Stalin's point of view and in a telegram of April 26, he laid all the blame for these "leftist tendencies" on local CCP leaders, and informed the "Master-in-Chief" that these tendencies "have already been thoroughly corrected."[63] In September 1948, however, he again tried to radicalize the political course, this time approaching the question from the standpoint of economics. In his report to a Politburo meeting in Xibaipo from September 8 to 13, he asserted that the socialist sector would become the leading sector in the national economy during the period of New Democracy, since after the revolution bureaucratic capital as well as large enterprises belonging to bureaucratic capital would become the property of the state.[64] In January–February 1949, during his meetings with Mao, Mikoyan again expounded the Soviet position. He did so rather arrogantly, not so much advising as instructing. Mao was offended, but he concealed his dissatisfaction and affirmed his acceptance of Stalinist directives. To Mikoyan he presented what was essentially a compromise variation of his ideas. In a rambling talk with his guest in early February on current and future policies of the CCP, in referring to cooperation with the national bourgeoisie and carrying out land reform without confiscating "kulak" property he emphasized that even though the coalition government would include several "democratic parties," the future

Chinese state would be in essence "a dictatorship of the proletariat." He also asserted that the construction of New China would take place on the foundation of the Soviet experience.[65]

In order to win over the "Master-in-Chief," Mao asserted to Stalin's emissary that his ideological formulations derived from Stalin's theses concerning the nature of the Chinese revolution.[66] In reality, his compromise position did not fundamentally contradict Stalin's views. In the final analysis, Stalin was himself hardly a moderate. He merely worried about whether the communists' power in a future unified China would be sufficiently camouflaged and worried, too, about the potential rapidity of China's modernization. Therefore, he was quite satisfied to learn that his directives had been formally accepted.[67]

Meanwhile, in early 1949, anticipating victory over the Guomindang, Mao again tried to return to his radical ideas, striving to escape from the bounds of New Democracy. In his report to the Second Plenum of the Central Committee meeting in Xibaipo in March 1949, Mao almost entirely avoided mentioning the term "New Democracy," employing instead the formula of the popular democratic revolution. The resolution of the Second Plenum indicated how Mao distinguished between these two terms, namely, that in the countries of Eastern Europe that were termed people's democracies "the existence and development of capitalism . . . the existence and development of free trade and competition . . . was limited and constrained."[68] The concept of New Democracy, by contrast, implied considerable economic freedom.[69] After the plenum the concept of New Democracy virtually disappeared from the texts of Mao's speeches and articles. His new programmatic text, which he would publish on June 30, 1949, would be titled "On the People's Democratic Dictatorship."[70] Many years later, Mao acknowledged, "In essence, the basic proposition about destroying the bourgeoisie was contained in the decisions of the Second Plenum of the Seventh Central Committee."[71]

Stalin was able to correct this position in December 1949, after the victory of the Chinese revolution. Nevertheless, his tactical maneuvers helped Mao Zedong achieve an impressive victory over Chiang Kai-shek. In late 1947 and early 1948, the Chinese communists, masquerading as New Democrats, even succeeded in splitting the Guomindang with the aid of Song Qingling, the widow of Sun Yat-sen, who had long collaborated with the CCP and Moscow. On January 1, 1948, leftists within the Guomindang, meeting in Hong Kong, declared the formation of the so-called Revolutionary Committee of the Guomindang. Song Qingling herself became its honorary chairman and such well-known persons as Feng Yuxiang and Tan Pingshan were among its leaders.

On March 23, Mao and other Central Committee officials left Xibaipo for Beiping, two months after its capture by PLA troops. Before departing, Mao laughingly said to Zhou Enlai, "We're going to the capital to take our exams."

"We must pass them," Zhou replied. "We won't give up."

"Giving up would be equivalent to defeat," Mao said seriously. "However, we will not become like Li Zicheng.* Let's hope that we pass the exams with flying colors."[72]

The communists managed to do everything they wanted to. On September 30, 1949, they organized a multiparty coalition government;† Mao became the chairman and Liu Shaoqi, Zhu De, and Song Qingling were his deputies. On October 1, in Beiping, which ten days earlier the CCP had restored to its former name of Beijing, Mao Zedong proclaimed the establishment of the People's Republic of China.

This was his finest hour. He stood in the rostrum of Tiananmen Gate, its palace tower behind him rising above the entrance to the Forbidden City of the emperors. He gazed out at the gigantic crowd that filled the central square beneath him to overflowing. (More than four hundred thousand people took part in the celebration.) Before his feet lay a great country with an ancient history and culture, and now he was its all-powerful master. What was he thinking about? Power? The years of painful struggle? His friends and comrades who had perished? Perhaps he was thinking about what lay in the future for him and the long-suffering people of China? We don't know.

Standing next to him were his comrades-in-arms: Zhou Enlai, Liu Shaoqi, Zhu De, and many other members of the communist leadership and of the coalition government, among them Song Qingling. Mao was cheerful and lighthearted, smiling continuously, showing his even teeth. He did not want to conceal his triumph. Fastened with a safety pin to the left side of his new dark brown jacket was a red ribbon with two yellow characters—*zhuxi*—Chairman. For many long years this word would be of utmost importance in the lives of all those living in the PRC.

---

* Li Zicheng (1605 or 1606–1645) was the leader of a vast popular uprising at the end of the Ming dynasty. In 1644 he captured Beijing and was proclaimed emperor, but he could not maintain control in the city—that is, in Mao's figure of speech, he couldn't pass the exams. Under the blows of the Manchus he had to retreat, and he was killed in the summer of 1645.

† Ever since then in the PRC, in addition to the ruling CCP there have been eight minuscule so-called democratic parties that formed a united front with the communists. They have never constituted a real opposition to the CCP one-party dictatorship and have been a kind of democratic window-dressing. In the early 1950s some of their members even held positions in the so-called coalition government.

PART THREE

THE DICTATOR

24

VISIT TO THE RED MECCA

After coming to Beijing, Mao initially lived in a country villa, Shuangqing, in the picturesque Fragrant Hills northwest of the city. This district had long served as a place of solitude for many Chinese rulers, who had adorned it with elegant pavilions and pagodas. In the eighteenth century the Manchu emperor Qianlong had transformed it into an astonishingly beautiful park complex. The pure mountain air redolent of pine needles, the light breezes, the swaying of the pine branches, the smooth surface of the blue lakes: all created a peaceful atmosphere.

Mao arrived there in late March 1949, when Beiping was in the grip of sandstorms. The scorching dust, driven by winds from the Mongolian plains, made breathing difficult. But in the Fragrant Hills one could sense the approach of spring. Flowers exuded their fragrance and birds sang. Shuangqing, a one-story villa that got its name ("Double pure springs") from two mountain springs that flowed nearby, was particularly lovely. In communist circles, for security reasons, Mao's residence soon came to be called the Labor University (*laodong daxue*) or simply *laoda*. It is not known who thought up this name, but it was surprisingly suitable to the place. Simply by changing the tone of the word *lao,* the characters *lao* and *da* signify "respected" and "great." No one deserved this epithet more than the Chairman! But war was still going on, and the location of the head of the CCP was a secret.

At fifty-six Mao was no longer the fit and trim young man with an iron constitution whom Edgar Snow had met in 1936. He had put on weight, become rather heavy, and slowed down. He began to cut his hair short. He suffered increasingly from insomnia and frequently caught colds. For many years he had had angioneurosis, a functional disorder of enervation of the blood vessels that often caused sweating and hot flashes as well as headaches and dizziness, lumbago, and neuropathy in his joints, fingers, and toes. He became irritable and lost self-control. When his illness flared up he complained to his relatives and doctors, "I have the feeling that I'm walking on cotton."[1] Sometimes while walking he would suddenly lose coordination. He would begin waving his arms about as if he were clutching at the air. At these times it seemed to him that he had "lost the earth," as if the ground had gone out from under his legs.[2]

He continued to work hard—fifteen to sixteen hours a day—but he grew more and more tired. He never changed the daily regimen he had begun many years earlier. He slept till two or three in the afternoon, in the evenings he held meetings, and then he read and wrote till morning. He chain-smoked, about three packs a day, preferring American Chesterfields, British 555s, and Chinese Red Star.

Growing older, he became ever more attached to the young and energetic Jiang Qing, who was not only a passionate lover but also an exacting secretary and housekeeper. She looked after his health and daily regimen, his schedule of visitors, his clothes, diet, and walks. Even during the dances that he and she both adored, and which Mao continued to arrange on a regular basis, she steered young girls to him. Unlike Zizhen she was more savvy than jealous. "Sex is engaging in the first rounds, but what sustains interest in [a man] in the long run is power," she said later to her biographer.[3] During her absences, Mao simply could not manage on his own. Being separated from his wife was very distressing. Contact with his younger son, Anqing, and his eldest daughter, Jiaojiao, to whom, it will be recalled, he had given the new name of Li Min, did not help. These children came to live with him shortly after Jiang Qing and Li Na's departure. Ivan Kovalev brought them from Manchuria.*

Mao's meeting with his children was quite warm.

"Comrade Mao Zedong, here are your beloved children," Kovalev said to Mao, tugging at the timid Anqing and Jiaojiao.

"Come closer, children, this is your father, Chairman Mao," said one of the attending officials.

"I raised my head and saw someone I didn't know at all," recalled Li Min. "He was dressed in a loose-fitting gray tunic and simple black cloth slippers. He was so ordinary and simple, not at all like the Leader." Li Min writes that the meeting was very affectionate. Mao put his face to hers and began to kiss her, but she laughed because she couldn't understand his Chinese, especially his Hunanese accent.

Soon, however, there was a certain cooling off between them. It started when Li Min, strolling through the park once with her father, asked, "Papa, won't Jiang Qing beat me?" Mao was dumbstruck; he looked at his daughter with a strange expression on his face and for a long time did not reply. "Step-mothers often beat their stepchildren," Li Min continued.[4]

---

* In her reminiscences, Li Min writes that it was the special plenipotentiary of the Soviet Union, Pavel Yudin; however, Yudin did not come to China until 1950. Stalin's special representative in China in 1949 was Kovalev.

Jiang Qing did not beat her, but Jiang Qing never developed close, family relations with Mao's children from his previous marriages. They did not want to call her "Mama," and Jiang Qing felt they were unfriendly toward her. She paid them back in kind. She was unable to conceal her feelings toward Li Min even from the young American Roxane Witke, who had come to Beijing to write Jiang Qing's biography. "Li Min," Jiang Qing said to Witke, "did not grow up to be 'quick in action' [i.e., 'prompt to act']." What she had in mind, however, remains unclear.[5]

Mao had no time to delve into the nuances of family relations. He simply took Jiang Qing's side. The result was that he spent most of his free time playing with his youngest daughter, Li Na. He treated the children of his previous two wives almost indifferently, although he kept them in his household.[6]

In September 1949, he finally moved downtown with them and members of the leadership into the old imperial palace complex Zhongnanhai (Central and southern seas), surrounded by a brick wall and adjoining the western side of the Forbidden City. He settled into the so-called Pavilion of Chrysanthemum Fragrance, in the Garden of Abundant Reservoirs. Li Min described it:

> The Garden of Abundant Reservoirs was a traditional rectangular courtyard (*siheyuan*) with buildings around the perimeter and ancient cypresses in the center. From north to south and east to west the courtyard was bisected by two small paths, dividing the lawn into four equal quadrants. It was very quiet and peaceful in this beautiful courtyard. The plan of the courtyard had been precisely symmetrical. On the north side in the center was the drawing-room, and there were rooms to the left and right. Jiang Qing occupied one of them, and the other was for father. The rooms on the north side were high and spacious. In father's room were a large bed, a divan, easy chairs, bookcases, and a writing desk. There were also three rooms in the east wing. In the middle was a living room that also served as a dining room. In this room there was a coat rack for guests' and father's clothes. At one end of the structure was a study and at the other end a reception room. On the south side was a foyer in the middle and on either side Kolya's (Anqing's) room and my sister Li Na's room. On the west side of the pavilion, the central room had an entrance onto the street; one of the corner rooms first served as Jiang Qing's reception room, and then as our playroom where we spent our free time and played Ping-Pong. In the other corner room was father's library.[7]

Mao spent most of his time in his enormous bedroom. Lying on his spacious wooden bed, with books scattered about, he read a lot, worked on documents, and even received members of the Politburo, including his first deputy, Liu Shaoqi, and Zhou Enlai, who from the establishment of the PRC had served as the premier of the State Administrative Council, the highest organ of executive power. In that room Mao decided the fate of the country during the years of New Democracy and of socialist construction, during the Great Leap Forward with its dreadful consequences, and in the period of terrible crisis in the early 1960s, right up to the so-called Great Proletarian Cultural Revolution. Mao lived in the Pavilion of Chrysanthemum Fragrance until August 1966 when he moved to another building called the Swimming Pool Pavilion. (In the code words of the secret service, he, his family, and his closest associates were known as Group I.) [8]

It was there during the first months of the new government that he defined the main direction for the development of the PRC, a plan for creating a Stalinist state. Although during the first three years after the revolutionary victory the PRC formally remained a New Democratic republic and officially did not copy the Stalinist model of economic and political development, China maintained particularly close relations with the Soviet Union and its satellites, fiercely opposed imperialism, and took an active part in the armed conflict with United Nations forces in Korea during the war from 1950 to 1953. Behind the façade of New Democracy a very harsh communist order was being put into place modeled on the USSR. The only kind of socialism Mao knew was that laid out in *The History of the Communist Party of the Soviet Union, Short Course.* He looked upon Stalin as his teacher and the Soviet Union, which inspired fear throughout the world, as a model to imitate. This is why he tried to implant Stalinism in his country, understanding full well that this sociopolitical system meant strictly centralized and hierarchical totalitarian control by the Communist Party, an unlimited, nationwide cult of the party leader, all-encompassing control of the political and intellectual life of the citizens by the security organs, nationalization of private property, strict centralized planning, priority development for heavy industry, and enormous expenditures on national defense.

The Stalinization of the PRC, however, was constrained by the Soviet Union's ambivalent policy toward China from 1949 to 1953. With the establishment of the PRC, Stalin became more fearful of the emergence of a powerful industrialized China that might threaten his hegemony, and his maniacal suspiciousness concerning Mao Zedong and, in general, all Chinese, grew. "Stalin was suspicious of us, he placed a question mark over us," Mao Zedong recalled later.[9] He clearly grasped that the Kremlin dictator did not want to allow the CCP to build socialism, at least not until the USSR itself had become so strong that it would have nothing to fear from socialist rivals.

From the outside it seemed that Stalin was scrupulously following the canons of Marxism, according to which how long it would take to reach socialism depended upon the level of socioeconomic development of any particular country that had a revolution. Thus states that were economically less developed than Russia would have to traverse a longer path to socialism than the Soviet Union. The transitional period in such countries would be like the Soviet New Economic Policy (NEP) of the 1920s, a transitional stage to full-fledged socialism.

Finally, Stalin invited Mao Zedong to Moscow, graciously allowing Mao to come and tender him congratulations on the seventieth anniversary of the birth of the "Father of Peoples." [10] Stalin, who personally controlled the USSR's China policy, treated the visit of the Chinese leader very seriously. [11] On the eve of Mao's visit in December 1949, he again requested information about the "cave Marxist." This time, by a happy coincidence, along with negative reports he received positive information from Andrei Orlov, Mao's physician. "His attitude toward the Soviet Union is very good," Orlov reported on December 10. "This has an enormous influence on the entire communist party. . . . The role of the Soviet Union and of Comrade Stalin himself with regard to the victory of the Chinese revolution and the victory of the Chinese people are especially valued. . . . Now Mao Zedong places all his hopes upon the USSR, the CPSU, and, especially, on Comrade Stalin."

Even these dispatches could not entirely quiet Stalin's fear, since it was not in Stalin's character to trust his informants. Orlov also noted that Mao was extremely cautious and quick to take offense, as well as a great actor. "He is able to conceal his feelings, and play the role that is his; he talks about this with intimates (sometimes with well-known persons) and laughingly asks whether he has pulled it off well." [12] Was "this actor" deceiving Comrade Stalin?

On December 1, the Soviet Politburo adopted "A Plan Concerning the Arrival, Sojourn, and Send-off of the Chinese Government Delegation." Attention was paid to even the slightest details. A special train was arranged for the border station of Otpor consisting of a saloon car for Mao Zedong; one for the people accompanying him; one for the Soviet ambassador to China, Nikolai Roshchin; a car for Stalin's representative in China, Ivan Kovalev, and his retinue; two international cars; one soft sleeper; and one dining car. The Politburo assigned the Ministry of State Security (MGB) of the USSR and Minister Viktor Abakumov personally the responsibility for arrangements for feeding the arriving guests and their security personnel on the way from and to the border. The MGB was also given responsibility for housing Mao Zedong and his entourage in Moscow in a private house at No. 8 Ostrovskii Street. Moreover, the suburban dacha Zareche, where Jiang Qing had lived just recently, was also put at Mao's disposal. [13]

Anatolii Lavrent'ev, the deputy foreign minister of the USSR, and Fedor Matveev, chief of the Protocol Division of the Ministry of Foreign Affairs, were assigned to greet the delegation on the border at Otpor station. Initially it was decided that Mao Zedong would be met at the Yaroslav Station in Moscow by the deputy chairman of the Council of Ministers of the USSR, Nikolai Bulganin; Foreign Affairs Minister Andrei Vyshinsky; Armed Forces Minister Aleksandr Vasilevskii; as well as high-ranking officials of the Ministry of Foreign Affairs and the Ministry of the Armed Forces.[14] At the last minute, however, Stalin decided to upgrade the level of the reception. He also sent Vyacheslav Molotov, who was now first deputy chairman of the Council of Ministers of the USSR, to the station.

Mao Zedong likewise made preparations for meeting the Great Teacher. He was very nervous. Various thoughts, including the most far-fetched, bounced around in his head. Sometimes he thought an attempt would be made on his life in Moscow, and several times he asked Kovalev what measures were being taken to provide for his security. He wanted very much to see Stalin, congratulate him on his seventieth birthday, and present him with the many gifts that he had personally selected. He intended to spend a lot of time with him as well as to meet with Molotov and the Soviet Communist Party Secretary Andrei Zhdanov. He also wanted to rest and receive medical treatment. Above all, he counted on concluding a Treaty of Friendship, Alliance, and Mutual Assistance between the PRC and the Soviet Union and receiving a loan of US $300 million. He brought with him a small working group of officials headed by Chen Boda and including one other secretary, Ye Zilong; his chief bodyguard, Wang Dongxing; bodyguard Li Jiaji; and interpreter Shi Zhe, who had lived for many years in the Soviet Union in the 1920s and 1930s and knew Russia well. Kovalev suggested including Anying, who knew Russian very well, in the group as an interpreter, but Mao refused.[15] He was still unable to forgive his eldest son for his disrespectful behavior in Xibaipo despite the fact that he had formally forgiven the "mutineer" and even welcomed him and his young wife to Zhongnanhai every Saturday. (Anying had married in 1949; Liu Shaoqi had served as matchmaker.)[16]

Mao left Beijing in early December accompanied by Ambassadors Roshchin and Kovalev. The latter recalled: "The PLA provided a stepped-up guard along the entire rail route from Beijing to the Soviet border. On both sides of the railroad right-of-way, facing outwards at a distance of 50 meters from each other and from the right-of-way . . . in a continuous chain from Beijing to Otpor Station were soldiers bearing automatic weapons."[17] Such a guard was not unwarranted. Notwithstanding the heightened security measures, a grenade, bombs, and other explosives were discovered at the Tianjin station.[18]

At noon on December 16, Mao Zedong's train, decorated with the flags of the USSR and the PRC, pulled in to Yaroslavl Station. It was cold, and the reception came off as excessively dry and formalistic. Those greeting him obviously did not know how to act. Should they embrace and kiss Mao or should they limit themselves to simple handshakes? Mao was confused and insulted. Appearing on the platform, he turned to Molotov and the other Soviet government officials and said, "Dear comrades and friends!"[19] But he experienced no warmth in return. Everyone was constrained; the weather reflected the meeting: the hard frost stung at one's cheeks, and a sharp wind was blowing. The ceremony had to be curtailed because of the cold.[20]

That same evening he was received by Stalin in Moscow at 6 P.M. The reception was brief but remarkable. After initially speaking of the "prospects for peace" in the world, Stalin talked about what was troubling him most, namely, New Democracy and its relationship to socialism. He clearly emphasized that "the Chinese Communists must take the national bourgeoisie into consideration." He also tried to soften Mao's harsh position toward the Western world, pointing out that "there is no need for you [the Chinese] to create conflicts with the British. . . . The main point is not to rush and to avoid conflicts." Mao had to reassure Stalin that they would not touch the national bourgeoisie and foreign enterprises "so far."[21]

Afterward, he languished for four and a half days at the suburban dacha. Stalin did not invite him anymore, and Mao did not know what to think. Molotov, Bulganin, Mikoyan, and Vyshinsky paid him courtesy calls, but these meetings did not satisfy him. They were brief and merely according to official protocol. The behavior of his Soviet hosts betrayed a certain mistrust, a strange caution. "They [Molotov and the others] came for a short time, and sat on the edge of their chairs," Kovalev recalled later. "Moreover, whenever Mao suggested that they *chifan* [dine], they courteously refused and left. This also insulted and offended him."[22]

On December 21, Stalin's birthday, when Mao had to go to the Bolshoi Theater for the celebration, he became terribly agitated. He even needed to down several doses of atropine to keep his head from spinning. He felt even worse just before he delivered a brief speech praising the "Great Leader and Teacher." The only thing that calmed Mao and gave him at least some reassurance was that Stalin seated him on his immediate right. He took little pleasure from the reception and dinner, however. Unlike Stalin's entourage, Mao drank little and he found Russian food uninspiring.

What really devastated him was that after the banquet he was escorted back to his dacha and did not see Stalin for the next thirty days. During this time he visited the Moscow automobile factory and went to Leningrad, where he paid a visit to the cruiser *Aurora* and the Hermitage museum, and viewed a large number of Soviet films on historical themes. He also went to see Kremlin doctors. Three days before New Year's he developed a toothache. Mao never cleaned his teeth, considering it sufficient to rinse them with green tea, which is why even though his teeth were even they had an obvious greenish tint and almost all of them were riddled with cavities. He also went to a dermatologist.

His wrists had itched for a long time, and in spots they were covered in rashes. But his main reason for seeking medical assistance was his angioneurosis, for which the doctors could do little. They advised him to stop smoking, get body massages, take pine-needle baths at night, take vitamin B₁, take regular walks outdoors, periodically undergo a course of Pantokrin injections,* and eat regularly and often.[23]

The consultative committee that examined the patient on January 2, 1950, came to the following conclusion:

> The patient displays moderately expressed generalized arteriosclerosis; predominantly affected are the blood vessels in the brain and the arteries supplying the heart. Because of this the patient periodically and suddenly experiences vascular interferences in the brain that are expressed in a sensation of general weakness and instability in the legs. The stated vascular interferences sometimes last for several hours.
>
> The lungs have moderately manifested emphysema with residual evidence of the inflammation of the lungs and pleura experienced in 1948.[24]

Mao was furious about wasting so much time. Of course, what exasperated him most of all were not the physicians, but rather Stalin's ignoring him. "You invited me to Moscow and you do nothing. Why have I come?" he asked Kovalev angrily. "Why have I come here to spend whole days just eating, sleeping, and defecating?" He tried calling Stalin but was told that Stalin was not at home and that he should see Mikoyan. "I was insulted by all of this," Mao recalled, "and I decided to do nothing else but just sit it out at the dacha." He was offered excursions around the country, but he "sharply refused this suggestion," replying that he would prefer to "catch up on his sleep at the dacha."[25] Taking for granted that there were listening devices in his residence,[26] he blurted out anything that was on his mind.[27]

"Denied any meetings with Stalin, Mao was very nervous, and in a rage he uttered sharply critical statements about his sojourn in Moscow," Kovalev recalled later.

> More than once he emphasized that he had come not only as a head of state, but as the chairman of the CCP in order to strengthen the ties between two fraternal parties. But this was not what was happening. He was just sitting alone with nothing to do. Nobody phoned him, nobody came to visit or, if they did, they stayed only briefly on proto-

---

* A medicine made from Siberian stag antlers.

col calls. Once he asserted that he would give up his earlier plan for a three-month visit, and that he intended to return to China very soon, leaving to Zhou Enlai, whom he had already summoned to Moscow, the job of drawing up and signing the treaty and other Soviet-Chinese documents. It was my job to inform Stalin, sometimes in writing, about Mao's moods as expressed in these declarations of his.

Stalin did nothing to correct the situation. Finally, Mao said to Kovalev, "I simply can't stand it anymore; I'm in such a state that I can no longer control myself." He locked himself in his bedroom and would let no one in. In Kovalev's words, he "was very afraid that his trip to Moscow would produce no results. This would confirm the truth of those who had opposed his making the trip, and would lower his authority in the eyes of the Chinese people."[28]

Stalin was deliberately doing things his way. He wanted to humiliate Mao, teach him a lesson for the future, bring him down a notch. He was telling Mao in effect, I am everything here. I am the Great Leader of the world communist movement and you are nothing, you are my wretched pupil, and you will do what I tell you to do. Stalin behaved this way not only with Mao, but with all the other communist leaders, although he overdid it with respect to the Chairman. "Probably, we went too far," he finally observed to Kovalev when the latter next reported to him on Mao's mood.

Only then did negotiations resume on the highest level. Stalin again invited Mao to the Kremlin, and then called him to his nearby dacha in Kuntsevo. But these meetings did not bring Mao peace of mind. Stalin remained reserved and on guard, and said little. "Occasionally he threw sideways glances at his guest from afar," recalled Stalin's interpreter Nikolai Fedorenko. "The room where the conversations took place . . . reminded one of a stage where a demonic play was being presented."[29] None of this escaped Mao's attention, but what oppressed him most was Stalin's openly imperialist policy toward China. In the words of Mao's personal interpreter Shi Zhe, he sensed Stalin's "pan-Russianism" very clearly, since Stalin expressed it "even more strongly than the Russian people in general."[30] Mao found particularly insulting Stalin's refusal to conclude an official intergovernmental treaty with him, because Stalin felt that his existing treaty with the Guomindang regime was adequate.[31] This latter treaty, it will be recalled, was an unequal treaty that disfavored the Chinese side and was very advantageous for the USSR. Stalin changed his position and agreed to conclude a Treaty of Friendship, Alliance, and Mutual Aid only after he learned of Great Britain's decision to recognize the PRC at the beginning of January 1950. But this historic document was not signed until February 14. Mao was now satisfied, but still he could not restrain himself from registering his "surprise" at Stalin's decision. "But changing this agreement goes against the decisions of the Yalta Conference?!" he noted, not without malice, reminding Stalin of the very argument Stalin himself had used to object to signing a treaty with the PRC. "True, it does," Stalin replied, "and to hell with it!"[32]

The joy of the Chinese communists at the signing of this treaty was clouded by Stalin's unmistakable desire to control not only Mao's political course of action, but also the economy of New China. Additional secret protocols were appended to the treaty that revealed Stalin's real intentions. The first of these afforded the USSR a number of privileges in Northeast China and Xinjiang. All non-Soviet foreigners were removed from these territories. Stalin even wanted to conclude separate commercial agreements with these border regions to strengthen Soviet control over them, but he encountered determined resistance from Mao and Zhou Enlai, who had come to Moscow at Mao's request on January 20.[33] Two additional agreements aimed at creating four joint enterprises on Chinese territory to secure Soviet interests in exploiting Chinese economic resources. These were the so-called joint Soviet-Chinese stock companies, two of which were in Xinjiang for rare and nonferrous metals and for petroleum, and two others in Dalian for civil aviation and ship repair and construction. The Soviet side owned 50 percent of the capital investment, received 50 percent of profits, and exercised overall leadership.[34]

The Chinese communists were also dismayed by the new agreement that Stalin imposed upon them concerning the Chinese Changchun Railroad. Mao and Zhou had thought to establish a commission to run the railroad in which the posts of chairman and director would be filled by Chinese. They had also hoped to change the proportion of the shares of capital that each side invested, and increase the Chinese share to 51 percent. Stalin and Molotov rejected these proposals, insisting on parity, with both partners sharing equally both in investment and management.[35] In connection with the new agreement on the Chinese Changchun Railroad,* Lüshun, and Dalian, Soviet control over the railroad and the naval base in Lüshun was preserved until the end of 1952.[36] The status of Dalian was to be determined after the signing of a peace treaty with Japan.[37]

The more Stalin intervened in Chinese affairs, the greater his appetite grew, as did his mistrust of Mao. Stalin's successor Nikita Khrushchev said that after meetings with Mao, Stalin "was never ecstatic" and referred to Mao in a not very complimentary fashion. "You could feel a kind of haughty attitude on his part toward Mao," Khrushchev noted.[38] On one occasion, the Kremlin boss even tried to provoke Mao Zedong by saying, whether as a joke or seriously, that "in China communism is nationalistic, and that although Mao Zedong was a communist, he was inclined toward nationalism." Stalin also said that there was a danger that a "Chinese Tito" might emerge. According to Mao, he

---

* On March 22, 1950, the Politburo of the CPSU approved the draft by the Soviet Council of Ministers, "On Securing Joint Administration of the Chinese Changchun Railroad."

replied to Stalin curtly, "Everything that was said just now does not conform to reality."[39] He obviously did not understand that Stalin possessed, in the words of the Soviet novelist Konstantin Simonov, a "semi-inscrutable sense of humor that could be dangerous for his interlocutor."[40] Trying to dispel Stalin's doubts, Mao asked Stalin to send a "Soviet comrade" to China to review and edit his works.[41] Mao really wanted Stalin to send one of his trusted confidants to China to see with his own eyes just how scrupulously Marxist the Chinese communists were.[42]

After concluding the treaty and agreements, Mao and Zhou departed from Moscow on February 17. Once again the businesslike and focused Molotov escorted them to the station, but this time Mao was very formal, although he still insisted on calling his Soviet hosts "comrades and friends." Prior to entering the railroad car, he declared, "On departing from the Great Socialist capital, we sincerely express our heartfelt gratitude to Generalissimo Stalin, to the Soviet government and the Soviet people. Long live the eternal friendship and eternal cooperation between China and the Soviet Union!"[43] But Stalin's mistrust and greed weighed upon him. He could not sleep, felt terrible, and became very nervous and extremely irritable.[44]

Stalin actually did send a well-known Soviet expert in Marxist philosophy, academician Pavel Yudin, to China in the spring of 1950 to verify Mao's credentials. Yudin was charged with undertaking an "accurate and tactically correct" editing of a new edition of Mao's *Selected Works* that was supposed to come out shortly in Russian and Chinese. An earlier Chinese edition that had not been vetted by Soviet specialists had been published in Harbin in 1949 and then translated and published in Moscow.

Yudin sojourned in China for two years, and during this time made five hundred notes on Mao's works, but all of these were private in character. In his words, he "did not uncover . . . any serious anti-Marxist or anti-Leninist propositions" in Mao Zedong's articles and books.[45] Upon his return, Yudin was summoned to a meeting of the Politburo, at which Stalin questioned him closely: "Well, are they Marxists?" (Stalin put particular stress on the last word.) Yudin replied, "They are Marxists, Comrade Stalin!"[46] After this, according to Yudin, "the Master-in-Chief" summed up, "This is good! We can relax. They grew up themselves without our help."[47] We do not know whether Stalin really set his mind at ease, but shortly thereafter Mao Zedong again demonstrated his loyalty to the Kremlin chief.

25

THE KOREAN ADVENTURE

On October 19, 1950, in accordance with Stalin's wishes, Mao sent the Chinese army to assist the North Korean communists, who several months earlier had invaded South Korea, an ally of the United States. Mao's decision had great significance for Stalin, and the Chairman certainly knew this. He would often say later that only after the PRC entered the Korean War on the side of the North Korean leader Kim Il Sung did Stalin remove the label of "suspected Titoist" from him and come to believe that "the Chinese communists are not pro-American, and the Chinese revolution is not an example of 'nationalist communism.' "[1] This was confirmed by China's foreign minister Chen Yi, who said that Stalin shed tears on hearing of Mao's decision to send troops. "The Chinese comrades are so good!" the aged dictator said twice.[2] Mao's entry into the Korean War appears at least in part to have been a conscious demonstration of the PRC leaders' devotion to the Kremlin boss.

This bloody war was unleashed by the North Korean communists on June 25, 1950. The Chinese entered at the critical moment when the Korean communists were on the verge of defeat. Kim's army encountered resistance not only from South Korean soldiers, but also from the armed forces of the UN that had been sent by the Security Council to stop the aggressor. The main contingent of UN forces was made up of Americans, who also exercised overall command in the person of General Douglas MacArthur, the head of the Allied army.

An agreement between Kim Il Sung and Stalin had preceded the beginning of the war, which Stalin provoked by supporting Kim's adventurist plan that envisioned seizing the south in no more than twenty-seven days.[3] Without approval from the Kremlin dictator, the North Korean leader would never have crossed the 38th parallel, which divided the two Koreas. The Kremlin boss deliberately dragged the Americans into this war. On the eve of the decisive vote in the Security Council regarding North Korea's aggression, Stalin ignored First Deputy Foreign Minister Andrei Gromyko's request that Stalin instruct the Soviet representative, Yacov Malik, to participate in the Security

Council session in order to veto any resolutions it might adopt.* The USSR had been boycotting sessions of the Security Council since January 1950 on the pretext that the council had refused to recognize the PRC's lawful rights to UN membership. To Gromyko's suggestion that Malik return to the council in order to block any resolution harmful to North Korea or the Soviet Union, Stalin categorically asserted, "In my opinion, the Soviet representative must not take part in the Security Council meeting." Gromyko tried to object, explaining that the absence of a Soviet representative would enable the Security Council to dispatch UN troops to South Korea, but Stalin remained implacable. He even personally dictated instructions to Gromyko forbidding Malik's presence at the Security Council session.[4]

Stalin thereby abandoned the opportunity to veto the resolution adopted by the council, even though "[o]n the very day the war began, it became clear that the United States would intervene."[5] This enabled the United States and its allies to condemn the North Koreans on June 25. (In the absence of the representative from the USSR, the resolution censuring North Korea was adopted by a vote of 9–0 with Yugoslavia abstaining.) Two days later, on June 27, the Security Council, with Malik still absent, sanctioned the use of international force against the North Korean People's Army (NKPA), and soon fifteen countries joined in repelling the aggressor. (Fifty-three states approved the use of force.)[6]

In explaining his reasoning to his associates, Stalin was completely cynical about why he dragged the "imperialists" into the war in Korea. Here is what he wrote to the Soviet ambassador to Czechoslovakia, Mikhail A. Silin, on August 27, 1950, for transmission to Czechoslovakian president Klement Gottwald:

> We temporarily absented ourselves from the Security Council for four reasons: First to demonstrate the Soviet Union's solidarity with New China; second to emphasize the stupidity and idiocy of U.S. policy which recognizes the Guomindang scarecrow as the representative of China in the Security Council; third to render the decisions of the Security Council illegal in the absence of representatives of two great powers [in addition to the USSR, Stalin had the PRC in mind]; fourth to untie the hands of the American government and provide it an opportunity, using its majority in the Security Council, to commit new stupidities so that public opinion can view the true face of the American government.
>
> I think we have succeeded in achieving all of these objectives.
>
> After our departure from the Security Council America has got-

---

* At this time the Security Council consisted of eleven members, including the five permanent members possessing the right of the veto. These five were the United States, the USSR, Chiang Kai-shek's Republic of China, Great Britain, and France.

ten mixed up in a military intervention in Korea and is now squandering its military prestige and its moral authority. Can any honest person now doubt that in military terms it is not as strong as it claims to be? Moreover, it is clear that the United States of America has been distracted from Europe to the Far East. Does this help us out in terms of the balance of world power? Absolutely it does.

Let us suppose that the American government will become even more bogged down in the Far East and that China will be dragged into the struggle for the freedom of Korea and for its own independence. What might come out of this? First, America, like any other state, will be unable to cope with China which has at the ready large military forces. Probably, America will be weighted down by this conflict. Second, because of its being weighted down, in the short term America will be unable to fight a Third World War. Probably, a Third World War will be put off to some indefinite future; this will ensure us the time needed to strengthen socialism in Europe. I am not even addressing the fact that a struggle between America and China will bring about revolution throughout Far Eastern Asia. Does this help us out in terms of the balance of world forces? Absolutely it does.

As you can see, the question of whether or not the Soviet Union participates in the Security Council is not such a simple question as it may appear at first glance.[7]

From the very beginning, Stalin intended to use the Korean War to weaken the United States by involving it in a conflict not only with North Korea, *but also with China*. "One should keep in mind that we also are not without sin," Khrushchev would later say to Mao Zedong. "It was we who drew the Americans to South Korea."[8] In other words, for Stalin the Korean War seemed to be only an element in a new global plan for world revolution. Lenin's "Great Pupil" had never renounced the idea of a world socialist takeover, although unlike Lenin, who would not have hesitated to sacrifice Russia for the world revolution, he considered the world revolution a means to spread Russian hegemony. Now in the early 1950s it seemed that a new chance had appeared—the last one, as it happened—to achieve this ambitious goal. Stalin had possessed nuclear weapons since August 1949. Half of Europe lay at his feet. The red flag flew over China, Mongolia, and North Korea. In Indochina, Moscow's satellites were waging war against French imperialists supported by the United States. The victory of the world revolution seemed not far distant.

Mao's position in this regard, however, was not a simple one. Prior to the conflict he apparently fully supported Kim Il Sung and Stalin. He had learned of Kim's plans a year before the invasion, from North Korean representatives who had visited him in Shuangqing. He had unequivocally promised his neighbors help, including troops, but only after the end of the civil war with Chiang Kai-shek.[9] In late January 1950, during one of their talks, Stalin himself had raised the question of the "need and possibility of providing help to the DPRK [North Korea] in order to augment its military potential and strengthen its defenses."[10] However, he said nothing to Mao about a possible North Korean invasion of South Korea. This omission was yet another slight to his guest.[11] Mao kept mum, although he was offended by Stalin's mistrust. Instead of a vague discussion about "providing help to the DPRK," "the Great Leader" might have told Mao directly what he wanted. But Stalin thought it possible to discuss the planned invasion only with Kim Il Sung. He made Kim promise not to reveal the plan for now, whether to the "Chinese comrades" or even to other North Korean leaders. "This is dictated by the need to keep the enemy in darkness," he wrote to Kim.[12]

Nonetheless, even without Stalin's explanations, Mao understood: the idea had long since been mooted. By this time Stalin had already made his decision, but Mao's agreement was indispensable and was forthcoming. The Chairman promised to help the DPRK "strengthen its defenses," not only because the guest did not want to contradict the host, but because Mao himself desired a united Korea that was building socialism. Perhaps he understood that Stalin was preparing him for the role of "shock force" in the world revolution. In any case, he was unafraid of the Americans; he was convinced that "the Americans would not become engaged in a Third World War for such a small territory [as Korea]."[13]

After talking with Mao, on January 30, 1950, Stalin telegraphed the Soviet ambassador to the DPRK, Terentii Shtykov: "He [Kim Il Sung] must understand that such a large matter in regard to South Korea such as he wants to undertake needs considerable preparation. The matter must be organized so that there would not be too great a risk. If he wants to discuss this matter with me, then I will always be ready to receive him and discuss with him. Transmit all this to Kim Il Sung and tell him that I am ready to help him in this matter."[14]

On March 30 a jubilant Kim left for Moscow, where he met with Stalin secretly three times during April. Stalin confirmed that, "[i]n case of emergency, the PRC will send troops." He added a reservation calculated to calm Kim: "We must be absolutely certain that Washington will not get involved in the fight." Stalin seemed to be informing his guest that the Soviet Union would do everything possible to prevent American intervention. In reality, as we have seen, Stalin wanted to draw the Americans into the conflict.

The bedazzled Kim was apparently blind to the double game his teacher was playing. In the presence of the "Great" Stalin, this former captain in the Soviet Army lost his capacity for critical thought. He happily assured his host that "the Americans will not risk getting entangled in a large war because of the Soviet-Chinese alliance." He did not understand Stalin's geopolitical plans, and so remarked, "The Koreans prefer to rely on their own strength in uniting the country and we believe we will succeed." Stalin, however, again counseled, "You must rely upon Mao who has an excellent grasp of Asian affairs."[15]

Kim needed Mao's help but did not want to become too dependent upon the Chinese. He was not only a communist but a Korean nationalist, and he was wary of China. For too many centuries his country had endured the imperial hegemony of its large neighbor. Kim wanted to avoid such a fate. Moreover, he really was certain of victory. The armed forces of North Korea were clearly superior to the army of South Korean president Syngman Rhee. Kim had twice as many troops and artillery pieces, seven times as many machine guns, thirteen times as many automatic rifles, six and a half times as many tanks, and six times as many planes.[16] It was impossible to disobey Stalin, but Kim played his hand shrewdly.

After returning to Pyongyang, he sent a chief aide to Beijing to inform Mao, Zhu De, and Zhou Enlai of the results of his talks with the "Father of Nations" and tell the "Chinese brothers" that he would like to receive from them only the three Korean divisions in the PLA. The CCP had formed these units, each ten thousand strong, from local Koreans in Manchuria during the civil war. Kim's was a clever gambit. Mao, pretending that he did not fully understand the real meaning of the request, not only indicated his approval to Kim's emissary, but also amicably added, "In case of need we can also throw in Chinese soldiers; they are all black [this is how it is written in the text; obviously, it should be "yellow"] [and] nobody will be able to tell the difference."[17] Mao immediately informed Kovalev of this conversation and the latter reported everything to Stalin.

On May 13, Mao received Kim Il Sung, who arrived in Beijing on a Soviet airplane. The following day Stalin belatedly informed Mao of his secret meetings with the North Korean leader:

> Comr[ade] Mao-Tse-Tung [Mao Zedong]! In a conversation with the Korean comrades Filippov [Stalin] and his friends expressed the opinion, that, in light of the changed international situation, they agree with the proposal of the Koreans to move toward reunification. In this regard a qualification was made, that the question should be decided finally by the Chinese and Korean comrades together, and in case of disagreement by the Chinese comrades the decision on the question should be postponed until a new discussion. The Korean comrades can tell you the details of the conversation. Filippov.[18]

Stalin sent this telegram only after Mao, piqued that talks between Stalin and Kim Il Sung had taken place in the Kremlin without his knowledge, had requested on May 13 "personal clarifications" from the Boss regarding the understanding he had come to with Kim.[19] From the Chairman's perspective this was no more than a formality, since he had long since understood Stalin's intentions to start a war in Korea, but he still resented Stalin's failure to level with him in January.

Nevertheless, Mao again gave his full agreement to support the unification of Korea by military means. Kim Il Sung acquainted Mao with his overall plan of operation, and the Chairman fully approved it. Of course he did—the basic contours of the plan had already been coordinated in Moscow. On parting, however, Mao remarked to Kim that "the Americans might still get involved in the fighting," but as before Mao was not particularly anxious on this score. "If the Americans take part in military actions, then China will provide troops to North Korea," he summed up.[20]

Just like Kim Il Sung, however, Mao miscalculated. Stalin alone came out a winner. From the outset everything went just as he had supposed. The Americans rushed to defend South Korea. By the time they first landed on June 29, however, the North Korean People's Army had succeeded in routing the main force South Korean divisions and had occupied the capital city of Seoul just three days after the war began. Soon, however, the UN troops reversed the situation and the North Korean armies all but disintegrated. Trying to avoid encirclement, they quickly retreated toward the Chinese border.[21] By the end of September, South Korean forces were approaching the 38th parallel; encountering no resistance, they crossed it on October 1. That same day General MacArthur demanded that the NKPA high command surrender immediately and unconditionally. The time for Mao Zedong to act had arrived. This was the moment Stalin had been awaiting. Soon the world revolution would begin.

On October 1, Stalin, who was then in Sochi, on the Black Sea coast, sent Mao and Zhou Enlai an urgent secret telegram:

> I think that if in the current situation you consider it possible to send troops to assist the Koreans, then you should move at least five–six divisions toward the 38th parallel at once so as to give our Korean comrades an opportunity to organize combat reserves north of the 38th parallel under the cover of your troops. The Chinese divisions could be considered as volunteers, with Chinese in command at the head, of course.[22]

Stalin was certain that Mao was merely waiting for his order. He knew from Ambassador Roshchin that the Chinese had deployed three armies with 120,000 troops in the vicinity of Shenyang in case UN troops crossed the 38th parallel.

Now that the decision point was at hand, the Chairman suddenly hesitated. Weighing all the reasons for and against intervening, he now realized that he had underestimated America. China was not prepared for a full-scale war with the United States. His country lay in ruins; the people were tired of fighting. Moreover, the Americans ruled the skies over Korea, and Stalin had made no promises to provide air cover for a Chinese offensive. The PRC had no air force of its own. Would it be an act of folly to throw oneself on the altar of world revolution for Moscow's benefit? On October 1 and 2, Mao discussed the situation in Korea with his closest associates; the majority of the leaders of the PRC, with Zhou Enlai being the most outspoken, opposed sending troops. Many military men, including Lin Biao, likewise did not support intervention. "It is better not to fight this war except as a last resort," they asserted.[23]

The Chinese were also offended by Kim Il Sung's behavior. He had neither requested their armed intervention nor even considered it necessary to inform them about how the resistance was going. Kim was obviously revealing his mistrust of the CCP leaders and preferred to beg Stalin for assistance. Zhou, evidently at Mao's request, had repeatedly complained about this to the Soviet ambassador. Stalin also considered this behavior "abnormal," but Kim persisted. Even at the end of September, in response to a Chinese offer to help, he merely replied that "the Korean people are prepared for a protracted war."[24] Soviet ambassador Shtykov reported to Gromyko on September 22, 1950 (the coded telegram was intended for Stalin):

> On September 21, 1950 the Secretary of the Central Committee of the Workers' Party, [Aleksei Ivanovich] Hegai, a Soviet Korean, paid me a visit.
>
> At the outset of the discussion, Hegai asserted that he wanted to inform me about a session of the Political Council of the party that had taken place on September 21.
>
> For two and a half hours there was a discussion about how to reply to the Chinese comrades in regard to ZHOU ENLAI'S inquiry about the Chinese government's proposal to the Korean government on the developing situation. . . . Those who spoke . . . came to the same conclusion, that the situation was difficult and that obviously they could not cope with the Americans on their own. Therefore, they concluded it was necessary to ask the Chinese government to send troops to Korea.
>
> After this KIM IL SUNG spoke, saying that What then? We had figured that with so many people we could manage with our own forces. The Soviet Union gave us as much armaments as we requested. On what basis can we request aid from the Chinese[?].
>
> Then KIM IL SUNG raised the question of what consequences might follow if the Chinese entered the war on the side of the Koreans. Might this not lead to a Third World War. . . .

He proposed for now to defer a decision about asking the Chinese government for help, instead to write a letter to Comrade STALIN and ask his advice as to whether to request that the Chinese send troops. In this connection, he allegedly emphasized that the Soviet Union might be offended on the grounds that its assistance in the form of advisers and armaments was insufficient.

Further, KIM IL SUNG declared that if we had time, we would expedite the formation of new units, then it would not be necessary to turn to the Chinese. But they were afraid this was not to be.

No decisions were taken as a result of the discussions.[25]

After heated debates, on September 28 the Politburo of the Central Committee of the Korean Workers' Party finally decided to send a letter to Beijing, which contained only "a hint of aid."[26] The North Koreans still placed their primary hopes "personally on Comrade Stalin," to whom they sent a letter on September 29 imploring him to intervene directly in the conflict.[27] To this the "Leader and Teacher" irritably replied that the best solution for the Korean question would be entry of Chinese troops onto Korean territory, and he advised the leaders of the DPRK to begin consultations with the Chinese as soon as possible.[28] After this Kim could no longer ignore reality. Late on the night of October 1, he asked the Chinese ambassador to transmit to Mao immediately his request to send Chinese troops to Korea. Furthermore, he sent a parallel telegram to Beijing through his own channels.[29]

On October 2, however, Mao sent a message to Stalin via Soviet ambassador Roshchin, which Stalin received the following day:

We originally planned to move several volunteer divisions to North Korea to render assistance to the Korean comrades when the enemy advanced north of the 38th parallel.

However, having thought this over thoroughly, we now consider that such actions may entail extremely serious consequences.

In the first place, it is very difficult to resolve the Korean question with a few divisions (our troops are extremely poorly equipped, there is no confidence in the success of military operations against American troops), the enemy can force us to retreat.

In the second place, it is most likely that this will provoke an open conflict between the USA and China, as a consequence of which the Soviet Union can also be dragged into war, and the question would thus become extremely large. Many comrades in the CC CPC [Central Committee of the Communist Party of China] judge that it is necessary to show caution here.

Of course, not to send out troops to render assistance is very bad for the Korean comrades, who are presently in such difficulty, and we ourselves feel this keenly; but if we advance several divisions and the enemy forces us to retreat; and this moreover provokes an open conflict between the USA and China, then our entire plan for peaceful construction will be completely ruined, and many people in the country will be dissatisfied (the wounds inflicted on the people by the war have not yet healed, we need peace).

Therefore it is better to show patience now, refrain from advancing troops, [and] actively prepare our forces, which will be more advantageous at the time of war with the enemy.

Korea, while temporarily suffering defeat, will change the form of the struggle to guerrilla war.

We will convene a meeting of the CC, at which will be present the main comrades of various bureaus of the CC. A final decision has not been taken on this question. This is our preliminary telegram, we wish to consult with you. If you agree, then we are ready immediately to send by plane Comrades ZHOU ENLAI and LIN BIAO to your vacation place, to talk over this matter with you and to report the situation in China and Korea.

We await your reply.

MAO ZEDONG

2.10.50[30]

Of course, it was dangerous to quarrel with Stalin, but Mao thought he could persuade the Boss on the basis of objective difficulties. In any case, on the same day, October 2, he drafted a completely different telegram to Stalin in which he said, "We [the Central Committee of the CCP] have decided to send a detachment of troops under the name of the Volunteer Army to Korea."[31] For now he held on to this telegram,[32] after deciding first to probe Stalin's frame of mind. Who could tell—perhaps Stalin might buy his argument?

On the afternoon of October 4, Mao convened an enlarged meeting of the Politburo attended by "the main comrades from various bureaus of the CC." He asked those attending the meeting "to list the disadvantages involved in dispatching troops to Korea." At the same time, he added, "We'd feel bad if we stood idly by."[33] A discussion ensued during which a majority of the leaders again voiced their opposition to intervention.

But then Mao received Stalin's reply, which revealed the Boss's extreme irritation over Mao's telegram. Stalin now bluntly explained that an open clash between China and America was precisely what he was aiming for. The text of his coded telegram, sent to Beijing in reply to Mao Zedong's message of October 2, bristled with sinister candor:

Of course, I took into account . . . [the possibility] that the USA, despite its unreadiness for a big war, could still be drawn into a big war out of [considerations of] prestige, which, in turn, would drag China into the war, and along with this draw into the war the USSR, which is bound with China by the Mutual Assistance Pact. Should we fear this? In my opinion, we should not, because together we will be stronger than the USA and England, while the other European capitalist states (with the exception of Germany which is unable to provide any assistance to the United States now) do not present serious military forces. If a war is inevitable, then let it be waged now, and not in a few years when Japanese militarism will be restored as an ally of the USA and when the USA and Japan will have a ready-made bridgehead on the continent in a form of the entire Korea run by Syngman Rhee.[34]

Juxtaposing this top-secret coded telegram with Stalin's telegram cited above to the Soviet ambassador to Czechoslovakia on August 27, 1950, leaves no doubt about Stalin's true geopolitical intentions. For the sake of world revolution he was ready to provoke World War III. All of his earlier peace-loving talk was simply a pretense.

On October 5, a crestfallen Mao convened another enlarged plenum of the Politburo at which he called on Peng Dehuai, a strong advocate of intervention. Peng implored the assembled to "send troops to help Korea," emphasizing that if this were not done, the United States might next attack China from two bases, from Taiwan and from Korea. "The tiger wanted to eat human beings," he asserted, "when it would do so would depend on its appetite."[35] Peng's impassioned speech broke the impasse, and the plenum took the decision that Stalin required. Then Mao appointed Peng commander of the Volunteer Army, which had yet to be established. (At first Mao had wanted to give this position to Lin Biao, but Lin turned down the assignment, pleading illness.)[36] Then the Chairman telegraphed Stalin to "express solidarity with the fundamental positions" discussed in Stalin's telegram and, trying to mollify the Boss, said he would "send to Korea nine, not six, divisions." He explained that he would "send them not now, but after some time" and he requested that Stalin "receive his representatives and discuss some details of the mission with them."[37]

Stalin agreed to this proposal, and Mao dispatched Zhou Enlai and Lin Biao, both opponents of the war, to Sochi on October 8. He waited impatiently for word on what the Boss would say. Meanwhile, trying to ingratiate himself with Stalin, Mao ordered Peng Dehuai and the chairman of the Northeast regional government, Gao Gang, who was concurrently commander and political commissar of the Northeast Military Region, to reorganize the troops deployed in Manchuria into the Chinese People's Volunteer Army. He requested that the CPVA promptly enter Korea.[38] On October 8, Mao informed Kim Il Sung of his order,[39] although he understood that neither Peng Dehuai nor Gao Gang could "act quickly," despite the fact that they were both proponents of intervention. They needed time to reorganize the army.

On October 10, at 7 P.M., Zhou Enlai and Lin Biao met with Stalin in Sochi. The talks, in which other members of the Soviet leadership—Vyacheslav Molotov, Georgii Malenkov, Lavrentii Beria, Lazar Kaganovich, Nikolai Bulganin, and Anastas Mikoyan—also participated, were difficult. As always, Zhou was calm and collected, but toward the end, after hours of debate, even he felt tired. Lin looked just like a corpse, according to Shi Zhe. At 5 A.M., when Stalin suggested they celebrate the conclusion of the talks with a banquet, Lin was horrified. Unlike Zhou Enlai, who could outdrink anyone, Lin was a teetotaler, but he could not refuse to attend. Thus, despite their fatigue the guests accepted the invitation. What exactly, however, was there to celebrate? Stalin had not agreed to provide air cover to the CPVA, saying that the Soviet Air Force was not yet ready. He promised to send airplanes only after two or two and a half months. He wrote the same thing to Mao after the talks.[40] He demanded self-sacrifice from the Chinese, but he was in no hurry to send his airplanes.

Meanwhile, the fighting on the Korean peninsula continued. Then, on October 12, Mao, disheartened, again informed Stalin that he could not send troops to Korea. That same day he countermanded his order to Peng Dehuai and Gao Gang to take the field, and he summoned them back to Beijing for consultations.[41]

Here was an insurrection. The specter of Chinese "Titoism" once more loomed before Stalin. Infuriated with Mao as well as with Kim, about whose ambiguous behavior Zhou and Lin had had much to say, that same day Stalin ordered the North Korean leader to withdraw the remnants of his armies from North Korea: "The Chinese have again refused to send troops. In this connection you must evacuate North Korea and withdraw Korean troops to the north."[42] On October 13, he reiterated: "We believe that continued resistance is hopeless. The Chinese comrades are refusing to take part in military action. In these circumstances, you must prepare to evacuate completely into China and/or the USSR. . . . The potential to engage the enemy in the future must be preserved."[43] Then he said to his entourage, "Well, what of it? We didn't send our troops in there, and so now the Americans will be our neighbors on our Far Eastern border, that's all."[44] The world revolution had ended before it began.

Then suddenly a miracle occurred. On the same day Stalin told Kim Il Sung he considered Kim's struggle "hopeless," October 13, Mao unexpectedly informed Ambassador Roshchin that "the CC CCP [actually it was the Central Committee Politburo] discussed the situation again and decided after all to render military assistance to the Korean comrades, regardless of the insufficient armament of the Chinese troops."[45] He sent the same message to Zhou Enlai, who was still in Moscow. Both Roshchin and Zhou quickly informed the Soviet leadership.[46] Ultimately Mao was unable to oppose Stalin and retreated at the final moment, even though the "Leader and Teacher" refused to provide air cover. Stalin's influence upon him was too great: the shadow of the all-powerful Kremlin dictator continued to hang over Zhongnanhai.

Receiving this good news from Roshchin, Stalin immediately ordered Kim Il Sung to "postpone temporarily the implementation of the telegram sent to you yesterday about the evacuation of North Korea and the retreat of the Korean troops to the north."[47] He did not bother to conceal his joy. Everything was again going according to plan.

Six days later, four field armies and three artillery divisions of the PLA, under the overall command of Peng Dehuai, finally intervened in the Korean conflict. UN troops faltered and then started rolling south, but soon the situation stabilized. The South Koreans and the Americans began to put up stiff resistance, which led Peng Dehuai to halt the offensive. The front lines stretched out in the general vicinity of the 38th parallel.

The initial successes of the Chinese Army had inspired Mao, who even began to think that the war might end in victory if, like his own earlier war in China, it became protracted. He wrote to Stalin to this effect on March 1, 1951. Stalin for his part insisted that "there is no need to accelerate the war, since in the first place a protracted war will provide an opportunity for Chinese troops to learn modern warfare under field conditions and, second, it will shake Truman's regime in America and discredit the military prestige of Anglo American forces."[48]

In February 1951, Stalin, via the CCP, had instructed the Indonesian communist party (PKI) to launch a struggle to seize power by armed force as well. "The fundamental task of the Communist Party of Indonesia in the near future," he emphasized in a telegram to Liu Shaoqi intended for the Central Committee of the PKI, is not " 'to create the broadest possible united national front' against the imperialists to 'achieve the genuine independence of Indonesia,' but to eliminate feudal property on land and the transfer of land to the peasants."[49] The world conflagration continued to rage.

Neither Stalin nor Mao was concerned about the numerous victims of war. In this same letter of March 1, Mao informed the "Teacher" that Chinese forces had already suffered 100,000 dead and wounded and that during this and the following year battle losses were projected at 300,000. "Thus," Mao concluded, "we will need another 300,000 to fill the ranks."[50] That's all he had to say. It is as if he were speaking not of people, but of inanimate statistical units.

As time passed, however, the war began to seem hopeless. The Chinese People's Volunteers, whose numbers swelled to one million men (another one million men took part in transporting supplies to Korea), poured out its lifeblood, and Mao finally began to think about how to extricate them from Korea. In early summer 1951, insistently but cautiously, he began to broach this thought in his correspondence with Stalin.[51] Stalin, however, would not give his blessing to ending the conflict. He still needed the war. On the Korean peninsula Chinese and North Korean troops were attending the school of contemporary warfare, preparing themselves for new battles and, moreover, "bringing about revolution throughout Far Eastern Asia" and "strengthening socialism in Europe."

By the summer of 1951, however, the North Koreans also began to realize that the war had to be ended. On June 10, with Mao's consent, Kim Il Sung and Gao Gang flew to Moscow, where they were joined by Lin Biao, who was in the Soviet Union for medical treatment. The three of them succeeded in convincing Stalin to agree to talks with the enemy. However, the Kremlin dictator did not grant Kim and Mao the power to conclude peace in Korea. The armistice talks, begun on July 10, 1951, moved slowly while the flames of war continued to burn.

Mao then began to complain to Stalin about the economic difficulties caused by the war. On November 14, 1951, for example, he wrote:

> In the current year, in view of our assistance to Korea and the strug-
> gle against American imperialism, the Chinese government's budget
> has increased by 60 percent over last year's. Thirty-two percent of
> the overall budget goes directly to the Korean military theater (the
> military credits supplied to us by the Soviet Government are not in-
> cluded in this calculation). Thus, if we do not now practice economy,
> next year the budget will grow even more which will inevitably influ-
> ence our financial situation and lead to a large increase in commodity
> prices which, in turn, will create problems at the front as well as in
> economic reconstruction in the rear. Achieving peace through nego-
> tiations would surely benefit us.[52]

In January 1952, news reached Moscow that 10 percent of the population in North Korea was suffering from hunger, and that by April or May a majority of peasants would be in the grip of famine. Mao decided to help the Koreans by shipping them grain, despite the fact that the food situation in the PRC itself was far from ideal. Stalin, it seems, deliberately took no notice. During his meeting in the Kremlin on August 20, 1952, with Zhou and other members of the Chinese delegation, he was adamant:

> This war is getting on America's nerves. The North Koreans have lost
> nothing, except for casualties. . . . Americans understand that this
> war is not advantageous and they will have to end it, especially after

it becomes clear that our troops will remain in China. Endurance and patience is needed here. . . . The war in Korea has shown America's weakness. . . . [A]mericans are not capable of waging a large-scale war at all, especially after the Korean war. . . . America cannot defeat little Korea . . . [and] they have lost the capability to wage a large-scale war. They are pinning their hopes on the atom bomb and air power. But one cannot win a war with that. One needs infantry, and they don't have much infantry; the infantry they do have is weak. They are fighting with little Korea, and already people are weeping in the USA. What will happen if they start a large-scale war? Then, perhaps, everyone will weep.[53]

Mao was able to extricate himself "with honor" from this difficult situation only after Stalin died in 1953. In the meantime the war on the Korean peninsula was a colossal burden for China. The PLA could no longer wage such a costly war. Kim Il Sung was also happy to end it. On March 11, 1953, six days after the dictator's death, Zhou Enlai, who had arrived in Moscow for the funeral, conveyed to Soviet leaders Malenkov, Beria, and Khrushchev an urgent request from the PRC to accelerate the armistice negotiations. The new Soviet leaders also favored ending the war.[54] On March 19, the Council of Ministers of the USSR resolved to change Stalin's line and seek a way out of Korea.[55] A special representative was dispatched from Moscow to Pyongyang to convey the new Soviet instructions to Kim Il Sung.

At 10 A.M. on July 27, 1953, representatives of North Korea and the PRC on one side and the UN command on the other signed a cease-fire agreement. The Chinese People's Volunteers remained in Korea until October 1958, when, under pressure from Kim Il Sung, they returned home.[56]

In this war, according to official data, China lost 148,000 killed and more than 300,000 wounded, POWs, and MIA. (According to other sources, the number of deaths was 152,000 or even 183,000 while the overall number of casualties reached 900,000.)[57] At the same time the North Korean People's Army lost 520,000 dead, the South Koreans 415,000, and the Americans 142,000 killed and wounded, including 36,516 KIA. The Soviet Union lost 299 men, including 138 officers and 161 sergeants and soldiers. The greatest number of victims were peaceful Korean citizens; according to various data between three and four million of them died.[58]

Among those killed was Mao Zedong's eldest son, Mao Anying. In the summer of 1950, when the war in Korea began he applied to join the army. Again, as he had during the war against fascism, he rushed to the front. Perhaps he wanted to show his father, who was still cool to him, that he was worth something. In any case, he went to Korea, where he was assigned to the General Staff of the Chinese People's Volunteers. Commander in Chief Peng Dehuai tried to keep him by his side, but was unable to protect Anying from harm. On November 25, 1950, Anying died during an American air raid on Peng Dehuai's headquarters. He was only twenty-eight years old. That same day Peng wrote to Mao, but Ye Zilong, the Chairman's secretary, with the approval of Zhou Enlai, withheld the telegram from Mao. Only after several days did Mao learn the bitter truth.

According to those in his entourage, Mao shed no tears. "He . . . did not express his feelings at all," Ye Zilong recalled, "but his face looked very pinched. He waved his hand and said, 'In such a war there have been and always will be sacrifices. This is nothing.' "[59] He repeated the same thing to Peng Dehuai when they next met. "Chairman," Peng said to him, "I did not safeguard Anying, it is my fault. I request that you punish me!" But Mao merely closed his eyes. "There can be no revolutionary war without sacrifices. . . . A simple soldier died, and one need not make a big deal out of this just because he was my son."[60] It was obvious, however, that he was taking the loss hard. For several days he ate almost nothing and was unable to sleep. He sat alone in his armchair and smoked one cigarette after another.

By then he had lost many family members. His youngest brother, Zetan, fell in battle with the Nationalists in western Fujian in 1935. His middle brother, Zemin, suffered a cruel death in 1943 in Xinjiang, where he had gone to work in 1940 for the militarist Sheng Shicai. For quite some time Sheng passed himself off as a friend of Stalin and had even applied for membership in the Soviet Communist Party. But in 1942 he severed his relations with the Soviet Union, suspecting, apparently with good reason, that the Comintern and the CCP were plotting to overthrow him. Sheng seized Mao Zemin and other leaders of the Xinjiang branch of the CCP and threw them in prison. They were interrogated and tortured for several months, and on September 27, 1943, they were executed. They were first beaten with truncheons, then suffocated, and their bodies were stuffed into sacks and buried on a remote mountainside. Mao Zedong later heard rumors that three days later Sheng supposedly ordered the bodies to be dug up and photographed, and had the photos sent to Song Meiling to give to Chiang Kai-shek.[61]

In August 1929, Mao's foster sister, Zejian, died at the hands of the Nationalists, just a year and three months before Kaihui's death. In June 1946, nineteen-year-old Mao Chuxiong, one of his nephews and the only son of his brother Zetan, was killed. In Changsha in 1930, Kaihui's cousin Kaiming was shot, and in 1935, during the Long March, Mao lost another brother-in-law, He Meiren, the younger brother of Zizhen. He was killed by Tibetans for defiling a Lamaist temple.

Of the families of Mao's two brothers, only the children of Zemin were alive: Yuanzhi, his daughter from his first marriage, who was a year older than the deceased Anying, and his son, Yuanxin. The latter had been born on February 14, 1941, in Xinjiang soon after the lustful Zemin left his second wife, Xijun, and married his new passion. His third wife, Zhu Danhua, was also an actress, like Jiang Qing. In February 1943, she was arrested and imprisoned along with her young son. She was not released until May 1946; in July she and Yuanxin arrived in Yan'an, where Mao greeted them. He showed great warmth and even sentimentality toward his small nephew, who was just half a year younger than his daughter Li Na. He may have felt it his duty to be more concerned about him than he was about his own children. He also paid attention to his niece Yuanzhi, but she was already grown up. She had married in 1945 and a year later gave birth to a son, so Mao began to feel like a grandfather. From 1951 on Yuanxin grew up under the supervision of Mao. Zhu Danhua remarried and lived and worked with her new husband in Nanchang, leaving her son at Mao and Jiang Qing's request to live in Zhongnanhai.

Mao's grief at the death of Anying, however, did not pass, and neither his daughter nor his younger son nor his beloved nephew could deaden it. It was as if something between him and his fallen son had not been resolved and periodically tormented him.

Anying's death was particularly troubling for Anqing. More than just brothers, they had been bound by grief over their dead mother, memories of their hunger-ridden childhood and their adventurous journey from Hong Kong to Moscow, their sojourn in the International Orphanage, and their lives together with Mama He. Anqing was a very nervous young man, prone to anxiety, and with an unbalanced psychology. The terrible blow to the head that the soldier had dealt him when his mother had been arrested had left its mark. The death of his brother pushed him over the edge. He lost sleep, began to wander about the house, and talked to himself. Soon the doctors delivered the terrible diagnosis of schizophrenia. Anqing was no longer able to work. Mao sent Anqing to the Soviet Union for treatment, but he was beyond help. Returning to China, he was taken to a military sanatorium in Dalian, where he lived under medical supervision. His brother's widow, Liu Songlin, and her younger sister Shao Hua were very solicitous toward him. The latter even moved to Dalian to look after the sick man. In 1960 Anqing and Shao Hua were married. Two years later they returned to Beijing. Anqing began to feel better, but he never fully recovered.[62]

Mao, of course, was very upset by the illness of his son, but he was even more disappointed. "Shall I be deprived of descendants . . . (one son was killed, one went mad)," he said bitterly.[63] To be sure, as usual he had little time for emotions. Power and politics displaced his paternal feelings.

26

THE CONTRADICTIONS
OF NEW DEMOCRACY

Mao wanted China to develop rapidly into a modern socialist country. But in the early years of the PRC, Stalin's suspicious nature, urge to dominate, and dogmatism combined to limit his provision of Soviet aid to China. Even had he really wanted to do more, the war-devastated Soviet economy would have prevented him from substantially increasing assistance to the PRC. The available documents indicate, however, that political rather than economic reasons motivated Stalin to limit aid to the PRC. The reminiscences of Konstantin Koval, Soviet deputy minister of foreign trade, concerning Stalin's negotiations with Zhou Enlai in August–September 1952 are eloquent in this regard.[1] Stalin ignored Zhou when the latter suggested, "You will help us to build a socialist China, and we will help you to build a communist Soviet Union."[2] Stalin likewise disapproved of China's efforts to draft a five-year plan for 1951–55, deeming it unrealistic.[3] The financial aid he provided the People's Republic, judging from the agreement signed on February 14, 1950, was US $300 million in credits over a five-year period at a favorable annual interest rate of 1 percent.[4] It is true that this is the amount Mao requested, supposing it "better for us to borrow less than to borrow more at present and for several years."[5] Yet Stalin did not offer any more and during the Korean War the Chinese were forced to apply the loan to buy Soviet arms. Naturally, they considered this unfair since the loan had initially been intended to help with domestic economic problems, and the Chinese believed they were fulfilling their "internationalist duty" in Korea.[6]

By the time of Stalin's death on March 5, 1953, the Soviet government had formally approved only 50 of the 147 industrial projects that Beijing had proposed,[7] and it had been in no hurry to fulfill these obligations.[8] Stalin rebuffed all Chinese requests to accelerate the pace of assistance, consistently advising the leaders of the CCP not to force the pace of modernization. At a meeting with Zhou Enlai on September 3, 1952, to discuss the proposed Five-Year Plan,

Stalin expressed dissatisfaction with the Chinese desire to establish an annual 20 percent industrial growth rate. He could not agree since, according to official statistics, the Soviet economy during the First Five-Year Plan had grown at only 18.5 percent per annum.* For competitive reasons Stalin advised Zhou to lower the overall rate of growth to 15 percent and agreed to consider the 20 percent limit for annual plans only as a propaganda slogan.[9] In early February 1953, Mikhail Saburov, chairman of the State Planning Committee of the USSR, sent Li Fuchun, deputy chairman of the PRC Financial-Economic Commission, who was in Moscow at the time, a set of comments by Soviet experts on the PRC's draft Five-Year Plan. Following Stalin's precepts, Saburov advised the Chinese comrades to set an even lower rate of industrial growth of between 13.5 and 15 percent.[10] The State Administrative Council of the PRC was forced to agree.[11] Ultimately, the figure for the annual industrial growth rate was set at 14.7 percent.[12]

Stalin's meeting with Liu Shaoqi, a member of the Politburo and deputy chairman of the Central People's Government of the PRC, held in October 1952 during the Nineteenth Congress of the CPSU, likewise demonstrated Moscow's caution with respect to building socialism in China. At this time, Stalin firmly opposed Mao's idea of introducing the cooperativization and collectivization of the Chinese peasantry over a period of ten to fifteen years, an idea Mao had first expressed at a meeting of the Secretariat of the Central Committee one month earlier.[13] Liu Shaoqi informed Stalin of this when he presented a report on the policies of the CCP Central Committee.[14] As Liu Shaoqi recalled in a conversation with Soviet ambassador Vasily Kuznetsov in November 1953, "Comrade Stalin advised not to hasten cooperativization and collectivization of agriculture inasmuch as conditions in the PRC were more favorable than in the USSR during the period of collectivization."[15] Liu conveyed Stalin's opinion to Beijing, and Mao was forced to take it into account.

But Mao did not always follow Stalin's directives. Between 1949 and 1953, on his own initiative he undertook a number of measures directed toward accelerating the Stalinization of China. After the proclamation of the PRC and the expulsion of the remnant Guomindang army to Taiwan, the communist regime continued regular military actions against various social forces that had not consistently supported the Guomindang during the civil war. Among these were the traditional rural elites, representatives of some local power structures who had remained on the sidelines during the civil war, hoping to wait out this time of troubles. After the complete defeat of the Guomindang, Mao gradually but surely began to establish his power at the local level, dis-

---

* According to the majority of Western specialists, during the First Five-Year Plan, Soviet industry grew by an annual rate of 12 percent. It is doubtful, however, that Stalin trusted Western statistics.

placing local elites and empowering new pro-communist supporters during the course of establishing new organs of power.

Now the CCP encountered fierce resistance from its social antagonists and the civil war acquired a mass character, affecting millions of persons. According to probably conservative official figures, by the end of 1951 more than two million people had been killed in the course of the struggle. Another two million had been imprisoned and sent to labor camps.[16] This war continued, but no further statistics were published on the number of victims. According to data compiled by the Russian China specialist Colonel B. N. Gorbachev, 39 corps of the PLA, or more than 140 divisions numbering some 1.5 million troops, participated in these battles.[17] One of the cruelest acts was the purge of unreliable elements among former Guomindang officers who had gone over to the CCP side during the war. According to the reminiscences of General Georgii Semenov, adviser to the commander of the North China Military District, among the former units of General Fu Zuoyi of the Beijing Garrison that had defected to the PLA side, 22,014 criminals were "unmasked" during "peacetime," among whom, by decision of the political commissar, 1,272 deserved an immediate death sentence, 1,415 a delayed death sentence, and 6,223 exile.[18] The situation was complicated by the fact that during the first years of the PRC there was no law that regulated punishment for civil crimes. Between 1949 and 1954, the CCP ruled the country by means of political campaigns and mass mobilization.

The sharpest struggle took place in the countryside during the agrarian reform. By 1948 Mao had shelved the slogan not only of land redistribution, but also those of rent and interest reduction, thereby guaranteeing the party the neutrality of the landholders in the countryside and expediting the Guomindang's defeat by isolating it from its social roots. The day of reckoning, however, came quickly. Over approximately three years, progressing from north to south, the CCP gradually carried out an agrarian reform that might better be termed an agrarian revolution "from above." The passivity of the peasantry was remedied by the dispatch of special teams to the countryside composed of party activists, approximately three hundred thousand yearly, who organized peasant unions, implanted new local elites, and dealt harshly with everyone labeled as landlords and counterrevolutionaries. Popular tribunals dispensing rough justice were established in the villages and given the power to impose death sentences. Many who resisted were summarily shot or sent to concentration camps. Despite the CCP's avowed policy of protecting rich peasants, their numbers declined sharply. Power in the countryside and a number of economic privileges were conferred upon a new "communist" elite.

After the rural rich were eliminated, urban property owners were the next target. In December 1951, Mao launched campaigns directed against the bourgeoisie: the Sanfan (Three Anti) campaign against corrupt officials, and the Wufan (Five Anti) campaign against private entrepreneurship. Popular tribunals empowered to pronounce death sentences were established in the cities. Public trials were held that often resulted in on-the-spot public executions. The main form of repression applied to the bourgeoisie was the imposition of staggering indemnities that seriously weakened their economic position. The result was that by September 1952, at a meeting of the Secretariat of the CCP Central Committee, Mao Zedong was able to assert that the state share of industry was 67.3 percent and of trade 40 percent; thus the socialist sector occupied the dominant and leading position in the Chinese economy.[19]

Gradually, the intelligentsia became the target of the ideological campaign. In 1951, on Mao's initiative, a campaign of Marxist indoctrination began under the pretext of discussing a film called *The Life of Wu Xun*. This film about a well-known nineteenth-century Confucian educator who had risen from desperate poverty to prominence first evoked the fury of Jiang Qing, a self-proclaimed specialist on cinematic art. "Continued veneration of Wu Hsun's [Wu Xun's] model," she said to Mao, "was dangerous because his actions discredited present national imperatives: overthrow the landlord class, bury Confucian scholars, and put down the reformist . . . tenet that education dissolves class contradictions and leads to social and political success."[20] Mao agreed. The campaign quickly transmuted into an ideological condemnation of dissent, kicking off a movement for the ideological remolding of intellectuals in which the methods of ideological terror that played a sinister role in the subsequent development of spiritual life in the PRC were already evident.

According to some data, during these campaigns in the early years of the PRC more than four million "counterrevolutionaries" were repressed.[21] The ruling party itself did not escape the sharpening struggle. In 1951, Mao already had decided to conduct a verification and reregistration of CCP members that led to a new "purge" of "alien" elements. By 1953, 10 percent of the party members had been expelled.

During the period of New Democracy, intended as a transitional period to socialism, however, not all the leaders of the PRC agreed with Mao's policies. Several high-ranking leaders conceived of New Democracy differently from Mao. Liu Shaoqi was the most important. We know that as early as 1949, Stalin was receiving confidential information on Liu Shaoqi from another member of the CCP Politburo, Gao Gang, chairman of the Northeast regional government, who accused Liu of "right deviation" and "overestimating the Chinese bourgeoisie." Some of Gao's assertions, albeit without direct reference to Gao himself, were contained in a critical secret report from Kovalev to Stalin titled "On several questions regarding policies and practice in the CC Chinese Communist Party." The report also contained accusations against Zhou Enlai and such Central Committee members as Peng Zhen, Li Fuchun, Li Lisan,* Bo Yibo, and Lin Feng.[22] Stalin, however, did not accept all these accusations, and asserted that "regarding the question of democratic parties in China and the necessity to reckon with their leaders Com. Gao Gang . . . is wrong, but Coms. Zhou Enlai and Liu Shaoqi are certainly right." During one of his meetings with Mao Zedong at his dacha in the vicinity of Moscow, Stalin even gave Mao a copy of Kovalev's report and some other documents received from Kovalev and Gao Gang.[23] Kovalev, who was in the hospital at this time, learned this from Shi Zhe, Mao's personal interpreter, who was present at the meeting.[24]

Mao Zedong viewed Stalin's conduct as yet another demonstration of his "mistrust and suspicion" of the Central Committee of the CCP.[25] One may also discern other motives in Stalin's actions. In the first place, he may not have believed Gao, who had earlier also provided him information on members of the Chinese communist leadership that seemed suspicious. Among those whom the regional CCP leader "unmasked" was Mao himself. In late 1949, for example, Gao Gang informed Stalin via Kovalev of the anti-Soviet and "right Trotskyite" tendencies of Mao and his associates in the Chinese Communist Party.[26] He repeated his accusations against the CCP leaders, albeit in a "restrained and cautious form," in a conversation with Yudin, who returned to the Soviet Union in 1952 via Manchuria and visited Gao en route.[27] Stalin might have considered all these accusations evidence of intraparty struggle within the CCP and simply paid no attention to them.

Second, from the summer of 1949, Stalin was deeply disappointed in Gao, who he thought had behaved very stupidly during one of the Kremlin leader's meetings with the Chinese delegation headed by Liu Shaoqi. Trying to appear "holier than the Pope," Gao, a member of the delegation, made in the presence of the others some very far-reaching proposals, including that the USSR should increase the number of its troops in Dalian and station naval forces at Qingdao, and, most important of all, that Manchuria should become a republic of the Soviet Union. Irritated, Stalin cut him off, calling him "Comrade Zhang Zuolin."[28] (Zhang Zuolin, it will be recalled, was a Chinese militarist who ruled Manchuria independent of the Chinese central government up to 1928.) †

---

* Li Lisan was elected a member of the CCP Central Committee on Mao's initiative in June 1945 at the Seventh Party Congress. It is worth mentioning that at the time he was still in Moscow and he was not even a member of the party because he had been expelled. But Mao wanted to play the role of unifier of the CCP; that is why he forgave Li.

† Kovalev mistakenly asserts that this took place at an enlarged plenum of the Politburo on July 27, 1949. On July 27, however, a Politburo meeting was not held but rather there was an exchange of opinions among Stalin, Bulganin, and Vyshinsky on one side and Liu Shaoqi, Gao Gang, and Wang Jiaxiang on the other. The Politburo meeting was held on July 11.

Third, if Stalin trusted the information he had received, he might have considered Liu's "deviation" useful insofar as it could help in his own policy of "containing" Mao Zedong's radicalism.

Finally, Gao was not Stalin's sole source of information within the Chinese leadership. According to some sources, Liu Shaoqi himself provided Stalin some confidential information. Petr Deriabin, a former official of the Ministry of State Security (MGB), claims that Liu Shaoqi began to work for the Soviet secret service in the 1930s when he was in Moscow as a representative of the All-China Federation of Trade Unions to the Trade Union International (Profintern). Liu continued to supply secret information to Stalin in the 1940s.[29] If Deriabin's account is accurate, then it is logical to suppose that Liu must have been more valuable to Stalin than Gao, since he was the second-ranking person in the CCP after Mao. By sacrificing Gao Gang, Stalin could strengthen the position of his more important informant.

In any case, Gao Gang was correct. The leadership of the CCP was not united on the question of New Democracy. Unlike Mao, who had abandoned the term "New Democracy," several other CCP leaders continued to use the terminology of the New Democratic revolution. Zhou Enlai as well as Liu Shaoqi apparently took seriously Stalin's admonitions concerning a gradual transition to socialism in the PRC, and spoke of the New Democratic state, of the construction of New Democracy, of New Democratic trends in literature and art, and so on.[30] They formed at the time a cautious opposition to Mao, who was interpreting New Democracy in an extremely radical fashion.

This is why CCP policies were somewhat contradictory during these years. The concept of a democratic transformation of society was reflected in the Common Program of the united front, whose organizational embodiment was the Chinese People's Political Consultative Council (CPPCC), convened by the communists in Beijing in late September 1949. The CPPCC as the organizational form of the united front took upon itself the functions of a constituent assembly, with Mao as its chairman. It was in the name of the CPPCC that the communists established the new organs of state power and adopted the Common Program, which became the main programmatic document of the new state authority, functioning like a provisional constitution. The program proclaimed democratic values but emphasized the leading role of the CCP within a multiparty system in which eight political parties that acknowledged the leading role of the CCP received legal status. The program guaranteed the people's right to own private property and contained clauses supporting private national entrepreneurship and the mutually beneficial regulation of relations between labor and capital. The document proclaimed a policy of democratic development for the country. The idea of the socialist reconstruction of Chinese society was entirely absent, as was the very word "socialism."[31]

The Agrarian Reform Law, adopted by the government on June 28, 1950, likewise corresponded fully to the spirit of people's democracy. Land was given to the peasant as private property, and the rich-peasant economy was preserved.[32] "The policy of preserving the rich-peasant economy," Liu Shaoqi said in his report to a session of the All-China Committee of the CPPCC in June 1950, "is not a temporary policy but one intended for the long term. In other words, the rich-peasant economy will be preserved for the duration of the entire period of New Democracy."[33]

The policies of the new government were supported by democratic and patriotic circles that welcomed the transformation and development of the system of popular education aimed at liquidating or, more accurately, reducing illiteracy, opening new higher education institutions and creating the preconditions for their democratization, training scientists, and establishing a system of modern scientific institutes.[34] The law on marriage and the family adopted in 1950 received broad public support; it provided women with full civil rights and was aimed at achieving their actual equality.[35] Chinese public opinion was also impressed by the independent and, in the cases of Korea and Tibet,* even aggressive foreign policy of the new government.

Between 1949 and 1953, not only Liu Shaoqi and Zhou Enlai, but Chen Yun and several other leading CCP officials expressed moderate views regarding New Democracy, even in unofficial conversations with representatives of other communist parties.[36] In their muted opposition to Mao, these leaders relied upon the authority of Stalin, whose advice was not to hasten the construction of socialism. Such political support, independent of its actual goals, was particularly important since it provided an ideological foundation for the ideas they were putting into practice. Stalin's position also exercised influence over Mao and his associates, who had no choice but to pay heed to the viewpoint of the "Elder Brother." It is revealing that Liu Shaoqi appealed to the authority of Stalin during his conversations with the Soviet ambassador in November 1953, even after he had suffered a defeat in his discussions with Mao.

Both Mao and his opponents accepted socialist ideals, but they differed in the methods of achieving them. Here are just a few examples. In the spring of 1951, the Provincial Party leaders of Shanxi proposed accelerating the pace of rural cooperativization. Liu Shaoqi not only criticized these ideas at a meeting of propagandists, but in July 1951 issued a document in the name of the Central Committee calling the provincial undertaking "an erroneous, dangerous and utopian notion of agrarian socialism." However, Mao protected the local activists and two months later disavowed the document that Liu had prepared.[37] At a session of the State Administrative Council chaired by Zhou Enlai in December 1952, a new draft tax system prepared by Finance Minis-

---

* Tibet, which had retained its formally independent status under the Guomindang, was conquered by the PLA in 1950–51.

ter Bo Yibo was presented and approved. Its principal innovation was that all forms of property were subjected to uniform taxation. State and cooperative property lost their tax advantages, and the private capitalist sector was granted favorable conditions for competition. The draft law had not been cleared with the Central Committee apparatus and Mao did not know about it. Soon afterward, on January 15, 1953, Mao sent an angry letter to the leaders of the State Council—Zhou Enlai, Chen Yun, Deng Xiaoping, and Bo Yibo—saying that their aim of creating conditions for a revival of private entrepreneurship was ill-founded.[38] This dispute led to an intensive ideological-political campaign against those who disagreed with Mao's line. In an informal talk with leaders of the Central South Bureau of the Central Committee in Wuhan in mid-February, Mao observed, "There are people who say, 'We must strengthen the New Democratic order'; there are also people who speak in favor of the 'four big freedoms' [i.e., freedom for peasants to take out loans, to rent land, to hire labor, and to engage in trade]. I think both of these are wrong. New Democracy is a transitional stage toward socialism."[39]

By the summer of 1953, Mao's struggle against "moderate" leaders of the CCP intensified. The last link in a chain of ideological debates, it reached its climax at the All-China Conference on Financial and Economic Work, held in Beijing from June 14 to August 12. Almost all of the high-level officials of the party and the government participated in the conference, which formally was dedicated to discussing the new tax system. In fact it addressed the entire political strategy of the CCP. In addition to Zhou Enlai and Deng Xiaoping, Gao Gang presided over the forum. Despite Mao's personal dislike of Gao, in ideological terms they were very close and Gao did his utmost to discredit the position of Liu Shaoqi and his supporters. In a conversation with the Soviet consul general Andrei Ledovsky in Shenyang, Gao Gang asserted not only that Liu Shaoqi supported "the erroneous bourgeois line of Bo Yibo," but that in fact the line actually derived from Liu.[40]

The ideological key of the meeting was supplied by Mao Zedong in his speech at a session of the Politburo on June 15, 1953. Mao sharply criticized party leaders who were striving to "firmly establish the new-democratic social order."[41] They "have remained," Mao said of Liu and his supporters,* "where they were after the victory of the democratic revolution. They fail to realize there is a change in the character of the revolution and they go on pushing their 'New Democracy' instead of socialist transformation. This will lead to Right deviationist mistakes."[42] Mao was particularly exasperated by the effort of these leaders to "[s]ustain private property."[43] This was the first time that

---

* No names are mentioned in the published text of Mao's speech. However, the Chinese publishers of his speech supplied notes to the published text that indicate the target was Liu Shaoqi and his supporters.

Mao had so clearly and directly dissociated himself from the concept of New Democracy and expressed himself in favor of a swift transition to the socialist revolution.

Reports by Gao Gang and Li Fuchun on economic construction and by Li Weihan on private capital were delivered at this lengthy conference. A majority of the top leadership took part in the discussion.

Gao was the most active. Subjecting Bo to criticism, not only for the "mistakes" he had committed but for "struggling against the Party line," which was like handing down a death sentence, Gao repeatedly cited the "erroneous" pronouncements of Liu as proof of the finance minister's guilt. To be sure, he did not quote Liu himself, but pretended that it was Bo Yibo who had spoken this way.[44] In other words, while openly denouncing Bo he was covertly attacking Liu. (Mao would not allow him to criticize Liu openly.) Everyone present, including Liu himself, understood these tactics perfectly well.

The situation for the "moderates" became ominous since no one knew whether Gao Gang was being egged on by Mao. Then, on July 7, Zhou wrote a letter to Mao, who was absent from the conference, informing him of what had happened at the sessions and requesting instructions. Clearly understanding that Liu and Zhou were terrified, Mao decided to act the peacemaker. In reality, he had no intention of removing them from their posts despite his disagreements with them. He simply wanted to teach them who was the master of the house. Having achieved this result, he could now take pleasure in his victory. This is why, hearing of Gao Gang's actions, he replied to Zhou: "We must conduct the struggle openly and solve the problems; we should not act boorishly. It is wrong to be silent face-to-face, but to prattle behind another's back, not to speak directly, but to beat about the bush, not to point to a specific person, but to engage in innuendos."[45] (One might suppose that Mao himself always conducted his struggles openly and that he never criticized Liu Shaoqi in veiled form.)

Zhou immediately transmitted this "revelation" to all interested persons. Bo Yibo, Liu Shaoqi, Deng Xiaoping, and Zhou himself quickly understood just what had to be done. Liu, Deng, and Bo took the floor and openly engaged in self-criticism, the latter on two occasions.[46] Zhou acknowledged his "political and organizational errors" and his "isolation from the party leadership," and he severely and extensively censured Bo Yibo. He accused the latter of "failing to acknowledge his errors over a certain period of time."[47] Bo's "right deviation," according to Zhou, "originated from his not taking Marxism-Leninism, the policy of the party, and the interests of the working people as his point of departure, but from consciously and unconsciously reflecting many of the outlooks, opinions, and habits of the capitalist class."[48] Zhou reproached Bo for "insincerity towards the party."[49]

Mao Zedong pronounced the work of the conference "a success," praised

Liu and Deng for their self-criticism, and supported criticism of the "bour-geois line." In this and several other speeches he emphasized the enormous political and ideological significance of the work that had been accomplished. It was evident from his statements that he considered the conference a definite turning point in the development of the CCP and the PRC, and he emphasized the decisive importance of the tax issue. "That [tax] system, if allowed to de-velop, would have led inevitably to capitalism, in contradiction of Marxism-Leninism and the Party general line for the transition period," he asserted.[50] The conference, as Mao supposed, could remove this threat from China, lead to the liberation from New Democratic illusions, and open the way to the so-cialist development of the country. Mao also noted subsequently that the work of the conference was the most important factor in affirming the general line for the construction of socialism that was formulated at precisely this time: "But for the Conference on Financial and Economic Work held in July and August, the question of the general line would have remained unsettled for many comrades."[51] Thus Mao imposed his views on the leadership of the CCP. The course for "constructing socialism on the Soviet model" was officially proclaimed.

27

SOCIALIST
INDUSTRIALIZATION

Stalin's death facilitated Mao's victory at the Conference on Financial and Economics Work. Only now could Mao accelerate the tempo of revolutionary transformation, in other words, the complete and decisive Stalinization of China. Naturally, he never displayed his innermost feelings. On the contrary, arriving at the embassy of the USSR to pay his respects to the late Kremlin boss, he was almost in tears. "He tried to maintain his self-control and not display any emotions, but he did not succeed," recalled an eyewitness. "There were tears in [his] eyes." Zhou Enlai cried along with the new Soviet ambassador, Alexander Panyushkin.[1]

Mao, however, did not wish to attend the funeral of the "Father of Nations." Perhaps he was afraid of catching pneumonia—there was frost in Moscow in early March. Perhaps it was because just two months earlier he had discovered that Stalin had been listening in on his conversations with members of the Politburo in Zhongnanhai itself. At the end of 1950, Stalinist technicians from the MGB who were working in Beijing installed microphones in Mao's bedroom and several other rooms in Mao's residence, obviously with the help of their Chinese agents. When this was discovered, Mao was furious and even sent Stalin a note of protest. The latter replied disingenuously that he had no idea what sorts of unseemly activities these MGB agents were up to in China. He conveyed to Mao his formal apology.[2] In his last year Stalin caused one more unpleasant incident that again clouded his relations with Mao. This resulted from the screening in the Soviet Union of *Przheval'skii*, a film that depicted the Chinese people in an unfavorable light, according to the CCP leadership. The screenwriters may have tried to create an objective picture of the great traveler Nikolai Przheval'skii who disliked the Chinese on account of their "hypocrisy, craftiness, and cunning."[3] But Stalin, who was the chief censor in matters of cinematography, saw nothing amiss, and not only approved showing the film in the USSR, but also sent a copy to an international film festival in Czechoslovakia. Dissatisfied, the Chinese requested that their Soviet comrades not show the film. Then Stalin, in the name of Minister of Cinematography Ivan Bol'shakov, sent a sharply worded telegram to Beijing saying that he considered the Chinese criticism "incorrect and deeply mistaken." The dictator, unaccustomed to criticism, accused the Chinese of nationalism. "It must be said," he noted,

> that here in the Soviet Union at a certain time among a certain number of historians and artists of a nationalist persuasion we also observed and still encounter attempts to embellish history as well as to conceal historical truth. . . . We Russian communists view such persons as dangerous, as chauvinists who infect the masses with the poison of nationalism and undermine the bases of criticism and self-criticism that are the foundation of the communist method of educating the masses.[4]

Mao was of course offended by the tone of the telegram and the reproaches it contained.

A meeting of the Central Committee selected Zhou Enlai to head the Chinese delegation to Stalin's funeral. He would also convey the Chairman's condolences to the new leadership of the CPSU. "Everyone knows that Comrade Stalin greatly loved the Chinese people and believed that the forces of the Chinese revolution were amazing," Mao Zedong wrote. "He displayed the greatest wisdom on questions relating to the Chinese revolution. . . . We have lost a great teacher and a most sincere friend. . . . This is a great sorrow. It is impossible to express our grief in words."[5]

Mao was also unofficially represented by his wife, Jiang Qing, who was in the USSR again for rest and treatment. She was also very upset by Stalin's death and visited the Hall of Columns in the House of Soviets where she was allowed to stand guard at the bier of the deceased.[6] On March 9, Zhou marched in the funeral procession; alone among the foreign guests he was given the honor of carrying Stalin's coffin along with the leaders of the CPSU.

On March 11, Zhou and other members of his delegation held talks with the new Kremlin leaders Georgii Malenkov, Lavrentii Beria, and Nikita Khrushchev on economic assistance to the PRC.[7] These talks culminated in the signing on March 21 of an important protocol on the exchange of goods between the USSR and the PRC for 1953 as well as an agreement regarding Soviet assistance to the PRC in the construction of electricity-generating stations.[8] Then, on May 15, 1953, the USSR and China signed an even more important agreement, by which the Soviet Union undertook the responsibility of furnishing all the technical documentation and complete sets of equipment for constructing ninety-one large industrial enterprises in China by the end of 1959.[9]

The negotiations between Zhou Enlai and Malenkov, Beria, and Khrushchev also led to the acceleration of work on the construction of fifty projects that the Soviet side had already undertaken to build. In a telegram to Malenkov on this occasion Mao expressed his heartfelt gratitude to the Soviet government for its agreement to provide economic and technical aid to China. "This will have extraordinary importance for the industrialization of China, for China's gradual transition to socialism, as well as for strengthening the forces of the camp of peace and democracy headed by the Soviet Union," Mao wrote.[10]

The negotiations in March signified a sharp turn in the Soviet leadership's attitude toward Chinese plans for socialist industrialization. In the complicated post-Stalin period, the leaders of the CPSU quickly abandoned Stalin's cautious policy toward the PRC. Malenkov, Beria, and Khrushchev were striving to gain Mao's support, fearing that he might take advantage of Stalin's death to cast off Soviet tutelage. Sensing danger, they went all out to indulge Mao. They wanted to preclude the possibility that China might go the way of Yugoslavia, an independent communist state. Khrushchev, at least, understood very well that the late dictator had pursued an imperialist foreign policy. To all appearances, he genuinely tried to change this.[11] Beria and Malenkov probably were in the same boat. Unlike Molotov and Mikoyan, none of the three had been directly involved with Stalin's China policy and therefore bore no responsibility for Stalin's denigration of Mao.

Moscow's new position meant that Mao could now seriously depend upon wide-scale Soviet assistance for the construction of an industrialized socialist China. With Soviet political support and economic cooperation he could finally crush the intraparty opposition that had opposed his plans to abandon New Democracy. The discussions at the Conference on Financial and Economic Work and its decisions reflected this new ideological-political situation.

After Mao's victory over the "moderates" in the summer of 1953, any polemic in the Chinese Communist Party could occur only within the framework of the dominant ideological tendency, aimed at constructing a powerful socialist state. The general line of the party on constructing socialism did not replace the political program of the CCP, but it did define its concrete social and political objectives and clarified the means of achieving them.

The adoption of the general line provoked additional conflict within the party leadership. The discussion generated by the formulation of the new course clearly indicated the positions of the contending sides. Mao provided the initial definition of the general line in early June 1953 while familiarizing himself with the draft report on the relationship between the party and capitalist industry and commerce, prepared by Li Weihan, secretary of the State Council and head of the United Front Department of the Central Committee.[12] During a Politburo discussion of this draft on June 15, 1953, Mao said: "The general line or general task of the Party for the transition period is basically to accomplish the industrialization of the country and the socialist transformation of agriculture, handicrafts, and capitalist industry and commerce *in ten to fifteen years, or a little longer.*[13] Obviously, for the time being he was still rather cautious, apparently trying to secure formal support of his new course from all the members of the Politburo. He did not want to frighten the "moderates," and he even mentioned in passing a "step-by-step" transition to socialism.[14] However, he severely criticized those who had failed to understand that a shift in the character of the revolution had occurred (the "right" deviation) while mildly admonishing the "mistakes" of those who "had gone too fast" (the "left" deviation).

The Politburo supported Mao's ideas, but "moderates" like Liu Shaoqi tried to attenuate their revolutionary impulse by changing several key words in the text. On June 23, 1953, speaking at the Conference on Financial and Economic Work, Li Weihan, in the name of the Politburo, offered the following proposition:

> From the time of the creation of the People's Republic of China our country has entered into a transitional period, a time of *gradual* transition to socialist society. The general line and the general task during the transitional period consists of *gradually* achieving the basic industrialization of the country and *gradually* achieving the basic transformation of agriculture and handicraft industry as well as of capitalist industry and commerce *in the course of a protracted period of time.*[15]

The new formulation did not indicate the time frame of the new course ("ten to fifteen years, or a little longer") and the word "gradual," repeated three times, apparently was of particular significance.

Toward the end of the conference, Mao again attempted to change economic policy radically. On August 10, during a Politburo discussion of the text of the Concluding Report, which Zhou Enlai intended to deliver at the conference and which contained the Politburo's formulation, he proposed a third formula that carefully avoided the term "gradually." At the same time he agreed not to provide a specific time frame. Although the remainder of the text was unaltered, its general meaning changed. Mao's new version read:

> The time between the founding of the People's Republic of China and the basic completion of socialist transformation is a period of transition. The Party's general line or general task for the transition period is basically to accomplish the country's industrialization and the socialist transformation of industry of agriculture, handicrafts and capitalist industry and commerce *over a fairly long period of time.*[16]

Accepting this definition, Zhou Enlai made the appropriate corrections to his Concluding Report.[17] On September 8, 1953, he unveiled this formulation at an enlarged plenum of the Standing Committee of the All-China Committee of the CPPCC.[18] However, other "moderates" continued to maneuver, and in December 1953 they presented yet another version of the general line. They added the word "gradually" to the verb "accomplish" in Mao's formula, and this new definition of the general line was inserted into the Central Committee's thesis for propagating the party's general line during the transitional period, which thesis was titled, "Struggle to Mobilize All Forces to Transform Our Country into a Great Socialist State."[19] On February 10, 1954, the final formulation calling for the *"step by step"* implementation of industrialization and socialist transformation was adopted by the Fourth Plenum of the CCP Central Committee.[20]

Mao was absent from the plenum, resting up at Hangzhou while Liu Shaoqi directed the forum. Liu had to engage in self-criticism for having mistakenly asserted that "China was suffering from the underdevelopment of capitalism."[21] Thus a compromise was achieved. Mao accepted the cautious formulation of the general line while the "moderates" in the person of Liu apologized for their "right deviation." But as soon became evident, the Chairman had no intention of maintaining this balance of power. New Democracy became obsolete, and China began to move forward along the path of constructing Stalinist socialism. Moscow adopted a benevolent attitude.

Meanwhile, Mao had to resolve myriad problems, including intraparty ones. Chief among them in 1953–54 was "unmasking" Gao Gang, the same "Comrade Zhang Zuolin" whom Stalin had compromised during the Moscow summit. Stalin, however, would not allow anyone to get at Gao, and only the death of the dictator and the establishment of equal relations with the Soviet leadership helped Mao get rid of the traitor who "provide[d] foreigners with information behind the back of the Central Committee."[22] Gao was not among Mao's ideological opponents. On the contrary, he was one of the most fervent partisans of the leftist course. In the late 1940s, in one of his telegrams to Kovalev, Stalin even criticized Gao for excessive leftism, and in the early 1950s Mao used Gao in his struggle against the "moderates." On February 16, 1952, for example, Mao published a private letter to Gao Gang in the main party newspaper *Renmin ribao* (People's daily) that contained a detailed critique of the "right deviation."[23] Moreover, in private conversations with Gao, Mao often complained about the "conservatism" of Liu Shaoqi and Zhou Enlai.[24] He was unwilling, however, to forgive Gao his role as an informer for Stalin.

Not suspecting Mao's true feelings, Gao Gang treasured his "intimate" conversations with the Chairman as a mark of special trust. Therefore, he actively sought ways to eliminate the "moderates" from the higher echelons of party leadership. He actively circulated rumors in the party that the Central Committee contained "two groups that cannot be trusted: Liu Shaoqi heads one of them and Zhou Enlai the other."[25] He succeeded in winning over Rao Shushi, the head of the Organizational Department of the Central Committee, who had earlier been the boss of the Shanghai region, as well as several other leading officials. The conspirators had already begun to divide up the positions—Gao Gang intended to occupy Liu's place, and Rao Shushi the post of prime minister—when Mao learned of their plans from Chen Yun and Deng Xiaoping, both of whom Gao had unwisely tried to win over to his side.[26] He was furious. Mao had no desire to replace Liu and Zhou with Gao and Rao despite the differences between himself and "the moderates." During his meeting with Deng, restraining his rage, Mao asked Deng what he thought about all this and how he would advise him to proceed. Deng, knowing of Mao's fondness for classical aphorisms, replied with the words of Confucius: "If a gentleman forsakes humanity, how can he make a name for himself?"[27] Mao could not but agree. At a Politburo meeting on December 24, 1953, Mao attacked Gao and Rao, accusing them of "conspiratorial" activity. On Mao's initiative, in February 1954, Liu Shaoqi presented the so-called Gao Gang–Rao Shushi Affair to the Fourth Plenum of the Central Committee. Both conspirators were accused of "sectarianism" and "factionalism," of establishing "independent kingdoms," and of organizing a plot to seize power. The Fourth Plenum censured Gao and Rao but did not expel them from the party. Nonetheless, Gao committed suicide on August 17, 1954, apparently because he became convinced that Mao had betrayed him. After all, while concocting the plot against Liu and Zhou, he assumed he was acting with the Chairman's tacit approval.[28] In March 1955, the All-China Conference of the CCP considered the Gao Gang–Rao Shushi Affair. It expelled Gao Gang and Rao Shushi from the party and affirmed the political line of Mao Zedong, in effect calling for the uprooting of all of his enemies.[29] (Rao would be imprisoned and died in his cell in March 1975 from pneumonia.)

Mao's triumph in the Gao-Rao Affair, the first purge of top leaders in the history of the PRC, created a dangerous precedent that doomed a significant part of the party leadership to defeat in battles with the Chairman. The affair was an extraordinarily important episode. Thereafter the countrywide promotion of the Mao cult constituted the basic direction of ideological work in the Communist Party. The campaign to exalt Chairman Mao Zedong was well organized and extremely effective. The *Selected Works* of the Leader were the primary means of ideological indoctrination, and studying them became the duty of every citizen. In 1954, it is true, Mao suggested removing the term "Mao Zedong Thought" from circulation. He did this for tactical reasons in the context of evolving active relations with the USSR. The Propaganda Department of the Central Committee explained it as follows:

Their [Mao Zedong Thought] content and the content of Marxism-Leninism is identical. . . . In expounding the party statutes and the most important party documents that were adopted earlier, as before we must proceed from the original, and not substitute the latter. However, to avoid the possibility of false interpretations regarding differences in the content of both terms, it is necessary to indicate that Mao Zedong Thought is synonymous with the ideas of Marxism-Leninism.[30]

The purge of Gao, Rao, and their confederates provoked an intense and widespread campaign inside and outside the party to uproot "hidden" counter-revolutionaries. The politically active part of Chinese society, including many *ganbu* (party cadres) and intellectuals, could not easily accept abandoning New Democracy. They supported the New Democratic slogans of the CCP and were disoriented by the sharp turn of 1953. The party leadership resorted to ideological terror, employing the method of "study" that had been approved more than once, starting from the notorious *zhengfeng* (rectification of style) movement that had unfolded in the party in the early 1940s. During the Marxist indoctrination of 1951, Mao had used these same methods. He initially presented each of these campaigns as "pedagogic," supposedly directed at educating backward intellectual cadres, and afterward he resorted to repression.

The next campaign began in 1954 as a scholarly discussion of the eighteenth-century novel *Dream of the Red Chamber* (incidentally, Mao's favorite novel). It quickly developed into a political witch hunt aimed at Yu Pingbo, a scholar who was the best-known expert on this novel. But this was only the beginning. Soon Mao attacked Hu Shi, a leading philosopher of pragmatism who had fled to Taiwan. Hu, whom Mao at one time had treated with great reverence, was now inscribed on his enemies' list. Hu's liberal philosophy undermined the ideological bases of the communist regime. Yu Pingbo and other cultural figures were accused of sympathy toward Hu Shi and Western bourgeois ideology.[31] In late 1954, a struggle unfolded against Hu Feng, a poet, essayist, and literary critic who was a member of the CCP and one of the leaders of the League of Chinese Writers. As a well-known nonconformist among left-wing writers, Hu Feng, who defended freedom of speech, was accused of counterrevolunationary activity and of seeking to restore the Guomindang regime. The Maoists were no longer willing to tolerate him or his supporters, who criticized their harsh methods of guiding culture. In 1955 Hu Feng and seventy-seven other liberal intellectuals were arrested. In all, more than two thousand persons in Beijing, Shanghai, Tianjin, and Nanjing were swept up in this affair.[32] (All of them were rehabilitated only twenty-five years later.)

At the same time, a so-called doctors' plot was concocted involving physicians who treated the leaders of the CCP. Several doctors in Zhongnanhai were accused of attempting to poison high-ranking patients. In the words of an eyewitness, "this campaign was a hard lesson. Chinese had no rights. Everyone had to obey their 'superiors' unconditionally. . . . A given individual was merely a tiny gear in an enormous and complicated machine. The slightest sign of dissatisfaction or deviation from established norms and the gear would be discarded."[33]

Mao's campaign against intellectuals was merely the prologue to a nation-wide movement against counterrevolutionaries that commenced in March 1955 and was aimed at uprooting all those who doubted his course in constructing socialism. During the next two years more than eighty thousand "counterrevolutionaries" were subjected to repression. According to information from a party leader in Canton that came to the attention of the Soviet embassy, no less than 7 percent of the officials of the local administrative and party apparatus were "involved in counterrevolutionary affairs to one degree or another."[34] The atmosphere of terror was such that in the latter half of 1955 more than 190,000 party members, fearing public humiliation, voluntarily appeared at the security organs with false self-accusations.[35] More than four thousand people committed suicide. The ideological campaign among intellectuals also accelerated. Among the new targets of criticism was Liang Shuming, a leading Chinese philosopher renowned for his ideas of reforming rural China. Liang, who lived and worked in Beijing, supported the new government, but he tried to defend his independent point of view. Characteristically, he was one of a few social scientists who maintained his convictions in an atmosphere of ideological terror. Meanwhile, several other leading cultural figures, including Guo Moro, Mao Dun, and Zhou Yang, acted as a shock force of the ideological terror during these initial large-scale ideological campaigns. The wave of repression reached the countryside as well when in 1954–55 a number of former landlords and rich peasants were subjected to preemptive repression.

Ultimately, Mao triumphed. His general line aimed at the Stalinization of China along a Soviet model was supported both by the party and broad strata of the population. This was assisted not only by the campaigns of repression but by the economic successes that the communist regime, aided by the Soviet Union, had achieved in the first half of the 1950s. By 1953 the communists had managed to establish order in the country, accomplish land reform, and recover a national economy that had been wrecked during the long period of wars. They increased production of steel by approximately 80 percent, coal and cotton by 50 percent, and grain by 25 percent over 1950–53. As a result they reached the levels attained in 1936. They could even tackle inflation "by restraining demand and by stimulating supply." The rate of inflation "declined from one in the hundreds of thousands to 20 percent in 1951 and well below 10 per cent in 1952."[36] Mao was so enthusiastic that he even included the formulation of the general line and an additional sentence regarding the significance for China of the Soviet experience in the Constitution of the People's Republic of China, which replaced the Common Program of the Chinese People's Political Consultative Council, which had functioned as the basic law up until then.

He introduced a suitable sentence in the revised version of Liu Shaoqi's report on the draft constitution.[37]

This constitution was adopted on September 20, 1954, by the first session of the new parliament, the National People's Congress (NPC). The highest state organs of the PRC were reorganized and the post of chairman of the People's Republic of China, in effect the president of the country, was established. Mao of course occupied it and Zhu De was his deputy. Liu Shaoqi was chosen as chairman of the Standing Committee of the NPC. Zhou Enlai was confirmed as premier of the State Council.[38]

The new parliament was chosen as a result of elections that, while not universal, were still of a mass character. ("Class enemies" of the regime, as well as landlords and other "counterrevolutionaries," were denied voting rights.) Thus the CCP derived its power from a "popular mandate," and that is why the event was greeted so ecstatically in the USSR.

Nikita S. Khrushchev, who headed the Central Committee of the CPSU from September 1953, played the decisive role in defining Soviet policy toward the PRC. While Khrushchev was fighting for power, support from China was essential, and Mao helped him out at critical moments. CCP leaders fully accepted the absurd accusations, arrest, and physical elimination of Stalin's closest associate, Lavrentii Beria, the minister of internal affairs. They likewise quickly accepted the elimination of Malenkov. Mao was pragmatic about this. His interpreter Shi Zhe recalled him saying, "We will support whoever comes out on top [in the Soviet leadership]."[39] Nevertheless, this did not diminish the significance of such support.

Khrushchev initially responded in kind, accepting post facto the resolution on Gao Gang and Rao Shushi. Zhou Enlai and Liu Shaoqi informed Soviet ambassador Yudin about this matter only in early February 1954.[40] Prior to this, conversing in Hangzhou on January 2 with Ivan Tevosian, deputy chairman of the Council of Ministers of the USSR, and Yudin, Mao merely hinted at what had occurred. He told his guests a story about how in antiquity the kingdom of Qin had destroyed the kingdom of Chu. Mao noted that had this not happened "disorders might have arisen in China."[41] His Soviet guests, of course, did not understand this ancient story, but Mao was in no hurry to enlighten them. He personally informed Khrushchev about the matter several months later, on September 1, after the death of Gao.[42] Even though the Chinese had acted without Moscow's sanction, Mao was not rebuked. The Chairman and his associates presented the purge of Gao and Rao as a parallel to the Beria affair in the Soviet Union, and the Soviets did not object.[43]

Soon, however, Soviet-Chinese cooperation entered a new phase. After receiving a request from the PRC government in 1954 to increase the size of Soviet loans for the construction of Chinese heavy industrial enterprises, Khrushchev responded with such enormous enthusiasm that he directed the appropriate ministries of the USSR to work up plans for furnishing such assistance on an unprecedented scale. He decided to make Mao a present, offering him a new long-term credit and broad-scale economic cooperation in various fields. Aid to China was placed under the direct control of the first secretary of the Soviet Communist Party,[44] thereby becoming a priority item.[45] At the same time, Khrushchev began to purge Soviet-Chinese relations of all the past misunderstandings and tried to put them on a true basis of equality. "We will live like brothers with the Chinese," he reiterated. "If it comes to that, we will divide in half our last piece of bread."[46] He needed Mao's unconditional recognition of him as Stalin's successor and as the most authoritative leader not only of the CPSU, but also of the world communist movement. The chairman of the CCP enjoyed an extraordinarily high reputation throughout the communist world. Moreover, a close friendship with Mao would strengthen the eastern borders of the Soviet Union, by no means insignificant in the context of a worsening Cold War.

In late September 1954, Khrushchev convened a special meeting of the Presidium of the Central Committee of the CPSU to secure approval of his China policy from the Soviet leadership. He declared, "We will let slip an historic opportunity to build and strengthen our friendship with China if . . . we do not help to implement the most important projects in the forthcoming Five-Year Plan for the socialist industrial development of China."[47] It was Khrushchev's enthusiasm that compelled other leaders of the USSR to drop their objections.

Shortly after, on September 29, Khrushchev headed a Soviet party and government delegation to Beijing to participate in the celebration of the fifth anniversary of the founding of the People's Republic. During high-level meetings a number of agreements were signed by which the Soviet side extended to China a long-term foreign currency loan equal to 520 million rubles, expanded technical assistance in the sum of 400 million rubles for the construction of 141 industrial enterprises, and offered assistance in constructing an additional 15 industrial projects. Moreover, Khrushchev relinquished the Soviet share of four joint enterprises* and returned the Soviet naval base in Lüshun, where Soviet troops had been stationed, to China. (During the Korean War, the USSR and China had agreed on September 15, 1952, to extend the stay of Soviet troops in Lüshun. Their withdrawal was scheduled for completion by May 26, 1955.) He also annulled the secret agreements that gave the USSR privileges in Manchuria and Xinjiang. Finally, he agreed to help China develop atomic weapons and to train nuclear specialists.[48] In sum, Khrushchev's visit

---

* The Soviet Union agreed to return its shares to China on January 1, 1955, in exchange for Chinese goods.

greatly helped accelerate the implementation of Chinese plans for socialist industrialization.[49]

At first sight, Mao was pleased. As he later conceded, "[T]he first time I met with Comrade Khrushchev, we had very pleasant conversations . . . and established mutual trust."[50] He also acknowledged that "[W]e are thankful to him for this. . . . Comrade Khrushchev abolished the [previous] 'cooperatives.'"[51] Khrushchev, however, went too far in his generosity. Where he should have been guided by reason, he was instead ruled by emotion. He had always wanted to see the world, but Stalin had not allowed him to go abroad. Now, at the first opportunity, Khrushchev giddily plunged into this new business. He made a fatal mistake at the very outset. Under no circumstances should he have paid Mao a visit first; he should have arranged for Mao to visit him. But the opportunity to visit China excited Khrushchev and he was unable to suppress his playful and enthusiastic impulses. He was happy as a child.[52] At the departure from Moscow, he was making puns, teasing Mikoyan, and suggesting to Nikolai Shvernik, chairman of the Soviet Labor Union Association, that he "prepare himself to eat snake."[53] He was in the same elevated mood during his stay in China. He did not observe protocol, went around embracing and kissing Mao, which shocked the Chinese, joked around, told stories about Beria's sexual escapades, promised a lot, and gave a lot in the fashion of a merchant.

His conduct, like his excessively expensive gifts, in fact provoked a negative response from Mao, who, like Stalin, respected only force. Mao was unable to appreciate Khrushchev's cordiality, took it as a sign of weakness, and became convinced that the new Soviet leader was "a big fool."[54] This feeling led Mao to believe that Khrushchev was in need of his moral support.[55] During the summit meetings, Mao and Zhou constantly tested Khrushchev, bombarding him with innumerable requests. Mao even asked him for the secrets of the atomic bomb and asked him to build China a submarine fleet.[56] Although Khrushchev rebuffed most of these requests, the impression remained that he was a weak partner. For his part Mao was in no hurry to be effusive. He did not even want to introduce Khrushchev to his wife. When Zhou Enlai, following protocol, tried to steer Jiang Qing over to Khrushchev on the rostrum of Tiananmen Gate during the October 1 parade, Mao quickly took her by the hand and led her to the far side of the platform.[57]

The summit meeting signified the beginning of Mao's emancipation, of his deliverance from Soviet tutelage, as Khrushchev himself sensed by the end of his visit. Many years later he recalled:

When we made our trip to China in 1954 and held several meetings with Mao, I said to the comrades afterward: "A conflict between China and us is inevitable." I drew this conclusion from remarks Mao had made and from the way our delegation was treated. A kind of

Oriental atmosphere of sickly sweet politeness was created around us. They were unbelievably attentive, but it was all insincere. We lovingly hugged and kissed with Mao, swam in a pool with him, chatted away on various subjects, and spent the whole time like soul mates. But it was all so sickly sweet it turned your stomach. Some particular questions, on the other hand, that came up and confronted us put us on our guard. Most important, I had the feeling—and I said something about this to all my comrades even then—that Mao had not resigned himself to having any Communist Party other than the Chinese party be predominant in the world Communist movement, not even to the slightest extent. That he could not tolerate.[58]

For the time being, Mao's moods did not surface. Even he could not so easily free himself from respecting the "elder brother." Moreover, China still wanted to receive Soviet assistance in building socialism.

Yet, after returning to Moscow, Khrushchev decided in December 1954 to furnish China at no cost 1,400 technical blueprints of major industrial enterprises and more than 24,000 sets of various scientific-technical documents.[59] In March 1955, the Soviets signed a new agreement with China in which they promised to finance an additional sixteen industrial projects.[60] A month later the Soviet Union and the PRC officially reached agreement on Soviet assistance to China in developing nuclear technology for peaceful means.[61] Soon afterward, in August, the Soviet government sent the PRC a memorandum in which it offered to help in the construction of fifteen defense industry enterprises and fourteen new industrial complexes. Sometime earlier, in late 1954, the Chinese government had directed a request to Moscow concerning the possibility of increasing the Soviet role in developing China's defense and fuel industries.[62]

The Soviets continued to cooperate with the PRC in working out the final draft of their First Five-Year Plan, an economic program the Chinese had begun to discuss with them back in 1952. This draft was completed in February 1955, and on March 21, Deputy Premier Chen Yun introduced its main features to delegates at the National Party Conference. On March 31, the final draft was approved, and on July 5–6, Li Fuchun, chairman of the State Planning Commission, presented it to the deputies of the Second Session of the National People's Congress. On July 30, the Second Session of the NPC adopted the document as the official economic development plan of the PRC for 1953–57, embodying the CCP's policies of industrialization and socialist construction.[63] The plan envisioned the completion of 694 major industrial projects including large electricity-generating stations, metallurgical enterprises, machine-building plants, and other complexes that would lay the foundation for the rapid development of heavy and defense industries. The Five-Year Plan was also intended to promote the cooperative movement in the countryside. The intention was to organize about one-third of peasant households into so-called semi-socialist lower-level agricultural producers' cooperatives by the end of 1957. In these cooperatives peasant proprietors would work together only in the joint economy while preserving private property rights with respect to the shares of land, cattle, and major agricultural equipment they brought into the cooperative. Income distribution would be done according to the amount of labor as well as their share of property. Moreover, there were plans to organize about two million urban handicraft workers into cooperatives. Finally, the majority of private factories and plants as well as commercial enterprises would be converted into state enterprises or enterprises under the control of the state. The government planned to raise the pay of industrial workers by one-third.[64]

The close cooperation between the Soviet leadership and the leaders of the PRC in the post-Stalin era enabled the PRC to develop the Five-Year Plan, which fit the needs of the Chinese national economy as well as the economic capabilities of the USSR. By this time the industrialization of China was already under way, and the overwhelming majority of specialists considered that China could successfully achieve the objectives laid out in the plan.

The results exceeded all expectations. The rate of growth of Chinese industry was much higher than what had been planned. According to various estimates, the annual growth rate was actually on the order of 16–18 percent. The gross industrial output more than doubled while the production of pig iron and steel even tripled.[65] Soviet aid was of enormous significance. Although direct Soviet investment in the economy of the PRC was not that great—1.57 billion yuan, constituting just 3 percent of the total Chinese investment capital of 49.3 billion yuan[66]—it is difficult to overestimate the importance of Soviet aid. Besides providing China a certain amount of financial support, the USSR furnished at no cost an enormous volume of technical information that would have cost at least hundreds of millions of American dollars on the world market. While helping China construct a significant portion of its key industrial projects, the USSR also played a vital role in training scientific and technical personnel for the PRC. In the 1950s China sent more than 6,000 students and about 7,000 workers to study in the USSR. More than 12,000 specialists and advisers from the Soviet Union and Eastern Europe came to China.[67]

Still, despite the importance of Soviet aid, it was the state investment in economic modernization that secured the rapid growth of Chinese industry. State capital investment constituted 97 percent of total investment in the basic branches of the economy. As in the USSR under Stalin, the countryside was the source for the primary accumulation of capital for financing urban industrialization. In building socialism the Chinese communists made use of Soviet experience, which, however brutal, had demonstrated enormous economic effectiveness.

28

THE GREAT TURNING POINT

Achieving the First Five-Year Plan for agricultural production and the social transformation of the countryside was at the center of the party's work. The completion of agrarian reform in 1950–53 radically changed the majority of peasants into middle-ranking individual peasant proprietors, a status that largely freed them from the arbitrariness of the authorities. The post-reform countryside, however, was unable to supply society with sufficient produce and raw materials. The basic reasons were the backwardness of production forces in China; agrarian overpopulation; the shortage of arable land and, as a consequence, the existence of small-scale households; the underdevelopment of the agricultural infrastructure; and archaic social relations. The social leveling consequent to the agrarian reform exacerbated the crisis of underproduction since it led to an increase in peasant consumption and diminished the marketable surplus. As Liu Shaoqi remarked to the new Soviet ambassador, Vasily Kuznetsov, on November 9, 1953, "if the peasants are sufficiently well-fed, then grain production in the country suffices only to meet their needs, but the cities are without grain. . . . In the present circumstances we are still not in a position to allow the peasants to eat as much as they want." [1]

The party leadership faced the task of devising new forms of rural cooperation. They had already discarded a market approach. The idea of a socialist utopia began to guide policy. In the fall of 1953, Mao Zedong launched an attack against New Democratic market relations in the countryside. His goal was utterly clear, namely, to collectivize the peasantry and nationalize private property in order, on this foundation, to achieve the industrialization of an economically backward country. None of the Chinese leaders demurred. To implement this program they had established the strictest control over the socioeconomic, political, and ideological life of the Chinese people. Intraparty discord concerned only the methods and tempo of executing this plan.

On October 16, on Mao's initiative, the Central Committee decided to introduce a monopoly on grain as of November 16, 1953. [2] This meant the compulsory purchase of grain from peasants at low fixed prices. [3] Individuals were forbidden to purchase grain or sell it on the market. The following year state monopolies were introduced on trade in cotton and cotton goods and vegetable oil. Peasants were thereby reduced to being tenants of the state and completely deprived of any property rights. These measures profoundly desta-bilized the market economy throughout China and soon led to the introduc-tion of rationing for basic consumer goods among the urban population. This made it possible to guarantee a supply of essential provisions, albeit at a low level. Urban residents could now purchase provisions only in state stores and only by presenting ration coupons.

The powerful state repressive machine tried to control the flow of all basic goods. If in 1952 the state stockpiled 33 million tons of grain, between 1953 and 1955 the authorities succeeded in raising this to 48, 53, and 50 million tons. The grain was collected by means of a high tax in kind as well as by com-pulsory grain purchases; the ratio between the former and the latter was usu-ally about 2:3. In 1954 and 1955, the PRC harvested about 160 million tons of grain per annum. Of that amount 31 percent was extracted from the peasantry, which was 6–11 percent more than the peasants themselves usually sold on the market.[4] According to the Russian economist L. D. Bony, the likely result was that "the physically necessary consumption level of the Chinese peasant must have been infringed upon, which is attested to by peasant disturbances in many districts around the country."[5] Mao and Zhou Enlai later admitted that the communists "purchased a little more grain" from the peasants than they should have.[6] Peasant disturbances continued in the spring of 1955.

The concentration of provisions in the hands of the state did not solve the problem of hunger. According to official figures, in 1952 China produced on average 250 kilograms of grain per person, a situation that did not improve in 1953 or 1954. Ten percent of peasant households were not self-sufficient in grain and depended upon state assistance. In reality, more than half of the rural population lived in a state of semi-starvation and millions of families could survive only with direct state support.[7] The situation was paradoxical. On one hand, by implementing the centralized procurement of grain and other products the authorities controlled a significant proportion of the rural production and created the appearance of state economic power. On the other hand, they had to return almost two-thirds of the grain to the countryside to save millions of peasants in the poorer districts from starvation. The state's capacity to assist the development of agriculture gradually diminished. The in-crease in state requisitions undercut peasant interest in boosting production, and the number of those requiring state assistance constantly grew. Their own anti-market policy created a vicious circle in which Mao and his associates were trapped.

The country was deeply divided: the authorities strived to increase the extraction of goods from the countryside while the peasantry actively resisted.

Mao Zedong began to lose the support of the peasantry. In October 1955 he was forced to admit:

> The peasants are no longer satisfied with the alliance we formed with them in the past on the basis of the agrarian revolution. They are beginning to forget about the benefits they reaped from the alliance. They should now be given new benefits, which means socialism. . . . The old alliance to oppose landlords, overthrow the local despots and distribute land was a temporary one; it has become unstable after a period of stability.[8]

This situation helped launch the cooperative movement.

During the period of agrarian reform from 1950 to 1953, the Chinese communists had done almost nothing to accelerate cooperativization. By the end of 1951 there were only three hundred or more so-called lower-stage cooperatives, with between twenty and forty households each.[9] The New Democratic political atmosphere restrained the active proponents of the socialist transformation of agriculture. Conceptually and in practice the CCP was very cautious in approaching the transformation of the countryside. Typical in this regard was "The Resolution on Mutual Labor Aid and Cooperation in Agricultural Production," adopted by the Central Committee on February 13, 1953. The draft document, prepared by the Rural Work Department of the Central Committee, was presented to the committee by its director, the veteran communist Deng Zihui, concurrently a deputy premier of the State Council. It was party practice to indicate the danger of both right and left policy deviations, but Deng pointed to the left deviation as the main danger. "At present," Deng Zihui noted, "haste and racing forward are the main deviation and the main danger on a national scale."[10] His report, approved by the Central Committee, served as the guiding document on the basis of which struggles against various "leftist" errors were conducted.

Meanwhile, the party accumulated experience with the cooperative movement during the period of New Democracy. Supply and marketing co-ops and credit co-ops, which had begun during the Guomindang era, became an organic part of the development of market relations in the reformed villages. By the end of 1952, 40 percent of peasant households had joined mutual aid teams.[11] These were special forms of cooperation that had first been approved in the communist-controlled "liberated areas" during the Sino-Japanese War of 1937–45. The party leadership, especially Liu Shaoqi, viewed these teams as the definitive organizational and economic foundation of the voluntary cooperative movement. The semi-socialist "lower-stage" cooperatives likewise expanded, although in 1953 the Central Committee conducted a "massive disbandment" of nonviable cooperatives that had been created by violating the principle of voluntary membership. By the end of 1953, there were more than fourteen thousand cooperatives.

Mao's victory over the "moderates" in the summer of 1953 encouraged him to force the pace of collectivization. The question of the tempo of the socialist transformation of the peasantry became a central theme in intraparty discussions. "We struck while the iron was hot," Mao recalled later on. "This was a tactical necessity, it was impossible to 'take a breather' or to establish a 'New Democratic order.' If we had undertaken to create that, later we would have wasted our energies on breaking it up." [12]

In the fall of 1953, Mao held meetings with officials of the Rural Work Department to persuade them to counteract the increasingly "dangerous" strengthening of "capitalist tendencies" in the Chinese countryside and to accelerate socialist transformation. [13] He did not succeed, however, in suppressing the resistance of some party functionaries. Therefore, on December 16, 1953, a compromise Resolution of the CCP Central Committee on Developing Agricultural Producers' Cooperatives was adopted and briefly became the programmatic document for the socialist reconstruction of the countryside. [14] The resolution envisioned the planned and gradual cooperativization of peasant households along with the mechanization of agriculture. Central Committee officials considered it dangerous to implement cooperativization apart from the technical transformation of the countryside. The document indicated that by the end of 1954, the number of "lower-stage" cooperatives would be 35,800, or less than 1 percent, of all peasant households. The tasks set for the First Five-Year Plan were equally moderate. Initially, the draft envisioned the cooperativization of 20 percent of peasant households by the end of 1957; [15] later, in the final version, this was increased to 33 percent. This referred only to "lower-stage" cooperatives. "Higher" or "advanced" cooperative farms, meaning fully "socialist" collectives, based on the complete collectivization of peasant property and aggregating 100–300 households, were to be established only on an experimental basis.

Mao was dissatisfied with these plans. At the same time he was not bothered by the extreme technical backwardness of the countryside, evident in the underdevelopment of the forces of production. "We must carry out the socialist revolution before anything else, that is, agricultural cooperativization," he wrote in July 1954 to Liu Shaoqi and Deng Xiaoping. "Carrying out the technical revolution, that is, the gradual introduction of mechanization and the implementation of other technical transformations in the countryside is a secondary task. . . . Various possible technical changes [should be introduced] on the foundation of cooperativization." [16]

He continued to express dissatisfaction with the "slow tempo" despite the fact that by the end of 1954 the number of cooperatives had increased sevenfold to 100,000. In October 1954, on Mao's initiative, the Central Committee adopted a resolution to further speed up the organization of cooperatives. A new, accelerated program was drafted calling for a leap forward in the cooperative movement. In 1955 the number of lower-stage cooperatives was slated to increase sixfold to 600,000. However, by the spring of 1955, their number had already grown to 670,000.[17] In the province of Zhejiang alone in the winter of 1954–55, 42,000 cooperatives were organized, seven times as many as existed before.[18]

Naturally, the cadres who were mobilized to achieve accelerated collectivization used violence, harsh orders, and arbitrariness in fulfilling the party's tasks. In many villages peasants who refused to join the cooperatives were forced into the street and made to stand in the broiling sun or freezing cold for hours or even days until, exhausted, they agreed to submit their applications "voluntarily." In many districts peasants began to slaughter their livestock and poultry in protest. In Zhejiang, for example, the number of hogs dropped by 1.2 million, or 30 percent. In one region famous for its ham, the drop was 40 percent. In other places a shortage of fodder caused an outbreak of cattle plague. At the beginning of 1955, a large number of rural inhabitants who had lost their land were starving to death. Some of the middle peasants committed suicide; others fled from their homes and headed for the cities. Many openly expressed their dissatisfaction. "The communist party is worse than the Guomindang," they said. "The CCP has led [us] to the brink of death, the CCP has degenerated."[19]

Meanwhile, several party leaders were still trying to restrain the Chairman's radicalism. Deng Zihui, director of the Rural Work Department of the Central Committee, insisted that the program of cooperativization be implemented in accordance with the Five-Year Plan. His department proposed slowing the pace to organize no more than 350,000 cooperatives in a year and a half. Deng Zihui also intended to dissolve 120,000 nonviable cooperatives.[20] Liu Shaoqi, Deng Xiaoping, and many other Politburo members, especially Zhou Enlai, supported his position.

Mao vacillated for a while and thought that perhaps "the relations of production must correspond to the needs of the development of the forces of production; otherwise, the forces of production might rebel. Now the peasants are killing their hogs and sheep. This is a rebellion of the forces of production."[21] He decided to halt cooperativization for half a year, until the fall. Liu Shaoqi supported this decision and suggested cutting the number of cooperatives by 170,000. In the spring of 1955, the Rural Work Department decided to dissolve cooperatives that had been established through administrative means rather than voluntarily.

This decision provoked opposition from local leaders who tried to continue forcing the pace of the movement. "There is no need," they said, "to curtail the number of cooperatives."[22] The head of the Shanghai Bureau of the

CCP, the veteran Bolshevik Ke Qingshi, was particularly indignant, charging that as many as 30 percent of the party cadres did not support socialism, and expressing his dissatisfaction directly to the Chairman when he visited Shanghai in April 1955.[23] At this time Mao went on a sixteen-day inspection tour of the eastern and southern provinces, during which many other provincial and county officials also voiced leftist sentiments.

Meanwhile, in Beijing, Deng Zihui convened a National Conference on Rural Work at which he advocated slowing the tempo of cooperativization. He and other "moderates" were out of step with the times and Mao no longer wanted to listen to them. The Chairman returned from his tour inspired by the Bolshevik mood of the provincial leaders, which revived his interest in achieving a rapid "breakthrough" to socialism. He abandoned his doubts and stood firm. He met with Deng Zihui and warned him, "Do not repeat the mistake of mass dissolution of cooperatives made in 1953, or otherwise you will . . . have to make a self-criticism."[24] Several days later he added, "The peasants want 'freedom.' But we want socialism. . . . There is a group of . . . officials who reflect the mood of the peasantry and who do not want socialism."[25]

In mid-May he held a meeting in Zhongnanhai with the leaders of fifteen provincial and municipal party committees to impress upon officials of the Rural Work Department what he believed the people wanted. He called for discarding "pessimistic moods" with regard to cooperativization. "If we don't discard [them]," Mao gloomily observed, "we will be making a big mistake."[26] Soon he departed again to "conduct an investigation," this time to Hangzhou.

Deng Zihui, however, did not heed these words and, relying on the support of Liu Shaoqi, clung to his own views. In mid-June a Politburo meeting chaired by Liu Shaoqi thoroughly discussed the issue and a majority of its members supported the proposals of the Rural Work Department. Liu Shaoqi noted, "By next spring [i.e., a whole year later] we will raise the number of cooperatives [only] to one million, i.e. we will screen access to them. This is good. Let the middle peasants come and knock on the door. By keeping the door closed, we will guarantee that middle peasants enter voluntarily."[27] The Rural Work Department then disbanded more than 20,000 nonviable co-ops by the middle of 1955, including more than 15,000 cooperatives embracing 400,000 peasant households in Zhejiang alone.[28]

Mao had no intention of surrendering. He simply circumvented the Politburo, which had rebuffed him, and appealed directly to party cadres throughout the country. At a meeting he convened on July 31, 1955, he called on provincial, municipal, and district party secretaries to support his plans. Mao's report, "On the Co-operative Transformation of Agriculture," aimed at convincing party activists of the need to accelerate rural cooperativization. Contrary to the Five-Year Plan just adopted by the National People's Congress, which envisioned 33 percent of peasant households enrolled in cooperatives by the end of 1957, Mao insisted on a figure of 50 percent. By the fall of 1956 the number of cooperatives should double from the 650,000 that remained after the disbandment of nonviable cooperatives, to 1.3 million.[29]

Mao's speech contained the usual positive assessment of the Soviet development path, including the assertion that the Soviet experience demonstrated that large-scale collectivization in a short time was fully possible.[30] Yet it was evident that while the Chairman was still inspired by the Soviet model, he had already begun to contemplate even higher rates of socialist construction than in the USSR. He condemned "several comrades" who invoked Stalin's well-known criticism of the errors of "hastiness" and "running ahead" committed in the course of Soviet collectivization and added, "[O]n no account should we allow these comrades to use the Soviet experience as a cover for their ideas of moving at a snail's pace."[31] Formulating the principle of building socialism "more, better, faster" for the first time, Mao did not yet enshrine it as the new general line. He still embraced the Soviet model but wanted to achieve it more rapidly. In irritation he told his personal physician,* "When I say 'Learn from the Soviet Union,' we don't have to learn how to shit and piss from the Soviet Union, too, do we?"[32] Khrushchev asked him not to accelerate the pace of co-operativization, but Mao had stopped listening.[33] He was optimistic about the powerful upsurge of the cooperative movement. The conference marked the first time in the history of the party that Mao had appealed to local cadres over the head of the Politburo and had openly expressed his disagreement with its decisions. He would return to this practice many times.

On the whole his maneuver succeeded. Having received the support "from below" that he had anticipated, the Chairman was now able to compel the party leadership to accept his program of accelerated Stalinization. In October 1955, he convened the Sixth Enlarged Plenum of the Central Committee in Beijing to secure formal support for his political course. The number of middle- and low-ranking party officials invited was ten times greater than the number of Central Committee members, ensuring that the plenum would approve his policy prescriptions, which indeed it did. "We are facing a steady upsurge of the movement for cooperativization in the countryside," the resolution asserted, and "the task of the party is boldly to advance this movement. . . . Meanwhile, some comrades persist in adhering to old ideas. . . .

---

* This physician was named Li Zhisui. He worked in Mao's entourage for more than twelve years. In 1988 by some miracle he was able to leave China for the United States, where six years later he published his memoirs. In them he revealed many secrets of the private life of Mao Zedong and other leaders of the CCP, which evoked a storm of indignation in the PRC. Afterward, in an interview with U.S. television in January 1995, Dr. Li announced his intention to publish one more work of biography. He was unable, however, to carry out this intention. Several weeks after the interview, he died in Carol Stream, Illinois.

[T]hey do not see the activity of the majority of the peasants who want to take the socialist path." [34]

Deng Zihui, Bo Yibo, and Li Fuchun engaged in self-criticism while Zhou Enlai unconditionally supported Mao. [35] The Chairman, still agitated, grumbled that "Deng Zihui supported us during the democratic revolution . . . but after liberation he went another way. He is like a girl walking on bound feet. She walks, swaying back and forth, sometimes to the east, sometimes to the west." [36] Only in retrospect did he note with satisfaction that "1955 was the year in which basic victory was won as regards the aspect of ownership in the relations of production." [37]

After the plenum Mao Zedong launched what proved to be an effective propaganda campaign to rally the party behind him. Rank-and-file communists actively threw themselves into the struggle to achieve the utopian plans of their leader. They believed in Mao, worshipped him, even deified him. A leader-centered party could not exist without such a cult. Mao was the embodiment of New China, of the general line for constructing socialist society, of the bright future of equality and abundance. It is understandable, therefore, why participation in all-around collectivization was a matter of honor for a majority of ordinary communists.

By the beginning of 1956 Mao and his supporters had sharply accelerated the tempo of cooperativization, which now entered a new stage of basically completing collectivization in the first half of 1956. Local party cadres skillfully exploited the egalitarian mood of the poor peasants who accounted for the majority of small-scale households. The communists still enjoyed great prestige among them, and the masses of poor peasants supported the communists enthusiastically, hoping that the policy of the CCP would be to their advantage as it had been during the agrarian reform. At the same time, following Stalin, the Chinese government freely employed repressive methods. In 1956, it forcefully bound the peasants to the land by forbidding rural inhabitants to move anywhere outside their immediate cooperative. [38] From then on peasants had to get permission from village authorities even to travel to a nearby city or a neighboring cooperative.

In sum, agrarian socialism triumphed. By June 1956, 110 million peasant households (about 92 percent of the total number) had joined agricultural producers' cooperatives. Of these, 63 million had become members of "higher-stage" ("socialist") cooperatives. This process continued in the second half of the year until practically all peasants were included in cooperatives. Meanwhile, small cooperatives were consolidated and primary cooperatives transformed into higher-stage cooperatives. By the end of 1956, there were 756,000 agricultural producers' cooperatives embracing 96 percent of all peasant households throughout the country; 88 percent of peasant households belonged to higher-stage cooperatives. [39]

Mao Zedong's father,
Mao Yichang.

Mao Zedong's mother,
Wen Qimei.

The house in Shaoshanchong village where Mao Zedong was born.

The room where he was born.

The first photograph of Mao Zedong, taken in Changsha, spring of 1913.

Mao Zedong's favorite professor, Yang Changji.

Professor Li Dazhao, the first Chinese Bolshevik.

Professor Chen Duxiu, founder of the Chinese Communist Party.

The First CCP Congress took place in this house in Shanghai.

Members of the Central Committee Bureau of the Soviet areas, Ruijin, November 1931.
Left to right: Gu Zuolin, Ren Bishi, Zhu De, Deng Fa, Xiang Ying, Mao Zedong, and Wang
Jiaxiang.

CCP leaders in Yan'an, December 1937. Front row (left to right): Xiang Ying, Kai Feng, Wang Ming, Chen Yun, Liu Shaoqi. Rear row (left to right): Kang Sheng, Peng Dehuai, Luo Fu, Zhang Guotao, Lin Boqu, Bo Gu, Zhou Enlai, and Mao Zedong.

Presidium of the Sixth Enlarged CCP Central Committee Plenum, Yan'an, Fall of 1938. Front row (left to right): Kang Sheng, Mao Zedong, Wang Jiaxiang, Zhu De, Xiang Ying, Wang Ming. Rear row (left to right): Chen Yun, Bo Gu, Peng Dehuai, Liu Shaoqi, Zhou Enlai, and Luo Fu.

Mao Zedong reads Stalin, Yan'an, 1939.

Yang Kaihui, Mao's second wife, and their sons, Anying (right) and Anqing, Shanghai, 1924.

Mao and He Zizhen, his third wife, Bao'an, 1936.

Jiang Qing, Mao's fourth wife,
Moscow, 1949.

Mao and his son Anying, Yan'an, 1946.

Mao's son Mao Anqing,
Moscow, 1950s.

Mao and his daughter Li Min, Xiangshan, 1949.

Mao and his daughter Li Na (far left), Beijing, early 1950s.

CCP-Guomindang negotiations, Chongqing, fall 1945. Front row (left to right): Patrick J. Hurley, Chiang Kai-shek, and Mao Zedong. Rear row (left to right): Chiang Kai-shek's son Chiang Ching-kuo, General Zhang Qun, and China's foreign minister Wang Shijie.

Wang Jiaxiang, Liu Shaoqi, and Gao Gang in Moscow, July 1949.

Mao Zedong proclaims the founding of the People's Republic of China, Beijing, October 1, 1949. At far left is Lin Boqu; at far right is Zhou Enlai.

Mao at Tiananmen Palace wearing a ribbon that says *zhuxi* (Chairman), Beijing, October 1, 1949.

Mao and Joseph Stalin, Moscow, December 21, 1949.

Nikita Khrushchev, Mao, and Nikolai Bulganin. Moscow, November 7, 1957.

Mao Zedong floating in the Yangzi River, Wuhan, July 16, 1966.

Zhou Enlai, Mao Zedong, and Lin Biao celebrate the Cultural Revolution, Beijing, late 1960s.

Red Guards assault
a victim during the
Cultural Revolution.

Mao and Richard Nixon. Mao's last mistress, Zhang Yufeng, is in the center, Beijing,
February 21, 1972.

Mao Zedong and Deng Xiaoping, 1974.

Mao lies in state following his death on September 9, 1976.

Mao's enormous political victory came at a great personal price. During the sharp conflict within the CCP, especially toward the end of 1955, Mao was almost unable to sleep. He had suffered before from periodic insomnia and at such times was simply unable to close his eyes for several days straight. "His waking hours grew longer and longer," his physician wrote, "until he would stay awake for twenty-four or even thirty-six or forty-eight hours, at a stretch. Then he could sleep ten or twelve hours continuously." He took sleeping pills (barbiturates) in unimaginably large doses, but they did not help. He would become exhausted, rock from side to side, suffer from unbearable itching, and grow dizzy. But his doctor was powerless to help him. His "sleeplessness . . . was a result of . . . political battle."[40]

The triumph of collectivization had an additional cost. It made Mao and the entire party hostages of the unfulfilled promises of prosperity that had lured peasants into the cooperatives. Soon disappointed, many peasants began to express their dissatisfaction.[41] Two years later, Mao himself acknowledged that cooperativization had not solved the contradiction between the CCP and the "great mass of intermediate elements."[42] On the contrary, according to data from Soviet experts, social tensions that had begun to accumulate after the introduction of the grain monopoly now intensified. "The collectivization of agriculture [in China] encountered resistance on the part of peasants," Soviet economists concluded in early 1957.[13] Disturbances racked the newly formed cooperatives but Mao was convinced that it was impossible to build "the bright future" without trials and tribulations. "On this matter we are quite heartless!" he said. "On this matter Marxism is indeed cruel and has little mercy, for it is determined to exterminate imperialism, feudalism, capitalism, and small production to boot. . . . Our aim is to exterminate capitalism, obliterate it from the face of the earth and make it a thing of the past. What emerges in history is bound to die out."[44] The scale of peasant resistance, however, was nowhere near that in the Soviet Union during collectivization. On the whole, socialism came rather peacefully to the Chinese countryside.

At the same time, in 1955–56, the CCP, on Mao Zedong's initiative, carried out the large-scale socialist transformation of industry and commerce. These reforms were the continuation of measures taken in 1951 and 1952 that had been directed against the urban bourgeoisie. In 1953–54 the CCP had established state control over the sale of all important consumer goods, thereby sharply limiting the market economy. State industrial and commercial companies squeezed out private firms. The communists made use of various kinds of so-called lower forms of state capitalism. To a certain degree they repeated what the Guomindang regime had already done in the 1930s and 1940s. This included such things as the government buying up the products of private enterprises and state orders for the compulsory delivery of raw materials at fixed prices. In 1955 the state placed about 80 percent of small and medium enterprises under its control. The large enterprises, those employing five hundred workers and staff, were transformed into joint state-private enterprises by having the state invest capital through purchasing stock in the companies. By mid-1956 private property had been basically destroyed throughout the country.[45] Mao valued this as a victory of the socialist revolution in the economic realm, an early fulfillment of the party's general line; at this time he believed that the general line was aimed at resolving the question of property.[46]

The upshot was that the CCP succeeded in radically transforming Chinese society in the shortest possible time. Its tactics were effective in both the cities and the countryside and did not encounter significant opposition from wealthier Chinese. The resistance of the bourgeoisie was weakened by the decision of the Chinese government to "buy out" private industrial property. On October 29, 1955, Mao offered the Chinese capitalists significant monetary compensation and full employment as well as high social status in exchange for their promise not to sabotage the socialist reforms. The capitalists had to surrender their property to the government voluntarily.[47] A subsequent government decision established that they would be paid 5 percent annual interest over a seven-year period.[48] (In reality, the payments continued for an even longer period, up until 1966.)

It was actually the working class that demonstrated the most resistance to CCP policies, something that came as a shock to a party that proclaimed its fidelity to the cause of the proletariat. The socialist transformation, however, led to deterioration in the material condition of workers. They lost a number of privileges they had previously enjoyed while exercising control over the entrepreneurs. The system of workers' control that had been introduced following the communist victory in 1949 served to defend the interests of workers. But this system was short-lived. The establishment by the CCP of official trade unions in place of actual workers' control, a transformation that took place after the state took over the means of production, led to a reduction in the living standards of manual laborers. The official trade unions, controlled by the state, defended the government, not the workers. The latter began to express their dissatisfaction by means of strikes, which the local authorities managed to suppress with considerable difficulty. According to official data, between August 1956 and January 1957 there were more than 10,000 large and small strikes by workers and more than 10,000 strikes by students and pupils.[49] Judging from available Chinese archives, workers in the former private companies in Shanghai were particularly active. In the spring of 1957, there were "large disturbances" at 587 enterprises in Shanghai involving about 30,000 workers and less serious disturbances at more than 700 mills and factories. About 90 percent of the incidents took place at factories newly brought under state control.[50]

By the end of 1956, as a result of accelerated industrial development and forced socialist reforms, the Chinese economy began to experience a number of economic difficulties connected to shortages of raw materials, electricity, and qualified workers. At the same time a triumph of socialism strengthened the CCP rigid dictatorship over the society. The party bureaucracy now enjoyed not only absolute political authority but also total economic power. Under these circumstances, with a national economy now completely under state control, the communist elite could launch even more dangerous experiments in an effort to resolve all economic difficulties by its iron will. Here Mao still followed Stalin, who had asserted: "There are no fortresses that the working people, the Bolsheviks, cannot capture."[51]

29

THE EMANCIPATION
OF CONSCIOUSNESS

Another event in 1956 profoundly shook China and the whole world. At a closed session of the Twentieth Congress of the Communist Party of the Soviet Union in Moscow on February 25, Nikita Khrushchev delivered a report in which he condemned the cult of personality of Stalin. The deceased dictator was accused of numerous crimes. Khrushchev asserted that Stalin had committed serious errors in the early period of World War II, had violated the principle of collective leadership, and had established a personal dictatorship. He spoke about Stalin's errors in nationality and agrarian policies as well as in the international relations of the USSR. Nothing was said, however, about Stalin's mistrust of Mao Zedong; however, Khrushchev did speak of Stalin's errors with respect to Tito.[1]

Mao was not at the congress. Zhu De, Deng Xiaoping, and some other party officials represented the CCP, and it was they who first informed the Chairman of this "staggering news." Mao was stunned. In the name of the Central Committee he had sent greetings to the Twentieth Congress in which, as always, he had sung the praises of the late Stalin. The letter spoke about the "invincible Communist Party of the Soviet Union, created by Lenin and nurtured by Stalin."[2] The "venerable Zhu" was no less embarrassed; he had read the letter from the rostrum of the congress to stormy applause in the hall. The impression arose that Khrushchev did not care how his speech would be received in the communist world. He even did not give a text of his report to foreign communists, and Mao had to read a Chinese translation done by Xinhua (New China) News Agency from a copy published in the *New York Times* on March 10.[3] Khrushchev simply wanted to resolve his own problems. In other words, in condemning Stalinism, the new Soviet leader acted like Stalin, doubting not at all that Moscow's satellites would accept everything that came out of the Kremlin.[4] They had accepted the inconceivable Molotov-Ribbentrop

Pact of 1939, which completely reversed relations with Hitler's Germany and they would also accept the censure of Stalin.

After reflecting for a while, however, Mao suppressed his first unpleasant feeling. Be that as it may, the censure of the Kremlin ex-dictator emancipated him once and for all. The process that had begun with Khrushchev's visit in 1954 had now reached its logical conclusion.[5]

Some time later official information arrived from Khrushchev, and Mao could not help notice that the "demolisher of Stalin" was not fully confident. He was obviously trying to elicit Mao's favor. This pleased the Chairman; it confirmed his initial impressions of Khrushchev as a weak partner. Informing Mao in a private letter of the resolution adopted with respect to Stalin, the first secretary of the CPSU offered to help the Chinese build fifty-one military projects and three scientific research institutes. He also expressed willingness to cooperate in building a railroad from Urumqi in Xinjiang to the Soviet-Chinese border. In other words, Khrushchev was trying to win Mao over. On April 7, 1956, Khrushchev's personal representative Anastas Mikoyan and the Chinese signed an agreement regarding Soviet assistance in building fifty-five new industrial enterprises, including plants to produce rockets and atomic weapons.[6]

All of this radically altered the balance of forces in relations between China and the USSR. From now on Mao no longer had to look to the Soviet Union and feel obliged to copy its experience. If in 1955 and early 1956, while carrying out a Stalinist collectivization like that in the USSR, he had dared only to call for a faster tempo of cooperativization than the Soviets, now he was fully able to grope toward his own path of development. He could even try to catch up with and overtake the Soviet Union and turn China into the mightiest industrial power.

Soon after familiarizing himself with Khrushchev's report, on March 31, Mao invited Soviet ambassador Yudin, who had returned to China from Moscow after taking part in the Twentieth Congress, for a visit. Yudin himself had wanted a meeting with Mao. Khrushchev, who again badly needed the support of the Chinese Communist Party, had requested this of the ambassador. Mao, however, pleading illness, put Yudin off for a long time before he finally agreed to see him. The conversation lasted three hours. Mao was in an exhilarated frame of mind, and despite the serious subject matter he was constantly making jokes. He wanted to give the impression of a man who had grown wise from his experience in life, and who calmly faced the storms of the world. It was obvious, however, that he found it difficult to talk about Stalin.

He started off by telling Yudin that, as before, he considered his former mentor "unquestionably . . . a great Marxist, a good and honest revolutionary." At the same time, according to Yudin, Mao said that "the materials from the congress had produced a strong impression upon him." Mao emphasized that "the spirit of criticism and self-criticism and the atmosphere following the congress had also helped us . . . to express our view more freely on a number of questions. It was good that the CPSU had posed these questions. It would have been . . . difficult for us to take the initiative in this matter."[7]

Mao was well aware of what he was saying. As we have seen, throughout the entire history of the communist movement in China, its leaders, including Mao Zedong, had been almost invariably dependent ideologically, organizationally, and politically on Moscow. Although what Mao knew of Stalin's perfidy was more than enough for him to feel relief after Stalin's death, naturally he could not undertake to criticize openly his "leader and teacher." It is true that he was unaware of the full scope of Stalin's perfidy. For example, he did not know that in 1938 the Kremlin dictator was planning to stage a massive political trial of Comintern officials. In this connection, pondering those to be targeted, he included on the list of those who would be accused such communists as Zhou Enlai, Liu Shaoqi, Kang Sheng, Chen Yun, Li Lisan, Luo Fu, Wang Jiaxiang, Ren Bishi, Deng Fa, Wu Yuzhang, Yang Shangkun, Dong Biwu, and even Qu Qiubai, who had already been executed by the Guomindang in 1935.[8] NKVD investigator Aleksandr Ivanovich Langfang beat accusations against these persons out of an official of the Personnel Department of the ECCI, Guo Zhaotang, who was arrested in March 1938.[9] There is no doubt that Langfang did not do this on his own initiative.*

Stalin proposed to stage a Comintern show trial in late spring 1938, in addition to the three that had already taken place against Zinoviev and Kamenev, against Radek and Piatakov, and against Bukharin and Rykov. This time the main accused would be the secretary of the Executive Committee of the Comintern, Josef Aronovich Piatnitsky. Other leading targets would be ECCI officials Bela Kun and Wilhelm Knorin,[10] while the Chinese were supposed to play supporting roles. The decision to arrest massive numbers of Comintern officials was taken back in May 1937. At 1 A.M. on May 26, Dimitrov was summoned to the office of People's Commissar Yezhov, who told him, "Important spies are at work in the Comintern." Arrests took place during the second half of 1937 and the early part of 1938; however, the majority of Chinese working in Moscow were not arrested. There's no way of knowing, but had Stalin not dropped his plan to stage a trial, it is possible that many CCP leaders would have become his victims. He did not include Mao Zedong on his "blacklist," but who really knows how many such lists there were?

Knowing nothing about this proposed trial, in his conversation with the ambassador Mao devoted most of his attention to Stalin's mistaken policy toward China and the Chinese communist movement. He also shared several

---

* That NKVD investigators did not conduct inquiries on their own say-so is attested to in Khrushchev's report "On the Cult of Personality and Its Consequences."

of the insults that had piled up during his contacts with Stalin.[11] In conclusion, he informed Yudin of the forthcoming publication in *People's Daily* of an editorial devoted to the question of the cult of personality in the USSR.

This article, written by Chen Boda[12] and edited by Mao himself and several others, only some of whom were Politburo members,[13] was published on April 5, 1956. It was titled "On the Historical Experience of the Dictatorship of the Proletariat," and since it was intended for a broad audience it did not contain unusual criticism of the former communist idol. The leaders of the CCP, Mao in the first instance, did not want anyone to oppose their own dictatorship by waving an anti-Stalinist banner. Later, on April 28, at an enlarged meeting of the Politburo, Mao Zedong acknowledged that "we do not intend to divulge . . . to the masses" everything "bad that Stalin and the Third International did."[14] For now Mao also did not want to reveal his own plans regarding his search for his own development path. Stalin's merits and demerits were summed up in a ratio of 70:30, but the Soviet Union was praised nevertheless for its "selfless criticism . . . of past mistakes."

The next day Mao spoke on this theme to Khrushchev's personal representative Mikoyan, who had come to China on April 6 for a two-day visit. In the spirit of the article he devoted a lot of attention to criticizing Stalin's "serious mistakes" with regard to the Chinese revolution; however, he noted that "Stalin's achievements surpass his mistakes."[15] In reply, Mikoyan invited Mao to come to Moscow. The Chairman asked, "What for?" Mikoyan parried, "There must be something to do there."[16] Mao was not pleased by his guest's paternalistic tone.

On May 1, during the traditional May Day parade in Tiananmen Square, the marchers carried giant portraits of the late head of the Soviet Union just as they had the year before.[17] It was the same in cities all over China.

The next day, on his own initiative, Mao paid a call on Yudin. According to the recollections of Soviet diplomat Konstantin Krutikov, once again Mao expressed the Politburo's position regarding the "merits and mistakes" of Stalin; however, he observed that after his last meeting with Mikoyan, "it had become clearer why Stalin did not trust him. . . . Apparently, Stalin considered even his closest associates Voroshilov, Molotov, and Mikoyan as scarcely better than foreign protégés."[18] His main reason for coming, however, was something else. Mao had come to Yudin to express his disagreement with Khrushchev's position set forth in his report to the Twentieth Congress on "peaceful coexistence of the two systems" and on "the possibility of preventing war in the present era." Up till then the CCP Politburo had quietly let it be known that it simply did not agree with the thesis contained in the same report regarding the possibility of a "peaceful transition from capitalism to socialism."[19] In an article on the Twentieth Congress published in *People's Daily* on February 19, 1956, this latter idea of Khrushchev's had been deliberately ignored.[20]

Now Mao decided to express his views on "peaceful coexistence" as well. He did this, to be sure, in a very circumspect manner, not making a direct attack. He told the ambassador that during the period of the Three Kingdoms (220–280 CE), as a result of constant warfare the population of China had diminished by forty million people, and that during the rebellion of An Lushan (755–63 CE) against Xuanzong, the emperor of the Tang dynasty, it had shrunk even more. His meaning was that there was no need to fear a nuclear war with imperialism. Even if the imperialists succeeded in seizing the European part of the USSR and the coastal regions of China, socialism would still ultimately triumph. Imperialism, he concluded, was just a "paper tiger." [21] For some reason, he liked the expression "paper tiger" (in Chinese *zhilaohu*), and he used it on various occasions. He even playfully called Jiang Qing a "paper tiger." [22] In this instance, he was simply repeating in veiled form what he had already said in late January 1955 to Carl-Johan Sundstrom, the Finnish ambassador to China:

> The Chinese people are not to be cowed by U.S. atomic blackmail. Our country has a population of 600 million and an area of 9,600,000 square kilometres. The United States cannot annihilate the Chinese nation with its small stack of atom bombs. . . . Should the United States launch a third world war and supposing it lasted eight or ten years, the result would be the elimination of the ruling classes in the United States, Britain and the other accomplice countries and the transformation of most of the world into countries led by Communist Parties. . . . [T]he sooner they make war, the sooner they will be wiped from the face of the earth. [23]

He had expressed himself more simply on this same subject earlier, in October 1954, in conversation with Jawaharlal Nehru, the Indian prime minister, who was paying a friendly visit to China. "If your government is destroyed by an atomic bomb," Mao "reassured" his flabbergasted guest, "the people will establish a new government, and it will be able to conduct peace negotiations." [24] He wanted now to communicate this to Khrushchev, who, from Mao's perspective, had overestimated the power of American imperialism.

Just recently, in late April, Mao Zedong had delivered an unusual speech at a four-day enlarged meeting of the Politburo. Presented on April 25 and titled "On the Ten Major Relationships," it had far-reaching consequences. In essence, this speech marked a critical turn in Mao Zedong's entire worldview, reflecting a new atmosphere of the emancipation of consciousness taking shape in the CCP. In general terms it defined the party's new policy with respect to building socialism, a course that differed from the Soviet model. First, the Chairman offered a devastating critique of the Soviet experience and called openly for the party to take a new path:

[T]here are some problems in our work that need discussion. Particularly worthy of attention is the fact that in the Soviet Union certain defects and errors that occurred in the course of their building socialism have lately come to light. Do you want to follow the detours they have made? It was by drawing lessons from their experience that we were able to avoid certain detours in the past, and there is all the more reason for us to do so now.[25]

It was clear that he had begun to reexamine the Stalinist model, deeming it insufficiently radical and the Soviet pace of development too slow.

Mao did not present a detailed program for building Chinese-style socialism; however, he designated a number of strategic elements and emphasized the need to follow the principles of "more, faster, better, and more economically."* What he had in mind was a substantial increase in capital investment in light industry and agriculture, the rapid development of interior provinces, and curtailment of investment in the defense sector, as well as an acceleration of economic construction as a whole. Mao spoke also about strengthening spiritual rather than material incentives for work, reducing the scope of the economy under centralized bureaucratic administration, and developing relatively autonomous production complexes. He did not conceal the difference between the new strategy and the Soviet strategy:

[W]e must learn with an analytical and critical eye, and we mustn't copy everything indiscriminately and transplant mechanically. . . . Some people never take the trouble to analyze, they simply follow the "wind." Today, when the north wind [i.e., the Soviet Union] is blowing, they join the "north wind" school. . . . It would lead to a mess if every single sentence, even of Marx's, were followed. . . . [I]n those cases where we already have clear knowledge, we must not follow others in every detail. . . . [M]any people in the Soviet Union are conceited and very arrogant.[26]

That Mao's speech was not published at the time is hardly surprising. The Chairman was not simply openly criticizing the Soviet Union. His

---

* Two versions of Mao's speech exist, the uncorrected stenographic report and a partially edited canonical text. A translation of the first appeared in the West and in the Soviet Union in the 1970s. The official document was published in the PRC in 1976. The formula "build socialism more, faster, better, and more economically" is only in the stenographic account. In a note, however, the editors of the fifth volume of the *Selected Works of Mao Zedong* confirm that in his speech Mao did indeed propose this idea as the general line for socialist construction.

ideas ran directly counter to the concepts of many Chinese leaders themselves. Among these latter were Liu Shaoqi, Zhou Enlai,* and Chen Yun.
Deng Xiaoping also failed to understand it.[27] In late April 1956, for example, Zhou Enlai openly took issue with Mao at an enlarged Politburo meeting when Mao called for increasing investments in capital construction by
two billion yuan. Zhou asserted that this would make it very difficult to supply the population with essential commodities and lead to an extraordinary
growth of the urban population. Mao was stung by this observation,[28] and on
May 2 he presented most of his new ideas to members of the Supreme State
Council.[29]

In this situation, the Central Committee felt obligated to distribute the
text of his April 25 speech, but only to upper- and mid-level party cadres.† At
this time, Zhou Enlai, Chen Yun, and other economists were busy drawing
up the Second Five-Year Plan, and they did not fully grasp Mao's unortho-
dox ideas. In essence, they ignored them. Liu Shaoqi and Deng Xiaoping did
likewise. All of them were preoccupied with daily party and government affairs, and they had no time for further discussions with the "great theoretician"
about his new ideas.

Mao was offended by the lack of response to his ideas, and in mid-1956 he
flew from Beijing south to Canton to undertake a new inspection tour, hoping, as before, to elicit support from local cadres. The heat was unbearable and
the Cantonese were plagued by mosquitoes. There was no air-conditioning
in the villa where Mao was staying, but he was in no hurry to return to Beijing. He had to solve a pile of problems, meet with people he needed, assess
their frame of mind, and secure their support in his ongoing struggle with
the "die hard moderates." These persons, taking advantage of the Leader's absence, published an editorial in *People's Daily* that criticized "voluntarism" and
"blind advances." Mao's reaction was touchingly childish: "I will not read it.
Why should I read an article in which they abuse me?"[30]

How wearisome he found these "zombies with a slave psychology" who
entirely lacked "courage and determination."[31] No, he had to show them that
he was more powerful than all of them put together.

Thus he decided to fulfill an old dream, to swim across three great rivers,

---

* Zhou Enlai was the first to put forward the formula of "socialist construction according
to the principle of 'more, faster, better, and more economically.' " He did this on January 14,
1956, in a report to a conference about intellectuals convened by the Central Committee
at which he developed Mao's ideas presented on December 6, 1955. However, he did not
impart any "revolutionary" meaning to this formula.

† Nevertheless, it soon became known outside China. For example, members of a delegation from the Yugoslavian Communist Union referred to "The Ten Major Relationships"
during their talk with Mao Zedong in September 1956.

the Pearl River in Canton, the Xiang River in Changsha, and the Yangzi River in Wuhan. He was indeed an excellent swimmer, but the idea that had entered his head seemed like true folly. All three of the rivers were unusually wide, and the Yangzi had numerous whirlpools and a swift current to boot. But trying to get him to change his mind was a waste of time. In late May 1956, he plunged into the turbid waters of the Pearl River, which was more than 1.5 miles across. "The water . . . was filthy," recalled his doctor, who was duty-bound to swim with him. "I saw occasional globs of human waste float by. The pollution did not bother Mao. He floated on his back, his big belly sticking up like a round balloon, legs relaxed, as though he were resting on a sofa. The water carried him downstream, and only rarely did he use his arms or legs to propel himself forward."[32] For two hours he floated with the current a distance of more than six miles. Soon afterward he left Canton and headed for Changsha, where he swam across the one-mile-wide Xiang River, which was no cleaner than the Pearl River, twice. His delight knew no bounds. "The Xiang River is too small," he cried. "I want to swim in the Yangtze [Yangzi]. On to the Yangtze River!"[33]

Mao finally arrived in Wuhan in early June. Soon, accompanied by his forty-odd bodyguards, he was on the bank of the famous river. He was unable, to be sure, to swim across it; that would have been a nonsensical undertaking. The power of the stream was so great that Mao was simply carried along by the current. Therefore, as in the Pearl River, he simply let himself go with the flow, which carried him more than eighteen miles. Nonetheless, he was inexpressibly happy, the more so since the journalists, who were prepared for anything, immediately disseminated the "good" news of the conquest of the mighty river "by our beloved helmsman." During the several days Mao spent in Wuhan, he swam in the Yangzi River three times.[34] "There is nothing you cannot do if you are serious about it," he said enthusiastically afterward.[35] It was understood that what he had in mind were the "moderates" in the Politburo.

Full of enthusiasm, he turned again to his Muse:

Just drank Changsha water.
Now eating Wuchang fish.
I swim across the thousands-of-miles long Yangtze [Yangzi],
looking as far as the endless Chu skies,
ignoring wind's blowing and waves' beating:
better than walking slowly
in the quiet courtyard.
Today I am relaxed and free.
Confucius said by the river:
All passing things flow away like the river.

Boats sail with the wind.
Turtle and Snake mountains stay,
while great plans grow.
A bridge flies across north to south,
natural barrier turns into an open road.
High in the gorges a rock dam will rise,
cutting off Wu Mountain's cloud and rain.
A still lake will climb in the tall gorges.
Mountain goddess—
I hope she is still well—
will be startled at a changed world.[36]

A new disappointment awaited him in Beijing, however. The "moderates" in the Politburo who were busy making preparations for the forthcoming Eighth Congress of the Chinese Communist Party were ready to place the question of the cult of personality on the agenda. The atmosphere in Beijing was supercharged, and Mao for a time stayed away from party affairs, in the quiet resort town of Beidaihe, on the shore of the Yellow Sea. He gave his opponents carte blanche, having decided to put them to the test on the entire program. "Do you want to show what you are capable of? Go right ahead, we'll see!" is how he probably reasoned, again adopting his favorite tactic: "The enemy advances, we retreat; the enemy camps, we harass; the enemy tires, we attack; the enemy retreats, we pursue." It was not for nothing that one of his pseudonyms was Desheng—"Retreat in the Name of Victory." At the end of the summer, he declared to his associates that he intended to give up the post of chairman of the PRC for "reasons of health," keeping for himself only the position of chairman of the Central Committee of the CCP.[37]

Liu Shaoqi and several other members of the Politburo, not wishing to ignore Mao, also went off to Beidaihe. As before, the Chairman remained their leader. All they wanted from him was a somewhat more collective leadership. But this was precisely what Mao could not agree with. He was convinced that with Khrushchev's thaw, which threatened not only China but the entire socialist cause with unpredictable consequences, the CCP needed to unite around him as never before.

The Eighth Congress was convened in this setting of conflict between two points of view. Its official sessions took place in Beijing from September 15 to 27. There were 1,026 voting delegates and 107 alternates representing almost 11,730,000 members of the party. The formal sessions were preceded by closed discussions (a so-called preparatory conference) from August 29 to September 12. It was during these discussions that all of the basic decisions of the forum were made. Behind closed doors the delegates discussed and adopted drafts of all the resolutions and texts of all the basic reports and speeches. They also settled personnel matters.

During this time Mao was extremely cautious. As before, feeling out his opponents, he presided over none of the sessions and made not even a single report. He gave the most active roles to Liu Shaoqi, Zhou Enlai, and Deng Xiaoping. He himself demonstrated his "modesty." He greeted the assembled delegates with just two brief speeches, one at the first session of the preparatory conference on August 30 and the second at the opening of the congress on September 15.[38] At the same time, he did everything he could to popularize his ideas. In particular, in both of his brief speeches he returned to the ideas in "The Ten Major Relationships" and, correcting the draft "Political Report of the Central Committee" that Liu Shaoqi was supposed to deliver, he added the following paragraph:

> The Chinese revolution and [socialist] construction in China are naturally in the hands of the Chinese people themselves in the first instance. It must be clear. The need for foreign assistance is secondary. It is completely incorrect to lose faith and suppose that you yourself can do nothing on your own; it is wrong to suppose that the fate of China is not in the hands of the Chinese themselves, and to rely wholly on foreign assistance.[39]

Consciously demonstrating his rejection of Soviet paternalism, Mao even refused to attend the September 17 session of the congress at which Khrushchev's representative Mikoyan gave a speech.[40]

The basic tone of the congress was different from Mao's intentions, however. Under the leadership of Liu Shaoqi, Zhou Enlai, and Deng Xiaoping, the delegates gave the Soviet model its due and supported only those social experiments of Mao's that were aimed at accelerating the achievement of Stalinization. The congress officially proclaimed that the "proletarian-socialist revolution" in China was basically victorious. All the speakers enthusiastically praised the results of the socialist transformation of the countryside and the cities.

The most important thing, however, was that the congress adopted a resolution that must have been particularly painful for Mao. In the new atmosphere created by Khrushchev's speech, the delegates agreed to remove from the party statutes the sentence that the Chinese Communist Party "guides its entire work" by Mao Zedong Thought.[41] It was replaced with the following statement: "The Chinese Communist Party is guided by Marxism-Leninism."[42] In his report "On Changes in the Party Statutes," Deng Xiaoping placed special emphasis on the need to struggle "against the intrusion of personality, against its glorification." "Our party," he declared, "rejects the alien concept of deifying personalities." To be sure, he noted that Mao Zedong was playing an important role in the fight against the cult of personality in the CCP; however, it was very difficult to take these words seriously.[43] The congress reinstated the post of general secretary of the CCP, which was also quite remarkable. Mao himself proposed that Deng be promoted to the position. Even though Deng did not understand "The Ten Major Relationships," Mao considered him "quite an honest man"[44] since Deng did not display his opposition to Mao's adventurism as overtly as Liu and Zhou.

The opponents of Mao's voluntarist experiments prepared a resolution of the congress on Liu Shaoqi's report, inserting in this document the thesis that from now on, following the construction of a socialist society,

> the main contradiction inside our country has become the contradiction between the demand of the people to build an advanced industrial country and the backward condition of our agrarian nation, as well as the contradiction between the rapidly growing economic and cultural demands of the people and the incapacity of the contemporary economy and culture of our country to satisfy these demands of the people.[45]

After the congress, in November 1956 at a meeting of officials from the Ministry of Trade, Deputy Premier Chen Yun and several other economists spoke of the need for a rational combination of economic construction with an improvement in the lives of the people.[46]

Mao was understandably dissatisfied with many of the resolutions of the congress. The issue of the cult of personality was among the most troublesome. Soon after the congress he decided to counterattack. Receiving a delegation from the Yugoslavian Communist Union he noted, as if in passing, that "[f]ew people in China have ever openly criticized me. The [Chinese] people are tolerant of my shortcomings and mistakes. It is because we always want to serve the people and do good things for the people." These words sounded as a warning to Mao's opponents, the more so since, as the Chairman explained, "bossism" was not an actual problem in China. He also added, "When some people criticize me, others would oppose and accuse them of disrespecting the leader."[47] At this time, within his close circle of intimates he began to express caustic criticism of Khrushchev's anti-Stalin policy. Stalin should have been "criticized but not killed," he complained to his interpreter Li Yueran. Khrushchev is not "mature enough to lead such a big country," he said in a fit of temper to another interpreter, Yan Mingfu. People like Khrushchev "do not adhere to Marxism-Leninism," he said to others of his associates.[48]

Quickly reacting to the slightest change in the political climate, on October 1, Zhou Enlai expounded Mao's new, critical position regarding the cult of personality to Boris Nikolaevich Ponomarev, a member of the Central Committee of the CPSU who had attended the Eighth Congress. Zhou criticized the CPSU for the "mistakes" it had made during its debunking of Stalin: in the first place, he said, "no preliminary consultation was carried out with fraternal parties"; secondly, "an all-around historical analysis was completely lacking"; and, finally, the leading comrades of the CPSU "lacked self-criticism." [49]

The anti-Stalinist events in Poland and in Hungary in 1956 greatly increased the cultlike mood in the Chinese leadership and consequently strengthened Mao's position. In October 1956, the new communist leader of Poland, Władysław Gomułka, who had come to power on a wave of workers' demonstrations, expelled the Stalinists from the Politburo of the Polish Workers' Party. Among them was Marshal Konstantin Konstantinovich Rokossowski, Poland's minister of defense and concurrently deputy chairman of the Council of Ministers. He had been appointed to these posts by Stalin. The anti-Soviet mood, which was already strong among the Poles, began to grow rapidly. Meanwhile, in Hungary, as a result of a democratic revolution power in the government passed to a popular liberal communist, Imre Nagy. The crisis of socialism in Eastern Europe was undoubtedly triggered by Khrushchev's speech against Stalin.

Mao understood this very well, and he did not hide his dissatisfaction with Khrushchev's actions. On the evening of October 20 Mao convened an enlarged session of the Politburo, at which for the first time he condemned the Soviet Union for "great power chauvinism." News had reached him that Khrushchev intended to use force against Gomułka, and he did not want to see this happen. Soviet intervention against Poland might explode the whole socialist camp. After the session, Mao immediately summoned Soviet ambassador Pavel Yudin, whom Mao received in his bedroom dressed in his bathrobe, contrary to all protocol. Extremely irritated, Mao asserted, "We resolutely condemn what you are doing. I request that you telephone Khrushchev right away to convey our opinion: if the Soviet Union moves troops we will support Poland." [50]

Having received Yudin's information, Khrushchev panicked and on October 21 decided "considering the circumstances . . . [fully] to refrain from armed intervention. Show patience." [51]

Mao felt victorious. Around 1 A.M. on October 23, he again summoned the unfortunate Yudin to his bedroom; in the presence of Liu Shaoqi, Zhou Enlai, Chen Yun, and Deng Xiaoping, the entire leadership of the Politburo, he noted with irritation that the Russians had completely discarded the sword of Stalin. The result, he added, was that enemies had taken up the sword to kill communists. This, he continued, was the same as lifting a rock and dropping it on one's own feet. [52]

That same night, Mao, Liu, Zhou, Chen and Deng decided to help the leadership of the CPSU manage the situation. They did this in response to a telegram about "the need for consultation," sent to the Central Committee of the CCP from Moscow on October 21. Khrushchev sent similar requests to the central committees of the communist parties of Czechoslovakia, Bulgaria, and the German Democratic Republic.[53] Early on the morning of October 23, a Chinese delegation including Liu, Deng, Wang Jiaxiang, who was then the director of the International Liaison Department of the Central Committee, and Hu Qiaomu, a member of the Secretariat of the Central Committee, flew off to Moscow.* The delegation stayed on for eleven days. From October 23 to 31, Liu and the others held conversations with Khrushchev, Molotov, and Bulganin at Stalin's former dacha in Lipki. On several occasions Khrushchev invited Liu, Deng, and other members of the Chinese delegation to meetings of the Presidium of the Central Committee of the CPSU. On the very first evening Liu Shaoqi conveyed Mao's point of view on the "discarded sword" and on "great power chauvinism" to Khrushchev, who was forced to swallow all of this.[54] By this time the Soviet leadership had decided on its own not to intervene in Poland.[55]

The main thing now bothering Mao was the situation in Hungary. It had gotten much tenser on October 23. A genuine popular revolution had begun in Budapest. Thus the issue of Hungary was at the center of Khrushchev's discussions with Liu. Liu was in constant contact with Mao, and Mao initially recommended to Khrushchev that he adopt the same peaceful position he had taken in Poland. He believed that "the working class of Hungary" would be able to "regain control of the situation and to put down the uprising on its own."[56] But everything changed on the afternoon of October 30. It was then that Mao received reports from his ambassador in Hungary as well as from Liu Shaoqi that state security officers were being lynched in Budapest,† and his patience was exhausted. He decided that it was impossible just to let things go. The revolution in Hungary differed, it seemed, from the liberal communist reforms of Gomułka. It might fundamentally affect the situation throughout the socialist camp. Liu informed Khrushchev and other members of the Presidium of the CPSU Central Committee of Mao's new point of view: "[Soviet] troops should remain in Hungary and Budapest."[57] This was a green light for the suppression of the Hungarian democratic movement.

At the same time, Mao and Liu pressured the Presidium of the CPSU Central Committee, demanding that it adopt a special "Declaration on the Foun-

---

* In his memoirs, Khrushchev mistakenly asserts that Kang Sheng was a member of Liu Shaoqi's delegation.

† Liu learned of this from information provided him by Khrushchev, who had received it from Mikoyan and KGB head Ivan Aleksandrovich Serov, then in Hungary.

dation and Further Strengthening of Friendship and Cooperation between the Soviet Union and Other Socialist Countries." They did this in order to avert further manifestations of Soviet great power chauvinism with regard to the socialist countries. It was just such chauvinism they deemed one of the main reasons for the "unhealthy" situation that had occurred in Eastern Europe. The declaration stated, "The countries of the great community of socialist nations can construct their mutual relations only on the basis of the principles of full equality, respect for territorial integrity, state independence and sovereignty, and noninterference in each other's internal affairs." [58]

Seeing off the Chinese delegation at the airport on the evening of October 31, Khrushchev, evidently heeding Mao's changed position, informed Liu Shaoqi that the Presidium of the Central Committee of the CPSU had decided "to restore order in Hungary." "There were no arguments," Khrushchev recalled later. "Liu Shaoqi said that if in Beijing it turned out people were thinking differently, he would notify us." [59] But Mao did not change his position. The result was that the Soviet leader decided "to pull out all the stops," especially since it soon became known that the Hungarian government, having declared its intention to withdraw Hungary from the Warsaw Pact, had turned to Western countries and the Pope for aid. On November 4, Soviet tanks entered Budapest. The Hungarian popular revolution was drowned in blood.

Despite this, Mao Zedong and other Chinese leaders were profoundly shaken by the very fact of a liberal democratic movement in the socialist countries. In mid-November, at the Second Plenum of the Eighth Central Committee, Mao developed his idea about the "discarded sword." His attack on the USSR was without precedent. Unable to restrain his indignation, he even asserted that a number of Soviet leaders had discarded "the sword of Lenin . . . to a considerable extent." Moreover, he outlined another sphere of disagreement with Moscow, for the first time openly criticizing Khrushchev's thesis about the possibility of a "peaceful transition from capitalism to socialism." "Khrushchev's report at the Twentieth Congress of the Communist Party of the Soviet Union says it is possible to seize state power by the parliamentary road, that is to say," Mao emphasized, "it is no longer necessary for all countries to learn from the October Revolution. Once this gate is opened, by and large Leninism is thrown away." [60]

Of course, the polemic that he unleashed was obviously contrived: after all, no one could predict the future. Nonetheless, from then until the late 1970s the Soviet and Chinese leaderships would engage in pointed discussions about the possibility of "peaceful transition from capitalism to socialism."

Mao also made claims to leadership in a number of Eastern European countries whose basic problem, he believed, was that their communists were not waging class struggle properly. The result was that in these countries they "left so many counter-revolutionaries at large." [61]

Taking advantage of the situation, at the same time he tried to push his ideas concerning acceleration of the tempo of economic development in the PRC by renewing his attack on the group of "moderates" who, as before, were oriented toward the Soviet economic experience. "Something good came out of the Twentieth Congress of the CPSU," he noted in this connection on the eve of the plenum, "namely, that [the congress] revealed the true state of affairs, emancipated consciousness, and led to a situation in which people stopped thinking that everything that was done in the Soviet Union was the absolute truth which was not subject to change and must be implemented as is. We must use our own wits and decide questions of the revolution and construction in our country."[62]

At this same plenum, after again criticizing the "moderates," Mao called for a new rectification campaign in the CCP to take place next year.[63] He did not name these "moderates," but the delegates understood that he had in mind Liu Shaoqi, Zhou Enlai, and Chen Yun, who presented key reports at the plenum.[64] Mao's dissatisfaction was aroused by the fact that Liu, Zhou, and Chen tried to set a course for "temporary retreat" in the sphere of industrial construction, fearing that the "economy would overheat."[65] What irritated him most of all, however, was that the reports by Liu and Zhou linked the events in Eastern Europe with the "miscalculations" of Polish and Hungarian leaders regarding the economy, in particular their persistent attempts to force the pace of industrialization and collectivization.[66] Typically, on the opening day of the plenum, November 10, *People's Daily* published an article that, in keeping with the ideas of Liu and Zhou, asserted that Hungarian leaders had mistakenly pushed industrialization and forcefully implemented collectivization. And although everyone who spoke at the plenum, including the "moderates," shared Mao's indignation regarding the "mistakes" of the Soviet leadership, the Chairman remained dissatisfied.

In early November he had already voiced the need to prepare a new article on Stalin—"particularly in connection with the Hungarian events."[67] In December the Politburo had assigned this task to the editors of *People's Daily*. Six versions were prepared. All of them were discussed at an enlarged meeting of the Politburo. Mao made a number of revisions, the most important of which was deletion of the following phrase from the sixth draft: "Rapid progress in the matter of socialist construction in China is largely the result of learning from the Soviet experience." At the same time, he wrote in the margins, "The future will tell whether the path taken in construction in China was correct. As of now it is impossible to say."[68] The article, titled "Once More on the Historical Experience of the Dictatorship of the Proletariat," was published in the *People's Daily* on December 29, 1956. In it the criticism of Stalin was significantly curtailed. If the initial publication in April spoke of "the great contributions" of the Soviet people and the CPSU to the history of humanity, the new article emphasized "the great contributions" of Stalin "to the development of the Soviet Union and . . . the international communist movement."

Following this, Mao sent a delegation headed by Zhou Enlai to the Soviet Union, Poland, and Hungary in January 1957.[69] Its mission included cooperating in the further management of problems linked to the crisis in Eastern Europe. Zhou had to explain to Khrushchev once again that "those in the Soviet Union who may wish again to pursue [a policy] of great power chauvinism will inevitably confront difficulties." "These people," Mao told Zhou, "are blinded by their thirst for gain. The best way to deal with them is by giving them a dressing-down."

Zhou energetically followed Mao's "advice" even though up till then he had maintained a noncommittal stance regarding the issue of relations with the USSR. Meeting with Khrushchev, Bulganin, and Mikoyan, who gave him a "splendid grandiose reception," on the very next day he went on the attack. He began with the new position of his Politburo on the question of Stalin, and he drew their attention to the recent article in *People's Daily*. But, as he reported later to Mao, all three of them asserted that "the criticism of Stalin" contained in this article "made them displeased (or put them in a difficult position, I can't remember the exact words)."[70]

Nonetheless, sensing danger, Khrushchev tried to soften his position in relation to Stalin. On January 17, in a welcoming speech at a PRC embassy reception on the occasion of the arrival of Zhou's delegation, he unexpectedly began to speak about Stalin. According to Lev Petrovich Deliusin, a *Pravda* correspondent who was standing not far from him, Khrushchev was quite drunk and often tripped over his words.[71] Nonetheless, he was able to convey his main thought to those around him. It was that Soviet communists, as before, were Stalinists. "We criticized Stalin not for being a bad communist," Khrushchev said. "The name of Stalin is inseparable from Marxism-Leninism."[72] This did not move Zhou, however. This is what he reported later to Mao: "Spelling out a good deal of inappropriate words [we can only guess at what Zhou was referring to], however, he made no self-criticism. We then pushed him . . . how can those comrades, especially those [Soviet] Politburo members, who had worked with Stalin, decline to assume any responsibility?" At this Khrushchev and Bulganin simply replied that they were afraid of being shot, and therefore, "they could not do anything to persuade Stalin or prevent his mistakes." However, Zhou persisted: "I . . . expressed our Chinese Party's conviction that open self-criticism will do no harm to, but will enhance, the Party's credibility and prestige." Underlining everything that had been said, Khrushchev, arriving at the airport, explained to Zhou "that [the Soviets] could not conduct the same kind of criticism as we [Chinese] do; should they do so, their current leadership would be in trouble."[73]

Mao reacted to this in a measured fashion. And although he did not change his negative opinion of Khrushchev, he issued instructions not to go overboard in the propaganda. "In the future," he indicated, "we shall always remain cautious and modest, and we shall tightly tuck our tails between our legs. We still need to learn from the Soviet Union. However, we shall learn from them rather selectively; only accept the good stuff, while at the same time avoiding picking up the bad stuff."[74] Still, in late January and early February he stepped up his attacks against the Soviet Union in a series of closed-door speeches.[75] At this same time, a large amount of negative information began to appear in classified information bulletins about life in the USSR and Soviet foreign policy, especially on the eve of World War II (the incursions into Poland, Finland, and Romania).[76]

At the end of February, however, Mao toned down the criticism somewhat. In an open speech "On the Correct Handling of Contradictions among the People," given at an enlarged meeting of the Supreme State Conference on February 27, he again called for learning "conscientiously from the advanced experience of the Soviet Union." To be sure, he made it clear that he had in mind only that experience that was relevant to Chinese conditions.[77] In a conversation on March 17 with top officials from Tianjin, Mao explained that he put special emphasis on the word "advanced."[78] At this time, however, the Soviet Union was not his major theme. In his speech at the conference, Mao expounded the theoretical foundations of his review of the political and economic course set out by the Eighth Congress. Once again going over the heads of the higher party organs, he appealed to mid-level *ganbu,* the kind of party functionaries who attended the conference. He tried to win them over to his side by discussing, if briefly, the further acceleration of modernization. His speech was inconsistent: on one hand he affirmed the victory of socialism; on the other he expressed doubts about the ability of the party to transform China into a great military and economic power in a historically brief period of time. In order to reinvigorate the party, he called upon the masses of nonparty persons, especially members of the "democratic" parties and other intellectuals, to criticize Marxism and the members of the CCP and provide bold and honest assessments of party policy. He called for a broad-scale ideological campaign directed against bureaucratism. He probably hoped to channel criticism from below against his opponents in the communist leadership. He proposed that the campaign develop under the slogan "Let a Hundred Flowers Bloom, Let a Hundred Schools of Thought Contend."[79]

Mao had first introduced this slogan in December 1955, at a Politburo meeting, but at that time it did not catch on because of opposition from the party apparatus and skepticism on the part of intellectuals.[80] Now Mao made one more attempt to launch the campaign. Although his speech was not published until June, on April 27, 1957, the Central Committee adopted measures to implement Mao's instructions by making them the basis of its "Resolution on a Rectification Movement." This resolution became a program of renewal for the CCP, which, Mao believed, had become too conservative and bureaucratized and therefore incapable of adopting his radical political and economic principles. Intraparty bureaucratism, subjectivism, and sectarianism became the targets of intensive criticism.

On May 10, the Central Committee published a new resolution calling upon party cadres to return to the populist practices of the "Yan'an Way" in order to overcome "bourgeois ways." The Yan'an Way meant harmonious relations between party cadres and the masses, which, according to Mao, had been characteristic of the Sino-Japanese War period of 1937–45. As a means of reviving the "Yan'an spirit," the Central Committee proposed that all *ganbu* regardless of their positions devote a certain amount of time to physical labor together with the workers and peasants.[81] On the eve of the new and unprecedented upsurge in the realm of economic and social development that Mao had already anticipated, the party had to be wholly prepared to reexamine the traditional Soviet model of social development.

In May, the new Hundred Flowers campaign was officially launched. Mao, apparently, had granted complete freedom of speech to the people. He spoke now in favor of ideological and political pluralism. From early May and continuing for almost a month all Chinese newspapers and other means of mass propaganda were open to anyone who wanted to express critical views on political issues. Many, however, criticized not "individual mistakes" but the entire system of communist dictatorship. The very ideological foundation of the CCP, namely, Marxism-Leninism, was subjected to a withering fire of criticism. Members of the democratic parties such as Zhang Naiqi, Zhang Bojun, and Luo Longji were particularly active. Their anticommunist articles won the sympathy of many university instructors. Unrest gripped the student population.

The leadership of the CCP and Mao himself had obviously not expected such a passionate response. They were not ready for serious discussions with their opponents, who, it appeared, enjoyed considerable popularity. Mao had apparently miscalculated. The intellectuals were not so much helping him as they were demonstrating their rejection of communism. There was nothing to do but terminate the campaign. On June 8, at Mao's initiative, the Central Committee adopted an inner party directive, "Master Our Forces to Repulse the Rightists' Wild Attacks." Freedom of speech was liquidated and the communists returned to their previous methods of political and ideological terror. On the same day, an editorial in *People's Daily* tried to explain such an unexpected turn of events as follows:

From May 8 to June 7, our newspaper and the entire party press, upon orders of the Central Committee, almost without exception did not speak out against incorrect views. This was done so that . . . the venomous weeds could grow luxuriantly and the people could see this and shudder at the realization that such things existed in the world. Then the people would destroy such vile things with their own hands.

In essence, the paper was acknowledging a massive political provocation staged by the leadership.

A new campaign of repression, unprecedented in scale, was now launched against the intellectuals. For the first time in the history of the CCP, the label of "rightist bourgeois elements" was affixed to millions of educated people. About half a million were incarcerated in labor reform camps.[82] Not all of them had criticized the regime; many were loyal to the new authorities but had fallen victim to intrigue and "the logic of class struggle."

The atmosphere of terror enabled Mao to overcome his main opponents in the sphere of economic construction, Zhou Enlai in the first instance. In late summer 1957, Mao attacked Zhou, saying that the premier had committed serious errors in trying to pursue balanced economic development in China. The Chairman proclaimed that he himself was an adventurist at heart and that he was not afraid of upsetting things in order to accelerate China's transition to socialism and communism.[83]

In the autumn of 1957 the Third Enlarged Plenum of the Central Committee summed up some of the results of the massive political campaigns. It assessed them as having been entirely successful. Even Mao was satisfied. "No one refuted me, I got the upper hand and was encouraged," he said sometime afterward. "The Third, September, plenum of the CC in 1957 heartened us. The party and the whole people rather clearly defined the path of development."[84] Toward the end of the plenum Mao decided to attenuate the Rectification Movement. Now he could address a rhetorical question to the party: "Can't we avoid the Soviet Union's detours and do things faster and better?" The answer was foreordained: "We should of course strive for this."[85]

It was at this plenum that Mao first began to speak of the possibility of colossal growth in agricultural production, and proposed to revive the forgotten slogan of "more" and "faster." "If we carefully work the earth, our country will become the most productive in the world," he asserted. "Already . . . there are districts where they harvest 1,000 *jin* [1 *jin* is 1.1. pounds] of grain per mu [0.16 acre]. Can the indicators of 400, 500, and 800 be raised to 800, 1,000, and 2,000? I think it is possible. . . . Earlier I also believed that man could not fly to the moon, but now I believe."[86]

What made him believe was not only his personal bent toward adventurism ("I am the kind of person who is inclined [to assess events] adventuristically," Mao loved to say), but also the Soviet launch on October 5, 1957, of the first artificial satellite, Sputnik. Although Mao still believed that one should not copy the Soviet Union in all respects, he was shaken by this event. To be sure, he saw this not so much as an indicator of the power of the USSR as of the superiority of socialism in general. The Americans with their 100 million tons of steel "have thus far not launched so much as a sweet potato into space," he rejoiced, secretly dreaming of the time when his country, too, would soar into the cosmos.[87]

In the meantime, the anti-rightist movement continued to pick up steam. A struggle was launched against party cadres who acted according to the principle of the "Three Many, and the Three Few." They spoke a lot, but unmasked few counterrevolutionaries; they were excessively tolerant but rarely exposed "those who had crawled into the revolutionary ranks"; they often exposed those in the lower ranks, but very rarely those in the leading organs. A competition began in party organizations to see who could unmask the largest number of covert rightists. The higher party organs began to send out detailed orders specifying the precise number of those who had to be called to account. Posters appeared all over the country demanding that the rightists be punished.

Meanwhile, Mao received an invitation from Khrushchev to attend the celebration of the fortieth anniversary of the October Revolution, following which it was proposed to convene a conference of representatives of communist and workers' parties. Mao Zedong's presence at both the celebration and the conference was of vital importance to Khrushchev. The Moscow congress of communists was intended to demonstrate the "monolithic unity" of the socialist camp around the ideals of the Great October.

After thinking it over, Mao decided to visit the Soviet Union for a second time.[88] Khrushchev was overjoyed and sent two TU-104 planes to ferry Mao and the members of his delegation.

At 8 A.M. on November 2, Mao and his retinue, including Madame Song Qingling, Deng Xiaoping,[89] and Peng Dehuai, and some others, flew out of Beijing.

On the eve of his departure Mao asked his interpreter Li Yueran:

"How do you say *zhilaohu* in Russian?"

"*Bumazhnyi tigr* [paper tiger]," Li replied.

Mao repeated the same expression in English in a heavy Hunanese accent and burst out laughing.[90] He was prepared for the summit meeting of communist leaders.

Khrushchev himself, looking hale, hearty, and sleek, greeted his guests at Vnukovo Airport. With him were Voroshilov, Bulganin, Mikoyan, and a crowd of lesser dignitaries. They all radiated cordiality. Several months earlier, in June, Khrushchev had smashed the "anti-party" group of Molotov; therefore he again was in need of Mao's support. He knew of the Chinese leader's dissatisfaction with his "arbitrariness," but he tried not to attach too much significance to this. He felt he could do this because just before the arrival of the

PRC delegation, Averkii Borisovich Aristov, a member of the CPSU Presidium, had visited China in September–October 1957 and informed him that in their conversation Mao had emphasized the "unity of the PRC and the USSR." To be sure, the head of the CCP had expressed his perplexity regarding the June events, but had done so only in passing. "We are always with you," he said to Aristov, "but sometimes one shouldn't hasten to resolve certain problems. Now, for example, we were very fond of Molotov [Stalin's right-hand man], and the decision of the June plenum of the Central Committee of the CPSU concerning Molotov produced some confusion among us." On this occasion he said nothing more on this theme,[91] but, as usual, returned to the question of Stalin. "Today you have seen a big portrait of Stalin displayed in our square," Mao said to his guest from Moscow. "Do you think we bear no grudge against Stalin? No, we bear him a huge grudge. Stalin was the cause of many difficulties for the Chinese revolution. . . . Nevertheless, Stalin's portrait is hung on the occasion of important holidays in the PRC. This is done not for the leaders, but for the people." Mao added, "In my home I have no portrait of Stalin."[92]

Khrushchev was troubled by the peculiar position of the Chinese on the question of Stalin. Nevertheless, he probably hoped that in private conversations he would succeed in mollifying Mao.

But the Chairman had not come to the USSR to make friends with Khrushchev. He already understood the Soviet leader's meaning very well. Mao felt that time was on his side. Socialism in China had been basically constructed, industry had developed, and the dictatorship of the Communist Party in the world's most populous country was absolute. It seemed that Moscow, once all-powerful, had irretrievably forfeited its authority in the communist world; the Polish and Hungarian events were graphic examples. Of course, Khrushchev possessed nuclear weapons, and in October 1957 the Russians launched Sputnik. Still, Mao wanted to show all these communist comrades just where the center of the world communist movement was now.

Khrushchev pulled out all the stops for Mao, housing him and all of the Chinese in the Kremlin despite the fact that a majority of the delegates from other communist parties were lodged in dachas outside Moscow; he called on the Chinese every morning, showered them with gifts, escorted them to all the cultural events, and held "intimate friendly" conversations. He was beside himself with joy and was relishing the role of chief host. But Mao was "reserved and even a bit cool."[93] Of course, he was pleased to receive the royal treatment this time. The contrast between Stalin's and Khrushchev's treatment of him was striking. "Just look how differently they treat us," he said with a contemptuous smile to his entourage.

But he did not reciprocate Khrushchev's feelings. The more Khrushchev courted Mao, the more Mao thumbed his nose at him. From time to time he did not even bother to conceal his contempt for the leader of the CPSU who was fussing over him. Thus, arriving at the Bolshoi Theater with Khrushchev to see *Swan Lake,* after the second act he suddenly got up and left. "Why did they dance that way, prancing around on their toes?" he said to the perplexed Khrushchev. "It made me uncomfortable. Why don't they just dance normally?"[94]

On his first visit to Moscow, he did not indulge himself like that even when Stalin was absent. As Shi Zhe, his interpreter on that earlier occasion, recalled, Mao sat through the ballet *Baiaderka* in the Kirov Theater, and after the performance he even presented a bouquet of flowers to the prima ballerina.[95]

On occasion Mao was even quite rude. According to the reminiscences of his interpreter Li Yueran, once during a banquet Mao sharply interrupted Khrushchev, who, oblivious to the world, was enthusiastically talking about what a major role he had played during the war. "Comrade Khrushchev," Mao said, throwing down his napkin after wiping his lips, "I have already finished eating, but have you finished the history of the Southwest front?"[96]

But the main surprise awaited Khrushchev at the conference of representatives of communist and workers' parties. It was not for nothing that Mao had asked his interpreter how to say "paper tiger" in Russian. This was the theme he talked about, asserting that all reactionaries were paper tigers. This would have been quite enough, but he then added the following:

> Let's try to suppose, how many people would die if war breaks out? Of the 2.7 billion people on earth, the losses might be one-third, or perhaps, somewhat more, say half of mankind. . . . As soon as war begins, atomic and hydrogen bombs will be used in abundance. I once argued about this with a foreign political leader. He said that in case of an atomic war absolutely everyone would die. I said that in the worst case half the people would die, but the other half would survive, and that imperialism would be wiped off the face of the earth and the whole world would become socialist. A certain number of years would pass, and the population would again reach 2.7 billion and most likely even more.[97]

Obviously, he was developing ideas that he had expressed earlier to Nehru, the Finnish ambassador Carl-Johan Sundstrom, and to Yudin as well in veiled form. On this occasion, to be sure, his figures were more concrete, and his offhand juggling with hundreds of millions of lives produced a horrible impression on everyone. There was silence in the hall. Everyone felt uncomfortable.

Later, at the banquet, he again turned the conversation to the utility of nuclear war in advancing the cause of socialism. Khrushchev did not know what to think. Then the head of the Italian communist party, Palmiro Togliatti, asked, "Comrade Mao Zedong? And how many Italians will survive an atomic war?" Mao calmly replied, "None at all. But why do you think that Italians are so important to humanity?"[98] Oleg Aleksandrovich Grinevskii, one of Khrushchev's speechwriters, who was in the hall at the time serving as an interpreter, recalls that Mao did not even smile when he said these words. (Grinevskii, who did not know Chinese, was interpreting from Russian to English for the English-speaking audience after a Soviet Sinologist, Vasilii Sidikhmenov, had first translated Mao's remarks from Chinese into Russian.)

What did this mean? Could Mao really have been so ignorant as not to know that his argument was nonsense? No, of course not. He was knowledgeable enough, at least with respect to politics and military affairs. So why did he say this? Many who have pondered this question have expressed the thought that he obviously wanted to push the USSR into a nuclear conflict with the United States. Others disagree: Mao was just behaving too rudely. They conjecture that Mao simply wished to head off a rapprochement between the superpowers. However, neither of these explanations of Mao's behavior is correct. In reality, he was simply shocking his public, openly mocking both Khrushchev as well as the old Comintern warhorses who only recently had fawned upon Stalin. He hated all of these Togliatti types, who had once been assigned to the ECCI, where they had befriended Wang Ming and had sneered at the likes of Mao.* At one time they had been ready to applaud any stupidity on the part of the "Leader of Peoples" and tried to decipher his riddles and jokes. Now it was his turn.

Mao felt his greatness and wanted everyone else to acknowledge it. He wanted to take his revenge for all the humiliation he had endured at the hands of the sullen Kremlin tyrant who liked to indulge his black humor. This is why he tried so obviously to imitate Stalin. He spoke in a patronizing tone, played the role of Boss, and tried to make savage and strange jokes just like Stalin. Consequently, he returned to the theme of nuclear war and the prospects for victory over imperialism on more than one occasion. He would also expound on this theme during his official talks with Khrushchev. And each time Khrushchev would ponder Mao's views and "what he based them on."[99] Thus he never understood what Mao Zedong was up to.[100]

Before his departure, Khrushchev gave his guest many souvenirs as well as a large jar of granular caviar. It was of excellent quality, but Mao could not eat it since Chinese generally do not include raw fish in their diet. He took the jar, however, and brought it with him to Beijing. Several days later he invited his secretaries and bodyguards to dinner, and urged them to taste the exotic food, which had been carefully arranged on a porcelain plate. "Try it, try it," he said laughing. "This is socialist caviar!" One of the invitees picked some caviar

---

* Palmiro Togliatti (pseudonym Mario Ercoli) (1893–1964) was a member of the Presidium of the ECCI from 1938 to 1943 and also a member of the Secretariat of the ECCI from 1935 to 1943.

up with his chopsticks and put it in his mouth. It was obvious that he was not eager to eat it, but he got control of himself and swallowed it. He almost threw up.

"Well, how is it? Delicious?" Mao asked, and a burst of laughter shook his corpulent body.

"It looks so beautiful," the unfortunate one replied, "but it doesn't taste good. I don't like it, and I can't eat it."

"Well, okay! If you can't gobble it down, then don't!" Mao said to him simply.[101]

He was especially pleased that the people in his entourage found Khrushchev's gift not to their liking. This was all very symbolic.

After he returned to China, Mao began to develop the ideas for a special, Chinese road to socialism that he had first expressed in "The Ten Major Relationships." He pondered over and over variations of a Great Leap, a new model of accelerated economic development grounded fundamentally in the utilization of China's comparative advantages, in the first place its inexhaustible human resources. "Our country produces too little steel," he lamented. "We have to do everything we can to increase our material strength. Otherwise, people will look down on us."[102]

In Moscow he had already begun to boast that after fifteen years China would overtake Great Britain in the production of metal. "England annually produces 20 million tons of steel," he said to the representatives of communist and workers' parties. "In 15 years it may achieve a production of 30 million tons of steel annually. And China? In 15 years China may produce 40 million tons. So won't it overtake England?"[103] Mao was inspired to such boasting by none other than Khrushchev who, as is well known, was boastful by nature. About two weeks prior to Mao's speech, at an anniversary meeting of the Supreme Soviet of the USSR, Khrushchev had loudly proclaimed that in the coming fifteen years the USSR would be able not only to catch up with but to overtake America.[104] Thus Mao Zedong's speech was a response to "Elder Brother."

Mao, speaking generally, was being modest. In reality he was overcome by the desire to overtake the Soviet Union itself, to show everyone, and especially Khrushchev who had now launched two Sputniks, that he, Mao, was not born yesterday. Just how much sarcasm and anger permeated the words he spoke to his comrades in early 1957: "What is their [Soviet leadership's] asset. It involves nothing more than 50 million tons of steel, 400 million tons of coal, and 80 million tons of oil. How much does this count? It does not count for a thing. With this asset, however, their heads have gotten really big. How can they be communists [by being so cocky]? How can they be Marxists?"[105] Thus Mao's new path was fraught with the inevitable further deterioration of relations between China and the Kremlin traditionalists.

At conferences in Hangzhou (Zhejiang province) and Nanning (Guangxi Zhuang Autonomous Region) in January 1958, Mao intensified his criticism of those who opposed "haste" and "blindly rushing forward." He again censured those who followed the Soviet model. "If we did everything like the Soviet Union did after the October Revolution," he declared, "then we would have no textiles, and we would have no foodstuffs (when there are no textiles there is nothing to exchange for foodstuffs), there would be no coal, no electricity, no nothing." In Hangzhou he declared that the Rectification Movement, which he had only recently, at the Third Plenum, decided to relax, would be carried through to the end. In Nanning on January 18, he warned party cadres that the struggle against "blindly rushing forward" would inevitably "dampen the enthusiasm . . . of 600 million people."[106] Moreover, he also informed Zhou Enlai that he and several other "comrades were only some 50 meters distance from the rightists."[107] The *ganbu* supported Chairman Mao and the premier was forced to engage in self-criticism. Later Zhou explained to his secretary that the main reason he had made mistakes was that ideologically he lagged behind Comrade Mao Zedong. "I must carefully study Mao Zedong Thought," he said sadly.[108] However, Mao even proposed replacing Zhou with Ke Qingshi, head of the Shanghai Bureau of the Central Committee. Sometime later Zhou agreed to step down, but in the end Mao generously forgave him.[109]

Once more Mao triumphed. On January 31 he summed up the results of both conferences in an important document, "Sixty Theses on Work Methods," which basically laid out the course for the Great Leap and put forward the slogan of "Three Years of Persistent Work."[110] This became the most important part of his program for Chinese socialism.

Thus, Mao's concept of a special Chinese path of development, initially expressed in April 1956 and subsequently developed in 1957–58, could arise only in the post-Stalin environment that Khrushchev created in the world communist movement. It was Khrushchev who stimulated Mao not only to accelerate Stalinization, but also, against his (Khrushchev's) intentions, to reject the Soviet path of development decisively.

The Stalinist model of socialist construction that had earlier inspired Mao had run out of steam. The result was that the entire epoch of Stalinization, beginning with the establishment of New China in 1949, had come to an end. From now on it was no longer appropriate to talk about Stalinization, but rather about the Maoization of the People's Republic of China. At the same time, we should not forget that in the sphere of politics and ideology Maoism itself was nothing more than a Chinese form of Stalinism, in other words Chinese national communism. And even though the Soviet Stalinization of the PRC was concluded, the influence of Stalinism as a totalitarian political and economic system of power remained unchanged in the PRC.

30

THE GREAT LEAP FORWARD

Throughout the winter of 1957–58 Mao was elated. The trip to Moscow had apparently revitalized him. He had no doubts that China would soon become the leading country in the world. He rushed around the country, urging on the laggards, venting his anger at the skeptical fence-sitters, and telling off those who blindly imitated the Soviet Union. Even before his trip to the USSR, he had begun writing an article, published in *People's Daily* on December 12, in which he called upon the party and the country to "boldly follow the course of 'more, faster, better, and more economically.' " It was imperative to catch up with and overtake England as well as other leading countries in the basic indicators of economic development. For whatever reason he focused on two: steel and grain.

He knew nothing of economics, but this did not bother him. He was not alone in his ignorance of economics. Many other world leaders had a poor grasp of economics, as did almost all the members of the Chinese Politburo. Aware of this, the Chairman even trumpeted his ignorance. "The majority of Politburo members," he said at the Nanning Conference in January 1958, "are 'red,' but 'unqualified.' . . . I am the most uneducated, I am unsuited to be a member of any committee."[1]

Mao's deficiencies, however, were more than compensated for by his enormous enthusiasm, his belief in his own infallibility, his will, and his power. "Our method is to put politics in command," he asserted. "Politics is the commanding force."[2] This was precisely how he had acted all his life in the party: by relying on political and, of course, military levers. At the very beginning of the year he provoked a confrontation with his fellow Hunanese Zhou Xiaozhou, first secretary of the Hunan party committee.

"Why can't Hunan increase its agricultural production[?] . . . Why do the Hunan peasants still plant only one crop of rice a year?" he asked, as if he himself did not know that in his native province anything more was impossible. "You're not even studying other experiences. That's the trouble."

"We will study the matter, then," replied Zhou, timidly.

"What do you mean study? . . . You won't get anywhere with your study. You can go now," the Chairman roared.[3] He acted like this everywhere.

Mao's pressure and threats were effective. Zhou Enlai proposed to call Mao's new course the Great Leap, and Liu Shaoqi took part in preparing the Sixty Theses, drafting one of the sections of this important document articulating the principles of the Great Leap.[4] Years later Deng Xiaoping, who also became excited about the Great Leap, recalled,

> Comrade Mao got carried away when we launched the Great Leap Forward, but didn't the rest of us go along with him? Neither Comrade Liu Shaoqi nor Comrade Zhou Enlai nor I for that matter objected to it, and Comrade Chen Yun didn't say anything either. We must be fair on these questions and not give the impression that only one individual made mistakes while everybody else was correct, because it doesn't tally with the facts.[5]

In January 1958, Mao began to call for the implementation of a "permanent revolution" in the country. In simple terms, it meant that the people must advance to communism without the slightest pause, via an endless series of alternating revolutionary campaigns and reforms. Otherwise, Mao said, "People would . . . be covered in mold."[6] There was the scent of fear in the air; permanent revolution meant the exacerbation of class conflict.

The entire party leadership became involved in the pursuit of this mirage. The leadership began feverishly searching for means to fulfill the plans. Communiqués flew into the center reporting an unusual upsurge of popular enthusiasm. At an enlarged meeting of the Politburo on February 18, with the support of all assembled Mao proclaimed the course of "more, faster, better, and more economically" as the party's new general line for socialist construction.[7] The line would be officially adopted in May at the Second Session of the Eighth Congress of the CCP, in the following formulation: "Exerting all our efforts, advancing forward to build socialism more, faster, better, and more economically."[8]

Mao had no concrete plans for the Great Leap. He did not know how to increase the production of steel and grain; therefore, at all the conferences all he did was repeat the incantation "We can catch up with England in fifteen years." He demanded that leading officials engage in experimentation, try out various methods, including the most improbable. He promised there would be no punishment for leftism or subjectivism.[9] He understood that China had an enormous advantage compared to other countries: a huge reservoir of cheap labor.

As early as the autumn of 1957, at the Third Plenum, Mao had proposed attracting the people with another campaign, the success of which, he thought, would substantially advance agricultural production. He envisioned a campaign against the so-called Four Pests—rats, mosquitoes, flies, and sparrows—which harmed not only the production of grain, but also the health of the producers. The task of destroying these "vermin" had been posed even earlier, in January 1956 in the special Program for Developing Agriculture in the PRC in 1956–57, but it had not taken hold.[10] "I am very interested in the struggle against the 'Four Pests,' but no one shares this interest," the Chairman complained.[11] He returned to this issue in early December, calling upon the Central Committee and the State Council to issue appropriate decrees and even composing a draft himself a month later. Ultimately, he succeeded in convincing everyone, and in mid-February 1958 such a decree was promulgated.[12]

Throughout the country a "hunt for pests" got under way in which both young and old took part. No one could dispute the need to struggle for cleanliness. Most Chinese paid little attention to hygiene. They lived amid horrendous filth and ignored the hordes of rats that roamed the courtyards and trash dumps and were just as oblivious to the clouds of flies. Rats, flies, and mosquitoes, of course, were carriers of infections that could engender epidemics. Sparrows made the list of pests because they liked to eat grain in the field. Thus the struggle against pests was justifiable; however, the executors of Mao's directives took things too far. An eyewitness provides a description of how the campaign proceeded:

> I was awakened in the early morning by a woman's bloodcurdling screams. Rushing to my window I saw that a young woman was running to and fro on the roof of the building next door, frantically waving a bamboo pole with a large sheet attached to it. Suddenly, the woman stopped shouting, apparently to catch her breath, but a moment later, down below in the street, a drum started beating, and she resumed her frightful screams and the mad waving of her peculiar flag. This went on for several more minutes; then the drums stopped and the women fell silent. I realized that in all the upper stories of the hotel, white-clad females were waving sheets and towels that were supposed to keep the sparrows from alighting on the building. . . . During the whole day, it was drums, gun shots, screams, and waving bedclothes. . . . [T]he battle went on without abatement until noon, with all the manpower of the hotel mobilized and participating— bellboys, desk managers, interpreters, maids, and all. . . . The strategy behind this war on the sparrows boiled down to keeping the poor creature from coming to rest on a roof or tree. . . . [I]t was claimed that a sparrow kept in the air for more than four hours was bound to drop from exhaustion.[13]

The campaign against the other pests was similar. Aroused by the propaganda, people rushed about after the terrified rodents, striking at flies and mosquitoes with rags; someone might have supposed that the entire country had gone mad. Tens of millions of people participated in the campaign. In the city of Chongqing, Sichuan province, alone, over a period of several days more than 230,000 rodents were killed, more than two tons of fly larvae were destroyed, and six hundred tons of trash collected.[14] The corpses of tens of thousands of tormented sparrows were presented to the state.

Mao insisted that the destruction of the Four Pests would strengthen the health of the nation:

> We will be able to open schools in the hospitals, and doctors will go to cultivate the land: the numbers of sick people will decrease greatly, this will raise the moral spirit of the people, the percentage of those working will increase significantly. . . . On the day the Four Pests are eliminated in China, there can be a celebration. These events will be inscribed in the chronicles of history. Bourgeois governments are unable to cope with the Four Pests. They consider themselves civilized countries, yet they have huge numbers of flies and mosquitoes.[15]

The results of the campaign were horrendous. The extermination of sparrows as well as other "vermin" destroyed the ecological balance. At a certain point the boundary was crossed where a reasonable beginning turned into a calamity. Insects began to reproduce rapidly and destroy crops. As a result, the Chinese even had to import sparrows from the Soviet Union. To be sure, they did not import rats, flies, and mosquitoes, but they slowed their persecution.

During the Nanning Conference another plan emerged: to enlarge the cooperatives by expanding each one to embrace ten thousand households or more. This expansion would enable mobilizing the masses to construct irrigation projects, including reservoirs that were needed for agriculture. The idea of deep plowing and dense planting of grain to wrest multiple harvests from the land was also put forward. By these means the state could increase the amount of grain that it received in taxes and earn more hard currency through grain exports. (At this time China was one of the largest exporters of grain, mainly to the Eastern European countries.) The upsurge in agriculture would guarantee enormous industrial growth via constantly increasing investments in steel mills and the machine-building industry.

The idea of establishing very large cooperatives had been first expressed by Mao in 1955, but it failed to gain support. It was proposed again at Nanning in January 1958, but it was not until April that Liu Shaoqi and Zhou Enlai came up with the name of "commune" for these giant complexes during an inspection tour in South China.[16] Everyone liked it.

The first commune, Weixing (Sputnik), was established in April, near the district town of Suiping in southern Henan. It embraced twenty-seven cooperatives, or 43,000 people. The next one was organized in northern Henan in Xinxiang county. Its members, striving for originality, called it a people's commune.

Once more Mao tried to use practice as his point of departure; he was convinced that practice was the criterion of truth. This was why he spent eight of the twelve months of 1958 traveling around the country.[17] He familiarized himself with "leading" practices, conversed with party officials as well as simple peasants, and inspected reservoirs and other projects. He "conducted investigations so as to have the right to speak." But he failed to take into account that since he was now the "Great Leader," local officials did everything possible to create a good impression on him. They knew very well what he wanted. Mao himself had told them repeatedly it was better to be too leftist than rightist.

Naturally, an upsurge of popular enthusiasm was evident throughout the country. Millions of people believed the communists, because much of what they had talked about had actually come to pass. The doors of universities and institutes had been opened to the children of peasants and workers, free medical care had been introduced, a large number of factories and mills had been constructed, and illiteracy was being wiped out. The poor were particularly happy; for the first time in their lives they felt they enjoyed equal rights. The rest of the population, too, demonstrated "fervent enthusiasm"; they understood very well the dangerous consequences of not participating in party campaigns. Nobody wanted to be branded a rightist.

Thus the "investigation" that the Chairman was conducting inevitably created an illusory picture that strengthened his belief in voluntarism. "In my view, we must resort to 'blindly rushing forward,' " Mao proclaimed after a routine inspection. "We must work energetically and joyfully, and not apathetically and sullenly. . . . Everything that can be done quickly, we must do as quickly as possible."[18] The phantom of the Great Leap drove him to make increasingly leftist adjustments in the plans and methods of socialist construction. It was as if all one had to do was mobilize the population of 600 million and any dream would become reality.

He was particularly interested in the experience of the communes. The Chinese "communards" began to organize production in new ways, shifting to the optimal division of labor. In order to maximize labor efficiency, Weixing Commune and other such cooperatives began to establish communal dining halls. Household kitchens were done away with. This freed up working women to work overtime in the fields, saved on fuel, and improved nutrition. Liu Shaoqi enthusiastically supported the "communards," saying that their initiative created the opportunity to increase by one-third the number of working hands in the countryside. "If previously more than two-hundred [of every five hundred people] were engaged in preparing food, now no more than forty do so," he said.[19] The "communards" also promoted communist relations by doing away with wage labor and dowries, introducing free dining, and adopting the communist principle "from each according to his ability, to each according to his need." They socialized domestic poultry and even household utensils. "Why do we need bowls and cups now that we have communal dining halls where we can eat our fill?" they wondered, actually believing that free communal food signified the arrival of communism. They were so eager to escape from poverty.

Mao was ecstatic. On July 16, in the journal *Hongqi* (Red flag), the new theoretical organ of the CCP, editor in chief Chen Boda published a directive from the Chairman: "We must gradually transform industry, agriculture, trade, culture and education, as well as the militia, i.e. the people's armed forces, into one large commune that will form the basic unit of our society."[20] At the beginning of August, Mao visited a people's commune in Henan and could not conceal his delight. Communism was being built before his eyes! "This name, 'people's commune,' is great!" Mao said. "French workers created the Paris commune when they seized power. Our farmers have created the people's commune as a political and economic organization in the march toward communism. The people's commune is great!"[21] At once dozens of newspapers and magazines printed special editions to disseminate this "wonderful revelation," following which a campaign to establish people's communes swept the country.

A little later Mao explained the significance of people's communes:

> People's communes are distinguished, on the one hand, by their large size, and on the other by their degree of collectivization. . . . In both the countryside and the cities we must infuse communist ideas into the socialist order everywhere. . . . Now we are building socialism, but also have the shoots of communism. We can establish people's communes everywhere, in educational institutions, in factories, in urban neighborhoods. In just a few years everything will be united into one large commune.

Mao was attracted by the notion that such large complexes, with thousands of people, could become fully self-sufficient by virtue of their internal division of labor. "Such gigantic cooperatives," he exulted, "can engage in industry as well as agriculture, trade, education, and military affairs, and this can be done in conjunction . . . with forestry, cattle-breeding, and sideline fish farming."[22]

Mao was happy that the people "grasped" his enthusiasm for the Great Leap. That is how it appeared on the surface, at least in the places to which he traveled. Increasingly, Mao was sensing his own greatness. With a wave of his hand, hundreds of millions of people rushed to execute his instructions, "put their brains in gear," think up new forms of organization, toil indefatigably night and day. He could do whatever he wanted with these poor and uneducated people who were full of hope for the future. "[T]he 600 million people of China have one outstanding [advantage]: it is poverty and backwardness," Mao said candidly. "At first glance this is bad, but actually it is good. Poverty arouses them to change, to action, to revolution. On a blank sheet of paper one can write the newest, most beautiful characters, one can create the newest, most beautiful pictures." [23]

In 1958 Mao suddenly sensed that communism was not something for the distant future. "It will not take 100 years to build communism in China, 50 will suffice," he declared. "The first condition of communism is an abundance of goods, the second is the existence of a communist spirit." Although not everything was going well with respect to the first condition, the second was already at hand. "An era of perpetual happiness is approaching," he argued at an enlarged Politburo meeting.

> We will organize a world-wide committee and institute unified planning for the entire earth. . . . In about ten years there will be an abundance of goods and morale will rise to unprecedented heights. . . . In the future everything will be called a commune. . . . Every large commune will build a highway or a wide concrete or asphalt road. If trees are not planted along the sides, airplanes can use them as landing strips. Here is your airport. In the future every province will have 100–200 airplanes, each county will have an average of two airplanes.

"We are not crazy," he added. [24]

The communist ideal was so good that even Mao could not fully believe in the capability of people to achieve it on their own without some prodding. For that reason he warmly welcomed the experience of those people's communes that supplemented their communist profile by introducing "a military organization of labor, a militarized work style, and a military discipline." "The concept of 'military' and the concept of 'democracy' appear to be mutually exclusive," he said, "but it is actually quite the opposite. Democracy arises in the army. . . . When everyone is a soldier, then people will become inspired and bolder."

In response to the Leader's call the country began to transform itself into a military camp. Mao continually provided inspiration: "Control is indispensable. One cannot simply adhere to democracy. We need to combine Marx with Qin Shi Huangdi." (The latter, it will be recalled, was the notoriously cruel ancient Chinese emperor whom Mao had loved to read about during his school years in Dongshan.) "Qin Shihuang buried alive 460 Confucian scholars," he reminded people.

> But he was nowhere near us. . . . We have acted like ten Qin Shi-
> huangs. I assert that we are stronger than Qin Shihuang. He buried
> 460 people, but we have buried 46,000, a hundred times more. To
> kill someone, then dig a grave and bury them is the same as burying
> them alive! They curse us as partisans of Qin Shihuang, as usurpers.
> We admit all this and say that we still haven't done much along these
> lines; there's much more we can do. . . . Earlier during the revolution
> many people perished; this was a demonstration of the spirit of self-
> sacrifice. Why can't we proceed upon the same principles now?[25]

Therefore, enthusiasm was not the only basis on which the communes were organized. Mao himself knew that his "society of people's prosperity" very closely resembled war communism, which Lenin and Trotsky had instituted in the early days of the Bolshevik revolution.[26] But he saw nothing wrong in this and, like the leaders of the October Revolution, he also insisted that all white-collar workers spend at least one month a year doing physical labor in order to assist the workers and peasants to carry out the Great Leap.[27]

With each passing day these tasks became more urgent. In May 1958, Mao suddenly declared that it was possible to overtake England in steel production in seven years rather than fifteen, and in coal production in just two or three years. In June he said that in the near future, specifically, in 1959, England would be left behind, and that in five years China would already draw close to the USSR in smelting steel. This meant that in 1958 the PRC had to double its steel production over 1957, to 10.7 million tons, and in 1959 reach 20–25 million, and 60 million tons in 1962. A while later he revisited these figures: now he wanted 30 million tons in 1959, 60 million in 1960, and 80–100 or even 120 million tons in 1962, which would overtake America. After fifteen years, that is, in the mid-1970s, Mao figured on annually producing 700 million tons, twice England's per capita production. At this time Liu Shaoqi developed plans that were no less absurd.[28]

If one considers that the draft Second Five-Year Plan of National Economic Development adopted by the Eighth Party Congress in September 1956 set the target for steel production in 1962 at 10.5–12 million tons, one can grasp what an enormous "leap" Mao and Liu wanted to make. The spurt in agriculture was to be no less dramatic: in 1958 the production of grain was supposed to double to 300–350 million tons, whereas the First Five-Year Plan had envisioned a 1962 target of barely 250 million tons.[29]

In August Mao declared, "Industry is the main line today. The entire party, the entire people must grasp industry." [30] People were enrolled in a campaign "for a larger number of open hearth furnaces." A "battle for steel" was launched that assumed truly monstrous forms. Everywhere, in village and urban court-yards, in sports fields, in parks and city squares, primitive blast furnaces were erected. People lugged everything they could to these furnaces—scrap iron and steel, door handles, shovels, household utensils—entirely unaware that such pitifully small and primitive furnaces could not produce any real steel. Ignorance was exalted to a virtue.

Knowledgeable engineers kept quiet, and if they did object, no one paid them any heed. Mao had long found intellectuals irritating. Skeptical and con-scientious, they aroused in him, as well as in other Bolshevik leaders, hatred and revulsion. Everything about them irritated Mao, not just their knowledge that he did not possess. After launching the Great Leap, he proclaimed, "Intel-lectuals must bow down before the working people. In some respects intel-lectuals are wholly illiterate." [31] After such talk how could the engineers object?

At Mao's request, Premier Zhou himself headed the campaign for steel smelting. By mid-September more than 20 million people had already smelted steel, and by October 90 million.* In a month the share of the metal smelted in backyard furnaces rose from 14 percent to 49 percent. Peasants, workers, teachers, students, elementary and middle school pupils, doctors and nurses, sales clerks and accountants all took part in the campaign. Columns of black smoke rose above cities and villages. The strains of the campaign song "We Will Overtake England and Catch Up to America" boomed out of loudspeakers.

Soon it became clear that the task assigned by the Great Helmsman would be fulfilled. By the end of the year China would produce 11 million tons of metal. Even Mao was astounded. "If these small backyard furnaces can really produce so much steel," he said to his entourage, "why do foreigners build such gigantic steel mills? Are foreigners really so stupid?" [32] He received an answer to this question very soon. The metal smelted in these backyard furnaces was useless. Even though Mao supposed that an "uneducated person was stronger than an educated one," [33] he could not deceive technology.

In pursuing the phantom of the Great Leap in industry, the Chinese leadership had slackened its attention to the grain problem. The harvesting of rice and other grains was thrust onto the shoulders of women, old men, and children. Although they worked without rest, they could not succeed in gathering the entire harvest. Meanwhile, leaders everywhere, fearing Mao's wrath, were reporting amazing growth in the quantity of agricultural products and sending inflated figures to their superiors. "[S]ome comrades said that the grain output was more than 500 million tons while others said that it was

---

* The first primitive blast furnaces were established in China in the spring of 1958. By June there were 12,680. But the real epidemic of steel making began in August.

450 million tons," recalled Minister of Defense Peng Dehuai. "Later Chairman suggested 375 million tons as the figure to be released."[34] In reality, only 200 million tons were harvested, just 5 million more than in 1957.[35] When the time came to settle accounts with the state, almost everything was taken from the peasants. As in 1955, the countryside again faced famine. Mao, however, refused to acknowledge there was a crisis and was in no hurry to ask for assistance. Therefore, all the contracts to export grain abroad were fulfilled so the "foreign devils" would have no reason to suspect he had erred. This had a serious effect on the domestic food supply.

Most of all, Mao did not want to ask help from Khrushchev. This would have been the most terrible "loss of face." At the very height of the Great Leap, July 31, 1958, Khrushchev suddenly flew to Beijing on an unofficial visit and the Chairman had to receive him, making a special trip from the resort at Beidaihe for this purpose. This time Mao was not merely rude to Khrushchev; he positively radiated malice.

The reason was that ten days before Khrushchev's arrival, Ambassador Yudin had transmitted to Mao a proposal from the Soviet leadership to establish a joint Pacific naval fleet with the PRC. This was in response to a Chinese request for Soviet assistance in developing its own naval fleet. Mao had high hopes that Khrushchev would respond positively to his request, but he was mistaken. Instead, Khrushchev offered something else. Moreover, the Soviet leader did not even explain to Yudin the principles on which such a joint fleet would be organized. When Mao expressed interest in whether the fleet would be some sort of Soviet-Chinese "cooperative," and who would control it, the ambassador did not know the answer. Mao was indignant, especially since four months earlier China had received a letter from Soviet defense minister Malinovsky containing another appeal from the Soviet government for China and the USSR to establish a joint radar station in China for communicating with the Soviet Pacific Fleet.[36]

Mao and other Chinese leaders viewed these proposals as violations of Chinese sovereignty. Mao, recalling all the insults he had suffered at Stalin's hands, told the ambassador that China would never again allow the establishment of foreign military bases like Port Arthur on its territory. When Yudin timidly noted that it would be "desirable" under the circumstances "in view of the importance" of these questions for Mao and Khrushchev to speak in person, Mao expressed doubts about such a meeting.[37]

This is why Khrushchev came to Beijing, along with Malinovsky and several leading officials in the Ministry of Defense, the Ministry of Internal Affairs, and the Central Committee of the CPSU. He was very upset and could not understand why Mao had suddenly flown into a rage. Khrushchev thought that a joint fleet and radar station would be in "the common interests" of the USSR and the PRC.[38] But grasping what was at issue, Khrushchev immediately withdrew his proposals. He said, "It was a misunderstanding. . . . Let's write: there neither was, is, nor will be a question."[39] But Mao would not calm down for a long time and he expressed his indignation in the most capricious manner.

Characteristic of his rudeness toward Khrushchev, Mao, a chain smoker, smoked one cigarette after another during their conversations, and blew the smoke right into Khrushchev's face. Khrushchev could not stand tobacco smoke. Mao tried to stay calm, but periodically he lost self-control, poked his finger at his interlocutor's nose, started yelling, and during the breaks between sessions berated his interpreter for not conveying the whole gamut of the emotions that were gripping him. Then he shifted the negotiations to his swimming pool. Mao was an excellent swimmer while Khrushchev, hardly a swimmer at all, felt quite humiliated in the pool.[40] The diaries of the famous film director Mikhail Romm contain an interesting entry regarding Khrushchev's revelations about his reception in the pool:

> "Just where do you think Mao Zedong received me?" Khrushchev blurted out between sessions of a regular plenum of the Central Committee. "In a swimming pool. He received me in a swimming pool!"
>
> There was nothing he could do. Mao was the host. The head of the Soviet government had to strip off his suit and hand it to his bodyguard, and clad in satin swimming trunks, quite contrary to protocol, flop into the water. Chairman Mao was swimming, and Khrushchev floundered after him—"I am a miner, and, just between us, not much of a swimmer, and I got tired"—with the interpreter between them. Mao Zedong, apparently intentionally, pretended not to notice how difficult it was for his distinguished guest to keep up with him, and deliberately expounded upon current politics, asked various questions, to which Khrushchev, having swallowed some water, could not respond clearly. . . . Nikita Sergeevich soon got fed up with this situation. "I swam and swam, and was thinking, to hell with you, I am getting out. I climbed onto the ledge and dangled my legs. Now I was above and he was swimming below. The interpreter did not know whether to swim with him or sit next to me. He was swimming, and I was above, looking down on him. He was looking up at me and saying something about communes, about their communes. I had already caught my breath and answered him about the communes. 'Well, we shall see what comes out of your communes.' I felt much better once I had sat down. He was offended. Comrades, that's how we got started."[41]

During their exchange Mao conveyed to Khrushchev a basket of complaints he had accumulated against the Soviet Union during the period of Stalin's leadership. The list was so long that Khrushchev lost his composure. "You defended Stalin. I have been attacked for criticizing Stalin. And now everything is reversed." But he was unable to say anything particularly good about Stalin. He merely noted, "We speak of Stalin's achievements and we are also among those achievements." [42] Mao, of course, agreed with this. However, his meeting with Khrushchev left a very bad impression that he did not hide from his entourage. "Their real purpose," Mao said, "is to control us. They're trying to tie our hands and feet, but they're full of wishful thinking, like idiots talking about their dreams." [43]

Mao was displeased by Khrushchev's skeptical attitude toward the people's communes. Popular enthusiasm for the Great Leap was at its height, but his distinguished Soviet guest allowed himself to express doubts. Mao told Khrushchev that for the first time since the establishment of the PRC he felt happy, and proudly informed him of the unprecedented harvest of grain that was waiting to be gathered. Not bothering to restrain himself he even "taunted" Khrushchev. Knowing there was not enough grain in the USSR, he asked him, as if in passing, "We have accumulated a solid surplus of wheat, and we are now puzzled as to what to do with it. Can you give us some helpful advice?"

"We have never had a grain surplus," Khrushchev shot back, and suddenly exploded, "The Chinese are not idiots. You will think of something to do with it." [44] For a moment Mao was dumbstruck, but then he composed himself and burst out laughing. When he soon encountered serious economic problems he could not help but remember Khrushchev's wicked joke.

Another of the Soviet leader's crude witticisms also stuck in Mao's throat. During one of their conversations Khrushchev laughed that Russian engineers in China called the Chinese workers who carried dirt from construction sites in woven baskets "walking excavator[s]." Mao roared with laughter, but he nursed yet another grievance. [45]

Soon, at the end of August, Mao ordered an artillery bombardment of the Nationalist-held offshore islands of Quemoy and Matsu in the Taiwan Strait. Khrushchev immediately offered to send a "division of planes" to help the "Chinese brothers," but Mao let Khrushchev know he found the offer "insulting." "We can solve our own problems," he explained to Khrushchev.

Mao did not intend to take the islands. The presence of Chiang Kai-shek's forces off the shores of the PRC was to Mao's advantage. It could help unite the Chinese people in the struggle to achieve the party's plans. The military action had a single goal: to demonstrate the martial spirit and growing power of the Chinese army to the whole world, including the leaders of the CPSU.*

Not grasping any of this, [46] Khrushchev warned the American president,

---

* The Chinese communists continued the bombardment on alternate days for the next twenty years.

Dwight Eisenhower, that if he had any desire to interfere in the conflict, the USSR would consider an attack against the PRC as an attack upon the Soviet Union. He even hinted that he might not refrain from launching a nuclear counterattack against the "aggressor." He so informed Mao Zedong,* and this time Mao expressed his "sincere gratitude." [47]

Meanwhile, in early November 1958, encountering initial economic difficulties, Mao gave the order to slow down the pace of the Great Leap. Later he added, "What's the hurry? So we can report to Marx and hear praise from his own lips?" Now the plan was to smelt not 30 million tons of steel in 1959 but 20 million (in May 1959 this target was further reduced to 13 million tons). Mao still wanted to harvest a great deal of grain, no less than 525 million tons, that is, two and a half times more than in 1958. [48]

At a regular plenum of the Central Committee held in late November to early December 1958, Mao submitted a request to retire from the post of chairman of the PRC. He could finally relieve himself of the ceremonial duties he had long found onerous. The plenum unanimously accepted his proposal that Liu Shaoqi replace him. Several months later, in April 1959, the National People's Congress officially confirmed this change of leadership. Mao retained only the main post of chairman of the Central Committee of the CCP. [49]

Meanwhile, a catastrophe was brewing in the country. Serious imbalances were arising in the development of the economy. From mid-December 1958, interruptions in the food supply began to occur everywhere. Meat disappeared even from the state dining room in Zhongnanhai. In cities everywhere people were standing in line for days. In Beijing the monthly ration of peanut oil was just 11.6 ounces (the norm for party officials was a little more than a pound) and, if you were really lucky, one pound of meat per person. The rice ration was thirty-one pounds. A family of three received a little more than a pound of sugar. [50] In Anhui, Gansu, and Sichuan famine had already taken hold and it soon had several other provinces in its grip. According to several sources, 25 million people were starving. [51] By the spring of 1959, Mao finally grasped that the Great Leap had failed to achieve its objectives. He angrily blamed the local cadres for all the misfortunes, for having misled him. "There are so many lies," he said indignantly. "When there is pressure from the top, there will be lies from the bottom." [52]

He now cursed the party cadres for "worrying only about production, not about the lives of the people." [53] He had no intention, however, of abandoning the people's communes. He simply wanted a time-out so that in the new year of 1959 an even greater leap could be accomplished. The economic targets for

---

* Khrushchev conveyed this information via China's ambassador Liu Xiao, who was specially summoned to Yalta for four days where Khrushchev was resting.

1959 remained very high: steel smelting was slated to increase by 41 percent and coal by 62 percent.[54]

At the end of June 1959, Mao decided to visit his native place of Shaoshan-chong. He had not been there for thirty-two years. He hoped that there, among his fellow countrymen, he would learn what was really going on. He was not mistaken. He passed two days there and saw and heard things that apparently profoundly disturbed him. The gravestone over his parents' grave was missing, and the small Buddhist temple where his mother used to pray was in ruins. "The tiny shrine, like the tombstone had disappeared, torn down only months before with the establishment of the commune," wrote Mao's physician, who accompanied him on the journey. "The bricks were needed to build the back-yard steel furnaces, and the wood had been used as fuel." Dropping in on his relatives, Mao also saw ruin. The house was completely empty. There were no household utensils, no clay stove. He listened to the complaints of the local inhabitants, looked at the chunks of misshapen metal that had been smelted from saucepans and iron cooking vessels, sighed, and left. "If you can't fill your bellies at the public dining hall, then it's better just to disband it," he concluded. "[I]t's a waste of food. . . . And if you cannot produce good steel, you might as well quit."[55]

The only thing that made him happy was the new harvest. And so before departing he composed the following optimistic verses:

> *The past is a vague accursed dream,*
> *thirty-two years gone by since I left home.*
> *Under the red banner slaves and peasants rose,*
> *weapons in blackened hands they smashed the landlords.*
> *Their sacrifice tempered our iron will*
> *as we lit the sun and moon in a newborn sky.*
> *How I rejoice to see endless waves of grain.*
> *Dusk falls, smoke curls up, labor heroes homeward bound.*[56]

But Mao celebrated prematurely. The entire country and he himself soon faced new trials and tribulations. Quite innocent of this, he set out from Shaoshan to Wuhan and from there by boat to Jiujiang (in Jiangxi province). He decided to convene an enlarged meeting of the Politburo at the mountain resort of Lushan (a "convocation of the 'saints,' " as he jokingly called it).[57]

He arrived in Lushan on July 1 and settled into a two-story stone villa, Meilu (Beautiful hut), in the Gulin district (180 Hedong Street). This house had once belonged to Chiang Kai-shek's wife, Song Meiling, and she loved to go there on holiday. Mao strolled around the vicinity, happily swam in the small reservoir with its crystal waters, enjoyed the beautiful mountains, and inhaled the pure air with pleasure. But then unexpectedly he thought of He

Zizhen. A long time ago, amid just such green mountains he had met her, youthful, willowy, like the stem of a lotus. Now more than thirty years had passed. How quickly time had flown by. He suddenly had a burning desire to see Zizhen again, but he restrained himself and only several days later did he order the wife of his bodyguard to go and fetch her and bring her to Lushan.

Jiang Qing was then in Beijing. For the past four years Mao had had only formal relations with her. They lived their own lives and did not bother each other. His previous attachment to his once-beloved wife had passed and all that remained was habit. Jiang was preoccupied with her health and spent several months a year in health resorts. In late 1956, it was discovered that she had cancer. After treatment in the Soviet Union and China she finally conquered the illness, but her ordeal had profoundly affected her character. She became irritable and nervous, was forever tangling with her doctors, nurses, and guards, and the only thing she would talk about was her illnesses.[58] Mao tried not to cause her any stress. He satisfied his sexual needs with innumerable charming young women whom he encountered during his travels. Most of all he loved dancers from the People's Liberation Army Song and Dance Ensemble.

His desire to see Zizhen came to him suddenly under the influence of the Jiangxi scenery. His former wife was living in Nanchang, a four-hour ride from Lushan. She did not look well, and meeting with her Mao could not conceal his sadness. Zizhen was obviously not herself and from time to time spoke in a confused manner. It is not known what they spoke about, but when her visit was over Mao told his bodyguard, "He Zizhen is not quite in her right mind. , , . We need to pay attention to her condition and tomorrow send her back from Lushan. . . . Until she leaves stay by her side all the time. It would be unfortunate if she met somebody she knows."[59] They never saw each other again.

Several days later, at the conference, Mao experienced additional stress. On July 14, he received a letter from his minister of defense, Peng Dehuai, containing criticism of the Great Leap. Peng expressed himself very cautiously, did not deny the "great achievements," and naturally did not directly attack the Chairman himself, but his obvious dissatisfaction with Mao Zedong's voluntarism showed through his entire argument. He wrote about "a certain confusion" with respect to ownership, about "rather large losses" from "the nation-wide smelting of steel" (almost two billion yuan), about the "epidemic of bragging" that had gripped the leading cadres, and of "petty bourgeois fanaticism." Summing up, he said, "All of this was a kind of leftist deviation," and he called for "drawing a clear line between truth and lies."

Mao was enraged. A hidden enemy had come out into the open! The folk saying *Lushan zhen mianmu* (Lushan uncovers the true face) was correct. Of course, Mao himself understood that there were many problems in the country, but the tenor of Peng's letter was that the entire Great Leap had been mistaken. "We were thinking of entering a communist society in one stride," Peng wrote. "So we banished from our minds the mass line and the working style of seeking truth from facts. . . . In the eyes of comrades . . . everything could be done by putting politics in command. . . . [But] putting politics in command cannot replace economic laws, let alone concrete measures in economic work." [60] This criticism was certainly targeted at the Chairman. How could Peng have dared to write something like this? Mao's mood was ruined and he even lost his appetite.

Late on the evening of July 16, Mao convened a meeting of the Standing Committee of the Politburo and presented Peng's letter to its members. (In attendance were Liu Shaoqi, Zhou Enlai, Zhu De, and Chen Yun.) Everyone was depressed, and Mao indignantly declared that if there was a split in the party, he would go off to the mountains and create a new communist party and a new Red Army from among the peasantry. [61] A decision was made to punish the "splittist" severely. After writing "Comrade Peng Dehuai's opinion" on the letter, Mao had it delivered to the Office of the Central Committee to make copies and distribute them to participants in the conference.

Now it was Peng's turn to become exasperated with the Chairman's backstage maneuvering. He had written a confidential letter not intended for general discussion and had not always been careful in his choice of words. Now everyone had been informed of his tactlessness. On the morning of July 17, his closest associate, PLA chief of staff Huang Kecheng, to whom Peng had shown the letter, expressed his concern about its "sharp style," but then added, "[However], you and the Chairman are bound together by long years of struggle, so that you probably understand each other very well." [62] That was way off the mark. The years of guerrilla "brotherhood" had long since passed, and was there really ever any brotherhood?

On July 18, despite protests from Peng, who had requested the Office of the Central Committee to withdraw the copies of the letter "written in haste" from circulation, the participants in the conference began discussing the missive to the Chairman. The overwhelming majority, foaming at the mouth, began to accuse the unfortunate Peng of all kinds of mortal sins. Everyone well understood what kind of mood the Great Helmsman was in.

A few voiced support for Peng, among them the first secretary of the Hunan Provincial Party Committee, Zhou Xiaozhou. Another was the former general secretary of the Central Committee, Luo Fu, who was serving as deputy foreign minister; a third was Huang Kecheng, and also the Chairman's new secretary, Li Rui. They were immediately included along with Peng in an "anti-party group," and on the morning of July 23 Mao, as he put it, "turned up the heat"; he said that his whole life he had followed the principle of "If someone beats up on me I will answer in kind; if they beat up on me first, I will give as good as I get."

He criticized Peng's letter as a "program of right opportunism," which was also supposedly "purposeful in design and organization." He called the group of "comrades" who supported Peng a choir that accompanied the lead singer. "I feel as if there are two tendencies," he declared, and this sounded like he was pronouncing a sentence. Once again, but this time to everyone attending the conference, Mao proclaimed that "if ruin is inevitable" he would go off to the countryside and rally the peasantry to overthrow the government. "If the People's Liberation Army does not follow me," he asserted, hinting at the fact that Peng was minister of defense, "then I will mobilize a Red Army. But in my opinion the PLA will follow me." In this connection, to be sure, he acknowledged several errors of his own, the greatest of which was calling for the smelting of 10.7 million tons of steel, but at the same time he called upon everyone there to be conscious of their own responsibility.

"I can hardly find suitable words to describe my heavy feelings as I listened to the speech of the Chairman," Peng recalled. "I could not be convinced at all. My resentment was very strong."[63]

During a break in the session Mao came up to him.

"Minister Peng, let's have another talk," he said offhandedly.

"There's nothing more to talk about," replied Peng, crimson from anger and barely able to restrain himself. "Talk is useless."[64] Waving his arm, he headed for the door. All conversations with Mao were useless.

On August 2, a plenum of the Central Committee was convened in Lushan to examine "the matter of the anti-party group headed by Peng." Mao spoke again, subjecting the "splittists" to an even more withering critique. "We are talking about a struggle . . . against the rightists who have launched a pernicious attack against the party, against the victorious march toward socialism of 600 million people," he summed up.[65]

After this everyone knew that the careers of Peng Dehuai, Luo Fu, Huang Kecheng, Zhou Xiaozhou, and Li Rui were finished. Peng offered a self-criticism in true Chinese communist style, but he was accused of being "dishonest, insincere, and deceitful."[66] The other members of the "group" also made self-criticisms, but also to no avail. "I advise you," Mao said to Peng and his "confederates," "that you learn to eat pepper, how else will you be able to understand that pepper is hot?"[67]

One month after the Lushan Plenum, Peng was relieved of his post as minister of defense. Mao appointed Lin Biao in his place. Luo Ruiqing, until then the minister of public security, was appointed chief of the general staff, in place of Huang Kecheng. All the other "conspirators" likewise lost their posts. Peng addressed a request to Mao to be sent somewhere to a people's commune, but the Chairman would not agree and advised him to engage in self-study. Mao could never forgive Peng and his supporters. After Peng's dismissal, the unfortunate marshal was ousted from Zhongnanhai, not just anywhere, but to the half-ruined house of the famous traitor Wu Sangui, who had surrendered China to the Manchus in 1644.[68]

For Mao, however, it was a Pyrrhic victory. He was entirely unaccustomed to criticism, and the thought that Peng might be correct gave him no peace. He clearly saw the results of the Great Leap, but he stubbornly continued to insist the general line was correct, the accomplishments enormous, and the prospects bright. Knowing there were people in the party and in the leadership who considered him an "ignoramus" gnawed at him. After Lushan he became particularly suspicious.

Conditions in the country did not help to strengthen his authority. Unlike in 1958, the harvests were bad everywhere in 1959. The single exception perhaps was Shaoshan, where waving fields made Mao happy. In August Mao urgently revised the plans. In the current year he would now be satisfied with 275 million tons of grain instead of 525 million, and 12 million tons of steel instead of 13 million.[69]

By now it was already too late. Famine had assumed the proportions of a national disaster. Something had to be done at once to avert a catastrophe, but Mao was now worrying only about saving face. The suffering of millions barely bothered him. He asserted, "When there is not enough to eat people starve to death. It is better to let half of the people die so that the other half can eat their fill."[70] He even found time for jokes: "Sometimes . . . there are very few vegetables, there are no hairpins or very few hairpins, no soap, things are out of whack, markets are disturbed. Everyone is nervous and feels ill at ease, but I think there is no reason to get agitated. . . . If you are worried during the first half of the night, take a sleeping pill, and you'll be fine."[71]

After the Lushan Plenum he decided to strengthen the cult of personality around him. "There are two kinds of personal reverence," he believed. "One kind is proper, for example, reverence shown to Marx, Engels, Lenin, and Stalin is quite proper. We cannot treat them with a lack of reverence. And why shouldn't we revere them since they had truth on their side. . . . The other kind is improper reverence, blind reverence without an analytic approach. That is unsuitable."[72] Naturally, he believed his cult was an example of the former.

A new outpouring of sycophantic emotions inundated China right after the Lushan Plenum. The loudest voices in the chorus of flatterers belonged to Liu Shaoqi and Lin Biao, who jump-started the unrestrained adoration of Mao at an enlarged session of the Military Affairs Council of the Central Committee in Beijing. "The leadership of Comrade Mao Zedong," Liu declared, "is in no way inferior to the leadership of Marx and Lenin. I am convinced that if Marx and Lenin lived in China, they would have guided the Chinese revolution in just the same way. . . . The party needs an authority figure; the proletariat needs an authority figure. If we did not have a single figure as an authority, how could we accomplish our construction?"[73] Lin Biao was so obsequious that he called contemporary Marxism-Leninism—not just in China but throughout the world—"Mao Zedong Thought."[74] These words acted like the finest balm for Mao's wounded psyche. He gradually regained his confidence.

Just then Khrushchev angered him again. In September 1959, the Soviet leader was intending to travel to the United States, where, in the spirit of his theory of peaceful coexistence, he was to hold talks with Eisenhower, whom Mao, quite logically, viewed as his main adversary. On the eve of his visit Khrushchev was trying to stabilize the world situation and to avoid damaging Soviet-American relations. Just then, as bad luck would have it, in late August an armed conflict erupted on the Sino-Indian border. The border, which ran through the mountains, was a fiction; it had been drawn a long time before by the British. The government of India did not consider it lawful, which is why Indian border troops crossed beyond it. Sino-Indian relations were already tense because of Chinese suppression in March 1959 of an uprising by Tibetans demanding independence. The spiritual leader of Tibet, the Dalai Lama, fled to India, disguised as a common soldier, and India's Prime Minister Nehru spoke out in his defense. The Sino-Indian border conflict was something that Khrushchev could have done without prior to his meeting with the American president. Nor did he wish to spend a lot of time on this complex problem. But since the U.S. government had come out on the side of Tibet and India he had to do something. He instructed the Ministry of Foreign Affairs to compose the text of a TASS statement regarding the situation on the Sino-Indian border. The text, edited by Foreign Minister Andrei Gromyko himself, turned out to be completely unsatisfactory since Khrushchev wanted to please both sides. Thus the Foreign Ministry made it clear that the USSR was maintaining "neutrality." As the Soviet diplomat Konstantin Krutikov recalls, "In Beijing the TASS statement was judged to be unfavorable to China. They believed that the USSR had shifted away from supporting its ally. . . . And, of course, they were irritated that Khrushchev had put pressure on China while cultivating relations with the United States."[75]

It was obvious that the humiliation that had accumulated during his "swimming pool negotiations" had stretched Khrushchev's patience beyond the breaking point. He began to act so crudely with respect to China that Mao seethed with indignation. On the eve of the Lushan Plenum, June 20, 1959, Khrushchev suddenly declared that he was annulling the agreement to provide China the technology to produce a nuclear weapon.[76] This agreement had been in force since October 1957, when a Soviet-Chinese protocol regarding this matter was signed in Moscow. According to its terms, the USSR promised to furnish China a working model of an atom bomb and assign Soviet scientists to instruct Chinese specialists in how to make one. In August 1958, right after he returned from Beijing, Khrushchev had dispatched a special delegation to the PRC to make preparations for transferring the bomb.[77] Suddenly he backed off. Later he explained that this was an act of retaliation. "[T]hey were denouncing us so hard . . . how could we at a time like that supply them with an atomic bomb, as though we were unthinking, obedient slaves?"[78]

Soon afterward, news reached Mao that on July 18, 1959, while in the Polish city of Poznan, Khrushchev sharply criticized the communes, saying that those who were playing with this idea "had a poor understanding of what Communism is and how it is to be built."[79] It is difficult to say what suddenly got into the Soviet leader at this time. He was often tipsy, especially during diplomatic receptions, and therefore often talked nonsense.[80] He might have been drunk this time, too, but Mao was not about to forgive him. Nor did Khrushchev wish to apologize. He had just lost patience. Arriving in Beijing on September 30 for the tenth anniversary of the People's Republic of China, he no longer even tried to check his emotions. Following his lead, the other members of the Soviet delegation behaved just as crudely. Mao too began to display his hostility openly, as did the other Chinese leaders with him. The era of the Great Friendship rapidly drew to a close.[81]

There were two main issues during the negotiations on October 2: Soviet and Chinese relations with the United States, including the Taiwan question, and the Sino-Indian border conflict. Mao exploded when Khrushchev, who had just returned from America, suggested on Eisenhower's behalf that Mao demonstrate "goodwill" and return to the United States five Americans whom the Chinese army had taken captive during the Korean War. Mao concluded that for the sake of improving relations with the imperialists the Soviet leader was ready to betray the cause of socialism.

He reacted the same way to Khrushchev's assertion that the USSR could not allow a new world war to erupt over Taiwan.[82] After all, it was only recently that Khrushchev had assured Mao that in a conflict between the PRC and the Chinese Nationalists he would not refrain from striking a nuclear counterattack against the "aggressor" (meaning the United States) if it dared to attack the People's Republic of China. Now he was suddenly going back on his word.* What was this if not treachery?

Khrushchev's statement regarding India and Tibet evoked even greater irritation on the part of Mao and the Chinese leadership. Khrushchev said bluntly, "If you will allow me to say what it is not permitted for a guest to say, the events in Tibet are your fault." Then he made it clear that he did not believe the Chinese version of the border conflict with India. PRC minister of foreign affairs Chen Yi responded with unconcealed hostility that the policy of the

---

* At that time the main advocate within the leadership of the CPSU of a hard line toward the PRC was Mikhail Andreevich Suslov, the secretary for ideology in the Central Committee. It was he who convinced Khrushchev that the Chinese should be harshly condemned for exacerbating tensions in the Taiwan Strait.

USSR was one of "opportunism and time-serving." Khrushchev flared up and began shouting at Chen, "If, as you say, we are time-servers, Comrade Chen Yi, then don't extend your hand to me. I will not shake it!" Little by little they got involved in a real verbal brawl. The Soviet guest lost his self-control and said something absurd, but very crude. "You," he barked at Chen Yi, "don't spit at me from the heights of your marshal's baton! You don't have enough spittle. You can't scare us."[83] Chen Yi, according to Khrushchev's memoirs, "kept repeating over and over, as though he had been wound up like a machine: 'Nehru, Nehru, Nehru!'"[84]

After the meeting the Soviet leader said to the members of his delegation, "Our road is one with that of the Chinese Communists. We consider them our friends. However, we cannot live with even our friends talking down to us."[85] Then he suddenly began to mock the Chinese cruelly, rhyming their names with unprintable Russian words and calling Mao himself an "old galosh."[86] The mudslinging match continued the next day at the airport prior to Khrushchev's departure. The Soviet leader had been in Beijing for a week, but after the difficult negotiations he decided to break off his visit. This time Mao did not get involved in the polemics. He had made up his mind that it was impossible to repair the broken thread. Three months later, looking back on this visit, he summed up:

> Starting in March 1959 our friends [the Soviet leadership] began singing in a powerful anti-Chinese chorus along with the imperialists and the reactionary nationalists as well as with revisionists like Tito. On one hand, China will be isolated for a long time, but on the other hand it will garner support of many communist parties, countries, and peoples. And after eight years, surviving every test, China will become a very powerful country. . . . The darker the clouds, the brighter the dawn.[87]

Once more, as he had two years earlier, he called upon the Chinese people to carry out "permanent revolution." The approaching economic catastrophe, however, caused problems for his ambitious plans.

31

FAMINE AND FEAR

Throughout the summer of 1959 drought gripped Northeast China while torrential rains fell in the south. The exhausted population lost its enthusiasm for the Great Leap, but Mao still believed that the difficulties were temporary. He placed high hopes on 1960 and announced grandiose plans. "The situation in the country is excellent," he insisted.[1] Now he demanded 300 million tons of grain and 20–22 million tons of steel despite the fact that the grain harvest in 1959 was only 170 million tons and steel 13 million tons. In the spring of 1960 Chinese newspapers heralded a "New Great Leap."[2]

But in 1960 the entire country was in the grip of a terrible drought. There had been nothing like it since the beginning of the century. Rivers and canals dried up, and even the mighty Yellow River shrank. Following the drought came a period of torrential rains and typhoons. Rivers overflowed their banks. Weak dams collapsed and terrible flooding ensued. On more than half of the cultivated land the harvest either shriveled to the roots or was drowned. The grain harvest was a mere 143.5 million tons, more than 50 million less than in 1957, the year preceding the Great Leap. A humanitarian crisis unfolded throughout the country. China had never witnessed such a terrible famine in its entire history. Tens of thousands of people were dying every day in the countryside and in the cities.

The ones who suffered worst were peasants from whom the state had seized their last crumbs. In many villages there was simply nothing to eat. Emaciated villagers roamed the countryside, stripping off leaves and bark from trees, collecting worms, beetles, frogs, wild plants, and grasses. In many places they even ate dirt mixed with weeds, a concoction called *Guan Yin tu* (Goddess of Mercy earth). Death was the result of eating such food even though in some places it was boiled before being eaten. An eyewitness recalled, "People mixed it [the *Guan Yin* soil] with corn flour and the bread made of this mixture was . . . very filling. . . . But once in the stomach, the soil dried out all the moisture in the colon. . . . Many people never made it to the hospital and others died on the operating table."[3]

Once more, as in 1957–58, people began to hunt for sparrows, only now it was to relieve their hunger. Nor were other birds spared. Another eyewitness related that

> we began to eat anything that flew. I practiced with a sling to shoot sparrows. After I caught one, I would take it home to my mother, and she would cook some soup for my grandmother. . . . That is why my grandmother did not die. . . . After the birds became scarce, we stripped tree leaves. . . . People even drained the ponds and ate practically everything that could be found there, even water snakes. . . . When there was almost nothing left, many people starved to death. . . . During the great famine, it was common to have two or three members of the family starve to death.[4]

In several provinces the population of entire villages died. A doctor who visited western Gansu with a group of inspectors reported:

> Early one morning, we stopped at a big village but found few signs of life around the low mud huts. A few people could be seen who were so weak, they could hardly beg for food. The team leader raised his voice, shouting "Old folks, come out now! Chairman Mao and the Communist Party have sent doctors to rescue you!" He shouted over and over again. Eventually, those still alive crawled out of their houses. These were people struggling on the edge of death. If they fell over, they were unable to get up again. The team found one group of dead bodies after another. I pushed open the door of one hut and had to draw back because of the stink. A low groan came from inside and I saw two or three people lying still in the darkness on a *kang*. At the front lay an old man and one of his hands pointed at something. Together with him lay a woman who had long been dead and whose decomposing body was the source of the stench. The old man's hand was pointing at a small human body, four limbs spread out, mouth open wide. It looked as if the child was crying out but in fact the body had been lying dead for days.[5]

The situation in southeastern Fujian was no less horrifying. "We were so weak that we could not work," recalled one of the local inhabitants. "Not long afterwards my brother starved to death. I still remember what he looked like before his death. He was too weak to walk. He lay in bed, uttering the same word, 'eat, eat, eat.' He continued to groan until his last breath."[6]

"Is Chairman Mao going to allow us to starve to death?" asked members of communes in letters to their sons who were serving in the army.[7] In some places people rose up and attacked railroad grain cars, warehouses, and granaries, often under the leadership of party secretaries. Elsewhere peasants took to the roads and entered the cities, where they naïvely supposed the people had ample supplies of rice and meat. In 1958–61 approximately 1 million people outmigrated from the villages of Anhui, 1.5 million from the people's communes in Hunan, 1.6 million from villages in Shandong. In all, more than 10 million people took part in this exodus. Many died along the roads, famished and emaciated. "The road from the village to the neighboring province was strewn with bodies," recalled someone from Northeast China, "and piercing wails came from holes on both sides of the road. Following the cries, you could see the tops of the heads of children who were abandoned in these holes. A lot of parents thought their children had a better chance of surviving if they were adopted by somebody else. The holes were just deep enough so that the children could not get out to follow them but could be seen by passers-by who might adopt them." [8]

Life was hardly better in the cities. The crowds of rural poor with glassy eyes and sunken cheeks elicited little sympathy from malnourished city folk. They, too, were stripping trees of their leaves and bark, catching birds, and gathering wild vegetables and grasses. The situation was no better in the capital. A Beijing resident recalled, "It was extremely hard to find anything to eat. But once a friend and I managed to get hold of some sugar. We were overjoyed! We really wanted to eat it all on the spot. However, after feasting our eyes on the sweet lumps, we decided to bring it to our colleague. He was in such a bad state that he had been hospitalized. But there was no food in the hospital either. He was so happy when we presented the sticky sugar to him. But he did not manage to eat it. He simply smiled and died." [9]

Even within Zhongnanhai the famine made itself known. "Our rations had been reduced to sixteen pounds of grain a month," recalled Mao's personal physician. "Meat, eggs, and cooking oil were nowhere to be had. We were allowed to buy vegetables on the open market, but there were hardly any for sale. Some people organized expeditions to hunt wild goats, but soon goats became extinct too. . . . Our stomachs were always half empty." [10]

Mao resolved to suffer with everyone else. He gave up eating meat. "Everyone is starving. I can't eat meat," he said to those in his entourage. Zhou Enlai gave up meat and eggs and curtailed his monthly consumption of rice to fifteen pounds. Many party leaders and their wives began to grow vegetables in the inner courtyards of their luxurious houses, to travel outside of town to gather wild grasses and edible roots, and to drink tea brewed from the leaves of trees. None of this, of course, had any impact upon the problem of hunger.

At this point, Khrushchev recalled all the Soviet specialists from China. He could not have administered a heavier or more ruthless blow to a starving nation. The meanest enemy is he who only recently was proclaiming friendship and brotherhood. Khrushchev was actually no less cruel than Stalin.

In six weeks 1,390 Soviet engineers and technicians, scientists, industrial designers, and other experts left China for the Soviet Union, taking with them all their scientific documents, plans, and blueprints. Many building sites were shut down and many scientific projects were halted. This exodus exacerbated China's economic crisis.

Khrushchev's decision was made hastily, in mid-July 1960, right after the congress of the Romanian Communist Party at which he had clashed with Peng Zhen, the head of the Chinese delegation.[11] During the nine months since Khrushchev's last unsuccessful visit to Beijing, relations between the two parties and the two countries had rapidly deteriorated. Thus Khrushchev's emotional outburst in Bucharest and his subsequent recall of experts from China were far from fortuitous. A covert sniping in the press and at various party forums continued throughout the winter and spring of 1959–60. Finally it emerged openly in late April 1960 on the ninetieth anniversary of Lenin's birth, April 22. On that date *Red Flag*, the theoretical journal of the CCP, published a lengthy editorial, "Long Live Leninism!" and *People's Daily* published a somewhat shorter lead article, "Forward along the Path of the Great Lenin!" These polemical articles took aim against Khrushchev's policy of "peaceful co-existence between two systems" as well as his thesis about "peaceful transition from capitalism to socialism." Mao himself had done the final editing on the article in *Red Flag*, which was buttressed with quotations from Lenin, Marx, and Engels. Its main point was to demonstrate that Lenin had always considered war an inevitable consequence of imperialism. The Russian response was drafted by the old Comintern apparatchik Otto Kuusinen, who quoted Lenin's widow, Nadezhda Krupskaia, to the effect that her late husband had believed a time would come when wars would become so destructive it would be impossible to fight them.[12] The recollections of Krupskaia, however, could hardly persuade Mao and the other leaders of the CCP.

In June 1960, the Chinese emphasized their hard-line viewpoint at a session of the General Council of the World Federation of Trade Unions meeting in Beijing. They were unwittingly assisted by the Americans, who stressed on the eve of the forum their continuing commitment to contain communism. On May 1, in the sky over Sverdlovsk, a city in the Ural Mountains, a Soviet rocket downed a U-2 plane engaged in intelligence gathering. Its pilot, Gary Powers, wound up in the hands of the Soviet authorities. Without deliberating, the choleric Khrushchev puffed up a spy scandal, not realizing this played into Mao's hands. Khrushchev wanted to confront Eisenhower, who had deceived him. The Chinese took advantage of the opportunity to intensify their criticism of what they regarded as Khrushchev's softheaded policy toward the imperialists, a policy that had brought about this situation. On May 12, Khrushchev, wishing to discuss this question with Mao, invited him to visit Moscow, but Mao refused.[13]

Now in Bucharest, clashing with Peng Zhen at the Congress of the Romanian Communist Party, Khrushchev exploded. He discarded his prepared text and suddenly poured invective on Mao personally. He called him an "ultraleftist, an ultra-dogmatist, indeed, a left revisionist," "a Buddha who gets his theory out of his nose," and "an old galosh." He also accused him of being "oblivious of any interests other than his own."[14] Peng responded in kind, accusing Khrushchev of blowing hot and cold in foreign policy. Khrushchev now switched to the subject of Stalin and the cult of personality. Fedor Burlatsky, who attended the congress, recalls that Khrushchev began to yell at the head of the Chinese delegation,* "If you want Stalin, you can have him in a coffin! We'll send him to you in a special railway car!"[15] Khrushchev returned to Moscow greatly agitated. It is quite unlikely that he seriously considered the impact his decision to recall Soviet experts would have on the Chinese economy. He simply wanted to punish Mao.

Meanwhile, people in China were continuing to starve. Mao adopted extreme measures, agreeing to the purchase of grain from abroad. In 1961 the PRC imported four million tons of grain from Australia, Canada, and the United States via third parties, and the next year it imported even more.[16] But the crisis remained severe. Even Khrushchev suddenly grasped this, and on February 27, 1961, in a personal letter to Mao he offered to supply one million tons of grain—300,000 tons of wheat and 700,000 tons of rye—to China as well as 500,000 tons of Cuban sugar. He received a reply from Zhou Enlai who agreed to accept only the sugar. "The USSR itself is now experiencing difficulties," Zhou declared, "therefore we do not want to burden the Soviet Union."[17]

The Chinese authorities denied the existence of famine and did everything they could to conceal it. In the latter half of 1960, on Mao's instructions Edgar Snow, an "old friend" of the Chinese Communist Party, was invited on a five-month visit to China. Mao always believed that Snow was a CIA agent, so he permitted Snow to visit many interior regions, including the poorest ones, because he wanted to use him as a channel to inform Americans and the whole world about the absence of famine in China. Toward the end of Snow's visit he met with Mao twice and Zhou Enlai once. Mao was simple, sociable, and friendly, just as he had been in Baoan twenty-four years earlier. He told Snow about the "remarkable successes" of the Great Leap, especially in the production of steel, but he added that China as before was still a "poor and backward country." However, he expressed no anxiety about this, simply noting that "people must become acquainted with difficulties, shortages, and struggle." He said nothing about mass famine; Mao only indulged in black humor by saying that "the Chinese people are mostly vegetarians, and although they eat little meat, there is not enough."[18] Snow reported to the world just what the Great

---

* Burlatsky mistakenly wrote that this was Liu Shaoqi.

Helmsman wanted him to say. "I must assert that I saw no starving people in China, nothing that looked like old-time famine. . . . I do not believe there is famine in China."[19]

Of course, the millions of Chinese dying of malnutrition had no inkling of what Snow said. Neither did the starving hear Field Marshal Bernard Law Montgomery, who visited China twice, in May 1960 and September 1961. After meeting with Mao he asserted, "Talks of large-scale famine, of thousands dying from hunger, of grim want, of apathy, of a restless nation, are totally untrue, they are lies spread by those who want the regime of Mao Tse-tung [Mao Ze-dong] and his government to fail. All such talk is nonsense, maybe even dangerous."[20] Nor did ordinary Chinese citizens know what Mao said to the French socialist François Mitterrand in February 1961: "I repeat in order to be clearly understood: there is no famine in China."[21] All this was repeated abroad.

Only in 1980, after the death of Mao, did China officially acknowledge the massive loss of life from famine during and after the Great Leap. Hu Yao-bang, the general secretary of the Central Committee of the CCP, gave a figure of 20 million dead; however, according to various estimates this figure is too low. A more realistic figure would be 30 million, perhaps as high as 40 million or even more. The most recent Western study of the Great Famine based on Chinese local archives puts the number of deaths at a minimum of 45 million while a book by a Chinese dissident writer indicates deaths of 36 million.[22] In the single province of Sichuan, with a 1957 population of 70 million, one out of every eight persons died, and in Anhui with 33 million and Gansu 12 million, one out of every four perished.[23] The overall economic loss from the Great Leap amounted to 100–120 billion yuan, which was twice as much as the capital investment in the PRC during the entire First Five-Year Plan.[24]

In a democratic country after such a catastrophe the entire government would be replaced. But in the PRC all power belonged to the party-state bureaucracy, which relied upon the army, the police, and the extended bureaucratic apparatus. The party penetrated every cell of society, and dissenters were persecuted. The bureaucracy was recruited from the people itself, more precisely from its lowest social classes—the poorest peasantry, the Hakka, as well as former lumpens, paupers, and other proletarians. But the bureaucracy expressed its own corporate interests and cared most about protecting its own privileges and power. At the summit of power was a group of "old revolutionaries" who had taken part in the class struggles of the 1920s through the 1940s. "Today there are about 800 survivors of all those years," Mao said to Edgar Snow in October 1960. "By and large the country is still being run and for some time will depend upon these 800."[25]

In such circumstances opposition could emerge only from within this narrow stratum of the party elite. It was the mood within this group that caused Mao the greatest anxiety, particularly after the Peng Dehuai affair. Famine and economic crisis might again cause dissatisfaction among his old comrades, many of whom still clung to their New Democratic inclinations.

He understood that something had to be done about the economy and perhaps politics, too, but he refused to acknowledge his fundamental errors. He needed to seize the initiative, but throughout the spring and most of the summer of 1960 Mao was terribly depressed. Not until August was he able to snap out of it. By this time there were voices in the government calling for an end to the Great Leap. In July 1960, the head of the State Planning Commission, Li Fuchun, suggested a new economic policy of "adjustment, consolidation, and raising standards." He was supported by Zhou Enlai, who added to this formula one word, namely, "replenishment." Chen Yun also expressed his strong approval for such a policy.[26]

Mao understood the need to act promptly. He insisted on investigations but continued to blame the famine on local cadres. "In some communes, the cadres went too far; they lost any concept of discipline; without authorization from higher authorities they engaged in egalitarianism and redistribution," he said shamelessly.[27] These were the cadres who needed to be investigated.

At the same time, he believed that vast numbers of city dwellers should be mobilized to help the peasants. Millions of industrial workers and intellectuals should be relocated to the countryside. During the Great Leap the urban population of China had doubled through an influx of working hands from the countryside. Now Mao decided to return at least some of them to the villages. Of course, "rightists and guilty persons" were swept up in this mobilization; many of those sent to the countryside, including intellectuals, had never actually worked there before. This did not bother Mao. "Man must eat every day whether engaged in industry, communication, education, capital construction, or any other enterprise; no one can do without grain," the Chairman declared, demanding to "adopt all effective measures" in order to "strengthen the first line of agricultural production" by squeezing out "all of the labor force that can be squeezed out" for the rural people's communes.[28] His instructions immediately became the guide to action. Hundreds of thousands of city people were sent to work in the fields.

His main proposal, however, impacted basic policies. In September 1960, he demanded that the members of the Politburo Standing Committee make the "production brigade" or the "team" consisting of twenty or so households the basic accounting unit. The people's communes would remain only as the basic administrative units as well as one of the elements in the tripartite system of property in the countryside. This system, which had come into effect after the establishment of the people's commune, was one in which a part of the means of production—for example, almost all of the land—had belonged to a commune consisting of 40,000–50,000 persons while another part was divided up among the big production brigades consisting of some 6,000 persons, and the production brigades or teams at the lowest level consisting of some 200 or so people. Thus, each level of property corresponded to a certain level of collectivization.

In early November the Central Committee issued a twelve-point directive titled "Emergency Directives on Current Policies regarding Rural People's Communes," which also allowed peasants to have small personal plots and to engage in sideline handicraft enterprises on a small scale. Zhou Enlai authored this document.[29]

Soon, in the name of the Central Committee, Mao directed provincial, municipal, and district party committees to ensure that "the five epidemics be thoroughly eliminated," meaning the collectivization of personal belongings, deception, commandism, the isolation of cadres, and blind command of production. Emphasis was to be put on eliminating the "epidemic of collectivizing [personal] property."[30]

Mao's tilt to the right was palpable, but the Chairman did not even consider capitulating to the "moderates." He simply wanted to be seen as the source of the reforms, and he succeeded. The next regular plenum of the Central Committee, held in January 1961, approved the reform of the communes. The party retreated to the era of higher-level agricultural producers' cooperatives of the mid-1950s. But Mao was satisfied because the participants in the plenum echoed his ideas.

At the end of the meeting he again called upon everyone to engage in investigations. "We must look at everything through our own eyes, not others', listen with our own ears, and touch things with our own hands. . . . In all we must proceed from practice," he urged them. He also gently admonished the Central Committee, noting that "last fall . . . it did not see the situation clearly, did not grasp things well and did not make full corrections." In this way he underscored that he was the initiator of the new policy of adjustment, having sized up the situation in good time. "1961 must become the year of a realistic approach to our affairs," Mao declared and added, "There is no need to be discouraged if you made a mistake."[31] He easily dodged a crisis in the party.

Nevertheless, he still had a very poor grasp of economics. "There are many issues of economic construction I do not understand," he said in a moment of frankness. "I am not well-versed in industry and commerce; I know a little about agriculture, but only to a certain degree, that is, I understand a little."[32] This is precisely why he fell into deep depression in the spring of 1960, when he finally understood that the famine was catastrophic. Although he resumed activity in the autumn, his mood remained depressed. He knew that the Great Leap had failed but he had no clear plan for correcting the errors. To return to New Democracy would have meant repudiating the entire experience of building socialism, to admit having been wrong in his dispute with the "moderates," and to lose face. Yet to bulldoze one's way forward to communism was to risk a powerful explosion of popular indignation. "You know, we have a lot of experience when it comes to policy, political directives, political methods, military affairs, and class struggle," he said to Snow in October 1960, "but as far as socialist construction is concerned, we had never been engaged in it, and we still don't have much experience. You might ask, haven't you been doing it now for eleven years? Indeed, we have, but we still lack knowledge, our experience is insufficient, and one might say we have just begun to accumulate some experience, but it is still only a little."

This is why the first thing he thought of was to return for a time, at least for the next seven years, to the pre–Great Leap forms of organizing production. Beyond that he had no idea whatsoever. When Snow asked him about his long-term plans for economic development in China, Mao replied, "I don't know." Snow was astounded. "You are speaking too cautiously." But Mao reiterated, "It's not a question of whether I'm being cautious or not, it's simply that I don't know; we simply lack experience." [33]

Abandoning his ambitious Great Leap plans, he now believed it would be impossible to build a powerful socialist economy in China in the next fifty years. "In order to catch up with and overtake the most advanced capitalist countries," he said entirely without enthusiasm, "it will take a hundred years or more in my opinion." [34] In the middle of April 1961, he issued instructions to shutter the communal dining halls, which, in his words, had developed into "fatal tumors." [35]

Feeling dispirited, he decided to retreat to the "second line" and allow other members of the party to lead. He entrusted Liu Shaoqi, who of course was a "moderate" but still supporting Mao fanatically, to implement the new eight-character line, that is, "adjustment, consolidation, raising standards, and replenishment." Chen Yun, Deng Xiaoping, and other members of the Politburo were to help Liu, whom Mao now began to speak of as his successor. Several years later, he explained: "What I am responsible for is the division [of the leadership] into first and second lines. Why did we make this division into first and second lines? The first reason is that my health is not very good [here Mao was being cunning]; the second was the lesson of the Soviet Union. Malenkov was not mature enough, and before Stalin died he had not wielded power. Every time he proposed a toast, he [Liu] fawned and flattered. I wanted to establish their prestige before I died." [36]

Mao did not stop attending conferences and meetings, but his speeches now became perfunctory. He continued to call upon administrators to conduct "systematic investigations and study of reality," and not "to view flowers from horseback." He grumbled that "cadres at all levels still do not really understand what socialism is," and he called for a struggle against the "evil wind of [excessive] collectivization." [37] He could do nothing more.

Epochal events were occurring throughout the country. In Anhui and elsewhere peasants began adopting so-called household contracts that meant actually dividing the land and assigning responsibility for production to families. They signed agreements with the local authorities to rent land de facto from the brigade or the team, promising to fulfill grain quotas to the state during the harvest season. This happened spontaneously ("rather suddenly," as Mao Zedong would say later on) and then began to spread like a chain reaction.[38] Some party leaders perceived no danger in this undertaking. The first secretary of the Anhui party committee even supported it. Some believed that "[p]easants were very concerned about their own profit. If the profit is to be shared with ten thousand people, they will not work; if it is shared with one thousand, they will work a little bit; if shared with one hundred, they will work a bit more; if shared by ten, they will work even better; and if shared only by their own family, they work the most."[39]

Of course, no one in the party thought of distributing land to the peasants as their private property. The small sideline plots were alloted only for short-term use and even then not everywhere. Thus it is not surprising that the secretary of the Anhui party committee considered this a temporary expedient that would not damage socialism but would solve the short-term problem of hunger. By midsummer 1961, 5 percent of the land in Anhui was being cultivated by individual peasant households.[40]

Many Central Committee leaders reacted positively to the Anhui initiative. "The peasants are doing nothing now but complain," Chen Yun said in exasperation. "They are saying that under Chiang Kai-shek they 'suffered' but had plenty to eat. Under Mao Zedong everything is 'great' but they eat only porridge. All we have to do is give the peasants their own land. Then everyone will have plenty to eat."[41] What could it mean for Mao? It doesn't matter if it is socialism or capitalism as long as the economy develops and the people are living well?

Liu Shaoqi, who just a month before had seemed to be a fanatical supporter of Mao, drew the most unwelcome conclusions from Mao's perspective. Returning from a trip to his native district of Ningxiang in Hunan, at a working session of the Central Committee in May 1961 he said, "The peasants in Hunan have a saying, 'Three-tenths of misfortune comes from Heaven, seven-tenths from man.' . . . There are some places in the country where the main reason [for difficulties] was natural disasters, but I'm afraid there are not many such places. In most places the main reason is shortcomings and mistakes in our work." He went on, "There are comrades who consider this a matter of one finger and nine fingers. But I'm afraid that it is obvious now . . . that if we talk all the time about nine fingers and one finger and do not change this equation, this will contradict reality."[42] This remark was essentially an attack against Mao since everyone knew that the Chairman loved to compare achievements and failures according to the principle of "nine healthy fingers and one sick one," a formula he even applied to the Great Leap. But Liu could not restrain himself. The visit to his native village really shook him. Over the course of forty days,

Liu had become acquainted with conditions on the spot. Prior to his departure, on saying farewell to the peasants of his native village, he was unable to cover up how upset he felt. "I have not been home for forty years, and I wanted very much to come here and see how things are. Now that I have returned I can see that the lives of my fellow villagers are very difficult. We have done our work badly; please forgive us!"[43]

At this meeting Deng Xiaoping supported Liu Shaoqi. Many others were similarly inclined. Not expecting such a blow, Mao looked embarrassed. Taking the floor, he acknowledged mistakes. "And now they are taking retribution upon us," he said. "The soil is not fertile, people and livestock are emaciated. The retribution is for the policies of the past three years. And who is guilty? The Central Committee and I bear the heaviest responsibility. I bear the major responsibility."[44] He also noted that for a long time he had "profoundly not understood how to build socialism in China."[45] For a time, in mid-1961, Mao was even ready to recognize the Anhui experiment, but not for long.

He was greatly demoralized. "All the good party members are dead. The only ones left are a bunch of zombies," he said to his physician. "What we want, though, is socialism," Mao said in a moment of frankness. "We are facing difficulties in agricultural production now, so we have to make concessions to the peasants. But this is not the direction we should take in the future."[46]

The intraparty opposition continued to gain strength. Indirect criticism directed at Mao grew continuously and once more he felt isolated as he had many years before in southern Jiangxi. Again he felt like chucking it all and going off into the mountains. Let them send messengers imploring him to return!

Meeting Field Marshal Montgomery for a second time, Mao raised the subject of death. Mao was then in his sixty-ninth year, his guest was seventy-five, but the Chairman ignored etiquette. He observed that one might die at any moment from any number of causes, but he considered death from illness the most likely. He told the field marshal that a popular belief existed in China that seventy-three and eighty-four were the critical years in life. If a person survived these milestones he would live to be one hundred. Mao said that he himself had no desire to live past seventy-three. He intended "to join Karl Marx" since "he had much to discuss with Marx." He again referred to Liu Shaoqi as his successor.[47]

Throughout the second half of 1961, Mao's mood was gloomy, and it did not improve in 1962. At an enlarged meeting of the Central Committee in January and February, Mao encountered the most serious criticism he had been subjected to recently. More than seven thousand leaders had assembled from all over China. It is no wonder that some of them "went too far," particularly since members of the Politburo set the tone. Peng Zhen raised the question of the personal responsibility of top leaders for the failures of the Great Leap, and suggested that blame should be put on the Central Committee, including the

Chairman, Liu Shaoqi, and other members of the Politburo Standing Committee if they deserved it. He even added, "If Chairman Mao's prestige isn't as high as Mt. Everest, it is certainly as high as Mt. Taishan, so much so that even if you remove a few tons of earth away, it is still very high. It is like the East China Sea (even if you remove several buckets of water, there is still a lot left). . . . But if Chairman Mao has committed a 1 per cent error or even a one in a thousand error, it would be odious to our Party if he did not self-criticize." [48]

Mao should have blamed himself. He had to be more careful in selecting leading cadres. After deciding that he would provoke everyone else, he determined to include in the conference agenda the question of democratic centralism and criticism and self-criticism, standard CCP techniques to assess the loyalty of party members. His intent was to test the soundness of his comrades by giving them a chance to "let off steam." He wanted to lure the venomous snakes from their holes by once more using the tried and true tactic of "Let a Hundred Flowers Bloom," but this time applied to the party.

He got more than he bargained for in Liu Shaoqi's astounding speech. "Earlier we invariably said that the ratio between shortcomings and mistakes and successes was one to nine," Liu began, repeating the conclusion about the unfavorable relationship between subjective and objective factors responsible for economic crisis, and then added, "Now, I'm afraid, we cannot say that this applies to all regions, but only to a few." At this point Mao interrupted. "There are quite a few such regions," he muttered, but Liu Shaoqi continued. "If one speaks of the country as a whole we cannot say that the ratio between shortcomings and successes is one finger to nine fingers. I'm afraid we have to say three fingers to seven fingers."

Mao was unhappy, but Liu was not finished. "There are even some regions in the country," he noted, "in which the shortcomings and mistakes outweigh the successes." [49] According to an eyewitness, Liu Shaoqi's speech completely ruined Mao's mood. [50]

At this point local representatives entered the fray. One declared that subjectivism was the main problem that had arisen in recent years. Others questioned Mao's thesis that shortcomings derived from lack of experience. Everyone knew that the CCP had also lacked much experience during the struggle to fulfill the First Five-Year Plan. "Why then did not as many problems arise as they have now?" several party cadres asked sharply. [51]

How could Mao respond? All he could say was that he was to blame. And he did. "I bear responsibility for all of the errors directly committed by the Central Committee," he said. "I also will answer in part for the indirect errors of the Central Committee for I am the chairman of the Central Committee." That is as far as his self-criticism went, although he also acknowledged that for him economics remained "an unknown realm of necessity." Almost everyone knew this. Mao directed his main fire against other party leaders who, in his words, "commit errors but remain silent, fearing that others will talk about it." He warned such persons "the more you are afraid, the more you will be pursued by devils. . . . All those who shun responsibility, who fear responsibility, who do not allow others to speak out, who are afraid to stroke the tiger, all those who cling to such a position, will undoubtedly fail." He even managed to joke to the assembled, "Are you really afraid to stroke the tiger?" adding, "In my speech I criticized various phenomena and criticized various comrades, but I did not name any names. . . . You yourselves can figure it out."[52]

Everyone laughed, although many were in no mood for humor. After the Chairman's speech, numerous party leaders engaged in self-criticism, but only a few enthusiastically supported Mao's speech, Lin Biao among them. He said that he "felt strongly that when our work was going well it was a period when we were implementing the ideas of Chairman Mao, a period when the ideas of Chairman Mao were not being obstructed. . . . If we encounter any problem, any difficulty, it is because we have not followed the instructions of the Chairman closely enough, because we ignored or circumscribed the Chairman's advice. Such is the history of our party over several decades." Based on this logic, Lin explained that the mistakes of the Great Leap occurred because "we did not heed the warnings of Chairman Mao." The secretary of Mao's native county party committee, the able and efficient Hua Guofeng, also delivered a panegyric to the Chairman. Mao remembered this fine fellow from his trip to Shaoshan in 1959. He had liked him then and he liked him now. But it was Lin's speech that was balm to his wounded soul. This was hardly an accident since Mao had edited the speech himself.[53]

The Great Helmsman was irritated by most of the other speeches and increasingly disappointed with his associates. He was tired, looked somewhat pinched, and had aged a lot. The atmosphere in the Politburo sickened him. On February 8, the day after the forum, he turned daily affairs over to Liu Shaoqi and left Beijing, intending not to return for a long time. He wanted to see how these "big headed know-it-alls" would cope with running the state. He did not view them as enemies, of course, but his resentment toward them was constantly growing. He had intentionally relinquished his power, retreated to the "second line" in order to bolster their influence in the country prior to his death, and now suddenly everything moved "in the opposite direction."[54] Let them suffer without him!

That same evening his associates convened a working meeting, chaired by Liu Shaoqi, at which they analyzed the economic situation in the country. The budget deficit was more than 300 million yuan and prospects for the future were disturbing, to put it mildly. Chen Yun, who was considered the best economist among the members of the Politburo, shouldered the task of working out concrete proposals for dealing with the situation. In essence, his plan, presented two weeks later, was to curtail the urban population, the army, and the administrative apparatus significantly, and to shift the center of gravity of economic construction from industry to agriculture. That is as far as he went. He offered no radical ideas. Liu Shaoqi warned that China might be on the threshold of civil war if the leadership did not promptly adopt concrete measures to improve the food situation. They all recognized the gravity of the economic situation.[55]

Meanwhile, after withdrawing to Hangzhou, Mao was nursing his wounds. On February 25, he instructed his secretary, Tian Jiaying, to assemble a small commission and travel to the same places in Hunan where Liu Shaoqi had recently been. They should also visit Shaoshan and the neighboring village of Tangjiatuo, the birthplace of Mao's mother, to talk with the people and assess the situation. Liu's assertion that people, that is, the Chairman himself, were chiefly responsible for the failure of the Great Leap gnawed at Mao. He wanted to refute this calumny. Tian Jiaying suited this purpose better than anyone else. Mao recalled how Tian had sharply condemned the contract system in March 1961 after a trip to Anhui, where, on assignment from Mao, he had conducted his first investigation of this innovation. Tian had considered the contract system inhumane because there was no place in it for widows and orphans. Just thinking of what would become of the latter if the contract system was extended throughout the whole country distressed Mao's good-hearted secretary.[56] Now he was charged with collecting material that would enable the Chairman to refute his associates.

Arriving in Hunan, Tian was genuinely shocked by what the peasants told him. Most of them cursed the Great Leap and praised the contract system. Some even wished to return to New Democracy. The secretary had no choice but to report all this to Mao, who made a wry face and said, "We are among those people who follow the mass line, but sometimes it is impossible to listen to everything that the masses say. For example, it is impossible for us to listen to what they say about the contract system."[57]

Tian also spoke with Chen Yun and Liu Shaoqi and was pleased that they took the side of the peasants. Deng Xiaoping also supported the contract system. Liu, Deng, and Chen worked hard all spring to restore the economy. Slowly the situation began to improve due to extension of the contract system. By the summer of 1962, between 20 and 30 percent of the land was in the hands of the peasants.[58] This was enough to enable the country gradually to overcome the profound food crisis. In 1961, the production of grain increased by 4 million tons, and in 1962 by 12.5 million tons.[59] Liu, Deng, and Chen concluded that without the widespread division of land among households, there would be no way to secure steady economic growth. Chen was particularly radical in this respect. "This is an emergency measure for an unusual time," he said. "You may call it 'household division of land,' or 'assignment of tasks by household,' either way is fine. . . . The state has encountered colossal disasters brought about both by nature and by man, and we must let all the peasants, following the words of *The International,* 'save' themselves and 'decree the common salvation.' They will restore production faster than anyone else." [60]

Liu and Deng supported Chen. Deng even asserted by using an old Sichuan and Anhui proverb, "It does not matter if it is a black cat or yellow cat, as long as it catches mice it is a good cat." [61] Zhou Enlai offered no objections. Deng Zihui, head of the Central Committee's Rural Work Department, did all he could to promote the contract system.

Moreover, in March, Liu and Deng had begun working to rehabilitate the hundreds of thousands of so-called rightists targeted by the purges of the late 1950s. "Beginning in 1959," Liu wrote to the minister of public security, "many local organs of the Ministry of Public Security and even communes and brigades, using methods of long-term detention and lengthy reeducation through labor, actually deprived a large number of people of their freedom, some of whom died of hunger or were tortured to death. . . . This was not stopped completely even in 1961. I encountered such a situation last year in Hunan. You must seriously investigate, disclose, criticize, and correct this lawlessness." [62] Neither Liu nor Deng spoke of rehabilitating Peng Dehuai and his "confederates." These men were too important. They did succeed in vindicating more than 3,500 rank-and-file rightists. [63]

Buoyed by support from Liu and other leaders, Tian Jiaying told Mao that if peasants were allowed to choose, the number of households on the contract system would soon grow to 40 percent, and only 60 percent of families would remain in the cooperatives. He cautiously added that when production was restored at a later date, the peasants might be induced to return to the collectives. Mao calmly inquired, "Is this only your personal opinion or do others also think this way?" Tian replied, "It's just mine." [64] He did not want to betray Liu and Chen. But Mao knew very well what was going on in his absence. He understood that the loyalty the "moderates" showed him was just a formality. He now decided to strike the intraparty opposition a crushing blow from which it would never recover.

He returned to Beijing in early July 1962 and immediately summoned Liu, Zhou, Deng, and Tian. He also invited Chen Boda, the editor in chief of *Red Flag,* knowing that Chen would always take his side. Mao raged against the contract system and instructed Chen Boda to prepare a draft Central Committee resolution to strengthen the collective economy of the people's communes. [65] Chen Yun was absent from this meeting. Mao had met with Chen earlier and expressed his indignation at his plan to divide up the land. "Comrade Mao Zedong was incensed," Chen Yun subsequently recalled. [66]

All of Mao's associates retreated. Chen Yun complained about his poor health. Deng Xiaoping, who just the day before had repeated his favorite phrase about different-colored cats at a Communist Youth League meeting, urgently called the first secretary of its Central Committee to demand that his unfortunate remark be deleted from the stenographic record of his speech.[67]

As always, the cautious Zhou Enlai supported Mao. The Great Helmsman said that Zhou had been taught a lesson when he had opposed "blindly rushing forward" back in 1956–57.[68] Liu Shaoqi also tried to alter course; he began defending collective property passionately just a few days after the "cold shower" that Mao Zedong had administered. On July 18, the Central Committee issued a circular prohibiting propagating family contracts.[69]

Mao continued to rage. He repeatedly summoned first Liu and then Zhou and vented his anger upon them. "I feel that the situation is very serious!! Very unsettled!" one of the Central Committee leaders wrote in his diary in these days, and he underlined these words.[70]

Mao sharply criticized Chen Yun, Deng Zihui, Tian Jiaying, and other Party cadres. "Are you for socialism or for capitalism?" he shouted. "Now some people speak out in favor of introducing the contract system on a national scale, including even dividing up the land. Is the communist party in favor of dividing up the land?"[71]

From the end of July to the end of August, Mao held another Central Committee work conference and tongue-lashed the terrified party officials. "You have also pressured me for a long time," he said menacingly. "Since 1960, one may say, that is, for more than two years. I can also pressure you in return."[72] He simply seethed with rage. "Some persons are suffering from ideological confusion; they have lost their way, they have lost their faith. This is no good," he fulminated. At this conference he raised for the first time the issue of antagonistic classes in socialist society, interpreting the disagreements within the party in class terms. This made his speech truly ominous.

Mao apparently achieved his goal of inspiring terror in his auditors. In his struggle against the "moderates," he had seemingly gone as far as he could go. Now they were all his class enemies, and settling scores with them was just a matter of time. He wanted to warn the waverers just how dangerous a road they were treading in arguing about contracts and other "bourgeois things."

He was incredulous that other communists did not see that the family contracts had resulted in "polarization, corruption, thievery, speculation, the taking of concubines, and usury. On one hand is the growth of wealth, on the other the poverty of the families of military men, heroes who fell in battle, workers, and cadres. . . . Even Khrushchev did not dare to disband the collective farms."

"Counterrevolution still exists," Mao summed up, even raising the specter that the Communist Party might be overthrown if it continued to pander to the bourgeoisie within its ranks. "If people became too choosy," he gloomily concluded, "revolution is necessary."[73]

He had arrived at these conclusions after lengthy deliberation, influenced not only by what had recently occurred in his country and party, but also by growing tension in the international situation. An important factor that had helped shape these views was the Sino-Soviet split. Naturally, Mao blamed the leadership of the CPSU, which he believed had simply degenerated or, to be more precise, had undergone a bourgeois transformation. This was the source of all of Khrushchev's "revisionist" talk about peaceful coexistence between two systems, the possibility of averting war in the present epoch, and peaceful transition from capitalism to socialism. It also explained his flirtation with the American imperialists and the Indian "reactionaries." "The Soviet Union has already existed for several decades," he declared to the participants in the work conference, "and yet revisionism, which serves international capitalism and is, in essence, a counterrevolutionary phenomenon, has appeared there. . . . The bourgeoisie may revive. This is what has happened in the Soviet Union."[74]

Such talk scotched any hope of improving relations with the CPSU. In Mao's mind the USSR now represented what might happen to China if it did not permanently uproot the sprouts of capitalism. In August 1962, he sanctioned the initiation of a massive propaganda campaign against the "Soviet revisionists," the central argument being that the universal striving for material well-being in the USSR had wholly extinguished the revolutionary enthusiasm of the masses. After this, the severance of ties with the CPSU was inevitable.

At the next regular meeting of the Central Committee, which quickly followed the work conference, Mao also raised the possibility that the Communist Party might degenerate. This time, however, he did not loose any thunderbolts and even graciously observed, "If the comrades who have committed mistakes will understand their deficiencies and return to the positions of Marxism-Leninism, we will close ranks with them. . . . There is no need to resort to chopping off heads."

Once more he felt in control since he had chased the opposition into a corner. All that remained was to create a supercharged atmosphere, educate the cadres in an antirevisionist spirit, and administer a decisive blow against all his "enemies" at a time of his choosing. "One can say now with assurance that classes exist in socialist countries," he continued.

After the overthrow of feudalism there was restoration everywhere. . . . This sort of recidivism can occur in socialist countries, too. Thus, Yugoslavia has degenerated, and become revisionist . . . a state ruled by reactionary nationalist elements. In our own country we must grasp, understand, and study this problem. It is necessary to recognize that . . . reactionary classes can bring about restoration. . . . Therefore, starting today we must speak of class struggle every year, every month, every day, at meetings, party congresses, at plenums, at every session, so that with regard to this issue we have a more or less clear Marxist-Leninist line.[75]

This became the main theme of his speeches. Following the plenum, Mao launched a new campaign: *fan xiu, fang xiu* (oppose revisionism from abroad, guard against revisionism at home). It became a component of the mass movement for socialist education.

The countryside became the primary arena for the movement. Because of the contract system, it was there, Mao believed, that the threat of restoration originated. But the urban population was also targeted. Everywhere, both in the provinces and at the center, it was necessary to reject money-grubbing and to substitute moral and revolutionary incentives in place of material ones. Only then, according to Mao, would an inspired people be able "to move mountains."

His immediate circle fully shared his ideas, first among them Jiang Qing, who understood that only by unconditional devotion to Mao could she retain her spouse, who no longer was interested in her as a woman. In late September 1962, Mao first allowed her into the political arena by entrusting her with control over the sphere of culture. Jiang enthusiastically assumed her new role, resolved, like Ibsen's Nora, to strike another blow against bourgeois society. Her goal was to achieve the total revolutionary transformation of "rotten" literature and "degraded" art.

Again, as during the Yan'an period, Kang Sheng became an intimate of the Chairman, who once again assigned him the job of vetting cadres. Mao also relied upon the fanatically loyal Chen Boda, who was ready to provide a Marxist foundation for whatever the Chairman said, no matter how absurd. He found faithful assistants in Shanghai, among them Ke Qingshi, whom Mao had wanted to install as premier back in 1958. In early 1965, he was designated Zhou Enlai's deputy, but this dedicated anti-rightist warrior soon died of pancreatic cancer. But Ke's people were still in Shanghai, including two talented journalists, one of whom, the forty-eight-year-old Zhang Chunqiao, was secretary of the Municipal Committee in charge of propaganda, and the other, the thirty-four-year-old Yao Wenyuan, on the staff of the local party newspaper *Jiefang ribao* (Liberation daily).

Even though he had opposed Mao in the past, Zhou Enlai now demonstrated his selfless devotion to the Chairman. Zhou must have been pleased that the Leader's ire was directed against Liu Shaoqi and his assistants. He bore an ancient grudge against Liu, rooted in jealousy. Each of them had wanted to be second in the pecking order under Mao. Sometimes their rivalry assumed comic form. Ivan Kovalev, Stalin's former representative in China, recalled, "Zhou Enlai and Liu Shaoqi really disliked each other. . . . It was rather comical: if I toasted Liu at a banquet after Mao then Zhou would stalk out of the hall, and vice versa."[76]

Everyone on Mao's team occupied a definite place. First in the lineup was Lin Biao, the minister of defense, who since the late 1950s had been turning the army into a "School of Mao Zedong Thought." In 1961 the PLA newspaper *Jiefangjun ribao* (People's Liberation Army daily) began to publish a quotation from Mao every day as an epigraph. Soldiers were ordered to cut out these epigraphs and compile their own collections of Mao quotations, which they then studied assiduously. In January 1964 the General Political Administration of the PLA issued the first mimeographed book of quotations, a little red book or, as it was called in China, the *hongbaoshu* (the precious red book). It included 200 quotations arranged in twenty-three sections. Then in May 1964, a new, expanded edition was published with 326 quotations in thirty chapters, and in August 1965, yet another edition with 427 quotations grouped in thirty-three chapters. The third edition became a classic and more than a billion copies were printed in the next eleven years. The dimensions of this 270-page pocket-sized book were 4.1 by 3 inches. (Some editions were slightly larger, 5.1 by 3.5 inches.)

Other forms of Maoist propaganda were developed in the army, including the cult of the rank-and-file model soldier, the communist Lei Feng, whose core virtue was his boundless loyalty to Chairman Mao. Orphaned as a child, Lei owed everything in his life to the Communist Party. Entering the army, he became a model soldier and ideal citizen. In August 1962, at the age of twenty-two, he died as the result of an accident. To enumerate his "feats" would exhaust our patience. Among them were remitting his scanty salary to the parents of his comrades in arms, serving tea to officers and new recruits, and washing the feet of his comrades who were tired out from long marches, as well as washing and darning their socks and bedclothes. Above all, what made him a national hero was the diary in which he poured out his deep feelings of love for his motherland, the party, and most of all for Chairman Mao. From his earliest childhood he had dreamed of the "great friend of all orphans," and the first five Chinese characters that Lei learned in school were *Mao zhuxi wansui* (Long live Chairman Mao).

Deeply moved when he was told about the diary, on March 5, 1963, Mao ordered everyone to learn from Lei Feng and from the PLA.[77] He was satisfied with Lin Biao, who had transformed the army into the most reliable stronghold of the Chairman. The life of the country became militarized. Political departments modeled on those of the army were set up in various institutions.[78]

Jiang Qing also scored some great successes. The "revolutionary operas" and "ballets" that had been created and then imposed on the artistic bureaucrats squeezed out the "wretched feudal" productions. The "progressive" movement for "socialist education" continually gathered steam, while in the economy, thanks to the efforts of Zhou and Chen Boda, collective property was once more strongly affirmed. No more leaps were attempted and there were no more natural disasters, but the peasants, now aggregated in production brigades rather than the mammoth communes, apparently were reconciled to their fate. For three straight years (1962–64) the grain harvest was fairly good. In 1964 an epochal event occurred that signaled China's debut as a potential world power. A successful test of a nuclear weapon was carried out at 3 P.M. on October 16 at the Malan Testing Ground, in the Lop Nor desert of Xinjiang. The entire country celebrated this great victory.

Now everything seemed to be going Mao's way. The country was developing, if slowly, and the masses were immersed in the struggle against the danger of capitalist restoration. The "moderates," whom the Leader now called "the capitalist roaders," were fast losing ground. With Mao's encouragement, the cult of the Chairman was in full flower, especially after the inglorious fall of Khrushchev, who had been ousted in October 1964 at a plenum of the Central Committee of the CPSU. Mao thought that one of the reasons for Khrushchev's downfall was that, unlike Stalin, the Soviet leader had no cult of personality at all.[79]

In these eventful years Mao experienced ever-growing psychological agitation. Like a beast tirelessly tracking its prey, he burned with lethal desire. That Liu, Deng, and other apostates had done nothing "wrong" for a long time only strengthened his fervor. He viewed their loyalty as a sign of weakness and therefore he did everything in his power to isolate his former friends. Each of their initiatives, even if it was in accord with his own views, he looked upon with a jaundiced eye as an attempt by his "enemies" to strengthen their authority.

During this tempestuous period he made a new personal conquest of lasting importance. At the end of 1962, in the compartment of his special railroad car he met a young woman who soon became his closest lover, and then his most trusted secretary. Her name was Zhang Yufeng ("Jasper Phoenix"), and she was then just eighteen years old. Mao generally loved young girls, but he was particularly taken by her. There was something unusual about her. She was naïve and shy like many young Chinese girls, yet she possessed a very strong character and was quick-witted and sharp-tongued. Most of all, she was a real beauty. She melted the heart of the old man.

She came from the town of Mudanjiang in the north of China and served as a conductor on Mao's special train. She was introduced to Mao by his head bodyguard, who knew of his chief's passion for young girls. The Chairman asked her to write her given name and family name, but Yufeng's hand trembled from agitation. So he wrote the characters himself and showed them to her. She blushed. Then the chief bodyguard asked the Chairman whether he would like Comrade Zhang to service his compartment. Mao nodded. The affair quickly assumed the form of an impetuous romance.[80] There can be no doubt whatsoever that the eighteen-year-old girl was flattered. Could such a thing be imagined? She had become the lover of the Great Helmsman himself! So what if he was nearing seventy and false iron teeth glittered in his mouth? His sexual energy was enormous.

In May 1965, reinvigorated by his love, Mao decided to embark on a journey by rail to the places from his heroic youth. Preparing for his final battle against the "moderates" whom he found increasingly irritating, he set off for the Jinggang Mountains, where thirty-eight years earlier he had led a guerrilla war.[81] The journey clearly had symbolic significance for him. Gazing at the eternal green mountains, he ecstatically composed some new verses:

> *A long-time cherished hope:*
> *to fly through clouds*
> *and once more visit Chingkangshan [Jinggang Mountains].*
> *Coming a thousand miles*
> *to search for the old place,*
> *all changed by a new look.*
> *Orioles singing, swallows dancing, everywhere,*
> *flowing water bubbling,*
> *tall trees climbing into the sky,*
> *Huangyangchieh [Huangyangjie]'s paths, then deadly,*
> *now not even steep.*
>
> *Wind and thunder were violent,*
> *powerful flags were waving.*
> *Now unshakeable on the earth,*
> *the passing of thirty years*
> *a moment's snap of the thumb.*
>
> *Now we can pick up the moon*
> *in the nine-leveled sky,*
> *and catch turtles in all five oceans.*
> *Triumphant return with talk and laughter:*
> *nothing difficult in this world*
> *if you can keep climbing.*[82]

Mao had reason to be proud. He had become the ruler of a great country. With a snap of his fingers he could command the obedience of hundreds of millions of people. But the higher he reached on the pinnacle of power the less peace of mind he enjoyed. He was incapable of understanding the wisdom of the Daoists, who said that only "emptiness and stillness reached throughout 'Heaven and Earth.'" As the ancient Daoist philosopher Zhuangzi said, "[T]he kings of the world in ancient times . . . though their abilities outshone all within the four seas . . . did not of themselves act."[83]

32

"THE DISMISSAL OF
HAI RUI FROM OFFICE"

Returning to Beijing in June 1965, Mao encountered disorder. The Socialist Education campaign uncovered scandalous instances of "bourgeois degeneration" in most party organizations. In at least half of them "class enemies" had seized power. Mao loyalists had been informing him of the "threatening situation" at the local levels since late 1964, and now it had come to a head. This was inevitable since every party official able to fathom the Helmsman's mood reported up the chain of command only that information he knew Mao wanted to hear. Such was the totalitarian system Mao himself had created. By an irony of fate he became its greatest victim.

The world of terrible illusions in which he lived aroused him to real actions. Even though he was past seventy, he was quite unlike Confucius, who said, "At seventy, I follow all the desires of my heart without breaking any rules." This was not the only way in which Mao differed from the great sage. Confucius had also said, "At sixty, my ear was attuned."[1] The Chairman was unable to do this to the end of his days.

In Beijing he had a long conversation with Jiang Qing about cultural affairs. Earlier she had already convinced him of the need to unmask as "counterrevolutionary" a play by Wu Han about a courageous and noble sixteenth-century official, Hai Rui, who had dared to speak the truth to a depraved Ming dynasty emperor. Wu Han had written this play in January 1961, and it had been playing to small audiences in China ever since. In it Hai Rui addressed these words to the emperor: "In the past you did some good things, but what are you doing now? Rectify your mistakes! Let the people live in happiness. You have committed too many mistakes, yet you believe that you are always correct and therefore reject all criticism." Jiang Qing believed that Wu Han was drawing a parallel between the cases of Hai Rui and Peng Dehuai. The purpose of his "malicious" play was to strike at the authority of the Great Helmsman. Other

Chinese theatergoers, however, saw no "criminal" intent in the play and did not consider Wu Han, a loyal follower of Mao, perfidious.

Jiang Qing had early doubts about the play, but neither Mao nor anyone else supported her initially. Even Kang Sheng was skeptical of Jiang's claim. Everyone knew that Mao was fond of Hai Rui. In Hai Rui he saw himself, "an honest and upright revolutionary" who fought against the vices of the degenerate classes. In late 1961, Mao even presented Wu Han an autographed copy of the third volume of his *Selected Works*.[2]

By 1965, however, Mao had begun seeing enemies everywhere; now Jiang Qing succeeded in arousing his suspicions about Wu Han. The scholar and playwright was also the deputy mayor of Beijing and a direct subordinate of Peng Zhen. Peng, in turn, was one of the closest associates of Liu Shaoqi and Deng Xiaoping. In the Chairman's fevered brain, all four of them—Wu Han, Peng Zhen, Liu Shaoqi, and Deng Xiaoping—were united in a single "malevolent band."

At the very end of December 1964, Mao had vented his discontent with Liu and Deng at a Politburo Work Conference. His emotional outburst was occasioned by the fact that on the eve of the conference Deng had suggested Mao not take part in it. There was nothing unusual about this suggestion, since at the time Mao was feeling indisposed and Deng felt sorry for him. But Mao had shown up in the conference hall anyway and had spoken, as always, about class struggle. He had even said that at present the main contradiction in the countryside was the one between those in authority taking the capitalist road on one hand, and the broad masses on the other. Liu attempted to oppose this view because he had long since feared that the struggle against revisionism was exceeding all limits and that he himself might be targeted. He sensed that the Leader was turning against him. Mao became so incensed that he decided to make a scene. In a few days he arrived at the meeting with the texts of the Constitution of the PRC and of the Party Statutes and shouted at his comrades that he had here two books and they both granted him the right to express himself, one as a citizen and the other as a party member. But, according to Mao, "one of you" (Deng Xiaoping) did not allow him into this meeting, and the other (Liu Shaoqi) did not let him speak.[3]

Soon after this he recalled Jiang Qing's comment about Wu Han. Finally, everything fell into place. Wu Han wrote a play on orders from Peng Zhen, Liu Shaoqi, and Deng Xiaoping, who were dreaming of crushing me! he must have thought. Several years later he would tell Edgar Snow that the decision to replace Liu was made in January 1965, because Liu "had strenuously opposed" the ongoing Socialist Education campaign aimed at the removal of "those in the Party in authority" who were "taking the capitalist road." At this time, based on what Mao had told him, Snow wrote, "a great deal of power—over propaganda work within the provincial and local party committees, and especially within the Peking [Beijing] Municipal Party Committee—had been out of his control." Therefore, he decided "there was need for more personality cult, in order to stimulate the masses to dismantle the anti-Mao Party bureaucracy."[4]

In February 1965 Mao sent Jiang Qing to Shanghai "to arrange for the publication of an article criticizing the play *The Dismissal of Hai Rui from Office.*"[5] His faithful wife carried out her assignment with help from local party journalist Yao Wenyuan. The article went through eleven drafts that Jiang Qing and the Shanghai leftist Zhang Chunqiao had secretly delivered to Mao in Beijing by special courier.[6] Only toward the end of the summer did he find "it mostly to his liking." He delivered the final text to Jiang Qing and suggested that other leading figures on the Central Committee read it, but his wife said, "It's better to publish the article as is. In my opinion, it's just as well if Comrades Zhou Enlai and Kang Sheng are not given a chance to read it." Jiang was afraid that if Zhou and Kang got hold of the article then Liu Shaoqi and Deng Xiaoping would also want to read it.[7] They decided to proceed as Jiang suggested. The article, which appeared on November 10, 1965, in the Shanghai newspaper *Wenhui bao* (Literary reports), initiated a new mass movement that was soon dubbed the Great Proletarian Cultural Revolution.

Mao had conceived the idea of a radical revolution in the sphere of culture in December 1963 while reading a report by Jiang Qing's confederate the Shanghai leader Ke Qingshi, who painted a dire picture of the cultural situation. Mao drafted a resolution asserting that "scoundrels" in the cultural realm were propagating feudal and bourgeois rather than socialist values.[8] He had earlier expressed his dismay that creative intellectuals, including party members, were avoiding class struggle. Not until early July 1964, however, did he demand that a special Five-Member Group be organized in the Central Committee to deal with cultural revolutionary affairs.[9] Wishing to avoid conflict with the Chairman, the "moderates" backed this idea, and the group was headed by Peng Zhen, a supporter of Liu Shaoqi; Kang Sheng represented the hard-line Maoists. However, Mao was dissatisfied with the group. Peng and his associates tried to limit party interference in the sphere of culture by organizing academic discussions, but the Chairman was convinced that a class purge of the creative circles was imperative.

All summer Mao had kept the draft article about Wu Han a secret. He did not consider publishing the article in Beijing because he did not yet want to precipitate an open conflict. He intended to strike Wu, Peng Zhen, and their behind-the-scenes supporters Liu Shaoqi and Deng Xiaoping on the sly. Liu and Deng seemed oblivious to the Great Helmsman's mood and may have considered themselves invulnerable. In late September, at the new meeting of the cultural affairs group, Peng Zhen declared, "In truth, all persons are equal, regardless of whether they are on the party Central Committee or [are] the Chairman."[10] Mao could not forgive this. He soon signaled Yao Wenyuan to publish the article. Yao condemned Wu Han's drama as a weapon in the struggle of the bourgeoisie against the dictatorship of the proletariat and the socialist revolution. In Mao's China such an accusation was the equivalent of a death sentence.

In November 1965, two days after publication of the article, Mao set out for Shanghai, the leftist fiefdom, stopping in Tianjin, Jinan, Xuzhou, Bengfu (Anhui province), and Nanjing. He was very dissatisfied with the local leaders whom he met en route. Everyone enthused over the "enormous successes" achieved during the Socialist Education movement. No one was gripped by the struggle against revisionism or worried about the danger of capitalist restoration.

Only in Shanghai was the air saturated with radicalism. Yet even there he could not slacken his efforts. The news from Beijing was alarming. Peng Zhen's first response to the article in *Literary Reports* was to prohibit its republication in the central press and reframe the discussion of the play as an academic matter. Wu Han replied to the Shanghai journalist's critique by pointing out a number of factual inaccuracies in the *Literary Reports* article. "I am not afraid of Yao Wenyuan's criticism," Wu Han wrote, "but it seems to me that pseudo-criticism of this sort, which is decked out with false labels, is an improper form of behavior. Who [after this] will be bold enough to write anything? Who will dare to study history?" [11]

After reading this response, Mao could not fall asleep. Peng Zhen and the Beijing Municipal Committee, which controlled the central press, refused to surrender. The struggle was intensifying. "I could do nothing in Peking [Beijing]," Mao later recalled.[12] Peng Zhen and his supporters failed to understand who was actually behind Yao Wenyuan. But Zhou Enlai intervened in the matter, informing Peng that Mao intended to publish Yao's work as a separate brochure if Beijing's mass media continued to ignore it.[13] Only then, on November 29, did *People's Daily* reprint the malicious libel, adding its own commentary, which, in the spirit of Peng Zhen, referred to it as part of a polemic among scholars.

Now Mao celebrated. He composed heroic verses about a bird that yearns for the storm.

> *Unfurling his wings Kun Peng**
> *traverses ninety thousand* li,†
> *lets loose a whirlwind everywhere he goes.*
> *Gripping Heaven in his talons*
> *the giant bird surveys the world below.*

---

* Kun Peng (the roc) is a gigantic bird referred to in Chapter One of *Zhuangzi*.

† *Li* is a traditional Chinese unit of distance, an equivalent of 1,640.42 feet.

The roar of cannons shakes the earth.
Swirling crows blacken the sky.
A frightened sparrow cowers in a bush,
"A holocaust! What's going on?" she cries.
"I really must fly off."
"And may I ask, where to?"
"To the Fairyland above
*where three drew up a pact last fall.**
Besides, there's much to eat,
Potatoes roasted with a side of beef."†
"You've farted quite enough you clown,
do you not know the world is turning upside down?"[14]

Indeed, in the world that Mao inhabited, heaven and earth had really changed places. He desired to turn the whole country upside down.

His mood uplifted, Mao set out from Shanghai for Hangzhou, where, on the banks of placid Xili Lake, he could finally relax. Now everything was going his way. After ten days, however, he took to the road again, unable to sit still. He thirsted for combat. In Shanghai he held another meeting of the Politburo Standing Committee, then returned to Hangzhou, where Chen Boda, Kang Sheng, and other close confidants awaited him. Then he traveled to Lushan, Canton, and Nanning before returning to Hangzhou after New Year. In early February he left for Wuhan via Changsha.[15]

There, in the Donghu Guest House on the shore of East Lake in Wuhan, he received four members of the Five-Member Cultural Revolution Group: Peng Zhen, Kang Sheng, Lu Dingyi, head of the Propaganda Department of the Central Committee, and Wu Lengxi, director of the Xinhua News Agency and the editor in chief of *People's Daily,* who brought him their "Outline Report Concerning the Current Academic Discussion." One of the participants described the meeting:

> Mao asked Peng Zhen a question, "Is Wu Han really an anti-party and anti-socialist [element]?" But before Peng Zhen could reply, Kang Sheng jumped in, saying that Wu Han's play was an "anti-party, anti-socialist venomous weed." No one dared contradict him. "Of course, if anyone has a contrary point of view, they should express it," Mao

---

* Mao is referring to the treaty banning nuclear testing in the atmosphere, outer space, and under water signed in Moscow by the U.S., USSR, and Great Britain on August 5, 1963.

† Mao is mocking Khrushchev's description in April 1964 that communism is a plateful of goulash for everybody.

said in the silence that followed. . . . Finally, Peng Zhen spoke. He wanted to defend the document that he had brought with him.[16]

He said, "I think that we must proceed from the Chairman's instructions to let one hundred schools contend and one hundred flowers bloom when it comes to discussing the academic issues raised in the play." Lu Dingyi supported Peng Zhen. Mao summed up: "You people work it out. I don't need to see it."[17]

Neither Peng nor Lu nor Wu, believing that Mao approved their theses, was aware this was a trap. Right after their conversation with the Chairman, with light hearts they made their way to the antiquarian bookshops for which Wuchang and Hankou were famous.[18] Several days later the Central Committee adopted and disseminated the theses classified "top secret."

Now Mao, again seized by a passion for combat, sprang into action. In mid-May, piqued at Peng Zhen, he approved a "Summary of the Army Forum on Literature and Art Work" prepared by Jiang Qing, based on a February PLA conference that Lin Biao had sanctioned.[19] Unlike the theses in Peng Zhen's report, this document spoke of the "anti-party, anti-socialist black line" opposed to Mao Zedong Thought, propagated by literature and art officials since the founding of the PRC. "Such theories as 'Write the Truth' are characteristic of this line," the "Summary" emphasized. It called for "resolutely carrying out a great socialist revolution on the cultural front to liquidate this black line completely."[20]

In mid-March, Mao held an enlarged meeting of the Politburo Standing Committee to which he invited Liu Shaoqi, Zhou Enlai, and provincial, autonomous region, and province-level municipal first party secretaries. Some Central Committee members also attended. Many were shocked by what they heard. Not only did Mao attack Peng Zhen, Wu Han, and Wu Lengxi for disseminating bourgeois culture, but he also called for unleashing class struggle in all of the universities, high schools, and primary schools throughout the whole country. "Let the students . . . make a ruckus. We don't need blind faith or restraint. We need a new intelligentsia, new points of view, a new creative approach. What we need, then, is for the students to overthrow the professors."[21]

A week later, in Hangzhou, Mao Zedong told his closest collaborators, including Jiang Qing and Kang Sheng, that the Beijing Municipal Committee and the Propaganda Department of the Central Committee were defending bad people and not supporting the leftists. "The situation in the Beijing Municipal Committee is well-described in the proverb, 'A needle can't be stuck into it nor a drop of water permeate it,'" he said. "It needs to be dissolved. As for the Propaganda Department, it is the 'Palace of the King of Hell.' We need to overthrow the King of Hell and set the little devils free." Again he branded Wu Han "anti-party and anti-socialist." He also criticized Deng Tuo, the former editor in chief of *People's Daily*, and Liao Mosha, the former head of the United Front Work Department of the Beijing Municipal Committee, for publishing satirical feuilletons in the capital press, many of which, incidentally, were coauthored with Wu Han.[22]

Pressured by Mao, the Central Committee circulated Jiang Qing's "Summary." Six days later the Chairman convened an enlarged plenum of the Standing Committee of the Politburo in Hangzhou at which he demanded that Peng Zhen's report be repudiated and the Five-Member Cultural Revolution Group be disbanded, to be replaced by a new group attached to the Politburo Standing Committee.[23] Wang Renzhong, the first secretary of the Hubei Party Committee, who participated in the meeting, wrote down the Chairman's angry words in his diary: "Revisionism has surfaced not only in the cultural sphere, but also in the party, the government, and the army. Revisionism is particularly rife in the party and the army."[24]

Mao had no intention of returning to Beijing now, so he asked Liu Shaoqi of all people to convene an enlarged plenum of the Politburo in Zhongnanhai to implement these decisions. "The west wind [from the 'revisionist' Soviet Union] is blowing fallen leaves into Chang'an [the capital of ancient China, in the given situation a reference to Beijing]," he said to his associates. "If we don't sweep them up, the dust will not disappear by itself."[25] Trying to protect himself, Liu betrayed Peng; in May his loyal associate was removed from all his posts and accused of disseminating the "bourgeois" slogan of "Everybody is equal before the truth." In late April Peng was placed under house arrest.[26]

Lu Dingyi was simultaneously purged, not only because he had supported Peng Zhen in Wuhan during the discussion of the April theses. In early 1966, Ye Qun, Lin Biao's wife, discovered that Lu's spouse, Yan Weibing, whom she had long considered a "comrade in arms," actually hated her with a passion. Whether this hatred derived from envy or some other reason is unknown. (Later Lu Dingyi would assert that his wife suffered from schizophrenia.) Beginning in 1960, right after "Comrade Ye" became the head of her husband's office in the Ministry of Defense, "Comrade Yan" began to inundate her and other members of Lin Biao's family with anonymous letters. Most asserted that Ye Qun had always been dissolute and had repeatedly cuckolded Lin Biao. In letters to Lin Biao's daughter Doudou, Yan Weibing asserted that Ye Qun was not her biological mother.

Infuriated, Ye Qun and Lin Biao demanded that the responsible authorities punish the slanderer and handed over several dozen of these anonymous letters to the Ministry of Public Security, which initiated a criminal case against Lu Dingyi's wife. On April 28, 1966, she was arrested on charges of "counterrevolutionary activity." After several days the unfortunate Lu, like Peng Zhen, was put under house arrest.[27]

At Mao's insistence they were lumped together in a single "anti-party" group along with Luo Ruiqing, the chief of the General Staff, and Yang Shangkun, head of the General Affairs Department of the Central Committee, who had been fired earlier for entirely unrelated reasons.[28] Aggregating them was intended to demonstrate that the unfolding Cultural Revolution was aimed not only at bureaucrats in the fields of culture and propaganda, but also against other "representatives of the bourgeoisie who had infiltrated the party, the government, and the army," in other words, against everyone who was prepared "to seize power at the first convenient opportunity and transform the dictatorship of the proletariat into a dictatorship of the bourgeoisie."

On May 16, at the enlarged Politburo meeting, Lin Biao grilled Lu Dingyi: "You and your wife conspired for a long time and slandered Comrade Ye Qun and my whole family, inundating us with anonymous letters. What were you trying to accomplish? Speak!"

Everyone present turned toward Lu. Before the session had begun, each of them had found on the table in front of them a sheet of paper written in Lin's hand: "I certify that (1) when she and I got married, Ye Qun was a pure virgin, and she has remained faithful ever since; (2) Ye Qun and Wang Shiwei [a writer executed in Yan'an] had never been lovers; (3) Laohu [a son of Lin Biao] and Doudou are Ye Qun's and my own flesh and blood; and (4) Yan Weibing's counterrevolutionary letters contain nothing but rumors. Lin Biao, May 14, 1966."[29]

The terrified Lu Dingyi hastened to disown his once greatly beloved wife: "Yan Weibing [indeed] wrote anonymous letters, but I knew [nothing of this]. She did not discuss them with me, did not give them to me to read, and I suspected nothing."

"You are lying," Lin Biao exploded, banging his fist on the table. "How could you not know what your wife was up to?"

"Is it really so unusual for husbands not to know what their wives are up to?" Lu Dingyi, perplexed, finally blurted out, barely conscious of what he was saying.

Everyone sat rigidly, but Lin Biao lost his head entirely. "I will shoot you!" he roared. Following this Kang Sheng pronounced the verdict "Lu Dingyi is a spy."[30]

Kang also accused Peng Zhen, the main figure among the "four traitors," of espionage, asserting that Peng had maintained secret ties with Chiang Kai-shek's agents throughout the entire existence of the PRC. He also listed Peng Zhen's father-in-law as "a big traitor."[31]

On May 16, the same enlarged meeting of the Politburo, acting in the name of the Central Committee, adopted the text of a special communiqué to party organizations throughout the country announcing the disbanding of the Group of Five and the establishment of a new Cultural Revolution Group directly under the Standing Committee of the Politburo. This communiqué for the first time called upon the entire party to "hold high the great banner of the proletarian cultural revolution."

A few paragraphs of this communiqué, including that on the establishment of a new Cultural Revolution Group directly under the Standing Committee of the Politburo, were written by Mao himself. The most important was the following:

> Those representatives of the bourgeoisie who have sneaked into the Party, the government, the army and various cultural circles are a bunch of counter-revolutionary revisionists. Once conditions are ripe, they will seize political power and turn the dictatorship of the proletariat into a dictatorship of the bourgeoisie. Some of them we have already seen through, others we have not. Some are still trusted by us and are being trained as our successors, persons like Khrushchev, for example, who are still nestling beside us. Party committees at all levels must pay full attention to this matter.[32]

This communiqué invited popular involvement in the Cultural Revolution, its distinguishing characteristic. Heretofore all party purges had occurred behind tightly closed doors.[33] Now the Chairman had granted the people the right to judge "revisionist party members," including "big party tyrants." Yet no one knew just whom the Great Helmsman had in mind when talking about persons like Khrushchev who "are being trained as our successors" and "who are still nestling beside us."

Everyone knew that Mao's heir was Liu Shaoqi, but no one imagined him to be a traitor, except, perhaps, a few persons from the Chairman's inner circle. Kang Sheng recalled: "On May 16, 1966, Chairman Mao stressed: revisionists, reactionaries, and traitors are hiding among us and enjoying our friends' trust. At that time, many cadres did not understand what Chairman Mao really meant, thinking that the allusion was to Luo [Ruiqing] and Peng [Zhen]. But in fact, Peng Zhen had been exposed. No one dared to think of who were traitors among us."[34] "I," Kang Sheng added, "did not sense [either] that the reference was to Liu Shaoqi, but had only a very superficial understanding of this important instruction from Chairman Mao."[35] Zhang Chunqiao, the Shanghai leftist, said the same: "When the movement began, quite a few people had a very poor understanding of—and responded very ineffectively to—the Chairman's words, in particular the passage about 'persons like Khrushchev, for example, who are still nestling beside us.' At that time, I did not really understand this passage. I could only think of Peng Zhen and did not fully anticipate Liu Shaoqi."[36]

Mao considered his thesis about "China's Khrushchev" the main point of the communiqué and quickly informed Kang Sheng and Chen Boda. He wanted his communiqué to "explode" not only the party but Chinese society as a whole.

Kang Sheng, enlightened by Mao, later explained:

The Great Cultural Revolution originated from the idea that classes and class struggle still exist in the socialist system. This idea is both theoretical and empirical. Experiences have shown that even in the Soviet Union—the homeland of Lenin—the Bolshevik party adopted revisionism. Our experiences over the past 20 years in building a proletarian dictatorship, and especially the recent incidents in Eastern Europe where bourgeois liberalism and capitalism were restored, also pose the question of how to conduct a revolution in the context of the proletarian dictatorship and under socialist conditions. To solve the problem, Chairman Mao himself initiated the Great Cultural Revolution in China.

According to Kang Sheng, the Great Helmsman initially proposed a three-year plan for the Cultural Revolution. The task of the first year (June 1966–June 1967) was "mobilization of the people," that of the second year (June 1967–June 1968) was "to gain significant victories," and that of the last year (until June 1969) was "to conclude the Revolution." "As for a great revolution like this," the faithful adherent of Mao claimed, "three years is not a long period of time."[37]

At a Politburo meeting on May 18, 1966, Lin Biao delivered a major report on the Cultural Revolution. For the first time he implied criticism of Liu Shaoqi, "who has never publicized the thoughts of Mao Zedong."[38] Kang Sheng raised the question of changing the term "Mao Zedong Thought" to "Mao Zedongism." However, Mao again rejected this change.

The country plunged into chaos, yet Mao was unconcerned. On the contrary, he himself stirred the pot. Apparently the aging Leader was energized by directing the mass movement. He staked everything on this game, feeling that he was surrounded by enemies. In order to crush the "conspirators" he again turned to the people. This time he issued the call to the inexperienced youth—students in colleges and technical institutes as well as middle schools—who were fanatically devoted to him. In mid-March 1966, he had already concluded that students should "overthrow their professors." Now, after "unmasking" Peng Zhen and other intraparty capitalist roaders, he clearly sensed that the enthusiasm of the youthful students was higher than ever before. All he had to do was give the signal and a revolutionary conflagration would envelop the educational institutions. He received daily reports from the omniscient public security organs, the Shanghai branch of the Central Cultural Revolution Group, headed by Zhang Chunqiao, and from student activists. One student who, incidentally, was the son of a cadre, wrote: "Who could have supposed that such old party stalwarts such as Peng Zhen and Luo Ruiqing, were actually dangerous persons? Now I feel that we can trust only Chairman Mao, only the Central Committee (I am talking about the Party), we must suspect everyone and everybody, and if someone fails to carry out Chairman Mao's directives, that person must be attacked."[39] This "cannon fodder" would become his new guard. Not a single bureaucrat "taking the capitalist road" could possibly withstand their powerful pressure.

For a long time he had been pondering the need to draw young people more deeply into "a genuine socialist revolution." He considered "class struggle" the main focus and most of the subjects taught in higher educational institutions "harmful." Therefore, the number of classroom hours devoted to lectures should be sharply curtailed and instead of having students "listen to all kinds of rubbish," they should spend their time actively participating in "class battles." "The present method [of education] cripples talent, cripples the youth," he asserted indignantly. "I do not approve of this. A stop must be put to reading so many books!" He also disliked the system of academic exams. "The current method of conducting exams [treats students] like the enemy," he said, referring to the method of administering tests according to the rule "If I can't do it, you can write, and I will copy it from you. There's nothing terrible in that." Some exams, he believed, should be done away with entirely. "The current system of education, of programs, methodology, methods of administering exams all need to be changed, because they cripple people," he summed up at a meeting more than two years before the Cultural Revolution.[40]

He also broached this theme in a letter to Lin Biao dated May 7, 1966, nine days before the Politburo's communiqué announcing the beginning of the Cultural Revolution.[41] In sum, purging educational institutions of the "capitalist roaders" and mobilizing youth to take part in "class struggle" became one of the main tasks of the newly organized Central Cultural Revolution Group. As its head, Mao appointed Chen Boda, with Jiang Qing as a deputy. Kang Sheng was an adviser to the group.

Kang dispatched his wife to Peking University, where one of her acquaintances, Nie Yuanzi, served as secretary to the party committee of the Department of Philosophy. Kang's wife incited Nie to mobilize several students to criticize the Municipal Party Committee and the party leadership of Beida, as Chinese habitually referred to Peking University. The forty-five-year-old Nie jumped at the chance and on May 25, with six students, she posted a *dazibao* (big character poster) on the dining room wall. She accused several leaders of the University Work Department of the Beijing Municipal Committee as well as the rector of Beida, who was also the secretary of the Beida party committee, of "carrying out a revisionist line that was aimed against the Central Committee and Mao Zedong Thought."[42] In terms of the prevailing party norms, this was an insurrection. But Nie and her students, of course, had nothing to fear; they were backed by the Cultural Revolution Group.

As soon as he received the text of the *dazibao* Kang Sheng immediately printed and sent it to Mao, who was still in Hangzhou. Mao immediately praised this calumny as "the first Marxist-Leninist *dazibao*," ordering Kang Sheng and Chen Boda to disseminate it via the mass media. He wrote to them: "To Comrades Kang Sheng and Boda! It is very important that this text be broadcast in its entirety by the Xinhua News Agency and published in all the nation's newspapers. Now the smashing of the reactionary stronghold that is Peking University can begin. Mao Zedong. June 1."[43] A couple of hours later, he phoned both of his confederates in Beijing to add that the *dazibao* was a manifesto of the Beijing Commune of the 1960s and was "even more significant than the Paris Commune."[44] By then Chen had already dispatched a so-called work team to the editorial offices of *People's Daily* to take over the newspaper. Mao had long expressed dissatisfaction with this paper, saying that no one should read it because it was under the influence of Liu Shaoqi, Deng Xiaoping, and Peng Zhen.[45] Now, finally, it was in the hands of orthodox Maoists who also began to exercise control over the Xinhua News Agency. So Chen had no problem implementing the Leader's instructions.[46]

Liu, Deng, and many other Politburo leaders were nonplussed. In the Chairman's absence, they simply did not know what to do. Their consternation was increased by the fact that upon Mao's demand the Beijing garrison had been bolstered with two more divisions from the Ministry of Public Security that Lin Biao had ordered not to confront the revolutionary students.[47] The armed forces wholly supported the Chairman, and the leftist youth had nothing to fear.

Meanwhile, marking time, Liu and Deng slowly reorganized the Beijing Municipal Committee and replaced the rector of Beida. These actions immediately echoed throughout the whole country. Students at many institutions of higher education followed Nie Yuanzi's example by attacking their own rectors and party committees. The universities were seized by an epidemic of *dazibao* and students stopped attending class.

Regaining a grip on themselves, on June 9, Liu and Deng along with Zhou, Chen Boda, Kang Sheng, and Tao Zhu, the new head of the CC Propaganda Department, left for Hangzhou to persuade Mao to return to Beijing. But Mao refused. Then they sought his permission to send party work teams to all universities throughout the country to "reestablish order,"[48] a suggestion that Chen Boda, who was taking part in the conversation, opposed. Mao was noncommittal. He behaved exactly as he had in his meeting with Peng Zhen in Wuhan. "[T]hey may be sent, they may not be sent. But they should not be dispatched hastily," he asserted inscrutably.[49] As before, he simply wanted to provide his "enemies" an opportunity to emerge in the open. He acted according to the old principle "Let everything repulsive crawl completely out since if they come out only half-way, they can hide themselves again."[50] It is amazing that such experienced politicians as Liu and Deng did not see through this.

Perplexed, they returned to Beijing, where they immediately took two contradictory decisions: on one side, they "temporarily, for six months" terminated study at all schools and universities throughout the country, canceling academic exams, and on the other, they acknowledged as correct the dispatch of work teams to all the universities to "restore order." "The CC considers that the measures adopted by the work team at Peking University with regard to the disturbances are correct and timely," they asserted. "The same measures adopted at Beida may be applied in any organization where similar occurrences appear."[51] Soon more than ten thousand persons were included in work teams in Beijing and other districts throughout China.[52]

They could not have committed a greater mistake. This is precisely what Mao Zedong needed in order to accuse his "enemies" of "suppressing" the masses. He understood that no sooner would the work teams appear on campuses than the rabble-rousing leftists would stage provocations, after which clashes between the two sides would develop into bloody encounters. Anticipating this, from his lofty heights he observed the events unfolding below. "A single *dazibao* at Peking University ignited the conflagration of the Cultural Revolution!" he exulted.[53]

In the middle of June he left Hangzhou for his ancestral home, Shaoshan, but he spent only eleven days there. By the end of the month he was already back in Wuhan, where he again lodged at the Donghu Guest House on the shore of East Lake. It was there amid the peace and quiet, under the shade of the cherry trees, enjoying the cool light breeze, that he finally decided the time had come to strike a decisive blow against the "black gang of capitalist roaders who were ensconced in the leadership of the communist party." On July 8 he revealed his rebellious thoughts in a letter to his wife in which he welcomed "chaos":

> Complete disorder under Heaven will lead to universal order. This repeats itself every seven or eight years. All sorts of vermin will crawl out into the open. They cannot help doing this, because it is determined by their class nature. . . . Our task now in the whole party and the whole country is to basically overthrow the rightists (it is impossible to do it completely). After seven or eight years we will again start a movement to clean out the vermin. It will be necessary to clean them out many times.[54]

He sent this letter to Jiang Qing in Beijing and then wanted once more to surprise the Chinese people and indeed the whole world. In his seventy-second year he decided to take one of his periodic swims in the Yangzi River.

He entered its waters on July 16. Of course, he did not try to swim across the great river, but as he had done before he swam with its mighty current, which carried him a distance of some nine miles. The whole "swim" took just one hour and five minutes. But it made millions of Chinese immeasurably happy. The Xinhua News Agency reported: "On July 16, 1966, the Great Leader of the Chinese people Chairman Mao Zedong with a favoring wind rippling the waves took a swim in the Yangzi River. In an hour and five minutes he swam about fifteen kilometers. . . . The joyful news . . . quickly flew all over Wuhan. The whole city was overjoyed, and the news passed from mouth to mouth. The people said, 'Our Beloved Leader Chairman Mao Zedong is so healthy. This is the greatest happiness for the entire Chinese people. This is the greatest happiness for the revolutionary peoples of the whole world.' "

On the day Mao chose to swim

a forest of colorful flags lined the banks of the Yangzi, large posters with slogans were hung, exultant crowds of people milled around, loudspeakers broadcast the majestic strains of *The East Is Red*, singing the praises of our Beloved Leader Chairman Mao Zedong. . . . Thunderous joyful exclamations and sirens merged into a single sound. Chairman Mao Zedong, looking healthy and radiant, stood on the deck of the motor-launch. . . . On the river one could see red flags held aloft, and enormous banners bearing quotations from the works of Chairman Mao, "Unity, Intensity, Seriousness, and Liveliness," "The imperialists condescend toward us; we must take this very seriously," "Filled with resolve, we fear no sacrifice, we shall overcome all difficulties to achieve victory." . . . Chairman Mao Zedong waved his hand at the enthusiastic masses . . . [and] responding to their reception he said loudly, "Hello, comrades! Hooray, comrades!" A detachment of more than two hundred young swimmers, primary school pupils, especially drew Chairman Mao's attention. These Pioneers who were eight to fourteen years old [were swimming and holding] in their hands signs saying "Learning is good, every day we make progress!" and they sang a song, "We are the communist successor generation," demonstrating the revolutionary enthusiasm of the Pioneers of the era of Mao Zedong. . . . The cutter approached the great Wuchang dike. Chairman Mao Zedong entered the water and swam. It was precisely eleven o'clock in the morning. During the summer the currents of the Yangzi are swifter. Chairman Mao swam first using one stroke and then another. He swam on his side, then on his back. . . . When the hands of the clock showed that one hour and five minutes had passed . . . Chairman Mao Zedong climbed on board; he was hale and hearty, and showed no trace of fatigue.[55]

News of Mao's triumphal feat also astonished many persons abroad. But not everyone believed the propaganda that the seventy-two-year-old Mao had covered a distance of nine miles in a little over an hour. No one had publicized the fact that Mao had simply been carried along by the current.

Professional swimmers made particular sport of the leader of the CCP. The president of the International Swimming Association (FINA), William Berge Phillips, even wrote Mao Zedong a letter inviting him to take part in two competitions in Canada. "We have been told that on July 16, you swam 9 miles in the brilliant time of one hour and five minutes," he wrote sarcastically. "This would give you the opportunity to take part in these two competitions since the record for swimming ten miles, established last year in a traditional competition in Quebec by one of the fastest swimmers in the world, Herman Willemse (Germany)* was 4 hours and 35 minutes." The president further noted that in February 1966 Giulio Travaglio (Italy) established a new record on Lake El Quillén in Argentina, but even his time of 3 hours and 56 minutes was not as impressive as the result achieved by the Chairman. The time attributed to Mao indicates that on average he swam 100 yards in 24.6 seconds, whereas even today no one has yet succeeded in swimming that distance any faster than in 45.6 seconds. "Perhaps Mao Zedong would like to represent Red China at the next Olympic Games before turning professional," the president wrote tongue-in-cheek. "But if he would like to earn some easy money, I suggest that he take part in the professional swimmers' competitions this summer and give some swimming lessons to Willemse, Travaglio, and others who obviously cannot hold a candle to him."[56]

On July 18, Mao returned to Beijing and immediately showed Liu and Deng who was boss. When he returned, he temporarily settled into the former diplomatic residence Diaoyutai (Fishing pavilion) on the western edge of the city. He deliberately refused to live in Zhongnanhai, where Deng and Liu dwelled. Liu immediately rushed over, but Mao did not want to receive him. "The Chairman is resting," Mao's secretary said to the dumbfounded Liu. In reality, Mao was talking behind closed doors to Kang Sheng and Chen Boda, who, of course, used the opportunity to depict Liu's and Deng's actions in the darkest hues. Not until the following evening was Liu able to see Mao. For Liu the meeting was rather unpleasant. Mao came down hard, asserting that his "work teams were completely unsuitable, that the former [Beijing] Municipal Committee was rotten, that the Propaganda Department of the Central Committee was rotten, that the Ministry of Higher Education likewise was rotten, and that People's Daily was good for nothing." Liu was like an ant in a frying pan. Meanwhile, Mao pressed on, skillfully playing the role of the Great Leader whose hopes had been deceived. In eight days he convened seven conferences

---

* This was mistaken. Herman Willemse was actually from Holland.

in which he demanded that the work teams, which "are actually acting like a brake and helping the counterrevolution," be recalled.[57] "Who suppressed student movements?" he raged. "Only the northern warlords did. . . . We must not restrict the masses. . . . Those who suppress the student movement will come to no good end!"[58]

Under pressure from the incensed Chairman, who accused the Politburo leadership of sabotaging the Great Cultural Revolution, Liu and Deng, with the help of Zhou Enlai and the new leaders of the Beijing Municipal Committee, convened a large-scale meeting of activists from student organizations on July 29, in the Great Hall of the People on Tiananmen Square. More than ten thousand persons were present. Liu and Deng had to try to justify their actions, which they did rather awkwardly. Liu was particularly pitiful; he acknowledged that "I . . . honestly . . . don't know . . . how to carry out the proletarian 'Cultural Revolution.'"[59] There was dead silence in the hall. Deng Xiaoping's daughter, who was present, began to sob.

"The childish babble" of his "enemy," however, only inflamed Mao, who now smelled the scent of blood. While Liu was speaking, Mao stayed behind the scenes out of sight. He was also hiding while listening to Deng and to the loyal Zhou. Only when everyone had finished did he part the curtain and to everyone's surprise step to the podium. The crowd let out an ecstatic roar, "Long Live Chairman Mao! Long Live Chairman Mao!" He walked back and forth along the stage, waving his arm in greeting.[60]

A great performer was giving a premier performance. The disgraced Deng and Liu had no choice but to take part in the spectacle, applauding their tormentor with all their strength.

33

TO REBEL IS JUSTIFIED

The work teams were withdrawn, but Mao did not calm down. "The dispatch of work teams was in fact an act in opposition to the proletarian revolution from the bourgeois stand," he thundered, demanding that the Cultural Revolution be carried out only with the support of the young people and revolutionary teachers. "If we cannot rely upon them, then on whom can we rely?" he inquired.[1]

On August 1, he sent a greeting to one of the youth organizations that had been founded on May 29, in a middle school attached to Tsinghua University. This organization called itself *hongweibing* (Red Guards), a name Mao liked very much. He praised its members: "No matter where they are, in Peking [Beijing] or anywhere else in China, I will give enthusiastic support to all who take an attitude similar to yours in the Cultural Revolution movement."[2]

When the letter was made public, Red Guard groups were organized among young students all over the country. Mao rubbed his hands with glee: with such an army he could "storm Heaven." "We believe in masses," he acclaimed. "To become teachers of the masses we must first be the students of the masses. The present great Cultural Revolution is a heaven-and-earth-shaking event. Can we, dare we, cross the pass into socialism? This pass leads to the final destruction of classes, and the reduction of the three great differences."[3]

In early August he convened an enlarged regularly scheduled plenum of the Central Committee, to which he invited "revolutionary teachers and students" from various institutions of higher education. In all there were 188 persons present, among them 75 Central Committee members and 67 alternates. The author of the "first Marxist-Leninist" *dazibao*, Nie Yuanzi, also attended.

The plenum, which opened on August 1, had been scheduled for five days but stretched to thirteen. Mao, who was responsible for extending the plenum, cursed the work teams, accusing them now of "terrorism." At the first session he rudely interrupted Liu Shaoqi, who was making a political report. Mao said that 90 percent of the teams had made mistakes of line, had stood on the side of the bourgeoisie, and opposed proletarian revolution.[4] That same day, August 1, he distributed his letter to the Red Guards at the middle school attached to Tsinghua University.

Trying to calm the enraged Chairman, the next evening the terrified Liu visited one of the universities in Beijing to see what the work teams were up to. He continued his investigation the following two evenings, and invited the members of the work team to visit him in Zhongnanhai, where he mildly criticized them. "If you don't permit them [students] to rebel, they will get rid of you for sure."[5] Meanwhile, at the plenum on August 2 and 3, his supporters timidly tried to soften the extremely harsh criticism Mao had leveled at Liu and the work teams.

The Great Helmsman, however, became even more furious. On August 4, he abruptly interrupted the plenum and hastily convened an enlarged meeting of the Politburo Standing Committee. There he castigated Liu and the other "capitalist roaders," comparing them not only with the northern militarists, but also with the CCP's main enemy, the Guomindang, which had also suppressed the students. He told the cowed members of the Standing Committee and the others, "There are monsters and demons among the people present here!" He said this in response to a rejoinder by the party veteran Marshal Ye Jianying: "We have a multi-million man army, and we are not afraid of evil spirits." To Liu Shaoqi, who took responsibility for everything that had happened in Beijing, Mao irritably noted, "You have established [here] in Beijing your own dictatorship. Good for you!"[6]

The following day, at Mao's behest, Zhou Enlai informed Liu that he was no longer to appear in public or receive foreign guests as head of the PRC. Afterward Liu called the first secretary of the Beijing Municipal Party Committee, Li Xuefeng, and told him he was no longer to visit higher educational institutions. "[I]t seems that I am not qualified to lead the Cultural Revolution," he said.[7] Obviously Liu felt very bitter and realized he was doomed.

What he did not yet know was that on the same day, August 5, while the plenum was in session, Mao wrote his own *dazibao* titled "Bombard the Headquarters—My Big Character Poster," which caused many party officials to tremble in fear.[8] Everyone now understood that the Cultural Revolution was aimed against Liu Shaoqi. Revising its agenda, the plenum investigated the personal affairs of Liu and his closest associate, Deng Xiaoping.[9]

On August 8, the plenum adopted a special "Decision of the Central Committee of the Communist Party of China Concerning the Great Proletarian Cultural Revolution" (the so-called Sixteen Points). Chen Boda and his Central Cultural Revolution Group had drafted the text in July, but Mao approved it only during the plenum after having corrected it thirty times. Its key paragraph said:

Although the bourgeoisie has been overthrown, it is still trying to use the old ideas, culture, customs and habits of the exploiting classes to corrupt the masses, capture their minds and endeavor to stage a come-back. The proletariat must do just the opposite: it must meet head-on every challenge of the bourgeoisie in the ideological field and use the new ideas, culture, customs, and habits of the proletariat to change the mental outlook of the whole of society. At present, our objective is to struggle against those persons in authority who are taking the capitalist road, to criticize and repudiate the reactionary bourgeois academic "authorities" and the ideology of the bourgeoisie and all other exploiting classes and to transform education, literature and art and all other parts of the superstructure that do not correspond to the socialist economic base, so as to facilitate the consolidation and development of the socialist system.[10]

The exhilarated Red Guards memorized this excerpt.

The resolution did not pass without some opposition. As Mao subsequently recalled, "[O]nly after discussion did I succeed in gathering scarcely more than half of the delegates. It goes without saying that, as before, many did not accept this point of view."[11]

Striving to eliminate resistance from Liu's supporters, Mao reorganized the leading organs of the Politburo and added his associates Lin Biao, Kang Sheng, and Chen Boda to the Politburo Standing Committee. Lin filled the post of the sole deputy chairman* and became Mao's newly designated successor in place of the discredited Liu Shaoqi.[12] In order to weaken Deng Xiaoping's influence the post of general secretary of the Central Committee was abolished and the Secretariat itself was shorn of any influence whatsoever in the party. After the plenum its functions were given to the Cultural Revolution Group.

On August 18, five days after the plenum, standing on the rostrum of the Gate of Heavenly Peace (Tiananmen Gate), Mao, Lin Biao, and others greeted hundreds of thousands of ecstatic Red Guards assembled on the square below. Many of the students, overcome with emotion, began sobbing with joy. Enthusiastic shouts of "Long Live Chairman Mao!" and the songs "The East Is Red," "Sailing the Seas Depends on the Helmsman," and "I Love Chairman Mao's Books Best of All" floated across the square. Many young men and young women, bearing bouquets and garlands of flowers, danced together. Red banners fluttered above the sea of people and gigantic portraits of the Leader were held aloft.

The greatest outburst of emotion occurred when a young female Red

---

* Prior to this, besides Lin Biao there were four other deputy chairmen: Liu Shaoqi, Zhou Enlai, Zhu De, and Chen Yun.

Guard, invited onto the rostrum, tied a scarlet armband with the inscription "Red Guard" around the Leader's left arm. The crowd roared. Numerous cameras snapped pictures and television and movie cameramen recorded this historic moment. Mao, smiling slightly at the slender girl with big glasses, softly asked, "What's your name?"

"Song Binbin ["Well-mannered Song"]," she replied, and froze on the spot.

Mao raised his eyebrows. "You must become a warrior [*yao wu ma*]," he said and burst out laughing.

The embarrassed young girl became completely tongue-tied. But after her historic meeting with the Great Helmsman, she changed her name to Song Yaowu ("Song Who Will Be a Warrior").[13] Her comrades took the Chairman's words as a direct summons to more resolute actions.

That same day, Mao met with Peng Xiaomeng, an eighteen-year-old female student at the middle school attached to Peking University, renowned throughout China for having beaten the leader of the work team, the party veteran Zhang Chengxian, with a copper-buckled leather belt. The fifty-one-year-old Zhang was deputy director of the Propaganda Department of the North China Bureau of the Central Committee, but neither his age nor the lofty position of her victim bothered the girl. Mao was immediately informed of Peng's "feat" and was delighted by this hooliganism. On August 1, 1966, in his aforementioned letter to the Red Guards of the middle school attached to Tsinghua University, he referred to "little" Peng, giving her "enthusiastic support."[14]

The meeting with Peng on August 18 was brief but significant. Mao was in excellent spirits; he was making jokes, and teasing Peng Xiaomeng, he taught her how to swim by making comical swimming motions with his arms in the air. But suddenly, at an instant, he turned serious when Peng asked him what the Red Guards should do from now on. He responded passionately, "Of course, rebel! Without rebellion nothing that is bad can be fixed. First you must struggle, second you must criticize, and third you must carry out transformation. All this must be done in accordance with the Sixteen Points."[15] The political crisis further intensified, and the Cultural Revolution was increasingly stained blood red. After the parade in Tiananmen on August 18, 1966, the Red Guards emerged from the university and school campuses onto the streets of the cities.

A wave of violence swiftly inundated the country. In this bloody drama the main role was not played by university students, but by juveniles, middle school and even primary school kids who were delirious from the atmosphere of total permissiveness.[16] These were children who had not yet grown up, wolf cubs who scented the smell of blood, ignorant fanatics who fancied themselves titans rebelling against the "Four Olds" behavioral norms—old ideas, culture, customs, and habits—and the capitalist roaders. There were some thirteen million of them throughout the country. It was on them that Mao placed his immoral wager in fanning the wild conflagration of the Cultural Revolution. With his "directives," appeals, and *dazibao* he poisoned the souls of these children and committed the most egregious of crimes. What could be more criminal than the molestation of the young?

In Beijing in just two months (August–September) the crazed youngsters killed 1,773 persons suspected of being capitalist roaders. In Shanghai during the same period 1,238 people perished, of whom 704 took their own lives, unable to bear the insults of the juvenile Red Guards. The Ministry of Public Security did not intervene. "In the final analysis, bad people are bad people, so if they are beaten to death it is not a tragedy!" the minister of public security, strictly following the instructions of the Great Helmsman, informed his subordinates.[17] On August 21, 1966, the CCP Central Committee adopted a resolution prohibiting the Ministry of Public Security from interfering with the actions of the "revolutionary students." A similar resolution with respect to the PLA was confirmed that same day by the General Staff and the General Political Administration of the Chinese army.[18]

The young people persecuted their teachers as their primary targets. In some schools individual classrooms were turned into prisons, where the students tormented teachers they had arrested on the charge of belonging to the "black gang of bourgeois reactionary authorities." These teachers were humiliated, beaten, and tortured, many to the point of death. One such jail was directly across the street from Zhongnanhai, in the music classroom of Beijing No. 6 Middle School. On the wall they wrote with the blood of their teachers: "Long live the red terror."[19] This is how the youth understood the slogan "In this great cultural revolution, the phenomenon of our schools being dominated by bourgeois intellectuals must be completely changed."[20]

Excited by the impunity they had been granted, starting in September 1966 the Red Guards of the capital and other cities began to spread out around the country, sowing misfortune and terror everywhere. In their travels they invariably visited Shaoshanchong and Jinggang, Zunyi and Yan'an to pay their respects to these "sacred places." They saw their main objective everywhere as enlightening the backward masses and uprooting capitalist-road vermin. Mao was overjoyed to hear of these "revolutionary initiatives":

> Let them travel about! They can relieve each other, taking turns looking after their parents [who remain at home]. They should be given letters of introduction, let them all travel about. The members of the Cultural Revolution Group can give them permission to travel. . . . The departing students should be given provisions. Some people say the students have nowhere to sleep. Where are there places without lodging? There are homes everywhere. This is just a pretext [not to allow the students to go].

Animated by the good news, at the end of August he observed to the staff of the *People's Daily,* "It is not necessary to wrap up the Cultural Revolution by the end of the year. At first we'll keep it going until lunar New Year [i.e., the beginning of February 1967], and then we'll talk about [ending] the revolution."[21]

The "revolutionary students" were enormously enthusiastic about the Great Helmsman's support. "We were not tourists," one participant recalls. "We were soldiers going out to war against an old world.... From now on, we no longer need envy our parents for their heroic deeds in revolutionary wars and feel sorry because we were born too late.... We will enlighten and organize the masses, dig out hidden enemies, shed our blood, and sacrifice our lives for the final victory of the Cultural Revolution."[22] In 1966, the author of these reminiscences was barely fifteen years old, so it is impossible to doubt that her juvenile outburst was sincere. However, she did not have to shed her own blood, unlike those whom she and her comrades consigned to the ranks of capitalist roaders. It was useless for these people, like all the others who were "adherents of old culture," to beg for mercy. The young "missionaries" of the new were proud that their revolution was no less merciless than their parents' revolution before them.

In cities and hamlets across China, the Red Guards mounted didactic performances in which the leading actors were the "capitalist roaders" they had arrested. Terror-stricken elderly people, their arms broken, were led along the streets to the jeers and malicious shouts of the mob. They were crowned with dunce caps just as the village extremists in the 1920s had done to their targets. Placards were hung around their necks reading, "Counterrevolutionary revisionist element so-and-so," and "Member of the anti-party black gang so-and-so." The victims' faces were smeared with tar or ink, their clothes ripped, and they were forced to bow before the "revolutionary masses," confessing all of their "sins" until they were exhausted. Meanwhile, the gawking onlookers shouted imprecations and thrust their clenched fists in the air to shouts of "Down with!"

The hearts of those crushed under the "Red Wheel" were filled with terror. If those doomed to such tortures managed to survive, the dismal pictures of these tribunals remained in their memories for the rest of their lives:

Fiery red armbands set flames to young hearts. Resounding quotations urged children to fight. Charge, fight, smash, go out with red in your eyes and build a red, red world. But they still didn't know who their opponents were....

"Answer: you hate the Party, don't you? What kind of dreams do you dream about recovering your lost paradise?"

"Answer: what kind of anti-revolutionary plots have you hatched? How are you now preparing to overthrow the Party?"

"Answer: what kind of old documents have you kept, hoping to get back all your old property? You want Chiang Kai-shek to come back to power so you can get revenge and kill off the Party, don't you. . . ."

A leather belt snapped, a chain clanked, and an anguished cry rang out.

"Answer, answer, answer!"

"I love the Party!"

"Bullshit! How could you love the Party? How could you possibly love the Party? How dare you say you love the Party? How could you deserve to love the Party? You're a stubborn mule with a head of granite!"

Swish, clank, belt and chain, fire and ice, blood and sweat.[23]

Robbery, too, was an indivisible component of the red terror to which the "backward" teachers and "black" party officials were subjected. All movable property was dragged from the homes of the "evil" person, and what could not be moved was destroyed. In Beijing alone, in late August and early September the Red Guards pillaged 33,695 homes from which they carried off 5.7 tons of gold, more than 19 tons of silver, about 55.5 million yuan in cash, and 613,600 jade objects. During this same time the "bearers of the new culture" in Shanghai robbed 84,222 homes; in addition to a large number of precious stones and metals they confiscated $3.24 million in American dollars, $3.3 million in other currencies, 2.4 million in Chinese Nationalist currency, and 370 million in PRC currency. Throughout China, by October 1966 about 65 tons of gold alone had been confiscated. (Of course, these figures do not give a complete picture of the scale of the theft; they represent only the amounts that the Red Guards surrendered to the Bank of China. No one knows how much they appropriated for themselves. Nonetheless, even the volume of stolen goods that was reported impressed the leaders of the CCP. In October 1966, a regular working session of the CCP Central Committee showered praise upon the new "heroes of the Liangshanbo.")*[24]

It was not only the homes of ordinary citizens that were pillaged and robbed; state institutions—cultural institutions in the first instance such as museums, libraries, and exhibition halls—also fell victim to the Red Guards. Wherever possible, historical monuments were destroyed. In November 1966, students from Beijing Normal University, who traveled to the birthplace of Confucius in the city of Qufu, Shandong province, destroyed roughly seven thousand monuments, including a thousand ancient stone steles, and smashed two thousand graves. They defiled the burial place of the great philosopher. Three months earlier, a group of Red Guards in Shandong defiled the grave of

---

* This was the name of the base of the rebellious peasants in the novel *Water Margin*.

Wu Xun, a nineteenth-century Confucian educator. The remains of the scholar were exhumed and burned while the crowd whooped and hollered. The bones of Hai Rui, exhumed from his grave on Hainan, were likewise destroyed.[25]

Not all party leaders welcomed the Red Guards. Many, including quite a few members of the Central Committee, were dismayed. A struggle within the party leadership continued throughout September. Those who still managed to preserve their reason tried to contain the chaos in the hope of avoiding another economic crisis. In mid-September, sober-minded Central Committee officials headed by Zhou Enlai convinced Mao to approve a prohibition against worker and peasant involvement in the Red Guard movement.[26] But soon the orthodox Maoists administered a new blow against Liu's group. At a Central Committee work conference in mid-October, Lin Biao attacked Liu and Deng by name, accusing them of pursuing "a line of repression of the masses and opposition to the revolution."[27] His speech was obviously vetted by Mao. Jiang Qing took part in the conference even though she was not a member of the Central Committee. Starting in late August she functioned as head of the Cultural Revolution Group, in place of Chen Boda, who was overloaded with work.[28]

Liu had to engage in self-criticism. On October 23, at the work conference he delivered a speech that ended his political career. Deng followed, also acknowledging his mistakes.

Mao did not attend the first two weeks of the conference, but he controlled its proceedings through Lin, Zhou, Chen, and Kang Sheng. It was not until October 25, two days after Liu's and Deng's self-flagellation, that he appeared in the hall. He began circuitously, even mildly criticizing himself for "not paying attention to day-to-day affairs" since he was not on the front line, but on the so-called second line in the rear for a long time. Then he took the offensive.

> This meeting has had two stages. In the first stage the speeches were not quite normal, but during the second stage, after speeches and the exchange of experience by comrades at the Centre, things went more smoothly and the ideas were understood a bit better. It has only been five months. Perhaps the movement may last another five months, or even longer. . . . [T]he five months of the Great Cultural Revolution, the fire . . . I kindled. It has been going on only five months, not even half a year, a very brief span compared to the twenty-eight years of democratic revolution and the seventeen years of socialist revolution. So one can see why it has not been thoroughly understood and there were obstacles. . . . I think that there are advantages in being assailed. For so many years you had not thought about such things, but as soon as they burst upon you, you began to think.[29]

Some time later, after the conference, Mao, obviously savoring his victory over the silenced Central Committee, added:

The babies want to rebel—we must support them. Let them make their own way; we should not be afraid they will make mistakes. . . . If we don't start to learn from the little generals, then we are done for. . . . As soon as the masses come on the scene, the evil spirits will vanish. Strictly speaking, there are no evil spirits; it is only in the cerebral cortex of certain people that an evil spirit dwells, and the name of this evil spirit is "fear of the masses." . . . Disorders are caused by people, and those who create disorder are not guilty of any crimes. . . . The young create great things in the world.[30]

We already know just how great these things were, but Mao evidently hoped for even more. He seemed unconcerned that the wild outbursts of the Red Guards would threaten China's economy.

But the economic situation began to suffer when young workers in Shanghai and other cities ignored the Central Committee's September resolution prohibiting workers and peasants from getting involved in the movement. They began to organize revolutionary groups spontaneously. In early November, delegates of working youth from seventeen industrial enterprises formed the so-called Shanghai Workers' Revolutionary Rebels General Headquarters (*Shanghai gongren geming zaofan zong silingbu*), with a young guard at one of the textile plants by the name of Wang Hongwen as the leader. He had already come to the attention of the Maoists in June 1966, when he became the first Shanghai worker who posted an extremist *dazibao* criticizing the factory administration. This militant and energetic young man fulfilled all the revolutionary criteria. By his thirty-first year, he had already served in the army, fought in Korea, and joined the party.

Wang Hongwen's organization, however, was not recognized by the Shanghai Municipal Party Committee, which had not yet reoriented itself and viewed the actions of Wang and his comrades as harmful to production. Then, Wang, acting impetuously, had provoked an incident at the Anting railroad station in suburban Shanghai that shut down the rail line to Nanjing for thirty hours. His followers, numbering more than two thousand, lay down on the tracks, demanding they be provided a train to take them to Beijing to meet the Great Helmsman and inform him of the "outrages" committed by the municipal authorities. Wang Hongwen's "revolutionary action" was supported by Zhang Chunqiao, Jiang Qing, and Yao Wenyuan, who, after condemning the Shanghai Municipal Committee, began to make use of the workers. Thereafter, all across China organizations of young workers and employees were established parallel to the Red Guards. These were called *zaofan* (Rebels), after the Shanghai organization.

This appellation was borrowed from a famous phrase Mao had formulated in Yan'an when speaking on the occasion of Stalin's sixtieth birthday. "The laws of Marxism are intricate and complex, but in the final analysis they boil down to one thing: 'To rebel is justified' (*zaofan youli*)."[31] On June 5, 1966, *People's Daily* reminded its readers of this phrase, after which the same Red Guards from the middle school attached to Tsinghua University used the expression "To rebel is justified" in their *dazibao*. They sent these publications to Mao, who, in his reply that we have already noted, exclaimed, "You say it is right to rebel against reactionaries; I enthusiastically support you."[32] Thereafter, the expression "To rebel is justified" became the main slogan of the Cultural Revolution.

In early December an enlarged Politburo plenum chaired by Lin Biao repudiated the September resolution that prohibited Red Guards from expanding into people's communes and industrial enterprises. China's economy was once again threatened. The transportation system was in crisis. Inspired by Mao's greetings to the Red Guards on August 18, fanatical youth and adolescents jammed onto trains bound for Beijing. Every Red Guard and Rebel wanted to see the Great Helmsman. Mao welcomed this, explaining to the Central Cultural Revolution Group that the more people would see him the better for the revolution. "One of the reasons why the Soviet Union had discarded Leninism was that too few people had seen Lenin alive," he said.[33]

By the end of November he had presided over eight receptions cum parades on Tiananmen Square involving more than 11 million people. The largest were those of November 25 and 26 in which 2.5 million revolutionary students took part.

It is impossible now to read the Xinhua News Agency reports of these parades with a straight face.

"Yesterday at 11:30 A.M.," an anonymous correspondent reported breathlessly,

> to the solemn strains of *The East Is Red* our Great Teacher, Great Leader, and Great Commander, the Great Helmsman Chairman Mao Zedong and his close comrade-in-arms Lin Biao mounted the central rostrum on Tiananmen Square. . . . At this moment all of Tiananmen Square and the streets adjoining it on the east were transformed into a triumphal human ocean. . . . Everyone jumped up and down from excitement and joy. Waves of never ending exclamations of "Long live Chairman Mao! A long life to him! A long, long life to him!" rolled through the human sea. . . . Then to the tune of *Sailing the Seas Depends on the Helmsman* more than 600,000 youthful revolutionaries passed through Tiananmen Square. . . . They continuously declaimed the slogan in honor of the Great Leader, "Long Live Chairman Mao!" . . . On November 25, the temperature in the capital fell to minus seven Celsius. Nevertheless, our most respected and most beloved Great Leader Chairman Mao Zedong, coatless, in

a khaki-colored uniform, ascended the central rostrum from which he cordially waved his hand and applauded the young revolutionaries, inspiring them to carry out the Great Cultural Revolution to the end. . . . On the afternoon of November 26 Chairman Mao Zedong reviewed a parade of more than 1.8 million revolutionary teachers, employees, and Red Army men who had gathered on Tiananmen Square. . . . To the sound of ardent and joyful exclamations, Chairman Mao Zedong, his close comrade-in-arms Comrade Lin Biao, and other leading comrades from the party center set out in open cars from Tiananmen Square to the west, into the heart of the army of the Cultural Revolution.[34]

Among those present on the rostrum of Tiananmen were both Liu and Deng who were still included among the party leadership. But their days were already numbered. As early as October 21, *dazibao* had been posted at Beida that openly proclaimed: "Liu Shaoqi is China's Khrushchev!" On October 24, the day after Liu's and Deng's self-criticism, a *dazibao* saying "Deng Xiaoping is also China's Khrushchev!" appeared at the Central Committee's Organizational Department. It asserted for the first time that in the early 1960s Deng Xiaoping had proclaimed: "The color of the cat does not matter, as long as it catches mice."[35]

On December 18, one of Jiang Qing's deputies, the Shanghai leftist Zhang Chunqiao, instructed the leader of the Tsinghua University Red Guards: "You, the little revolutionary generals, must unite, fill yourselves with revolutionary spirit, and beat the dog in the water, dethrone them [Liu and Deng], and do not stop at half measures." He added that Liu and Deng, "these two upholders of the bourgeois reactionary line in the Central Committee, have still not surrendered." Seven days later a five-thousand-person demonstration took place in Beijing under the slogan of "Down with Liu Shaoqi! Down with Deng Xiaoping! Carry out the bloody battle against Liu and Deng to the end!"[36]

Soon similar demonstrations were being held throughout the country. Liu and Deng instantly disappeared from the political stage. On January 1, 1967, on the wall of Liu's house in Zhongnanhai appeared the inscription "Down with China's Khrushchev Liu Shaoqi!" Two days later a "criticism and struggle meeting" was organized at the offices of the Central Committee, where Liu and his wife were subjected to public censure. Subsequently such "meetings" became commonplace. One of the participants described the meeting:

Soldiers and officers from the Central Garrison Corps were there, too, watching. No one was offering even the slightest help to Liu Shaoqi. Liu and his wife Wang Guangmei were standing in the center of the crowd, being pushed and kicked and beaten by staff members from the Bureau of Secretaries. Liu's shirt had already been torn open, and a couple of buttons were missing, and people were jerking him around by the hair. When I moved closer for a better look, someone held his arms behind his back while others tried to force him to bend forward from the waist in the position known as "doing the airplane." Finally, they forced him down and pushed his face toward the ground until it was nearly touching the dirt, kicking him and slapping him in the face. Still the soldiers from the Central Garrison Corps refused to intervene. I could not bear to watch. Liu Shaoqi was already an old man by then, almost seventy, and he was our head of state.[37]

After numerous requests for an audience, on January 13, Mao finally received his defeated enemy. Liu asked only that he be allowed to resign and to withdraw to the countryside to live out his life as an ordinary peasant. But Mao turned him down.[38]

By then the Cultural Revolution had entered its bloodiest phase. On December 27, 1966, Jiang Qing dispatched Red Guards from Beijing to Sichuan, where the disgraced Peng Dehuai was living. A band of thugs burst into his house, seized him, and brought him to the capital, where he was thrown into prison. Peng was tortured and beaten more than a hundred times, his ribs were broken, his face maimed, and his lungs damaged. He was repeatedly dragged to criticism and struggle meetings. The elderly marshal groaned continuously and could barely speak. From prison he wrote to Mao, "I send you my final greeting. I wish you a long life!" In 1973 he was transferred to a prison hospital. He died on November 29, 1974.[39]

Another hero of the Chinese revolution, Marshal He Long, was also subjected to horrible tortures. A convivial jokester and ladies' man, he was one of the few who had gladly supported Mao when he began living with Jiang Qing in Yan'an. His earlier friendship with the wife of the Leader did not save him. In the early 1960s he fell out with Lin Biao, openly expressing his contempt for Lin, whom he considered an ignoramus in the sphere of modern weaponry. This is what led to his downfall. On December 30, 1966, Jiang Qing summoned students at Tsinghua University to strike a blow at He Long. He Long sought protection from Zhou Enlai, asking the premier to give him shelter in Zhongnanhai. But the frightened premier replied, "Even in Zhongnanhai the situation is tense. You need to find a quiet place farther away to rest up." But there were no longer any such places in China. Several months later the exhausted marshal was arrested and passed through the circles of hell. Tired of trying to vindicate himself, he finally stopped eating and died on June 9, 1969. Not long before he died he said to his wife, "I have only one wish, that Chairman Mao would pronounce a single sentence, 'He Long is our comrade.'"[40]

Not long after He died, on June 22, Li Lisan, who had been terribly persecuted by the Rebels, took his own life. This was the same Li Lisan who had headed the Communist Party in the early 1930s. He had returned to China from the Soviet Union in early 1946, served on the Central Committee, and had held leading posts in the party, the trade unions, and the government. In late 1966, young people dragged him to a criticism and struggle meeting, then left him alone for a time, but in late January 1967 he was picked on again. He was beaten and tortured for two and a half years, until he could no longer endure it and took a large dose of sleeping pills. "My spiritual and physical tortures are unbearable," he wrote to Mao.[41] The day after Li's death, his Russian wife and their two daughters, who had also gone through countless "criticism and struggle meetings," were arrested.[42] Li's widow recalled that when she found herself locked in a quiet cell she was so relieved after all the stress that she thought to herself, "I am free, I am saved."[43]

On August 24, 1966, Li Da, the rector of Wuhan University and one of the founders of the CCP, died, unable to endure the torture to which he had been subjected. That same year, Tian Jiaying, Mao Zedong's secretary who had once told the Leader the truth about the mood of the peasantry, committed suicide. On September 19, 1966, Wang Xiaotang, first secretary of Tianjin Municipal Committee, died soon after the Red Guards forced him to stand for several hours under the scorching sun. In January 1967, Zhang Lingzhi, minister of the coal industry, died under torture during an interrogation. At the same time Zhao Erlu, deputy director of the Defense Industry Committee of the Central Committee Military Council, and Wei Heng and Yan Hongyan, first secretaries of the Shanxi and Yunnan provincial party committees respectively, committed suicide.

Liu Shaoqi, too, succumbed to persecution. Throughout most of 1967 he was mocked at meetings both in Zhongnanhai and elsewhere in Beijing. In mid-September his wife was imprisoned, after which the grief-stricken Liu suffered from hypertension and elevated blood sugar levels. This was accompanied by disruption in the functions of his autonomous nervous system. Then he came down with pneumonia. Terribly ill, he was kept under house arrest and practically refused any medical attention. In mid-October 1969 he was secretly transported to Kaifeng under the fictitious name of Liu Weihuang and left there to die, completely without hope, in a building belonging to the local "revolutionary" authorities. There was no furniture in the room where he was put except the dirty stretcher on the floor that served as his bed. A month later, at 6:45 A.M., the former chairman of the PRC expired. An ambulance arrived two hours after he died.[44] On his death certificate in the space for "Occupation," the doctor wrote, "unemployed." The cause of death was listed as "illness." Many other lesser-known CCP leaders also became victims of the Red Guard and Rebel terror. The Cultural Revolution spread across the country like a firestorm.

Did Mao know about all of this? Did the groans of his former comrades reach his ears? There can be no doubt about this. It was he who made the ultimate decisions regarding the fate of individual party leaders. It was he who removed them from their government and party positions. It is true that unlike Stalin, he did not personally sign their death warrants. But isn't driving someone to suicide the equivalent of execution? And wasn't his connivance with the fiends who tortured and brutalized the arrested likewise the equivalent of issuing a death sentence? Is it possible that Mao could not conceive of the scale of the lawlessness, that he could have failed to understand where the universal permissiveness would lead? No, he understood everything perfectly, and that is why he bears responsibility for the miserable fates of the victims. He was the chief culprit of the senseless and merciless mass terror. More than a million persons were tortured, shot, or driven to suicide during these years of "complete chaos under Heaven," [45] and a hundred million suffered to one degree or another. Only a small fraction of them were party members or cadres. Mao knew everything and understood everything.

Over a long period not only did Mao fail to try to stop the outburst of anarchy; on the contrary he encouraged it any way he could. An irrepressible lust for violence, clearly evident as far back as his *Report on an Investigation of the Peasant Movement in Hunan,* was never extinguished in Mao. How could it have slackened when it was constantly reinforced by revolutionary struggles and reading of Marxist literature? All his life Mao believed in the false formula that "without destruction there can be no creation." He was unaffected by the life-and-death dramas of the victims of the Cultural Revolution. Even when his daughter Li Min complained to him that the insane warriors against revisionism were beginning to level idiotic accusations against her and her husband, Mao did not lift a finger. He simply laughed and replied, "There's nothing terrible about it, you're just gaining some experience." [46] On December 26, 1966, celebrating his seventy-third birthday with his inner circle, Mao gave a toast: "To the unfolding of nationwide all-round civil war!" [47]

He lived in his own world, where there was no place for human suffering. He spent his free hours in the company of pretty seventeen- and eighteen-year-old girls; from time to time he traded them in for Zhang Yufeng, whom he still found attractive. At night he shut himself in with them in the spacious and well-furnished Room 118 in the Great Hall of the People, and from late 1966 he began to hold group "pajama parties" in Zhongnanhai in a building with an indoor swimming pool. He now preferred this to his study in the Pavilion of Chrysanthemum Fragrance. [48] Meanwhile, he constantly kept his hand on the pulse of the enormous country. Not a single important question was decided without his knowledge. He, the Chairman, was the ultimate arbiter of truth. Acting on a whim he alone could save someone who had been condemned.

This is how he dealt with Deng Xiaoping, whose "case" he finally distinguished from that of Liu Shaoqi. Although Mao cursed him repeatedly at various meetings, grumbling that for six years "starting in 1959, [Deng] had not reported" to him "about his work," he would not allow anyone to destroy Deng. No matter how angry he was at the "diminutive Deng," he still valued his phenomenal organizational abilities. "When Deng Xiaoping was denounced and overthrown, he was protected by Mao, both physically and politically," his younger daughter, Deng Rong (Maomao), wrote. In July 1967 he even blurted out to one of his comrades in arms, "If Lin Biao's health gets worse I intend to call Deng back. I'll make him at least a member of the Standing Committee of the Politburo."[49]

The former general secretary experienced the horrors of privileged imprisonment. He was forced to engage in self-criticism, to wear a dunce cap, and get down on his knees, but he was not killed. On October 22, 1969, together with his wife and stepmother, Deng was sent to Jiangxi province, where he spent three and a half years in a labor reform school for cadres. Meanwhile, his spiritual sufferings were immense. It was not so much because he had been deprived of his positions and his power. The Cultural Revolution struck a heavy blow at Deng Xiaoping's family. At the end of August 1968, his eldest son, Pufang, a student at Peking University, unable to endure the mockery directed at him, jumped out of an upper-story window in one of the university buildings. Miraculously, he did not die, but he broke his spine and remained paralyzed the rest of his life.

Liu Shaoqi's son, Yunpin, was not as fortunate; he succeeded in his attempt at suicide. The ferocious explosion of terror in 1966–68 prompted many people to commit suicide. Artists and writers, university professors, and officials in party organizations unable to endure inhumane treatment resorted to suicide. At the end of August 1966, following a savage criticism and struggle meeting, Lao She, a brilliant writer, drowned himself in Taiping Lake in Beijing.

In late December 1966, egged on by Zhang Chunqiao, the Red Guards and Rebels of Shanghai stormed the headquarters of the Shanghai Municipal Party Committee and in early January 1967 occupied it. This uprising was led by the head of the Shanghai Rebels, Wang Hongwen. The battle for the committee lasted more than four hours and caused lots of casualties. The Maoists celebrated victory. As Zhang Chunqiao said, after the "revolutionary" actions of Wang Hongwen and his fellows "the Municipal Party Committee was paralyzed and toppled and nobody will listen to it anymore."[50]

Mao was ecstatic upon learning of the seizure of the Municipal Party Committee in Shanghai. "This is one class overthrowing another," he asserted. "This is a great revolution."[51] The only thing that worried him was the relative weakness of the Red Guards and the Rebels; so he ordered Lin Biao to send PLA troops to aid the "leftists." After this the seizure of power by young rascals from ultrarevolutionary organizations accelerated everywhere.

34

THE RED GUARD TRAGEDY

The January revolution in Shanghai led to the creation throughout China of new organs of power, the so-called revolutionary committees including representatives of three sides: Red Guard and Rebel leaders, PLA officers, and some "revolutionary" old cadres who survived. Local party organizations stopped functioning. Friction that not infrequently escalated into bloody confrontations developed between the military and the radicals regarding the division of provincial and municipal portfolios. In some places army units suppressed the leftists instead of supporting them at the same time that the Red Guards and the Rebels were trying to "revolutionize" the army by inciting the youthful soldiers against their commanders. Particularly heated clashes took place in Chengdu (Sichuan province) and Xining (Qinghai province), where about two hundred people died. More than ten thousand Sichuanese Red Guards and a sizable number from Qinghai were imprisoned.[1]

The first provincial revolutionary committee was established in Heilongjiang on January 31, 1967, but efforts to form new organs of power elsewhere dragged on for a long time. The Rebels and the Red Guards were unable to create anything new; all they could do was destroy. Thus revolutionary students from several universities in Beijing seized control of the Municipal Party Committee in January, but all they could do was to carry out a pogrom. Not until three months later, on April 20, 1967, did the CCP Central Committee and the Cultural Revolution Group succeed in establishing a Beijing Revolutionary Committee.[2] The Great Helmsman appointed Xie Fuzhi, the minister of public security, to head it.

Mao was probably unconcerned, believing that everything would take care of itself. The people would sort out who was right and who was guilty. However, the radicals' attack on the army, the crisis in the party, and the Red Guards' seizure of power everywhere distressed a group of veteran Politburo members, including five deputy premiers, Tan Zhenlin, Chen Yi, Li Fuchun, Li Xiannian, and Nie Rongzhen, as well as Xu Xiangqian, deputy head of the

Military Committee of the Central Committee, and Ye Jianying, the secretary of the Military Committee. Four of them—Chen, Nie, Xu, and Ye—were also marshals. At two meetings of the central leadership that included both Politburo members and members of the Central Cultural Revolution Group in early and mid February 1967 they sharply criticized the seizures of power and the Cultural Revolution as a whole.

Mao was responsible for creating this opportunity to criticize the Cultural Revolution. On the eve of the "anti-party" speeches of the Politburo members, he personally criticized Chen Boda and Jiang Qing at one of the meetings of the Cultural Revolution Group. He had long ago noticed that instead of efficiently handling the tasks assigned to them, the members of the CRG were perpetually squabbling with each other. Kang Sheng never agreed with Chen Boda, who in turn could not stand the "honorable" Kang. Jiang Qing often tried to bring Chen around but frequently failed. The imperious and hysterical Jiang was no diplomat, and she was not well versed in politics, let alone economics. Mao was also annoyed that Jiang and Chen sometimes took matters into their own hands and did not always consult with him. Irritated, he shouted at his instantly cowed associates.

"You, Chen Boda," he flung at Chen. "In the past, as far as relations between [Liu] Shaoqi and myself have been concerned, you've always been an opportunist. As many years as I know you, you've never sought me out unless the matter involved you personally."

The mortified Chen immediately asked permission to speak in order to engage in self-criticism, but Mao waved him off and attacked his wife.

"As for you, Jiang Qing, you have grandiose aims but puny abilities, great ambition but little talent. You look down on everyone else."

Then, turning to Lin Biao, he added, "See, it's still just like it was before! I don't get reports. Things are being kept secret from me. The sole exception is the premier. Whenever there's something important going on, let it be not so important, he always reports to me."[3]

Li Fuchun and Ye Jianying, who were present at this meeting, reported this outburst to their comrades in the Politburo. Because of this scent of change in the air, they spoke out against the Cultural Revolution.

At the following meeting of the central leadership in Zhongnanhai on February 11, 1967, the day after the Chairman's blow-up against Chen Boda and Jiang Qing, the party veteran Ye Jianying attacked the unfortunate Chen, whom he considered a convenient target. (Mao normally did not attend such meetings, although he followed them through trusted confidants.) Ye accused Chen of "making a mess of the party, a mess of the government, a mess of factories and the countryside," and "still you're not satisfied. You insist on making a mess of the army as well! What are you up to, going on like this?"

Xu Xiangqian supported Ye Jianying: "The army is a pillar of the dictatorship of the proletariat, but the way you're making a mess of it, it's as if you didn't want this pillar. Are you suggesting that none of us are worth saving? What do you want? For people like Kuai Dafu [the Red Guard leader at Tsinghua University who in December 1966 organized the first mass demonstration against Liu Shaoqi] to lead the army?" Zhou Enlai, chairing the meeting, became nervous, and the initiative passed to Kang Sheng: "The army does not belong to you, Xu Xiangqian." He wanted to add something, but he was cut off by Ye Jianying: "Can the revolution do without the party leadership? Does one not need an army?" He was backed by Nie Rongzhen: "Only persons with despicable intentions could persecute veterans and strike them from behind."

An oppressive silence hung over the hall. Kang Sheng, Chen Boda, and Wang Li, another member of the Cultural Revolution Group, looked daggers at the party veterans sitting across from them. Zhou Enlai abruptly ended the session, after which Deputy Premier Chen Yi whispered to Ye Jianying, "My duke, you are truly courageous!" Zhou resumed the discussion five days later, after emotions had supposedly cooled. It was a huge mistake. Party veteran Tan Zhenlin immediately attacked Zhang Chunqiao and defended the first secretary of the Shanghai Municipal Committee, who had been overthrown by the Rebels. Zhang calmly replied that the masses would sort out this question by themselves. Tan interrupted, "What masses? Always the masses, the masses. There's still the leadership of the party! [You] don't want the leadership of the party, but keep talking from morning till late about the masses liberating themselves, educating themselves, and making revolution by themselves. What is this stuff? It's metaphysics!"

Taking a breath, he continued with increasing agitation:

> Your aim is to purge the old cadres. You're knocking them down one by one, until there's not a single one left. . . . The children of high-level cadres are all being persecuted, every one of them. . . . Of all the struggles in the history of the party, this is by far the cruelest. . . . Had I known at the outset that we would live to see something like this, I would never have joined the revolution or entered the communist party. I would not have had to live till 65 and follow Chairman Mao for forty-one years.

He wanted to leave, but Chen Yi spoke out: "Don't go. We must fight!"

For the next three hours, the veterans and the members of the Cultural Revolution Group yelled at each other while the powerless Zhou vainly tried to make them come to their senses. Chen Yi was the most aggressive. He told the snarling radicals:

If you seize power you will be practicing revisionism. Already back in Yan'an Liu Shaoqi, Deng Xiaoping, and Peng Zhen . . . pretended to be the most energetic bearers of Chairman Mao Thought! They never came out openly against Chairman Mao. . . . It is we who came out against Chairman Mao for which we were criticized. Wasn't the premier likewise criticized? Didn't history [in the end] prove who [in reality] opposed Chairman Mao!? The future will prove it again. Khrushchev seized power soon after Stalin's death. But didn't he viciously attack Stalin once he himself was in power?[4]

Chen had gotten carried away. None of the other Politburo members engaged in such sharp criticism. Again, Zhou had to terminate the meeting. Zhang Chunqiao, Yao Wenyuan, and Wang Li hastened to inform Jiang Qing, who immediately ordered them to report everything to Mao. Zhang Chunqiao contacted the Leader and requested an audience.

Mao listened attentively but apparently did not attach great significance to the rebellion of the Politburo members. He even laughed several times, finding some of the veterans' words amusing. His mood darkened only when he heard what Chen Yi had said, but it was not merely the insult that ruined his mood. He suddenly realized that he was confronting the most implacable opposition, and that it would be difficult to crush it.

But his long experience of political intrigue made it virtually impossible to gain the upper hand over him. He understood that he could conquer the Oppositionists by dividing them, which is exactly what he did. He instructed Zhou Enlai to publish an editorial in *People's Daily* and *Red Flag* stating that no blows should be directed against any of the veterans. "Cadres must be handled properly," the article said. Then he invited Zhou Enlai, Kang Sheng, minister of public security Xie Fuzhi, Lin Biao's wife, Ye Qun (Lin was again unwell), and three of the "disturbers of the peace," namely, Li Fuchun, Ye Jianying, and Li Xiannian, to his private quarters late at night.[5] Quite a scene ensued. Mao began shouting at the top of his lungs:

The CCRG [Central Cultural Revolution Group] has been implementing the line adopted by the Eleventh Plenum [i.e., the August (1966) plenum]. Its errors amount to 1, 2, maybe 3 percent, while it's been correct up to 97 percent. If someone opposes the CCRG, I will resolutely oppose him! You attempt to negate the Great Cultural Revolution, but you shall not succeed! Comrade Ye Qun, you tell Lin Biao that he's not safe either. Some people are trying to grab his power, and he should be prepared. If this Great Cultural Revolution fails, he and I will withdraw from Beijing and go back to the Jinggang Mountains to fight a guerrilla war. You say that Jiang Qing and Chen Boda are

no good; let's make you, Chen Yi, the head of the CCRG, and arrest
Chen Boda and Jiang Qing and have them executed! Let's send Kang
Sheng into exile! I'll step down, too, and then we can ask Wang Ming
to return to be Chairman.[6]

Not until dawn did Mao calm down. He ordered Zhou Enlai to force Chen Yi
to engage in self-criticism, Li Fuchun and Xie Fuzhi to pressure Tan Zhenlin,
and Ye Jianying, Li Xiannian, and Xie Fuzhi to lean on Xu Xiangqian. He did
not ask for any apologies from Li Fuchun, Ye Jianying, or Li Xiannian.

Thus Mao aimed his blows at the most active of the "plotters" of division.
Chen, Tan, and Xu found themselves in a crossfire. On one side were Li Fuchun, Ye Jianying, and Li Xiannian, who had betrayed them; on the other side
were the members of the Cultural Revolution Group. Naturally, Jiang Qing,
Kang Sheng, and Chen Boda were the most vicious, labeling their enemies as
"capitalist roaders." No less aggressive was Zhang Chunqiao, who labeled the
veterans' attacks as the "February reverse current." Tan, Chen, and Xu, totally
isolated, had no recourse but to admit their guilt. Zhou Enlai also engaged in
self-criticism for failing to control the refractory members of the Politburo.[7]

The Politburo and State Council practically ceased to exist. The Chairman assigned their functions to the Cultural Revolution Group.[8] Jiang
Qing, triumphant, could not resist taking a jab at Zhou: "You, Zhou Enlai,
also have to come over to our meetings, because your meetings do not work
anymore."[9]

Rumors about the statements of the marshals and major party leaders
against the Cultural Revolution loudly echoed throughout the country and
evoked an upsurge of resistance against the Red Guards and the Rebels on the
part of the military and civilians who were indignant at the hooliganism of the
leftists. Consequently, a real civil war erupted in 1967 between the radicals and
members of the Cultural Revolution Group and those who were trying to rein
in Red Guard outrages. Anti-extremist groups emerged in all the cities.

Such organizations had also surfaced in 1966 but at that time had not
enjoyed popular support. One such anti-leftist organization was the United
Action Committee, established in Beijing by the children of high-ranking cadres. Members of the committee swore loyalty to "Marxism-Leninism and Mao
Zedong Thought prior to 1960" and called for the "complete destruction of left
opportunism." In late January 1967, 139 members of this organization were
arrested on charges of slandering Jiang Qing and Chen Boda and defending
Liu Shaoqi, but they were freed three months later on Mao's orders, because he
feared a massive outburst of dissatisfaction from party cadres.[10]

In the spring of 1967, similar organizations sprang up everywhere. Their
members attacked Red Guards and Rebels, arrested and beat them up, and
sometimes even killed them. They reviled the leaders of the Cultural Revolu-

tion, Jiang Qing, Zhang Chunqiao, Yao Wenyuan, and others, but they excepted Mao, whom they continued to regard as the great and infallible helmsman. The situation was complicated by the fact that the Red Guard movement had long since splintered into a multitude of mutually hostile groups and factions that accused each other of being capitalist roaders and revisionists.

Mao continued to believe that everything was going in the right direction. "You are constantly talking about disorders," he observed to one of his body-guards. "But you did not see what is most important, that this is a movement, a revolution taking place under the leadership of the proletariat. There's no need to be afraid of it. . . . Let the masses learn something in the course of the movement, acquire experience."

He offered the same explanation to foreign guests.

> Disorders are a result of class struggle, struggle between two fac-tions. The leftist faction is struggling against the rightist faction. The disorders are not a calamity; the sky will not fall down. I once told some other foreign friends, "First, the sky will not fall down, second, the grass and the trees on the mountain slopes will continue to grow as before, if you do not believe, go up there and you will see, third, fish will continue to swim in the rivers, fourth, women will continue to give birth to children." . . . Our government depends upon the masses. One can do nothing without the masses.[11]

By early summer, the Chairman's insouciance notwithstanding, the civil war intensified. (Mao acknowledged this fact only six months later, in Decem-ber 1967, when in a conversation with one of the foreign delegations, he inad-vertently let slip, "Armed conflict employing fire-arms began [in our country] in June 1967.")[12]

The focal point of clashes was Wuhan, where in late May, fifty-three anti-extremist organizations united to form an organization called A Million Heroes. It had a large and very militant membership. Eighty-five percent of them were party members, and in turn many of them were simultaneously part of the so-called Red People's Militia—armed workers' detachments in Wuhan. Chen Zaidao, commander of the Wuhan and Hubei military districts, a straight-talking warrior who was a hero of the anti-Japanese and civil wars, provided direct moral and material support to the alliance.[13] In the summer of 1967, the Million Heroes instigated a series of bloody incidents in which more than a hundred Red Guards and Rebels were killed and about two thousand seriously wounded.

Mao decided to intervene. In mid-July he traveled to Wuhan, against the objections of most party leaders, who were unsure his safety could be guar-anteed in the turbulent city. Mao brushed off their doubts. "I'm not afraid of disturbances," he declared. "I will go."[14] On the eve of his departure he sent the faithful Zhou to Wuhan to make arrangements for his visit.

He stayed in his beloved Donghu Guest House, but this time he did not feel quite himself. The situation in Wuhan was complicated and the city had slipped out of his control. Here and there posters plastered on the walls proclaimed, "Down with Chen Zaidao, the old Wuhan Tan [Zhenlin]! Let us completely liberate the Central plain!" Bitter clashes among the warring sides continued. On the day following Mao's arrival a bloody fight took place between the radicals and the moderates in which ten people were killed and forty-five wounded. Zhou increased the guard in the hotel, although the situation there was itself cause for alarm as the hotel staff was divided into two factions.[15]

After analyzing the situation Mao understood that "[a]t present the party and the government are powerless; only the army can resolve the task [of restoring order]." On the evening of July 18, meeting with Chen Zaidao and the political commissar of the district, Zhong Hanhua, he was much more patient than during his conversation with the February Oppositionists. It might be dangerous to yell at Chen and Zhong. Might they arrest him, as Zhang Xueliang had done with Chiang Kai-shek? He had to act cautiously.

He focused on the unification of the army with the revolutionary students, and chastised both the military and the insurgents for committing mistakes. He even condemned the Red Guards of the capital for their excessively rough treatment of Liu Shaoqi, which elicited sympathy on the part of the politically inexperienced generals. Only once during the conversation did he play with fire. "Why can't we arm the workers and students?" he suddenly asked his nonplussed guests, and not waiting for a reply, he said, "I say we should arm them!"[16] Then, turning to the attendants in the room, some of whom were Red Guards, he laughed, "You won't try to overthrow your commander again, will you? I personally have no intention of doing so."[17] Toward the end of the conversation he gently but firmly persuaded the generals to engage in self-criticism, which they did the next morning at the headquarters of the Wuhan Military Region.

Their self-flagellation, however, angered not only the Wuhan Heroes but also many army officers who despised the leftists. Early on the morning of July 20, about two hundred Heroes burst into the Donghu Guest House, where Wang Li and Minister of Public Security Xie Fuzhi, radicals from Beijing who had just arrived in town, were staying. (They did not know that Mao was also in the hotel, since the Chairman's visit to Wuhan was a secret.) Loudly shouting and gesticulating, they seized Wang Li and dragged him to their headquarters. There they cruelly beat him, breaking his leg in the process.[18]

Mao, incensed, ordered Chen Zaidao to return Wang Li. Then he hurriedly flew to Shanghai, not entirely certain that the general would execute his orders, since he did not yet know whether Chen himself was behind the arrest of Wang. The situation was critical. Arriving in Shanghai and lodging at one of the best hotels in town, the Hongqiao binguan (Rainbow), he stayed up all night, discussing the crisis with the officials who had accompanied him. He vacillated between the supposition that Chen himself had raised the rebellion and his feeling that General Chen was actually a good comrade.

"Could he have acted against me?" he anxiously asked Yang Chengwu, chief of the general staff.

Yang emphatically argued against the worst-case scenario.

"Chairman, no one could oppose you. The army, the cadres, the party members and the people all view you as their great liberator. All the old comrades in the army made the revolution with you."

"That's true. That's what I also think," Mao agreed. "If Chen and Zhong had wanted to have done with me, they wouldn't have allowed us to leave Wuhan!"[19]

He calmed down only two days later after deciding to disband the Million Heroes immediately as well as the Wuhan garrison that had supported them. Then he promptly demanded that Zhou Enlai summon Chen Zaidao and Zhong Hanhua to Beijing.

Meanwhile, General Chen, who had no intention of rebelling against the Great Helmsman, succeeded in freeing Wang Li, who returned to the capital. On July 25, a mass rally against capitalist roaders in the army was organized by Jiang Qing in Beijing.[20] Afterward, Chen Zaidao and Zhong Hanhua, who had come to Beijing, were reprimanded at an enlarged meeting of the Politburo Standing Committee chaired by Zhou.[21] On July 27 they were removed from all their positions, and soon thereafter troops dispatched by Lin Biao forcibly disarmed the Wuhan garrison. The arrested soldiers and officers were sent to labor camps. Next the Million Heroes were smashed.[22]

Emboldened, on July 31, Zhang Chunqiao requested Mao's permission to establish a workers' militia in Shanghai to defend the leftists. Assenting, Mao promptly wrote to the other members of the Cultural Revolution Group as well as Lin Biao and Zhou Enlai, welcoming Zhang's initiative. Then, on August 4, he sent another letter to Jiang Qing expressing his conviction that 75 percent of the officers in the PLA were unreliable because they stood on the side of the rightists. He called for establishing a dictatorship of the masses in the country, seizing power in the organs of public security and justice, establishing "revolutionary" courts and arming the leftists everywhere. Jiang quickly passed this message to the Politburo Standing Committee and soon armed Red Guard units were formed throughout the country.[23]

Before three weeks had passed, Mao, to his own surprise, understood he had gone too far. Buoyed by his support, the most frenzied members of the Cultural Revolution Group, Wang Li and a certain Guan Feng, had initiated the seizure of power in the Ministry of Foreign Affairs, where armed Red Guards had destroyed valuable diplomatic papers. Then the same two had provoked rebels to storm the Beijing office of the British chargé d'affaires. The more than ten thousand young anti-imperialist warriors beat up the diplomats in the building, smashed precious furniture, and burned the office and car of the chargé d'affaires. This is how they expressed their protest against the British occupation of Hong Kong.[24]

The formation of armed Red Guard detachments did not put an end to civil war. On the contrary, it only exacerbated the conflict. On average in August around thirty bloody clashes between the radical and the moderate rebels occurred daily in the provinces.[25] Both radicals and moderates continued to be involved in conflicts with the army.

Grasping that the Red Guards would not calm down on their own, Mao finally initiated action against them. In late August 1967, at the request of Zhou Enlai, who was mortified by the attacks on the Ministry of Foreign Affairs and the office of the British representative, Mao ordered the arrest of Wang Li and Guan Feng. Six months later, Qi Benyu, another ultraleftist member of the Cultural Revolution Group, was taken into custody. At Mao's request, an investigation into their "counterrevolutionary activity" revealed that all three were supposedly Guomindang and Soviet spies.[26] Indignant at this "revelation," Mao wrote on a document related to the Wang Li affair, "Big, big, big poisonous weed!" Afterward he carried out a sweeping purge of leftist organizations as well as another periodic purge of all state and public institutions. This time, on his orders, extremists were ferreted out and held to account.

Now Mao's rhetoric changed sharply. He asserted that "[t]he overwhelming majority of our cadres are good and only a tiny minority are not. True, those persons in power taking the capitalist road are our targets, but they are a mere handful."[27] In early September 1967, Mao began to mention the possibility of rehabilitating the majority of repressed party cadres, and in mid-September, setting out from Shanghai to Beijing, he elaborated this theme in all the places he visited en route.[28] In Wuhan he even hinted at the likely return of Deng Xiaoping to high office. "Do we need to protect Deng Xiaoping?" He addressed this provocative question to the perplexed new leaders of Wuhan and, as if thinking out loud, he continued, "First, he has already endured a number of blows, second, he is not a Guomindang agent, third, he does not harbor any black thoughts."[29] He said nothing more specific, but everyone supposed that the Chairman was thinking about "pardoning" Liu Shaoqi's main associate. In mid-October, the Chairman ordered the prompt resumption of studies in schools and universities. At the end of October he ordered the Central Committee and the Cultural Revolution Group to issue a directive reviving the party organizations in all places where Revolutionary Committees existed.[30]

By this time, revolutionary committees had been formed in only seven of the twenty-nine provinces, autonomous regions, and provincial-level municipalities. By March 1968, they would be established in an additional eleven provinces. The process of forming revolutionary committees did not conclude until September. (The last Provincial Revolutionary Committee was set up in Xinjiang.) The army took the lead in the creation of new organs of power and sought to establish its control in the revolutionary committees. There was no equality in the participation of the "three sides." The overwhelming majority of the 48,000 members of the new organs of power above the district level were serving PLA officers. Six of the twenty-nine chairs of provincial-level revolutionary committees were colonel generals, five were lieutenant generals, and nine were major generals. The rest were political commissars. Twenty-two of the twenty-nine first secretaries of the newly reorganized provincial, autonomous region, and provincial-level municipal party committees were likewise high-ranking PLA officers.[31]

Since the fall of 1967, after returning to Beijing from Shanghai, the Chairman also began to talk about "Grasping Revolution and Stimulating Production."[32] The faithful Zhou and the former Oppositionist Li Fuchun, who were responsible for working up the Third Five-Year Plan (1966–70), regularly delivered reports about the catastrophic fall in production, caused not only by the "sabotage of the capitalist roaders" but by the idleness of the "revolutionary" workers.[33]

Calming the impassioned young people turned out to be difficult. Having tasted "freedom," no one wanted to return to the "kingdom of necessity." Detachments of young people marched through the cities and villages shouting, "Long Live Chairman Mao!" "We Will Smash the Dog's Head of Liu Shaoqi, Chief of the Black Gang!" and "Down with Revisionism!" They continued to drag out the "capitalist roaders" and their families, set up kangaroo courts, shouted, and created an uproar. They dragged elderly professors and party officials from their apartments and paraded them in front of improvised tribunals under the burning sun or the fierce cold, crowned them with dunce caps, and hung humiliating placards around their necks. The ignorant youngsters were still battling the Four Olds—old ideas, culture, customs, and habits. In many cities the leftists introduced new rules, for example, crossing the street when the light is red, because red is the color of revolution. Ancient monuments were demolished; archives destroyed; veteran specialists, including medical personnel, engineers, and technicians, not allowed to work. The mass chaos increasingly threatened catastrophe.

On July 3, 1968, Mao demanded that disturbances cease immediately. On July 27 more than thirty thousand workers from more than sixty industrial enterprises in Beijing, organized into so-called Mao Zedong Thought Propaganda Teams, entered into Tsinghua University. Clashes occurred and ten people were killed, but the frenzied Red Guards refused to surrender.

Mao was infuriated. The next day he convened a meeting of the party leadership in the Great Hall of the People, including Lin Biao, Zhou Enlai, Jiang Qing, Kang Sheng, Chen Boda, Xie Fuzhi, and the new chief of the general staff of the PLA, Huang Yongsheng. The Red Guard chiefs of Beijing were summoned to serve as scapegoats.

Mao seemed outwardly calm, and he even tried to crack jokes, but his humor was sinister.

"Kuai Dafu," he began,

> wants to seize the black villain. After all so many workers "suppress" and "oppress" Red Guards. But just who is this black villain? This black villain has still not been captured. This black villain is none other than I. . . . I am the one who dispatched the guard regiment of the CC and the Xinhua typographers and the knitwear factory workers. I said, "Go, do your work, observe, and figure out how to resolve the question of armed struggle in the higher education institutions." Thus, 30,000 persons set out.

"Peking University [also] wants to seize the black villain," he said, turning to Nie Yuanzi, the author of the "first Marxist-Leninist *dazibao*," "but this black villain is not I but Xie Fuzhi. I do not suffer from such ambition."

The Red Guard leaders listened, their heads downcast. Mao continued:

> You have been engaged in the Cultural Revolution for two years by now. With respect to struggle, criticism, and reforms, first, you do not struggle, second, you do not criticize, and third, you have not achieved any reforms. It's true that you struggle, but you conduct armed struggle. The people don't like this, the workers don't like this, the peasants don't like this, the people of [Beijing] don't like this, the majority of students at educational institutions don't like this, and even some people in groups that support you don't like this. And is this how you wish to unite our country?

"Important events are taking place in the country," Lin Biao observed portentously and then paraphrased the beginning of the *Romance of the Three Kingdoms:* "That which was long broken up must be united; and that which was long united must be broken up.[34] The fortifications that were built for armed struggle [in the higher education institutes must] be completely dismantled; all firearms and side-arms, knives, and rifles [must be] handed over to the depots."

The Red Guard leaders understood this was the end. None of them, except for Kuai Dafu, who began sobbing, even tried to justify themselves. Nie

Yuanzi, who had suddenly seen the light, even asked the Chairman to dispatch the PLA to Peking University.

Mao concluded:

Confusion and bitter struggle are rife. . . . Perhaps this time you will expel me from the party? Expel me for bureaucratism, moreover I am a black villain and I suppress the Red Guards. . . . The masses do not like engaging in civil war. . . . We must address . . . an appeal . . . to the whole country. And if anyone continues to destroy order, attack the Liberation Army, destroy communications, kill people or commit arson, then he will be treated as a criminal. If a handful of people do not heed these warnings, and stubbornly refuse to mend their ways, they will turn into robbers and Guomindang elements, and they will have to be surrounded on all sides. If they resist they will have to be destroyed.

"Progress cannot be achieved instantaneously, history always takes a zigzag path," he added, ending the meeting.[35]

In August, PLA troops went into action. Only they were able to restore order and gain control of the universities, which, in the Chairman's words, had become " 'independent kingdoms,' big or small."[36]

Of course, there were now new victims. Sensing the Chairman's inclinations, the military began to suppress the Red Guards in the cruelest manner. The clashes that took place in August 1968 between the army and young people in Nanning, the capital of the Guangxi Zhuang Autonomous Region, were particularly bloody. The streets of the city literally ran in blood; the urban districts controlled by the young people's organizations were wiped from the face of the earth. The number of victims was 2,324; about 10,000 were imprisoned and more than 50,000 people were left homeless.[37] Hearing of this, Mao placed all the responsibility on the extremists among the Red Guards and Rebels, asserting that their uprising against the army was "a kind of death throes of the class enemies."[38]

Beginning in the second half of 1968, some twelve million disillusioned youth were deported to the countryside over the next seven years, most of them to education-through-labor camps where the overwhelming majority remained until the death of the Great Helmsman in 1976. Theirs was a bitter education. Many of them could have spoken the words of the hero of one of the writer Wang Meng's stories: "It's just rotten luck to be born Chinese. . . . The Chinese race, so great and yet so tragic."[39]

In October 1968, the next enlarged plenum of the Central Committee summed up the period of Sturm und Drang. By then more than 70 percent of the members and alternate members of the Central Committee had been

labeled "anti-party elements," "traitors," and "spies" who were "maintaining secret ties with abroad." Ten of the ninety-seven members of the Central Committee had died since August 1966.

Only 40 members and 19 alternates of the 87 members and 96 alternates
chosen at the Eighth Party Congress were present at the plenum. To attain a
quorum, Mao gave full voting rights to 10 alternates from the Central Committee, of which 9 were high-ranking military officers. He also granted voting rights to 74 members from the Cultural Revolution Group, the Military
Commission of the Central Committee, as well as leaders of provincial revolutionary committees and military regions together with a number of Central
Committee officials. The plenum expelled Liu Shaoqi "forever" from the party
and emphasized that the "unmasking" of his "counterrevolutionary physiog-
nomy" was a "great victory" for Mao Zedong Thought. The former head of
state was called a "hidden provocateur and scab, a running dog of imperialism, contemporary revisionism, and Guomindang reaction who had committed egregious crimes against the masses."[40]

Yet, under pressure from Mao, the plenum allowed Deng Xiaoping to
remain a member of the party. "You all want to kick him out, [but] I'm not
keen on the idea," Mao Zedong said.[41] This was enough. Mao also did not allow
the radicals to expel the former February Oppositionists, the marshals and
party officials who had opposed Red Guard mayhem in February 1967. Moreover, he insisted they be "chosen" as delegates to the party congress scheduled
for the following year. This despite the considerable attention devoted at the
plenum to criticism of the February reverse current. "Comrade Chen Yi," Mao
said to the "ideologue" of the February Oppositionists, "you will participate
[in the congress] as the representative of the Right."[42] No sooner said than
done. The plenum enthusiastically supported Chen.

The battle first with the "moderates" and then with the Red Guards was
practically over. Mao now decided to convene a new party congress, the Ninth,
which took place April 1–24, 1969, in Beijing. It was attended by 1,512 delegates representing almost 22 million communists. It resulted in the unanimous adoption of new party statutes in which Mao Zedong Thought was
again declared to be the theoretical foundation of the CCP. Now it was called
"Marxism-Leninism of the era in which imperialism is heading for total collapse and socialism is advancing to world-wide victory."[43]

The composition of the leading organs of the CCP underwent a radical
change. The new Central Committee, consisting of 170 members and 109 alternates, followed the principle of combining "three sides," namely the leading
figures of the Cultural Revolution, the main commanders of the PLA, and the
"revolutionary" party leaders who were the most loyal to Mao. He also retained on the Central Committee several former opponents, including Deng

Zihui, and the February Oppositionists—Chen Yi, Ye Jianying, Xu Xiangqian, Nie Rongzhen, Li Fuchun, and Li Xiannian. All the "comrades" named by the Leader received the requisite number of votes.

At the First Plenum of the newly chosen Central Committee, the power-hungry wives of Mao and Lin Biao, Jiang Qing and Ye Qun, were included in the Politburo, as were the heroes of Shanghai, Zhang Chunqiao and Yao Wenyuan. Chen Boda, Zhou Enlai, and Kang Sheng were included in the Politburo Standing Committee along with Mao and Lin. Lin Biao was returned as the sole deputy chairman, and the entire country began to learn from the army with renewed enthusiasm, especially since it was PLA troops that ultimately had restored order in the country.

The plenum concluded with stormy applause. The cries of "Long Live the Victory of the Great Proletarian Cultural Revolution," "Long Live the Chinese Communist Party," "Long Live Invincible Mao Zedong Thought," "Long Live Chairman Mao, Wan sui! Wan wan sui! (10,000 years, 100 million years!)" long echoed in the hall.

One of the important themes emphasized at the congress and the plenum was the struggle against Soviet revisionism. Mao said:

> The Soviet revisionists now attack us. Some TASS broadcast or other, the Wang Ming material, and the long screed in *Kommunist* [a Soviet Party journal] all say we are no longer a party of the proletariat, and call us a "petit-bourgeois party." They say we have imposed a monolithic order and have returned to the time of the bases, which means we have retrogressed. What is this thing they call becoming monolithic? They say it is a military-bureaucratic system. . . . I say let them talk. They can say whatever they want. But their words have one characteristic: they avoid branding us a bourgeois party, instead they label us a "party of the petit bourgeoisie." We, on the other hand, say that they are a bourgeois dictatorship, and are restoring the dictatorship of the bourgeoisie.[44]

The Central Committee report that Lin Biao delivered at the congress was also sharply anti-Soviet. In 1969 the polemics that had ignited in the early 1960s reached their apogee.

In March, on the eve of the congress, armed clashes occurred on the Far Eastern border between the USSR and the PRC. Soviet and Chinese border troops fought over Damansky (Zhenbao) Island in the Ussuri River. There were dead on both sides: on the first day alone, March 2, twenty-nine soldiers and two officers on the Soviet side and seventeen servicemen on the Chinese side. Forty-nine persons were wounded and one Soviet soldier was taken prisoner and later died in captivity.[45] Some in the West exulted over the "first socialist war."

Relations between China and the USSR had gone steadily downhill after the sudden withdrawal of Soviet specialists in 1960. At various meetings Soviet and Chinese representatives engaged in sharp exchanges regarding the nature of the current era and the question of Stalin's cult of personality. The Chinese accused the leaders of the CPSU of being "social democrats," while the Soviet communists screamed about the "ultra-leftism" of the CCP leaders.

Finally, in 1963, Khrushchev had had enough. In response to a letter from the Central Committee of the CCP, dated June 14, 1963, and titled "A Proposal Concerning the General Line of the International Communist Movement," the Central Committee of the CPSU on July 14 sent an open letter to all communists in the Soviet Union. It referred to the "erroneous and fatal" policy of the Chinese Communist Party, the "glaring contradiction" in the actions of the Chinese leadership "not only to the principles of mutual relations among socialist countries, but, in a number of cases, to the accepted rules and norms all states should abide by."[46]

In response, *People's Daily* and the journal *Red Flag* erupted with a joint editorial in which they excoriated the shameful united front of Moscow, Washington, New Delhi, and Belgrade "against socialist China and against all Marxist-Leninist Parties." "Khrushchev revisionists" were condemned as betrayers "of Marxism-Leninism and proletarian internationalism."[47] The Chinese press then published eight more so-called critical articles developing this theme. In May 1964, at one of the meetings of the Chinese leadership, Mao, making no attempt to check his anger, asserted, "In the Soviet Union there is now a dictatorship of the bourgeoisie, a dictatorship of the big bourgeoisie, a German-fascist dictatorship of the Hitler type. This is a gang of bandits who are worse than De Gaulle."[48]

At the same time, both sides raised contentious new issues. The Chinese asserted territorial claims vis-à-vis the Soviets. "In discussions with our advisors in China, the Beijing leadership stated in a very hostile way that the Russians had taken what was then the Soviet Far Eastern region from China, along with other adjacent territories," Khrushchev recalled.

> Some misunderstandings arose between us in regard to the border along the Ussuri River and along some other rivers. As is generally known, rivers tend to change course over time, and new islands are sometimes formed. Under the treaty signed between China and the tsarist government, the Chinese bank of the river formed the border, not the middle of the river channel, as is the usual practice under international law. Thus, if new islands were formed they were considered Russian. . . . Later the situation became more strained.[49]

In 1962 Moscow agreed to secret border talks with Beijing which began in February 1964. Khrushchev broke them off in October, however, because the Chinese, in addition to the question about the river channel, insisted on discussing the problem of czarist expansion in Siberia and the Far East. Nevertheless, the Soviet side agreed that a new border treaty with the PRC should replace the czarist one. According to this treaty, Damansky Island should go to the Chinese since it was west of the main channel of the Ussuri River. In other words, if one followed international practice, it was in Chinese territorial waters. A treaty was not signed, however, but the Chinese, noting that the USSR had agreed to conclude it according to international principles, began to consider Damansky theirs.[50]

For a time, following Khrushchev's ouster in October 1964, there was hope that a constructive dialogue might be revived. In early November, a Chinese delegation headed by Zhou Enlai came to Moscow by invitation of the Soviet side to celebrate the anniversary of the October Revolution. It was greeted by the Soviet premier Alexei Kosygin, the most active supporter of normalizing ties with China. However, the chance to arrange even normal businesslike relations with what had once been a good neighbor collapsed. In the words of Andrei Aleksandrov-Agentov, an assistant to Khrushchev's successor, Leonid Brezhnev, this occurred because of "an absurd incident or under the influence of the military leadership which was infuriated at the Chinese. In any event, at a festive banquet in the Kremlin, a highly intoxicated Marshal Malinovsky, the minister of defense, approached the Chinese premier and in the hearing of everyone said, 'Well, we have done our part, we got rid of our old galosh Khrushchev. Now if you will chuck out your old galosh Mao, then our problems will be over.' Outraged, Zhou Enlai immediately stalked out of the banquet."[51] The following day Brezhnev tried to smooth over the matter: "Malinovsky is not a member of the Presidium [of the CPSU], he drank too much and blurted out something. Moreover, the translation was imprecise. We are prepared to apologize."[52] But Zhou said, "There is nothing for us to talk about."[53]

Kosygin and several other members of the Soviet leadership who favored improving relations with China were shaken by this. They advised Brezhnev to pay a visit to Mao, but Brezhnev was obdurate. Finally, he challenged Kosygin: "If you consider this so essential, then go yourself." Kosygin actually did. In February 1965, he met in Beijing with Zhou and then with Mao and Liu. "The conversation was pointed and rather unpleasant," writes Aleksandrov-Agentov. "Our comrades were reminded of all the injustices Khrushchev committed vis-à-vis China, and the accusations about the CPSU's 'revision of Leninism' were repeated. In a word, it became clear that there was no possibility of returning to the former 'fraternal friendship,' and that China would never again play the role of 'younger brother' to the Soviet Union."[54] Mao expressed his wish to continue the polemics with the CPSU even if they lasted another ten thousand years, and only when he was wrapping up the talks did he soften and shorten this by one thousand years.[55]

A year later, however, when the Cultural Revolution commenced, Mao sharply intensified attacks on the USSR, even accusing the Soviet leadership of wishing to unleash a war against China. "The Soviet Union is planning . . . to violate the state border in Siberia and Mongolia, to carry out incursions into Inner Mongolia and Northeast China and to occupy China," he declared to the whole world. "This may result in a situation in which the People's Liberation Army and the Soviet Army will face each other across opposite sides of the Yangzi River."[56]

Attempting to force the government of the USSR to sign a border treaty, the Chinese side began acting in an increasingly threatening manner. From 1964 to 1969, there were 4,189 incidents—not armed, it is true—along the Soviet-Chinese border. The situation deteriorated sharply after the dispatch of Soviet troops to Czechoslovakia in late August 1968, and the assertion by the Soviet leadership of the so-called Brezhnev Doctrine, which stated that the USSR had the right to intervene in the internal affairs of any socialist country where socialism was in danger. In October 1968, PRC minister of defense Lin Biao put the armed forces of the PRC on alert. Mao Zedong and Zhou Enlai were initially skeptical of Lin Biao's anxiety, but they raised no objections to these precautionary measures.[57]

Thus the gunfire on Damansky was no accident. Who fired the first shot is still not known to this day. Most likely everything happened spontaneously. Someone's nerves simply snapped. But the incident brought Sino-Soviet relations to a new level. The gunshots echoed in both capitals. Each side loudly accused the other of provocations. According to several sources, the Soviet government was in a state of panic. Minister of Defense Andrei Grechko was insisting on an atomic attack against the PRC's industrial centers. Others suggested blowing up Chinese atomic sites. Instead Brezhnev authorized a massive strike on Chinese territory with Grad rockets to a depth of 20 kilometers. This was done on the night of March 14–15 in the same vicinity of Damansky. More than eight hundred Chinese died.

Speaking soon afterward at the First Plenum of the Ninth Central Committee, Mao devoted a significant portion of his speech to the question of preparing for war with the USSR.[58] He really thought a Soviet armed attack against China was likely. After the plenum he even issued secret instructions for preparing to evacuate the majority of party leaders from Beijing.[59]

If only he had known that in late January 1967, in a conversation with officials of the Department of Socialist Countries of the Central Committee of the CPSU, Wang Ming, who lived in the Soviet Union, had advised the Soviet leaders to carry out armed intervention in the affairs of the PRC. "The current situation in China is even more dangerous for the socialist camp and the international communist movement than the events in Hungary in 1956," Wang said. "We cannot let the opportunity pass by . . . we [must] provide them [the healthy forces in the Chinese Communist Party] not only political, but also material support via arms and possibly by sending a force composed of the proper nationalities from Central Asia and the Mongolian People's Republic." Wang was even prepared to hold secret talks with the leaders of Xinjiang and Inner Mongolia, whom he considered his secret supporters.[60]

Of course, no such incursion took place. In April, May, June, and August 1969, however, new clashes occurred both in the Far East and along the Xinjiang sector of the border. The situation was soon brought under control during another meeting between Kosygin and Zhou Enlai at the Beijing airport on September 11.[61] Following this, negotiations over the contentious border issues commenced. The Soviets had to give up Damansky. Yet until his death Mao continued to view the Soviet Union as China's worst enemy. The uncompromising struggle against "frenzied" revisionism continued at home and abroad.

35

THE MYSTERY OF
PROJECT 571

On December 10, 1970, when Edgar Snow interviewed Mao Zedong for the fifth and final time, Mao was two weeks shy of his seventy-seventh birthday. Snow found him in reasonably good physical condition. Mao seemed to be suffering from a cold but otherwise looked quite well. He had even lost weight since their last meeting, in January 1965. Of course, his age was showing, but the Chairman's mind was still lively. The Great Helmsman observed to his guest that he would "soon be going to see God," but he did not seem upset. It was inevitable, Mao said: everyone eventually had to see God. Snow knew that even earlier Mao had liked to speak about death. The Chairman had been talking about going to see Marx ever since 1961, when he spoke with Field Marshal Montgomery. On the eve of the Cultural Revolution in 1965, he had talked about the approach of death with Snow and first said that "very soon" he would meet with God. (No one knows why he no longer referred to Marx, but rather to the Almighty.)[1] Old age and death had long since become favorite themes of his.

Of course, there was a significant element of intrigue in this. Mao loved to pretend that he was sick or unwell in order to gauge the impression this would produce upon his entourage.[2] In February 1963, for example, he played the role of a seriously ill old man before Stepan Chervonenko, the Soviet ambassador. "He first rehearsed his act several times in front of me and other members of his staff, covering himself with a terry-cloth blanket, feigning lethargy and pain," his physician recalled. " 'Do I look like I'm sick?' he wanted to know. Then he called the Soviet envoy to his bedside and staged an excellent dramatic performance."[3] The Soviet representatives were truly stunned:

> We were struck by an unexpected contrast: in the middle of the poorly lighted room stood a tall bed on which Mao Zedong was half-lying. Around it sat Liu Shaoqi, Zhou Enlai, Deng Xiaoping, and the inter-

preter in respectful poses. . . . The Chairman said that he could no longer decipher small characters and that large character texts were specially printed for him; he asserted that he no longer presided over sessions of the Politburo and did not read all the important papers. "Now they are the ones conducting the affairs of the party," Mao Zedong said, pointing to the leaders of the CCP who were sitting in his bedroom.[4]

In December 1970, Mao really felt unwell. It took a considerable effort for him to appear healthy to Snow. On the eve of their meeting he had barely begun to recover from a serious bout of pneumonia that had confined him to bed for almost two months. That is why he looked thinner.

Eventually he regained his full strength. Parting with Snow, Mao left him with the words that he was "a monk holding an umbrella, without hair, without sky."[5] This meant that he was subject neither to the laws of man nor those of heaven. In other words, he lived as he liked, and he would live as long as he desired. (The words for "hair" and "law" are pronounced similarly in Chinese [fa], although the tones differ.)

Snow understood none of this, because the young interpreter, Nancy Tang (Tang Wensheng), born in America and unfamiliar with classical philosophy, translated the expression as if Mao were "only a lone monk walking the world with a leaky umbrella."[6] No one knows how she came up with this phrase, but Snow trusted her implicitly and conveyed Mao's message to the whole world. People everywhere tried to guess just what he had in mind. Why was he so alone!

Mao boasted in vain about living as long as he liked. At his age pneumonia was very dangerous. Previously he had suffered only from bronchitis, which he could not fully overcome because he continued to smoke two packs of cigarettes a day. His favorite brands were no longer Chesterfields or 555s, but domestic cigarettes like Zhonghua (China), Xiongmao (Panda), and Luojiashan (Mount Luojia). Possibly he chose these for patriotic reasons. Shortly before Snow's arrival, Mao switched to Northern Star, a higher-quality cigarette manufactured in Canton from foreign tobacco.[7]

Mao's health was also compromised by his abnormal habits. He went to bed well past midnight, often around 5 A.M., and slept only until 11 A.M. He ate just twice a day, around 2 or 3 P.M. and again between 8 and 9 P.M. His favorite dish was fatty roast pork cut into small pieces and prepared with hot Hunan pepper sauce. However, he drank in moderation, on rare occasions allowing himself some Chinese grape wine. Only on major holidays did he drink a little *maotai*, a pungent rice liquor.

The unrelenting political struggle also had a devastating impact on his health. After the Red Guards were crushed, political struggle shifted from the streets back to the party. The sharply increasing role of the leading generals in the army, who were directly responsible for restoring order, provoked dissatisfaction on the part of those in Jiang Qing's faction who were the main leaders of the Cultural Revolution. Relations among the various factions of the once-united left became increasingly strained. Jiang Qing and her associates began to express indignation at the actions of the PLA. Lin Biao and his generals, as well as his wife, Ye Qun, who had an enormous influence on her husband and his entourage, reacted irritably. They believed that the era of Sturm und Drang was over and that production and military modernization were the top priorities. Zhou Enlai supported them.

The first signs of conflict had already appeared in late 1967. This is how Soviet intelligence reported the situation to the Central Committee of the CPSU:

> Information from Comrade TSVIGUN* Entry No. 4761 from December 7, 1967. . . . Inside the new ruling group [in the Chinese Communist Party our agents] have witnessed a growing strain in relations between ZHOU ENLAI and LIN BIAO on one hand, and the leaders of the CC Cultural Revolution Group, especially KANG SHENG and JIANG QING on the other. The criticism and sidelining of many figures who are representatives of the "new forces," supported by KANG SHENG and JIANG QING, indicates that the position of these latter figures has become somewhat weakened at present. The termination of the purge in the army, the reining in of the Red Guards and the Rebels with respect to seizing power by force, the refusal to arm them, and the greater attention paid to economic questions, all these actions undoubtedly have increased the authority of ZHOU ENLAI and LIN BIAO.[8]

This information was accurate. Jiang Qing was encouraging anti–Lin Biao sentiment within the party leadership in an increasingly open manner. Initially she was unable to lure Mao into her intrigues. He continued to trust his close comrade in arms (such was Lin's official title). At the Ninth Party Congress a statement that Lin Biao was Mao Zedong's successor was even included in the party's statutes.[9]

Mao refused to hear anything bad about Lin, whom he had known since April 1928, when Zhu De's forces, in which Lin Biao served, joined with Mao's insurgents in the Jinggang Mountains. They had been introduced by Chen Yi, the chief political commissar in Zhu De's army who had described Lin as a

---

* Semyon Kuz'mich Tsvigun (1917–1982) was first deputy chairman of the KGB from November 1967.

brilliant officer that knew how to rout the enemy. Mao was ecstatic. "You're so young and you fight so boldly. That's great!" he exclaimed.[10]

Lin then was just going on twenty-one. He had been born on December 5, 1907, in Huanggang county, Hubei, into a family of weavers. He had a middle school education and in 1924, under the influence of two communist cousins joined the Socialist Youth League. In the winter of 1925 he was admitted to the Whampoa Academy in revolutionary Canton and found his career. He joined the Communist Party in late 1925 and was sent to the communist regiment of Ye Ting. Lin Biao participated in the Nanchang Uprising of August 1, 1927, along with Ye Ting and Zhu De. After its defeat he went to the Jinggang Mountains.[11]

He quickly fell under the influence of Mao, whom he began to treat with filial deference. The older man valued his junior acolyte. For Lin Biao, who was weak in Marxist theory, Mao was an encyclopedia of knowledge, a genius of science and politics as well as a military leader. Modest and shy, Lin was not a natural leader although he was a talented military commander. Among the leaders of the Chinese Communist Party he was called "the Maiden."[12] Thin and diminutive with thick, almost astonishingly raised eyebrows, he reminded one of a beauty from some Beijing opera in which men play the female roles. The name Lin Biao, which means "Forest Snow Leopard," did not fit well with his looks and behavior.

His obedience, devotion, and lack of ambition, combined with his brilliant military abilities,* impressed Mao Zedong, who easily bent Lin to his own strong will. Mao began to nominate Lin to leading positions, because he did not discern a rival in this taciturn and unassertive military commander who was always ready to execute his orders. By 1949 Lin was already a member of the Central Committee and commander of the Fourth Field Army. That year he was chosen as a member of the Central People's Government Council as well as deputy chairman of the People's Revolutionary Military Council of the PRC. In 1954 he was made deputy premier of the State Council. A year later, Mao brought Lin into the Politburo and awarded him the rank of marshal. In May 1958, he became a member of the Politburo Standing Committee and one of Mao's deputy chairmen. Following the dismissal of Peng Dehuai in 1959, Mao quickly appointed Lin Biao as his new minister of defense.

The one thing that occasionally annoyed even Mao was the extraordinary adulation Lin accorded him. "I never believed that several of my little books could possess such great magical power," Mao wrote to Jiang Qing in July 1966. "Now, after his [Lin Biao's] laudatory words, the entire country has begun to

---

* Even Otto Braun, who despised Lin Biao, was compelled to point out in one of his reports to the ECCI that "I personally consider him [Lin Biao] to be the best field commander in the Eighth Route Army."

extol them; this is truly a case of 'Old Woman Wang sells her pumpkins, and says how good they are.' . . . He [Lin Biao] spoke even more forcefully in the press. He worshiped me as if I were like the holiest of the saints. So, I just have to play along. But . . . the higher the praise, the more painful the fall." [13] Lin Biao's toadying, however, was not a significant transgression. Although Mao might grumble over this, it also pleased him. Moreover, there were any number of people prepared to idolize the Chairman, so many that by the late 1960s the aging Leader himself began to feel he was a god. The number of copies of the *Quotations* was exceeded only by the number of Bibles, and *People's Daily* and other newspapers were constantly writing about inconceivable miracles wrought by Mao Zedong Thought. Correspondents of the Xinhua News Agency reported the resurrection of the dead after physicians uttered quotations from the Great Helmsman over their bodies, the blind recovering their sight and the dumb their ability to speak as well as other absurdities. [14] Lin Biao was not responsible for such nonsense. Jiang Qing and Chen Boda controlled the mass media.

Much more inconvenient for Mao was that his future successor was always ill. The nature of his illness remains a mystery. We know only that it was psychological rather than physical in nature. Possibly it was the consequence of the four wounds he had suffered during the civil war and the Sino-Japanese War. As early as his first trip to Moscow in 1939–41, Lin Biao complained about severe headaches, vomiting, heart palpitations, insomnia, and nervous disorders. [15] He was treated at Monino and Kislovodsk, but to no avail. In his own words, every time he did a "little mental labor" he developed severe headaches and insomnia. [16] From July to October 1951, he and his wife, Ye Qun, and their daughter Liheng—her pet name was Doudou, a diminutive from the word for "bean" *—sojourned in the Soviet Union, where he again underwent treatment that was ineffective. He stopped trusting in doctors and developed a serious persecution complex. He believed that his doctors were plotting to kill

---

* Lin Biao was married twice. His first wife, Liu Xingmin (she was also known both as Liu Xinmin and as Zhang Mei), was twelve years younger than he. She was a simple, unlettered girl from northern Shaanxi. In 1939 she went with her husband to the Soviet Union. But after two years, Lin broke with her. He returned to China in August 1941, leaving her pregnant in Moscow. Liu gave birth to a daughter, whom she named Xiaolin. Until September 1948 Liu worked in the International Orphanage in Ivanovo, where, it will be recalled, Mao's former wife Zizhen was for a time. Then she returned to China. Xiaolin was able to leave for China only in 1950 after Lin Biao himself interceded on her behalf. However, he saw this daughter only rarely. He now had a different family. During the anti-Japanese war he married a native of Fujian named Ye Qun, who was also twelve years his junior. He had two children from this marriage: Lin Liheng (Doudou), the daughter born in 1944, and a son, Lin Liguo, born in 1946.

him by poisoning the baths they prescribed for him. He stopped seeing them and thereafter his wife became his physician.[17] She was a woman of amazingly strong character, so it is not surprising that the weak-willed Lin was completely under her power. She did not love her husband, who was constantly languishing in depression, especially since Lin, who cycled through his illnesses, had lost any interest in sex. The marriage was her springboard to higher power, which is why she tried her utmost to indulge her sick spouse.

Meanwhile, Lin Biao's psychological attacks worsened with each passing year. Although he formally held various leading positions, for months at a time Lin was absent from work.[18] Mao's personal physician, who was asked to visit Lin in his residence, described one of these attacks: "When we were escorted into his room, Lin Biao was in bed, curled in the arms of his wife, Ye Qun, his head nestled against her bosom. Lin Biao was crying, and Ye Qun was patting him and comforting him as though he were a baby." Lin's wife told the doctor that in the 1940s her husband had become addicted to opium and had then switched to morphine. He had been cured of this habit in the Soviet Union, but

> his behavior continued to be strange. Lin Biao was . . . so afraid of wind and light that he rarely went outside, often missing meetings. His fear of water was so extreme that even the sound of it would give him instant diarrhea. He would not drink liquids at all. Ye Qun made sure he received liquid by dipping steamed buns in water and feeding them to her husband. That and the water in his food were the only liquids he got.
>
> Lin Biao never used a toilet. When moving his bowels, he would use a quilt, as if it were a tent, to cover himself, and would squat over a bedpan that his wife would place on his bed.
>
> I was astonished. Lin Biao was obviously mentally unsound.[19]

Another Chinese physician who examined the minister of defense gave a similar diagnosis. He "could find nothing functionally wrong" with him, but he recognized "a plenitude of symptoms of psychological disorientation and plain evidence of drug usage."[20]

According to the reminiscences of Lin Biao's daughter Doudou and his son-in-law, Zhang Qinglin, the sick marshal invariably took some kind of "medicine" before he dared to venture out of his house, which was surrounded by a high stone wall, to attend public events during the Cultural Revolution. This "medicine," which was kept in ampules labeled as vitamin C, could keep him going for several hours, but afterward the wretched man's illness would get worse for weeks at a time.[21]

This was precisely the kind of "close comrade in arms" that Mao, who feared strong individuals, needed. Or might the Chairman simply have pitied the unfortunate Lin, and cut him the slack to be sick? In any case, he did not wish to listen to Jiang Qing and her confederates slander the minister of defense.

But flowing water sculpts even the hardest rock. Ultimately the perfidious Jiang succeeded in toppling the sick marshal. In the deadly struggle for power between the two factions the aging Helmsman supported his wife. In early May 1970, while resting in Hangzhou, Mao thought of changing the constitution of the PRC by deleting the Second Article, which designated the chairman of the People's Republic of China as the formal head of state. Following the purge of Liu Shaoqi this post had remained vacant; now Mao decided it was superfluous. He informed the members of the Politburo, adding, however, that if they wanted to preserve this position they should know that he (Mao) did not wish to be the chairman of the PRC. "If [the Politburo] decides to maintain such a position, it is Lin Biao who should hold the position," he summed up.[22] Many years later this is how General Wu Faxian, commander of the PLA Air Force and a member of the Politburo, recalled Mao's instructions.[23]

After this communication, the members of the Politburo established a six-member commission that soon began drafting a new constitution. Meanwhile, Lin Biao, who had not attended the Politburo meeting, informed both Mao and the others that he did not wish to become the chairman of the PRC. However, he thought it "would be wrong for such a large country" like China "not to have a symbolic head to represent it." Therefore, he insisted that Mao himself should accept this position. Possibly, Lin did not understand what the Great Helmsman actually wanted, and decided to flatter him just in case. Of course, according to the rules of proper Chinese behavior, he should decline even if he really wanted the position. But he actually was horrified at the thought of the numerous duties, of the need to attend diplomatic events and to travel abroad frequently. For someone in his condition this would be an inordinate burden.

Mao, it seems, understood Lin Biao's fears or toadying. At any rate, he informed Lin that the post of chairman of the PRC could be maintained in the constitution. But he added, "I will not hold the position, and neither will you. Let Old Dong [Biwu]* be the state chairman and, at the same time, put several younger people in the position of vice-chairmen."[24] There, it seems, the matter might have ended.

Just then, however, heated disputes flared up among the members of the commission preparing a draft constitution over how to fathom the intentions of the Great Helmsman. Kang Sheng and Zhang Chunqiao argued that Mao

---

* It will be recalled that in the early 1930s Dong Biwu (1886–1975) was the secretary of the Party Control Commission. From 1959 on he and Song Qingling were vice chairmen of the PRC.

really did not want the post of chairman of the PRC, while Wu Faxian and another general from Lin Biao's faction thought the opposite. Moreover, there was disagreement over whether to include in the text of the constitution the sentence "Mao Zedong Thought is the guiding force of our country." The generals favored this, but their opponents were against it. The latter were probably just egging on Lin Biao's supporters, trying to provoke a scandal. Zhang Chunqiao even said, "There are some people who are constantly mouthing off about Marxism and Mao Zedong Thought. But this doesn't mean that they are actually Marxists." He was obviously hinting at Lin Biao and alluding to Mao's grumbling about flattery. Chen Boda, who was also participating in the work of the commission, defended the generals. The sixth member of the group kept mum.

The apostasy of Chen Boda, who had been one of the closest confederates of Jiang Qing and Kang Sheng, was deeply rooted. Chen had long conceived a dislike for Mao's wife. He had even confided to several friends that he wanted to do away with himself because he could no longer tolerate this hysterical and power-hungry woman. By switching to the side of Lin Biao and Ye Qun he chose betrayal rather than suicide. In late 1968 he had begun to openly support Jiang Qing's rivals, which step, of course, she could not forgive.[25]

In these circumstances the Second Plenum of the Central Committee convened in Lushan in August–September 1970. The issue of a new constitution was on the agenda. Lin Biao took advantage of this to strike a blow against Zhang Chunqiao and the entire Jiang Qing faction. Zhou supported him, and then Mao, indicating his agreement, merely advised Lin not to criticize Zhang by name. "It must be Jiang Qing who backed Zhang Chunqiao," he noted.[26]

Lin did everything that he had agreed to with Mao. He did not name Zhang but he asserted that the Great Helmsman was a genius, which justified inserting a passage about Mao's Thought in the constitution. Then the participants in the plenum divided into small groups to discuss Lin's speech. Then something happened that Lin would soon have occasion to regret. Many of those speaking, the generals in the first instance, enthusiastically supported their commander, especially when they grasped that his speech was aimed against Zhang, Jiang Qing, and their ilk. The Long March veterans also supported Lin.

Jiang Qing's tragedy was that few people in the party liked her. The enmity of many party leaders and their wives pursued Jiang throughout her marriage, which she repaid with malice, envy, and hatred. It was a vicious circle. The more they despised her, the more she hated them all; the more keenly she persecuted her enemies, the more fiercely they despised her. When she headed the Cultural Revolution Group she conceived a particular hatred for the party veterans. Now those who had managed to survive the Red Guard terror were savoring revenge. They willingly began singing the praises of Lin to spite Jiang. Chen Boda plunged into this effort.

The discussions continued for two days. Jiang, Zhang, and the other left-ists were terribly frightened. So they did the only thing they could do: they turned to Mao for help. One can only imagine what dark hues they used to paint Lin Biao, Ye Qun, and the generals. Judging by what was to come, they must have presented their opponents as "plotters" seeking to undo the Cul-tural Revolution. Moreover, because Lin thought it necessary to preserve the post of chairman of the PRC, they accused him of an attempt to seize power in the state. They were not at all dissuaded by the fact that the naïve marshal had suggested that Mao be given this position. They interpreted everything their enemy had said as a vile attempt of this "inveterate intriguer" to deceive the Leader. The Great Helmsman could not abide this.

He reacted instantaneously by convening a meeting of the Politburo Standing Committee, at which he firmly took Zhang's side. Then he aborted the plenum and prepared to deliver a counterblow against Jiang Qing's en-emies. He followed through six days later, concentrating all his critical fire on Chen Boda, who had betrayed Jiang and, by association, the Cultural Revolu-tion. Mao wanted to force Chen to make a self-criticism.

Lin had not expected such a gambit from the Great Helmsman. This was the first occasion during their "friendship" that Mao had so shamelessly betrayed him. Departing Lushan, Lin gloomily told his colleagues, "We are generals, and we only know how to fight wars," meaning neither he nor his subordinates had ever learned how to engage in political intrigues.[27]

Lin, who had really been offended by Mao, ordered his generals not to engage in self-criticism. He realized he had lost a power struggle with Jiang and Zhang but he did not want to take part in this dirty brawl anymore. Mao, however, could not calm down. As had happened repeatedly before, he was gripped by the passion of the hunt. Sensing this, the bloodthirsty Jiang Qing fed Mao's rage by hammering home to him the idea of a military plot. Feeling the ground slipping from under his feet, Lin reluctantly gave permission to his generals to make self-criticisms in front of the Leader. He did not admit any fault of his own. He simply hid his head in the sand.

Ye Qun understood the urgency of finding a way out of this dangerous situation. The most active and strong-willed of those in Lin Biao's entourage, she was the first to contemplate countermeasures. The fate of Liu Shaoqi and his wife haunted her. Knowing what could happen to her, Lin, and their family if the Leader continued to listen to Jiang Qing, she could not sit idly by. Her son, Liguo, shared her anxiety. He was an air force officer, and although he was very young (in 1970 he was just twenty-four years old), he enjoyed great influ-ence in the PLA Air Force. Since October 1969 Liguo had served as deputy director of the Operations Department of the air force and concurrently as a leading staff member in the office of the air force chief of staff Wu Faxian. Not surprisingly, he was extremely vain and cocky. From childhood he had been treated like a prince by his mother, who loved him so much that she had no love left for her firstborn child, Doudou. The daughter grew up a pariah, did the heavy housework, and endured constant humiliation from her mother. She accumulated these insults in her heart.

In October 1970, Lin Liguo and several of his closest comrades who revered him and addressed him as "commander" in English formed a secret group they called the Joint Fleet.[28] This organization aimed to seize power in the country. Ye Qun became the éminence grise. (The members of the group called her the viscountess.)[29]

The plotters began to discuss several variants of a rescue plan. Lin Liguo, extremely decisive, was even more radical than his mother. With his approval, in March 1971, one of the air force officers drafted several versions of a plan to assassinate Mao Zedong. Liguo was ecstatic when he saw it. He promptly named the document "Theses of Project 571." (In Chinese this number is pronounced wu qiyi. The words for "armed rebellion" are pronounced the same though with somewhat different tones.) Mao appeared in the draft plan under the code name B-52 after the famous American bomber. These were naïve children playing at war.

Of course, they were doomed. Not a single version of their plan was realistic. For example, one of the means for getting rid of Mao was to send aloft an entire air corps to bomb the Great Helmsman's special train. Another entailed blowing up an oil storage tank in Shanghai at the moment the Chairman's train approached. A third was to arrange an accident on a bridge between Shanghai and Nanjing.[30] The conspirators were convinced a surprise attack was essential.[31]

The plotters were racing against time, lacking the leisure to work out a detailed plan for a putsch. They expected to be arrested at any moment. "[W]e must use a violent, revolutionary coup," wrote the author of the plan. B-52 "is wary of us. It is better to burn our bridges behind us rather than to sit and wait to be captured. . . . This is a life-or-death struggle—either we devour them, or they devour us."[32]

Meanwhile, Mao, who suspected nothing, increased the pressure on Lin Biao. In his own words, he used three methods: "throwing stones," "mixing sand into soil," and "undermining the wall."[33] In other words, he criticized, brought his own people into the Military Commission, and restructured organizations loyal to Lin. In late 1970 and early 1971 he reorganized the Northeast Bureau of the Central Committee and the command of the Beijing Military Region, purging from them well-known supporters of Lin and Chen Boda. At the same time a hysterical campaign spread across the country to criticize Chen, who was accused of "treason and espionage." (No one in the country except for Mao and the members of the Cultural Revolution Group understood what these crimes were actually about.) Meanwhile, Mao let Lin know that he had better come crawling to him on his knees. But his mentally ill comrade in arms was depressed and aggrieved. He no longer had the strength to pull himself together. Even when, at Mao's request, Zhou Enlai visited him and informed him of the Leader's mood, Lin could only mutter through clenched teeth a single sentence: "One often harvests what he did not sow." [34] He did not move from his place.

Mao assumed that the marshal, who was avoiding him, would make a self-criticism at the forthcoming Central Committee Work Conference on education, scheduled for April–June. But Lin, pleading illness, ignored this event. By now the Chairman had run out of patience. In July 1971, barely containing his rage, he told Zhou Enlai, "Their mistakes are different from your past mistakes because they were conspirators." [35]

Less than a month later, on August 14, Mao secretly departed the capital to feel out the mood in the provinces. From August 15 to September 11, he visited Wuhan, Changsha, Nanchang, Hangzhou, and Shanghai, meeting with regional party officials and military commanders. Prior to his departure he observed to his doctor, "I don't think the regional commanders will side with Lin Biao. The People's Liberation Army won't rebel against me, will it? Anyway, if they don't want my leadership, I'll go to Jinggangshan and start another guerrilla war." [36]

Now things began to take an abrupt turn. It is not entirely clear whether Mao by this time knew about the real plot by Lin Liguo and Ye Qun. Some eyewitnesses answer in the affirmative; others express doubt. Most likely he was unaware, and by "conspirators" he supposed that Lin Biao and his supporters were simply engaging in intraparty intrigues. Otherwise, it is unlikely he would have allowed the conspirators to remain at liberty while he left Beijing. Nevertheless, at every meeting with local cadres he openly attacked the "new Lushan conspirators," even naming them. His words sounded like a death sentence.

> At the 1970 Lushan Conference they [Lin Biao and the others] made a surprise attack and carried out underground activity. Why didn't they dare to act openly? Clearly they had something to hide. So they first dissembled and then made a surprise attack. They concealed things from three of the five members of the Standing Committee of the Politburo. They also concealed things from the great majority of comrades on the Politburo. . . . They said not a word and then launched a surprise attack.

Mao was furious. Red-hot with rage, he continued: "A certain person was anxious to become state chairman, to split the Party and to seize power. The question of 'genius' is a theoretical question. Their theory was idealist apriorism." At this point, the majority of his auditors sighed deeply and no longer doubted the "counterrevolutionary" essence of the heretofore respected "close comrade-in-arms of the Great Leader." One wonders if any of them understood the meaning of the awful-sounding word "apriorism." Yet Mao was not done. "Comrade Lin Biao did not discuss that speech of his with me," Mao shame-lessly prevaricated. He also demonstrated his contempt for Lin as a worthless man and father. "I never approved of someone's wife [Mao used the colloquial expression *lao po* (old woman)] becoming the office manager in one's own work unit," he flung at Lin. Regarding Lin Biao's son Liguo, Mao said: "It does a person under thirty no good at all if you call him a 'super-genius.' "

After such words, the only options remaining to Lin's family and his gen-erals was to beg for forgiveness, shoot themselves, or rise in rebellion. Mao provided them an apparent opportunity to turn over a new leaf by repeating his familiar formula, "We should still operate a policy of educating them, that is, 'learning from past mistakes to prevent future ones and curing the disease to save the patient.' We still want to protect Lin." Yet he characterized his dis-agreements with his new "enemies" as a struggle between two lines and two headquarters, placing the "new Lushan conspirators" on the same footing not only with Peng Dehuai, but also with Liu Shaoqi.[37]

Ye Qun and Lin Liguo were promptly informed of Mao's speeches. They panicked and could not decide what to do. They did have sufficient wit to real-ize that launching Project 571 was impossible. The only thing left was to flee for their lives. Tension built as Mao traveled from one city to another. Finally, on September 12, when he returned to Beijing, they had arrived at the critical point. Ye and Lin Liguo suggested to Lin Biao that they flee. They did not want to take Doudou with them. Ye Qun's relations with her daughter remained venomous. Lin Liguo was also on very bad terms with his sister. She repaid him in kind, and was sometimes so deeply depressed that once, during her early adolescence, she had even attempted suicide. She persisted in thinking that Ye Qun was not her biological mother, a suspicion that grew into certainty when the poor girl began receiving anonymous letters confirming her fears.

In September 1971 the entire family was vacationing in the resort of Bei-daihe. At the nearby airport of Shanhaiguan a Trident No. 256 was at the dis-posal of the minister of defense. It was on this plane that Lin Biao, Ye Qun, and Lin Liguo finally decided to flee the country. All their conversations were held behind closed doors, but on the evening of September 12, Liguo divulged their intentions to his sister. Doudou did not hesitate to denounce her parents and brother. At 10 P.M. she barged into the guardhouse to inform the deputy com-mander of the PLA unit 8341, which served the high-ranking party leaders, about everything she knew. She was absolutely convinced that her mother and brother had decided to "kidnap" her father.

The deputy commander quickly contacted his superior in Beijing, who informed Zhou Enlai. The premier rushed to Zhongnanhai to inform the Leader. Mao grimaced in fury. Zhou advised the Chairman to leave his residence at once and move to the Great Hall of the People, where he would be more secure.[38]

Meanwhile, Lin Biao and his wife and son grabbed their porcelain ware, place mats, cameras, and tape recorder and rushed to the airport in an armored car. Once on board, they ordered the pilot to take off, without checking on how much fuel was in the tank. There was barely a ton. In their haste, they did not take a copilot, navigator, or radio operator. On takeoff their plane grazed a fuel tanker, resulting in the undercarriage tearing away, an inauspicious beginning to a doomed flight.

An eyewitness informs us of what was going on at this time in Room No. 118 of the Great Hall of the People, where Mao, his mistress Zhang Yufeng, and others of his entourage were gathered:

> Zhou Enlai suggested to Mao that they order a missile attack against the plane. Mao refused. "Rain will fall from the skies. Widows will remarry. What can we do? Lin Biao wants to flee. Let him. Don't shoot," he said. We waited. . . . Chinese radar was tracking the plane's route. . . . It was heading northwest, in the direction of the Soviet Union. . . . At about 2:00 A.M. word came that Lin Biao's plane had left China and entered Outer Mongolian airspace. The plane had disappeared from Chinese radar. Zhou Enlai reported this to Mao. "So we've got one more traitor," Mao said, "just like Zhang Guotao and Wang Ming." The next big news came that afternoon, when Zhou Enlai received a message from Xu Wenyi, the Chinese ambassador to Outer Mongolia. A Chinese aircraft with nine persons on board— one woman and eight men—had crashed in the Undur Khan area of Outer Mongolia. Everyone on board had been killed. . . . "That's what you get for running away," Mao said.[39]

The Mongolian and Soviet investigators working at the crash site concluded that the airplane had exploded while attempting a crash landing. On touching down it became unbalanced, dragged its right wing along the ground, and caught fire. Its remains were scattered across an area of four square miles. Ambassador to Mongolia Xu Wenyi, who arrived in Undur Khan on September 15, described the scene of the accident:

> Most of the corpses were laid on their backs, their arms and legs apart, the heads were so burned that the corpses could not be identified. We laid out all nine corpses from north to south, numbered them, and photographed them from various positions in order to try and

identify them later on. According to a subsequent inquest, Lin Biao was identified as corpse No. 5. A small bald patch was preserved, the skin on the head was abraded, the bones stuck out, the eyebrows were scorched, and the eyes transformed into dark orifices. Corpse No. 8 was Lin Biao's wife Ye Qun. . . . She had been burned relatively little, her hair was almost totally preserved, her left side was injured. Corpse Number 2 was Lin Biao's son, Lin Liguo: tall, the face was charred and had a look of excruciating torture as if it had gone through flames. Among the items belonging to the deceased was uncovered pass No. 002 for the Air Force Academy in the name of Lin Liguo.

Per agreement with the Mongolians, Soviet representatives severed the heads of Lin Biao and his wife and brought them to Moscow for forensic examination.[40] The remains of the deceased were buried at the site of the accident.

On that same night of September 13, three of Lin Liguo's assistants tried to flee the PRC in a helicopter, but they were forced to land not far from Beijing. Two of them committed suicide after first shooting the pilot. The only surviving member of the plotters soon began to give evidence.[41]

The flight and death of Lin Biao shook the members of the Chinese leadership. No matter how hard Mao tried to stay calm, he also was deeply affected. His first reaction was to keep the betrayal of his "close comrade-in-arms" a secret. After instructing the faithful Zhou to investigate what had happened, he shut himself up in Zhongnanhai. He became apathetic. He stopped doing anything, lapsed into silence, and did not emerge from his bedroom for days on end. Two months later, when he finally reappeared in public, everyone noted how he had suddenly grown infirm. He shuffled around the house, constantly coughing and spitting on the floor. He complained about headaches and heaviness in his legs. His blood pressure was elevated—180 over 100—and he suffered from arrhythmia.

Meanwhile, Zhou's people uncovered details of the plot. During their search of the home of one of the conspirators they found a notebook outlining the "Theses of Project 571." Not until twenty days after the accident were the top PLA commanders and high-ranking party officials informed of the betrayal by "the close comrade-in-arms of the Leader" at closed meetings.[42] Afterward came the turn of ordinary party members and only then finally the broad masses. A new hysterical campaign to criticize Lin Biao unfolded throughout the country. The Chairman's former "close comrade-in-arms" now was criticized as an "ultra-leftist."[43]

Mao continued to feel awful. He was often feverish, his pulse rate increased to 140 per minute. Unexpectedly he became sentimental. He was drawn to the friends of his youthful struggles, many of whom had been in disgrace during the Cultural Revolution because of his own will. He was extremely distressed when he learned of the death on January 6, 1972, of Marshal Chen Yi, his comrade from the Jinggang Mountains and his minister of foreign affairs. On January 10, the day of Chen Yi's funeral, despite his own poor health and the bad weather, Mao went to express his condolences to Chen Yi's widow. Afterward he ordered Zhou to rehabilitate those party veterans, victims of the Cultural Revolution, who could still be saved.

His condition deteriorated by the day. Mao's doctors diagnosed congestive heart failure. His brain was getting insufficient oxygen, he gasped for breath, periodically opening his mouth, greedily inhaling air, and then noisily exhaling. "The Chairman's life was in danger," writes his former physician. "His arms and legs were sprawled motionless on the sofa, as though paralyzed."

On the night of January 21, he felt worse than ever. In the presence of several persons from his entourage, he turned to Zhou Enlai. " 'No. Cannot make it. I cannot make it. You take care of everything after my death. Let's say this is my will.' " Jiang Qing turned pale. "Her eyes opened wide, her hands curled into fists." But Mao was adamant. " 'It's done now,' Mao finally said. 'You can all go.' "[44] Although he did not die then, he was unable to make a full recovery from his illness. During his last five years his life gradually ebbed away.

The system of barracks communism was dying with him. Its collapse was still some time off, but the political crisis of the early 1970s demonstrated with exceptional clarity the bankruptcy of the Maoist system of power. An ever larger circle of people in China began to lose faith in its rationality. The era of Mao Zedong was drawing to a close.

36

DEATH OF THE RED EMPEROR

Why did Mao choose Zhou Enlai? Why did he not appoint Kang Sheng or Zhang Chunqiao as his successor? Or Jiang Qing herself? It is difficult to say. Probably influenced by the funeral of the disgraced Chen Yi, Mao felt irritated toward the leftists. The old cadres who had been at his side for decades were gone. He alone remained. He was at the pinnacle of power, but now he was truly alone, having severed his ties with many comrades who had been devoted to him. Among those with whom he had started out only Zhou still had regular access to him. The others he had either brought down or alienated.

Mao did not want to blame himself. It was simpler to vent his bad mood on those who on his orders or of their own free will had entered the front ranks of the pioneers of "universal disorder." Thus he had attacked Jiang Qing to let her know what her place would be.

But his solitude grew increasingly acute and not even the beautiful Zhang Yufeng could relieve it. Perhaps solitude was the fate of all Great Helmsmen? The postulates of socialism, including class warfare and settling accounts, were designed to inspire fear and terror by setting people against each other. Is it any wonder that Lenin, Stalin, and Mao were so isolated? How could it have been otherwise if in the mind of their type of radical revolutionaries, as Dostoevsky wrote, "[t]he spiritual world, the higher part of man's being" was "rejected altogether, dismissed with a sort of triumph, even with hatred"? [1]

Throughout his life in the revolution Mao manipulated the basest of human emotions. It was not brotherly love that he conveyed, but rather enmity and universal suspicion. "Down with landlords!" "Down with rich peasants!" "Down with the bourgeoisie, merchants and intellectuals!" "Down with those who are not like us!" "Down with the educated, with businesspersons, with the talented!" Down with all of them, down with them, down. Class struggle has not ended. "Dragons beget dragons, phoenixes beget phoenixes, and rats beget rats" was a common saying in Maoist China. Mao proclaimed that there was no end to struggle. "When we reach Communism will there be no struggles?" he asked, and replied, "I don't believe that. Even when we reach Communism there will still be struggles, but they will be between the new and the old, the correct and the incorrect. After tens of millennia have passed by, the incorrect will still be no good and will fail."[2] Thus the lonely and sick emperor was forced to partake of the fruits of his own tyranny.

But Mao still clutched at life and tried to control everything. There was still much to accomplish. China had not achieved world recognition. In the UN, China was represented by Taiwan, backed by the United States. Mao needed a diplomatic breakthrough in the early 1970s after the border war with the USSR. Relations between China and the Soviet Union—the erstwhile Elder Brother—turned out to be very dangerous; improving relations between the PRC and America could go a long way toward changing the balance of power in East Asia. Rapprochement with the United States and entry into the UN became another idée fixe for Mao. He took the first steps to achieve this result in the second half of 1970 when Snow arrived in China, as it turned out for the last time. As we remember, Mao always believed that Snow was a CIA agent, although he was mistaken. On this occasion, too, he resorted to this same "channel of communication." On October 1, 1970, he invited Snow and his wife to stand beside him on the rostrum at Tiananmen Gate during the celebration of the founding of the PRC and was photographed with them. No other American had ever been accorded this honor. Mao was obviously sending a signal to Washington.

But he got no reply to his message. The White House simply did not understand. Several years later President Nixon's national security advisor Henry Kissinger wrote, "Eventually, I came to understand that Mao intended to symbolize that American relations now had his personal attention, but it was by then a purely academic insight: we had missed the point when it mattered. Excessive subtlety had produced a failure of communication."[3]

Leaders in Washington still remembered Mao's words just six months earlier, in May 1970, after U.S. troops had made an incursion into Cambodia. Mao had called Nixon a "fascist" and asserted that "American imperialism kills people in foreign countries" as well as "whites and Negroes at home." "Nixon's fascist crimes ignited the raging flames of a mass revolutionary movement in the U.S.," he proclaimed. "The Chinese people firmly support the revolutionary struggle of the American people. I am certain that the heroic struggles of the American people will ultimately achieve victory, and that fascist rule in the U.S. will inevitably collapse."[4] But now Mao wanted Nixon to come to China. A visit by the president would serve to vastly elevate the prestige of the PRC as well as of the Chairman himself.

Until the early 1970s Chinese officials had only intermittent contact with Americans, via ambassadorial meetings in Warsaw that yielded little. After

Nixon's inauguration in January 1969, however, the meetings continued on the suggestion from the PRC. Mao knew that in August 1968, right after he was nominated, Nixon had declared, "We must not forget China. We must always seek opportunities to talk with her. . . . We must not only watch for changes. We must seek to make changes."[5]

Nixon was genuinely interested in negotiations with Mao for his own reasons. By the early 1970s, the American war in Vietnam had reached a stalemate. Nixon badly needed the Chairman's help to enable him to withdraw U.S. troops from Indochina while avoiding the appearance of defeat. He wanted Mao to lean on his Vietnamese comrades to make concessions. Thus there was a reciprocal aspiration to improve relations between the two countries. In an interview with *Time* magazine in early October 1970, Nixon expressed his desire to visit the PRC. "If there is anything I want to do before I die, it is to go to China," he said. "If I don't, I want my children to."[6] In early December, Zhou Enlai sent a letter via a Pakistani intermediary inviting Washington to send a "special envoy" to Beijing "to discuss the subject of the vacation of Chinese territories called Taiwan." The White House understood correctly that raising the question of Taiwan was of no significance; it was simply a "standard formula." This was really a question concerning Nixon's visit. Kissinger responded, "[T]he meeting in Beijing would not be limited only to the Taiwan question."[7]

Meanwhile, Mao invited Snow, who was still in Beijing, for breakfast, during which he said, in part, "between Chinese and Americans there need be no prejudices. There could be mutual respect and equality." He expressed his respect for the people of the United States and said that he placed his hopes on them. Then he said straight out that he "would be happy to talk" with Richard Nixon.[8] On December 25, *People's Daily* published a photograph of Mao and Snow taken on October 1 on the rostrum of Tiananmen Gate during the celebration of the founding of the PRC. A quotation from Mao Zedong was printed on the upper right-hand corner of the page: "The people of the whole world, including the American people, are our friends."

Mao was certain that Snow would immediately transmit this invitation for Nixon to the CIA, but, of course, he did not. He did not publish the interview until April 1971, by which time it was no longer of any use to Nixon and Kissinger.[9] By then an American table tennis team, responding to an invitation from the Chinese, had come to China from Nagoya, Japan, where the 31st World Table Tennis Championship had taken place. Obviously, the decision to invite these athletes had been taken at the highest levels. On April 14, the Americans, as well as table tennis champions from other countries, were received at the Great Hall of the People. Zhou Enlai said to the president of the American table tennis association, Graham B. Steenhoven, "To have friends come from afar; is this not a delight?"[10] This famous quotation from Confucius, coming from the lips of the premier, did not pass unnoticed by the foreign journalists who began predicting the possible establishment of "friendly ties" between the PRC and the United States.

Soon after, on July 9, Henry Kissinger, Nixon's special representative, arrived in Beijing via Pakistan. He held three days of intensive talks with Zhou and officials in the Ministry of Foreign Affairs of the PRC. Mao, naturally, did not meet with Nixon's envoy and not merely for protocol reasons. At the time he had a very low opinion of the former Harvard professor. "Kissinger is a stinking scholar," he said to Pham Van Dong, one of the leaders of North Vietnam, several months before Kissinger's visit to Beijing.[11] Kissinger's visit was secret, but both sides agreed to issue a communiqué on the results of the talks. In Zhou's words, it would "shake the world."[12]

And so it did. An announcement concerning Kissinger's trip was made simultaneously in both capitals on July 15. President Nixon emphasized that his national security advisor had brought him an invitation from Premier Zhou that he gladly accepted.[13] The whole world held its breath.

Finally, on October 25, 1971, the United States removed all obstacles to the PRC taking its place in the UN. On February 21, 1972, the president of the United States and his wife arrived in Beijing. They were met at the airport by Zhou Enlai. Mao was impatiently awaiting Nixon in his own residence. In the three weeks leading up to Nixon's arrival he had been undergoing intensive medical treatment. By the time of the historic meeting he was feeling much better. "His lung infection was under control, and his heart irregularities had subsided," writes his doctor. "His edema was better. . . . His throat was still swollen, and he had difficulty talking. His muscles had atrophied from weeks of immobility."[14] Mao was very anxious prior to the meeting, and he greedily devoured telephoned reports of the progress of the president's cortège that came constantly to his office. The medical equipment was removed from his room to the foyer, and the oxygen cylinders and anything that he might need in case of emergency were concealed either in an enormous lacquer trunk or behind large potted plants.

At 2:50 P.M., Nixon arrived at Zhongnanhai accompanied by Zhou and Kissinger. Kissinger's assistant Winston Lord (a future U.S. ambassador to China), Mao's grandniece Wang Hairong, who, at the time, was deputy chief of the Protocol Department in the Ministry of Foreign Affairs, and the interpreter Nancy Tang entered Mao's study. Nixon and Kissinger found the room to be untidy. "Several of the books were open to various pages on the coffee table next to where he was sitting," Nixon later noted in his diary.[15] "Mao's study . . . looked more the retreat of a scholar than the audience room of the all-powerful leader of the world's most populous nation," Kissinger recalled.[16] Supported by Zhang Yufeng, Mao rose to greet his guests and with difficulty took several steps toward them.[17] He took Nixon's hands in his and squeezed them. "I can't talk very well," he said.[18] "Words seemed to leave his bulk as if with great reluctance," Kissinger wrote. "They were ejected from his vocal cords in gusts, each of which seemed to require a new rallying of physical force until enough strength had been assembled to tear forth another round of pungent declaration."[19] He looked swollen, whether from dropsy or something else. In reality, he was suffering from congestive heart failure.

Nonetheless, one could sense that Mao was pleased by the meeting. He was cracking jokes nonstop and trying to create a relaxed atmosphere. At all of Nixon's attempts to turn the conversation toward business Mao waved his hand in the direction of Zhou. "These are not questions we need to discuss here. They should be broached with the premier. I discuss philosophical issues." Nixon thrice tried to draw Mao into a discussion of the Soviet threat to China, but the Chairman deflected him each time.

Consequently, the conversation skipped from one extraneous topic to another. Mao was particularly tickled by Nixon's joke about Kissinger's "girlfriends." The president recalled:

> Mao remarked on Kissinger's cleverness in keeping his first trip to Beijing secret.
>
> "He doesn't look like a secret agent," I said. "He is the only man in captivity who could go to Paris twelve times and Peking [Beijing] once, and no one knew it—except possibly a couple of pretty girls." [Zhou laughed.]
>
> "They didn't know it," Kissinger interjected. "I used it as a cover."
>
> "In Paris?" Mao asked with mock disbelief.
>
> "Anyone who uses pretty girls as a cover must be the greatest diplomat of all time," I said.
>
> "So you often make use of your girls?" Mao asked.
>
> "*His* girls, not mine," I replied. "It would get me into great trouble if I used girls as a cover."
>
> "Especially during an election," Chou [Zhou] remarked as Mao joined in the laughter.[20]

Such was their joking on "philosophical issues." Several of the remarks, however, were serious. "Our common old friend, Generalissimo Chiang Kai-shek, doesn't approve of this," said Mao, sweeping his arm in a circle. "He calls us communist bandits."[21] He wondered what Nixon would answer, but the president parried: "Chiang Kai-shek calls the Chairman a bandit. What does the Chairman call Chiang Kai-shek?" In such a casual fashion was the Taiwan question set aside. The president made it clear that he would not abandon old friends for the sake of new ones.

The meeting lasted sixty-five minutes instead of the scheduled fifty. The Chairman was showing signs of fatigue, and Zhou was glancing impatiently at his watch. Nixon noted this and wrapped up the conversation. Mao stood up to see off his guests. On parting Nixon said that Mao looked good. "Appearances are deceiving," Mao replied.[22]

After this Nixon held talks with Zhou, at the end of which a joint communiqué was published on February 28. In addition to setting forth the positions of the two sides on various international issues, it emphasized that "progress toward the normalization of relations between China and the United States is in the interests of all countries."[23] Subsequently, during regularly scheduled talks with the Vietnamese communists on July 12, 1972, Zhou Enlai skillfully pressed the leaders of the Democratic Republic of Vietnam (North Vietnam) to make concessions to the Americans by withdrawing their demand that Saigon's president, Nguyen Van Thieu, be removed from power.[24] A wave of diplomatic recognitions of the PRC by Japan, West Germany, and many other countries followed. Official relations with the United States at the ambassadorial level took longer but were accomplished on January 1, 1979.

Mao was ecstatic about Nixon's visit and even began to recover more quickly. "His edema subsided, his lungs cleared, and his coughing stopped," writes his doctor. "He had given up smoking during his illness, and his coughing and bronchitis did not return." Of course, he was still weak, he walked slowly, his hands and feet trembled, and he sometimes drooled uncontrollably.[25] Nevertheless, his mind remained clear, and his power unlimited. He continued to control the party and the state and was ready for a new battle.

Once again Jiang Qing, who now saw Zhou Enlai as her main enemy, tried to take advantage of Mao's "fighting" mood. She could not reconcile herself to Mao's designation of Zhou as his successor, and wanted the Chairman to appoint to leading positions in the leadership, including the premiership, persons who were loyal to her. Toward this end she used an old and tested method, namely, blackening the name of her enemy in the Chairman's eyes as a "counterrevolutionary" and "traitor" who was "intriguing" behind his back. She also struck a new blow against Zhou's supporters, the old party officials who had survived or had been rehabilitated following the high tide of the Cultural Revolution.

Her first step was to champion the young Shanghai radical Wang Hongwen, the leader of the Rebels, as Mao's successor. Wang was loyal to a fault, young and energetic, and also within easy reach so that Jiang could easily rule China through him. He was already a member of the Ninth Central Committee, but Jiang wanted him elevated to deputy chairman. In September 1972, she convinced Mao to assign Wang to work in the Central Committee headquarters.[26] This marked the beginning of his rapid ascension. The denizens of Zhongnanhai took to calling Jiang's favorite "the Rocket." Jiang's closest confederates—Zhang Chunqiao and Yao Wenyuan—supported all of her undertakings. Kang Sheng, already ill with terminal bladder cancer, also supported Mao's wife.

Chance favored Jiang Qing. Not long after Kang had been diagnosed with cancer, cancerous cells were detected in the premier's urine and doctors said that Zhou did not have long to live. At this point the Chairman's wife went into high gear. She could not rest even when Mao appointed Wang Hongwen as his successor on December 28.[27] She wanted to finish off the enfeebled Zhou by depriving him of the premiership and awarding it to her faithful confederate Zhang Chunqiao.

There were quite a few obstacles, however, on Jiang's path. Zhou Enlai was supported by many in the party leadership, among them the powerful Marshal Ye Jianying, a longtime member of the Politburo and one of the leaders of the Military Committee. Moreover, the Chairman himself was not prepared to indulge her every whim. In the summer of 1972 Mao began seriously thinking about rehabilitating the disgraced Deng Xiaoping, someone Jiang loathed. On August 3, Deng had sent a letter to the Chairman in which as usual he engaged in self-criticism, but also asked to be given some work to do even if only technical in nature. Eleven days later, Mao drafted a resolution saying, "Comrade Deng Xiaoping committed serious mistakes, but he is different from Liu Shaoqi. . . . He . . . won distinction."[28] Jiang could only grind her teeth.

Zhou, sensing an opportunity, went on the offensive. In early October he made two speeches in which he sharply criticized ultraleftism. He spoke generally about Lin Biao but many of his more engaged listeners knew clearly whom he had in mind. Several days later, on October 14, *People's Daily,* supporting Zhou's positions, published three articles opposing anarchism in which it labeled this tendency as a "counterrevolutionary weapon of fraudulent pseudo-Marxists." Jiang and her confederates immediately turned to Mao. They succeeded in browbeating Mao so that the Great Leader had to intervene. In his wheezy voice, he proclaimed that Lin was an "ultra-Right who practiced revisionism, tried to split the Party by means of conspiracy, and betrayed the Party and the nation."[29] Now everyone was properly placed.

However, Mao did not back away from his plan to rehabilitate Deng and return him to power. On March 9, 1973, he appointed Deng as Zhou's deputy. Later Mao explained this to his colleagues on the Military Committee, "We had persons in the party who did nothing yet still managed to commit mistakes, but Deng Xiaoping made mistakes while actually doing things. . . . In my opinion, he appears to be soft like cotton, but he is actually sharp as a needle."[30] At this same meeting, Mao observed that Deng's actions "should be thought of as three and seven fingers." He meant that only 30 percent had been erroneous and 70 percent successful.[31]

Jiang now understood that she had to act more energetically. In May 1973 the leftists succeeded in obtaining Mao's agreement to have Wang Hongwen and Wu De, the mayor of Beijing, who was also a radical, take part in the work of the Politburo. Another person granted this privilege was Hua Guofeng, the former secretary of the party committee in Mao's home county, whom the Chairman had kept in mind ever since his fiery speech glorifying the Leader and Teacher at the Seven Thousand Cadre Conference in the winter of 1962. At the outset of the Cultural Revolution Mao had elevated Hua to secretary of the Hunan Provincial Party Committee. Hua was then appointed acting chairman of the Hunan Revolutionary Committee. In 1969, at the Ninth Congress, Mao included him in the Central Committee, and in 1971 he was transferred to work in the State Council.

Jiang decided to intensify her struggle for power in anticipation of the Tenth Party Congress, scheduled to take place in late August 1973. Six weeks prior to it, on July 4, Wang Hongwen and Zhang Chunqiao paid a visit to Mao, having secured permission from Zhang Yufeng. A meek-looking but very strong woman, Zhang had by then turned into the main intermediary between the Chairman and the outside world. Even Jiang could not see her husband without Zhang's approval. The importance of Xiao Zhang ("Little Zhang," as the residents of Zhongnanhai called her) grew especially in early 1973, when the Great Helmsman's speech became almost inarticulate. Mao wheezed terribly and periodically gasped for breath so that it was difficult to understand what he was saying. But Zhang understood him very well, which added to her political influence.

The first subject of conversation was Zhou Enlai. The leftist leaders drew the darkest picture of Zhou's activities in international relations. Mao agreed with them despite the fact that China was doing very well diplomatically. He noticed that Zhou was not "firm enough" in dealing with Americans. At the end of the conversation, Mao irritably remarked, "[Zhou] no longer discusses big issues with me; every day he drags in trivial matters. If the situation does not change revisionism will inevitably appear." This was all that Jiang Qing's comrades in arms needed to hear. They immediately switched the conversation to what seemed to be a "philosophical" topic, telling Mao that during a search of Lin Biao's house an entire index file of quotations from Confucius had been found. Who would have imagined that the half-mad Lin Biao was attracted to ancient Chinese philosophy? Mao knew about this, but only now did he express interest in this discovery. He compared Lin to the Guomindang leaders who, like his former marshal, revered Confucius. They "worshiped Confucius and opposed the Legalist School," he said contemptuously.[32] Wang and Zhang departed completely satisfied.

Prior to their visit they and Jiang Qing had had a long talk about how to mobilize the people for an open struggle against the "new capitulationists" in the party leadership. It would be dangerous to finger the influential Zhou and

Deng by name, as Mao was not yet ready to cast them aside. Therefore, they cunningly resolved to unleash a campaign of criticism ostensibly against Lin that was really directed against Zhou. The discovery in Lin Biao's home of quotations from Confucius was opportune.[33] Mao's grumbling about Lin and the Nationalists both worshipping Confucius was another stroke of good fortune. Now they could easily weave a new theme into the old anti-Lin campaign, one aimed against Confucius, and direct it against the unsuspecting premier.

To understand their strategy one must recall that Confucius (551 BCE–479 BCE) lived at the end of the Zhou dynasty, a time of great social and economic crisis. Traditional social relations were rapidly disintegrating, many people were questioning the cult of ancestors, and a class of nouveaux riches had emerged that disregarded the communal clan laws and the authority of the dynasty. China was rent by civil wars. The humanist philosopher Confucius spoke in defense of the fading order, saying, "Let the lord be a lord; the subject a subject; the father a father; the son a son."[34] In this order he discerned the essence of proper rule. From his perspective, relations within the clans should remain unchanging and any attempt to destroy the balance of social forces could only exacerbate chaos. His teachings were opposed by the Legalists, the followers of Shang Yang whom Mao Zedong had once admired. They reflected the interests of the wealthy landowners and they had contempt for the moribund clan aristocracy.

Jiang Qing and her confederates extrapolated this ancient situation onto China in the early 1970s. Since Confucius defended the old society, it followed that he was "reactionary." Since the Legalists opposed him, obviously they were "progressives" or even revolutionaries. This was from the perspective of Marxism-Leninism and Mao Zedong Thought. Thus the past struggle between the Legalists and Confucius was merely an episode in the eternal struggle between revolutionaries and reactionaries. The battle between good and evil was ongoing and in China, and in the CCP in particular, there were still many "Confucians" who dreamed of turning back the clock.

Of course, Jiang and her leftist allies could apply the label of contemporary Confucian to whatever enemy they chose. Their main objective was to evoke a negative reaction among the popular masses toward Zhou Enlai, whose surname was written with the same character as the name of the "reactionary" Zhou dynasty whose interests Confucius had supposedly defended. For most Chinese in the 1970s, the Chinese character "zhou" in newspapers and magazines signified the premier in the first instance. Therefore, the constant repetition of this character in a negative context constituted a well-veiled attack against Jiang's main enemy.

The intrigues of the leftists, however, failed. Among most people their abstruse and tedious articles about the struggle between the Legalists and the Confucians evoked only boredom and apathy. The image of the beloved premier not only remained untarnished, it in fact shone even brighter as worrisome rumors about his terrible illness circulated around the country.

The Tenth Party Congress, which took place in Beijing on August 24–28, 1973, was likewise not a triumph for the leftists. Attending the sessions were 1,249 delegates representing 28 million party members. Only some of them belonged to Jiang Qing's faction. Zhou's supporters still retained a lot of influence. It was the premier whom Mao entrusted with delivering the main report. At the same time, Wang Hongwen's star was shining brightly. The Chairman seated him to his right (Zhou sat on Mao's left), and after the premier finished his speech, Wang delivered a report on the party constitution. The Congress affirmed all of the directives of the Cultural Revolution, lauded the Great Helmsman, condemned Lin Biao and deleted his name from the party constitution, and chose a new Central Committee. In the main elected organ, the Politburo, the two factions were represented in roughly equal proportions. A majority of the nine members of the Politburo Standing Committee were on Zhou's side.[35] Of course, this meant nothing. One man alone still made the major decisions.

Soon after the congress, Mao again put Zhou in his place.

On the evening of November 10, Henry Kissinger, who had just been appointed the U.S. Secretary of State, arrived in Beijing for a three-and-a-half-day official visit. He was greeted by Zhou and Ye Jianying. Mao also met with him (once, on November 12), but basically followed the negotiations by means of stenographic reports. Then, after the negotiations had concluded, Mao suddenly suspected the premier of having concealed something from him, some details of his conversations with the American envoy. This accusation was concocted, since at the time Zhou had come to report to Mao (according to other information he had tried to call him), the Chairman, who was not feeling well, was asleep, and his lover cum secretary Zhang Yufeng did not want to disturb him. After waking up, Mao was very displeased and immediately suspected the premier of engaging in some intrigue. He became even more incensed when just a bit later he looked through the final stenographic reports and again noted that Zhou had been insufficiently firm in dealing with the imperialists. Kissinger had tried in every which way to win Beijing over to a military alliance against Moscow, but Zhou had not resolutely defended the PRC's independent policy.[36] (In this case, the premier really was excessively diplomatic, and rather than put the exceedingly importunate Kissinger in his place, gave him to understand "that the proposal would have to be implemented in 'a manner so that no one feels we are allies.' ")[37] Mao, via his closest collaborators, his grandniece Wang Hairong and Nancy Tang, who were serving as his intermediaries with other leaders, at once informed the members of the Politburo that in his view Zhou had entered into military collaboration with the United States, having agreed that the Americans would place China under its "nuclear umbrella." Of course, Zhou had done nothing of the sort (he generally was unable to make decisions on his own), still Mao was terribly irritated. "Some people," he grumbled, "want to lend us an umbrella, but we don't want it."[38] Mao was also displeased with Zhou's spinelessness regarding the Taiwan question. It seemed to Mao that the premier was ready to agree to the United States maintaining special relations with Chiang Kai-shek and company.

Always suspicious, now that he was sick Mao no longer trusted anyone. At Mao's request, Zhou's conduct was scrutinized in the Politburo, where Jiang and her followers did not hesitate to slander the premier. There the matter ended. Mao cooled off; his rage turned to mercy.[39] In December he voiced the thought that he wanted to see Deng Xiaoping as chief of the General Staff of the PLA. (He did not officially make this decision until January 1975.)

Moreover, after the congress, Mao, with increasing frequency and insistence, criticized Jiang Qing for attempting to sow discord in the Politburo, advised her not to "blow up trifles," and even accused her—publicly at a session of the Politburo—of cobbling together a "Gang of Four" consisting of herself, Wang Hongwen, Zhang Chunqiao, and Yao Wenyuan.[40]

Obviously Mao was tacking from side to side. But this was not a chaotic movement. Mao consciously did not want to yield excessive power to one faction or the other. Even in his difficult physical condition, he had not lost the capacity to control the balance of forces in the leadership, maintaining a relative balance between the rival sides. He was such a master of political maneuvering that the leaders of the different factions were compelled to seek the truth in him alone. Even an experienced politician like Kissinger, meeting with an ill Mao, sensed the powerful magnetic field of his will.[41]

The only factor that worked against him was time. From 1974 on he was no longer able to attend all the meetings of the Politburo. At the beginning of the year, Mao lost sight in both of his eyes due to cataracts. He could distinguish only between light and dark. But this was only a minor misfortune. Far worse was that in the summer of 1974 he began to show symptoms of Lou Gehrig's disease, or amyotrophic lateral sclerosis (ALS). This fatal disease, caused by sclerosis of the nerve cells of the spinal cord, initially manifests itself via weakness in the wrists or legs and then gradually spreads through the entire body. Its victims lose their ability to move, to speak, to swallow, and finally, to breathe. In Mao ALS first appeared in the progressive paralysis of his right arm and right leg, and after a while it affected his throat, larynx, tongue, and intercostal muscles. According to his doctors the Chairman had less than two years to live.[42]

In addition, Mao continued to suffer from congestive heart failure. Both of his lungs were badly infected, and he also developed emphysema in his left lung. His blood oxygen level was low. Mao coughed constantly and could lie down only on his left side. He could no longer swallow solid food, and Zhang Yufeng fed him chicken or beef bouillon.

Yet the Great Helmsman clung to life. His brain still worked energetically, and the world continued to pay heed to his maxims. The concept he announced in February 1974 that all of humanity was divided into three worlds produced a particularly deep impression. Mao assigned the two superpowers, the United States and the USSR, to the First World; Japan, Europe, Australia, and Canada to the Second World; and all the other countries to the Third World. Calling upon the peoples of the Third World to unite, Mao asserted that China also belonged to the Third World.[43] At Mao's behest, Deng Xiaoping elaborated this concept in some detail at a session of the UN General Assembly on April 10, 1974.[44]

Mao's bursts of activity were not infrequent, but they could not wholly deaden his suffering. In the summer, no longer trusting in his doctors, Mao decided to cure himself. "He said that one could 'trust the doctors' words only one-third of the time or at most half,'" recalled Zhang Yufeng. "He believed that he could cope with the blows of his diseases by relying on his own powers of resistance that were in his own body."[45] He wanted to change his surroundings and breathe in the fresh air of the provinces. In mid-July, right after the Politburo meeting at which he had tongue-lashed Jiang Qing, Mao set out on a new trip around the country. It turned out to be his last. On July 18 he arrived in Wuhan, where he stayed until mid-October. Afterward he went to his native Changsha, where he spent the entire winter. There he even tried swimming in a pool, but could not.

In addition to the devoted Zhang, who could understand the decrepit Chairman only "by reading his lips and . . . gestures," two other women continued to help him during this period. One was his grandniece Wang Hairong, then a deputy foreign minister; the other was his English-language interpreter, Nancy Tang, who already headed one of the departments in the Foreign Ministry.[46] They shuttled back and forth between Beijing and Wuhan, and then Beijing and Changsha, bringing the Chairman information from Zhou Enlai and Deng Xiaoping, and sometimes from Jiang Qing as well. Their sympathies were entirely with Zhou and it was he whom they consulted on each of their trips even though on June 1, 1974, the premier entered the hospital. He faced a difficult operation for cancer, which had invaded his bladder, large intestine, and lungs.

Realizing that Zhou had little time left, Mao decided to appoint Deng to the post of first deputy premier. At the same time, faithful to his principle of balancing the factions, he entrusted the day-to-day running of the party to Wang Hongwen. Neither faction was satisfied. Jiang Qing felt the need to act quickly. On the evening of October 17, she convened a secret meeting of her closest confederates at which it was decided to send Wang Hongwen to Mao without informing the other members of the Politburo. Wang was to inform the Chairman that "[t]he atmosphere in Beijing now is very much like that at the Lushan Meeting [of 1970]."[47] What was being suggested was that Zhou Enlai, Marshal Ye Jianying, and Deng Xiaoping were ready to go the way of Lin Biao. In such circumstances, the Gang of Four thought it impossible to award the post of first deputy premier to the "counterrevolutionary" Deng.

Wang carried out his assigned mission flawlessly. According to Zhang Yufeng's recollections, which Wang himself confirmed, he said to Mao, "Although the Premier is ill and hospitalized, he is busy summoning people far into the night. Almost every day someone goes to his place."[48] But Mao became enraged, and Little Zhang conveyed his words to the frightened Wang. "If you have an opinion, you should say it directly to one's face, but this way is no good. You must unite with Comrade Xiaoping." Then Mao added, "Go back and talk things over with the premier and Comrade Jianying. Don't act together with Jiang Qing. Be on guard with her."[49]

Later, in mid-November, he explained indignantly to Wang Hairong and Nancy Tang, who were visiting him, that "Jiang Qing is ambitious. She'd like to make Wang Hongwen Chairman of the Standing Committee [of the National People's Congress] and make herself Chairman of the Communist Party."[50]

Possibly Jiang really did nurture such hopes at this time. But in January 1975, the Second Plenum of the Tenth Central Committee, acting on a proposal by Mao, who was still in Changsha, chose Deng Xiaoping as one of the deputy chairmen of the Central Committee and a member of the Politburo Standing Committee. At a subsequent meeting of the NPC, Deng was confirmed as first deputy premier. On April 18, Mao, who had returned to Beijing, said to Kim Il Sung, the head of North Korea who was paying him a visit,

> I am 82, this year . . . I don't want to talk about political affairs. You can talk with him [Mao waved his hand in the direction of Deng, who was taking part in the meeting] about them. His name is Deng Xiaoping. He knows how to fight wars, and he knows how to fight revisionism. The Red Guards attacked him, but now there's no problem. He was forced out of the office for several years, but today he's back. We need him.[51]

From July 1975 on, Deng, with Mao's blessing, became the leader in the Politburo. Jiang Qing and her confederates were beside themselves. But they had no intention of giving up. After their torpid campaign to criticize Lin Biao and Confucius revealed their ideological bankruptcy, they initiated several more ideological movements: to study the theory of the dictatorship of the proletariat, against empiricism, and, finally, against "capitulationism," which was supposedly exemplified by the classical novel *Water Margin*. None of these ideological campaigns, however, could change the balance of power in the Politburo[52] as long as the Chairman himself did not want this to happen. Thus all the efforts of the "leftists" aimed at mobilizing the masses against the intra-party "revisionists" led nowhere.

Jiang Qing had to conquer Mao. But access to Mao was limited by Zhang Yufeng, who, toward the end of 1974, was officially named by the Politburo as the Chairman's Secretary for Essential and Confidential Matters. Moreover, the inseparable Wang Hairong and Nancy Tang, supporters of Zhou, served as links between Mao and the Politburo. Jiang attempted to win over Yufeng by giving her gifts, ingratiating herself with her, and trying to strike up a friend-ship, but she failed. Little Zhang did not indulge her very much. Then a new young woman made her appearance in Mao's entourage, Meng Jinyun, who assumed the duties of assistant to Yufeng. Stunningly beautiful, she had no reason to love the "leftists." She had been imprisoned from 1968 to 1973 after being slandered by the Red Guards. With Yufeng's help she came to Mao seek-ing rehabilitation. At one time, in the 1960s, she had danced in the PLA Air Force Song and Dance Ensemble, and had first met the Great Helmsman at one of its performances. Mao took an immediate fancy toward her and wanted to dance with her. During their dance he asked her "not to be so prim," and after a few steps he took her off to his bedroom. Their affair did not last long, and Zhang Yufeng was not jealous. Quite the opposite—she sympathized with Meng, who was four years her junior. Afterward, Meng Jinyun worked as a nurse in Wuhan, and was then arrested.

Meeting Yufeng again at the very end of May 1975, Meng asked her help in arranging an audience with Mao. Mao was saddened to hear about the misad-ventures of his former lover, "rehabilitated" her, and kept her by his side. Jiang Qing was unhappy but had to reconcile herself to it.[53]

Suddenly, in early October, Jiang and her confederates got lucky. For some reason, the decrepit dictator decided to make his nephew Mao Yuanxin his go-between with the Politburo in place of Wang Hairong and Nancy Tang. Apparently, he simply missed him. The clever and cunning Yuanxin, however, knew how to take advantage of the situation to pressure his uncle to tilt in the direction Jiang Qing desired. He was her ardent supporter and made no at-tempt to conceal this.

The leftists got a second wind. Through Mao's beloved nephew, they began an intensified effort to turn the Chairman against Deng. "I am worried about the Central Committee. I'm afraid some of them will want to go back to the way things were before," Yuanxin whispered to his uncle. "I've been paying close attention to the speeches of Comrade Xiaoping. I sense a question. He rarely mentions the accomplishments of the Cultural Revolution. He rarely criticizes Liu Shaoqi's revisionist line. This year I haven't once heard him talk about how to study theory [of the dictatorship of the proletariat], or criticize *Outlaws of the Marsh* [*Water Margin*], or criticize revisionism."[54] And further,

"There are two attitudes towards the Cultural Revolution: one is to complain about it and the other is to settle accounts with it."[55]

This softening up lasted for a month. Finally, Mao succumbed. He became enraged and began to be exasperated by Deng. At his request, members of the Politburo began to criticize Deng. In the country as a whole a new campaign to "criticize Deng Xiaoping and struggle against the right deviationist wind to reverse correct verdicts" began to gather steam. Deng Xiaoping was relieved of most of his duties, allowed only to open and close meetings of the Politburo and deal with foreign policy matters.

At the very height of this struggle, Zhou Enlai passed away at 9:57 A.M. on January 8, 1976. Many mourned his passing. The majority of Chinese remembered the premier as wise, honest, and humane. Very few persons in China were interested in whether he really was or not. The image of a noble leader reigned in the minds of the masses. On January 11 a funeral cortège with his ashes made its way to the cemetery of revolutionary heroes, accompanied by the lamentations and mournful cries of the inhabitants of Beijing. Everyone who braved the frost that day on the central thoroughfare of Chang'an Avenue—and there were more than a million—remembered for the rest of their lives the white and blue bus carrying the beloved Zhou to eternity.

Soon rumors floated around the city that the premier had fallen victim to the leftists who hated him. These rumors intensified in March after the Shanghai paper *Literary Reports* hinted that Zhou had been a "capitalist roader." Immediately, handbills and big character posters appeared in Nanjing calling on people to protest. This quickly became known in Beijing. People began streaming into Tiananmen Square to lay flowers and wreaths in Zhou's memory at the Monument to Revolutionary Heroes. This action occurred spontaneously over a period of two weeks, and finally on April 4, on the traditional day of remembrance of the dead, the square filled to overflowing. The people were very indignant. Here and there were shouts of "Defend Premier Zhou with our lives!" "Long live the great Marxist Zhou Enlai!" "Down with all those who oppose Premier Zhou!" Many sang the "Internationale."[56]

Jiang Qing and her retinue were frightened. They feared an uncontrolled mass movement. Their opponents were no less anxious. They were all unaccustomed to democracy. At an emergency session of the Politburo on the evening of April 4, they adopted a joint resolution to suppress the unsanctioned meetings. "A batch of bad people had come up with writing, some directly attacking Chairman Mao," asserted Hua Guofeng, who on Mao's orders was serving as acting premier, "while many others attacking the Central Committee."[57] On April 5, the police attacked the demonstrators. From the Great Hall of the People on the western side of the square, Jiang observed through binoculars the assault against the crowds.

Mao too supported the suppression of this "counterrevolutionary uprising," which he learned of "objectively" via Yuanxin, who placed all the blame for these popular demonstrations on Deng Xiaoping. The Great Leader became resolute after hearing his nephew's report. "Bold fighting spirit. Good, good, good." Then he issued a directive: "Remove Deng from all posts."[58] With this same order he appointed the fifty-five-year-old Hua Guofeng first deputy chairman of the Central Committee and premier of the State Council. Three weeks later, no longer able to speak, he wrote the following to his final successor: "Go slowly, do not be anxious. Keep on course. With you in charge, I am at ease."[59]

Jiang and the other radicals exulted while the majority of people in Beijing grieved. As a sign of silent protest, people began to display small bottles in the windows of their homes. This was because the characters *xiaoping* in Deng Xiaoping's name are homonyms for the characters *xiaoping,* meaning "small bottle," while the *tai* in the word *chuangtai* (windowsill) can be translated as "the top." By placing small bottles in their windows, opponents of the Gang of Four were signifying that "Deng Xiaoping is still on top!"

Thus the campaign to criticize Deng, lacking support from the people, was doomed to failure. The majority of party cadres only went through the motions of taking part in it. Mao's last flash of political activity fizzled out.

But it is doubtful that the Great Helmsman was fully aware of his actions. He already had one foot in the grave. His terrible physical condition weighed upon his mood. Mao was constantly irritable and excitable. He had great difficulty breathing. His lungs, heart, and kidneys failed to function normally. He was perpetually bathed in sweat and greedily gulped for air. He was in constant need of oxygen. Since he always lay on his left side, he ultimately developed bedsores.

The only improvement was in his vision. On July 23, 1975, he had had a successful operation on his left eye. In order to ensure that all went smoothly, several ophthalmologists practiced on forty old men who were used as experimental subjects. Only after they had settled on the correct method did they operate, with considerable trepidation, on the Great Leader.[60] Zhang Yufeng recalled, "When . . . the gauze bandages were removed from the Chairman's eye, he opened his eyes and glanced around. Suddenly, excitedly pointing to one of his attendants, he correctly indicated the color and pattern of her clothing. Similarly, pointing to the wall, he said, 'It is white.'"[61]

But there were no other positive changes in the progression of his illness. Some days he was so weak that, according to Zhang's reminiscences, "he found it very difficult even 'to open his mouth when he was being fed,' and to swallow."[62] At other times, however, he felt somewhat better. He even had the courage to greet foreign guests. On April 30, 1976, for example, Mao met with Robert Muldoon, the prime minister of New Zealand. Of course, he did not discuss any serious issues with him; he only complained about his health. "My feet are bothering me," he said. Then after a moment of silence, he added, "There is great disorder in the world." [63]

On May 11, he suffered his first heart attack. Zhang Yufeng and Meng Jinyun did not leave his side. The doctors did all that they could, but it was two weeks before Mao felt a little better. On May 20, he wanted to meet with Lee Kuan Yew, the prime minister of Singapore, who was visiting China, and on May 27 with Ali Bhutto, the prime minister of Pakistan, and his wife. But after ten minutes of small talk on both occasions, he became very tired and had to terminate the conversations.* Nevertheless, his guests were not disappointed. "He is not a young man," Bhutto informed the journalists. "I was not expecting to meet Tarzan." [64] Afterward, the Ministry of Foreign Affairs of the PRC officially announced that the Chairman would no longer meet with foreign visitors since he "is very busy now, and has a lot of work." [65]

In mid-June, Mao summoned Hua Guofeng; the Gang of Four, headed by Jiang Qing; and his grandniece Wang Hairong. Lying in bed, he wheezed:

> Since ancient times, it has been rare for a man to live to seventy. I am now more than eighty. In my old age I have thought often of death. In China it is said, "You can judge a man only after they close the lid of his coffin." Although my "coffin lid" is not yet closed, it will happen soon, so it is a time to sum up. During my life I have accomplished two things. First, over the course of several decades, I fought against Chiang Kai-shek and chased him to the islands. During eight years of the war against Japan, I requested that the Japanese soldiers return home. We conquered Beijing and ultimately seized the Forbidden City. There are few people who do not acknowledge this. And there are only a few people who buzz into my ears that I should retake these islands quickly. The second thing you all know about. This is the launching of the Great Cultural Revolution. There are not many who support it, and not a few who oppose it. Both of these tasks are unfinished. This "legacy" must be handed down to the next generation. How should that be done? If it can't be done peacefully, then it must be done via shock tactics. If we really do not engage in this, then "the wind and rain will turn red with blood." How will you deal with this? Only Heaven knows. [66]

Zhang Yufeng had great difficulty conveying this monologue.

---

* At a press conference Bhutto said the meeting had lasted twenty-one minutes, but the Chinese said later that Mao met with the Pakistani premier for no more than ten minutes. This is just how long he spoke with Lee Kuan Yew.

On June 26, Mao had a second, more serious heart attack. He was in such a bad state that he could no longer eat on his own. He began to be fed through a tube inserted in his nostril. Four members of the Politburo, headed by Hua Guofeng, designated as a commission to oversee the doctors, took turns keeping vigil by the bed of the Leader. In early July the famous Austrian nephrologist Walter Birkmayer came to examine Mao, but he too was unable to help the Chairman.[67]

Mao was dying, but even in this condition he tried to hold on to power. Barely having come to, he would ask Zhang Yufeng to read him party documents, if only for a few minutes a day. On July 6 he was informed of the passing of Zhu De, his old comrade in arms. He took the news calmly.

He often watched Taiwanese and Hong Kong films with Little Zhang. They distracted him and enabled him to doze off. He did not alter this routine even after he was transferred on the night of July 27–28 to an earthquake-proof building near the Swimming Pool Pavilion in the wake of a terrible earthquake (7.8 on the Richter Scale) that completely destroyed the city of Tangshan, not far from Beijing. More than 240,000 persons died in the ruins, and more than 160,000 were injured. The shocks were so strong they were felt in Zhongnanhai. Even the bed on which Mao was lying in the Swimming Pool Pavilion shook.

The new building to which the Chairman was moved was quickly refitted and Mao's room filled with medical equipment. A room for viewing films was set up with a projector and a television. Thus Mao spent his last days watching "enemy" films and taking nourishment through a tube.

On September 2, he suffered a third heart attack. This was the most serious one. The doctors were no longer able to battle to save his life, but his powerful will to live would not let go. Mao constantly asked his doctors how serious was his condition.[68] They tried to console him, but they no longer held out any hope.

Just after 8 P.M. on September 8, his face began to turn noticeably blue. In another few minutes, he lost feeling in his extremities, and he became groggy. The doctors tried to pump out the fluid through his nose, but there was no response. By 9:16 P.M. his tachycardia increased, and a half hour later his blood pressure fell perilously. At 10:15 P.M. he slipped into a coma. Soon afterward his pupils dilated widely, and he no longer responded to light. At 12:04 A.M. on September 9 he began to have convulsions. Two minutes later he stopped breathing on his own. At ten minutes after midnight, Mao's heart ceased beating. The great dictator, revolutionary, and tyrant had died in his eighty-third year.

EPILOGUE

Chinese are famous for their energy and industriousness. In a country with just one time zone, hundreds of millions of people wake up at the same time, at 6 A.M., perform *qigong* breathing exercises, eat breakfast, and go about their daily business to offices, to shops, to fields, to schools.

The people of Beijing arise before dawn and crowd onto the subway, buses, and trains. Bells ringing, they pedal along on their bicycles while the richer among them ride in taxis or private automobiles. They mill about noisily on the shopping streets, stare at foreign tourists, and fly dragon kites above Tiananmen Square.

From early in the morning, city markets seethe with activity, and the aromatic odors of marvelous dishes waft from innumerable hole-in-the-wall restaurants. In the lanes, the *hutong*, that have miraculously survived, old men and old women warm themselves in the morning sun, and children play nearby. One can hear the sharp sounds of Beijing speech and the cries of peddlers shouting their wares.

On the stretch of Wangfujing, one of the main shopping streets, recently turned into a pedestrian mall, there are especially large numbers of people. Crowds move about in every direction, but if you walk south you will come out onto the broad avenue of Chang'an, the main street of the city. Turn right and you will pass the massive Beijing Hotel, and in ten minutes you will come to the historic center of Beijing, Tiananmen Square. On the right is the Forbidden City, and on the left is the square itself.

The first thing that strikes your eyes is an enormous portrait of Chairman Mao adorning the entrance to the former palace of the emperor, the Gate of Heavenly Peace. There are his penetrating eyes, the domed forehead, and the distinctive mole under his lower lip. The Great Helmsman looks calm and dignified. It seems that for a long time he has no longer been concerned with what is going on in the Chinese Communist Party, the country, and the world. He is not bothered by the fact that contrary to the wishes he expressed in April 1956, his body was not cremated, but instead embalmed shortly after his death. It reposes right there on the square in a majestic mausoleum in the Chairman Mao Memorial Hall. The white and sand-colored building is 110 feet high and covers 300,000 square feet. The body of Mao Zedong rests in the central hall, in a crystal coffin set on top of a pedestal of black Shandong granite. The Chairman is dressed in a grayish-blue jacket and covered with a red flag with the hammer and sickle. Around the pedestal are fresh flowers in white porcelain vases with blue patterns. At the head of the coffin, inscribed on a white marble wall are the gold characters "Eternal Glory to the Great Leader and Teacher Chairman Mao Zedong!"

The renascence of a market economy in the PRC in the late 1970s and early 1980s, facilitated by the "reincarnation" of the "moderate" faction soon after Mao's death, and most of all the return to power in July 1977 of Deng Xiaoping, led to the commercialization of the Mao cult. Hawkers and sellers in the souvenir shops in various parts of the city, including Tiananmen, do a brisk trade in kitsch: Mao badges and posters, busts, and *Quotations of Chairman Mao.* The transformation of the former leader into a souvenir of history was aided by the more than condescending assessment of his rule by the new leaders of the CCP. "Comrade Mao Zedong was a great Marxist and a great proletarian revolutionary, strategist and theorist. It is true that he made gross mistakes during the 'cultural revolution,' but, if we judge his activities as a whole, his contributions to the Chinese revolution far outweigh his mistakes. His merits are primary and his errors secondary," the party leaders asserted in 1981.[1] Since then they have not revisited this assessment, which, incidentally, fully accords with China's cultural tradition. Chinese, like Japanese, Vietnamese, and many other peoples of the East, lack a concept of "repentance." For the West this is a great Christian sacrament without which there can be neither absolution nor purification. But for those who dwell in All-Under-Heaven, the main thing is not to lose face.

In Mao's case, a number of other factors likewise explain this attitude. Unlike Lenin and Stalin, who destroyed a great and powerful Russia that prior to the October Revolution had been one of the leading world powers, Mao transformed China from a semi-colony into an independent and powerful state. He was not only a revolutionary who transformed social relations, but also a national hero who brought to fruition the mighty anti-imperialist revolution begun by Sun Yat-sen, compelling the entire world to respect the Chinese people. He united mainland China after a long period of disintegration, power struggle, and civil wars. It was during Mao's rule that China was finally able to become one of the main geopolitical centers of the world, politically equidistant from both superpowers, and, therefore, attracting increased attention from world public opinion. Of course, during Mao's rule the Chinese people remained poor, and the Chinese economy backward, but it was precisely during this time that Chinese began to take pride in their country's present as well as its past. This is why the Chinese people will never forget the "Great Helmsman."

Mao brought to the Chinese not only national liberation, but social servitude. It was he and the Chinese Communist Party he directed that, through deceit and violence, imposed totalitarian socialism upon the long-suffering people of China, driving them into the abyss of bloody social experiments. The lives of hundreds of millions of people were thereby maimed, and several tens of millions perished as a result of hunger and repression. Entire generations grew up isolated from world culture. Mao's crimes against humanity are no less terrible than the evil deeds of Stalin and other twentieth-century dictators. The scale of his crimes was even greater.

Still, Mao is distinguished from the ideologists and practitioners of Russian Bolshevism even in his totalitarianism. His personality was much more complex, variegated, and multifaceted. No less suspicious or perfidious than Stalin, still he was not as merciless. Almost throughout his entire career, even during the Cultural Revolution, in intraparty struggle he followed the principle of "cure the illness to save the patient," compelling his real or imagined opponents to confess their "guilt" but not sentencing them to death. This is precisely why the "moderate" faction, despite the repeated purge of its members, was ultimately able to stand its ground and come to power after the Chairman's death. Mao did not cure the "illness" of Deng Xiaoping and his supporters, but neither did he eliminate them physically. He did not even order the death of Liu Shaoqi. The chairman of the PRC was hounded to his death by enraged Red Guards. Moreover, Mao did not take revenge on his former enemies. He neither killed Bo Gu, nor Zhou Enlai, nor Ren Bishi, nor Zhang Guotao, nor even Wang Ming. He tried to find a common language with all of them after forcing them to engage in self-criticism. In other words, he forced them to "lose face" but also kept them in power.

In all of this, Mao was an authentically Chinese leader and ideologist who was able to combine the principles of foreign Bolshevism not only with the practice of the Chinese revolution, but also with Chinese tradition.

A talented Chinese politician, an historian, a poet and philosopher, an all-powerful dictator and energetic organizer, a skillful diplomat and utopian socialist, the head of the most populous state, resting on his laurels, but at the same time an indefatigable revolutionary who sincerely attempted to refashion the way of life and consciousness of millions of people, a hero of national revolution and a bloody social reformer—this is how Mao goes down in history. The scale of his life was too grand to be reduced to a single meaning.

And that is why he reposes in an imperial mausoleum in the center of China, in the square adorned with his gigantic portrait. He will be there for a long time, perhaps forever. In essence, the phenomenon of Mao reflects the entire trajectory of twentieth-century China in all its complexity and contradictions, the trajectory of a great but socially and economically backward Eastern country that made a gigantic break from the past to the present over the course of eight decades.

The achievements of Mao Zedong are indisputable. So are his errors and crimes. However, the Chinese poured out all of their righteous anger vis-à-vis Mao's dictatorial socialism against the closest comrades in arms of the Great Helmsman. His wife was arrested one month after the Chairman's death by Hua Guofeng, who "betrayed" her. Jiang Qing and other leaders of the Cultural Revolution were brought before a court in late 1980 and early 1981. Jiang did not confess her guilt, and she loudly declaimed before the whole world: "Everything I did, Mao told me to do. I was his dog; what he said to bite, I bit." [2] She was given a death sentence, suspended for two years. The same verdict was handed down to Zhang Chunqiao. The other leftist leaders, Wang Hongwen, Yao Wenyuan, and Chen Boda, received respectively life, twenty years, and eighteen years in prison.[3] After two years, however, the death sentences for Jiang Qing and Zhang Chunqiao were converted into life sentences.

Jiang was imprisoned until early May 1984, after which she was held under house arrest. But in 1989, after the suppression of the student protests on Tiananmen Square, she was returned to prison, this time for having criticized Deng for the killing of students. Yet she was soon let out again and placed under guard in a two-story villa in Jiuxianqiao, in the northeast section of Beijing. In mid-March 1991, when her health deteriorated, Jiang was taken to a hospital operated by the Ministry of Public Security. There, tiring of a meaningless life, she committed suicide late on the night of May 14, 1991. She made a rope out of handkerchiefs she had knotted together and hanged herself in her bathroom. Before doing this she penned a note, "Chairman, your student and co-fighter is coming to see you now."[4]

Mao's previous wife, Zizhen, had passed away several years earlier, on April 19, 1984, in Shanghai. His sole surviving son, Anqing, died in Beijing on March 23, 2007. Mao's daughters Li Min and Li Na are still living in the Chinese capital. Mao's children have long since had their own children. Anqing and Li Na had sons, and Li Min had both a son and a daughter. Mao's niece Yuanzhi and his nephew Yuanxin also have children. The grandchildren are already grown up and among them is a direct descendant—Dongdong, Anqing's grandson. He is already nine years old. Symbolically, he was born on December 26, 2003, the 110th anniversary of the birth of his great-grandfather.

New life swirls around them. Chinese society is rapidly modernizing. Many young Chinese are acquiring the latest technology; they engage in business, and go abroad for their education. Mao's heirs are no exception. Li Min's daughter, Kong Dongmei, received an M.A. in the United States in May 2001. Li Min's son, Kong Jining, is a businessman.

None of the reformers of the post-Mao era is still among us, yet China continues to push forward. The era of social experiments is long since gone. China is developing a new society with a mixed economy. The face of this enormous country is changing with astonishing speed. The reforms begun after Mao's death stimulated an outburst of activity on the part of the Chinese people. The success of these reforms is a sign that the influence of Maoism on the political and ideological life of China, which is still rather strong for now, will not last long.

★

At the start of the Cultural Revolution, Mao sent Jiang Qing a letter in which he welcomed "complete disorder under Heaven." At that time, he wrote,

> I believe in myself, but in some things I don't believe. In my youth I said, "A human life will last two hundred years, and the waves created will roll on for three thousand years." That is more than enough arrogance, but at the same time I am unsure of myself, I always have the feeling that if there is no tiger on the mountain, then the monkey will become the king of the beasts. I have become such a king, but this is not a case of eclecticism. I have the spirit of a tiger, this is primary, and the spirit of a monkey is secondary. In the past I made use of the following several sentences from a letter by Li Gu, who lived during the Han dynasty, to Huang Qiong [the biographies of both men are included in the 5th century CE chronicle of the Later Han dynasty]: "Solid things are easily broken, light things are easily soiled. He who can sing the *yangchun baixue* [an ancient melody that was very difficult to perform] may easily wind up in solitude. Will he merit great fame?" The last two sentences apply directly to me.[5]

Was Mao's self-analysis correct? Or was he simply playing his usual role? Perhaps he was sharing his innermost secrets with his wife? This we cannot know. The Chairman has long since gone to speak with Marx.

ACKNOWLEDGMENTS

It gives us great pleasure to express our deep appreciation to those persons without whose attention and friendly assistance this work would never have seen the light of day. We want to express our thanks to Kirill Mikhailovich Anderson, Bob Bender, Peter W. Bernstein, Ekaterina Borisovna Bogoslovskaia, Cao Yunshan—Mao Zedong's grandnephew, Chen Yung-fa, Georgii Iosifovich Cherniavskii, Laura Deal, Hua-ling Nieh Engle, Friedrich Igorevich Firsov, Fujishiro Kaori, Geng Bao, Aleksandr Vladimirovich Gordon, Oleg Aleksandrovich Grinevskii, Michael H. Hunt, Liudmila Konstantinovna Karlova, Elizaveta Pavlovna Kishkina (Li Sha)—a widow of Li Lisan, Tamara Mikhailovna Kolesova, Kong Jining—the grandson of Mao Zedong, Liudmila Mikhailovna Kosheleva, Madeline G. Levine, Li Danhui, Li Huayu, Inna Li—a daughter of Li Lisan, Li Yuzhen, Lin Liheng (Doudou)—the daughter of Lin Biao, William H. Magginis, Larisa Nikolaevna Malashenko, Aleksei Aleksandrovich Maslov, Arlen Vaagovich Meliksetov, Nina Nikolaevna Mel'nikova, Andrew J. Nathan, Christian F. Ostermann, Nina Stepanovna Pantsova, Larisa Aleksandrovna Rogovaia, Svetlana Markovna Rozental', Peter Sillem, Valentina Nikolaevna Shchetilina, Shen Zhihua, Valerii Nikolaevich Shepelev, Stephen Smith, Irina Nikolaevna Sotnikova, Daria Aleksandrovna Spichak, Elena Konstantinovna Staroverova, Ivan Aleksandrovich Tikhoniuk, Yurii Tikhonovich Tutochkin, Ezra F. Vogel, Wang Fanxi, Wang Fuzeng, Yu Minling, Zi Zhongyun—one of Mao's interpreters, and to many citizens of the People's Republic of China who shared their reminiscences of their lives under Mao Zedong, but who prefer to remain anonymous.

ILLUSTRATION
CREDITS

The photographs reproduced in this book are from five sources. The photograph on the title page is © Swim Ink/Corbis. Photographs nos. 1–6, 8, 10, 11, 14, 17, 19–21, 23–25, and 33 come from the excellent collection *In Memory of Mao Zedong,* edited by Museum of the Chinese Revolution (Beijing: Wenwu chubanshe, 1986). Photographs nos. 7, 12, 13, 15, 16, 18, 22, 26–29, 31, and 32 are preserved in the Russian State Archive of Social and Political History. Photograph no. 9 was taken by our colleague and friend Dr. Daria A. Spichak of the Russian Higher School of Economics. Finally, photo no. 30 is from the National Security Archive website at http://www.gwu.edu/~nsarchiv/NSAEBB/ NSAEBB145/index.htm

We express our gratitude to Mr. Geng Bao, deputy director and editor of Wenwu chubanshe, Dr. Valerii N. Shepelev, deputy director of the Russian State Archive of Social and Political History, and Dr. Daria A. Spichak for granting us permission to reproduce these photographs.

MAO ZEDONG'S CHRONOLOGY

1893, December 26—a son Zedong (his second, unofficial name is Runzhi) is born into the family of a prosperous peasant Mao Yichang and his wife, Wen Qimei, in the village of Shaoshanchong, Xiangtan county, Hunan province.

1913, Spring–June 1918—attends the Provincial Fourth (later First) Normal School in Changsha.

1918, April—takes part in organizing the educational liberal-democratic Renovation of the People Study Society.

1918, October–March 1919—works as an assistant to the librarian of Peking University. First becomes acquainted with Marxism-Leninism.

1921, January 1–3—founds a communist organization in Changsha.

July 23–31—takes part in the First Congress of the Chinese Communist Party (CCP) in Shanghai and Jiaxing as a representative of the Hunan organization.

1923, June 12–20—takes part in the Third Congress of the CCP in Canton. He is elected as a member and secretary of the CEC and director of the Organizational Department of the CEC. After the congress, in keeping with the united front policy, he joins the Guomindang.

1924, January 20–30—takes part in the sessions of the First Congress of the Guomindang in Canton. He is chosen as a candidate member of the CEC Guomindang.

1925, February–August—takes leave due to illness, leads the movement of the poorest peasants and paupers in Shaoshan and neighboring villages.

1925, October–May 1926—serves as acting director of the Propaganda Department of the Guomindang CEC in Canton. He edits the Guomindang journal *Zhengzhi zhoubao* (Political weekly).

1927, January 4–February 5—undertakes research on the peasant movement in Hunan, after which he calls for a radical agrarian revolution.

April 12—Chiang Kai-shek unleashes a bloody white terror in Shanghai and other regions in eastern China.

April 27–May 9—takes part in the Fifth Congress of the CCP in Wuhan. He is chosen as a candidate member of the Central Committee.

July 15—Wang Jingwei, the leader of the Guomindang leftists, breaks the united front with the communists.

August 7—takes part in an emergency conference of the CCP Central Committee in Hankou. He is chosen as a candidate member of the Provisional Politburo of the CC.

September 9–19—organizes a communist uprising in eastern Hunan, and, after its failure, goes to the high mountain area of Jinggang on the Hunan-Jiangxi border, where, with the help of local bandits, he founds the first soviet area.

1928, April 20 or 21—Zhu De's forces and Mao's detachments unite in eastern Hunan and soon are designated the Fourth Corps of the Chinese Worker-Peasant Revolutionary Army. In June 1928, Mao founds the Red Army.

June 18–July 11—at the Sixth Congress of the CCP he is chosen in absentia as a member of the Central Committee.

1929, January–February—leads troops to the Jiangxi-Fujian border region.

1930—Mao becomes the general political commissar of the First Front Army and twice attacks Changsha.

September—at an enlarged plenum of the Central Committee in Shanghai he is co-opted as a candidate member of the Politburo.

October—establishes a guerrilla base in south Jiangxi; it is called the Central Soviet Area (CSA).

December—provokes the Futian Incident.

1930, end–September 1931—Mao's forces repel Chiang Kai-shek's three punitive expeditions against the CSA.

1931, November 7–20—Mao presides over the First All-China Congress of Soviets in Ruijin. He is chosen as chairman of the CEC and head of the Council of People's Commissars of the Chinese Soviet Republic (CSR).

1931–1932—is subjected to single-minded attacks from the CCP Central Committee that he rejects. He is stripped of all his positions in the Red Army.

1933, February–October 1934—the Red Army of the Central Soviet Area fights against Chiang Kai-shek's fourth and fifth punitive expeditions.

1934, January 15–18—on Moscow's insistence he is transferred from a candidate member to a member of the Politburo at an enlarged plenum of the CCP Central Committee.

January 22–February 1—takes part in the work of the Second All-China Congress of Soviets. He is reelected chairman of the CEC of the CSR, but is stripped of his post as head of the Council of People's Commissars.

October—departs on the Long March with troops of the Red Army.

1935, January 15–17—takes part in an enlarged Politburo meeting at Zunyi. He criticizes the party and army leadership. He is co-opted into the Politburo Standing Committee and is appointed assistant to the general political commissar of the Red Army.

March 4—appointed front political commissar of the Red Army.

July–August—Stalin starts to promote Mao's cult of personality.

1935, September–November 1936—split with Zhang Guotao, who establishes a second "CCP Central Committee."

1935, October—completion of the Long March. Mao begins to establish a soviet area in northern Shaanxi.

1937, July 7—Japan launches a full-scale war against China.

September 22–23—formation of a new united front with the Guomindang.

1938, July—Georgii Dimitrov, general secretary of the Executive Committee of the Comintern, transmits to the CCP Central Committee Moscow's decision to recognize Mao Zedong as the leader of the Chinese people. The Comintern insists that Chinese communists unite around Mao.

1939, December–January 1940—formulates his theory of New Democracy.

1942, February—begins a wide-scale purge in the party, the *zhengfeng* campaign.

1945, April 23–June 11—presides over the Seventh Congress of the CCP in Yan'an. The congress adopts new party statutes that say "Mao Zedong Thought" "guides its entire work." He is chosen as a member of the Central Committee, and at the First Plenum as chairman of the Central Committee, of the Politburo, and of the Secretariat of the Central Committee.

August 14 (15)—Japan surrenders.

End of August–mid-October—conducts peace talks with Chiang Kai-shek and other Guomindang leaders in Chongqing.

1946, June—start of a new civil war with the Guomindang.

1949, January 31—PLA troops enter Beiping (Beijing).

September 30—chosen as chairman of the Central People's Government.

October 1—proclaims the founding of the People's Republic of China.

1949, December 16–February 17, 1950—pays an official visit to the Soviet Union. He conducts negotiations with Stalin and signs a Treaty of Friendship, Alliance, and Mutual Assistance with the USSR.

1950, June—starts the New Democratic agrarian reform.

October 19—sends PLA troops to Korea to take part in the war against United Nations forces.

1953, January—start of implementation of the First Five-Year Plan.

Summer—formulates the party's general line to build socialism on the Soviet model.

1953–1954—concocts the Gao Gang–Rao Shushi Affair.

1954, September 15–28—presides over the First Session of the National People's Congress, which adopts the Constitution of the People's Republic of China. He is chosen as chairman of the PRC.

1955–1956—the socialist transformation of agriculture, industry, and commerce.

1956, April 25—delivers a speech at an enlarged plenum of the Politburo, "On the Ten Major Relationships," which lays the foundation for the new policy of the CCP regarding socialist construction distinct from the Soviet model.

1957, February 27—delivers a speech at an enlarged meeting of the Supreme State Council, "On the Correct Handling of Contradictions among the People," in which he calls for a campaign, "Let a Hundred Flowers Bloom, Let a Hundred Schools of Thought Contend." The campaign is cut off on June 8 and followed by a struggle against "rightist bourgeois elements."

1958, February 18—at an enlarged meeting of the Politburo he announces the policy of "more, faster, better, and more economically" as the new general line of the party in socialist construction. Three months later the Second Session of the Eighth Congress of the CCP confirms this policy. The Great Leap Forward begins.

November–December—submits request to the plenum of the CCP Central Committee that he be relieved of his post as chairman of the PRC. Four months later his request, approved by the plenum, is confirmed by the National People's Congress. Liu Shaoqi replaces him.

1959, July 2–August 16—presides over the Lushan enlarged meeting of the Politburo and the plenum of the CCP Central Committee. Unleashes a campaign against Peng Dehuai and his supporters, who had criticized the horrendous results of the Great Leap Forward.

1960, April—the beginning of public polemics between the CCP and the Communist Party of the Soviet Union.

1961, Spring—Mao retreats to the "second line," transferring daily leadership of the Central Committee to the "moderate" Liu Shaoqi, who implements a program of "adjustment."

1962, January–February—at an enlarged meeting of the Central Committee attended by seven thousand cadres in Beijing, Mao's policies are subjected to criticism. He makes a self-criticism.

July—returns to the "first line" and initiates a struggle against the "moderates" in the party.

1965, November 10—on his initiative the Shanghai newspaper *Literary Reports* publishes Yao Wenyuan's critical article about Wu Han's play *The Dismissal of Hai Rui from Office.*

1966, May 16—on Mao's initiative an enlarged plenum of the Politburo acting in the name of the Central Committee adopts the text of a special communiqué to all party organizations throughout the country calling for the entire party to hold high the banner of the Great Proletarian Cultural Revolution.

August 5—writes a *dazibao,* "Bombard the Headquarters," directing the Red Guards to strike against the "moderates" in the highest echelon of the party leadership.

August–November—greets parades of Red Guards on Tiananmen Square.

1967, February—a group of Politburo members come out in opposition to the Cultural Revolution.

May–July—mass disturbances in Wuhan directed against Red Guard extremists.

1968, July 3—demands the prompt cessation of Red Guard outrages. Over the next two months the PLA restores order.

1969, March 2–15—armed conflicts occur on Damansky (Zhenbao) Island between Soviet and Chinese border guards.

1970, August 23–September 6—a new Lushan plenum of the CCP Central Committee takes place. Mao strikes a blow against minister of defense Lin Biao and his subordinates.

1971, September 13—an airplane carrying Lin Biao, his wife, and son crashes in the territory of the Mongolian People's Republic. All aboard die.

October 25—the PRC becomes a member of the United Nations.

Autumn—Mao is seriously ill. His doctors diagnose congestive heart failure.

1972, February 21—receives President Richard Nixon on an official visit to the PRC and has a "philosophical discussion" with him lasting sixty-five minutes.

February 28—a joint Sino-American communiqué is published in Shanghai signifying progress toward the normalization of relations between the two countries.

1974, January—Mao loses his vision because of cataracts on both eyes.

February—formulates the theory of the "Three Worlds."

Summer—doctors diagnose him with Lou Gehrig's disease (amyotrophic lateral sclerosis).

1976, January—after the death of Zhou Enlai, he names Hua Guofeng acting premier and entrusts him with daily leadership of the work of the Central Committee.

March 19–April 5—demonstrations and meetings on Tiananmen Square. Chinese citizens express grief at the passing of Zhou Enlai. The Politburo deploys the police against the demonstrators and disperses them. Mao supports the suppression of the "counterrevolutionary rebellion."

April 7—appoints Hua Guofeng first deputy chairman of the Central Committee and premier of the State Council.

September 9, 12:10 A.M.—Mao dies.

MAO ZEDONG'S GENEALOGY

PARENTS

Father (nineteenth generation of the Mao clan named "yi"—"bestowing")—**Mao Yichang** (October 15, 1870–January 23, 1920).

Mother—**Wen Qimei** (February 12, 1867–October 5, 1919)

WIVES

First wife—**Luo Yigu** (October 20, 1889–February 11, 1910). Married in late 1907 or early 1908.

Second wife—**Yang Kaihui** (November 6, 1901 November 14, 1930) Married in December 1920.

Third wife—**He Zizhen** (September 1909–April 19, 1984). Married either May 25 or May 26, 1928.

Fourth wife—**Jiang Qing** (March 1914–May 14, 1991). Married November 19, 1939.

CHILDREN

First child (from his second wife)—a son **Mao Anying** *(twenty-first generation of the Mao clan named "yuan"—"remote")* (October 24, 1922–November 25, 1950)

> *Mao Anying's wife*—**Liu Enqi**, who later changed her name to **Liu Songlin** (born March 2, 1930). Married October 15, 1949.

Second child (from his second wife)—a son **Mao Anqing** *(twenty-first generation of the Mao clan named "yuan"—"remote")* (November 13, 1923–March 23, 2007).

Mao Anqing's wife—**Zhang Shaohua,** who later changed her name to **Shao Hua** (October 30, 1938–June 24, 2008). Married in 1960.

Third child (from his second wife)—a son **Mao Anlong** *(twenty-first generation of the Mao clan named "yuan"—"remote")* (April 4, 1927–May 1931).

Fourth child (from his third wife)—a daughter **Mao Jinhua** (late May 1929–?).

Fifth child (from his third wife)—a son **Mao Anhong** *(twenty-first generation of the Mao clan named "yuan"—"remote")* (early November 1932–?).

Sixth child (from his third wife)—a son *(twenty-first generation of the Mao clan named "yuan"—"remote")* (late autumn 1933 or early winter 1933–?).

Seventh child (from his third wife)—a daughter (February 1935–?).

Eighth child (from his third wife)—a daughter **Jiaojiao;** Mao Zedong later changed her name to **Li Min** (born January 1937).

> *Li Min's husband*—**Kong Linghua** (1934–January 20, 1999). Married August 29, 1958.

Ninth child (from his third wife)—a son **Lyova** *(twenty-first generation of the Mao clan named "yuan"—"remote")* (April 6, 1938–December 1938).

Tenth child (from his fourth wife)—a daughter **Li Na** (born August 3, 1940).

> *Li Na's first husband*—**Xu Ning** (?–?). Married in 1970. The marriage ended in either 1974 or 1976.

> *Li Na's second husband*—**Wang Jingqing** (born 1932). Married in early 1984.

GRANDSONS AND GRANDDAUGHTER

Grandson (from Mao Anqing)—**Mao Xinyu** ("New world") *(twenty-second generation of the Mao clan named "shi"—"dear")* (born January 17, 1970).*

> *Mao Xinyu's first wife*—**Hao Mingli** (January 1972–December 29, 2003). Married December 7, 1997. Marriage ended in May 2002.†

---

* The name was created by Mao Zedong, who did not want to give his grandson one more name, which would meet the requirements of the genealogical chronology of his clan. In general, after the communist takeover the tradition to name children in accordance with the clan chronologies disappeared. For a long time the Mao family called the little boy Maomao ("Fine Hairs"). As we know, it was also an informal name of one of Mao Zedong and He Zizhen's sons, Mao Anhong.

† Hao Mingli passed away in Qincheng municipal prison (Jiangxi province). She had been imprisoned in May 2002, when she began to quarrel with Mao Xinyu after learning that he wanted to divorce her.

Mao Xinyu's second wife—**Liu Bin** (born early 1977). Married in 2002.

Grandson (from Li Min)—**Kong Jining** ("Successor to Lenin's Cause") * (born October 27, 1962).

> *Kong Jining's wife*—**Shen Rong** (birth and marriage dates unknown).

Granddaughter (from Li Min)—**Kong Dongmei** ("Eastern Plum Blossom") †
(born 1972).

Grandson (from Li Na and Xu Ning)—**Xu Xiaoning;** later, after Li Na and Xu Ning divorced, his name was changed to **Li Xiaoyu,** but after Li Na married Wang Jingqing in 1984, his name was changed again to **Wang Xiaozhi** ("Modeled on Mao Runzhi," i.e., Mao Zedong) ‡ (born 1972).

> *Wang Xiaozhi's wife*—Married in 2007.

GREAT-GRANDSONS AND GREAT-GRANDDAUGHTERS

Great-grandson (from Mao Xinyu and Liu Bin)—**Mao Dongdong** (literally: "Winter East"); later the name was changed to **Dongdong** ("Inheritor of Mao Zedong's Legacy"), because a sister of his grandmother, Li Na, observed that Winter East was a very "cold name" *(twenty-third generation of the Mao clan named "dai"—"epochal")* (born December 26, 2003).

Great-granddaughter (from Kong Dongmei)—(born 2005).

Great-grandson (from Kong Dongmei)—(born October 2007).

BROTHERS

(Twentieth generation of the Mao clan named "ze"—"benefactor")

Brother—**Mao Zemin** (April 3, 1896–September 27, 1943).

> *Mao Zemin's first wife*—**Wang Shulan** (February 5, 1896–July 7, 1964). Married in 1919 or 1920.

> *Mao Zemin's second wife*—**Qian Xijun** (1905–September 11, 1989). Married in 1926.

---

* The name was devised by Mao Zedong and the infant's paternal grandfather.

† Mao named her. He took the character *dong* (east) from his own name and combined it with the character *mei* (plum blossom). He had a lifelong love for plum blossoms.

‡ Li Na came up with this name.

Mao Zemin's third wife—**Zhu Danhua** (December 26, 1911–May 29, 2010). Married in May 1940.

Younger brother—**Mao Zetan** (September 25, 1905–April 25, 1935).

Mao Zetan's first wife—**Zhao Xiangui** (September 5, 1905–June 1932). Married in 1924.

Mao Zetan's second wife—**Zhou Wennan** (October 1910–September 1992). Married in late 1926.

Mao Zetan's third wife—**He Yi** (1910–November 22, 1949). Married July 20, 1931.

FOSTER SISTER

Mao Zejian (October 1905–August 20, 1929).

Mao Zejian's first husband—Married in 1919 (?). Marriage ended in 1920.

Mao Zejian's second husband—**Chen Fen** (1903–May 1, 1928). Married in 1925.

NOTES

INTRODUCTION: MYTHS AND REALITIES

1. Edgar Snow, *Journey to the Beginning* (New York: Random House, 1958), 167.
2. See John King Fairbank, *The United States and China* (Cambridge, MA: Harvard University Press, 1948); Benjamin I. Schwartz, *Chinese Communism and the Rise of Mao* (Cambridge, MA: Harvard University Press, 1951); Conrad Brandt, Benjamin Schwartz, and John K. Fairbank, *A Documentary History of Chinese Communism* (Cambridge, MA: Harvard University Press, 1952); Robert C. North, *Moscow and Chinese Communists* (Stanford, CA: Stanford University Press, 1953).
3. George Pálóczi Horváth, *Mao Tse-tung: Emperor of the Blue Ants* (London: Secker & Warburg, 1962).
4. Stuart R. Schram, *Mao Tse-tung* (New York: Simon & Schuster, 1966).
5. Nikita S. Khrushchev, *Memoirs of Nikita Khrushchev*, vol. 3, trans. George Shriver (University Park: Pennsylvania State University Press, 2007), 401.
6. See B. N. Vereshchagin, *V starom i novom Kitae: Iz vospominanii diplomata* (In Old and New China: Reminiscences of a Diplomat) (Moscow: IDV RAN, 1999), 123; "Mao Tszedun o Kominterne i politike Stalina v Kitae" (Mao Zedong on the Comintern and Stalin's China policy), *Problemy Dal'nego Vostoka* (Far Eastern affairs), no. 5 (1994): 107; O. Arne Westad, ed., *Brothers in Arms: The Rise and Fall of the Sino-Soviet Alliance, 1945-1963* (Stanford, CA: Stanford University Press, 1998), 338–39, 340, 348, 350, 354–55; Li Zhisui, *The Private Life of Chairman Mao: The Memoirs of Mao's Personal Physician*, trans. Tai Hung-chao (New York: Random House, 1994), 117.
7. See Gregor Benton and Lin Chun, eds., *Was Mao Really A Monster? The Academic Response to Chang and Halliday's "Mao: The Unknown Story"* (London: Routledge, 2010). For Chang and Halliday's book itself, see Jung Chang and Jon Halliday, *Mao: The Unknown Story* (London: Jonathan Cape, 2005).

1. THE FOSTER CHILD OF THE BODHISATTVA

1. See Jin Chongji, ed., *Mao Zedong zhuan (1893–1949)* (Biography of Mao Zedong [1893–1949]) (Beijing: Zhongyang wenxian chuban she, 2004), 1; *Shaoshan Mao shi zupu* (The Chronicle of the Shaoshan Mao Clan), vol. 1 (Beijing: Quanguo tushuguan wenxian sowei fuzhi zhongxin, 2002), 181.
2. See Jin, *Mao Zedong zhuan (1893–1949)* (Biography of Mao Zedong [1893–1949]), 1; Ma Shexiang, *Hongse diyi jiazu* (The First Red Family) (Wuhan: Hubei renmin chubanshe, 2004), 4–5; *Mao Zedong shenghuo dang'an* (Archives of Mao Zedong's Life), vol. 1 (Beijing: Zhonggong dangshi chubanshe, 1999), 60.

3. Philip Short, *Mao: A Life* (New York: Henry Holt, 1999), 19.

4. Li Min, *Moi otets Mao Tszedun* (My Father Mao Zedong) (Beijing: Izdatel'stvo literatury na inostrannykh yazykakh, 2004), 87.

5. "Anketnyi list na Mao Tszeduna zapolnennyi ego bratom Mao Tszeminem v Moskve 28 dekabria 1939 goda" (Questionnaire about Mao Zedong Filled Out by His Brother Mao Zemin in Moscow, December 28, 1939), *Rossiskii gosudarstvennyi arkhiv sotsial'no-politicheskoi istorii* "Russian State Archive of Social and Political History" [hereafter RGASPI], collection 495, inventory 225, file 71, vol. 1, sheet 265.

6. See Jin, *Mao Zedong zhuan (1893–1949)* (Biography of Mao Zedong [1893–1949]), 2.

7. Edgar Snow, *Red Star Over China* (London: Victor Gollancz, 1937), 131.

8. Li, *Moi otets Mao Tszedun* (My Father Mao Zedong), 89.

9. Ibid., 90.

10. Ibid., 89.

11. Snow, *Red Star Over China*, 127–29.

12. For more details, see A. V. Pantsov, *Iz istorii ideinoi bor'by v kitaiskom revoliutsionnom dvizhenii 20–40-kh godov* (On the History of Ideological Struggle in the Chinese Revolutionary Movement, 1920s–1940s) (Moscow: Nauka, 1985), 12–25.

13. Statistical data from V. G. Gel'bras, *Sotsial'no-politicheskaiia struktura KNR, 50–60-e gody* (The Social-Political Structure of the PRC in the 1950s and 1960s) (Moscow: Nauka, 1980), 27, 33–34, 38.

14. Chang Kuo-t'ao, *The Rise of the Chinese Communist Party 1921–1927*, vol. 1 (Lawrence: University Press of Kansas, 1971), 2.

15. Snow, *Red Star Over China*, 132–33.

16. Ibid., 132.

17. Ibid., 130.

18. Ibid., 129.

19. Ibid.

2. ON THE THRESHOLD OF A NEW WORLD

1. Li, *Moi otets Mao Tszedun*, 91.

2. See Zheng Guanying, *Shengshi weiyan* (Words of Warning to an Affluent Age) (Beijing: Huaxia chubanshe, 2002).

3. Snow, *Red Star Over China*, 135.

4. See Kong Dongmei, *Gaibian shijiede rizi: yu Wang Hairong tan Mao Zedong waijiao wangshi* (Days that Changed the World: Talking to Wang Hairui about Mao Zedong's Foreign Policy) (Beijing: Zhongyang wenxian chubanshe, 2006), 16–17.

5. Snow, *Red Star Over China*, 145.

6. Ibid., 144–45.

7. See *Shaoshan Mao shi zupu* (The Chronicle of the Shaoshan Mao Clan), vol. 7, 387.

8. Pang Xianzhi, ed., *Mao Zedong nianpu, 1893–1949* (Chronological Biography of Mao Zedong, 1893–1949), vol. 1 (Beijing: Renmin chubanshe and Zhongyang wenxian chubanshe, 2002), 6.

9. Snow, *Red Star Over China*, 133.

10. Short, *Mao*, 29, 649.

11. See Ma, *Hongse diyi jiazu* (The First Red Family), 11.

12. Li, *Moi otets Mao Tszedun* (My Father Mao Zedong), 94.

13. Mao Zedong, *Oblaka v snegu. Stikhotvoreniia v perevodakh Aleksandra Pantsova* (Clouds in the Snow. Poems in Trans. Alexander Pantsov) (Moscow: "Veche," 2010), 11.

14. Stuart R. Schram, ed., *Mao's Road to Power: Revolutionary Writings 1912–1949*, vol. 1 (Armonk, NY: M. E. Sharpe, 1992), 60.

15. Snow, *Red Star Over China*, 134.

16. Ibid., 135; *Lichnoe delo Mao Tszeduna* (Personal File of Mao Zedong), RGASPI, collection 495, inventory 225, file 71, vol. 1, sheets 290–91.

17. Quoted from L. N. Borokh, *Konfutsianstvo i evropeiskaia mysl' na rubezhe XIX–XX vekov: Lian Tsichao i teoriia obnovleniia naroda* (Confucianism and European Thought at the Turn of the Nineteenth–Twentieth Centuries. Liang Qichao and the Renovation of the People Theory) (Moscow: Nauka, 2001), 98.

18. Quoted from Pang, *Mao Zedong nianpu, 1893–1949* (Chronological Biography of Mao Zedong, 1893–1949), vol. 1, 9.

19. Snow, *Red Star Over China*, 135.

20. See, for example, Short, *Mao*, 38.

3. "I THINK, THEREFORE, I AM"

1. See William Edgar Geil, *Eighteen Capitals of China* (Philadelphia: Lippincott, 1911), 273.

2. Snow, *Red Star Over China*, 136.

3. Edward H. Hume, *Doctors East, Doctors West: An American Physician's Life in China* (London: Allen & Unwin, 1949), 35.

4. For more details, see Joseph W. Esherick, *Reform and Revolution in China: The 1911 Revolution in Hunan and Hubei* (Berkeley: University of California Press, 1976).

5. Snow, *Red Star Over China*, 136.

6. Ibid., 139.

7. Ibid., 141.

8. Mao Tse-tung, *Selected Works of Mao Tse-tung*, vol. 3 (Beijing: Foreign Languages Press, 1967), 73.

9. See *Lichnoe delo Mao Tszeduna* (Personal File of Mao Zedong), RGASPI, collection 495, inventory 225, file 71, vol. 1, sheet 291.

10. Siao-yu, *Mao Tse-tung and I Were Beggars* (Syracuse, NY: Syracuse University Press, 1959).

11. Ibid., 31.

12. Emi Hsiao, *Mao Tszedun, Chzhu De: Vozhdi kitaiskogo naroda* (Mao Zedong, Zhu De: Leaders of the Chinese People) (Moscow: Gosizdat, 1939), 7; *Lichnoe delo Mao Tszeduna* (Personal File of Mao Zedong), RGASPI, collection 495, inventory 225, file 71, vol. 1, sheet 292.

13. Snow, *Red Star Over China*, 138, 143.

14. Liao Gailong, ed., *Mao Zedong baike quanshu* (Encyclopedia of Mao Zedong), vol. 1 (Beijing: Guangming ribao chubanshe, 2003), 37.

15. Snow, *Red Star Over China*, 143.

16. Schram, *Mao's Road to Power*, vol. 1, 60.

17. Siao-yu, *Mao Tse-tung and I Were Beggars*, 38–39.

18. See Li Jui, *The Early Revolutionary Activities of Comrade Mao Tse-tung* (White Plains, NY: International Arts & Sciences Press, 1977), 17.

19. Quoted from ibid., 17.

20. Schram, *Mao's Road to Power*, vol. 1, 181, 185, 187–89, 200, 208, 211, 251, 255, 277.

21. Ibid., 273.

22. Ibid., 263–64.

23. Ibid., 6.

24. Snow, *Red Star Over China*, 145.

25. Li, *The Early Revolutionary Activities of Comrade Mao Tse-tung*, 18.

26. Schram, *Mao's Road to Power*, vol. 1, 113.

27. Ibid., 120. Emphasis (bold) in the original.

28. Snow, *Red Star Over China*, 143.

29. Siao-yu, *Mao Tse-tung and I Were Beggars*, 129–30, 132.

30. Quoted from Pang, *Mao Zedong nianpu, 1893–1949* (Chronological Biography of Mao Zedong, 1893–1949), vol. 1, 17.

31. See Hume, *Doctors East, Doctors West*, 239.

32. Ibid., 241.

33. Li, *The Early Revolutionary Activities of Comrade Mao Tse-tung*, 47.

34. Schram, *Mao's Road to Power*, vol. 1, 94, 95.
35. Ibid., 199, 241.
36. Ibid., 237–38, 250.
37. Ibid., 139.
38. Quoted from Liao, *Mao Zedong baike quanshu* (Encyclopedia of Mao Zedong), vol. 5, 2662; Stuart Schram, *Mao Tse-tung* (Harmondsworth, UK: Penguin, 1974), 43.

4. THE SOUND OF FOOTSTEPS IN A DESERTED VALLEY

1. Liao, *Mao Zedong baike quanshu* (Encyclopedia of Mao Zedong), vol. 5, 2663; Li, *Moi otets Mao Tszedun* (My Father Mao Zedong), 99.
2. Snow, *Red Star Over China*, 144; Schram, *Mao's Road to Power*, vol. 1, 81–82, 84; Li, *The Early Revolutionary Activities of Comrade Mao Tse-tung*, 74.
3. See Schram, *Mao's Road to Power*, vol. 1, 84.
4. Quoted from Snow, *Red Star Over China*, 144.
5. See Alexander V. Pantsov's interview with Inna Li in Beijing, June 14, 2010; Tang Chunliang, *Li Lisan zhuan* (Biography of Li Lisan) (Harbin: Heilongjiang renmin chubanshe, 1984), 8.
6. Li, *The Early Revolutionary Activities of Comrade Mao Tse-tung*, 74–75.
7. *Lichnoe delo Mao Tszeduna* (Personal File of Mao Zedong), RGASPI, collection 495, inventory 225, file 71, vol. 1, sheet 294.
8. Li, *The Early Revolutionary Activities of Comrade Mao Tse-tung*, 75.
9. Snow, *Red Star Over China*, 144–45.
10. Liao, *Mao Zedong baike quanshu* (Encyclopedia of Mao Zedong), vol. 5, 2661; Li, *The Early Revolutionary Activities of Comrade Mao Tse-tung*, 52–53.
11. Liao, *Mao Zedong baike quanshu* (Encyclopedia of Mao Zedong), vol. 5, 2662.
12. Ibid.
13. Schram, *Mao's Road to Power*, vol. 1, 146.
14. See Liao, *Mao Zedong baike quanshu* (Encyclopedia of Mao Zedong), vol. 5, 2662.
15. Quoted from Robert Payne, *Portrait of a Revolutionary: Mao Tse-tung* (London: Abelard-Schuman, 1961), 54.
16. Li, *The Early Revolutionary Activities of Comrade Mao Tse-tung*, 50–51; Schram, *Mao Tse-tung*, 43.
17. Quoted from Li, *The Early Revolutionary Activities of Comrade Mao Tse-tung*, 48.
18. See Payne, *Portrait of a Revolutionary*, 54.
19. Snow, *Red Star Over China*, 147.
20. *Lichnoe delo Mao Tszeduna* (Personal File of Mao Zedong), RGASPI, collection 495, inventory 225, file 71, vol. 1, sheet 292.
21. See Snow, *Red Star Over China*, 145.
22. Pang, *Mao Zedong nianpu, 1893–1949* (Chronological Biography of Mao Zedong, 1893–1949), vol. 1, 40.
23. Stuart R. Schram, ed., *Mao's Road to Power: Revolutionary Writings, 1912–1949*, vol. 2 (Armonk, NY: M. E. Sharpe, 1994), 20.
24. Li, *Moi otets Mao Tszedun* (My Father Mao Zedong), 97; Li, *The Early Revolutionary Activities of Comrade Mao Zedong*, 71–72.
25. *Lichnoe delo Mao Tszeduna* (Personal File of Mao Zedong), RGASPI, collection 495, inventory 225, file 71, vol. 1, sheet 298.
26. Zhou Shizhao et al., *Wusi yundong zai Hunan* (The May Fourth Movement in Hunan) (Changsha: Hunan renmin chubanshe, 1959), 38.
27. Schram, *Mao's Road to Power*, vol. 2, 20.
28. *Lichnoe delo Mao Tszeduna* (Personal File of Mao Zedong), RGASPI, collection 495, inventory 225, file 71, vol. 1, sheet 295.
29. Snow, *Red Star Over China*, 145–46.
30. Schram, *Mao's Road to Power*, vol. 2, 19.

31. See Li Weihan, *Huiyi yu yanjiu* (Reminiscences and Studies), vol. 1 (Beijing: Zhonggong dangshi ziliao chubanshe, 1986), 3.

32. Ibid.

33. *Lichnoe delo Mao Tszeduna* (Personal File of Mao Zedong), RGASPI, collection 495, inventory 225, file 71, vol. 1, sheet 295.

34. Snow, *Red Star Over China,* 146.

35. Li, *Moi otets Mao Tszedun* (My Father Mao Zedong), 99.

36. Schram, *Mao's Road to Power,* vol. 1, 450.

37. Li, *The Early Revolutionary Activities of Comrade Mao Zedong,* 78.

38. Mao Zedong, *Poems of Mao Tse-tung,* trans., introd., and notes by Hua-ling Nieh Engle and Paul Engle (New York: Simon and Schuster, 1972), 32.

39. Schram, *Mao's Road to Power,* vol. 2, 21.

40. Siao-yu, *Mao Tse-tung and I Were Beggars,* 164.

41. Ibid., 165.

42. For more details, see Marilyn A. Levine, *The Found Generation: Chinese Communists in Europe during the Twenties* (Seattle: University of Washington Press, 1993).

43. See Daria A. Spichak, *Kitaitsy vo Frantsii* (Chinese in France) (manuscript), 13–14.

44. Ibid., 23–24.

45. Ibid., 23.

46. Pang, *Mao Zedong nianpu, 1893–1949* (Chronological Biography of Mao Zedong, 1893–1949), vol. 1, 174.

47. Schram, *Mao's Road to Power,* vol. 1, 174.

48. Siao-yu, *Mao Zedong and I Were Beggars,* 165–66.

49. Pang, *Mao Zedong nianpu, 1893–1949* (Chronological Biography of Mao Zedong, 1893–1949), vol. 1, 174.

5. DREAMS OF A RED CHAMBER

1. Siao-yu, *Mao Tse-tung and I Were Beggars,* 166.

2. Liao, *Mao Zedong baike quanshu* (Encyclopedia of Mao Zedong), vol. 1, 25, 36.

3. Ma, *Hongse diyi jiazu* (The First Red Family), 17–18.

4. Ibid., 30.

5. Siao-yu, *Mao Tse-tung and I Were Beggars,* 41.

6. Quoted from Ma, *Hongse diyi jiazu* (The First Red Family), 22.

7. Schram, *Mao's Road to Power,* vol. 2, 23; Snow, *Red Star Over China,* 149.

8. Siao-yu, *Mao Tse-tung and I Were Beggars,* 166.

9. See David Strand, *Rickshaw Beijing: City People and Politics in the 1920s* (Berkeley: University of California Press, 1989), 13.

10. See Ellen N. La Motte, *Peking Dust* (New York: Century, 1919), 20.

11. Strand, *Rickshaw Beijing,* 20–21; Snow, *Red Star Over China,* 148.

12. Schram, *Mao's Road to Power,* vol. 2, 17–22; Chang, *The Rise of the Chinese Communist Party,* vol. 1, 39.

13. Snow, *Red Star Over China,* 149.

14. On Li Dazhao, see the Exposition of Li Dazhao Museum in Laoting, Hebei Province; Han Yide et al., *Li Dazhao shengping jinian* (Biographical Chronicle of Li Dazhao) (Harbin: Heilongjiang renmin chubanshe, 1987); *Li Dazhao zhuan* (Biography of Li Dazhao) (Beijing: Renmin chubanshe, 1979); *Li Dazhao guju* (Li Dazhao's Birthplace) (Shijiazhuang: Hebei renmin chubanshe, 1996); *Li Dazhao jinianguan* (Museum of Li Dazhao) (Shijiazhuang: Hebei renmin chubanshe, 1999); Maurice Meisner, *Li Ta-chao and the Origins of Chinese Marxism* (New York: Atheneum, 1979).

15. Chang, *The Rise of the Chinese Communist Party,* vol. 1, 90, 265, 335.

16. Snow, *Red Star Over China,* 148.

17. See Schram, *Mao's Road to Power,* vol. 1, 317.

18. For more details, see L. N. Borokh, *Obshchestvennaia mysl' Kitaia i sotsialism (nachalo*

XX v.) (Social Thought in China and Socialism in the Early Twentieth Century) (Moscow: Nauka, 1984); M. A. Persits, "O podgotovitel'nom etape kommunisticheskogo dvizheniia v Azii" (On the Preparatory Stage of the Communist Movement in Asia), in R. A. Ul'anovsky, ed., *Revoliutsionnyi protsess na Vostoke: Istoriia i sovremennost'* (The Revolutionary Process in the East: Past and Present) (Moscow: Nauka, 1982), 38–76; Martin Bernal, *Chinese Socialism to 1907* (Ithaca, NY: Cornell University Press, 1976); *Makesi Engesi zhuzuo zhongyiwen zonglu* (Catalogue of Chinese Translations of Marx and Engels's Works) (Beijing: Shumu wenxian chubanshe, 1988), 1119–21.

19. Mao Zedong, "Qida gongzuo fangzhen" (Work Report at the Seventh Congress), *Hongqi* (Red flag), no. 14 (1981): 4.

20. Li Dazhao, *Izbrannye proizvedeniia* (Selected Works) (Moscow: Nauka, 1989), 147.

21. Ibid., 155, 156, 158–61.

22. See Han, *Li Dazhao shengping jinian* (Biographical Chronicle of Li Dazhao), 59.

23. See Liao, *Mao Zedong baike quanshu* (Encyclopedia of Mao Zedong), vol. 5, 2662.

24. Li, *Izbrannye proizvedeniia* (Selected Works), 164.

25. See Liao, *Mao Zedong baike quanshu* (Encyclopedia of Mao Zedong), vol. 5, 2664.

26. Snow, *Red Star Over China*, 151.

27. Schram, *Mao's Road to Power*, vol. 1, 139.

28. See Lee Feigon, *Chen Duxiu: Founder of the Chinese Communist Party* (Princeton, NJ: Princeton University Press, 1983), 23–112.

29. Schram, *Mao's Road to Power*, vol. 1, 329.

30. Chen Duxiu, *Chen Duxiu wenzhang xuanbian* (Selected Writings of Chen Duxiu), vol. 1 (Beijing: Shenghuo. Dushu. Xinzhi sanlian shudian, 1984), 170.

31. See Li, *Izbrannye proizvedeniia* (Selected Works), 192; Feigon, *Chen Duxiu*, 142; Chang, *The Rise of the Chinese Communist Party*, vol. 1, 90, 110, 694.

32. See *Lichnoe delo Mao Tszeduna* (Personal File of Mao Zedong), RGASPI, collection 495, inventory 225, file 71, vol. 1, sheet 296.

33. Snow, *Red Star Over China*, 149.

34. Spichak, *Kitaitsy vo Frantsii* (Chinese in France) (manuscript), 23–24; Luo Shaozhi, "Cai mu Ge Jianhao" (Mama Cai, Ge Jianhao), in Hu Hua, ed., *Zhonggongdang shi renwu zhuan* (Biographies of Persons in the History of the CCP), vol. 6 (Xi'an: Shaanxi renmin chubanshe, 1982), 47–57.

35. Snow, *Red Star Over China*, 148.

36. Ibid., 150.

37. See Schram, *Mao's Road to Power*, vol. 1, 85.

38. Snow, *Red Star Over China*, 148.

39. Schram, *Mao Tse-tung*, 48.

40. Snow, *Red Star Over China*, 149.

41. Schram, *Mao's Road to Power*, vol. 1, 317.

42. Ibid., 317.

43. Snow, *Red Star Over China*, 147.

44. Mao, *Oblaka v snegu* (Clouds in the Snow), 13.

45. See Pang, *Mao Zedong nianpu, 1893–1949* (Chronological Biography of Mao Zedong, 1893–1949), vol. 1, 52.

6. THE GREAT UNION OF THE POPULAR MASSES

1. See Zhou, *Wusi yundong zai Hunan* (The May Fourth Movement in Hunan), 9.

2. L. P. Deliusin, ed., *Dvizhenie 4 maia 1919 goda v Kitae: Dokumenty i materialy* (The May Fourth Movement of 1919 in China: Documents and Materials) (Moscow: Nauka, 1969), 45.

3. Ibid., 50–51.

4. Ibid., 54–55.

5. See ibid., 96.

6. Ibid., 107; Pang, *Mao Zedong nianpu, 1893–1949* (Chronological Biography of Mao Zedong, 1893–1949), vol. 1, 41.

7. Schram, *Mao's Road to Power*, vol. 1, 211.

8. Ibid., vol. 2, 24.

9. Pang, *Mao Zedong nianpu, 1893–1949* (Chronological Biography of Mao Zedong, 1893–1949), vol. 1, 41.

10. Deliusin, *Dvizhenie 4 maia 1919 goda v Kitae: Dokumenty i materialy* (The May Fourth Movement of 1919 in China: Documents and Materials), 71, 84.

11. Ibid., 42.

12. Zhou, *Wusi yundong zai Hunan* (The May Fourth Movement in Hunan), 13.

13. Ibid.; Pang, *Mao Zedong nianpu, 1893–1949* (Chronological Biography of Mao Zedong, 1893–1949), vol. 1, 42.

14. V. I. Lenin, *Selected Works*, vol. 2 (New York: International, 1943), 19.

15. Schram, *Mao's Road to Power*, vol. 1, 320.

16. Ibid., 318, 319.

17. Ibid., 329–30.

18. Ibid., 332.

19. Ibid., vol. 2, 172.

20. *Wusi shiqi qikan jieshao* (Survey of May Fourth Era Publications), vol. 1 (Beijing: Shenghuo. Dushu. Xinzhi sanlian shudian, 1979), 144, 547–49.

21. Zhou, *Wusi yundong zai Hunan* (The May Fourth Movement in Hunan), 17.

22. Schram, *Mao's Road to Power*, vol. 1, 378, 381.

23. Ibid., 380, 385–86.

24. Ibid., 319.

25. Li, *The Early Revolutionary Activities of Comrade Mao Tse-tung*, xxix; Short, *Mao*, 95; Zhou, *Wusi yundong zai Hunan* (The May Fourth Movement in Hunan), 15–16.

26. Zhou, *Wusi yundong zai Hunan* (The May Fourth Movement in Hunan), 29.

27. Schram, *Mao's Road to Power*, vol. 1, 418.

28. See Zhou, *Wusi yundong zai Hunan* (The May Fourth Movement in Hunan), 21.

29. Schram, *Mao's Road to Power*, vol. 1, 445.

30. Ibid., 491; Short, *Mao*, 115.

31. Schram, *Mao's Road to Power*, vol. 1, 422. In this connection, the following assertion by Jung Chang and Jon Halliday, the English biographers of Mao Zedong, is astonishing. They write that Mao's works on the woman question composed in 1919 prove only one thing: "Evidently, as a man, Mao did not want to have to look after women. He wanted no responsibility towards them. . . . He felt little tenderness towards them." Chang and Halliday, *Mao*, 18. This is precisely the opposite of the truth.

32. See Pang, *Mao Zedong nianpu, 1893–1949* (Chronological Biography of Mao Zedong, 1893–1949), vol. 1, 47.

33. Zhou, *Wusi yundong zai Hunan* (The May Fourth Movement in Hunan), 29–30.

34. See Pang, *Mao Zedong nianpu, 1893–1949* (Chronological Biography of Mao Zedong, 1893–1949), vol. 1, 49.

35. Ibid.; Wu Qinjie, ed., *Mao Zedong guanghui licheng dituji* (Atlas of Mao Zedong's Glorious Historical Path) (Beijing: Zhongguo ditu chubanshe, 2003), 18.

36. See *Lichnoe delo Mao Tszeduna* (Personal File of Mao Zedong), RGASPI, collection 495, inventory 225, file 71, vol. 1, sheet 297.

37. See Schram, *Mao's Road to Power*, vol. 1, 487.

38. See Pang, *Mao Zedong nianpu, 1893–1949* (Chronological Biography of Mao Zedong, 1893–1949), vol. 1, 76.

39. Schram, *Mao's Road to Power*, vol. 1, 492.

40. See Ibid., 491–95.

41. Ibid., 488–89.

42. Ibid., 476.

43. Ibid., 473.

44. Ibid., 496.

45. See Edward A. McCord, *The Power of the Gun: The Emergence of Modern Chinese War-lordism* (Berkeley: University of California Press, 1993), 296–300.

46. Schram, *Mao's Road to Power,* vol. 1, 518–19.

47. Ibid., 522.

48. Snow, *Red Star Over China,* 153.

49. See Pang, *Mao Zedong nianpu, 1893–1949* (Chronological Biography of Mao Zedong, 1893–1949), vol. 1, 57; Alexander Pantsov, *The Bolsheviks and the Chinese Revolution, 1919–1927* (Honolulu: University of Hawai'i Press, 2000), 33–35.

50. For more detailed treatment, see Feigon, *Chen Duxiu,* 138–46.

51. See Yu. M. Garushiants, *Dvizhenie 4 maia v Kitae* (The May Fourth Movement in China) (Moscow: Nauka, 1959); Deliusin, *Dvizhenie 4 maia 1919 goda v Kitae: Dokumenty i materialy* (The May Fourth Movement of 1919 in China: Documents and Materials); Chow Tse-tsung, *The May Fourth Movement: Intellectual Revolution in Modern China* (Cambridge, MA: Harvard University Press, 1960).

52. Li, *Izbrannye proizvedeniia* (Selected Works), 204.

53. Mao Tse-tung, *Selected Works of Mao Tse-tung,* vol. 4 (Beijing: Foreign Languages Press, 1969), 413.

54. See Luosu (Russell), "You E ganxiang" (Impressions of a Journey to Russia), *Xin qing-nian* (New youth) 8, no. 2 (1920): 1–12.

55. See L. P. Deliusin, *Spor o sotsializme: Iz istorii obshchestvenno-politicheskoi mysli Kitaia v nachale 20-kh godov* (The Dispute over Socialism: From the History of Sociopolitical Thought in China in the Early 1920s) (Moscow: Nauka, 1970), 31–34.

56. Quoted from Schram, *Mao's Road to Power,* vol. 2, 8.

57. Ibid., vol. 1, 505.

58. Ibid., 506.

59. Ibid., 534.

60. Ibid., 519.

61. Ibid.

7. BREATHING WORLD REVOLUTION, OR THE MAGIC OF DICTATORSHIP

1. Ibid., 518; vol. 2, 26.

2. See Li, *The Early Revolutionary Activities of Comrade Mao Tse-tung,* 134.

3. Schram, *Mao's Road to Power,* vol. 1, 518.

4. See Pan Ling, *In Search of Old Shanghai* (Hong Kong: Joint, 1983), 19; Betty Peh-t'i Wei, *Old Shanghai* (Hong Kong, 1991), 13, 14, 15; *All About Shanghai and Environs: A Standard Guide Book: Historical and Contemporary Facts and Statistics* (Shanghai: University Press, 1934); Tang Zhentang, ed., *Jindai Shanghai fanhualu* (Lively Notes on Modern Shanghai) (Hong Kong: Shangwu yinshuguan, 1993), 12.

5. See Li, *The Early Revolutionary Activities of Comrade Mao Tse-tung,* 134.

6. See Schram, *Mao's Road to Power,* vol. 1, 473, 514–16.

7. Snow, *Red Star Over China,* 152.

8. See A. M. Grigoriev, *Antiimperialisticheskaia programma kitaiskikh burzhuaznykh revo-liutsionerov (1895–1905)* (The Anti-imperialist Program of the Chinese Bourgeois Revolutionaries [1895–1905]) (Moscow: Nauka, 1966), 65.

9. Schram, *Mao's Road to Power,* vol. 1, 501.

10. Ibid., 599.

11. Ibid., 523.

12. Ibid., 523, 526.

13. Ibid., 511, 527, 529.

14. Ibid., 572.

15. Snow, *Red Star Over China,* 151.

16. Ibid., 154.

17. See V. I. Glunin, "Grigorii Voitinsky, 1893–1953," in G. V. Astafiev et al., eds., *Vidnye sovietskie kommunisty—uchastniki kitaiskoi revoliutsii* (Prominent Soviet Communists—Participants in the Chinese Revolution) (Moscow: Nauka, 1970), 66–67; Pantsov, *The Bolsheviks and the Chinese Revolution, 1919–1927*, 295.

18. See M. L. Titarenko et al., eds., *VKP(b), Komintern i Kitai: Dokumenty* (The CPSU, the Comintern and China: Documents), vol. 1 (Moscow: AO "Buklet," 1994), 48; M. L. Titarenko, ed., *Istoriia Kommunisticheskoi partii Kitaia* (History of the Communist Party of China), vol. 1 (Moscow: IDV AN SSSR, 1987), 48–49; Chang, *The Rise of the Chinese Communist Party*, vol. 1, 122–23.

19. Schram, *Mao's Road to Power*, vol. 1, 589.

20. See *Lichnoe delo Mao Tszeduna* (Personal File of Mao Zedong), RGASPI, collection 495, inventory 225, file 71, vol. 1, sheets 296–97.

21. Schram, *Mao's Road to Power*, vol. 1, 584–86.

22. Shao Piaoping, *Xin Eguo zhi yanjiu* (A Study of the New Russia) (n.p.: Riben daban naqu dongying bianyishe, 1920).

23. Schram, *Mao's Road to Power*, vol. 1, 534, 585–86, 589–91; vol. 2, 48–49.

24. Pang, *Mao Zedong nianpu, 1893–1949* (Chronological Biography of Mao Zedong, 1893–1949), vol. 1, 63.

25. Schram, *Mao's Road to Power*, vol. 1, 554–55.

26. See Chang and Halliday, *Mao*, 16.

27. See Schram, *Mao's Road to Power*, vol. 1, 493–94, 506–7, 518.

28. Qiwu lao-ren (Bao Huiseng), "Do i posle obrazovaniia Kommunisticheskoi partii Kitaia" (Before and After the Formation of the Communist Party of China), *Rabochii klass i sovremennyi mir* (The working class and the contemporary world), no. 2 (1971): 120; *Renmin ribao* (People's daily), August 14, 1983; Xiao Jingguang, "Fusu xuexi qianhou" (Before and After Studying in the Soviet Union), *Gemingshi ziliao* (Materials on revolutionary history), Beijing, no. 3 (1981): 6; Donald Klein and Anne Clark, *Biographic Dictionary of Chinese Communism*, vol. 1 (Cambridge, MA: Harvard University Press, 1971), 241; vol. 2, 982.

29. See Xiao, "Fusu xuexi qianhou" (Before and After Studying in the Soviet Union), 6; Exposition of the Shanghai Socialist Youth League Museum.

30. Schram, *Mao's Road to Power*, vol. 1, 536–37, 539–40, 575–76, 615.

31. See Short, *Mao*, 108.

32. Schram, *Mao's Road to Power*, vol. 2, 16.

33. See *Lichnoe delo Mao Tszeduna* (Personal File of Mao Zedong), RGASPI, collection 495, inventory 225, file 71, vol. 1, sheets 296–97.

34. Snow, *Red Star Over China*, 152.

35. Schram, *Mao's Road to Power*, vol. 2, 167.

36. Ibid., vol. 1, 595.

37. Ibid.

38. Zhang Yunhou et al., *Wusi shiqi de shetuan* (Societies During the May Fourth Era), vol. 1 (Beijing: Shenghuo. Dushu. Xinzhi sanlian shudian, 1979), 28–29. In this connection, Jung Chang and Jon Halliday's assertion that the idea of forming the Communist Party "did not stem . . . from any . . . Chinese" is mistaken. Chang and Halliday, *Mao*, 19. Cai Hesen decided that it was necessary to establish the CCP independently of Voitinsky or of any other representatives of Moscow.

39. See Titarenko, *VKP(b), Komintern i Kitai: Dokumenty* (The CPSU, the Comintern and China: Documents), vol. 1, 30.

40. See K. V. Shevelev, *Iz istorii obrazovaniia Kommunisticheskoi partii Kitaia* (From the History of the Establishment of the Communist Party of China) (Moscow: IDV AN SSSR, 1976), 63.

41. Schram, *Mao's Road to Power*, vol. 1, 600.

42. Ibid.

43. Ibid., vol. 2, 26–27.

44. Ibid., 8.

45. Ibid., 8, 9.

46. Ibid., 11.

47. Ibid., vol. 1, 544.

48. See V. I. Glunin, *Komintern i stanovlenie kommunisticheskogo dvizheniia v Kitae, 1920–1927* (The Comintern and the Rise of the Communist Movement in China, 1920–1927), in R. A. Ulianovskii, ed., *Komintern i Vostok: Bor'ba za leninskuiu strategiiu i taktiku v natsional'no-osvoboditel'nom dvizhenii* (The Comintern and the East: The Struggle for Leninist Strategy and Tactics in the National Liberation Movement) (Moscow: Nauka, 1968), 249.

49. Chen Duxiu, "Shehuizhuyi piping" (A Critique of Socialism), *Xin qingnian* (New youth) 9, no. 3 (1921): 11, 13.

50. See, for example, their selected works, included in the following collections: *Makesizhuyi zai Zhongguo—cong yingxiang chuanru dao chuanbo* (Marxism in China—From Influence to Dissemination), vol. 2 (Beijing: Qinghua daxue chubanshe, 1983); *Gongchan xiaozu* (Communist Cells), 2 vols. (Beijing: Zhonggong dangshi ziliao chubanshe, 1987).

51. See Wu, *Mao Zedong guanghui licheng dituji* (Atlas of Mao Zedong's Glorious Historical Path), 21.

52. Pang, *Mao Zedong nianpu, 1893–1949* (Chronological Biography of Mao Zedong, 1893–1949), vol. 1, 70.

53. Ibid.

54. Quoted from Schram, *Mao's Road to Power*, vol. 1, 594.

55. See Pang, *Mao Zedong nianpu, 1893–1949* (Chronological Biography of Mao Zedong, 1893–1949), vol. 1, 75.

56. Ibid., 73; Chang, *The Rise of the Chinese Communist Party*, vol. 1, 105, 129.

57. See Li, *Moi otets Mao Tszedun* (My Father Mao Zedong), 134.

58. Quoted from Pang, *Mao Zedong nianpu, 1893–1949* (Chronological Biography of Mao Zedong, 1893–1949), vol. 1, 76.

59. Ibid.

60. Li, *Moi otets Mao Tszedun* (My Father Mao Zedong), 135.

61. Short, *Mao*, 226.

62. In 1920 Mao Zedong had rescued this woman from the family of her unloved husband, having convinced her to dissolve her "feudal marriage." Zejian was fifteen years old at the time and her name was Jumeizi ("Younger Sister Chrysanthemum"). Mao himself created a new name for her: Zejian means "Beneficent Creation." See Li, *Moi otets Mao Tszedun* (My Father Mao Zedong), 127–28; Kong Dongmei, *Fankai wo jia laoyingji: Wo xinzhongde waigong Mao Zedong* (Opening the Old Photo Albums of My Family: My Grandfather Mao Zedong Is In My Heart) (Beijing: Zhongyang wenxian chubanshe, 2003), 189; Pei Jian, *Xiang hun—Mao Zedongde jiashi* (The Spirit of Hunan—Generations of Mao Zedong's Family) ([Beijing]: Qunzhong chubanshe, 1992), 56–58; *Mao zhuxi yijia liu lieshi* (Six Martyrs from the Chairman Mao's Family) (Changsha: Hunan renmin chubanshe, 1978), 93–110.

63. See Pang, *Mao Zedong nianpu, 1893–1949* (Chronological Biography of Mao Zedong, 1893–1949), vol. 1, 82.

64. See Li, *Moi otets Mao Tszedun* (My Father Mao Zedong), 135.

8. "FOLLOWING THE RUSSIAN PATH"

1. Schram, *Mao's Road to Power*, vol. 2, 61.

2. Ibid., 67–70.

3. Ibid., 37–38.

4. Ibid., 38. Bold in the original.

5. Titarenko, *VKP(b), Komintern i Kitai: Dokumenty* (The CPSU, the Comintern and China: Documents), vol. 1, 27.

6. Chang, *The Rise of the Chinese Communist Party,* vol. 1, 137, 139.

7. Titarenko, *VKP(b), Komintern i Kitai: Dokumenty* (The CPSU, the Comintern and China: Documents), vol. 1, 743.

8. Ibid., 60.

9. See *Shanghai diqu jiandang huodong yanjiu ziliao* (Materials for the Study of Party Building in the Shanghai Region) (Shanghai: Shanghai shi diyi renmin jingcha xuexiao, 1986), 120; Pang, *Mao Zedong nianpu, 1893–1949* (Chronological Biography of Mao Zedong, 1893–1949), vol. 1, 84.

10. Quoted from M. A. Persits, "Iz istorii stanovleniia Kommunisticheskoi partii Kitaia (Doklad podgotovlennyi Chzhang Taileem dlia III Kongressa Kominterna kak istoricheskii istochnik)" (From the History of the Founding of the Communist Party of China [Zhang Tailei's Report to the Third Congress of the Comintern as an Historical Source]), *Narody Azii i Afriki* (Peoples of Asia and Africa), no. 4 (1971): 51.

11. See *Shanghai diqu jiandang huodong yanjiu ziliao* (Materials for the Study of Party Building in the Shanghai Region), 120–21; Chen Gongbo and Zhou Fohai, *Chen Gongbo, Zhou Fohai huiyilu* (Reminiscences of Chen Gongbo, Zhou Fohai) (Hong Kong: Chunqiu chubanshe, 1988), 116.

12. *Shanghai diqu jiandang huodong yanjiu ziliao* (Materials for the Study of Party Building in the Shanghai Region), 131.

13. See "Novye materialy o pervom s"ezde Kommunisticheskoi partii Kitaia" (New Materials on the First Congress of the Communist Party of China), *Narody Azii i Afriki* (Peoples of Asia and Africa), no. 6 (1972): 151.

14. Chang and Halliday write that Zhang Guotao had been chosen because "he had been to Russia and had links with the foreigners." Chang and Halliday, *Mao,* 26. This is untrue. Zhang Guotao first visited Russia only half a year after the founding congress of the CCP. As for "the foreigners" (emissaries of the Comintern?) his ties with them were no greater than those of the majority of the other delegates. He was chosen as chair of the congress because he had been particularly active prior to the first session.

15. Chang, *The Rise of the Chinese Communist Party,* vol. 1, 140, 141.

16. C. Martin Wilbur, ed., *The Communist Movement in China: An Essay Written in 1924 by Ch'en Kung-po* (New York: Columbia University Press, 1960), 106.

17. Ibid.

18. Ibid., 109.

19. Ibid., 83.

20. See "Kongress Kommunisticheskoi partii v Kitae" (Congress of the Communist Party of China), *Narody Azii i Afriki* (Peoples of Asia and Africa), no. 6 (1972): 151–52.

21. See Shen Dechun and Tian Haiyan, "Zhongguo gongchandang 'Yi Da' de zhuyao wenti" (Main Questions Connected to the First Congress of the Communist Party of China), *Renmin ribao* (People's daily), June 30, 1961.

22. V. I. Lenin, *Polnoe sobranie sochinenii* (Complete Collected Works), vol. 39 (Moscow: Politizdat, 1974), 327.

23. V. I. Lenin, *Selected Works,* vol. 10 (New York: International, 1943), 231–44.

24. "Kongress Kommunisticheskoi partii v Kitae" (Congress of the Communist Party in China), 153. See also *Shanghai diqu jiandang huodong yanjiu ziliao* (Materials for the Study of Party Building in the Shanghai Region), 9, 122–24; Wu, *Mao Zedong guanghui licheng dituji* (Atlas of Mao Zedong's Glorious Historical Path), 23; Chen and Zhou, *Chen Gongbo, Zhou Fohai huiyilu* (Reminiscences of Chen Gongbo and Zhou Fohai), 40, 117; Chang, *The Rise of the Chinese Communist Party,* vol. 1, 136–52; Qiwu, *Do i posle obrazovaniia Kommunisticheskoi partii Kitaia* (Before and After the Establishment of the Communist Party of China), 117–27; Chen Pang-qu (Chen Tanqu), "Vospominaniia o I s"ezde Kompartii Kitaia" (Reminiscences of the First Congress of the CCP), *Kommunisticheskii Internatsional* (Communist International), no. 14 (1936): 96–99; Siao-yu, *Mao Tse-tung and I Were Beggars,* 196–203. Chang and Halliday ignore these generally known facts and assert that the CCP was founded not at its founding congress in July 1921, but a year earlier, in

August 1920. See Chang and Halliday, *Mao,* 19. They do so, in their own words, in order to explode the "myth" that Mao Zedong was one of the founders of the party. But what was founded in the summer of 1920 was not the party, but only the first, Shanghai, communist circle.

9. THE LESSONS OF BOLSHEVIK TACTICS

1. See Tony Saich, *The Origins of the First United Front in China: The Role of Sneevliet (Alias Maring),* vol. 1 (Leiden: Brill, 1991), 309–10.
2. *Shanghai diqu jiandang huodong yanjiu ziliao* (Materials on Party Building in the Shanghai Region), 10.
3. See *Otchet tov. G. Maringa Kominternu. Iul' 1922 g.* (Comrade G. Maring's Report to the Comintern, July 1922), RGASPI, collection 514, inventory 1, file 20, sheets 85–91; Zhang Tailei, *Zhang Tailei wenji* (Works of Zhang Tailei) (Beijing: Renmin chubanshe, 1981), 330; Harold Isaacs, "Documents on the Comintern and the Chinese Revolution," *China Quarterly,* no. 45 (1971): 103–4; Lin Hongyuan, "Zhang Tailei," in Hu Hua, ed., *Zhonggongdang shi renwu zhuan* (Biographies of Persons in the History of the Chinese Communist Party), vol. 4 (Xi'an: Shaanxi renmin chubanshe, 1982), 81–82; *Zhonggong "sanda" ziliao* (Materials from the Third Congress of the CCP) (Guangzhou: Guangdong renmin chubanshe, 1985), 12; Saich, *The Origins of the First United Front,* vol. 1, 216–46, 252, 317–23.
4. Saich, *The Origins of the First United Front in China,* vol. 1, 323.
5. Jiang Xuanhua, "Dangde minzhu geming gangling de tichu he guogong hezuo celüede jige wenti" (Several Questions Regarding the Party Program for the Democratic Revolution and the Strategy of Cooperation Between the Guomindang and the CCP), *Jindaishi yanjiu* (Studies in modern history), no. 2 (1985): 116.
6. See *"Erda" he "sanda": Zhongguo gongchandang di' er san ci daibiaodahui ziliao xuanbian* (The Second and Third Congresses: Selected Documents from the Second and Third Congresses of the CCP) (Beijing: Zhongguo shehui kexue chubanshe, 1985), 36.
7. See Saich, *The Origins of the First United Front in China,* vol. 1, 284.
8. See Glunin, *Komintern i stanovlenie kommunisticheskogo dvizheniia v Kitae (1920–1927)* (The Comintern and the Rise of the Communist Movement in China [1920–1927]), 252.
9. Pang, *Mao Zedong nianpu, 1893–1949* (Chronological Biography of Mao Zedong, 1893–1949), vol. 1, 85.
10. Ibid., 86.
11. See Schram, *Mao's Road to Power,* vol. 2, 100.
12. Ibid.
13. Ibid., 134.
14. Mao Zedong, *Mao Zedong shici duilian jizhu* (Collection of Mao Zedong's Poems). (Changsha: Huwan wenyi chubanshe, 1991), 161. Lake Dongting is a big lake north of Changsha. The Xiao and Xiang are rivers in Hunan.
15. Pang, *Mao Zedong nianpu, 1893–1949* (Chronological Biography of Mao Zedong, 1893–1949), vol. 1, 91.
16. Schram, *Mao's Road to Power,* vol. 2, 107.
17. Ibid., 174–75; Snow, *Red Star Over China,* 155.
18. See Wu, *Mao Zedong guanghui licheng dituji* (Atlas of Mao Zedong's Glorious Historical Path), 27.
19. Schram, *Mao's Road to Power,* vol. 2, 174, 175; *Zhonggong "sanda" ziliao* (Materials from the Third Congress of the CCP), 128.
20. Snow, *Red Star Over China,* 155.
21. Schram, *Mao's Road to Power,* vol. 2, 177.
22. Pang, *Mao Zedong nianpu, 1893–1949* (Chronological Biography of Mao Zedong, 1893–1949), vol. 1, 92–103; Wu, *Mao Zedong guanghui licheng dituji* (Atlas of Mao Zedong's Glorious Historical Path), 27–29.
23. Pang, *Mao Zedong nianpu, 1893–1949* (Chronological Biography of Mao Zedong,

1893–1949), vol. 1, 119, 128; Ma, *Hongse diyi jiazu* (The First Red Family), 310–12, 334–35.

24. Mao Zemin, "Avtobiografiia" (Autobiography), RGASPI, collection 495, inventory 225, file 477, sheet 12; Li, *Moi otets Mao Tszedun* (My Father Mao Zedong), 108; Ma, *Hongse diyi jiazu* (The First Red Family), 259, 286.

25. Schram, *Mao's Road to Power*, vol. 2, 136, 137, 177.

26. Pang, *Mao Zedong nianpu, 1893–1949* (Chronological Biography of Mao Zedong, 1893–1949), vol. 1, 103–4.

27. Schram, *Mao's Road to Power*, vol. 2, 132–40.

28. Ibid., 136.

29. Titarenko, *VKP(b), Komintern i Kitai: Dokumenty* (The CPSU, the Comintern and China: Documents), vol. 1, 236.

30. Snow, *Red Star Over China*, 152.

31. Schram, *Mao's Road to Power*, vol. 2, 136.

32. See Wu, *Mao Zedong guanghui licheng dituji* (Atlas of Mao Zedong's Glorious Historical Path), 26; Pang, *Mao Zedong nianpu, 1893–1949* (Chronological Biography of Mao Zedong), vol. 1, 95.

33. Pang, *Mao Zedong nianpu, 1893–1949* (Chronological Biography of Mao Zedong, 1893–1949), vol. 1, 95–96.

34. See Wu, *Mao Zedong guanghui licheng dituji* (Atlas of Mao Zedong's Glorious Historical Path), 26.

35. See Saich, *The Origins of the First United Front in China*, vol. 1, 344–45.

36. Schram, *Mao's Road to Power*, vol. 2, 103.

37. Ibid., 93.

38. Pang, *Mao Zedong nianpu, 1893–1949* (Chronological Biography of Mao Zedong, 1893–1949), vol. 1, 87; Li, *Moi otets Mao Tszedun* (My Father Mao Zedong), 119.

39. RGASPI, collection 5, inventory 3, file 31, sheet 56.

40. See V. I. Lenin, *Polnoe sobranie sochinenii* (Complete Collected Works), vol. 44 (Moscow: Politizdat, 1977), 702; Chang, *The Rise of the Chinese Communist Party*, vol. 1, 207–9.

41. See "Yuandong geguo gongchandang ji minzu geming tuanti diyi ci dahui xuanyan" (Manifesto of the First Congress of Communist Parties and National Liberation Organization of the Countries of the Far East), *Xianqu* (Pioneer), no. 10 (1922): 4.

42. See Chang, *The Rise of the Chinese Communist Party*, vol. 1, 220.

43. For more details, see M. I. Sladkovskii, ed., *Noveishaia istoriia Kitaia, 1917–1927* (Contemporary History of China, 1917–1927) (Moscow: Nauka, 1983), 108–9.

44. "Zhongguo gongchandang duiyu shiju de zhuzhang" (Statement of the Chinese Communist Party on the Current Situation), *Xianqu* (Pioneer), no. 9 (1922): 2, 3.

45. Quoted from Glunin, *Komintern i stanovlenie kommunisticheskogo dvizheniia v Kitae* (The Comintern and the Rise of the Communist Movement in China), 252; Jiang Xuanhua, "Dangde minzhu ganglingde tichu he guogong hezuo celüede jige wenti" (Several Questions Regarding the Party Program for the Democratic Revolution and the Strategy of Cooperation Between the Guomindang and the CCP), 116.

46. Snow, *Red Star Over China*, 156.

47. Chang and Halliday assert that Mao did not take part because "he was dropped from" the congress (Chang and Halliday, *Mao*, 31), but they provide no source for this assertion.

48. See *Zhongguo gongchandang jiguan fazhan cankao ziliao* (Reference Materials on the History of the Development of the CCP Organization), vol. 1 (Beijing: Zhonggong dangxiao chubanshe, 1983), 38.

49. See *Zhongguo gongchandang wunian lai zhi zhengzhi zhuzhang* (Political Declarations of the Chinese Communist Party over the Past Five Years) (Guangzhou: Guoguan shuju, 1926), 1–23; *Zhonggong "sanda" ziliao* (Materials from the Third Congress of the CCP), 5–7; Wilbur, *The Communist Movement in China*, 105–17.

50. Wilbur, *The Communist Movement in China*, 119–20.

51. Saich, *The Origins of the First United Front in China,* vol. 1, 327.

52. Chang, *The Rise of the Chinese Communist Party,* vol. 1, 250.

53. See Dov Bing, "Sneevliet and the Early Years of the CCP," *China Quarterly,* no. 48 (1971): 690–91.

54. Cited from S. A. Dalin, *Kitaiskie memuary, 1921–1927* (Chinese Memoirs, 1921–1927) (Moscow: Nauka, 1975), 134.

55. See Wang Jianmin, *Zhongguo gongchandang shigao* (A Draft History of the Chinese Communist Party), vol. 1 (Taibei: Author Press, 1965), 94.

56. See Saich, *The Origins of the First United Front in China,* vol. 1, 53.

57. Ibid., 310; Chang, *The Rise of the Chinese Communist Party,* vol. 1, 138.

58. See Yang Kuisong, "Obshchaia kharakteristika otnoshenii mezhdu VKP(b) (KPSS), Kominternom i KPK do 1949 goda" (The General Nature of Relations Between the VKP(b) [CPSU], and the CCP to 1949), *Problemy Dal'nego Vostoka* (Far Eastern affairs), no. 6 (2004): 103.

IO. ENTERING THE GUOMINDANG

1. See S. Kalachev (S. N. Naumov), "Kratkii ocherk istorii Kitaiskoi kommunisticheskoi partii" (Brief History of the Chinese Communist Party), *Kanton* (Canton), no. 10 (1927): 51; Chang, *The Rise of the Chinese Communist Party,* vol. 1, 260.

2. Chang, *The Rise of the Chinese Communist Party,* vol. 1, 260; Xu Yuandong et al., *Zhongguo gongchandang lishi jianghua* (Lectures on CCP History) (Beijing: Zhongguo qingnian chubanshe, 1982), 36.

3. See *Biulleten' IV Kongressa Kommunisticheskogo Internatsionala* (Bulletin of the Fourth Congress of the Communist International), no. 20 (November 29, 1922), 18.

4. See Zou Lu, *Zhongguo guomindang shigao* (An Outline History of the Chinese Guomindang) (Changsha: Minzhi shuju, 1931), 345–48.

5. I. F. Kurdiukov et al., eds., *Sovetsko-kitaiskie otnosheniia, 1917–1957: Sbornik dokumentov* (Soviet-Chinese Relations, 1917–1957: A Documentary Collection) (Moscow: Izd-vo vostochnoi literatury, 1959), 64–65.

6. Quoted from Ma, *Hongse diyi jiazu* (The First Red Family), 29.

7. See Pang, *Mao Zedong nianpu, 1893–1949* (Chronological Biography of Mao Zedong, 1893–1949), vol. I, 111.

8. See Wu, *Mao Zedong guanghui licheng dituji* (Atlas of Mao Zedong's Glorious Historical Path), 29.

9. Saich, *The Origins of the First United Front in China,* vol. 1, 345.

10. Wu, *Mao Zedong guanghui licheng dituji* (Atlas of Mao Zedong's Glorious Historical Path), 31, 32.

11. Schram, *Mao's Road to Power,* vol. 2, 157, 159, 161.

12. Saich, *The Origins of the First United Front in China,* vol. 1, 448–49; vol. 2, 589–90, 616–17.

13. See *Zhonggong "sanda" ziliao* (Materials from the Third Congress of the CCP), 155.

14. See Ibid., 128.

15. For more details, see Daria A. Spichak, *Kitaiskii avangard Kremlia: Revoliutsionery Kitaia v moskovskikh shkolakh Kominterna (1921–1939)* (Chinese Vanguard of the Kremlin: Revolutionaries of China in Moscow Comintern Schools [1921–1939]) (Moscow: "Veche," 2012), 58–59.

16. *Zhonggong "sanda" ziliao* (Materials from the Third Congress of the CCP), 62.

17. Alexander V. Pantsov's interview with former Chinese communist Wang Fanxi in Leeds, England, July 17, 1992.

18. Cai He-sen, "Istoriia opportunizma v Kommunistecheskoi partii Kitaia" (The History of Opportunism in the Communist Party of China), *Problemy Kitaia* (Problems of China), no. 1 (1929): 4.

19. Quoted from Sladkovskii, *Noveishaia istoriia Kitaia, 1917–1927* (Contemporary History of China, 1917–1927), 140.

20. See Chang, *The Rise of the Chinese Communist Party,* vol. 1, 308.

21. Saich, *The Origins of the First United Front in China,* vol. 2, 580.

22. Chang, *The Rise of the Chinese Communist Party,* vol. 1, 311.

23. *Zhonggong "sanda" ziliao* (Materials from the Third Congress of the CCP), 81, 82.

24. See ibid., 132.

25. Pang, *Mao Zedong nianpu, 1893–1949* (Chronological Biography of Mao Zedong, 1893–1949), vol. 1, 114.

26. See Titarenko, *VKP(b), Komintern i Kitai: Dokumenty* (The CPSU, the Comintern and China: Documents), vol. 1, 238. See also *Soviet Plot in China* (Peking: Metropolitan Police Headquarters, 1927), document no. 13.

27. Quoted from Chang, *The Rise of the Chinese Communist Party,* vol. 1, 309.

28. *Zhonggong "sanda" ziliao* (Materials from the Third Congress of the CCP), 88.

29. M. L. Titarenko, ed., *Kommunisticheskii Internatsional i kitaiskaia revoliutsiia: Dokumenty i materialy* (The Communist International and the Chinese Revolution: Documents and Materials) (Moscow: Nauka, 1986), 39.

30. Peng Pai, *Zapiski Pen Paia* (Notes of Peng Pai), trans. A. Ivin (Moscow: Zhurnal'no-gazetnoe ob'edinenie, 1938), 9.

31. See Sladkovskii, *Noveishaia istoriia Kitaia, 1917–1927* (Contemporary History of China, 1917–1927), 166.

32. *Zhonggong "sanda" ziliao* (Materials from the Third Congress of the CCP), 103–4.

33. Ibid., 157.

34. See Schram, *Mao's Road to Power,* vol. 2, xxx.

35. See Pang, *Mao Zedong nianpu, 1893–1949* (Chronological Biography of Mao Zedong, 1893–1949), vol. 1, 115.

36. See *Voprosy istorii KPSS* (Problems of history of the Communist Party of the Soviet Union), no. 10 (1966): 34; Saich, *The Origins of the First United Front in China,* vol. 2, 526.

37. Schram, *Mao's Road to Power,* vol. 2, 165.

38. See Titarenko, *VKP(b), Komintern i Kitai: Dokumenty* (The CPSU, the Comintern and China: Documents), vol. 1, 240.

39. Jiang Song Meiling (Madame Chiang Kai-shek), *Yu Baoluoting tanhua huiyilu* (Conversations with Mikhail Borodin) (Taibei: Yuancheng wenhua tushu gongyingshe, 1976), 12–13.

40. Dalin, *Kitaiskie memuary, 1921–1927* (Chinese Memoirs, 1921–1927), 149.

41. Chang, *The Rise of the Chinese Communist Party,* vol. 1, 519.

42. See Titarenko, *VKP(b), Komintern i Kitai: Dokumenty* (The CPSU, the Comintern and China: Documents), vol. 1, 255–314; Chiang Chung-cheng (Chiang Kai-shek), *Soviet Russia in China: A Summing Up at Seventy,* trans. under the direction of Madame Chiang Kai-shek, revised, enlarged edition, with maps (New York: Farrar, Straus & Cudahy, 1958), 21–27; Ch'en Chieh-ju, *Chiang Kai-shek's Secret Past: The Memoirs of His Second Wife* (Boulder, CO: Westview Press, 1993), 130–37.

43. Titarenko, *VKP(b), Komintern i Kitai: Dokumenty* (The CPSU, the Comintern and China: Documents), vol. 1, 261.

44. Chen Chieh-ju, *Chiang Kai-shek's Secret Past,* 131, 133, 136.

45. See *Kommunist* (Communist), no. 4 (1966): 12–14.

46. See A. I. Cherepanov, *Zapiski voennogo sovetnika v Kitae* (Notes of a Military Adviser in China), 2nd ed. (Moscow: Nauka, 1976), 30–72. See also Alexander Ivanovich Cherepanov, *Notes of a Military Adviser in China,* trans. Alexandra O. Smith (Taipei: Office of Military History, 1970), 10–37.

47. Sun Yat-sen, *Izbrannye proizvedeniia* (Selected Works), 2nd ed., revised and expanded (Moscow: Nauka, 1985), 327.

48. Pang, *Mao Zedong nianpu, 1893–1949* (Chronological Biography of Mao Zedong, 1893–1949), vol. 1, 116, 118.

49. Chang, *The Rise of the Chinese Communist Party*, vol. 1, 315.

50. Schram, *Mao's Road to Power*, vol. 2, 179, 181, 182.

51. Pang, *Mao Zedong nianpu, 1893–1949* (Chronological Biography of Mao Zedong, 1893–1949), vol. 1, 118.

52. Schram, *Mao's Road to Power*, vol. 2, 193.

53. See Pang, *Mao Zedong nianpu, 1893–1949* (Chronological Biography of Mao Zedong, 1893–1949), vol. 1, 119; Angus W. McDonald Jr., *The Urban Origins of Rural Revolution: Elites and the Masses in Hunan Province, China, 1911–1927* (Berkeley: University of California Press, 1978), 58, 120, 205; Short, *Mao*, 144.

54. Schram, *Mao's Road to Power*, vol. 2, 194.

55. *Zhonggong "sanda" ziliao* (Materials from the Third Congress of the CCP), 103–4, 120.

56. Ibid., 121.

57. See Pang, *Mao Zedong nianpu, 1893–1949* (Chronological Biography of Mao Zedong, 1893–1949), vol. 1, 118.

58. See McDonald, *The Urban Origins of Rural Revolution*, 137.

59. Mao, *Oblaka v snegu* (Clouds in the Snow), 14–15.

I I . HOPES AND DISAPPOINTMENTS

1. Dalin, *Kitaiskie memuary, 1921–1927* (Chinese Memoirs, 1921–1927), 89.

2. V. V. Vishniakova-Akimova, *Two Years in Revolutionary China, 1925–1927*, trans. Steven I. Levine (Cambridge, MA: East Asian Research Center, Harvard University, 1971), 191.

3. Chang, *The Rise of the Chinese Communist Party*, vol. 1, 328.

4. Dalin, *Kitaiskie memuary, 1921–1927* (Chinese Memoirs, 1921–1927), 86.

5. Vishniakova-Akimova, *Two Years in Revolutionary China*, 177–78.

6. Quoted from Saich, *The Origins of the First United Front in China*, vol. 2, 580.

7. "Guomindang yi da dangwu baogao xuanzai" (Selected Reports on Party Affairs Delivered at the First Congress of the Guomindang), *Gemingshi ziliao* (Materials on revolutionary history), Shanghai, no. 2 (1986): 29–30.

8. For more details, see M. F. Yuriev, *Revoliutsiia 1925–1927 gg. v Kitae* (The Revolution of 1925–1927 in China) (Moscow: Nauka, 1968), 17–28.

9. Li Dazhao, *Li Dazhao wenji* (Works of Li Dazhao), vol. 2 (Beijing: Renmin chubanshe, 1984), 704.

10. See Cherepanov, *Zapiski voennogo sovetnika v Kitae* (Notes of a Military Adviser in China), 99.

11. See Zheng Canhui, "Zhongguo guomindang di yi ci quanguo daibiao dahui" (First All-China Congress of the Chinese Guomindang), *Gemingshi ziliao* (Materials on revolutionary history), Shanghai, no. 1 (1986): 119–20; Schram, *Mao's Road to Power*, vol. 2, 202–3.

12. Quoted from Cherepanov, *Notes of a Military Adviser in China*, 103.

13. See Sun Yat-sen, *Zhongshan quanji* (Complete Works of [Sun] Yat-sen), vol. 2 (Shanghai: Liangyou tushu yinshua gongsi, 1931), 1171–73.

14. See Pantsov and Levine, *Chinese Comintern Activists: An Analytic Biographic Dictionary* (manuscript), 266; Ch'ü Chiu-pai, "My Confessions," in Dun J. Li, ed., *The Road to Communism: China Since 1912* (New York: Van Nostrand Reinhold, 1969), 159–67. See also Qu Qiubai, *Superfluous Words*, trans. and commentary by Jamie Greenbaum (Canberra: Pandanus, 2006).

15. Titarenko, *VKP(b), Komintern i Kitai: Dokumenty* (The CPSU, the Comintern and China: Documents), vol. 1, 446.

16. See Saich, *The Origins of the First United Front in China*, vol. 2, 611.

17. Alexander V. Pantsov's private archives.

18. See Yang Kuisong, "Obshchaia kharakteristika otnoshenii mezhdu VKP(b) (KPSS), Kominternom i KPK do 1949 goda" (The General Nature of the Relation Between the

AUCP(b) [the CPSU], the Comintern, and the CCP to 1949), 104; see also Chang, *The Rise of the Chinese Communist Party,* vol. 1, 408. Alexander V. Pantsov's private archives.

19. Alexander V. Pantsov's private archives; Pan Zuofu (A. V. Pantsov), "Xin faxian de Li Dazhao, Chen Duxiu, Ren Bishi xinjian" (Newly Discovered Letters of Li Dazhao, Chen Duxiu, and Ren Bishi), *Bainian chao* (Century tides), no. 1 (2005): 31–34.

20. Titarenko, *VKP(b), Komintern i Kitai: Dokumenty* (The CPSU, the Comintern and China: Documents), vol. 1, 425.

21. See Hans Van den Ven, *From Friend to Comrade: The Founding of the Chinese Communist Party, 1920–1927* (Berkeley: University of California Press, 1991), 150.

22. See Wu, *Mao Zedong guanghui licheng dituji* (Atlas of Mao Zedong's Glorious Historical Path), 32; Pang, *Mao Zedong nianpu, 1893–1949* (Chronological Biography of Mao Zedong, 1893–1949), vol. 1, 123; Titarenko, *VKP(b), Komintern i Kitai: Dokumenty* (The CPSU, the Comintern and China: Documents), vol. 1, 483–84.

23. Dalin, *Kitaiskie memuary, 1921–1927* (Chinese Memoirs, 1921–1927), 165.

24. Ibid. For more details, see V. I. Glunin, *Kommunisticheskaia partiia Kitaia nakanune i vo vremia natsional'noi revoliutsii 1925–1927 gg.* (The Communist Party of China on the Eve of and During the 1925–1927 National Revolution), vol. 1 (Moscow: IDV AN SSSR, 1975), 148–54.

25. See *Gongchandang zai Guomindang neide gongzuo wenti yijue'an* (Declaration on the Question of the Work of the Communist Party inside the Guomindang), *Dangbao* (Party paper), no. 3 (1924): 1–3; *Zhongguo gongchandang di sici quanguo daibiaodahui yijue'an ji xuanyan* (Resolutions and Declarations of the Fourth All-China Congress of the CCP) (n.p., 1925), 25.

26. Titarenko, *VKP(b), Komintern i Kitai: Dokumenty* (The CPSU, the Comintern and China: Documents), vol. 1, 458–59.

27. Schram, *Mao's Road to Power,* vol. 2, 215–17.

28. See Titarenko, *VKP(b), Komintern i Kitai: Dokumenty* (The CPSU, the Comintern and China: Documents), vol. 1, 328.

29. See Sladkovskii, *Noveishaia istoriia Kitaia, 1919–1927* (Contemporary History of China, 1917–1927), 159.

30. See A. I. Kartunova, ed., *V. K. Bliukher v Kitae, 1924–1927 gg.: Novye dokumenty glavnogo voennogo sovetnika* (V. K. Bliukher in China, 1924–1927: New Documents on the Chief Military Adviser) (Moscow: Natalis, 2003), 15.

31. See Pang, *Mao Zedong nianpu, 1893–1949* (Chronological Biography of Mao Zedong, 1893–1949), vol. 1, 128.

32. Quoted from Short, *Mao,* 149.

33. See Pang, *Mao Zedong nianpu, 1893–1949* (Chronological Biography of Mao Zedong, 1893–1949), vol. 1, 127; Ma, *Hongse diyi jiazu* (The First Red Family), 29; Wu, *Mao Zedong guanghui licheng dituji* (Atlas of Mao Zedong's Glorious Historical Path), 32.

34. See Titarenko, *VKP(b), Komintern i Kitai: Dokumenty* (The CPSU, the Comintern and China: Documents), vol. 1, 483–84. See also Chang, *The Rise of the Chinese Communist Party,* vol. 1, 378.

35. See Mao Zemin, "Avtobiografiia" (Autobiography), 124; Ma, *Hongse diyi jiazu* (The First Red Family), 259; Li, *Moi otets Mao Tszedun* (My Father Mao Zedong), 109, 120; Pang, *Mao Zedong nianpu, 1893–1949* (Chronological Biography of Mao Zedong, 1893–1949), vol. 1, 131.

36. Titarenko, *VKP(b), Komintern i Kitai: Dokumenty* (The CPSU, the Comintern and China: Documents), vol. 1, 520.

37. See Pang, *Mao Zedong nianpu, 1893–1949* (Chronological Biography of Mao Zedong, 1893–1949), vol. 1, 131.

38. Quoted from Short, *Mao,* 152.

39. Titarenko, *VKP(b), Komintern i Kitai: Dokumenty* (The CPSU, the Comintern and China: Documents), vol. 1, 425.

40. See Peng, *Zapiski Peng Paia* (Notes of Peng Pai), 13.

41. See McDonald, *The Urban Origins of Rural Revolution*, 224.

42. Snow, *Red Star Over China*, 157.

43. Quoted from Ma, *Hongse diyi jiazu* (The First Red Family), 259.

44. See Pang, *Mao Zedong nianpu, 1893–1949* (Chronological Biography of Mao Zedong, 1893–1949), vol. 1, 133; McDonald, *The Urban Origins of Rural Revolution*, 225; Liu Renzhong, "Mao Zetan," in Hu Hua, ed., *Zhonggongdang shi renwu zhuan* (Biographies of Persons in the History of the CCP), vol. 3 (Xian: Shaanxi renmin chubanshe, 1981), 290.

12. PLAYING WITH CHIANG KAI-SHEK

1. See Yuriev, *Revoliutsiia 1925–1927 gg. v Kitae* (The Revolution of 1925–1927 in China), 159–67.

2. Ibid., 169, 174.

3. Ibid., 239–41; see Pantsov and Levine, *Chinese Comintern Activists: An Analytic Biographic Dictionary* (manuscript), 290.

4. See McDonald, *The Urban Origins of Rural Revolution*, 225.

5. See Pang, *Mao Zedong nianpu, 1893–1949* (Chronological Biography of Mao Zedong, 1893–1949), vol. 1, 132–34.

6. Ibid., 135–37.

7. See Li, *Moi otets Mao Tszedun* (My Father Mao Zedong), 120.

8. Zheng Chaolin, *An Oppositionist for Life: Memoirs of the Chinese Revolutionary Zheng Chaolin*, trans. Gregor Benton (Atlantic Highlands, NJ: Humanities Press, 1997), 142–43.

9. See ibid., 145–47.

10. See Pang, *Mao Zedong nianpu, 1893–1949* (Chronological Biography of Mao Zedong, 1893–1949), vol. 1, 147.

11. Schram, *Mao's Road to Power*, vol. 2, 237.

12. Snow, *Red Star Over China*, 157.

13. "Pis'mo G. N. Voitinskogo L. M. Karakhanu ot 22 aprelia 1922 g." (G. N. Voitinsky's Letter to L. M. Karakhan, April 22, 1925), RGASPI, collection of unsorted documents. The text of the letter was first published in 1994. See Titarenko, *VKP(b), Komintern i Kitai: Dokumenty* (The CPSU, the Comintern and China: Documents), vol. 1, 549–53.

14. See RGASPI, collection 495, inventory 163, file 177, sheets 1–4.

15. RGASPI, collection 558, inventory 1, file 2714, sheets 17–18. *Pravda* (Truth), May 22, 1925. Emphasis added.

16. Titarenko, *Kommunisticheskii Internatsional i kitaiskaia revoliutsiia* (The Communist International and the Chinese Revolution), 58, 61. Emphasis added.

17. For more details, see Pantsov, *The Bolsheviks and the Chinese Revolution*, 211–12.

18. See Chang, *The Rise of the Chinese Communist Party*, vol. 1, 484–85.

19. Schram, *Mao's Road to Power*, vol. 2, 227–29, 234–36, 320.

20. Quoted from ibid., 235.

21. Ibid., 265, 266.

22. See Ch'ü, *My Confessions*, 166.

23. Schram, *Mao's Road to Power*, vol. 2, 249, 260, 261–62.

24. See V-n [S. N. Belen'kii], "Rets. Mao Tsze-dun: Analiz klassov kitaiskogo obshchestva, 'Kitaiskii krest'ianin,' no. 2, 1 fevralia 1926 g." (Review of Mao Zedong's "Analysis of Classes in Chinese Society," *Kitaiskii krest'ianin* [Chinese Peasant], no. 2, February 1, 1926), *Kanton* (Canton), 8–9 (1926): 37–43.

25. See Pang, *Mao Zedong nianpu, 1893–1949* (Chronological Biography of Mao Zedong, 1893–1949), vol. 1, 150, 152; Schram, *Mao's Road to Power*, vol. 2, 310–19.

26. Vishniakova-Akimova, *Two Years in Revolutionary China*, 175.

27. See Chang, *The Rise of the Chinese Communist Party*, vol. 1, 479.

28. Vishniakova-Akimova, *Two Years in Revolutionary China*, 175.

29. See Pang, *Mao Zedong nianpu, 1893–1949* (Chronological Biography of Mao Zedong, 1893–1949), vol. 1, 152, 155, 156.

30. *Shestoi rasshirennyi plenum Ispolkoma Kominterna: Stenograficheskii otchet, 17 fevralia–15 marta 1926* (Sixth Enlarged Plenum of the ECCI: Stenographic Report, February 17–March 15, 1926) (Moscow and Leningrad: Gospolitizdat, 1927), 8.

31. RGASPI, collection 514, inventory 1, file 168, sheet 219.

32. See *Ob'edinennoe zasedanie Prezidiuma Ispolkoma Kominterna i Mezhdunarodnoi Kontrol'noi Komissii, 27 sentiabria 1927 g.: Stenograficheskii otchet* (Joint Session of the Presidium of the Executive Committee of the Comintern and the International Control Commission, September 27, 1927: Stenographic Report), RGASPI, collection 505, inventory 1, file 65, sheet 21. See also L. Trotsky, "Stalin i Kitaiskaia revoliutsiia: Fakty i dokumenty" (Stalin and the Chinese Revolution: Facts and Documents), *Biulleten' oppozitsii bol'shevikov-lenintsev* (Bulletin of the opposition of the Bolsheviks and Leninists), nos. 15–16 (1925): 8.

33. See RGASPI, collection 514, inventory 1, file 171, sheets 7–9. See also file 168, sheet 219; "Spravka Raita 'O vkhozhdenii Gomin'dana v Komintern' " (Information from Rait "On the entry of the Guomindang into the Comintern"), *Ob'edinennoe zasedanie Prezidiuma Ispolkoma Kominterna i Mezhdunarodnoi Kontrol'noi Komissii, 27 sentiabria 1927 g.: Stenograficheskii otchet* (Joint Session of the Presidium of the Executive Committee of the Comintern, and the International Control Commission, September 27, 1927: Stenographic Report), sheet 33.

34. RGASPI, collection 514, inventory 1, file 171, sheets 7–9. The text of the letter is also in M. L. Titarenko et al., eds., *VKP(b), Komintern i Kitai: Dokumenty* (The CPSU, the Comintern and China: Documents), vol. 2 (Moscow: AO "Buklet," 1996), 131–32.

35. Chiang, *Soviet Russia in China,* 24.

36. Chen Chieh-ju, *Chiang Kai-shek's Secret Past,* 135–36.

37. See Dan N. Jacobs, *Borodin: Stalin's Man in China* (Cambridge, MA: Harvard University Press, 1981), 278.

38. Vishniakova-Akimova, *Two Years in Revolutionary China,* 210.

39. See Yuriev, *Revoliutsiia 1925–1927 gg. v Kitae* (The Revolution of 1925–1927 in China), 312–13.

40. Quoted from Cherepanov, *Zapiski voennogo sovetnika v Kitae* (Notes of a Military Adviser in China), 376.

41. See RGASPI, collection of unsorted documents. The text adopted by the plenum may be found in *Zhongguo guomindang di yi di er ci quanguo daibiao dahui huiyi shiliao* (Materials on the History of the First and Second Congresses of the Guomindang), vol. 2 (Nanjing: Jiangsu guji chubanshe, 1986), 714–15.

42. Yuriev, *Revoliutsiia 1925–1927 gg. v Kitae* (The Revolution of 1925–1927 in China), 320–21; Pang, *Mao Zedong nianpu, 1893–1949* (Chronological Biography of Mao Zedong, 1893–1949), vol. 1, 165.

43. For more details, see Pantsov, *The Bolsheviks and the Chinese Revolution,* 92–93.

44. RGASPI, collection 17, inventory 162, file 3, sheet 55. The text of the Politburo resolution was first published in 1996. See Titarenko, *VKP(b), Komintern i Kitai: Dokumenty* (The CPSU, the Comintern and China: Documents), vol. 2, 202. Emphasis added.

45. Chang, *The Rise of the Chinese Communist Party,* vol. 1, 508.

46. RGASPI, collection 17, inventory 162, file 3, sheets 59, 74; Titarenko, *VKP(b), Komintern i Kitai: Dokumenty* (The CPSU, the Comintern and China: Documents), vol. 2, 205.

47. See Chang, *The Rise of the Chinese Communist Party,* vol. 1, 510.

48. See Yuriev, *Revoliutsiia 1925–1927 gg. v Kitae* (The Revolution of 1925–1927 in China), 320–21.

49. See ibid., 250; Pang, *Mao Zedong nianpu, 1893–1949* (Chronological Biography of Mao Zedong, 1893–1949), vol. 1, 158, 161, 162–63; Li, *The Early Revolutionary Activities of Comrade Mao Tse-tung,* 283–84.

50. Schram, *Mao's Road to Power,* vol. 2, 319, 343, 358.

51. Quoted from A. S. Titov, *Materialy k politicheskoi biografii Mao Tsze-duna* (Materials for a Political Biography of Mao Zedong), vol. 1 (Moscow: IDV AN SSSR, 1969), 123.

52. Schram, *Mao's Road to Power*, vol. 2, 308–9.

53. Ibid., 321, 325.

54. See Glunin, *Kommunisticheskaia partiia Kitaia nakanune i vo vremia natsional'noi revoliutsii 1925–1927 gg. v Kitae* (The Communist Party of China Before and During the 1925–1927 National Revolution), vol. 1, 280–81; Tony Saich, ed., *The Rise to Power of the Chinese Communist Party: Documents and Analysis* (Armonk, NY: M. E. Sharpe, 1996), 152–58.

55. Wang Jianying, ed., *Zhongguo gongchandang zuzhi shi ziliao huibian—lingdao jigou yange he chengyuan minglu* (Collection of Documents on the History of the CCP Organizations—The Evolution of Leading Organs and Their Personal Composition) (Beijing: Hongqi chubanshe, 1983), 32.

56. See Pang, *Mao Zedong nianpu, 1893–1949* (Chronological Biography of Mao Zedong, 1893–1949), vol. 1, 156, 157.

57. Schram, *Mao's Road to Power*, vol. 2, 370.

58. See Yuriev, *Revoliutsiia 1925–1927 gg. v Kitae* (The Revolution of 1925–1927 in China), 323–38; Chang, *The Rise of the Chinese Communist Party*, vol. 1, 520–36; McDonald, *The Urban Origins of Rural Revolution*, 229–36.

59. See Pang, *Mao Zedong nianpu, 1893–1949* (Chronological Biography of Mao Zedong, 1893–1949), vol. 1, 165–69.

60. Mao Zedong, *Mao Zedong wenji* (Works of Mao Zedong), vol. 1 (Beijing: Renmin chubanshe, 1993), 37, 39.

13. THE COLLAPSE OF THE UNITED FRONT

1. See Pang, *Mao Zedong nianpu, 1893–1949* (Chronological Biography of Mao Zedong, 1893–1949), vol. 1, 169–72; Yuriev, *Revoliutsiia 1925–1927 gg. v Kitae* (The Revolution of 1925–1927 in China), 416; Vishniakova-Akimova, *Two Years in Revolutionary China*, 261–325; Chang, *The Rise of the Chinese Communist Party*, vol. 1, 532–72.

2. See Pang, *Mao Zedong nianpu, 1893–1949* (Chronological Biography of Mao Zedong, 1893–1949), vol. 1, 172–73; Wang, *Zhongguo gongchandang zuzhi shi ziliao huibian* (Collection of Documents on the History of the CCP Organizations), 32.

3. Pang, *Mao Zedong nianpu, 1893–1949* (Chronological Biography of Mao Zedong, 1893–1949), vol. 1, 169; Short, *Mao*, 168.

4. See Glunin, *Kommunistechkaia partiia Kitaia nakanune i vo vremia natsional'noi revoliutsii 1925–1927 gg.* (The Communist Party of China Before and During the 1925–1927 National Revolution), vol. 2, 192.

5. Chang, *The Rise of the Chinese Communist Party*, vol. 1, 529.

6. *Zhongguo gongchandang di san ci zhongyang kuoda zhixing weiyuanhui yijue'an* (Resolutions of the Third Enlarged Plenum of the CEC CCP) (n.p., 1926), 66.

7. Chang, *The Rise of the Chinese Communist Party*, vol. 1, 529.

8. See *Mao Zedong shenghuo dang'an* (Archives of Mao Zedong's Life), vol. 1, 93.

9. See RGASPI, collection 495, inventory 165, file 71, sheets 27–31.

10. See Glunin, *Kommunisticheskaia partiia Kitaia nakanune i vo vremia natsional'noi revoliutsii 1925–1927 gg.* (The Communist Party of China Before and During the 1925–1927 National Revolution), vol. 2, 198–201.

11. Schram, *Mao's Road to Power*, vol. 2, 411–13.

12. Ibid., 414–19.

13. Chang, *The Rise of the Chinese Communist Party*, vol. 1, 534–35, 542, 547.

14. Quoted from ibid., 557.

15. Ibid., 572.

16. Ibid., 562.

17. Chen Duxiu, "Political Report," in Saich, *The Rise to Power of the Chinese Communist Party*, 219–23; Glunin, *Kommunisticheskaia partiia Kitaia nakanune i vo vremia*

natsional'noi revoliutsii 1925–1927 gg. (The Communist Party of China Before and During the 1925–1927 National Revolution), vol. 2, 153–57.

18. See Pang, *Mao Zedong nianpu, 1893–1949* (Chronological biography of Mao Zedong, 1893–1949), vol. 1, 174.

19. Quoted from Glunin, *Kommunisticheskaia partiia Kitaia nakanune i vo vremia natsional'noi revoliutsii 1925–1927 gg.* (The Communist Party of China Before and During the 1925–1927 National Revolution), vol. 2, 160.

20. Quoted from Chang, *The Rise of the Chinese Communist Party,* vol. 1, 573.

21. See Cherepanov, *Zapiski voennogo sovetnika v Kitae* (Notes of a Military Adviser in China), 517; Jonathan Fenby, *Chiang Kai-shek: China's Generalissimo and the Nation He Lost* (New York: Carroll & Graf, 2004), 127.

22. Pang, *Mao Zedong nianpu, 1893–1949* (Chronological Biography of Mao Zedong, 1893–1949), vol. 1, 173.

23. Schram, *Mao's Road to Power,* vol. 2, 421, 422; "Soveshchanie Dal'biuro i Ts[i]k KPK, 18 ianvaria 1927 goda" (Conference of the Far Eastern Bureau and the CEC of the CCP, January 18, 1927), RGASPI, collection 495, inventory 154, file 294, sheet 3; A. V. Bakulin, *Zapiski ob wuhan'skom periode kitaiskoi revoliutsii (iz istorii kitaiskoi revoliutsii 1925–1927 gg.)* (Notes on the Wuhan Period of the Chinese Revolution [From the History of the Chinese Revolution of 1925–1927]) (Moscow and Leningrad: Giz, 1930), 51.

24. "Soveshchanie Dal'biuro i Ts[i]k KPK, 18 ianvaria 1927" (Conference of the Far Eastern Bureau and the CEC of the CCP, January 18, 1927), 3.

25. See A. A. Pisarev, *Guomindang i agrarno-krest'ianskii vopros v Kitae v 20-30-e gody XX v.* (The Guomindang and the Agrarian-Peasant Question in China in the 1920s and 1930s) (Moscow: Nauka, 1986), 17–53; L. P. Deliusin and A. S. Kostiaeva, *Revoliutsiia 1925–1927 gg. v Kitae: Problemy i otsenki* (The Revolution of 1925–1927 in China: Problems and Assessment) (Moscow: Nauka, 1985), 132–38; McDonald, *The Urban Origins of Rural Revolution,* 217–315; Roy Hofheinz Jr., *The Broken Wave: The Chinese Communist Peasant Movement* (Cambridge, MA: Harvard University Press, 1977), 3–53; Fernando Galbiati, *P'eng P'ai and the Hai-lu-feng Soviet* (Stanford, CA: Stanford University Press, 1985), 16–20, 41–42; Lucien Bianco, *Peasants without the Party: Grass-roots Movements in Twentieth-Century China* (Armonk, NY: M. E. Sharpe, 2001), 175–214; Mary S. Erbaugh, "The Secret History of the Hakkas: The Chinese Revolution as a Hakka Enterprise," *China Quarterly,* no. 132 (1992): 937–68.

26. See A. S. Kostiaeva, *Krest'ianskie soiuzy v Kitae 20-e gody XX veka* (Peasant Unions in China in the 1920s) (Moscow: Nauka, 1978), 57; Deliusin and Kostiaeva, *Revoliutsiia 1925–1927 gg. v Kitae: Problemy i otsenki* (The Revolution of 1925–1927 in China: Problems and Assessment), 134.

27. See Glunin, *Kommunisticheskaia partiia Kitaia nakanune i vo vremia natsional'noi revoliutsii 1925–1927 gg.* (The Communist Party of China Before and During the 1925–1927 National Revolution), vol. 2, 186; McDonald, *The Urban Origins of Rural Revolution,* 303.

28. See Kostiaeva, *Krest'ianskie soiuzy v Kitae 20-e gody XX veka* (Peasant Unions in China in the 1920s), 57; McDonald, *The Urban Origins of Rural Revolution,* 272–73.

29. See Mao Zedong, *Selected Works,* vol. 1 (Beijing: Foreign Languages Press, 1969), 24; McDonald, *The Urban Origins of Rural Revolution,* 271; Li, *The Early Revolutionary Activities of Comrade Mao Tse-tung,* 295.

30. Quoted from McDonald, *The Urban Origins of Rural Revolution,* 308.

31. Mao Zedong, *Mao Zedong nongcun diaocha wenji* (Works of Mao Zedong on Rural Investigation) (Beijing: Renmin chubanshe, 1982), 1.

32. Schram, *Mao's Road to Power,* vol. 2, 429–64.

33. Ibid., 426.

34. See Wu, *Mao Zedong guanghui licheng dituji* (Atlas of Mao Zedong's Glorious Historical Path), 35; Pang, *Mao Zedong nianpu, 1893–1949* (Chronological Biography of Mao Zedong, 1893–1949), vol. 1, 181.

35. Titarenko, *Kommunisticheskii Internatsional i kitaiskaia revoliutsiia* (The Communist International and the Chinese Revolution), 94, 96, 97–99.

36. RGASPI, collection 17, inventory 162, file 4, sheet 34. See also Titarenko, *VKP(b), Komintern i Kitai: Dokumenty* (The CPSU, the Comintern and China: Documents), vol. 2, 571.

37. RGASPI, collection 17, inventory 162, file 4, sheet 64.

38. Ibid., 71–72; see Titarenko, *VKP(b), Komintern i Kitai: Dokumenty* (The CPSU, the Comintern and China: Documents), vol. 2, 632–33.

39. Quoted from McDonald, *The Urban Origins of Rural Revolution*, 310.

40. Schram, *Mao's Road to Power*, vol. 2, 467–75.

41. See Chang, *The Rise of the Chinese Communist Party*, vol. 1, 581–82.

42. See Wu, *Mao Zedong guanghui licheng dituji* (Atlas of Mao Zedong's Glorious Historical Path), 35.

43. Ibid.; Pang, *Mao Zedong nianpu, 1893–1949* (Chronological Biography of Mao Zedong, 1893–1949), vol. 1, 190; Schram, *Mao's Road to Power*, vol. 2, 486.

44. Snow, *Red Star Over China*, 158.

45. See "Zapis' besedy t. Grigoriia s Chan Kai-shi ot 22 fevralia 1927 g." (Record of Conversation between Comrade Grigorii and Chiang Kai-shek, February 22, 1927), RGASPI, collection 514, inventory 1, file 240, sheets 12–13; see also Titarenko, *VKP(b), Komintern i Kitai: Dokumenty* (The CPSU, the Comintern and China: Documents), vol. 2, 630–31.

46. RGASPI, collection 17, inventory 162, file 4, sheets 90–93; see also Titarenko, *VKP(b), Komintern i Kitai: Dokumenty* (The CPSU, the Comintern and China: Documents), vol. 2, 658–59.

47. Quoted from Pang, *Mao Zedong nianpu, 1893–1949* (Chronological Biography of Mao Zedong, 1893–1949), vol. 1, 193.

48. Ibid., 193–97.

49. Quoted from Jiang Yongjing, *Baoluoting yu Wuhan zhengquan* (Borodin and the Wuhan Government) (Taibei: Zhongguo xueshu zhuzuo jiangzhu weiyuanhui, 1963), 278, 280.

50. Quoted from Bakulin, *Zapiski ob ukhanskom periode kitaiskoi revoliutsii* (Notes on the Wuhan Period of the Chinese Revolution), 201.

51. See Robert C. North and Xenia Eudin, *M. N. Roy's Mission to China: The Communist-Kuomintang Split of 1927* (Berkeley: University of California Press, 1963), 59.

52. Chang, *The Rise of the Chinese Communist Party*, vol. 1, 619.

53. Ibid.

54. Snow, *Red Star Over China*, 158–59.

55. See *Lichnoe delo Zhao Xiangui* (Personal File of Zhao Xiangui), RGASPI, collection 495, inventory 225, file 2682.

56. See Mao, "Avtobiografiia" (Autobiography), 125; Ma, *Hongse diyi jiazu* (The First Red Family), 266–68, 315–17; Li, *Moi otets Mao Tszedun* (My Father Mao Zedong), 109–10, 120; "Mao Zemin," in Hu Hua, ed., *Zhonggongdang shi renwu zhuan* (Biographies of Persons in the History of the CCP), vol. 9 (Xi'an: Shaanxi renmin chubanshe, 1983), 50–51; Liu, "Mao Zetan," 290–91.

57. See Han, *Li Dazhao shengping jinian* (Biographical Chronicle of Li Dazhao), 203–6.

58. See Chang, *The Rise of the Chinese Communist Party*, vol. 1, 630–31.

59. RGASPI, collection 17, inventory 162, file 5, sheets 8–9, 30.

60. Ibid., 30. This telegram was first published in 1996 in Titarenko, *VKP(b), Komintern i Kitai: Dokumenty* (The CPSU, the Comintern and China: Documents), vol. 2, 763–64.

61. Chang, *The Rise of the Chinese Communist Party*, vol. 1, 637.

62. Quoted from Cai, *Istoriia opportunizma v Kommunistecheskoi partii Kitaia* (The History of Opportunism in the Communist Party of China), 63.

63. Liu, "Mao Zetan," 291; Li, *Moi otets Mao Tszedun* (My Father Mao Zedong), 120–21.

64. Chang, *The Rise of the Chinese Communist Party*, vol. 1, 640.

65. Snow, *Red Star Over China*, 160. Chang and Halliday assert that in the summer of 1927

Mao "pondered his alternatives" whether to take the side of the Guomindang or remain in the CCP. Chang and Halliday, *Mao*, 46–47. But Mao remained 100 percent communist and tried his utmost to radicalize the situation.
66. Mao, *Poems of Mao Tse-tung*, 35.

14. THE PATH TO THE SOVIETS

1. Chang, *The Rise of the Chinese Communist Party*, vol. 1, 486, 652.
2. See McDonald, *The Urban Origins of Rural Revolution*, 316.
3. Schram, *Mao's Road to Power*, vol. 2, 515–16.
4. See *Mao Zedong: Biography—Assessment—Reminiscences* (Beijing: Foreign Languages Press, 1986), 236–37.
5. See Li, *The Early Revolutionary Activities of Comrade Mao Tse-tung*, 315.
6. Stuart R. Schram, ed. *Mao's Road to Power: Revolutionary Writings 1912-1949*, vol. 3 (Armonk, NY: M. E. Sharpe, 1995), 31; Pang, *Mao Zedong nianpu, 1893-1949* (Chronological Biography of Mao Zedong, 1893–1949), vol. 1, 208.
7. Schram, *Mao's Road to Power*, vol. 3, 11; Pang, *Mao Zedong nianpu, 1893-1949* (Chronological Biography of Mao Zedong, 1893–1949), vol. 1, 205.
8. Chang, *The Rise of the Chinese Communist Party*, vol. 1, 656.
9. Ibid., 656–77; Pang, *Mao Zedong nianpu, 1893-1949* (Chronological Biography of Mao Zedong, 1893–1949), vol. 1, 206; A. M. Grigoriev, *Kommunisticheskaia partiia Kitaia v nachal'nyi period sovetskogo dvizheniia (iul' 1927 g.–sentyabr' 1931g.)* (The Communist Party of China in the Initial Soviet Movement Period [July 1927–September 1931]) (Moscow: IDV AN SSSR, 1976), 14–16.
10. M. L. Titarenko et al., eds., *VKP(b), Komintern i Kitai: Dokumenty* (The CPSU, the Comintern and China: Documents), vol. 3 (Moscow: AO "Buklet," 1999), 73, 75.
11. Lars T. Lih et al., eds., *Stalin's Letters to Molotov 1925-1936*, trans. Catherine A. Fitzpatrick (New Haven, CT: Yale University Press, 1995), 141, 142.
12. See Titarenko, *VKP(b), Komintern i Kitai: Dokumenty* (The CPSU, the Comintern and China: Documents), vol. 2, 503, 505.
13. Ibid., vol. 3, 72–74.
14. See M. Buber-Neiman, *Mirovaia revoliutsiia i stalinskii rezhim: Zapiski ochevidtsa o deiatel'nosti Kominterna v 1920-1930-kh godakh* (The World Revolution and the Stalinist Regime: Notes of an Eyewitness About Comintern Activity in the 1920s and 1930s), trans. A. Yu. Vatlin (Moscow: AIRO-XX, 1995), 39.
15. Chang, *The Rise of the Chinese Communist Party*, vol. 1, 669–70.
16. Titarenko, *VKP(b), Komintern i Kitai: Dokumenty* (The CPSU, the Comintern and China: Documents), vol. 3, 72.
17. Pang, *Mao Zedong nianpu, 1893-1949* (Chronological Biography of Mao Zedong, 1893–1949), vol. 1, 206.
18. See Chang, *The Rise of the Chinese Communist Party*, vol. 2, 13; Pang, *Mao Zedong nianpu, 1893-1949* (Chronological Biography of Mao Zedong, 1893–1949), vol. 1, 208; Chen Geng, "Ot Nanchana do Svatou" (From Nanchang to Swatow), in *Vsiudu krasnye znamena: Vospominaniia i ocherki o vtoroi grazhdanskoi revoliutsionnoi voine* (Red Banners Everywhere: Reminiscences and Sketches of the Second Revolutionary Civil War) (Moscow: Voenizdat, 1957), 13–20.
19. Chang, *The Rise of the Chinese Communist Party*, vol. 1, 489.
20. Tang Baolin and Li Maosheng, *Chen Duxiu nianpu* (Chronological Biography of Chen Duxiu) (Shanghai: Shanghai renmin chubanshe, 1988), 335.
21. See Zheng Chaolin, *Zheng Chaolin huiyilu* (Memoirs of Zheng Chaolin) ([Hong Kong], 1982), 149–52; *Baqi huiyi* (The August 7 Conference) (Beijing: Zhonggongdang shi ziliao chubanshe, 1986), 3–4, 161–72, 175–80, 195–201; Li Weihan, *Huiyi yu yanjiu* (Reminiscences and Studies), vol. 1 (Beijing: Zhonggongdang shi ziliao chubanshe, 1986), 156–69; Marcia R. Ristaino, *China's Art of Revolution: The Mobilization of Discontent, 1927-1928*

(Durham, NC: Duke University Press, 1987), 39–55; Alexander V. Pantsov's interview with staff member of RGASPI, Iu. T. Tutotchkin in Moscow, October 11, 2005.

22. In 1960, Mao will say, "People later used to say that we [Deng and I] met in Wuhan, but I do not remember at all. We might have met, but we certainly did not talk." Quoted from Leng Buji, *Deng Xiaoping zai Gannan* (Deng Xiaoping in Southern Jiangxi) (Beijing: Zhongyang wenxian chubanshe, 1995), 85.

23. *Baqi huiyi* (The August 7 Conference), 57, 58; Schram, *Mao's Road to Power,* vol. 3, 30–31.

24. *Baqi huiyi* (The August 7 Conference), 73; Schram, *Mao's Road to Power,* vol. 3, 32.

25. *Baqi huiyi* (The August 7 Conference), 74.

26. Cai, *Istoriia opportunizma v Kommunistecheskoi partii Kitaia* (The History of Opportunism in the Communist Party of China), 68; *Baqi huiyi* (The August 7 Conference), 44, 200.

27. Alexander V. Pantsov's interview with the former Chinese communist Wang Fanxi in Leeds, England, July 19, 1992.

28. Quoted from Pang, *Mao Zedong nianpu, 1893–1949* (Chronological Biography of Mao Zedong, 1893–1949), vol. 1, 209.

29. Chang, *The Rise of the Chinese Communist Party,* vol. 1, 659; vol. 2, 13.

30. See Titarenko, *VKP(b), Komintern i Kitai: Dokumenty* (The CPSU, the Comintern and China: Documents), vol. 3, 79.

31. Hsü K'e-hsiang, "The Ma-Jih Incident," in Li, *The Road to Communism,* 91.

32. *Baqi huiyi* (The August 7 Conference), 112.

33. Alexander V. Pantsov's interview with Iu. T. Tutochkin, staff member of the RGASPI, Moscow, December 19, 2005.

34. See Peng Gongda, "Report on the Progress of the Autumn Harvest Uprising in Hunan," in Saich, *The Rise to Power of the Chinese Communist Party,* 322; Schram, *Mao's Road to Power,* vol. 3, 33.

35. Pang, *Mao Zedong nianpu, 1893–1949* (Chronological Biography of Mao Zedong, 1893–1949), vol. 1, 209–10.

36. Schram, *Mao's Road to Power,* vol. 3, 35. See also Peng, "Report on the Progress of the Autumn Harvest Uprising in Hunan," 323.

37. Schram, *Mao's Road to Power,* vol. 3, 40. See also Peng, "Report on the Progress of the Autumn Harvest Uprising in Hunan," 324, and Snow, *Red Star Over China,* 163.

38. See Schram, *Mao's Road to Power,* vol. 3, 39, and Peng, "Report on the Progress of the Autumn Harvest Uprising in Hunan," 326.

39. Schram, *Mao's Road to Power,* vol. 3, 36. See also Peng, "Report on the Progress of the Autumn Harvest Uprising in Hunan," 324.

40. Quoted from Peng, "Report on the Progress of the Autumn Harvest Uprising in Hunan," 323.

41. Ibid., 325, 326. See also Schram, *Mao's Road to Power,* vol. 3, 39–40.

42. Schram, *Mao's Road to Power,* vol. 3, 37–42; Pang, *Mao Zedong nianpu, 1893–1949* (Chronological Biography of Mao Zedong, 1893–1949), vol. 1, 210–14.

43. Many years later Mao would tell Edgar Snow, "[T]he general programme of the Hunan Committee and of our army was opposed by the Central Committee of the Party, which seemed, however, to have adopted a policy of wait-and-see rather than of active opposition." Snow, *Red Star Over China,* 163.

44. See Peng, "Report on the Progress of the Autumn Harvest Uprising in Hunan," 328, 504.

45. Mao, *Oblaka v snegu* (Clouds in the Snow), 103.

46. See Li, *Moi otets Mao Tszedun* (My Father Mao Zedong), 110–11, 138–39; Ma, *Hongse diyi jiazu* (The First Red Family), 32–36; *Lichnoe delo Yun Shu* (Personal File of Yong Shu), RGASPI, collection 495, inventory 225, file 2799, sheet 4; *Mao Zedong shenghuo dang'an* (Archives of Mao Zedong's Life), vol. 1, 93–98.

15. RED BANNER OVER THE JINGGANG MOUNTAINS

1. Mao, *Oblaka v snegu* (Clouds in the Snow), 23.

2. Snow, *Red Star Over China,* 164.

3. Peng, "Report on the Progress of the Autumn Harvest Uprising in Hunan," 328–29.

4. See Chang, *The Rise of the Chinese Communist Party,* vol. 2, 3–35; Grigoriev, *Kommunisticheskaia partiia Kitaia v nachal'nyi period sovetskogo dvizheniia* (The Communist Party of China in the Initial Soviet Movement Period), 39.

5. Snow, *Red Star Over China,* 164.

6. Ibid., 167.

7. Liu Xing, "Do i posle 'vosstaniia osennego urozhaia'" (Before and After the "Autumn Harvest Uprising"), in *Vsiudu krasnye znamena* (Red Banners Everywhere), 26.

8. See Pang, *Mao Zedong nianpu, 1893–1949* (Chronological Biography of Mao Zedong, 1893–1949), vol. 1, 216–20; Wu, *Mao Zedong guanghui licheng dituji* (Atlas of Mao Zedong's Glorious Historical Path), 39–40; Li, *Moi otets Mao Tszedun* (My Father Mao Zedong), 155, 162.

9. Schram, *Mao's Road to Power,* vol. 3, 109.

10. See Chen Yi, "Chen Yi tongzhi guanyu Zhu Mao jun de lishi ji qi zhuangkuang de baogao" (Comrade Chen Yi's Report on the History of the Zhu-Mao Army and Its Present Situation), in *Jinggangshan geming genjudi shiliao xuanbian* (Collection of Selected Materials on the Revolutionary Base Area in the Jinggang Mountains) (Nanchang: Jiangxi renmin chubanshe, 1986), 176; [Chen Yi], *Istoriia boevykh deistvii 4-go korpusa* (History of the Military Engagements of the Fourth Corps), in Pavel Mif, ed., *Sovety v Kitae: Sbornik materialov i dokumentov* (Soviets in China: Collection of Materials and Documents) (Moscow: Partizdat, 1934), 187.

11. Wu, *Mao Zedong guanghui licheng dituji* (Atlas of Mao Zedong's Glorious Historical Path), 40.

12. Quoted from Pang, *Mao Zedong nianpu, 1893–1949* (Chronological Biography of Mao Zedong, 1893–1949), vol. 1, 236.

13. See Li, *Moi otets Mao Tszedun* (My Father Mao Zedong), 147–61; Short, *Mao,* 225–27; Ma, *Hongse diyi jiazu* (The First Red Family), 39–45; Pang, *Mao Zedong nianpu, 1893–1949* (Chronological Biography of Mao Zedong, 1893–1949), vol. 1, 223–26.

14. Zheng, *An Oppositionist for Life,* 137.

15. *Ren Bishi nianpu, 1904–1950* (Chronological Biography of Ren Bishi, 1904–1950) (Beijing: Zhongyang wenxian chubanshe, 2004), 78; see Ristaino, *China's Art of Revolution,* 71–72.

16. *Gongfei huoguo shiliao huibian* (Collection of Materials on the History of the Communist Bandits Who Brought Misfortune to the Country), vol. 1 (Taipei: Zhonghua minguo kaiguo wushinian wenxian biancuan weiyuanhui, 1964), 568–70; *Zhonggong zhongyang wenjian xuanji* (Collection of CCP CC Selected Documents), vol. 3 (Beijing: Zhonggong zhongyang dangxiao chubanshe, 1989), 481, 483–84.

17. See Pang, *Mao Zedong nianpu, 1893–1949* (Chronological Biography of Mao Zedong, 1893–1949), vol. 1, 226; Schram, *Mao's Road to Power,* vol. 3, 51; John E. Rue, *Mao Tse-tung in Opposition, 1927–1935* (Stanford, CA: Stanford University Press, 1966), 84.

18. *Lichnoe delo Mao Tszeduna* (Personal File of Mao Zedong), RGASPI, collection 495, inventory 225, file 71, vol. 2, sheet 256.

19. Schram, *Mao's Road to Power,* vol. 3, 94.

20. See Titarenko, *VKP(b), Komintern i Kitai: Dokumenty* (The CPSU, the Comintern and China: Documents), vol. 3, 333.

21. See Schram, *Mao's Road to Power,* vol. 3, 84; Liao Gailong et al., eds., *Zhongguo gongchandang lishi da cidian. Zengdingben. Zonglu. Renwu* (Great Dictionary of the History of the Chinese Communist Party. Expanded edition. General section. Personnel) (Beijing: Zhonggong zhongyang dangxiao chubanshe, 2001), 277.

22. Quoted from Titov, *Materialy k politicheskoi biografii Mao Tsze-duna* (Materials for a Political Biography of Mao Zedong), vol. 1, 166.

23. See Schram, *Mao's Road to Power*, vol. 3, 84; Pang, *Mao Zedong nianpu, 1893–1949* (Chronological Biography of Mao Zedong, 1893–1949), vol. 1, 227–28; 236–40.

24. See Lois Wheeler Snow, *Edgar Snow's China: A Personal Account of the Chinese Revolution Compiled from the Writings of Edgar Snow* (New York: Random House, 1981), 72.

25. Agnes Smedley, *The Great Road: The Life and Times of Chu Teh* (New York: Monthly Review Press, 1956), 10.

26. Helen Foster Snow (Nym Wales), *Inside Red China* (New York: Da Capo Press, 1977), 113, 116.

27. Snow, *Edgar Snow's China*, 73.

28. See Snow (Wales), *Inside Red China*, 110–12.

29. Snow, *Red Star Over China*, 166.

30. Schram, *Mao's Road to Power*, vol. 3, 57.

31. Ibid., 51.

32. Ibid., 128–30.

33. Ibid., 104, 111.

34. Ibid., 104, 96.

35. Ibid., 92.

36. Ibid., 74.

37. Ibid., 94.

38. Mao, *Poems of Mao Tse-tung*, 38.

39. See Li, *Moi otets Mao Tszedun* (My Father Mao Zedong), 162.

40. Schram, *Mao's Road to Power*, vol. 3, 57.

41. Peng Dehuai, *Memoirs of a Chinese Marshal: The Autobiographical Notes of Peng Dehuai (1898–1974)*, trans. Zheng Longpu (Beijing: Foreign Languages Press, 1984), 231.

42. Ibid.; see also Schram, *Mao's Road to Power*, vol. 3, 149.

43. Schram, *Mao's Road to Power*, vol. 3, 149–51; Pang, *Mao Zedong nianpu, 1893–1949* (Chronological Biography of Mao Zedong, 1893–1949), vol. 1, 261–62; Ma, *Hongse diyi jiazu* (The First Red Family), 48.

44. Quoted from Schram, *Mao's Road to Power*, vol. 3, 151.

45. Quoted from Peng, *Memoirs of a Chinese Marshal*, 228–29.

46. Chang and Halliday, *Mao*, 61.

16. A SINGLE SPARK CAN START A PRAIRIE FIRE

1. See "Heben Dazuo wei cehua 'Huanggutun shijian' zhi Jigu Lianjie deng han liangjian (1928 nian 4 yue)" (Two Messages from Komoto Daisaku to Isogai Rensuke Planning to Create the Huanggutun Incident [April 1928])," *Minguo dang'an* (Republican Archives), no. 3 (1998): 3–5; Heben Dazuo (Komoto Daisaku) et al., *Wo shasila Zhang Zuolin* (I Killed Zhang Zuolin) (Changchun: Jilin wenshi chubanshe, 1986). A few years ago some Russian authors claimed that Zhang Zuolin indeed was killed by Stalin's secret agents, but their arguments seem unconvincing. See Dmitrii Prokhorov, " 'Liternoe delo' marshala Zhang Zuolinya" (The "Lettered File" of Marshal Zhang Zuolin), *Nezavisimoe voennoe obozrenie* (Independent military review), no. 21 (2003): 5.

2. See Grigoriev, *Kommunisticheskaia partiia Kitaia v nachal'nyi period sovetskogo dvizheniia* (The Communist Party of China in the Initial Soviet Movement Period), 107, 121.

3. *Stenograficheskii otchet VI s"ezda Kommunisticheskoi partii Kitaia* (Stenographic Record of the Sixth Congress of the Communist Party of China), book 2 (Moscow: Institute of Chinese Studies Press, 1930), 80–81.

4. Ibid., book 1, 98.

5. Ibid., 13.

6. Schram, *Mao's Road to Power*, vol. 3, 114, 151.

7. Ibid., 106, 115.

8. *Stenograficheskii otchet VI s'ezda Kommunisticheskoi partii Kitaia* (Stenographic Record of the Sixth Congress of the Communist Party of China), book 1, 5–6, 8–10.

9. Peng, *Memoirs of a Chinese Marshal,* 274–76; *Jinggangshan douzheng dashi jieshao* (Survey of Main Events in the Struggle in the Jinggang Mountains) (Beijing: Jiefangjun chubanshe, 1985), 187–91.

10. See Léonard Lévesque, *Hakka Beliefs and Customs,* trans. J. Maynard Murphy (Taichung: Kuang Chi Press, 1969), 70.

11. Snow, *Red Star Over China,* 166.

12. See, for example, Liao, *Zhongguo gongchandang lishi da cidian* (Great Dictionary of the History of the Chinese Communist Party), 118, 405.

13. Schram, *Mao's Road to Power,* vol. 3, 351.

14. *Stenograficheskii otchet VI s'ezda Kommunisticheskoi partii Kitaia* (Stenographic Record of the Sixth Congress of the Communist Party of China), book 5, 12, 13.

15. Ibid., book 2, 151; book 4, 183; Zhou Enlai, *Selected Works of Zhou Enlai,* vol. 1 (Beijing: Foreign Languages Press, 1981), 195–96.

16. Schram, *Mao's Road to Power,* vol. 3, 139.

17. Ibid., 173–74.

18. See Ma, *Hongse diyi jiazu* (The First Red Family), 54; Short, *Mao,* 254; *Jiefang ribao* (Liberation daily), March 7, 2005; Wen Fu and Zhang Haishen, *Mao Zedong yu He Zizhen* (Mao Zedong and He Zizhen) (Beijing: Tuanjie chubanshe, 2004).

19. See Schram, *Mao's Road to Power,* vol. 3, 150.

20. See Saich, *The Rise to Power of the Chinese Communist Party,* 471–72.

21. Schram, *Mao's Road to Power,* vol. 3, 155–56.

22. Pavel Mif, ed., *Strategiia i taktika Kominterna v natsional'no-kolonial'noi revoliutsii na primere Kitaia* (The Comintern's Strategy and Tactics in National-Colonial Revolution, for Example, China) (Moscow: IWEIP Press, 1934), 236–44.

23. Schram, *Mao's Road to Power,* vol. 3, 256, 257, 504.

24. Quoted from Mao, *Mao Zedong wenji* (Works of Mao Zedong), vol. 1, 206.

25. See Pang, *Mao Zedong nianpu, 1893–1949* (Chronological Biography of Mao Zedong, 1893–1949), vol. 1, 278.

26. *Lichnoe delo Liu Tsilana (Anguna)* (Personal File of Liu Jilang [Angong]), RGASPI, collection 495, inventory 225, file 1656; Liao, *Mao Zedong baike quanshu* (Encyclopedia of Mao Zedong), vol. 3 (Beijing: Guangming ribao chubanshe, 2003), 1401; Pang, *Mao Zedong nianpu, 1893–1949* (Chronological Biography of Mao Zedong, 1893–1949), vol. 1, 274–77.

27. Schram, *Mao's Road to Power,* vol. 3, 419, 420, 421.

28. Ibid., 188.

29. See Chen, "Chen Yi tongzhi guanyu Zhu Mao jun de lishi ji qi zhuangkuang de baogao" (Comrade Chen Yi's Report on the History of the Zhu-Mao Army and Its Present Situation), 176–93.

30. A. Ivin, *Sovietskii Kitai* (Soviet China) (Moscow: "Molodaia gvardiia," 1931), 43–44.

31. Pang, *Mao Zedong nianpu, 1893–1949* (Chronological Biography of Mao Zedong, 1893–1949), vol. 1, 285.

32. Li, *Moi otets Mao Tszedun* (My Father Mao Zedong), 169.

33. Mao Zedong, "Da Li Shuyi" (A Reply to Li Shuyi), in Mao, *Mao Zedong shici duilian jizhu* (Collection of Mao Zedong's Poems), 96.

34. Schram, *Mao's Road to Power,* vol. 3, 192.

35. Ibid., 194.

36. Ibid., 195–230.

37. See, for example, Huang Ping, *Wangshi huiyilu* (Reminiscences of the Past) (Beijing: Renmin chubanshe, 1981).

38. Wang Fanxi, *Memoirs of a Chinese Revolutionary,* trans. Gregor Benton (New York: Columbia University Press, 1977), 109.

39. See Titarenko, *VKP(b), Komintern i Kitai: Dokumenty* (The CPSU, the Comintern and China: Documents), vol. 3, 457.

40. Ibid., 1048, 1075.

41. See Yang Kuisong, *Zouxiang polie: Mao Zedong yu Mosike enen yuanyuan* (Heading for a Split: Concord and Discord in Relations Between Mao Zedong and Moscow) (Hong Kong: Sanlian shudian, 1999), 189.

42. *Pravda* (Truth), December 29, 1929.

43. See Titarenko, *VKP(b), Komintern i Kitai: Dokumenty* (The CPSU, the Comintern and China: Documents), vol. 3, 482–88; Grigoriev, *Kommunisticheskaia partiia Kitaia v nachal'nyi period sovetskogo dvizheniia* (The Communist Party of China in the Initial Soviet Movement Period), 287–88.

44. See Hsiao Tso-liang, *Power Relations within the Chinese Communist Party, 1930–1934,* vol. 2 (Seattle: University of Washington Press, 1967), 26–29.

45. See Schram, *Mao's Road to Power,* vol. 3, 157–58.

46. Ibid., 261.

47. Ibid., 240, 245, 246.

48. Quoted from Grigoriev, *Kommunisticheskaia partiia Kitaia v nachal'nyi period sovetskogo dvizheniia* (The Communist Party of China in the Initial Soviet Movement Period), 308, 309.

49. Saich, *The Rise to Power of the Chinese Communist Party,* 429.

50. Schram, *Mao's Road to Power,* vol. 3, 455–502, 508–23, 529–32; Pang, *Mao Zedong nianpu, 1893–1949* (Chronological Biography of Mao Zedong, 1893–1949), vol. 1, 310–16.

51. See Grigoriev, *Kommunisticheskaia partiia Kitaia v nachal'nyi period sovetskogo dvizheniia* (The Communist Party of China in the Initial Soviet Movement Period), 338.

52. Schram, *Mao's Road to Power,* vol. 3, 459.

53. Ibid., 234–36; Pang, *Mao Zedong nianpu, 1893–1949* (Chronological Biography of Mao Zedong, 1893–1949), vol. 1, 275.

54. Schram, *Mao's Road to Power,* vol. 3, 235.

17. UNDER THE COMINTERN'S WING

1. See Titarenko, *VKP(b), Komintern i Kitai: Dokumenty* (The CPSU, Comintern and China: Documents), vol. 3, 1273.

2. Titarenko, *Kommunisticheskii Internatsional i kitaiskaa revoliutsiia* (The Communist International and the Chinese Revolution), 204, 205.

3. Titarenko, *VKP(b), Komintern i Kitai: Dokumenty* (The CPSU, Comintern and China: Documents), vol. 3, 1019.

4. Ibid., 1029, 1037; Zhang Qiushi, *Qu Qiubai yu gongchan guoji* (Qu Qiubai and the Comintern) (Beijing: Zhonggong dangshi chubanshe, 2004), 314–17.

5. Chang, *The Rise of the Chinese Communist Party,* vol. 2, 86.

6. See Wang, *Zhongguo gongchandang zuzhi shi ziliao huibian* (Collection of Documents on the History of the CCP Organizations), 145–46.

7. Meng Qingshu, "Vospominaniia o Van Mine" (Reminiscences of Wang Ming) (manuscript), 66–67. For more details, see Spichak, *Kitaiskii avangard Kremlia* (Chinese Vanguard of the Kremlin), 104.

8. "Zapis' besedy tt. Chzhou Enlaia, Chzhen Lina [Ren Bishi] i [G. I.] Mordvinova 16 noiabria 1939 goda" (Record of a Conversation between Zhou Enlai, Zheng Ling [Ren Bishi], and [G. I.] Mordvinov, November 16, 1939), RGASPI, collection 495, inventory 225, file 71, vol. 1, sheet 35.

9. See Titarenko, *VKP(b), Komintern i Kitai: Dokumenty* (The CPSU, Comintern and China: Documents), vol. 3, 817, 1079–80, 1139, 1323.

10. Titarenko, *Kommunisticheskii Internatsional i kitaiskaia revoliutsiia* (The Communist International and the Chinese Revolution), 205.

11. A. Ivin, *Ocherki partizanskogo dvizheniia v Kitae, 1927–1930* (Sketches of the Guerrilla Movement in China, 1927–1930) (Moscow and Leningrad: GIZ, 1930), 90.

12. See Titarenko, *VKP(b), Komintern i Kitai: Dokumenty* (The CPSU, the Comintern and China: Documents), vol. 3, 48, 1067.

13. Ibid., 1108–9.

14. Schram, *Mao's Road to Power,* vol. 3, 377–78.

15. Of course, for tactical reasons Mao might still on occasion renounce the rural lumpens. In June 1930, for example, at a joint conference of the Front Committee of the Fourth Corps and the Special West Jiangxi Committee, trying to shake off the repeated accusation that he adhered to a "lumpen proletarian ideology," he secured passage of a resolution on the question of "drifters." It said, "The Red Army and the Red Guard are the important tools of the revolutionary masses in seizing state power and protecting it. . . . No vagabonds can be allowed to penetrate into these organizations." See ibid., 453. This thesis, however, was not worth the paper it was written on; it was impossible to implement. In 1930, according to estimates by the Far Eastern Bureau of the ECCI, the Red Army consisted basically of déclassé elements. See Titarenko, *VKP(b), Komintern i Kitai: Dokumenty* (The CPSU, the Comintern and China: Documents), vol. 3, 817.

16. Schram, *Mao's Road to Power,* vol. 3, 636, 638.

17. [Liu Shiqi], *Sovetskii raion iugo-zapadnoi Tsiansi v 1930 g.: Doklad instruktora TsK kompartii Kitaia ot 7 oktiabria 1930 g.* (The Soviet District of Southwest Jiangxi in 1930: Report of a CCP Central Committee Instructor, October 7, 1930), in Mif, *Sovety v Kitae* (Soviets in China), 237.

18. Schram, *Mao's Road to Power,* vol. 3, 269.

19. See [Liu Shiqi], *Sovetskii raion iugo-zapadnoi Tsziansi v 1930 g.* (The Soviet District of Southwest Jiangxi in 1930), 227–44; Titarenko, *VKP(b), Komintern i Kitai: Dokumenty* (The CPSU, the Comintern and China: Documents), vol. 3, 1272–74; Chen, "Chen Yi tongzhi guanyu Zhu Mao jun de lishi ji qi zhuangkuang de baogao" (Comrade Chen Yi's Report on the History of the Zhu-Mao Army and Its Present Situation), 192; *Zhongguo renmin jiefangjun zuzhi yange he geji lingdao chengyuan minglu* (Organizational Evolution and Personnel of the Leading Organs at All Levels of the PLA) (Beijing: Junshi kexue chubanshe, 1987), 35; Erbaugh, "The Secret History of the Hakkas," 937–38; Stephen C. Averill, "The Origins of the Futian Incident," in Tony Saich and Hans J. van de Ven, eds., *New Perspectives on the Chinese Communist Revolution* (Armonk, NY: M. E. Sharpe, 1995), 79–115.

20. Titarenko, *VKP(b), Komintern i Kitai: Dokumenty* (The CPSU, the Comintern and China: Documents), vol. 3, 1349, 1368.

21. See Averill, "The Origins of the Futian Incident," 83–84, 86–92.

22. See Short, *Mao,* 268.

23. Several days later Mao asserted that "two-thirds of the personnel of the leading organs of the southwest Jiangxi soviet government and of the technical workers are AB Corps elements." Schram, *Mao's Road to Power,* vol. 3, 560. Where he got this figure is a mystery.

24. Ibid., 554.

25. *Lichnoe delo Mao Tszeduna* (Personal File of Mao Zedong), RGASPI, collection 495, inventory 225, file 71, vol. 2, sheets 257, 258.

26. See *Zhongguo renmin jiefangjun zuzhi yange he geji lingdao chengyuan minglu* (Organizational Evolution and Personnel of the Leading Organs at All Levels of the PLA), 38.

27. Quoted from Short, *Mao,* 273.

28. *Lichnoe delo Mao Tszeduna* (Personal File of Mao Zedong), RGASPI, collection 495, inventory 225, file 71, vol. 2, sheet 261.

29. Ibid., 260–61; Titov, *Materialy k politicheskoi biografii Mao Tsze-duna* (Materials for a Political Biography of Mao Zedong), vol. 1, 310, 311.

30. *Lichnoe delo Mao Tszeduna* (Personal File of Mao Zedong), RGASPI, collection 495, inventory 225, file 71, vol. 2, sheets 258, 259, 261; vol. 3, sheets 18, 19; P. P. Vladimirov, *Osobyi raion Kitaia, 1942–1945* (Special Region of China, 1942–1945) (Moscow: APN, 1975), 224, 225.

31. Schram, *Mao's Road to Power,* vol. 3, 713.

32. See Titarenko, *VKP(b), Komintern i Kitai: Dokumenty* (The CPSU, the Comintern and China: Documents), vol. 3, 1276–81.

33. Ibid., 1348–52; Xu Zehao, ed., *Wang Jiaxiang nianpu, 1906–1974* (Chronological Biography of Wang Jiaxiang, 1906–1974) (Beijing: Zhongyang wenxian chubanshe, 2001), 52; *Ren Bishi nianpu, 1904–1950* (Chronological Biography of Ren Bishi, 1904–1950), 165–66; *Zhou Enlai nianpu (1898–1949)* (Chronological Biography of Zhou Enlai [1898–1949]), rev. ed. (Beijing: Zhongyang wenxian chubanshe, 1998), 212.

34. Titarenko, *VKP(b), Komintern i Kitai: Dokumenty* (The CPSU, the Comintern and China: Documents), vol. 3, 1067.

35. Titov, *Materialy k politicheskoi biografii Mao Tsze-duna* (Materials for a Political Biography of Mao Zedong), vol. 1, 329.

36. See "Beseda [G. I.] Mordvinova s t. Chzhou Enlaem 4 marta 1940 g." (Conversation Between [G. I.] Mordvinov and Comrade Zhou Enlai, March 4, 1940), RGASPI, collection 495, inventory 225, file 71, vol. 1, sheet 32.

37. See Saich, *The Rise to Power of the Chinese Communist Party,* 530–35.

38. See Wang, *Zhongguo gongchandang zuzhi shi ziliao huibian* (Collection of Documents on the History of the CCP Organizations), 159, 161.

39. Quoted from Averill, "The Origins of the Futien Incident," 108.

40. Liao, *Zhongguo gongchandang lishi da cidian* (Great Dictionary of the History of the Chinese Communist Party), 260.

41. See Pang, *Mao Zedong nianpu, 1893–1949* (Chronological Biography of Mao Zedong, 1893–1949), vol. 1, 330–31; Short, *Mao,* 257.

42. Mao, *Poems of Mao Tse-tung,* 53. Buzhou (Imperfect) Mountain is a mythical mountain that was leveled by the ancient Chinese hero Gonggong.

43. See Titarenko, *VKP(b), Komintern i Kitai: Dokumenty* (The CPSU, the Comintern and China: Documents), vol. 3, 1147, 1258, 1273.

44. Li, *Moi otets Mao Tszedun* (My Father Mao Zedong), 163.

45. See Chang, *The Rise of the Chinese Communist Party,* vol. 2, 175.

46. *Lichnoe delo Mao Tszeduna* (Personal File of Mao Zedong), RGASPI, collection 495, inventory 225, file 71, vol. 2, sheet 256.

47. See Frederick S. Litten, "The Noulens Affair," *China Quarterly,* no. 138 (1994): 492–512; Frederic Wakeman, *Policing Shanghai 1927–1937* (Berkeley: University of California Press, 1995), 151–60, 253–54; Nie Rongzhen, *Inside the Red Star: The Memoirs of Marshal Nie Rongzhen* (Beijing: New World Press, 1983), 97–98, 104–6.

48. See M. L. Titarenko et al., eds., *VKP(b), Komintern i Kitai: Dokumenty* (The CPSU, the Comintern and China: Documents), vol. 4 (Moscow: AO "Buklet," 2003), 146.

49. See Yang, *Zouxiang polie* (Heading Toward a Split), 189.

50. "Zapis' besedy tt. Chzhou Enlaia, Chzhen Lina [Ren Bishi] i [G. I.] Mordvinova 16 noiabria 1939 goda" (Record of Conversation Among Comrades Zhou Enlai, Zheng Ling [Ren Bishi], and [G. I.] Mordvinov, November 16, 1939), 33–34; Wakeman, *Policing Shanghai, 1927–1937,* 156.

51. See *Zhou Enlai nianpu (1898–1949)* (Chronological Biography of Zhou Enlai [1898–1949]), 218.

52. See Li Chongde, "Escorting Mao Zedong's Sons to Shanghai," in *Mao Zedong: Biography—Assessment—Reminiscences,* 222–26; Zhu Weiyang, "Qian Xijun he Mao Zemin" (Qian Xijun and Mao Zemin), in *Mao Zedong de jiashi* (Mao Zedong's Family Affairs) (Beijing: Chunqiu chubanshe, 1987), 14–15; "Zhongguo gongchandang chuang-bande di yige youzhiyuan" (First Children's Home Organized by the CCP), *Xinmin wanbao* (The renovation of people evening newspaper), June 13, 2004; "Mao Anying san xiongdi zai Shanghai shide qingkuang" (What Happened to Mao Anying and His Brothers During Their Sojourn in Shanghai), ibid., December 23, 2004; Ma, *Hongse diyi jiazu* (The First Red Family), 136–37; Titarenko, *VKP(b), Komintern i Kitai: Dokumenty* (The CPSU, the Comintern and China: Documents), vol. 4, 1052.

53. See Wang, *Zhongguo gongchandang zuzhi shi ziliao huibian* (Collection of Documents on the History of the CCP Organizations), 163.

54. Agnes Smedley, *China's Red Army Marches* (New York: International, 1934), 314–15.

18. DOG EAT DOG, COMMUNIST-STYLE

1. Hsiao, *Power Relations within the Chinese Communist Movement, 1930–1934,* vol. 2, 382–89.

2. See Pang, *Mao Zedong nianpu, 1893–1949* (Chronological Biography of Mao Zedong, 1893–1949), vol. 1, 319, 320.

3. Titarenko, *VKP(b), Komintern i Kitai: Dokumenty* (The CPSU, the Comintern and China: Documents), vol. 3, 893, 938, 939, 940.

4. See Hsiao, *Power Relations within the Chinese Communist Movement, 1930–1934,* vol. 2, 391–407; Jin, *Mao Zedong zhuan (1893–1949)* (Biography of Mao Zedong [1893–1949]), 280–81.

5. See Pang, *Mao Zedong nianpu, 1893–1949* (Chronological Biography of Mao Zedong, 1893–1949), vol. 1, 358.

6. See ibid., 360; Wang, *Zhongguo gongchandang zuzhi shi ziliao huibian* (Collection of Documents on the History of the CCP Organizations), 164; *Zhongguo renmin jiefangjun zuzhi yange he geji lingdao chengyuan minglu* (Organizational Evolution and Personnel of the Leading Organs at All Levels of the PLA), 48–52.

7. See *Zhou Enlai nianpu (1898–1949)* (Chronological Biography of Zhou Enlai [1898–1949]), 220; Wang Song [Liu Yalou], Li Ting [Lin Biao], and Zhou Den [Mao Zemin], *Doklad general'nomu sekretariu IKKI G. Dimitrovu, 8 ianvaria 1940 g.* (Report to the General Secretary of the ECCI G. Dimitrov, January 8, 1940), RGASPI, collection 495, inventory 225, file 477, sheet 48.

8. Saich, *The Rise to Power of the Chinese Communist Party,* 558–66.

9. Ibid.; Pang, *Mao Zedong nianpu, 1893–1949* (Chronological Biography of Mao Zedong, 1893–1949), vol. 1, 364; Jin, *Mao Zedong zhuan (1893–1949)* (Biography of Mao Zedong [1893–1949]), 289–90; Wang [Liu], Li [Lin] i Zhou [Mao], *Doklad general'nomu sekretariu IKKI G. Dimitrovu, 8 ianvaria 1940 g.* (Report to the General Secretary of the ECCI G. Dimitrov, January 8, 1940), 48.

10. See Li Ruilin, "Vosstanie v Ningdu" (Uprising in Ningdu), in *Vsiudu krasnye znamena* (Red Banners Everywhere), 52–58.

11. See Wen and Zhang, *Mao Zedong yu He Zizhen* (Mao Zedong and He Zizhen), 75–79; Pang, *Mao Zedong nianpu, 1893–1949* (Chronological Biography of Mao Zedong, 1893–1949), vol. 1, 365; Jin, *Mao Zedong zhuan (1893–1949)* (Biography of Mao Zedong [1893–1949]), 290–91.

12. Titarenko, *Kommunisticheskii internatsional i kitaiskaia revoliutsiia: Dokumenty* (The Communist International and the Chinese Revolution), 628–29.

13. Ibid., 240, 242. See also Titarenko, *VKP(b), Komintern i Kitai: Dokumenty* (The CPSU, the Comintern and China: Documents), vol. 4, 96.

14. See also Titarenko, *VKP(b), Komintern i Kitai: Dokumenty* (The CPSU, the Comintern and China: Documents), vol. 4, 100–102.

15. See Donald A. Jordan, *China's Trial by Fire: The Shanghai War of 1932* (Ann Arbor: University of Michigan Press, 2001).

16. See Mif, *Sovety v Kitae* (Soviets in China), 454–56; Stuart R. Schram, ed., *Mao's Road to Power: Revolutionary Writings, 1912–1949,* vol. 4: (Armonk, NY: M. E. Sharpe, 1997), 209–14.

17. Otto Braun, *A Comintern Agent in China 1932–1939,* trans. Jeanne Moore (Stanford, CA: Stanford University Press, 1982), 30.

18. See Nie, *Inside the Red Star,* 114–28.

19. Titarenko, *VKP(b), Komintern i Kitai: Dokumenty* (The CPSU, the Comintern and China: Documents), vol. 4, 146–47. This telegram is rather confusing. One senses that the

members of the Bureau themselves did not fully comprehend what the Provisional Politburo wanted from them, but they wanted very much to show their loyalty. "It goes without
saying," they wrote, "that we must struggle against Li Lisan's adventurist line of attacking
large cities. The current situation is in our favor, however. We must fight against right opportunistic excessive fear before attacks on the most important cities."

20. Pang, *Mao Zedong nianpu, 1893–1949* (Chronological Biography of Mao Zedong,
1893–1949), vol. 1, 375.
21. Titarenko, *VKP(b), Komintern i Kitai: Dokumenty* (The CPSU, the Comintern and
China: Documents), vol. 4, 153.
22. Ibid., 158.
23. Ibid., 159.
24. See Pang, *Mao Zedong nianpu, 1893–1949* (Chronological Biography of Mao Zedong,
1893–1949), vol. 1, 377; *Zhongguo renmin jiefangjun zuzhi yange he geji lingdao chengyuan
minglu* (Organizational Evolution and Personnel of the Leading Organs at All Levels of the
PLA), 58–61.
25. See Pang, *Mao Zedong nianpu, 1893–1949* (Chronological Biography of Mao Zedong,
1893–1949), vol. 1, 342.
26. See ibid., vol. 1, 379–80; Schram, *Mao's Road to Power,* vol. 4, 242–44.
27. See Wang [Liu], Li [Lin], and Zhou [Mao], *Doklad General'nomu sekretariu IKKI G.
Dimitrovu, 8 ianvaria 1940 g.* (Report to ECCI General Secretary G. Dimitrov, January 8,
1940), 49; Titarenko, *VKP(b), Komintern i Kitai: Dokumenty* (The CPSU, the Comintern
and China: Documents), vol. 4, 146–48, 152–53, 158–59, 193; *Lichnoe delo Mao Tszeduna*
(Personal File of Mao Zedong), RGASPI, collection 495, inventory 225, file 71, vol. 3, sheets
176–79.
28. Wang [Liu], Li [Lin], and Zhou [Mao], *Doklad General'nomu sekretariu IKKI G. Dimitrovu, 8 ianvaria 1940 g.* (Report to ECCI General Secretary G. Dimitrov, January 8, 1940), 49.
29. Titarenko, *VKP(b), Komintern i Kitai: Dokumenty* (The CPSU, the Comintern and
China: Documents), vol. 4, 187–88.
30. Quoted from Jin, *Mao Zedong zhuan (1893–1949)* (Biography of Mao Zedong [1893–
1949]), 309.
31. Titarenko, *VKP(b), Komintern i Kitai: Dokumenty* (The CPSU, the Comintern and
China: Documents), vol. 4, 191, 192.
32. See Jin, *Mao Zedong zhuan (1893–1949)* (Biography of Mao Zedong [1893–1949]), 309.
33. Ibid., 334.
34. Quoted from Wen and Zhang, *Mao Zedong yu He Zizhen* (Mao Zedong and He Zizhen),
92; Jin, *Mao Zedong zhuan (1893–1949)* (Biography of Mao Zedong [1893–1949]), 310.
35. See Titarenko, *VKP(b), Komintern i Kitai: Dokumenty* (The CPSU, the Comintern and
China: Documents), vol. 4, 194, 223, 225.
36. See Wang, *Zhongguo gongchandang zuzhi shi ziliao huibian* (Collection of Documents
on the History of the CCP Organizations), 188.
37. Titarenko, *VKP(b), Komintern i Kitai: Dokumenty* (The CPSU, the Comintern and
China: Documents), vol. 4, 199.
38. See Pang, *Mao Zedong nianpu, 1893–1949* (Chronological Biography of Mao Zedong, 1893–1949), vol. 1, 393; "Zapis' besedy tt. Chzhou Enlaia, Chzhen Lina [Ren Bishi] i
[G. I.] Mordvinova, 16 noiabria 1939 goda" (Notes on a Conversation Among Comrades
Zhou Enlai, Zheng Ling [Ren Bishi], and [G. I.] Mordvinov, November 16, 1939), 34.
39. Titarenko, *VKP(b), Komintern i Kitai: Dokumenty* (The CPSU, the Comintern and
China: Documents), vol. 4, 295.
40. Ibid., 295, 298, 309, 323.
41. See "Dokladnaia zapiska o provalakh i provokatsiiakh v tsentral'nykh organizatsiiakh
KP Kitaia v Shanhae za poslednie tri goda i o dele 'Osobogo otdela' " (Reportorial Notes on
the Failures and Provocations in the Central Organs of the CP of China in Shanghai for the
Past Three Years and of the Matter of the 'Special Section'), RGASPI, collection 495, inventory 74, file 299, sheets 1–60; Litten, "The Noulens Affair," 492–512.

42. Jin, *Mao Zedong zhuan (1893–1949)* (Biography of Mao Zedong [1893–1949]), 311.

43. See Wen and Zhang, *Mao Zedong yu He Zizhen* (Mao Zedong and He Zizhen), 91.

44. See Deng Maomao, *Deng Xiaoping: My Father* (New York: Basic Books, 1995), 210–17.

45. Quoted from Wen and Zhang, *Mao Zedong yu He Zizhen* (Mao Zedong and He Zizhen), 99; Jin, *Mao Zedong zhuan (1893–1949)* (Biography of Mao Zedong [1893–1949]), 333.

46. Quoted from Jin, *Mao Zedong zhuan (1893–1949)* (Biography of Mao Zedong, 1893–1949), 334.

47. See Braun, *A Comintern Agent in China 1932–1939*, 1–79.

48. Titarenko, *VKP(b), Komintern i Kitai: Dokumenty* (The CPSU, the Comintern and China: Documents), vol. 4, 1145.

49. Ibid., 1146. See also Bo Gu, "Moia Predvaritel'naia ispoved'" (My Preliminary Testimony), RGASPI, collection 495, inventory 225, file 2847, sheets 1–111.

50. See Titarenko, *VKP(b), Komintern i Kitai: Dokumenty* (The CPSU, the Comintern and China: Documents), vol. 3, 1306–27; vol. 4, 103–4.

51. See ibid., vol. 4, 243, 427.

52. Braun, *A Comintern Agent in China 1932–1939*, 49.

53. See the unpublished proofs of the book Pavel Mif, ed., *Soviety v Kitae: Materialy i dokumenty, Sbornik vtoroi* (Soviets in China: Materials and Documents, Second Collection) (Moscow: Partizdat TsK VKP(b), 1935), 183–258. This book was never published, due to a radical change in the policy of Stalin's Comintern in 1935. One of the surviving copies of the proofs is in Alexander V. Pantsov's private library.

54. See Wang, *Zhongguo gongchandang zuzhi shi ziliao huibian* (Collection of Documents on the History of the CCP Organizations), 198.

55. See Titarenko, *VKP(b), Komintern i Kitai: Dokumenty* (The CPSU, the Comintern and China: Documents), vol. 3, 49.

56. Ibid., vol. 4, 585.

57. Ibid., 586.

58. Quoted from Jin, *Mao Zedong zhuan (1893–1949)* (Biography of Mao Zedong [1893–1949]), 339.

59. See *Kommunisticheskii Internatsional* (Communist International), no. 20 (1934): 21–29; no. 23 (1934): 32–51; *Za rubezhom* (Abroad), no. 27 (59) (1934): 1, 4–9; Mao Zedong, *Tol'ko soviety mogut spasti Kitai: Doklad na 11-m s ezde Sovetov Khula* (Only Soviets Can Save China: Report at the Second Congress of Chinese Soviets) (Moscow and Leningrad: Izdatel'stvo inostrannykh rabochikh v SSSR, 1934); Mao Zedong, *Ekonomicheskoe stroitel'stvo i itogi proverki razdela zemli v Kitaiskoi Sovietskoi Respublike (Izbrannye rechi i stat'i)* (Economic Construction and the Results of the Verification of Land Redistribution in the Chinese Soviet Republic [Selected Speeches and Articles]) (Moscow and Leningrad: Izdatel'stvo inostrannykh rabochikh v SSSR, 1934).

60. See *Pravda* (Truth), February 11, 1930.

61. Titarenko, *VKP(b), Komintern i Kitai: Dokumenty* (The CPSU, the Comintern and China: Documents), vol. 4, 693.

62. See Nie, *Inside the Red Star*, 158–59; Braun, *A Comintern Agent in China 1932–1939*, 40–43, 75–76; Violet Cressy-Marcks, *Journey into China* (New York: Dutton, 1942), 166.

63. Stuart R. Schram, *Mao's Road to Power: Revolutionary Writings, 1912–1949*, vol. 5 (Armonk, NY: M. E. Sharpe, 1999), 528–29.

64. Titarenko, *VKP(b), Komintern i Kitai: Dokumenty* (The CPSU, the Comintern and China: Documents), vol. 4, 602.

65. Ibid., 614.

66. See Pang, *Mao Zedong nianpu, 1893–1949* (Chronological Biography of Mao Zedong, 1893–1949), vol. 1, 428.

67. Braun, *A Comintern Agent in China 1932–1939*, 76.

68. See Titarenko, *VKP(b), Komintern i Kitai: Dokumenty* (The CPSU, the Comintern and China: Documents), vol. 4, 613.

69. See Helen Foster Snow (Nym Wales), *The Chinese Communists: Sketches and Autobiographies of the Old Guard* (Westport, CT: Greenwood, 1972), 245, 246.
70. See Wen and Zhang, *Mao Zedong yu He Zizhen* (Mao Zedong and He Zizhen), 95–97; Ma, *Hongse diyi jiazu* (The First Red Family), 323–24.

19. THE LONG MARCH

1. Braun, *A Comintern Agent in China 1932–1939*, 83.
2. See Pang, *Mao Zedong nianpu, 1893–1949* (Chronological Biography of Mao Zedong, 1893–1949), vol. 1, 435–36; Braun, *A Comintern Agent in China 1932–1939*, 81–82; Li, *Huiyi yu yanjiu* (Reminiscences and Studies), vol. 1, 344–45; A. A. Martynov et al., eds., *Velikii pokhod 1-go fronta Kitaiskoi raboche-krest'ianskoi krasnoi armii: Vospominaniia* (The Long March of the First Front Chinese Worker-Peasant Red Army: Reminiscences), trans. A. A. Klyshko et al. (Moscow: Izd-vo inostrannoi literatury, 1959), 43.
3. See "Dokladnaia zapiska o provalakh i provokatsiiakh v tsentral'nykh organizatsiiakh KP Kitaia v Shanghae za poslednie tri goda i o dele 'Osobogo otdela' " (Report on the Failures and Provocations Within the Central Organizations of the CP of China in Shanghai over the Past Three Years and on the Matter of the "Special Department"), 30–32.
4. Braun, *A Comintern Agent in China 1932–1939*, 90.
5. See Erbaugh, "The Secret History of the Hakkas," 937–68.
6. See Pantsov and Levine, *Chinese Comintern Activists: An Analytic Biographic Dictionary* (manuscript), 533–35; Snow (Wales), *Inside Red China*, 227–29.
7. Braun, *A Comintern Agent in China 1932–1939*, 71; see also *Zunyi huiyi wenxian* (Documents of the Zunyi Conference) (Beijing: Renmin chubanshe, 1985), 37.
8. See Jin, *Mao Zedong zhuan (1893–1949)* (Biography of Mao Zedong [1893–1949]), 342–43; Pang, *Mao Zedong nianpu, 1893–1949* (Chronological Biography of Mao Zedong, 1893–1949), vol. 1, 434–35.
9. Braun, *A Comintern Agent in China 1932–1939*, 98.
10. Nie, *Inside the Red Star,* 210; See also *Zunyi huiyi wenxian* (Documents of the Zunyi Conference), 41, 111–14.
11. See Nie, *Inside the Red Star,* 211–12.
12. Quoted from ibid., 210.
13. See Braun, *A Comintern Agent in China 1932–1939*, 98–103; *Zunyi huiyi wenxian* (Documents of the Zunyi Conference), 116–17; Jin, *Mao Zedong zhuan (1893–1949)* (Biography of Mao Zedong [1893–1949]), 353–54; Yang Shangkun, *Yang Shangkun huiyilu* (The Memoirs of Yang Shangkun) (Beijing: Zhongyang wenxian chubanshe, 2001), 117–21.
14. "Pis'mo Li Tina [Lin Biao] v Otdel kadrov IKKI i IKK ot 29 ianvaria 1940 g." (Letter from Li Ting [Lin Biao] to the Department of Personnel of the ECCI and the ICC, January 29, 1940), RGASPI, collection 495, inventory 225, file 53, vol. 1, sheet 180.
15. Jin, *Mao Zedong zhuan (1893–1949)* (Biography of Mao Zedong [1893–1949]), 354; see also Nie, *Inside the Red Star,* 211.
16. See *Zunyi huiyi wenxian* (Documents of the Zunyi Conference), 117.
17. Braun, *A Comintern Agent in China 1932–1939*, 104.
18. See Zhang Wentian, *Zhang Wentian xuanji* (Selected Works of Zhang Wentian) (Beijing: Renmin chubanshe, 1985), 37–59.
19. *Zunyi huiyi wenxian* (Documents of the Zunyi Conference), 42–43, 132–36.
20. Quoted from Li, *Moi otets Mao Tszedun* (My Father Mao Zedong), 171.
21. Quoted from Kong Dongmei, *Mao Zedong, He Zizhen fufu: Wei geming tongshi wu ge zinü* (A Couple Mao Zedong and He Zizhen: They Painfully Sacrificed Five Sons and Daughters for the Revolution), *Jiefang ribao* (Liberation daily), March 7, 2005.
22. See ibid.
23. See *Zunyi huiyi wenxian* (Documents of the Zunyi Conference), 134.
24. Quoted from *Zhou Enlai nianpu (1898–1949)* (Chronological Biography of Zhou Enlai [1898–1949]), 280.

25. See *Zunyi huiyi wenxian* (Documents of the Zunyi Conference), 134–35; Jin, *Mao Zedong zhuan (1893–1949)* (Biography of Mao Zedong [1893–1949]), 361.

26. Mao, *Poems of Mao Tse-tung*, 63.

27. Braun, *A Comintern Agent in China 1932–1939*, 111.

28. See Li, *Moi otets Mao Tszedun* (My Father Mao Zedong), 173.

29. Braun, *A Comintern Agent in China 1932–1939*, 113–14.

30. Ibid., 120.

31. Chang, *The Rise of the Chinese Communist Party*, vol. 2, 378.

32. See *Lichnoe delo Liu Tina* (Personal File of Liu Ting), RGASPI, collection 495, inventory 225, file 3078, n.p.

33. See Schram, *Mao's Road to Power*, vol. 5, xlii; Braun, *A Comintern Agent in China 1932–1939*, 123; A. S. Titov, *Iz istorii bor'by i raskola v rukovodstve KPK 1935–1936 gg.* (From the History of Struggle and Split in the Leadership of the CCP, 1935–1936) (Moscow: Nauka, 1979), 39–40.

34. See K. O. Wagner [Otto Braun], "Spravka o Chzhan Gotao i sobytiiakh 1935–1936 gg." (Information About Zhang Guotao and the Events of 1935–1936), RGASPI, collection 495, inventory 4, file 298, sheet 75; Braun, *A Comintern Agent in China 1932–1939*, 125–26.

35. See Pang, *Mao Zedong nianpu, 1893–1949* (Chronological Biography of Mao Zedong, 1893–1949), vol. 1, 462–63.

36. Braun, *A Comintern Agent in China 1932–1939*, 126.

37. Pang, *Mao Zedong nianpu, 1893–1949* (Chronological Biography of Mao Zedong, 1893–1949), vol. 1, 463–66; Schram, *Mao's Road to Power*, vol. 5, xliv.

38. Braun, *A Comintern Agent in China 1932–1939*, 136–37.

39. Schram, *Mao's Road to Power*, vol. 5, 24.

40. See Pang, *Mao Zedong nianpu, 1893–1949* (Chronological Biography of Mao Zedong, 1893–1949), vol. 1, 471; Wagner, "Spravka o Chzhan Gotao i sobytiiakh 1935–1936 gg." (Information About Zhang Guotao and the Events of 1935–1936), 77.

41. Schram, *Mao's Road to Power*, vol. 5, xlvii.

42. See Pang, *Mao Zedong nianpu, 1893–1949* (Chronological Biography of Mao Zedong, 1893–1949), vol. 1, 475–76.

43. Chang and Halliday write that "Mao and the core leaders had known about this base before the Long March," but they cite no evidence for this statement. At the same time, they assert that the entire march of the communists to northern Shaanxi was planned by Chiang Kai-shek. Chang and Halliday, *Mao*, 140, 171.

44. Quoted from Nie, *Inside the Red Star*, 248.

45. See Schram, *Mao's Road to Power*, vol. 5, 36; Pang, *Mao Zedong nianpu, 1893–1949*, (Chronological Biography of Mao Zedong, 1893–1949), vol. 1, 482.

46. Mao, *Poems of Mao Tse-tung*, 70.

20. THE XI'AN INCIDENT

1. See Pang, *Mao Zedong nianpu, 1893–1949* (Chronological Biography of Mao Zedong, 1893–1949), vol. 1, 478.

2. See Wagner, "Spravka o Chzhan Gotao i sobytiiakh 1935–1936 gg." (Information About Zhang Guotao and the Events of 1935–1936), 77–78.

3. Braun, *A Comintern Agent in China 1932–1939*, 143, 146.

4. See Agnes Smedley, *China Fights Back: An American Woman with the Eighth Route Army* (New York: Vanguard Press, 1938), 8–9, 19–20; Janice R. MacKinnon and Stephen R. MacKinnon, *Agnes Smedley: The Life and Times of an American Radical* (Berkeley: University of California Press, 1988), 183.

5. See Wu, *Mao Zedong guanghui licheng dituji* (Atlas of Mao Zedong's Glorious Historical Path), 62.

6. See Pang, *Mao Zedong nianpu, 1893–1949* (Chronological Biography of Mao Zedong, 1893–1949), vol. 1, 617.

7. Chang, *The Rise of the Chinese Communist Party,* vol. 2, 474.

8. Molotov's reminiscences are particularly frank in this regard. See Felix Chuev, *Molotov Remembers: Inside Kremlin Politics: Conversations with Felix Chuev,* trans. Albert Resis (Chicago: I. R. Dee, 1993).

9. Wang Ming, *Sobraniie sochinenii* (Collected Works), vol. 3 (Moscow: IDV AN SSSR, 1985), 364.

10. See Titarenko, *VKP(b), Komintern i Kitai: Dokumenty* (The CPSU, the Comintern and China: Documents), vol. 3, 49.

11. See Qing Shi (Yang Kuisong), *Gongchan guoji yazhi Mao Zedong le ma? Mao Zedong yu Mosike de enen yuanyuan* (Did the Comintern Suppress Mao Zedong? Concord and Discord in the Relations Between Mao Zedong and Moscow), *Bainian chao* (Century tides), no. 4 (1997): 33.

12. Quoted from Titov, *Materialy k politicheskoi biografii Mao Tsze-duna* (Materials for a Political Biography of Mao Zedong), vol. 2, 137.

13. *Lichnoe delo Mao Tszeduna* (Personal File of Mao Zedong), RGASPI, collection 495, inventory 225, file 71, vol. 1, sheets 242–43.

14. *Lichnoe delo Van Mina* (Personal File of Wang Ming), RGASPI, collection 495, inventory 225, file 6, vol. 1, sheets 62, 63.

15. See Titov, *Materialy k politicheskoi biografii Mao Tsze-duna* (Materials for a Political Biography of Mao Zedong), vol. 2, 613.

16. Ibid., 619.

17. See *Kommunisticheskii Internatsional* (Communist International), no. 33–34 (1935): 83–88.

18. A. Khamadan, "Vozhd' kitaiskogo naroda—Mao Tszedun" (The Leader of the Chinese People—Mao Zedong), *Pravda* (Truth), December 13, 1935.

19. See A. Khamadan, *Vozhdi i geroi kitaiskogo naroda* (Leaders and Heroes of the Chinese People) (Moscow: Ogiz-Sotsekgiz, 1936).

20. See *Lichnoe delo Chzhan Khao (Li Fushen)* (Personal File of Zhang Hao [Li Fusheng]), RGASPI, collection 495, inventory 225, file 2850; Wang Xingfu, *Linshi sanxiongdi: Lin Yuying, Lin Yunan, Lin Biao* (The Three Lin Brothers: Lin Yuying, Lin Yunan, Lin Biao) (Wuhan: Hubei renmin chubanshe, 2004), 73–75.

21. Schram, *Mao's Road to Power,* vol. 5, 66–67.

22. See Zhang, *Zhang Wentian xuanji* (Selected Works of Zhang Wentian), 66–70; Zhang Peisen, ed., *Zhang Wentian nianpu* (Chronological Biography of Zhang Wentian), vol. 1 (Beijing: Zhongyang wenxian chubanshe, 2000), 278–79, 286–87.

23. See Schram, *Mao's Road to Power,* vol. 3, 73–74.

24. See Zhang, *Zhang Wentian xuanji* (Selected Works of Zhang Wentian), 71–79; Mao, *Mao Zedong wenji* (Works of Mao Zedong), vol. 1, 376–82; Schram, *Mao's Road to Power,* vol. 3, 86–102.

25. Schram, *Mao's Road to Power,* vol. 3, 89, 91.

26. See Mao, *Mao Zedong wenji* (Works of Mao Zedong), vol. 1, 490.

27. James Bertram, *Crisis in China: The Story of the Sian Mutiny* (London: Macmillan & Co., 1937), 108; Harriet Sergeant, *Shanghai* (London: Jonathan Cape, 1991), 5.

28. See Li, *Moi otets Mao Tszedun* (My Father Mao Zedong), 2; Chang, *The Rise of the Chinese Communist Party,* vol. 2, 474–75.

29. Schram, *Mao's Road to Power,* vol. 5, 249.

30. See Titarenko, *VKP(b), Komintern i Kitai: Dokumenty* (The CPSU, the Comintern and China: Documents), vol. 4, 1068; Fenby, *Chiang Kai-shek,* 279.

31. See Titarenko, *VKP(b), Komintern i Kitai: Dokumenty* (The CPSU, the Comintern and China: Documents), vol. 4, 1055–58.

32. See Georgi Dimitrov, *Dnevnik 9 mart 1933–6 fevruari 1949* (Diary, March 9, 1933–February 6, 1949) (Sofia: Universitetsko izdatelstvo "Sv. Kliment Okhridski," 1997), 117.

33. Titarenko, *Kommunisticheskii Internatsional i kitaiskaiia revoliutsiia* (The Communist International and the Chinese Revolution), 266–69.

34. See Schram, *Mao's Road to Power*, vol. 5, 323–32.

35. Ibid., 334.

36. Dimitrov, *Dnevnik* (Diary), 117.

37. Snow, *Red Star Over China*, 409.

38. Bertram, *Crisis in China*, 134–37; see also Snow, *Red Star Over China*, 412.

39. See Tang Peiji, ed., *Zhongguo lishi da nianbiao: Xiandaishi juan* (Chronology of Chinese Historical Events: Contemporary History Volume) (Shanghai: Shanghai cishu chubanshe, 1997), 320; see also Chiang Kai-shek, "The Day I Was Kidnapped," in Li, *The Road to Communism*, 135–41.

40. Ye Zilong, *Ye Zilong huiyilu* (Memoirs of Ye Zilong) (Beijing: Zhongyang wenxian chubanshe, 2000), 38–39.

41. Braun, *A Comintern Agent in China 1932–1939*, 183.

42. Edgar Snow, *Random Notes on Red China (1936–1945)* (Cambridge, MA: East Asian Research Center, Harvard University, 1957), 1.

43. Pang, *Mao Zedong nianpu, 1893–1949* (Chronological Biography of Mao Zedong, 1893–1949), vol. 1, 621.

44. Short, *Mao*, 347.

45. Chang, *The Rise of the Chinese Communist Party*, vol. 2, 481.

46. Ivo Banac, ed., *The Diary of Georgi Dimitrov 1933–1949*, trans. Jane T. Hedges et al. (New Haven, CT: Yale University Press, 2003), 41. See also RGASPI, collection 146, inventory 2, file 3, sheet 29.

47. Banac, *The Diary of Georgi Dimitrov*, 41–42. See also RGASPI, collection 146, inventory 2, file 3, sheets 29–30.

48. Banac, *The Diary of Georgi Dimitrov*, 42. See also RGASPI, collection 146, inventory 2, file 3, sheet 30.

49. Banac, *The Diary of Georgi Dimitrov*, 42. See also RGASPI, collection 146, inventory 2, file 3, sheet 30. Dmitrii Manuilsky at the time was secretary of the ECCI.

50. Titarenko, *Kommunisticheskii internatsional i kitaiskaiia revoliutsiia* (The Communist International and the Chinese Revolution), 270.

51. Snow, *Random Notes on Red China*, 2.

52. Short, *Mao*, 719–20; Jin, *Mao Zedong zhuan (1893–1949)* (Biography of Mao Zedong [1893–1949]), 433.

53. Chiang, *Soviet Russia in China*, 79.

54. Jin, *Mao Zedong zhuan (1893–1949)* (Biography of Mao Zedong [1893–1949]), 431, 432.

55. Pang, *Mao Zedong nianpu, 1893–1949* (Chronological Biography of Mao Zedong, 1893–1949), vol. 1, 639.

56. Titarenko, *Kommunisticheskii Internatsional i kitaiskaiia revoliutsiia* (The Communist International and the Chinese Revolution), 270–71.

57. Ibid., 272; Dimitrov, *Dnevnik* (Diary), 122.

58. *Kangri minzu tongyi zhanxian zhinan* (Directives of the Anti-Japanese National United Front), vol. 1 (n.p., n.d.), 79–81.

59. Li, *Moi otets Mao Tszedun* (My Father Mao Zedong), 1, 5, 39–40, 259.

60. Quoted from Ye, *Ye Zilong huiyilu* (Memoirs of Ye Zilong), 40.

2 I . THE FLIRTATIOUS PHILOSOPHER

1. Braun, *A Comintern Agent in China 1932–1939*, 190.

2. See Cressy-Marcks, *Journey into China*, 156–59; Nym Wales, *My Yenan Notebooks* (Madison, CT: n.p., 1961), 135; Helen Foster Snow, *My China Years* (New York: Morrow, 1984), 231–32.

3. See Evans Fordyce Carlson, *Twin Stars of China: A Behind-the-Scenes Story of China's Valiant Struggle for Existence by a U.S. Marine Who Lived and Moved with the People* (New York: Hyperion Press, 1940), 162.

4. See "Pis'mo Agnes Smedli I. A. Piatnitskomu ot 1 marta 1935 goda" (Letter from Agnes Smedley to I. A. Piatnitsky, March 1, 1935), RGASPI, collection 495, inventory 74, file 287, sheets 1–14; MacKinnon and MacKinnon, *Agnes Smedley*, 146–49, 182–87; Harvey Klehr, John Earl Haynes, and Fridrikh Igorievich Firsov, *The Secret World of American Communism* (New Haven, CT: Yale University Press, 1995), 60–70.

5. See Agnes Smedley, *Battle Hymn of China* (New York: Knopf, 1943), 170–71; Nym Wales, *My Yenan Notebooks,* 62–63; Snow (Wales), *Inside Red China,* 186–87; Snow (Wales), *The Chinese Communists,* 250–61; Snow, *My China Years,* 265, 274–76, 278–79; MacKinnon and MacKinnon, *Agnes Smedley,* 182–89, 192; Wen and Zhang, *Mao Zedong yu He Zizhen* (Mao Zedong and He Zizhen), 110–20.

6. Snow (Wales), *The Chinese Communists,* 252.

7. Quoted from MacKinnon and MacKinnon, *Agnes Smedley,* 190.

8. Ibid., 190–91; Wen and Zhang, *Mao Zedong yu He Zizhen* (Mao Zedong and He Zizhen), 121–22.

9. See Smedley, *China Fights Back,* 4, 8–10; Snow (Wales), *The Chinese Communists,* 254; Snow, *My China Years,* 281–82.

10. Banac, *The Diary of Georgi Dimitrov,* 40.

11. See Titarenko, *VKP(b), Komintern i Kitai: Dokumenty* (The CPSU, the Comintern and China: Documents), vol. 4, 1092; Schram, *Mao's Road to Power,* vol. 4, 356–57.

12. See Yang Kuisong, "Sulian da guimo yuanzhu zhongguo hongjun de yici changshi" (Large-Scale Efforts of Soviet Aid to the Chinese Red Army), in Huang Xiurong, ed., *Sulian, gongchanguoji yu zhongguo geming de guanxi xintan* (New Research on [the History of] Relations Between the Soviet Union, the Comintern, and the Chinese Revolution) (Beijing: Zhonggong dangshi chubanshe, 1995), 324–26.

13. Banac, *The Diary of Georgi Dimitrov,* 36, 57.

14. *Zhou Enlai nianpu (1898–1949)* (Chronological Biography of Zhou Enlai [1898–1949]), 366–67.

15. Pang, *Mao Zedong nianpu, 1893–1949* (Chronological Biography of Mao Zedong, 1893–1949), vol. 1, 677.

16. Quoted from Wales, *My Yenan Notebooks,* 63.

17. *Zhou Enlai nianpu (1898–1949)* (Chronological Biography of Zhou Enlai [1898–1949]), 373–74.

18. According to Chang and Halliday, it was Stalin who unleashed the Sino-Japanese War by making use of General Zhang Zhizhong, "a long-term Communist agent in the heart of the Nationalist army" who provoked the Japanese bombardment of Shanghai. General Zhang supposedly had become a mole of the CCP starting in the summer of 1925, when he was teaching at the Whampoa Academy. Chang and Halliday consider this school the seedbed of communism in China inasmuch as it was organized by Russians. Chang and Halliday, *Mao,* 208–9. On this basis, one should also deem Chiang Kai-shek himself an "agent" of the communist party since he was head of the school.

19. See Vladimirov, *Osobyi raion Kitaia 1942–1945* (Special Region of China, 1942–1945), 239–40.

20. See Pang, *Mao Zedong nianpu, 1893–1949* (Chronological Biography of Mao Zedong, 1893–1949), vol. 1, 654–55; *Lin Boqu zhuan* (Biography of Lin Boqu) (Beijing: Hongqi chubanshe, 1986), 195; Stuart R. Schram, ed., *Mao's Road to Power: Revolutionary Writings, 1912–1949,* vol. 6 (Armonk, NY: M. E. Sharpe, 1999), xxxv.

21. Schram, *Mao's Road to Power,* vol. 6, 11, 12, 14; see also Vladimirov, *Osobyi raion Kitaia 1942–1945* (Special Region of China 1942–1945), 519, 600.

22. Schram, *Mao's Road to Power,* vol. 6, 11, 12; Braun, *A Comintern Agent in China 1932–1939,* 212.

23. Braun, *A Comintern Agent in China 1932–1939,* 211–13; Chang, *The Rise of the Chinese Communist Party,* vol. 2, 533–41; A. V. Pantsov, "Obrazovaniie opornykh baz 8-i Natsional'no-revoliutsionnoi armii v tylu iaponskikh voisk v Severnom Kitae" (Establishment of Eighth Route Army Base Areas in the Japanese Rear in North China), in

M. F. Yuriev, ed., *Voprosy istorii Kitaia* (Problems of Chinese History) (Moscow: Izdatel'stvo MGU, 1981), 39–41.

24. See Wang Shi, ed., *Zhongguo gongchandang lishi jianbian* (Short History of the CCP) (Shanghai: Shanghai renmin chubanshe, 1959), 178–79.

25. Pang Xianzhi, ed., *Mao Zedong nianpu, 1893–1949* (Chronological Biography of Mao Zedong, 1893–1949), vol. 2 (Beijing: Renmin chubanshe, 2002), 17.

26. Mao Zedong, *Mao Zedong wenji* (Works of Mao Zedong), vol. 2 (Beijing: Renmin chubanshe, 1993), 8–10.

27. Schram, *Mao's Road to Power,* vol. 6, 43, 44–45, 51–52, 57.

28. Banac, *The Diary of Georgi Dimitrov,* 67–69.

29. Quoted from Short, *Mao,* 360.

30. Banac, *The Diary of Georgi Dimitrov,* 67.

31. Jin, *Mao Zedong zhuan (1893–1949)* (Biography of Mao Zedong [1893–1949]), 521.

32. Ibid., 522–23.

33. See I. Shirokov and A. Aizenberg, eds., *Materialisticheskaia dialektika* (Materialist Dialectics) (Moscow, 1932); M. Mitin and I. Razumovskii, eds., *Dialekticheskii i istoricheskii materialism v dvukh chastiakh. Uchebnik dlia komvuzov i vuzov* (Dialectical and Historical Materialism, in Two Parts. Textbook of Communist Higher Educational Institutions and Higher Educational Institutions) (Moscow: Partiinoe izdatel'stvo, 1932); M. B. Mitin, ed., "Dialekticheskii materialism" (Dialectical Materialism), *Bolshaia Sovetskaia Entsiklopediia* (Large Soviet Encyclopedia), vol. 22 (Moscow: Sovetskaia entsiklopediia, 1935), 45–235. Mao read translations of the following Chinese texts: Shiluokefu (Shirokov), Ailunbao (Aizenberg), *Bianzhengfa weiwulun jiaocheng* (Textbook on Dialectical Materialism), trans. Li Da and Lei Zhujian, 3rd ed. (Shanghai: Bigengtang shudian, 1935) and 4th ed. (Shanghai: Bigengtang shudian, 1936); Mitin deng (Mitin et al.), *Bianzheng weiwulun yu lishi weiwulun* (Dialectical and Historical Materialism), trans. Shen Zhiyuan, vol. 1 ([Changsha], 1935); Mitin, *Xin zhexue dagang* (Outline of New Philosophy), trans. Ai Siqi and Zheng Yili (Shanghai: Dushu shenhuo chubanshe, 1936).

34. M. B. Mitin, "Predislovie" (Preface), in M. B. Mitin, *Boevye voprosy materialisticheskoi dialektiki* (Urgent Problems of Materialist Dialectics) (Moscow: Partizdat TsK VKP(b), 1936), 3.

35. See Schram, *Mao's Road to Power,* vol. 6, 672, 729, 741; Nick Knight, ed., *Mao Zedong on Dialectical Materialism: Writings on Philosophy* (Armonk, NY: M. E. Sharpe, 1990), 17.

36. Schram, *Mao's Road to Power,* vol. 6, 673.

37. Ibid., 580.

38. Pang, *Mao Zedong nianpu, 1893–1949* (Chronological Biography of Mao Zedong, 1893–1949), vol. 1, 671–72; Schram, *Mao's Road to Power,* vol. 6, 573.

39. Quoted from Pang, *Mao Zedong nianpu, 1893–1949* (Chronological Biography of Mao Zedong, 1893–1949), vol. 2, 41.

40. See Jin, *Mao Zedong zhuan (1893–1949)* (Biography of Mao Zedong [1893–1949]), 522–26.

41. Quoted from Schram, *Mao's Road to Power,* vol. 6, xl.

42. See Cressy-Marcks, *Journey into China,* 162–63.

43. Schram, *Mao's Road to Power,* vol. 6, 193.

44. See *Lichnoe delo Ven Yun* (Personal File of Wen Yun), RGASPI, collection 495, inventory 225, file 420, n.p.

45. Ibid.

46. See Kong Dongmei, *Ting waipo jiang neiguoqude shiqing—Mao Zedong yu He Zizhen* (Listening to Grandmother's Stories About Her Past—Mao Zedong and He Zizhen) (Beijing: Zhongyang wenxian chubanshe, 2005), 172; Kong, *Fankai wo jia laoyingji* (Opening the Old Photo Albums of My Family), 67, 106, 189.

47. See Wen and Zhang, *Mao Zedong yu He Zizhen* (Mao Zedong and He Zizhen), 127.

48. Cressy-Marcks, *Journey into China,* 165.

49. Evans Fordyce Carlson, *Evans F. Carlson on China at War, 1937–1941* (New York: China and US Publications, 1993), 37–38.

50. Carlson, *Twin Stars of China*, 168, 169.

51. Carlson, *Evans F. Carlson on China at War, 1937–1941*, 22, 49.

52. See Frederick C. Teiwes and Warren Sun, "From a Leninist to a Charismatic Party: The CCP's Changing Leadership, 1937–1945," in Saich and van de Ven, *New Perspectives on the Chinese Communist Revolution*, 343.

22. CONSOLIDATING CONTROL OVER THE CCP

1. See Ren Bishi, *Ren Bishi xuanji* (Selected Works of Ren Bishi) (Beijing: Renmin chuban-she, 1987), 164–207; Gao Hua, *Hong taiyang shi zen me yang shengqi de: Yan'an zhengfeng yundong lailong qumai* (How the Red Sun Rose: Analysis of the Yan'an Rectification Move-ment (Hong Kong: Zhongwen daxue chubanshe, 2000), 164–66.

2. See Titarenko, *Kommunisticheskii internatsional i kitaiskaia revoliutsiia* (The Commu-nist International and the Chinese Revolution), 283; *Ren Bishi nianpu, 1904–1950* (Chrono-logical Biography of Ren Bishi, 1904–1950), 370–72.

3. See *Lichnoe delo Mao Tszeduna* (Personal File of Mao Zedong), RGASPI, collection 495, inventory 225, file 71, vol. 1, sheet 185; *Ren Bishi nianpu, 1904–1950* (Chronological Biog-raphy of Ren Bishi, 1904–1950), 372; Xu, *Wang Jiaxiang nianpu, 1906–1974* (Chronological Biography of Wang Jiaxiang, 1906–1974), 190.

4. Quoted from Xu, *Wang Jiaxiang nianpu, 1906–1974* (Chronological Biography of Wang Jiaxiang, 1906–1974), 190; *Ren Bishi nianpu, 1904–1950* (Chronological Biography of Ren Bishi, 1904–1950), 372; Yang, *Zouxiang polie* (Heading for a Split), 76.

5. Xu, *Wang Jiaxiang nianpu, 1906–1974* (Chronological Biography of Wang Jiaxiang, 1906–1974), 196; Pang, *Mao Zedong nianpu, 1893–1949* (Chronological Biography of Mao Zedong, 1893–1949), vol. 2, 90; Jin, *Mao Zedong zhuan (1893–1949)* (Biography of Mao Zedong [1893–1949]), 531.

6. Li, *Huiyi yu yanjiu* (Reminiscences and Studies), vol. 1, 415–16.

7. Quoted from Teiwes and Sun, "From a Leninist to a Charismatic Party," 344.

8. Quoted from Vladimirov, *Osobyi raion Kitaia 1942–1945* (Special Region of China, 1942–1945), 603.

9. See Titov, *Iz istorii bor'by i raskola v rukovodstve KPK 1935–1936 gg.* (From the History of Struggle and Split in the Leadership of the CCP, 1935–1936), 140–43.

10. See M. I. Kalinin, "O Kitae" (On China), in *Kitai: Rasskazy* (China: Stories) (Moscow and Leningrad: Detgiz, 1938), 34–35.

11. E. Snow, *Geroicheskii narod Kitaia* (The Heroic People of China), trans. L. Mirtseva (Moscow: Molodaia gvardiia, 1938), 72, 74; Snow, *Red Star Over China*, 69, 70.

12. Mao Zedong, "Moia zhizn' " (My Life), *Internatsional'naia literatura* (International lit-erature), no. 11 (1937): 101–11; no. 12 (1937): 95–101.

13. *Mao Tsze-dun: Biograficheskii ocherk* (Mao Zedong: Biographical Sketch) (Moscow: OGIZ, 1939).

14. Emi, *Mao Tszedun, Chzhu De* (Mao Zedong, Zhu De).

15. Schram, *Mao's Road to Power*, vol. 6, 534–35.

16. Ibid., 529.

17. Ibid., 538–39.

18. See "Doklad tov. Mao Tsze-duna na VI rasshirennom plenume TsK kompartii Kitaia ot 12–14 oktabria 1938 goda: O novom etape razvitiia antiiaponskoi natsional'noi voiny i edi-nogo antiiaponskogo natsional'nogo fronta" (Report of Comrade Mao Zedong at the Sixth Enlarged Plenum of the CC of the Chinese Communist Party, October 12–14, 1938: On the New Stage of Development of the Anti-Japanese National War and the Anti-Japanese Na-tional United Front), RGASPI, collection 495, inventory 225, file 71, vol. 1, sheets 66–215; see also *Lichnoe delo Lin Biao* (Personal File of Lin Biao), RGASPI, collection 495, inventory 225, file 53, vol. 1, sheet 207.

19. On Hatem see Sidney Shapiro, *Ma Haide: The Saga of American Doctor George Hatem in China* (Beijing: Foreign Languages Press, 2004).

20. R. Karmen, "God v Kitae" (A Year in China), *Znamia* (Banner), no. 8 (1940): 75.

21. See Braun, *A Comintern Agent in China 1932–1939*, 248–50; Shapiro, *Ma Haide*, 55–57; Roxane Witke, *Comrade Chiang Ch'ing* (Boston: Little, Brown, 1977), 145; Helen Foster Snow, *My China Years*, 262–63.

22. See Li, *The Private Life of Chairman Mao*, 175.

23. See *Lichnoe delo Mao Tsze-duna* (Personal File of Mao Zedong), RGASPI, collection 495, inventory 225, file 71, vol. 1, sheet 17; Karmen, *God v Kitae* (A Year in China), 77; Schram, *Mao's Road to Power*, vol. 6, 297–300; Witke, *Comrade Chiang Ch'ing*, 155; Wen Songhui, "Mao Zedong chushi Jiang Qing" (Mao Zedong's First Meeting with Jiang Qing), *Renmin zhengxie bao* (Newspaper of the Chinese people's political consultative conference), September 10, 2004; Roger Faligot and Rémi Kauffer, *The Chinese Secret Service*, trans. Christine Donougher (New York: Morrow, 1989), 14–15, 81–83, 122–28; John Byron and Robert Pack, *The Claws of the Dragon: Kang Sheng—The Evil Genius Behind Mao and His Legacy of Terror in People's China* (New York: Simon & Schuster, 1992), 145–49; Ross Terrill, *Madam Mao: The White-Boned Demon*, rev. ed. (Stanford, CA: Stanford University Press, 1999), 14–142; Braun, *A Comintern Agent in China 1932–1939*, 250.

24. See "Vypiska iz materiala vkh. no. 8497 ot 10 Dekabria 1949 g. (Doklad t. Terebina, nakhodivshegosia v Kitae v kachestve vracha pri rukovodstve TsK KPK s 1942 po 1949 g." (Excerpt from Material Incoming No. 8497, December 10, 1949 [Report of Comrade Terebin, Who Was in China as a Physician Attached to the Leadership of the CC CCP from 1942 to 1949), RGASPI, collection 495, inventory 225, file 71, vol. 4, sheet 71; I. V. Kovalev, "Rossiia v Kitae (s missiei v Kitae)" (Russia in China [My Mission to China]), *Duel'* (Duel), November 5, 1997.

25. See *Lichnoe delo Ven Yun* (Personal File of Wen Yun), n.p.; *Lichnoe delo Mao Anyina (Yun Fu)* (Personal File of Mao Anying [Yong Fu]), RGASPI, collection 495, inventory 225, file 71, vol. 10, sheets 2–17.

26. Quoted from Li, *Moi otets Mao Tszedun* (My Father Mao Zedong), 15.

27. *Lichnoe delo Mao Anying (Yun Fu)* (Personal file of Mao Anying [Yong Fu]), 27–28; *Lichnoe delo Yun Shu* (Personal file of Yong Shu), 23; Mao Zedong, *Mao Zedong shuxin xuanji* (Selected Letters of Mao Zedong) (Beijing: Renmin chubanshe, 1983), 166–67.

28. See Mao, *Mao Zedong shuxin xuanji* (Selected Letters of Mao Zedong), 157.

29. Li, *Moi otets Mao Tszedun* (My Father Mao Zedong), 40; Ma, *Hongse diyi jiazu* (The First Red Family), 70; Pang, *Mao Zedong nianpu, 1893–1949* (Chronological Biography of Mao Zedong, 1893–1949), vol. 2, 201.

30. See Pantsov, "Obrazovanie opornykh baz 8-i Natsional'no-revoliutsionnoi armii v tylu iaponskikh voisk v Severnom Kitae" (Establishment of Eighth Route Army Base Areas in the Japanese Rear in North China), 41–48.

31. Vladimirov, *Osobyi raion Kitaia* (Special Region of China), 77–78.

32. See Zhang, *Zhang Wentian nianpu* (Chronological Biography of Zhang Wentian), vol. 1, 624.

33. Stuart R. Schram, ed., *Mao's Road to Power: Revolutionary Writings 1912–1949*, vol. 7 (Armonk, NY: M. E. Sharpe, 2005), 330–69.

34. Ibid., 262–64.

35. Milovan Djilas, *Conversations with Stalin*, trans. Michael B. Petrovich (New York: Harcourt, Brace & World, 1962), 33.

36. Ibid. See also Vladimir Dedijer, *The War Diaries of Vladimir Dedijer*, vol. 3 (Ann Arbor: University of Michigan Press, 1990), 313.

37. See Djilas, *Conversations with Stalin*.

38. *Lichnoe delo Mao Tszeduna* (Personal File of Mao Zedong), RGASPI, collection 495, inventory 225, file 71, vol. 3, sheet 189.

39. Ibid., 186–89; RGASPI, collection 495, inventory 74, file 314.

40. Banac, *The Diary of Georgi Dimitrov*, 295.

41. See Pantsov and Levine, *Chinese Comintern Activists: An Analytic Biographic Dictionary* (manuscript), 302.

42. RGASPI, collection 17, inventory 162, file 36, sheet 41.

43. Banac, *The Diary of Georgi Dimitrov*, 172, 176.

44. To be sure, such generosity after the Nazi attack on the USSR might be explained by Stalin's gratitude to Mao, who on June 15, 1941, had informed the Kremlin leader via the Soviet military attaché Nikolai Roshchin of the forthcoming invasion, giving the precise date, June 22. Mao had received this information from his secret agent in Chongqing, Yan Baohang. In his return telegram after the outbreak of the war, Stalin thanked Mao, emphasizing that his accurate information had helped the Russians initiate their supposed military preparations on time. "Letter from Yan Mingfu, a son of Yan Baohang, to the Russian Ministry of Foreign Affairs, September 9, 2005," Alexander V. Pantsov's private archives.

45. Dimitrov, *Dnevnik* (Diary), 101.

46. See Raymond F. Wylie, *The Emergence of Maoism: Mao Tse-tung, Ch'en Po-ta, and the Search for Chinese Theory 1935–1945* (Stanford, CA: Stanford University Press, 1980), 227; Li Hua-Yu, "Stalin's *Short Course* and Mao's Socialist Economic Transformation of China in the Early 1950s," *Russian History* 29, nos. 2–4 (Summer–Fall–Winter 2002): 357–76.

47. See Pang, *Mao Zedong nianpu, 1893–1949* (Chronological Biography of Mao Zedong, 1893–1949), vol. 2, 326.

48. Schram, *Mao's Road to Power*, vol. 7, 810.

49. Ibid., 826–32; Pang, *Mao Zedong nianpu, 1893–1949* (Chronological Biography of Mao Zedong, 1893–1949), vol. 2, 349–51.

50. Quoted from Vladimirov, *Osobyi raion Kitaia 1942–1945* (Special Region of China, 1942–1945), 123.

51. Ibid., 40, 41.

52. Liu Shaoqi, *Selected Works of Liu Shaoqi*, vol. 1 (Beijing: Foreign Languages Press, 1984), 136.

53. See Liu Chongwen and Chen Shaochou, eds., *Liu Shaoqi nianpu, 1898–1969* (Chronological Biography of Liu Shaoqi, 1898–1969), vol. 1 (Beijing: Zhongyang wenxian chubanshe, 1998), 360.

54. See Li Min et al., eds., *Jenshide Mao Zedong: Mao Zedong shenbian gongzuo renyuan de huiyi* (The Real Mao Zedong: Reminiscences of Persons Who Worked by Mao's Side) (Beijing: Zhongyang wenxian chubanshe, 2004), 2; Wang, *Zhongguo gongchandang zuzhi shi ziliao huibian* (Collection of Documents on the History of CCP Organizations), 424–26.

55. See Zhou Guoquan et al., *Wang Ming nianpu* (Chronological Biography of Wang Ming) ([Hefei]: Anhui renmin chubanshe, 1991), 121, 123.

56. Ibid., 120.

57. Banac, *The Diary of Georgi Dimitrov*, 256.

58. Ibid.

59. See *Lichnoe delo Van Mina* (Personal File of Wang Ming), RGASPI, collection 495, inventory 225, file 6, vol. 2, sheet 6.

60. Banac, *The Diary of Georgi Dimitrov*, 259.

61. Ibid., 260.

62. Ibid., 288.

63. Titarenko, *Kommunisticheskii Internatsional i kitaiskaia revoliutsiia* (The Communist International and the Chinese Revolution), 296.

64. RGASPI, collection 146, inventory 2, file 13, sheets 4, 5.

65. Ibid., sheet 16; see also Vladimirov, *Osobyi raion Kitaia 1942–1945* (Special Region of China 1942–1945), 251–53.

66. RGASPI, collection 146, inventory 2, file 13, sheet 8.

67. Ibid., 26–27. Wang Ming's daughter who lived in Moscow was adopted by Dimitrov.

68. Quoted from Wang Ming, *Mao's Betrayal*, trans. Vic Schneierson (Moscow: Progress, 1979), 157.

69. See Mao Zedong, *Selected Works*, vol. 3 (Beijing: Foreign Languages Press, 1969), 205–70.

70. See Vladimirov, *Osobyi raion Kitaia 1942–1945* (Special Region of China 1942–1945), 487.

71. See "Resolution of the CCP CC on Certain Historical Questions," in Saich, *The Rise to Power of the Chinese Communist Party,* 1164–79.

72. Liu Shao-chi, *On the Party* (Beijing: Foreign Languages Press, 1950), 157.

73. Mao Zedong, *Mao Zedong wenji* (Works of Mao Zedong), vol. 5 (Beijing: Renmin chubanshe, 1996), 260–61.

74. Quoted from Mao, "Qida gongzuo fangzhen" (Work Report at the Seventh Congress), 8.

75. See A. V. Pantsov, "K diskussii v KPK vokrug 'idei Mao Tsze-duna' " (On the Discussion Within the CCP of "Mao Zedong Thought"), *Rabochii klass i sovremennyi mir* (The working class and the contemporary world), no. 3 (1982): 61–64.

76. See Pang, *Mao Zedong nianpu, 1893–1949* (Chronological Biography of Mao Zedong, 1893–1949), vol. 2, 607, 617; vol. 3 (Beijing: Renmin chubanshe, 2002), 10–12.

23. STALIN, MAO, AND THE NEW DEMOCRATIC REVOLUTION IN CHINA

1. See Freda Utley, *China at War* (New York: John Day, 1939); Claire and William Band, *Dragon Fangs: Two Years with Chinese Guerrillas* (London: Allen & Unwin, 1947); T. A. Bisson, "China's Part in a Coalition War," *Far Eastern Survey,* no. 12 (1939): 139; Harrison Forman, *Report from Red China* (New York: Henry Holt, 1945). See also Kenneth Shewmaker, *Americans and Chinese Communists, 1927–1945* (Ithaca, NY: Cornell University Press, 1971), 239–62.

2. See David D. Barrett, *Dixie Mission: The United States Army Observer Group in Yenan, 1944* (Berkeley, CA: Center for Chinese Studies, 1970); Carrole J. Carter, *Mission to Yenan: American Liaison with the Chinese Communists 1944–1947* (Lexington: University Press of Kentucky, 1997); Vladimirov, *Osobyi raion Kitaia 1942–1945* (Special Region of China 1942–1945), 306–7, 313, 626.

3. Joseph Esherick, ed., *Lost Chance in China: The World War II Dispatches of John S. Service* (New York: Random House, 1974), 308, 309.

4. See *United States Relations with China: With Special Reference to the Period 1944–1949* (New York: Greenwood Press, 1968), 92–93, 94–96; "Statement by General Patrick J. Hurley on December 5 & 6, 1945," *United States–China relations. Hearings before the Committee on Foreign Relations, United States Senate, Ninety-second Congress, First Session on the Evolution of U.S. Policy Toward Mainland China (Executive Hearings Held July 21, 1971; Made Public December 8, 1971) and Hearings Before the Committee on Foreign Relations, United States Senate, Seventy-ninth Congress, First Session on the Situation in the Far East, Particularly China. December 5, 6, 7, and 10, 1945* (Washington: U.S. Government Printing Office, 1971), 78, 122.

5. Lyman P. Van Slyke, ed., *The Chinese Communist Movement: A Report of the United States War Department, July 1945* (Stanford, CA: Stanford University Press, 1968), 1, 258.

6. See Mao, *Selected Works of Mao Tse-tung,* vol. 3, 219.

7. See Dieter Heinzig, *The Soviet Union and Communist China, 1945–1950: The Arduous Road to the Alliance* (Armonk, NY: M. E. Sharpe, 2004), 51–125.

8. See A. V. Torkunov, *Zagadochnaia voina: Koreiskii konflikt 1950–1953* (The Enigmatic War: The Korean Conflict 1950–1953) (Moscow: ROSSPEN, 2000), 6–29.

9. O. Arne Westad et al., eds., "77 Conversations Between Chinese and Foreign Leaders on the Wars in Indochina," *CWIHP Working Paper,* no. 22 (May 1998): 105.

10. Quoted from A. M. Ledovsky, *SSSR i Stalin v sud'bakh Kitaia: Dokumenty i svidel'stva uchastnika sobytii, 1937–1952* (The USSR and Stalin in China's Fate: Documents and Witness of a Participant, 1937–1952) (Moscow: Pamiatniki istoricheskoi mysli, 1999), 61. See

also "Zapis' besedy tovarishcha Stalina I. V. s Predsedatelem Tsentral'nogo narodnogo pravitel'stva Kitaiskoi Narodnoi Respubliki Mao Tsze-dunom 16 dekabria 1949 g." (Record of Comrade J. V. Stalin's Conversation with the Chairman of the Central People's Government of the Chinese People's Republic Mao Zedong, December 16, 1949), RGASPI, collection 55, inventory 11, file 329, sheets 9–17; "Zapis' besedy tovarishcha Stalina I. V. s Predsedatelem Tsentral'nogo narodnogo pravitel'stva Kitaiskoi Narodnoi Respubliki Mao Tsze-dunom 22 ianvaria 1950 g." (Record of Comrade J. V. Stalin's Conversation with the Chairman of the Central People's Government of the Chinese People's Republic Mao Zedong, January 22, 1950), ibid., 29–38; *CWIHP Bulletin,* nos. 6–7 (1995/1996): 5–9; Niu Jun, "The Origins of the Sino-Soviet Alliance," in Westad, *Brothers in Arms,* 70.

11. See Kurdiukov, *Sovetsko-kitaiskie otnosheniia, 1917–1957: Sbornik dokumentov* (Soviet-Chinese relations, 1917–1957: A Collection of Documents), 196–203.

12. See Yugoslav and Bulgarian records of the secret Soviet-Bulgarian-Yugoslav meeting in the Kremlin, February 10, 1948, at which Stalin referred to this fact. The texts of the records are published in *CWIHP Bulletin,* no. 10 (March 1998): 128–34. See also Vladimir Dedijer, *Tito Speaks* (London: Weidenfeld & Nicolson, 1953), 331; "Minutes, Mao's Conversation with a Yugoslavian Communist Union Delegation, Beijing, September [undated] 1956," *CWIHP Bulletin,* nos. 6–7 (1995/1996): 149; Shi Zhe, *Zai lishi juren shenbian* (At the Side of Historical Titans), rev. ed. (Beijing: Zhongyang wenxian chubanshe, 1995), 308; "Mao Tszedun o kitaiskoi politike Kominterna i Stalina" (Mao Zedong on the China Policy of the Comintern and of Stalin), *Problemy Dal'nego Vostoka* (Far Eastern affairs), no. 5 (1998): 107; Vladislav Zubok, "The Mao-Khrushchev Conversations, July 31–August 3, 1958 and October 2, 1959," *CWIHP Bulletin,* nos. 12/13 (Fall/Winter 2001): 255; David Wolff, " 'One Finger's Worth of Historical Events': New Russian and Chinese Evidence on the Sino-Soviet Alliance and Split, 1948–1959," *CWIHP Working Paper,* no. 30 (August 2000): 54, 77; Westad, "77 Conversations between Chinese and Foreign Leaders on the Wars in Indochina," 105–6.

13. "Mao Tszedun o kitaiskoi politike Kominterna i Stalina" (Mao Zedong on the China Policy of the Comintern and of Stalin), 107.

14. Pang, *Mao Zedong nianpu, 1893–1949* (Chronological Biography of Mao Zedong, 1893–1949), vol. 3, 10.

15. See Westad, "77 Conversations Between Chinese and Foreign Leaders on the Wars in Indochina," 106.

16. O. Borisov [O. B. Rakhmanin] and M. Titarenko, eds., *Vystupleniia Mao Tsze-duna, ranee ne publikovavshiesia v kitaiskoi pechati* (Mao Zedong's Speeches Previously Unpublished in the Chinese Press), series 2 (Moscow: Progress, 1975), 168.

17. Quoted from *Peng Zhen nianpu, 1902–1997* (Chronological Biography of Peng Zhen, 1902–1997), vol. 1 (Beijing: Zhongyang wenxian chubanshe, 2002), 280.

18. "Pismo I. V. Stalina V. M. Molotovu, L. P. Beria, G. M. Malenkovu, A. I. Mikoyanu, 10 noiabria, 1945 g." (Letter from J. V. Stalin to V. M. Molotov, L. P. Beria, G. M. Malenkov, A. I. Mikoyan, November 10, 1945), RGASPI, collection 558, inventory 11, file 98, sheet 81.

19. Odd Arne Westad, *Cold War and Revolution: Soviet-American Rivalry and the Origins of the Chinese Civil War, 1944–1946* (New York: Columbia University Press, 1993), 152.

20. See Heinzig, *The Soviet Union and Communist China, 1945–1950,* 98.

21. Ibid., 98–101; Westad, *Cold War and Revolution,* 161.

22. Dean Acheson, "Letter of Transmittal," in *United States Relations with China,* xv.

23. See Witke, *Comrade Chiang Ch'ing,* 199; Wu, *Mao Zedong guanghui licheng dituji* (Atlas of Mao Zedong's Glorious Historical Path), 75.

24. See Peng, *Memoirs of a Chinese Marshal,* 453.

25. General Hu Zongnan, one of Chiang Kai-shek's most faithful officers, was at the head of the Guomindang troops that took Yan'an. Based just on the fact that he, like General Zhang Zhizhong, had been at the Whampoa Academy in the mid-1920s, Chang and Halliday conclude that he, too, was a "Red 'sleeper.' " Chang and Halliday, *Mao,* 312.

26. Quoted from Huang Zheng, "Mao Anying," in Hu Hua, ed., *Zhonggongdang shi renwu*

zhuan (Biographies of Persons in the History of the CCP), vol. 21 (Xi'an: Shaanxi renmin chubanshe, 1985), 151.

27. See *Lichnoe delo Mao Anyina (Yun Fu)* (Personal File of Mao Anying [Yong Fu]), 22.

28. See Huang, "Mao Anying," 152.

29. *Lichnoe delo Mao Tszeduna* (Personal File of Mao Zedong), RGASPI, collection 495, inventory 225, file 71, vol. 1, sheet 25.

30. Quoted from Li, *The Private Life of Chairman Mao*, 82.

31. Quoted from Li, *Moi otets Mao Tszedun* (My Father Mao Zedong), 59.

32. Ibid., 21.

33. See Xu, *Wang Jiaxiang nianpu, 1906–1974* (Chronological Biography of Wang Jiaxiang, 1906–1974), 348; Zhu Zhongli, *Cancan hongye* (A Bright Red Leaf) (Changsha: Hunan renmin chubanshe, 1985), 115–17, 124.

34. Li, *Moi otets Mao Tszedun* (My Father Mao Zedong), 23–24.

35. See Deng Xiaoping, *Deng Xiaoping zishu* (Autobiographic Notes of Deng Xiaoping) (Beijing: Jiefangjun chubanshe, 2004), 118.

36. See Wu, *Mao Zedong guanghui licheng dituji* (Atlas of Mao Zedong's Glorious Historical Path), 81.

37. *Lichnoe delo Mao Tszeduna* (Personal File of Mao Zedong), vol. 1, 26.

38. Mao Zedong, *Selected Works*, vol. 4 (Beijing: Foreign Languages Press, 1969), 100, 101.

39. Ibid., 133–34.

40. See Wu, *Mao Zedong guanghui licheng dituji* (Atlas of Mao Zedong's Glorious Historical Path), 81.

41. Acheson, "Letter of Transmittal," vi.

42. Li, *The Private Life of Chairman Mao*, 37.

43. See A. V. Meliksetov, ed., *Istoriia Kitaia* (History of China) (Moscow: Izdatel'stvo MGU, 1998), 582–88; Jonathan D. Spence, *The Search for Modern China* (New York: Norton, 1990), 473–80.

44. See Brian Murray, "Stalin, the Cold War, and the Division of China: A Multi-Archival Mystery," *CWIHP Working Paper*, no. 12 (June 1995): 1–17.

45. See Westad, "77 Conversations Between Chinese and Foreign Leaders on the Wars in Indochina," 108.

46. See RGASPI, collection 17, inventory 162, file 40, sheets 1–2.

47. Ibid.

48. RGASPI, collection of unsorted documents.

49. Quoted from Westad, "77 Conversations Between Chinese and Foreign Leaders on the Wars in Indochina," 108; see also *Problemy Dal'nego Vostoka* (Far Eastern affairs), no. 1 (1989), 141; record of Kang Sheng's speech at the meeting of the CPSU and CCP delegations, July 13, 1963, published in *CWIHP Bulletin*, no. 10 (1998): 182.

50. See John W. Garver, *Chinese-Soviet Relations, 1937–1945: The Diplomacy of Chinese Nationalism* (New York: Oxford University Press, 1988), 261.

51. Khrushchev, *Memoirs of Nikita Khrushchev*, vol. 3, 409.

52. Chuev, *Molotov Remembers*, 81.

53. *Lichnoe delo Mao Tsze-duna* (Personal File of Mao Zedong), RGASPI, collection 495, inventory 225, file 71, vol. 2, sheets 249, 250.

54. See RGASPI, collection 17, inventory 162, file 40, sheet 183; *Lichnoe delo Tszian Tsin* (Personal File of Jiang Qing), RGASPI, collection 495, inventory 225, file 3217, n.p.

55. See A. I. Kartunova, "Vstrechi v Moskve s Tszian Tsin, zhenoi Mao Tszeduna" (Meetings in Moscow with Jiang Qing, the Wife of Mao Zedong), *Kentavr* (Centaur) 1–2 (1992): 121–27.

56. See "Zapis' priema tovarishchem Stalinym delegatsii TsK KPK" (Report on Comrade Stalin's Reception of a CC CCP Delegation), RGASPI, collection 558, inventory 11, file 329, sheets 1–7.

57. See RGASPI, collection 17, inventory 162, file 41, sheet 49.

58. RGASPI, collection of unsorted documents.

59. "Minutes, Mao's Conversation with a Yugoslavian Communist Union Delegation," 151.

60. Quoted from Ledovsky, *SSSR i Stalin v sud'bakh Kitaia* (The USSR and Stalin in China's Fate), 53.

61. Quoted from Westad, *Brothers in Arms*, 298.

62. Quoted from telegram, "Stalin to Mao Zedong, April 20, 1948," ibid., 298–99.

63. Quoted from Westad, *Brothers in Arms*, 300.

64. Mao, *Mao Zedong wenji* (Works of Mao Zedong), vol. 5, 140–41, 145.

65. See Pang, *Mao Zedong nianpu, 1893–1949* (Chronological Biography of Mao Zedong, 1893–1949), vol. 2, 449; Sergei Goncharov, John W. Lewis, and Xue Litai, *Uncertain Partners: Stalin, Mao, and the Korean War* (Stanford, CA: Stanford University Press, 1993), 40; Wolff, "One Finger's Worth of Historical Events," 55; B. N. Vereshchagin, *V starom i novom Kitae. Iz vospominanii diplomata* (In Old and New China: Reminiscences of a Diplomat) (Moscow: IDV RAN, 1999), 124; Heinzig, *The Soviet Union and Communist China 1945–1950*, 135–56.

66. See Ledovsky, *SSSR i Stalin v sud'bakh Kitaia* (The USSR and Stalin in China's Fate), 65.

67. See A. I. Mikoyan, *Tak bylo: Razmyshleniia o minuvshem* (How It Was: Reflections on the Past) (Moscow: Vagrius, 1999), 528–29.

68. Quoted from Zhou Enlai, "Rech' na Vsekitaiskom finansovo-ekonomicheskom soveshchanii" (Speech at the All-China Financial-Economic Conference), *Arkhiv vneshnei politiki Rossiiskoi Federatsii* (Archives on the Foreign Policy of the Russian Federation) [hereafter AVP RF], collection 0100, inventory 46, file 374, folder 121, sheet 9.

69. Ibid.

70. See Mao, *Selected Works of Mao Tse-tung*, vol. 4, 411–24.

71. Borisov and Titarenko, *Vystupleniia Mao Tsze-duna, ranee ne publikovavshiesia v kitaiskoi pechati* (Mao Zedong's Speeches Previously Unpublished in the Chinese Press), series 2, 181.

72. Pang, *Mao Zedong nianpu, 1893–1949* (Chronological Biography of Mao Zedong, 1893–1949), vol. 3, 469.

24. VISIT TO THE RED MECCA

1. See "Vypiska iz materiala vkh. no. 8497 ot 10 dekabria 1949 g. (Doklad t. Terebina, nakhodivshegosia v Kitae v kachestve vracha pri rukovodstve TsK KPK s 1942 po 1949 g.)" (Excerpts from Material Incoming No. 8497, December 10, 1949 [Report of Comrade Terebin Assigned to China as Physician Attached to the Leadership of the CC CCP from 1942 Through 1949]), 72.

2. See Kartunova, *Vstrechi v Moskve s Tsian Tsin, zhenoi Mao Tszeduna* (Meetings in Moscow with Jiang Qing, Mao Zedong's wife), 127.

3. Witke, *Comrade Chiang Ch'ing*, 449.

4. Li, *Moi otets Mao Tszedun* (My Father Mao Zedong), 29, 30, 32, 33.

5. Witke, *Comrade Chiang Ch'ing*, 166.

6. See "Vypiska iz materiala vkh. no. 8497 ot 10 dekabria 1949 g. (Doklad t. Terebina, nakhodivshegosia v Kitae v kachestve vracha pri rukovodstve TsK KPK s 1942 po 1949 g.)" (Excerpts from Material Incoming No. 8497, December 10, 1949 [Report of Comrade Terebin Assigned to China as Physician Attached to the Leadership of the CC CCP from 1942 Through 1949]), 71.

7. Li, *Moi otets Mao Tszedun* (My Father Mao Zedong), 38.

8. See Li, *Zhenshide Mao Zedong*, 750–56; Li, *The Private Life of Chairman Mao*, 66.

9. Quoted from O. B. Rakhmanin, "Vzaimnootnosheniia mezhdu I. V. Stalinym i Mao Tszedunom glazami ochevidtsa" (Relations Between J. V. Stalin and Mao Zedong Through the Eyes of an Eyewitness), *Novaia i noveishaia istoriia* (Modern and contemporary history), no. 1 (1998): 85.

10. See "Zapis' besedy tovarishcha Stalina I. V. s predsedatelem Tsentral'nogo narodnogo pravitel'stva Kitaiskoi Narodnoi Respubliki Mao Tsze-dunom 16 dekabria 1949 g." (Rec-

ord of the Conversation Between Comrade J. V. Stalin and the Chairman of the Central People's Government of the Chinese People's Republic Mao Zedong, December 16, 1949), 9–17; "Zapis' besedy I. V. Stalina s Predsedatelem Tsentral'nogo narodnogo pravitel'stva Kitaiskoi Narodnoi Respubliki Mao Tsze-dunom 22 ianvaria 1950 g." (Record of Conversation Between J. V. Stalin and the Chairman of the Central People's Government of the Chinese People's Republic Mao Zedong, January 22, 1950), 29–38; *CWIHP Bulletin*, nos. 6–7 (1995/1996): 5–19.

11. I. V. Kovalev, "Dialog Stalina s Mao Tszedunom" (Stalin's Dialogue with Mao Zedong), *Problemy Dal'nego Vostoka* (Far Eastern affairs), no. 6 (1991): 84.

12. "Vypiska iz materiala vkh no. 8497 ot 10 dekabria 1949 g. (Doklad t. Terebina, nakhodivshegosia v Kitae v kachestve vracha pri rukovodstve TsK KPK s 1942 po 1949 g.)" (Excerpt from Material Incoming No. 8497, December 10, 1949 [Report of Comrade Terebin Assigned to China as Physician Attached to the Leadership of the CC CCP from 1942 Through 1949]), 69–70; *Lichnoe delo Mao Tszeduna* (Personal File of Mao Zedong), RGASPI, collection 495, inventory 225, file 71, vol. 3, sheet 289.

13. See RGASPI, collection 17, inventory 162, file 41, sheets 50–51; file 42, sheet 163.

14. Ibid., collection 17, inventory 162, file 42, sheet 163.

15. See I. V. Kovalev, "Rossiia i Kitai (s missiei v Kitae)" (Russia and China [My Mission to China]), *Duel'* (Duel), February 25, 1997.

16. See *Lichnoe delo Mao Anina (Yun Fu)* (Personal File of Mao Anying [Yong Fu]), 31; Ma, *Hongse diyi jiazu* (The First Red Family), 141–43.

17. Kovalev, "Rossiia i Kitai (s missiei v Kitae)" (Russia and China [My Mission to China]), *Duel'* (Duel), February 25, 1997.

18. See "Zapiska I. V. Kovaleva ot 24 dekabria 1949 g.," *Novaia i noveishaia istoriia* (Modern and contemporary history), no. 1 (1998): 139; Shi Zhe and Shi Qiulang, *Wode yisheng— She Zhe zishu* (My Life—She Zhe's Reminiscences) (Beijing: Renmin chubanshe, 2002), 323.

19. *Pravda* (Truth), December 17, 1949.

20. See I. V. Kovalev, "Rossiia i Kitai (s missiei v Kitae)" (Russia and China [My Mission to China]), *Duel'* (Duel), March 25, 1997; K. I. Krutikov, *Na kitaiskom napravleniiu: Iz vospominanii diplomata* (Pointed Toward China: A Diplomat's Reminiscences) (Moscow: IDV RAN, 2003), 123.

21. *CWIHP Bulletin*, nos. 6–7 (1995/1996): 5, 6.

22. Kovalev, "Rossiia i Kitai (s missiei v Kitae)" (Russia and China [My Mission to China]), *Duel'* (Duel), March 25, 1997.

23. See *Lichnoe delo Mao Tszeduna* (Personal File of Mao Zedong), RGASPI, collection 495, inventory 225, file 71, vol. 1, sheets 180–84.

24. Ibid., sheets 182 reverse–183.

25. "Mao Tszedun o kitaiskoi politike Kominterna i Stalina" (Mao Zedong on the China Policy of the Comintern and Stalin), 106; Mao, *Mao Zedong on Diplomacy* (Beijing: Foreign Languages Press, 1998), 253.

26. Several years later, in conversation with Mao Zedong, Khrushchev confirmed that Stalin did eavesdrop on him. "Yes. . . . He had bugged us as well, he even bugged himself. Once, when I was on vacation with him, he admitted that he mistrusted himself. I am good-for-nothing, he said, I mistrust myself." Zubok, "The Mao-Khrushchev Conversations" (Beijing: Foreign Languages Press, 1998), 255.

27. See Vereshchagin, *V starom i novom Kitae* (In Old and New China), 124; see also Wang Dongxing, *Wang Dongxing riji* (Diary of Wang Dongxing) (Beijing: Zhongguo shehui kexue chubanshe, 1993), 156–212.

28. Kovalev, "Rossiia i Kitai (s missiei v Kitae)" (Russia and China [My Mission to China]), *Duel'* (Duel), March 25, 1997.

29. N. T. Fedorenko, "Stalin i Mao: Besedy v Moskve" (Stalin and Mao: Conversations in Moscow), *Problemy Dal'nego Vostoka* (Far Eastern affairs), no. 1 (1989): 152, 156.

30. Shi, *Zai lishi juren shenbian* (At the Side of History's Giants), 446–47.

31. See "Zapis' besedy tovarishcha Stalina I. V. s Predsedatelem Tsentral'nogo narodnogo pravitel'stva Kitaiskoi Narodnoi Respubliki Mao Tsze-dunom 16 dekabria 1949 g." (Report on Comrade J. V. Stalin's Conversation with the Chairman of the Central People's Government of the Chinese People's Republic Mao Zedong, December 16, 1949), 9–17; *CWIHP Bulletin*, nos. 6–7 (1995/1996): 5–7.

32. *CWIHP Bulletin*, nos. 6–7 (1995/1996), 8. See also "Zapis' besedy I. V. Stalina s Predsedatelem Tsentral'nogo narodnogo pravitel'stva Kitaiskoi Narodnoi Respubliki Mao Tsze-dunom 22 ianvaria 1950 g." (Record of J. V. Stalin's Conversation with the Chairman of the Central People's Government of the Chinese People's Republic Mao Zedong, January 22, 1950), 32.

33. See *CWIHP Bulletin*, nos. 6–7 (1995/1996), 9; "Zapis' besedy I. V. Stalina s Predsedatelem Tsentral'nogo narodnogo pravitel'stva Kitaiskoi Narodnoi Respubliki Mao Tsze-dunom 22 ianvaria 1950 g." (Record of J. V. Stalin's conversation with the Chairman of the Central People's Government of the Chinese People's Republic Mao Zedong, January 22, 1950), 37.

34. See RGASPI, collection 17, inventory 17, file 1080, sheets 65, 252; inventory 163, file 1595, sheets 115, 116; file 1607, sheets 70, 71; Kurdiukov, *Sovetsko-kitaiskie otnosheniia* (Soviet-Chinese Relations), 227–29; G. Ganshin and T. Zazerskaia, "Ukhaby na doroge 'bratskoi druzhby' " (Potholes on the Road of "Fraternal Friendship"), *Problemy Dal'nego Vostoka* (Far Eastern affairs), no. 6 (1994): 67–72; Shu Guang Zhang, "Sino-Soviet Economic Cooperation," in Westad, *Brothers in Arms*, 198; Li Ping and Ma Zhisun, eds., *Zhou Enlai nianpu (1949–1976)* (Chronological Biography of Zhou Enlai [1949–1976]), vol. 1 (Beijing: Zhongyang wenxian chubanshe, 1997), 22–25.

35. See "Zapis' besedy I. V. Stalina s Predsedatelem Tsentral'nogo narodnogo pravitel'stva Kitaiskoi Narodnoi Respubliki Mao Tsze-dunom 22 ianvaria 1950 g." (Memorandum of Conversation between J. V. Stalin and the Chairman of the Central People's Government of the Chinese People's Republic Mao Zedong, January 22, 1950), 34–35; *CWIHP Bulletin*, nos. 6–7 (1995/1996): 8–9. See also Mao Zedong's January 25, 1950, telegram to Liu Shaoqi concerning the Soviet-Chinese negotiations and drafts of various documents in *CWIHP Bulletin*, nos. 8–9 (1996/1997): 235.

36. See RGASPI, collection 17, inventory 3, file 1080, sheets 61, 192–242.

37. See ibid., 82, 260, 261; Kurdiukov, *Sovetsko-kitaiskie otnosheniia* (Soviet-Chinese Relations), 221–22.

38. Khrushchev, *Memoirs of Nikita Khrushchev*, vol. 3, 412, 414.

39. Quoted from B. T. Kulik, *Sovetsko-kitaiskii raskol: Prichiny i posledstviia* (The Sino-Soviet Split: Causes and Consequences) (Moscow: IDV RAN, 2000), 31, 32.

40. Konstantin Simonov, *Istorii tiazhelaia voda* (The Heavy Water of History) (Moscow: Vagris, 2005), 382.

41. See "Zapis' besedy tovarishcha Stalina I. V. s Predsedatelem Tsentral'nogo narodnogo pravitel'stva Kitaiskoi Narodnoi Respubliki Mao Tsze-dunom 16 dekabria 1949 g." (Memorandum of Conversation between Comrade J. V. Stalin and the Chairman of the Central People's Government of the Chinese People's Republic Mao Zedong, December 16, 1949), 34; *CWIHP Bulletin*, nos. 6–7 (1995/1996): 7.

42. See "Record of Conversation: Mao Zedong and Soviet Ambassador to China Pavel Yudin, July 22, 1958," in Westad, *Brothers in Arms*, 350.

43. *Pravda* (Truth), February 18, 1950.

44. "Tekst besedy lechashchego vracha Mao Tszeduna L. I. Mel'nikova s poslom V. N. Roshchinym o sostoianii zdorov'ia Mao Tszeduna. 15 iyunia 1950 g." (Text of Conversation Between Dr. L. I. Mel'nikov, Physician in Charge of Mao Zedong's Treatment, and Ambassador N. V. Roshchin About Mao Zedong's Health, June 15, 1950), RGASPI, collection 495, inventory 225, file 71, vol. 1, sheets 187–187 reverse.

45. *Lichnoe delo Mao Tszeduna* (Personal File of Mao Zedong), RGASPI, collection 495, inventory 225, file 71, vol. 1, sheets 54, 55. See also Shi Zhe and Li Haiwen, *Zhongsu guanxi jianzheng lu* (Notes of an Eyewitness to Sino-Soviet Relations) (Beijing: Dangdai Zhong-

guo chubanshe, 2005), 89–98; N. Fedorenko, "Kak academik P. F. Yudin redaktiroval Mao Tszeduna" (How Academician P. F. Yudin Edited Mao Zedong), *Problemy Dal'nego Vostoka* (Far Eastern affairs), no. 6 (1992): 75.

46. Quoted from Vereshchagin, *V starom i novom Kitae* (In Old and New China), 75.

47. "Mao Tszedun o kitaiskoi politike Kominterna i Stalina" (Mao Zedong on the China Policy of the Comintern and of Stalin), 106–7.

25. THE KOREAN ADVENTURE

1. See notes of Mao's conversation with Khrushchev's ambassador Pavel Fedorovich Yudin, March 31, 1956, and July 22, 1958, and with a delegation from the Yugoslavian Communist Union in September 1956 and the Soviet minister of foreign affairs, Gromyko, on November 19, 1957, published or cited in "Mao Tszedun o kitaiskoi politike Kominterna i Stalina" (Mao Zedong on the China Policy of the Comintern and of Stalin), 107; Mao, *Mao Zedong on Diplomacy,* 252, 253; "Minutes, Mao's Conversation with a Yugoslavian Communist Union Delegation," 148–49; Kulik, *Sovetsko-kitaiskii raskol,* 95. See also Westad, *Brothers in Arms,* 201, 350.

2. Quoted from Goncharov, Lewis, and Xue, *Uncertain Partners,* 195.

3. From 1948 to 1950, Kim sent forty-eight telegrams to Stalin on this subject. See Kathryn Weathersby, "New Findings on the Korean War," *CWIHP Bulletin,* no. 3 (1993): 14, 15–16.

4. A. A. Gromyko, *Pamiatnoe* (Remembered), book 1, 2nd, enlarged ed. (Moscow: Politizdat, 1990), 248–49. "Indeed, the decision [to ignore the session of the UN Security Council at the time of voting on Korea] was taken at the Politburo level," write Sergei N. Goncharov, John W. Lewis, and Xue Litai, referring to an eyewitness. Goncharov, Lewis, and Xue, *Uncertain Partners,* 161, 334.

5. "Stalin knew that the lack of the Soviet representation on the Security Council would ensure both North Korea's being branded the aggressor and the UN's endorsement of U.S. actions in Korea," write Sergei N. Goncharov, John W. Lewis, and Xue Litai, referring to a former Soviet military adviser in North Korea. Ibid., 161, 334.

6. *The Korean War,* vol. 1 (Lincoln: University of Nebraska Press, 2000), 244–73; Gordon F. Rottman, *Korean War Order of Battle: United States, United Nations, and Communist Ground, Naval, and Air Forces, 1950–1953* (Westport, CT: Praeger, 2002), 117–24.

7. "Telegramma Filippova sovetskomu poslu v Chekhoslovakii dlia Klementa Gotval'da" (Telegram from Filippov [J. V. Stalin] to the Soviet Ambassador to Czechoslovakia [Mikhail Alexandrovich Silin] for [the President of the Czechoslovakian Republic] Klement Gottwald, August 27, 1950), RGASPI, collection 558, inventory 11, file 62, sheets 71–72. Emphasis added. The telegram was first published by A. M. Ledovsky in his "Stalin, Mao Zedong i koreiskaia voina 1950–1953 godov" (Stalin, Mao Zedong, and the Korean War of 1950–1953), *Novaia i noveishaia istoriia* (Modern and contemporary history) 5 (2005): 96–97, and the first English translation, made by Gary Goldberg, appeared in the Cold War International History Project [hereafter CWIHP] virtual archives.

8. Zubok, *The Mao-Khrushchev Conversations,* 265.

9. See Torkunov, *Zagadochnaia voina* (The Enigmatic War), 35–36, 51, 52, 59.

10. Ibid., 56. See also Khrushchev, *Memoirs of Nikita Khrushchev,* 425–26; Nikita S. Khrushchev, *Vremia, Liudi, Vlast': Vospominaniia* (Time, People, Power: Reminiscences) (Moscow: Moskovskie novosti, 1999), 164, 434; and the memoirs of Mao's interpreter Shi Zhe, cited in Chen Jian, *China's Road to the Korean War: The Making of the Sino-American Confrontation* (New York: Columbia University Press, 1994), 87–88.

11. See "Mao Tszedun o kitaiskoi politike Kominterna i Stalina" (Mao Zedong on the China Policy of the Comintern and of Stalin), 101–10.

12. Torkunov, *Zagadochnaia voina* (The Enigmatic War), 56.

13. Ibid., 67. See also Weathersby, "New Findings of the Korean War," 16.

14. Ciphered Telegram from Stalin to Shtykov, January 20, 1950, *CWIHP Bulletin,* no. 5

(1995): 9. Translated for CWIHP by Kathryn Weathersby. In exchange for his promise to support Kim Il Sung's plan, Stalin demanded that the North Koreans annually supply the USSR with 25,000 tons of graphite.

15. Torkunov, *Zagadochnaia voina* (The Enigmatic War), 58, 59.

16. See Weathersby, "New Findings of the Korean War," 16.

17. Torkunov, *Zagadochnaia voina* (The Enigmatic War), 62.

18. Ciphered telegram from Filippov (Stalin) to Mao Tse-Tung (Mao Zedong), May 14, 1950, *CWIHP Bulletin*, no. 4 (1994): 61. Translated for CWIHP by Vladislav Zubok.

19. *CWIHP Bulletin*, no. 4 (1994): 61.

20. Torkunov, *Zagadochnaia voina* (The Enigmatic War), 70.

21. See Weathersby, "New Findings of the Korean War," 16.

22. Ciphered Telegram from Stalin to Mao Zedong and Zhou Enlai, October 1, 1950, *CWIHP Bulletin*, nos. 6–7 (1995/1996): 114; Torkunov, *Zagadochnaia voina* (The Enigmatic War), 113.

23. Quoted from Nie, *Inside the Red Star*, 634.

24. Torkunov, *Zagadochnaia voina* (The Enigmatic War), 108–9. See also RGASPI, collection of unsorted documents; Chen, *China's Road to the Korean War*, 177; *CWIHP Bulletin*, nos. 8–9 (1996/1997): 239, 242.

25. "Telegramma posla SSSR v KNDR T. F. Shtykova l-mu zamestiteliu ministra innostrannykh del SSSR A. A. Gromyko dlia instantsii, 22 sentiabria 1950 goda" (A Telegram from the Soviet Ambassador to the DPRK, T. F. Shtykov, to the First Deputy Minister of Foreign Affairs of the USSR, A. A. Gromyko, for the Higher Authority, September 22, 1950), RGASPI, collection of unsorted documents.

26. Torkunov, *Zagadochnaia voina* (The Enigmatic War), 90. See also "New Evidence on the Korean War," *CWIHP Bulletin*, nos. 6–7 (1995/1996): 111; Shen Zhihua, "Sino–North Korean Conflict and Its Resolution during the Korean War," *CWIHP Bulletin*, nos. 14–15 (2003/2004): 11.

27. See "New Evidence on the Korean War," 111–12; Torkunov, *Zagadochnaia voina* (The Enigmatic War), 92–93.

28. See Shen, "Sino–North Korean Conflict and Its Resolution during the Korean War," 11.

29. See Pang Xianzhi and Jin Chongji, eds., *Mao Zedong zhuan (1949–1976)* (Biography of Mao Zedong [1949–1976]), vol. 1 (Beijing: Zhongyang wenxian chubanshe, 2003), 113.

30. Letter from Mao Zedong to Stalin on October 2, 1950, *CWIHP Bulletin*, nos. 6–7 (1995/1996): 114–15. Emphasis added.

31. Mao Zedong, *Jianguo yilai Mao Zedong wengao* (Manuscripts of Mao Zedong from the Founding of the PRC) [hereafter cited as Mao's Manuscripts], vol. 1 (Beijing: Zhongyang wenxian chubanshe, 1997), 539. For a photocopy of the first page of the draft manuscript of this letter, see Pang and Jin, *Mao Zedong zhuan (1949–1976)* (Biography of Mao Zedong [1949–1976]), vol. 1, 116.

32. See Mao Zedong, *Mao Zedong wenji* (Works of Mao Zedong), vol. 6 (Beijing: Renmin chubanshe, 1999), 99; Pang and Jin, *Mao Zedong zhuan (1949–1976)* (Biography of Mao Zedong [1949–1976]), vol. 1, 116–18. See also *CWIHP Bulletin*, nos. 8–9 (1996/1997): 239.

33. Quoted from Peng, *Memoirs of a Chinese Marshal*, 472.

34. "Letter from Stalin to Mao Zedong, October 2, 1950," *CWIHP Bulletin*, nos. 6–7 (1995/1996): 116; Torkunov, *Zagodochnaia voina* (The Enigmatic War), 116. Emphasis added.

35. Peng, *Memoirs of a Chinese Marshal*, 473.

36. See Nie, *Inside the Red Star*, 636. See also Pang and Jin, *Mao Zedong zhuan (1949–1976)* (Biography of Mao Zedong [1949–1976]), vol. 1, 118–19; Li and Ma, *Zhou Enlai nianpu (1949–1976)* (Chronological Biography of Zhou Enlai [1949–1976]), vol. 1, 84.

37. "New Evidence on the Korean War," 116; Torkunov, *Zagadochnaia voina* (The Enigmatic War), 117.

38. See Mao, *Jianguo yilai Mao Zedong wengao* (Mao's Manuscripts), vol. 1, 543–44.

39. Ibid., 545.

40. See Chen, *China's Road to the Korean War,* 197–200; Goncharov, Lewis, and Xue, *Uncertain Partners,* 188–92. See also the memoirs of the interpreter Shi Zhe, who took part in the talks. Shi, *Zai lishi juren shenbian* (At the Side of Historical Titans), 496–99. The compilers of *Zhou Enlai nianpu (1949–1976)* (Chronological Biography of Zhou Enlai [1949–1976]), however, give a different date for the talks, namely, October 11, which is evidently according to the Chinese time zone (vol. 1, 85).

41. See Mao, *Jianguo yilai Mao Zedong wengao* (Mao's Manuscripts), vol. 1, 552–53. See also Pang and Jin, *Mao Zedong zhuan (1949–1976)* (Biography of Mao Zedong [1949–1976]), vol. 1, 121.

42. Torkunov, *Zagadochnaia voina* (The Enigmatic War), 117.

43. Ibid., 97.

44. Quoted from Khrushchev, *Memoirs of Nikita Khrushchev,* vol. 2, 426.

45. "Ciphered telegram from Fyn Si [Stalin] to Kim Il Sung [via Shtykov], October 13, 1950," *CWIHP Bulletin,* nos. 6–7 (1995/1996): 119. Torkunov, *Zagadochnaia voina* (The Enigmatic War), 117–18.

46. See Mao, *Mao Zedong wenji* (Works of Mao Zedong), vol. 6, 103–4; Pang and Jin, *Mao Zedong zhuan (1949–1976)* (Biography of Mao Zedong [1949–1976]), vol. 1, 121–22; Li and Ma, *Zhou Enlai nianpu (1949–1976)* (Chronological Biography of Zhou Enlai [1949–1976]), vol. 1, 85–86.

47. "New Evidence on the Korean War," 119; Torkunov, *Zagadochnaia voina* (The Enigmatic War), 118–19.

48. RGASPI, collection of unsorted documents. This document was first published by Torkunov in his book, 163–64.

49. RGASPI, collection of unsorted documents.

50. Torkunov, *Zagadochnaia voina* (The Enigmatic War), 44.

51. Ibid., 162.

52. Ibid., 248.

53. *CWIHP Bulletin,* nos. 6–7 (1995/1996): 12–13. See also "Zapis' besedy tovarishcha Stalina I. V. s Zhou Enlaem 20 avgusta 1952 goda" (Record of a Conversation Between Comrade Stalin and Zhou Enlai, August 20, 1952), RGASPI, collection 558, inventory 11, file 329, sheets 66–68. See also Torkunov, *Zagadochnaia voina* (The Enigmatic War), 252, 259–60.

54. See Li and Ma, *Zhou Enlai nianpu (1949–1976)* (Chronological Biography of Zhou Enlai [1949–1976]), vol. 1, 289; Weathersby, "New Findings of the Korean War," 16.

55. "New Evidence on the Korean War," 80; Torkunov, *Zagadochnaia voina* (The Enigmatic War), 272–73.

56. See Weathersby, "New Findings of the Korean War," 16, 17.

57. See Xu Yan, "Chaoxian zhanzheng zhong jiaozhan gefang sunshi duoshao junren" (What Are the Casualties of All Sides During the Korean War?), *Wenshi cankao* (History reference), no. 12 (June 2010); Shu Guang Zhang, *Military Romanticism: China and the Korean War, 1950–1953* (Lawrence: University Press of Kansas, 1995), 247. The number 900,000 was estimated by the UN. See Rottman, *Korean War,* 212.

58. See Michael H. Hunt and Steven I. Levine, *Arc of Empire: America's Wars in Asia from the Philippines to Vietnam* (Chapel Hill: University of North Carolina Press, 2012), 172; G. F. Krivosheev, ed., *Grif sekretnosti sniat: Poteri Vooruzhennykh Sil SSSR v voinakh, boevykh deistviyakh i voennykh konfliktakh: Statisticheskoe issledovanie* (The Stamp of Secrecy Is Removed: Losses of the Armed Forces of the USSR in Wars, Battles, and Armed Conflicts: A Statistical Analysis) (Moscow: Voennoe izdatel'stvo, 1993), 395; Max Hastings, *The Korean War* (New York: Simon & Schuster, 1987), 329; Burton I. Kaufman, *The Korean Conflict* (Westport, CT: Greenwood Press, 1999), 15, 43.

59. Ye, *Ye Zilong huiyilu* (Memoirs of Ye Zilong), 197. See also the reminiscences of Mao's bodyguard, Li Yingqiao, in Quan Yanchi, *Mao Zedong. Man, Not God* (Beijing: Foreign Languages Press, 1992), 43.

60. Li, *Moi otets Mao Tszedun* (My Father Mao Zedong), 145, 146.

61. Ibid., 117–19; *Lichnoe delo Mao Tszeminia* (Personal File of Mao Zemin), 2; "Mao Zemin," 71–75; Ma, *Hongse diyi jiazu* (The First Red Family), 281.

62. See *Lichnoe delo Yun Shu* (Personal File of Yong Shu), 31–35, 37; Ma, *Hongse diyi jiazu* (The First Red Family), 155–56, 181–91, 273–89, 301–3; Liao, *Mao Zedong baike quanshu* (Encyclopedia of Mao Zedong), vol. 1, 26–39.

63. Stuart R. Schram, ed., *Chairman Mao Talks to the People: Talks and Letters: 1956–1971* (New York: Pantheon Books, 1974), 143.

26. THE CONTRADICTIONS OF NEW DEMOCRACY

1. See K. I. Koval, "Moskovskiie peregovory I. V. Stalina s Chzhou En'laem v 1952 g. i N. S. Khrushcheva s Mao Tszedunom v 1954 g." (J. V. Stalin's Negotiations in Moscow with Zhou Enlai in 1952 and N. S. Khrushchev's with Mao Zedong in 1954), *Novaia i noveishaia istoriia* (Modern and contemporary history), no. 5 (1989): 104–7. Koval gives the wrong months for these negotiations.

2. Quoted from ibid., 107; see also Westad, *Brothers in Arms*, 145, 197–200, 257.

3. See M. L. Titarenko, ed., *Istoriia Kommunisticheskoi partii Kitaia* (History of the Chinese Communist Party), vol. 2, part 1 (Moscow: IDV AN SSSR, 1987), 130; see also Heinzig, *The Soviet Union and Communist China 1945–1950*, 263–384.

4. See Kurdiukov, *Sovetsko-kitaiskie otnosheniia* (Soviet-Chinese Relations), 223. Mao asked Stalin to shorten from five to four years the period for the provision on credit of industrial equipment and arms, but Stalin did not agree. See "Zapis' besedy I. V. Stalina s Predsedatelem Tsentral'nogo narodnogo pravitel'stva Kitaiskoi Narodnoi Respubliki Mao Tsze-dunom 22 janvaria 1950 g." (Memorandum of Conversation Between J. V. Stalin and the Chairman of the Central People's Government of the Chinese People's Republic Mao Zedong, January 22, 1950), 36; *CWIHP Bulletin*, nos. 8–9 (1996/1997): 229.

5. "Mao Zedong's Telegram to CCP CC, January 4, 1950," *CWIHP Bulletin*, nos. 8–9 (1995/1996): 229; see also Ledovsky, *SSSR i Stalin v sud'bakh Kitaia* (The USSR and Stalin in China's Fate), 78.

6. See Zhang, *Sino-Soviet Economic Cooperation*, 197.

7. In this connection, the assertion by the Russian historian B. T. Kulik that Stalin supposedly agreed to fulfill all of Zhou Enlai's requests, including a request to plan for and build 151 (?) industrial enterprises in China, does not correspond to the historical facts. See Kulik, *Sovetsko-kitaiskii raskol* (The Soviet-Chinese Split), 95.

8. See "Zapis' besedy tovarishcha Stalina I. V. s Chzhou En'laem 3 sentiabria 1952 goda" (Memorandum of Conversation between Comrade J. V. Stalin and Zhou Enlai, September 3, 1952), RGASPI, collection 558, inventory 11, file 329, sheet 81; *CWIHP Bulletin*, nos. 6–7 (1995/1996): 15–16; Kurdiukov, *Sovetsko-kitaiskie otnosheniia* (Soviet-Chinese Relations), 285; Chen Zhiling, "Li Fuchun," in Hu Hua, ed., *Zhonggongdang shi renwu zhuan* (Biographies of Persons in the History of the CCP), vol. 44 (Xi'an: Shaanxi renmin chubanshe, 1990), 62–63, 67; Koval, "Moskovskiie peregovory I. V. Stalina s Chzhou En'laem v 1952 g. i N. S. Khrushcheva s Mao Tszedunom v 1954 g." (J. V. Stalin's Negotiations in Moscow with Zhou Enlai in 1952 and N. S. Khrushchev's with Mao Zedong in 1954): 107.

9. "Zapis' besedy tovarishcha Stalina I. V. s Chzhou Enlaiem 3 sentiabria 1952 goda" (Memorandum of Conversation between Comrade J. V. Stalin and Zhou Enlai, September 3, 1952), 75, 85; *CWIHP Bulletin*, nos. 6–7 (1995/1996): 14, 16. See also Li and Ma, *Zhou Enlai nianpu (1949–1976)* (Chronological Biography of Zhou Enlai [1949–1976]), vol. 1, 258; Maurice Meisner, *Mao's China and After: A History of the People's Republic of China*, 3rd ed. (New York: Free Press, 1999), 127.

10. See Kulik, *Sovetsko-kitaiskii raskol* (The Soviet-Chinese Split), 126; Chen, "Li Fuchun," 63.

11. See Li and Ma, *Zhou Enlai nianpu (1949–1976)* (Chronological Biography of Zhou Enlai [1949–1976]), vol. 1, 284–85; Kulik, *Sovetsko-kitaiskii raskol* (The Soviet-Chinese Split), 126.

12. See Li Fu-ch'un [Li Fuchun], "Report on the First Five-Year Plan, 1953–1957, July 5–6,

1955," in Robert Bowie and John K. Fairbank, eds., *Communist China 1955-1959: Policy Documents with Analysis* (Cambridge, MA: Harvard University Press, 1962), 53, 61.

13. See *Kratkaia istoriia KPK (1921-1991)* (A Short History of the CCP [1921-1991]) (Beijing: Izdatel'stvo literatury na inostrannykh iazykakh, 1993), 530.

14. See Liu and Chen, *Liu Shaoqi nianpu, 1898-1969* (Chronological Biography of Liu Shaoqi, 1898-1969), vol. 2, 304-5.

15. Quoted from "Dnevnik sovetskogo posla v Kitae V. V. Kuznetsova. Zapis' besedy s Liu Shaoqi. 9 noiabria 1953 g." (The Diary of Soviet Ambassador to China V. V. Kuznetsov: Memorandum of Conversation with Liu Shaoqi, November 9, 1953), AVP RF, collection 0100, inventory 46, file 12, folder 362, sheet 185.

16. See Stéphane Courtois et al., *The Black Book of Communism: Crimes, Terror, Repression,* trans. Jonathan Murphy and Mark Kramer (Cambridge, MA: Harvard University Press, 1999), 481; Meisner, *Mao's China and After,* 72.

17. Arlen V. Meliksetov's interview with B. N. Gorbachev in Moscow, November 25, 1999.

18. G. G. Semenov, *Tri goda v Pekine: Zapiski voennogo sovetnika* (Three Years in Beijing: Notes of a Military Adviser) (Moscow: Nauka, 1978), 47-48, 60-62.

19. See Yang Kuisong, "Mao Zedong weishenma fangqi xinminzhuyi? Guanyu Eguo moshide yingxiang wenti" (Why Did Mao Zedong Abandon New Democracy? On the Influence of the Russian Model), *Jindaishi yanjiu* (Studies in contemporary history), no. 4 (1997): 182-83.

20. Witke, *Comrade Chiang Ch'ing,* 239.

21. See Jerome Cooper, "Lawyers in China and the Rule of Law," *International Journal of the Legal Profession,* 6, no. 1 (1999): 71-89.

22. "Zapiska I. V. Kovaleva ot 24 dekabria 1949 g." (I. V. Kovalev's Note of December 24, 1949), 135, 138, 139.

23. "[W]e members of the Politburo of the AUCP(B) were indignant over Stalin's action," Khrushchev wrote in this connection, noting that it was Gao who accused not only Liu Shaoqi, but also Zhou Enlai as well as a number of other leaders of the country, of "especially expressions of displeasure" toward "the USSR." Khrushchev, *Memoirs of Nikita Khrushchev,* vol. 3, 412-14. The report, however, contains an indication that Zhou Enlai himself criticized Bo Yibo for economic mistakes in a talk with Kovalev.

24. See Kovalev, *Dialog Stalina s Mao Tszedunom* (Stalin's Dialogue with Mao Zedong), 91; Khrushchev, *Memoirs of Nikita Khrushchev,* vol. 3, 412-14; Bo Yibo, *Ruogan zhongda juece yu shijian de huigu* (Recollections of Several Important Political Decisions and Their Implementation), vol. 1 (Beijing: Zhonggong zhongyang dangxiao, 1991), 40-41; Ye, *Ye Zilong huiyilu* (Memoirs of Ye Zilong), 201; Chen Aifei and Cao Zhiwei, *Zouchu guomende Mao Zedong* (Mao Zedong Abroad) (Shijiazhuang: Hebei renmin chubanshe, 2001), 88-91; Heinzig, *The Soviet Union and Communist China 1945-1950,* 157, 158, 285-86, 296-97.

25. "Mao Tszedun o kitaiskoi politike Kominterna i Stalina" (Mao Zedong on the China Policy of the Comintern and Stalin), 106.

26. See Kovalev, *Dialog Stalina s Mao Tszedunom* (Stalin's Dialogue with Mao Zedong), 89; I. V. Kovalev, "Rossiia i Kitai (s missiei v Kitae)" (Russia and China [My Mission to China]), *Duel'* (Duel), November 19, 1997.

27. *Lichnoe delo Mao Tszeduna* (Personal File of Mao Zedong), RGASPI, collection 495, inventory 225, file 71, vol. 1, sheet 57.

28. See Kovalev, "Dialog Stalina s Mao Tszedunom" (Stalin's Dialogue with Mao Zedong), 89.

29. Peter S. Deriabin and Joseph Culver Evans, *Inside Stalin's Kremlin: An Eyewitness Account of Brutality, Duplicity, and Intrigue* (Washington: Brassey's, 1998), 110, 229-30.

30. See Liu Shaoqi, *Selected Works of Liu Shaoqi,* vol. 1 (Beijing: Foreign Languages Press, 1984); Zhou Enlai, *Selected Works of Zhou Enlai,* vol. 1 (Beijing: Foreign Languages Press, 1981).

31. See *Obrazovanie Kitaiskoi Narodnoi Respubliki: Dokumenty i materialy* (Establishment

of the Chinese People's Republic: Documents and Materials) (Moscow: Gospolitizdat, 1950), 30–49.

32. See N. G. Sudarikov, ed., *Konstitutsiia i osnovnye zakonodatel'nye akty Kitaiskoi Narodnoi Respubliki* (Constitution and Founding Legislative Acts of the People's Republic of China) (Moscow: Izdatel'stvo inostrannoi literatury, 1955), 381–92.

33. Quoted from L. P. Deliusin, ed., *Agrarnye preobrazovaniia v narodnom Kitae* (Agrarian Transformation in People's China) (Moscow: Izdatel'stvo inostrannoi literatury, 1955), 39.

34. See Sudarikov, *Konstitutsiia i osnovnye zakonodatel'nye akty Kitaiskoi Narodnoi Respubliki* (Constitution and Founding Legislative Acts of the People's Republic of China), 493–523.

35. Ibid., 475–81.

36. See A. V. Meliksetov, " 'Novaia demokratiia' i vybor Kitaem putei sotsial'no-ekonomicheskogo razvitiia (1949–1953)" ("New Democracy" and China's Choice of a Socioeconomic Development Path [1949–1953]), *Problemy Dal'nego Vostoka* (Far Eastern affairs), no. 1 (1996): 82–95.

37. See Mao Tse-tung, *Selected Works of Mao Tsetung,* vol. 5 (Beijing: Foreign Languages Press, 1977), 71; Sladkovskii, *Informatsionnyi biulleten'. Seriia A. "Kulturnaiia revoliutsiia" v Kitae. Dokumenty i materialy (perevod s kitaiskogo). Vypusk 1: Hongveibinovskaia pechat' o Liu Shaotsi* (Information Bulletin. Series A. The "Cultural Revolution" in China. Documents and Materials [Translated from Chinese]. The First Installment: The Red Guard Press on Liu Shaoqi) (Moscow: IDV AN SSSR, 1968), 73–74.

38. Bo, *Ruogan zhongda juece yu shijian de huigu* (Recollections of Several Important Political Decisions and Their Implementation), vol. 1, 234–35.

39. Pang and Jin, *Mao Zedong zhuan (1949–1976)* (Biography of Mao Zedong [1949–1976]), vol. 1, 247.

40. A. M. Ledovsky, *Delo Gao Gana-Zhao Shushi* (The Gao Gang-Rao Shushi Affair) (Moscow: IDV AN SSSR, 1990), 99.

41. Mao, *Selected Works of Mao Tsetung,* vol. 5, 93.

42. Ibid.

43. Ibid., 94.

44. See Frederick C. Teiwes, *Politics at Mao's Court: Gao Gang and Party Factionalism* (Armonk, NY: M. E. Sharpe, 1990), 163.

45. Quoted from Bo, *Ruogan zhongda juece yu shijian de huigu* (Recollections of Several Important Political Decisions and Their Implementation), vol. 1, 247.

46. See ibid., 93–94, 101–11, 247–48; Zhou, "Rech' na Vsekitaiskom finansovo-ekonomicheskom soveshchanii" (Speech at the All-China Financial-Economic Conference), 8–19; Ledovsky, *Delo Gao Gana-Zhao Shushi* (The Gao Gang-Rao Shushi Affair), 99.

47. Zhou, "Rech' na Vsekitaiskom finansovo-ekonomicheskom soveshchanii" (Speech at the All-China Financial-Economic Conference), 18.

48. Ibid.

49. Ibid.

50. Mao, *Selected Works of Mao Tsetung,* vol. 5, 103.

51. Ibid., 138.

27. SOCIALIST INDUSTRIALIZATION

1. Rakhmanin, "Vzaimnootnosheniia mezhdu I. V. Stalinym i Mao Tszedunom glazami ochevidtsa" (An Eyewitness Account of Relations Between J. V. Stalin and Mao Zedong), 80.

2. See Deriabin and Culver, *Inside Stalin's Kremlin,* 111–13.

3. See N. M. Przheval'skii, *Puteshestvie v Ussuriiskom krae: Mongolia i strana tangutov* (Travels in the Ussuri Region: Mongolia and the Country of Tanguts) (Moscow: Drofa, 2007).

4. See RGASPI, collection of unsorted documents.

5. *Pravda* (Truth), March 11, 1953.

6. See Kartunova, *Vstrechi v Moskve s Tszian Tsin, zhenoi Mao Tszeduna* (Encounters in Moscow with Jiang Qing, Mao Zedong's wife), 126; Witke, *Comrade Chiang Ch'ing,* 257.

7. See Li and Ma, *Zhou Enlai nianpu (1949–1976)* (Chronological Biography of Zhou Enlai [1949–1976]), vol. 1, 289–90.

8. See Kurdiukov, *Sovetsko-kitaiskie otnosheniia* (Soviet-Chinese Relations), 284; Li and Ma, *Zhou Enlai nianpu (1949–1976)* (Chronological Biography of Zhou Enlai [1949–1976]), vol. 1, 290.

9. See Kurdiukov, *Sovetsko-kitaiskie otnosheniia* (Soviet-Chinese Relations), 284–85; Li and Ma, *Zhou Enlai nianpu (1949–1976)* (Chronological Biography of Zhou Enlai [1949–1976]), vol. 1, 290.

10. Kurdiukov, *Sovetsko-kitaiskie otnosheniia* (Soviet-Chinese Relations), 285.

11. See Khrushchev, *Memoirs of Nikita Khrushchev,* vol. 3, 401–4. Subsequently, in conversations with Mao, Khrushchev repeatedly asserted that he had opposed Stalin's "senile stupidity." See Zubok, *The Mao-Khrushchev Conversations,* 250, 261.

12. See Titarenko, *Istoriia Kommunisticheskoi partii Kitaia* (History of the Chinese Communist Party), vol. 2, part 1, 118.

13. Mao, *Selected Works of Mao Tsetung,* vol. 5, 93. Emphasis added.

14. Ibid., 94.

15. Quoted from Titarenko, *Istoriia Kommunisticheskoi partii Kitaia* (History of the Chinese Communist Party), vol. 2, part 1, 119–20. Emphasis added.

16. Mao, *Selected Works of Mao Tsetung,* vol. 5, 102. Emphasis added.

17. See Li and Ma, *Zhou Enlai nianpu (1949–1976)* (Chronological Biography of Zhou Enlai [1949–1976]), vol. 1, 317.

18. See Zhou Enlai, *Zhou Enlai xuanji* (Selected Works of Zhou Enlai), vol. 2 (Beijing: Renmin chubanshe, 1980), 104–5.

19. *Borot'sia za mobilizatsiiu vsekh sil dlia prevrashcheniia nashei strany v velikoe sotsialisticheskoe gosudarstvo: Tezisy dlia izucheniia i propagandy general'noi linii partii v perekhodnyi period (Razrabotany otdelom agitatsii i propagandy TsK KPK i utverzhdeny TsK KPK v dekabre 1953 g.)* (Struggle to Mobilize All Forces to Transform Our Country into a Socialist State: Theses for Studying and Propagandizing the Party's General Line in the Transitional Period [Prepared by the Department of Agitation and Propaganda of the CC CCP and Affirmed by the CC CCP in December 1953]) (Moscow: Gospoliizdat, [1957]), 10.

20. "Excerpt from the Communiqué of the Fourth Plenum (February 18, 1954)," In Telwes, *Politics at Mao's Court,* 237. Emphasis added.

21. Quoted from K. V. Shevelev, "O nekotorykh aspektakh raboty 4-go plenuma TsK KPK 7-ogo sozyva" (On Several Aspects of the Work of the Fourth Plenum of the Seventh Central Committee of the CCP), in *Perspektivy sotrudnichestva Kitaia, Rossii i drugikh stran Severo-vostochnoi Azii v kontse XX-nachale XXI veka. Tezisy dokladov VIII Mezhdunarodnoi nauchnoi konferentsii "Kitai. Kitaiskaia tsivilizatsiia i mir. Istoriia, sovremennost', perspektivy," Moskva, 7–9 oktiabria 1997 g.* (Prospects for Cooperation Among China, Russia, and Other Countries of Northeast Asia at the End of the Twentieth and Beginning of the Twenty-first Century. Papers from the VIII International Scholarly Conference on China, Chinese Civilization, and the World: History, the Present, and the Future, Moscow, October 7–9, 1997) (Moscow: IDV RAN, 1997), 151.

22. Mao, *Selected Works of Mao Tsetung,* vol. 5, 340.

23. See Gao Gang, *Izbrannoe* (Selections) (Moscow: IDV AN SSSR, 1989), 226–31.

24. See Short, *Mao,* 442.

25. Paul Wingrove, "Mao's Conversations with the Soviet Ambassador, 1953–1955," *CWIHP Working Paper,* no. 36 (April 2002): 40.

26. See Deng Xiaoping, *Selected Works of Deng Xiaoping (1975–1982),* 2nd ed. (Beijing: Foreign Languages Press, 1995), 292–93.

27. See Teiwes, *Politics at Mao's Court,* 308–9. For the quotation from Confucius, see Confucius, *The Analects of Confucius,* trans. Simon Leys (New York: Norton, 1997), 17.

28. See Short, *Mao,* 442, 444, 737; Zhao Jialiang and Zhang Xiaoji, *Banjie mubei xiade*

wangshi: Gao Gang zai Beijing (A Story Dug from Underneath a Half-Destroyed Tombstone: Gao Gang in Beijing) (Hong Kong: Dafeng chubanshe, 2008), 203–6, 238–45; Teiwes, *Politics at Mao's Court,* 240–52.

29. See Wingrove, "Mao's Conversations with the Soviet Ambassador, 1953–1955," 28–29, 34–35, 40–41; Teiwes, *Politics at Mao's Court;* Short, *Mao,* 441–45.

30. *Hongqi* (Red flag), no. 2 (1981): 32.

31. Mao, *Selected Works of Mao Tsetung,* vol. 5, 150–51. See also Wingrove, "Mao's Conversations with the Soviet Ambassador, 1953–1955," 21–23.

32. See Cheng Bo, *Zhonggong "bada" juece neimu* (Behind the Scenes Decision-Making at the Eighth Congress of the CCP) (Beijing: Zhonggong dang'an chubanshe, 1999), 54–55; Wingrove, "Mao's Conversations with the Soviet Ambassador, 1953–1955," 38–40.

33. Li, *The Private Life of Chairman Mao,* 65.

34. Krutikov, *Na kitaiskom napravleniu* (Pointed Toward China), 183.

35. He Ganzhi, *Istoriia sovremennoi revoliutsii v Kitae* (History of the Contemporary Revolution in China) (Moscow: Izdatel'stvo literatury na inostrannykh iazykakh, 1959), 682.

36. Richard Evans, *Deng Xiaoping and the Making of Modern China,* rev. ed. (London: Penguin, 1997), 112. See also Titarenko, *Istoriia Kommunisticheskoi partii Kitaia* (History of the Communist Party of China), vol. 2, part 1, 36; Meisner, *Mao's China and After,* 107.

37. See Mao Zedong, *Jianguo yilai Mao Zedong wengao* (Mao's Manuscripts), vol. 4 (Beijing: Zhongyang wenxian chubanshe, 1998), 548.

38. See *Pervaia sessiia Vsekitaiskogo sobraniia narodnykh predstavitelei Kitaiskoi Narodnoi Respubliki pervogo sozyva (dokumenty i materialy)* (The First Session of the First National People's Congress of the PRC [Documents and Materials]) (Beijing: Izdatel'stvo literatury na inostrannykh iazykakh, 1956).

39. See Shi Zhe, *Feng yu gu—Shi Zhe huiyilu* (Summit and Abyss: Reminiscences of Shi Zhe) (Beijing: Hongqi chubanshe, 1992), 103; see also Wingrove, "Mao's Conversations with the Soviet Ambassador, 1953–1955," 10–12.

40. See Westad, *Brothers in Arms,* 38.

41. Ye, *Ye Zilong huiyilu* (Memoirs of Ye Zilong), 202.

42. See Mao's telegram to the Central Committee of the CPSU, September 1, 1954, published in Mao, *Jianguo yilai Mao Zedong wengao* (Mao's Manuscripts), vol. 4, 537–38.

43. See Wingrove, "Mao's Conversations with the Soviet Ambassador, 1953–1955," 13–18; Mao, *Selected Works of Mao Tsetung,* vol. 5, 337–38. See also the reminiscences of the former Soviet foreign minister Dmitrii Timofeevich Shepilov about Mao Zedong's meeting with a Soviet delegation, September 30, 1954, in Beijing. D. T. Shepilov, "Vospominaniia" (Reminiscences), *Voprosy Istorii* (Problems of history), no. 9 (1998): 26.

44. See Koval, "Moskovskiie peregovory I. V. Stalina s Chzhou En'laem v 1952 g. i N. S. Khrushcheva s Mao Tszedunom v 1954 g." (J. V. Stalin's Negotiations in Moscow with Zhou Enlai in 1952, and N. S. Khrushchev's with Mao Zedong in 1954), 108–13.

45. See Westad, *Brothers in Arms,* 16.

46. D. T. Shepilov, "Vospominaniia" (Reminiscences), *Voprosy istorii* (Problems of history), no. 10 (1998): 25.

47. Quoted from Koval, "Moskovskiie peregovory I. V. Stalina s Chzhou En'laem v 1952 g. i N. S. Khrushcheva s Mao Tszedunom v 1954 g." (J. V. Stalin's Negotiations in Moscow with Zhou Enlai in 1952 and N. S. Khrushchev's with Mao Zedong in 1954), 113.

48. See Westad, *Brothers in Arms,* 16, 39.

49. See Khrushchev, *Memoirs of Nikita Khrushchev,* vol. 3, 420–27; D. T. Shepilov, "Vospominaniia" (Reminiscences), *Voprosy istorii* (Problems of history), no. 9 (1998): 18–31; no. 10 (1998), 3–30; Koval, "Moskovskiie peregovory I. V. Stalina s Chzhou En'laem v 1952 g. i N. S. Khrushchev s Mao Tszedunom v 1954 g." (J. V. Stalin's Negotiations with Zhou Enlai in 1952 and N. S. Khrushchev's with Mao Zedong in 1954), 113–18; Shi, *Feng yu gu* (Summit and Abyss), 106–15.

50. Cited in Chen Jian and Yang Kuisong, "Chinese Politics and the Collapse of the Sino-Soviet Alliance," in Westad, *Brothers in Arms*, 285.

51. Mao, *Mao Zedong on Diplomacy*, 251, 256.

52. Many years later, he himself said that he "had literally looked with the innocent eyes of children on our relations with our Chinese brothers." Khrushchev, *Memoirs of Nikita Khrushchev*, vol. 3, 445.

53. Quoted from D. T. Shepilov, "Vospominaniia" (Reminiscences), *Voprosy istorii* (Problems of history), no. 9 (1998): 18.

54. Witke, *Comrade Chiang Ch'ing*, 272.

55. See Shi, *Feng yu gu* (Summit and Abyss), 101–5; Li Yueran, *Waijiao wutai shang de xin Zhongguo lingxiu* (Leaders of New China on the Diplomatic Stage) (Beijing: Waiyu jiaoxue yu yanjiu chubanshe, 1994), 69–70.

56. See Nikita S. Khrushchev, *Vospominaniia. Izbrannye fragmenty* (Reminiscences: Selected Fragments) (Moscow: Vagrius, 1997), 336, 356–57; see also D. T. Shepilov, "Vospominaniia (Reminiscences), *Voprosy istorii* (Problems of history), no. 10 (1998): 28–29.

57. Witke, *Comrade Chiang Ch'ing*, 262.

58. Khrushchev, *Memoirs of Nikita Khrushchev*, vol. 3, 399–400.

59. See Titarenko, *Istoriia kommunisticheskoi partii Kitaia* (History of the Communist Party of China), vol. 2, part 1, 137.

60. See Zhang, *Sino-Soviet Economic Cooperation*, 202.

61. See Chen and Yang, "Chinese Politics and the Collapse of the Sino-Soviet Alliance," 257.

62. See Goncharenko, "Sino-Soviet Military Cooperation," in Westad, *Brothers in Arms*, 147.

63. *Materialy vtoroi sessii Vsekitaiskogo sobraniia narodnykh predstavitelei (5–30 iulia 1955 g.)* (Materials from the Second Session of the National People's Congress, [July 5–30, 1955]) (Moscow: Gospolitizdat, 1956), 256.

64. See Li, *Report on the First Five-Year Plan*, 43–91.

65. See "Memo, PRC Foreign Ministry to the USSR Embassy in Beijing, March 13, 1957," *CWIHP Bulletin*, nos. 6–7 (1995/1996): 160; Meisner, *Mao's China and After*, 113; Bo, *Ruogan zhongda juece yu shijian de huigu* (Recollections of Several Important Political Decisions and Their Implementation), vol. 1, 295–96.

66. See *China Quarterly*, no. 1 (1960): 38.

67. See Meisner, *Mao's China and After*, 113. According to other statistics, more than 8,000 Soviet and East European advisers and experts worked in China in the 1950s while 7,000 Chinese were receiving special training and education in the USSR and Eastern Europe. See Zhang, *Sino-Soviet Economic Cooperation*, 202. Shepilov asserts that more than 11,000 Chinese students and more than 8,000 workers and technicians were trained in the Soviet Union. See D. T. Shepilov, "Vospominaniia" (Reminiscences), *Voprosy istorii* (Problems of history), no. 10 (1998): 26.

28. THE GREAT TURNING POINT

1. Quoted from "Dnevnik sovetskogo posla v Kitae V. V. Kuznetsova" (Diary of the Soviet Ambassador to China V. V. Kuznetsov), 184–85.

2. A partial, experimental system of state monopoly over basic consumer goods was introduced in January 1951. On January 5, 1951, the head of the Planning Department of the East China Military-Administrative Committee, Luo Gengmo, informed the Soviet consul-general in Shanghai, Vladimirov, that centralized state purchase of all products from private spinning and weaving mills had been introduced in Shanghai on January 4. "Luo stressed that all of this information was top secret," Vladimirov, a veteran intelligence agent, reported to Moscow. See AVP RF, collection 0100, inventory 44, file 15, folder 322, sheets 146–47.

3. See ibid.

4. See L. D. Bony, "Mekhanizm iz"iatiia tovarnogo zerna v KNR (50'e gody)" (The Mechanism of Grain Acquisition in the PRC [in the 1950s]), in L. P. Deliusin, ed., *Kitai: gosudarstvo i obshchestvo* (China: State and Society) (Moscow: Nauka, 1977), 27, 28.

5. Ibid., 33–34.

6. See Mao, *Selected Works of Mao Tsetung*, vol. 5, 217–18, 290–91; Chou En-lai [Zhou Enlai], "Report on the Proposals for the Second Five-Year Plan for Development of the National Economy," in *Eighth National Congress of the Communist Party of China*, vol. 1, *Documents* (Beijing: Foreign Language Press, 1956), 270.

7. See Gel'bras, *Sotsial'no-ekonomicheskaia struktura KNR: 50–60-e gody* (The Socioeconomic Structure of the PRC: 1950s and 1960s), 60.

8. Mao, *Selected Works of Mao Tsetung*, vol. 5, 212.

9. Ibid., 186.

10. Quoted from Jiang Boying et al., "Deng Zihui," in Hu Hua, ed., *Zhonggongdang shi renwu zhuan* (Biographies of Persons in the History of the CCP), vol. 7 (Xi'an: Shaanxi renmin chubanshe, 1990), 367.

11. See Deliusin, *Agrarnye preobrazovaniia v narodnom Kitae* (Agrarian Transformation in People's China), 345.

12. Borisov and Titarenko, *Vystupleniia Mao Tsze-duna, ranee ne publikovavshiesia v kitaiskoi pechati* (Mao Zedong's Speeches Previously Unpublished in China), series 2, 111.

13. Mao, *Selected Works of Mao Tsetung*, vol. 5, 131–40, 186, 189–90.

14. See Deliusin, *Agrarnye preobrazovaniia v narodnom Kitae* (Agrarian Transformation in People's China), 361–86.

15. *Borot'sia za mobilizatsiiu vsekh sil* (Struggle to Mobilize All Forces), 33.

16. Mao, *Jianguo yilai Mao Zedong wengao* (Mao's Manuscripts), vol. 4, 497, 498.

17. Mao, *Selected Works of Mao Tsetung*, vol. 5, 186.

18. See Krutikov, *Na kitaiskom napravleniu* (Pointed Toward China), 169.

19. Quoted from Shevelev, *Formirovaniie sotsial'no-ekonomicheskoi politiki rukovodstva KPK v 1949–1956 godakh* (The Formulation of the CCP's Socioeconomic Policy in 1949–1956 (manuscript), VI-13.

20. See Jiang, "Deng Zihui," 369–70; Mao, *Selected Works of Mao Tsetung*, vol. 5, 187; Meliksetov, *Istoriia Kitaia* (History of China), 640. See also Frederick C. Teiwes and Warren Sun, eds., *The Politics of Agricultural Cooperativization in China: Mao, Deng Zihui and the "High Tide" of 1955* (Armonk, NY: M. E. Sharpe, 1993).

21. Quoted from Pang and Jin, *Mao Zedong zhuan (1949–1976)* (Biography of Mao Zedong [1949–1976]), vol. 1, 370.

22. Quoted from Shevelev, *Formirovaniie sotsial'no-ekonomicheskoi politiki rukovodstva KPK v 1949–1956 godakh* (The Formulation of the CCP's Socioeconomic Policy in 1949–1956) (manuscript), VI-22.

23. See Pang and Jin, *Mao Zedong zhuan (1949–1976)* (Biography of Mao Zedong [1949–1976]), vol. 1, 374.

24. Mao, *Selected Works of Mao Tse-tung*, vol. 5, 190.

25. Quoted from Pang and Jin, *Mao Zedong zhuan (1949–1976)* (Biography of Mao Zedong [1949–1976]), vol. 1, 375.

26. Quoted from ibid., 376.

27. Quoted from Liu and Chen, *Liu Shaoqi nianpu, 1898–1969* (Chronological Biography of Liu Shaoqi, 1898–1969), vol. 2, 340.

28. According to Soviet estimates, the Chinese communists disbanded about 200,000 cooperatives. This figure corresponds to data cited in various *dazibao* (big character wall newspapers) from the Cultural Revolution years of 1966–69 that criticized Liu Shaoqi and his opposition to Mao. See Mao, *Selected Works of Mao Tsetung*, vol. 5, 189–90; Jiang, "Deng Zihui," 369–70; Shevelev, *Formirovanie sotsial'no-ekonomicheskoi politiki rukovodstva KPK v 1949–1956 godakh* (The Formulation of the CCP's Socioeconomic Policy in 1949–1956), VI-24.

29. Mao, *Selected Works of Mao Tsetung,* vol. 5, 187.

30. Ibid., 213; Mao Zedong, *Jianguo yilai Mao Zedong wengao* (Mao's Manuscripts), vol. 5 (Beijing: Zhongyang wenxian chubanshe, 1991), 251.

31. Mao, *Selected Works of Mao Tse-tung,* 198; Mao, *Jianguo yilai Mao Zedong wengao* (Mao's Manuscripts), vol. 5, 251.

32. Quoted from Li, *The Private Life of Chairman Mao,* 136.

33. See Westad, *Brothers in Arms,* 17.

34. *Reshenie shestogo (rasshirennogo) plenuma TsK Kommunisticheskoi partii Kitaia sed'-mogo sozyva po voprosu o kooperirovanii v sel'skom khoziastve* (Decision of the Sixth [enlarged] Plenum of the Seventh CC of the Communist Party of China on the Question of Agricultural Cooperation) (Moscow: Gospolitzdat, 1955), 4–5.

35. See Jiang, "Deng Zihui," 371.

36. Quoted from Li, *The Private Life of Chairman Mao,* 111, and Li Youjiu, "Deng Zihui yu nongye hezuohua yundong" (Deng Zihui and the Movement for Agricultural Cooperativization), in Lu Lin and Chen Dejin, eds., *Hongse jiyi: Zhongguo gongchandang lishi koushu shilu (1949–1978)* (Red Reminiscences: True Oral Stories of the History of the Chinese Communist Party [1949–1978]) (Jinan: Shandong renmin chubanshe, 2002), 245.

37. Mao, *Selected Works of Mao Tsetung,* vol. 5, 243.

38. See Jasper Becker, *Hungry Ghosts: Mao's Secret Famine* (New York: Free Press, 1996), 52.

39. Figures calculated from *Zhongguo gongchandang lishi jiangyi* (Lectures on CCP History), vol. 2 (Changchun: Liaoning renmin chubanshe, 1981), 590–91.

40. Li, *The Private Life of Chairman Mao,* 106, 107, 110.

41. See *Zhongguo gongchandang lishi jiangyi* (Lectures on CCP History), vol. 2 (Jinan: Shandong renmin chubanshe, 1982), 120; Jiang, "Deng Zihui," 369.

42. Borisov and Titarenko, *Vystupleniia Mao Tsze-duna, ranee ne publikovavshiesia v kitaiskoi pechati* (Mao Zedong's Speeches Previously Unpublished in China), series 2, 110.

43. To be sure, the Chinese side objected to this assertion. See "Memo, PRC Foreign Ministry to the USSR Embassy in Beijing," 159–60.

44. Mao, *Selected Works of Mao Tsetung,* vol. 5, 214.

45. See A. S. Perevertailo et al., eds., *Ocherki istorii Kitaia v noveishee vremia* (An Outline History of Contemporary China) (Moscow: Nauka, 1959), 576.

46. See *Borotsia za mobilizatsiiu vsekh sil* (Struggle for the Mobilization of All Forces), 12.

47. See *Zhongguo gongchandang lishi jiangyi* (Lectures on CCP History) Jinan, 138–39.

48. See Perevertailo, *Ocherki istorii Kitaia v noveishee vremia* (An Outline History of Contemporary China), 573.

49. See Xiao Xiaoqin, ed., *Zhonghua renmin gongheguo sishi nian* (Forty Years of the People's Republic of China) (Beijing: Beijing shifan xueyuan chubanshe, 1990), 109.

50. See Elizabeth J. Perry, "Shanghai's Strike Wave of 1957," *China Quarterly,* no. 137 (March 1994): 1, 9.

51. J. V. Stalin, *Works,* vol. 11 (Moscow: Foreign Languages Publishing House, 1954), 62.

29. THE EMANCIPATION OF CONSCIOUSNESS

1. See N. S. Khrushchev, *Speech Before a Closed Session of the XXth Congress of the Communist Party of the Soviet Union on February 25, 1956* (Washington: U.S. Government Printing Office, 1957).

2. *Stenographicheskii otchet XX s"ezda KPSS* (Stenographic Report of the Twentieth Congress of the CPSU), vol. 1 (Moscow: Gospolitzdat, 1956), 230.

3. See Wu Lengxi, *Shinian lunduan: Zhongsu guanxi huiyilu (1956–1966)* (The Ten Year Debate: Memoirs of Sino-Soviet Relations [1956–1966]), vol. 1 (Beijing: Zhongyang wenxian chubanshe, 1999), 4–5.

4. See K. Aimermakher, ed., *Doklad N. S. Khrushcheva o kul'te lichnosti Stalina na XX s"ezda KPSS. Dokumenty* (N. S. Khrushchev's Report on Stalin's Cult of Personality at the Twentieth CPSU Congress: Documents) (Moscow: ROSSPEN, 2002), 24, 37; see also Vittorio

Vidali, *Diary of the Twentieth Congress of the Communist Party of the Soviet Union*, trans. Nell Amter Cattonar and A. M. Elliot (Westport, CT: Lawrence Hill, 1974), 26–27.

5. See "Mao Tszedun o kitaiskoi politike Kominterna i Stalina" (Mao Zedong on the China Policy of the Comintern and Stalin), 103; M. S. Kapitsa, *Sovetsko-kitaiskie otnosheniia* (Moscow: Izd-vo vostochnoi literatury, 1958), 357, 364; *Zhanhou zhongsu guanxi zouxiang (1945–1960)* (The Development of Sino-Soviet Relations After the War [1945–1960]) (Beijing: Shehui kexue wenhua chubanshe, 1997), 78.

6. See M. S. Kapitsa, *Na raznykh paralleliakh. Zapiski diplomata* (On Various Parallels: Notes of a Diplomat) (Moscow: Kniga i biznes, 1996), 63.

7. "Mao Tszedun o kitaiskoi politike Kominterna i Stalina" (Mao Zedong on the China Policy of the Comintern and Stalin), 107, 108.

8. See Pantsov and Levine, *Chinese Comintern Activists: An Analytic Biographic Dictionary*, 48.

9. Ibid., 48, 71–72.

10. See Boris A. Starkov, "The Trial That Was Not Held," *Europe-Asia Studies* 46, no. 8 (1994): 1297–1316; Reinhard Müller, "Der Fall des Antikomintern-Blocks—ein vierter Moskauer Schaoprozeβ," *Jahrbuch für Historishce Kommunismusforschung*, 1996, 187–214.

11. Later, in conversations with Soviet representatives, Mao would often say that he himself would write a book about Stalin's errors and crimes. "It will be so terrible that I will not allow it to be published in 10,000 years." See, for instance, Mao, *Mao Zedong on Diplomacy*, 257.

12. Concerning Chen Boda's authorship, see Mao Zedong, *Jianguo yilai Mao Zedong wengao* (Mao's Manuscripts), vol. 6 (Beijing: Zhongyang wenxian chubanshe, 1992), 59.

13. For Mao's corrections and additions to the text of the article, see ibid., 59–67. Concerning the Politburo's discussion of Khrushchev's speech and different versions of the article, see the reminiscences of the former director of the New China News Agency Wu Lengxi, who took part in several of the sessions. The discussion stretched from March 17 to April 4. Wu Lengxi, *Yi Mao zhuxi: Wo qinshen jinglide ruogan zhongda lishi shijian pianduan* (Remembering Chairman Mao: Some Important Historical Events from My Own Life) (Beijing: Xinhua chubanshe, 1995), 2–7; Wu, *Shinian lunduan* (The Ten-Year Debate), vol. 1, 12–33.

14. Borisov and Titarenko, *Vystupleniia Mao Tsze-duna, ranee ne publikovavshiesia v kitaiskoi pechati* (Mao Zedong's Speeches Previously Unpublished in China), series 1, 93.

15. Quoted from Chen and Yang, "Chinese Politics and the Collapse of the Sino-Soviet Alliance," 263.

16. Mao, *Mao Zedong on Diplomacy*, 251.

17. William Taubman, *Khrushchev: The Man and His Era* (New York: Norton, 2003), 339.

18. Krutikov, *Na kitaiskom napravleniu* (Pointed Toward China), 212–13.

19. See N. S. Khrushchev, *Report of the Central Committee of the Communist Party of the Soviet Union to the 20th Party Congress* (Moscow: Foreign Languages Publishing House, 1956), 38–46.

20. See the analysis of Mao's speech on this subject at an enlarged Politburo meeting on March 12, 1956, published in Wu, *Yi Mao zhuxi*, 4–5.

21. Krutikov, *Na kitaiskum napravleniu* (Pointed Toward China), 212.

22. Li, *The Private Life of Chairman Mao*, 238.

23. Mao, *Selected Works of Mao Tsetung*, vol. 5, 152–53.

24. Quoted from O. E. Vladimirov (O. B. Rakhmanin), ed., *Maoizm bez prikras: Nekotorye uzhe izvestnye, a takzhe ranee ne opublikovannye v kitaiskoi pechati vyskazyvaniia Mao Tszeduna: Sbornik* (Maoism Unembellished: Some Already Known Sayings of Mao Zedong and Others Previously Unpublished in the Chinese Press: A Collection) (Moscow: Progress, 1980), 238; Mao Zedong, *Mao Zedong wenji* (Works of Mao Zedong), vol. 7 (Beijing: Renmin chubanshe, 1999), 412; see also Mao, *Mao Zedong wenji* (Works of Mao Zedong), vol. 6, 367–70; Mao's recollection of his conversation with Nehru published in Edgar Snow, *The Long Revolution* (New York: Random House, 1972), 208.

25. Mao, *Selected Works of Mao Tsetung*, vol. 5, 284.

26. Ibid., 303–6; see also Schram, *Chairman Mao Talks to the People*, 61–83.

27. See Yang Shengqun and Yan Jianqi, eds., *Deng Xiaoping nianpu, 1904–1974* (Chronological Biography of Deng Xiaoping, 1904–1974), vol. 3 (Beijing: Zhongyang wenxian chubanshe, 2010), 1421.

28. See Li Ping, *Kaiguo zongli Zhou Enlai* (Zhou Enlai, the First Premier) (Beijing: Zhonggong zhongyang dangxiao chubanshe, 1994), 356. See also Chen and Yang, "Chinese Politics and the Collapse of the Sino-Soviet Alliance," 287.

29. See Mao, *Jianguo yilai Mao Zedong wengao* (Mao Zedong's Manuscripts), vol. 6, 105.

30. Borisov and Titarenko, *Vystupleniia Mao Tsze-duna, ranee ne publikovavshiesia v kitaiskoi pechati* (Mao Zedong's Speeches Previously Unpublished in the Chinese Press), series 2, 123.

31. Li, *The Private Life of Chairman Mao*, 234.

32. Ibid., 158.

33. Ibid., 154.

34. See ibid., 162–68, 177; Liao Gailong et al., eds., *Mao Zedong baike quanshu* (Encyclopedia of Mao Zedong), vol. 6 (Beijing: Guangming ribao chubanshe, 2003), 3108.

35. Quoted from Li, *The Private Life of Chairman Mao*, 165.

36. Mao, *Poems of Mao Tse-tung*, 97.

37. See Li, *The Private Life of Chairman Mao*, 181, 183, 192.

38. See Mao, *Selected Works of Mao Tsetung*, vol. 5, 312–23; *Materialy VIII Vsekitaiskogo s'ezda Kommunisticheskoi partii Kitaia* (Materials from the Eighth Congress of the Communist Party of China) (Moscow: Gospolitizdat, 1956), 3–6.

39. Mao, *Jianguo yilai Mao Zedong wengao* (Mao's Manuscripts), vol. 6, 148.

40. Mao, *Mao Zedong on Diplomacy*, 251–52.

41. It was suggested by Peng Dehuai (see *The Case of Peng Dehuai 1959–1968* [Hong Kong: Union Research Institute, 1968], 445), who may have recalled that on numerous occasions Mao himself had balked at the term "Mao Zedong Thought." See Shen Zhihua, "Zhonggong bada weishenma bu ti 'Mao Zedong sixiang' " (Why did the Eighth Congress not Raise "Mao Zedong Thought"?), *Lishi jiaoxue* (Teaching of history), no. 5 (2005): 6. However, Mao did not suggest removing the sentence from the party statutes.

42. *Materialy VIII Vsekitaiskogo s'ezda Kommunisticheskoi partii Kitaia* (Materials from the Eighth Congress of the Communist Party of China), 508.

43. Ibid., 98.

44. Mao, *Mao Zedong wenji* (Works of Mao Zedong), vol. 7, 110. See also Mao, *Jianguo yilai Mao Zedong wengao* (Mao's Manuscripts), vol. 6, 165; Wingrove, *Mao's Conversations with the Soviet Ambassador, 1953–1955*, 36.

45. *Materialy VIII Vsekitaiskogo s'ezda Kommunisticheskoi partii Kitaia* (Materials from the Eighth Congress of the Communist Party of China), 472.

46. See Meliksetov, *Istoriia Kitaia*, 647.

47. "Minutes, Mao's Conversation with a Yugoslavian Communist Union Delegation," 151.

48. Quoted from Taubman, *Khrushchev*, 339.

49. Quoted in Westad, *Brothers in Arms*, 378.

50. Quoted from Wu, *Shinian lunduan* (The Ten-Year Debate), vol. 1, 35.

51. A. A. Fursenko, ed., *Prezidium TsK KPSS, 1954–1964* (Presidium of the Central Committee of the CPSU, 1954–1964), *Chernovye protokol'nye zapisi zasedanii. Stenogrammy. Postanovleniia* (Draft Notes of the Sessions. Stenograms. Resolutions), vol. 1 (Moscow: ROSSPEN, 2003), 174–75; A. A. Fursenko, ed., *Prezidium TSK KPSS, 1954–1964* (The Presidium of the CC of the CPSU, 1954–1964), vol. 2, *Postanovleniia 1954–1958* (Resolutions of 1954–1958) (Moscow: ROSSPEN, 2006), 471–72.

52. Quoted from Li and Ma, *Zhou Enlai nianpu (1949–1976)* (Chronological Biography of Zhou Enlai [1949–1976]), vol. 1, 631; "Records of Meetings of the CPSU and CCP Delegations, Moscow, July 5–20, 1963," 378. See also Wu, *Shinian lunduan* (The Ten-Year Debate), vol. 1, 42–45.

53. See *Istoricheskii arkhiv* (Historical archive), nos. 4–5 (1996): 184–85.

54. See Pang and Jin, *Mao Zedong zhuan (1949–1976)* (Biography of Mao Zedong [1949–1976]), vol. 1, 602–3; *Vozniknoveniie i razvitiie raznoglasii mezhdu rukovodstvom KPSS i nami: Po povodu otkrytogo pis'ma TsK KPSS* (The Origin and Development of Disagreements Between the Leadership of the CPSU and Us: On the Open Letter of the CC CPSU) (Beijing: Izdatel'stvo literatury na inostrannykh iazykakh, 1963), 12; "Records of Meeting of the CPSU and CCP Delegations, Moscow, July 5–20, 1963," 378.

55. See Fursenko, *Prezidium TsK KPSS, 1954–1964* (Presidium of the Central Committee of the CPSU, 1954–1964), vol. 1, 175.

56. Quoted from Taubman, *Khrushchev*, 297.

57. Fursenko, *Prezidium TsK KPSS, 1954–1964* (Presidium of the CC CPSU, 1954–1964), vol. 1, 188.

58. Kurdiukov, *Sovietsko-Kitaiskie otnosheniia* (Soviet-Chinese Relations), 319.

59. Khrushchev, *Memoirs of Nikita Khrushchev*, vol. 3, 651. See also the remarks of Liu Shaoqi on this subject at the Second Plenum of the Eighth Central Committee of the CCP, November 10, 1956, published in Pang and Jin, *Mao Zedong zhuan (1949–1976)* (Biography of Mao Zedong [1949–1976]), vol. 1, 603–5.

60. Mao, *Selected Works of Mao Tsetung*, vol. 5, 341. It is interesting that in maneuvering prior to the Eighth Congress, in August 1956, he did not oppose inclusion in the draft of Liu Shaoqi's Political Report a statement asserting that "[t]he Twentieth Congress of the Communist Party of the Soviet Union . . . has made an outstanding contribution to the slackening of international tension and the struggle for world peace and the progress of mankind." Mao, *Jianguo yilai Mao Zedong wengao* (Mao's Manuscripts), vol. 6, 137–38. This statement, somewhat revised, was also in the final text of the report.

61. Mao, *Selected Works of Mao Tsetung*, vol. 5, 342.

62. Quoted from Pang and Jin, *Mao Zedong zhuan (1949–1976)* (Biography of Mao Zedong [1949–1976]), vol. 1, 606.

63. Mao, *Selected Works of Mao Tsetung*, vol. 5, 347–49.

64. See Bo, *Ruogan zhongda juece yu shijian de huigu* (Recollections of Several Important Political Decisions and Their Implementation), vol. 1, 555–59.

65. Ibid., 556–57; Zhou, *Zhou Enlai xuanji* (Selected Works of Zhou Enlai), vol. 2, 229–38. For a more detailed treatment see Shevelev, *Formirovanie sotsial'no-ekonomicheskoi politiki rukovodstva KPK v 1949–1956 godakh* (The Formation of the CCP's Socioeconomic Policy in 1949–1956), X-2-10.

66. See Shevelev, *Formirovanie sotsial'no-ekonomicheskoi politiki rukovodstva KPK v 1949–1956 godakh* (The Formation of the CCP's Socioeconomic Policy in 1949–1956), X-9-10.

67. Pang and Jin, *Mao Zedong zhuan (1949–1976)* (Biography of Mao Zedong [1949–1976]), vol. 1, 606.

68. See Mao, *Jianguo yilai Mao Zedong wengao* (Mao's Manuscripts), vol. 6, 285.

69. See Liu and Chen, *Liu Shaoqi nianpu, 1898–1969* (Chronological Biography of Liu Shaoqi, 1898–1969), vol. 2, 378; Li and Ma, *Zhou Enlai nianpu (1949–1976)* (Chronological Biography of Zhou Enlai [1949–1976]), vol. 2, 4–14; *CWIHP Bulletin*, nos. 6–7 (1995/1996): 153–54; Khrushchev, *Vremia, Liudi, Vlast'* (Time, People, Power), Book 3, 49–52.

70. *CWIHP Bulletin*, nos. 6–7 (1995/1996): 152, 154.

71. See Taubman, *Khrushchev*, 339.

72. Kurdiukov, *Sovetsko-kitaiskie otnosheniia* (Soviet-Chinese Relations), 329.

73. *CWIHP Bulletin*, nos. 6–7 (1995/1996): 153.

74. Ibid.

75. Mao, *Selected Works of Mao Tsetung*, vol. 5, 350–83; Borisov and Titarenko, *Vystupleniia Mao Tsze-duna, ranee ne publikovavshiesia v kitaiskoi pechati* (Mao Zedong's Speeches Previously Unpublished in the Chinese Press), series 1, 117–19, 124, 126–28, 138, 139; Chen and Yang, "Chinese Politics and the Collapse of the Sino-Soviet Alliance," in Westad, *Brothers in Arms*, 266.

76. See Krutikov, *Na kitaiskom napravleniu* (Pointed Toward China), 226–27.

77. Mao, *Selected Works of Mao Tsetung*, vol. 5, 420.

78. Borisov and Titarenko, *Vystupleniia Mao Tsze-duna, ranee ne publikovavshiesia v kitaiskoi pechati* (Mao Zedong's Speeches Previously Unpublished in the Chinese Press), series 1, 242–43.

79. Mao, *Selected Works of Mao Tsetung*, vol. 5, 408–14.

80. See Roderick MacFarquhar, *The Hundred Flowers Campaign and the Chinese Intellectuals* (New York: Praeger, 1960).

81. See Meliksetov, *Istoriia Kitaia* (History of China), 647–48.

82. Ibid., 649.

83. See Chen and Yang, "Chinese Politics and the Collapse of the Sino-Soviet Alliance," in Westad, *Brothers in Arms*, 265.

84. Borisov and Titarenko, *Vystupleniia Mao Tsze-duna, ranee ne publikovavshiesia v kitaiskoi pechati* (Mao Zedong's Speeches Previously Unpublished in the Chinese Press), series 2, 122, 273.

85. Mao, *Selected Works of Mao Tsetung*, vol. 5, 491.

86. Borisov and Titarenko, *Vystupleniia Mao Tsze-duna, ranee ne publikovavshiesia v kitaiskoi pechati* (Mao Zedong's Speeches Previously Unpublished in the Chinese Press), series 2, 50, 55–56.

87. Ibid., 93.

88. Li, *The Private Life of Chairman Mao*, 218.

89. During this trip Mao introduced Deng Xiaoping to Khrushchev with these words: "See that little fellow over there? . . . He's a very wise man, sees far into the future." Quoted from Khrushchev, *Memoirs of Nikita Khrushchev*, vol. 3, 439. Then he added: "He is not only a man of principle, but also versatile, he is a rare talent." Quoted from Li, *Waijiao wutai shang de xin Zhongguo lingxiu* (Leaders of the New China in the Diplomatic Arena), 143.

90. Li Yueran, "Mao zhuxi di erci fangwen Sulian" (Chairman Mao's Second Visit to the Soviet Union), in Li, *Zhenshide Mao Zedong* (The Real Mao Zedong), 567; Li, *Waijiao wutai shang de xin Zhongguo lingxiu* (Leaders of the New China in the Diplomatic Arena), 125. On Mao's visit to the USSR in 1957, see also Yang Shangkun, *Yang Shangkun riji* (Yang Shangkun's Diary), vol. 1 (Beijing: Zhongyang wenxian chubanshe, 2001), 284–96.

91. He returned to the question of Molotov later, just before his departure to Moscow, in conversation with Ambassador Yudin. "Talking about what's going on in our party," he observed, "many comrades cannot understand how such an old party veteran, who fought for the revolution over the course of several decades, could become an anti-party element." Yudin heard the same thing from Peng Dehuai, who queried the ambassador, "Why did you put it ['anti-party group'] that way? Couldn't you think of something wiser?" Quoted from Taubman, *Khrushchev*, 340.

92. Quoted from Vereshchagin, *V starom i novom Kitae* (In Old and New China), 94–95.

93. Li, *The Private Life of Chairman Mao*, 220.

94. Quoted from ibid., 221, 222.

95. Shi and Li, *Zhongsu guanxi jiancheng lu* (Eyewitness Notes on Sino-Soviet Relations), 56.

96. Li, *Waijiao wutai shang de xin Zhongguo lingxiu* (Leaders of the New China in the Diplomatic Arena), 142–43; Lu Zhen and Liu Qingxia, "Mao Zedong chong Heluxiaofu fahuo" (How Mao Zedong Got Angry at Khrushchev), *Zhuanji wenxue* (Biographical literature), no. 4 (2004): 25.

97. Borisov and Titarenko, *Vystupleniia Mao Tsze-duna, ranee ne publikovavshiesia v kitaiskoi pechati* (Mao Zedong's Speeches Previously Unpublished in the Chinese Press), series 2, 94.

98. Alexander V. Pantsov's interview with O. A. Grinevskii, Columbus, Ohio, April 4, 2004.

99. Khrushchev, *Memoirs of Nikita Khrushchev*, vol. 3, 461.

100. In 1965, in response to Edgar Snow's question, "[D]o you still believe as before that the

[atomic] bomb is a paper tiger?" Mao replied that all of his talks on this theme were "just a way of talking . . . a figure of speech." Quoted from Snow, *The Long Revolution,* 208; see also Mao, *Mao Zedong wenji* (Works of Mao Zedong), vol. 8, 401.

101. Quoted from Ye, *Ye Zilong huiyilu* (Memoirs of Ye Zilong), 190.

102. Li, *The Private Life of Chairman Mao,* 224.

103. Borisov and Titarenko, *Vystupleniia Mao Tsze-duna, ranee ne publikovavshiesia v kitaiskoi pechati* (Mao Zedong's Speeches Previously Unpublished in the Chinese Press), series 2, 94. Mao said essentially the same thing in his meeting with Andrei Gromyko, minister of foreign affairs of the USSR, that took place during this time. See A. A. Gromyko, *Pamiatnoe* (Remembered), vol. 2 (Moscow: Politizdat, 1988), 131.

104. See *Pravda* (Truth), November 7, 1957.

105. *CWIHP Bulletin,* nos. 6–7 (1995/1996): 152.

106. Borisov and Titarenko, *Vystupleniia Mao Tsze-duna, ranee ne publikovavshiesia v kitaiskoi pechati* (Mao Zedong's Speeches Previously Unpublished in the Chinese Press), series 2, 102, 105, 106.

107. Ibid., 123; Li, *Kaiguo zongli Zhou Enlai* (Zhou Enlai, the First Premier), 359.

108. Quoted from Li, *Kaiguo zongli Zhou Enlai* (Zhou Enlai, the First Premier), 361.

109. See ibid., 362–63.

110. Borisov and Titarenko, *Vystupleniia Mao Tsze-duna, ranee ne publikovavshiesia v kitaiskoi pechati* (Mao Zedong's Speeches Previously Unpublished in the Chinese Press), series 2, 134–55.

30. THE GREAT LEAP FORWARD

1. Ibid., 120, 121.

2. Ibid., 112, 377; series 3 (Moscow: Progress, 1976), 40.

3. Quoted from Li, *The Private Life of Chairman Mao,* 226.

4. See Roderick M. MacFarquhar, *The Origins of the Cultural Revolution,* vol. 2, *The Great Leap Forward 1958–1960* (New York: Columbia University Press, 1983), 34, 347; Frederick C. Teiwes, *Politics and Purges in China: Rectification and the Decline of Party Norms, 1950–1965,* 2nd ed. (Armonk, NY: M.E. Sharpe, 1993), 266; Mobo G. G. Gao, *Gao Village: A Portrait of Rural Life in Modern China* (Honolulu: University of Hawai'i Press, 1999), 123.

5. Deng, *Selected Works of Deng Xiaoping (1975–1982),* 295. For more details about Deng's excitement in regard to the Great Leap, see Yang and Yan, *Deng Xiaoping nianpu, 1904–1974* (Chronological Biography of Deng Xiaoping, 1904–1974), vol. 3, 1463–68.

6. Borisov and Titarenko, *Vystupleniia Mao Tsze-duna, ranee ne publikovavshiesia v kitaiskoi pechati* (Mao Zedong's Speeches Previously Unpublished in the Chinese Press), series 2, 111–12, 131; Mao Zedong, *Jianguo yilai Mao Zedong wengao* (Mao's Manuscripts), vol. 7 (Beijing: Zhongyang wenxian chubanshe, 1998), 25–26.

7. Pang and Jin, *Mao Zedong zhuan (1949–1976)* (Biography of Mao Zedong [1949–1976]), vol. 1, 766.

8. *Vtoraia sessiia VIII Vsekitaiskogo s"ezda Kommunisticheskoi partii Kitaia* (Second Session of the Eighth Congress of the Communist Party of China) (Peking: Izdatel'stvo literatury na inostrannykh iazykakh, 1958), 68.

9. Borisov and Titarenko, *Vystuplenia Mao Tsze-duna, ranee ne publikovavshiesia v kitaiskoi pechati* (Mao Zedong's Speeches Previously Unpublished in the Chinese Press), series 2, 156, 158.

10. Ibid., 103; Bowie and Fairbank, *Communist China 1955–1959: Policy Documents with Analysis,* 125.

11. Borisov and Titarenko, *Vystupleniia Mao Tsze-duna, ranee ne publikovavshiesia v kitaiskoi pechati* (Mao Zedong's Speeches Previously Unpublished in the Chinese Press), series 2, 52.

12. Mao, *Jianguo yilai Mao Zedong wengao* (Mao's Manuscripts), vol. 6, 666–69; vol. 7, 4.

13. Mikhail A. Klochko, *Soviet Scientist in Red China*, trans. Andrew MacAndrew (New York: Praeger, 1964), 68–69.

14. See MacFarquhar, *The Origins of the Cultural Revolution*, vol. 2, 22–23.

15. Borisov and Titarenko, *Vystupleniia Mao Tsze-duna, ranee ne publikovavshiesia v kitaiskoi pechati* (Mao Zedong's Speeches Previously Unpublished in the Chinese Press), series 2, 125, 339.

16. See Huang Lingjun, "Liu Shaoqi yu dayuejin" (Liu Shaoqi and the Great Leap Forward), *Zhongguo xiandaishi* (Contemporary history of China), no. 7 (2003): 107.

17. See Ye, *Ye Zilong huiyilu* (Memoirs of Ye Zilong), 213.

18. Borisov and Titarenko, *Vystupleniia Mao Tsze-duna, ranee ne publikovavshiesia v kitaiskoi pechati* (Mao Zedong's Speeches Previously Unpublished in the Chinese Press), series 2, 158, 170.

19. Quoted from Huang, "Liu Shaoqi yu dayuejin" (Liu Shaoqi and the Great Leap Forward), 107.

20. Mao, *Jianguo yilai Mao Zedong wengao* (Mao's Manuscripts), vol. 7, 317.

21. Quoted from Li, *The Private Life of Chairman Mao*, 269.

22. Borisov and Titarenko, *Vystupleniia Mao Tsze-duna, ranee ne publikovavshiesia v kitaiskoi pechati* (Mao Zedong's Speeches Previously Unpublished in the Chinese Press), series 2, 310, 311, 315, 329.

23. Mao, *Jianguo yilai Mao Zedong wengao* (Mao's Manuscripts), vol. 7, 177–78.

24. Borisov and Titarenko, *Vystupleniia Mao Tsze-duna, ranee ne publikovavshiesia v kitaiskoi pechati* (Mao Zedong's Speeches Previously Unpublished in the Chinese Press), series 2, 201, 237, 238, 312, 314, 316, 319, 329.

25. Ibid., 241, 307, 319, 336.

26. See ibid., 327–28, 333–34.

27. For the Bolshevik perspective on war communism see "Pis'mo L. D. Trotskogo [V. I. Leninu] ot 19 dekabria 1919 g." (Letter from L. D. Trotsky [to V. I. Lenin]. December 19, 1919), RGASPI, collection 5, inventory 1, file 1408, sheets 1–2.

28. See Huang, "Liu Shaoqi yu dayuejin" (Liu Shaoqi and the Great Leap Forward), 107–8.

29. See Borisov and Titarenko, *Vystupleniia Mao Tsze-duna, ranee ne publikovavshiesia v kitaiskoi pechati* (Mao Zedong's Speeches Previously Unpublished in the Chinese Press), series 2, 264, 275, 281; MacFarquhar, *The Origins of the Cultural Revolution*, vol. 2, 83, 90.

30. Borisov and Titarenko, *Vystupleniia Mao Tsze-duna, ranee ne publikovavshiesia v kitaiskoi pechati* (Mao Zedong's Speeches Previously Unpublished in the Chinese Press), series 2, 337.

31. Ibid., 317, 334.

32. Quoted from Li, *The Private Life of Chairman Mao*, 276.

33. Borisov and Titarenko, *Vystupleniia Mao Tsze-duna, ranee ne publikovavshiesia v kitaiskoi pechati* (Mao Zedong's Speeches Previously Unpublished in the Chinese Press), series 2, 266.

34. Peng Dehuai, *Memuary marshala* (Memoirs of a Marshal), trans. A. V. Pantsov, V. N. Usov, and K. V. Sheveliev (Moscow: Voenizdat, 1988), 486–87; see also Borisov and Titarenko, *Vystupleniia Mao Tsze-duna, ranee ne publikovavshiesia v kitaiskoi pechati* (Mao Zedong's Speeches Previously Unpublished in the Chinese Press), series 2, 360, 383, 403.

35. See MacFarquhar, *The Origins of the Cultural Revolution*, vol. 2, 328.

36. See Mao, *Mao Zedong on Diplomacy*, 247, 250–58; Zhang, "Sino-Soviet Economic Co-operation," 207.

37. See Vereshchagin, *V starom i novom Kitae* (In Old and New China), 119–29.

38. Khrushchev, *Memoirs of Nikita Khrushchev*, vol. 3, 454–58.

39. Quoted from Wolff, "One Finger's Worth of Historical Events," 54, 55; Zubok, "The Mao-Khrushchev Conversations," 256.

40. See Lu and Liu, "Mao Zedong chong Heluxiaofu fahuo" (How Mao Zedong Got An-

gry at Khrushchev), 27; Li, *Waijiao wutai shang de xin Zhongguo lingxiu* (Leaders of New China in the Diplomatic Arena), 154–58; N. Fedorenko, "Vizit N. Khrushcheva v Pekin" (N. Khrushchev's Visit to Beijing), *Problemy Dal'nego Vostoka* (Far Eastern affairs), no. 1 (1990): 123; Taubman, *Khrushchev*, 390–92.

41. Quoted from *Ogonek* (Little light), no. 14 (1999): 28–29. See also M. Romm, *Ustnye rasskazy* (Oral Tales) (Moscow: "Kinotsentr," 1991), 154; Khrushchev, *Memoirs of Nikita Khrushchev*, vol. 3, 456–62.

42. Quoted from Wolff, "One Finger's Worth of Historical Events," 53; Zubok, "The Mao-Khrushchev Conversations," 268.

43. Li, *The Private Life of Chairman Mao*, 261.

44. Quoted from Fedorenko, "Vizit N. Khrushcheva v Pekin" (N. Khrushchev's Visit to Beijing), 123; Vereshchagin, *V starom i novom Kitae* (In Old and New China), 130. See also Ye, *Ye Zilong huiyilu* (Memoirs of Ye Zilong), 215. Mao's translator Li Yueran, however, recalled that it was Liu Shaoqi who asked Khrushchev what to do with the surplus of grain in China. See Li, *Waijiao wutai shang de xin Zhongguo lingxiu* (Leaders of the New China in the Diplomatic Arena), 149–50.

45. See Khrushchev, *Memoirs of Nikita Khrushchev*, vol. 3, 441.

46. Ibid., 442–43.

47. *CWIHP Bulletin*, nos. 6–7 (1995/1996): 219, 226–27; Pang and Jin, *Mao Zedong zhuan (1949–1976)* (Biography of Mao Zedong [1949–1976]), vol. 1, 856–84; Liu Xiao, *Chushi Sulian ba nian* (Eight Years as Ambassador to the USSR) (Beijing: Zhonggong dangshi chubanshe, 1998), 74–78. See also Chen Jian, *Mao's China and the Cold War* (Chapel Hill: University of North Carolina Press, 2001), 163–204.

48. Borisov and Titarenko, *Vystupleniia Mao Tsze-duna, ranee ne publikovavshiesia v kitaiskoi pechati* (Mao Zedong's Speeches Previously Unpublished in the Chinese Press), series 2, 414, 419–20; series 3, 164–65; MacFarquhar, *The Origins of the Cultural Revolution*, vol. 2, 247.

49. See *Lichnoe delo Mao Tszeduna* (Personal File of Mao Zedong), RGASPI, collection 495, inventory 225, file 71, vol. 1, sheets 117–18; *Materialy 6-go plenuma Tsentral'nogo Komiteta Kommunisticheskoi partii Kitaia vos'mogo sozyva* (Materials of the Sixth Plenum of the Eighth Central Committee) (Beijing: Izdatel'stvo literatury na inostrannykh iazykakh, 1959), 55.

50. Some of these statistics are presented in the survey "The contemporary economic situation in the PRC" (in Russian), prepared in early July 1959 by the State Committee on International Economic Relations of the USSR Council of Ministers. Excerpts from them are in Wolff, "One Finger's Worth of Historical Events," 63–64. See also MacFarquhar, *The Origins of the Cultural Revolution*, vol. 2, 202.

51. See Becker, *Hungry Ghosts*, 85.

52. Quoted from Li, *The Private Life of Chairman Mao*, 295.

53. Borisov and Titarenko, *Vystupleniia Mao Tsze-duna, ranee ne publikovavshiesia v kitaiskoi pechati* (Mao Zedong's Speeches Previously Unpublished in the Chinese Press), series 2, 413.

54. See Wolff, "One Finger's Worth of Historical Events," 63.

55. Li, *The Private Life of Chairman Mao*, 302, 304. For a different and radiant account of Mao's visit to Shaoshan, see the one written in 1965 by Zhou Lipo, head of the Hunan Federation of Writers, "A Visit to His Hometown," in *Mao Zedong: Biography—Assessment—Reminiscences*, 233–38.

56. Mao, *Oblaka v snegu* (Clouds in the Snow), 75.

57. Borisov and Titarenko, *Vystupleniia Mao Tsze-duna, ranee ne publikovavshiesia v kitaiskoi pechati* (Mao Zedong's Speeches Previously Unpublished in the Chinese Press), series 3, 109.

58. See Li, *The Private Life of Chairman Mao*, 109, 142, 143, 349, 353, 401, 452; Kartunova, "Vstrechi v Moskve s Tszian Tsin, zhenoi Mao Tszedun" (Meetings in Moscow with Jiang

Qing, the Wife of Mao Zedong), 127; Witke, *Comrade Chiang Ch'ing*, 30–31, 48, 124, 164, 169, 172–73, 225–26, 227–28, 241, 242, 254–56, 259, 260, 268–71, 303, 445.

59. Quoted from Li, *Moi otets Mao Tszedun* (My Father Mao Zedong), 189; see also the memoirs of Li Min's daughter, Kong, *Ting waipo jiang neiguoqu de shiqing—Mao Zedong yu He Zizhen* (Listening to Grandmother's Stories about Her Past—Mao Zedong and He Zizhen).

60. "Comrade Peng Dehuai's Letter to Chairman Mao (July 14, 1959)," in Peng, *Memoirs of a Chinese Marshal*, 517–18.

61. See Li, *The Private Life of Chairman Mao*, 315. See also Li and Ma, *Zhou Enlai nianpu (1949–1976)* (Chronological Biography of Zhou Enlai [1949–1976]), vol. 2, 243.

62. Huang Kecheng, "Lushan fengyun" (The Lushan Events), in Lu and Chen, *Hongse jiyi* (Red Reminiscences), 423–24.

63. Peng, *Memoirs of a Chinese Marshal*, 504.

64. Quoted from Li, *The Private Life of Chairman Mao*, 317.

65. Borisov and Titarenko, *Vystupleniia Mao Tsze-duna, ranee ne publikovavshiesia v kitaiskoi pechati* (Mao Zedong's Speeches Previously Unpublished in the Chinese Press), series 3, 111.

66. Peng, *Memoirs of a Chinese Marshal*, 508. See also Li Rui, *Lushan huiyi shilu* (The True Record of the Lushan Plenum) (Beijing: Chunqiu chubanshe/Hunan jiaoyu chubanshe, 1989); Pang and Jin, *Mao Zedong zhuan (1949–1976)* (Biography of Mao Zedong [1949–1976]), vol. 2, 953–1010; Zhang, *Zhang Wentian nianpu* (Chronological Biography of Zhang Wentian), vol. 2, 1147–56; *Zhou Xiaozhou zhuan* (Biography of Zhou Xiaozhou) (Changsha: Hunan renmin chubanshe, 1985), 58–71, 93–94; Yu. N. Galenovich, *Peng Dehuai i Mao Tszedun: Politicheskie lidery Kitaia XX veka* (Peng Dehuai and Mao Zedong: Political Leaders of 20th Century China) (Moscow: Ogni, 2005).

67. Quoted from Galenovich, *Peng Dehuai i Mao Tszedun* (Peng Dehuai and Mao Zedong), 101.

68. See Peng, *Memuary marshala* (Memoirs of a Marshal), 14.

69. See *Dokumenty VIII Plenuma Tsentral'nogo Komiteta Kommunisticheskoi partii Kitaia vos'mogo sozyva* (Documents of the Eighth Plenum of the Eighth Central Committee of the Communist Party of China) (Beijing: Izdatel'stvo literatury na inostrannykh iazykakh, 1959), 33.

70. Quoted from Frank Dikötter, *Mao's Great Famine: The History of China's Most Devastating Catastrophe, 1958–1962* (New York: Walker, 2010), 88, 134.

71. Borisov and Titarenko, *Vystupleniia Mao Tsze-duna, ranee ne publikovavshiesia v kitaiskoi pechati* (Mao Zedong's Speeches Previously Unpublished in the Chinese Press), series 3, 92.

72. Ibid., series 2, 165.

73. Quoted from Huang, "Liu Shaoqi yu dayuejin" (Liu Shaoqi and the Great Leap Forward), 108.

74. See *Hongqi* (Red flag), no. 2 (1981): 33.

75. Krutikov, *Na kitaiskom napravleniu* (Pointed Toward China), 281. See also Khrushchev, *Memoirs of Nikita Khrushchev*, vol. 3, 464–69; Vereshchagin, *V starom i novom Kitae* (In Old and New China), 145–48; Kapitsa, *Na raznykh parallelakh* (On Various Parallels), 63–65; MacFarquhar, *The Origins of the Cultural Revolution*, vol. 2, 256–60.

76. See "Records of Meeting of the CPSU and CCP Delegations, Moscow, July 5–20, 1963," 379; MacFarquhar, *The Origins of the Cultural Revolution*, vol. 2, 225–26; Shu Guang Zhang, "Between 'Paper' and 'Real Tigers': Mao's View of Nuclear Weapons," in John Lewis Gaddis et al., eds., *Cold War Statesmen Confront the Bomb: Nuclear Diplomacy Since 1945* (Oxford: Oxford University Press, 1999), 208.

77. See Zhang, "Sino-Soviet Economic Cooperation," 207; MacFarquhar, *The Origins of the Cultural Revolution*, vol. 2, 11–15; Wu, *Shinian lunduan* (The Ten-Year Debate), 205–8.

78. Khrushchev, *Memoirs of Nikita Khrushchev*, vol. 3, 480–81.

79. Quoted from MacFarquhar, *The Origins of the Cultural Revolution*, vol. 2, 226–27.

80. In May 1955, for example, during a visit to Yugoslavia, Khrushchev drank so much that he started to kiss everyone, especially Tito, and reeking of alcohol, said, "Iosya, quit being angry! What a thin skinned one you are! Let's drink up, and may whoever brings up the past lose his sight!" Quoted from Galina Vishnevskaia, *Galina: Istoriia zhizni* (Galina: A Life Story) (Moscow: Gorizont, 1991), 179. A year later at an air show in Tushino near Moscow, quite intoxicated, he began to bad-mouth all foreign countries, and did not even notice when several foreign diplomats got up from their seats and walked out. Taubman, *Khrushchev*, 348.

81. See Dong Wang, "The Quarreling Brothers: New Chinese Archives and a Reappraisal of the Sino-Soviet Split, 1959–1962," *CWIHP Working Paper*, no. 36 (April 2002): 1–80.

82. For excerpts from the stenographic report of the negotiations between N. S. Khrushchev and Mao Zedong on October 2, 1959, as well as the report by M. A. Suslov, secretary of the Central Committee of the CPSU, see Wolff, "One Finger's Worth of Historical Events," 64–72; also Zubok, "The Mao-Khrushchev Conversations," 262–70.

83. Quoted from Wolff, "One Finger's Worth of Historical Events," 65; Zubok, "The Mao-Khrushchev Conversations," 266, 267, 269.

84. Khrushchev, *Memoirs of Nikita Khrushchev*, vol. 3, 468. See also Liu, *Chushi Sulian ba nian* (Eight Years as Ambassador to the USSR), 88–91; Li, *Waijiao wutai shang de xin Zhongguo lingxiu* (Leaders of the New China in the Diplomatic Arena), 159–64.

85. Quoted from Wolff, "One Finger's Worth of Historical Events," 70. On the Sino-Soviet rift, see in detail Lorenz M. Lüthi, *The Sino-Soviet Split: Cold War in the Communist World* (Princeton, NJ: Princeton University Press, 2008).

86. Taubman, *Khrushchev*, 394.

87. Mao Zedong, *Jianguo yilai Mao Zedong wengao* (Mao's Manuscripts), vol. 8 (Beijing: Zhongyang wenxian chubanshe, 1993), 600–601.

31. FAMINE AND FEAR

1. Borisov and Titarenko, *Vystupleniia Mao Tsze-duna, ranee ne publikovavshiesia v kitaiskoi pechati* (Mao Zedong's Speeches Previously Unpublished in the Chinese Press), series 3, 163.

2. See MacFarquhar, *The Origins of the Cultural Revolution*, vol. 2, 301, 305; V. N. Usov, *KNR: Ot "bol'shogo skachka" k "kul'turnoi revoliutsii" (1960–1966)* (The PRC: From the Great Leap to the "Cultural Revolution," [1960–1966]), part 1 (Moscow: IDV RAN, 1998), 13.

3. Quoted from Becker, *Hungry Ghosts*, 208.

4. Leung Laifong, *Morning Sun: Interviews with Chinese Writers of the Lost Generation* (Armonk, NY: M. E. Sharpe, 1994), 201, 202, 204.

5. Quoted from Becker, *Hungry Ghosts*, 159–60.

6. Leung, *Morning Sun*, 243.

7. Quoted from MacFarquhar, *The Origins of the Cultural Revolution*, vol. 2, 329.

8. Quoted from Becker, *Hungry Ghosts*, 153–54.

9. Alexander V. Pantsov's interview with a Beijing resident, October 28, 2004.

10. Li, *The Private Life of Chairman Mao*, 339, 340.

11. For details, see Lüthi, *The Sino-Soviet Split*, 167–80.

12. See *Hongqi* (Red flag), no. 8 (1960); *Renmin ribao* (People's daily), April 22, 1960; *Pravda* (Truth), April 23, 1960.

13. See "The Letter of the Central Committee of the CPSU to the Central Committee of the CPC, March 30, 1963," in *The Polemic on the General Line of the International Communist Movement* (Beijing: Foreign Languages Press, 1965), 496–97; Fursenko, *Prezidium TsK KPSS, 1954–1964* (Presidium of the CC CPSU, 1954–1964), vol. 1, 443.

14. Quoted from *The Sino-Soviet Dispute* (New York: Charles Scribner's Sons, 1969), 28; Taubman, *Khrushchev*, 471.

15. *Moskovskii komsomolets* (Moscow young communist), February 6, 2002.

16. See Gao, *Gao Village,* 138.

17. Quoted from Liu, *Chushi sulian ba nian* (Eight Years as Ambassador to the USSR), 128.

18. Mao Zedong, "Tong Sinuode tanhua (1960 nian 10 yue 22 ri)" (Conversation with Snow [October 22, 1960]), in Mao Zedong, *Mao Zedong wenji* (Works of Mao Zedong), vol. 8 (Beijing: Renmin chubanshe, 1999), 215, 216–17; excerpts from Snow's notes of his conversations with Mao cited in S. Bernard Thomas, *Season of High Adventure: Edgar Snow in China* (Berkeley: University of California Press, 1996), 299.

19. Edgar Snow, *The Other Side of the River: Red China Today* (New York: Random House, 1962), 619.

20. Bernard Law Montgomery, *Three Continents: A Study of the Situation and Problems in Asia, Africa, and Central America, and the Relationship of Those Areas to Defence Policies in the 1960's and to the British Commonwealth* (London: Collins, 1962), 17.

21. Quoted from Becker, *Hungry Ghosts,* 293.

22. See Dikötter, *Mao's Great Famine,* x, 324–34; Yang Jisheng, *Mubei: Zhongguo liushi nian dai da jihuang jishi* (Tombstone: Unforgettable Facts about the Great Famine in the 1960s), 2 vols. (Hong Kong: Tian di tushu youxian gongsi, 2008).

23. See Dudley L. Poston Jr. and David Yaukey, eds., *The Population of Modern China* (New York: Plenum Press, 1992), 170, 226, 252; Michael Dillon, ed., *China: A Cultural and Historical Dictionary* (Richmond, UK: Curzon Press, 1998), 122; Becker, *Hungry Ghosts,* 149, 161, 162, 164.

24. See MacFarquhar, *The Origins of the Cultural Revolution,* vol. 2, 330; Usov, *KNR: Ot "bol'shogo skachka" k "kul'turnoi revoliutsii"* (The PRC: From the "Great Leap" to the "Cultural Revolution"), 15.

25. Quoted from Thomas, *Season of High Adventure,* 300.

26. See MacFarquhar, *The Origins of the Cultural Revolution,* vol. 2, 323.

27. Borisov and Titarenko, *Vystupleniia Mao Tsze-duna, ranee ne publikovavshiesia v kitaiskoi pechati* (Mao Zedong's Speeches Previously Unpublished in the Chinese Press), series 3, 162.

28. Mao Zedong, *Miscellany of Mao Tse-tung Thought (1949–1968),* part 1 (Springfield, VA: Joint Publications Research Service, 1974), 232.

29. See MacFarquhar, *The Origins of the Cultural Revolution,* vol. 2, 324; Li and Ma, *Zhou Enlai nianpu (1949–1976)* (Chronological Biography of Zhou Enlai [1949–1976]), vol. 1, 366.

30. Borisov and Titarenko, *Vystupleniia Mao Tsze-duna, ranee ne publikovavshiesia v kitaiskoi pechati* (Mao Zedong's Speeches Previously Unpublished in the Chinese Press), vol. 3, 167.

31. Ibid., 268, 269, 271, 272.

32. Ibid., series 4 (Moscow: Progress, 1976), 19.

33. Ibid., 17–18.

34. Ibid., 18–19. See also Mao Zedong, "Tong Mengemalide tanhua, 1960 nian 5 yue 27 ri" (Conversation with Montgomery, May 27, 1960), in Mao, *Mao Zedong wenji* (Works of Mao Zedong), vol. 8, 189; Mao, "Tong Sinuode tanhua (1960 nian 10 yue 22 ri)" (Conversation with Snow [October 22, 1960]), 215.

35. Mao Zedong, *Jianguo yilai Mao Zedong wengao* (Mao's Manuscripts), vol. 9 (Beijing: Zhongyang wenxian chubanshe, 1996), 467–70.

36. Schram, *Chairman Mao Talks to the People,* 266.

37. Borisov and Titarenko, *Vystupleniia Mao Tsze-duna ranee ne publikovavshiesia v kitaiskoi pechati* (Mao Zedong's Speeches Previously Unpublished in the Chinese Press), series 3, 273–74; 285–88.

38. Ibid., series 4, 36.

39. Leung, *Morning Sun,* 204–5.

40. Becker, *Hungry Ghosts,* 242.

41. Li, *The Private Life of Chairman Mao,* 378.

42. See Liu Shaoqi, *Liu Shaoqi xuanji* (Selected Works of Liu Shaoqi), vol. 2 (Beijing: Renmin chubanshe, 1985), 337.

43. Ibid., 328.

44. Quoted from Usov, *KNR: Ot "bol'shogo skachka" k "kul'turnoi revoliutsii"* (The PRC: From the "Great Leap" to the "Cultural Revolution"), 47.

45. Mao, *Mao Zedong wenji* (Works of Mao Zedong), vol. 8, 273.

46. Quoted from Li, *The Private Life of Chairman Mao*, 377, 380.

47. See Montgomery, *Three Continents*, 33, 34.

48. Quoted from Bo, *Ruogan zhongda juece yu shijian de huigu* (Recollections of Several Important Political Decisions and Their Implementation), vol. 2, 1026. See also MacFarquhar, *The Origins of the Cultural Revolution*, vol. 3, 158.

49. Liu, *Liu Shaoqi xuanji* (Selected Works of Liu Shaoqi), vol. 2, 421. See also Usov, *KNR: Ot "bol'shogo skachka" k "kul'turnoi revoliutsii"* (The PRC: From the "Great Leap" to the "Cultural Revolution"), 78; Huang, "Liu Shaoqi yu dayuejin" (Liu Shaoqi and the Great Leap Forward), 110.

50. Xue Muqiao, "Huainian weidade makesizhuyizhe Liu Shaoqi tongzhi" (Remembering the Great Marxist Comrade Liu Shaoqi), *Guangming ribao* (Enlightenment daily), November 24, 1988.

51. Quoted from Usov, *KNR: Ot "bol'shogo skachka" k "kul'turnoi revoliutsii"* (The PRC: From the "Great Leap" to the "Cultural Revolution"), 77.

52. Borisov and Titarenko, *Vystupleniia Mao Tsze-duna ranee ne publikovavshiesia v kitaiskoi pechati* (Mao Zedong's speeches previously unpublished in the Chinese press), series 4, 6, 12.

53. See Li, *The Private Life of Chairman Mao*, 387–88; Usov, *KNR: Ot "bolsh'ogo skachka" k "kul'turnoi revoliutsii"* (The PRC: From the "Great Leap" to the "Cultural Revolution"), 85–87; MacFarquhar, *The Origins of the Cultural Revolution*, vol. 3, 166–68, 545.

54. Schram, *Chairman Mao Talks to the People*, 266.

55. See Pang and Jin, *Mao Zedong zhuan (1949–1976)* (Biography of Mao Zedong [1949–1976]), vol. 2, 1207–8, 1218; Zhu Jiamu, ed., *Chen Yun nianpu, 1905–1995* (Chronological Biography of Chen Yun, 1905–1995), vol. 3 (Beijing: Zhongyang wenxian chubanshe, 2000), 107–10; Becker, *Hungry Ghosts*, 156.

56. See Dong Bian et al., eds., *Mao Zedong he tade mishu Tian Jiaying* (Mao Zedong and His Secretary Tian Jiaying) (Beijing: Zhongyang wenxian chubanshe, 1989), 62–65.

57. Quoted from Bo, *Ruogan zhongda juece yu shijian de huigu* (Recollections of Several Important Political Decisions and Their Implementation), vol. 2, 1084.

58. Borisov and Titarenko, *Vystupleniia Mao Tsze-duna, ranee ne publikovavshiesia v kitaiskoi pechati* (Mao Zedong's Speeches Previously Unpublished in the Chinese Press), series 4, 36.

59. See MacFarquhar, *The Origins of the Cultural Revolution*, vol. 3, 282.

60. Quoted from Zhu, *Chen Yun nianpu, 1905–1995* (Chronological Biography of Chen Yun, 1905–1995), vol. 3, 115.

61. Deng used this phrase for the first time at the end of June 1962 at a meeting of the CCP Central Committee Secretariat. Quoted from Bo, *Ruogan zhongda juece yu shijian de huigu* (Recollections of Several Important Political Decisions and Their Implementation), vol. 2, 1084.

62. Quoted from Liu and Chen, *Liu Shaoqi nianpu, 1898–1969* (Chronological Biography of Liu Shaoqi, 1898–1969), vol. 2, 551.

63. See Peng, *Memuary marshala* (Memoirs of a Marshal), 16.

64. Quoted from Pang and Jin, *Mao Zedong zhuan (1949–1976)* (Biography of Mao Zedong [1949–1976]), vol. 2, 1230.

65. Ibid., 1232.

66. Quoted from Zhu, *Chen Yun nianpu, 1905–1995* (Chronological Biography of Chen Yun, 1905–1995), vol. 3, 120.

67. See Deng Xiaoping, *Selected Works of Deng Xiaoping (1938–1965)* (Beijing: Foreign Languages Press, 1992), 293; Roderick MacFarquhar, *The Origins of the Cultural Revolution*,

vol. 3, *The Coming of the Cataclysm, 1961–1966* (New York: Oxford University Press and Columbia University Press, 1997), 268.

68. Borisov and Titarenko, *Vystupleniia Mao Tsze-duna, ranee ne publikovavshiesia v kitaiskoi pechati* (Mao Zedong's Speeches Previously Unpublished in the Chinese Press), series 3, 97.

69. See Pang and Jin, *Mao Zedong zhuan (1949–1976)* (Biography of Mao Zedong [1949–1976]), vol. 2, 1232–33.

70. Yang, *Yang Shangkun riji* (Yang Shangkun's Diary), vol. 2, 196.

71. Quoted from Pang and Jin, *Mao Zedong zhuan (1949–1976)* (Biography of Mao Zedong [1949–1976]), vol. 2, 1234.

72. Borisov and Titarenko, *Vystupleniia Mao Tsze-duna, ranee ne publikovavshiesia v kitaiskoi pechati* (Mao Zedong's Speeches Previously Unpublished in the Chinese Press), series 4, 40.

73. Borisov and Titarenko, *Vystupleniia Mao Tsze-duna, ranee ne publikovavshiesia v kitaiskoi pechati* (Mao Zedong's Speeches Previously Unpublished in the Chinese Press), series 4, 35–40, 44.

74. Ibid., 38–39.

75. Ibid., 47.

76. Kovalev, "Rossiia i Kitai (S missiei v Kitae)" (Russia and China [My Mission to China]), *Duel'* (Duel), November 5, 1997.

77. *Renmin ribao* (People's daily), March 5, 1963.

78. Borisov and Titarenko, *Vystupleniia Mao Tsze-duna, ranee ne publikovavshiesia v kitaiskoi pechati* (Mao Zedong's Speeches Previously Unpublished in the Chinese Press), series 4, 74–75.

79. See Mao's interview with Edgar Snow, January 9, 1965, published in Snow, *The Long Revolution*, 70, 205, and Mao, *Mao Zedong on Diplomacy*, 424–25.

80. See Ye Yonglie, *Jiang Qing zhuan* (Biography of Jiang Qing) (Beijing: Zuojia chubanshe, 1998), 340–41.

81. See Wang, *Wang Dongxing riji* (Diary of Wang Dongxing), 214–16.

82. Mao, *Poems of Mao Tse-tung*, 130.

83. Zhuangzi, *The Complete Works of Chuang-tsu*, trans. Burton Watson (New York: Columbia University Press, 1968), 144–45.

32. "THE DISMISSAL OF HAI RUI FROM OFFICE"

1. Confucius, *The Analects of Confucius*, 6.

2. See MacFarquhar, *The Origins of the Cultural Revolution*, vol. 3, 252–56, 443–47.

3. See Borisov and Titarenko, *Vystupleniia Mao Tsze-duna, ranee ne publikovavshiesia v kitaiskoi pechati* (Mao Zedong's Speeches Previously Unpublished in the Chinese Press), series 4, 183–86, 192–93, 206; Bo, *Ruogan zhongda juece yu shijian de huigu* (Recollections of Several Important Political Decisions and Their Implementation), vol. 2, 1128–31; Pang and Jin, *Mao Zedong zhuan (1949–1976)* (Biography of Mao Zedong [1949–1976]), vol. 2, 1366–75; Li, *The Private Life of Chairman Mao*, 416–17.

4. Snow, *The Long Revolution*, 17, 67, 169, 170.

5. O. Borisov [O. B. Rakhmanin] and M. Titarenko, eds., *Vystupleniia Mao Tsze-duna, ranee ne publikovavshiesia v kitaiskoi pechati* (Mao Zedong's Speeches Previously Unpublished in the Chinese Press), series 5 (Moscow: Progress, 1976), 194.

6. See Roderick MacFarquhar and Michael Schoenhals, *Mao's Last Revolution* (Cambridge, MA: Belknap Press of Harvard University Press, 2006), 17.

7. Borisov and Titarenko, *Vystupleniia Mao Tsze-duna, ranee ne publikovavshiesia v kitaiskoi pechati* (Mao Zedong's Speeches Previously Unpublished in the Chinese Press), series 5, 154, 194–95. See also Snow, *The Long Revolution*, 87.

8. Borisov and Titarenko, *Vystupleniia Mao Tsze-duna, ranee ne publikovavshiesia v kitaiskoi pechati* (Mao Zedong's Speeches Previously Unpublished in the Chinese Press), series 5, 71.

9. See *History of the Chinese Communist Party—A Chronology of Events (1919–1990)* (Beijing: Foreign Languages Press, 1991), 311.

10. Quoted from Andrew Hall Wedeman, *The East Wind Subsides: Chinese Foreign Policy and the Origins of the Cultural Revolution* (Washington, DC: Washington Institute Press, 1988), 176.

11. Quoted from Pang and Jin, *Mao Zedong zhuan (1949–1976)* (Biography of Mao Zedong [1949–1976]), vol. 2, 1399.

12. Schram, *Chairman Mao Talks to the People,* 270.

13. See MacFarquhar and Schoenhals, *Mao's Last Revolution,* 18; Wedeman, *The East Wind Subsides,* 223–24.

14. Mao, *Oblaka v snegu* (Clouds in the Snow), 99.

15. See Wu, *Mao Zedong guanghui licheng dituji* (Atlas of Mao Zedong's Glorious Historical Path), 122, 125. According to another source, Mao arrived in Wuchang January 5, 1966. See Pang and Jin, *Mao Zedong zhuan (1949–1976)* (Biography of Mao Zedong [1949–1976]), vol. 2, 1402.

16. For the text of the theses, see *CCP Documents of the Great Proletarian Cultural Revolution 1966–1967* (Hong Kong: Union Research Institute, 1968), 7–12.

17. Quoted from Li, *The Private Life of Chairman Mao,* 448.

18. See MacFarquhar and Schoenhals, *Mao's Last Revolution,* 31.

19. Chang and Halliday believe that Lin Biao "held back about helping Mao" at the beginning of the Cultural Revolution. Chang and Halliday, *Mao,* 527. But their assertion is contradicted by the facts.

20. *Velikaia Proletarskaia kul'turnaia revolitsiia (vazhneishie dokumenty)* (The Great Proletarian Cultural Revolution [Key Documents]) (Beijing: Izdatel'stvo literatury na inostrannykh iazykakh, 1970), 191–92.

21. Borisov and Titarenko, *Vystupleniia Mao Tsze-duna, ranee ne publikovavshiesia v kitaiskoi pechati* (Mao Zedong's Speeches Previously Unpublished in the Chinese Press), series 5, 62–63, 66, 68.

22. *History of the Chinese Communist Party—A Chronology of Events,* 320–21. See also Borisov and Titarenko, *Vystupleniia Mao Tsze-duna, ranee ne publikovavshiesia v kitaiskoi pechati* (Mao Zedong's Speeches Previously Unpublished in the Chinese Press), series 5, 69.

23. See Liao, *Mao Zedong baike quanshu* (Encyclopedia of Mao Zedong), vol. 6, 3212.

24. Quoted from Pang and Jin, *Mao Zedong zhuan (1949–1976)* (Biography of Mao Zedong [1949–1976]), vol. 2, 1408.

25. Borisov and Titarenko, *Vystupleniia Mao Tsze-duna, ranee ne publikovavshiesia v kitaiskoi pechati* (Mao Zedong's Speeches Previously Unpublished in the Chinese Press), series 5, 73.

26. See MacFarquhar and Schoenhals, *Mao's Last Revolution,* 34.

27. See Chen Qingquan and Song Guangwei, *Lu Dingyi zhuan* (Biography of Lu Dingyi) (Beijing: Zhonggong dangshi chubanshe, 1999), 485–502; MacFarquhar and Schoenhals, *Mao's Last Revolution,* 34–35; Jin Qiu, *The Culture of Power: The Lin Biao Incident in the Cultural Revolution* (Stanford, CA: Stanford University Press, 1999), 153–54.

28. See Chen and Song, *Lu Dingyi zhuan* (Biography of Lu Dingyi), 496–508; Westad, "77 Conversations Between Chinese and Foreign Leaders on the Wars in Indochina," 131.

29. According to some other sources, the statement concluded as follows: "The Chairman can testify to Ye Qun's virginity!" Quoted from MacFarquhar and Schoenhals, *Mao's Last Revolution,* 35. See also Chen and Song, *Lu Dingyi zhuan* (Biography of Lu Dingyi), 501.

30. Quoted from Chen and Song, *Lu Dingyi zhuan* (Biography of Lu Dingyi), 500.

31. Westad, "77 Conversations Between Chinese and Foreign Leaders on the Wars in Indochina," 131.

32. *CCP Documents of the Great Proletarian Cultural Revolution 1966–1967,* 27, 28.

33. See Liu Guokai, *A Brief Analysis of the Cultural Revolution* (Armonk, NY: M. E. Sharpe, 1987), 16; Barbara Barnouin and Yu Changgen, *Ten Years of Turbulence: The Chinese Cultural Revolution* (London: Kegan Paul International, 1993), 73–74.

34. Westad, "77 Conversations Between Chinese and Foreign Leaders on the Wars in Indochina," 132.

35. Quoted from MacFarquhar and Schoenhals, *Mao's Last Revolution*, 48.

36. Quoted from ibid.

37. Westad, "77 Conversations Between Chinese and Foreign Leaders on the Wars in Indochina," 130–31.

38. Ibid., 132.

39. Quoted from Pang and Jin, *Mao Zedong zhuan (1949–1976)* (Biography of Mao Zedong [1949–1976]), vol. 2, 1413.

40. Borisov and Titarenko, *Vystupleniia Mao Tsze-duna, ranee ne publikovavshiesia v kitaiskoi pechati* (Mao Zedong's Speeches Previously Unpublished in the Chinese Press), series 4, 94, 95, 97, 98, 103.

41. Ibid., series 5, 74–75.

42. Nie Yuanzi et al., "Song Shuo, Lu Ping, Peng Peiyuan zai wenhua gemingzhong jiujing gan shenma" (What Are Song Shuo, Lu Ping, and Peng Peiyuan Really Doing with Respect to the Cultural Revolution), *Renmin ribao* (People's daily), June 2, 1966.

43. Quoted from Pang and Jin, *Mao Zedong zhuan (1949–1976)* (Biography of Mao Zedong [1949–1976]), vol. 2, 1414, and MacFarquhar and Schoenhals, *Mao's Last Revolution*, 58.

44. Quoted from MacFarquhar and Schoenhals, *Mao's Last Revolution*, 58.

45. Borisov and Titarenko, *Vystupleniia Mao Tsze-duna, ranee ne publikovavshiesia v kitaiskoi pechati* (Mao Zedong's Speeches Previously Unpublished in the Chinese Press), series 4, 105.

46. See Chao Feng, ed., *"Wenhua da geming" cidian* (Dictionary of the "Great Cultural Revolution") (Taibei: Taiwan donghua shuju gufen youxian gongsi, 1993), 429, 436–37; *History of the Chinese Communist Party—A Chronology of Events*, 325. See also Borisov and Titarenko, *Vystupleniia Mao Tsze-duna, ranee ne publikovavshiesia v kitaiskoi pechati* (Mao Zedong's Speeches Previously Unpublished in the Chinese Press), series 5, 154.

47. See MacFarquhar and Schoenhals, *Mao's Last Revolution*, 42–51, 62.

48. The new Beijing Municipal Party Committee had already sent a party work team to Peking University on June 2. It was approved by Liu and Deng. The next day, the enlarged meeting of the Politburo Standing Committee decided to send the work teams to all other Beijing schools. They numbered 7,239 party cadres. See Liu and Chen, *Liu Shaoqi nianpu, 1898–1969* (Chronological Biography of Liu Shaoqi, 1898–1969), vol. 2, 640; MacFarquhar and Schoenhals, *Mao's Last Revolution*, 65, 66.

49. Quoted from Barnouin and Yu, *Ten Years of Turbulence*, 75; Lowell Dittmer, *Liu Shao-ch'i and the Chinese Revolution: The Politics of Mass Criticism* (Berkeley: University of California Press, 1974), 81. See also Liu and Chen, *Liu Shaoqi nianpu, 1898–1969* (Chronological Biography of Liu Shaoqi, 1898–1969), vol. 2, 641.

50. Borisov and Titarenko, *Vystupleniia Mao Tsze-duna, ranee ne publikovavshiesia v kitaiskoi pechati* (Mao Zedong's Speeches Previously Unpublished in the Chinese Press), series 4, 114.

51. Quoted from Pang and Jin, *Mao Zedong zhuan (1949–1976)* (Biography of Mao Zedong [1949–1976]), vol. 2, 1415.

52. See M. I. Sladkovskii, ed., *Informatsionnyi biulleten': Seriia A: "Kulturnaia revoliutsiia" v Kitae: Dokumenty i materialy (perevod s kitaiskogo)*, Vypusk 7, *Vystupleniia Zhou Enlaia v period "kul'turnoi revoliutsii"* (Information Bulletin: Series A: The "Cultural Revolution" in China: Documents and Materials Translated from Chinese, 7th Installment, Zhou Enlai's Speeches During the "Cultural Revolution" (Moscow: IDV AN SSSR, 1971), 6.

53. Quoted from Pang and Jin, *Mao Zedong zhuan (1949–1976)* (Biography of Mao Zedong [1949–1976]), vol. 2, 1417.

54. O. Borisov [O. B. Rakhmanin] and M. Titarenko, eds., *Vystupleniia Mao Tsze-duna, ranee ne publikovavshiesia v kitaiskoi pechati* (Mao Zedong's Speeches Previously Unpublished in the Chinese Press), series 6 (Moscow: Nauka, 1976), 212–14.

55. *Dosie k lichnomu delu Mao Tszeduna* (Dossier to the Personal File of Mao Zedong), RGASPI, collection 495, inventory 225, file 71, vol. 4, sheets 88–90, 93.

56. Ibid., 86–87.

57. Borisov and Titarenko, *Vystupleniia Mao Tsze-duna, ranee ne publikovavshiesia v kitaiskoi pechati* (Mao Zedong's Speeches Previously Unpublished in the Chinese Press), series 5, 84, 85.

58. Quoted from MacFarquhar and Schoenhals, *Mao's Last Revolution,* 84.

59. Liu Shaoqi, *Liu Shaoqi zishu* (Autobiographical Notes of Liu Shaoqi) (Beijing: Jiefangjun wenyi chubanshe, 2002), 177.

60. See Deng Rong, *Deng Xiaoping and the Cultural Revolution: A Daughter Recalls the Critical Years,* trans. Sidney Shapiro (New York: Random House, 2005), 18–19; Li, *The Private Life of Chairman Mao,* 469–70.

33. TO REBEL IS JUSTIFIED

1. Quoted from *History of the Chinese Communist Party—A Chronology of Events,* 328; Borisov and Titarenko, *Vystupleniia Mao Tsze-duna, ranee ne publikovavshiesia v kitaiskoi pechati* (Mao Zedong's Speeches Previously Unpublished in the Chinese Press), series 5, 84, 129.

2. Schram, *Chairman Mao Talks to the People,* 260.

3. Ibid., 254. The three great differences are those between workers and peasants, city and countryside, and mental and physical labor.

4. See MacFarquhar and Schoenhals, *Mao's Last Revolution,* 87; Liao, *Mao Zedong baike quanshu* (Encyclopedia of Mao Zedong), vol. 6, 3216; Liu and Chen, *Liu Shaoqi nianpu, 1898–1969* (Chronological Biography of Liu Shaoqi, 1898–1969), vol. 2, 647.

5. Quoted from MacFarquhar and Schoenhals, *Mao's Last Revolution,* 89.

6. Borisov and Titarenko, *Vystupleniia Mao Tsze-duna, ranee ne publikovavshiesia v kitaiskoi pechati* (Mao Zedong's Speeches Previously Unpublished in the Chinese Press), series 6, 216–17; Pang and Jin, *Mao Zedong zhuan (1949–1976)* (Biography of Mao Zedong [1949–1976]), vol. 2, 1427–28; *History of the Chinese Communist Party—A Chronology of Events,* 328; Liao, *Mao Zedong baike quanshu* (Encyclopedia of Mao Zedong), vol. 6, 3216.

7. Quoted from MacFarquhar and Schoenhals, *Mao's Last Revolution,* 89.

8. For the text of this *dazibao,* see ibid., 90.

9. See Pang and Jin, *Mao Zedong zhuan (1949–1976)* (Biography of Mao Zedong [1949–1976]), vol. 2, 1428–29; Liao, *Mao Zedong baike quanshu* (Encyclopedia of Mao Zedong), vol. 6, 3215; Liu and Chen, *Liu Shaoqi nianpu, 1898–1969* (Chronological Biography of Liu Shaoqi, 1898–1969), vol. 2, 649.

10. *CCP Documents of the Great Proletarian Cultural Revolution 1966–1967,* 42–43.

11. Borisov and Titarenko, *Vystupleniia Mao Tsze-duna, ranee ne publikovavshiesia v kitaiskoi pechati* (Mao Zedong's Speeches Previously Unpublished in the Chinese Press), vol. 5, 195.

12. See *Lichnoe delo Mao Tsze-duna* (Personal File of Mao Zedong), RGASPI, collection 495, inventory 225, file 71, vol. 3, sheets 104–5; Liao, *Mao Zedong baike quanshu* (Encyclopedia of Mao Zedong), vol. 6, 3215; *History of the Chinese Communist Party—A Chronology of Events,* 329.

13. See Wu Liping, "Wenhua da geming zhongde nü hongweibing" (Women-Hongweibings in the Great Cultural Revolution), *Ershiyi shiji* (Twenty-first century), no. 68 (2007): 57.

14. Schram, *Chairman Mao Talks to the People,* 260.

15. Borisov and Titarenko, *Vystupleniia Mao Tsze-duna, ranee ne publikovavshiesia v kitaiskoi pechati* (Mao Zedong's Speeches Previously Unpublished in the Chinese Press), series 5, 96.

16. See MacFarquhar and Schoenhals, *Mao's Last Revolution,* 104.

17. Quoted from ibid., 125.

18. See Pang and Jin, *Mao Zedong zhuan (1949–1976)* (Biography of Mao Zedong [1949–1976]), vol. 2, 1438.

19. See MacFarquhar and Schoenhals, *Mao's Last Revolution*, 126.

20. *CCP Documents of the Great Proletarian Cultural Revolution 1966–1967*, 50.

21. Quoted from Pang and Jin, *Mao Zedong zhuan (1949–1976)* (Biography of Mao Zedong [1949–1976]), vol. 2, 1439.

22. Rae Yang, *Spider Eaters: A Memoir* (Berkeley: University of California Press, 1997), 131.

23. Wang Meng, *Bolshevik Salute: A Modernist Chinese Novel*, trans. Wendy Larson (Seattle: University of Washington Press, 1989), 12–14.

24. See Elizabeth J. Perry and Li Xun, *Proletarian Power: Shanghai in the Cultural Revolution* (Boulder, CO: Westview Press, 1997), 12; Wang Shaoguang, *Failure of Charisma: The Cultural Revolution in Wuhan* (Hong Kong: Oxford University Press, 1995), 72; MacFarquhar and Schoenhals, *Mao's Last Revolution*, 115.

25. See MacFarquhar and Schoenhals, *Mao's Last Revolution*, 113–16, 118–22.

26. See *CCP Documents of the Great Proletarian Cultural Revolution 1966–1967*, 73–74, 77–78.

27. Quoted from *History of the Chinese Communist Party—A Chronology of Events*, 331.

28. See *Lichnoe delo Mao Tszeduna* (Personal File of Mao Zedong), RGASPI, collection 495, inventory 225, file 71, vol. 3, sheet 77; *History of the Chinese Communist Party—A Chronology of Events*, 324–25.

29. Schram, *Chairman Mao Talks to the People*, 271, 273.

30. Borisov and Titarenko, *Vystupleniia Mao Tsze-duna, ranee ne publikovavshiesia v kitaiskoi pechati* (Mao Zedong's Speeches Previously Unpublished in the Chinese Press), series 5, 136–37.

31. *Xin Zhonghua bao* (New China), December 30, 1939.

32. Schram, *Chairman Mao Talks to the People*, 260.

33. Quoted from MacFarquhar and Schoenhals, *Mao's Last Revolution*, 107.

34. *Dosie k lichnomu delu Mao Tszeduna* (Dossier to the Personal File of Mao Zedong), RGASPI, collection 495, inventory 225, file 71, vol. 4, sheets 10, 11–13.

35. See MacFarquhar and Schoenhals, *Mao's Last Revolution*, 146.

36. Quoted from Liu and Chen, *Liu Shaoqi nianpu, 1898–1969* (Chronological Biography of Liu Shaoqi, 1898–1969), vol. 2, 652.

37. Li, *The Private Life of Chairman Mao*, 489–90.

38. See MacFarquhar and Schoenhals, *Mao's Last Revolution*, 147.

39. See *History of the Chinese Communist Party—A Chronology of Events*, 333; Peng, *Memuary marshala*, 18–20; *Peng Dehuai nianpu* (Chronological Biography of Peng Dehuai) (Beijing: Renmin chubanshe, 1998), 851.

40. Quoted from *He Long nianpu* (Chronological Biography of He Long) (Beijing: Zhonggong zhongyang dangxiao chubanshe, 1988), 455. See also M. I. Sladkovskii, ed. *Informatsionnyi biulleten': Seriia A: "Kulturnaiia revoliutsiia" v Kitae: Dokumenty i materialy (perevod s kitaiskogo), Vypusk 2, "Hunveibinovskaia pechat" o Den Siaopine, Pen Chzhene, Yan Shankune, i Khe Lune* (Information Bulletin: Series A: The "Cultural Revolution" in China: Documents and Materials Translated from Chinese, 2nd Installment, The Red Guard Press on Deng Xiaoping, Peng Zhen, Yang Shangkun, and He Long) (Moscow: IDV AN SSSR, 1968), 225–329.

41. Quoted from Tang, *Li Lisan zhuan* (Biography of Li Lisan), 168.

42. For details see Li Sha, *Wode zhongguo yuanfen: Li Lisan furen Li Sha huiyilu* (My Chinese Fate: Memoirs of Li Lisan's Wife Li Sha) (Beijing: Waiyu jiaoxue yu yanjiu chubanshe, 2009).

43. Alexander V. Pantsov's interview with Elizaveta Pavlovna Kishkina (Li Sha) in Beijing, June 14, 2010.

44. See Liu, *Liu Shaoqi zishu* (Autobiographical Notes of Liu Shaoqi), 179–254; Wang Guangmei and Liu Yuan, *Ni suo bu zhidao de Liu Shaoqi* (The Unknown Liu Shaoqi)

(Zhengzhou: Henan renmin chubanshe, 2000); Liu and Chen, *Liu Shaoqi nianpu, 1898–1969* (Chronological Biography of Liu Shaoqi, 1898–1969), vol. 2, 653–61; Yen Chia-chi and Kao Kao, *The Ten-Year History of the Chinese Cultural Revolution* (Taipei: Institute of Current China Studies, 1988), 168.

45. According to some estimates, the toll killed in rural China alone is between 750,000 and 1.5 million. The number of people killed in cities is still unknown. See MacFarquhar and Schoenhals, *Mao's Last Revolution,* 262.

46. Quoted from Li, *Moi otets Mao Tszedun* (My Father Mao Zedong), 265.

47. Quoted from MacFarquhar and Schoenhals, *Mao's Last Revolution,* 155.

48. See Li, *The Private Life of Chairman Mao,* 478–81.

49. Quoted from Deng, *Deng Xiaoping and the Cultural Revolution,* 39, 53.

50. Quoted from *History of the Chinese Communist Party—A Chronology of Events,* 334.

51. Schram, *Chairman Mao Talks to the People,* 275.

34. THE RED GUARD TRAGEDY

1. See MacFarquhar and Schoenhals, *Mao's Last Revolution,* 177–83.

2. See ibid., 94–99, 156–61, 171–73; Borisov and Titarenko, *Vystupleniia Mao Tsze-duna, ranee ne publikovavshiesia v kitaiskoi pechati* (Mao Zedong's Speeches Previously Unpublished in the Chinese Press), series 5, 180; Pang and Jin, *Mao Zedong zhuan (1949–1976)* (Biography of Mao Zedong [1949–1976]), vol. 2, 1470–71.

3. Quoted from Chen Xiaonong, ed., *Chen Boda zuihou koushu huiyi* (The Last Oral Reminiscences of Chen Boda) (Hong Kong: Xingke'er chuban youxian gongsi, 2006), 325–26; Pang and Jin, *Mao Zedong zhuan (1949–1976)* (Biography of Mao Zedong [1949–1976]), vol. 2, 1480; MacFarquhar and Schoenhals, *Mao's Last Revolution,* 189.

4. Quoted from MacFarquhar and Schoenhals, *Mao's Last Revolution,* 191–94; Li and Ma, *Zhou Enlai nianpu (1949–1976)* (Chronological Biography of Zhou Enlai [1949–1976]), vol. 3, 125–27; *Ye Jianying zhuanlüe* (Short Biography of Ye Jianying) (Beijing: Junshi kexueyuan chubanshe, 1987), 269; Nie, *Inside the Red Star,* 740–42; Pang and Jin, *Mao Zedong zhuan (1949–1976)* (Biography of Mao Zedong [1949–1976]), vol. 2, 1481–82.

5. See Li and Ma, *Zhou Enlai nianpu (1949–1976)* (Chronological Biography of Zhou Enlai [1949–1976]), vol. 3, 129. Li Fuchun and Li Xiannian were also active in the debate during the second meeting at Zhongnanhai.

6. Quoted from MacFarquhar and Schoenhals, *Mao's Last Revolution,* 195–96. See also Pang and Jin, *Mao Zedong zhuan (1949–1976)* (Biography of Mao Zedong [1949–1976]), vol. 2, 1482–83. Wang Ming had lived since early 1956 in the Soviet Union, where he had received medical treatment. He would pass away in Moscow from a heart attack on March 27, 1974.

7. See MacFarquhar and Schoenhals, *Mao's Last Revolution,* 196; Pang and Jin, *Mao Zedong zhuan (1949–1976)* (Biography of Mao Zedong [1949–1976]), vol. 2, 1483; Li and Ma, *Zhou Enlai nianpu (1949–1976)* (Chronological Biography of Zhou Enlai [1949–1976]), vol. 3, 129–30.

8. See *History of the Chinese Communist Party—A Chronology of Events,* 336.

9. Quoted from Jin, *The Culture of Power,* 105.

10. See MacFarquhar and Schoenhals, *Mao's Last Revolution,* 197–98; Borisov and Titarenko, *Vystupleniia Mao Tsze-duna, ranee ne publikovavshiesia v kitaiskoi pechati* (Mao Zedong's Speeches Previously Unpublished in the Chinese Press), series 5, 188.

11. Pang and Jin, *Mao Zedong zhuan (1949–1976)* (Biography of Mao Zedong [1949–1976]), vol. 2, 1486–87.

12. Quoted from ibid., vol. 2, 1490.

13. See MacFarquhar and Schoenhals, *Mao's Last Revolution,* 203.

14. Quoted from Pang and Jin, *Mao Zedong zhuan (1949–1976)* (Biography of Mao Zedong [1949–1976]), vol. 2, 1491.

15. See ibid., 1493, 1494.

16. Quoted from MacFarquhar and Schoenhals, *Mao's Last Revolution*, 215.

17. Quoted from Pang and Jin, *Mao Zedong zhuan (1949–1976)* (Biography of Mao Zedong [1949–1976]), vol. 2, 1495.

18. See ibid., 1496; MacFarquhar and Schoenhals, *Mao's Last Revolution*, 204–12.

19. Quoted from Pang and Jin, *Mao Zedong zhuan (1949–1976)* (Biography of Mao Zedong [1949–1976]), vol. 2, 1496–97.

20. See *History of the Chinese Communist Party—A Chronology of Events*, 338.

21. See Li and Ma, *Zhou Enlai nianpu (1949–1976)* (Chronological Biography of Zhou Enlai [1949–1976]), vol. 3, 173.

22. See Wang, *Failure of Charisma*, 159–60; MacFarquhar and Schoenhals, *Mao's Last Revolution*, 213–14.

23. See MacFarquhar and Schoenhals, *Mao's Last Revolution*, 215.

24. See *History of the Chinese Communist Party—A Chronology of Events*, 338.

25. See MacFarquhar and Schoenhals, *Mao's Last Revolution*, 216.

26. See ibid., 232; Pang and Jin, *Mao Zedong zhuan (1949–1976)* (Biography of Mao Zedong [1949–1976]), vol. 2, 1502–4.

27. *History of the Chinese Communist Party—A Chronology of Events*, 340.

28. See Pang and Jin, *Mao Zedong zhuan (1949–1976)* (Biography of Mao Zedong [1949–1976]), vol. 2, 1500, 1504–6.

29. Quoted from ibid., 1506.

30. See *History of the Chinese Communist Party—A Chronology of Events*, 338–40.

31. See MacFarquhar and Schoenhals, *Mao's Last Revolution*, 240, 245–46; Pang and Jin, *Mao Zedong zhuan (1949–1976)* (Biography of Mao Zedong [1949–1976]), vol. 2, 1450, 1512, 1519.

32. Pang and Jin, *Mao Zedong zhuan (1949–1976)* (Biography of Mao Zedong [1949–1976]), vol. 2, 1455–56.

33. See MacFarquhar and Schoenhals, *Mao's Last Revolution*, 174.

34. "The empire, long divided, must unite; long united, must divide. Thus it has ever been," says this book. Luo Guangzhong, *Three Kingdoms: A Historical Novel*, abridged ed., trans. Moss Roberts (Berkeley: University of California Press, 1999), 3.

35. See Borisov and Titarenko, *Vystupleniia Mao Tsze-duna, ranee ne publikovavshiesia v kitaiskoi pechati* (Mao Zedong's Speeches Previously Unpublished in the Chinese Press), series 6, 226–28, 237–38, 244, 245, 256.

36. *History of the Chinese Communist Party—A Chronology of Events*, 342.

37. See MacFarquhar and Schoenhals, *Mao's Last Revolution*, 244–45.

38. Borisov and Titarenko, *Vystupleniia Mao Tsze-duna, ranee ne publikovavshiesia v kitaiskoi pechati* (Mao Zedong's Speeches Previously Unpublished in the Chinese Press), series 6, 239.

39. Wang, *Bolshevik Salute*, 55, 95.

40. *Velikaia Proletarskaia kul'turnaia revolitsiia (vazhneishie dokumenty)* (The Great Proletarian Cultural Revolution [Key Documents]), 165–67.

41. Quoted from Deng, *Deng Xiaoping and the Cultural Revolution*, 75.

42. Quoted from Barnouin and Yu, *Ten Years of Turbulence*, 175.

43. James T. Myers et al., eds., *Chinese Politics: Documents and Analysis*, vol. 1 (Columbia: University of South Carolina Press, 1986), 393.

44. Schram, *Chairman Mao Talks to the People*, 282.

45. In the period of March 2–21, 1969, the Soviet army total loss was 54 soldiers and four officers dead, and 85 soldiers and nine officers wounded. The exact number of Chinese casualties is unknown. According to Chinese sources, 29 servicemen were killed, 62 wounded, and one missing. According to Soviet sources, 800 Chinese were killed. See *Geroi ostrova Damanskii* (Heroes of Damansky Island) (Moscow: Molodaia gvardiia, 1969); Krivosheev, *Grif sekretnosti sniat* (The Stamp of Secrecy Is Removed), 398; Christian F. Ostermann, "East German Documents on the Border Conflict, 1969," *CWIHP Bulletin*, nos. 6–7 (1995/1996): 188–90; Michael Clodfelter, *Warfare and Armed Conflict: A Statistical Encyclopedia of*

Casualty and Other Figures, 1494–2007, 3rd ed. (Jefferson, NC: McFarland, 2008), 676; D. S. Riabushkin, *Mify Damanskogo* (Damansky's Myths) (Moscow: AST, 2004), 73–75, 78–81.

46. *The Polemic on the General Line of the International Communist Movement,* 573, 576.

47. Ibid., 57.

48. Borisov and Titarenko, *Vystupleniia Mao Tsze-duna, ranee ne publikovavshiesia v kitaiskoi pechati* (Mao Zedong's Speeches Previously Unpublished in the Chinese Press), series 4, 119.

49. Khrushchev, *Memoirs of Nikita Khrushchev,* vol. 3, 471–72.

50. See Ostermann, *East German Documents on the Border Conflict,* 186–87.

51. A. M. Aleksandrov-Agentov, *Ot Kollontai do Gorbacheva: Vospominaniia diplomata, sovetnika A. A. Gromyko, pomoshchnika L. I. Brezhneva, Iu. V. Andropova, K. U. Chernenko i M. S. Gorbacheva* (From Kollontai to Gorbachev: The Reminiscences of a Diplomat, and Adviser to A. A. Gromyko, and Assistant to L. I. Brezhnev, Iu. V. Andropov, K. U. Chernenko, and M. S. Gorbachev) (Moscow: Mezhdunarodnye otnosheniia, 1994), 169.

52. Quoted from Li and Ma, *Zhou Enlai nianpu (1949–1976)* (Chronological Biography of Zhou Enlai [1949–1976]), vol. 2, 686.

53. Quoted from *Lichnoe delo Mao Tszeduna* (Personal File of Mao Zedong), RGASPI, collection 495, inventory 225, file 71, vol. 4, sheet 149.

54. Aleksandrov-Agentov, *Ot Kollontai do Gorbacheva* (From Kollontai to Gorbachev), 169–70.

55. See Snow, *The Long Revolution,* 175. See also *Lichnoe delo Mao Tszeduna* (Personal File of Mao Zedong), RGASPI, collection 495, inventory 225, file 71, vol. 4, sheets 49, 51–52, 149.

56. *Lichnoe delo Mao Tszeduna* (Personal File of Mao Zedong), RGASPI F. 495, inventory 225, file 71, vol. 3, sheet 80.

57. See Ostermann, "East German Documents on the Border Conflict, 1969," 187.

58. Borisov and Titarenko, *Vystupleniia Mao Tsze-duna, ranee ne publikovavshiesia v kitaiskoi pechati* (Mao Zedong's Speeches Previously Unpublished in the Chinese Press), series 6, 266.

59. See Barnouin and Yu, *Ten Years of Turbulence,* 91.

60. *Lichnoe delo Van Mina* (Personal File of Wang Ming), vol. 2, 48, 49.

61. See A. Elizavetin, "Peregovory A. N. Kosygina i Chzhou En'laia v Pekinskom aeroportu" (Talks between A. N. Kosygin and Zhou Enlai at the Beijing Airport), *Problemy Dal'nego Vostoka* (Far Eastern affairs), no. 5 (1992): 39–63; no. 2 (1993): 107–19. For a version of the talks by the PRC Ministry of Foreign Affairs, see "Meeting between Zhou Enlai and Kosygin at the Beijing Airport," http://www.fmprc.gov.cn/eng/5691.html.

35. THE MYSTERY OF PROJECT 571

1. See Snow, *The Long Revolution,* 4, 89, 168, 170, 194, 219, 220; "Statement of Edgar Snow," RGASPI, collection 495, inventory 225, file 71, vol. 6, sheet 379; Mao, *Mao Zedong wenji* (Works of Mao Zedong), vol. 8, 400.

2. See Snow, *The Long Revolution,* 89.

3. Li, *The Private Life of Chairman Mao,* 105.

4. Rakhmanin, *Vzaimnootnosheniia mezhdu I. V. Stalinym i Mao Tszedunom glazami ochevidtsa* (Relations between J. V. Stalin and Mao Zedong through the Eyes of an Eyewitness), 80, 81.

5. Quoted from Thomas, *A Season of High Adventure,* 326; Li, *The Private Life of Chairman Mao,* 120.

6. Snow, *The Long Revolution,* 175.

7. *Lichnoe delo Mao Tszeduna* (Personal File of Mao Zedong), RGASPI, collection 495, inventory 225, file 71, vol. 6, sheet 440.

8. *Lichnoe delo Lin Biao* (Personal File of Lin Biao), RGASPI, collection 495, inventory 225, file 53, vol. 1, sheets 197–200, 204–6.

9. See *IX Vsekitaiskii s'ezd Kommunisticheskoi partii Kitaia (dokumenty)* (Ninth Congress of the Communist Party of China [Documents]) (Beijing: Izdatel'sto literatury na inostrannykh iazykakh, 1969), 102–3.

10. Quoted from Wang, *Linshi san xiongdi* (The Three Lin Brothers), 314.

11. Lin Biao, "Avtobiografiia" (Autobiography), RGASPI, collection 495, inventory 225, file 53, vol. 1, 197–200, sheets 204–6.

12. See *Lichnoe delo Lin Biao* (Personal File of Lin Biao), ibid., 201.

13. Borisov and Titarenko, *Vystupleniia Mao Tsze-duna, ranee ne publikovavshiesia v kitaiskoi pechati* (Mao Zedong's Speeches Previously Unpublished in the Chinese Press), series 6, 212, 213.

14. See George Urban, ed., *The Miracles of Chairman Mao: A Compendium of Devotional Literature 1966–1970* (Los Angeles: Nash, 1971); *Lichnoe delo Mao Tszeduna* (Personal File of Mao Zedong), RGASPI, collection 495, inventory 225, file 71, vol. 5, sheets 267–77.

15. See *Lichnoe delo Lin Biao* (Personal File of Lin Biao), RGASPI, collection 495, inventory 225, file 53, vol. 1, sheets 167, 177.

16. Ibid., sheet 178.

17. Alexander V. Pantsov's interview with Lin Liheng (Doudou) in Beijing, October 31, 2004.

18. *Lichnoe delo Mao Tszeduna* (Personal File of Mao Zedong), RGASPI, collection 495, inventory 225, file 71, vol. 7, sheet 211.

19. Li, *The Private Life of Chairman Mao*, 453, 454.

20. Quoted from Jin, *The Culture of Power*, 147.

21. Ibid., 129.

22. Quoted from ibid., 121.

23. The unpublished memoirs of Wu Faxian are widely cited in his daughter's book *The Culture of Power: The Lin Biao Incident in the Cultural Revolution*, published by Stanford University Press in 1999.

24. Quoted from Jin, *The Culture of Power*, 122.

25. Ibid., 101, 117.

26. Ibid., 123.

27. Ibid., 131.

28. See Chao, *"Wenhua da geming" cidian* (Dictionary of the "Great Cultural Revolution"), 404; Yen and Kao, *The Ten-Year History of the Chinese Cultural Revolution*, 312–22.

29. See Michael Y. M. Kau, ed., *The Lin Piao Affair: Power Politics and Military Coup* (White Plains, NY: International Arts and Sciences Press, 1975), 81.

30. See *A Great Trial in Chinese History: The Trial of the Lin Biao and Jiang Qing Counter-Revolutionary Cliques, Nov. 1980–January 1981* (Oxford: Pergamon Press, 1981), 24–25; Li, *The Private Life of Chairman Mao*, 540.

31. See "Outline of 'Project 571,' " in Kau, *The Lin Piao Affair*, 88.

32. Ibid., 83, 85.

33. Schram, *Chairman Mao Talks to the People*, 295.

34. Quoted from Jin, *The Culture of Power*, 134.

35. Ibid., 135.

36. Li, *The Private Life of Chairman Mao*, 533.

37. Schram, *Chairman Mao Talks to the People*, 290–99. See also *Lichnoe delo Mao Tszeduna* (Personal File of Mao Zedong), RGASPI, collection 495, inventory 225, file 71, vol. 7, sheet 286–94.

38. Jin, *The Culture of Power*, 173–80, 186; Li, *The Private Life of Chairman Mao*, 534–37.

39. Li, *The Private Life of Chairman Mao*, 537, 538.

40. See V. Skosyrev, "Golovu Lin Biao general KGB privez v Moskvu" (A KGB General Brought Lin Biao's Head to Moscow), *Izvestiia* (News), February 17, 1994.

41. See *A Great Trial in Chinese History,* 89–100, 216; Chao, *"Wenhua da geming" cidian* (Dictionary of the "Great Cultural Revolution"), 405; Jin, *The Culture of Power,* 237; Yen and Kao, *The Ten-Year History of the Chinese Cultural Revolution,* 343–45.

42. Alexander V. Pantsov's interview with a Beijing resident, October 31, 2004. According to another source, it took five to ten days to inform the top party officials about the incident. See Deng, *Deng Xiaoping and the Cultural Revolution,* 182.

43. See Barnouin and Yu, *Ten Years of Turbulence,* 252–53.

44. Li, *The Private Life of Chairman Mao,* 552.

36. DEATH OF THE RED EMPEROR

1. Fyodor Dostoevsky, *The Brothers Karamazov,* trans. Constance Garnett (New York: Modern Library, 1996), 350, 353.

2. Borisov and Titarenko, *Vystupleniia Mao Tsze-duna, ranee ne publikovavshiesia v kitaiskoi pechati* (Mao Zedong's Speeches Previously Unpublished in the Chinese Press), series 6, 280. See also notes of Mao's conversation with Pol Pot, the leader of the Khmer Rouge, June 21, 1975, in Westad, "77 Conversations Between Chinese and Foreign Leaders on the Wars in Indochina," 191.

3. Henry A. Kissinger, *White House Years* (Boston: Little, Brown, 1979), 699.

4. Borisov and Titarenko, *Vystupleniia Mao Tsze-duna, ranee ne publikovavshiesia v kitaiskoi pechati* (Mao Zedong's Speeches Previously Unpublished in the Chinese Press), series 6, 270.

5. Quoted from Kissinger, *White House Years,* 164.

6. Richard Nixon, *RN: The Memoirs of Richard Nixon* (New York: Grosset & Dunlap, 1978), 546.

7. Kissinger, *White House Years,* 700–702.

8. Snow, *The Long Revolution,* 171, 172. See also Mao, *Mao Zedong wenji* (Works of Mao Zedong), vol. 8, 436–37.

9. Edgar Snow, "A Conversation with Mao Tse-tung," *Life,* April 30, 1971, 46–48.

10. Quoted from Li and Ma, *Zhou Enlai nianpu (1949–1976)* (Chronological Biography of Zhou Enlai [1949–1976]), vol. 2, 451. See also *The Analects of Confucius,* 3; Kissinger, *White House Years,* 708–10; Li, *The Private Life of Chairman Mao,* 558; Liao, *Mao Zedong baike quanshu* (Encyclopedia of Mao Zedong), vol. 1, 36.

11. Westad, "77 Conversations Between Chinese and Foreign Leaders on the Wars in Indochina," 175.

12. Kissinger, *White House Years,* 163, 755.

13. Nixon, *RN,* 544.

14. Li, *The Private Life of Chairman Mao,* 563.

15. Nixon, *RN,* 560.

16. Kissinger, *White House Years,* 1058.

17. See Zhang Yufeng, "Neskol'ko shtrikhov k kartine poslednikh let zhizni Mao Tszeduna, Chzhou Enlaia" (Some Brushstrokes Toward a Picture of the Last Years of Mao Zedong and Zhou Enlai), in Yu. N. Galenovich, ed., *Smert' Mao Tszeduna* (The Death of Mao Zedong) (Moscow: Izd-vo "Izograf," 2005), 89.

18. Quoted from Nixon, *RN,* 560.

19. Kissinger, *The White House Years,* 1059.

20. Nixon, *RN,* 561–62. See also William Burr, ed., *The Kissinger Transcripts: The Top Secret Talks with Beijing and Moscow* (New York: New Press, 1998), 60.

21. Ibid.

22. Nixon, *RN,* 561–64; Burr, *The Kissinger Transcripts,* 65.

23. Quoted from Kissinger, *White House Years,* 1492.

24. See Westad, "77 Conversations Between Chinese and Foreign Leaders on the Wars in Indochina," 179–82.

25. Li, *The Private Life of Chairman Mao,* 566, 569.

26. See Liao, *Mao Zedong baike quanshu* (Encyclopedia of Mao Zedong), vol. 6, 3249.

27. See Barnouin and Yu, *Ten Years of Turbulence*, 249.

28. Quoted from Deng, *Deng Xiaoping and the Cultural Revolution*, 209.

29. Quoted from *History of the Chinese Communist Party—A Chronology of Events*, 358.

30. Borisov and Titarenko, *Vystupleniia Mao Tsze-duna, ranee ne publikovavshiesia v kitaiskoi pechati* (Mao Zedong's Speeches Previously Unpublished in the Chinese Press), series 6, 283.

31. *Vremia novostei* (News hour), August 23, 2004.

32. Quoted from *History of the Chinese Communist Party—A Chronology of Events*, 360.

33. Jin, *The Culture of Power*, 78.

34. *The Analects of Confucius*, 57.

35. See *Zhongguo gongchandang di shici quanguo daibiaodahui wenjian huibian* (Collection of Documents from the Tenth Congress of the Chinese Communist Party) (Beijing: Renmin chubanshe, 1973); *The Tenth National Congress of the Communist Party of China (Documents)* (Beijing: Foreign Languages Press, 1973); *Lichnoe delo Mao Tszeduna* (Personal File of Mao Zedong), RGASPI, collection 495, inventory 225, file 71, vol. 6, sheets 257–60.

36. See Burr, *The Kissinger Transcripts*, 166–216; Li and Ma, *Zhou Enlai nianpu (1949–1976)* (Chronological Biography of Zhou Enlai [1949–1976]), vol. 3, 632–34; Gao Wenqian, *Zhou Enlai. The Last Perfect Revolutionary. A Biography*, trans. Peter Rand and Lawrence R. Sullivan (New York: PublicAffairs, 2007), 239–42.

37. Burr, *The Kissinger Transcripts*, 205.

38. Quoted from Gao, *Zhou Enlai*, 241.

39. Deng, *Deng Xiaoping and the Cultural Revolution*, 255–56.

40. See Liao, *Mao Zedong baike quanshu* (Encyclopedia of Mao Zedong), vol. 6, 3253.

41. Kissinger, *White House Years*, 1058.

42. Li, *The Private Life of Chairman Mao*, 581–82.

43. See Mao, *Mao Zedong on Diplomacy*, 454. This concept had been maturing in his mind since the fall of 1963. See ibid., 387–88.

44. See *History of the Chinese Communist Party—A Chronology of Events*, 363.

45. Zhang, "Neskol'ko shtrikhov k kartine poslednikh let zhizni Mao Tszeduna, Chzhou En'laia" (Some Brushstrokes Toward a Picture of the Last Years of Mao Zedong and Zhou Enlai), 81.

46. Ibid., 99; *Lichnoe delo Mao Tszeduna* (Personal File of Mao Zedong), RGASPI, collection 495, inventory 225, file 71, vol. 7, sheet 170; *A Great Trial in Chinese History*, 49–50.

47. Ibid., 159.

48. Ibid., 47.

49. Quoted from Pang and Jin, *Mao Zedong zhuan (1949–1976)* (Biography of Mao Zedong [1949–1976]), vol. 2, 1704.

50. Quoted from Deng, *Deng Xiaoping and the Cultural Revolution*, 282–83.

51. Ibid., 300.

52. See Pang and Jin, *Mao Zedong zhuan (1949–1976)* (Biography of Mao Zedong [1949–1976]), vol. 2, 1739.

53. For details see the book by Guo Jinrong based on Meng Jinyun's memoirs: Guo Jinrong, *Zoujin Mao Zedongde zuihou suiyue* (Entering Mao Zedong's Last Months) (Beijing: Zhonggong dangshi chubanshe, 2009).

54. Quoted from Deng, *Deng Xiaoping and the Cultural Revolution*, 353.

55. *History of the Chinese Communist Party—A Chronology of Events*, 373.

56. See *Rethinking the "Cultural Revolution"* (Beijing: Foreign Languages Press, 1987), 22–23; Yen and Kao, *The Ten Year History of the Chinese Cultural Revolution*, 553.

57. Quoted from *History of the Chinese Communist Party—A Chronology of Events*, 375.

58. Quoted from Deng, *Deng Xiaoping and the Cultural Revolution*, 398.

59. Quoted from Pang and Jin, *Mao Zedong zhuan (1949–1976)* (Biography of Mao Zedong [1949–1976]), vol. 2, 1778.

60. See ibid., 1745–1746; Li, *The Private Life of Chairman Mao*, 601–2, 604–5.

61. Zhang, "Neskol'ko shtrikov k kartine poslednikh let zhizni Mao Tszeduna, Chzhou En'laia" (Some Brushstrokes Toward a Picture of the Last Years of Mao Zedong and Zhou Enlai), 98.

62. Ibid., 102.

63. *Lichnoe delo Mao Tszeduna* (Personal File of Mao Zedong), RGASPI, collection 495, inventory 225, file 71, vol. 6, sheet 114.

64. Ibid., sheet 107.

65. Ibid., sheet 201. See also Pang and Jin, *Mao Zedong zhuan (1949–1976)* (Biography of Mao Zedong [1949–1976]), vol. 2, 1778.

66. Pang and Jin, *Mao Zedong zhuan (1949–1976)* (Biography of Mao Zedong [1949–1976]), vol. 2, 1781–82. For slightly different translations see Barnouin and Yu, *Ten Years of Turbulence,* 291; Michael Schoenhals, ed., *China's Cultural Revolution, 1966–1969: Not a Dinner Party* (Armonk, NY: M. E. Sharpe, 1996), 293.

67. See *Lichnoe delo Mao Tszeduna* (Personal File of Mao Zedong), RGASPI, collection 495, inventory 225, file 71, vol. 6, sheet 81.

68. See Li, *The Private Life of Chairman Mao,* 614, 618, 624; Li, *Moi otets Mao Tszedun* (My Father Mao Zedong), 296–97.

EPILOGUE

1. *Resolution on CPC History (1949–81)* (Beijing: Foreign Languages Press, 1981), 56.

2. Quoted from Terrill, *Madam Mao,* 9.

3. See *A Great Trial in Chinese History,* 128.

4. Quoted from Terrill, *Madam Mao,* 353.

5. Borisov and Titarenko, *Vystupleniia Mao Tsze-duna, ranee ne publikovavshiesia v kitaiskoi pechati* (Mao Zedong's Speeches Previously Unpublished in the Chinese Press), series 6, 212–13, 214.

BIBLIOGRAPHY

PRIMARY SOURCES

ARCHIVAL SOURCES

RUSSIAN STATE ARCHIVES OF SOCIAL AND POLITICAL
HISTORY (RGASPI IN RUSSIAN ABBREVIATION)

Collection 5. Inventory 1. Secretariat of Chairman of Council of People's Commissars and Council of Labor and Defense Vladimir Ilich Lenin. 1917–23: Documents on State Activity of Vladimir Ilich Lenin.

Collection 5. Inventory 2. Secretariat of Chairman of the Council of People's Commissars and Council of Labor and Defense Vladimir Ilich Lenin. 1917–23: Documents on Party and Public Activity of Vladimir Ilich Lenin.

Collection 5. Inventory 3. Secretariat of Chairman of Council of People's Commissars and Council of Labor and Defense Vladimir Ilich Lenin. 1917–23: Documents on Vladimir Ilich Lenin's Leadership of the International Labor and Communist Movement (1917–23).

Collection 17. Inventory 2. Plenums of the Central Committee of the Russian Communist Party (Bolsheviks) and the All-Union Communist Party (Bolsheviks). 1918–41.

Collection 17. Inventory 3. Minutes of Sessions of the Politburo of the Central Committee of the Russian Communist Party (Bolsheviks) and the All-Union Communist Party (Bolsheviks)

Collection 17. Inventory 162. Special Papers of the Politburo of the Central Committee of the Russian Communist Party (Bolsheviks) and the All-Union Communist Party (Bolsheviks).

Collection 146. Inventory 2. File 3. The Diary of Georgii Dimitrov (March 9, 1933–February 6, 1949).

Collection 495. Inventory 3. Political Secretariat of the Executive Committee of the Communist International.

Collection 495. Inventory 65a. Personal Files of Employees of the Executive Committee of the Communist International Apparatus.

Collection 495. Inventory 154. Eastern Secretariat of the Executive Committee of the Communist International.

Collection 495. Inventory 163. The Fifth Enlarged Plenum of the Executive Committee of the Communist International.

Collection 495. Inventory 164. The Sixth Enlarged Plenum of the Executive Committee of the Communist International.

Collection 495. Inventory 165. The Seventh Enlarged Plenum of the Executive Committee of the Communist International.

Collection 495. Inventory 225. File 71. Dossier to the Personal File of Mao Zedong. 5 vols.

Collection 495. Inventory 225. File 71. Personal File of Mao Zedong. 10 vols.

Collection 495. Inventory 225. Personal Files of 3,327 Members of the Chinese Communist Party and the Guomindang.

Collection 505. International Control Commission of the Communist International.

Collection 508. Delegation of the All-Soviet Communist Party (Bolsheviks) on the Executive Committee of the Communist International.

Collection 514. Central Committee of the Chinese Communist Party.

Collection 514. Inventory 3. Collection of Mao Zedong's Documents of 1923–40.

Collection 530. Communist University of the Toilers of China.

Collection 532. Communist University of the Toilers of the East and the Research Institute of National and Colonial Problems.

Collection 558. Joseph Vissarionovich Stalin.

Collection of unsorted documents.

ARCHIVES ON THE FOREIGN POLICY OF THE RUSSIAN
FEDERATION (AVP RF IN RUSSIAN ABBREVIATION)

Collection 0100. Inventory 46. File 12. The Diary of Soviet Ambassador to China Vasily Vasilevich Kuznetsov. Miscellaneous papers.

Collection 0100. Inventory 46. File 374. Folder 121. Zhou Enlai Speech at the Financial-Economic Conference.

BUREAU OF INVESTIGATION OF THE MINISTRY OF LEGISLATION ON TAIWAN

Miscellaneous papers on Chinese communist movement.

PRIVATE ARCHIVES

Archives of Alexander V. Pantsov. Miscellaneous papers.

Archives of Meng Qingshu. Meng Qingshu. *Vospominaniia o Van Mine* (Reminiscences of Wang Ming). Manuscript.

Archives of Wang Fanxi. Miscellaneous papers.

HOUGHTON LIBRARY, HARVARD UNIVERSITY

Trotsky Papers.

PRINTED DOCUMENTS

Acheson, Dean. "Letter of Transmittal." In *United States Relations with China: With Special Reference to the Period 1944–1949,* iii–xvii. New York: Greenwood Press, 1968.

Aimermakher, K., ed. *Doklad N. S. Khrushcheva o kul'te lichnosti Stalina na XX s'ezde KPSS: Dokumenty* (N. S. Khrushchev's Report on Stalin's Cult of Personality at the 20th CPSU Congress: Documents). Moscow: ROSSPEN, 2002.

" 'All Under the Heaven Is Great Chaos': Beijing, the Sino-Soviet Clashes, and the Turn to Sino-American Rapprochement, 1968–69." *CWIHP Bulletin,* no. 11 (March 1998): 155–75.

Bakulin, A. V. *Zapiski ob ukhan'skom periode kitaiskoi revoliutsii (iz istorii kitaiskoi revoliutsii 1925–1927 gg.)* (Notes on the Wuhan Period of the Chinese Revolution: From the History of the Chinese Revolution of 1925–1927). Moscow-Leningrad: Giz, 1930.

Banac, Ivo, ed. *The Diary of Georgi Dimitrov 1933–1949.* Translated by Jane T. Hedges et al. New Haven, CT: Yale University Press, 2003.

Baqi huiyi (The August 7 Conference). Beijing: Zhonggongdang shi ziliao chubanshe, 1986.

Benton, Gregor, ed. *Chen Duxiu's Last Articles and Letters, 1937–1942.* Richmond, UK: Curzon Press, 1999.

Biulleten' IV Kongressa Kommunisticheskogo Internatsionala (Bulletin of the Fourth Congress of the Communist International), no. 20 (November 29, 1922).

Borisov, O. [O. B. Rakhmanin] and M. Titarenko, eds. *Vystupleniia Mao Tsze-duna, ranee ne publikovavshiesia v kitaiskoi pechati* (Mao Zedong's Speeches Previously Unpublished in the Chinese Press). 6 series. Moscow: Progress, 1975–76.

Borot'sia za mobilizatsiiu vsekh sil dlia prevrashcheniia nashei strany v velikoe sotsialisticheskoe gosudarstvo. Tezisy dlia izucheniia i propagandy general'noi linii partii v perekhod-

nyi period (Razrabotany otdelom agitatsii i propagandy TsK KPK i utverzhdeny TsK KPK v dekabre 1953 g.) (Struggle to Mobilize All Forces to Transform Our Country into a Socialist State. Theses for Studying and Propagandizing the Party's General Line in the Transitional Period [Prepared by the Department of Agitation and Propaganda of the CC CCP and Affirmed by the CC CCP in December 1953]). Moscow: Gospolitizdat, [1957].

Bowie, Robert R., and John K. Fairbank, eds. *Communist China 1955–1959: Policy Documents with Analysis.* Cambridge, MA: Harvard University Press, 1962.

Brandt, Conrad, Benjamin Schwartz, and John K. Fairbank. *A Documentary History of Chinese Communism.* Cambridge, MA: Harvard University Press, 1952.

Burr, William, ed. *The Kissinger Transcripts: The Top Secret Talks with Beijing and Moscow.* New York: New Press, 1998.

The Case of Peng Te-huai. 1959–68. Hong Kong: Union Research Institute, 1968.

CCP Documents of the Great Proletarian Cultural Revolution 1966–1976. Hong Kong: Union Research Institute, 1968.

Chen Duxiu. *Chen Duxiu wenzhang xuanbian* (Selected Writings of Chen Duxiu). 3 vols. Beijing: Shenghuo. Dushu. Xinzhi sanlian shudian, 1984.

———. "Political Report." In Tony Saich, ed. *The Rise to Power of the Chinese Communist Party. Documents and Analysis,* 219–23. Armonk, NY: M. E. Sharpe, 1996.

———. "Shehuizhuyi piping" (A Critique of Socialism). *Xin qingnian* (New youth) 9, no. 3 (1921): 1–13.

Chen Jian. "Deng Xiaoping, Mao's 'Continuous Revolution,' and the Path towards the Sino-Soviet Split." *CWIHP Bulletin,* no. 10 (March 1998): 162–64.

Chen Yi. "Chen Yi tongzhi guanyu Zhu Mao jun de lishi ji qi zhuangkuang de baogao" (Comrade Chen Yi's Report on the History of the Zhu-Mao Army and Its Present Situation). In *Jingganshan geming genjudi shiliao xuanbian* (Collection of Selected Materials on the Revolutionary Base Area in the Jinggang Mountains), 176–93. Nanchang: Jiangxi renmin chubanshe, 1986.

———. "Istoriia boevykh deistvii 4-go korpusa" (History of the Military Engagements of the Fourth Corps). In Pavel Mif, ed. *Sovety v Kitae: Sbornik materialov i dokumentov* (Soviets in China: Collection of Materials and Documents), 186–92. Moscow: Partizdat, 1934.

Chiang Kai shek. *China's Destiny.* New York: Macmillan, 1947.

Chou En-lai [Zhou Enlai]. "Report on the Proposals for the Second Five-Year Plan for Development of the National Economy." In *Eighth National Congress of the Communist Party of China,* vol. 1, *Documents,* 261–328. Beijing: Foreign Language Press, 1956.

"Comrade Peng Dehuai's Letter to Chairman Mao (July 14, 1959)." In Peng Dehuai, *Memoirs of a Chinese Marshal: The Autobiographical Notes of Peng Dehuai (1898–1974),* 510–20. Translated by Zheng Longpu. Beijing: Foreign Languages Press, 1984.

Dallin, Alexander, and F. I. Firsov. *Dimitrov and Stalin 1934–1943: Letters from the Soviet Archives.* Translated by Vadim A. Staklo. New Haven: Yale University Press, 2000.

Dedijer, Vladimir. *The War Diaries of Vladimir Dedijer.* 3 vols. Ann Arbor: University of Michigan Press, 1990.

Degras, Jane, ed. *The Communist International: 1919–1943: Documents.* 3 vols. London: Oxford University Press, 1960.

Deliusin, L. P., ed. *Agrarnye preobrazovania v narodnom Kitae* (Agrarian Transformation in People's China). Moscow: Izdatel'stvo inostrannoi literatury, 1955.

———, ed. *Dvizheniie 4 maia 1919 v Kitae. Dokumenty i materialy* (The May Fourth Movement of 1919 in China: Documents and Materials). Moscow: Nauka, 1969.

Deng Xiaoping. *Selected Works of Deng Xiaoping (1938–1965).* Beijing: Foreign Languages Press, 1992.

———. *Selected Works of Deng Xiaoping (1975–1982).* 2nd ed. Beijing: Foreign Languages Press, 1995.

———. *Selected Works of Deng Xiaoping (1982–1992)*. Beijing: Foreign Languages Press, 1994.

"Deng Xiaoping's Talks with the Soviet Ambassador and Leadership, 1957–1963." *CWIHP Bulletin*, no. 10 (March 1998): 165–82.

Deng Zhongxia. *Deng Zhongxia wenji* (Works of Deng Zhongxia). Beijing: Renmin chubanshe, 1983.

Dimitrov, Georgii. *Dnevnik 9 mart 1933–6 fevruari 1949* (Diary, March 9, 1933–February 6, 1949). Sofia: Universitetsko izdatelstvo "Sv. Kliment Okhridski," 1997.

Dokumenty VIII Plenuma Tsentral'nogo Komiteta Kommunisticheskoi partii Kitaia vos'mogo sozyva (Documents of the Eighth Plenum of the Eighth Central Committee of the Communist Party of China). Beijing: Izdatel'stvo literatury na inostrannykh iazykakh, 1959.

Dong Bian et al., eds. *Mao Zedong he tade mishu Tian Jiaying* (Mao Zedong and His Secretary Tian Jiaying). Beijing: Zhongyang wenxian chubanshe, 1989.

"12 sovetov I. V. Stalina rukovodstvu Kompartii Kitaia" (J. V. Stalin's Twelve Advices to the Chinese Communist Party Leadership). *Novaia i noveishaia istoriia* (Modern and contemporary history), no. 1 (2004): 125–39.

Eighth National Congress of the Communist Party of China. 2 vols. Beijing: Foreign Languages Press, 1956.

Elizavetin, A. "Peregovory A. N. Kosygina i Chzhou En'laia v Pekinskom aeroportu" (Talks Between A. N. Kosygin and Zhou Enlai at the Beijing Airport). *Problemy Dal'nego Vostoka* (Far Eastern affairs), no. 5 (1992): 39–63; no. 2 (1993): 107–19.

"The Emerging Disputes between Beijing and Moscow: Ten Newly Available Chinese Documents, 1956–1958." *CWIHP Bulletin*, nos. 6–7 (1995/1996): 148–63.

"Erda" he "sanda": Zhongguo gongchandang di' er san ci daibiaodahui ziliao xuanbian (The Second and Third Congresses: Selected Documents from the Second and Third Congresses of the CCP). Beijing: Zhongguo shehui kexue chubanshe, 1985.

Esherick, Joseph, ed. *Lost Chance in China: The World War II Dispatches of John S. Service*. New York: Random House, 1974.

Eudin, Xenia, and Robert C. North. *Soviet Russia and the East: 1920–1927: A Documentary Survey*. Stanford, CA: Stanford University Press, 1957.

"Excerpt from the Communiqué of the Fourth Plenum (February 18, 1954)." In Frederick C. Teiwes, *Politics at Mao's Court: Gao Gang and Party Factionalism*, 236–37. Armonk, NY: M. E. Sharpe, 1990.

Fremantle, Anne, ed. *Mao Tse-tung: An Anthology of His Writings*. Updated and Expanded, with Additional Writings of Chiang Ching and Lin Piao. New York: New American Library, 1971.

Fursenko, A. A., ed. *Prezidium TSK KPSS: 1954–1964* (The Presidium of the CC of the CPSU: 1954–1964). Vol. 1. *Chernovye protokolnye zapisi zasedanii, stenogrammy, postanovleniia* (Drafts of Minutes of Sessions, Stenographic Records, Decisions). Moscow: ROSSPEN, 2003.

———. *Prezidium TSK KPSS: 1954–1964* (The Presidium of the CC of the CPSU: 1954–1964). Vol. 2. *Postanovleniia 1954–1958* (Resolutions of 1954–1958). Moscow: ROSSPEN, 2006.

———. *Prezidium TSK KPSS: 1954–1964* (The Presidium of the CC of the CPSU: 1954–1964). Vol. 3. *Postanovleniia 1959–1964* (Resolutions of 1959–1964). Moscow: ROSSPEN, 2008.

Gao Gang. *Izbrannoe* (Selections). Moscow: IDV AN SSSR, 1989.

Geming lieshi shuxin (Letters of Revolutionary Martyrs). 2 vols. Beijing: Zhongguo qingnian chubanshe, 1983.

Geroi ostrova Damanskii (Heroes of Damansky Island). Moscow: "Molodaia gvardiia," 1969.

Gongchan xiaozu (Communist Cells). 2 vols. Beijing: Zhonggong dangshi ziliao chubanshe, 1987.

Gongchandang zai Guomindang neide gongzuo wenti yijue'an (Declaration on the Question of the Work of the Communist Party inside the Guomindang). *Dangbao* (Party paper), no. 3 (1924): 1–3.

Gongfei huoguo shiliao huibian (Collection of Materials on the History of the Communist Bandits Who Brought Misfortune to the Country). 4 vols. Taipei: Zhonghua minguo kaiguo wushinian wenxian biancuan weiyuanhui, 1964.

The Great Cultural Revolution in China. Rutland, VT: C. E. Tuttle, 1968.

The Great Socialist Cultural Revolution in China. Vols. 1–6. Beijing: Foreign Languages Press, 1966.

A Great Trial in Chinese History: The Trial of the Lin Biao and Jiang Qing Counter-Revolutionary Cliques, Nov. 1980–Jan. 1981. Oxford: Pergamon Press, 1981.

"Guomindang yi da dangwu baogao xuanzai" (Selected Reports on Party Affairs, Submitted to the First Guomindang Congress). *Gemingshi ziliao* (Materials on revolutionary history). Shanghai, no. 2 (1986): 28–35.

"Heben Dazuo wei cehua. 'Huanggutun shijian' zhi Jigu Lianjie deng han liangjian (1928 nian 4 yue)" (Two Messages from Komoto Daisaku to Isogai Rensuke Planning to Create the Huanggutun Incident [April 1928])." *Minguo dang'an* (Republican archives), no. 3 (1998): 3–5.

Hsiao Tso-liang. *Power Relations Within the Chinese Communist Movement, 1930–1934*. Vol. 2. Seattle: University of Washington Press, 1967.

Isaacs, Harold. "Documents on the Comintern and the Chinese Revolution." *China Quarterly*, no. 45 (1971): 103–12.

Jiang Jiannong, and Wang Benqian. *Sinuo yu Zhongguo* (Snow and China). Harbin: Heilongjiang renmin chubanshe, 1993.

Jinggangshan geming genjudi shiliao xuanbian (Collection of Selected Materials on the Revolutionary Base Area in the Jinggang Mountains). Nanchang: Jiangxi renmin chubanshe, 1986.

Kangri minzu tongyi zhanxian zhinan (Directives of the Anti-Japanese National United Front). Vol. 1. N.p., n.d.

Kartunova, A. I., ed. *V. K. Bliukher v Kitae: 1924–1927 gg.: Novye dokumenty glavnogo voennogo sovetnika* (V. K. Bliukher in China: 1924–1927: New Documents on the Chief Military Adviser). Moscow: Natalis, 2003.

Kau, Michael Y. M., ed. *The Lin Piao Affair: Power Politics and Military Coup*. White Plains, NY: International Arts and Sciences Press, 1975.

Khrushchev, N. S. *Report of the Central Committee of the Communist Party of the Soviet Union to the 20th Party Congress*. Moscow: Foreign Languages Publishing House, 1956.

———. *Speech before a closed session of the XXth Congress of the Communist Party of the Soviet Union on February 25, 1956*. Washington, DC: U.S. Government Printing Office, 1957.

"Khrushchev's Nuclear Promise to Beijing During the 1958 Crisis." *CWIHP Bulletin*, nos. 6–7 (1995/1996): 219, 226–27.

Klehr, Harvey, John Earl Haynes, and Fridrikh Igorievch Firsov. *The Secret World of American Communism*. New Haven, CT: Yale University Press, 1995.

Knight, Nick, ed. *Mao Zedong on Dialectical Materialism: Writings on Philosophy, 1937*. Armonk, NY: M. E. Sharpe, 1990.

"Kongress Kommunisticheskoi partii v Kitae" (Congress of the Communist Party in China). *Narody Azii i Afriki* (Peoples of Asia and Africa), no. 6 (1972): 151–55.

Kovalev, I. V. "Zapiska I. V. Kovaleva ot 24 dekabria 1949 g." (I. V. Kovalev's Note of December 24, 1949). *Novaia i noveishaia istoriia* (Modern and contemporary history), no. 1 (1998): 132–39.

Kramer, Mark. "The USSR Foreign Ministry's Appraisal of Sino-Soviet Relations on the Eve of the Split, September 1959." *CWIHP Bulletin*, nos. 6–7 (1995/1996): 170–85.

Kurdiukov, I. F., et al., eds. *Sovetsko-kitaiskie otnosheniia, 1917–1957: Sbornik dokumentov* (Soviet-Chinese Relations, 1917–1957: A Documentary Collection). Moscow: Izd-vo vostochnoi literatury, 1959.

Laoyibei gemingjia shuxin xuan (Selected Letters of the Old Generation Revolutionaries). Changsha: Hunan renmin chubanshe, 1984.

Ledovsky, A. M. *SSSR i Stalin v sud'bakh Kitaia: Dokumenty i svidel'stva uchastnika sobytii: 1937–1952* (The USSR and Stalin in China's Fate: Documents and Witness of a Participant: 1937–1952). Moscow: Pamiatniki istoricheskoi mysli, 1999.

———. "Stalin, Mao Zedong i koreiskaia voina 1950–1953 godov" (Stalin, Mao, and the Korean War of 1950–1953). *Novaia i noveishaia istoriia* (Modern and contemporary history), no. 5 (2005): 79–113.

Lenin, V. I. *Polnoe sobranie sochinenii* (Complete Collected Works). 55 vols. Moscow: Politizdat, 1963–78.

———. *Selected Works.* 12 vols. New York: International, 1943.

Li Da. "Makesi huanyuan" (Marx's Revival). *Xin qingnian* (New youth) 8, no. 5 (1921): 1–8.

Li Dazhao. *Izbrannye proizvedeniia* (Selected Works). Moscow: Nauka, 1989.

———. *Li Dazhao wenji* (Works of Li Dazhao). 2 vols. Beijing: Renmin chubanshe, 1984.

Li, Dun J., ed. *The Road to Communism: China Since 1912.* New York: Van Nostrand Reinhold, 1969.

Li Fu-ch'un [Li Fuchun]. "Report on the First Five-Year Plan, 1953–1957, July 5–6, 1955." In Robert R. Bowie and John K. Fairbank, eds. *Communist China 1955–1959: Policy Documents with Analysis,* 43–91. Cambridge, MA: Harvard University Press, 1962.

Li Xiaobing, et al., eds. "Mao Zedong's Handling of the Taiwan Straits Crisis of 1958: Chinese Recollections and Documents." *CWIHP Bulletin,* nos. 6–7 (1995/1996): 208–26.

Lih, Lars T., et al., eds. *Stalin's Letters to Molotov 1925–1936.* Translated by Catherine A. Fitzpatrick. New Haven, CT: Yale University Press, 1995.

Lin Guliang. "Gongchan guoji daibiao lai Hua qingkuang ziliao zhaibian" (Digest of Materials on the Comintern Representatives' Trips to China). *Dangshi yanjiu ziliao* (Study materials on party history), no. 13 (1979): C. 5–28.

Liu Shao-chi. *On the Party.* Beijing: Foreign Languages Press, 1950.

Liu Shaoqi. *Selected Works of Liu Shaoqi.* 2 vols. Beijing: Foreign Languages Press, 1984.

———. *Liu Shaoqi xuanji* (Selected Works of Liu Shaoqi). 2 vols. Beijing: Renmin chubanshe, 1985.

[Liu Shiqi]. "Sovetskii raion iugo-zapadnoi Tsiansi v 1930 g.: Doklad instruktora TsK kompartii Kitaia ot 7 oktiabria 1930 g." (The Soviet District of Southwest Jiangxi in 1930: Report of a CCP Central Committee Instructor, October 7, 1930). In Pavel Mif, ed. *Sovety v Kitae: Sbornik materialov i dokumentov* (Soviets in China: Collection of Materials and Documents), 227–44. Moscow: Partizdat, 1934.

MacFarquhar, Roderick, ed. *The Secret Speeches of Chairman Mao: From the Hundred Flowers to the Great Leap Forward.* Cambridge, MA: Council on East Asian Studies/ Harvard University, 1989.

Makesizhuyi zai Zhongguo—cong yingxiang chuanru dao chuanbo (Marxism in China— From the Ideological Penetration to Its Dissemination). 2 vols. Beijing: Qinghua daxue chubanshe, 1983.

Mao shi zupu (Chronicle of the Mao Clan). Tianjin: Tianjin guji chubanshe, 1999.

"Mao's Dispatch of Chinese Troops to Korea: Forty-six Telegrams, July–October 1950." *Chinese Historians* 5, no. 1 (Spring 1992): 63–86.

"Mao Tszedun o kitaiskoi politike Kominterna i Stalina" (Mao Zedong on the China Policy of the Comintern and of Stalin). *Problemy Dal'nego Vostoka* (Far Eastern affairs), no. 5 (1998): 101–10.

Mao Zedong. *Ekonomicheskoe stroitel'stvo i itogi proverki razdela zemli v Kitaiskoi Sovietskoi Respublike: Izbrannye rechi i stat'i* (Economic Construction and the Results of the Verification of Land Redistribution in the Chinese Soviet Republic: Selected Speeches and Articles). Moscow and Leningrad: Izdatel'stvo inostrannykh rabochikh v SSSR, 1934.

———. *Jianguo yilai Mao Zedong wengao* (Manuscripts of Mao Zedong from the Founding of the PRC). 13 vols. Beijing: Zhongyang wenxian chubanshe, 1987–98.

———. *Mao Zedong junshi wenji* (Military Works of Mao Zedong). 6 vols. Beijing: Junshi kexue chubanshe, Zhongyang wenxian chubanshe, 1993.

———. *Mao Zedong nongcun diaocha wenji* (Works of Mao Zedong on Rural Investigation). Beijing: Renmin chubanshe, 1982.

———. *Mao Zedong on Diplomacy.* Beijing: Foreign Languages Press, 1998.

———. *Mao Zedong shici duilian jizhu* (Collection of Mao Zedong's Poems). Changsha: Hunan wenyi chubanshe, 1991.

———. *Mao Zedong shici ji* (Collection of Mao Zedong's Poems). Beijing: Xianzhuang shuju, 1997.

———. *Mao Zedong shuxin xuanji* (Selected Letters of Mao Zedong). Beijing: Renmin chubanshe, 1983.

———. *Mao Zedong sixiang wansui* (Long Live Mao Zedong Thought). 2 vols. Beijing: s.n., 1967–69.

———. *Mao Zedong wenji* (Works of Mao Zedong). 8 vols. Beijing: Renmin chubanshe, 1993–99.

———. *Mao Zedong xinwen gongzuo wenxuan* (Mao Zedong's Selected Works on the Information Work). Beijing: Xinhua chubanshe, 1983.

———. *Mao Zedong xuanji* (Selected Works of Mao Zedong). 3 vols. Beijing: Renmin chubanshe, 1951–52.

———. *Mao Zedong xuanji* (Selected Works of Mao Zedong). Vol. 4. Beijing: Renmin chubanshe, 1960.

———. *Mao Zedong xuanji* (Selected Works of Mao Zedong). Vol. 5. Beijing: Renmin chubanshe, 1977.

———. *Mao Zedong zai qi dade baogao he jianghua ji* (Collection of Reports and Speeches of Mao Zedong at the Seventh Congress). Beijing: Zhongyang wenxian chubanshe, 2000.

———. *Mao Zedong zhuzuo xuandu* (Source Book of Mao Zedong). 2 vols. Beijing: Renmin chubanshe, 1986.

———. *Mao zhuxi shici* (Poems of Chairman Mao). Beijing: Renmin wenxue chubanshe, 1976.

———. *Miscellany of Mao Tse-tung Thought (1949–1968).* 2 parts. Springfield, VA: Joint Publications Research Service, 1974.

———. *Oblaka v snegu: Stikhotvoreniia v perevodakh Aleksandra Pantsova* (Clouds in the Snow: Poems in Translation by Alexander Pantsov). Moscow: "Veche," 2010.

———. *Poems of Mao Tse-tung.* Translation, introd., and notes by Hua-ling Nieh Engle and Paul Engle. New York: Simon & Schuster, 1972.

———. "Qida gongzuo fangzhen" (Work Report at the Seventh Congress). *Hongqi* (Red flag), no. 11 (1981): 1–7.

———. *Selected Works of Mao Tse-tung.* Vols. 1–3. Beijing: Foreign Languages Press, 1967.

———. *Selected Works of Mao Tse-tung.* Vol. 4. Beijing: Foreign Languages Press, 1969.

———. *Selected Works of Mao Tsetung.* Vol. 5. Beijing: Foreign Languages Press, 1977.

———. "Tol'ko soviety mogut spasti Kitai: Doklad na II-m s'ezde Sovetov Kitaia" (Only Soviets Can Save China: Report at the Second Congress of Chinese Soviets). Moscow and Leningrad: Izdatel'stvo inostrannykh rabochikh v SSSR, 1934.

Mao Zedong shenghuo dang'an (Archives of Mao Zedong's life). 3 vols. Beijing: Zhonggong dangshi chubanshe, 1999.

Martynov, A. "Komintern pered sudom likvidatorov" (The Comintern Before the Court of the Liquidationists). *Kommunisticheskii Internatsional* (Communist International), no. 30 (104) (1927): 9–21.

———. "Problema kitaiskoi revoliutsii" (The Problem of the Chinese Revolution). *Pravda* (Truth), April 10, 1927.

Materialy 6-go plenuma Tsentral'nogo Komiteta Kommunisticheskoi partii Kitaia vos'mogo sozyva (Materials of the Sixth Plenum of the Eighth Central Committee of the Chinese Communist Party). Beijing: Izdatel'stvo literatury na inostrannykh iazykakh, 1959.

Materialy VIII Vsekitaiskogo s"ezda Kommunisticheskoi partii Kitaia (Materials from the Eighth Congress of the Communist Party of China). Moscow: Gospolitizdat, 1956.

Materialy vtoroi sessii Vsekitaiskogo sobraniia narodnykh predstavitelei (5–30 iulia 1955 g.) (Materials from the Second Session of the National People's Congress [July 5–30, 1955]). Moscow: Gospolitizdat, 1956.

"Meeting Between Zhou Enlai and Kosygin at the Beijing Airport." http://www.fmprc.gov .cn/eng/5691.html.

"Memo, PRC Foreign Ministry to the USSR Embassy in Beijing, March 13, 1957." *CWIHP Bulletin,* nos. 6–7 (1995/1996): 159–60.

Mif, Pavel, ed. *Sovety v Kitae: Materialy i dokumenty. Sbornik vtoroi* (Soviets in China: Materials and Documents. Collection Two). Moscow: Partizdat TSK VKP(b), 1935. Unpublished proofs.

———, ed. *Sovety v Kitae: Sbornik materialov i dokumentov* (Soviets in China: Collection of Materials and Documents). Moscow: Partizdat, 1934.

———, ed. *Strategiia i taktika Kominterna v natsional'no-kolonial'noi revoliutsii na primere Kitaia* (Strategy and Tactics of the Comintern in National and Colonial Revolution: The Case of China). Moscow: IWEIP Press, 1934.

"Minquan yundong datongmeng xuanyan" (Declaration of the Alliance of Democracy Movements). *Xianqu* (Pioneer), no. 20 (1922): 1–2.

"Minutes, Mao's Conversation with a Yugoslavian Communist Union Delegation, Beijing, September [undated] 1956." *CWIHP Bulletin,* nos. 6–7 (1995/1996): 148–52.

Myers, James T., et al., eds. *Chinese Politics: Documents and Analysis.* Vols. 1 and 2. Columbia: University of South Carolina Press, 1986.

"Nepublikovavshaiasia rech' I. V. Stalina o Kitae" (Josef V. Stalin's Unpublished Speech on China). *Problemy Dal'nego Vostoka* (Far Eastern affairs) 1 (2001): 149–59.

"A New 'Cult of Personality': Suslov's Secret Report on Mao, Khrushchev, and Sino-Soviet Tensions, December 1959." *CWIHP Bulletin,* nos. 8–9 (1996/1997): 244, 248.

"New East Bloc Documents on the Sino-Indian Conflict, 1959 & 1962." *CWIHP Bulletin,* nos. 8–9 (1996/1997): 258–69.

"New Evidence on the Korean War." *CWIHP Bulletin,* nos. 6–7 (1996/1997): 30–125.

Nie Yuanzi, et al. "Song Shuo, Lu Ping, Peng Peiyuan zai wenhua gemingzhong jiujing gan shenma" (What Are Song Shuo, Lu Ping, and Peng Peiyuan Really Doing with Respect to the Cultural Revolution). *Renmin ribao* (People's daily), June 2, 1966.

IX Vsekitaiskii s"ezd Kommunisticheskoi partii Kitaia (dokumenty) (Ninth Congress of the Communist Party of China [Documents]). Beijing: Foreign Languages Press, 1969.

North, Robert C., and Xenia Eudin. *M. N. Roy's Mission to China: The Communist-Kuomintang Split of 1927.* Berkeley: University of California Press, 1963.

"Novye materialy o pervom s"ezde Kommunisticheskoi partii Kitaia" (New Materials on the First Congress of the Communist Party of China). *Narody Azii i Afriki* (Peoples of Asia and Africa), no. 6 (1972): 150–58.

Obrazovanie Kitaiskoi Narodnoi Respubliki: Dokumenty i materialy (Establishment of the Chinese People's Republic: Documents and Materials). Moscow: Gospolitizdat, 1950.

Ostermann, Christian F. "East German Documents on the Border Conflict, 1969." *CWIHP Bulletin,* nos. 6–7 (1995/1996): 186–93.

Pan Zuofu (Pantsov, A. V.). "Xin faxian de Li Dazhao, Chen Duxiu, Ren Bishi xinjian" (Newly Discovered Letters of Li Dazhao, Chen Duxiu, and Ren Bishi). *Bainian chao* (Century tides), no. 1 (2005): 31–34.

Peng Gongda. "Report on the Progress of the Autumn Harvest Uprising in Hunan." In Tony Saich, ed. *The Rise to Power of the Chinese Communist Party: Documents and Analysis,* 322–31. Armonk, NY: M. E. Sharpe, 1996.

Pervaiia sessiia Vsekitaiskogo sobraniia narodnykh predstavitelei Kitaiskoi Narodnoi Respubliki pervogo sozyva (dokumenty i materialy) (The First Session of the First National People's Congress of the PRC [Documents and Materials]). Beijing: Izdatel'stvo literatury na inostrannykh iazykakh, 1956.

The Polemic on the General Line of the International Communist Movement. Beijing: Foreign Languages Press, 1965.

Polemika o general'noi linii mezhdunarodnogo kommunisticheskogo dvizheniia (The Polemic on the General Line of the International Communist Movement). Peking: Izdatel'stvo literatury na inostrannykh iazykakh, 1965.

Politburo TSK VKP(b) i Sovet ministrov SSSR 1945–1953 (The Politburo of the CC of the AUCP(b) and the USSR Council of Ministers 1945–1953). Moscow: ROSSPEN, 2002.

"Record of Conversation, Mao Zedong and Soviet Ambassador to Beijing Pavel Yudin, July 22, 1958." In O. Arne Westad, ed. *Brothers in Arms: The Rise and Fall of the Sino-Soviet Alliance, 1945–1963,* 347–56. Stanford, CA: Stanford University Press, 1998.

Ren Bishi. *Ren Bishi xuanji* (Selected Works of Ren Bishi). Beijing: Renmin chubanshe, 1987.

Reshenie shestogo (rasshirennogo) plenuma TsK Kommunisticheskoi partii Kitaia Sed'mogo sozyva po voprosu o kooperirovanii v sel'skom khoziaistve (Decision of the Sixth [enlarged] Plenum of the Seventh CC of the Communist Party of China on the Question of Agricultural Cooperation). Moscow: Gospolitzdat, 1955.

"Resolution of the CCP CC on Certain Historical Questions." In Tony Saich, ed. *The Rise to Power of the Chinese Communist Party: Documents and Analysis,* 1164–84. Armonk, NY: M. E. Sharpe, 1996.

Resolution on CPC History (1949–81). Beijing: Foreign Languages Press, 1981.

Saich, Tony. *The Origins of the First United Front in China: The Role of Sneevliet (Alias Maring).* 2 vols. Leiden: Brill, 1991.

———, ed. *The Rise to Power of the Chinese Communist Party: Documents and Analysis.* Armonk, NY: M. E. Sharpe, 1996.

Schoenhals, Michael, ed. *China's Cultural Revolution, 1966–1969: Not a Dinner Party.* Armonk, NY: M. E. Sharpe, 1996.

Schram, Stuart, ed. *Chairman Mao Talks to the People: Talks and Letters: 1956–1971.* New York: Pantheon, 1974.

———, ed. *Mao's Road to Power: Revolutionary Writings 1912–1949.* 7 vols. Armonk, NY: M. E. Sharpe, 1992–2005.

Shanghai diqu jiandang huodong yanjiu ziliao (Materials for the Study of Party Building in the Shanghai Region). Shanghai: Shanghai shi diyi renmin jingcha xuexiao, 1986.

Shao Piaoping. *Xin Eguo zhi yunjiu* (A Study of the New Russia). N.p.. Riben daban naqu dongying bianyishe, 1920.

Shaoshan Mao shi zupu (The Chronicle of the Shaoshan Mao Clan). 7 vols. Beijing: Quanguo tushuguan wenxian sowei fuzhi zhongxin, 2002.

Shestoi rasshirennyi plenum Ispolkoma Kominterna: Stenografischeskii otchet. 17 fevralia–15 marta 1926 g. (Sixth Enlarged Plenum of the ECCI: Stenographic Report: February 17–March 15, 1926). Moscow and Leningrad: Gospolitizdat, 1927.

Shi Cuntong. "Makeside gongchanzhuyi" (Marx's Communism). *Xin qingnian* (New youth) 9, no. 4 (1921): 1–11.

The Sino-Soviet Dispute. New York: Charles Scribner's Sons, 1969.

Sladkovskii, M. I., ed. *Informatsionnyi biulleten': Seriia A: "Kulturnaia revoliutsiia" v Kitae: Dokumenty i materialy (perevod s kitaiskogo)* (Information Bulletin: Series A: The "Cultural Revolution" in China: Documents and Materials [Translated from Chinese]). 12 installments. Moscow: IDV AN SSSR, 1968–72.

Soviet Plot in China. Peking: Metropolitan Police Headquarters, 1927.

Stalin, J. V. *Works.* 13 vols. Moscow: Foreign Languages Publishing House, 1954.

"Stalin's Conversations with Chinese Leaders: Talks with Mao Zedong, 1949–January 1950, and with Zhou Enlai, August–September 1952." *CWIHP Bulletin,* nos. 6–7 (1995/1996): 5–19.

Statement by General Patrick J. Hurley on December 5 & 6, 1945. United States–China Relations. Hearings Before the Committee on Foreign Relations, United States Senate, Ninety-second Congress, First Session on the Evolution of U.S. Policy Toward Mainland China

(Executive Hearings Held July 21, 1971; Made Public December 8, 1971) and Hearings Before the Committee on Foreign Relations, United States Senate, Seventy-Ninth Congress, First Session on the Situation in the Far East, Particularly China. December 5, 6, 7, and 10, 1945. Washington, DC, 1971.

Stenograficheskii otchet VI s'ezda Kommunisticheskoi partii Kitaia (Stenographic Record of the Sixth Congress of the Communist Party of China). 6 vols. Moscow: NII po Kitaiu, 1930.

Stenograficheskii otchet XX s'ezda KPSS (Stenographic Report of the Twentieth Congress of the CPSU). 2 vols. Moscow: Gospolitizdat, 1956.

Sudarikov, N. G., ed. *Konstitutsiia i osnovnye zakonodatel'nye akty Kitaiskoi Narodnoi Respubliki* (The Constitution and Founding Legislative Acts of the People's Republic of China). Moscow: Izdatel'stvo inostrannoi literatury, 1955.

Sun Yat-sen. *Izbrannye proizvedeniia* (Selected Works). 2nd ed., revised and expanded. Moscow: Nauka, 1985.

————. *Zhongshan quanji* (Complete Works of [Sun] Yat-sen). 2 vols. Shanghai: Liangyou tushu yinshua gongsi, 1931.

The Tenth National Congress of the Communist Party of China (Documents). Beijing: Foreign Languages Press, 1973.

Tikhvinsky, S. L. "Perepiska I. V. Stalina s Mao Tszedunom v ianvare 1949 g." (Correspondence Between J. V. Stalin and Mao Zedong in January 1949). *Novaia i noveishaia istoriia* (Modern and contemporary history), nos. 4–5 (1994): 132–40.

————, ed. *Russko-kitaiskie otnosheniia v XX veke: Dokumenty i materialy* (Russo-Chinese Relations in the Twentieth Century). Vols. 4–5. Moscow: Pamiatniki istoricheskoi mysli, 2000–2005.

Titarenko, M. L., et al., eds. *Kommunisticheskii Internatsional i kitaiskaia revoliutsiia: Dokumenty i materialy* (The Communist International and the Chinese Revolution: Documents and Materials). Moscow: Nauka, 1986.

————, eds. *VKP(b), Komintern i Kitai: Dokumenty* (The CPSU, the Comintern, and China: Documents). 5 vols. Moscow: AO "Buklet," 1994–2007.

Torkunov, A. V. *Zagadochnaia voina: Koreiskii konflikt 1950–1953 gg.* (The Enigmatic War: The Korean Conflict 1950–1953). Moscow: ROSSPEN, 2000.

Trotsky, L. "Stalin i Kitaiskaia revoliutsiia: Fakty i dokumenty" (Stalin and the Chinese Revolution: Facts and Documents). *Biulleten' oppozitsii (bol'shevikov-lenintsev)* (Bulletin of the opposition of the Bolsheviks and Leninists), nos. 15–16 (1925): 7–19.

Tsiui Tsiu-bo (Qu Qiubai). *Ocherki i stat'i* (Essays and Articles). Moscow: Gosizdat khudozhestvennoi literatury, 1959.

United States Relations with China: With Special Reference to the Period 1944–1949. New York: Greenwood Press, 1968.

Urban, George, ed. *The Miracles of Chairman Mao: A Compendium of Devotional Literature 1966–1970*. Los Angeles: Nash, 1971.

Van Slyke, Lyman P., ed. *The Chinese Communist Movement: A Report of the United States War Department, July 1945*. Stanford, CA: Stanford University Press, 1968.

Velikaia proletarskaia kul'turnaia revoliutsiia (vazhneishie dokumenty) (The Great Proletarian Cultural Revolution [Key Documents]). Beijing: Izdatel'stvo literatury na inostrannykh iazykakh, 1970.

Vladimirov, O. E. (O. B. Rakhmanin), ed. *Maoizm bez prikras: Nekotorye uzhe izvestnye, a takzhe ranee ne opublikovannye v kitaiskoi pechati vyskazyvaniia Mao Tszeduna: Sbornik* (Maoism Unembellished: Some Already Known Sayings of Mao Zedong and Others Previously Unpublished in the Chinese Press: A Collection). Moscow: Progress, 1980.

Vozniknovenie i razvitie raznoglasii mezhdu rukovodstvom KPSS i nami: Po povodu otkrytogo pis'ma TsK KPSS (The Origin and Development of Disagreements Between the Leadership of the CPSU and Us: On the Open Letter of the CC CPSU). Beijing: Izdatel'stvo literatury na inostrannykh iazykakh, 1963.

Vtoraia sessiia VIII Vsekitaiskogo s'ezda Kommunisticheskoi partii Kitaia (Second Session of the Eighth Congress of the Communist Party of China). Peking: Izdatel'stvo literatury na inostrannykh iazykakh, 1958.

Wang Dongxing. *Wang dongxing riji* (Diary of Wang Dongxing). Beijing: Zhongguo shehui kexue chubanshe, 1993.

Wang Ming. *Sobranie sochinenii* (Collected Works). 4 vols. Moscow: IDV AN SSSR, 1984–87.

Weathersby, Katheryn. "New Findings of the Korean War." *CWIHP Bulletin,* no. 3 (1993): 1, 14–18.

———. "To Attack, or Not to Attack? Stalin, Kim Il Sung, and the Prelude to War." *CWIHP Bulletin,* no. 5 (1995): 1–9.

Westad, O. Arne, ed. *Brothers in Arms: The Rise and Fall of the Sino-Soviet Alliance, 1945–1963.* Stanford, CA: Stanford University Press, 1998.

Westad, O. Arne, et al., eds. "77 Conversations Between Chinese and Foreign Leaders on the Wars in Indochina, 1964–1977." *CWIHP Working Paper,* no. 22 (May 1998).

Wilbur, C. Martin, ed. *The Communist Movement in China: An Essay Written in 1924 by Ch'en Kung-po.* New York: Octagon Books, 1960.

Wilbur, C. Martin, and Julie Lian-ying How. *Missionaries of Revolution: Soviet Advisers and Nationalist China, 1920–1927.* Cambridge, MA: Harvard University Press, 1989.

Wingrove, Paul. "Mao's Conversations with the Soviet Ambassador, 1953–1955." *CWIHP Working Paper,* no. 36 (April 2002).

Wishnick, Elizabeth. "In the Region and in the Center: Soviet Reactions to the Border Rift." *CWIHP Bulletin,* nos. 6–7 (1995/1996): 194–201.

———. "Sino-Soviet Tensions, 1980: Two Russian Documents." *CWIHP Bulletin,* nos. 6–7 (1995/1996): 202–6.

Wolff, David. " 'One Finger's Worth of Historical Events': New Russian and Chinese Evidence on the Sino-Soviet Alliance and Split, 1948–1959." *CWIHP Working Paper,* no. 30 (August 2000).

Wusi shiqi qikan jieshao (Survey of May Fourth Era Publications). 4 vols. Beijing: Shenghuo. Dushu, Xinzhi sanlian shudian, 1979.

Yang Kaihui. *Ougan* (Random Feelings). In Mao Zedong. *Mao Zedong shici duilian jizhu* (Collection of Mao Zedong's Poems), 99–100. Changsha: Hunan wenyi chubanshe, 1991.

Yang Shangkun. *Yang Shangkun riji* (Yang Shangkun's Diary). 2 vols. Beijing: Zhongyang wenxian chubanshe, 2001.

"Yuandong geguo gongchandang ji minzu geming tuanti diyi ci dahui xuanyan" (Manifesto of the First Congress of Communist Parties and National Liberation Organizations of the Countries of the Far East). *Xianqu* (Pioneer), no. 10 (1922): 4–5.

Zhang Tailei. *Zhang Tailei wenji* (Works of Zhang Tailei). Beijing: Renmin chubanshe, 1981.

Zhang Wentian. *Zhang Wentian xuanji* (Selected Works of Zhang Wentian). Beijing: Renmin chubanshe, 1985.

Zhang Yunhou, et al. *Wusi shiqi de shetuan* (Societies During the May Fourth Era). 4 vols. Beijing: Shenghuo. Dushu. Xinzhi sanlian shudian, 1979.

Zhang Zhichao. *Mao Zedong yijia ren—Cong Shaoshan dao Zhongnanhai* (Mao Zedong in His Family—From Shaoshan to Zhongnanhai). 2 vols. Beijing: Zhongyang wenxian chubanshe, 2000.

Zheng Guanying. *Shengshi weiyan* (Words of Warning to an Affluent Age). Beijing: Huaxia chubanshe, 2002.

Zhonggong "sanda" ziliao (Materials from the Third Congress of the CCP). Guangzhou: Guangdong renmin chubanshe, 1985.

Zhonggong zhongyang wenjian xuanji (Collection of CCP CC Selected Documents). 18 vols. Beijing: Zhonggong zhongyang dangxiao chubanshe, 1989.

Zhongguo gongchandang di sanci zhongyang kuoda zhixing weiyuanhui yijue' an (Resolution of the Third Enlarged Plenum of the CEC CCP). N.p., 1926.

Zhongguo gongchandang di sici quanguo daibiaodahui yijue'an ji xuanyan (Resolutions and Declarations of the Fourth All-China Congress of the CCP). N.p., 1925.

Zhongguo gongchandang di shici quanguo daibiaodahui wenjian huibian (Collection of Documents from the Tenth Congress of the Chinese Communist Party). Beijing: Renmin chubanshe, 1973.

"Zhongguo gongchandang duiyu shiju de zhuzhang" (Statement of the Chinese Communist Party on the Current Situation). *Xianqu* (Pioneer), no. 9 (1922): 1–3.

Zhongguo gongchandang jiguan fazhan cankao ziliao (Reference Materials on the History of the Development of the CCP Organization). Vol. 1. Beijing: Zhonggong dangxiao chubanshe, 1983.

Zhongguo gongchandang wunian lai zhi zhengzhi zhuzhang (Political Declarations of the Chinese Communist Party over the Past Five Years). Guangzhou: Guoguan shuju, 1926.

Zhongguo guomindang di yi di er ci quanguo daibiao dahui huiyi shiliao (Materials on the History of the First and Second Guomindang Congresses). 2 vols. Nanjing: Jiangsu guji chubanshe, 1986.

Zhou Enlai. *K voprosu ob intelligentsii (Doklad na soveshchanii po voprosu ob intelligentsii, sozvannom TSK KPK 14 ianvaria 1956 g.)* (On the Issue of Intelligentsia [A Report at the Meeting on Intelligentsia Held by the CCP CC on January 14, 1956]). Beijing: Izdatel'stvo literatury na inostrannykh iazykakh, 1956.

———. *Selected Works of Zhou Enlai.* 2 vols. Beijing: Foreign Languages Press, 1981.

———. *Zhou Enlai xuanji* (Selected Works of Zhou Enlai). 2 vols. Beijing: Renmin chubanshe, 1980.

Zubok, Vladislav. " 'Look what Chaos in the Beautiful Socialist Camp!' Deng Xiaoping and the Sino-Soviet Split, 1956–1963." *CWIHP Bulletin,* no. 10 (March 1998): 152–62.

———. "The Mao-Khrushchev Conversations, July 31–August 3, 1958 and October 2, 1959." *CWIHP Bulletin,* nos. 12–13 (Fall/Winter 2001): 244–72.

Zunyi huiyi wenxian (Documents of the Zunyi Conference). Beijing: Renmin chubanshe, 1985.

MEMOIRS

Aleksandrov-Agentov, A. M. *Ot Kollontai do Gorbacheva: Vospominaniia diplomata, sovetnika A. A. Gromyko, pomoshchnika L. I. Brezhneva, Iu. V. Andropova, K. U. Chernenko i M. S. Gorbacheva* (From Kollontai to Gorbachev: The Reminiscences of a Diplomat and Adviser to A. A. Gromyko, and Assistant to L. I. Brezhnev, Iu. V. Andropov, K. U. Chernenko, and M. S. Gorbachev). Moscow: Mezhdunarodnye otnosheniia, 1994.

Band, Claire, and William Band. *Dragon Fangs: Two Years with Chinese Guerrillas.* London: Allen & Unwin, 1947.

Barrett, David D. *Dixie Mission: The United States Army Observer Group in Yenan, 1944.* Berkeley: University of California Press, 1970.

Bertram, James M. *Crisis in China: The Story of the Sian Mutiny.* London: Macmillan, 1937.

Bisson, T. A. *Yenan in June 1937: Talks with the Communist Leaders.* Berkeley: Center for Chinese Studies, University of California, 1973.

Blagodatov, A. V. *Zapiski o kitaiskoi revoliutsii 1925–1927 gg.* (Notes on the 1925–1927 Chinese Revolution). 3rd ed. Moscow: Nauka, 1979.

Bliukher, G. *Vospominaniia o muzhe—marshale V. K. Bliukhere* (Reminiscences of My Husband—Marshal V. K. Bliukher). Tiumen: Institut problem osvoeniia Severa SO RAN, 1996.

Bo Yibo. *Ruogan zhongda juece yu shijiande huigu* (Recollections of Several Important Political Decisions and Their Implementation). 2 vols. Beijing: Zhonggong zhongyang dangxiao, 1991.

Braun, Otto. *A Comintern Agent in China 1932–1939.* Translated by Jeanne Moore. Stanford, CA: Stanford University Press, 1982.

Brezhnev, A. A. *Kitai: ternistyi put' k dobrososedstvu: vospominaniia i razmyshleniia* (China: The Arduous Way to Neighborliness: Reminiscences and Thoughts). Moscow: Mezhdunarodnye otnosheniia, 1998.

Buber-Neiman, M. *Mirovaia revoliutsiia i stalinskii rezhim: Zapiski ochevidtsa o deiatel'nosti Kominterna v 1920–1930-kh godakh* (The World Revolution and the Stalinist Regime: Notes of an Eyewitness about Comintern Activity in the 1920s and 1930s). Translated by A. Yu. Vatlin. Moscow: AIRO-XX, 1995.

Cadart, Claude, and Cheng Yongxiang, eds. *Mémoires de Peng Shuzhi: L'Envol du Communisme en Chine*. Paris: Gallimard, 1983.

Cai He-sen. "Istoriia opportunizma v Kommunistecheskoi partii Kitaia" (The History of Opportunism in the Communist Party of China). *Problemy Kitaia* (Problems of China), no. 1 (1929): 1–77.

Carlson, Evans Fordyce. *Evans F. Carlson on China at War, 1937–1941*. New York: China and US Publications, 1993.

———. *Twin Stars of China: A Behind-the-Scenes Story of China's Valiant Struggle for Existence by a U.S. Marine Who Lived and Moved with the People*. New York: Hyperion Press, 1940.

Carter, Carrole J. *Mission to Yenan: American Liaison with the Chinese Communists 1944–1947*. Lexington: University Press of Kentucky, 1997.

Chang Kuo-t'ao. *The Rise of the Chinese Communist Party: Volumes One & Two of Autobiography of Chang Kuo-t'ao*. Lawrence: University Press of Kansas, 1972.

Chen Boda. *Chen Boda yi gao: yuzhong zishu ji qita* (Chen Boda's Manuscripts: Prison Autobiographical Notes and Other [Materials]). Hong Kong: Tiandi tushu youxian gongsi, 1998.

———. *Chen Boda zuihou koushu huiyi* (The Last Oral Reminiscences of Chen Boda). Rev. ed. Hong Kong: Xingke'er chubanshe youxian gongsi, 2005.

Ch'en Chieh-ju. *Chiang Kai-shek's Secret Past: The Memoirs of His Second Wife, Ch'en Chieh-ju*. Boulder, CO: Westview Press, 1993.

Chen Geng. "Ot Nanchana do Svatou" (From Nanchang to Swatow). In *Vsiudu krasnye znamena: Vospominaniia i ocherki o vtoroi grazhdanskoi revoliutsionnoi voine* (Red Banners Everywhere: Reminiscences and Sketches of the Second Revolutionary Civil War), 13–20. Moscow: Voenizdat, 1957.

Chen Gongbo, and Zhou Fohai. *Chen Gongbo, Zhou Fohai huiyilu* (Reminiscences of Chen Gongbo, Zhou Fohai). Hong Kong: Chunqiu chubanshe, 1988.

Chen Pang-qu (Chen Tanqu). "Vospominaniia o I s"ezde Kompartii Kitaia" (Reminiscences of the First Congress of the CCP). *Kommunisticheskii Internatsional* (Communist International), no. 14 (1936): 96–99.

Cherepanov, Alexander Ivanovich. *Notes of a Military Adviser in China*. Translated by Alexandra O. Smith. Taipei: Office of Military History, 1970.

———. *Zapiski voennogo sovetnika v Kitae* (Notes of a Military Adviser in China). 2nd ed. Moscow: Nauka, 1976.

Chiang Ching-kuo. *My Days in Soviet Russia*. [Taipei, 1963].

Chiang Chung-cheng (Chiang Kai-shek). *Soviet Russia in China*. Translated under the direction of Madame Chiang Kai-shek. Rev., enlarged ed., with maps. New York: Farrar, Straus & Cudahy, 1958.

Chiang Kai-shek. "The Day I was Kidnapped." In Dun J. Li ed., *The Road to Communism: China Since 1912*, 135–41. New York: Van Nostrand Reinhold, 1969.

Ch'ü Chiu-pai. "My Confessions." In Dun J. Li, ed., *The Road to Communism: China Since 1912*, 159–76. New York: Van Nostrand Reinhold, 1969.

Chuev, Felix. *Molotov Remembers: Inside Kremlin Politics: Conversations with Felix Chuev*. Translated by Albert Resis. Chicago: I. R. Dee, 1993.

Cressy-Marcks, Violet. *Journey into China*. New York: Dutton, 1942.

Dalin, S. A. *Kitaiskie memuary, 1921–1927* (Chinese Memoirs, 1921–1927). Moscow: Nauka, 1975.

———. *V riadakh kitaiskoi revoliutsii* (In the Ranks of the Chinese Revolution). Moscow and Leningrad: Moskovskii rabochii, 1926.

Dedijer, Vladimir. *Tito Speaks.* London: Weidenfeld & Nicolson, 1953.

Deng Maomao. *My Father Deng Xiaoping.* New York: Basic Books, 1995.

Deng Rong. *Deng Xiaoping and the Cultural Revolution: A Daughter Recalls the Critical Years.* Translated by Sidney Shapiro. New York: Random House, 2005.

Deng Xiaoping. *Deng Xiaoping zishu* (Autobiographic Notes of Deng Xiaoping). Beijing: Jiefangjun chubanshe, 2004.

Deriabin, Peter S., and Joseph Culver Evans. *Inside Stalin's Kremlin: An Eyewitness Account of Brutality, Duplicity, and Intrigue.* Washington, DC: Brassey's, 1998.

Din-Savva, L. *Iz Moskvy da v Pekin: Vospominaniia* (From Moscow to Beijing: Memoirs). Tenafly, NJ: Hermitage, 2000.

Djilas, Milovan. *Conversations with Stalin.* Translated by Michael B. Petrovich. New York: Harcourt, Brace & World, 1962.

Emi Hsiao. *Mao Tszedun, Chzhu De: Vozhdi kitaiskogo naroda* (Mao Zedong, Zhu De: Leaders of the Chinese People). Moscow: Gosizdat, 1939.

Fedorenko, N. T. "Besedy s Mao Tszedunom na puti v Moskvu, Dekabr' 1949 g." (Talks with Mao Zedong on the Way to Moscow, December 1949). *Novaia i noveishaia istoriia* (Modern and contemporary history), no. 6 (1996): 124–35.

———. "Kak akademik P. F. Yudin redaktiroval Mao Tszeduna" (How Academician P. F. Yudin Edited Mao Zedong). *Problemy Dal'nego Vostoka* (Far Eastern affairs), no. 6 (1992): 74–78.

———. "Stalin i Mao: Besedy v Moskve" (Stalin and Mao: Conversations in Moscow). *Problemy Dal'nego Vostoka* (Far Eastern affairs), no. 1 (1989): 149–64.

———. "Vizit N. Khrushcheva v Pekin" (N. Khrushchev's Visit to Beijing). *Problemy Dal'nego Vostoka* (Far Eastern affairs), no. 1 (1990): 121–28.

Fedotov, V. P. *Polveka vmeste s Kitaem: Vospominaniia, zapisi, razmyshleniia* (A Half Century Together with China: Reminiscences, Notes, Thoughts). Moscow: ROSSPEN, 2005.

Fischer, Louis. *Men and Politics: An Autobiography.* New York: Duell, Sloan & Pearce, 1941.

Forman, Harrison. *Report from Red China.* New York: Henry Holt, 1945.

———. *V Novom Kitae* (In New China). Moscow: Izdatel'stvo inostrannoi literatury, 1948.

Gromyko, A. A. *Pamiatnoe* (Remembered). 2 vols. Moscow: Politizdat, 1988.

———. *Pamiatnoe* (Remembered). 2 vols. 2nd, enlarged ed. Moscow: Politizdat, 1990.

Guo Shaotang. *Istoriko-memuarnie zapiski kitaiskogo revoliutsionera* (Historical Memoir Notes of a Chinese Revolutionary). Moscow: Nauka, 1990.

Heben Dazuo (Komoto Daisaku) et al. *Wo shasila Zhang Zuolin* (I Killed Zhang Zuolin). Changchun: Jilin wenshi chubanshe, 1986.

Hsü K'e-hsiang. "The Ma-jih Incident." In Dun J. Li, ed. *The Road to Communism: China Since 1912,* 91–95. New York: Van Nostrand Reinhold, 1969.

Huang Hua. "My Contacts with John Leighton Stuart After Nanjing's Liberation." *Chinese Historians* 5, no. 1 (Spring 1992): 47–56.

Huang Kecheng. "Lushan fengyun" (The Lushan Events). In Lu Lin and Chen Dejin, eds. *Hongse jiyi: Zhongguo gongchandang lishi koushu shilu (1949–1978)* (Red Reminiscences: True Oral Stories of the History of the Chinese Communist Party [1949–1978]), 422–44. Jinan: Shandong renmin chubanshe, 2002.

Huang Ping. *Wangshi huiyilu* (Reminiscences of the Past). Beijing: Renmin chubanshe, 1981.

Hume, Edward H. *Doctors East, Doctors West: An American Physician's Life in China.* London: Allen & Unwin, 1949.

Jiang Kanghu. *Xin E youji* (A Journey to the New Russia). Shanghai: Shangwu yingshuguan, 1923.

Jiang Song Meiling (Madam Chiang Kai-shek). *Yu Baoluoting tanhua huiyilu* (Conversations with Mikhail Borodin). Taibei: Yuancheng wenhua tushu gongyingshe, 1976.

Kapitsa, M. S. *Na raznykh paralleliakh: Zapiski diplomata* (On Various Parallels: Notes of a Diplomat). Moscow: Kniga i biznes, 1996.

Karmen, R. "God v Kitae" (A Year in China). *Znamia* (Banner), no. 8 (1940): 3–122.

Kartunova, A. I. "Vstrechi v Moskve s Tszian Tsin, zhenoi Mao Tszeduna" (Meetings in Moscow with Jiang Qing, the Wife of Mao Zedong). *Kentavr* (Centaur), 1–2 (1992): 121–27.

Kazanin, M. I. *V shtabe Bliukhera: Vospominaniia o kitaiskoi revoliutsii* (On Bliukher's Staff: Reminiscences of the Chinese Revolution). Moscow: Nauka, 1966.

Khrushchev, Nikita S. *Memoirs of Nikita Khrushchev.* 3 vols. Translated by George Shriver. University Park: Pennsylvania State University Press, 2007–2008.

———. *Vospominaniia: Izbrannye fragmenty* (Reminiscences: Selected Fragments). Moscow: Vagrius, 1997.

———. *Vremia, Liudi, Vlast': Vospominaniia* (Time, People, Power: Memoirs). 4 vols. Moscow: Moskovskie novosti, 1999.

Kissinger, Henry A. *White House Years.* Boston: Little, Brown, 1979.

———. *Years of Upheaval.* Boston: Little, Brown, 1982.

Klochko, Mikhail A. *Soviet Scientist in Red China.* Translated by Andrew MacAndrew. New York: Praeger, 1964.

Kong Dongmei. *Fankai wo jia laoyingji: Wo xinzhongde waigong Mao Zedong* (Opening the Old Photo Albums of My Family: My Grandfather Mao Zedong Is in My Heart). Beijing: Zhongyang wenxian chubanshe, 2003.

———. *Gaibian shijiede rizi: yu Wang Hairong tan Mao Zedong waijiao wangshi* (Days that Changed the World: Talking to Wang Hairong about Mao Zedong's Foreign Policy). Beijing: Zhongyang wenxian chubanshe, 2006.

———. "Mao Zedong, He Zizhen fufu: wei geming tongshi wu ge zinü" (A Couple Mao Zedong and He Zizhen: They Painfully Sacrificed Five Sons and Daughters for the Revolution). *Jiefang ribao* (Liberation daily), March 7, 2005.

———. *Ting waipo jiang neiguoqude shiqing—Mao Zedong yu He Zizhen* (Listening to Grandmother's Stories About Her Past—Mao Zedong and He Zizhen). Beijing: Zhongyang wenxian chubanshe, 2005.

Koval, K. I. "Moskovskiie peregovory I. V. Stalina s Chzhou En'laem v 1952 g. i N. S. Khrushcheva s Mao Tszedunom v 1954 g." (J. V. Stalin's Negotiations in Moscow with Zhou Enlai in 1952 and N. S. Khrushchev's with Mao Zedong in 1954). *Novaia i noveishaia istoriia* (Modern and contemporary history), no. 5 (1989): 104–19.

Kovalev, I. V. "Dialog Stalina s Mao Tszedunom" (Stalin's Dialogue with Mao Zedong). *Problemy Dal'nego Vostoka* (Far Eastern affairs), no. 6 (1991): 83–93; nos. 1–3 (1992): 77–91.

———. "Rossiia v Kitae (S missiei v Kitae)" (Russia in China: My Mission to China). *Duel'* (Duel), November 5, 11, 19, 25, December 3, 17, 1996, January 14, February 11, 25, March 25, April 8, 1997.

Krutikov, K. I. *Na kitaiskom napravleniu: Iz vospominanii diplomata* (Pointed Toward China: A Diplomat's Reminiscences). Moscow: IDV RAN, 2003.

Lamotte, Ellen N. *Peking Dust.* New York: Century, 1920.

Leung, Laifong. *Morning Sun: Interviews with Chinese Writers of the Lost Generation.* Armonk, NY: M. E. Sharpe, 1994.

Li Chongde. "Escorting Mao Zedong's Sons to Shanghai." In *Mao Zedong: Biography—Assessment—Reminiscences,* 222–26. Beijing: Foreign Languages Press, 1986.

Li Genqiao. *Zouxiang shentande Mao Zedong* (Mao Zedong Raised Up to the Sacred Throne). Beijing: Zhongwei wenhu chuban gongsi, 1989.

Li Jiaji, and Yang Qingwang. *Lingxiu shenbian shisan nian—Mao Zedong weishi Li Jiaji fangtan lu* (Thirteen Years at the Side of the Leader—Records of Conversations with Mao Zedong's Bodyguard Li Jiaji). 2 vols. Beijing: Zhongyang wenxian chubanshe, 2007.

Li Jing, ed. *Shihua shishuo Fengzeyuan* (True Stories About the Garden of Abundant Reservoirs). 2 vols. 4th ed. Beijing: Zhongguo qingnian chubanshe, 2010.

Li Min. *Moi otets Mao Tszedun* (My Father Mao Zedong). Beijing: Izdatel'stvo literatury na inostrannykh iazykakh, 2004.

Li Min, et al., eds. *Zhenshide Mao Zedong: Mao Zedong shenbian gongzuo renyuande huiyi* (The Real Mao Zedong: Recollections of People Who Worked with Mao Zedong). Beijing: Zhongyang wenxian chubanshe, 2004.

Li Rui. *Lushan huiyi shilu* (The True Record of the Lushan Plenum). Beijing: Chunqiu chubanshe/Hunan jiaoyu chubanshe, 1989.

Li Ruilin. "Vosstanie v Ningdu" (Uprising in Ningdu). In *Vsiudu krasnye znamena: Vospominaniia i ocherki o vtoroi grazhdanskoi revoliutsionnoi voine* (Red Banners Everywhere: Reminiscences and Sketches of the Second Revolutionary Civil War), 52–58. Moscow: Voenizdat, 1957.

Li Sha. *Wode zhongguo yuanfen: Li Lisan furen Li Sha huiyilu* (My Chinese Fate: Memoirs of Li Lisan's Wife Li Sha). Beijing: Waiyu jiaoxue yu yanjiu chubanshe, 2009.

Li Weihan. *Huiyi yu yanjiu* (Reminiscences and Studies). 2 vols. Beijing: Zhonggong-dang shi ziliao chubanshe, 1986.

Li Youjiu. "Deng Zihui yu nongye hezuohua yundong" (Deng Zihui and the Movement for Agricultural Cooperativization). In Lu Lin and Chen Dejin eds., *Hongse jiyi: Zhongguo gongchandang lishi koushu shilu (1949–1978)* (Red Reminiscences: True Oral Stories of the History of the Chinese Communist Party [1949–1978]), 241–50. Jinan: Shandong renmin chubanshe, 2002.

Li Yueran. "Mao zhuxi di erci fangwen Sulian" (Chairman Mao's Second Visit to the Soviet Union). In Li Min et al., eds. *Zhenshide Mao Zedong: Mao Zedong shenbian gongzuo renyuande huiyi* (The Real Mao Zedong: Recollections of People Who Worked with Mao Zedong), 566–78. Beijing: Zhongyang wenxian chubanshe, 2004.

———. *Waijiao wutai shang de xin Zhongguo lingxiu* (Leaders of New China in the Diplomatic Arena). Beijing: Waiyu jiaoxue yu yanjiu chubanshe, 1994.

Li Zhisui. *The Private Life of Chairman Mao: The Memoirs of Mao's Personal Physician.* Translated by Tai Hung-chao. New York: Random House, 1994.

Liu Shaoqi. *Liu Shaoqi zishu* (Autobiographical Notes of Liu Shaoqi). Beijing: Jiefangjun wenyi chubanshe, 2002.

Liu Xiao. *Chushi Sulian ba nian* (Eight Years as Ambassador to the USSR). Beijing: Zhonggong dangshi chubanshe, 1998.

Liu Xing. "Do i posle 'vosstaniia osennego urozhaia' " (Before and After the "Autumn Harvest Uprising"). In *Vsiudu krasnye znamena: Vospominaniia i ocherki o vtoroi grazhdanskoi revoliutsionnoi voine* (Red Banners Everywhere: Reminiscences and Sketches of the Second Revolutionary Civil War), 21–27. Moscow: Voenizdat, 1957.

Lominadze, Sergo. "Deviatnadtsatoe ianvaria" (January 19). *Znamia* (Banner) 11 (1997): 149–63.

Lu Lin, and Chen Dejin, eds. *Hongse jiyi: Zhongguo gongchandang lishi koushu shilu (1949–1978)* (Red Reminiscences: True Oral Stories of the History of the Chinese Communist Party [1949–1978]). 3 vols. Jinan: Shandong renmin chubanshe, 2002.

Luosu (Russell). "You E ganxiang" (Impressions of a Journey to Russia). *Xin qingnian* (New youth) 8, no. 2 (1920): 1–12.

Mao Xinyu. *Qinqingde niudai: xie zai yeye Mao Zedong danchen 110 zhounian* (Dear Links: In Commemoration of the 110th Anniversary of My Grandfather Mao Zedong's Birthday). Beijing: Zhongyang wenxian chubanshe, 2003.

———. *Wode bofu Mao Anying* (My Uncle Mao Anying). Beijing: Changcheng chubanshe, 2000.

———. *Yeye jili wo chengzhang* (Grandfather Influenced My Raising). Beijing: Zhongguo mangwen chubanshe, 2006.

———. *Yeye Mao Zedong* (Grandfather Mao Zedong). Beijing: Zhongguo mangwen chubanshe, 2003.

———. *Yeye shuai hongjun zouguo: Mao Xinyu hua changzheng* (Grandfather Leads the Red Army: Mao Xinyu Talks About the Long March). Beijing: Huawen chubanshe, 2007.

Mao Zedong: Biography—Assessment—Reminiscences. Beijing: Foreign Languages Press, 1986.

Mao Zedong. *Avtobiografiia; Stikhi* (Autobiography; Poems). Translated by A. Pantsov. Moscow: Rubezhi XXI veka, 2008.

———. *Mao Zedong zishu* (Autobiographical Notes of Mao Zedong). Beijing: Jiefangjun wenyi chubanshe, 2001.

———. *Mao Zedong zizhuan* (Autobiography of Mao Zedong). Hong Kong, n.d.

———. "Moia zhizn'" (My Life). *Internatsional'naia literatura* (International literature), no. 11 (1937): 101–11; no. 12 (1937): 95–101.

Martynov, A. A., et al., eds. *Velikii pokhod 1-go fronta Kitaiskoi raboche-krest'ianskoi krasnoi armii: Vospominaniia* (The Long March of the First Front Chinese Worker-Peasant Red Army: Reminiscences). Translated by A. A. Klyshko et al. Moscow: Izd-vo inostrannoi literatury, 1959.

Mikoyan, A. I. *Tak bylo: Razmyshleniia o minuvshem* (How It Was: Reflections on the Past). Moscow: Vagrius, 1999.

Montgomery of Alamein, Bernard Law, Field-Marshal the Viscount. *Three Continents: A Study of the Situation and Problems in Asia, Africa, and Central America, and the Relationship of Those Areas to Defence Policies in the 1960's and to the British Commonwealth.* London: Collins, 1962.

Nanwangde huiyi: Huainian Mao Zedong tongzhi (Unforgettable Recollections: Warmly Remembering Comrade Mao Zedong). Beijing: Zhongguo qingnian chubanshe, 1985.

Nie Rongzhen. *Inside the Red Star: The Memoirs of Marshal Nie Rongzhen.* Beijing: New World Press, 1983.

Nixon, Richard. *In the Arena: A Memoir of Victory, Defeat and Renewal.* New York: Simon & Schuster, 1990.

———. *RN: The Memoirs of Richard Nixon.* New York: Grosset & Dunlap, 1978.

Paniushkin, A. S. *Zapiski posla: Kitai 1939–1955 gg.* (Notes of the Ambassador: China 1939–1955). Moscow: IDV AN SSSR, 1981.

Pantsov, A. V. "Sud'ba kitaiskogo trotskista" (The Fate of a Chinese Trotskyist). *Problemy Dal'nego Vostoka* (Far Eastern affairs), no. 3 (1998): 97–107; no. 4 (1998): 81–90.

Peng Dehuai. *Memoirs of a Chinese Marshal: The Autobiographical Notes of Peng Dehuai (1898–1974).* Translated by Zheng Longpu. Beijing: Foreign Languages Press, 1984.

———. *Memuary marshala* (Memoirs of a Marshal). Translated by A. V. Pantsov, V. N. Usov, and K. V. Sheveliev. Moscow: Voenizdat, 1988.

Peng Pai. *Zapiski Pen Paia* (Notes of Peng Pai). Translated by A. Ivin. Moscow: Zhurnal'no-gazetnoe ob"edinenie, 1938.

Pu Yi. *From Emperor to Citizen.* Translated by W. J. F. Jenner. New York: Oxford University Press, 1987.

Qiwu lao-ren (Bao Huiseng). "Do i posle obrazovaniia Kommunisticheskoi partii Kitaia" (Before and After the Formation of the Communist Party of China). *Rabochii klass i sovremennyi mir* (The working class and the contemporary world), no. 2 (1971): 117–27.

Qu Qiubai. *Superfluous Words.* Translated by Jamie Greenbaum. Canberra: Pandanus Books, 2006.

Quan Yanchi. *Mao Zedong: Man, Not God.* Beijing: Foreign Languages Press, 1992.

Rakhmanin, O. B. "Vzaimnootnosheniia mezhdu I. V. Stalinym i Mao Tszedunom glazami ochevidtsa" (Relations between J. V. Stalin and Mao Zedong Through the Eyes of an Eyewitness). *Novaia i noveishaia istoriia* (Modern and contemporary history), no. 1 (1998): 78–91.

Rittenberg, Sidney, and Amanda Bennett. *The Man Who Stayed Behind.* New York: Simon & Schuster, 1993.

Romm, M. *Ustnye rasskazy* (Oral Tales). Moscow: "Kinotsentr," 1991.

Russell, Bertrand. *The Autobiography of Bertrand Russell: 1914–1944.* Boston: Little, Brown, 1956.

Semenov, G. G. *Tri goda v Pekine: Zapiski voennogo sovetnika* (Three Years in Beijing: Notes of a Military Adviser). Moscow: Nauka, 1978.

Shao Hua. *Mao Zedong zhilu—zhuixun fuqinde zuji* (Mao Zedong's Road—Following in Father's Footsteps). Kunming: Yunnan jiaoyu chubanshe, 2001.

Shepilov, D. T. "Vospominaniia" (Reminiscences). *Voprosy istorii* (Problems of history), no. 9 (1998): 18–33; no. 10 (1998): 3–31.

Shi Zhe. *Feng yu gu—Shi Zhe huiyilu* (Summit and Abyss—Reminiscences of Shi Zhe). Beijing: Hongqi chubanshe, 1992.

———. *Zai lishi juren shenbian* (At the Side of Historical Titans). Rev. ed. Beijing: Zhongyang wenxian chubanshe, 1995.

Shi Zhe, and Li Haiwen. *Zhongsu guanxi jianzheng lu* (Eyewitness Notes on Sino-Soviet Relations). Beijing: Dangdai Zhongguo chubanshe, 2005.

Shi Zhe, and Shi Qiulang. *Wode yisheng—She Zhe zishu* (My Life—She Zhe's Reminiscences). Beijing: Renmin chubanshe, 2002.

Shipman, Charles. *It Had to Be Revolution: Memoirs of an American Radical.* Ithaca: Cornell University Press, 1993.

Siao-yu. *Mao Tse-tung and I Were Beggars.* Syracuse, NY: Syracuse University Press, 1959.

Simonov, Konstantin. *Istorii tiazhelaia voda* (The Heavy Water of History). Moscow: Vagris, 2005.

Sinuo lu, Wang Heng yi (Snow's recording, Wang Heng's translation). *Mao Zedong zizhuan* (Autobiography of Mao Zedong). Shanghai: Liming shuju, 1937.

———. *Mao Zedong zizhuan* (Autobiography of Mao Zedong). Beijing: Jiefangjun wenyi chubanshe, 2001.

Smedley, Agnes. *Battle Hymn of China.* New York: Knopf, 1943.

———. *China Fights Back: An American Woman with the Eighth Route Army.* New York: Vanguard Press, 1938.

———. *The Great Road: The Life and Times of Chu Teh.* New York: Monthly Review Press, 1956.

Snow, Edgar. "A Conversation with Mao Tse-tung." *Life,* April 30, 1971, 46–48.

———. *Geroicheskii narod Kitaia* (Heroic People of China). Translated by L. Mirtseva. Moscow: "Molodaia gvardiia," 1938.

———. *Journey to the Beginning.* New York: Random House, 1958.

———. *The Long Revolution.* New York: Random House, 1972.

———. *The Other Side of the River: Red China Today.* New York: Random House, 1962.

———. *Random Notes on Red China (1936–1945).* Cambridge, MA: East Asian Research Center, Harvard University, 1957.

———. *Red Star Over China.* London: Victor Gollancz, 1937.

Snow, Helen Foster (Nym Wales). *The Chinese Communists: Sketches and Autobiographies of the Old Guard.* Westport, CT: Greenwood, 1972.

———. *Inside Red China.* New York: Da Capo Press, 1977.

———. *My China Years.* New York: Morrow, 1984.

Snow, Lois Wheeler. *A Death with Dignity: When the Chinese Came.* New York: Random House, [1975].

———. *Edgar Snow's China: A Personal Account of the Chinese Revolution Compiled from the Writings of Edgar Snow.* New York: Random House, 1981.

Sun Yong. *Zai Mao zhuxi shenbian ershi nian* (Twenty Years at the Side of Chairman Mao). Beijing: Zhongyang wenxian chubanshe, 2010.

Tikhvinsky, S. L. "Kitai v moei zhizni" (China in My Life). *Problemy Dal'nego Vostoka* (Far Eastern affairs), no. 3 (1989): 104–19; no. 4 (1989): 103–17; no. 4 (1990): 103–12; no. 5 (1990): 99–108.

Utley, Freda. *China at War.* New York: John Day, 1939.

Vereshchagin, B. N. *V starom i novom Kitae: Iz vospominanii diplomata* (In Old and New China: Reminiscences of a Diplomat). Moscow: IDV RAN, 1999.

Vidali, Vittorio. *Diary of the Twentieth Congress of the Communist Party of the Soviet Union.*

Translated by Nell Amter Cattonar and A. M. Elliot. Westport, CT: Lawrence Hill/ Journeyman Press, 1974.

Vishnevskaia, Galina. *Galina. Istoriia zhizni* (Galina: A Life Story). Moscow: Gorizont, 1991.

Vishniakova-Akimova, V. V. *Dva goda v vostavshem Kitae, 1925–1927: Vospominaniia* (Two Years in Revolutionary China, 1925–1927: Memoirs). Moscow: Nauka, 1965.

———. *Two Years in Revolutionary China, 1925–1927*. Translated by Steven I. Levine. Cambridge, MA: East Asian Research Center, Harvard University, 1971.

Vladimirov, P. P. *Osobyi raion Kitaia 1942–1945* (Special Region of China 1942–1945). Moscow: APN, 1975.

Voitinsky, G. "Moi vstrechi s Sun Yat-senom" (My Meetings with Sun Yat-sen). *Pravda* (Truth), March 15, 1925.

Vsiudu krasnye znamena: Vospominaniia i ocherki o vtoroi grazhdanskoi revoliutsionnoi voine (Red Banners Everywhere: Reminiscences and Sketches of the Second Revolutionary Civil War). Moscow: Voenizdat, 1957.

Wales, Nym. *My Yenan Notebooks*. Madison, CT: Morrow, 1961.

Wang Fanxi. *Shuangshan huiyilu* (Memoirs of Shuangshan). Hong Kong: Zhou, 1977.

Wang Guangmei, and Liu Yuan. *Ni suo bu zhidaode Liu Shaoqi* (The Unknown Liu Shaoqi). Zhengzhou: Henan renmin chubanshe, 2000.

Wang Hebin. *Jinshi shusheng—Mao Zedong mishu jiedu Maoti moji* (The Great, Internationally Recognized Master of Calligraphy—Mao Zedong's Secretary Deciphers Mao's Handwriting). Beijing: Changzheng chubanshe, 2004.

Wang Ming. *Mao's Betrayal*. Translated by Vic Schneierson. Moscow: Progress, 1979.

Witke, Roxane. *Comrade Chiang Ch'ing*. Boston: Little, Brown, 1977.

Wu Lengxi. *Shinian lunduan: Zhongsu guanxi huiyilu (1956–1966)* (The Ten-Year Debate: Memoirs of Sino-Soviet Relations [1956–1966]). 2 vols. Beijing: Zhongyang wenxian chubanshe, 1999.

———. *Yi Mao zhuxi: Wo qinshen jinglide ruogan zhongda lishi shijian pianduan* (Remembering Chairman Mao: Some Important Historical Events from My Own Life). Beijing: Xinhua chubanshe, 1995.

Wu Liangping. "Qianyan." In Wu Liangping, ed. *Mao Zedong yi jiu san liu nian tong Sinuode tanhua: guanyu zijide geming jingli he hongjun changzheng deng wenti* (Mao Zedong's 1936 Talks with Snow: On his Revolutionary road, the Red Army Long March, and Other Questions), 1–9. Beijing: Renmin chubanshe, 1979.

Xiao Jingguang. "Fusu xuexi qianhou" (Before and After Studying in the Soviet Union). *Gemingshi ziliao* (Materials on revolutionary history), Beijing, no. 3 (1981): 1–21.

Xue Muqiao. "Huainian weidade makesizhuyizhe Liu Shaoqi tongzhi" (Warmly Remembering the Great Marxist Comrade Liu Shaoqi). *Guangming ribao* (Enlightenment daily), November 24, 1988.

Yakovlev, M. I. *17 let v Kitae* (Seventeen Years in China). Moscow: Politizdat, 1981.

Yan Wen (A. G. Krymov). "Vospominanie o 'dvizhenii 4 maia'" (Reminiscences of the 'May Fourth Movement'). In A. G. Afanasiev (A. G. Krymov), ed., *Dvizhenie 4 maia 1919 goda v Kitae: Sbornik statei* (The May 4, 1919, Movement in China: Collected Articles), 128–31. Moscow: Nauka, 1971.

Yang, Rae. *Spider Eaters: A Memoir*. Berkeley: University of California Press, 1997.

Yang Shangkun. *Yang Shangkun huiyilu* (Memoirs of Yang Shangkun). Beijing: Zhongyang wenxian chubanshe, 2001.

Ye Zilong. *Ye Zilong huiyilu* (Memoirs of Ye Zilong). Beijing: Zhongyang wenxian chubanshe, 2000.

Yu Guangyuan. *Wo yi Deng Xiaoping* (I Remember Deng Xiaoping). Hong Kong: Shidai guoji chuban youxian gongsi, 2005.

Zhang Yaoci. *Zhang Yaoci huiyilu—Zai Mao zhuxi shenbiande rizi* (Memoirs of Zhang Yaoci—Days at the Side of Chairman Mao). Beijing: Zhonggong dangshi chubanshe, 2008.

Zhang Yufeng. "Neskol'ko shtrikhov k kartine poslednikh let zhizni Mao Tszeduna, Chzhou Enlaia" (Some Brushstrokes Toward a Picture of the Last Years of Mao Zedong and Zhou Enlai). In Yu. N. Galenovich, *Smert' Mao Tszeduna* (The Death of Mao Zedong), 79–106. Moscow: Izd-vo "Izograf," 2005.

Zhang Yunsheng, and Zhang Congkun. *"Wen ge" qijian wo gei Lin Biao dang mishu* (I Served as Lin Biao's Secretary during the "Cultural Revolution"). 2 vols. Hong Kong: Xianggang Zhonghua ernü chubanshe youxian gongsi, 2003.

Zheng Chaolin. *An Oppositionist for Life: Memoirs of the Chinese Revolutionary Zheng Chaolin.* Translated by Gregor Benton. Atlantic Highlands, NJ: Humanities Press, 1997.

———. *Zheng Chaolin huiyilu* (Memoirs of Zheng Chaolin). [Hong Kong], 1982.

Zhou Enlai. *Zhou Enlai zishu* (Autobiographical Notes of Zhou Enlai). Beijing: Jiefangjun wenyi chubanshe, 2002.

Zhou Lipo. "A Visit to His Hometown." In *Mao Zedong: Biography—Assessment—Reminiscences*, 233–38. Beijing: Foreign Languages Press, 1986.

Zhou Shizhao, et al. *Wusi yundong zai Hunan* (The May Fourth Movement in Hunan). Changsha: Hunan renmin chubanshe, 1959.

Zhu Zhongli. *Cancan hongye* (A Bright Red Leaf). Changsha: Hunan renmin chubanshe, 1985.

NEWSPAPERS AND JOURNALS

Bainian chao (Century tides). Beijing, 2001–2005.

Biulleten' IV Kongressa Kommunisticheskogo Internatsionala (Bulletin of the Fourth Congress of the Communist International). Moscow, 1922.

Biulleten' oppozitsii (bol'shevikov-lenintsev) (Bulletin of the opposition of the Bolsheviks and Leninists). Paris, New York, 1929–1941.

Bolshevik (Bolshevik). Moscow, 1925–1927.

The China Quarterly. London, 1960–2009.

Chinese Historians, College Park, MD, 1990–1996.

Cold War International History Bulletin. Washington, D.C., 1992–2008.

Dangbao (Party paper). Shanghai, 1923–1924.

Dangshi yanjiu (Studies on party history). Beijing, 1986–1987.

Dangshi yanjiu ziliao (Study materials on party history). Beijing, 1979–2009.

Duel' (Duel). Moscow, 1996–1997.

Ershiyi shiji (The Twenty-first century). Hong Kong, 2007.

Europe-Asia Studies. Glasgow, 1994.

Far Eastern Survey, New York, 1939.

Gemingshi ziliao (Materials on revolutionary history). Beijing, 1981.

Gemingshi ziliao (Materials on revolutionary history). Shanghai, 1986.

Guangming ribao (Enlightenment daily). Beijing, 1988.

Guoji gongyun (International communist movement). Beijing, 1983.

Hongqi (Red Flag). Beijing, 1981.

International Journal of the Legal Profession. Abingdon, Oxfordshire, U.K., 1999.

Internatsional'naia literatura (International literature). Moscow, 1937.

Istoricheskii arkhiv (Historical archive). Moscow, 1992–1996.

Izvestiia (News). Moscow, 1994.

Izvestiia TsK KPSS (News of the CPSU CC). Moscow, 1989–1991.

Issues & Studies. Taipei, 1994–2005.

Jiefang ribao (Liberation daily). Beijing, 2005.

Jindaishi yanjiu (Studies in modern history). Shanghai, 1985–2009.

Kanton (Canton). Canton, 1927.

Kentavr (Centaur). Moscow, 1992.

Kommunist (The Communist). Moscow, 1964–1966.

Kommunisticheskii Internatsional (Communist International). Moscow, 1920–1927, 1934, 1936.

Life. New York, 1971.
Lishi yanjiu (Studies in history). Beijing, 1998.
Lishi jiaoxue (Teaching of history). Tianjin, 2005.
Mao Zedong sixiang yanjiu (Studies in Mao Zedong Thought). Chengdu, 1990.
Minguo dang'an (Republican archives). Nanjing, 1998.
Minguo ribao (Republican daily). Shanghai, 1917.
Moskovskii komsomolets (Moscow Young Communist). Moscow, 2002.
Narody Azii i Afriki (Peoples of Asia and Africa). Moscow, 1972–1976.
Nezavisimoe voennoe obozrenie (Independent military review). Moscow, 2008.
Novaia i noveishaia istoriia (Modern and contemporary history). Moscow, 1989–2011.
Ogonek (Little light). Moscow, 1999.
Pravda, (Truth). Petrograd-Moscow, 1917–2009.
Problemy Dal'nego Vostoka (Far Eastern Affairs). Moscow.
Problemy Kitaia (Problems of China). Moscow, 1929.
Problemy vostokovedeniia (Problems of Oriental studies). Moscow, 1960.
Rabochii klass i sovremennyi mir (The working class and the contemporary world). Moscow, 1971–1982.
Renmin ribao (People's daily). Beijing, 1949–1983.
Renmin zhengxie bao (Newspaper of the Chinese People's Political Consultative Conference). Beijing, 2004.
Republican China. Urbana, IL, 1994.
Rossia. Kitai. XXI vek (Russia. China. The 21st Century). Moscow, 2006–2007.
Russian History. Pittsburgh, PA, 2002.
Segodnia (Today). Ukraine, 1989.
Shanghai shifan xueyuan xuebao (Herald of Shanghai Normal Institute). Shanghai, 1984.
Twentieth-Century China. Columbus, OH, 2008.
Vestnik Moskovskogo Universiteta (Herald of Moscow University). Series 13: *Vostokovedenie* (Oriental studies). Moscow, 2005.
Voprosy istorii (Problems of history). Moscow, 1990.
Voprosy istorii KPSS (Problems of history of the Communist Party of the Soviet Union). Moscow, 1958.
Vremia novostei (News hour). Moscow, 2004.
Wenshi cankao (History reference). Beijing, 2010.
Xianqu (Pioneer). Beijing, 1922–1923.
Xiangjiang pinglun (Xiang River review). Changsha, 1919.
Xin Hunan (New Hunan). Changsha, 1919.
Xin qingnian (New youth). Shanghai, 1919–1925.
Xin Zhonghua bao (New China). Yan'an, 1939.
Xinmin wanbao (The renovation of people evening newspaper). Shanghai, 2004.
Za rubezhom (Abroad). Moscow, 1934.
Zhongguo xiandaishi (Contemporary history of China). Beijing, 1989–2003.
Zhuanji wenxue (Biographical literature). Taipei, 2004.
Znamia (Banner). Moscow, 1940, 1997.

SECONDARY SOURCES

Afanasiev, A. G. (A. G. Krymov), ed. *Dvizhenie "4 maia" 1919 goda v Kitae. Sbornik statei* (The May 4, 1919, Movement in China: Collected Articles). Moscow: Nauka, 1971.
All About Shanghai and Environs: A Standard Guide Book: Historical and Contemporary Facts and Statistics. Shanghai: University Press, 1934.
Averill, Stephen C. "The Origins of the Futian Incident." In Tony Saich and Hans J. van de Ven, eds. *New Perspectives on the Chinese Communist Revolution,* 79–115. Armonk, NY: M. E. Sharpe, 1995.
Barnouin, Barbara, and Yu Changgen. *Ten Years of Turbulence: The Chinese Cultural Revolution.* London: Kegan Paul International, 1993.

Becker, Jasper. *Hungry Ghosts: Mao's Secret Famine.* New York: Free Press, 1996.

Benton, Gregor. *China's Urban Revolutionaries: Explorations in the History of Chinese Trotskyism.* Atlantic Highlands, NJ: Humanities Press, 1996.

Benton, Gregor, and Lin Chun, eds. *Was Mao Really a Monster? The Academic Response to Chang and Halliday's "Mao: The Unknown Story."* London: Routledge, 2010.

Bernal, Martin. *Chinese Socialism to 1907.* Ithaca, NY: Cornell University Press, 1976.

Bianco, Lucian. *Peasants Without the Party: Grass-roots Movements in Twentieth-Century China.* Armonk, NY: M. E. Sharpe, 2001.

Bing, Dov. "Sneevliet and the Early Years of the CCP." *China Quarterly,* no. 48 (1971): 687–95.

Bisson, T. A. "China's Part in a Coalition War." *Far Eastern Survey,* no. 12 (1939): 139.

Bony, L. D. "Mekhanizm iz"iatiia tovarnogo zerna v KNR (50'e gody)" (The Mechanism of Grain Acquisition in the PRC in the 1950s). In L. P. Deliusin, ed. *Kitai: Gosudarstvo i obshchestvo* (China: State and Society), 275–95. Moscow: Nauka, 1977.

Borisov, O. (O. B. Rakhmanin). *Iz istorii sovetsko-kitaiskikh otnoshenii v 50-kh godakh (k diskussii v KNR o Mao Tszedune)* (On the History of Sino-Soviet Relations in the 1950s: Regarding the Discussion in the PRC on Mao Zedong). Moscow: Mezhdunarodnye otnosheniia, 1981.

Borokh, L. N. *Konfutsianstvo i evropeiskaia mysl' na rubezhe XIX–XX vekov: Lian Tsichao i teoriia obnovleniia naroda* (Confucianism and European Thought at the Turn of the Nineteenth–Twentieth Centuries: Liang Qichao and the Renovation of the People Theory). Moscow: Nauka, 2001.

———. *Obshchestvennaia mysl' Kitaia i sotsialism (nachalo XX v.).* (Social Thought in China and Socialism in the Early Twentieth Century). Moscow: Nauka, 1984.

Burlatskii, F. *Mao Zedong.* Moscow: Ripol Classic, 2003.

———. *Mao Zedong i ego nasledniki* (Mao Zedong and His Successors). Moscow: Mezhdunarodnye otnosheniia, 1979.

———. *Mao Zedong: "Nash koronnyi nomer—eto voina, diktatura . . ."* (Mao Zedong: "Our Main Act Is War, and Dictatorship . . ."). Moscow: Mezhdunarodnye otnosheniia, 1976.

———. *Mao Zedong, Tsian Tsin and sovetnik Den* (Mao Zedong, Jiang Qing and the Adviser Deng). Moscow: Eksmo-press, 2003.

———. *Nikita Khrushchev.* Moscow: Ripol Classic, 2003.

Byron, John, and Robert Pack. *The Claws of the Dragon: Kang Sheng—The Evil Genius Behind Mao and His Legacy of Terror in People's China.* New York: Simon & Schuster, 1992.

Carter, Carrole J. *Mission to Yenan: American Liaison with the Chinese Communists 1944–1947.* Lexington: University Press of Kentucky, 1997.

Carter, Peter. *Mao.* New York: New American Library, 1980.

Chang, Jung, and Jon Halliday. *Mao: The Unknown Story.* London: Jonathan Cape, 2005.

Chang Kuo-hsing. *Mao Tse-tung and His China.* Hong Kong: Heinemann, 1978.

Chao Feng, ed. *"Wenhua da geming" cidian* (Dictionary of the Great Cultural Revolution). Taibei: Taiwan donghua shuju gufen youxian gongsi, 1993.

Cheek, Timothy, ed. *A Critical Introduction to Mao.* Cambridge: Cambridge University Press, 2010.

Chen Aifei, and Cao Zhiwei. *Zouchu guomende Mao Zedong* (Mao Zedong Abroad). Shijiazhuang: Hebei renmin chubanshe, 2001.

Chen, Jêrome. *Mao.* Englewood Cliffs, NJ: Prentice-Hall, [1969].

———. *Mao and the Chinese Revolution.* New York: Oxford University Press, [1970].

Chen Jian. *China's Road to the Korean War. The Making of the Sino-American Confrontation.* New York: Columbia University Press, 1994.

———. "A Crucial Step towards the Breakdown of the Sino-Soviet Alliance: The Withdrawal of Soviet Experts from China in July 1960." *CWIHP Bulletin,* nos. 8–9 (1996/1997): 246, 249–50.

———. *Mao's China and the Cold War.* Chapel Hill: University of North Carolina Press, 2001.

———. "The Sino-Soviet Alliance and China's Entry into the Korean War." *CWIHP Working Paper,* no. 1 (June 1992).

Chen Jian, and Yang Kuisong. "Chinese Politics and the Collapse of the Sino-Soviet Alliance." In O. Arne Westad, ed. *Brothers in Arms: The Rise and Fall of the Sino-Soviet Alliance, 1945–1963,* 246–94. Stanford, CA: Stanford University Press, 1998.

Chen Qingquan, and Song Guangwei. *Lu Dingyi zhuan* (Biography of Lu Dingyi). Beijing: Zhonggong dangshi chubanshe, 1999.

Chen Yutang. *Zhonggong dangshi renwu bieming lu (zihao, biming, huaming)* (Collection of Pseudonyms of CCP Historical Personalities [Aliases, Pen Names, Other Names]). Beijing: Hongqi chubanshe, 1985.

Chen Zhiling. "Li Fuchun." In Hu Hua, ed., *Zhonggongdang shi renwu zhuan* (Biographies of Persons in the History of the CCP), vol. 44, 1–112. Xi'an: Shaanxi renmin chubanshe, 1990.

Cheng Bo. *Zhonggong "bada" juece neimu* (Behind the Scenes Decision-making at the Eighth Congress of the CCP). Beijing: Zhonggong dang'an chubanshe, 1999.

Chow Tse-tsung. *The May Fourth Movement: Intellectual Revolution in Modern China.* Cambridge, MA: Harvard University Press, 1960.

Clodfelter, Micheal. *Warfare and Armed Conflicts: A Statistical Encyclopedia of Casualty and Other Figures, 1494–2007.* 3rd ed. Jefferson, NC: McFarland, 2008.

Confucius. *The Analects of Confucius.* Translated by Simon Leys. New York: Norton, 1997.

Cooper, Jerome. "Lawyers in China and the Rule of Law." *International Journal of the Legal Profession* 6, no. 1 (1999): 71–89.

Cormack, J. G. *Chinese Birthday, Wedding, Funeral, and Other Customs.* Peking and Tientsin: La Librairie française, 1923.

Courtois, Stéphane, et al. *The Black Book of Communism: Crimes, Terror, Repression.* Translated by Jonathan Murphy and Mark Kramer. Cambridge, MA: Harvard University Press, 1999.

Davin, Delia. *Mao Zedong.* Gloucestershire, UK: Sutton, 1997.

Deliusin, L. P. *Spor o sotsializme: Iz istorii obshchestvenno-politicheskoi mysli Kitaia v nachale 20-kh godov* (The Dispute over Socialism: From the History of Socio-Political Thought in China in the Early 1920s). Moscow: Nauka, 1970.

Deliusin, L. P., and A. S. Kostiaeva. *Revoliutsiia 1925–1927 v Kitae: Problemy i otsenki* (The Revolution of 1925–1927 in China: Problems and Assessment). Moscow: Nauka, 1985.

Dikötter, Frank. *Mao's Great Famine: The History of China's Most Devastating Catastrophe, 1958–1962.* New York: Walker, 2010.

Dillon, Michael, ed. *China: A Cultural and Historical Dictionary.* Richmond, UK: Curzon Press, 1998.

Dittmer, Lowell. *Liu Shao-ch'i and the Chinese Revolution: The Politics of Mass Criticism.* Berkeley: University of California Press, 1974.

Dong Wang. "The Quarreling Brothers: New Chinese Archives and a Reappraisal of the Sino-Soviet Split, 1959–1962." *CWIHP Working Paper,* no. 36 (April 2002): 1–80.

Dostoevsky, Fyodor. *The Brothers Karamazov.* Translated by Constance Garnett. New York: Modern Library, 1996.

———. *Crime and Punishment.* Translated by Constance Garnett. New York: Modern Library, 1994.

———. *Possessed.* Translated by Constance Garnett. 2 vols. New York: Dutton, 1960.

Ehrenburg, G. "K voprosu o kharaktere i osobennostiakh narodnoi demokratii v Kitae" (On the Nature and Characteristics of People's Democracy in China). In L. V. Simonovskaia and M. F. Yuriev, eds. *Sbornik statei po istorii stran Dal'nego Vostoka* (Collection of Articles on the History of the Countries of the Far East), 5–21. Moscow: Izdatel'stvo MGU, 1952.

———. "Mao Tszedun" (Mao Zedong). *Za rubezhom* (Abroad), no. 31 (63) (1992): 15.

———. *Sovetskii Kitai* (Soviet China). Moscow: Partizdat, 1933.

———. *Sovetskoe dvizhenie v Kitae* (The Soviet Movement in China). Moscow, 1933.

Erbaugh, Mary S. "The Secret History of the Hakkas: The Chinese Revolution as a Hakka Enterprise." *China Quarterly*, no. 132 (1992): 937–68.

Esherick, Joseph W. *Reform and Revolution in China: The 1911 Revolution in Hunan and Hubei*. Berkeley: University of California Press, 1976.

Evans, Richard. *Deng Xiaoping and the Making of Modern China*. Rev. ed. London: Penguin, 1997.

Fairbank, John King. *The United States and China*. Cambridge, MA: Harvard University Press, 1948.

Faligot, Roger, and Rémi Kauffer. *The Chinese Secret Service*. Trans. Christine Donougher. New York: Morrow, 1989.

Fang Daming, and Yang Busheng. "Yang Kaihui." In Hu Hua, ed. *Zhonggongdang shi renwu zhuan* (Biographies of Persons in the History of the CCP). Vol. 14, 246–59. Xi'an: Shaanxi renmin chubanshe, 1985.

Farnsworth, Robert M. *From Vagabond to Journalist: Edgar Snow in Asia 1928–1941*. Columbia: University of Missouri Press, 1996.

Feigon, Lee. *Chen Duxiu: Founder of the Chinese Communist Party*. Princeton, NJ: Princeton University Press, 1983.

———. *Mao. A Reinterpretation*. Chicago: Ivan R. Dee, 2002.

Fenby, Jonathan. *Chiang Kai-shek: China's Generalissimo and the Nation He Lost*. New York: Carroll & Graf, 2004.

Firsov, F. *Sekretnye kody Kominterna 1919–1943* (Secret Codes of the Comintern 1919–1943). Moscow: AIRO-XX/Kraft+, 2007.

Galbiati, Fernando. *P'eng P'ai and the Hai-lu-feng Soviet*. Stanford, CA: Stanford University Press, 1985.

Galenovich, Yu. N. *Peng Dehuai i Mao Tszedun: Politicheskie lidery Kitaia XX veka* (Peng Dehuai and Mao Zedong: Political Leaders of Twentieth Century China). Moscow: Ogni, 2005.

———. *Smert' Mao Tszeduna* (The Death of Mao Zedong). Moscow: Izd-vo "Izograf," 2005.

Galitskii, V. P. *Tszian Tszinguo: Tragedia i triumf syna Chan Kaishi* (Jiang Jingguo: The Tragedy and Triumph of Chiang Kai-shek's Son). Moscow: RAU-Universitet, 2002.

Gan Hailan, ed. *Lao She nianpu* (Chronological Biography of Lao She). Beijing: Shumu wenxian chubanshe/Xinhua shudian jingxiao, 1989.

Ganshin, G., and T. Zazerskaia. "Ukhaby na doroge 'bratskoi druzhby' " (Potholes on the Road of "Fraternal Friendship"). *Problemy Da'nego Vostoka* (Far Eastern affairs), no. 6 (1994): 67–72.

Gao Hua. *Hong taiyang shi zen me yang shengqi de: Yan'an zhengfeng yundong lailong qumai* (How the Red Sun Rose: Analysis of the Yan'an Rectification Movement). Hong Kong: Zhongwen daxue chubanshe, 2000.

Gao, Mobo G. G. *Gao Village: A Portrait of Rural Life in Modern China*. Honolulu: University of Hawai'i Press, 1999.

Gao Wenqian. *Zhou Enlai: The Last Perfect Revolutionary: A Biography*. Trans. Peter Rand and Lawrence R. Sullivan. New York: PublicAffairs, 2007.

Garushiants, Yu. M. *Dvizhenie 4 maia v Kitae* (The May Fourth Movement in China). Moscow: Nauka, 1959.

Garver, John W. *Chinese-Soviet Relations, 1937–1945: The Diplomacy of Chinese Nationalism*. New York: Oxford University Press, 1988.

Geil, William Edgar. *Eighteen Capitals of China*. Philadelphia: Lippincott, 1911.

Gel'bras, V. G. *Sotsial'no-politicheskaiia struktura KNR, 50–60-e gody* (The Social-Political Structure of the PRC in the 1950s and 1960s). Moscow: Nauka, 1980.

Glunin, V. I. "The Comintern and the Rise of the Communist Movement in China (1920–1927)." In R. A. Ulianovskii, ed. *The Comintern and the East: The Struggle for Leninist Strategy and Tactics in the National Liberation Movement*, 280–388. Moscow: Progress, 1969.

———. "Grigorii Voitinsky, 1893–1953." In G. V. Astafiev et al., eds. *Vidnye sovietskie kommunisty—uchastniki kitaiskoi revoliutsii* (Prominent Soviet Communists—Participants in the Chinese Revolution). Moscow: Nauka, 1970.

———. *Komintern i stanovlenie kommunisticheskogo dvizheniia v Kitae, 1920–1927* (The Comintern and the Rise of the Communist Movement in China, 1920–1927). In R. A. Ulianovskii, ed. *Komintern i Vostok: Bor'ba za leninskuiu strategiiu i taktiku v natsional'no-osvoboditel'nom dvizhenii* (The Comintern and the East: The Struggle for Leninist Strategy and Tactics in the National Liberation Movement). Moscow: Nauka, 1968.

———. *Kommunisticheskaia partiia Kitaia nakanune i vo vremia natsional'noi revoliutsii 1925–1927 gg.* (The Chinese Communist Party on the Eve and during the 1925–1927 National Revolution). 2 vols. Moscow: IDV AN SSSR, 1975.

Glunin, V. I., and A. S. Mugruzin. "Krest'ianstvo v kitaiskoi revoliutsii" (The Peasantry in the Chinese Revolution). In R. A. Ulyanovsky, ed. *Revoliutsionnyi protsess na Vostoke: Istoriia i sovremennost'* (The Revolutionary Process in the East: History and the Present), 111–65. Moscow: Nauka, 1982.

Gogol, N. V. *Dead Souls: A Poem*. Oxford: Oxford University Press, 1998.

Goncharenko, Sergei. "Sino-Soviet Military Cooperation." In O. Arne Westad, ed. *Brothers in Arms: The Rise and Fall of the Sino-Soviet Alliance, 1945–1963*, 141–64. Stanford, CA: Stanford University Press, 1998.

Goncharov, Sergei N., John W. Lewis, and Xue Litai. *Uncertain Partners: Stalin, Mao, and the Korean War*. Stanford, CA: Stanford University Press, 1993.

Gong Yuzhi, Pang Xiangzhi, and Shi Zhongquan. *Mao Zedongde dushu shenghuo* (Mao Zedong as a Reader). Beijing: Shenghuo. Dushu. Xinzhi sanlian shudian, 1986.

Grigoriev, A. M. *Antiimperialisticheskaiia programma kitaiskikh burzhuaznykh revoliutsionerov (1895–1905)* (The Anti-imperialist Program of the Chinese Bourgeois Revolutionaries [1895–1905]). Moscow: Nauka, 1966.

———. *Kommunisticheskaia partiia Kitaia v nachal'nyi period sovetskogo dvizheniia (iul' 1927 g.–sentiabr' 1931 g.)* (The Communist Party of China in the Initial Soviet Movement Period, July 1927–September 1931). Moscow: IDV AN SSSR, 1976.

Gu Ci. "Xiang Jingyu." In Hu Hua, ed. *Zhonggongdang shi renwu zhuan* (Biographies of Persons in the History of the CCP). Vol. 6, 58–90. Xi'an: Shaanxi renmin chubanshe, 1982.

Guo Jinrong. *Zoujin Mao Zedongde zuihou suiyue* (Entering the Last Years and Months of Mao Zedong's Life). Beijing: Zhonggong dangshi chubanshe, 2009.

Hai Lude. *Shenghuozhongde Mao Zedong* (Mao Zedong in Life). Beijing: Hualing chubanshe, 1989.

Hamilton, John Maxwell. *Edgar Snow: A Biography*. Bloomington: Indiana University Press, 1988.

Hamilton, Nigel. *Monty: Final Years of the Field-Marshal, 1944–1976*. New York: McGraw-Hill, 1987.

Han Yide, et al. *Li Dazhao shengping jinian* (Biographical Chronicle of Li Dazhao). Harbin: Heilongjiang renmin chubanshe, 1987.

Hastings, Max. *The Korean War*. New York: Simon & Schuster, 1987.

He Ganzhi. *Istoriia sovremennoi revoliutsii v Kitae* (History of the Contemporary Revolution in China). Moscow: Izdatel'stvo inostrannoi literatury, 1959.

He Long nianpu (Chronological Biography of He Long). Beijing: Zhonggong zhongyang dangxiao chubanshe, 1988.

Heinzig, Dieter. *The Soviet Union and Communist China 1945–1950: The Arduous Road to the Alliance*. Armonk, NY: M. E. Sharpe, 2004.

History of the Chinese Communist Party—A Chronology of Events (1919–1990). Beijing: Foreign Languages Press, 1991.

Hofheinz, Roy, Jr. *The Broken Wave: The Chinese Communist Peasant Movement*. Cambridge, MA: Harvard University Press, 1977.

Holubnychy, Lydia. *Michael Borodin and the Chinese Revolution, 1923–1925*. New York: Columbia University Press, 1979.

Horváth, George Pálóczi. *Mao Tse-tung: Emperor of the Blue Ants*. London: Secker & Warburg, 1962.

Hsiao Tso-liang. *Power Relations within the Chinese Communist Movement, 1930–1934: A Study of Documents*. Seattle: University of Washington Press, 1967.

Hu Sheng, et al. *Zhongguo Gongchandang qishi nian* (Seventy Years of the Chinese Communist Party). Beijing: Zhonggong dangshi chubanshe, 1991.

Huang Lingjun, "Liu Shaoqi yu dayuejin" (Liu Shaoqi and the Great Leap Forward). *Zhongguo xiandaishi* (Contemporary history of China), no. 7 (2003): 107–11.

Huang Qijun. "Wang Jiaxian 1937 nian qu gongchan guojide jianyao jingguo" (A Brief History of Wang Jiaxiang's Trip to the Comintern in 1937). *Dangshi yanjiu* (Studies on party history), no. 6 (1987): 184–85.

———. "Yi jiu san liu nian Deng Fa qu gongchan guojide jianyao jingguo" (Brief Summary of Deng Fa's Trip to the Comintern in 1936). *Dangshi yanjiu* (Studies on party history), no. 5 (1986): 73–74.

Huang Zheng. "Mao Anying." In Huang Hua, ed. *Zhonggongdang shi renwu zhuan* (Biographies of Persons in the History of the CCP). Vol. 21, 145–58. Xian: Shaanxi renmin chubanshe, 1985.

Hunt, Michael, and Steven I. Levine. *Arc of Empire: America's Wars in Asia from the Philippines to Vietnam*. Chapel Hill: University of North Carolina Press, 2012.

Ivin, A. *Ocherki partizanskogo dvizheniia v Kitae, 1927–1930* (Sketches of the Guerrilla Movement in China, 1927–1930). Moscow and Leningrad: GIZ, 1930.

———. *Sovietskii Kitai* (Soviet China). Moscow: "Molodaia gvardiia," 1931.

Jacobs, Dan N. *Borodin: Stalin's Man in China*. Cambridge, MA: Harvard University Press, 1981.

Jiang Boying, et al. "Deng Zihui." In Hu Hua, ed. *Zhonggongdang shi renwu zhuan* (Biographies of Persons in the History of the CCP). Vol. 7, 296–380. Xi'an: Shaanxi renmin chubanshe, 1990.

Jiang Xuanhua. "Dangde minzhu geming gangling de tichu he guogong hezuo celüede jige wenti" (Several Questions Regarding the Party Program for the Democratic Revolution and the Strategy of Cooperation Between the Guomindang and the CCP). *Jindaishi yanjiu* (Studies in modern history), no. 2 (1985): 111–26.

Jiang Yihua. *Guomindang zuopai qizhi—Liao Zhongkai* (The Banner of the Left Guomindang—Liao Zhongkai). Shanghai: Shanghai renmin chubanshe, 1985.

Jiang Yongjing. *Baoluoting yu Wuhan zhengquan* (Borodin and the Wuhan Government). Taibei: Zhongguo xueshu zhuzuo jiangzhu weiyuanhui, 1963.

Jin Chongji, ed. *Liu Shaoqi zhuan 1898–1969* (Biography of Liu Shaoqi 1898–1969). 2 vols. Beijing: Zhongyang wenxian chubanshe, 2008.

———. *Mao Zedong zhuan (1893–1949)* (Biography of Mao Zedong [1893–1949]). Beijing: Zhongyang wenxian chubanshe, 2004.

———. *Zhou Enlai zhuan. 1898–1976* (Biography of Zhou Enlai. 1898–1976). 2 vols. Beijing: Zhongyang wenxian chubanshe, 2009.

Jin Qiu. *The Culture of Power: The Lin Biao Incident in the Cultural Revolution*. Stanford, CA: Stanford University Press, 1999.

Jing Fuzi. *Mao Zedong he tade nürenmen* (Mao Zedong and His Women). 6th ed. Taipei: Lianjing chuban shiye gongsi, 1993.

Jinggangshan douzheng dashi jieshao (Survey of Main Events in the Struggle in the Jinggang Mountains). Beijing: Jiefangjun chubanshe, 1985.

Jordan, Donald A. *China's Trial by Fire: The Shanghai War of 1932*. Ann Arbor: University of Michigan Press, 2001.

Kalachev, S. (S. N. Naumov). "Kratkii ocherk istorii Kitaiskoi kommunisticheskoi partii" (Brief History of the Chinese Communist Party). *Kanton* (Canton), no. 10 (1927): 13–66.

Kalinin, M. I. "O Kitae" (On China). In *Kitai: Rasskazy* (China: Stories), 5–35. Moscow and Leningrad: Detgiz, 1938.

Kampen, Thomas. *Mao Zedong, Zhou Enlai and the Evolution of the Chinese Communist Leadership*. Copenhagen: NIAS, 2000.

Kapitsa, M. S. *Sovetsko-kitaiskie otnosheniia* (Soviet-Chinese Relations). Moscow: Gospolitizdat, 1958.

Karnow, Stanley. *Mao and China: From Revolution to Revolution*. New York: Viking Press, [1972].

———. *Mao and China: A Legacy of Turmoil*. 3rd ed. Rev. and updated. New York: Penguin Books, 1990.

Kaufman, Burton I. *The Korean Conflict*. Westport, CT: Greenwood Press, 1999.

Kerry, Tom. *The Mao Myth and the Legacy of Stalinism in China*. New York: Pathfinder Press, 1977.

[Khamadan, A. M.]. "Mao Tszedun—Vozhd' kitaiskogo trudovogo naroda" ("Mao Zedong—The Leader of the Chinese Toiling People"). *Kommunisticheskii Internatsional* (Communist International), nos. 33–34 (1935): 83–88.

———. "Vozhd' kitaiskogo naroda—Mao Tszedun" (The Leader of the Chinese People—Mao Zedong). *Pravda* (Truth). December 13, 1935.

———. *Vozhdi i geroi kitaiskogo naroda* (Leaders and Heroes of the Chinese People). Moscow: Ogiz-Sotsekgiz, 1936.

———. *Zapiski korrespondenta* (Notes of a Correspondent). Moscow: "Sovetskii pisatel'," 1968.

Klein, Donald, and Anne Clark. *Biographic Dictionary of Chinese Communism: 1921–1969*. 2 vols. Cambridge, MA: Harvard University Press, 1971.

Kolpakidi, A., and D. Prokhorov. *Imperiya GRU: Ocherki istorii rossiiskoi voennoi razvedki* (The GRU Empire: An Outline History of the Russian Military Intelligence Service). Moscow: "Olma-Press," 1999.

———. *Vneshnaia razvedka Rossii* (Russian Foreign Intelligence Service). St. Petersburg: Neva, Olma-Press, 2001.

Kolpas, Norman. *Mao*. New York: McGraw-Hill, 1981.

The Korean War. Vol. 1. Lincoln: University of Nebraska Press, 2000.

Kostiaeva, A. S. *Krest'ianskie soiuzy v Kitae (20-e gody XX veka)* (Peasant Unions in China in the 1920s). Moscow: Nauka, 1978.

Kratkaia istoria KPK (1921–1991) (A Short History of the CCP [1921–1991]). Beijing: Izdatel'stvo literatury na inostrannykh iazykakh, 1993.

Krivosheev, G. F., ed. *Grif sekretnosti snyat: Poteri Vooruzhennykh Sil SSSR v voinakh, boevykh deistviyakh i voennykh konfliktakh: Statisticheskoe issledovanie* (The Stamp of Secrecy Is Removed: Losses of the Armed Forces of the USSR in Wars, Battles, and Armed Conflicts: A Statistical Analysis). Moscow: Voennoe izdatel'stvo, 1993.

Kulik, B. T. *Sovetsko-kitaiskii raskol. Prichiny i posledstviia* (The Sino-Soviet Split. Causes and Consequences). Moscow: IDV RAN, 2000.

Kurchatkin, A. N. *Pobeditel': Istinnaia zhizn' legendarnogo razvedchika* (Victor: A Real Life of a Legendary Secret Service Man). Moscow: "Molodaia gvardiia," 2005.

Lawrance, Alan. *Mao Zedong: A Bibliography*. New York: Greenwood Press, 1991.

Ledovsky, A. M. *Delo Gao Gana–Rao Shushi* (The Gao Gang–Rao Shushi Affair). Moscow: IDV AN SSSR, 1990.

Lee, Frederic E. *Currency, Banking, and Finance in China.* Washington, DC: U.S. Government Printing Office, 1926.

Leng Buji. *Deng Xiaoping zai Gannan* (Deng Xiaoping in Southern Jiangxi). Beijing: Zhongyang wenxian chubanshe, 1995.

Leng Rong, and Wang Zuoling, eds. *Deng Xiaoping nianpu: 1975–1997* (Chronological Biography of Deng Xiaoping: 1975–1997). 2 vols. Beijing: Zhongyang wenxian chubanshe, 2004.

Lévesque, Léonard. *Hakka Beliefs and Customs.* Trans. J. Maynard Murphy. Taichung: Kuang Chi Press, 1969.

Levine, Marilyn A. *The Found Generation: Chinese Communists in Europe during the Twenties.* Seattle: University of Washington Press, 1993.

Levine, Steven I. *Anvil of Victory: The Communist Revolution in Manchuria, 1945–1948.* New York: Columbia University Press, 1987.

Li Danhui. "Mao Zedong dui Su renshi yu Zhongsu guanxide yanbian" (Mao Zedong's Knowledge of the Soviet Union and Changes in His Views on Sino-Soviet Relations). In *Zhanhou zhongsu guanxi zouxiang (1945–1960)* (The Development of Sino-Soviet Relations after the War [1945–1960]), 61–90. Beijing: Shehui kexue wenhua chubanshe, 1997.

Li Dazhao guju (Li Dazhao's Birthplace). Shijiazhuang: Hebei renmin chubanshe, 1996.

Li Dazhao jinianguan (Museum of Li Dazhao). Shijiazhuang: Hebei renmin chubanshe, 1999.

Li Dazhao zhuan (Biography of Li Dazhao). Beijing: Renmin chubanshe, 1979.

Li, Hua-Yu. "Stalin's *Short Course* and Mao's Socialist Economic Transformation of China in the Early 1950s." *Russian History* 29, nos. 2–4 (Summer–Fall–Winter 2002): 357–76.

Li Jie, and Yu Jundao. *Dongfang juren Mao Zedong* (A Titan of the East Mao Zedong). Beijing: Jiefangjun chubanshe, 1996.

Li Jinzeng. "Changzheng diyi shu jin an zai?" (Where Is the First Book on the Long March Now?). http://www.crt.com.cn/news/Html/lijin/00008746.html.

Li Jui. *The Early Revolutionary Activities of Comrade Mao Tse-tung.* White Plains, NY: International Arts & Sciences Press, 1977.

Li Ping. *Kaiguo zongli Zhou Enlai* (Zhou Enlai, the First Premier). Beijing: Zhonggong zhongyang dangxiao chubanshe, 1994.

Li Ping, and Ma Zhisun, eds. *Zhou Enlai nianpu (1949–1976)* (Chronological Biography of Zhou Enlai [1949–1976]). 3 vols. Beijing: Zhongyang wenxian chubanshe, 1997.

Li Rui. "Mao Tsze-dun v poslednie gody zhizni" (Mao Zedong in the Last Years of His Life). *Problemy Dal'nego Vostoka* (Far Eastern affairs), no. 1 (1990): 129–32.

———. *Sanshi sui yiqiande Mao Zedong* (Mao Zedong Before Thirty). Taipei: Shibao wenhua, 1993.

Li Ying, ed. *Cong yida dao shiliu da* (From the First to the Sixteenth Congress). 2 vols. Beijing: Zhongyang wenxian chubanshe, 2002.

Li Yuan, ed. *Mao Zedong yu Deng Xiaoping* (Mao Zedong and Deng Xiaoping). Beijing: Zhonggong dangshi chubanshe, 2008.

Liao Gailong, et al., eds. *Mao Zedong baike quanshu* (Encyclopedia of Mao Zedong). 7 vols. Beijing: Guangming ribao chubanshe, 2003.

———. *Zhongguo gongchandang lishi da cidian. Zengdingben. Shehui geming shiqi* (Great Dictionary of the History of the Chinese Communist Party. Expanded edition. The Period of the Socialist Revolution). Rev. ed. Beijing: Zhonggong zhongyang dangxiao chubanshe, 2001.

———. *Zhongguo gongchandang lishi da cidian. Zengdingben. Xin minzhu zhuyi geming shiqi* (Great Dictionary of the History of the Chinese Communist Party. Expanded edition. The Period of the New Democratic Revolution). Rev. ed. Beijing: Zhonggong zhongyang dangxiao chubanshe, 2001.

———. *Zhongguo gongchandang lishi da cidian. Zengdingben. Zonglu. Renwu.* (Great Dictionary of the History of the Chinese Communist Party. Expanded Edition. General

Section. Personnel). Rev. ed. Beijing: Zhonggong zhongyang dangxiao chubanshe, 2001.

———. *Zhongguo renwu da cidian* (Great Dictionary of China's Personalities). Shanghai: Shanghai cishu chubanshe, 1992.

Lin Boqu zhuan (Biography of Lin Boqu). Beijing: Hongqi chubanshe, 1986.

Lin Hongyuan. "Zhang Tailei." In Hu Hua, ed. *Zhonggongdang shi renwu zhuan* (Biographies of Persons in the History of the CCP), 62–108. Vol. 4. Xi'an: Shaanxi renmin chubanshe, 1982.

Litten, Frederick S. "The Noulens Affair." *China Quarterly*, no. 138 (1994): 492–512.

Liu Chongwen, and Chen Shaochou, eds. *Liu Shaoqi nianpu: 1898–1969* (Chronological Biography of Liu Shaoqi: 1898–1969). 2 vols. Beijing: Zhongyang wenxian chubanshe, 1998.

Liu Guokai. *A Brief Analysis of the Cultural Revolution*. Armonk, NY: M. E. Sharpe, 1987.

Liu Jianping. "Sugong yu Zhongguo gongchandang renmin minzhu zhuanzheng lilunde queli" (The CPSU and the Setting Forth of the CCP New Democratic Theory). *Lishi yanjiu* (Studies of history) 1 (1998): 78–96.

Liu Jiecheng. *Mao Zedong yu Sidalin huiwu jishi* (Unforgettable Facts about Mao Zedong's Meetings with Stalin). Beijing: Zhonggong dangshi chubanshe, 1997.

Liu Renzhong. "Mao Zetan." In Hu Hua, ed. *Zhonggongdang shi renwu zhuan* (Biographies of Persons in the History of the CCP), 283–332. Vol. 3. Xi'an: Shaanxi renmin chubanshe, 1981.

Lu Ren, and Liu Qingxia. "Mao Zedong chong Heluxiaofu fahuo" (How Mao Got Angry at Khrushchev). *Zhuanji wenxue* (Biographical literature), no. 4 (2004): 21–28.

Lu Sin (Lu Xun). *Izbrannye proizvedeniia* (Selected Works). Moscow: Khudozhestvennaia literatura, 1981.

Luo Guangzhong, *Three Kingdoms: A Historical Novel*. Abridged ed. Trans. Moss Roberts. Berkeley: University of California Press, 1999.

Luo Shaozhi. "Cai mu Ge Jianhao" (Mama Cai, Ge Jianhao). In Hu Hua, ed. *Zhonggongdang shi renwu zhuan* (Biographies of Persons in the History of the CCP). Vol. 6, 47–57. Xi'an: Shaanxi renmin chubanshe, 1982.

Luo Shaozhi, et al. "Cai Hesen." In Hu Hua, ed. *Zhonggongdang shi renwu zhuan* (Biographies of Persons in the History of the CCP). Vol. 6, 1–46. Xi'an: Shaanxi renmin chubanshe, 1982.

Lüthi, Lorenz M. *The Sino-Soviet Split: Cold War in the Communist World*. Princeton, NJ: Princeton University Press, 2008.

Lynch, Michael. *Mao*. London: Routledge, 2004.

Ma Shexiang. *Hongse diyi jiazu* (The First Red Family). Wuhan: Hubei renmin chubanshe, 2004.

MacFarquhar, Roderick. *The Hundred Flowers Campaign and the Chinese Intellectuals*. New York: Praeger, 1960.

———. *The Origins of the Cultural Revolution*. Vol. 1, *Contradictions Among the People, 1956–1957*. New York: Columbia University Press, 1974.

———. *The Origins of the Cultural Revolution*. Vol. 2, *The Great Leap Forward, 1958–1960*. New York: Columbia University Press, 1983.

———. *The Origins of the Cultural Revolution*. Vol. 3, *The Coming of the Cataclysm, 1961–1966*. New York: Columbia University Press, 1997.

MacFarquhar, Roderick, and Michael Schoenhals. *Mao's Last Revolution*. Cambridge, MA: Belknap Press of Harvard University Press, 2006.

MacKinnon, Janice R., and Stephen R. MacKinnon. *Agnes Smedley: The Life and Times of an American Radical*. Berkeley: University of California Press, 1988.

Makesi Engesi zhuzuo zhongyiwen zonglu (Catalogue of Chinese Translations of Marx and Engels's works). Beijing: Shumu wenxian chubanshe, 1988.

Maliavin, V. V. *Kitaiskaia tsivilizatsiia* (Chinese Civilization). Moscow: Astrel', 2004.

"Mao Anying san xiongdi zai Shanghai shide qingkuang" (What Happened to Mao Anying and His Brothers During Their Sojourn in Shanghai). *Xinmin wanbao* (The renovation of people evening newspaper), December 23, 2004.

Mao Tsze-dun: Biograficheskii ocherk (Mao Zedong: Biographical Sketch). Moscow: OGIZ, 1939.

Mao Zedong de jiashi (Mao Zedong's Family Affairs). Beijing: Chunqiu chubanshe, 1987.

Mao Zedong sixiang lunwenji (Collection of Essays about Mao Zedong Thought). Shanghai: Shanghai renmin chubanshe, 1984.

"Mao Zemin." In Hu Hua, ed. *Zhonggongdang shi renwu zhuan* (Biographies of Persons in the History of the CCP). Vol. 9, 47–75. Xi'an: Shaanxi renmin chubanshe, 1981.

Mao zhuxi yijia liu lieshi (Six Martyrs from Chairman Mao's Family). Changsha: Hunan renmin chubanshe, 1978.

Marx, Karl. *Capital.* Vol. 1, *The Process of Production of Capital.* In Karl Marx and Friedrich Engels, *Collected Works,* Vol. 35. Translated by Richard Dixon et al. New York: International, 1996.

———. "Critique of the Gotha Program." In Karl Marx and Friedrich Engels, *Collected Works,* Vol. 24. Translated by Richard Dixon et al. New York: International, 1989.

Mayakovsky, V. V. *Polnoe sobranie sochinenii* (Complete Collected Works). 13 vols. Moscow: Khudozhestvennaia literatura, 1961.

McCord, Edward A. *The Power of the Gun: The Emergence of Modern Chinese Warlordism.* Berkeley: University of California Press, 1993.

McDonald, Angus W., Jr. *The Urban Origins of Rural Revolution: Elites and the Masses in Hunan Province, China, 1911–1927.* Berkeley: University of California Press, 1978.

Meisner, Maurice. *Li Ta-chao and the Origins of Chinese Marxism.* New York: Atheneum, 1979.

———. *Mao Zedong: A Political and Intellectual Portrait.* Malden, MA: Polity, 2007.

———. *Mao's China and After: A History of the People's Republic.* 3rd ed. New York: Free Press, 1999.

Meliksetov, A. V., ed. *Istoriia Kitaia* (History of China). Moscow: Izdatel'stvo MGU, 1998.

———. " 'Novaia demokratiia' i vybor Kitaem putei sotsial'no-ekonomicheskogo razvitiia (1949–1953)" ("New Democracy" and China's Choice of a Socio-economic Development Path [1949–1953]). *Problemy Dal'nego Vostoka* (Far Eastern affairs), no. 1 (1996): 82–95.

Meliksetov, A. V., and Alexander Pantsov. "Stalinization of the People's Republic of China." In William C. Kirby, ed. *Realms of Freedom in Modern China,* 198–233. Stanford, CA: Stanford University Press, 2003.

Mitin, M. B., ed. "Dialekticheskii materialism" (Dialectical Materialism). *Bolshaia Sovetskaia Entsiklopediia* (Large Soviet Encyclopedia). Vol. 22, 45–235. Moscow: Sovetskaia Entsiklopediia, 1935.

———. "Predislovie" (Preface). In M. B. Mitin. *Boevye voprosy materialisticheskoi dialektiki* (Urgent Problems of Materialist Dialectics), 3–5. Moscow: Partizdat TsK VKP(b), 1936.

———. *Xin zhexue dagang* (Outline of New Philosophy). Translated by Ai Siqi and Zheng Yili. Shanghai: Dushu shenghuo chubanshe, 1936.

Mitin, M. B., and I. Razumovskii, eds. *Dialekticheskii i istoricheskii materialism, v dvukh chastiakh. Uchebnik dlia komvuzov i vuzov* (Dialectical and Historical Materialism, in Two Parts. Textbook of Communist Higher Educational Institutions and Higher Educational Institutions). Moscow: Partiinoe izdatel'stvo, 1932.

Mitin, M. B., et al. *Bianzheng weiwulun yu lishi weiwulun* (Dialectical and Historical Materialism). Translated by Shen Zhiyuan. Vol. 1. [Changsha], 1935.

Moss, George Donelson. *Vietnam: An American Ordeal.* 6th ed. Upper Saddle River, NJ: Prentice-Hall, 2006.

Müller, Reinhard. "Der Fall des 'Antikomintern-Blocks'—ein vierter Moskuaer Schauprozeß?" *Jahrbuch für Historische Kommunismusforschung 1996,* 187–214.

Murray, Brian. "Stalin, the Cold War, and the Division of China: A Multi-Archival Mystery." *CWIHP Working Paper,* no. 12 (June 1995).

Nathan, Andrew J. *Peking Politics, 1918–1923: Factionalism and the Failure of Constitutionalism.* Ann Arbor: Center for Chinese Studies, University of Michigan, [1998].

Niu Jun. "The Origins of the Sino-Soviet Alliance." In O. Arne Westad, ed. *Brothers in Arms: The Rise and Fall of the Sino-Soviet Alliance, 1945–1963,* 47–89. Stanford, CA: Stanford University Press, 1998.

North, Robert C. *Moscow and Chinese Communists.* Stanford, CA: Stanford University Press, 1953.

Pan Ling. *In Search of Old Shanghai.* Hong Kong: Joint, 1983.

Pang Xianzhi, ed. *Mao Zedong nianpu, 1893–1949* (Chronological Biography of Mao Zedong, 1893–1949). 3 vols. Beijing: Renmin chubanshe/Zhongyang wenxian chubanshe, 2002.

Pang Xianzhi, and Jin Congji, eds. *Mao Zedong zhuan (1949–1976)* (Biography of Mao Zedong [1949–1976]). 2 vols. Beijing: Zhongyang wenxian chubanshe, 2003.

Pantsov, Alexander V. "Bolshaia igra kremlevskogo 'otsa narodov': Stalin prednamerenno zatiagival voinu na Koreiskom poluostrove" (The Big Gamble of the Kremlin "Father of Nations": Stalin Deliberately Protracted the War on the Korean Peninsula). *Nezavisimoe voennoe obozrenie* (Independent military review), no. 24 (2008): 10–11.

——. *The Bolsheviks and the Chinese Revolution, 1919–1927.* Honolulu: University of Hawai'i Press, 2000.

——. "Chen Duxiu (1879–1942)." *Collier's Encyclopedia.* Vol. 6, 180–80A. New York: Collier's, 1996.

——. "How Stalin Helped Mao Zedong Become the Leader: New Archival Documents On Moscow's Role in the Rise of Mao." *Issues & Studies* 41, no. 3 (September 2005): 181–207.

——. *Iz istorii ideinoi bor'by v kitaiskom revoliutsionom dvizhenii 20–40-x godov* (On the History of Ideological Struggle in the Chinese Revolutionary Movement, 1920s–1940s). Moscow: Nauka, 1985.

——. "K diskussii v KPK vokrug 'idei Mao Tsze-duna' " (On the Discussion Within the CCP of "Mao Zedong Thought"). *Rabochii klass i sovremennyi mir* (Working class and the contemporary world), no. 3 (1982): 61–64.

——. "Kak possorilis' Nikita Sergeevich s Mao Tsze-dunom" (How Nikita Sergeevich Quarreled with Mao Zedong). *Rossiia, Kitai, XXI vek* (Russia, China, the twenty-first century), no. 7 (July 2007): 60–64; no. 8 (August 2007): 68–72.

——. " 'Lazurnaia reka': vzlet i padenie Tsian Tsin" ("Azure River": The Rise and Fall of Jiang Qing). *Rossiia, Kitai, XXI vek* (Russia, China, the twenty-first century), no. 8 (2006): 26–31.

——. *Mao Tszedun* (Mao Zedong). Moscow: "Molodaia gvardiia," 2007.

——. "Mao Tsze-dun i 'delo Lin Biao' (Mao Zedong and the "Lin Biao Affair"). *Problemy Dal'nego Vostoka* (Far Eastern affairs), no. 5 (2006): 111–23.

——. "Mao Tsze-dun: poslednie gody" (Mao Zedong: The Last Years). *Problemy Dal'nego Vostoka* (Far Eastern affairs), no. 6 (2006): 101–14.

——. "Obrazovaniie opornykh baz 8-i Natsional'no-revoliutsionnoi armii v tylu iaponskikh voisk v Severnom Kitae" (Establishment of Eighth Route Army Base Areas in the Japanese Rear in North China). In M. F. Yuriev, ed. *Voprosy istorii Kitaia* (Problems of Chinese History), 39–41. Moscow: Izdatel'stvo MGU, 1981.

——. "Priemnyi Syn Bodkhisattvy: Detskie gody Mao Tsze-duna" (The Foster Child of the Bodhisattva). *Rossiia, Kitai, XXI vek* (Russia, China, the twenty-first century), no. 1 (2007): 50–55.

——. *Rasskazy o Mao Tszedune* (Stories about Mao Zedong). 2 vols. Rostov-na-donu, Krasnodar: Feniks, Neoglori, 2009.

——. " 'Ya poteryal svoi gordyi topol': Zhizn' i sud'ba 'Zoriushki' Kaihui, zheny Mao Tsze-duna" ("I Lost My Majestic Poplar": A Life and Fate of "Little Dawn" Kaihui, Mao

Zedong's Wife). *Rossiia, Kitai, XXI vek* (Russia, China, the twenty-first century), no. 1 (2007): 42–46.

Pantsov, Alexander V., and Gregor Benton. "Did Trotsky Oppose Entering the Guomindang 'From the First'?" *Republican China* 19, no. 2 (April 1994): 52–66.

Pantsov, Alexander V., and Steven I. Levine. *Chinese Comintern Activists: An Analytic Biographic Dictionary.* Manuscript.

Pantsov, Alexander V., and Daria A. Spichak. "Light from the Russian Archives: Chinese Stalinists and Trotskyists at the International Lenin School, 1926–1938." *Twentieth-Century China,* no. 2 (2008): 29–50.

Payne, Robert. *Portrait of a Revolutionary: Mao Tse-tung.* London: Abelard-Schuman, 1961.

Pei Jian. *Xiang hun—Mao Zedongde jiashi* (The Spirit of Hunan—Generations of Mao Zedong's Family). [Beijing]: Qunzhong chunbanshe, 1992.

Peng Dehuai nianpu (Chronological Biography of Peng Dehuai). Beijing: Renmin chubanshe, 1998.

Peng Zhen nianpu, 1902–1997 (Chronological Biography of Peng Zhen, 1902–1997). Vol. 1. Beijing: Zhongyang wenxian chubanshe, 2002.

Pepper, Suzanne. *Civil War in China: The Political Struggle, 1945–1949.* Lanham, MD: Rowman & Littlefield, 1999.

Perelomov, L. S. *Konfutsii: "Lun yu"* (Confucius: "Lun yu"). Moscow: Vostochnaia literatura RAN, 1998.

Perevertailo, A. S., et al., eds. *Ocherki istorii Kitaia v noveishee vremia* (An Outline History of Contemporary China). Moscow: Izd-vo vostochnoi literatury, 1959.

Perry, Elizabeth J. "Shanghai's Strike Wave of 1957." *China Quarterly,* no. 137 (March 1994): 1–27.

Perry, Elizabeth, and Li Xun. *Proletarian Power: Shanghai in the Cultural Revolution.* Boulder, CO: Westview Press, 1997.

Persits, M. A. "Iz istorii stanovleniia Kommunisticheskoi partii Kitaia (Doklad podgotovlennyi Chzhan Taileem dlia III Kongressa Kominterna kak istoricheskii istochnik" (From the History of the Founding of the Communist Party of China [Zhang Tailei's Report to the Third Congress of the Comintern as an Historical Source]). *Narody Azii i Afriki* (Peoples of Asia and Africa), no. 4 (1971): 47–58.

———. "O podgovotel'nom etape kommunisticheskogo dvizheniia v Azii" (On the Preparatory Stage of the Communist Movement in Asia). In R. A. Ul'anovsky, ed. *Revoliutsionnyi protsess na Vostoke: Istoriia i sovremennost* (The Revolutionary Process in the East: Past and Present), 38–76. Moscow: Nauka, 1982.

Pisarev, A. A. *Guomindang i agrarno-krest'ianskii vopros v Kitae v 20–30-e gody XX v.* (The Guomindang and the Agrarian-Peasant Question in China in the 1920s and 1930s). Moscow: Nauka, 1986.

Poston, Dudley L., Jr., and David Yaukey, eds. *The Population of Modern China.* New York: Plenum Press, 1992.

Price, Ruth. *The Lives of Agnes Smedley.* New York: Oxford University Press, 2005.

Prokhorov, Dmitrii. " 'Liternoe delo' marshala Zhang Zuolinia" (The "Lettered File" of Marshal Zhang Zuolin). *Nezavisimoe voennoe obozrenie* (Independent military review), no. 21 (2003): 5.

Prozumeschikov, M. Y. "The Sino-Soviet Conflict, the Cuban Missile Crisis, and the Sino-Soviet Split, October 1962: New Evidence from the Russian Archives." *CWIHP Bulletin,* nos. 8–9 (1996/1997): 251–57.

Przheval'skii, N. M. *Putesheshestvie v Ussuriiskom krae: Mongolia i strana tangutov* (Travels in the Ussuri Region: Mongolia and the Country of Tanguts). Moscow: Drofa, 2007.

Qing Shi (Yang Kuisong). "Gongchan guoji yazhi Mao Zedong le ma?—Mao Zedong yu Mosike de enen yuanyuan" (Did the Comintern Suppress Mao Zedong?—Concord and Discord in the Relations between Mao Zedong and Moscow). *Bainian chao* (Century tides), no. 4 (1997): 21–33.

Qiu Ke'an, ed. *Sinuo zai Zhongguo* (Snow in China). Beijing: Shenghuo. Dushu. Xinzhi san-lian shudian, 1982.

Ren Bishi nianpu, 1904–1950 (Chronological Biography of Ren Bishi, 1904–1950). Beijing: Zhongyang wenxian chubanshe, 2004.

Ren Jianshu. "Chen Duxiu." In Wang Qi and Chen Zhiling, eds. *Zhonggongdang shi renwu zhuan* (Biographies of Persons in the History of the CCP). Vol. 51, 1–129. Xi'an: Shaanxi renmin chubanshe, 1992.

Ren Wuxiong. " 'Xi xing man ji' zhongde Xiao Zheng ji qita" (Xiao Zheng and Others in "The Trip to the West"). *Dangshi yanjiu ziliao* (Study materials on party history), no. 2 (2004): 25–35.

Rethinking the "Cultural Revolution." Beijing: Foreign Languages Press, 1987.

Riabushkin, D. S. *Mify Damanskogo* (Damansky's Myths). Moscow: AST, 2004.

Ristaino, Marcia R. *China's Art of Revolution: The Mobilization of Discontent, 1927 and 1928.* Durham, NC: Duke University Press, 1987.

Rottman, Gordon F. *Korean War Order of Battle: United States, United Nations, and Communist Ground, Naval, and Air Forces, 1950–1953.* Westport, CT: Praeger, 2002.

Rue, John E. *Mao Tse-tung in Opposition, 1927–1935.* Stanford, CA: Stanford University Press, 1966.

Rule, Paul. *Mao Zedong.* St. Lucia, AU: University of Queensland Press, 1984.

Saich, Tony, and Hans J. van de Ven, eds. *New Perspectives on the Chinese Communist Revolution.* Armonk, NY: M.E. Sharpe, 1995.

Salisbury, Harrison E. *The New Emperors: China in the Era of Mao and Deng.* Boston: Little, Brown, 1992.

Schram, Stuart R. *Mao Tse-tung.* New York: Simon & Schuster, 1966.

———. *Mao Tse-tung.* Harmondsworth, UK: Penguin, 1974.

———. *Mao Zedong: A Preliminary Reassessment.* Hong Kong: Chinese University Press, 1983.

Schwartz, Benjamin I. *Chinese Communism and the Rise of Mao.* Cambridge, MA: Harvard University Press, 1951.

———. "The Legend of the 'Legend of "Maoism." ' " *China Quarterly*, no. 2 (April–June 1960): 35–42.

Sergeant, Harriet. *Shanghai.* London: Jonathan Cape, 1991.

Shaffer, Lynda. *Mao and the Workers: The Hunan Labor Movement, 1920–1923.* Armonk, NY: M. E. Sharpe, 1982.

Shapiro, Judith. *Mao's War Against Nature: Politics and the Environment in Revolutionary China.* Cambridge: Cambridge University Press, 2001.

Shapiro, Sidney. *Ma Haide: The Saga of American Doctor George Hatem in China.* Beijing: Foreign Languages Press, 2004.

Shen Dechun, and Tian Haiyan. "Zhongguo gongchandang 'Yi Da' de zhuyao wenti" (Main Questions Connected to the First Congress of the Communist Party of China). *Renmin ribao* (People's daily), June 30, 1961.

Shen Zhihua. "Sino–North Korean Conflict and Its Resolution during the Korean War." *CWIHP Bulletin*, nos. 14–15 (Winter 2003–Spring 2004): 9–24.

———. "Zhonggong bada weishemma buti 'Mao Zedong sixiang'?" (Why did the Eighth CCP Congress not Raise "Mao Zedong Thought"? *Lishi jiaoxue* (Teaching of history), no. 5 (2005): 6–7.

———. "Zhongsu lianmeng yu Zhongguo chubing Chaoxiande juece—dui Zhongguo he Eguo wenxian ziliaode bijiao yanjiu" (The Sino-Soviet Alliance and China's Decision to Despatch Troops to Korea—A Comparative Analysis of Chinese and Soviet Documents). In *Zhanhou zhongsu guanxi zouxiang (1945–1960)* (The Development of Sino-Soviet Relations after the War [1945–1960]), 26–60. Beijing: Shehui kexue wenhua chubanshe, 1997.

Shevelev, K. V. *Formirovaniie sotsial'no-ekonomicheskoi politiki rukovodstva KPK v 1949–*

1956 godakh (rukopis') (The Formulation of the CCP's Socioeconomic Policy in 1949–1956). Manuscript.

———. *Iz istorii obrazovaniia Kommunisticheskoi partii Kitaia* (From the History of the Establishment of the Communist Party of China). Moscow: IDV AN SSSR, 1976.

———. "O nekotorykh aspektakh raboty 4-go plenuma TsK KPK 7-ogo sozyva" (On Several Aspects of the Work of the Fourth Plenum of the Seventh Central Committee of the CCP). In *Perspektivy sotrudnichestva Kitaia, Rossii i drugikh stran Severovostochnoi Azii v kontse XX-nachale XXI veka. Tezisy dokladov VIII Mezhdunarodnoi nauchnoi konferentsii "Kitai, Kitaiskaia tsivilizatsiia i mir: Istoriia, sovremennost', perspektivy," Moskva, 7–9 oktiabria 1997 g.* (Prospects for Cooperation Among China, Russia, and Other Countries of Northeast Asia at the End of the Twentieth and Beginning of the Twenty-First Century. Papers from the VIII International Scholarly Conference on "China, Chinese Civilization, and the World: History, the Present, and the Future," Moscow, October 7–9, 1997). Moscow: IDV RAN, 1997, 150–51.

Shewmaker, Kenneth. *Americans and Chinese Communists, 1927–1945.* Ithaca: Cornell University Press, 1971.

Shi Yongyan. *He Zizhen yu Mao Zedong* (He Zizhen and Mao Zedong). Beijing: Zhonggong dangshi chubanshe, 2008.

Shi Zhifu. "Wu Yuzhang zai gongchan guoji 'qi da' " ("Wu Yuzhang at the Seventh Congress of the Comintern"). *Dangshi yanjiu ziliao* (Study materials on party history), no. 9 (1982): 2–5.

Shiluokefu (Shirokov) and Ailunbao (Aizenberg). *Bianzhengfa weiwulun jiaocheng* (Textbook on Dialectical Materialism). Translated by Li Da and Lei Zhongjian. 3rd ed. Shanghai: Bigengtang shudian, 1935: 4th ed. Shanghai: Bigengtang shudian, 1936.

Shinuo (Snow). *Er wan wu qian li changzheng* (The Twenty-five Thousand Li Long March). Hong Kong: Xinsheng shudian, n.d.

Shirokov, I., and A. Aizenberg, eds. *Materialisticheskaia dialektika* (Materialist Dialectics). Moscow, 1932.

Short, Philip. *Mao: A Life.* New York: Henry Holt, 1999.

Skosyrev, V. "Golovu Lin Biao general KGB privez v Moskvu" (A KGB General Brought Lin Biao's Head to Moscow). *Izvestia* (News), February 17, 1994.

Sladkovskii, M. I., ed. *Noveishaiia istoriia Kitaia: 1917–1927* (Contemporary History of China: 1917–1927). Moscow: Nauka, 1983.

———. *Noveishaiia istoriia Kitaia: 1928–1949* (Contemporary History of China: 1928–1949). Moscow: Nauka, 1984.

Smedley, Agnes. *China's Red Army Marches.* New York: International, 1934.

Sokolov, V. V. " 'Zabytii diplomat' D. V. Bogomolov (1890–1938)" ("Forgotten Diplomat" D. V. Bogomolov [1890–1938]). *Novaia i noveishaia istoriia* (Modern and contemporary history), no. 3 (2004): 165–95.

Solzhenitsyn, A. *Bodalsia telenok s dubom: Ocherki literaturnoi zhizni* (The Oak and the Calf: Sketches of Literary Life). Moscow: Soglasie, 1996.

Song Pinsheng. "Xin faxiande 'Shaoshan Mao shi zupu' xunlüe ji Mao Zedong jiazu shishi kaoding" (A Brief Analysis of the Newly Discovered "Chronicle of the Shaoshan Mao Clan" and the Study of a History of Mao Zedong's Family). *Mao Zedong sixiang yanjiu* (Studies in Mao Zedong Thought) 2 (1990): 56–57.

Sorkin, G. Z. "S"ezd narodov Dal'nego Vostoka" (Congress of Peoples of the Far East). *Problemy vostokovedeniia* (Problems of Oriental studies), no. 5 (1960): 76–86.

Spence, Jonathan D. *Mao Zedong.* New York: Viking, 1999.

———. *The Search for Modern China.* 2nd ed. New York: Norton, 1999.

Spichak, Daria A. "Kitaiskie studenty Moskvy i stalinskie repressii 30-kh gg." (Chinese Students of Moscow and the 1930s Stalin Purges). *Vestnik Moskovskogo Universiteta* (Herald of Moscow University). Series 13: *Vostokovedenie* (Oriental studies), no. 2 (2005): 43–55.

———. *Kitaiskii avangard Kremlia: Revoliutsionery Kitaia v moskovskikh shkolakh Komin-*

terna (1921–1939) (Chinese Vanguard of the Kremlin: Revolutionaries of China in Moscow Comintern Schools [1921–1939]). Moscow: "Veche," 2012.

———. *Kitaitsy vo Frantsii* (Chinese in France). Manuscript.

Stanley, Margaret. *Foreigners in Areas of China Under Communist Jurisdiction Before 1949: Biographical Notes and a Comprehensive Bibliography of Yenan Hui.* Lawrence: Center for East Asian Studies, University of Kansas, 1987.

Starkov, Boris A. "The Trial That Was Not Held." *Europe-Asia Studies* 46, no. 8 (1994): 1297–1316.

Strand, David. *Rickshaw Beijing: City People and Politics in the 1920s.* Berkeley: University of California Press, 1989.

Sun Kexin, et al. *Mao Zedong diaocha yanjiu huodong jianshi* (A Brief History of Mao Zedong's Investigation and Study Activity). Beijing: Zhongguo shehui kexue chubanshe, 1984.

Sun Wuxia. "Qu Qiubai zai di san guoji huodong jilüe" (A Brief Sketch of Qu Qiubai's Activity in the Third International). *Shanghai shifan xueyuan xuebao* (Herald of Shanghai Normal Institute), no. 1 (1984): 106–11.

Sun Wuxia, and Ding Changjiang. "Zhou Enlai tongzhi zai gongchan guoji" (Comrade Zhou Enlai in the Comintern). *Guoji gongyun* (International communist movement), no. 1 (1983): 14–17.

Tang Baolin. *Zhongguo tuopai shi* (History of Trotskyite Groups in China). Taibei: Dongda tushu gongsi, 1994.

Tang Baolin, and Li Maosheng. *Chen Duxiu nianpu* (Chronological Biography of Chen Duxiu). Shanghai: Shanghai renmin chubanshe, 1988.

Tang Chunliang. *Li Lisan quanzhuan* (A Complete Biography of Li Lisan). Hefei: Anhui renmin chubanshe, 1999.

———. *Li Lisan zhuan* (Biography of Li Lisan). Harbin: Heilongjiang renmin chubanshe, 1984.

Tang Peiji, ed. *Zhongguo lishi da nianbiao: Xiandaishi juan* (Chronology of Chinese Historical Events: Contemporary History Volume). Shanghai: Shanghai cishu chubanshe, 1997.

Tang Zhentang. *Jindai Shanghai fanhualu* (Lively Notes on Modern Shanghai). Beijing: Shangwu yinshuguan, 1993.

Taubman, William. *Khrushchev: The Man and His Era.* New York: Norton, 2003.

Taylor, Jay. *The Generalissimo: Chiang Kai-shek and the Struggle for Modern China.* Cambridge, MA: Belknap Press of Harvard University Press, 2009.

Teiwes, Frederick C. *Politics and Purges in China: Rectification and the Decline of Party Norms, 1950–1965.* 2nd ed. Armonk, NY: M. E. Sharpe, 1993.

———. *Politics at Mao's Court: Gao Gang and Party Factionalism.* Armonk, NY: M. E. Sharpe, 1990.

Teiwes, Frederick C., and Warren Sun. "From a Leninist to a Charismatic Party: The CCP's Changing Leadership, 1937–1945." In Tony Saich and Hans J. van de Ven, eds. *New Perspectives on the Chinese Communist Revolution,* 339–87. Armonk, NY: M. E. Sharpe, 1995.

———, eds. *The Politics of Agricultural Cooperativization in China: Mao, Deng Zihui and the "High Tide" of 1955.* Armonk, NY: M. E. Sharpe, 1993.

Terrill, Ross. *Madam Mao: The White-Boned Demon.* Rev. ed. Stanford, CA: Stanford University Press, 1999.

———. *Mao: A Biography.* Stanford, CA: Stanford University Press, 1999.

Thomas, S. Bernard. *Season of High Adventure: Edgar Snow in China.* Berkeley: University of California Press, 1996.

Tikhvinsky, S. L. "O 'sekretnom demarshe' Zhou Enlaya i neofitsial'nykh peregovorakh KPK s amerikantsami v iyune 1949 g." (On Zhou Enlai's "Secret Démarche" and Nonofficial Negotiations Between the CCP and Americans in June 1949). *Problemy Dal'nego Vostoka* (Far Eastern affairs), no. 3 (1994): 133–38.

——, ed. *Novaia istoriia Kitaia* (Modern History of China). Moscow: Nauka, 1972.

Titarenko, M. L., ed. *Istoriia Kommunisticheskoi partii Kitaia* (History of the Communist Party of China). 2 vols. Moscow: IDV AN SSSR, 1987.

Titov, A. S. *Iz istorii bor'by i raskola v rukovodstve KPK 1935–1936 gg.* (From the History of Struggle and Split in the Leadership of the CCP, 1935–1936). Moscow: Nauka, 1979.

——. *Materialy k politicheskoi biografii Mao Tsze-duna* (Materials for a Political Biography of Mao Zedong). 3 vols. Moscow: IDV AN SSSR, 1969.

Ulianovskii, R. A., ed. *The Comintern and the East: The Struggle for Leninist Strategy and Tactics in the National Liberation Movement.* Moscow: Progress, 1969.

Usov, V. N. *KNR: Ot "bol'shogo skachka" k "kul'turnoi revoliutsii" (1960–1966)* (The PRC: From the "Great Leap" to the "Cultural Revolution" [1960–1966]). 2 parts. Moscow: IDV RAN, 1998.

Ven, Hans Van de. *From Friend to Comrade: The Founding of the Chinese Communist Party, 1920–1927.* Berkeley: University of California Press, 1991.

Vladimirov, O. (O. B. Rakhmanin) and V. Ryazantsev (B. T. Kulik). *Stranitsy politicheskoi biografii Mao Tse-tunga* (Pages from the Political Biography of Mao Zedong). 4th enlarged ed. Moscow: Mezdunarodnye otnosheniia, 1980.

V-n [S. N. Belen'kii], "Rets. Mao Tsze-dun,' Analiz klassov Kitaiskogo obshchestva, 'Kitaiskii krest'ianin,' No. 2,1 fevrarlia 1926 g." (Review of Mao Zedong's "Analysis of Classes in Chinese Society"). *Kitaiskii krest'ianin* [Chinese peasant], no. 2, February 1, 1926, *Kanton* (Canton), 8–9 (1926): 37–43.

Vogel, Ezra F. *Canton under Communism: Programs and Politics in a Provincial Capital.* Cambridge, MA: Harvard University Press, 1969.

Voitinsky, G. "Kolonial'nyi vopros na rasshirennom plenume IKKI" (The Colonial Question at the Enlarged Plenum of the ECCI). *Kommunisticheskii Internatsional* (Communist International), no. 4 (41) (1925): 64–71.

——. "Peregruppirovka sil v Kitae" (The Regrouping of Forces in China). *Pravda* (Truth), March 24, 1926.

——. "Sun Yat-sen i osvoboditel'noe dvizheniie v Kitae" (Sun Yat-sen and the Liberation Movement in China). *Bol'shevik* (Bolshevik), nos. 5–6 (21–22) (1925): 44–52.

——. "Tendentsii revoliutsionnogo dvizheniia v Kitae i Guomindang" (Trends in the Revolutionary Movement in China and the Guomindang). *Kommunisticheskii Internatsional* (Communist International), no. 3 (40) (1925): 153–58.

Volkogonov, Dmitrii. *Trotsky.* 2 vols. Moscow: Novosti, 1992.

Wakeman, Frederic, Jr. *Policing Shanghai 1927–1937.* Berkeley: University of California Press, 1995.

Wang Jianmin. *Zhongguo gongchandang shigao* (A Draft History of the Chinese Communist Party). 3 vols. Taibei: Author Press, 1965.

Wang Jianying, ed. *Zhongguo gongchandang zuzhi shi ziliao huibian—lingdao jigou yange he chengyuan minglu* (Collection of Documents on the History of the CCP Organizations—The Evolution of Leading Organs and Their Personal Composition). Beijing: Hongqi chubanshe, 1983.

Wang Meng. *Bolshevik Salute: A Modernist Chinese Novel.* Trans. Wendy Larson. Seattle: University of Washington Press, 1989.

Wang Shaoguang. *Failure of Charisma: The Cultural Revolution in Wuhan.* Hong Kong: Oxford University Press, 1995.

Wang Shi, ed. *Zhongguo gongchandang lishi jianbian* (Short History of the CCP). Shanghai: Shanghai renmin chubanshe, 1959.

Wang Xingfu. *Linshi sanxiongdi: Lin Yuying, Lin Yunan, Lin Biao* (The Three Lin Brothers: Lin Yuying, Lin Yunan, Lin Biao). Wuhan: Hubei renmin chubanshe, 2004.

Wedeman, Andrew Hall. *The East Wind Subsides: Chinese Foreign Policy and the Origins of the Cultural Revolution.* Washington, DC: Washington Institute Press, 1988.

Wei, Betty Peh-t'i. *Old Shanghai.* Hong Kong: Oxford University Press, 1993.

Wen Fu, and Zhang Naishen. *Mao Zedong yu He Zizhen* (Mao Zedong and He Zizhen). Beijing: Tuanjie chubanshe, 2004.

Wen Songhui. "Mao Zedong chushi Jiang Qing" (Mao Zedong's First Meeting with Jiang Qing). *Renmin zhengxie bao* (Newspaper of the Chinese People's Political Consultative Conference). September 10, 2004.

Westad, Odd Arne, ed. *Brothers in Arms: The Rise and Fall of the Sino-Soviet Alliance, 1945–1963.* Stanford, CA: Stanford University Press, 1998.

———. *Cold War and Revolution: Soviet-American Rivalry and the Origins of the Chinese Civil War, 1944–1946.* New York: Columbia University Press, 1993.

———. "Fighting for Friendship: Mao, Stalin, and the Sino-Soviet Treaty of 1950." *CWIHP Bulletin,* nos. 8–9 (1996/1997): 224–36.

Wittfogel, Karl A. "The Legend of 'Maoism.' " *China Quarterly,* no. 1 (January–March 1960): 72–86; no. 2 (April–June 1960): 16–33.

Wittfogel, Karl A., Benjamin Schwartz, and Henryk Sjaardema. " 'Maoism'—'Legend' or 'Legend of a "Legend" '?" *China Quarterly,* no. 4 (October 1960): 88–101.

Wu Liping. "Wenhua da geming zhongde nü hongweibing" (Women Red Guards in the Great Cultural Revolution). *Ershiyi shiji* (Twenty-first century), no. 68 (2007): 50–67.

Wu Qinjie, ed. *Mao Zedong guanghui licheng dituji* (Atlas of Mao Zedong's Glorious Historical Path). Beijing: Zhongguo ditu chubanshe, 2003.

Wu Zhengyu and Li Jie, eds. *Tusho Mao Zedong* (An Illustrated Biography of Mao Zedong). Beijing: Zhongguo qingnian chubanshe, 2009.

Wylie, Raymond F. *The Emergence of Maoism: Mao Tse-tung, Ch'en Po-ta, and the Search for Chinese Theory 1935–1945.* Stanford, CA: Stanford University Press, 1980.

Xiao Xiaoqin, et al., ed. *Zhonghua renmin gongheguo sishi nian* (Forty Years of the People's Republic of China). Beijing: Beijing shifan xueyuan chubanshe, 1990.

Xin Ziling. *Mao Zedong quanzhuan* (Complete Biography of Mao Zedong). 4 vols. [Hong Kong]: Liwen chubanshe, 1993.

Xu Xiaobing, et al. *Mao Zedongzhi lu—Huashuo Mao Zedong he tade zhunyou* (Mao Zedong's Road—An Illustrated Biography of Mao Zedong and His Comrades-in Arms). Wuhan: Changjiang wenyi chubanshe, 2009.

Xu Yan. "Chaoxian zhanzheng zhong jiaozhan gefang sunshi duoshao junren" (What Are the Casualties of All Sides During the Korean War?). *Wenshi cankao* (History reference). No. 12 (June 2010).

Xu Yuandong, et al. *Zhongguo gongchandang lishi jianghua* (Lectures on the History of the CCP). Beijing: Zhongguo qingnian chubanshe, 1982.

Xu Zehao, ed. *Wang Jiaxiang nianpu, 1906–1974* (Chronological Biography of Wang Jiaxiang, 1906–1974). Beijing: Zhongyang wenxian chubanshe, 2001.

Yang Jisheng. *Mubei: Zhongguo liushi nian dai da jihuang jishi* (Tombstone: Unforgettable Facts about the Great Famine in the 1960s). 2 vols. Hong Kong: Tian di tushu youxian gongsi, 2008.

Yang Kuisong. "Mao Zedong weishenma fangqi xinminzhuyi? Guanyu Eguo moshide yingxiang wenti" (Why Did Mao Zedong Discard New Democracy? On the Influence of the Russian Model). *Jindaishi yanjiu* (Studies in contemporary history), no. 4 (1997): 139–83.

———. "1920–1940 niandai Mosike wei Zhonggong tigong caizheng yuanzhu qingkuang gaishu" (On Moscow's Financial Aid to the CCP in the 1920–40s). *Ershiyi shiji* (The twenty-first century), no. 27 (2004): 1–18; 28 (2004): 1–17.

———. "Obshchaia kharakteristika otnoshenii mezhdu VKP(b) (KPSS), Kominternom i KPK do 1949 goda" (The General Nature of Relations Between the AUCP(b), (the CPSU), the Comintern, and the CCP to 1949), *Problemy Dal'nego Vostoka* (Far Eastern affairs), no. 6 (2004): 99–107.

———. "Sulian da guimo yuanzhu zhongguo hongjun de yici changshi" (Large-Scale Efforts of Soviet Aid to the Chinese Red Army). In Huang Xiurong, ed. *Sulian, gongchanguoji yu zhongguo geming de guanxi xintan* (New Research on [the History of] Relations Between the Soviet Union, the Comintern, and the Chinese Revolution), 324–26. Beijing: Zhonggong dangshi chubanshe, 1995.

———. *Zhonggong yu Mosike guanxi (1920–1960)* (Relations between the CCP and Moscow [1920–1960]). Taibei: Sanmin shuju, 1997.

———. *Zouxiang polie: Mao Zedong yu Mosike enen yuanyuan* (Heading for a Split: Concord and Discord in Relations between Mao Zedong and Moscow). Hong Kong: Sanlian shudian, 1999.

Yang Shengqun, and Yan Jianqi, eds. *Deng Xiaoping nianpu, 1904–1974* (Chronological Biography of Deng Xiaoping, 1904–1974). 3 vols. Beijing: Zhongyang wenxian chubanshe, 2010.

Ye Jianying zhuanlüe (Short Biography of Ye Jianying). Beijing: Junshi kexueyuan chubanshe, 1987.

Ye Yonglie. *Jiang Qing zhuan* (Biography of Jiang Qing). Beijing: Zuojia chubanshe, 1998.

———. *Mao Zedongde mishumen* (Secretaries of Mao Zedong). Shanghai: Shanghai renmin chubanshe, 2005.

Yen Chia-chi, and Kao Kao. *The Ten-Year History of the Chinese Cultural Revolution.* Taipei: Institute of Current China Studies, 1988.

Yuriev, M. F. *Revoliutsiia 1925–1927 gg. v Kitae* (The Revolution of 1925–1927 in China). Moscow: Nauka, 1968.

Zhang Chunhou, and C. Edwin Vaughan. *Mao Zedong as Poet and Revolutionary Leader: Social and Historical Perspectives.* Lanham, MD: Lexington Books, 2002.

Zhang Jingru, et al. *Wusi yilai lishi renwu biming, bieming lu* (Collection of Pen Names and Pseudonyms of Historical People since the May Fourth Movement). Xi'an: Shaanxi renmin chubanshe, 1986.

Zhang Peisen, ed. *Zhang Wentian nianpu* (Chronological Biography of Zhang Wentian). 2 vols. Beijing: Zhongyang wenxian chubanshe, 2000.

Zhang Qiushi. *Qu Qiubai yu gongchan guoji* (Qu Qiubai and the Comintern). Beijing: Zhonggong dangshi chubanshe, 2004.

Zhang Shu Guang. "Between 'Paper' and 'Real Tigers': Mao's View of Nuclear Weapons." In John Lewis Gaddis et al., eds. *Cold War Statesmen Confront the Bomb: Nuclear Diplomacy Since 1945,* 194–215. Oxford: Oxford University Press, 1999.

———. *Mao's Military Romanticism: China and the Korean War, 1950–1953.* Lawrence: University Press of Kansas, 1995.

———. "Rise and Fall of the Sino-Soviet Alliance. 1945–1963," in O. Arne Westad, ed. *Brothers in Arms,* 189–225. Stanford, CA: Stanford University Press, 1998.

Zhanhou zhongsu guanxi zouxiang (1945–1960) (The Development of Sino-Soviet Relations after the War [1945–1960]). Beijing: Shehui kexue wenhua chubanshe, 1997.

Zhao Chang'an, et al. *Lao gemingjiade lian'ai, hunyin he jiating shenghuo* (Love, Marriages, and Family Life of the Old Generation Revolutionaries). Beijing: Gongren chubanshe, 1985.

Zhao Jialiang, and Zhang Xiaoji. *Banjie mubei xiade wangshi: Gao Gang zai Beijing* (A Story Dug from Underneath of a Half-Destroyed Tombstone: Gao Gang in Beijing). Hong Kong: Dafeng chubanshe, 2008.

Zhemchugov, A. A. *Kitaiskaia golovolomka* (A Chinese Puzzle). Moscow: OLMA-Press/ OAO PF "Krasnyi proletarii," 2004.

Zheng Canhui. "Zhongguo Guomindang di yici quanguo daibiao dahui" (The First All-China Congress of the Chinese Guomindang). *Gemingshi ziliao* (Materials on revolutionary history), Shanghai no. 1 (1986): 113–26.

"Zhongguo gongchandang chuangbande di yige youzhiyuan" (The First Orphanage Organized by the CCP). *Xinmin wanbao* (The renovation of people evening newspaper), June 13, 2004.

Zhongguo gongchandang lishi jiangyi (Lectures on CCP History). 2 vols. Changchun: Liaoning renmin chubanshe, 1981.

Zhongguo gongchandang lishi jiangyi (Lectures on CCP History). 2 vols. Jinan: Shandong renmin chubanshe, 1982.

Zhongguo renmin jiefangjun zuzhi yange he geji lingdao chengyuan minglu (Organizational Evolution and Personnel of the Leading Organs at All Levels of the PLA). Beijing: Junshi kexue chubanshe, 1987.

Zhou Enlai nianpu (1898–1949) (Chronological Biography of Zhou Enlai [1898–1949]). Rev. ed. Beijing: Zhongyang wenxian chubanshe, 1998.

Zhou Guoquan, et al. *Wang Ming nianpu* (Chronological Biography of Wang Ming). [Hefei]: Anhui renmin chubanshe, 1991.

Zhou Xiaozhou zhuan (Biography of Zhou Xiaozhou). Changsha: Hunan renmin chubanshe, 1985.

Zhou Yiping. *Mao Zedong shenghuo yanjiu qishinian* (Seventy Years of Study of Mao Zedong's Life). Taiyuan: Shanxi renmin chubanshe, 1993.

Zhu De nianpu (Chronological Biography of Zhu De). Beijing: Renmin chubanshe, 1986.

Zhu Jiamu, ed. *Chen Yun nianpu: 1905–1995* (Chronological Biography of Chen Yun: 1905–1995). 3 vols. Beijing: Zhongyang wenxian chubanshe, 2000.

Zhu Ruizhen. "Zhongsu fenliede genyuan" (Causes of the Sino-Soviet Split). In *Zhanhou zhongsu guanxi zuoxiang (1945–1960)* (The Development of Sino-Soviet Relations After the War [1945–1960]), 91–116. Beijing: Shehui kexue wenhua chubanshe, 1997.

Zhu Weiyang. "Qian Xijun he Mao Zemin" (Qian Xijun and Mao Zemin). In *Mao Zedong de jiashi* (Mao Zedong's Family Affairs), 14–15. Beijing: Chunqiu chubanshe, 1987.

Zhuangzi. *The Complete Works of Chuang Tsu*. Translated by Burton Watson. New York: Columbia University Press, 1968.

Zou Lu. *Zhongguo guomindang shigao* (An Outline History of the Chinese Guomindang). Changsha: Minzhi shuju, 1931.

INDEX

AB Corps (AB *tuan*), 240–44
Abakumov, Viktor, 367
Africa, 222
  communist organizations in, 88
agrarian reform, 392, 395–96, 413, 420, 585
  crisis of underproduction under, 413
  overpopulation and, 413
  rural hunger and, 414, 417
Agrarian Reform Law, 395–96
agrarian revolution, 136, 175, 178, 179,
    182–83, 191–93, 194–96, 212, 216,
    218–19, 224, 239, 240, 252*n*, 254, 304,
    320, 392, 415, 583
  in USSR, 223, 227
agriculture, 483, 585
  collectivization of, *see* collectivization
  cooperativization of, *see* cooperatives;
    cooperativization
  growth in production, 442, 449–52, 454
  household contracts and, 478–80, 483–85
  socialist transformation of, 403
  see also grain
Aisenberg, Arnold, 317
Al'brecht, Alexander, 206–7
Aleksandrov-Agentov, Andrei, 537
All-China Conference on Financial and
    Economic Work, 397–99, 400, 402, 403
All-China Federation of Trade Unions
    (ACFTU), 219, 336, 395
All-China Peasant Association, 177
All-China Secretariat of Trade Unions, 109,
    111
All-China Workers' Secretariat, Hunan, 108,
    109
American Observer Group, 344
amyotrophic lateral sclerosis (ALS, Lou
    Gehrig's disease), 565, 587
An Lushan, 428
Analects (Confucius), 14–15

"Analysis of Classes in Chinese Society"
    (Mao), 151–52, 177*n*
"Analysis of Various Classes of the Chinese
    Peasantry and Their Relationship to
    Revolution" (Mao), 157
anarchism, 94, 99, 520
  Chinese, 60, 64, 73, 76, 108
  as counterrevolutionary, 561
  French study abroad program and, 53–54,
    91
  Japanese, 64
anarcho-syndicalism, 64
Anderson, Mr., *see* Maring
Andreev, Andrei, 302
angioneurosis, 370
Anhui province, 63, 88, 285, 484, 494
  communists in, 112, 221
  famine in, 461, 472, 475
  household contracts in, 478–80, 483
  soviet in, 248
Anqing (Huaining), 63
anti-imperialism, 52, 113–14, 115, 119, 120,
    121–22, 126, 132, 135, 138, 144, 145,
    148, 151, 152, 154, 166, 167, 231–32,
    357, 366, 574
Anti-Japanese Military-Political University,
    318
anti-rightist movement, 442–43
Anting railroad station, 515
Anyuan, 109, 110–12, 120, 140, 197, 200,
    336
  communism in, 123
  Guomindang cell in, 129
  workers' club in, 110
arbitration commissions, 111
Argentina, 505
Aristov, Averkii Borisovich, 444
Armed Forces Ministry, Soviet, 368
Art of War, The (Sun Zi), 279

Asia, 222
  Central, 539
  communist organizations in, 88
  East, 556
Assembly of Workers, Peasants, and Soldiers'
    Deputies, 202
Association for the Revival of Hunan, 87
August First Declaration, 294
Australia, 474, 566
automobiles, 57–58
Autumn Harvest Uprising, 192, 194–98,
    200–201, 207–8, 584

Bai Fan, 242
Bai Huizhang, 278
Baiaderka, 445
baihua (common speech), 59
Bakunin, Mikhail, 64
Ban Gu, 27
Bancang, 96, 141, 195, 198–99, 249
Band, Claire and William, 343
bandits, 171, 193, 202–3, 206, 212, 220, 247,
    260, 584
  Red Army as, 221
Bank of China, 513
Bao Huisen, 102
Baoan, 2, 296, 299, 301, 302, 304, 305
Baoding, 54, 65
barracks communism, 8
Barrett, David D., 344
Barvikha Sanatorium, 355
Beida Student Union, 66
Beidaihe, 432, 551
Beijing, 2, 5, 49, 54, 65, 66, 67, 77, 82, 85, 87,
    90, 115, 127, 134, 143, 378, 389, 395,
    397, 400, 406, 407, 409, 418, 419, 431,
    466, 482, 491, 492, 493, 494, 497, 502,
    507, 511, 518, 519, 521, 526, 528, 530,
    531, 534, 537, 558, 562, 564, 566, 567,
    569, 572, 573
  in Boxer Rebellion, 24
  characteristics of, 57–58
  communism in, 92, 100, 101, 102, 108, 123
  food shortages in, 461, 472
  Forbidden City in, 3, 6, 24, 57, 58, 69, 359,
    365, 571, 573
  Khrushchev in, 409–11, 467, 469, 473
  Legation Quarter in, 69
  Mao as out of place in, 65–66, 68
  Mao in, 55, 56–59, 73, 79–80, 363
  as PRC capital, 356, 358–59, 390
  Red Guards in, 511, 516, 530
  renamed Beiping, 216
  student protests in, 69–70, 71
  Summer Palace in, 58
  Three-Eyed Well district of, 57, 59
Beijing Commune, 502

Beijing Garrison, 392
Beijing Military Region, 549
Beijing Municipal Party Committee, 402, 493,
    494, 496, 502, 505–6, 508, 522
  student takeover of, 522
  United Front Work Department of, 497
Beijing Normal Universal, Red Guards from,
    513
Beijing No. 6 Middle School, 511
Beijing Revolutionary Committee, 522
Beijing-Hankou railroad, 161, 184*n*
Beiping (Beijing), 287, 350, 351, 356
  CCP's restoration of name Beijing to, 359
  Japanese capture of, 315
  Japanese forces outside, 312
  PLA capture of, 351–52, 585
Beiyang Army, 34, 44
Beiyang Political-Legal Academy, 59
Bengfu, 494
Berger, Harry, *see* Ewert, Arthur Ernst
Bergson, Henri, 84
Beria, Lavrentii, 384, 387, 401–2, 408, 410
Bewhiskered He, *see* He Shuheng
Bhutto, Ali, 571
Biography of the Ever Faithful Yue Fei, The, 20
Birkmayer, Walter, 572
Bisson, T. A., 343
Black Sea, 379
Bliukher, Vasilii, 139, 155, 158, 188
Bo Gu (Qin Bangxian), ix, 235, 249, 273, 278,
    284, 302, 313, 314, 333–34, 340, 575
  Mao opposed by, 252–53, 256–57, 262–67,
    269–72, 276, 281
  Mao's reconciliation with, 290
  Mao's supplanting of, 277, 278–79
  in right column, 287, 289
  Wang Ming supported by, 321
Bo Yibo, ix, 394
  criticized as moderate, 398, 420
  as Finance Minister, 396–97
Bodhisattva Guan Yin, 12, 20
Bogomolov, Dmitrii, 297, 312
Bol'shakov, Ivan, 401
Bolshevik Revolution, 81, 97, 192, 456
  China's version of, 196
Bolsheviks, Bolshevism, 4, 61–62, 64, 73–74,
    77, 81–84, 87, 91, 97, 210, 227, 332, 353,
    418, 423, 500
  archive of, 4
  in China, 88, 89, 92–97, 102, 104–5, 108,
    113, 141, 339, 575
  cynicism of, 151
  in the East, 103–4
  and eternal suspicion, 284
  philosophy of, 317–19
  in Russia, 113, 116, 119, 126, 127, 150, 154,
    312, 316

Russian, 575
socialist revolution and, 104
Bolshoi Theater, 369, 445
Bony, L. D., 414
Border Area Soviet Government of Workers,
Peasants, and Soldiers, 212
Borodin, Mikhail Markovich (Bao Luoting;
Baoguwen; Mikhail Markovich
Gruzenberg), ix, 126–28, 134, 136–38,
140, 175, 179, 183, 185
Chiang opposed by, 164–65
on Guomindang, 135, 154, 156, 157, 161,
311
report on Mao to Stalin, 354–55
Stalin's lack of trust in, 188
bourgeois intellectuals, 442, 511
bourgeois-democratic revolution, 104, 217,
219, 318
bourgeoisie, 115, 121, 132, 157, 193, 229, 315,
357, 369, 399, 441, 498
campaigns against, 392–93, 585
in class conflict, 105
democracy and, 104, 219
dictatorship of, 498
economic weakening of, 393
and government buyouts, 422
Guomindang, 123–24, 149, 182
ideology of, 406
Mao's analysis of, 152
national, 342
party infiltration by, 498, 499, 508–9
peasant petit, 241
petty, 148, 150, 219, 221, 463
revolutionary movement "betrayed" by,
217
Boxer Rebellion, 24–25, 69
Boxers, 24–25
Brandt, Conrad, 3
Braun, Otto (K. O. Wagner), ix, 268–70,
272–73, 281, 543n
Li Lilian's marriage to, 326–27
on Long March, 275–76, 282, 286
Mao's supplanting of, 277, 278–79, 326
on Wayaobao, 289
on Xi'an Incident, 299–300
on Yan'an, 305
Brezhnev, Leonid Ilich, ix, 537–38
Brezhnev Doctrine, 538
Bu Shiji, 134n
Bucharest, 473, 474
Budapest, 436
Buddhism, 11, 12, 14, 18, 20, 84
Bukharin, Nikolai Ivanovich, ix, 125, 175,
188, 223, 258, 426
Bulganin, Nikolai, 368, 369, 384, 394n, 436,
439, 443
Bulgaria, 7, 291, 353, 436

bureaucratic capital, 357
bureaucratism:
intraparty, 441
opposition to, 440
Burlatsky, Fedor, 474
Burma, 27
Butcher Tang, see Tang Xiangming

Cai Chang (Rosa Nikolaeva), 321
Cai Hesen (Cailin Bin; Cailin Hexian), ix, 6,
12, 38, 40, 50–54, 65, 92, 109, 115, 119,
123, 124, 138, 140, 183, 187, 193, 217,
250, 321
execution of, 256
as Mao's closest friend, 180
separation between Xiang Jingyu and,
146–47
Cai Yuanpei, 53–54, 58–60, 199
Cambodia, 556
Canada, 474, 505, 566
Canton, 23, 54, 79, 101, 103, 107, 113–15,
120–21, 122, 126, 127, 128, 133, 136,
138, 139, 141, 147, 163, 177, 181, 190,
256, 407, 431, 495, 541, 543, 583
atmosphere and character of, 131–32
Canton Commune uprising in, 205
at center of anti-imperialist struggle, 144
Chiang's coup in, 154–56, 178–80
communism in, 100, 101, 112, 120, 131
Guomindang government in, 140, 143,
150, 159–60, 161, 352, 353, 583
Japanese defeat of, 330
Canye School, 51
Cao Pi, emperor of Wei, 55
Cao Rulin, 69–70, 73
Cao Xueqin, 59
Cao Yi'ou (Lina), 316
capital, private ownership of, 103
Capital (Marx), 90, 127, 354
capital construction, 430
capitalism, capitalists, 95, 99, 332, 398, 421,
479
aggression and Western, 22, 258
in China, 17, 23, 36, 157
class relations under, 152
compensation given to, 422
dangers of, 486
in Europe, 383
Great Depression and, 228–29
overthrow of, 103
peaceful transition to socialism from, 427
and people's democracy, 358
restoration of, 494, 500
state, 421–22
taxation and, 396–97, 399
tendencies towards, 416
workers exploited by, 61

capitalist industry, 403
capitalist roaders, 489, 501, 510, 511, 512, 527,
    529, 531, 569
  Liu and allies seen as, 492, 508
  Red Guard killings of suspected, 511
  unmasking of, 500
capitulationism, 567
Carlson, Evans, 320–21, 343
caves, 306, 348, 355
  as residences for CCP leaders, 289, 304,
    318
Central Chamber of Commerce, Beijing, 70
Central Committee of CCP, 4, 5, 180, 183,
    188, 209, 213, 215, 224, 239, 256, 261,
    264, 275, 305, 310, 316, 319, 323, 334,
    336, 340, 342, 351, 381, 432, 479, 501,
    519, 522, 530, 543, 560, 562, 564, 567,
    569, 570, 584, 587
  abolition of general secretary position of,
    509
  Action Committee, 197–98
  adventurism by, 255
  Braun as military adviser to, 269
  Bureau for the Soviet areas of, 237, 238,
    255
  Bureau of, 254, 256, 257–58, 259, 261, 262,
    263, 264, 265–66
  Central China Bureau of, 336
  Central South Bureau of, 397
  Changjian (Yangzi River) Bureau of, 321
  Comintern critique of, 233–37
  Comintern's special resolution on right
    opportunism to, 258–59
  Defense Industry Committee, 519
  Department of Agitation and Propaganda
    of, 230
  ECCI criticism of, 233–34
  ECCI personnel recommendations
    regarding, 333–34
  Eighth Plenum of, 437
  Extraordinary Conference of, 190
  First Plenum following the Seventh
    Congress of, 342
  Five-Member Cultural Revolution Group
    in, 493, 495–98
  Fourth Plenum of, 333, 335, 336, 404, 405
  Front Committee of, 197–98, 206, 207,
    211, 224, 225, 226
  General Affairs Department of, 498
  grain monopoly introduced by, 413–14
  Guomindang CEC approached by, 303–4
  Hunan Committee's request for aid to,
    189
  Internal Liaison Department of, 436
  intraparty conflict in, 281
  Investigation Bureau of, 337
  Korean War and, 381–82

Liu Shaoqi's accusation against Mao at,
    479–80
Lominadze's criticism of, 188–95
Mao as chairman of, 461
Mao as general secretary of, 323
Mao criticized by, 231, 584
Mao on, 180, 218, 583, 584
Mao on agrarian reform to, 195–96
Mao supported by, 244, 246
on Mao-Zhu troop unification, 210
Mao's sons sent to Soviet Union by, 250–51
membership of, 533–34
Mif's dominance of, 235–36
Military Affairs Council of, 466
Military Committee of, 189, 191, 206, 523,
    534, 561
Military Council of the, 342
Military Department of, 224
Ninth, 538
North China Bureau of, 510
Northeast Bureau of, 549
Office of, 464
Organizational Department of, 313,
    336–37, 405, 517
on peasant question, 223
people's communes and, 477
plenum on education of, 550
Politburo of, 182, 183, 193, 205, 231,
    233–37, 244, 246–48, 252, 255, 268, 270,
    276–79, 281, 285, 286, 288, 289, 291,
    292, 302, 312, 314, 317, 318, 321, 333,
    335–37, 340, 342, 346, 356, 366, 382–84,
    402–3, 405, 417, 418, 427, 428, 430–32,
    435, 439, 449, 455, 462, 482, 497, 498,
    501, 509, 516, 523, 525, 526, 535, 541,
    543, 546, 561, 562, 564–66, 568, 569,
    572, 584, 585, 586, 587
Politburo Standing Committee of, 183, 187,
    234, 270, 279–80, 303, 314, 316, 464,
    476, 481, 495, 496, 497, 498–99, 508,
    509, 521, 529, 535, 543, 548, 564, 567,
    584
Politburo Work Conference of, 492
Propaganda Committee of, 496
Propaganda Department of, 349, 405–6,
    495, 502, 505
Provisional Bureau of, 187, 190, 191
Provisional Politburo of, 194, 197, 205–6,
    217, 255, 256, 258, 259, 262, 263, 264,
    266, 584
Publication and Literature Distribution
    Department of, 181
radical change to, 534
Red Army and, 190, 210, 222, 223, 226–32,
    239–40, 241, 243–44
Red Guard resolution in, 511
Red Guards and, 513, 514, 522

relocation to Yan'an by, 304–5
resolution on cooperatives adopted by, 416–17
right column supported by, 287
Rural Work Department of, 415, 416, 417, 418, 484
Russian domination of, 185
Second Plenum of the Seventh, 341, 358
Second Plenum of the Tenth, 567
Second Session of the First Plenum of, 342
secret section of, 247
Secretariat of, 273, 333, 335, 336, 342, 391, 393, 436, 509, 585
Seventh Enlarged Plenum of, 340
Shanghai Bureau of, 448
Sixth Enlarged Plenum of, 324, 326n, 419
South Hunan Committee of, 194
South Hunan Military Department of, 206
Special Hunan Provincial Committee, 210
Special Work Committee of, 247, 250
Special Xiang District Committee, 120–21
Stalin's mistrust of, 394
Standing Committee of, 28, 235, 286
Standing Committee of the bureau for the soviet areas, 244
struggle against Japan supported by, 291
students and teachers at plenum of, 507–8
technical secretariat of, 191, 267–68
Third Enlarged Plenum of, 442, 450
United Front Department of, 402
Working Committee of, 350
Central Committee Special Sector, 311
Central Cultural Revolution Group, 498–502, 509, 514, 522–27, 529–30, 534, 549
  Jiang as head of, 516, 547
  Shanghai branch of, 500
Central Europe, communist parties in, 7
Central Executive Committee (CEC), CSR, 251, 255–56, 260, 271, 273, 275, 294, 584
Central Executive Committee (CEC), Guomindang, 134, 142–44, 153–54, 156, 163, 312
  CCP proposal to cooperate against Japan with, 296–97
  Chiang's anti-leftist speech to, 155–56
  Land Committee of, 178, 179
  Mao's medical leave from, 140
  Mao's return to, 148
  Organizational Department of, 156, 583
  Peasant Department of, 152, 156, 159
  on peasant question, 164–65
  Political Council of, 161, 301
  Propaganda Department of, 140, 143, 148, 153, 156, 158, 162, 180, 583
  Standing Committee of the, 153, 155, 177–78, 301

Third Plenum of the, 176–77
  Workers' Department of, 144
Central Peasant Training Institute, 177, 182
Central People's Government Council of the PRC, 391, 543
Central Red Army, 278, 281, 283, 284
Central Revolutionary Military Council (CRMC), 237–38, 244, 251, 256, 275, 281, 285, 290
  General Political Administration of, 256, 258
Central Soviet Area (CSA), 244, 251, 255, 256, 257, 263, 266, 268, 272, 277, 285, 290, 584
  dismissal of Mao's relatives from positions in, 267
  Long March from, 273–74, 283, 288
  retreat from, 278–79
centralized planning, 366
Chairman Mao Memorial Hall, 574, 575
Chang Jung, 5
Chang'an, 497
Changchun, 257
Changde, 79
Changsha, 1, 11, 30, 31–33, 36–37, 39, 45, 47, 48, 52, 56, 65, 74, 77, 78, 80, 88, 90, 91, 114, 132, 140, 141, 159, 163, 176, 183, 190, 197, 198, 199, 200, 201, 208, 252, 327, 336, 431, 495, 550, 566, 567, 584
  anti-imperialism in, 145
  communism in, 100, 101, 102, 108, 123, 166–67, 186
  Guomindang destruction of Hunan party committee in, 206
  Guomindang organizing in, 128–29, 167, 186
  insurrection in, 19
  Mao in, 68, 71, 166–67, 172, 174
  Mao's organizing in, 95–96, 98–99, 110, 112, 120, 122, 583
  NRA attack on, 182
  Red Army seizure of, 231, 234
  strikes in, 108
  Xu's coup in, 182, 185, 194
Changsha-Wuchang railroad, 120
Changxingdian railroad station, 123
Chao Chao, Tanya, see Li Min
Chen, "bloodsucker," 145
Chen Bilan, 147
Chen Boda, ix, 331, 351, 368, 427, 454, 484, 495, 499, 547, 548, 549
  in Cultural Revolution, 501, 505, 508, 509, 514, 523, 524–26, 532, 535
  imprisonment of, 576
  loyalty of, 487
  mass media controlled by, 544
Chen Changhao, 333–34

Chen Congying (Zheng Song), 321
Chen Duxiu (T. S. Chen; Tu-siu Chen; the
    Old Man), ix, 72, 82, 83, 88, 89–90,
    91–93, 95–96, 100–102, 103, 106,
    121–22, 123, 124, 128, 129, 134, 135,
    140, 146–48, 162, 163, 180, 182, 183,
    193, 194, 340
  arrest of, 73
  Borodin supported by, 179
  on Chiang's coup, 155–56
  conversion to communism of, 81
  departure from Peking University of, 79
  on Guomindang alliance, 107–8, 111–12,
    113–16, 119–20, 123–24, 133, 137–39
  as hampered by Comintern, 185, 187
  Mao's opposition to cautious policies of,
    191
  October directive followed by, 165–66
  at Peking University, 59–60, 63–65
  retirement from power of, 187, 191
  Right opportunism of, 325
Chen Fen, 592
Chen Gongbo, 66, 105–6
Chen Guang, 334
Chen Jiongming, 100–101, 107, 115, 120, 125
Chen Shaoyu, see Wang Ming
Chen Tianhua, 27
Chen Wangdao, 81, 91
Chen Yannian, 162, 187
Chen Yi, ix, 225, 226, 334, 374, 542–43
  death of, 554, 555
  opposition to Red Guards by, 522–23,
    524–26, 534–35
  Soviets criticized by, 468–69
Chen Yu (Polevoi), 6, 248
Chen Yuandao, 235
Chen Yun (Liao Chenyun), x, 266, 281, 291,
    316, 318, 405, 411, 426, 435–36, 464,
    476, 509n
  on Great Leap Forward, 478, 479, 482–84,
    485
  as moderate, 396–97, 430, 434, 438
Chen Zaidao, x, 528–29
Chen Zuoxin, 33–34
Chenbao (Morning news), 134
Cheng Qian, 176–77
Chengdu, 54, 337, 522
  Guomindang government in, 352
Chervonenko, Stepan, 540
Chiang Ching-kuo (Nikolai Vladimirovich
    Elizarov), 181, 312
Chiang Kai-shek, x, 151, 163, 176, 183, 312,
    332, 337, 343, 375n, 388, 462, 479, 498,
    559, 565, 571, 583, 585
  arrest of, 298–304, 528
  assassination attempt against, 247
  attack on Jiangxi by, 240

broad attack launched by, 348
Canton coup of, 154–55, 158
CCP opposed by, 294, 297, 298, 350–54,
    377, 584
  in clashes between NRA and worker-
    peasant forces, 178
  as commandant of Guomindang Army, 138
  as commander of NRA First Corps, 144
  conflict with Guomindang left by, 176–77
  counterrevolution of, 180–81
  death of, 302
  defeat of, 352, 358
  domestic policies of, 352
  Japanese invasion of Manchuria not
    contested by, 257
  Mao opposed by, 2, 243, 249, 291, 313
  Mao's and Stalin's negotiations with,
    346–47
  military successes of, 143, 152–53
  on mission to USSR, 127, 154
  National government established in
    Nanjing by, 179
  Northern Expedition and, 158–60, 216
  opposition to, 159, 164–65
  power consolidated by, 216
  power struggle between Tang and, 175
  Provisional Central Political Council
    founded by, 166
  Red Army fought by, 245–46, 268, 272,
    276, 296, 297–98
  rightward evolution of, 154–55, 158, 164
  shortsighted USSR policy of, 347
  Soviet aid to, 312, 315
  Soviet nonaggression treaty of, 313
  Stalin's insistence that CCP work with,
    296–97
  in Taiwan, 460
  united front policy and, 296–97, 312–15,
    317, 321
  Voitinsky's talks with, 166
  Zhang's forces attacked by, 285
Chicherin, Georgy, 127
Chief Medical Administration, 273
children, 209
China:
  in 19th century, xx–xxi
  ancient, 27, 497
  anti-foreign sentiments in, 32
  anti-Japanese feelings in, 290–91
  antimonarchical revolution in, 32–33
  archives in, 4
  civil society absent in, 23
  civil war in, 346–59, 377, 378, 388, 391–92,
    527, 544, 585
  class structure of, 151–52
  despotic monarchy in, 30
  dialects in, 28–29

divided territory of, 345
eastern, 351
economic modernization of, 354
economy of, 24, 34, 59, 202, 229, 352, 372, 407, 412, 422, 574
federalism for, 87–88
India's border conflict with, 467–68
industrialization and modernization of, 22
infancy traditions in, 12–13
inflation in, 352
liberalism in, 35–36
liberation movement in, 331
literature of, 19–20
under Mao, xxiv–xxv
as militarized, 186–87
military power in, 80, 112
modernization of, 358
national debt of, 25
National Government of, 2
national revival in, 37
nationalism in, 104, 401
nationalist revolution in, 144
North, 24, 287, 347
Northeast, 346, 347, 372, 470, 472, 538
patriarchal society in, 122
patriotism in, 290–91
peasant revolution in, 3
personal connections important in, 89
polygamy in, 209
population of, 428
poverty in, 132
power in, 83
public executions in, 19
puritanical social norms in, 309
reform movements in, 23, 25, 27, 29, 32, 33, 50, 52, 98, 393
revolutionary organizations in, 24
semicolonial economic dependency in, 22, 25, 43, 216, 232, 331, 574
South, 11, 22, 100–101, 107, 114, 120, 128, 131, 132, 154
sovereignty of, 458
split between communist parties in Soviet Union and, 3, 7
tariffs of, 22
traditional cultural values of, 8
traditional laws in, 202
transformation of, 98–99
unification of, 160, 574
united front policy for, see united front policy
war industry in, 316
see also People's Republic of China (PRC); Republic of China
China Revival Society (Xingzhonghui), 23–24
Chinese Anarchist Group, Paris, 53
Chinese Changchun Railroad, 372
Chinese Communist Party (CCP), 1, 2, 3, 5, 6, 39, 53, 63, 110, 111, 142, 167, 181, 203, 210, 283, 285, 292, 327, 388, 399, 406, 440, 473, 519, 527, 536, 539, 541, 573, 575
adventurist policies of, 205, 233
All-China Conference of, 405
anti-Japanese stance of, 290–91
autonomy and self-reliance of, 2
base areas established behind Japanese lines by, 331
Beijing name restored by, 359
"bourgeois degeneration" in, 491
cadres in, 325
canonical history of, 325–26, 335–36, 339, 340, 342
Central Bureau of, 106, 112, 113, 162, 165, 174, 180, 270
Central Committee of, see Central Committee of CCP
Central Executive Committee of (CEC), 106, 114, 115, 116, 119, 121, 124, 126, 128, 136–37, 139, 140, 146–47, 148, 158, 162, 167, 174, 176, 178, 179
on Chiang's arrest, 299–300
children of leaders in, 209
Committee on the Peasant Movement of, 161–63, 181
defeat of, 183, 185–86
deteriorating situation in, 181–83
dictatorship of, 427, 441, 444
distancing from USSR by, 319–21
Eighth Congress of, 432, 435, 440, 450, 456, 534, 586
emancipation of consciousness in, 428
establishment of, 37, 66
European branch of, 29, 134, 138, 140
execution of Northern Bureau leaders in, 182
Executive Committee Plenum of, 129
false self-accusations by members of, 407
Fifth Congress of, 177, 179–80, 583
Fifth Plenum of, 325
financial dependence on Moscow by, 6, 116, 135–36
First Congress of, 50, 100–106, 108, 113, 583
founders of, 18, 276
Fourth Congress of, 139–40, 180
free love and conflicts within, 146–47
Guomindang alliance and, see united front policy
at Guomindang conference, 133–34
Guomindang conflict with, 302, 347–48
Hunan committee of, 112
ideological foundations of, 441

Chinese Communist Party (CCP) (*cont.*)
  intraparty conflicts in, 209, 267, 285, 319,
    321–24, 332–42, 480–83, 541–42
  Japan opposed by, 294
  Kremlin policy for, 148–49
  leaders of, 289
  left opportunism and, 325, 335, 357, 415,
    526
  Mao as main leader of, 322–26
  Mao criticized by, 217–19
  Mao on militarization and, 196–97
  Mao Zedong as ideological foundation of,
    340–42
  Mao's advocacy of a military force for,
    186–87
  Mao's control over, 330
  Mao's desire to radicalize policy of, 181–83
  Mao's provocation within, 481
  Mao's rise to power in, 7, 211, 218
  Mao's speeches to, 36–37
  membership of, 122–23, 129, 180, 205, 217
  Nanchang Uprising sponsored by, 189–90
  as nationalist force, 260
  need to win masses over to, 217
  new party constitution of, 340–41, 342, 564
  Ninth Congress of, 534, 562
  Ninth Party Congress of, 542
  Organizational Department of, 124
  Party Statutes of, 492
  peasants and, 164, 417, 420, 421
  political changes in, 112–14
  and position of USSR in world arena, 343
  principles of, 102–3, 106
  proletarian resistance to, 422
  purge of, 335–40, 585
  putschism condemned by, 217–18, 228,
    340
  radio link reestablished with Moscow by,
    296
  rectification campaign for, 438
  rewards for leaders of, 272
  right opportunism in, 314, 325, 415, 465
  rumors of Mao's expulsion from, 207
  rupture between Guomindang and, 183,
    185–90
  Second Congress of, 114–16, 122
  secret archives of, 4
  self-criticism in, 481–82
  Seventh Congress of, 316*n*, 323, 333–34,
    337, 340–42, 394*n*, 585
  shaming as tactic of, 227
  Shanghai Bureau of, 417–18
  Sixth Congress of, 193, 217–20, 584
  Soviet control over, 155–56, 163, 178, 185,
    187–88, 194, 197, 205, 318; *see also*
    Communist International, CCP
    dominated by

Soviet funding of, 151, 188–89, 228, 248,
    293, 296, 311, 334, 346
Soviet Union seen as not influencing,
    344–45
special commission on the Futian Incident
    of, 244
Special Xiang District Committee of, 112
Stalinization of, 47, 323–24, 356
struggle against Guomindang by, 260
tensions in, 163
Tenth Congress of, 562, 564
Third Congress of, 122–25, 132, 134, 583
transformation of Chinese society by, 422
united front policy of, 114–16, 119,
    294–304, 311–21, 322–23, 328, 332
unofficial Moscow visit by delegation from,
    356
uprisings policy of, 217–18
victory of, 352–53, 359
withdrawal from Guomindang of, 204
Zhang Xueliang and, 296
zhengfeng movement in, 406
"Chinese Communist Party and China's Path
    to Liberation, The" (Wang Jiaxiang), 341
Chinese Communist Youth League, 136–37,
    142, 181, 191, 218–19, 235, 241, 263,
    279, 345
  Archives of, 4
  Central Committee of, 228, 485
  in Hunan, 171
  Soviet funding of, 248
  see also Socialist Youth League
Chinese Eastern Railroad, 346
Chinese Mint, 69
Chinese People's Liberation Army (PLA), 348,
    465, 471, 532, 534, 538, 542, 550, 553
  Air Force of, 546, 548, 549
  in continuing civil war, 392
  Cultural Revolution and, 502, 532
  Deng and, 565
  fervor of, 352
  Fourth Field Army of, 543
  General Political Administration of, 511
  Korean War and, 378, 387
  lack of technology and arms of, 351
  Mao Zedong Thought in, 488
  order restored by, 532, 535, 586
  purge of former Guomindang officers in,
    392
  Red Guards and Rebels supported by, 511,
    521, 522, 524
  in revolutionary committees, 531
  rightist officers in, 528, 529
  size of, 350, 351
  Tibet captured by, 396*n*
Chinese People's Political Consultative
    Council (CPPCC), 395

All-China Committee of, 396, 404
Chinese People's Volunteer Army (CPVA),
    382–87
  Mao Anying's death in, 387–89
"Chinese Revolution and the Chinese
    Community Party" (Mao et. al), 331
Chinese Revolutionary Alliance (Zhongguo
    geming tongmenghui), *see*
    Revolutionary Alliance
Chinese Revolutionary Military Council,
    237*n*, 336
Chinese Revolutionary Party, 333
Chinese Society for Frugal Study in France,
    53–54
Chinese Soviet Republic (CSR), 251, 271,
    273
  Central Executive Committee of, *see*
    Central Executive Committee
  Chiang's plan to exterminate, 272
  constitutional program of, 252
  Council of People's Commissars of, *see*
    Council of People's Commissars
  Northwest Office of the Central
    Government of, 290, 313
  Party control of, 256
  struggle against Japan supported by, 291
  war declared on Japan by, 260
Chinese Worker-Peasant Revolutionary
    Army, 584
  General Political Administration of, 258
Chinese Worker-Peasant Revolutionary
    Council, 237*n*
Chongqing, 54, 452
  Guomindang government in, 330–31, 346
  U.S. embassy in, 311
Christianity:
  Boxer Rebellion and, 24
  Taiping Rebellion and, 22
Chronicle of the Shaoshan Mao Clan, 27
Chu, kingdom of, 408
Ci Xi, Empress Dowager of China, 12, 22–25
CIA, 474, 556, 557
Ciano, Count, 295
Ciping, 202, 208, 211
civil aviation, 372
clans:
  Mao, 5, 11–12, 13, 141
  in rural villages, 168–70
  wealthy, 169
class:
  abolition of, 103
  Mao's theorizing of, 168, 294
  in rural China, 168
class enemies, 227, 253, 408
  moderates as, 485
  in party organization, 491
class morality, 41

class struggle, 41, 95, 105, 243, 258, 291, 320,
    492, 527
  in education, 496, 501
  under socialism, 500–501
Class Struggle (Kautsky), 81
class warfare, 555
coal, 407, 456
Cold War, 348, 354
collective leadership, 424, 432
collectivization, 454
  agricultural, 320, 391, 413, 438, 488–89
  as belief of ordinary communists, 420
  dissatisfaction with, 421
  excessive, 478
  pace of, 416
  and people's communes, *see* people's
    communes
  of personal property, 477
  Soviet, 419, 421, 485
Comintern International Organization for
    Aid to Revolutionary Fighters, 250
commerce, socialization of, 403, 585
commodities, 430
Common Program of the Chinese People's
    Political Consultative Council, 395, 407
communism, 38, 81, 99, 352–53, 556
  barracks, 8, 554
  beginnings of true, 454–55, 477
  in China, 89, 92–93, 366, 583
  Chinese national, 448
  elite of, 392
  growth of, 94
  hypocrisy and, 166
  intellectuals in rejection of, 441–42
  liberal, 135, 136
  Mao's conversion to, 77, 81–84, 87–88
  nationalist, 374
  radical vs. moderate, 99
  revolutionary allure of, 105
  in Russia, 83
  Russian, 95, 104
  Soviet, 88
  war, 456
  world, 88–89, 444
Communist Academy, 317
Communist Information Bureau
    (Cominform), 4
Communist International (Comintern), 93,
    153, 160, 183, 191, 194, 195, 248, 269,
    270, 316, 388, 427, 446, 473
  agents of, 5
  agrarian policy of, 223
  anticolonial revolution and, 104
  anti-Japanese sentiment supported by, 291
  attempt to contact by Long Marchers, 287
  battle with Trotskyism in, 140
  Bukharin's dismissal from, 223

Communist International (Comintern) (*cont.*)
  CCP delegation to, 292, 293, 323
  CCP dominated by, 116, 121, 125–26,
    133–38, 140, 163, 171, 175, 179, 185,
    187–89, 217–19, 223, 228–29, 233–37,
    243–44, 248, 258–59, 261, 301–4, 318,
    323, 332–35, 585
  Chiang and, 127
  Chiang's arrest and, 300–304
  and Chinese communism, 88–89
  Chinese loyalists to, 249
  Congress of the Peoples of the Far East
    sponsored by, 113
  CP dominated by, 266
  critiques of Mao by, 205
  emissaries of, 266
  Executive Committee (ECCI) of, *see*
    Executive Committee of the Comintern
  First Congress of the, 81
  Fourth World Congress of, 119, 134
  funding by, 247–48
  German-Japanese pact against, 301
  Guomindang alliance supported by, 107–8,
    111–16, 119, 138
  Guomindang and, 151, 153–54, 175
  internationalism supported by, 104
  on Manchurian invasion, 258
  Mao supported by, 7, 236–37, 265–66
  Mao's cult of personality initiated by,
    291–93
  New Epoch funded by, 105
  Politburo of, 294
  Presidium of, 322
  radicalization of policy of, 227–29
  reliance on masses not military by, 192
  representatives to CCP from, 100–106,
    107–8
  rightist danger feared by, 258
  Second Congress of, 100, 103, 104
  secret archives of, 4
  Seventh Congress of, 7, 291–93
  Sixth Congress of, 154, 265
  Smedley and, 306
  Stalin's control of, 6–7
  Stalin's dissolution of, 332
  Stalin's plans for show trial for, 426
  united front policy of, 294
  Youth, 219
  Zhang Guotao thought well of in, 284
Communist Manifesto, The (Marx and Engels),
  60, 81–82, 91, 95
Communist Party, German, 265
Communist Party of the Soviet Union
  (CPSU), 4, 304, 332, 334, 367, 388, 401,
  438, 460, 536
  Central Committee of, 356, 408, 409, 435,
    436, 444, 458, 536, 542
  China's alienation from, 486, 586
  and Chinese response to Eastern European
    crisis, 436
  Department of Socialist Countries of the
    Central Committee of, 538
  Khrushchev's leadership of, 408, 409
  Khrushchev's ouster and, 489
  Nineteenth Congress of, 391
  Presidium of Central Committee of,
    436–37, 444, 537
  purges of, 335
  Twentieth Congress of, 424–27, 437
Communist Party of the USA (CPUSA),
  306
Communist University of the Toilers of
  China (KUTK), 228, 234, 235–36, 284
Communist University of the Toilers of the
  East (KUTV), 123, 134*n*, 146–47, 149,
  191, 210, 336
Communist Youth International, 136
communists, popularity of, 453
Confucianism, 14–15, 21, 31, 32, 52, 55, 59,
  77, 330, 393, 456, 514, 563
  opposition to, 59
Confucius, 14–15, 20, 84, 304, 327, 405, 431,
  491, 513, 557
  Lin Biao's interest in, 562–63, 567
Congress of the Peoples of the Far East, 113,
  114
Constitution of 1912, 332
Constitution of the People's Republic of
  China, 407–8, 492, 546, 585
constitutional monarchy, 21, 23, 29–30, 34, 39
consumer goods, state control of, 414, 421
Contemporary Socialism (Shinzō), 60
cooperatives:
  higher-stage ("socialist"), 420, 477
  large, *see* people's communes
  lower-level agricultural producers', 412,
    415
  moderates on, 415, 417, 418
  nonviable, 415–16, 417, 418, 419
  peasant resistance to, 417, 418
cooperativization:
  of agriculture, 391, 396, 412, 415–21
  tempo of, 416–20, 425
cotton, 407
  state monopoly on, 414
Council of Ministers of the USSR, 368, 408
Council of People's Commissars, 251, 252,
  255–56, 260, 270, 271, 273, 275, 584
counterrevolutionaries, 392, 393, 406–7, 408,
  443, 485, 506, 512, 530, 551, 560, 567,
  570, 587
  Liu as, 534
Cressy-Marcks, Violet, 320
Crimea, 355

"Critique of Socialism, A" (Chen Duxiu), 95
Critique of the Gotha Programme, The (Marx),
    81, 95
Cuba, 474
cult of personality, 432, 434–35
    commercialization of Mao's, 574
    Khrushchev's lack of, 489
    of Lei Feng, 488
    of Mao, 291–93, 323, 332, 335–36, 340,
        350–51, 355, 366, 420, 466, 493, 584
    of Stalin, 424–25, 466, 489, 536
    in the USSR, 427
Cultural Book Society, 90, 98
Cultural Revolution, 7–8, 366, 507–38, 540,
        542, 545, 547–48, 562, 564, 568–69, 571,
        574, 575, 577, 586
    critics of, 522–23
    extension of time for, 512
    initial three-year plan for, 500
    Mao's change of heart on, 529–33
    origins of, 493–501
    rehabilitation of party veterans after,
        553–54, 560
    student activists in, 500–503, 506, 507–8;
        see also Red Guards
    suicide epidemic in, 521
    "To rebel is justified" as slogan of, 516
    trial of leaders of, 576
Czechoslovakia, 356, 375, 383, 401, 436, 538

Dabie, 350
Dadu River, 283
Dagong bao (Justice), 62, 74, 77, 111
Daheito, 59
Dalai Lama, 467
Dalian, 121, 389
    Soviet control of, 346, 372, 392
Dalin, Sergei, 126, 131, 136–37
Damansky (Zhenbao) Island, 535–39, 586
Daoism, 13, 18, 490
Darwin, Charles, 36, 90
dazibao, 517, 569
    Mao's, 508, 511, 586
    Nie's, 501–2, 516, 532
    Wang's, 515
de Gaulle, Charles, 536
death sentences:
    in agrarian reform, 392
    for bourgeoisie, 393
December Ninth Movement of 1935, 290,
        297, 299
"Declaration of the Citizens of Beijing"
        (Chen), 73
defense industry, 411
Defense Ministry, Soviet, 458
Dekanozov, Vladimir, 337
Deliusin, Lev Petrovich, 439

democracy, 24, 36, 52, 64, 73, 77, 101, 114,
        120, 455, 475
    advocated by CCP, 319–21
    bourgeois, 104, 217
    Chinese traditions of, 331–32
    ECCI's promotion of, 303–4
    in Hungary, 435–37
    liberal, 321, 583
    Mao's dismissal of, 455
    New, *see* New Democracy
    popular, 332, 358
    social, 99, 321
    Sun's three-step transition to, 216
    transition to socialism from, 315
    types of, 103
    Western, 331
democratic parties, 440, 441
democratic revolution, 313, 358
Deng Fa (Fang Ling), 333, 426
    Mao opposed by, 263–64
Deng Pei, 113
Deng Pufang, 521
Deng Rong (Maomao), 521
Deng Tuo, 496
Deng Xiaoping (Deng Xixian; Deng
        Xiansheng), x, 5, 191, 334, 397, 405, 416,
        424, 433, 435–36, 443, 478, 540, 566, 570
    character of, 268–69
    disgrace of, 502–3, 505–6, 508–9, 514, 517,
        520–21, 525
    failed campaign against, 569–70
    as first deputy premier, 566–67
    Gang of Four's opposition to, 568–70
    on Great Leap, 450, 480, 483–85
    Mao's protection of, 521, 530, 534
    as moderate, 417, 430
    rehabilitation of, 530, 561, 563, 565
    return to power of, 574–75
    rise to power of, 566–67
    seen by Mao as enemy, 489, 492–93
    Tiananmen Square incident and, 576
    at UN, 566
Deng Xixian, *see* Deng Xiaoping
Deng Yingchao, 304, 330, 333*n*, 334
Deng Zhongxia (Deng Kang), x, 6, 62–63, 71,
        80–81, 82, 144, 219*n*
    on Provisional Politburo, 193
Deng Zihui, x, 415, 417, 418, 420, 484–85,
        535
Deriabin, Petr, 395
Descartes, René, 41
despotic monarchy, 29–30
Dewey, John, 84
dialectical materialism, 318, 326*n*
Diaoyutai, 505
dictatorships, 319
    ideological foundation for, 324–26

Diligent Work and Frugal Study movement, 109

Dimitrov, Georgii (G. M.), x, 291–92, 300–303, 311, 315–16, 317, 322–23, 333, 426, 585
  attempt to protect Wang Ming by, 335, 337–40

Dimitrova, Roza, 340

Ding Ling, 308, 310

Dismissal of Hai Rui from Office (Wu Han), 491–96, 586

Dixie Mission, 344

doctors' plot, 406–7

Doll's House, A (Ibsen), 328, 487

Dong Biwu, 267, 281*n*, 426, 546

Dong Jianwu (Pastor Wang), 250–51

Donggu, 239, 242, 243, 267

Donghu Guest House, 495, 503, 528

Dongshan Higher Primary School, 28–30, 35

Dongshan Hospital, 145

Dostoevsky, Fyodor, 555

Dream of the Red Chamber (Cao Xueqin), 59, 406

Dutch East Indies, 100

East Asia, 556

East Lake, 503

Eastern Europe:
  Chinese grain exported to, 452
  communist parties in, 7
  crisis in socialism in, 435–39, 444, 500, 539
  people's democracies in, 358

economics:
  Jiang Qing's ignorance of, 523
  Mao's lack of understanding of, 449, 464, 515

economy, market, 413, 414, 421, 574

education, 98
  class struggle in, 496, 501
  European, 54
  in Japan, 63
  Mao's, 15, 21, 26, 27, 28–30, 32–46, 48, 52, 62
  for the poor, 453
  revolution and, 53
  socialist, 488
  work teams and, 507–8, 510

egalitarianism, 105, 212, 476

Egypt, 149

Ehrenburg, Georgii Borisovich, x, 271

Eighth Route Army, 313–14, 316, 321, 334, 347, 543*n*

Eisenhower, Dwight, 460–61, 467, 468, 473

Eisler, Gerhard, 234

Elder Brother Society, 19, 34, 171, 210

electricity:
  generating stations for, 401, 411
  shortages of, 423

"Energy of the Mind, The" (Mao), 42

Engels, Friedrich, x, 60–61, 81, 95, 325, 335, 466, 473

England, 36, 68, 126, 383
  coal production in, 456
  constitutional monarchy in, 30
  in Opium Wars, 22, 58
  steel production in, 456
  see also Great Britain

Enlightenment, New Culture Movement and, 59

entrepreneurship, private, 393, 397

Europe, 566
  communist organizations in, 88
  political ideas from, 36

Ewert, Arthur Ernst (Arthur; Harry Berger; Jim), x, 265–66, 269–71, 272–73

Executive Committee of the Comintern (ECCI), 4, 88, 100, 113, 115–16, 119, 122, 123, 125, 126, 127, 146, 179, 205, 218, 219*n*, 264, 284, 291, 292–93, 311, 543*n*
  anti-kulak policy of, 239
  on Bo-Mao rivalry, 270–71
  CCP delegation to, 315–16
  CCP representation on, 248, 333*n*
  CCP's ties to, 304
  Central Committee criticized by, 233–34, 236
  Eighth Plenum of, 175
  Eleventh Plenum of, 258–59
  Far Eastern Bureau of, 162, 163, 167, 206, 234–35, 237, 246–48, 266–67, 268, 269, 275
  Far Eastern Secretariat of, 100, 115, 234, 265, 269–70
  Fifth Enlarged Plenum of, 149
  on Guomindang alliance, 134, 137, 138, 149–51, 153–54
  International Liaison Department of, 206–7, 228, 247–48
  lack of radio contact with, 275
  Mao supported by, 261–62, 264, 265–66, 322–23, 327, 585
  Ninth Enlarged Plenum of, 217–20
  organizational recommendations by, 333–35
  Personnel Department of, 333–34, 426
  Political Commission of the Political Secretariat of, 261, 271, 273, 293
  political journal of, 174
  Political Secretariat of, 223, 266
  Presidium of, 322
  Secretariat of, 296, 303, 446*n*

Seventh Enlarged Plenum of, 175
Shaanxi-Gansu brigade and, 287
Shanghai favored by, 194
show trials planned against, 426
Sixth Enlarged Plenum of the, 147, 150,
    153, 154
Tenth Plenum of, 227–28
on Xi'an Incident, 301

Fairbank, John King, 3
Fang Ruilin, 133
Fang Weixia, 39
Fang Zhimin, 177, 293
Far East, 537
fascism, 291, 295, 387
February Oppositionists, 528, 531, 534, 535
Fedorenko, Nikolai, 371
Feng Guifen, 27
Feng Xi, see Stalin, Joseph Vissarionovich
Feng Yuxiang, 143, 159, 183, 358
Feng Ziyou, 133
Fenghuangshan (Mount Phoenix), 305–6
Filippov, see Stalin, Joseph Vissarionovich
Financial-Economic Commission, PRC, 391
Finland, 428, 440
First All-China Congress of Soviets, 251–52,
    255, 584
First Bandit Suppression Campaign, 240–45
First Peasant Congress of Hunan, 166
First Silk Factory, 109
Five-Member Cultural Revolution Group,
    493, 495–98
Five-Year Plan, First Chinese, 390–91, 409,
    411–13, 416–19
Five-Year Plan, First Soviet, 391
Five-Year Plan, Second Chinese, 430, 456
Five-Year Plan, Third Chinese, 531
Foreign Affairs, 2
Foreign Affairs Ministry, Soviet, 368, 467
    Protocol Division of, 367
Fori River, 283
Forman, Harrison, 343
Formosa, 27
four big freedoms, 397
Four Olds, 510, 531
Four Pests, 451–52
Fragrant Hills, 363
France, 29, 36, 68, 131–32, 210, 295, 454
    China's 1885 war with, 23
    Chinese laborers in, 54
    in Indochina, 376
    in Second Opium War, 22, 58
    in Shanghai, 86
    on UN Security Council, 375n
    Wang Jingwei in, 165
    work-study visits to, 47, 53–55, 64–66, 71,
        92, 93, 109, 115, 138

free love, 77, 146, 147, 307
free trade, 22, 358
freedom of speech, 406, 492
    in Hundred Flowers campaign, 440–41
Freier, Boris (Bu Lici), 167
Fu Daqing, 134n
Fu Liangzuo, 45, 49
Fu Sinian, 66
Fu Zuoyi, 352, 392
fuel industry, 411
Fujian province, 88, 168, 203, 215, 220, 221,
    224, 225, 227, 230, 231, 240, 245, 246,
    251, 261, 293, 388, 584
    famine in, 471
    soviet in, 230
Futian, 241, 242, 243
Futian Incident, 239–45, 584

Gang of Four, 565–71
Ganjiang River, 233, 241, 243, 245
Gansu province, 285, 287, 290, 313, 319, 321
    famine in, 461, 471, 475
Ganxian, 260
Ganzhou:
    plan to attack, 257, 259, 263
    siege of, 259, 260
Gao Gang, x, 6, 334, 585
    in Korean War, 383–84, 386
    moderates accused of right deviation by,
        393–95, 397–98
    purge and suicide of, 404–6, 408
Gao Gang–Rao Shushi Affair, 404–6, 585
Gao Junyu, 115
Gao Shuangcheng, 296
Gao Zili, 271
Garden of Abundant Reservoirs, 365
Gauss, Clarence, 344
Ge Jianhao (Ge Lanying), 65
Geming (Revolution), 152
General Trade Union Council, 144
Germany, 39, 70, 210, 295, 383, 436
    Chiang's advisers from, 272
    Chinese holdings of, 44, 68–69
    communists from, 205, 265, 268
Germany, East, 7, 436
Germany, Nazi, 349, 425
    Anti-Comintern Pact with Japan of, 301
    USSR attacked by, 334
Germany, West, PRC recognized by, 560
Goering, Hermann, 295
Golden Mean, 15
Gomułka, Władysław, 435, 436
Gong, Prince, 22
Gongchan (Common property), 223
Gongchandang (Communist), 93
Goodnow, Frank, 44
Gorbachev, B. N., 392

Gorky, Maxim, 307
Gottwald, Klement, 375
grain, 386, 407, 489
    centralized procurement of, 413–14
    exports of, 452, 458
    imports of, 474
    production of, 450–52, 457–58, 461, 466
    quotas on, 479
    shortages of, 413, 458, 480
    Soviet shortage of, 460
    state monopoly on, 413–14, 421
    stockpiles of, 352, 414, 460
Great Britain, 131, 132, 302, 369, 428
    in nuclear test ban treaty, 495n
    PRC recognized by, 371
    Red Guard attack on diplomatic office of,
        530
    in Shanghai, 85–86
    Shanghai investments of, 312–13
    in Shanghai Massacre, 143–44
    in shelling of Nanjing, 178
    Sino-Indian border determined by, 467
    steel production in, 447
    on UN Security Council, 375n
    see also England
Great Depression, 228–29
Great Famine, 456, 461, 470–77, 484
    concealment of, 475
Great Hall of the People, 506, 520, 532, 552,
    557, 569
Great Leap Forward, 7, 366, 447–48, 449–66,
    470, 475–83, 586
Great Learning, 15
Great Proletarian Cultural Revolution, see
    Cultural Revolution
Great Revolution, 231, 315
Great Soviet Encyclopedia, 317
"Great Union of the Popular Masses, The"
    (Mao), 74–76, 77, 80
Grechko, Andrei, 538
Grinevskii, Oleg Aleksandrovich, 446
Gromyko, Andrei Andreevich, x, 374–75,
    380, 467
Group I, 366
Gu Shunzhang, 247, 250
Gu Zhenghong, 143
Gu Zuolin, Mao opposed by, 263–64
Guan Feng, 529–30
Guan Xiangying, 333
Guangdong province, 23, 100–101, 105, 108,
    120, 121, 131, 144, 159, 203, 220, 229,
    240, 261
    CCP armed ventures in, 187
    communism in, 123, 162, 166, 221
    defeat of Second National Revolutionary
        Army in, 190
    eastern, Chiang's capture of, 143

    Guomindang in, 133, 160
    Mao's organizing in, 156, 160
    NRA attacks in, 186
    peasant unions in, 125, 155, 158, 161–62,
        164, 181
    soviet area attacked by militarists in, 262
Guangdong Provisional Education
    Committee, 101, 107
Guangdong-Jiangxi border, 207
Guangxi province, 22, 45, 107, 143, 276
    communists in, 221
    soviet in, 230
Guangxi Zhuang Autonomous Region, 448,
    533
Guangxu (Bright Beginning) Emperor of
    China, 12, 23, 25
guerrilla warfare:
    in Chinese civil war, 348, 352
    in Korean War, 382
    in Red Army, 222, 223, 229, 233, 249,
        253–55, 259, 262–64, 267, 269, 271, 276,
        290, 584
    in Sino-Japanese war, 313–14, 315, 319,
        323, 324, 330, 336
Guide Weekly, 174
Guilin, 107
Guizhou army, 278
Guizhou province, 45, 276–78, 280, 283
Guo Moro, 407
Guo Zhaotang (Afanasii Gavrilovich
    Krymov), 292, 426
Guomindang (GMD; Nationalist Party), 2, 44,
    45, 187, 280, 353, 357, 406, 417, 426,
    508, 530, 533, 534, 562, 585
    AB Corps and, 240–41
    air force of, 282, 283, 301, 348
    army of, see National Revolutionary Army,
        Guomindang
    attacks against and by, 185–86
    blockade by, 307
    Canton under, 131
    CCP battles with, 347–48
    CCP opposition to, 302
    CCP struggle against, 260
    Central Control Commission of, 153
    Central Government of, 345
    collapse of troops of, 352
    communist alliance with, 107–8, 113–16,
        119–29, 145, 148–51, 153–56, 167, 183
    communist attitude towards politics of,
        136–38
    control lost by, 330–31
    cooperatives under, 415
    defeat of, 392
    ECCI's radio confiscated by, 275
    execution of Northern Bureau leaders of,
        182

feelings against appeasement of Japan within, 291
Fifth Encirclement and Suppression campaign of, 325
First All-China Conference of the, 129, 131–36, 141, 153, 583
Fourth Expedition of, 268
goal to unite China under, 139
Hakka feared by, 276
industrial centers controlled by, 215
infantry of, 348
internal struggles in, 229
joint action against Japan with, 294–97
leftists in, 143, 148, 151, 153, 154–56, 157, 161, 174, 175, 176, 179–80, 181, 182, 183, 188, 189, 197, 311n, 343, 358, 584
Mao and, 108, 121–22, 583
Mao in fight against, 267
Nineteenth Army of, 259
Northeast Army of, 294–95, 298
peace with, 305
power struggle within, 143
Red Army battles with, 248, 265, 268, 272, 277, 296
red terror in cities controlled by, 247
Revolutionary Committee of the, 358
right wing of, 133–34, 138, 140, 143, 148, 151, 154–55, 157, 163, 164–66, 171
rupture between CCP and, 183, 185–90
Second Congress of the, 152–54
Seventeenth Field Army of, 297
shaming as tactic of, 227
Shanghai bureau of, 136, 139–40
Shanghai strikers supported by, 144
spies from, 240–41
Standing Committee (Politburo) of, 134
troops of, 348, 350, 351
Twenty-Sixth Army of, 257
UN recognition of, 375
Unification Congress of the GMD held by, 129
unification of China under, 216
united front between CCP and, 311–21, 332, 585
U.S. support for, 345
withdrawal of CCP from, 204
Zhao Xiangui executed by, 208n
Zhou Lu executed by, 211
Guominjun (Nationalist Army), 143
Gutian, 225, 227

Hai Rui, 491–92, 514
Haifeng district, 160
Hainan, Red Guards in, 514
Hakka, 168–70, 193, 196, 203, 210, 212, 220, 224, 226, 241, 260, 276, 277, 289, 475
country of, 215, 225–26, 240, 245, 246, 289

Halliday, Jon, 5
Han Chinese, 280
Han dynasty, 28, 29, 43, 577
handicrafts, 403, 477
cooperatives for, 412
Hangzhou, 106, 115–16, 312, 404, 408, 448, 483, 495, 502–3, 546, 550
communism in, 123
Hankou, 32, 79, 121, 161, 166, 174, 177, 187, 190, 195, 204, 234, 247, 256, 496
CEC in, 179
communism in, 123
Guomindang in, 133
railway workers' strike in, 121–22, 159
Hankou Republic daily (Hankou minguo ribao), 181
Hanyang, 32, 161
Hao Mingli, 590
Harbin, 350, 373
Harriman, W. Averill, 345
Hatem, George (Ma Haide), 326–27
Hawaii, 23
He Jian, 179, 186, 198–99
He Long, x, 189–90, 207, 308, 313, 334
death of, 518–19
Second and Sixth Front Army groups commanded by, 275–76, 290
He Meiren, 388
He Meixue, 267, 273
He Minfan, 96–97
He Shizhen, 133
He Shuheng (Bewhiskered He), x, 50, 71, 78, 112–13
and the Bolshevization of the Renovation of the People Study Society, 96, 98–99
at CCP Founding Congress, 101–2
He Tingying, 207
He Yi, 208, 267, 268, 281n, 592
death of, 274
He Yingqin, 246, 268, 301
He Zizhen (Guiyuan; Wen Yun) (Mao's third wife), x, 204, 208, 225, 258, 264, 268, 281n, 289, 388, 589
Anqing and Anying's friendship with, 329–30, 349, 389
breakdown of, 349–50
character and personality of, 226, 364
death of, 576
on Long March, 273, 275
with Mao on Red Army campaigns, 215, 260
Mao's final visit with, 462–63
pregnancies and childbirth of, 215, 221–22, 265, 267, 280–81, 304, 319
"reeducation" of, 267
separation of Mao and, 215, 311, 318, 326, 329

He Zizhen (Guiyuan; Wen Yun) (*cont.*)
  Smedley and Lily opposed by, 307–11
  in Soviet Union, 319, 329, 544*n*
  wounded in Guomindang air strike, 282, 319
  in Yan'an, 305–6
health care, 453
heavy industry, 408–9, 411–12
  prioritization of, 366
Hebei province, 120, 121, 229, 287, 350, 355
Hegai, Aleksei Ivanovich, 380
Heilongjiang, 522
Henan province, 55, 120, 121, 159, 183, 285, 453
  peasant movement in, 164
Hengjiang River, 245
Hengyang, 79, 110, 112
History of Socialism, A (Kirkup), 81, 90
History of the Communist Party of the Soviet Union, Short Course, 335, 366
History of the Former Han Dynasty (Ban Gu), 27
Hitler, Adolf, 295, 425
Hong Kong, 23, 121, 131, 190, 205, 209, 251, 329, 389, 520
  Shanghai supported by, 144
Hong Xiuquan, 22
hongbaoshu (Precious Red Book; Little Red Book), 488, 544, 574
Hongjiang (Prosperity) society, 17–19
Hongmeng (Red Brotherhood), 17
Hongqi (Red flag), 454, 473, 484, 525, 536
Hongse Zhonghua (Red China), 260
House of Soviets, Hall of Columns in, 401
Hu Feng, 406
Hu Hanmin, 134, 153–54
Hu Qiaomu, 436
Hu Shi, x, 59, 66, 76, 90, 408
Hua Guofeng, x, 482, 562, 569–72, 576, 587
Huaining (Anqing), 63
Huang Ai, 108–9
Huang Di, 312
Huang Gonglüe, 243–44
Huang Huiguan, 250
Huang Kecheng, 464–65
Huang Ping, 134*n*, 219*n*
Huang Qiong, 577
Huang Shaolan, 102
Huang Yongsheng, 532
Huanggang county, 543
Huangpu River, 85, 144
Huangyang Pass, battle of, 213
Huaqingchi, 297
Hubei Party Committee, 497
Hubei province, 32–33, 108, 121, 133, 159, 161, 183, 191, 276, 285, 527, 543

CCP armed ventures in, 187, 229
communists in, 221, 247
NRA attacks in, 185–86
peasant movement in, 164, 178
peasant violence in, 186
soviet in, 230, 248
taxes in, 170*n*
humanism, 64
Hume, Edward, 32
Hunan Army, 34–35
Hunan Commercial Institute, 96
Hunan Federation of Trade Unions (HFTU), 111, 129
Hunan Higher Provincial Middle School, *see* Provincial First Middle School
Hunan Institute of Higher Education, 32–35
Hunan party committee, 201, 205, 206
Hunan province, 11, 13, 17, 18, 19, 28–29, 30, 31, 37, 43, 49, 109, 120, 126, 144, 175, 186, 191, 196, 198, 201, 202, 208*n*, 261, 273, 276, 284, 290, 336, 479, 483, 484, 495, 583
  agricultural production in, 449–50
  army of, 159
  campaign against Shang in, 78–80
  CCP armed ventures in, 187, 229
  citywide strike in, 71–72
  communists in, 50, 108, 111, 112, 121, 126, 128, 166, 171, 174, 183, 186, 191
  after death of Yuan Shikai, 45
  famine in, 472
  Guomindang Army in, 198
  Guomindang in, 125–26, 128–29, 133, 157, 171, 186
  local character of, 16
  Mao's organizing for Autumn Uprising in, 194–98, 584
  military government in, 33–34
  NRA attacks in, 185–86
  NRA liberation of, 160, 161
  peasant movement in, 158, 159, 164, 167, 178, 186, 187, 209
  popular self-rule for, 87–88, 90–91
  Provincial Constitution of, 91–92
  revolution in, 34–35, 37, 49
  soviet in, 248
  support for Mao in, 243
  taxes in, 170*n*
  tense political situation in, 68, 70–72
Hunan Provincial Fourth Normal School, 37, 50
Hunan Provincial Party Committee, 464, 562
Hunan Revolutionary Committee, 562
Hunan Students Association, 71–72, 76, 77, 79

Hunan-Jiangxi Special Border Area
    Committee, 211
Hunan-Jiangxi-Guangdong border, 211
Hundred Flowers campaign, 440–41, 481,
    585
    as political provocation, 442
Hungary, democratic revolution in, 435–37,
    438–39, 444, 539
Huns (Xiongnu nomads), 29
Hurley, Patrick J., 345, 346

Ibsen, Henrik, 328, 487
ideological campaigns, against intelligentsia,
    393, 406–7
ideological indoctrination, 405–6
imperial examination system, 21, 50
imperialism, 428, 445, 534
income distribution, 412
India, 149, 179, 428, 468, 486, 536
    China's border conflict with, 467–68
individualism, 40–41
Indochina, 27, 222, 376, 557
Indonesia, national liberation struggle in,
    100
Indonesia communist party (PKI), 385
industrial development, 422–23
industrialization:
    and buyouts of private property, 422
    of PRC, 390–91, 401–3, 407, 408–9,
        411–12, 425, 438, 444, 452, 453, 456–57,
        483, 538, 585
    socialist, 402, 408–10
industry, 516, 585
    heavy, 366, 408–9, 411–12
    state share of, 393
inflation, 407
Institute of Marxism-Leninism, 336
intellectuals, 36, 218
    campaign of repression against, 442–43
    Hundred Flowers campaign and, 440–41
    ideological remolding of, 393
    Mao's annoyance at, 457
    relocation to countryside of, 476
    as rightist bourgeois elements, 442
intelligentsia, 332, 393
    Mao's proposal for a new, 496
interest reduction, 392
Internal Affairs Ministry, Soviet, 458
"International," 252, 484, 569
International Organization for Aid to
    Revolutionary Fighters (MOPR), 228,
    319, 329
International Orphanage, 329, 349, 389,
    544n
International Swimming Association
    (FINA), 505
internationalism, 104, 390

Internatsional'naia literatura (International
    literature), 324
Iolk, Evgenii Sigismundovich (York; Johan;
    Johanson), 177n
Irkutsk, 100
Italy, 68, 295, 445–46
    in Shanghai massacre, 144
Ivanov, Alexei (Ivin), 271
Ivanovo, 329, 350

Japan, 33, 39, 88, 102, 276, 557, 566
    anarchism in, 64
    Anti-Comintern Pact with Germany of,
        301
    bombing of Yan'an by, 348
    Boxer Rebellion and, 25
    CCP opposition to, 294
    China as viewed by, 6
    Chinese conflict with, 311–21
    Chinese opposition to, 69–73, 332
    communism in, 113
    constitutional monarchy in, 30
    CSR declaration of war on, 260
    education in, 63
    expansionism of, 257–58
    feelings against, 290–91
    films against, 328
    German holdings in China retained by, 44,
        68–69
    Imperial Army of, 287–88, 315, 330–31
    imperialism of, 296
    Korea and Formosa occupied by, 27
    Kwantung Army of, 257, 295, 347
    Manchuria and, 216
    Manchuria invaded and occupied by,
        257–58, 260, 287
    militarism in, 383
    opposition to imperialism of, 294–303
    peace treaty with, 372
    potential invasion of USSR by, 258
    PRC recognized by, 560
    protests against and boycott of goods from,
        70–73, 77, 78, 120–21, 143–44
    Russia defeated by, 30
    seizure of Chinese territory by, 330–31
    in Shanghai, 86
    Shanghai attacked by, 259–60
    Sino-Japanese War and, 23
    Soviet fears of aggression by, 291, 296
    on Soviet Union, 302
    surrender of, 346, 585
    threat of invasion by, 287–88
    threats against China by, 297
    in World War I, 44
    zhuyi concept borrowed by, 341
Java, 100, 103
Ji'an, 230, 233, 251, 257

Jiang Jihuan, 90
Jiang Qing (Li Yunhe; Lan Ping; Marianna
    Yusupova; Li Shumeng; Mao's fourth
    wife), x–xi, 326–29, 348, 350, 351, 389,
    410, 428, 546, 555, 589
  in Central Cultural Revolution Group,
    501–3, 514, 515, 517–18, 523, 525–27,
    529, 532, 535, 542, 547, 554, 577
  on cultural affairs, 487, 488, 491–94,
    496–97
  in Gang of Four, 565
  ill health of, 463
  imprisonment of, 576
  Life of Wu Xun criticized by, 393
  Mao's changed relations with, 463, 487
  Mao's children and, 349, 365
  Mao's criticism of, 565, 566
  Mao's passing over of, 554, 555
  Mao's relationship with, 364, 543–44
  mass media controlled by, 544
  power struggle of, 560–61, 562–71
  pregnancy and childbirth of, 330
  on Stalin's death, 401
  suicide of, 576
  in USSR, 355–56, 367, 463
Jiangsu province, 164, 229, 247, 284
Jiangxi province, 11, 17, 18, 109, 112, 159,
    160, 183, 190, 201, 202, 220, 221,
    223–24, 229–31, 240, 246, 248, 251, 256,
    257, 259, 260, 261, 312, 336, 462–63,
    480, 521, 584
  CCP armed ventures in, 187, 209, 584
  Guomindang in, 133
  land law in, 219
  local CCP organization in, 239, 241–43,
    246, 248
  natives (bendi) of, 240
  NRA attacks in, 186
  party leadership in, 262, 264, 266
  peasant movement in, 164, 177
  Red Army base in, 233, 246
  Red Army in, 215, 259
  soviet in, 230, 233, 237n, 238, 240, 241, 245
  Zhou in, 238
Jiangxi Provincial Committee, 211
Jiangxi Provincial Soviet Government, 233
Jiao Dafeng, 33–34
Jiaojiao, see Li Min
Jiaozhou Bay, 44, 68, 69
Jiaxing, 106, 583
Jiefang ribao (Liberation daily), 341
Jiefangjun ribao (People's Liberation Army
    daily), 488
Jilin province, 257
Jinan, 44, 84, 208n, 327, 494
  communism in, 100, 101, 112, 123
Jing bao (Capital news), 62

Jinggang, 202–3, 206–12, 214–15, 216–20,
    230, 233, 246, 257, 258, 490, 511, 525,
    542, 550, 554, 584
Jinggangshan Land Law, 212, 219
Jinsha River, 283
Jiujiang, 183, 350, 462
  failed attack on, 231
Jiuxianqiao, 576
Joffe, Adolf, 119–20, 121
Joint Fleet conspiracy, 549–51
joint Soviet-Chinese stock companies, 372
joint state-private enterprises, 421–22
Journey to the West, 20
Juewu (Awakening) society, 138

Kaganovich, Lazar, 384
Kai Feng, xi, 278, 279, 281, 284
Kaifeng, 519
Kamenev, Lev, 127
Kang Keqing, 307
Kang Sheng (Zhao Yun; Zhang Zongke), xi,
    7, 271, 315, 318, 332, 333, 334, 336,
    337, 426, 436n, 487, 492–93, 495, 542,
    546–47, 555
  and Cultural Revolution, 458, 493, 495,
    499–501, 505, 509, 514, 523–26, 532,
    535
  Jiang supported by, 561
  Lan Ping's relationship with, 326, 327–29
  return to China by, 316
  Wang Ming supported by, 321
Kang Youwei, xi, 23, 29–30, 33
Kantianism, 52
Karakhan, Lev Mikhailovich, xi, 127, 135,
    136, 149, 166
Kartunova, Anastasia, 356
Kautsky, Karl, 81
Ke Qingshi, 418, 448, 487
KGB, 5, 296, 355, 436n, 542n
Khamadan, Aleksandr Moiseevich (Faingar,
    Mikhailov), 293
Khrushchev, Nikita Sergeevich, xi, 5, 276,
    372, 387, 432, 433, 485, 499, 517
  drunkenness of, 439, 468
  fall from power of, 489, 537
  Mao's lack of respect for, 7, 410, 419, 425,
    427, 434–37, 439–40, 443–48, 458–61,
    467–69, 473–74, 495n, 537
  and Mao's second Moscow visit, 443–47
  on peaceful coexistence of the two systems,
    427–28, 437, 467, 473, 485
  on peaceful transition from capitalism to
    socialism, 427, 473, 486
  rise to leadership by, 401–2, 408, 409, 525
  Soviet relations with PRC under, 408–12
  Soviet specialists recalled from China by,
    472–73, 536

Stalin censured by, 424–25, 427, 434–35, 439, 448, 460, 525
   on USSR-PRC border dispute, 537
   visits to Beijing by, 409–11, 458–60
Kim Il Sung, xi, 374, 376–81, 384–87, 567
Kirkup (Kirkupp), Thomas, 81, 90
Kirov Theater, 445
Kislovodsk, 544
Kissinger, Henry A., xi, 556–59, 564, 565
Knorin, Wilhelm, 426
Kommunist, 535
Kommunisticheskii Internatsional (Communist International), 174, 271, 293
Kong Dongmei (Mao's granddaughter), 26n, 576, 591
Kong Jining (Mao's grandson), 576, 591
Kong Linghua, 520, 590
Kong Yuan, 334
Korea, 27, 29, 396
   communism in, 113
Korea, North (DPRK), 7, 374–87, 567
Korea, South, 374–79, 383, 385, 387
Korean War, 7, 374–89, 390, 409, 468, 515, 585
Korean Workers' Party, Politburo of Central Committee of, 381
Kosygin, Alexei Nikolaevich, xi, 537, 539
Koval, Konstantin, 390
Kovalev, Evgenii, 356
Kovalev, Ivan Vladimirovich, xi, 353, 356, 364, 367–71, 378, 393–94, 404, 487
Kremlin, 100, 116
Kropotkin, Peter, 64, 75, 76, 90
Krupskaya, Nadezhda, 473
Krutikov, Konstantin, 427, 467
Kuai Dafu, xi, 524, 532
Kuchino, 319
Kuchumov, Vladimir (Mayer; Meyer; Ma Kefu), 194, 196, 205
Kuibyshev, Nikolai V. (Kisanka), 154–55
kulaks, 223, 230, 239, 240, 248, 252n, 254, 259, 294, 357
Kun, Bela, 426
Kunming, 210
Kuntsevo, 371
Kuusinen, Otto, 261, 473
Kuznetsov, Vasily, 391, 413
Kuznetsova, Maria (Nora), 89

Labor Association, 108–9
labor movement, Chinese, 48, 109–12
labor reform camps, 442
Labor University, 363
laborers, seasonal, 110

Lake Nanhu, 106
Lan Ping, *see* Jiang Qing
land:
   distribution of, 169, 239
   nationalization of, 24
   redistribution of, 392
   reform of, 357, 407
   shortages of, 413
land laws, 212, 219, 239, 240
landlords, 12, 157, 158, 160, 162, 164, 167, 168, 185, 189, 195, 212, 213, 223, 226, 229, 238, 239, 252n, 293, 304, 342, 392, 393, 408, 415, 563
   feudal (*dizhu*), 173, 174, 252n, 260
   in GMT and NRA, 151
   preemptive repression of, 407
Langfang, Aleksandr Ivanovich, 426
Lanzhou, 321
Lao She, 521
Laogong zhoukan (Labor weekly), 108
Latin America, 222
Lavrent'ev, Anatolii, 367
League of Chinese Writers, 406
Ledovsky, Andrei, 397
Lee Kuan Yew, 571
Legalist philosophy, 41–42, 562–63
LeHand, Marguerite "Missy," 320n
Lei Feng, 488
Lenin, Vladimir Ilich, xi, 4, 6, 35, 62, 72, 75, 81, 84, 100, 126, 217, 376, 424, 456, 466, 500, 516, 555, 574
   on Bolshevism in the East, 103–4
   Comintern created by, 88
   Guomindang cooperation supported by, 113
   policy of unfettered proletarian terror of, 83
   war and imperialism in thought of, 473
Leningrad, 369
Leninism, 3, 99, 153, 236, 279, 320, 325, 329, 335, 341, 373, 437, 473, 516, 537
   right to dishonesty in, 105
Li Chongde, 249–50
Li Da, xi, 101, 106
   death of, 519
Li Dazhao (T. C. Li; Ta-chao Li), xi, 19, 59–65, 72, 73, 75, 79, 80–82, 89–92, 101, 115, 123, 124, 125, 133–34, 135
   execution of, 181–82
Li Dewen, 327
Li Fuchun, xi, 391, 394, 398, 411, 420, 476, 522, 523, 525, 526, 531, 535
Li Gu, 577
Li Hanjun, xi, 102, 105–6
Li Jiaji, 368
Li Jinxi, 84
Li Lilian, 326–27

Li Lisan (Li Longzhi), xi, 6, 48, 109, 111, 133,
147, 176n, 217, 218, 226, 228, 250, 292,
336, 340, 394, 426
as CCP leader, 48, 230–31
Comintern defied by, 234–36, 256
criticized by Mif's proteges, 254–55
General Trade Union Council headed by,
144
Left opportunism of, 325
on Provisional Bureau of CCP, 187
on Provisional Politburo, 193
suicide of, 519
on Wang's undermining of Mao, 292–93
Li Lisanism, 339
Li Min (Jiaojiao; Tanya Chao Chao) (Mao's
daughter), xii, 226, 280, 304, 311,
349–50, 364–65, 576, 590
accused of revisionism, 520
in Moscow, 329
Li Na (Mao's daughter), xii, 330, 348, 365,
389, 576, 590
travel to USSR by, 355
Li Rui, 464–65
Li Shaojiu, xii, 241–45
Li Shizeng, 53–54
Li Si'an, 51
Li Weihan (Luo Mai; Luo Man), xii, 51, 121,
126, 133, 333–34, 398, 402–3
on Provisional Bureau of CCP, 187, 191
on Provisional Politburo, 193
Li Xiannian, 522, 525, 526, 535
Li Xuefeng, 508
Li Yuanhong, 32–33, 45, 101
Li Yueran, 434, 443, 445
Li Yunhe, see Jiang Qing
Li Zhilong, 155
Li Zhisui, 419n, 421, 431, 462, 472, 480, 554,
558, 560
Li Zhongwu, 134n
Li Zicheng, 359
Liang Qichao, xii, 23, 29, 30, 33, 34, 50, 61, 98,
134n
Liang Shuming, 407
Liangshanbo, 513
Liao Mosha, 496
Liao Zhongkai, 134, 138, 151
liberalism, liberals, 35–36, 40, 52, 73, 76, 77,
83–84, 90, 94, 101, 103, 406
Anglo-American, 82
bourgeois, 500
purge of, 406
lieshen (evil gentry), 18, 22, 125, 162, 164,
176n, 212
Life of Wu Xun, The, 393
Liling county, 176n
Lily Wu (Wu Guangwei), 306–10
Lin Biao (Li Ting), xii, 230, 279, 287, 308,

313, 326, 333n, 334, 407, 465, 496, 498,
518, 538, 542, 547
background and personality of, 542–43
Confucius quotes found in home of,
562–63, 567
in Cultural Revolution, 500, 501, 509,
516–17, 521, 523, 529, 532
fall from grace of, 547–51, 564, 586
flight and death of, 551–53, 587
Fourth Corps commanded by, 231, 232
ill health of, 521, 525, 544–46
Korean War and, 380, 382, 383–84, 386
Liu and Deng attacked by, 514
Mao supported by, 466–67, 482
as Mao's designated successor, 509, 542
as minister of defense, 488, 543
Lin Boqu, 119–20, 133, 134, 153, 156, 159
as chairman of Special Border Region, 313
Lin Feng, 394
Lin Liguo (Laohu), xii, 544n, 548–53
Lin Liheng (Doudou), 497, 498, 544–45, 549,
551
Lin Xiaolin, 544n
Lin Yuying (Zhang Hao), 293, 334
Lintong, 297
Linxian, 210
Liping, 277
Lipki, 436
Little Dawn, see Yang Kaihui
Little Zhang, see Zhang Yufeng
Litvinov, Maxim, 295
Liu Angong, 224–25
Liu Bang, emperor of China, 28, 43, 45
Liu Bin, 591
Liu Bocheng, 286, 313, 334
Liu Di, 242, 244–45
Liu Mingfu, 219n
Liu Renjing, 93, 102, 119, 134
Liu Shaoqi (Liu Weihuang), xii, 5, 6, 7,
336–37, 340, 350, 351, 353, 356, 359,
366, 368, 385, 416, 426, 433, 435–36,
464, 496, 540, 548
as chairman of Standing Committee of the
NPC, 408
on communes, 452, 453–54
in Cultural Revolution, 497
death of, 519, 575
disgrace of, 421, 502–3, 505–6, 507–9, 514,
517–18, 519, 524, 525, 526, 528, 530,
531, 534, 546, 551, 561, 568
on grain shortages, 413
Great Leap Forward and, 450, 479–80,
481–85
Mao enthusiastically supported by, 466,
478
as Mao's designated successor, 478, 480,
499

Mao's view of, 489, 492–93, 499, 500, 523
  as moderate, 393–99, 403, 404–5, 415,
    417–18, 430, 432, 434, 438, 478, 586
  as new chairman of PRC, 461, 586
  Peng betrayed by, 497
  report on the constitution by, 408
  self-criticism by, 398–99, 404
  as Soviet informer, 395
  Stalin's meeting with, 392, 394–95
  Zhou's dislike of, 487
Liu Shiqi, 240, 243
Liu Shucheng, 102
Liu Songlin (Liu Enqi), 368, 389, 589
Liu Xiao, 329, 334, 461n
Liu Xingmin (Liu Xinmin; Zhang Mei), 544n
Liu Yunpin, 521
Liu Zhidan, 287–89
livestock, 417
Lominadze, Vissarion Vissarionovich
    (Nikolai; Werner), xii, 188–95, 197,
    204–5, 284
Long March, xxiii–xxiv, 273, 275–88, 316,
    584, 585
  deaths on, 283, 288
  ending of, 288, 325
  first stage of, 276
  and goal to reunite with Zhang Guotao's
    forces, 282
  reunion with Zhang Guotao's army in,
    283–84
  veterans of, 547
  women on, 307
Longgang village, 245n
Longshi, 211
Longyan, 221
Lop Nor desert, 489
Lord, Winston, 558
Lu Dingyi, xii, 219n, 495–96
  purge of, 497–98
Lu Xun Academy of the Arts, 328
Lu Zongyu, 69, 70, 75
Ludden, Raymond P., 344
Lufeng county, 190
Lunar New Year, 97, 249
Luo Fu (Zhang Wentian), xii, 270, 273, 278,
    282, 284–85, 296, 306, 316, 317, 323,
    329, 331, 426
  Mao opposed by, 256–57, 263–66
  Mao's alliance with, 276–79, 314
  in new triumvirate, 281
  on peasant policy, 293–94
  Peng supported by, 464–65
  in right column, 286–87, 289
  Zhang called to account by, 285
Luo Helou, 25–26
Luo Jialun, 66, 76
Luo Longji, 441

Luo Mai, see Li Weihan
Luo Man, see Li Weihan
Luo Ming, 267, 268
Luo Ruiqing, 465, 497, 499, 501
Luo Xiaoying, 220
Luo Yigu (Mao's first wife), xii, 25–28, 589
Luo Yinong, 147
Luo Zhanglong (Tate Uchirō), xii, 47–48, 50,
    82n, 128, 340
Luochuan Conference, 314–15
  Wang Ming's condemnation of, 317
Luofuzhang, 220
Luoxiao range, 202, 211
Luoyang, 297
Lushan, 312, 463, 495, 547, 548
Lushan Plenum, 462, 465–66, 467, 550, 567,
    586
Lüshun (Port Arthur), 121
  return of Soviet naval base in, 409
  Soviet occupation of, 346, 372, 458

M. V. Frunze Military Academy, 269, 272
Ma Lin, see Maring
MacArthur, Douglas, 374
machine-building plants, 411, 452
Mad'iar, Ludwig, 270
Malan Testing Ground, 489
malaria, 225, 273, 286
Malenkov, Georgii, 384, 387, 401–2, 408, 478
Malik, Yacov, 374–75
Malinovsky, Rodion, 347, 458, 537
Manchu dynasty, see Qing dynasty
Manchuria, 216, 364, 378, 384, 394
  CCP troops in, 347
  Japanese invasion of, 257–58, 260
  Japanese occupation of, 287, 295
  PLA operations in, 351
  Soviet occupation of, 345, 347, 394, 409
  war in, 348
"Manifesto of the Communist International
    to the Proletariat of the World"
    (Trotsky), 81
Manifesto on Reorganizing the Guomindang,
    128
Manuilsky, Dmitry, 261, 300
Mao: The Unknown Story (Chang and
    Halliday), 5
Mao Anhong (son), 265, 273–74, 590
Mao Anlong (Mao Anmin; Yang Yongtai)
    (son), 178, 183, 195, 226, 249–50, 590
Mao Anqing (Kolya; Mao Yuanyi; Nikolai
    Yongshu; Yang Yongshu) (son), xii, 129,
    139–40, 147, 163, 172, 174, 183, 195,
    198, 226, 249–51, 349, 364–65, 589
  death of, 576
  mental illness of, 389
  in USSR, 250–51, 329–30

Mao Anying (Mao Yuanren; Sergei Yongfu; Yang Yongfu; Yong Fu) (son), xii, 120, 129, 139–40, 147, 163, 172, 174, 183, 195, 198–99, 226, 249–51, 368, 589
  death in Korean War of, 387–89
  Mao's relationship with, 348–49, 350–51
  in Soviet Army, 349, 387
  in USSR, 250–51, 329–30, 351
Mao Chuxiong, 208, 388
Mao clan, 5, 11–12, 13, 141
Mao Dongdong (Mao's great grandson), 591
Mao Dun (Shen Yanbing), 158, 407
Mao Enpu, 13
Mao Fuxuan, 141–42
Mao Huachu (Mao Yuanhuai; Wang Huachu), 209
Mao Jinhua (Mao's daughter), 199, 221–22, 590
Mao Lyova (son), 319, 590
Mao Taihua, 11
Mao Tse-tung and I Were Beggars (Xiao Yu), 37–38
Mao Xinyu (Mao's grandson), 590
Mao Yichang (Mao's father), xiii, 12, 25, 50, 141, 330, 583, 589
  character and personality of, 13–17, 28, 54–55
  Confucianism encouraged by, 14–15
  death of, 67, 110
  financial success of, 17, 19
  Mao's conflicts with, 21, 27, 28, 36
Mao Yuanxin, xiii, 388–89, 568–70, 576
Mao Yuanzhi, xiii, 111, 209, 388, 389, 576
Mao Zedong (Mao Runzhi), xiii, 284
  accused of Trotskyism, 337
  as activist and organizer, 47–50
  on agrarian policy, 178–79, 191–93, 195–96, 216, 239–40, 254–55
  ambition of, 28, 41, 42–43, 65–66
  anti-Japanese feelings of, 44
  appearance and personality of, 37–38, 102, 308, 309, 363
  arrest orders for, 121, 145
  articles and essays written by, 42, 59
  as avid newspaper reader, 49–50, 62
  bamboo flute of, 258, 260, 265
  biographies of, 1–2, 3, 27, 29
  birth of, 11–12, 583
  Bolshevism embraced by, 93–97
  cataracts of, 565, 570
  in CCP Central Committee, 180–81, 218
  on CCP Central Executive Committee, 124, 136–37, 153
  CCP controlled by, 330
  at CCP Founding Congress, 101–2, 106
  as Chairman, 359, 408, 432, 585
  as chairman of PRC, 546–47

character and personality of, 16, 292, 355
Chen Boda and Jiang Qing criticized by, 523
Chiang Kai-shek mistrusted by, 313–14
children of, 5, 27, 120, 129, 178, 221–22, 249–51, 265, 267, 273–74, 280–81, 304, 319, 329–30, 348–50, 364–65, 368
China's rapid socialist development desired by, 390–91, 396–99
Chinese political culture understood by, 342
in Chinese Soviet Republic, 251–52
cigarettes smoked by, 364, 459, 541, 560
class theory of, 151–52, 157–58, 162, 163, 164, 170, 172–76, 246, 294
in Committee on Peasant Movement, 161–63, 181
communist conversion of, 77, 81–84, 87–88
congestive heart failure of, 559, 565, 587
criticisms of, 205–7, 217–19, 224, 225, 237, 243, 254–74
cult of personality of, 3, 291–93, 323, 332, 335–36, 340, 350–51, 355, 366, 420, 466, 584
death of, 475, 572, 574, 587
in defense of Provincial First Normal School, 49
in defense of Wuhan, 182
demoralization of, 480
depressions of, 99, 122, 140, 224, 226, 258, 477, 480
discarded sword of Stalin as metaphor of, 435–37
dismissal from Politburo of, 206
dossier on, 5
economics not understood by, 449, 477
education of, 15, 21, 26, 27, 28–30, 32–46, 48, 52, 62
egalitarian view of, 224
emancipation from Soviet domination of, 410–11, 424–48
embalmed body of, 574
emotional nature of, 367
energy and confidence of, 249, 449
family's interest in communism, 110–11
on famine, 472
in fight against Guomindang, 267
first marriage of, 25–28
as founder of modern China, 1
frustration over failure of Great Leap Forward by, 480–87
frustration with opponents by, 264–65
on grain monopoly, 414
as great actor, 367
as guerrilla leader and advocate, 253, 254–55, 259, 262, 263, 264, 267, 269,

271, 313–14, 315, 323–24, 336, 352, 382, 584
in Guomindang CEC, 134, 139
at Guomindang conferences, 132–36, 152–53
on Guomindang cooperation, 108, 121–22, 123–24, 125–26, 128–29, 132–36, 139
Guomindang post resigned by, 156
Guomindang propaganda by, 148, 151
habit of leadership in, 196
He Jian's attempted revenge on, 186
heart attacks of, 571, 572
in Hunan revolutionary army, 34–35, 49
Hunanese self-rule favored by, 87–88
Hunan's request for return of, 189
ill health of, 139–40, 145, 147–48, 225, 267, 270, 271, 273, 363–64, 369–70, 421, 425, 432, 478, 482, 492, 540–41, 553–54, 556, 558–59, 560, 562, 565–66, 570–72, 583, 587
impulsiveness of, 140
inaccessibility of, 3
inspection tours of, 418, 430–31
interviews and pronouncements of, 3
iron will of, 112
isolation of, 555–56
on Japan, 257–58
Japan opposed by, 291
as journalist, 77, 108–9, 151–52, 164, 172–75
as journalist and editor, 72–76, 148, 158, 583
Khrushchev as viewed by, 7, 410, 419, 425, 427, 434–37, 439–40, 443–48, 458–61, 467–69, 473–74, 495n, 537
Korean War and, 374, 378–87
as landowner, 141
language gifts lacking in, 35, 65, 81
leadership of, 6, 65, 66, 71–72, 78, 108
as library assistant, 60, 65–66, 76
Lin Liguo's assassination plot on, 549–51, 553
on Liu's criticism, 479–81
on Long March, 275–88
long workdays of, 364
Lou Gehrig's disease suffered by, 565, 587
loyalists to, 491
lust for violence of, 520
as master of intrigue, 249
as master of political maneuvering, 565
at meeting on Guomindang split, 165–66
micromanaging by, 224
on militarization, 186–87, 191–93, 196–97, 218, 341
in military troika, 282
miscalculations of, 232
in Moscow, 367–73

Moscow Chinese opposed to, 224–25
Moscow's support for, 224
mother's death and, 66–67
multifaceted nature of, 5–6
naming of, 13
in national campaign to remove Zhang Jingyao, 79–80
nationalism of, 30, 42, 372
in new triumvirate, 281
nuclear war not feared by, 428, 445–46
as organizer, 141
organizing work done by, 251
overbearing character of, 29
patriotism of, 43, 48, 87, 148, 291
peasant background of, 39
peasant organizing by, 145, 156–60, 161–64, 167, 170–75, 177, 583
on peasant policy, 293–94
peasant question and, 19–20, 124–25, 192–93, 583
on peasants and workers, 36–37, 49, 74–75, 141
people's expectations of, 453
perceived independence of, 2–3
persecution against, 268
physical labor of, 85
poetry of, 52–53, 67, 109, 130, 184, 200, 213–14, 225, 245, 258, 282, 288, 310, 431–32, 462, 490, 494–95, 575
on Politburo, 236
power consolidated by, 342
as primary school director, 96
Project 571 assassination plot against, 549–51
as propagandist, 72, 152, 153, 158, 160, 224, 292, 331, 420, 486, 583
radicalism of, 395, 417
recalled to CCP central, 121
Red Army advocated by, 186–87
Red Army and, 198, 212–32, 233, 236–41, 243–49, 251–55, 257, 260–74, 275
Red Guards manipulated by, 510–11
refused permission to lead peasant insurgents in Nanchang Uprising, 190
Renovation of the People Study Society and, 50–51
reputation of, 304
return to power by, 276–80
as revolutionary, 33–34, 46
revolutionary program of, 192–93
reward for capture of, 272
rhetoric of, 291
in right column, 286, 287
rise to power of, 7
in role as unifier of CCP, 394n
romance rejected by, 48

Mao Zedong (Mao Runzhi) (*cont.*)
  romances of, 56–57, 77, 79–80, 96–97, 199,
    204, 307–10, 326–29, 364, 463, 489–90,
    520, 568
  Russia Study Group formed by, 90
  Russia trip envisioned by, 90–99, 112
  Second Congress of CCP missed by, 114
  second marriage of, 97
  self-assessment of, 99–100
  self-criticism of, 327, 481, 586
  self-improvement as obsession of, 42,
    51–52
  sense of own greatness of, 455
  in Shanghai Bureau of GMD, 136–37
  sick leave of, 258–59, 264, 267
  socioeconomic policies of, 245
  Soviet support for, 236–38
  Stalin as teacher of, 425
  Stalin's relationship with, 2–4, 5, 7, 44,
    236–37, 248–49, 270, 292, 296, 302,
    322–24, 334, 335, 342, 343, 345–47,
    353–58, 369–73, 395, 400–401, 424–26,
    459–60, 584, 585
  stepping back by, 478
  support for, 224
  swimming by, 430–31, 459, 503–5, 566
  on Tang Xiangming, 45–46
  as target of Futian Incident, 243–44
  as teacher, 37, 68
  Three Worlds concept of, 566, 587
  traps laid by, 496
  union organizing by, 109–12, 120–21
  on united front, 326
  U.S. talks with, 344–45
  victory over moderates by, 398–99, 402
  Wang Ming understood by, 316
  on Xi'an incident, 301–3
  Zhang Guotao criticized by, 285
"Mao Zedong, Zhu De" (Leaders of the
    Chinese people) (Xiao), 324
Mao Zedong Museum, 209*n*
Mao Zedong Thought, 340–42, 401, 405–6,
    433–34, 448, 467, 496, 500, 525, 526,
    534, 535, 544, 547, 563, 585
  in PLA, 488
Mao Zedong Thought Propagation Teams,
    531
Mao Zejian, 97, 110, 388, 592
Mao Zemin (Yang Ze; Zhou Den), xiii, 14, 16,
    55, 97, 110, 112, 141, 181, 183, 198, 226,
    256, 268, 333, 591
  in Anyuan colliery organizing, 111, 140
  death of, 388
  as emissary to contact ECCI, 287
  Mao's sons and, 249–50
  marriages of, 97, 208–9, 389
  as minister of economy of foreign trade, 290

Mao Zetan, xiii, 14, 16, 97, 110, 140, 141, 142,
    145, 181, 183, 256, 592
  death of, 273, 388
  dismissal from military work of, 267
  in Jinggang, 207–8
  marriages of, 110, 208
  in Red Army, 240
Mao Zuquan, 133
Maogong County, 283, 284
Maoists, Maoism, 493, 502, 515, 554, 577
Maoping, 203
Maoxian, 283
Maring (Ma Lin; Mr. Anderson; Hendricus
    Josephus Franciscus Marie Sneevliet;
    Philipp), xiii, 100–106, 121, 134, 135,
    136, 185, 284
  Guomindang cooperation supported by,
    107–8, 113, 115–16, 122, 123–24
market economy, 413, 414, 421, 574
Marseille, 251, 329
martial arts, 8, 24
Marx, Karl, xiii, 8, 60, 75, 81, 90, 95, 127, 354,
    429, 455, 461, 466, 473, 480, 540, 577
  economic teachings of, 102
Marxism, 2, 16, 60–61, 64, 81, 82, 87–88, 91,
    112, 153, 217, 224, 225, 263, 279, 320,
    329, 335, 341, 343, 354, 363, 366–67,
    373, 421, 447, 487, 515, 520, 543, 547,
    574
  Chinese, 3, 318, 325–26, 339
  classical, 95, 341
  criticism encouraged for, 440–41
  historical materialism of, 95
  indoctrination of, 405–6
  political economy in, 141
  Soviet, 2
  theory of capital and surplus value, 93
  working class in, 3, 109, 141
Marxism-Leninism, 47, 341, 343, 398, 399,
    434, 439, 486, 532, 536, 583
  Hundred Flowers critiques of, 441
  Mao Zedong Thought and, 405–6, 433–34,
    467, 526, 534, 563
  Nie Yuanzi's *dazibao* and, 502
Marxist Study Society, 62
masses, dictatorship of, 529
matchmakers, 26
Matveev, Fedor, 367
May Day parade, 427
May Fourth Movement of 1919, 82, 138, 143,
    276, 332
May Thirtieth Movement, 144
Meizhou pinglun (Weekly Review), 60, 72,
    81
Mencius, 84
Mencius, 15
Meng Jinyun, 568, 571

Meng Qingshu (Rosa Vladimirovna Osetrova), 236, 316
merchants, 221
metallurgical enterprises, 411
metals, rare and nonferrous, 372
Metropolitan Trading Company, 248
middle class, 24, 137
Mif, Pavel (Petershevskii), xiii, 234–36, 246, 259
  execution of, 333
  proteges of, 235–36, 238, 244, 248, 249, 252–55, 261, 262, 269–70, 276, 279, 284, 333
Mikoyan, Anastas Ivanovich (Andreev), xiii, 356–57, 369–70, 384, 402, 410, 425, 427, 433, 436n, 439, 443
military opportunism, 341
Mill, John Stuart, 36
Million Heroes, A, 527–29
Minbao (The People), 24, 43
Ming dynasty, 11, 17, 28, 34, 40, 58, 491
Minguo shibao (Republic news), 62
Ministry of Defense, PRC, 488, 497
Ministry of Education, Chinese, 54, 69
Ministry of Foreign Affairs, PRC, 530, 571
  Protocol Department of, 558
Ministry of Higher Education, PRC, 505
Ministry of Public Security, PRC, 484, 497, 502, 511, 576
Ministry of State Security (MGB), 367, 395, 400
Ministry of Trade, PRC, 434
Minli bao (People's independence), 33
mintuan (peasant self-defense forces), 185
Mitin, Mark Borisovich, 317–18
Mitkevich, Olga, 205
Mitterrand, François, 475
moderates, 393–99, 403–5, 415, 417–18, 430, 431–32, 434, 438, 476, 477–78, 485, 493, 586
  Mao's campaign against, 489–90, 534, 586
  return of, 574, 575
  see also capitalist roaders
Moiseenko-Velikaiia, Tatiana, 247
Molotov, Vyacheslav, 188, 300–302, 353, 354, 384, 402, 427, 436
  Americans manipulated by, 345
  fall from favor of, 443–44
  Mao's visit to Moscow and, 368–69, 372, 373
Molotov-Ribbentrop Pact of 1939, 424–25
monarchy:
  constitutional, 21, 23, 29–30, 34, 39
  despotic, 29–30
  monarchism, 332
Mongolia, 363, 376, 538
  Outer, 552

Mongolian People's Republic, 539, 587
Mongols, 11
Monino, 329, 544
Montesquieu, Baron de la Brède et de, 36
Montgomery, Bernard Law, xiii, 475, 480
Mordvinov, Georgii, 355
Moscow, 4, 89, 91, 100, 107, 108, 113, 114, 119, 146, 185, 248, 287, 291, 329, 355, 377, 389, 391, 400–401, 427, 436, 444, 537, 544, 553
  Chinese communists in, 3, 123, 134, 140, 181, 208n, 224, 225, 234, 235–36, 249, 253, 254–55, 269, 276, 284, 319, 321, 322, 327, 335
  Comintern headquarters in, 88, 101
  ECCI in, 217, 227, 270–71
  Mao's son born in, 5
  radio link reestablished with, 296
Moscow Institute of Oriental Studies, 349, 356
Moskvin, see Zhou Enlai
Mount Shao, 11, 29, 32
Mudanjiang, 489
Mukden, 257
Mukden Incident, 257, 295
Muldoon, Robert, 570–71
Museum of the First Congress of the CCP, 102
Mussolini, Benito, 295
Mussolini, Edda, 295
mutual aid, 64, 75, 76
mutual responsibility (baojia), 272
"My Hopes for the Labor Association" (Mao), 108–9

Nagy, Imre, 435
Nanchang, 160, 165, 207, 233, 245, 257, 350, 389, 463, 550
  Chiang's seat of power in, 165–66
  failed attack on, 231
Nanchang Uprising, 189–90, 206, 211, 543
Nanjing, 34, 58, 84, 108, 177, 208n, 301, 302, 303, 356, 406, 494, 515, 549, 569
  British and American shelling of, 178
  Chiang's national government in, 179, 246, 288, 303, 312, 314, 321, 350, 351
  communism in, 123
  fall of, 353
  as Guomindang capital, 216–17
  Japanese capture of, 321
  PLA capture of, 352
Nanning, 495, 533
Nanning Conference, 448, 449, 452
National Assembly, Chinese, 34–35, 39
National Congress of Peasant Unions, 177
National Party Conference, 411

National People's Congress (NPC), 408, 461,
    585
  Five-Year Plan adopted by, 418
  Mao's resignation as chairman of, 461, 586
  Second Session of, 411
  Standing Committee of, 408, 567
National Revolutionary Army (NRA),
    Guomindang, 126, 138, 144, 152, 164,
    185–86, 197, 245
  and Anglo-American attack on Nanjing,
    178
  atrocities by, 186
  attacks on peasants by, 185–86
  Autumn Harvest Uprising and, 207
  in clashes with worker-peasant forces, 178
  Eighth Corps of, 213
  Fourth Corps of, 181, 183, 187, 207, 210
  General Political Administration, 177
  increasing conservatism of, 165, 170
  Kuibyshev and, 154
  in Nanjing, 177, 183
  Ninth Corps of, 240
  Northern Expedition of, 158–60, 161,
    170–71
  officers from landlord class in, 151, 185–86
  Red Army and, 213–14, 245–46, 313
  Second Front Army of the, 189–90
  in Shanghai, 177, 183
  Wuhan captured by, 161
nationalism, 24, 30, 42, 104, 122, 372
  China accused of, 401
nationalist communism, 374
Nationalist Party, Chinese, see Guomindang
Nationalists, 563
Nehru, Jawaharlal, 428, 445, 467
Neiman, Vladimir (Vasilii Berg), see Nikolsky
Netherlands, 100
Neumann, Heinz (Moritz; Gruber), 205
neurasthenia, 140, 145, 147
New Army:
  Eighth Engineer Battalion of, 32
  Fiftieth Regiment of, 33, 34
  Forty-Ninth Regiment of, 33
  Twenty-First Brigade of, 33
New Culture Movement, 58–60, 84, 332
New Democracy, 331, 340, 342, 345, 354,
    356–58, 366, 369, 483, 585
  CCP's rise to power under advocacy of,
    352–53
  cooperative movement under, 415–16
  Mao's reluctant advocacy and later
    abandonment of, 354, 357–58, 395, 397,
    413
  moderates' approach to, 393–99, 402,
    415–16, 476–77
  multiparty system in, 357, 359
  obsolescence of, 404, 406
  as transition to socialism, 369, 393, 395,
    397–99, 415
New Democratic Youth League, 345
New Epoch, 105
New York stock market, 228
New York Times, 424
New Zealand, 570
Nguyen Van Thieu, 560
Nie Rongzhen, xiii, 278, 279, 334, 522–23,
    524, 535
Nie Yuanzi, xiii, 501–2, 516, 532–33
Nikolai, Werner, see Lominadze, Vissarion
    Vissarionovich
Nikolsky (Vladimir Neiman; Vasilii Berg),
    100–103, 106
Ningdu county, 221, 257, 264, 281
Ningxia province, 313
Ningxiang, 50, 129, 479–80
Nixon, Pat, 558
Nixon, Richard M., 556–60, 587
NKVD, 333, 337, 426
No. 1 Cotton Mill strike, 108
North, Robert, 3
North China Military District, 392
North Korean People's Army (NKPA), 375,
    379
  losses to, 387
North Sea (Beihai), 57, 58
Northeast Army, 295, 298
Northeast Military Region, Chinese, 383
Northern Expedition, 158–60, 161–63,
    170–71, 210, 216
Novy mir (New world), 293n

October Revolution, 4, 62, 82, 95, 251, 437,
    443, 448, 456, 537, 574
Office of Strategic Services (OSS), U.S., 344
OGPU, Foreign Department of, 296
Old Bachelor Wang, 328
Old Man, the, see Chen Duxiu
"On Coalition Government" (Mao), 357
On New Democracy (Mao), 331
On Renovation of the People (Liang Qichao),
    29–30
"On the Co-operative Transformation of
    Agriculture" (Mao), 418–19
"On the Correct Handling of Contradictions
    among the People" (Mao), 440, 585
"On the Cult of Personality and Its
    Consequences" (Khrushchev), 426
"On the Historical Experience of the
    Dictatorship of the Proletariat" (Chen
    Boda), 427
"On the People's Democratic Dictatorship"
    (Mao), 358
"On the Ten Major Relationships" (Mao),
    428–29, 430n, 433, 434, 447, 585

"On the Work of Investigation" (Mao), 225
Opium Wars, 22, 58
"Oppose Bookism" (Mao), 225
Orange Island, 31, 32
Orlov, Andrei, 337, 353, 367
Otpor Station, 367–68
Outer Mongolia, 552

Pacific Ocean, 348
Pakistan, 557, 558, 571
Pan Hannian, 311, 312
Pang Renquan, 108–9
Pantsov, Alexander V., 4–5
Panyushkin, Alexander, 337, 400
paper tiger (*zhilaohu*), 428, 443, 445
Paris, 68, 251, 329
Paris commune, 454, 502
party cadres (*ganbu*), 406, 417, 418, 440, 441,
    443, 461, 463, 478, 481, 487, 501, 521,
    524, 525, 526, 555, 570, 586
    famine blamed on, 476
    "revolutionary," 522
    upper- and mid-level, 430, 448
Paulsen, Friedrich, 40–41, 42, 71
Pavilion of Chrysanthemum Fragrance, 365,
    366, 520
Pavlov, Pavel, 139
Pearl River, 131, 132, 431
peasant associations, 173, 195
    armed actions by, 189
    terror attacks by, 185
peasant disturbances, 414
peasant militias (*mintuan*), 182, 197, 201, 272
peasant movement, 167–70, 176, 178, 179,
    180, 583
Peasant Movement Training Institute, 141,
    156, 160, 163, 181
peasant proprietors, 413
"Peasant Question, The" (Mao), 160
peasant resistance, 421
peasant unions, 125, 142, 145, 155, 171, 186,
    392
    bandit takeovers of, 171
peasants, 74–75, 92, 104, 115, 137, 138, 149,
    150, 151, 158–60, 193, 223, 315, 441, 519
    and agrarian reform, 392
    bendi, 168, 260, 289
    city dwellers mobilized for aid to, 476
    contract system preferred by, 483–84
    "counterrevolutionary," 217
    defection by, 213
    egalitarianism opposed by, 212
    four big freedoms for, 397
    government seen as enemy by, 169–70
    grain monopoly and, 414
    insurrections by, 17–20
    land distribution and, 478–80

land given to, 396
Mao's attitude towards, 36, 43, 124–25,
    136–37, 141–42
middle, 294, 417, 418
night schools for, 142
organizing of, 125
owner-, 192–93, 212, 219, 223
poverty of, 17–19, 43, 159, 294, 420, 475
in Red Army, 275
rich, 213, 221, 223, 238–39, 260, 293, 294,
    349, 392, 396, 407
rural lumpen proletariat as, 16, 157,
    167–70, 185–87, 193, 196, 209, 211, 213,
    239, 252*n*, 475
support lost from, 414–15, 421
tenant farmers and well-to-do, 168, 173
as tenants of the state, 414
violence against other peasants by, 185–86
well-to-do, 352
working, 246
Yihequan uprising by, 24–25
peasants (*bendi*), 168, 260, 289
Peking Normal University, 39
Peking University (Beida), 39, 47, 53, 54,
    57–60, 62, 64–66, 69, 79, 82*n*, 93, 101,
    105, 199, 583
    Cultural Revolution at, 501–3, 521, 532–33
    middle school at, 510
Peng Dehuai, xiii, 214, 215, 220, 237, 243,
    279, 287, 306, 308, 348, 383, 443, 484
    critical letter from, 463–66, 475
    in CRMC, 256
    disgrace and dismissal of, 465, 518, 543,
        551, 586
    in Eighth Route Army, 313–15
    on grain output, 457–58
    Hai Rui as parallel to, 491
    in Korean War, 383, 384–85, 387–88
    Third Army Group commanded by, 231,
        246, 259
Peng Gongda, xiii, 194, 197
    party criticism of, 201, 205–6
Peng Huang, 96, 99
Peng Pai, xiii, 125, 141, 161–62, 177
    death of, 256
    and Nanchang Uprising, 189–90
    on Provisional Politburo, 193
Peng Shuzhi, 139, 140, 146–47, 180
Peng Xiaomeng, 509
Peng Zhen, xiii, 394
    downfall of, 497–501, 502, 525
    Five-Member Group headed by, 493–94,
        495–96
    on Great Leap, 480
    Khruschev's clash with, 473
    Wu Han and, 492
People's Assembly, 202

People's Committee of the Central Executive
    Committee of the Chinese Soviet
    Republic (Council of People's
    Commissars), 251
People's Committee of the Central
    Government (Council of People's
    Commissars of the CSR), 270
people's communes, 452–55, 459, 461, 465,
    476–77, 478, 484, 516
    Khrushchev's criticism of, 468
    labor efficiency in, 453
    personal plots and handicraft enterprises
        allowed on, 477
People's Liberation Army Song and Dance
    Ensemble, 463
People's Livelihood, 24, 34
People's Republic of China (PRC), 5, 6, 220,
    399, 432, 548, 562
    air force lacked by, 380
    disputed rights to UN membership of, 375
    economic development plan of, 411–12
    economy of, 422, 423, 442, 473, 475, 476,
        479, 481–83, 515, 575, 577
    establishment of, 356, 359
    evolving Soviet relationship with, 366,
        408–12, 425–48, 467–69, 472–73, 486,
        535–39, 556, 559, 586
    famine in, 456, 461, 470–77, 484
    fifth anniversary of, 409
    Five-Year Plans of, see Five-Year Plans
    founding of, 585
    as independent and powerful state, 574
    industrialization of, 390–91, 401–3, 407,
        408–9, 411–12, 425, 438, 444, 452, 453,
        456–57, 483, 538, 585
    in Korean War, 374–89, 390, 409, 585
    Maoization of, 448
    market economy in, 574
    modernizing of society in, 576
    Nixon's visit to, 557–60, 587
    nuclear technology and, 411
    nuclear weapons for, 409, 410, 425, 467–68,
        489
    party-state bureaucracy's power in, 475
    population of, 455
    as potential world power, 489
    proclamation of, 356, 391
    purges in, 405–7
    resistance against, 391–92
    Soviet aid to, 401–2, 408–9, 411–12, 425
    spiritual life of, 393
    Stalinization of, 366, 391, 400, 404, 407,
        419, 423, 425, 433, 448
    Third World and, 566
    transportation system crisis in, 516
People's Revolutionary Military Council, 543
People's War, 222, 315

personal freedom, 64
Personal Protests from the Study of Jiao Bin, 27
Peter the Great, Emperor of Russia, 23
Petershevskii, see Mif, Pavel
Petrograd, 113, 114
petroleum, 372
Pham Van Dong, 558
Philipp, see Maring
Phillips, William Berge, 505
physical culture, 42
Piatnitsky, Josef, 261, 265–66, 270
Pieck, Wilhelm, 261
Pingxiang, 17, 111, 112
    Hongjang insurrection in, 18–19
Pitou, 223, 239, 240
PLA Air Force Song and Dance Ensemble,
    568
"Plan for Developing the National Movement,
    A," 129
"Plan to Develop the Peasant Movement at
    the Present Stage," 164
Plato, 90
Poland, 440, 468
    anti-Stalinism in, 435–36, 438–39, 444
Polevoi, Sergei A., 89, 90
Polish Workers' Party, 435
"Political Parties in Russia and the Tasks of
    the Proletariat" (Lenin), 81
polygamy, 209, 220
Ponomarev, Boris Nikolaevich, 435
popular democracy, 332
populism, 441
postcolonial world, 3
poverty, as incentive for change, 455
Powers, Gary, 473
Poznan, 468
pragmatism, 408
Pravda, 271, 293, 439
private capital, 398
private enterprise, state involvement with,
    421–22
private property, 397
    in agrarian reform, 395–96
    cooperatives and, 412
    destruction of, 422
    household contracts and, 478–80
    industrial, 422
    nationalization of, 366, 413
Program for Developing Agriculture in the
    PRC, 451
Progressive Society (Gongjinhui), 32
Project 571, 549–51, 553
proletarian revolution, 508
proletarian-socialist revolution, 433
proletariat, 115, 148, 218, 219, 339, 342, 509,
    535
    in class conflict, 105

dictatorship of the, 95, 102–3, 132, 229, 319, 358, 494, 498, 524, 567, 568
  hegemony of, 149
  Mao's analysis of, 152
  resistance to CCP policies by, 422
  rural lumpen, 16, 157, 167–70, 185–87, 193, 196, 209, 211, 213, 239, 252n, 475
propaganda, 72, 391
  anti-Khrushchev, 440
  anti-Soviet, 486
  communist, 108
  Cultural Revolution against, 498
  Mao's, 72, 152, 153, 158, 160, 224, 292, 331
  Mao's swimming in, 505
  in PLA, 488
property, state, 357
Proudhon, Pierre-Joseph, 64
Provincial First Middle School, 35, 96, 583
Provincial First Normal School, 37–39, 51–52, 63, 65, 96, 109
  evening workers' school at, 48–49
  primary school of, 96, 110, 112
  Student Union at, 48–49
Przheval'skii, 400–401
Przheval'skii, Nikolai, 400
Pu Yi, emperor of China, 25, 35, 57
Pukou railroad station, 123
Pyongyang, 378, 387

Qi Benyu, 530
Qian Xijun, 181, 209, 249–50, 268, 389, 591
Qianfeng (Vanguard), 134
Qianlong, emperor of China, 363
qigong, 18
Qin, kingdom of, 31, 408
Qin Bangxian, *see* Bo Gu
Qin Shi Huangdi, emperor of China, 29, 31, 455–56
Qing (Manchu) dynasty, 12, 17–18, 32–35, 37, 39, 210, 363, 466
  Beijing captured by, 58
  military forces of, 25
  Sun's opposition to, 24
  Taiping Rebellion against, 22
Qingbang (Green Gang), 178
Qingdao, 44, 68–69, 70, 143–44, 327, 394
  PLA capture of, 352
Qinghai province, 522
Qingnian (Youth), 63
Qingshuitang, 112
Qingtang, 246, 262
Qu Qiubai, xiii, 6, 134, 140, 146–47, 163, 190, 192, 217–18, 284
  and Central Committee self-criticism, 234–35
  Changsha action ordered by, 205
  in Chinese Soviet Republic, 252

  death of, 426
  Lominadze and, 188–89
  as Mao's ally, 162, 174, 180, 187, 189
  ordered to withdraw CCP from Guomindang, 204
  on Provisional Bureau of CCP, 187
  on Provisional Politburo, 193–94
  tuberculosis suffered by, 190, 252
  in USSR, 218–19
Qufu, 84, 513
  Red Guards in, 513
Quotations of Chairman Mao, 488, 544, 574

Radek, Karl, 166
railroads, 31, 55, 110, 111, 121, 425
  Beijing-Hankou, 161
  Changsha-Wuchang, 111, 120, 161
Rao Shushi, xiv, 404–6, 408, 585
Rasputin, 356
rationing, 352
raw materials, shortages of, 423
Razumov, Mikhail, 190
Razumovskii, Isaak Petrovich, 317
reactionaries, 221
Rebels, 515–16, 519, 521, 522, 524, 526–27, 533, 560
Reclus, Élisée, 53
Records of the Grand Historian (Sima Qian), 27
Rectification Movement, 442, 448
Red Army, Chinese, 2, 198, 220–32, 264, 274, 293, 299, 306, 325, 584
  First Army Group of, 231, 237, 241, 275
  First Corps of, 273
  First Division of, 200, 202, 207
  First Front Army of, 231–32, 233, 237, 243, 244, 245, 256, 262, 271, 285, 290
  Second Front Army Group of, 275–76, 290
  Third Army Group of, 231, 246, 256, 259, 275
  Third Corps of, 243
  Fourth Corps of, 210, 212, 215, 222, 225, 227, 229, 230, 231, 239, 240, 258
  Fourth Front Army Group of, 276, 284, 285, 286, 290
  Fifth Army Group of, 256, 275
  Fifth Corps of, 215, 239
  Sixth Corps of, 231, 239
  Sixth Front Army Group of, 275
  Eighth Army Group of, 275
  Ninth Army Group of, 275
  Twelfth Corps of, 231
  Twentieth Corps of, 241–43, 244
  agrarian revolution, 212–13
  amalgamation of units in, 231
  attacks by Yi on, 280
  banditry ascribed to, 247, 260

Red Army, Chinese (*cont.*)
  bandits allied with, 212
  Bo Gu and Luo Fu's letter to, 256–57
  Braun on strategy of, 269
  Central, *see* Central Red Army
  Central Committee of CCP and, 190, 210, 222, 223, 226–32, 239–40, 241, 243–44
  Changsha overrun by, 206
  Chiang fought by, 276, 299
  defeats of, 234, 277
  formal uniforms of, 252
  Front Command of, 281
  Futian Incident and, 239–45, 584
  goal to reunite with Zhang Guotao's forces, 282
  against Guangdong militarists, 262
  guerrilla tactics of, 222, 223, 229, 233, 249, 254, 259, 276, 290
  Guomindang battles with, 213–14, 221, 248, 254, 265, 268, 272, 277, 296
  Hakka's view of, 215
  Jiangxi base of, 233, 246
  joint party conference of, 223
  on Long March, 273, 275–88
  Mao's and Zhu's troops united in, 209–11
  Moscow on, 234
  National Revolution Army and, 313
  numbers of, 283
  opium sales by, 212, 221
  propaganda by, 224
  proposed renaming of, 304
  question of, 206–7
  reorganization of, 285
  reserve division of, 275
  right and left columns of, 285–87
  in Shaanxi, 289–90
  Shaanxi-Gansu Brigade of, 287–88
  Sixth Congress' directions ignored by, 220–21
  size of, 214–15, 222, 232, 259, 275, 284, 287, 288, 290, 296
  songs by, 246
  in southeastern Hunan, 275
  split between right and left columns of, 285–87
  Stalin's support for, 237
  subject to CRMC, 256
  supplies and provisions shortages of, 214, 221, 273, 277, 285, 296
  urban attacks proposed for, 229, 257, 259
  welcomed by poor, 215, 239, 240
  withdrawal from Central Soviet Area by, 273–74
Red Army, Russian, 82
Red Army Academy, 267
Red Army Intelligence Directorate, 337

Red Guards, 507–19, 521–22, 524, 526–34, 568, 575, 586
  armed units of, 529–30
  hostile groups and factions among, 527
  military suppression of, 533, 541
  numbers of, 510
  scapegoating of Beijing chiefs of, 532
  songs of, 509, 516
  teachers persecuted by, 511
  terrorism by, 511–13, 519, 547
  at Tsinghua University middle school, 507–8
Red International of Trade Unions, 205
Red Order, 275
Red People's Militia, 527
Red Spears, 171
Red Star, 275
Red Star Over China (Snow), 1–2, 324
red terror, 185, 247
Red Zone, 257
redistribution, 476
Rehe, 287
Ren Bishi (Zheng Ling; Chen Lin), xiv, 136, 205, 244, 255, 262, 290, 333*n*, 334, 336, 426, 575
  Mao opposed by, 263–64
  in Moscow, 321, 322, 323, 328, 356
Renmin ribao (People's daily), 404, 427, 430, 438, 439–41, 449, 494–95, 496, 505, 512, 516, 525, 536, 544, 557, 561
Renovation of the People Study Society (Xinmin xuehui), 50–51, 62, 64–65, 68, 71, 77–79, 121, 583
  Bolshevism adopted by, 96–97, 98–99
rent reduction, 392
Report of an Investigation of the Peasant Movement in Hunan (Mao), 171–76, 520
Republic Day, 161
Republic of China, 34–35, 44, 87, 101
  Ministry of Foreign Affairs of, 347
  National government of, 144, 216–17
  in Taiwan, 302, 352, 383, 391, 406, 460, 557, 559, 565
  in UN, 375*n*, 556
  U.S. recognition of, 468
  see also Chiang Kai-shek; Guomindang
republican government, 23, 24
Resolution of the CCP Central Committee on Developing Agricultural Producers' Cooperatives, 416
"Resolution on a Rectification Movement," 440–41
revisionism, 525, 527, 534, 561, 562, 568
  Mao's campaign against, 487, 492, 494, 497, 499, 501, 512, 531
  Soviet, 486, 497, 500, 535, 536, 539
  Yugoslavian, 486

Revoliutsionnyi Vostok (Revolutionary East), 175

Revolution of 1911, 32, 33, 39, 45, 58, 59, 112, 210, 332

Revolutionary Alliance (Tongmenghui), 24, 32–34, 39, 44, 120, 127, 210

Revolutionary Bureau, 92

revolutionary committees, 522–23, 530–31

Rexue ribao (Hot blood), 140

Rhee, Syngman, 383

rickshaw pullers, 110

Rokossowski, Konstantin Konstantinovich, 435

Romance of Sui and Tang, The, 20

Romance of the Three Kingdoms, The, 20, 55, 279, 532

Romania, 440, 473, 474

Romanian Communist Party, 473
   Congress of the, 474

Romm, Mikhail, 459

Roosevelt, Franklin D., 320–21, 343

Roshchin, Nikolai, 353, 367–68, 379, 381, 384

Roy, M. N., xiv, 179, 183, 185, 188

Rudnik, Yakov, 247

Ruijin, 246, 255, 260
   as capital of CSR, 252, 261, 263, 266, 268–70, 274
   Mao sent away from, 262
   withdrawal from, 273

Russell, Bertrand, 83–84, 90, 99

Russia, 36, 60–61, 63, 74, 82, 84, 89, 136, 574
   Bolshevik, 81
   Japan's defeat of, 30
   Mao's desire to study in, 90–91, 112

Russia Studies Society, 90

Russian civil war, 316

Russian Communist Party, 134, 151
   Central Committee of, 127

Russian revolution, 61–62, 82, 89, 94, 126

Russian Social Democratic Labor Party, Fourth Conference of, 126

Russian State Archive of Social and Political History, 4

Russians, in Shanghai, 86

Rylsky, Ignatii, 248

Saburov, Mikhail, 391

Sandianhui (Three-Dot Society), 240

Sanfan (Three Anti) campaign, 393

Schwartz, Benjamin I., 3

Scotland, 39

Second All Russian Congress of Soviets, 62

Second All-China Congress of Soviets, 270, 271, 292–93, 584

Second Byelorussian Front, 349

Second National Revolutionary Army, 190

secret service, PRC, 366

sectarianism, 441

security organs, control over political and intellectual life by, 366

Selected Works (Mao), 373, 405, 429n, 492

Self-Study University, 112, 122, 129

Semenov, Georgii, 392

Serov, Ivan Aleksandrovich, 436n

Service, John Stewart, 344

Seven Thousand Cadre Conference, 562

Shaanxi province, 88, 210, 285, 295, 299, 301, 304, 306, 313, 348, 349, 544n
   northern, 348
   soviet in, 287–88, 289–90, 296, 585

Shamian island, 132, 144

Shandong, 208n

Shandong peninsula, 44

Shandong province, 24, 44, 84, 159, 327
   famine in, 472
   Red Guards in, 513

Shang Yang, 41–42, 563

Shanghai, 17, 49, 54, 66, 70, 77, 79, 84, 91, 93, 108, 111, 114, 115, 119, 121, 122, 123, 127, 128, 131, 135, 136, 139, 162, 181, 187, 198, 204, 208n, 209, 252, 276, 295, 312, 327, 328, 329, 350, 405, 406, 487, 495, 528, 529, 530, 531, 549, 550, 569
   CCP Founding Congress in, 100–102, 105–6, 107, 583
   CCP in, 204–6, 222, 224, 225, 227, 228, 230, 234–35, 236, 243, 244, 246–48, 250, 254, 256, 259, 261, 264, 266–67, 271, 275, 584
   Chiang's defeat of worker forces in, 178, 179, 180
   communism in, 100, 101, 108, 112, 123, 267
   cooperativization in, 418–19
   Cultural Revolution Group branch in, 500
   districts of, 85–87
   ECCI in, 194, 237, 261, 275
   foreigners in, 86
   French police in, 105–6
   general strike in, 175
   Guomindang Bureau in, 136, 139–40
   January revolution in, 521, 522
   Japanese attack against, 259–60
   Japanese bombardment and capture of, 312–13, 315, 328
   Mao in, 85, 163
   Mao's sons sent to, 249–50
   massacre in, 143–44
   PLA capture of, 352
   popular uprising against Sun Chuanfang in, 177
   Provisional Central Committee in, 248
   radicalism in, 494, 517, 560
   Red Guard looting in, 513

Shanghai (*cont.*)
    Soviet spy ring in, 306
    strikes in, 352, 422
    trade union activists in, 144
    white terror in, 248, 266, 583
Shanghai Municipal Party Committee, Rebels
    and, 515, 521, 524
Shanghai Workers' Revolutionary Rebels
    General Headquarters, *see* Rebels
Shanhaiguan, 551
Shanxi province, 315, 321, 350, 355, 519
    rural cooperativization in, 396
Shao Hua, *see* Zhang Shaohua
Shao Lizi, 299
Shao Piaoping, 62, 65, 90
Shaoshan, 5, 11–12, 17, 25, 27, 28, 110–11,
    143, 156, 186, 209n, 482, 483, 503,
    583
    grain harvest in, 466
    Guomindang in, 145
    insurrection in, 1
Shaoshanchong, 6, 11–12, 97, 142, 145, 511,
    583
    CCP cell in, 142
    Mao's return after thirty-two years to,
    462
Shen Rong, 591
Shen Yanbing (Mao Dun), 158, 407
Shen Zemin, 235, 244
Sheng Shicai, 388
shenshi, 25
Shenyang, 379, 397
Shi Zhe, xiv, 368, 371, 384, 394, 408, 445
Shinzō, Fukuda, 60
ship repair and construction, 372
Shirokov, Ivan Mikhailovich, 317
Shishi xinbao (Factual news), 62
Short, Philip, 27
Shtykov, Terentii, 377, 380
Shuangqing, 363, 376
Shuikoushan, 110
Shun, sage-king, 29
Shvernik, Nikolai, 410
Siberia, 537, 538
Sichuan province, 88, 168, 183, 210, 229, 276,
    280, 282, 283, 285, 289, 290, 330, 452,
    484, 518, 522
    famine in, 461, 475
Sidikhmenov, Vasilii, 446
Sikang (Tibet), 283
Silin, Mikhail A., 375
Sima Qian, 27
Simonov, Konstantin, 373
Singapore, 571
Sino-American Xiangya Hospital, 76, 90
Sino-French Study Society, 54
Sino-Indian border conflict, 467–68

Sino-Japanese War of 1937–45, 23, 302,
    312–21, 330–31, 336, 342, 354, 415, 441,
    527, 544, 571, 585
Sixteen Points, 508–9, 510
"Sixty Theses on Work Methods" (Mao), 448,
    450
small production, 421
Smedley, Agnes (Anna), xiv, 210, 306–11, 327,
    343, 351n
Smith, Adam, 36
Sneevliet, Hendricus Josephus Franciscus
    Marie, *see* Maring
Snow, Edgar, xiv, 1–2, 16, 20, 27, 30, 31, 35,
    39, 42, 50, 57n, 63, 65, 66, 81, 87, 201,
    210, 220, 296, 308, 309–10, 324, 326,
    343, 363, 474–75, 476, 492–93, 540–41,
    556, 557
Snow, Helen Foster (Peg; Peggy; Nym Wales),
    xiv, 308–9, 311, 327, 343, 556
Sochi, 379, 384
social democracy, 99, 536
Social Democratic Association of the Dutch
    East Indies, 103
social sciences, 407
socialism, 109, 315, 331, 332, 352, 357, 415,
    420, 445, 468, 479, 507, 534, 555
    Brezhnev doctrine and, 538
    building of, 411–12, 454, 477–78, 480
    in China, 12, 64, 73, 104, 111, 319–21
    Chinese, 44, 444
    class struggle under, 500–501
    classes in, 485, 486–87
    dictatorial, 576
    in Europe, 376
    Fabian, 81
    Maoist, 7–8
    Mao's desire to accelerate development of,
    390–91, 396–99, 400, 402–4, 407,
    416–21
    Marxian, 60–61
    "more, better, faster, more economically,"
    419, 429, 430n, 442, 449, 586
    national economy and, 357
    Russian, 99
    socioeconomic development and, 366–67
    Soviet model of, 366, 399, 412, 585
    Sputnik as proof of superiority of, 443
    Stalinist, 404
    Stalin's discouragement of PRC's, 366–67
    totalitarian, 575
    triumph of, 428
    Utopian, 52, 413
socialist construction, 366, 453, 478, 585, 586
Socialist Education campaign, 488, 491–92,
    494
socialist reforms, forced, 423
socialist revolution, 218

Socialist Youth Group of China, 92
Socialist Youth League, 97, 129, 136, 543
  in Anyuan colliery, 112
  Beijing, 95
  in Canton, 131
  in Changde, 112
  First Congress of, 113–14
  in Hengyang, 112
  Hunan, 96, 109, 110, 112
  in Pingjiang, 112
  Shanghai, 92, 95
  see also Chinese Communist Youth League
Socialist Youth League of Changsha,
    Executive Committee of, 112
Society of Hunanese Residing in Shanghai, 87
Song dynasty, 32, 46, 116
Song Jiaoren, 44
Song Meiling, 126, 302, 388, 462
  as communist sympathizer, 311, 358
Song Qingling (Madame Suzy; Leah), xiv,
    359, 443, 546n
Song Yaowu (Song Binbin), 510
Song Ziwen, 302
Sorge, Richard, 306
South Manchurian Railroad, 257
Soviet Air Force, 384
Soviet Army, Chiang Kai-shek demands
    immediate withdrawal of, 347–48
Soviet Asian Studies Association, 175
Soviet Central Committee, 269
Soviet Communist Party:
  Central Committee of, 4
  Guomindang and, 153–54
  rightists in, 227
  secret archives of, 4
  Twentieth Congress of, 3
Soviet Council of Ministers, 372n
Soviet Far East, 89
Soviet General Staff, intelligence of, 269
Soviet Labor Association, 410
Soviet New Economy Policy (NEP), 367
Soviet Order of the Fighting Red Banner, 284
Soviet Pacific Fleet, 458
Soviet Politburo, 125, 156, 163, 175, 178, 189,
    234, 334, 367, 372n, 373
Soviet Russia, 69, 83, 90, 91, 97, 103, 107, 115,
    128, 134
  anti-imperialist and anticapitalist policy of,
    82
Soviet Union, 160, 191, 230, 234, 295, 326,
    327, 329–30, 337, 389, 452, 478, 516,
    519, 530, 540, 544, 545n, 552–53, 566
  agrarian collectivization in, 223, 227
  aid to China from, 126, 188–89, 190, 248,
    273, 287, 312, 315, 334, 346, 352, 368,
    390
  aid to PLA from, 467–68

aid to PRC by, 401–2, 408–9, 411–12, 425
boycott of UN Security Council by, 375–76
and CCP's victory, 353
Chiang Kai-shek's nonaggression treaty
    with, 313
China policy of, 367
China's relationship with, 115, 120, 122
Chinese agents of, 400
Chinese communists in, 210
compromised authority of, 444
in continued relations with Guomindang,
    190
diplomatic mission to China by, 119, 127,
    135, 149
economy of, 390
First Five-Year Plan of, 391
foreign policy of, 440
German attack on, 334
glorification campaign for Mao in, 237,
    271, 291–93, 322, 584
great power chauvinism of, 435, 437, 439
imperialist attitude towards China by,
    371–72
intelligence of, 542
Japan and, 258
Japanese aggression feared by, 296, 301,
    302, 313, 317
Korean War and, 7, 374–87, 409
Mao promoted by, 323–24
Mao's critique of, 428–29
Mao's first visit to, 369–73, 445, 585
as Mao's model, 366, 449
Mao's second visit to, 443–47, 449
Mao's sons in, 250–51, 328–29
Mao's wish to overtake, 447
military advisors from, 126, 127–28,
    138–39, 143, 158, 315
in nuclear test ban treaty, 495n
nuclear weapons of, 376, 444, 446, 461,
    467–68, 538
Party control of, 256
paternalism of, 433
PRC's evolving relationship with, 366,
    408–12, 425–48, 467–69, 472–73, 486,
    535–59, 586
revisionism in, 486, 497, 500, 535, 536, 539
secret service of, 247, 395
security police of, 296
Sixth Congress of CCP held in, 217
spies of, 306
split between communist parties in China
    and, 3, 7
Sputnik satellite launched by, 442–43, 444,
    447
steel production in, 456
Sun Yat-sen and, 127, 138
support for Mao in, 255

Soviet Union (*cont.*)
  U-2 spy plane incident and, 473–74
  worsening of China's relations with,
    535–39
Soviet Union, former, archives in, 1, 4
Soviet-Chinese border dispute, 535–39, 586
Soviet-Chinese Navy, proposed, 458
Soviet-Guomindang Treaty of Friendship and
    Alliance, 346
soviets, 212, 218, 261, 285, 584
  all-China conference of, 230
  base for, 232
  in China, 202, 205, 211
  ECCI's suggestion Mao democratize, 303–4
  in Shaanxi-Gansu-Sichuan, 285, 287
sparrows, 451–52, 471
Special Border Region of the Chinese
    Republic, 304, 313–14, 345
Special West Jiangxi Committee, 239
Spencer, Herbert, 36
spontaneous revolution, 64
Stalin, Joseph Vissarionovich (Filippov; Feng
    Xi), xiv, 4, 6, 35, 88, 228, 253, 264, 306,
    325, 388, 410, 423, 445, 446, 520, 555,
    574
  and agrarian policy, 182, 223
  ambivalence towards PRC by, 366–68, 402
  anti-Trotskyist campaign of, 63, 317
  attack on Guomindang demanded by, 183,
    185
  attempt to manipulate Americans by, 345
  Borodin sent to China by, 126
  campaign against Wang and, 333, 335,
    337–39
  CCP blamed by, 188, 191, 217
  and CCP victory, 353–58
  CCP withdrawn from Guomindang by, 204
  on Chiang's arrest, 300–304
  China policy of, 367, 402, 426–27
  Chinese communist armies assisted by,
    347–48
  on Chinese development plans, 390–91,
    396
  Chinese informers of, 356
  Chinese reassessment of, 426–27, 444
  Chinese Titoism feared by, 372, 374, 384
  Comintern controlled by, 6–7
  Comintern dissolved by, 332
  cruelty of, 472
  cult of personality of, 424–25, 466, 489, 536
  death of, 387, 390, 400–401, 402, 426, 474,
    478, 525
  distrustful nature of, 343, 356, 366–68,
    372–73, 377, 394, 395, 424, 427
  Gao Gang and, 393–94, 404
  German and Japanese aggression feared by,
    291, 301

on growth of socialism, 234
on Guomindang policy, 149–51, 156, 162,
    163, 175, 179
Guomindang policy shifts of, 175, 178–79
Khrushchev's censure of, 424–25, 427,
    434–35, 439, 448, 460, 525
Korean War and, 7, 374–87
Mao Anying and, 349
Mao's relationship with, 2–4, 5, 7, 44,
    236–37, 248–49, 270, 292, 296, 302,
    322–24, 334, 335, 342, 343, 345–47,
    353–58, 369–73, 395, 400–401, 424–26,
    459–60, 584, 585
Mao's sons brought to Soviet Union by,
    250–51
as Mao's teacher, 366, 368
New Democracy concept supported by,
    354, 356–57
October Directive of, 163–65, 167, 170–71
rightist danger feared by, 258–59
seventieth birthday of, 367–69
show trial of Comintern officials planned
    by, 7
suspicious nature of, 390
tactics based on deception by, 319
unforgiving attitude towards losers by, 234
united front policy of, 291, 295–97,
    311–17, 319
and U.S. nuclear weapons monopoly,
    345–46
Zhou Enlai and, 5
Stalinism, 3, 248, 261, 317–18, 325–26, 335,
    341
  in CCP, 47
  Chinese, 352
  Mao's critique of, 429
  in PRC, 366, 391, 400, 404, 407, 419, 423,
    425, 433, 448
Standard Oil Company, 306
State Administrative Council, PRC, 366, 391,
    396–97, 402, 408, 415, 526, 543, 562,
    570, 587
State Department, U.S., 344
State People's Bank, 268
State Planning Commission, PRC, 411, 476
State Planning Committee of the USSR, 391
State Publishing Association, 327
steel mills, 452
steel production, 407, 447, 450, 452, 457,
    461–63, 470
Steenhoven, Graham B., 557
stock market, 1929 crash of, 228
Stockholm, 126
strikes, 111, 120–21, 352, 422
Strong, Anna Louise, 351
"Study of Physical Education, A" (Mao), 42,
    59

Study of the New Russia, A (Shao), 90
Su Zhaozheng, 144
subjectivism, 441, 450
Suiping, 453
"Summary of the Army Forum on Literature
    and Art Work" (Jiang Qing), 496–97
Sun Chuanfang, 159, 175, 177
Sun Ke, 180
Sun Mingjiu, 297–98
Sun Yat-sen (Sun Wen), xiv, 23, 32, 43, 44,
    123, 133–34, 136, 153, 192, 193, 311,
    332, 354, 358, 574
  as centrist, 137
  Chinese nationalists under, 103, 210
  communist alliance with, 107–8, 114–15,
    119–21, 125–28, 137–40, 154, 156
  death of, 143
  legacy of, 149, 158, 165
  as president of National Assembly, 34–35
  as president of Republic of China, 101, 103
  return to China by, 101
  Three Principles of the People declared by,
    24, 33, 34, 120, 121, 127, 148, 312, 320,
    331
  three-step transition to democracy
    envisioned by, 216
Sun Yat-Sen University of the Toilers of
    China, 181, 191, 228, 234, 276, 312
Sun Zi, 279
Sundstrom, Carl-Johan, 428, 445
Supreme Soviet of the USSR, 447
Supreme State Conference, 440
Supreme State Council, 430, 585
Suslov, Mikhail Andreevich, 468
Suzhou Creek, 85
Sverdlovsk, 312, 473
Svoboda, Irena, 356
Svoboda, Ludvik, 356
Swan Lake, 445
Swatow, 190, 207
Swimming Pool Pavilion, 366, 572
Switzerland, 88
Sword Society (*madaodui*), 203
System der Ethik (Paulsen), 40–41, 42

T. C. Li, *see* Li Dazhao
Ta-chao Li, *see* Li Dazhao
Taiping, 22, 25
Taiping Heavenly Kingdom, 22
Taiping Lake, 521
Taiping Rebellion, 22, 25, 169*n*
Taishan mountain, 84, 481
Taiwan, 27, 302, 383, 406, 557, 559, 565, 571
  Guomindang move to, 352, 391
Taiyuan, Japanese capture of, 315
Tan Pingshan, xiv, 66, 120, 133–34, 153, 156,
    162, 358

Tan Yankai, xiv, 34, 39, 45, 80, 90, 91, 125,
    128–29, 176, 179–80
  as head of National government, 166
  as NRA Second Corps commander, 144,
    151
Tan Zhen, 125–26, 128
Tan Zhenlin, xiv, 522, 524, 526, 528
Tang, Nancy (Tang Wensheng), xiv, 541, 558,
    564, 566–67, 568
Tang dynasty, 46, 85, 297, 428
Tang Hualong, 32, 33
Tang Shengzhi, xiv, 159–60, 165, 183
  power struggle between Chiang and, 175,
    176
Tang Xiangming (Butcher Tang), xiv, 45
Tangjiatuo, 55, 483
Tangshan, communism in, 123
Tao Yi, xv, 51, 78, 83, 96
  Mao's affair with, 77, 79, 97, 108
Tao Zhu, 502
TASS, 467, 535
taxes, 169–70, 196, 226
  capitalism and, 396–97, 399
  grain, 414
  progressive land, 24
  Red Army and, 212
  uniform, 396–97
Temple of Heaven (Tiantan), 58
Tevosian, Ivan, 408
Three Kingdoms, period of, 428
Three Worlds, 566, 587
Tian Jiaying, xv, 483–85
  suicide of, 519
Tiananmen Gate, 359, 509, 556, 573
Tiananmen Square, 69, 573
  Great Hall of the People on, 506, 520, 532,
    552, 557, 569
  May Day parade in, 427
  Monument to Revolutionary Heroes in,
    569
  portrait and Chairman Mao Memorial Hall
    on, 573–74, 575
  Red Guards parades in, 509–10, 516–17,
    586
  student protests in, 576
  Zhou mourned in, 569–70, 587
Tianjin, 17, 59, 79, 84, 92, 134, 138, 287, 351,
    406, 440, 494
  Japanese capture of, 315
Tianyi bao (Heaven's justice), 60
Tibet, 388, 396, 467, 468
Time, 557
Tito, Josip Broz, 354, 424
Togliatti, Palmiro, 445–46
Tokyo, 24, 60, 69, 101
Tolstoy, Leo, 63
Tonggu, 200

torture, 241, 242, 247, 256, 388
totalitarianism, 366
Trade Union International (Profintern), 395
trade unions, 109–12, 121–22, 336, 519
    official, 422
    in Shanghai, 144
Treaty of Friendship, Alliance, and Mutual
        Assistance, PRC-USSR, 368, 371–73,
        383, 585
Treaty of Versailles, 68–70, 71
Triad Society, 17
Trotsky, Leon, 4, 62, 81, 88, 100, 127, 140,
    156, 456
Trotskyism, 3, 140, 236, 337, 338
    Chinese, 7, 63, 234–35, 284, 332–33
    Mao accused of, 337, 394
Truman, Harry S., 343, 385
Tsinghua University, 507–8, 516–18, 524,
    531
Tsvigun, Semyon Kuz'mich, 542n
tuhao (masters of land), 17, 18, 22, 162, 164,
    176n, 186, 212
Turkestan, 29
Twenty Cents, 328
Twenty-One Demands, 44, 69, 71, 121

Uchirō, Tate, see Luo Zhanglong
Ulbricht, Walter, 7
ultraleftism, 561
Union to Defend Native Goods, 72
United Action Committee, 526
united front policy, 339, 583, 584, 585
    of CCP, 114–16, 119, 294–304, 311–21,
        322–23, 328, 332
    Chiang Kai-shek and, 296–97, 312–15, 317,
        321
    Comintern's, 294
    Stalin's, 291, 295–97, 311–17, 319
United Nations (UN):
    armed forces of, 374–75, 379, 387
    PRC excluded from, 375, 556
    PRC in, 558, 586
    Security Council of, 374–76
    Taiwan in, 375n, 556
    Three Worlds concept at, 566
United States, 69, 76, 126, 276, 302, 419n, 474,
    536, 566, 576
    air force of, 380, 387, 388
    Boxer Rebellion and, 25
    Chiang Kai-shek criticized by, 348
    Chiang Kai-shek supported by, 351, 353
    China not prepared for war with, 380
    communist organizations in, 88
    Khrushchev's threats to, 460–61
    Korean War and, 7, 374, 376, 377, 379,
        381–82, 384–88
    Korean War losses of, 387

Monroe Doctrine and Open Door policies
    of, 87
New Democracy as an attempt to deceive,
    343–45
in nuclear test ban treaty, 495n
nuclear weapons of, 345–46, 387, 428, 446,
    468
political ideas from, 36
PRC's relations with, 468, 556–60, 562,
    564–65, 587
in Shanghai, 86
Shanghai investments of, 312–13
in Shanghai massacre, 144
in shelling of Nanjing, 178
Soviet competition with, 447
Soviet relations with, 467–68, 486
space program of, 443
Stalin's fear of nuclear conflict with, 354
Stalin's hope of provoking war between
    China and, 376–77, 380–83
steel production in, 456
and table tennis team visit to China, 557
U-2 spy plane incident and, 473
on UN Security Council, 375n
Wilson's Fourteen Points and, 69–70
Ural Mountains, 473
urban population, 430
urban property owners, 392–93
Uruguay, 37
Urumqi, 425
USSR-PRC border clashes, 535–39
Ussuri River, 535–38
Utley, Freda, 343

vagrants, 157
    see also proletariat, rural lumpen
Vasilevskii, Aleksandr, 368
vegetable oil, state monopoly on, 414
Vietnam, 29
    North, 558, 560
    South, 560
Vietnam War, 557
Vil'de, Solomon (Vladimir), 124
Vishniakova-Akimova, Vera, 131, 153, 154
Vladimirov, Petr Parfenovich, xx, 337, 339
Vladivostock, 189
Vnukovo Airport, 443
Voitinsky, Grigorii Naumovich (Wu
        Tingkang; Zarkhin), xv, 89, 91, 92,
        100–101, 108, 114, 115, 121, 124, 136,
        137, 138, 139, 140, 149, 156, 185
    as chairman of Far Eastern Bureau of
        ECCI, 162, 165, 166, 178
Volin, Mikhail (Semen Natanovich Belen'kii),
    177
voluntarism, 453
Voroshilov, Kliment, 353, 427, 443

voting rights, 408
Vyshinsky, Andrei, 368, 369, 394n

Wade-Giles system, 135n
Wagner, K. O., see Braun, Otto
Wales, Nym, see Snow, Helen Foster
Wang Chuanshan, 40
Wang Dongxing, 368
Wang Guangmei, 517–18, 519
Wang Hairong, xv, 558, 564, 566–67, 568, 571
Wang Hongwen, xv, 515, 521, 560–61, 562,
    564, 566, 567
  in Gang of Four, 565
  imprisonment of, 576
Wang Huiwu, 101–2, 106
Wang Jiaxiang (Communard; Zhang Li), xv,
    235, 244, 252, 255, 258, 261, 262, 268,
    278, 284, 340, 350, 394n, 426, 436
  in CCP delegation, 323, 325
  in CRMC, 256
  Mao Zedong thought as proposal of, 341
  Mao's winning over of, 262–63, 264, 277,
    279
  in military troika, 282
  in new triumvirate, 281
  in right column, 287
Wang Jingqing, 590
Wang Jingwei, xv, 134, 143, 179, 180, 182–83,
    187, 188, 229, 584
  in France, 165
  as head of National government, 144, 148,
    151, 153, 154–55
  return to China by, 175, 177
Wang Li, 524, 525, 528–30
Wang Meng, 533
Wang Ming (Chen Shaoyu), xv, 5, 235–36,
    248, 249, 262, 266, 269, 270, 329, 332,
    333, 336, 526, 535, 538–39, 575
  Mao opposed by, 252–53, 254–55, 271,
    292–93, 316–19, 322–23
  Mao's campaign against, 333–40, 352
  as representative to ECCI, 291, 292–93,
    300, 315
  return to China by, 316
  as Stalin's best pupil, 317
  Wuhan power base of, 321
Wang Renzhong, 497
Wang Ruofei, 6
Wang Shigu, 26n
Wang Shiwei, 498
Wang Shulan, 97, 111, 141, 142, 145, 208–9,
    591
Wang Xiaotang, death of, 519
Wang Xiaozhi (Xu Xiaoning; Li Xiaoyu);
    (Mao's grandson), 591
Wang Xiuzhen (Mao's daughter), 281
Wang Yangming, 40

Wang Zhengting, 69
Wang Zuo, xv, 202–4, 212, 215, 219
War Department, U.S., 344
  Military Intelligence Division of, 345
"War of Resistance and Culture, The" (Ye
    Qing), 341
Warsaw, 556
Warsaw Pact, 437
Waseda University, 60
Water Margin, 20, 46, 259, 567, 568
Wayaobao, 289, 294, 296
weddings, traditions of Chinese, 26–27
Wei, kingdom of, 55
Wei Heng, 519
Weixing (Sputnik) commune, 453
Wen Qimei (Wen Suqin) (Mao's mother), xv,
    13–16, 20, 26, 29, 54–55, 483, 583, 589
  death of, 66–67
Wen Yunchang, 28–29
Wenhui bao (Literary reports), 493–94, 569,
    586
Wenjiashi, 201, 207
West Lake, 115–16, 135
Western Jiangxi Special Committee of the
    CCP, 248
Western world, China as viewed by, 6
Whampoa Academy, 138, 144, 145, 155, 160,
    543
white terror, 185–86, 205, 217, 248, 266,
    583
Wilson, Woodrow, 70
Witke, Roxane, 329n, 365
women:
  in CCP, 122
  Chinese attitudes towards, 77, 209
  Red Army and, 273
  Yan'an conflict among, 307–11
Words of Warning to an Affluent Age (Zheng
    Guanying), 21
work teams, 507–8, 510
worker-peasant revolution, 218
workers, 92, 95, 137, 138, 149, 150, 151, 315,
    441
  in CCP, 122
  communism not instilled in, 111–12, 231
  revolutionary, 531
  rights of, 120
  shortage of qualified, 423
Workers, The, 90
Workers and Peasants Revolutionary Army,
    see Eighth Route Army; Red Army,
    Chinese
workers' control, 422
workers' militias, 177, 182
workers' movement, 62, 108, 121, 336
Workers' Tide, 90
workers' unions, 131

Workers' World (*Laodongjie*), 90, 93
working class, 36, 37, 74–75, 104, 109, 124,
    141, 398
  capitalism and exploitation of, 61
  industrial, 82, 109–10
  in Marxism, 3, 38, 82
  resistance to CCP policies by, 422
World Federation of Trade Unions, General
    Council of, 473
world revolution, 444
  Korean War in Stalin's plan for, 376–77,
    380–83
World Table Tennis Championship, 557
World War I, 44, 49, 54, 75
  Treaty of Versailles and, 68–71
World War II, 293*n*, 329, 345–46, 390, 424,
    440
  Mao Anying in, 349, 387
Wu De, 562
Wu Di, emperor of China, 29
Wu Faxian, 546, 547
Wu Han, xv, 491–97, 586
Wu Lengxi, 495–96
Wu Ma-you, 349
Wu Peifu, xv, 120, 121, 143, 159, 161
Wu Sangui, 466
Wu Xun, 393, 513–14
Wu Yuzhang, 426
Wu Zhihui, 53
Wuchang, 92, 111, 161, 177, 181, 183, 195,
    208, 229, 496
Wuchang uprising of 1911, 32, 33, 39, 45
Wuchang-Changsha railway, 161, 184*n*
Wufan (Five Anti) campaign, 393
Wuhan, 17, 32–33, 55, 160, 184*n*, 191, 208*n*,
    229, 250, 350, 431, 462, 497, 502, 503,
    529, 530, 550, 566, 568, 586
  CCP in, 190, 583
  Central South Bureau of Central
    Committee in, 397
  Chiang Kai-shek's seat of power moved to,
    321
  communism in, 100, 101
  Cultural Revolution clashes in, 527–29
  Guomindang left in, 161, 164–65, 174,
    175–78, 180, 354
  Japanese defeat of, 330
  local bureau of CCP in, 248
  NRA conquest of, 161
  politically complicated situation in, 183
  Provisional Joint Assembly of Party and
    Government Organizations convened
    in, 165
  Xia's attack on, 182
Wujianting, 297
Wuqizhen, 288
wushu, 18

Wusong river, 85
Wuzhishan (Five Peaks Mountain), 202

Xia, *see* Yang Kaihui
Xia Douyin, 182
Xia Minghan, 206
Xia Xi, 133
Xi'an, 297, 299–300, 307, 311
Xi'an Incident, 299–304, 322
Xiang Army, 13–14, 25
Xiang District Committee, 126, 141
Xiang Jingyu, xv, 51, 92, 128, 139
  death of, 256
  separation between Cai Hesen and, 146–47
Xiang River, 14, 31, 37, 50, 52, 72, 76, 172,
    200, 431
Xiang Ying, xv, 238, 244, 246, 249, 255, 256,
    258, 270
  in Chinese Soviet Republic, 252
  Mao approached to return by, 259–60
  Mao opposed by, 263–64
Xiang Zhenxi, 56, 97, 139, 140, 141, 147, 163,
    198, 199, 249–50
Xiang Zhongfa, xv, 218, 234, 247
Xiangdao zhoukan (Weekly guide), 114, 115
Xiangjiang pinglun (Xiang River review),
    72–77
Xiangxiang, 11, 29, 30, 39
Xiao Ke, 334
Xiao San (Emi Siao; Xiao Zizhang), xvi, 29,
    37–38, 40, 49, 50, 51–52, 327
Xiao Yu (Xiao Zisheng), xvi, 37–38, 40, 43,
    50, 51, 53, 56, 68, 106
  Bolshevism rejected by, 93–94
  in France, 66
  Mao's correspondence with, 45–46
Xiao Zhang, *see* Zhang Yufeng
Xiaoyuan, 264
Xibaipo, 368
  as communist capital, 350–51, 353, 356–58
Xie Fuzhi, 522, 525, 526, 528, 532
Xie Meixiang, 220
Xikang, 290
Xili Lake, 495
Xin Hunan (New Hunan), 76
Xin qingnian (New youth), 42, 43, 59–60,
    63–64, 83, 88, 89–90, 95, 134
Xin shidai (New age), 122
Xinhe, 110
Xinhua (New China) News Agency, 424, 495,
    502, 504, 516–17, 544
Xining, 522
Xinjiang, 287, 316, 319, 321, 372, 388, 389,
    425, 489
  CCP branch of, 388
  Provincial Revolutionary Committee in, 531
  Soviet privileges in, 409

Xinmin congbao (Renovation of the people), 29, 50
Xinxiang county, 453
Xiongnu nomads (Huns), 29
Xiuye Primary school, 68, 96
Xu Fosu, 87
Xu Haidong, 308
Xu Kexiang, 182, 186, 194, 208
Xu Ning, 590
Xu Qian, 180
Xu Shichang, 70
Xu Teli, xvi, 39, 65, 252, 334
Xu Wenyi, 552–53
Xu Xiangqian, 334, 522–24, 526, 535
Xuanzong, emperor, 297, 428
Xuchang, 55
Xunwu county, 223
Xuzhou, 494

Yale University, 32
Yalta, 461*n*
Yalta Agreement, 346, 371–72
Yan Hongyan, 519
Yan Mingfu, 434
Yan River, 305
Yan Weibing, 497–98
Yan Xishan, Beijing occupied by, 216
Yan'an, 304, 305–8, 311–12, 314–20, 326–29, 331, 333*n*, 335, 336–37, 340, 344, 346–49, 355, 389, 487, 511, 515, 518, 525
  abandonment of, 348
  bombing of, 348
  communist recapture of, 350
Yan'an Way, 441
Yang Changji ("Confucius"), xvi, 39–40, 42, 51, 77, 96, 196
  death of, 79–80
  at Peking University, 47, 53, 54, 56–57, 59, 65
Yang Chengwu, 529
Yang Guifei, 297
Yang Hucheng, 297, 299, 301
Yang Kaihui (Xia; "Dawn"; "Little Dawn") (Mao's second wife), xvi, 56–57, 77, 79–80, 96–97, 108, 129–30, 139–41, 147–48, 174, 181, 182–83, 195, 389, 589
  arrest and execution of, 198–99, 226, 231, 249–50, 388
  assistance with peasant movement report by, 171–72
  Mao's betrayal of, 204, 329
  Mao's regrets over, 226
  pregnancies and childbirths of, 110, 120, 121, 129, 163, 178, 183
Yang Kaiming, 198, 199, 388
Yang Kaizhi, 56
Yang Mingzhai, 89

Yang Shangkun, xvi, 333, 426, 489–90
Yangzi River, 70, 85, 161, 184, 283, 353, 431, 503–5, 538
Yao, sage-king, 29
Yao Wenyuan, xvi, 493–94, 515, 525, 527, 535, 560–61, 586
  in Gang of Four, 565
  imprisonment of, 576
Yaroslavl Station, 368
Ye Jianying, xvi, 207, 334, 508, 523–26, 535, 561, 564, 567
Ye Qing, 341
Ye Qun, xvi, 525, 535, 542, 544–45, 547–48, 550–53
  flight and death of, 551–53
  in Lin Liguo's plot, 549, 550–51
  Yan Weibing's accusations against, 497–98
Ye Ting, 189–90, 207, 543
Ye Zilong, xvi, 368, 388
Yellow Crane Tower, 184
Yellow Emperor, 58
Yellow River, 55, 350, 470
Yellow Sea, 432
Yeltsin, Boris, 4
Yeping, 246, 251, 255, 268
Yezhov, Nikolai, 302, 426
Yi Lirong, 189, 194–95, 196, 198, 206
Yi nationality, 280
Yihequan (Fists of Righteousness and Harmony), *see* Boxers
Yihequan uprising, 24–25
Yiheyuan, 58
Yingwan, 50
Yokohama, 29, 50
Yongle, emperor of China, 58
Young China, 62
Young China, 90
Yu Fei, 219*n*
Yu Pingbo, 406
Yu Shude, 134
Yu Xuxiong, 6
Yuan Jiliu (Yuan Zhongqian), 39
Yuan Shikai, xvi, 23, 34–35, 43–45, 54, 101, 332
Yuan Wencai, xvi, 202–3, 204, 212, 215, 219
Yuanmingyuan, 58
Yuanzhi, 27
Yudin, Pavel Fedorovich, xvi, 354*n*, 373, 394, 408, 425–27, 435, 445, 458
Yudu, 273
Yue Fei, general, 116
Yuelu Academy, 32
Yuelu Mountain, 31, 52, 76, 172
Yuezhou, 110
Yugoslavia, 353, 354, 357, 375, 486, 536
Yugoslavian Communist Union, 430*n*, 434
Yunnan Military Academy, 210

Yunnan province, 11, 45, 143, 210, 280, 283, 519
Yunnanfu, 210
Yunshan, 273
Yusupov, Prince Felix, 356
Yusupova, Marianna, *see* Jiang Qing

Za rubezhom (Abroad), 271
Zaitian, *see* Guangxu
Zarkhin, Grigorii Naumovich, *see* Voitinsky, Grigorii Naumovich
Zhang Bojun, 441
Zhang Chengxian, 510
Zhang Chunqiao, xvi, 493, 499, 500, 515, 517, 521, 524–27, 529, 535, 546, 547–48, 555, 560–61, 562
  in Gang of Four, 565
  imprisonment of, 576
Zhang Dongsun, 98
Zhang Fakui, 189
Zhang Guotao, xvi, 6, 18–19, 100, 102, 106, 113, 115, 123, 124, 131, 133, 134, 140, 146–47, 151, 162, 165, 166, 179, 182, 194, 217, 235, 244, 249, 270, 314, 325, 552, 575
  absolute power craved by, 284–85
  appearance and personality of, 284
  on Borodin, 126–27, 156
  in Central Soviet Area, 248
  in Chinese Soviet Republic, 252
  on Comintern domination of CCP, 185
  decision to march south by, 287–88, 289
  Fourth Front Army commanded by, 276, 284
  grab for power by, 284–85
  left column led by, 285–87
  Lominadze and, 188–89
  in Long March reunion with army, 282, 283–84
  Mao's rivalry with, 18, 288, 289, 306, 340, 584
  on Mif, 234
  and Nanchang Uprising, 189
  on Provisional Bureau of CCP, 187
  on Provisional Politburo, 193
  reconciliation sought by, 290
  in USSR, 218–19
  Wang Ming supported by, 321
Zhang Huizan, 245
Zhang Jingtang, 78–79
Zhang Jingyao, xvi, 45, 70, 74, 76–77, 78–80
  activism against, 78–80, 87
Zhang Li, *see* Wang Jiaxiang
Zhang Lingzhi, 519
Zhang Naiqi, 441
Zhang Qinglin, 545
Zhang Qiubai, 113

Zhang Shaohua (Shao Hua), 389, 590
Zhang Tailei, 116, 119–20, 123, 125, 127, 134
  death of, 205
  on Provisional Bureau of CCP, 187
  on Provisional Politburo, 193
Zhang Wenliang, 96
Zhang Wentian, *see* Luo Fu
Zhang Xueliang, xvii, 216, 294–302, 304, 528
Zhang Yufeng (Xiao Zhang; Little Zhang), xvii, 489–90, 520, 552, 555, 558, 565, 566, 567, 570–72
  as Mao's intermediary, 562, 564, 568
Zhang Zhizhong, 346
Zhang Zongke, *see* Kang Sheng
Zhang Zongxiang, 69–70, 75
Zhang Zuolin, 159, 216, 295, 394
Zhangjiakou, 135
Zhangjiawan, 200
Zhangzhou, 260
Zhanshi (Warrior), 174
Zhao Erlu, 519
Zhao Hengti, xvii, 91, 109, 111–12, 121, 125, 128–29
  order for Mao's arrest by, 145
Zhao Wuzhen, 77
Zhao Xiangui (Zhao Lingying), 110, 140, 141, 142, 181, 208*n*, 592
  Guomindang execution of, 208*n*
Zhao Yimin (Xiao Ai), 292
Zhao Yun, *see* Kang Sheng
Zhdanov, Andrei, 302, 368
Zhejiang province, 106, 164, 230, 448
  cooperatives in, 417, 418
Zheng Chaolin, 146
Zheng Guanying (Zheng Zhengxiang), 21, 23
Zheng Ling, *see* Ren Bishi
Zhengzhi zhoubao (Political weekly), 148, 151, 158, 582
Zhengzhou, Feng's coup in, 183
Zhihua (wife of Qu Qiubai), 146–47
Zhili province, 24, 159
Zhivkov, Todor, 7
Zhong Hanhua, 528, 529
Zhongguo nongmin (Chinese peasant), 152, 157
Zhongnanhai, 365, 368, 389, 400, 406, 418, 461, 465, 497, 505, 508, 511, 517, 518, 519, 520, 552, 553, 558, 560, 562, 572
  famine and, 472
Zhongshan (warship), 155
Zhou dynasty, 563
Zhou Enlai (Moskvin), xvii, 6, 42, 138–39, 207, 210, 217, 222, 225, 228, 230, 234, 236, 248, 249, 250, 268, 270, 281, 285, 295, 302, 304, 306, 308, 330, 333*n*, 334, 346, 351, 358–59, 366, 388, 394, 410, 433, 435–36, 464, 474, 476, 493, 494,

496, 502, 506, 508, 509*n*, 518, 535, 538, 539, 540, 550, 552, 566
on communes, 452
Cultural Revolution and, 524, 525, 526, 529, 530, 531
death of, 569, 575, 587
economic ideas of, 442
famine and, 472
final illness of, 561
as flexible and cautious, 273, 277, 321, 434–35
on Great Leap, 450, 484
as head of secret services, 247
ill health of, 564, 566–67
Jiang Qing's enmity towards, 560–61, 562–64
in Jiangxi, 238
Korean War and, 376, 379, 380, 382, 383–84, 387
leftist attacks on, 562–64
Liu's dislike of, 487
as loyal to Mao, 506, 528, 531, 553
malaria contracted by, 286
on Mao, 218
Mao opposed by, 206, 256, 257, 259, 261
Mao supported by, 225, 420, 485
Mao's criticism of, 564–65
as Mao's designated successor, 554, 555, 560–61
Mao's "winning over" of, 262–63, 264, 269
in military troika, 281
as moderate, 395–98, 403–5, 417, 430, 434, 438
Moscow delegation of, 537
in Nanchang Uprising, 189, 211
in negotiations with new Kremlin leaders, 401–2
and Nixon's visit to PRC, 557–60
in NRA Political Department, 144
on people's communes, 477
as premier of the State Council, 408, 487
on Provisional Bureau of CCP, 187
on Provisional Politburo, 193
on Red Guards, 514
rehabilitation of, 338, 340
in right column, 286, 287, 289
self-criticism by, 448
shift to support of Mao by, 278–79
Stalin and, 5, 7, 426
at Stalin's funeral, 387, 400–401
Stalin's negotiations with, 390–91
steel campaign led by, 457

and united front, 312, 314
U.S. talks with, 344–45
in USSR, 230, 233, 371–73
on USSR-Eastern Europe delegation, 439
Wang Hairong and Nancy Tang's support of, 566, 568
Wang Ming supported by, 321
Xi'an Incident and, 301–2
Zhou Fohai, 102, 106
Zhou Lu, 206
attempts to discredit Mao by, 207
execution by Guomindang of, 211, 219
Zhou Shizhao, 68, 72, 74, 78, 83
Zhou Wennan, 181, 208, 209, 592
Zhou Xiaozhou, 449–50, 464, 465
Zhou Yang, 407
Zhu Danhua, 389, 592
Zhu De (Danilov), xvii, 5, 26, 37, 190, 207–9, 220–21, 222, 223, 230, 237, 240, 243, 244, 246, 258, 269, 292, 293, 306, 321, 327, 350, 351, 424, 464, 509*n*, 542, 584
agrarian revolution and, 216
background and character of, 210–11
on Central Committee, 236
in Chinese Soviet Republic, 252
as commander in chief, 262, 281
as commander of Eighth Route Army, 313–15
in CRMC, 256
death of, 572
as deputy to Chairman, 408
left column led by, 285–86, 290
Mao's relations with, 224–25, 226–27, 264, 279
Smedley's love for, 307–8
troop unification between Mao and, 209–10, 211, 231
U.S. talks with, 344–45
Zhu Qianzhi, 64
Zhu Xi, 32
Zhu Yuanzhang, emperor of China, 11, 28
Zhu Zhixin, 61
Zhuangzi, 490
Zhucheng, 327, 328
Zhuzhou, 111, 200
Zinoviev, Grigorii, 88, 100, 113, 121, 127, 156, 182, 426
Zinovo, 350
Zoucheng, 84
Zunyi, 277–78, 282, 511
Zunyi Conference, 278–80, 283, 284, 289, 291, 325–26, 335, 336, 340, 584